Peterson's

Smart Choices:

Honors Programs & Colleges

4th Edition

Dr. Joan Digby

The Official Guide of the National Collegiate Honors Council

National Collegiate ┆ Honors Council
⋯❭ YOUR LINK TO UNDERGRADUATE
HONORS EDUCATION

Australia • Canada • Mexico • Singapore • Spain • United Kingdom • United States

THOMSON

PETERSON'S

About Thomson Peterson's

Thomson Peterson's (www.petersons.com) is a leading provider of education information and advice, with books and online resources focusing on education search, test preparation, and financial aid. Its Web site offers searchable databases and interactive tools for contacting educational institutions, online practice tests and instruction, and planning tools for securing financial aid. Thomson Peterson's serves 110 million education consumers annually.

For more information, contact Thomson Peterson's, 2000 Lenox Drive, Lawrenceville, NJ 08648; 800-338-3282; or find us on the World Wide Web at www.petersons.com/about.

Editor: Fern A. Oram; Production Editor: Susan W. Dilts; Copy Editors: Bret Bollmann, Jim Colbert, Michael Haines, Sally Ross, Jill C. Schwartz, Mark D. Snider, Pam Sullivan, Valerie Bolus Vaughan; Research Project Manager: Dan Margolin; Programmer: Phyllis Johnson; Manufacturing Manager: Ivona Skibicki; Composition Manager: Gary Rozmierski.

ISBN 0-7689-2141-4

Printed in the United States of America

10 9 8 7 6 5 4 3 2 1   07 06 05

Fourth Edition

Contents

Acknowledgments

All of us engaged in Honors education owe a great debt of thanks to our staff and students whose good work and good nature give life to our endeavors—among them, this book. I'd like to thank the hundreds of people around the country who contributed information to this collective project. Above all, I must thank my heroic assistant, Tracey Christy, whose meticulous attention to detail and thoughtful attention to people helped me in greater measure than I can express. Thanks as well to a number of congenial helpers: Lois Brown, Alicia Delano, Danielle Hindiéh, Sara Izquierdo, Robin Marshall, and Tiffany Vlack. I also wish to thank Gary Bell, Bernice Braid, Katherine Bruce, John Grady, Ada Long, Lydia Lyons, Virginia McCombs, Jon Schlenker, Peter Sederberg, Patricia Speelman, and Bob Spurrier for the important essays they contributed; the Executive Committee and Publications Board of NCHC, as well as my home institution, Long Island University, for supporting this edition; and, finally, our editor, Fern Oram, for thinking it through and making it happen.

Dr. Joan Digby
Director
Honors Program and Merit Fellowship
Long Island University—C.W. Post Campus
President, National College Honors Council, 1999–2000

Welcome to Honors!

President's Message

Dr. Virginia McCombs
Director, Honors Program
Oklahoma City University
President, National Collegiate Honors Council, 2005

As President of The National Collegiate Honors Council (NCHC), I bring you greetings from directors, deans, faculty, and students who all believe very strongly that an undergraduate Honors education can shape students' lives in extraordinary ways.

This book will be useful for students, parents, and others who seek information about the wide range of Honors opportunities found at American colleges and universities. Here you will find a wealth of information about programs that range from Honors Colleges in large, research universities to Honors Programs in private, liberal arts universities and two-year community colleges. All are members of the National Collegiate Honors Council. We are an organization of institutions, faculty, administrators, students, and others interested in supporting Honors education. Just recently we have moved to our new home on the campus of The University of Nebraska–Lincoln. You can reach us there and should not hesitate to call on us with specific questions you might have about Honors. The mission of NCHC is to serve Honors professionals and to advance excellence in undergraduate education. The organization values an atmosphere that promotes academic opportunity and challenge for exceptionally able, highly motivated undergraduate students. NCHC also recognizes the importance of lifelong learning in preparing individuals for an increasingly complex world.

Now let me speak directly to the students. Your college education and experiences will play a pivotal role in shaping your future—what you want to do professionally and who you will become as a mature person. Your professors, major, the courses you take, the opportunities you seize, the lively discussions inside class and out, and the diverse groups of people you encounter—all will challenge, stretch, and sculpt the person you become.

The decision to join an Honors Program or College can be a critical step in shaping the undergraduate experience for many students. Highly motivated, academically gifted students look for colleges and universities that will challenge and engage them in a wide-ranging education that will not only prepare them for their future careers but will prepare them for lifelong learning. Honors Programs and Colleges pride themselves in cultivating just the right balance of stimulation and excitement, nurturing, and community that allows students to stretch and grow.

Many of you may have participated in Honors classes in high school; others may not have been on an

Marymount University students visit Washington, DC.

Honors track. Either way, you may have a notion of what Honors education is like. Be prepared to be surprised as you read through this book, especially noting the photographs and student testimonials. Diverse experiences—in Program size, opportunities, and the students themselves—are a central feature of Honors education. Many Programs offer Honors sections of required courses, whereas others have a unique Honors curriculum composed of interdisciplinary courses. In either case, you will experience a smaller classroom setting than in a non-Honors course, more discussion and interaction with your professor, and highly motivated and engaging classmates.

Many other opportunities await you if you choose to make Honors part of your undergraduate education. Are you interested in being an active learner, someone who does more than just read and listen? Honors education emphasizes undergraduate research, and many Honors students present their research at regional and national Honors conferences, as well as at disciplinary meetings. Do you want to be involved in the real world? Honors education has been a leader in service-learning programs that combine course work with community involvement. Have you dreamed of studying in another country? Honors Programs and Colleges emphasize international education, and you will find many options to study abroad for a summer or a semester through your own university or through NCHC Honors Semesters.

Honors students participate in a wide range of cocurricular activities as well. At my own university, we have Honors students who have served as Student Senate president, played varsity sports, won prestigious awards (such as the Goldwater Scholarship), been selected for the USA Today All Academic Team, been cast as the lead in theater productions, and founded campus chapters of Habitat for Humanity. You will find the same at any of the Honors Programs or Colleges listed in this book.

One need go no further than to ask Honors students themselves about the value of an Honors education. An Honors student recently wrote to me the following: "The Honors Program is designed to give students a well-rounded education, particularly for those who want to become educated individuals, not just specialists in one particular field. College students should experience and learn as much as possible, and the Honors Program gives students an extra opportunity to make the most of their undergraduate education." When you join an Honors community on your home campus, you will be joining a community of scholars—both students and faculty—who want you to have the most challenging, thought-provoking undergraduate education possible.

So, as you consider all of the factors in your selection of a college or university, keep in mind that an Honors education at any of the institutions included in this book will provide you with an excellent foundation, not only for your career but also for a lifetime of learning and participation in your community. An Honors program gives you the same exceptional education that formerly was reserved for students at the most elite—and expensive—colleges and universities. Add an Honors Program or College to your list of "must-haves" at the next stop in your educational career. And, by all means, embrace your college or university experience as an opportunity to plunge into life and learning. Challenge yourself. Take risks. Attend that play or art exhibit. Join in the midnight rally before the athletic contest. Join campus organizations. Participate in a research conference. Write a poem or a song or paint a sunset. Discover who you are and how you can make a difference. This is the goal of your education.

Greetings from the NCHC Executive Director

Patricia Ann Speelman

Hello from Lincoln, Nebraska! This is the permanent home of the National Collegiate Honors Council. And just what is NCHC? It's a nonprofit organization dedicated to serving its members—nearly 600 Honors Programs and Colleges at universities and colleges nationwide (all the ones that are listed in this book)—with seminars and speakers, publications, and consulting. Why does that matter to you? If your Honors Program or College is an NCHC member, you can be sure that you're connected to that nationwide network of possibilities. You'll reap the benefits of Program and College Directors who stay on top of the best practices in Honors education today. You'll have opportunities to run for election to the national executive committee and serve with faculty and students from throughout the U.S. in policy-making for this important organization. You will be eligible to present your own research to 2,000 fellow Honors students and faculty during the NCHC Annual Conference. You'll be on the cutting edge of new developments in lifelong learning.

As Executive Director of this venerable group, and the one who gets to sit every day in its beautiful offices at the University of Nebraska–Lincoln, I hope you'll take advantage of all NCHC has to offer. And once you get to your new school and get involved in its Honors activities, I hope you'll call or write or e-mail me with your ideas about how NCHC can make your wonderful experience even better. I look forward to hearing from you!

National Collegiate Honors Council
1100 Neihardt Residence Center
University of Nebraska–Lincoln
540 N. 16th Street
Lincoln, Nebraska 68588-0627
Telephone: 402-472-9150
Fax: 402-471-9152
E-mail: nchc@unlserve.unl.edu
Web site: www.nchchonors.org

NATIONAL COLLEGIATE HONORS COUNCIL PUBLICATIONS NOW AVAILABLE THROUGH THE NATIONAL OFFICE

Journal of the National Collegiate Honors Council
A refereed periodical of research for Honors Programs and Colleges.

Honors in Practice
A refereed journal dedicated to nuts-and-bolts practices and ideas for Honors Programs and Colleges.

Monograph Series
Topics of high interest for Honors faculty, administrators, and students.

Beginning In Honors: A Handbook by Samuel Schuman
A Handbook for Honors Administrators by Ada Long
Honors Composition: Historical Perspective and Contemporary Practices by Annmarie Guzy
Honors Programs at Smaller Colleges by Samuel Schuman
Innovations in Undergraduate Research and Honors Education: Proceedings of the Second Schreyer National Conference
Place as Text: Approaches to Active Learning edited by Bernice Braid and Ada Long
Teaching and Learning in Honors edited by Cheryl L. Fuiks and Larry Clark
Evaluating Honors Programs and Honors Colleges: A Practical Handbook by Rosalie Otero and Robert Spurrier
Two-Year College Handbook by Theresa James

Alumni Profiles

"Each day in my business, new situations present themselves. Past experiences help shape my decisions, and my thought processes continually quicken and grow sharper. Several business advisers emphasize the importance of listening to my instincts and thinking logically. While attending Southern Illinois University Carbondale and participating in the University Honors Program, I was fortunate to learn about decision making and creative thinking from distinguished scholars and business people. Sitting next to John Updike at an Honors Program breakfast helped me to see creative possibilities. I dug for dinosaur fossils in an Honors class, and appreciated the history in which I was immersed. In another Honors class, I glimpsed strength and perseverance while I listened to a Nazi Concentration Camp survivor discuss his experiences. My experiences live with me as I make decisions, think creatively, and continue to grow my business."

Ben Weinberger
Southern Illinois University Carbondale, 2001
Entrepreneur, owner, Digitalsmiths

"As I finish another year in the Ecology, Evolution, and Behavior Ph.D. program at the University of Minnesota, I still recount events that directed my career goals while in the University of North Carolina Wilmington Honors Scholars Program. Through Honors, I was able to round out my education and supplement it with experiences ranging from individual research to unique field trips to places such as the Galapagos Islands. At UNCW, I earned a B.S. in marine biology, but my Honors education provided me with a broader background and the idea that, in terms of my career, I would focus on pertinent questions related to animal behavior. And I learned that the study system should be what works for the question. Now, I work with honey bees. I went from examining sexual selection in fish to mechanisms of disease recognition in bees. I would never have guessed that this is where I'd be, but the Honors Scholars Program opened up lots of possibilities."

Mike Simone
University of North Carolina at Wilmington

Smart Choices for an Undergraduate Education

Dr. Joan Digby
Director, Honors Program and Merit Fellowship
Long Island University–C.W. Post Campus
President, National Collegiate Honors Council, 1999–2000

This book is designed to help smart students make equally smart choices that will shape their education and their lives. It does so by explaining how and why to put Honors Programs and Honors Colleges right up front in the college decision process. Then it offers nearly 600 Honors opportunities around the country—and a few overseas! This book will help you find the Honors Program or Honors College that best suits your personal needs, financial situation, and intellectual goals. Whichever one you choose, you can be sure you'll enjoy an extraordinarily fulfilling undergraduate education.

It is important to note that this book does not offer the usual college selection process. Many times, people are guided toward a narrow selection of colleges and universities based on reputation, conversations with friends, or promotional material. Few people think to approach the college search focused on Honors opportunities. As a result, they miss out on a rich variety of untapped financial resources and exciting college experiences for students with extraordinary talents and interests. For bright students, the smarter approach is to seek out a distinctive education that caters to their great diversity of intellectual and creative strengths. I therefore invite you to put Honors first and make the smartest choice of your life.

WHAT IS HONORS?

If you are a student filled with ideas, longing for creative expression, and ready to take on career-shaping challenges, then an Honors education is just for you. Honors Programs and Colleges offer some of the finest undergraduate degrees available in the United States and do so with students in mind. The essence of Honors is personal attention, top faculty, enlightening seminars, illuminating study-travel experi-

ences, research options, and career-building internships—all designed to enhance a classic education and prepare you for life achievements. And here is an eye-opening bonus: Honors Programs and Colleges may reward your academic performance by giving you scholarships that will help you pay for your higher education.

"Operation Clothespin" Honors Composition students at Oklahoma City University researched the historical and symbolic significance of a 240-square memorial quilt and developed a digital exhibit.

Take your choice of institutions: community, state or private, two- or four-year college, or large research university. There are Honors opportunities in each. What they share in common is an unqualified commitment to academic excellence. Honors education teaches students to think and write clearly, to be excited by ideas, and to become independent, creative, and self-confident learners. It prepares exceptional students for professional choices in every imaginable sphere of life—arts and sciences, engineering, business, health, education, medicine, theater, music, film, journalism, media, law, politics. Invent your own professional goal and Honors will guide you to it!

WHO ARE HONORS STUDENTS?

Who are you? Perhaps a high school junior making out your first college applications, a community college student seeking to transfer to a four-year college, or possibly a four-year college student doing better than you had expected. You might be an international student, a varsity athlete, captain of the debate team, or second violin in the campus orchestra. Whether you are the first person in your family to attend college or an adult with a grown family seeking a new career, Honors might well be right for you. Honors Programs admit students with every imaginable background and educational goal.

How can Honors satisfy you and give you something special? Read what students in some of our member Programs say. Although they refer to particular colleges, their experiences are typical of what students find exciting about Honors education on hundreds of campuses around the country:

"Being an Honors Program student has been a life-changing experience for me. I have gained tremendously in knowledge, experience, and self-esteem. I have learned so much more in the Program than any textbook could teach about the value of encouraging support and positive thinking."

Cheri Becker
Mount Wachusett Community College

"I've been in a healing ceremony in Ecuador and have performed music on stage. I've guided my peers and Navajo children, hiked the Grand Canyon, and so much more. Sometimes, experience speaks for itself; always, it creates paths, opens eyes, and helps us find our places. Thanks to my Honors Program, I've experienced these wonders and accomplishments. Now I know that there are no greater lessons than how to learn and to love discovery."

April Fisher
University of North Florida

"The Honors College has been my home away from home. In the midst of a diverse, fairly large university, it has provided me with the intimacy that I needed. . . . My freshman year living situation on the Honors floor . . . allowed me to find like-minded students early in my college career."

Brian Leech
Davidson Honors College
University of Montana

"I was able to transition from an Honors Program at a two-year institution into an Honors Program at a four-year institution without any reservations or tribulations."

Rachel Jones Williams
Elizabethtown College

"Every single professor is in love with what they do and it shows in their research, amazing teaching, and interaction with students outside of the classroom. The undergraduate journey can be very difficult at times, but as an Honors College student, you're sure to have plenty of support every step of the way."

Walteria Tucker
Wilkes Honors College
Florida Atlantic University

"The class size is perfect and I've been able to make some of my closest relationships with students and teachers through the Program. The majority of Honors faculty I have encountered have been overwhelmingly helpful . . . and my favorite courses have been Honors classes."

Ellen Daschler
Eastern Illinois University

"Our professor met us at a local restaurant the last evening of class and we shared a wonderful dinner. It had such a familiar feel to it because these are students I have known throughout my four years in the Program."

Betsy Porter
University of La Verne

"For the last two years, I have investigated new synthetic methods under the direction of a Professor Emeritus. Through the university Honors College I am able to pursue this interest in chemistry and other academic endeavors . . . that have allowed me to develop my academic potential and contribute to the scientific body of knowledge."

Justin Chalker
University of Pittsburgh

"The most rewarding part of being a member of the Honors Program is the joy of doing creative, meaningful projects with faculty I love."

Meleia Egger
Hartwick College

"I would . . . like to add a word of praise for the way the curriculum is structured. It has deepened and enriched my thinking and helped me develop tools to negotiate the complex world we live in."

Monideepa Talukdar
Southeastern Louisiana University

"We have a better time . . . our discussions get rather heated. In a lot of classes, only one or two students will speak up. But in the Honors classes, it's a free-for-all."

Jonathan Post
Reinhardt College

"My internship at a major international bank gave me an in-depth look into the world of investment and accounting. Funded by the Honors College, I was able to study business and culture in Shanghai, China, for a month. These valuable experiences are helping me to develop professionally, academically, and personally."

Jenny Lam
Honors College
The College of Staten Island, CUNY

"The Honors thesis was the key factor during the selection process at my future employer. . . . It

Steffi Nenz, Theodore Roosevelt Scholars Program, Dickinson University, interned in horse-assisted therapy near Munich, Germany.

helped me to get the job and have an advantage over others. It is a lot of work but, in the end, it is worth it."

Olgierd Hinz
Lee Honors College
Western Michigan University

"What I've enjoyed most about the Honors Program is the one thing I was most dreading: the Honors thesis. Now that I have started mine in a breast cancer laboratory, I absolutely love it. It is incredibly rewarding to put different scientific methods that I have learned from my Honors courses into real life application."

Celynne Guilmette
University of New Hampshire

These portraits don't tell the whole story, but they should give you a sense of what it means to be part of an Honors Program or Honors College. Outside of class, Honors students often run track, run the student government, and write the college newspaper. They are everywhere on campus: in plays and concerts, in laboratories and libraries, and in sororities and fraternities. Some are clear about their majors and professions; others need direction and advice. One of the great strengths of Honors Programs is that they are nurturing environments that encourage students to be well-rounded and help students make life choices.

WHAT IS AN HONORS PROGRAM?

An Honors Program is a sequence of courses designed specifically to encourage independent and creative learning. For more than half a century "Honors" education—given definition by the National Collegiate Honors Council—has been an institution on American campuses. Although Honors Programs have many different designs, there are typical components. At two-year colleges, the Programs often concentrate on special versions of general education courses and may have individual capstone projects that come out of the students' special interests. At four-year colleges and universities, Honors Programs are generally designed for students of almost every major in every college on campus. In growing numbers, they are given additional prominence as Honors Colleges. Whether a Program or a College, Honors usually includes a general education or "core" component followed by advanced courses (often called colloquia or seminars). Some Programs have Honors contracts that shape existing courses into Honors components to suit the needs of individual students. Many have interdisciplinary or collaborative seminars that bring students of different majors together to discuss a complex topic with faculty from different disciplines. A good number have final thesis, capstone, or creative projects, which may or may not be in the departmental major. Almost always, the Honors curriculum is incorporated within whatever number of credits is required of every student for graduation. Honors very rarely requires students to take additional credits. Students who complete an Honors Program or Honors College curriculum frequently receive transcript and diploma notations, as well as certificates, medallions, or other recognition at graduation ceremonies.

Catering to the student as an individual plays a central role in Honors course design. Most Honors classes are small (fewer than 20 students); most are discussion oriented, giving students a chance to present their own interpretations of ideas and even teach a part of the course. Many classes are interdisciplinary, which means they are taught by faculty members from two or more departments, providing different perspectives on a subject. All Honors classes help students develop and articulate their own perspectives by cultivating both verbal and written style. They help students mature intellectually, preparing them to engage in their own explorations and research. Some Programs even extend the options for self-growth to study abroad and internships in science, government, and the arts or business related to the major. Other Programs encourage or require community service as part of the Honors experience. In every case, Honors is an experiential education that deepens classroom learning and extends far beyond.

Despite their individual differences, all Honors Programs and Honors Colleges rely on faculty who enjoy working with bright, independent students. The ideal Honors faculty members are open-minded, encouraging, master teachers. They want to see their students achieve at their highest level, and they are glad to spend time with students in discussions and laboratories, on field trips and at conferences, or online in e-mail. They often influence career decisions, provide inspiring models, and remain friends long after they have served as thesis advisers.

WHERE ARE HONORS PROGRAMS AND HONORS COLLEGES LOCATED?

Because Honors Programs and Honors Colleges include students from many different departments or colleges, they usually have their own offices and space on campus. Some have their own buildings. Most Programs have Honors centers or lounges, where students gather together for informal conversations, luncheons, discussions, lectures, and special projects.

Many Honors students have cultivated strong personal interests that have nothing to do with classes. They may be multilingual; they may be fine artists or poets, musicians or racing car enthusiasts, mothers or fathers. Some work in hospitals or do landscape gardening to pay for college. Many work in retail stores and catering. Some are avid sports enthusiasts, while others collect antiques. When they get together in Honors lounges, there is always an interesting mix of ideas.

In general, Honors provides an environment in which students feel free to talk about their passionate interests and ideas, knowing that they will find good listeners and, sometimes, arguers. There is no end to conversations among Honors students. Like many students in Honors, you may feel a great relief in finding a sympathetic group that respects your intelligence and creativity. In Honors, you can be eccentric; you can be yourself! Some lifelong friendships, even marriages, are the result of social relationships developed in Honors Programs. Of course you will make other friends in classes, clubs, and elsewhere on campus—even through e-mail! But the Honors Program will build strong bonds, too.

In the Honors center, whether Program or College, you will also find the Honors Director or Dean. The Honors Director often serves as a personal adviser to all of the students in the Program. Many Programs also have peer counselors and mentors who are upper class Honors students and know the ropes from a student's perspective and experience. Some have specially assigned Honors advisers who guide Honors students through their degrees, assist in registration, and answer every imaginable question. The Honors office usually is a good place to meet people, ask questions, and solve problems.

ARE YOU READY FOR HONORS?

Admission to Honors Programs and Honors Colleges is generally based on a combination of several factors: high school or previous college grades, experience taking AP or IB courses, SAT or ACT scores, personal essay, and extracurricular achievements. To stay in Honors, students need to maintain a certain GPA (grade point average) and show progress toward the completion of the specific Honors Program or College requirements. Since you have probably exceeded admissions standards all along, maintaining your GPA will not be as big a problem as it sounds. Your professors and your Honors Director are there to help you succeed in the Program. Most Honors Programs have very low attrition rates because students enjoy classes and do well. You have every reason to believe that you can make the grade.

Of course, you must be careful about how you budget your time. Honors encourages well-rounded, diversified students, and you should play a sport if you want to, work at the radio station, join the clubs that interest you, or pledge a sorority or fraternity. You might find a job in the student center or library that will help you pay for your car expenses and that also is reasonable. But remember that each activity takes time, and you must strike a balance that will leave you enough time to do your homework, write papers, prepare for seminar discussions, do your research, and do well on exams. Choose the jobs and activities that attract you, but never let them overshadow your primary purpose—which is to be a successful student.

Sometimes even the very best students who apply for Honors admissions are frightened by the thought of speaking in front of a group, presenting seminar papers, or writing a thesis. But if you understand how the Programs work, you will see that there is nothing about which to be frightened. The basis of Honors is confidence in the student and building the student's self-confidence. Being admitted to an Honors Program means you have already demonstrated your academic achievement in high school or college classes. Once in

Maressa Dixon, Miami University, Urban Leadership Internship Program at the National Underground Railroad Freedom Center in Cincinnati, Ohio.

an Honors environment, you will learn how to formulate and structure ideas so that you can apply critical judgment to sets of facts and opinions. In small seminar classes you practice discussion and arguments so that by the time you come to the senior thesis or project, the method is second nature. For most Honors students, the senior thesis, performance, or portfolio presentation is the project that gives them the greatest fulfillment and pride. In many Honors Programs and Colleges students present their work either to other students or to faculty members in their major departments. Students often present their work at regional and national Honors conferences. Some students even publish their work jointly with their faculty mentors. These are great achievements, and they come naturally with the training. There is nothing to be afraid of. Just do it! Honors will make you ready for life.

YOUR HONORS GUIDE

In the following pages you will hear from Honors educators and officers of the National Collegiate Honors Council (NCHC), who extend to you their greetings and share their experience. All of the Honors Programs listed in this guide are members of the NCHC, which has advocated Honors education for more than 50 years. NCHC holds meetings every year for Honors directors, faculty members, and students. Honors students play a large role in NCHC. They have representatives to cover student issues. Students serve on committees and present papers at the national convention. In fact, in some years, there are as many students as faculty members attending the annual meeting—leading discussions, sharing their research, and shaping the future of American Honors education. Many Honors Programs pay all or part of their students' travel both to the national convention and to regional Honors conventions, which also present excellent opportunities for student participation. I hope to meet you there!

Meanwhile, think of yourself as setting out on a great journey. Use your smarts! The information that we have provided in this book should give you the means and direction to discover Honors and make your undergraduate education a spectacular one.

Alumni Profiles

"The Honors College at Hampton University provided me with a foundation for educational and professional success. Participation in the Honors College exposed me to graduates of Ivy League graduate schools. This association propelled me to fix my eyes upon my future alma mater: Harvard Law School.

Honors College instilled the value of pursuing professional excellence for its own sake. I internalized this principle through participation in debate tournaments hosted by Honors conferences. I found fulfillment in developing reasoned, well-researched, and logically sound arguments. The pursuit of excellence and purpose has held me in good stead in my young legal career. Currently, I serve large, multinational, nonprofit organizations that depend on my judgment and knowledge to carry out their altruistic purposes. The writing, research, and verbal communication skills honed through preparation for debate tournaments now enable me to help charitable organizations deliver life-sustaining services throughout the world."

Courtney D. Jones, Esq.
Hampton University

"My association with the University Honors Program put me one step ahead of my peers from the day that I first set foot on the campus of Mississippi State University. Because of the UHP, I was able to participate in numerous organizations, from the John C. Stennis Conference for Southern Women in Public Service to the Institute for International Mediation and Conflict Resolution in the Hague, Netherlands. The rich educational and professional experiences that I was able to gain through a close working relationship with the UHP faculty and my other professors allowed me to develop both personally and intellectually. Their dedication and genuine interest in my pursuits contributed directly to my Truman Scholarship award in 2003. I have continued to use the competitive edge afforded me by the UHP as the foundation for a successful career as an officer in the United States Air Force."

Jennifer Phillips
Mississippi State University

NCHC and Its Partnerships in Honors Education

Dr. Jon A. Schlenker
Director, Honors Program
The University of Maine at Augusta
President, National Collegiate Honors Council, 2005–06

For many years, the National Collegiate Honors Council (NCHC) has developed a variety of relationships with organizations to foster the development of undergraduate Honors education. All of these endeavors enhance the recognition of the high-quality education Honors Programs and Colleges provide, as well as the academic excellence and achievement of their students.

NCHC is closely allied with the six regional, independently operating Honors councils in the United States. Many colleges and universities are members of both a regional council and the NCHC and, as such, much collaboration occurs between those institutions and their members. The regional associations are The Northeast Region–National Collegiate Honors Council, The Southern Regional Honors Council, The Mideast Regional Honors Association (MEHA), The Upper-Midwest Honors Council, The Western Regional Honors Council, and The Great Plains Regional Honors Council.

Another undergraduate Honors association that works with NCHC is the National Association of African-American Honors Programs (NAAAHP). NAAAHP members come from historically and predominantly black colleges and universities.

NCHC currently cooperates with several Honors societies that are devoted to recognizing and promoting academic excellence among undergraduate students. Phi Kappa Phi is the oldest and largest collegiate Honors society open to undergraduate students from all disciplines. Phi Theta Kappa is the international honor society for two-year college students. In particular, NCHC and Phi Theta Kappa have partnered to produce the NCHC/Phi Theta Kappa Honors Satellite Seminar Series. Nearly 200 two-year and baccalaureate institutions subscribe to these seminars every year, resulting in a substantial impact on undergraduate Honors education. The seminars offer an excellent means for Honors Programs to provide their students with access to topic experts and authors for a nominal cost. In addition, the Phi Theta Kappa Honors Study Topic is used by nearly 200 two-year colleges as the foundation for a credit course or as a capstone course in the Honors Program. The 2004–2006 Honors Study Topic is "Popular Culture: Shaping and Reflecting Who We Are," while the 2006–2008 Topic will be "Gold, God and Glory: The Global Struggle for Power."

Other prominent organizations affiliate with NCHC as institutional members. Each of these relationships is intended to increase Honors students' opportunities to expand their educational experience. The Kettering Foundation supports deliberative democracy in the classroom and has partnered with NCHC to prepare an issue book to energize public deliberations on the future of higher education. The Fund for American Studies sponsors five institutes in Washington, DC, to prepare students to assume leadership positions in their communities and the nation. The Washington Center for Internships and Academic Seminars (TWC) sponsors opportunities for students to work and learn in Washington, DC, for academic credit.

Other institutional members of NCHC include the National Society of Collegiate Scholars and the Association of College Honors Societies (ACHS). The National Society of Collegiate Scholars is the nation's only Honors organization that recognizes first- and second-year college students for their outstanding academic achievements. The ACHS is the certifying agency for college and university Honors societies.

Still another significant partnership is that with the University of Nebraska–Lincoln. In 2005, the National Collegiate Honors Council established a permanent national headquarters, with the newly created position of Executive Director to lead NCHC in the 21st century. The location of the national office is now in wonderful facilities on the campus of The University of Nebraska–Lincoln.

NCHC continues to seek partnerships that increase and enhance the undergraduate Honors experience for students and supports the continued development of strong, high-quality academic programs and activities on the campuses of our member institutions.

Honors Students and Scholarships

Dr. Gary M. Bell
Dean, University Honors College
Texas Tech University

Here's some really good news: Students who are considering an Honors Program or College are also the very people most likely to be eligible for scholarship assistance. As the costs for college have escalated dramatically in recent years, funding has become a critical and difficult, albeit educational, part of being a student. Let's face it: higher education is expensive and getting more expensive with each passing year!

FINANCING YOUR COLLEGE EDUCATION

Scholarships provide part of the solution to financing your undergraduate career. Honors students are precisely the ones who colleges recruit most eagerly. Having good students choose them adds to the prestige of an institution. Thus, there is an excellent chance that the school of your choice may provide scholarship assistance in order to encourage your enrollment and enhance their bragging rights!

Another way to view the next four (or more) years on the way to your bachelor's degree is to assume that learning will be your primary employment. It is helpful, therefore, to think of a scholarship as part of the salary for undertaking your job of learning. From this perspective, you then have the right, again as a potential Honors student, to seek the best pay, or scholarship, possible. Thus, one of your first inquiries, as you examine a potential college setting, should be about the type of assistance that may be provided to you, given your interests, your academic record, and your personal history. Talk to a financial aid officer or a scholarship coordinator at the school. Virtually all schools have brochures or other publications that list scholarship opportunities at their institution. Read this literature carefully so that you can ask the appropriate questions. Find out as much as you can about what the scholarship picture is like at the institutions you are interested in. For instance, is it possible that your father's or your mother's company may provide matching funds for employees' children at that particular institution?

In your search for monetary assistance, also visit either your local bookstore or your local public library, where there are books that have several hundred scholarships listed in different categories. (*Peterson's Scholarships, Grants & Prizes* is one example.) The Internet is a similarly useful tool in obtaining additional information. In addition, high school counselors have keen insight into resources available at colleges, especially at schools in your local area. These people are the key point of contact between institutions of higher education and high school students.

A word of caution: In general, it is not a particularly good practice to use a private company that promises you, frequently for a considerable fee, a list of scholarships for which you *might* be eligible, as such lists are often very broad. More important, you can secure the same results by using available high school, university, and published information—at little or no cost.

WHAT DO WE MEAN BY THE WORD *SCHOLARSHIP* ANYWAY?

In the very broadest sense, scholarships consist of outright grants of financial assistance to eligible students to help them attend college. The money is to be applied to tuition or the costs of living while in school. Scholarships typically do not have to be repaid. They do often carry stringent criteria for maintaining them, such as the achievement of a certain grade point average, carrying a given number of class hours, matriculation in a specific program, or membership in a designated group. At many schools, scholarships may be combined with work-study programs or with educational loan programs. Generally, scholarships fall into three major categories:

1. Need-based scholarships, which are based on family income;

2. Merit-based scholarships, which are based on your academic and/or extracurricular achievements; and

Think about it . . . Dr. Sherrill Begres teaches philosophy at Robert E. Cook Honors College at the Indiana University of Pennsylvania.

3. Association-based scholarships, which are dependent on as many different associations as you can imagine (for instance, the county or even country from which you come or your identification with a particular group).

Frequently, schools have endowed scholarships (scholarships based on a fund whose principal can never be used), given by alumni or others with a particular interest in supporting Honors students. Merit-based scholarships can come from a variety of sources: the university as a whole, individual departments or colleges within the university, or special donors who want to assist eligible students. This fact is worth remembering as you work with financial aid officers so that they understand the special opportunities that may be available to you as a petroleum engineering, agriculture, accounting, pre-veterinary, or performing arts major. You also need to understand that merit-based scholarships are typically designed to reward excellent high school grades as well as the very highest scores on such precollege measures as standardized tests (the SAT or ACT). Since taking a standardized test more than once often leads to higher scores, it may be financially advantageous for you to take these tests several times. Also be sensitive to the fact that

many scholarships can be "bundled" together to provide you with a very attractive financial aid package. Equally important, scholarships can also be "bundled" with low-interest-loan programs to make the school of your choice unexpectedly affordable.

Inquire specifically into each of the three previously mentioned categories of scholarships. The association-based scholarships can sometimes be particularly helpful and quite surprising. Corporations or organizations (churches, civic groups, special-interest clubs, even family-name associations) may provide little-known assistance for college students. Scholarship literature is the primary key to unlocking the mysteries of association-based financial assistance (and the other two categories as well), but personal interviews with financial aid officers are also helpful.

Thus, your acceptance to an Honors Program can carry with it not only enhanced educational benefits but also substantial monetary assistance. However, if you are joining an Honors Program for a financial advantage only, you are joining for the wrong reason. Honors education is about broadening your educational experiences, opening an array of academic opportunities, and challenging you to be better than you think you can be. If money is your only incentive in becoming associated with Honors, you probably need to look elsewhere for financial assistance.

SEEKING SCHOLARSHIP ASSISTANCE

Most scholarship opportunities require an application form. It is time well spent to make sure your application is neat, grammatically correct, and logical. Correct spelling is essential, as is having someone proofread your application. Keep in mind that if an application requires an essay, few students typically take the time to complete that requirement. So those students who are willing to write an essay do have a better chance of winning that particular scholarship. Always be truthful about yourself in your applications, but, at the same time, provide your most positive portrayal to enhance your chances of being considered. Be sensitive to the fact that most merit-based and association-based scholarships are awarded competitively.

Most important, find out any and all deadlines! It is always wise to begin your search early so that you have plenty of time to work on several applications at the same time. (Much of the information you will have to provide is useful for more than one application.) The summer before your senior year is not too early to begin your search!

Finally, as soon as your plans become firm, do let the people who offer you assistance know whether or not you will accept. Too many students simply assume that a scholarship offer means automatic acceptance. This is not the case! In virtually all instances, you must send a letter of acknowledgment and acceptance.

COST AND CHOOSING A COLLEGE

There are many elements to consider, such as reputation, programs offered, courses provided, and the school's success in placing graduates. Visit the prospective school to see if the student profile, campus amenities, and atmosphere of the campus fit your needs and aspirations. But it is imperative that you pay attention to cost. Where can you realistically afford to go, without incurring very large debts that could plague you after graduation? In the end, you must choose the college or university that seems best for you *and* that fits your family's budget. Scholarships should play a very big role in your decision-making matrix.

Many private institutions have a great deal of money to spend on scholarship assistance, so you might well find that going to a private college will cost no more than attending a state school. However, even a substantial scholarship from a private school may still leave you with a very large annual bill to cover the actual cost of tuition, fees, and living expenses. Therefore, when you evaluate a scholarship, do so by comparing what your final, projected costs will be. Another factor to consider is the length of time for which the school extends scholarship support. Be cautious about the school that promises substantial assistance for the first year—in order to get you there—but then provides little or nothing in the second through the fourth or later years. The most attractive and meaningful scholarships are offered for four to five years.

Incidentally, the scholarship search should continue even after you are enrolled at the school of your choice. There are often a number of opportunities for the enrolled student, especially as you prove your ability and interest in a given field. Also, Honors students have been particularly successful in national scholarship competitions, such as the Rhodes, the Gates/Cambridge, the Fulbright, the Goldwater, the Truman, and the Udall. Finally, your earned scholarship may well be applied to study abroad or NCHC Honors Semester Programs.

Alumni Profiles

"Critical thinking is the key to producing a newscast—knowing what goes where and when you should take a chance on a tip. Critical thinking is what I learned through the Missouri Southern Honors Program.

I came to the Program a shy teenager from a very small town in southwest Missouri. I immediately learned that in the MSSU Honors Program I was no longer defined by who I used to be but by who I wanted to become. The instructors in the Program took time out to not just teach me but to mentor me. These teachers shared their passion for their subject. The extra effort on their part has made me a successful producer. But the MSSU Honors Program didn't end with college. I can still call on former professors when I have questions about anything from major career decisions to a clarification of a point that was made in their class."

Phil Cross
Missouri Southern State University, 2003
Television News Producer
WHO-TV, Des Moines, IA

"My being in The Honors College placed me in a strategic position within the University, providing me with small class sizes and studious classmates and thereby helping me make the most of my college experience. The College's professors were among the best at the University of Houston. Through the partnership between the Honors College and the University of Glasgow, I studied religion and the arts in Scotland. Upon my graduation from the University of Houston, I married fellow Honors College classmate, Justin O'Neill, and we now run our own performance business, Two Violins. Studying business and the arts in the Honors College definitely gave me an upper hand when applying to graduate schools. I am currently a student in the M.B.A./M.A. Arts Administration program at Southern Methodist University in Dallas, Texas."

Magdalena O'Neill
University of Houston, 2002
B.M., music business and violin

At the Top of the World: NCHC Students Recognized as Prestigious Scholarship Winners

Dr. Robert L. Spurrier, Jr.
Director, The Honors College
Oklahoma State University
President, National Collegiate Honors Council, 1998–99

One of the most rewarding aspects of working with Honors students during their undergraduate careers is sharing their excitement when they receive major national and international scholarships to continue their education at the graduate or professional level. Some of these students may have aspired to such prestigious scholarships at the time they entered college, but for many it was the Honors Program or Honors College experience that led them to compete at this, the highest possible level. Working closely with faculty mentors and Honors administrators, they really did reach *the top of the world* in terms of recognition of their outstanding work and their potential for the future. Of course not every Honors student wins one of these scholarships, but many tell us that the process of preparing to compete is invaluable to their own development and preparation for the future, either for graduate or professional education or for immediate entry into their chosen professions.

The profiles that follow introduce you to a number of these students, coming from a wide range of colleges and universities. The NCHC Web site provides links to detailed information about many of these scholarships and fellowships. Look into them at http://www.nchchonors.org/scholarships.htm. It never is too early for you to start thinking about competing in this arena.

As you are considering Honors Programs and Honors Colleges for your undergraduate career, keep these students and their experiences in mind—and never sell yourself short!

CHURCHILL

Churchill Scholarships are awarded for one year of study at Churchill College, Cambridge, in the fields of mathematics, biology, biochemistry, physical anthropology, computer speech and language processing, computer science, physics, chemistry, and mathematical statistics.

"As a member of the Schreyer Honors College at Penn State University, I was surrounded by fellow students who truly believed that there was no limit to their success. I was given access to advisers who would take hours out of their days at a minute's notice to discuss everything from academic interests and personal experiences to global challenges. I had academic supervisors who became colleagues. I was invited to the social events of the university's elite, and conversed with the minds that sculpted the university, the community, the state, and the nation. I was given opportunities to take part in academic and personal experiences that had the potential to change lives across the world. I had a committee surrounding me that bolstered my success on a multitude of levels. These gifts not only shaped my future, but shaped my inner being. I look forward to living the remainder of my life upholding the values for which my mentors at the Schreyer Honors College lived and breathed."

Danielle Perry
Pennsylvania State University
National Institutes of Health—University of Cambridge
Graduate Partnerships Program
Churchill Scholarship recipient

COOKE

The Jack Kent Cooke Undergraduate Scholars Program has two separate competitions: one for continuing four-year college students and the other for students currently attending two-year/community colleges who plan to transfer to four-year institutions.

"Looking back from my first year in graduate school, I am beginning to understand how much the Honors experience at Prince George's Community College has prepared me for the rigor of a Ph.D. program. Being in the Honors Programs was like being on a team of athletes. Everyone was pulling for me, pushing me to reach past the limits I had set for myself and to achieve something better. The environment was really rewarding and the extra work was worth it. The guidance of Honors mentors and the company of Honors students nurtured my talents and challenged me to not only grow as a student, but as a person."

Ron Crouch
Prince George's Community College, 2002
Jack Kent Cooke Undergraduate
Scholarship recipient, 2002
George Washington University, 2004
Truman Scholar, 2004
Graduate student in Clinical Psychology
at DePaul University
Jack Kent Cooke Graduate Scholarship recipient, 2005

FULBRIGHT

This program for students from the United States is designed to give recent graduates, young professionals, and young artists opportunities for international experience and promotes cross-cultural interaction and mutual understanding on a person-to-person basis.

"I graduated from the Pennsylvania State University in May 2004 with a B.S. in physics and minor in math, with honors in physics from the Schreyer Honors College. My post-graduation options all included graduate study of various forms. As I had experience with German from several courses at PSU, I decided to accept a Fulbright to study at the Technical University of Munich (TUM) in Germany. I had visited the institution the previous summer with the dual assistance of a DAAD (German Academic Exchange Service) fellowship and a travel grant provided from the Schreyer Honors College. The TUM is an excellent choice for physics study because of its close cooperation with several Max Planck Institutes in and around Munich. As a part of my Honors study at PSU, I participated for several years in research on superconducting nanostructures with Dr. Ying Liu, culminating in my Honors thesis. The work I am involved with now is no longer in the realm of superconductivity and condensed matter. However, I gained experience in experimental methodology and have had little difficulty in adapting this knowledge to the optical experiments in which I am now involved. Upon completion of my studies with the Fulbright, I intend to begin doctoral studies at the University of Washington in Seattle."

Nathan Kurz
Pennsylvania State University
Fulbright Scholarship recipient

GATES CAMBRIDGE

This scholarship to Cambridge University in Great Britain seeks to create a network of future leaders from around the world who will bring new vision and commitment to improving the life circumstances of citizens in their respective countries.

"The world of tomorrow is one of multidisciplinary collaborations. The traditional borders of the sciences and humanities are being rewritten as professionals expand the limits of human understanding. My experiences at Texas Tech University's Honors College not only exposed me to these multidisciplinary endeavors but also allowed me to participate in them. By taking Honors courses spanning organic chemistry to American history to bioethics, I have been provided with the background to operate in 21st century academia. The Honors College has also provided the guidance and environment to apply for highly competitive scholarships, generating Goldwater and Gates Cambridge Trust funding for my higher education. Overall, the Honors College has provided me with a crossroads—a home to cultivate my diverse interests and see them work in harmony."

William Michael Henne
Texas Tech University, 2005
Goldwater Scholarship recipient, 2004
Gates Cambridge Scholarship recipient, 2005

GOLDWATER

The Goldwater Scholarship is designed to fund educational opportunities for students in the sciences, mathematics, and engineering.

"I can attribute nearly all of my success to the Honors College at Oklahoma State. It first inspired me to get involved in research, which resulted in publications and the Goldwater Scholarship. Honors then opened my eyes to the world outside of engineering and I fell in love with the humanities. The broad Honors education gave me the competitive edge in the Gates Cambridge Scholarship and has made me a much more balanced and fulfilled individual."

Ashleigh Hildebrand
Oklahoma State University
Gates Cambridge Scholarship recipient, 2005
Goldwater Scholarship recipient

MARSHALL

The British Marshall Scholarship finances study at any British university for two years of study in any discipline at the undergraduate or graduate level that leads to the awarding of a British university degree.

"The Advanced Academy of Georgia and the University of West Georgia's Honors College played no small role in my development as a scholar and budding scientist. Always available for thoughtful guidance, the professors took a personal stake in the success of their students and challenged everyone to reach beyond their grasp. Nestled in a quiet yet rapidly growing part of Georgia, UWG's modest image belies its capacity as an institution that can prepare committed students for the highest echelons of academic excellence. Marshall Scholarship, Goldwater Scholarship, and Medical Scientist Training Program Scholarship— these are just a few among the twenty-plus merit scholarships that I have been fortunate to receive with the encouragement and support of UWG's

Honors College. I cannot recommend the Program more highly to America's most ambitious students."

Yong D. Suh
University of West Georgia
Marshall Scholarship recipient

NATIONAL SCIENCE FOUNDATION

NSF awards are for graduate students in the sciences who will contribute significantly to research, teaching, and industrial applications in science, mathematics, and engineering.

"Throughout my undergraduate and graduate education, I have benefited greatly from the Honors Program at The Ohio State University. It started in the Freshman Engineering Honors Program, which helped me move quickly into the engineering curriculum, grow intellectually in a challenging environment, and meet similar-minded classmates with whom I have maintained college-long relationships. In graduate school, I have been honored with an NSF fellowship, which has allowed me to pursue in-depth advanced study in my field of civil engineering."

Eric Setzler
The Ohio State University, 2003
NSF Fellowship recipient

PICKERING

The Pickering Fellowship is designed to attract students interested in careers in diplomacy and foreign service. Those receiving the award (there are levels for undergraduates and graduates) are assured of significant educational support, training, and summer postings to U.S. embassies around the world.

"In The Honors College at Oklahoma State University, students challenge themselves. I was selected as a Pickering Foreign Affairs Fellow, one of 20 in the nation, because I chose to participate in The Honors College and its community of incredible students and professors. Students with diverse backgrounds and experiences find an intellectual lyceum in the Honors College's interactive classes. Honors students are challenged to synthesize abstract concepts under the supportive guidance of expert professors. The Honors College at OSU provides exceptional students incredible experiences for lifelong learning."

Kyle Jones
Oklahoma State University
Pickering Fellowship recipient

RHODES

Rhodes Scholars are selected for two years of study at the University of Oxford in Great Britain, with the possibility of renewal for a third year.

"As I work on my present thesis, I find myself frequently drawing on my undergraduate thesis experience in the Burnett Honors College. In this I have a clear advantage over fellow students who did not have the opportunity to develop, write, and defend a substantial piece of research. Within the context of a large university, the Honors College promoted my personal interaction with distinguished faculty and provided access to world-class resources. The Burnett Honors College introduced me to those thinkers, both in texts and behind the lectern, whom I strive to emulate."

Tyler Fisher
University of Central Florida
Rhodes Scholar

ROTARY

The purpose of the Cultural Ambassadorial Scholarship Program is to further international understanding and friendly relations among people of different countries. The Program sponsors several types of scholarships for undergraduate and graduate students as well as for qualified professionals pursuing vocational studies. While abroad, scholars serve as ambassadors of goodwill to the people of the host country and give presentations about their homelands to Rotary clubs and other groups.

"In 2003, I received a Rotary Cultural Ambassadorial Scholarship to study the Costa Rican language and culture. I spent three months in San Jose, the capital of Costa Rica, living with a host family and attending super-intensive Spanish language training. It was thanks to the support and inspiration of Honors friends, the incredible enthusiasm of my Honors Director, and the knowledge and self-determination acquired through Honors classes, conferences, and activities that I was selected for the prestigious scholarship. Throughout my college career, Honors has taught me to constantly seek challenges and search beyond the surface. Honors has provided me with exceptional opportunities for growth that have made me a competitive candidate for the Rotary recognition. As part of the Honors Program, I have shared my insights and observations from Costa Rica at Columbia College and the National Collegiate Honors Conference, and I know that my achievements will be an inspiration to others. I am thankful to Rotary for the incredible opportunity and to Honors for giving me the self-confidence, recognition, and wisdom that I can now spread to friends and colleagues across the world."

Natalia Miteva
Columbia College, 2004
Rotary Cultural Ambassadorial Scholarship
recipient, 2003–04
NCHC "Student of the Year" Runner-up, 2003

TRUMAN

The Truman Scholarship is awarded to undergraduates who wish to attend graduate or professional school to prepare for careers in government or the nonprofit sector or elsewhere in public service.

"The Honors College challenged me and enriched my college education. The classes were hard, the professors brilliant, and the peers exceptional. It is such an undeniably creative place. I still brag about taking fascinating classes like Artists and Cadavers and Nutritional Anthropology. I will never forget getting to travel to France to paint for my thesis. It was such a golden chance to do something completely different and the college encouraged it. The support and guidance that the Honors College and Fellowships Office gave me while I was preparing for the Truman Scholarship competition made me feel valued. Winning the Truman Scholarship and the opportunities that came with it were truly life-changing."

Lara Bratcher
University of South Carolina, 2004
Truman Scholarship recipient, 2003
Glamour Magazine Top Ten College Women, 2003
ODK National Leader of the Year, 2004

UDALL

The Udall Scholarship provides for two types of students: (1) college sophomores and juniors studying the environment and related fields and (2) Native American and Alaska Native college sophomores and juniors in fields related to health care or tribal public policy.

"My studies focus on the effects of anthropogenic (human-induced) climate change on local environments. As a 2005 Udall Scholar in National Environmental Policy, my goal is to promote ecologically appropriate conservation and social policy based on sound evolving science. I have been given the opportunity to pursue extensive undergraduate research in this field, with the extensive encouragement and support of the university Honors College, through field research in Mongolia and upcoming field seasons in Kazakhstan and Greece."

Marion Sikora
University of Pittsburgh
Udall Scholarship recipient, 2005

Alumni Profiles

"My teachers from freshman year until my final semester challenged me to develop and defend ideas on a range of topics, from current issues to age-old controversies. We were expected to do more than just regurgitate selections from famous works or theories from political thinkers; instead, we participated, analyzed, and thought together in a creative learning process. This process was enriched by the way the Honors College has students from disparate majors and concentrations in the same environment, learning from each other's studies and interests, instead of specializing within our own majors after freshman year. When people ask me about my educational experience at the university, my answer is inextricably tied to my experiences in the Honors College—to the point where it is difficult to talk about my time at Ole Miss separate from the SMBHC."

Thomas Joel Rutherford Fyke
University of Mississippi, 2004
B.A., international studies
Truman Scholar, 2004

"The Honors Program has certainly prepared me for life in the Peace Corps as much as anything could. The focus in the seminars on diversity and service-learning helped me understand my desire to know more and serve humanity. The Honors senior seminar, *Construction of the Self*, is now helping me as I prepare to return to the U.S. and choose a career and life path.

The things that we were encouraged to think about, like the role of our families, biology, and our faith in who we are, have helped me decide how to shape my own life and self. As an Honors peer mentor, I had experience with leading a class, which was a good start for my teacher training here in the Peace Corps. But there are two things that are truly great about the Honors Program at Colorado State University. The first is the interdisciplinary approach: You cannot live in a single discipline, so you should not learn in a single discipline. The second is the people: Honors staff, professors, and students. You could not ask for a better community."

Mindy Simonson
Colorado State University
Peace Corps volunteer in Cameroon

National Collegiate Honors Council's Basic Characteristics of a Fully Developed Honors Program

No one model of an Honors Program can be superimposed on all types of institutions. However, there are characteristics that are common to successful, fully developed Honors Programs. Listed below are those characteristics, although not all characteristics are necessary for an Honors Program to be considered successful and/or fully developed.

1. A fully developed Honors Program should be carefully set up to accommodate the special needs and abilities of the undergraduate students it is designed to serve. This entails identifying the targeted student population by some clearly articulated set of criteria (e.g., GPA, SAT scores, a written essay). A Program with open admission needs to spell out expectations for retention in the Program and for satisfactory completion of Program requirements.

2. The Program should have a clear mandate from the institutional administration, ideally in the form of a mission statement, stating the objectives and responsibilities of the Program and defining its place in both the administrative and academic structure of the institution. This mandate or mission statement should ensure the permanence and stability of the Program by guaranteeing an adequate budget and by avoiding the tendency to force the Program to depend on temporary or spasmodic dedication of particular faculty members or administrators. In other words, the Program should be fully institutionalized so as to build a genuine tradition of excellence.

3. The Honors director should report to the chief academic officer of the institution.

4. There should be an Honors curriculum featuring special courses, seminars, colloquia, and independent study established in harmony with the mission statement and in response to the needs of the Program.

5. The Program requirements themselves should include a substantial portion of the participants' undergraduate work, usually about 20% or 25% of their total course work but certainly no less than 15%.

6. The Program should be so formulated that it relates effectively both to all the college work for the degree (e.g., by satisfying general education requirements) and to the area of concentration, departmental specialization, and preprofessional or professional training.

7. The Program should be both visible and highly reputed throughout the institution so that it is perceived as providing standards and models of excellence for students and faculty across the campus.

8. Faculty participating in the Program should be fully identified with the aims of the Program. They should be carefully selected on the basis of exceptional teaching skills and the ability to provide intellectual leadership to able students.

9. The Program should occupy suitable quarters constituting an Honors center with such facilities as an Honors library, lounge, reading rooms, personal computers, and other appropriate decor.

10. The director or other administrative officer charged with administering the Program should work in close collaboration with a committee or council of faculty members representing the colleges and/or departments served by the Program.

11. The Program should have in place a committee of Honors students to serve as liaison to the Honors faculty committee or council, which must keep the student group fully informed on the Program and elicit their cooperation in evaluation and development. This student group should enjoy as much autonomy as possible, conducting the business of the committee in representing the needs and concerns of all Honors students to the administration; it should also be included in governance, serving on the advisory/policy committee as well constituting the group that governs the student association.

12. There should be provisions for special academic counseling of Honors students by uniquely qualified faculty and/or staff personnel.

13. The Honors Program, in distinguishing itself from the rest of the institution, serves as a kind of laboratory within which faculty can try things they have always wanted to try but for which they could find no suitable outlet. When such efforts are demonstrated to be successful, they may well become institutionalized thereby raising the general level of education within the college or university for all students. In this connection, the Honors curriculum should serve as a prototype for educational practices that can work campuswide in the future.

14. The fully developed Honors Program must be open to continuous and critical review and be prepared to change in order to maintain its distinctive position of offering distinguished education to the best students at the institution.

15. A fully developed Program will emphasize the participatory nature of the Honors educational process by adopting such measures as offering opportunities for students to participate in regional and national conferences, Honors semesters, international programs, community service, and other forms of experiential education.

16. Fully developed two-year and four-year Honors Programs should have articulation agreements by which Honors graduates from two-year colleges can be accepted into four-year Honors Programs when they meet previously agreed-upon requirements.

Honors Programs and Honors Colleges: What's the Difference?

Dr. Peter C. Sederberg
Dean, South Carolina Honors College
University of South Carolina

Congratulations! If you are browsing through this guide, you are probably an academically talented and motivated student, searching for the best school to fulfill your educational ambitions. All the schools represented here offer enriched opportunities and challenges that promise to fulfill those goals. The variety of institutions, though, may seem daunting. In addition to the range of size, structure, and location of the hundreds of colleges and universities offering Honors opportunities, you probably noticed that they present themselves as being either an Honors "Program" or a "College." How should this difference affect your choice? Permit me a rather surprising answer: perhaps not that much.

Honors *Programs* have been around for decades. The Honors phenomenon really took off with the upsurge in demand for higher education after World War II. Elite private schools could not accommodate this demand nor could most students afford that path. Public higher education responded and, with the burgeoning growth in their student populations, began to experiment with enriched opportunities for their pool of talented students. Private schools below the "top tier" also responded by creating such opportunities, but, not surprisingly, Harvard and Yale did not.

Honors *Colleges*, however, are a much more recent trend. While a few have been around several decades, in a recent survey conducted on behalf of the National Collegiate Honors Council, 60 percent of the Honors Colleges responding had been established since 1994 and 80 percent grew out of a preexisting Honors Program. All the respondents reported that one of the primary motivations for the establishment of a College was to recruit stronger students, like you.

Unfortunately, you cannot presume that an Honors College is necessarily "better" than an Honors Program. You cannot even conclude that a "new" Honors College is significantly better than an "old" Honors Program. Apart from considerations of your fit with the overall institution, you will have to dig deeper to determine whether an Honors College is right for you. You may find, for example, when comparing roughly equivalent institutions, the Honors Program at one seems to offer the same opportunities as the Honors College at the other. No standards define minimum thresholds for claiming "College" status.

On a more positive note, in the same survey, nearly 89 percent of the Honors Colleges reported that another primary motivation behind their creation was to improve the quality of Honors educational opportunities. So you can look for certain characteristics that will help you evaluate your alternatives. Some Honors Colleges exist as largely, even completely, autonomous academic entities. Recently, some large community colleges have developed two-year Honors Colleges for their most talented students.

The following characteristics focus mainly on Honors Colleges within comprehensive universities, which is the dominant model.

- Honors Colleges tend to be located within universities. They represent one college in a diverse, multicollegiate institutional setting that includes colleges of arts and sciences, business, engineering, and so forth. Honors Colleges, therefore, offer students a wider range of undergraduate degree programs than those typically found at a four-year, liberal arts college.

- Honors Colleges tend to have a greater number of participants, as the Colleges are mainly located at comprehensive universities with a larger undergraduate population. In my survey, two thirds of the respondent Honors Colleges were part of a total undergraduate student population of 10,000 or more and had an Honors student body of at least 500. In short, Honors Colleges tend to be larger and more diverse, reflecting the institutions of which they are a part.

- In a university, a Dean typically heads the Honors College. This title may not mean much to you, but it does to the faculty. In my survey, 86 percent of the Colleges indicated that a third motivation for their establishment was to raise the profile of Honors education within their institution. Often the transformation to College status signifies that Honors education has moved from the periphery to the center of undergradu-

ate academics at that university. When the leader of Honors education becomes a dean, he or she now "sits at the table" with other deans and more directly participates in academic decision making. The change in title may also indicate that Honors educational opportunities have been enhanced.

How, though, might you figure out whether enhanced structural positioning led to expanded academic opportunities? Start by scrutinizing the publicity surrounding Honors Colleges in university settings and, for that matter, highly developed university Honors Programs. This publicity typically uses the phrase "the best of both worlds." With this phrase, the claim is that if you participate in the Honors College, you will enjoy some of the best characteristics of a small liberal arts college, while also drawing upon the resources of a comprehensive research university. The advantages of a research university include greater range of curriculum and undergraduate degree programs, more comprehensive research resources, and a more diverse and richer campus culture.

The real test of the "best of both worlds" claim is the extent to which an Honors College provides the experience of a high-quality liberal arts college: small classes, top teachers, exciting and personalized educational opportunities, and an intimate living-learning environment.

Oklahoma State University Honors College community service project with Habitat for Humanity.

- Size matters, but in a tricky way. How large is large enough, but not too large? A high-quality liberal arts college must reach a critical mass, but at some point, it could grow to a size that dilutes the intellectual intimacy commonly expected. The size of the overall undergraduate population also affects the range of appropriate size for the Honors College: in a university with 10,000 undergraduates, a College of 200 may be too small to hold its own and one of 2,000 may be too large to provide comprehensive academic opportunities for its students.

- Expect a university Honors College to offer Honors academic opportunities across all four years. Many Honors Colleges emerged from essentially lower-division Honors Programs. One goal of the transition probably was to extend this foundation across all four years. You should carefully assess the comprehensiveness and range of the Honors curriculum.

- High-quality liberal arts colleges require a senior thesis or project. Is this opportunity required, or even available, at the Honors Colleges you are investigating?

- Honors Colleges within a comprehensive university are uniquely placed to facilitate cross-disciplinary studies. Does the College you are considering offer opportunities for such study, perhaps including an interdisciplinary degree program?

- A highly developed Honors College in a university, with significant on-campus housing, should provide Honors residential opportunities. You must determine just how extensive these opportunities might be. Are they just for freshmen or do they exist across all four years? What percentage of Honors students can be accommodated in these communities?

- Universities, earnest in transitioning their Honors Program to Honors College, generally invest in upgraded Honors facilities and staffing. While "bricks and mortar" are secondary to the quality of Honors students, faculty, and instruction, they physically embody the seriousness of an institution's rhetoric. Prospective students need to carefully scrutinize the real academic resources of an Honors College relegated to shabby quarters on the fringe of the campus.

In addition to providing opportunities similar to those you might find at a liberal arts college, an Honors College at a comprehensive university claims an advantage over the typical liberal arts college: the resources of a comprehensive university. You must test the validity of this claim. The Honors College, for example, should cultivate Honors opportunities for the students who are in colleges, like engineering and business, which fall outside the traditional arts and sciences. Increasingly, these students make up a significant proportion of the undergraduate student body at universities, and a comprehensive Honors College should provide avenues for them to participate as well.

Honors Colleges are commonly located within universities that pride themselves on their research/scholarship mission. You should investigate how these opportunities are being cultivated in the Honors College and how avenues of undergraduate research and scholarship are created and supported.

My final point may strike you as a bit odd, since I have emphasized what you might expect from a highly developed Honors College. I also suggest that you investigate what an Honors College expects of you. When we made the transition from Program to College at the University of South Carolina, we not only increased what we offered the students but we also raised our admission and retention standards and enhanced what students would be expected to accomplish to earn our Honors distinction. An Honors College that fails to do these things may well be swamped by enrollment growth resulting only from their high-profile recruitment campaign.

Two Plus Two Equals a Winning Combination

Dr. Lydia Lyons
Director, Honors Institute
Hillsborough Community College

For any freshman, starting college can be an extremely exciting, but sometimes frightening, experience. All freshmen can be overwhelmed by new social freedoms. Honors Programs and Colleges across the nation offer some very special opportunities for their talented students to ease into college, bolstered by the sense of community that comes from the Honors environment. One option that many thousands of students have benefited from is to spend the first two years of the university experience in a community college Honors Program and then transfer to a university of choice.

Smaller classes, combined with lower tuition, are motivating factors in students' college decision processes. Community colleges are typically charged with being teaching institutions that focus on the first two years; therefore, community colleges' regular courses tend to be capped at smaller numbers than classes in large four-year institutions. However, Honors students often worry that the community colleges' open-door policy may not meet their needs for challenging curricula. Many Honors students, who have worked hard for outstanding grades in high school academic courses and performed well on college placement tests, believe that if they choose a community college, they will be letting themselves, their parents, and even their friends down. Those students will do well, as thousands of Honors students before them have, to research the opportunities offered by Honors Programs in community colleges.

Rather than starting college away from home, students beginning at community colleges typically still live with their families because few community colleges have dormitories. They are not as likely to be lost in "freedom land" when they are still living at home. The financial advantage of living at home is obvious, but after completing their first two years and general education requirements, students also transfer with increased confidence and maturity. For Damir Sinovcic, a student in my own Program, the skills he learned at his community college's Honors Institute became a solid foundation upon which he could successfully build his bachelor's, and later his master's, degree. Damir understood that

> *Transferring to another school is a life-altering experience. It challenges students to adapt to new environments with the skills learned at their previous institution.*

For Damir, this meant relocation to a different city, meeting new people, completing his education, and later starting a professional career. Regardless of where students begin their college experiences, they will be taking general education courses and some electives. Majors are not declared until junior year. For students in community colleges, identifying the majors and completing the prerequisites for those majors are important activities usually overseen in the Honors Programs. Honors directors are very aware of the importance of their students' being active and having exposure to a variety of academic and social opportunities. Within the secu-

Damir Sinovcic teaching a class.

rity of the community colleges' Honors Programs, students can truly become risk takers, leading them to examine their world and themselves, further leading to the maturity and confidence that universities find attractive in transfer students. One of my students, Roopal Mehta, emphasizes that

> My community college experience played a central role in my development as an individual. At the Honors Institute, I found myself undergoing a transformation from self-centeredness to global awareness. In my different classes, I learned to analyze contextually different philosophies, works, and movements. The application of academic and intellectual skills through my research changed my perception and treatment of human beings, whether in school or community. Now, as a student of Wellesley College, I have constructed an individual major in Asian development studies, with a concentration in economic development. My hope is to be a part of a collaborative initiative financing rural development efforts in China and India.

Many four-year institutions have deliberately cultivated relationships with community colleges to provide a seamless transition. They accept all or most of the credits earned in the A.A. degree, offer transfer scholarships, and encourage eligible students to continue their Honors education or begin a new Honors experience. Lori Langdon, who graduated from North Harris College, writes

> In June of 2002, I was awarded the Jack Ken Cooke Foundation Transfer Scholarship. I believe this was due largely to my involvement in the Honors Program . . . When I transferred to my senior institution, I was more than prepared for participation in their Honors Program.

Students around the country have similar transition experiences and have gone on to equally great achievements. Desirée Gonzales of Pueblo Community College notes

> When I initially enrolled in college, I had decided to set what I considered reasonable and attainable goals. At that time, it meant an Associate Degree in paralegal studies at my local community college. I was sure that would suffice as a career goal—until I was recognized by the Honors Program adviser and selected as one of only eight students to participate in the introductory year of the Program. Nothing motivates a student more than recognition of this type, and my selection to the Honors Program eliminated all previous insecurities about my abilities and limitations. As a result of this highly respected instructor and his initiation of this Program, I have gained the confidence to pursue more challenging career goals.

> In the fall, I will begin pursuing a Juris Doctor degree, enrolling in my local university's prelaw program.

At the C. W. Post Campus of Long Island University, community college transfer students are among recent award winners and nominees. John Giacco, a graduating senior in criminal justice, has won the two-year participation award for his groundbreaking research on incarcerated women. Standing next to him at the ceremony was Jacqueline De Rosa, who won the Honors thesis prize for her original drama based on characters in American fiction. Stephen Wolf, a marketing major, has just completed his project on Starbucks and how it was able to transform a routine 99-cent purchase into a $4 experience. Indeed, community college students shine as stars in the four-year Honors setting. Unfortunately, many students and parents do not realize that most universities, including the Ivy Leagues, welcome transfer students, as they show themselves to have clear focus and drive. Community college graduates have proven that they have the academic ability to succeed. Therefore, universities often have large financial packages to entice transfer students coming from two-year colleges.

Wherever Honors students want to graduate from, they should consider beginning in a community college Honors Program. Not only will this ease the financial burden for the first two years of college, but it may also afford students such unique opportunities as cultural trips abroad. I have taken students to China, Ecuador, Greece, and Russia—eye-opening experiences subsidized by the College. A great diversity of cultural opportunities exists in many community colleges, which is all the more reason I encourage you to put two and two together for a great undergraduate Honors education.

Lawyer-to-be Desirée Gonzales.

Value Added:
On the Road with NCHC

Dr. Bernice Braid
Dean, Academic/Instructional Resources
Director, University Honors
Long Island University, Brooklyn Campus
Chair, NCHC Honors Semesters Committee

Honors Programs everywhere offer enhanced educational experiences, designed to deepen and broaden the insights of students with imagination, energy, and a sense of adventure. The chance to be an active representative of your own Honors Program in one of the many adventures hosted or cosponsored by The National Collegiate Honors Council is an opportunity not to be missed!

Let's take meetings. Regional meetings are scheduled in the spring, and your university belongs to one of six regional Honors organizations that are NCHC partners. National conferences take place in the fall. Both meeting circuits move around a lot. Attending conferences, whether to pick up ideas for your own Program, participate on a panel, or present a paper or poster, gives you the chance to not only meet students from up to forty-nine other states but also to explore new cities and sites throughout the country.

Some sessions are designed to help small teams of students and faculty map new territories. NCHC calls these adventures City as Text©. They are regular features of meetings structured to introduce methods of exploration that students can pursue both in their own Programs and in many NCHC projects. New Orleans, Chicago, St. Louis, San Francisco, Philadelphia—cities large and larger—have offered Honors students and faculty an invitation to hit the streets, eat new food, find out about neighborhood treasures and resources, and talk to local folks to get behind the public rhetoric of each site. In this process, teams begin to discover what REALLY makes these places tick and what it feels like to live, work, and play in each of these cities.

Extended Programs built on such principles of exploration are continuing projects of NCHC, which

After receiving his Cambridge degree, Villanova University's Ryan Costella plans to pursue a career involving relations between the United States and China.

cosponsors and hosts Semesters and Mini-semesters, opening doors to the world in places such as Greece, the Czech Republic, Spain, Mexico, Puerto Rico, New York City, Washington, DC, Appalachia, El Paso, Maine, and London. Twenty-seven of these extraordinary invitations-to-discovery have taken place so far and many more are in the works. Each provides a chance to

Christina Won, Long Island University, Brooklyn Campus, presents her paper on "The Modern Use of Medicinal Plants on the Eastern Aegean Island of Psara, Greece" at the North-East Regional Honors Society, 2005.

probe a theme—world hunger, local culture, city planning—and/or a way of probing a theme—uncovering, as in being a detective, and testing, as in seeing how "systems" work when embedded in the environments they are meant to protect. Each provides field laboratories in which participants chart a course and figure out how to follow it to interesting conclusions. Each setting presents new challenges—snorkeling off the East Coast or folklore studies conducted while snowed-in among the North Carolina mountains—and reveals secrets as students ask: What are the real boundaries between neighborhoods and cultures?

These are intense and heightened experiences for all who undertake them. Everyone who has been in an NCHC Semester has talked about the challenges, adventures, and triumphs. Above all, they talk about change—change in how they see the world and themselves by the end of the experience. NCHC provides a meta-experience for undergraduates through these projects. Students take all they can from their home setting into this new and foreign one. And then they take a new self and lots of fresh perceptions back into their home setting.

As one student from the 2001 "Reinventing Urban Culture: A National Collegiate Honors Council Honors Semester" at Long Island University, Brooklyn Campus, put it:

> Nowhere is normal here. No two communities are alike. Chinatown is as different from nearby Greenwich Village as Forest Hills Gardens is from midtown Manhattan. There is no epitome district here. If anything, I'm surprised that I haven't completely come to expect the unexpected, since that's what it's been so much about: the bizarre, the random, the unexpected.

What NCHC promises you is that if you join one of these experiments in exploration, you will not see the world the same again, ever, and it will feel as though you yourself have been reinvented.

Students engaged in sugar cane testing at the 2004 Coastal Honors Semester, cosponsored by NCHC and Hood College.

Travels with Charley and Mike and Becky and Nina and Melissa and Tauheed and Johanna and Matt and John and . . .

Dr. Katherine E. Bruce
Director, Honors Scholars Program
University of North Carolina at Wilmington

One of the benefits of Honors Programs and Colleges is that they encourage travel as a vehicle for learning. City as Text and the Honors Semesters are striking examples of this experiential learning approach. In addition, it is quite common to find that Honors courses at many schools and universities have field trips or longer excursions as components of the classes. Because class sizes are typically small in Honors courses and because experiential learning is so valued, travel is encouraged and relatively feasible.

The key feature of classes that involve extended travel is that the students and professor spend class time and out-of-class time preparing for the trip. Typically, the class is organized around a theme and students research the destination, culture, history, or whatever aspect is of particular interest. A common pedagogy is to have students explore aspects of the theme and location and present this information to the rest of the class. Students then become experts on a specific topic and find that others look to them for guidance on the trip itself. Thus, they do not just "happen" into a location and take what comes. By preparing for the journey, they then seek out particular locations, people, and animals and explore those aspects to the fullest. Honors students and instructors take their traveling seriously; traveling is an avenue to experience a subject and theme in a personal and significant way.

At the University of North Carolina at Wilmington, we have tried to offer at least one Honors experiential seminar every spring that included an international trip. This trip is often the first international plunge for

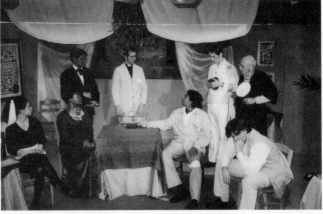

Honors Program students and faculty at Fairleigh Dickinson University in a performance of Murder on the Nile.

students and it is fortunate that many of them get the bug to learn through travel in these affordable classes. As a psychology faculty member teaching in Honors, I have traveled with Honors students to a number of exotic and no-so-exotic locations—our local roadside zoo, the Outer Banks of North Carolina, the Amazon Basin in Ecuador, and the Galapagos Islands—to study animal behavior and related topics. Without a doubt, the international travel has been the most meaningful, for a variety of reasons. With travel to the Amazon Basin and the Galapagos Islands, some students were living out lifelong dreams—traveling to places that they thought they might never see. (And for a few students, these international trips have involved first plane rides!) They often had particular themes already in mind, not just the theme of the class: a bent toward ecotourism as a career, pursing legal ramifications of offshore oil production, or understanding shamanism.

These personal dimensions always create a rich fabric for learning. For example, because of one student's particular interest in, and background research on, shamanism, we were able to add a daytrip to meet a local shaman and experience a curing ceremony as part of the Amazon Basin course. The research conducted by each student in preparation for the class and the trip was unique and, even though I was technically an instructor, I became a student. Everyone in this type of class benefits from the diverse perspectives and expectations.

The sense of community built on such a trip is remarkable. The adventures are not all positive ones: luggage gets lost and there are missed connections, lost passports, allergic reactions, pickpockets, lumpy beds, and long bus rides. However, we work through the rough spots and come out the better for it. From reading the journals students have kept, it is evident that they thrive on the spirit of community as well. Reticent students find new voices via shared experiences; extroverted students learn to listen to the discoveries made by others. Traveling with Honors students creates shared picture-perfect moments and memories and lifelong friendships.

Just another day in London for University of North Carolina Greensboro International Honors College students.

Honors: A Community for Life

Dr. Ada Long
University of Alabama at Birmingham
Editor, *Journal of the National Collegiate Honors Council*
and *Honors in Practice*

Students who join our Honors Program become members of our academic community not just for the next four years but, in most cases, for life, and I suspect the same is true for most Honors Programs. After our students graduate, they serve as mentors; participate in frequent reunions; help each other find scholarships, jobs, and housing; provide moral and financial support; and visit the Honors House whenever they're in the neighborhood. This community provides a sense of belonging and stability that helps each student find his or her bearings in an educational environment dedicated to challenge and change.

Today, many students see college as putting in time before they get to their "real lives" of life after college. Honors Programs are designed for the "other" students—those who see college as real life: a place and a time in their lives not just to prepare themselves for a career, but to learn about themselves and others, seek wisdom as well as knowledge, explore the unknown, and find what most excites them so that they may maintain this excitement for the rest of their lives. Above all, these students want to find a way to make a difference and leave a mark that is uniquely theirs.

What I think makes Honors Programs most honorable is their commitment to honoring the distinct gifts of their students within a context of high expectations. And what makes directing an Honors Program the best job in academia is watching those gifts develop, deepen, and then go to work in the world. Each student who has entered our Program has a story that illustrates this process—here are four.

Kellie skipped her senior year in high school and started college when she was 16. For an upper-level Honors project, she did a study of homelessness that included two weeks of living on the street and in shelters (scaring the daylights out of me and her parents—we checked on her constantly), leading to an extraordinarily moving and informative analysis of the

The Pennsylvania State University's Tom Bowler began his Fulbright Grant as an English teacher in a South Korean middle school.

daily lives of homeless women in Birmingham. She received a Truman Scholarship, which funded her last two years at the University of Alabama at Birmingham, and earned her master's degree at Johns Hopkins University. Since then, she has worked as a consultant for employment services for the homeless in Washington, DC, and traveled all over the world as a labor consultant. She is now in her second year of law school at Georgetown. Kellie helps all our students who are interested in public service careers, serves as an outside adviser on research projects, and spends every New Year's Eve at my house catching me up on the work she has done in Bulgaria and elsewhere.

I met Cedric when he was a student in my remedial English class. An immensely gifted and original young man, he was struggling to make up for twelve years in a rural Alabama school system. I invited him into the Honors Program, where he quickly became a favorite of his classmates. When he graduated, he took a test for the management training program at State Farm Insurance. An executive at State Farm called me to say that nobody from Cedric's county had ever performed so well on the test. Cedric married another student in the Honors Program (she is now a pediatrician), they have 2 sons, and they are regular visitors at the Honors House.

Katie was an anthropology major at UAB. During the summer, she went to Bali with her adviser to study macaques. She married a fellow Honors student, an engineering major, at the Honors House. The two of them moved to New York where Katie received a National Science Foundation Fellowship to study for her Ph.D. at the City University of New York (CUNY). She spent much of her time as a doctoral student studying chimpanzees in Cameroon (her work has been written up in the *New York Times*) while her husband was updating computer hardware for the National Oceanic and Atmospheric Administration at the South Pole. Now she is a post-doc at the NIH and he is a rocket scientist (for real). Both are regular mentors and research advisers for current students.

Andria joined the Honors Program after a 25-year career as a mother and retail sales manager. She was locally elected as a student representative on the Honors Council and nationally elected to serve on the Executive Committee of the National Collegiate Honors Council. She became an important mother figure to all the college-age students in the Honors Program, while at the same time doing excellent work within her major, English. Within weeks of graduating from UAB, she got a job at *Southern Living*, where she is now Foods Editor. Three months ago, she was appointed to the University of Alabama System's Board of Trustees; so she is now my boss, as well as close friend. Andria has long served on the Advisory Board of the Honors Program, has given at least five guest lectures, and has helped numerous students find internships and employment.

Many of our other Honors students have become lawyers, doctors, accountants, and every other kind of profession. When I or any of our students need any kind of service, there are always alumni out there to provide it. Our students—past, present, and future— contribute their unique gifts not just to the world at large, but to each other, helping to maintain a community that is always changing but always there as a home base. It is a community that is now global as well as local and welcomes each new student as an individual, as well a member of a shared lifelong support network. Surely this is what education is supposed to be, and it is what Honors Programs throughout the country foster in their special role in higher education.

Speaking as a Parent to Parents

John S. Grady
Director, University Honors Program
La Salle University

Having experienced the college selection process firsthand as a parent of 5 children, each of whom is a graduate of the La Salle University Honors Program, I can appreciate some of your concerns. Given the intellectual talents your child has demonstrated, the task of college selection can be even more formidable. In addition to addressing that challenge, I have attempted to respond to other parents' concerns throughout the three decades I have served as an Honors Program Director. With this dual perspective of parent and director, I hope what follows proves to be helpful.

Although each parent has concerns specific to his or her child and situation, I believe there are four major ones that parents and students have mentioned consistently over the years. In no particular order of importance, they are:

- the fear of taking on too much, too soon with participation in an Honors Program

- the fear of being labeled "elitist"

- the desire to participate to the fullest in the total undergraduate experience

- the parent's natural desire to be kept informed of the student's progress

Some students will be apprehensive about taking on the challenge participation in Honors presents. They might question their ability to compete with some of the most intellectually gifted students on the campus. But, if you reflect for a minute and recall their track record, these are students who have established a pattern of willingness to accept academic risks. They have been challenged by the best at every level and they have succeeded. Quite possibly, one of the factors that contributed significantly to that success was their acceptance of that challenge. Their history is not to be denied and, other things being equal, there is every reason to believe they will continue to excel at this next level.

No one would deny that different people have been blessed with different talents, and many have exceptional talents. There are differences among individuals and we would be remiss if we did not recognize and address them. Colleges and universities have long recognized differences in physical and athletic abilities. Some gifted athletes participate at one level, others less gifted at a somewhat different level. Is this anything more than the recognition and addressing of different endowments? Should this be any less true when the gifts are intellectual? That some students, such as your child, possess these intellectual gifts—that they constitute an academic elite, if you will—is simply a fact. One of the purposes of an Honors Program is to recognize this fact and provide those students with the means necessary to develop their talents. I do not see this as being elitist; I see it as being responsible.

If you examine the structure of most Honors Programs carefully, you will recognize that, in all cases, a student is only "part-time" in Honors. Typically, an Honors Program student will be completing core or general education requirements in Honors while pursuing major courses and electives in the general curriculum. Such a structure belies identification as separatist, since the vast majority of the students' class time will be outside Honors. Rather than encouraging withdrawal from the full undergraduate experience, the Honors Program student is encouraged to lead in broad areas that will further develop talents. Ironically, then, the Honors Program student is both part of the full community and the Honors community, reaping the varied benefits of full participation in each. Indeed, Honors Program students have been exceptional at building bridges that unite. Again, in most cases, this has been simply one more extension of a student's prior academic history.

For many, a child's advancement to college represents the first extended separation from family. As a parent or guardian, we want to be kept apprised of progress, as well as difficulty; we want to continue to parent. While this can certainly be accomplished, you must be cognizant of limitations imposed by law. Since most college students have reached the age of 18, their right to privacy, including college activities in and out of the classroom, is protected by law. As a professor or as an Honors Program Director, I am not permitted to reveal your child's academic, social, disciplinary, etc., records to you without his or her permission. So, as a parent like you, I want every possible assurance the environment in which my child will learn, socialize, and grow will be a nurturing and caring one, one that addresses the development of the whole person, as well as demanding the best of that person. This is what we attempt to create in the Honors communities.

I would like to conclude, as I began, on a personal note. Having seen more than 1,600 students complete their Honors education and move on to successful careers and productive lives has been most rewarding. This has been particularly so in the case of my own children, who often speak to how valuable their Honors experience was in strengthening their values and shaping their careers. My two daughters completed their legal studies and are now attorneys with major national law firms—one specializing in litigation and the other in employment law. One son had been a prosecutor for five years and now has his own practice; his brother completed his M.P.P. degree and works in economic development. Given my own experience, there is no doubt in my mind that the Honors Program experience was the best possible alternative to *in loco parentis*.

How to Use This Guide

QUICK-REFERENCE CHART

"Honors Colleges and Programs At-a-Glance" gives you an overview of all the Honors options contained in this guide. It can help you focus your choices in reading through the nearly 600 Honors Programs and Honors Colleges descriptions.

> **2** = Program is part of a two-year institution
> **4** = Program is part of a four-year institution
> **Pu** = public or state institution
> **Pr** = private college or university
> **G** = general Honors Program
> **D** = departmental Honors Program
> **Small** = Honors Program is under 100 students
> **Medium** = Honors Program is 100–500 students
> **Large** = Honors Program is more than 500 students
> **SC** = scholarships are available through the Honors Program
> **TR** = transfer students accepted
> **HBC** = categorized as a historically black college
> **AA** = Honors Program has special Honors academic advisers
> **GA** = Honors Program has special Honors graduate advisers
> **FA** = Honors Program has special Honors fellowship advisers

PROFILES OF HONORS PROGRAMS AND COLLEGES

Each entry is written by the Honors director or dean, providing such essential information as how long the Program or College has been in existence, how many Honors students are enrolled, what kinds of courses are offered, and what special features constitute Honors student life. Each description includes admissions and participation requirements. In the second section of each entry entitled, "Campus Overview," the publisher, Thomson Peterson's, has provided a description of the college or university as a whole, including cost of tuition and fees, as well as room and board. Finally, each entry ends with contact information and Web and e-mail addresses.

CAMPUS OVERVIEW

The "Campus Overview" contains basic data in capsule form for quick review and comparison. The following outline of the "Campus Overview" format shows the section headings and the items that each section covers. Any item that does not apply to a particular college or for which no information was supplied is omitted from that college's profile.

First Highlight

Institutional control: Each institution is classified as one of the following:

- **Private** institutions are designated as independent (nonprofit), proprietary (profit-making), or independent, with a specific religious denomination or affiliation. Nondenominational or interdenominational religious orientation is possible and would be indicated.

- **Public** institutions are designated by the source of funding. Designations include federal, state, province, commonwealth (Puerto Rico), territory (U.S. territories), county, district (an educational administrative unit often having boundaries different from units of local government), city, state and local (local may refer to county, district, or city), or state-related (funded primarily by the state but administratively autonomous).

Religious affiliation is also noted here.

Institutional type: Each institution is classified as one of the following:

- **Primarily two-year college:** Awards baccalaureate degrees, but the vast majority of students are enrolled in two-year programs.

- **Four-year college:** Awards baccalaureate degrees; may also award associate degrees; does not award graduate (postbaccalaureate) degrees.

- **Five-year college:** Awards a five-year baccalaureate in a professional field such as architecture or pharmacy; does not award graduate degrees.

- **Upper-level institution:** Awards baccalaureate degrees, but entering students must have at least two years of previous college-level credit; may also offer graduate degrees.

- **Comprehensive institution:** Awards baccalaureate degrees; may also award associate degrees; offers graduate degree programs, primarily at the master's, specialist's, or professional level, although one or two doctoral programs may be offered.

- **University:** Offers four years of undergraduate work plus graduate degrees through the doctorate in more than two academic or professional fields.

Founding date: If the year an institution was chartered differs from the year when instruction actually began, the earlier date is given.

System or administrative affiliation: Any coordinate institutions or system affiliations are indicated. An institution that has separate colleges or campuses for men and women but shares facilities and courses is termed a coordinate institution. A formal administrative grouping of institutions, either private or public, of which the college is a part, or the name of a single institution with which the college is administratively affiliated, is a system.

Second Highlight
Schools are designated as **urban** (located within a major city), **suburban** (a residential area within commuting distance of a major city), **small-town** (a small but compactly settled area not within commuting distance of a major city), or **rural** (a remote and sparsely populated area). The phrase *easy access to . . .* indicates that the campus is within an hour's drive of the nearest major metropolitan area that has a population greater than 500,000.

Third Highlight
Student body: An institution is **coed** (coeducational— admits men and women), **primarily** (80 percent or more) **women**, **primarily men**, **women only**, or **men only**.

Undergraduate students: Represents the number of full-time and part-time students enrolled in undergraduate degree programs as of fall 2004. The percentage of full-time undergraduates and the percentages of men and women are given.

Undergraduates
For fall 2004, the number of full- and part-time undergraduate students is listed. This list provides the number of states and U.S. territories, including the

District of Columbia and Puerto Rico (or, for Canadian institutions, provinces and territories), and other countries from which undergraduates come. Percentages are given of undergraduates who are from out of state; Native American, African American, and Asian American or Pacific Islander; international students; transfer students; and living on campus.

Faculty
Total: The total number of faculty members, the percentage of full-time faculty members, and the percentage of full-time faculty members who hold doctoral/first professional/terminal degrees are listed.

Student-faculty ratio: The school's estimate of the ratio of matriculated undergraduate students to faculty members teaching undergraduate courses.

Academic Programs
Details are given here on study options available at each college.

- **Accelerated degree program:** Students may earn a bachelor's degree in three academic years.

- **Academic remediation for entering students:** Instructional courses designed for students deficient in the general competencies necessary for a regular postsecondary curriculum and educational setting.

- **Adult/continuing education programs:** Courses offered for nontraditional students who are currently working or are returning to formal education.

- **Advanced Placement:** Credit toward a degree awarded for acceptable scores on College Board Advanced Placement (AP) tests.

- **Cooperative (co-op) education programs:** Formal arrangements with off-campus employers allowing students to combine work and study in order to gain degree-related experience, usually extending the time required to complete a degree.

- **Distance learning:** For-credit courses that can be accessed off-campus via cable television, the Internet, satellite, videotape, correspondence course, or other media.

- **Double major:** A program of study in which a student concurrently completes the requirements of two majors.

- **English as a second language (ESL):** A course of study designed specifically for students whose native language is not English.

- **External degree programs:** A program of study in which students earn credits toward a degree through a combination of independent study, college courses, proficiency examinations, and personal experience. External degree programs require minimal or no classroom attendance.

- **Freshmen honors college:** A separate academic program for talented freshmen.

- **Honors programs:** Any special program for very able students offering the opportunity for educational enrichment, independent study, acceleration, or some combination of these.

- **Independent study:** Academic work, usually undertaken outside the regular classroom structure, chosen or designed by the student with departmental approval and instructor supervision.

- **Internships:** Any short-term, supervised work experience usually related to a student's major field, for which the student earns academic credit. The work can be full- or part-time, on- or off-campus, paid or unpaid.

- **Off-campus study:** A formal arrangement with one or more domestic institutions under which students may take courses at the other institution(s) for credit.

- **Part-time degree program:** Students may earn a degree through part-time enrollment in regular session (daytime) classes or evening, weekend, or summer classes.

- **Self-designed major:** Program of study based on individual interests, designed by the student with the assistance of an adviser.

- **Services for LD students:** Special help for learning-disabled students with resolvable difficulties, such as dyslexia.

- **Study abroad:** An arrangement by which a student completes part of the academic program studying in another country. A college may operate a campus abroad or it may have a cooperative agreement with other U.S. institutions or institutions in other countries.

- **Summer session for credit:** Summer courses through which students may make up degree work or accelerate their program.

- **Tutorials:** Undergraduates can arrange for special in-depth academic assignments (not for remediation) working with faculty members one-on-one or in small groups.

- **ROTC:** Army, Naval, or Air Force Reserve Officers' Training Corps programs offered either on campus, at a branch campus [designated by a (b)], or at a cooperating host institution [designated by (c)].

- **Unusual degree programs:** Nontraditional programs such as a 3-2 degree program, in which 3 years of liberal arts study is followed by 2 years of study in a professional field at another institution (or in a professional division of the same institution), resulting in two bachelor's degrees or a bachelor's and a master's degree.

Athletics

Membership in one or more of the following athletic associations is indicated by initials:

- **NCAA:** National Collegiate Athletic Association

- **NAIA:** National Association of Intercollegiate Athletics

- **NCCAA:** National Christian College Athletic Association

- **NSCAA:** National Small College Athletic Association

- **NJCAA:** National Junior College Athletic Association

- **CIS:** Canadian Interuniversity Sports

The overall NCAA division in which all or most intercollegiate teams compete is designated by roman numeral I, II, or III. All teams that do not compete in this division are listed as exceptions.

Sports offered by the college are divided into two groups: **intercollegiate** (**M** or **W** following the name of each sport indicates that it is offered for men or women) and **intramural**. An **s** in parentheses following an **M** or **W** for an intercollegiate sport indicates that athletic scholarships (or grants-in-aid) are offered for men or women in that sport, and a **c** indicates a club team as opposed to a varsity team.

Costs

Costs are given for the 2005–06 academic year or for the 2004–05 academic year if 2005–06 figures were not yet available. Annual expenses may be expressed as a comprehensive fee (including full-time tuition, mandatory fees, and college room and board) or as separate figures for full-time tuition, fees, room and board, or room only. For public institutions where tuition differs according to residence, separate figures are given for area or state residents and for nonresidents. Part-time tuition is expressed in terms of a per-unit rate (per credit, per semester hour, etc.) as specified by the institution.

The tuition structure at some institutions is complex in that freshmen and sophomores may be charged a different rate from that for juniors and seniors, a professional or vocational division may have a different fee structure from the liberal arts division of the same institution, or part-time tuition may be prorated on a sliding scale according to the number of credit hours taken. Tuition and fees may vary according to academic program, campus/location, class time (day, evening, weekend), course/credit load, course level, degree level, reciprocity agreements, and student level. Room and board charges are reported as an average for one academic year and may vary according to the board plan selected, campus/location, type of housing facility, or student level.

Tuition payment plans that may be offered to undergraduates include tuition prepayment, installment payments, and deferred payment. A tuition prepayment plan gives a student the option of locking in the current tuition rate for the entire term of enrollment by paying the full amount in advance rather than year by year. Colleges that offer such a prepayment plan may also help the student to arrange financing.

The availability of full or partial undergraduate tuition waivers to minority students, children of alumni, employees or their children, adult students, and senior citizens may be listed.

Financial Aid

Financial aid information presented represents aid awarded to undergraduates for the 2003–04 or 2004–05 academic year. The number of Federal Work-Study and/or part-time jobs and average earnings are listed, as are the number of non-need-based awards that were made. Non-need-based awards are college-administered scholarships for which the college determines the recipient and amount of each award. These scholarships are awarded to full-time undergraduates on the basis of merit or personal attributes without regard to need, although they may be given to students who also happen to need aid. The average percent of need met for those determined to have need, the average financial aid package awarded to undergraduates (the amount of scholarships, grants, work-study payments, or loans (excluding PLUS) in the institutionally administered financial aid package divided by the number of students who received any financial aid), the average amount of need-based gift aid, and the average amount of non-need-based aid are given.

Contact

The name, title, and address of the Honors Program or Honors College contact are listed. In addition, if available, the telephone and fax numbers and e-mail and Web site addresses are also listed.

INDEX

The "Alphabetical Listing" allows you to quickly find a school by name.

DATA COLLECTION PROCEDURES

The data contained in the "Campus Overview" were researched between fall 2004 and spring 2005 through *Thomson Peterson's Annual Survey of Undergraduate Institutions*. Questionnaires were sent to the more than 2,000 colleges and universities that met the outlined inclusion criteria. All data included in this edition have been submitted by officials (usually admissions and financial aid officers, registrars, or institutional research personnel) at the colleges. In addition, many of the institutions that submitted data were contacted directly by the Thomson Peterson's research staff to verify unusual figures, resolve discrepancies, or obtain additional data. All usable information received in time for publication has been included. The omission of any particular item from the Campus Overview listing signifies that the information is either not applicable to that institution or not available. Because of Thomson Peterson's comprehensive editorial review and because all material comes directly from college officials, we believe that the information presented in the "Campus Overview" is guide is accurate. You should check with a specific college or university at the time of application to verify such figures as tuition and fees, which may have changed since the publication of this guide.

Quick-Reference Chart

Honors Programs and Colleges At-a-Glance

Name	Page Number	2-Year College	4-Year College	Public or State College	Private College	General Honors Program	Departmental Honors Program	Small Program (fewer than 100 students)	Midsize Program (100 to 500 students)	Large Program (more than 500 students)	Scholarships Available	Transfer Students Accepted	Historically Black College	Academic Advisers	Graduate Advisers	Fellowship Advisers
Abilene Christian University, Abilene, TX	492		X		X	X			X			X				
Adelphi University, Garden City, NY	327		X		X	X			X		X	X		X		
Albany State University, Albany, GA	153		X	X		X			X			X	X	X		
Albertus Magnus College, New Haven, CT	121		X		X	X	X					X		X		
Albion College, Albion, MI	265		X		X	X			X		X	X				
Alcorn State University, Alcorn State, MS	284		X	X		X			X		X	X	X			
Alfred University, Alfred, NY	328		X		X	X			X			X				
Allegany College of Maryland, Cumberland, MD	238	X		X		X		X			X	X				
Alvernia College, Reading, PA	429		X		X	X			X			X				
American River College, Sacramento, CA	92	X		X		X		X			X	X				
American University, Washington, DC	131		X		X	X			X		X	X				
Angelo State University, San Angelo, TX	493		X	X		X		X						X		
Appalachian State University, Boone, NC	375		X	X			X		X		X	X				
Arcadia University, Glenside, PA	430		X		X	X		X				X				
Arizona State University, Tempe, AZ	75		X	X						X	X	X		X		X
Arizona Western College, Yuma, AZ	76	X		X		X					X	X	X			
Arkansas State University, State University, AR	83		X	X		X		X			X	X				X
Arkansas Tech University, Russellville, AR	84		X	X		X					X	X		X		
Auburn University, Auburn University, AL	65		X	X						X	X	X				
Augusta State University, Augusta, GA	154		X	X		X						X				
Azusa Pacific University, Azusa, CA	92		X		X	X		X								
Ball State University, Muncie, IN	197		X	X		X	X		X			X		X		
Baylor University, Waco, TX	494		X		X	X			X		X	X		X		X
Bellarmine University, Louisville, KY	221		X		X	X		X			X	X		X		
Belmont University, Nashville, TN	481		X		X	X		X				X				
Bergen Community College, Paramus, NJ	312	X		X		X		X						X		
Bernard M. Baruch College of the City University of New York, New York, NY	329		X	X		X		X			X	X		X		
Berry College, Mount Berry, GA	155		X		X	X		X				X				
Birmingham-Southern College, Birmingham, AL	65		X		X	X	X					X				
Blinn College, Brenham, TX	495	X		X		X	X				X	X				
Bloomsburg University of Pennsylvania, Bloomsburg, PA	430		X	X		X			X		X	X				
Boise State University, Boise, ID	169		X	X		X	X				X	X				
Bowie State University, Bowie, MD	238		X	X			X				X	X	X		X	
Brenau University, Gainesville, GA	155		X		X	X		X				X				
Brevard Community College, Cocoa, FL	133	X		X		X			X		X	X		X		
Bridgewater State College, Bridgewater, MA	250		X	X		X	X		X			X				
Brigham Young University, Provo, UT	525		X		X	X				X		X		X		X
Brigham Young University–Hawaii, Laie, HI	168		X		X	X		X				X				

HONORS PROGRAMS AND COLLEGES AT-A-GLANCE

Name	Page Number	2-Year College	4-Year College	Public or State College	Private College	General Honors Program	Departmental Honors Program	Small Program (fewer than 100 students)	Midsize Program (100 to 500 students)	Large Program (more than 500 students)	Scholarships Available	Transfer Students Accepted	Historically Black College	Academic Advisers	Graduate Advisers	Fellowship Advisers
Brooklyn College of the City University of New York, Brooklyn, NY	330		X	X		X			X		X	X		X		X
Broome Community College, Binghamton, NY	331	X		X		X		X			X					
Broward Community College, Fort Lauderdale, FL	134	X		X		X				X	X	X				
Bryant University, Smithfield, RI	467		X		X	X		X			X					
Butler University, Indianapolis, IN	198		X		X	X			X		X					
Cabrini College, Radnor, PA	432		X		X	X		X			X					
California State Polytechnic University, Pomona, Pomona, CA	93		X	X		X			X		X	X				
California State University, Fullerton, Fullerton, CA	94		X	X		X			X		X	X		X		X
California University of Pennsylvania, California, PA	432		X	X		X			X		X	X				
Calvin College, Grand Rapids, MI	266		X		X				X		X					
Carroll Community College, Westminster, MD	239	X		X		X					X					
Carthage College, Kenosha, WI	553		X		X	X		X			X	X				X
Case Western Reserve University, Cleveland, OH	393		X	X		X		X								
Catawba College, Salisbury, NC	375		X	X				X			X					
Central Michigan University, Mount Pleasant, MI	267		X	X		X				X	X	X				
Cerritos College, Norwalk, CA	95	X		X		X			X		X	X		X		
Chaffey College, Rancho Cucamonga, CA	96	X		X					X		X	X				
Champlain College, Burlington, VT	531		X		X	X		X			X					
Chapman University, Orange, CA	97		X		X	X	X				X					
Chattanooga State Technical Community College, Chattanooga, TN	482	X		X		X			X·		X	X				
Chicago State University, Chicago, IL	171		X	X		X		X					X	X		
Christian Brothers University, Memphis, TN	483		X		X	X		X			X					
Cincinnati State Technical and Community College, Cincinnati, OH	394	X		X		X		X			X	X				
The Citadel, The Military College of South Carolina, Charleston, SC	470		X		X	X		X			X					
City College of the City University of New York, New York, NY	332		X	X		X			X		X			X		
City University of New York, New York, NY	333		X	X		X				X	X			X	X	X
Claflin University, Orangeburg, NC	471		X		X	X			X		X	X	X	X		
Clarion University of Pennsylvania, Clarion, PA	433		X	X		X		X			X	X				
Clarke College, Dubuque, IA	209		X		X	X		X			X					
Clarkson University, Potsdam, NY	334		X		X	X			X		X	X				
Clemson University, Clemson, SC	472		X	X		X	X		X		X			X		X
Cleveland State University, Cleveland, OH	395		X	X		X			X		X	X				
Cochise College, Sierra Vista, AZ	77	X		X		X			X		X					
Colby-Sawyer College, New London, NH	309		X		X	X		X								
College Misericordia, Dallas, PA	434		X		X	X		X								
College of Charleston, Charleston, SC	473		X	X		X			X		X	X				
College of DuPage, Glen Ellyn, IL	171	X		X		X			X		X	X				
College of Mount St. Joseph, Cincinnati, OH	396		X		X	X		X								

Name	Page Number	2-Year College	4-Year College	Public or State College	Private College	General Honors Program	Departmental Honors Program	Small Program (fewer than 100 students)	Midsize Program (100 to 500 students)	Large Program (more than 500 students)	Scholarships Available	Transfer Students Accepted	Historically Black College	Academic Advisers	Graduate Advisers	Fellowship Advisers
The College of New Rochelle, New Rochelle, NY	334		X		X	X		X				X	X			
College of Notre Dame of Maryland, Baltimore, MD	239		X		X			X				X				
College of Saint Benedict, Saint Joseph, MN	277		X		X				X			X				
College of St. Catherine, St. Paul, MN	277		X		X	X		X				X				
College of Saint Elizabeth, Morristown, NJ	313		X		X	X		X				X		X		
The College of St. Scholastica, Duluth, MN	278		X		X	X		X				X				
College of Staten Island of the City University of New York, Staten Island, NY	335		X	X				X			X	X		X		
College of the Redwoods, Eureka, CA	97	X		X		X		X				X		X		
Colorado State University, Fort Collins, CO	115		X	X		X				X	X	X				
Columbia College, Columbia, MO	291		X		X	X		X				X	X	X		
Columbia College, Columbia, SC	474		X		X	X			X			X	X			
Columbus State University, Columbus, GA	156		X	X		X		X				X	X	X		
The Community College of Baltimore County-Essex Campus, Baltimore, MD	240	X		X		X		X				X	X			
Community College of Southern Nevada, North Las Vegas, NV	306	X		X		X		X				X				
Concordia University, River Forest, IL	172		X		X	X		X				X	X			
Converse College, Spartanburg, SC	474		X		X	X			X			X	X		X		
Coppin State University, Baltimore, MD	241		X	X		X		X				X	X	X		
Corning Community College, Corning, NY	336	X		X		X		X								
Cuyahoga Community College, Cleveland, OH	396	X		X		X			X			X	X		X	
Delta College, University Center, MI	268	X		X		X			X			X	X			
Delta State University, Cleveland, MS	285		X	X		X		X				X			X	
Denison University, Granville, OH	397		X		X	X				X	X	X				
DePaul University, Chicago, IL	173		X		X			X				X		X		
DePauw University, Greencastle, IN	199		X		X	X		X				X	X			
Dickinson State University, Dickinson, ND	392		X	X		X		X				X	X		X		
Dominican University of California, San Rafael, CA	98		X		X	X		X				X	X		X		
Dordt College, Sioux Cener, IA	209		X		X	X		X				X	X		X		X
Dowling College, Oakdale, NY	337		X		X	X		X				X	X		X		
Drake University, Des Moines, IA	210		X		X	X		X				X				
Drexel University, Philadelphia, PA	435		X		X	X				X		X				
Duquesne University, Pittsburgh, PA	435		X		X	X			X							
Dutchess Community College, Poughkeepsie, NY	338	X		X		X		X				X	X			
East Carolina University, Greenville, NC	376		X	X		X				X		X				
East Central University, Ada, OK	415															
Eastern Connecticut State University, Willimantic, CT	122		X	X		X		X				X	X			
Eastern Illinois University, Charleston, IL	174		X	X		X	X				X	X		X		X
Eastern Kentucky University, Richmond, KY	222		X	X		X			X			X	X			
Eastern Michigan University, Ypsilanti, MI	268		X	X		X	X			X	X	X		X		
Eastern Oregon University, La Grande, OR	423		X	X				X				X		X		
Eastern University, St. Davids, PA	436		X		X	X		X				X	X			

Name	Page Number	2-Year College	4-Year College	Public or State College	Private College	General Honors Program	Departmental Honors Program	Small Program (fewer than 100 students)	Midsize Program (100 to 500 students)	Large Program (more than 500 students)	Scholarships Available	Transfer Students Accepted	Historically Black College	Academic Advisers	Graduate Advisers	Fellowship Advisers
Eastern Washington University, Cheney, WA	545		X	X		X	X		X		X	X		X		
East Stroudsburg University of Pennsylvania, East Stroudsburg, PA	437		X	X		X			X		X	X				
East Tennessee State University, Johnson City, TN	483		X	X		X	X	X			X	X				
Edinboro University of Pennsylvania, Edinboro, PA	438		X	X		X			X		X	X				
El Camino College, Torrance, CA	99	X		X		X		X								
Elgin Community College, Elgin, IL	175	X		X		X		X			X					
Elizabethtown College, Elizabethtown, PA	439		X		X	X		X			X					
Elmhurst College, Elmhurst, IL	176		X		X	X		X			X	X		X		
Elon University, Elon, NC	377		X		X	X			X		X	X		X		X
Embry-Riddle Aeronautical University, Daytona Beach, FL and Prescott, AZ	77		X		X	X			X		X			X		
Emerson College, Boston, MA	251		X		X	X		X			X			X		
Emporia State University, Emporia, KS	217		X	X		X		X			X					
Endicott College, Beverly, MA	251		X		X	X			X		X	X				
Erie Community College, Buffalo, NY	338	X		X		X		X								
Fairleigh Dickinson University, College at Florham, Madison, NJ	314		X		X	X			X		X			X		
Fairleigh Dickinson University, Metropolitan Campus, Teaneck, NJ	315		X		X	X			X		X			X		
Fashion Institute of Technology, New York, NY	339	X	X	X		X			X							
Fayetteville State University, Fayetteville, NC	378		X	X		X		X			X	X	X	X		
Felician College, Lodi, NJ	316		X		X	X		X			X					
Ferris State University, Big Rapids, MI	269		X	X		X			X		X			X		X
Florida Agricultural and Mechanical University, Tallahassee, FL	134		X	X		X			X		X	X	X			
Florida Atlantic University, Boca Raton, FL	135		X	X		X	X									
Florida Atlantic University, Jupiter, FL	136		X	X		X			X		X	X				
Florida International University, Miami, FL	137		X	X		X				X	X					
Florida State University, Tallahassee, FL	138		X	X		X				X	X	X				
Fordham University, New York, NY	339		X		X			X			X	X				
Framingham State College, Framingham, MA	252		X	X		X		X			X					
Francis Marion University, Florence, SC	475		X	X		X			X		X			X		
Frederick Community College, Frederick, MD	241	X		X		X	X	X			X			X		
Freed-Hardeman University, Henderson, TN	485		X		X				X		X					
Frostburg State University, Frostburg, MD	242		X	X		X			X		X	X				
Fullerton College, Fullerton, CA	100	X		X		X		X			X	X				
Gallaudet University, Washington, DC	132		X		X	X					X			X		
Gannon University, Erie, PA	440		X		X	X		X			X					
Gardner-Webb University, Boiling Springs, NC	379		X		X	X		X			X	X				
Georgetown College, Georgetown, KY	223		X		X	X		X			X					
Georgia College & State University, Milledgeville, GA	157		X	X		X			X		X	X		X		
Georgian Court University, Lakewood, NJ	316		X		X	X		X			X			X		
Georgia Perimeter College, Decatur, GA	157	X		X		X			X		X	X				
Georgia Southern University, Statesboro, GA	158		X	X		X		X			X					

Name	Page Number	2-Year College	4-Year College	Public or State College	Private College	General Honors Program	Departmental Honors Program	Small Program (fewer than 100 students)	Midsize Program (100 to 500 students)	Large Program (more than 500 students)	Scholarships Available	Transfer Students Accepted	Historically Black College	Academic Advisers	Graduate Advisers	Fellowship Advisers
Georgia State University, Atlanta, GA	159		X	X		X			X		X	X				
Golden West College, Huntington Beach, CA	100	X		X		X		X			X	X				X
Governors State University, University Park, IL	177			X		X		X			X	X				
Grand Valley State University, Allendale, MI	270		X	X		X				X	X	X		X		
Grayson County College, Denison, TX	496	X		X		X		X			X			X		
Greensboro College, Greensboro, NC	380		X		X	X		X			X	X				
Greenville Technical College, Greenville, SC	476	X		X			X	X			X	X				
Guilford College, Greensboro, NC	381		X		X	X			X		X	X				
Gwynedd-Mercy College, Gwynedd Valley, PA	440		X		X	X					X	X				
Hampden-Sydney College, Hampden-Sydney, VA	532		X		X	X	X		X		X	X				
Hampton University, Hampton, VA	533		X		X	X			X				X	X		
Harding University, Searcy, AR	84		X		X	X				X	X					
Hardin-Simmons University, Abilene, TX	496		X		X	X		X			X	X				
Harrisburg Area Community College, Harrisburg, PA	441	X		X		X		X								
Hartwick College, Oneonta, NY	340		X		X	X		X			X	X		X		
Heidelberg College, Tiffin, OH	398		X		X	X		X				X				
Henderson State University, Arkadelphia, AR	85		X	X				X			X	X				
Hilbert College, Hamburg, NY	341		X		X	X		X			X			X		
Hillsborough Community College, Tampa, FL	138	X		X		X		X			X	X		X		
Hinds Community College, Raymond, MS	285	X		X		X		X			X		X			
Hofstra University, Hempstead, NY	342		X		X	X		X			X	X		X	X	X
Holmes Community College, Goodman, MS	286	X		X		X		X			X	X		X		
Holy Cross College, Notre Dame, IN	200		X		X	X		X			X	X		X		
Holyoke Community College, Holyoke, MA	253	X		X		X		X			X	X				
Hunter College of the City University of New York, New York, NY	343, 344		X	X		X		X			X			X		
Illinois State University, Normal, IL	177		X	X		X				X	X	X				
Indiana University Bloomington, Bloomington, IN	201		X	X		X				X	X	X				
Indiana University of Pennsylvania, Indiana, PA	442		X	X		X			X		X	X				
Indiana University–Purdue University Indianapolis, Indianapolis, IN	202		X	X		X			X		X	X		X		
Indiana University South Bend, South Bend, IN	203		X	X		X			X		X	X		X		
Indiana Wesleyan University, Marion, IN	203		X		X	X		X			X					
Indian River Community College, Ft. Pierce, FL	139	X		X		X	X	X			X	X		X		
Iona College, New Rochelle, NY	345		X		X	X		X			X	X				
Iowa State University of Science and Technology, Ames, IA	211		X	X		X				X	X			X		
Ithaca College, Ithaca, NY	346		X		X	X		X			X					
Jackson State University, Jackson, MS	287		X	X		X			X		X	X	X			
Jacksonville State University, Jacksonville, AL	66		X	X		X			X		X	X				
James Madison University, Harrisonburg, VA	534		X	X		X				X	X	X				
John Brown University, Siloam Springs, AR	86		X		X	X			X		X					
John Carroll University, University Heights, OH	399		X		X	X			X		X					
Johnson & Wales University, Providence, RI	468		X		X	X				X	X	X				
Johnson County Community College, Overland Park, KS	218	X		X		X			X		X	X		X		

Name	Page Number	2-Year College	4-Year College	Public or State College	Private College	General Honors Program	Departmental Honors Program	Small Program (fewer than 100 students)	Midsize Program (100 to 500 students)	Large Program (more than 500 students)	Scholarships Available	Transfer Students Accepted	Historically Black College	Academic Advisers	Graduate Advisers	Fellowship Advisers
Joliet Junior College, Joliet, IL	178	X		X		X		X				X		X		
Kennesaw State University, Kennesaw, GA	160		X	X		X			X					X		X
Kent State University, Kent, OH	400		X	X		X				X	X	X				
Kentucky State University, Frankfort, KY	224		X	X		X		X			X	X	X			
Keystone College, LaPlume, PA	443		X		X			X			X					
Kingwood College, Kingwood, TX	497	X		X		X		X			X					
Kutztown University of Pennsylvania, Kutztown, PA	443		X	X		X		X			X	X				
Lake Land College, Mattoon, IL	179	X		X		X		X			X	X				
Lake Superior State University, Sault Sainte Marie, MI	271		X	X		X			X		X	X				
Lamar University, Beaumont, TX	498		X	X		X			X		X	X				
Laredo Community College, Laredo, TX	499	X		X		X		X			X			X		
La Salle University, Philadelphia, PA	444		X		X	X			X		X	X		X	X	X
Lasell College, Newton, MA	254		X		X	X		X			X					
La Sierra University, Riverside, CA	101		X		X	X			X		X					
Lee College, Baytown, TX	500	X		X		X		X			X	X				
Lehman College of the City University of New York, Bronx, NY	347		X	X		X		X			X	X		X	X	
Le Moyne College, Syracuse, NY	348		X		X	X		X			X					
Lenoir-Rhyne College, Hickory, NC	381		X		X	X			X		X	X		X		
LeTourneau University, Longview, TX	501		X		X	X		X								
Lincoln Land Community College, Springfield, IL	180	X		X		X		X			X	X				
Lipscomb University, Nashville, TN	485		X		X	X		X			X					
Lock Haven University of Pennsylvania, Lock Haven, PA	445		X		X	X		X			X	X				
Long Island University, Brooklyn Campus, Brooklyn, NY	349		X		X	X		X			X	X		X		X
Long Island University, C.W. Post Campus, Brookville, NY	350		X		X	X				X	X	X				
Longwood University, Farmville, VA	535		X	X		X			X		X	X				
Loras College, Dubuque, IA	212		X		X	X		X			X					
Los Medanos College, Pittsburg, CA	102	X		X		X		X			X					
Louisiana State University at Alexandria, Alexandria, LA	228	X		X		X					X					
Loyola Marymount University, Los Angeles, CA	103		X		X	X			X		X	X		X	X	X
Loyola University Chicago, Chicago, IL	180		X		X	X			X		X					
Loyola University New Orleans, New Orleans, LA	229		X		X	X		X			X					
Lubbock Christian University, Lubbock, TX	502		X		X	X		X				X				
Lynchburg College, Lynchburg, VA	536		X		X	X		X			X			X		
Malone College, Canton, OH	401		X		X	X		X			X					
Manchester College, North Manchester, IN	204		X		X	X			X		X	X		X		
Mansfield University of Pennsylvania, Mansfield, PA	446		X	X		X		X			X	X				
Maricopa Community Colleges, Tempe, AZ	78	X		X		X				X	X	X				
Marist College, Poughkeepsie, NY	351		X		X	X			X			X		X	X	X

Name	Page Number	2-Year College	4-Year College	Public or State College	Private College	General Honors Program	Departmental Honors Program	Small Program (fewer than 100 students)	Midsize Program (100 to 500 students)	Large Program (more than 500 students)	Scholarships Available	Transfer Students Accepted	Historically Black College	Academic Advisers	Graduate Advisers	Fellowship Advisers
Marquette University, Milwaukee, WI	554		X		X	X			X			X				
Marshall University, Huntington, WV	549		X	X		X			X		X	X				
Marymount College of Fordham University, Tarrytown, NY	352		X		X	X		X			X			X		
Marymount University, Arlington, VA	536		X		X	X		X			X	X		X		
Maryville University of Saint Louis, St. Louis, MO	292		X		X	X		X			X	X				
Marywood University, Scranton, PA	447		X		X	X		X			X			X		X
Massachusetts College of Liberal Arts, North Adams, MA	255		X	X		X		X				X				
McHenry County College, Crystal Lake, IL	181	X		X		X		X				X				
McKendree College, Lebanon, IL	182		X		X	X		X								
McNeese State University, Lake Charles, LA	230		X	X		X		X				X		X		
Medaille College, Buffalo, NY	353		X		X	X		X				X		X		
Mercer University, Macon, GA	161		X		X	X			X		X	X				
Mercy College, Dobbs Ferry, NY	354		X		X	X	X				X	X				
Mercyhurst College, Erie, PA	448		X		X	X		X			X	X		X		
Meredith College, Raleigh, NC	382		X		X	X		X			X	X		X		X
Mesa State College, Grand Junction, CO	116		X	X		X		X			X	X				
Messiah College, Grantham, PA	449		X		X	X		X			X					
Metropolitan State College of Denver, Denver, CO	117		X	X		X		X				X				
Miami University, Oxford, OH	402		X	X		X				X		X				
Michigan State University, East Lansing, MI	272		X	X		X				X	X	X		X		
Middle Tennessee State University, Murfreesboro, TN	486		X	X		X			X			X				
Midwestern State University, Wichita Falls, TX	502		X	X		X	X				X	X				
Millersville University of Pennsylvania, Millersville, PA	450		X	X		X		X			X	X				
Millikin University, Decatur, IL	183		X		X	X		X			X	X				
Minnesota State University Mankato, Mankato, MN	279		X	X		X		X				X				
Mississippi State University, Mississippi State, MS	287		X	X		X				X	X	X				
Mississippi University for Women, Columbus, MS	288		X		X	X										
Missouri Southern State University, Joplin, MO	293		X	X		X		X			X	X		X		
Missouri State University, Springfield, MO	294		X	X		X				X		X		X		X
Missouri Western State University, St. Joseph, MO	295		X	X		X	X	X			X	X				
Monmouth University, West Long Branch, NJ	317		X		X	X		X			X	X				
Monroe College, New Rochelle, NY	354		X		X	X		X			X	X		X		
Montana State University–Bozeman, Bozeman, MT	301		X	X		X		X			X	X				
Montgomery College, Conroe, TX	503	X		X		X				X	X	X		X		
Morehouse College, Atlanta, GA	162		X	X			X	X			X		X			
Motlow State Community College, Lynchburg, TN	487	X		X		X		X			X	X		X		
Mott Community College, Flint, MI	273	X		X		X		X			X	X		X		

Name	Page Number	2-Year College	4-Year College	Public or State College	Private College	General Honors Program	Departmental Honors Program	Small Program (fewer than 100 students)	Midsize Program (100 to 500 students)	Large Program (more than 500 students)	Scholarships Available	Transfer Students Accepted	Historically Black College	Academic Advisers	Graduate Advisers	Fellowship Advisers
Mount Mercy College, Cedar Rapids, IA	213		X		X	X		X			X	X				
Mt. San Antonio College, Walnut, CA	104	X		X		X			X			X				
Mount Vernon Nazarene University, Mount Vernon, OH	403		X		X	X		X			X	X				
Mount Wachusett Community College, Gardner, MA	255	X		X		X		X			X	X				
Murray State University, Murray, KY	225		X	X		X			X		X	X		X		
Nassau Community College, Garden City, NY	355	X		X		X			X		X	X				
Neosho County Community College, Chanute, KS	219	X		X		X		X			X					
Neumann College, Aston, PA	451		X		X			X			X	X				
Newberry College, Newberry, SC	476		X		X			X			X	X				
New Jersey Institute of Technology, Newark, NJ	318		X	X		X			X		X	X		X		
New Mexico State University, Las Cruces, NM	325		X	X			X		X			X				
Norfolk State University, Norfolk, VA	537		X	X		X			X			X	X			
Northampton Community College, Bethlehem, PA	451	X		X		X		X				X		X		
North Carolina Agricultural and Technical State University, Greensboro, NC	383		X	X		X			X			X	X	X		
North Carolina State University, Raleigh, NC	384		X	X		X	X			X	X	X				
North Central College, Naperville, IL	183		X		X	X			X		X	X		X		X
North Dakota State University, Fargo, ND	393		X	X		X		X			X	X				
Northeastern Illinois University, Chicago, IL	184		X	X		X			X		X	X				
Northeastern State University, Tahlequah, OK	416		X	X		X		X			X	X				
Northeastern University, Boston, MA	256		X		X	X				X	X	X		X		
Northeast State Technical Community College, Blountville, TN	487	X		X		X		X			X	X		X		
Northern Arizona University, Flagstaff, AZ	79		X	X		X				X	X	X		X		
Northern Illinois University, De Kalb, IL	185		X	X		X				X	X	X				
Northern Kentucky University, Highland Heights, KY	226		X	X		X			X		X	X				
Northern Michigan University, Marquette, MI	274		X		X	X		X			X	X				
North Harris College, Houston, TX	504	X		X		X		X			X	X				
North Hennepin Community College, Brooklyn Park, MN	280	X		X		X		X								
Northwestern State University of Louisiana, Natchitoches, LA	231		X	X		X			X		X	X		X		
Northwood Univeristy, Midland, MI	274		X		X	X			X		X	X				
Nova Southeastern University, Ft. Lauderdale, FL	140		X		X	X			X		X	X				
Oakton Community College, Des Plaines, IL	186	X		X		X			X		X					
Ohio Dominican University, Columbus, OH	404		X		X	X	X				X					
The Ohio State University, Columbus, OH	405		X	X		X				X	X	X				
Ohio University, Athens, OH	406		X	X		X			X		X	X				
Oklahoma Baptist University, Shawnee, OK	417		X		X	X		X			X			X		
Oklahoma City University, Oklahoma City, OK	417		X		X	X			X		X					
Oklahoma State University, Stillwater, OK	418		X	X		X	X			X	X			X		X

Name	Page Number	2-Year College	4-Year College	Public or State College	Private College	General Honors Program	Departmental Honors Program	Small Program (fewer than 100 students)	Midsize Program (100 to 500 students)	Large Program (more than 500 students)	Scholarships Available	Transfer Students Accepted	Historically Black College	Academic Advisers	Graduate Advisers	Fellowship Advisers
Oklahoma State University, Oklahoma City, Oklahoma City, OK	419	X		X		X		X			X	X				
Old Dominion University, Norfolk, VA	538		X	X		X				X	X	X				
Oral Roberts University, Tulsa, OK	420		X		X	X			X		X	X		X		
Orange County Community College, Middletown, NY	356	X		X				X			X	X		X		
Oregon State University, Corvallis, OR	424		X	X		X				X	X	X		X		
Pace University, New York, NY	357		X		X	X			X			X			X		X
Palm Beach Atlantic University, West Palm Beach, FL	141		X		X	X		X			X	X		X		
Palm Beach Community College, Lake Worth, FL	142	X		X		X			X			X				
Paradise Valley Community College, Phoenix, AZ	80	X		X		X			X			X				
Parkland College, Champaign, IL	187	X		X		X		X			X	X				
The Pennsylvania State University, University Park, PA	452		X	X		X				X	X	X				
Philadelphia Biblical University, Langhorne, PA	453		X		X	X		X			X	X		X		
Philadelphia University, Philadelphia, PA	454		X		X	X		X				X				
Pittsburg State University, Pittsburg, KS	219		X	X		X	X		X		X	X				
Point Park University, Pittsburgh, PA	455		X		X	X			X			X				
Polytechnic University, Brooklyn Campus, Brooklyn, NY	358		X		X	X		X			X	X		X	X	
Portland State University, Portland, OR	425		X	X		X			X		X	X				
Prairie State College, Chicago Heights, IL	187	X		X		X					X	X				
Prairie View A&M University, Prairie View, TX	504		X	X				X				X	X			
Prince George's Community College, Largo, MD	243	X		X		X			X		X	X		X		
Pueblo Community College, Pueblo, CO	117	X		X		X		X			X	X		X		
Purdue University, West Lafayette, IN	205		X	X						X	X	X				
Queens College of the City University of New York, Flushing, NY	359		X	X		X			X			X	X			
Quinnipiac University, Hamden, CT	123		X		X	X			X		X	X		X		
Radford University, Radford, VA	539		X	X		X			X			X				
Ramapo College of New Jersey, Mahwah, NJ	319		X	X		X		X				X		X		
Redlands Community College, El Reno, OK	421	X		X				X				X				
Reinhardt College, Waleska, GA	162		X		X	X		X			X	X		X		
Rhode Island College, Providence, RI	468		X	X		X			X		X	X				
The Richard Stockton College of New Jersey, Pomona, NJ	320		X	X		X		X				X		X		
Roanoke College, Salem, VA	540		X		X	X			X		X	X		X		
Rochester Community and Technical College, Rochester, MN	280	X		X		X		X				X				
Rochester Institute of Technology, Rochester, NY	360		X		X	X			X		X			X		
Roger Williams University, Bristol, RI	469		X		X	X			X		X			X		
Rollins College, Winter Park, FL	142		X	X		X		X				X		X		
Roosevelt University, Chicago, IL	188		X		X	X		X			X	X				
Rowan University, Glassboro, NJ	321		X	X		X			X			X		X		
Russell Sage College, Troy, NY	361		X		X	X			X			X				

HONORS PROGRAMS AND COLLEGES AT-A-GLANCE

Name	Page Number	2-Year College	4-Year College	Public or State College	Private College	General Honors Program	Departmental Honors Program	Small Program (fewer than 100 students)	Midsize Program (100 to 500 students)	Large Program (more than 500 students)	Scholarships Available	Transfer Students Accepted	Historically Black College	Academic Advisers	Graduate Advisers	Fellowship Advisers
Rutgers, The State University of New Jersey, Camden College of Arts and Sciences, Camden, NJ	322		X	X		X			X		X	X		X		
Rutgers, The State University of New Jersey, New Brunswick, New Brunswick, NJ	323		X	X		X				X	X	X		X		
Sacred Heart University, Fairfield, CT	124		X		X	X		X			X	X				
Sage College of Albany, Albany, NY	361		X		X	X		X			X	X				
Saint Anselm College, Manchester, NH	310		X		X	X		X			X					
St. Edward's University, Austin, TX	505		X		X		X		X							X
Saint Francis University, Loretto, PA	455		X		X	X			X			X		X		
Saint John's University, Saint Joseph, MN	281		X		X	X			X			X				
Saint Joseph College, West Hartford, CT	125		X		X	X		X				X		X		
Saint Joseph's University, Philadelphia, PA	456		X		X	X			X		X	X				
Saint Leo University, Saint Leo, FL	143		X		X	X		X			X	X				
St. Mary's College of Maryland, St. Mary's City, MD	244		X	X		X		X			X	X				
Saint Xavier University, Chicago, IL	188		X		X	X		X			X	X				
Salem State College, Salem, MA	257		X	X		X			X		X	X				
Salisbury University, Salisbury, MD	245		X	X		X			X		X	X				
Sam Houston State University, Huntsville, TX	506		X	X		X			X		X	X				
San Diego City College, San Diego, CA	104	X		X		X			X			X				
San Diego Mesa College, San Diego, CA	105	X		X		X			X		X	X				
San Diego State University, San Diego, CA	106		X	X		X			X							
San Jacinto College South, Houston, TX	507	X		X		X			X		X	X				
Santa Clara University, Santa Clara, CA	107		X		X	X			X			X				
Santa Fe Community College, Gainesville, FL	144	X		X		X			X			X				
Sauk Valley Community College, Dixon, IL	189	X		X		X		X			X					
Schreiner University, Kerrville, TX	507		X		X	X		X			X	X				
Scottsdale Community College, Scottsdale, AZ	80	X		X		X			X		X	X				
Seattle Pacific University, Seattle, WA	545		X		X	X			X					X		
Seminole Community College, Sanford, FL	145	X		X		X		X			X	X				
Shepherd University, Shepherdstown, WV	550		X	X		X			X		X	X				
Shippensburg University of Pennsylvania, Shippensburg, PA	457		X	X					X			X				
Simmons College, Boston, MA	257		X		X	X			X			X		X		X
Sinclair Community College, Dayton, OH	407	X		X		X		X				X				
Skyline College, San Bruno, CA	108	X		X					X		X	X		X		
South Dakota State University, Brookings, SD	479		X	X		X			X		X	X				
Southeastern Louisiana University, Hammond, LA	232		X	X		X			X		X	X				
Southeastern Oklahoma State University, Durant, OK	421		X	X		X			X		X					
Southeast Missouri State University, Cape Girardeau, MO	296		X	X		X			X			X				
Southern Arkansas University–Magnolia, Magnolia, AR	87		X	X		X		X						X	X	
Southern Connecticut State University, New Haven, CT	126		X	X		X			X		X	X				

Name	Page Number	2-Year College	4-Year College	Public or State College	Private College	General Honors Program	Departmental Honors Program	Small Program (fewer than 100 students)	Midsize Program (100 to 500 students)	Large Program (more than 500 students)	Scholarships Available	Transfer Students Accepted	Historically Black College	Academic Advisers	Graduate Advisers	Fellowship Advisers
Southern Illinois University Carbondale, Carbondale, IL	190		X	X		X				X	X	X		X	X	X
Southern New Hampshire University, Manchester, NH	311		X		X	X		X			X	X				
Southern Oregon University, Ashland, OR	426		X	X		X			X		X			X		
Southern Polytechnic State University, Marietta, GA	163		X	X		X		X			X	X				
Southern University and Agricultural and Mechanical College, Baton Rouge, LA	233		X	X		X				X	X	X	X	X		
Southern Utah University, Cedar City, UT	526	X		X		X			X		X	X				
South Florida Community College, Avon Park, FL	145	X		X		X		X			X	X				
South Mountain Community College, Phoenix, AZ	81	X		X		X		X			X	X				
Southwestern Illinois College, Belleville, IL	191	X		X		X			X		X	X				
Southwest Minnesota State University, Marshall, MN	282		X	X		X			X		X	X				
Spelman College, Atlanta, GA	164		X		X	X		X			X		X			
Springfield Technical Community College, Springfield, MA	258	X		X		X		X			X	X		X		
State University of New York at Binghamton, Binghamton, NY	362		X	X		X			X		X			X		
State University of New York at Buffalo, Buffalo, NY	363		X	X		X				X	X	X		X		
State University of New York at New Paltz, New Paltz, NY	364		X	X		X		X			X			X		
State University of New York at Oswego, Oswego, NY	365		X	X		X		X			X	X				
State University of New York at Plattsburgh, Plattsburgh, NY	366		X	X		X			X		X	X				
State University of New York College at Brockport, Brockport, NY	367		X	X		X			X		X	X				
State University of New York College at Cortland, Cortland, NY	368		X	X		X			X			X				
State University of New York College at Oneonta, Oneonta, NY	369		X	X		X		X				X				
State University of New York College at Potsdam, Potsdam, NY	369		X	X		X			X		X	X				
Stephen F. Austin State University, Nacogdoches, TX	508		X	X		X				X	X	X				
Stonehill College, Easton, MA	259		X		X	X			X			X		X		
Stony Brook University, State University of New York, Stony Brook, NY	370		X	X		X			X		X	X				
Sullivan County Community College, Loch Sheldrake, NY	371	X		X		X		X			X	X		X		
Susquehanna University, Selinsgrove, PA	458		X		X	X			X			X				
Sweet Briar College, Sweet Briar, VA	541		X		X	X		X			X	X				
Syracuse University, Syracuse, NY	372		X		X	X				X						
Temple University, Philadelphia, PA	459		X	X		X				X	X	X				

Name	Page Number	2-Year College	4-Year College	Public or State College	Private College	General Honors Program	Departmental Honors Program	Small Program (fewer than 100 students)	Midsize Program (100 to 500 students)	Large Program (more than 500 students)	Scholarships Available	Transfer Students Accepted	Historically Black College	Academic Advisers	Graduate Advisers	Fellowship Advisers
Tennessee Technological University, Cookeville, TN	488		X	X		X			X			X	X				
Texas A&M University, College Station, TX	509		X	X		X	X				X	X		X		
Texas A&M University–Corpus Christi, Corpus Christi, TX	510		X	X		X			X				X		X		
Texas Christian University, Fort Worth, TX	511		X		X	X			X				X				
Texas Lutheran University, Seguin, TX	512		X		X	X		X				X	X				
Texas Southern University, Houston, TX	513		X	X		X							X	X			
Texas State University–San Marcos, San Marcos, TX	514		X	X		X						X	X		X		X
Texas Tech University, Lubbock, TX	514		X	X		X						X	X				
Texas Woman's University, Denton, TX	516		X	X		X			X			X	X				
Thiel College, Greenville, PA	460		X		X	X		X				X	X				
Towson University, Towson, MD	246		X	X		X						X	X		X		
Trinity Christian College, Palos Heights, IL	191		X		X	X		X					X				
Trocaire College, Buffalo, NY	373	X			X	X		X				X	X		X		
Truman State University, Kirksville, MO	297		X	X		X		X					X				
Tulane University, New Orleans, LA	234		X		X	X			X						X	X	X
Tulsa Community College, Tulsa, OK	422	X		X		X		X				X	X				
Tyler Junior College, Tyler, TX	517	X		X		X		X				X	X		X		
Union College, Lincoln, NE	303		X		X	X		X				X	X				
The University of Akron, Akron, OH	408		X	X		X						X	X		X		X
The University of Alabama, Tuscaloosa, AL	67, 68, 69		X	X		X						X	X	X			
The University of Alabama at Birmingham, Birmingham, AL	70		X	X		X						X	X	X			
The University of Alabama in Huntsville, Huntsville, AL	71		X	X		X			X				X		X		
University of Alaska Anchorage, Anchorage, AK	73		X	X		X	X					X	X		X		
University of Alaska Fairbanks, Fairbanks, AK	74		X	X		X			X			X	X				
University of Amsterdam, Amsterdam, Netherlands	562		X	X		X			X				X		X		
The University of Arizona, Tucson, AZ	82		X	X		X						X	X		X		X
University of Arkansas, Fayetteville, AR	88		X	X		X						X	X	X	X		X
University of Arkansas at Fort Smith, Fort Smith, AR	89		X	X		X	X					X	X				
University of Arkansas at Little Rock, Little Rock, AR	89		X	X		X	X					X	X				
University of Arkansas at Pine Bluff, Pine Bluff, AR	90		X	X		X			X				X	X			
University of Baltimore, Baltimore, MD	247		X	X		X	X					X	X		X	X	X
University of California, Davis, Davis, CA	109		X	X		X			X								
University of California, Irvine, Irvine, CA	109		X	X		X			X				X				
University of California, Santa Barbara, Santa Barbara, CA	110		X	X		X						X	X				
University of Central Arkansas, Conway, AR	91		X	X					X			X	X				
University of Central Florida, Orlando, FL	146		X	X		X						X	X	X			
University of Cincinnati, Cincinnati, OH	409		X	X		X						X	X		X		

Name	Page Number	2-Year College	4-Year College	Public or State College	Private College	General Honors Program	Departmental Honors Program	Small Program (fewer than 100 students)	Midsize Program (100 to 500 students)	Large Program (more than 500 students)	Scholarships Available	Transfer Students Accepted	Historically Black College	Academic Advisers	Graduate Advisers	Fellowship Advisers
University of Colorado at Boulder, Boulder, CO	118		X	X		X				X	X	X		X		
University of Connecticut, Storrs, CT	127		X	X		X	X			X	X	X				
University of Dayton, Dayton, OH	410		X		X	X					X	X				
University of Delaware, Newark, DE	130		X	X		X				X	X	X				
University of Denver, Denver, CO	119		X		X	X			X		X	X				
University of Evansville, Evansville, IN	206		X		X	X			X							
The University of Findlay, Findlay, OH	411		X		X	X			X		X	X				
University of Florida, Gainesville, FL	147		X	X		X				X	X			X		X
University of Georgia, Athens, GA	165		X	X		X				X	X	X				
University of Hartford, West Hartford, CT	128		X		X	X	X		X			X				
University of Houston, Houston, TX	517		X	X						X	X	X				
University of Idaho, Moscow, ID	170		X	X		X			X		X	X				
University of Illinois at Chicago, Chicago, IL	192		X	X		X				X	X	X				
University of Illinois at Urbana–Champaign, Champaign, IL	193		X	X		X			X		X			X		X
The University of Iowa, Iowa City, IA	214		X	X		X				X	X	X		X		X
University of Kansas, Lawrence, KS	220		X	X		X				X	X	X				
University of La Verne, La Verne, CA	111		X		X	X		X			X	X		X		
University of Louisville, Louisville, KY	226		X	X						X		X		X	X	X
University of Maine, Orono, ME	235		X	X		X				X		X			X	
The University of Maine at Augusta, Augusta, ME	236		X	X		X		X			X	X				
University of Maryland, Baltimore County, Baltimore, MD	248		X	X		X			X		X	X				
University of Maryland, College Park, College Park, MD	249		X	X		X				X	X	X		X	X	X
University of Massachusetts Amherst, Amherst, MA	260		X	X		X				X	X	X		X		X
University of Massachusetts Boston, Boston, MA	262		X	X					X		X	X		X		X
University of Massachusetts Dartmouth, North Dartmouth, MA	263		X	X		X			X			X				
University of Massachusetts Lowell, Lowell, MA	264		X	X		X	X					X		X		
The University of Memphis, Memphis, TN	489		X	X		X	X			X	X	X				
University of Minnesota, Morris, Morris, MN	282		X	X		X					X	X				
University of Minnesota, Twin Cities Campus, Minneapolis, MN	283		X	X					X			X				
University of Mississippi, University, MS	289		X	X		X			X		X	X		X		
University of Missouri–Columbia, Columbia, MO	297		X	X		X				X		X		X		X
University of Missouri–Kansas City, Kansas City, MO	298		X	X		X			X			X		X		X
University of Missouri–St. Louis, St. Louis, MO	299		X	X		X					X	X				
The University of Montana–Missoula, Missoula, MT	302		X		X	X			X		X	X				
University of Nebraska at Kearney, Kearney, NE	303		X	X		X			X		X	X	X	X		
University of Nebraska at Omaha, Omaha, NE	304		X	X		X			X		X	X		X		X
University of Nebraska–Lincoln, Lincoln, NE	305		X	X		X	X			X	X	X				
University of Nevada, Las Vegas, Las Vegas, NV	307		X	X		X				X	X	X				

HONORS PROGRAMS AND COLLEGES AT-A-GLANCE

Name	Page Number	2-Year College	4-Year College	Public or State College	Private College	General Honors Program	Departmental Honors Program	Small Program (fewer than 100 students)	Midsize Program (100 to 500 students)	Large Program (more than 500 students)	Scholarships Available	Transfer Students Accepted	Historically Black College	Academic Advisers	Graduate Advisers	Fellowship Advisers
University of Nevada, Reno, Reno, NV	308		X	X		X	X		X		X	X				
University of New Hampshire, Durham, NH	311		X	X		X			X		X					
University of New Haven, West Haven, CT	129		X		X	X	X				X	X		X		
University of New Mexico, Albuquerque, NM	326		X	X		X				X	X					
University of North Alabama, Florence, AL	72		X	X		X		X			X	X		X	X	X
The University of North Carolina at Asheville, Asheville, NC	385		X	X			X		X		X	X				
The University of North Carolina at Chapel Hill, Chapel Hill, NC	386		X	X		X			X		X	X				
The University of North Carolina at Charlotte, Charlotte, NC	387		X	X		X	X		X		X	X		X		
The University of North Carolina at Greensboro, Greensboro, NC	388		X	X		X	X		X		X	X		X		X
The University of North Carolina at Pembroke, Pembroke, NC	390		X	X		X			X			X		X		
The University of North Carolina at Wilmington, Wilmington, NC	391		X	X		X	X		X		X	X				
University of Northern Colorado, Greeley, CO	120		X	X		X			X		X	X		X		
University of Northern Iowa, Cedar Falls, IA	215		X	X		X			X		X	X		X		
University of North Florida, Jacksonville, FL	148		X	X		X	X		X		X	X				
University of North Texas, Denton, TX	518		X	X		X				X	X	X				
University of Oklahoma, Norman, OK	423		X	X		X				X	X					
University of Oregon, Eugene, OR	427		X							X	X	X		X		
University of Pittsburgh, Pittsburgh, PA	460		X	X		X			X		X	X		X		
University of Portland, Portland, OR	428		X		X	X			X		X			X		X
University of Puerto Rico, Rio Piedras, San Juan, PR	466		X	X						X	X					
University of St. Francis, Joliet, IL	195		X		X	X		X			X	X		X		
University of St. Thomas, Houston, TX	519		X		X	X		X			X					
University of San Diego, San Diego, CA	112		X		X	X			X		X					
The University of Scranton, Scranton, PA	462		X		X	X			X					X		X
University of South Alabama, Mobile, AL	72		X	X		X	X		X		X	X				
University of South Carolina, Columbia, SC	477		X	X		X				X	X	X		X		X
The University of South Dakota, Vermillion, SD	480		X	X		X			X		X	X				
University of Southern California—Baccalaureate/MD Program, Los Angeles, CA	112		X		X	X		X			X			X		
University of Southern California—Thematic Option Honors Program, Los Angeles, CA	113		X		X	X			X		X					
University of Southern Indiana, Evansville, IN	207		X	X		X	X		X			X				
University of Southern Maine, Portland, ME	237		X	X		X		X			X	X				
University of Southern Mississippi, Hattiesburg, MS	290		X	X					X		X	X				
University of South Florida, Tampa, FL	149		X	X		X	X		X		X	X		X		X
The University of Tampa, Tampa, FL	150		X		X	X			X		X	X				
The University of Tennessee, Knoxville, TN	490		X	X		X				X	X			X	X	X
The University of Tennessee at Chattanooga, Chattanooga, TN	491		X	X		X			X		X	X		X	X	X

Name	Page Number	2-Year College	4-Year College	Public or State College	Private College	General Honors Program	Departmental Honors Program	Small Program (fewer than 100 students)	Midsize Program (100 to 500 students)	Large Program (more than 500 students)	Scholarships Available	Transfer Students Accepted	Historically Black College	Academic Advisers	Graduate Advisers	Fellowship Advisers
The University of Tennessee at Martin, Martin, TN	492		X	X		X			X		X	X				
The University of Texas at Arlington, Arlington, TX	520		X	X		X				X	X	X				
The University of Texas at Austin, Austin, TX	521		X	X		X	X		X		X	X		X		
The University of Texas at Dallas, Richardson, TX	522		X	X		X								X		X
The University of Texas at El Paso, El Paso, TX	523		X	X		X			X		X	X				
The University of Texas at San Antonio, San Antonio, TX	524		X	X		X				X	X	X		X		X
The University of Texas–Pan American, Edinburg, TX	524		X	X		X			X		X	X		X		
University of the Pacific, Stockton, CA	114		X		X	X		X			X			X		
The University of Toledo, Toledo, OH	411		X	X		X				X	X	X				
University of Utrecht, Utrecht, Netherlands	563		X (3-yr)	X			X	X			X			X	X	
University of Vermont, Burlington, VT	531		X	X					X		X	X				
University of Victoria, Victoria, BC, Canada	562		X	X		X			X		X	X		X	X	
University of Washington, Seattle, WA	546		X	X		X				X	X	X				
University of Washington, Tacoma, Tacoma, WA	547		X	X		X	X				X	X		X		
University of West Florida, Pensacola, FL	151		X	X		X			X		X	X				
University of West Georgia, Carrollton, GA	166		X	X		X			X		X	X				
University of Wisconsin–Eau Claire, Eau Claire, WI	554		X	X		X			X		X	X				
University of Wisconsin–Madison, Madison, WI	555		X	X		X	X			X	X	X				
University of Wisconsin–Milwaukee, Milwaukee, WI	556		X	X		X			X		X	X				
University of Wisconsin–Oshkosh, Oshkosh, WI	557		X	X		X			X			X				
University of Wisconsin–Stout, Menomonie, WI	558		X	X		X			X			X				
University of Wisconsin–Whitewater, Whitewater, WI	559		X	X		X			X		X	X		X	X	X
University of Wyoming, Laramie, WY	560		X	X		X				X	X	X		X	X	X
Utah State University, Logan, UT	527		X	X		X			X		X	X				
Utah Valley State College, Orem, UT	528	X	X	X		X			X		X					
Valdosta State University, Valdosta, GA	167		X	X		X			X		X	X				
Valencia Community College, Orlando, FL	152	X		X		X				X	X	X				
Valparaiso University, Valparaiso, IN	207															
Villanova University, Villanova, PA	463		X		X	X			X		X	X		X		X
Virginia Commonwealth University, Richmond, VA	542		X	X		X				X	X	X		X		
Virginia Military Institute, Lexington, VA	543		X	X		X	X				X	X				
Virginia Polytechnic Institute and State University, Blacksburg, VA	544		X	X		X				X	X	X				
Wagner College, Staten Island, NY	374		X		X	X			X		X	X				
Waldorf College, Forest City, IA	216		X		X	X		X			X	X				
Walsh University, North Canton, OH	412		X		X	X		X			X	X		X		
Wartburg College, Waverly, IA	217		X		X	X		X			X	X				
Washington State University, Pullman, WA	548		X	X		X				X	X	X				

Name	Page Number	2-Year College	4-Year College	Public or State College	Private College	General Honors Program	Departmental Honors Program	Small Program (fewer than 100 students)	Midsize Program (100 to 500 students)	Large Program (more than 500 students)	Scholarships Available	Transfer Students Accepted	Historically Black College	Academic Advisers	Graduate Advisers	Fellowship Advisers
Wayne State University, Detroit, MI	275		X	X		X	X		X			X				
Weber State University, Ogden, UT	529		X	X		X	X		X		X	X				
West Chester University of Pennsylvania, West Chester, PA	464		X	X		X			X		X	X		X		
Western Carolina University, Cullowhee, NC	391		X	X							X	X		X		
Western Illinois University, Macomb, IL	195		X	X		X					X	X		X		
Western Kentucky University, Bowling Green, KY	227		X	X		X					X	X		X		
Western Michigan University, Kalamazoo, MI	276		X	X							X	X		X		X
Western New Mexico University, Silver City, NM	327		X	X		X		X						X		
Western Washington University, Bellingham, WA	549		X	X		X			X		X	X				
Western Wyoming Community College, Rock Springs, WY	561	X		X		X		X				X				
Westminster College, Salt Lake City, UT	530		X	X	X	X		X						X		
West Virginia University, Morgantown, WV	551		X	X		X			X		X	X				
Wichita State University, Wichita, KS	221		X	X		X			X			X				
Widener University, Chester, PA	465		X	X	X				X		X	X				
William Paterson University of New Jersey, Wayne, NJ	324		X	X		X		X			X	X				
William Rainey Harper College, Palatine, IL	196	X		X		X			X		X	X				
William Woods University, Fulton, MO	300		X	X	X	X		X				X				
Winthrop University, Rock Hill, SC	478		X	X		X		X				X				
Wittenberg University, Springfield, OH	413		X	X	X	X			X			X				
Worcester State College, Worcester, MA	265		X	X		X			X		X	X		X		
Wright State University, Dayton, OH	414		X	X		X			X		X	X		X		
York College of Pennsylvania, York, PA	466		X	X	X	X		X			X	X		X		
Youngstown State University, Youngstown, OH	415		X	X		X				X	X	X				

Profiles of
Honors Programs and Colleges

ALABAMA

Auburn University
University Honors College
Auburn University, Alabama

The University Honors College offers students capable of academic excellence the advantages of a small college in the context of a large university. The College selects 200 entering freshmen each year. These students may be enrolled in any college or school of the University that has undergraduate programs or offerings. Students already enrolled in Auburn can also qualify for the College.

Participation in the Honors College exposes students to a wider range of intellectual and academic experience, gives students the opportunity to form lasting friendships with other students committed to academic excellence, and promotes more rewarding interaction between students and teachers. As a result of their special college experience, honors students have a distinct advantage in their future pursuits, whether they go on to graduate or professional school or go directly into their chosen professions.

Entering freshmen are introduced to the University Honors College through Summer Honors Orientation sessions where introductions to faculty members and fellow students are made and friendships begin. Amenities are provided in our Honors Residence Halls to encourage this interaction as well as to encourage individual intellectual growth. The mentor program, organized by upperclass honors students, further assists new students as they adjust to university life. From their second semester in the College, honors students are given priority at registration to ensure timely progress through their curricula. Most important, honors classes are taught in small sections and are designed to provide in-depth dialogue and interaction between students and faculty members. All honors sections are taught by professorial faculty members.

The staff of the Honors College has the responsibility for identifying and developing students to compete for prestigious national and international scholarships (Rhodes, Marshall, Mellon, Fulbright, Rotary, and others). These scholarships have different requirements ranging from a major emphasis on academic achievement to an emphasis on all-around ability.

The Honors Office is currently located in the Ralph B. Draughon Library and houses the offices of the director, assistant director, and secretary. Broun, Teague, Little, and Harper Halls are the Honors Residence Halls and are located in the Quad. They provide a place for the students to live, learn, and relax together. Computers and reference materials are available in the Honors Student Center, located in the basement of Broun Hall.

The 25-year-old program currently enrolls 630 students.

Participation Requirements: The University Honors College has two divisions. The curriculum of the lower division was developed to provide students with an opportunity for broad, enriching educational experiences and consists of honors sections of the required University core curriculum courses. Completion of these courses (24 hours) is recognized by a Junior Honors Certificate. The curriculum of the upper division consists of upper-level contract courses or reading/thesis courses, which provide opportunities for more focused and in-depth studies in the student's chosen discipline. Completion of these upper-level courses is recognized by a Senior Honors Certificate. Students can participate in either of these programs. Those who complete both programs with a minimum GPA of 3.4 will graduate as University Honors Scholars. This distinction is noted on students' diplomas and transcripts.

Admission Process: Entering freshmen and currently enrolled students who demonstrate the potential for academic excellence are eligible for admission into the University Honors College. Selection of incoming freshmen is based on ACT/SAT I scores (29/1280 minimum), high school GPA (3.5 minimum), and a record of leadership and service. Students currently enrolled at Auburn who have a 3.4 GPA may also be considered for admission.

Scholarship Availability: The Carolyn Brinson Reed Scholarships in the Arts and Humanities, the Raymond E. Sullivan Scholarships, the Compass Bank Scholarship, the Aldridge Honors Scholarship, the Boshell/Daniel Scholarships, the Sloan Y. Bashinsky Sr. Honors Scholarship, the Drummond Company Honors Scholarship, and the Wiatt Honors Scholarship are awarded annually to selected upperclassmen.

Campus Overview

State-supported university, founded 1856 • **Coed** 18,896 undergraduate students, 92% full-time, 48% women, 52% men.

Undergraduates 17,418 full-time, 1,478 part-time. Students come from 55 states and territories, 59 other countries, 32% are from out of state, 7% African American, 2% Asian American or Pacific Islander, 1% Hispanic American, 0.5% Native American, 0.8% international, 7% transferred in, 15% live on campus.

Faculty *Total:* 1,320, 89% full-time, 88% with terminal degrees. *Student/faculty ratio:* 16:1.

Academic Programs *Special study options:* accelerated degree program, adult/continuing education programs, advanced placement credit, cooperative education, distance learning, double majors, English as a second language, honors programs, independent study, internships, part-time degree program, services for LD students, study abroad, summer session for credit. *ROTC:* Army (b), Navy (b), Air Force (b).

Athletics Member NCAA. All Division I except football (Division I-A). *Intercollegiate sports:* baseball M(s), basketball M(s)/W(s), cross-country running M(s)/W(s), equestrian sports W(s), golf M(s)/W(s), gymnastics W(s), soccer W(s), softball W(s), swimming and diving M(s)/W(s), tennis M(s)/W(s), track and field M(s)/W(s), volleyball W(s). *Intramural sports:* badminton M/W, basketball M/W, bowling M/W, crew M(c)/W(c), football M/W, golf M/W, lacrosse M(c)/W(c), racquetball M/W, rugby M(c), sailing M(c)/W(c), soccer M(c)/W(c), softball M/W, swimming and diving M/W, table tennis M(c)/W(c), tennis M(c)/W(c), track and field M/W, volleyball M/W, wrestling M(c).

Costs (2004–05) *Tuition:* state resident $4610 full-time, $191 per credit hour part-time; nonresident $13,830 full-time, $573 per credit hour part-time. Full-time tuition and fees vary according to course load and program. Part-time tuition and fees vary according to course load and program. *Required fees:* $218 full-time. *Room and board:* $6686; room only: $2648. Room and board charges vary according to housing facility.

Financial Aid 564 Federal Work-Study jobs (averaging $2748). In 2003, 835 non-need-based awards were made. *Average percent of need met:* 51%. *Average financial aid package:* $7626. *Average need-based loan:* $3985. *Average need-based gift aid:* $3949. *Average non-need-based aid:* $3343.

Contact: Director: Dr. Jack W. Rogers Jr., RBD Library, Auburn University, Alabama 36849-5360; *Telephone:* 334-844-5860; *Fax:* 334-844-5885; *E-mail:* honors@mail.auburn.edu; *Web site:* http://www.auburn.edu//honors

Birmingham-Southern College
Honors Program
Birmingham, Alabama

The Honors Program at Birmingham-Southern College places a heavy influence on interdisciplinary learning. The program provides an alternative approach to meeting the general education

goals of the institution through a unique educational curriculum. The importance of viewing issues from many perspectives and of integrating as well as analyzing knowledge is a major focus. The curriculum is designed to foster students' intellectual curiosity beyond their major discipline, as well as to improve their oral and written communication skills and their ability to think and study independently.

Over the years, several small, interdisciplinary seminars have been developed specifically for the program. For example, Connections: Music, Mathematics and Structure in the Liberal Arts finds the math in music theory; Frankenstein meets "Snow White" takes into account cross-cultural studies in German and English romanticism; and Plural America teaches history through the literature of the time period being studied. The program typically offers three to four classes per semester, with class sizes ranging from 5 to 20. The average student-teacher ratio is 12:1.

Faculty involvement in both academic and nonacademic activities is high. Students are continually asking honors faculty members to speak or participate in discussion groups. There is an overall sense of rapport and camaraderie between students and teachers. The faculty members work intimately with senior honors students as sponsors for the students' independent study honors projects. Most professors are available to advise students at any hour, and many maintain contact with their honors students long after graduation.

Birmingham-Southern's Honors Program is more than the classes students take. Reminiscent of the European salons, the program strives to create an intellectual community in which its members can feel free to discuss ideas and concepts not tied to their major studies. Lecture series, book groups, and Provost forums have all been sponsored by the program in the past, with speakers and books chosen by honors students. Likewise, social events are planned according to the students needs and interests. The program provides study-break dinners at least once a month, usually in combination with tickets to one of the many on- and off-campus cultural events, for example, the latest Birmingham-Southern theater production of Hamlet *or* Amadeus *or directions and discounts to the Birmingham Film Festival.*

Honors Program facilities center on the Honors House. Located on Townhouse Row, the Honors House is three stories, complete with a full kitchen and laundry facilities. Furniture and electronic equipment, such as a television, VCR, and computer, are provided by the College. Up to 7 students can reside in the Honors House, alternately all men or all women, but it is open to all honors students for use at all times. In addition, the Honors Program works in conjunction with the International Studies Program, providing international and honors students alike with cooking facilities and a good place to "hang out."

Birmingham-Southern's Honors Program was founded circa 1980; currently, there are approximately 60 students enrolled.

Participation Requirements: The Honors Program component of an honors student's general education currently consists of 5 units of honors seminars and 1 unit of independent study, the Honors Project. Students may take one honors interim project, which counts toward the 5 units of honors seminars. The remaining general education requirements within the student's major field are completed according to the regular curriculum of the College. The specific general education requirements met by honors courses and those met by regular courses vary from student to student, depending on which honors courses the student elects to take. Students must maintain a minimum 3.5 GPA to stay enrolled in the program. Upon graduation from the program, the notation "Honors Program Scholar" is placed on the academic transcripts of graduating students.

Admission Process: The Honors Program at Birmingham-Southern College does not set a minimum GPA or SAT/ACT requirement. The College asks for a report of these figures on the application, but these are not the determining factors of admittance to the program. The application requests basic background, academic, and extracurricular information of the prospective student, as well as three letters of reference (one of which must be from a teacher) and an essay question. The applications are reviewed by the Program Director as well as the graduate assistant and other Honors Program faculty

members. Application deadlines are typically in February; students should know by April their admittance status to the program.

Scholarship Availability: There are no scholarships specific to the Honors Program, although exceptional students are invited by the College to participate in Scholarship Day. The scholarships awarded are based on academic achievement and merit. Individual departments also have performance/talent-based funding available.

Campus Overview

Independent Methodist comprehensive, founded 1856 • **Coed** 1,356 undergraduate students, 98% full-time, 58% women, 42% men.

Undergraduates 1,335 full-time, 21 part-time. Students come from 31 states and territories, 22 other countries, 25% are from out of state, 6% African American, 3% Asian American or Pacific Islander, 0.9% Hispanic American, 0.1% Native American, 0.1% international, 3% transferred in, 79% live on campus.

Faculty *Total:* 124, 77% full-time, 77% with terminal degrees. *Student/faculty ratio:* 12:1.

Academic Programs *Special study options:* advanced placement credit, double majors, honors programs, independent study, internships, off-campus study, part-time degree program, student-designed majors, study abroad, summer session for credit. *ROTC:* Army (c), Air Force (c). *Unusual degree programs:* 3-2 engineering with Auburn University, Columbia University, Washington University in St. Louis, University of Alabama at Birmingham; nursing with Vanderbilt University; environmental studies with Duke University.

Athletics Member NCAA. All Division I. *Intercollegiate sports:* baseball M(s), basketball M(s)/W(s), cross-country running M(s)/W(s), golf M(s)/W(s), riflery W(s), soccer M(s)/W(s), softball W(s), tennis M(s)/W(s), volleyball W(s). *Intramural sports:* basketball M/W, fencing M, football M/W, golf M/W, racquetball M, soccer M/W, softball M/W, tennis M/W, volleyball M/W.

Costs (2005–06) *Comprehensive fee:* $28,135 includes full-time tuition ($20,425), mandatory fees ($630), and room and board ($7080). Part-time tuition: $851 per credit hour. *College room only:* $5000. Room and board charges vary according to board plan and housing facility.

Financial Aid 142 Federal Work-Study jobs (averaging $1818). 157 state and other part-time jobs (averaging $1371). In 2003, 616 non-need-based awards were made. *Average percent of need met:* 82%. *Average financial aid package:* $16,015. *Average need-based loan:* $4560. *Average need-based gift aid:* $7342. *Average non-need-based aid:* $10,425.

Contact: Director: Dr. Susan K. Hagen, Box 549030, Birmingham-Southern College, Birmingham, Alabama 35254; *Telephone:* 205-226-7887; *E-mail:* shagen@bsc.edu

Jacksonville State University
College of Arts and Sciences Honors Program
Jacksonville, Alabama

*I*n keeping with the University's mission of serving the academic needs of a diverse student population, the Jacksonville State University Honors Program was established to provide academically gifted students with the opportunity to fully develop their intellectual potential. The Honors Program provides an enriched educational experience by fostering a strong grounding in the liberal arts and sciences, small classes, interaction with other outstanding and motivated students, instruction from some of JSU's most innovative and engaging faculty members, special activities, and special recognition for students successfully completing 18 hours or more of honors courses.

Participation Requirements: JSU offers honors courses in the arts, humanities, sciences, social sciences, and mathematics, which fulfill freshman and sophomore general studies requirements. Eligible students may take as many or as few honors classes as they wish.

Admission Process: For admissions information, students should contact the Director of the Honors Program at the address listed in this description.

Scholarship Availability: JSU offers scholarships to academically gifted students through its Faculty Scholars program. Alabama residents who score a minimum of 28 on the ACT or 1230 on the SAT may apply for a Faculty Scholarship. This scholarship pays full tuition and is renewable if the recipient maintains the necessary grade requirement. Students awarded this scholarship must reside in campus housing. Entering freshmen with an ACT score of 31 or above or SAT score of 1360 or above are eligible for an Elite Scholars award, which provides full tuition and housing. These scholarships are limited to Alabama residents. McGee Scholarships and Leadership Scholarships are available for non-Alabama residents. For a complete scholarship listing, students should call the Financial Aid Office at 256-782-5006 or consult the scholarship guide on the Web at http://www.jsu.edu.

Campus Overview

State-supported comprehensive, founded 1883 • **Coed** 7,138 undergraduate students, 80% full-time, 58% women, 42% men.

Undergraduates 5,700 full-time, 1,438 part-time. Students come from 43 states and territories, 70 other countries, 12% are from out of state, 22% African American, 1% Asian American or Pacific Islander, 1% Hispanic American, 0.7% Native American, 1% international, 10% transferred in, 20% live on campus.

Faculty *Total:* 412, 73% full-time, 53% with terminal degrees. *Student/faculty ratio:* 21:1.

Academic Programs *Special study options:* academic remediation for entering students, accelerated degree program, adult/continuing education programs, advanced placement credit, cooperative education, distance learning, double majors, honors programs, independent study, internships, part-time degree program, services for LD students, summer session for credit. *ROTC:* Army (b).

Athletics Member NCAA. All Division I except football (Division I-AA). *Intercollegiate sports:* baseball M(s), basketball M(s)/W(s), cross-country running M(s)/W(s), golf M(s)/W(s), riflery M(s)/W(s), softball W(s), tennis M(s)/W(s), volleyball W(s). *Intramural sports:* badminton M(c)/W(c), basketball M(c)/W(c), bowling M(c)/W(c), football M(c), golf M(c)/W(c), racquetball M(c)/W(c), soccer M(c)/W(c), softball M(c)/W(c), table tennis M(c)/W(c), tennis M(c)/W(c), volleyball M(c)/W(c).

Costs (2004–05) *Tuition:* state resident $4040 full-time, $169 per credit hour part-time; nonresident $8080 full-time, $338 per credit hour part-time. *Room and board:* $3312; room only: $1700. Room and board charges vary according to board plan and housing facility.

Financial Aid 304 Federal Work-Study jobs (averaging $2320).

Contact: Honors Program Director, College of Arts and Sciences, Jacksonville State University, 700 Pelham Road, North, Jacksonville, Alabama 36265; *Telephone:* 256-782-5649; *Fax:* 256-782-5689; *Web site:* http://www.jsu.edu/depart/cas/honors

The University of Alabama
Computer-Based Honors Program
Tuscaloosa, Alabama

*T*he Honors College was established by the University of Alabama (UA) Board of Trustees in 2004 to emphasize the importance of honors education at the University. The Honors College, which is overseen by its Dean, Dr. Bob Halli, is the administrative home of the University Honors Program, the Computer-Based Honors Program, and the International Honors Program. Students may apply for membership and complete the requirements for one, two, or three of the Honors Programs.

Administrators include the Dean, the 3 Honors Program directors, a registrar, a development officer, and a coordinator of prestige scholarships and awards. The coordinator of prestige scholarships and awards helps identify honors students to apply for and win distinctions at the University, national, and international levels.

A variety of services and enriching experiences are offered to all honors students. The Honors College offers weeklong pre–freshman year orientation programs for honors students. A Common Book Experience for honors freshmen further enhances their first year at UA. Authors and speakers are brought in to address honors students throughout the year. Honors students are the best and brightest at the University of Alabama, and the Honors College is designed to help them meet their great potential.

Whether one wants to be an English professor, a marketing executive, or an electrical engineer, not being able to apply computer technology to one's career field is a lot like not being able to read. The Computer-Based Honors Program (CBHP) is looking for 40 students who want to approach their fields of study, whatever they may be, with the best tools the Information Age has to offer. The CBHP, cited by the National Institute of Education as one of the six most intriguing honors programs in the United States, gives students opportunities to learn how to use computing technology in their major field of study. The program also gives 6 members of each entering class the chance to earn while they learn—six fellowships of $4000 per year, renewable for four years, are awarded on a competitive basis to CBHP students.

The Computer-Based Honors Program was founded in 1968 with a National Science Foundation grant. There is a maximum of 160 students in the program. The designation Computer-Based Honors Program appears on the honors student's diploma and transcript.

Participation Requirements: At the beginning of the freshman year, students take a highly accelerated course to introduce them to basic concepts of computing, to at least two computer languages, and to practical uses of the computer in problem solving. Although this course advances rapidly, it does not require any prior experience with computers.

When students are proficient in using the computer, they work as computer-oriented research assistants with faculty members or industry associates whose interests coincide with theirs. Projects in which CBHP students are involved usually entail researching a particular subject or experimenting with the computer as an instructional tool. The student participates in planning the project, in preparing the computer programs needed to complete the project, and in interpreting the results.

During the sophomore, junior, and senior years, students meet with other CBHP students in a weekly seminar with the program director. This systematic, long-term contact with students whose abilities are comparable to their own provides students with a forum for satisfying social and intellectual exchanges not readily available anywhere else.

Admission Process: The average ACT score is 32; the average SAT score is 1350. The average high school GPA is 3.9 to 4.0. The application, transcript, and essay are due by January 15. Twenty students are admitted based on their applications and are invited for a two-day visit to the campus.

Scholarship Availability: Six scholarships are awarded. Twenty-five total scholarships of $4000 are awarded per year; they are renewable based on continued superior performance. Three endowed scholarships from $2600 to $3000 are available to CBHP students on a competitive basis.

Campus Overview

State-supported university, founded 1831, part of The University of Alabama System • **Coed** 16,568 undergraduate students, 90% full-time, 53% women, 47% men.

Undergraduates 14,855 full-time, 1,713 part-time. Students come from 52 states and territories, 92 other countries, 20% are from out of state, 13% African American, 0.9% Asian American or Pacific Islander, 1% Hispanic American, 0.6% Native American, 1% international, 8% transferred in, 22% live on campus.

Faculty *Total:* 1,051, 80% full-time, 86% with terminal degrees. *Student/faculty ratio:* 20:1.

Academic Programs *Special study options:* academic remediation for entering students, accelerated degree program, adult/continuing education programs, advanced placement credit, cooperative education, distance learning, double majors, English as a second language, external degree program, freshman honors college, honors programs, independent study, internships, off-campus study, part-time degree program, services for LD students, student-designed majors, study abroad, summer session for credit. *ROTC:* Army (b), Air Force (b).

Athletics Member NCAA. All Division I except football (Division I-A). *Intercollegiate sports:* baseball M(s), basketball M(s)/W(s), cheerleading M(s)/W(s), cross-country running M(s)/W(s), golf M(s)/W(s), gymnastics W(s), soccer W(s), softball W(s), swimming and diving M(s)/W(s), tennis M(s)/W(s), track and field M(s)/W(s), volleyball W(s). *Intramural sports:* badminton M/W, basketball M/W, bowling M/W, crew M(c)/W(c), football M/W, golf M/W, lacrosse M(c)/W(c), racquetball M(c)/W(c), rugby M(c), soccer M(c)/W(c), softball M/W, squash M/W, table tennis M/W, tennis M(c)/W(c), track and field M/W, ultimate Frisbee M(c)/W(c), volleyball M/W, water polo M(c)/W(c), wrestling M(c)/W.

Costs (2004–05) *Tuition:* state resident $4630 full-time; nonresident $12,664 full-time. Full-time tuition and fees vary according to course load. Part-time tuition and fees vary according to course load. *Room and board:* $4734; room only: $2982. Room and board charges vary according to board plan and housing facility.

Financial Aid 700 Federal Work-Study jobs (averaging $3100). 1,500 state and other part-time jobs (averaging $4000). In 2002, 3978 non-need-based awards were made. *Average percent of need met:* 74%. *Average financial aid package:* $7902. *Average need-based loan:* $5025. *Average need-based gift aid:* $3664. *Average non-need-based aid:* $4659.

Contact: Director, Computer-Based Honors Program, Box 870169, Tuscaloosa, Alabama 35487-0169; *Telephone:* 205-348-5029; *Fax:* 205-348-5501; *E-mail:* cbhp@bama.ua.edu; *Web site:* http://www.cbhp.ua.edu

The University of Alabama
International Honors Program
Tuscaloosa, Alabama

The Honors College was established by the University of Alabama (UA) Board of Trustees in 2004 to emphasize the importance of honors education at the University. The Honors College, which is overseen by its Dean, Dr. Bob Halli, is the administrative home of the University Honors Program, the Computer-Based Honors Program, and the International Honors Program. Students may apply for membership and complete the requirements for one, two, or three of the Honors Programs.

Administrators include the Dean, the 3 Honors Program directors, a registrar, a development officer, and a coordinator of prestige scholarships and awards. The coordinator of prestige scholarships and awards helps identify honors students to apply for and win distinctions at the University, national, and international levels.

A variety of services and enriching experiences are offered to all honors students. The Honors College offers weeklong pre–freshman year orientation programs for honors students. A Common Book Experience for honors freshmen further enhances their first year at UA. Authors and speakers are brought in to address honors students throughout the year. Honors students are the best and brightest at the University of Alabama, and the Honors College is designed to help them meet their great potential.

Many honors students seek to excel in the classroom, lab, and studio—but may also desire to experience the larger world around them. The International Honors Program (IHP) at the University of Alabama is designed for students in any major who wish to internationalize their chosen course of study. IHP members study a foreign language for two years or more, take a cross-cultural communications course and upper-division courses with significant international content, and study abroad. Students become fully engaged in the international life of the UA campus through language conversation partnerships, activities hosted jointly with the International Student Association, and input into the campus's International Education Committee. IHP members have recently been distinguished as Rotary Ambassadorial Scholars, USA Today All-America Academic Team members, and Gilman Scholarship winners.

Founded in 1997, the program now enrolls 223 students.

Participation Requirements: All IHP students must complete the following: IHP 105 or 155, Culture and the Human Experience, a 3-credit seminar that exposes students to important world issues, raises global awareness, and develops cross-cultural communication skills; two upper-division courses (300- or 400-level) with significant international content, in which IHP students complete an additional project or assignment with prior arrangement with the instructor; two years of college-level foreign language courses or demonstration of proficiency in two languages; and international study or an international internship earning at least 6 hours of academic credit. IHP students must study abroad for a minimum of ten weeks; this can be completed in one semester or two standard summer terms abroad. Finally, a GPA of 3.0 or higher must be maintained.

Completion of the IHP is cited on students' transcripts and diplomas, is noted in the graduation program, and is distinguished by the wearing of a special IHP honor cord at the graduation ceremony.

Admission Process: Applications from incoming freshmen with an ACT composite score of 26 or higher or an SAT score of 1190 or higher are automatically accepted. Students not admitted as freshmen may apply after they have earned a GPA of 3.0 or higher for a semester's work at UA. Transfer students with at least a 3.0 GPA on courses transferred to UA are also automatically admissible.

Scholarship Availability: Support for study abroad is available from the McWane and Cox Endowments. The IHP actively assists members in locating scholarships and support for studying abroad.

Campus Overview

State-supported university, founded 1831, part of The University of Alabama System • **Coed** 16,568 undergraduate students, 90% full-time, 53% women, 47% men.

Undergraduates 14,855 full-time, 1,713 part-time. Students come from 52 states and territories, 92 other countries, 20% are from out of state, 13% African American, 0.9% Asian American or Pacific Islander, 1% Hispanic American, 0.6% Native American, 1% international, 8% transferred in, 22% live on campus.

Faculty *Total:* 1,051, 80% full-time, 86% with terminal degrees. *Student/faculty ratio:* 20:1.

Academic Programs *Special study options:* academic remediation for entering students, accelerated degree program, adult/continuing education programs, advanced placement credit, cooperative education, distance learning, double majors, English as a second language, external degree program, freshman honors college, honors programs, independent study, internships, off-campus study, part-time degree program, services for LD students, student-designed majors, study abroad, summer session for credit. *ROTC:* Army (b), Air Force (b).

Athletics Member NCAA. All Division I except football (Division I-A). *Intercollegiate sports:* baseball M(s), basketball M(s)/W(s), cheerleading M(s)/W(s), cross-country running M(s)/W(s), golf M(s)/W(s), gymnastics W(s), soccer W(s), softball W(s), swimming and diving M(s)/W(s), tennis M(s)/W(s), track and field M(s)/W(s), volleyball W(s). *Intramural sports:* badminton M/W, basketball M/W, bowling M/W, crew M(c)/W(c), football M/W, golf M/W, lacrosse M(c)/W(c), racquetball M(c)/W(c), rugby M(c), soccer M(c)/W(c), softball M/W, squash M/W, table tennis M/W, tennis M(c)/W(c), track and field M/W, ultimate Frisbee M(c)/W(c), volleyball M/W, water polo M(c)/W(c), wrestling M(c)/W.

Costs (2004–05) *Tuition:* state resident $4630 full-time; nonresident $12,664 full-time. Full-time tuition and fees vary according to course load. Part-time tuition and fees vary according to course load. *Room and board:* $4734; room only: $2982. Room and board charges vary according to board plan and housing facility.

Financial Aid 700 Federal Work-Study jobs (averaging $3100). 1,500 state and other part-time jobs (averaging $4000). In 2002, 3978 non-need-based awards were made. *Average percent of need met:* 74%. *Average financial aid package:* $7902. *Average need-based loan:* $5025. *Average need-based gift aid:* $3664. *Average non-need-based aid:* $4659.

Contact: Director, International Honors Program, Box 870169, Tuscaloosa, Alabama 35487-0169; *Telephone:* 205-348-5554; *Fax:* 205-348-5501; *E-mail:* ihp@bama.ua.edu; *Web site:* http://www.ihp.ua.edu

---

The University of Alabama
University Honors Program
Tuscaloosa, Alabama

The Honors College was established by the University of Alabama (UA) Board of Trustees in 2004 to emphasize the importance of honors education at the University. The Honors College, which is overseen by its Dean, Dr. Bob Halli, is the administrative home of the University Honors Program, the Computer-Based Honors Program, and the International Honors Program. Students may apply for membership and complete the requirements for one, two, or three of the Honors Programs.

Administrators include the Dean, the 3 Honors Program directors, a registrar, a development officer, and a coordinator of prestige scholarships and awards. The coordinator of prestige scholarships and awards helps identify honors students to apply for and win distinctions at the University, national, and international levels.

A variety of services and enriching experiences are offered to all honors students. The Honors College offers weeklong pre–freshman year orientation programs for honors students. A Common Book Experience for honors freshmen further enhances their first year at UA. Authors and speakers are brought in to address honors students throughout the year. Honors students are the best and brightest at the University of Alabama, and the Honors College is designed to help them meet their great potential.

Qualified students seeking a special academic challenge in their undergraduate work can find it in the University Honors Program (UH) at the University of Alabama. More than 1,600 students from all schools and colleges in the University participate in the program. The University Honors Program gives outstanding students the opportunity to work with their peers and with outstanding faculty members in an enriched academic environment. It also offers students the opportunity to combine some of the benefits of a small-college experience with the advantages of a major research university.

Honors courses have limited enrollment in order to facilitate interaction between students and faculty members. Honors courses often parallel regular University courses, but they offer enriched content and provide for more student input and creative writing. The University Honors Program fulfills core-curriculum and other requirements, allowing students to pursue their own specific degree and study objectives within the honors framework. Students in the program do not take a full schedule of honors courses. Most students take perhaps two honors courses each semester. However, all students are expected to take at least one honors course during each academic year of their first two years of the program in order to retain the privilege of priority registration. The evaluation of student work in honors courses neither penalizes nor unduly rewards students for their honors course work. Most students perform well in classes they find to be interesting and challenging.

Founded in 1987, the program now enrolls 1,635 students.

Participation Requirements: Students complete a total of 18 hours of honors credit, 3 to 6 of which may include an honors thesis. Students must choose two UH courses at the 100, 200, or 300 level in order to graduate with the Honors designation; they must also write an honors thesis in order to graduate with the Honors with Thesis designation.

The official transcript identifies honors courses, thereby enhancing an honors student's position in competing for employment or admission to professional schools. The University diploma indicates Honors status, with that distinction noted at graduation ceremonies. Each year, the Honors Program Student Association, a body of students who are also members of the Honors Program, gives the Outstanding Honors Program Graduate Award to a senior who has served the honors community faithfully and well over her or his undergraduate career at the University.

Admission Process: Students with an ACT score of at least 28 or an SAT score of at least 1240 are automatically admissible to the program. National Merit Finalists, National Achievement Finalists, National Hispanic Finalists, and UA Presidential Scholars are automatically admissible. Students not admitted to the program as freshmen may apply after they have earned a GPA of 3.3 or higher for a semester's work at UA. Transfer students with at least a 3.3 GPA on courses transferred to UA are also automatically admissible. All participants must maintain at least a 3.3 GPA and give evidence of actively pursuing the honors requirements to remain a member in good standing in the program.

Scholarship Availability: The Barrett C. and Tally Gilmer Shelton Scholarship and the Jo Nell Usrey Honors Scholarship are available to entering freshmen who are participating in the University Honors Program and who are receiving no other financial aid from the University. Other scholarships include seven John K. McKinley Student Excellence Awards and the Alton C. and Cecile C. Craig Scholarship. Support for research and study abroad is available from the McWane Endowment and the Cox Endowment.

Campus Overview

State-supported university, founded 1831, part of The University of Alabama System • **Coed** 16,568 undergraduate students, 90% full-time, 53% women, 47% men.

Undergraduates 14,855 full-time, 1,713 part-time. Students come from 52 states and territories, 92 other countries, 20% are from out of state, 13% African American, 0.9% Asian American or Pacific Islander, 1% Hispanic American, 0.6% Native American, 1% international, 8% transferred in, 22% live on campus.

Faculty *Total:* 1,051, 80% full-time, 86% with terminal degrees. *Student/faculty ratio:* 20:1.

Academic Programs *Special study options:* academic remediation for entering students, accelerated degree program, adult/continuing

education programs, advanced placement credit, cooperative education, distance learning, double majors, English as a second language, external degree program, freshman honors college, honors programs, independent study, internships, off-campus study, part-time degree program, services for LD students, student-designed majors, study abroad, summer session for credit. *ROTC:* Army (b), Air Force (b).

Athletics Member NCAA. All Division I except football (Division I-A). *Intercollegiate sports:* baseball M(s), basketball M(s)/W(s), cheerleading M(s)/W(s), cross-country running M(s)/W(s), golf M(s)/W(s), gymnastics W(s), soccer W(s), softball W(s), swimming and diving M(s)/W(s), tennis M(s)/W(s), track and field M(s)/W(s), volleyball W(s). *Intramural sports:* badminton M/W, basketball M/W, bowling M/W, crew M(c)/W(c), football M/W, golf M/W, lacrosse M(c)/W(c), racquetball M(c)/W(c), rugby M(c), soccer M(c)/W(c), softball M/W, squash M/W, table tennis M/W, tennis M(c)/W(c), track and field M/W, ultimate Frisbee M(c)/W(c), volleyball M/W, water polo M(c)/W(c), wrestling M(c)/W.

Costs (2004–05) *Tuition:* state resident $4630 full-time; nonresident $12,664 full-time. Full-time tuition and fees vary according to course load. Part-time tuition and fees vary according to course load. *Room and board:* $4734; room only: $2982. Room and board charges vary according to board plan and housing facility.

Financial Aid 700 Federal Work-Study jobs (averaging $3100). 1,500 state and other part-time jobs (averaging $4000). In 2002, 3978 non-need-based awards were made. *Average percent of need met:* 74%. *Average financial aid package:* $7902. *Average need-based loan:* $5025. *Average need-based gift aid:* $3664. *Average non-need-based aid:* $4659.

Contact: Director: University Honors Program, Box 870169, Tuscaloosa, Alabama 35487-0169; *Telephone:* 205-348-5500; *Fax:* 205-348-5501; *E-mail:* uhp@bama.ua.edu; *Web site:* http://www.uhp.ua.edu/

The University of Alabama at Birmingham
University Honors Program
Birmingham, Alabama

Since its founding in 1983, the University Honors Program at the University of Alabama at Birmingham (UAB) has offered an innovative and challenging curriculum for highly motivated, intellectually curious students. The program allows committed students representing a wide variety of majors, backgrounds, and interests to form close relationships with faculty members, explore new ideas, and share their ideas and interests, all in the friendly confines of the Spencer Honors House. The 33-hour honors curriculum, which replaces the core curriculum, consists of two 9-credit-hour interdisciplinary courses and five 3-credit-hour honors seminars. At the heart of the program is an interdisciplinary approach to learning. Each year, the fall interdisciplinary course is team-taught by 6 faculty members from different disciplines, who are carefully selected based on their excellence in teaching and scholarship. The 6 faculty scholars represent disciplines as diverse as English, engineering, biochemistry, psychology, economics, and theology. The courses are organized thematically, where a single subject (e.g., time, origins, human nature, beauty, or truth) is examined from multiple disciplinary perspectives, thus fostering critical thinking, mutual understanding, and interdisciplinary teamwork. Honors seminars cover topics not covered by courses offered in the regular undergraduate curriculum, are available in a variety of different fields, and focus on issues that are of major and topical interest within the field. The curriculum is always innovative, with no course offered more than once, so students are introduced to the latest information, methodologies, social trends, and technologies.

The program has a strong extracurricular focus that extends the undergraduate experience beyond academic course work to a way of life. The faculty and staff members and students of the University Honors Program make up a close community of active teachers and learners who share their energy and commitment not only to each other but with the larger community. Honors students organize and staff many community service projects, including those providing services to local public school children, homeless women and children, the elderly, and the sick.

The Spencer Honors House, a magnificent old church on the UAB campus built in 1902, houses a large lecture hall, two seminar rooms, a kitchen, a computer cluster, faculty offices, pool, table soccer, Ping Pong tables, and lots of places for studying and relaxing. Honors program students have access 24/7. The building has wireless Internet access. All honors course work takes place in the Spencer Honors House, as do the many lectures, films, social gatherings, and discussions sponsored by the program each year. Spencer Honors House is located at 1190 10th Avenue South.

Students in the University Honors Program are funded to attend state, regional, and national honors conferences, where they give formal presentations. Students are encouraged to get involved in undergraduate research and present their findings at regional and national honors and professional conferences. The vast majority of UAB students who have won prestigious national scholarships have been members of the University Honors Program. Students are also encouraged to participate in study-abroad opportunities.

The University Honors Program is limited to a total of about 200 students (about 50 students per year) and is open to students pursuing any major. Participation in the Honors Program does not delay progress toward a degree and promotes involvement in departmental honors programs, which are open to all qualified students.

Participation Requirements: In order to remain in the program, students must maintain a GPA of at least 3.0 in their honors course work. Students who complete the 33-hour curriculum graduate "With University Honors" on their transcript and are so acknowledged in the Commencement program. Students who go on to complete a departmental honors program graduate with the designation "With University Honors in (major)" on their transcripts and in the Commencement program. Graduates of the program are also honored at a special graduation for honors students

Admission Process: Students are selected for the program on the basis of national test scores, GPA, two letters of recommendation, an essay, a personal interview, and any special evidence a student chooses to submit. There is no cutoff used for standardized test scores or GPA, but the program seeks students with academic ability, creativity, talent, intellectual promise, and competence in basic skills. Although most students entering the program are full-time freshmen, part-time students are also eligible, and students may even enter the program as sophomores or juniors. Nontraditional students are encouraged to apply. The program admits a maximum of 50 students per year. Students wishing to enter the UAB Honors Program must complete a separate application in addition to the regular UAB application. The application deadline for the Honors Program is January 1.

Scholarship Availability: Most honors students are awarded scholarships by the University, for which they are automatically considered during the fall admissions process. The University Honors Program awards additional scholarships that can serve either to upgrade an existing UAB scholarship offer or offer scholarship to a student without a University scholarship. These include three University Scholarships (full tuition and fees plus $1000 per year for four years) for Alabama students with a minimum 28 ACT and 3.5 GPA; three Hess-Abroms Honors Scholarships ($5000 per year for four years) for students who best meet the general Honors Program admission criteria described above; three Juliet-Nunn Pearson Scholarships ($1000 each) for promising incoming students; and five Spencer Scholarships ($2000 each) on the basis of merit and need.

Campus Overview

State-supported university, founded 1969, part of University of Alabama System • **Coed** 11,441 undergraduate students, 70% full-time, 61% women, 39% men.

Undergraduates 7,995 full-time, 3,446 part-time. Students come from 43 states and territories, 76 other countries, 6% are from out of state, 33% African American, 3% Asian American or Pacific Islander, 1% Hispanic American, 0.4% Native American, 3% international, 9% transferred in, 11% live on campus.

Faculty *Total:* 881, 89% full-time, 87% with terminal degrees. *Student/faculty ratio:* 18:1.

Academic Programs *Special study options:* academic remediation for entering students, adult/continuing education programs, advanced placement credit, cooperative education, double majors, honors programs, independent study, internships, off-campus study, part-time degree program, services for LD students, student-designed majors, study abroad, summer session for credit. *ROTC:* Army (b), Air Force (c). *Unusual degree programs:* 3-2 accounting.

Athletics Member NCAA. All Division I except football (Division I-A). *Intercollegiate sports:* baseball M(s), basketball M(s)/W(s), cross-country running W(s), golf M(s)/W(s), riflery M/W, soccer M(s)/W(s), softball W(s), swimming and diving W(s), tennis M(s)/W(s), track and field W(s), volleyball W(s). *Intramural sports:* badminton M/W, baseball M, basketball M/W, bowling M/W, football M/W, golf M/W, racquetball M/W, soccer M/W, softball M/W, swimming and diving M/W, table tennis M/W, tennis M/W, track and field M/W, ultimate Frisbee M/W, volleyball M/W, wrestling M.

Costs (2004–05) *Tuition:* state resident $4662 full-time; nonresident $10,422 full-time. Full-time tuition and fees vary according to program. Part-time tuition and fees vary according to program. *Room only:* $3060. Room and board charges vary according to housing facility.

Financial Aid In 2004, 1254 non-need-based awards were made. *Average percent of need met:* 42%. *Average financial aid package:* $13,600. *Average need-based loan:* $4163. *Average need-based gift aid:* $3345. *Average non-need-based aid:* $8392.

Contact: Director: Dr. Mike Sloane, HOH, 1530 3rd Avenue South, Birmingham, Alabama 35294-4450; *Telephone:* 205-934-3228; *Fax:* 205-975-5493; *E-mail:* sloane@uab.edu; *Web site:* http://www.hp.uab.edu

---

The University of Alabama in Huntsville

University Honors Program

Huntsville, Alabama

The Honors Program at the University of Alabama in Huntsville (UAH) enhances the opportunity for academic excellence. It offers study of the scientific and humanistic accomplishments of the past and present in order to increase knowledge of the self and of the world. It provides academically talented undergraduate students with opportunities to develop their special talents and skills within an expanded and enriched version of the curriculum. Students in the Honors Program participate in structured enrichment activities that include honors course work parallel to regular offerings, special interdisciplinary seminars, field trips, and the option of independent study and research. First- and second-year students take Honors Forum, a course designed to introduce the multidisciplinary focus of the honors education. Seniors complete an Honors Senior Project directed by an adviser in their major and formally present their research findings in a public forum. In all of these specially designed classes and activities, students are assured an exciting academic career that will

also nurture their special talents. The Honors Program offers personalized academic guidance and counseling for all honors students, but especially for first- and second-year participants. The UAH Honors Program provides a path to a unique education.

The Honors Program is housed in a small complex that includes the director's and assistant's office and two comfortably outfitted study and lounge rooms. These rooms also include computers, basic reference books, and selected journals, newspapers, and other print media. This setting provides the opportunity for academic and social interaction among students, special campus guests, the director, and honors faculty members.

The 15-year-old program currently enrolls 130 students.

Participation Requirements: An honors student is required to maintain a cumulative GPA of 3.0 or above. Graduation from the program requires 24 hours of honors course work. Graduating honors students are awarded University Honors recognition at Honors Convocation and at Commencement. The title of the senior project is printed in the Commencement booklet and on official transcripts, and "University Honors" is printed on the diploma.

Admission Process: All academically eligible students are urged to participate in the Honors Program. The minimum requirement for first-year students is a high school GPA of 3.5. Minimum test scores for admission are as follows: ACT composite, 28; SAT I composite, 1200. Enrolled UAH students who complete 12 hours of course work with a GPA of 3.3 or higher may be invited to join the program based on outstanding performance.

Scholarship Availability: Scholarships are handled through the Financial Aid Office. Although no funds are designated specifically for honors students, many of them receive scholarships based on academic merit.

Campus Overview

State-supported university, founded 1950, part of University of Alabama System • **Coed** 5,523 undergraduate students, 73% full-time, 50% women, 50% men.

Undergraduates 4,033 full-time, 1,490 part-time. Students come from 42 states and territories, 66 other countries, 13% are from out of state, 15% African American, 4% Asian American or Pacific Islander, 2% Hispanic American, 1% Native American, 3% international, 12% transferred in, 16% live on campus.

Faculty *Total:* 459, 59% full-time, 70% with terminal degrees. *Student/faculty ratio:* 16:1.

Academic Programs *Special study options:* academic remediation for entering students, adult/continuing education programs, advanced placement credit, cooperative education, distance learning, double majors, English as a second language, honors programs, independent study, internships, off-campus study, part-time degree program, services for LD students, summer session for credit. *ROTC:* Army (c). *Unusual degree programs:* 3-2 engineering with Oakwood College, Morehouse College, Clark Atlanta University, Fisk University.

Athletics Member NCAA. All Division II except ice hockey (Division I). *Intercollegiate sports:* archery M(c)/W(c), badminton M(c)/W(c), baseball M(s), basketball M(s)/W(s), bowling M(c)/W(c), cheerleading M(s)/W(s), crew M(c)/W(c), cross-country running M(s)/W(s), ice hockey M(s), soccer M(s)/W(s), softball W(s), tennis M(s)/W(s), track and field M(s)/W(s), volleyball W(s). *Intramural sports:* badminton M/W, basketball M/W, football M/W, golf M/W, racquetball M/W, soccer M/W, softball M/W, table tennis M/W, ultimate Frisbee M/W, volleyball M/W.

Costs (2004–05) *Tuition:* state resident $4516 full-time, $1013 per term part-time; nonresident $9518 full-time, $2128 per term part-time. Full-time tuition and fees vary according to course load. Part-time tuition and fees vary according to course load. *Room and board:* $5200; room only: $3600. Room and board charges vary according to board plan and housing facility.

Financial Aid 108 Federal Work-Study jobs (averaging $2911). In 2004, 878 non-need-based awards were made. *Average percent of* *need met: 52%. Average financial aid package: $5848. Average need-based loan: $3618. Average need-based gift aid: $3240. Average non-need-based aid: $2208.*

Contact: Director: Dr. John S. Mebane, Honors Program, University of Alabama in Huntsville, Huntsville, Alabama 35899; *Telephone:* 256-824-6450; *Fax:* 256-824-7339; *Web site:* http://www.uah.edu/honors

University of North Alabama
Honors Program
Florence, Alabama

The University of North Alabama (UNA) Honors Program is a comprehensive four-year program open to majors in all areas of study. Honors education at UNA has four basic goals. The first goal is to provide the best possible environment for the learning process. The program also seeks to foster individual student growth in terms of creativity, imagination, and critical thinking. The third goal pertains to developing a commitment to service, to the University and, more importantly, to the larger communities—local, national, and global—in which the student lives. Finally, the UNA Honors Program has, as a part of its mission, the goal to train and enhance the leadership potential of its students.

The UNA Honors Program features small class sizes (15 students) taught by the most creative and dynamic faculty members on campus. Faculty members are recruited from all four campus colleges. Students complete two years of honors courses in a seminar format, including a first-year interdisciplinary seminar, world literature, world history, honors speech, and honors courses in the natural and social sciences. The UNA Honors Program was founded in 2005.

Participation Requirements: Honors students may major in any undergraduate program at UNA. Students who complete Honors Program requirements graduate with University Honors. The Honors Program curriculum consists of 42 credit hours of honors course work, including 34 credit hours of general education requirements. Honors students participate in the 1-credit hour Honors Forum during their first two years. The remaining 6 hours are fulfilled either through independent research in the major field or junior and senior seminars. To remain in the Honors Program, students must maintain a minimum 3.25 GPA.

Admission Process: Admissions are selective and ongoing throughout the spring. First-year students must have a minimum ACT score of 28 or minimum SAT score of 1260 (composite math and verbal scores) and a high school GPA of at least 3.5.

Scholarship Availability: All honors students at UNA attend on academic scholarships awarded through the Office of Admissions. Additional scholarships are also available in the 2005–06 academic year. Scholarships include National Merit and Achievement Finalists, National Merit and Achievement Semifinalists, full and partial academic scholarships, and Valedictorian and Salutatorian Scholarships. Students must be accepted into UNA by February 1 to qualify for these scholarships.

Campus Overview

State-supported comprehensive, founded 1830, part of Alabama Commission on Higher Education • **Coed** 5,200 undergraduate students, 82% full-time, 58% women, 42% men.

Undergraduates 4,240 full-time, 960 part-time. Students come from 40 states and territories, 43 other countries, 20% are from out of state, 10% African American, 0.7% Asian American or Pacific Islander, 0.8% Hispanic American, 2% Native American, 6% international, 12% transferred in, 19% live on campus.

Faculty *Total:* 298, 68% full-time, 51% with terminal degrees. *Student/faculty ratio:* 20:1.

Academic Programs *Special study options:* academic remediation for entering students, accelerated degree program, adult/continuing education programs, advanced placement credit, cooperative education, distance learning, double majors, English as a second language, independent study, internships, part-time degree program, services for LD students, summer session for credit. *ROTC:* Army (b).

Athletics Member NCAA. All Division II. *Intercollegiate sports:* baseball M(s), basketball M(s)/W(s), cross-country running M(s)/W(s), football M(s), golf M(s), soccer W(s), softball W(s), tennis M(s)/W(s), volleyball W(s). *Intramural sports:* badminton M/W, baseball M, basketball M/W, bowling M/W, cross-country running M/W, football M/W, golf M, racquetball M/W, softball W, swimming and diving M/W, table tennis M/W, tennis M/W, volleyball M/W, weight lifting M/W.

Costs (2004–05) *Tuition:* state resident $3528 full-time, $139 per credit hour part-time; nonresident $7055 full-time, $278 per credit hour part-time. Part-time tuition and fees vary according to course load. *Required fees:* $568 full-time. *Room and board:* $4140; room only: $1960. Room and board charges vary according to board plan and housing facility.

Financial Aid 240 Federal Work-Study jobs (averaging $1298). *Average percent of need met:* 41%. *Average financial aid package:* $3508. *Average need-based loan:* $4913. *Average need-based gift aid:* $2780.

Contact: Director: Dr. Vince Brewton, Honors Program, Lafayette Hall, University of North Alabama, Florence, Alabama 35632; *Telephone:* 256-760-9492; *E-mail:* vjbrewton@una.edu; *Web site:* http://www.una.edu/honors

University of South Alabama
Honors Program
Mobile, Alabama

The University of South Alabama (USA) Honors Program offers a curriculum of interdisciplinary excellence designed to stimulate analytical and critical thinking of exceptionally qualified and highly motivated students. In this effort, the USA Honors Program challenges the students with scholarly creative activities, exposes them to cultural enrichment, and requires them to engage in community service. The USA Honors Program aspires to instill in students the intellectual excitement that will better prepare them for productive careers and citizenship. Within the context and diversity of a midsized urban university, the USA Honors Program provides the academic and cultural atmosphere and setting expected of a small, personal campus community of excellence.

The main honors option, the University Honors Program, is a campuswide program that includes honors course work and extracurricular activities throughout the four years of a student's undergraduate career. In addition to general University curriculum requirements and degree requirements of the selected major, University honors students also complete enriched honors general studies courses, honors seminars, and a Senior Honors Project. A cornerstone of the program is that each student is assigned a faculty mentor, chosen from the student's major department or suggested by the Honors Program until a major has been identified, who directs the student through the research and scholarly experience that culminates in an Honors Senior Project. Mentors are outstanding faculty members of the University.

Honors classes are small (usually 20 or fewer students) and are taught by the University's most stimulating faculty members. Specially scheduled scholarly presentations involve honors students and the wider academic community in a format that includes the opportunity to debate various issues and to listen to and interact with invited speakers and performing artists.

In addition to challenging academic opportunities, the University Honors Program offers a variety of activities that extend learning beyond the classroom, including social and cultural activities and community service projects. All University honors students are required to participate on a continuing basis in community and campus service activities. University honors students are encouraged to participate in international programs and off-campus internships and are assisted by the program in applying for national or international scholarships (e.g., Fulbright and Rhodes scholarships and graduate and professional schools). University honors students are also given priority for registration and an option to select honors housing.

A second honors option, Departmental Honors, is available in many majors to transfer and upperclass students who enter with more than 32 semester hours. To receive a designation of With Distinction in the major, Departmental Honors students must complete the Senior Honors Project and meet the specific honors requirements of the major department.

Participation Requirements: Participants in the USA Honors Program take 30 semester hours of honors credit in a combination of special sections of selected general studies courses, honors seminars, and honors electives (often in their major). Only grades of C or better count toward the Honors Program. The culminating experience of the program is the Senior Honors Project, designed and conducted in close collaboration with a faculty mentor from the major field of study. The Senior Honors Project often results in a student-authored publication. Honors students are involved together in community and campus service projects and regularly attend cultural and scholarly events facilitated by the Honors Program Office.

University honors students must maintain satisfactory progress in the honors curriculum to remain in the program. Required overall GPAs for honors students are 3.0 or higher after the freshman year, 3.25 or higher after the sophomore year, and 3.5 or higher after the junior year and through completion of the requirements of the Honors Program. A student may be placed on honors probation for a period of one semester and must attain the required GPA at the end of the probationary semester in order to return to full status in the Honors Program.

Completion of the University Honors Program is signified by the notation of With University Honors on the transcript and special recognition in the graduation program. All honors courses are specifically noted on the transcript.

Admission Process: High school seniors with a minimum composite ACT score of 27 (or comparable SAT score) and a minimum 3.5 (of 4.0) high school GPA are invited to apply. USA students and transfer students who have completed no more than 32 semester hours with a GPA of at least 3.5 are also eligible to enter the program. Students without the above qualifications who feel they have strong potential for success in the University Honors Program are encouraged to submit an application package and documentation of evidence of their special qualifications for review by the Honors Admissions Committee. Transfer students applying for admission to the program should indicate any credit earned in other honors programs. An honors application package includes a completed honors application form, two letters of recommendation, and an essay on a topic specified annually by the USA Honors Program, in addition to a USA admission application and high school transcripts and standardized test scores.

Scholarship Availability: The University of South Alabama offers USA Honors Scholarships to qualified participants in the USA Honors Program. Scholarship award amounts are based upon ACT scores (or SAT equivalent) and range from $20,000 to $40,000 for four years.

Campus Overview

State-supported university, founded 1963 • **Coed** 10,350 undergraduate students, 73% full-time, 60% women, 40% men.

Undergraduates 7,590 full-time, 2,760 part-time. Students come from 48 states and territories, 102 other countries, 17% are from out of state, 18% African American, 3% Asian American or Pacific Islander, 2% Hispanic American, 0.9% Native American, 5% international, 10% transferred in, 19% live on campus.

Faculty *Total:* 978, 73% full-time. *Student/faculty ratio:* 18:1.

Academic Programs *Special study options:* academic remediation for entering students, accelerated degree program, adult/continuing education programs, advanced placement credit, cooperative education, distance learning, double majors, English as a second language, external degree program, freshman honors college, independent study, internships, part-time degree program, services for LD students, student-designed majors, study abroad, summer session for credit. *ROTC:* Army (b), Air Force (b).

Athletics Member NCAA. All Division I. *Intercollegiate sports:* baseball M(s), basketball M(s)/W(s), cross-country running M(s)/W(s), fencing M(c)/W(c), football M(c), golf M/W, soccer W(s), tennis M(s)/W(s), track and field M(s)/W(s), volleyball W(s). *Intramural sports:* badminton M/W, basketball M/W, bowling M/W, cheerleading M(c)/W(c), golf M/W, racquetball M/W, sailing M(c)/W(c), soccer M/W, softball M/W, table tennis M/W, tennis M/W, volleyball M/W, water polo M/W.

Costs (2004–05) *Tuition:* state resident $3810 full-time, $127 per credit hour part-time; nonresident $7620 full-time, $254 per credit hour part-time. *Required fees:* $480 full-time, $179 per term part-time. *Room and board:* $4222; room only: $2352. Room and board charges vary according to board plan, housing facility, and location.

Financial Aid In 2003, 890 non-need-based awards were made. *Average percent of need met:* 45%. *Average financial aid package:* $5702. *Average non-need-based aid:* $1978.

Contact: Honors Director: Dr. Bob Coleman, 1230 Seaman's Bethel Theater, 307 University Boulevard, North, Mobile, Alabama 36688-0002; *Telephone:* 251-461-1637; *Fax:* 251-460-7732; *E-mail:* honors@usouthal.edu; *Web site:* http://www.southalabama.edu/honors

ALASKA

University of Alaska Anchorage
University Honors Program
Anchorage, Alaska

The University Honors Program of the University of Alaska Anchorage (UAA) allows outstanding students from all disciplines to interact with one another through an interdisciplinary core curriculum and informal social activities. Honors classes have an intimate feel, generally range between 12 and 20 students, and are taught by faculty members with a strong commitment to innovative undergraduate education. All honors freshmen and sophomores take courses that allow them to participate in community service projects and heighten community and cultural awareness. University Honors also offers students the opportunity to participate in guided individual research within their chosen course of study. Honors seniors can choose from a variety of senior-year capstone experiences.

Outside of classes, Honors Program students receive a weekly honors newsletter and participate in various social events, including retreats, game nights, visiting speakers, and other functions. A floor in the campus residence halls is reserved for honors students. All students in the program have access to an honors computer lab, where they can study and socialize. Founded in 1998, the program currently enrolls approximately 180 students.

Participation Requirements: Students admitted into baccalaureate degree programs can participate in the program. Students must complete 9 credits of honors course work as freshmen and sophomores, a 1-credit thesis-preparatory course in the junior year, and a 6-credit senior capstone thesis, project, or seminar. Students who complete the required course work with a cumulative GPA of at least 3.5 have University Honors Scholar noted on their transcript and diploma, receive special recognition at commencement, and receive a certificate of achievement.

Admission Process: To join the program, students must have achieved a high school or college GPA of at least 3.0 and show strong evidence of ability to reach and maintain at least a 3.5 GPA level at UAA. Applications are judged based on the student's letter of application, writing sample, high school or college transcripts, SAT and/or ACT scores, and references.

Scholarship Availability: The University of Alaska system offers scholarships to the top 10 percent of all Alaska high school graduates (the University of Alaska Scholars Program, worth $1375 per semester in 2001–02). The UAA Honors Program also offers a limited number of full and partial tuition waiver scholarships to incoming freshmen and continuing students in the program, available to both resident and nonresident students. Other tuition waiver scholarships are available through the University of Alaska President's Office and the University of Alaska Anchorage Chancellor's Office. Other financial assistance, including scholarships, research support, grants, loans, and part-time employment, is available to qualified students at UAA.

Campus Overview

State-supported comprehensive, founded 1954, part of University of Alaska System • **Coed** 15,481 undergraduate students, 45% full-time, 61% women, 39% men.

Undergraduates 6,906 full-time, 8,575 part-time. Students come from 50 states and territories, 41 other countries, 6% are from out of state, 4% African American, 6% Asian American or Pacific Islander, 4% Hispanic American, 10% Native American, 2% international, 3% transferred in, 6% live on campus.

Faculty *Total:* 1,202, 44% full-time, 30% with terminal degrees. *Student/faculty ratio:* 18:1.

Academic Programs *Special study options:* academic remediation for entering students, accelerated degree program, adult/continuing education programs, advanced placement credit, cooperative education, distance learning, double majors, English as a second language, honors programs, independent study, internships, off-campus study, part-time degree program, services for LD students, student-designed majors, study abroad, summer session for credit. *ROTC:* Air Force (b).

Athletics Member NCAA. All Division II. *Intercollegiate sports:* basketball M(s)/W(s), cross-country running M(s), gymnastics W(s), ice hockey M(s), skiing (cross-country) M(s)/W(s), skiing (downhill) M(s)/W(s), swimming and diving M(s), volleyball W(s). *Intramural sports:* basketball M/W, field hockey M/W, ice hockey M/W, racquetball M/W, soccer M/W, volleyball M/W, weight lifting M/W.

Costs (2005–06) *Tuition:* state resident $2952 full-time, $116 per credit hour part-time; nonresident $9048 full-time, $370 per credit hour part-time. Full-time tuition and fees vary according to course level. Part-time tuition and fees vary according to course level. *Required fees:* $513 full-time. *Room and board:* $7810; room only: $4710. Room and board charges vary according to board plan and housing facility.

Financial Aid 129 Federal Work-Study jobs (averaging $2557). In 2003, 569 non-need-based awards were made. *Average percent of need met:* 71%. *Average financial aid package:* $9354. *Average need-based loan:* $6559. *Average need-based gift aid:* $3813. *Average non-need-based aid:* $2814.

Contact: Dean: Ronald Spatz, 3211 Providence Drive, Anchorage, Alaska 99508; *Telephone:* 907-786-1086; *Fax:* 907-786-1060; *E-mail:* ayhonor@uaa.alaska.edu; *Web site:* http://honors.uaa.alaska.edu

University of Alaska Fairbanks
Honors Program
Fairbanks, Alaska

The University of Alaska Fairbanks Honors Program is open to students in all majors. The program features the personalized attention of small classes with top professors within a larger research university. Specially selected faculty advisers guide honors students through their years as undergraduates.

The Honors Program offers an enriched core curriculum for approximately 200 talented students. Honors courses are offered in all disciplines with the availability of honors contract work in standard University courses. Many of these courses are designed specifically for the Honors Program and are frequently interdisciplinary. Honors students take at least one honors course per semester toward completion of the 27 credits of honors course work required for graduation in the program. Students may also earn honors credit for study abroad and internships.

The program emphasizes undergraduate research. In their senior research projects, all honors students have the opportunity to work directly with faculty members. All honors students must complete a senior honors thesis in their major discipline.

The Honors Student Advisory Committee organizes social events and fund-raising activities that contribute to a sense of community within the University.

Currently, there are 200 students in the program.

Admission Process: Students apply first to the University and then make application to the Honors Program. Students from other recognized college and university honors programs are welcomed as transfer students. There is no formal deadline.

Scholarship Availability: The Donald R. Theophilus Fund for Scholars, the Howard and Enid Cutler Scholarship, the Pat Andersen Scholarship, and the Helen Walker Memorial Scholarship are designated for honors students; the Usibelli Coal Mine Honors Scholarship, which is also designated for honors students, is awarded to about a dozen students. Many general University scholarships (that range from $1000 to $8000) are awarded to honors students.

Campus Overview

State-supported university, founded 1917, part of University of Alaska System • **Coed** 7,610 undergraduate students, 46% full-time, 60% women, 40% men.

Undergraduates 3,522 full-time, 4,088 part-time. Students come from 55 states and territories, 36 other countries, 15% are from out of state, 3% African American, 3% Asian American or Pacific Islander, 3% Hispanic American, 17% Native American, 2% international, 6% transferred in, 42% live on campus.

Faculty *Total:* 314, 98% full-time. *Student/faculty ratio:* 18:1.

Academic Programs *Special study options:* academic remediation for entering students, accelerated degree program, advanced placement credit, cooperative education, distance learning, double majors, English as a second language, external degree program, honors programs, independent study, internships, off-campus study, part-time degree program, services for LD students, student-designed majors, study abroad, summer session for credit. *ROTC:* Army (b). *Unusual degree programs:* 3-2 computer science.

Athletics Member NCAA. All Division II except ice hockey (Division I), men's and women's riflery (Division I). *Intercollegiate sports:* basketball M(s)/W(s), cross-country running M(s)/W(s), ice hockey M(s), riflery M(s)/W(s), skiing (cross-country) M(s)/W(s), volleyball W(s). *Intramural sports:* badminton M/W, basketball M/W, bowling M/W, cheerleading M(c)/W(c), cross-country running M/W, fencing

M(c)/W(c), ice hockey M/W, racquetball M/W, riflery M/W, skiing (cross-country) M/W, skiing (downhill) M/W, soccer M/W, softball M/W, swimming and diving M/W, table tennis M/W, tennis M/W, ultimate Frisbee M/W, volleyball M/W, water polo M/W, wrestling M/W.

Costs (2005–06) *Tuition:* state resident $3480 full-time, $116 per credit part-time; nonresident $11,100 full-time, $370 per credit part-time. Full-time tuition and fees vary according to course level, course load, and location. Part-time tuition and fees vary according to course level, course load, and location. *Required fees:* $1282 full-time. *Room and board:* $5580; room only: $2990. Room and board charges vary according to board plan and housing facility.

Financial Aid 95 Federal Work-Study jobs (averaging $3284). In 2004, 576 non-need-based awards were made. *Average percent of need met:* 70%. *Average financial aid package:* $8906. *Average need-based loan:* $6830. *Average need-based gift aid:* $3803. *Average non-need-based aid:* $3339.

Contact: Director: Dr. Roy K. Bird, P.O. Box 756282, Fairbanks, Alaska 99775; *Telephone:* 907-474-6612; *Fax:* 907-474-5559; *E-mail:* honors@uaf.edu; *Web site:* http://www.uaf.edu/honors/index.html

ARIZONA

Arizona State University
The Barrett Honors College
Tempe, Arizona

The Barrett Honors College at Arizona State University (ASU) is a selective, residential college that recruits academically outstanding undergraduates across the nation. Students enrolled in the Barrett Honors College are part of both the honors community of students and faculty and staff members and a disciplinary college. They may major in any field offered at ASU's three campuses. Honors classes are taught by honors faculty members within the Honors College as well as faculty members in departments and programs campuswide. The College establishes standards for admission, curriculum, and graduation through the Honors College, assuring University-wide transferability and quality for honors education. The Barrett Honors College Dean is Mark Jacobs.

The goal of the College's curriculum is to develop habits of mind that enable students to be lifelong learners, creative problem solvers, and participatory citizens in a democratic society. The College emphasizes small classes, generally limited to 19 students; seminars and other engaged modes of learning; and the development of critical reading, discussion, and writing skills. The College appoints faculty members who are responsible for offering the core honors curriculum, but the College otherwise uses the instructional and research resources of the University as a whole.

The Barrett Honors College offers students access to all of the human and physical resources of one of the nation's most rapidly rising research universities. Honors College students have access to honors advisers appointed by the College and to faculty advisers in the colleges and departments. Based in the Center Complex, nine buildings that include residence hall space for 850 students, the College promotes strong relationships among students, faculty members, and members of the College's administration.

The Honors College's residential space includes classrooms, meeting rooms, a writing lab, a thesis library, a state-of-the-art computing lab, and other student services. Arizona State University has more than 1,700 faculty members, including Faculty Honors Disciplinary Advisers, who enjoy working with strong undergraduates and assist honors students in navigating their major and honors thesis or other undergraduate research opportunities.

Honors students are strongly encouraged to participate in undergraduate research projects and internships. The staff members work closely with colleges and departments to ensure that appropriate programs are available and that honors students have preferential access to them. Many students participate in multiple internships and research projects. These experiences often provide the foundation for honors theses or creative projects.

The College offers four summer study-abroad programs: in London, Edinburgh, and Dublin; Paris, Amsterdam, and Brussels; Athens, Rome, and Dubrovnik; and Latin America. The summer study-abroad programs are restricted to honors students and are taught exclusively by honors faculty members. The programs are open to any college honors student in the nation, and all the courses carry honors credit.

The litany of success for the Barrett Honors College's Lorraine W. Frank Office of National Scholarship Advisement expands each year, with a distinguished record in such scholarship and fellowship competitions as the Rhodes, Marshall, Truman, Goldwater, NSEP, Woodrow Wilson, and Mellon. More than 200 of these fellowships and scholarships have been awarded to Barrett Honors College students since 1990.

The Barrett Honors College has been in existence for seventeen years, superseding a 27-year-old honors program. There are currently 2,700 students enrolled, with an entering freshman class of 750. The Barrett Honors College was created in 1988 by an act of the Arizona Board of Regents, signaling Arizona's commitment to providing outstanding undergraduates with exceptional educational opportunities. In 2000, Intel CEO Craig Barrett and his wife Barbara, an ASU alumna, endowed the Honors College with a $10-million gift for special programs. The Barrett Honors College was named in recognition of the gift, which, at the time, was the largest personal gift ever given to ASU. The College is scheduled to relocate to a new state-of-the-art residential complex, opening in 2007 on the ASU Tempe campus.

Participation Requirements: Graduation through the Barrett Honors College requires students to complete HON 171 and HON 172 (or HON 394 for transfer students), a bachelor's honors thesis or creative project, and additional honors curriculum course credit. Honors College students normally fulfill the requirements for their majors and for graduating through the Barrett Honors College without having to take additional hours. The College's courses meet a variety of general studies requirements, and course work in the major can be adapted to meet College requirements. Students must maintain at least a 3.4 GPA (on a 4.0 scale) for work completed at ASU. All work completed for honors credit is noted as such on the student's transcript. Graduation through the College is acknowledged at the University's commencement exercises and the College's convocation and is noted on the student's transcript. Students who complete their lower-division work (18 hours of honors course work with a minimum overall GPA of 3.4) also have that notation on their transcript.

Admission Process: Students are admitted to the Barrett Honors College as freshmen or may transfer into the College either from within the University or from other institutions at any time during their college career, as long as enough time remains to complete the requirements for graduating through the College. There is a separate Barrett Honors College application, and prospective honors students must apply and be accepted to the University before submitting the Barrett Honors College application. Applicants are evaluated on the basis of their high school GPA (Arizona Board of Regents GPA based on sixteen competency courses), performance on the SAT or ACT, and a required essay. Talents or achievements that contribute to academic leadership and community service or that reflect other academic values, including, though not limited to, engagement in scholarly activities, organizations, or an honors program, are also considered. Though not required, letters of recommendation are strongly encouraged. The typical first-year student in the Barrett Honors College has a high school GPA of 3.8, is in the top 6 percent of the graduating class, and earns a 29 composite on the ACT or 1310 on the SAT I.

Scholarship Availability: Students are eligible for a wide range of scholarships, including in- and out-of-state cash scholarship stipends that may cover all or part of tuition and other educational expenses, depending on the student's academic and cocurricular achievements; renewable cash awards for National Merit, National Hispanic, and National Achievement Finalists and other students whose performance on the SAT or ACT is especially strong; Gammage scholarships for National Merit Scholars in addition to the National Merit cash award; Leadership Scholar Scholarships for up to four years; and the Flinn Scholarship, awarded by the Flinn Foundation to Arizona residents attending an Arizona university.

Campus Overview

State-supported university, founded 1885, part of Arizona State University • **Coed** 39,377 undergraduate students, 80% full-time, 52% women, 48% men.

Undergraduates 31,570 full-time, 7,807 part-time. Students come from 53 states and territories, 96 other countries, 23% are from out of state, 4% African American, 5% Asian American or Pacific Islander, 12% Hispanic American, 2% Native American, 3% international, 10% transferred in, 18% live on campus.

Faculty *Total:* 2,184, 81% full-time, 73% with terminal degrees. *Student/faculty ratio:* 22:1.

Academic Programs *Special study options:* academic remediation for entering students, accelerated degree program, adult/continuing education programs, advanced placement credit, cooperative education, distance learning, double majors, honors programs, independent study, internships, off-campus study, part-time degree program, services for LD students, study abroad, summer session for credit. *ROTC:* Army (b), Air Force (b).

Athletics Member NCAA. All Division I except football (Division I-A). *Intercollegiate sports:* baseball M(s), basketball M(s)/W(s), cross-country running M(s)/W(s), golf M(s)/W(s), gymnastics W(s), soccer W(s), softball W(s), swimming and diving M(s)/W(s), tennis M(s)/W(s), track and field M(s)/W(s), volleyball W(s), water polo W, wrestling M(s). *Intramural sports:* badminton M(c)/W(c), basketball M/W, bowling M/W, crew M(c)/W(c), cross-country running M/W, equestrian sports M(c)/W(c), fencing M(c)/W(c), field hockey M(c), golf M/W, gymnastics M(c)/W(c), ice hockey M(c)/W(c), lacrosse M(c)/W(c), racquetball M/W, rugby M(c)/W(c), soccer M/W, softball M/W, swimming and diving M/W, table tennis M/W, tennis M/W, track and field M/W, ultimate Frisbee M(c)/W(c), volleyball M/W, water polo W(c), weight lifting M/W, wrestling M.

Costs (2004–05) *Tuition:* state resident $3973 full-time, $207 per credit part-time; nonresident $12,828 full-time, $535 per credit part-time. Full-time tuition and fees vary according to program. Part-time tuition and fees vary according to program. *Required fees:* $91 full-time, $23 per term part-time. *Room and board:* $6574; room only: $4178. Room and board charges vary according to board plan and housing facility.

Financial Aid 615 Federal Work-Study jobs (averaging $2228). 4,493 state and other part-time jobs (averaging $2892). In 2003, 3439 non-need-based awards were made. *Average percent of need met:* 61%. *Average financial aid package:* $7810. *Average need-based loan:* $3912. *Average need-based gift aid:* $4956. *Average non-need-based aid:* $4993.

Contact: Mark Jacobs, P.O. Box 871612, Tempe, Arizona 85287-1612; *Telephone:* 480-965-2354; *Fax:* 480-965-0760; *E-mail:* mark.jacobs@asu.edu; *Web site:* http://honors.asu.edu

Arizona Western College
Honors Program
Yuma, Arizona

The Honors Program at Arizona Western College (AWC) was established in the 1985–86 academic school year and currently has nearly 40 members. It offers three different courses of study that provide intellectual challenges and stimulation for academically talented and highly motivated students, encourage students to probe deeply into various subject areas, promote the synthesis of insights they have gained across the curriculum, and facilitate the sharing of their discoveries with faculty members and fellow students. Long-range goals include fostering a lifelong love of scholarly inquiry and independent thinking, building a sense of leadership and responsibility, and evoking an enhanced self-confidence that will result from having met the challenges offered in the program.

Honors courses enrich the regular curriculum with original source material or current research. Honors students have expanded opportunities for discussion and interaction with faculty members and outside experts in a variety of disciplines.

The deadline for submitting grant applications is March 16.

Scholarship Availability: Honors grant awards are available to students living on or off campus. Stipend recipients can receive tuition, fees, room, board, or partial grant awards. Honors students participate in service activities to the Honors Program. Students applying for an honors grant must qualify in one of three ways: graduate from high school in the upper 10 percent of their class, receive a composite score of at least 23 on the ACT or a composite score of 1000 or better on the SAT I, or complete 12 hours or more of college-level course work with a cumulative GPA of 3.5 or better on a 4.0 scale. All applicants must write a 500- to 750-word essay proposing a project to be completed during their time at AWC. Two letters of recommendation as well as secondary and postsecondary transcripts are also required.

Campus Overview

State and locally supported 2-year, founded 1962, part of Arizona State Community College System • **Coed** 6,450 undergraduate students, 28% full-time, 60% women, 40% men.

Undergraduates 1,830 full-time, 4,620 part-time. Students come from 26 states and territories, 7% are from out of state, 3% African American, 1% Asian American or Pacific Islander, 65% Hispanic American, 2% Native American, 0.6% international, 6% live on campus.

Faculty *Total:* 328, 32% full-time, 7% with terminal degrees. *Student/faculty ratio:* 16:1.

Academic Programs *Special study options:* academic remediation for entering students, adult/continuing education programs, advanced placement credit, cooperative education, distance learning, English as a second language, honors programs, independent study, part-time degree program, summer session for credit.

Athletics Member NJCAA. *Intercollegiate sports:* baseball M(s), basketball M(s), football M(s), soccer M(s), softball W(s), volleyball W(s). *Intramural sports:* badminton M/W, basketball M/W, football M, soccer M, softball M/W, swimming and diving M/W, table tennis M/W, volleyball M/W.

Costs (2005–06) *Tuition:* state resident $1140 full-time, $38 per credit hour part-time; nonresident $5700 full-time, $44 per credit hour part-time. Full-time tuition and fees vary according to course load, location, and reciprocity agreements. Part-time tuition and fees vary according to course load, location, and reciprocity agreements. *Room and board:* room only: $1740. Room and board charges vary according to board plan.

Financial Aid 350 Federal Work-Study jobs (averaging $1500). 100 state and other part-time jobs (averaging $1800).

Contact: Director: Dr. Michael Conway, P.O. Box 929, Yuma, Arizona 85366-0929; *Telephone:* 928-317-6022; *E-mail:* honors@azwestern.edu

Athletics Member NJCAA. *Intercollegiate sports:* baseball M, basketball M/W, equestrian sports M/W, soccer W.

Contact: Robert Atkinson, 901 Colombo, Sierra Vista, Arizona 85635; *Telephone:* 520-515-5409; *E-mail:* atkinson@cochise.edu

Cochise College
Honors Program
Sierra Vista, Arizona

The Cochise College Honors Program is designed to provide intellectual challenge and stimulation for motivated, creative, and academically talented students. A prime purpose of this program is to foster the lifelong love of scholarly inquiry, open-mindedness, and independent thinking. Meeting the challenges afforded by the program leads to confidence in intellectual ability and enhances the academic potential of all participants. Cochise College honors students create their own projects with the guidance of faculty mentors, within the context of established college courses. Honors contracts are available for courses in every academic, vocational, and technical discipline. The Cochise College Honors Program began in 1996 and continues to evolve. As of 2002, 202 students had successfully completed honors contracts and had taken Eng 102H.

Participation Requirements: At present, the Cochise College Honors Program consists of individual 1- to 4-unit contracts between instructors and students. Students must have a minimum 3.5 cumulative GPA, must have completed 12 credits in courses from the General Education curriculum leading to a degree, must be full-time and enrolled in a degree program, and must be approved by the Honors Committee. In addition, students must demonstrate the ability to initiate and follow through with a creative project above and beyond traditional classroom activities. In fall 2001, the following curriculum was available for honors students at Cochise College: Eng 102H (3 credits), Hon 251 Honors Seminar (1 credit), Hon 255 Leadership/Service (3 credits), and Hon 260 The Human Quest for Utopia (3 credits).

Scholarship Availability: The Honors Program offers scholarships for the honors contracts. Cochise College grants a variety of need- and merit-based scholarships to exceptional students in all fields of study. Incoming students are advised to contact the Financial Aid Office. In addition to participation in the College Honors Program, outstanding students are eligible to join Phi Theta Kappa, the international honors society for community college students.

Campus Overview

State and locally supported 2-year, founded 1977, part of Cochise College • **Coed** 4,446 undergraduate students, 28% full-time, 57% women, 43% men.

Undergraduates 1,257 full-time, 3,189 part-time. Students come from 27 states and territories, 8 other countries, 5% are from out of state, 7% African American, 4% Asian American or Pacific Islander, 31% Hispanic American, 1% Native American, 0.5% international, 6% transferred in.

Faculty Total: 394, 23% full-time. Student/faculty ratio: 14:1.

Academic Programs *Special study options:* academic remediation for entering students, accelerated degree program, adult/continuing education programs, cooperative education, distance learning, double majors, English as a second language, external degree program, honors programs, independent study, internships, part-time degree program, services for LD students, summer session for credit.

Embry-Riddle Aeronautical University
Embry-Riddle Honors Program
Prescott, Arizona, and Daytona Beach, Florida

The Embry-Riddle Honors Program, available at both its Prescott, Arizona, and Daytona Beach, Florida, residential campuses, is highly selective, offering enriched educational experiences and opportunities to exercise social and ethical responsibility through active, organized involvement on the campus and in the community. Emphasizing course work both in general education and in the majors, the program involves selected faculty members who formulate innovative courses and establish mentoring relationships with students. The program is designed to attract and retain top students and to develop their communicative, analytical, critical, and research skills, nurturing a love of lifelong learning, leadership, and service.

The Honors Program seeks to establish a sense of community among its members, foster a meaningful addition to campus life through the activities of its student organization, enhance the quality of the academic and cultural experience of the campus through its distinguished speakers series, and serve as a model of academic superiority and a seedbed of curricular innovation for the University.

Freshman students have common honors housing; continuing honors housing arrangements beyond the freshman year is optional. Students enjoy priority registration privileges, are active in community service, and participate in selecting faculty members for the monthly faculty lecture series. Students also have the opportunity to engage exclusively with guest speakers brought to campus from around the country, their areas of expertise tied directly to the theme of at least one of the honors seminars. The seminars are capped at 20 students (all members of the Honors Program); are discussion based; involve guest presentations by various faculty members from across the University campus; are designed to develop students' communicative, critical, research, and leadership skills; and require text and Web-based original research, written essays, and oral presentations. Honors work within the student's specific major may involve group projects or may be individually tailored to a student's specific research interests.

Participation Requirements: Honors courses are noted on the student's transcript, and successful completion of all Honors Program requirements is noted on the diploma. A total of 18 credit hours are required in the Honors Program, 9 of which are applicable to general education requirements, and 9 are within the student's major. Honors in general education emphasizes an interdisciplinary approach in each of three 3-credit-hour seminars. In lieu of the third honors seminar, students may select an independent study or travel-abroad option.

Individual degree programs establish, in coordination with Honors Program administration, the appropriate honors experience in the major, which may involve specified courses, or may involve individualized projects undertaken independently with a faculty mentor. Honors within the major may involve completion of an honors senior thesis, senior project, or senior portfolio.

Continuation in the program requires a minimum 3.0 cumulative GPA, as well as a minimum 3.0 GPA within the honors curriculum.

Admission Process: Members are admitted each fall. A limited number of University applicants are invited to apply to the Honors Program. Selection is based on SAT/ACT scores, a personal essay, rank in high school class, high school GPA, and a strong record of leadership, service, and cocurricular activity.

Scholarship Availability: The University awards a wide range of academic scholarships.

Campus Overview

Independent comprehensive, founded 1978 • **Small-town** 547-acre campus • **Coed, primarily men,** 1,637 undergraduate students, 90% full-time, 18% women, 82% men.

Undergraduates 1,467 full-time, 170 part-time. Students come from 52 states and territories, 31 other countries, 78% are from out of state, 2% African American, 6% Asian American or Pacific Islander, 7% Hispanic American, 0.9% Native American, 3% international, 6% transferred in, 49% live on campus.

Faculty *Total:* 106, 87% full-time, 58% with terminal degrees. *Student/faculty ratio:* 16:1.

Academic Programs *Special study options:* academic remediation for entering students, adult/continuing education programs, advanced placement credit, cooperative education, distance learning, double majors, English as a second language, independent study, internships, part-time degree program, services for LD students, study abroad, summer session for credit. *ROTC:* Army (b), Air Force (b).

Athletics Member NAIA. *Intercollegiate sports:* volleyball W(s), wrestling M(s). *Intramural sports:* archery M/W, badminton M/W, basketball M/W, bowling M/W, cross-country running M/W, fencing M(c)/W(c), lacrosse M(c)/W(c), racquetball M/W, rugby M(c)/W(c), skiing (cross-country) M(c)/W(c), skiing (downhill) M(c)/W(c), soccer M(c)/W(c), softball M/W, swimming and diving M/W, table tennis M/W, tennis M/W, track and field M/W, volleyball M/W, weight lifting M/W.

Costs (2005–06) *Comprehensive fee:* $30,006 includes full-time tuition ($22,820), mandatory fees ($670), and room and board ($6516). Part-time tuition: $955 per credit hour. *College room only:* $3580.

Financial Aid 79 Federal Work-Study jobs (averaging $2917). 496 state and other part-time jobs (averaging $1397). In 2004, 292 non-need-based awards were made. *Average financial aid package:* $6312. *Average need-based loan:* $2259. *Average need-based gift aid:* $4925. *Average non-need-based aid:* $3412.

Contact: Prescott campus, Dr. Monica Halka, Honors Program Director, Embry-Riddle Aeronautical University, Building 74, Suite 204, 3700 Willow Creek Road, Prescott, Arizona 86301; *Telephone:* 928-777-3876; *Fax:* 928-777-3827; *E-mail:* monica.halka@erau.edu. Daytona Beach campus, Dr. Geoffrey Kain, Honors Program Director, Embry-Riddle Aeronautical University, 600 South Clyde Morris Blvd., Daytona Beach, Florida 32114-3900; *Telephone:* 386-226-6650; *Fax:* 386-226-7210; *E-mail:* kaing@erau.edu

Maricopa Community Colleges
Honors Program
Tempe, Arizona

The mission of the Honors Program at Maricopa Community Colleges is to foster a climate of excellence in the colleges and the surrounding communities, to recognize and reward the talent and motivation of outstanding community college students and faculty members, to promote a sense of scholarship and community among program participants and among the colleges, and to raise the awareness of the high quality and variety of educational opportunities and services.

The Honors Program of Maricopa Community Colleges was initiated in January 1981 with an internal grant. The initial grant allowed a faculty committee to investigate the initiation of a community college honors program and to determine factors that were crucial to the design of such a program. In June 1981, the Governing Board allocated funds for the development and implementation of honors programs at each of the Maricopa Community Colleges. The Office of the Vice Chancellor for Student and Educational Development was assigned to provide coordination of the colleges' programs. Since 1981, the Governing Board has approved funds each year to support the colleges' programs. The Honors Committee at each campus is free within district guidelines to administer these funds according to its needs.

The Honors Forum Lecture Series features nationally known speakers who address specific issues related to an annual theme. The theme is generally adapted from the annual study topic and materials developed by Phi Theta Kappa, the two-year college honorary society.

An Honors Forum course offered at the colleges explores in greater depth the theme and issues discussed throughout the year. The Forum activities provide the opportunity for all honors students throughout Maricopa County Community College District (MCCCD) to have common learning experiences based on the topic chosen for the year. Honors students may be required to attend the lecture and write a synopsis for the honors forum class.

Three times each fall and spring semester a guest speaker visits two of the ten colleges for informal discussion and a question-and-answer period. A third college hosts dinner with the distinguished visitor. College faculty members and students are invited, as well as the Chancellor, Vice-Chancellors, and Governing Board members. All honors students, faculty members, staff members, administrators, and Governing Board members are invited to "Applaud and Celebrate" the activities and accomplishments of the year at an annual convocation held in the spring. Students are recognized and rewarded with special scholarships. This is also an opportunity to recognize and reward faculty members who have taught honors courses for three, five, eight, and twelve years.

Approximately 2,250 students and 400 faculty members participate.

Participation Requirements: Students who are Honors Fee Waiver Scholars and President's Scholars must complete a minimum of 12 hours (100-level and above) of course work each semester. This includes the completion of one honors course each semester. A GPA of 3.25 must be maintained and students must remain in good standing at one of the colleges/centers.

Awards, certificates, and diploma citations conferred upon program completion are issued under the individual jurisdiction of the ten colleges that make up the Maricopa Community Colleges. These colleges include Chandler-Gilbert Community College, Estrella Mountain Community College, GateWay Community College, Glendale Community College, Mesa Community College, Paradise Valley Community College, Phoenix College, Rio Salado College, Scottsdale Community College, and South Mountain Community College.

Admission Process: In the President's Scholar category, a student must be graduated (within the top 15 percent of the class at the end of the sixth, seventh, or eighth semesters) from a North Central Accredited (NCA) high school in Maricopa County and apply within one academic year from high school graduation. Enrollment in an MCCCD college/center must include at least one honors course per semester. The applicant may not be enrolled in another postsecondary institution, summer school excluded. College-preparatory schools are not included in this restriction. President's Scholars may enroll in the Honors Program at any MCCCD college/center. Enrollment must be for at least 12 credit hours per semester (fall/spring). The scholarship does not cover the cost of course work below 100-level and/or pass/fail classes (P/Z option). Remedial and/or pass/fail-option classes may be included in a student's schedule to meet the 12-credit-hour minimum requirement, but the award is prorated for the semester.

Scholarship Availability: A number of scholarships are available to honors students, including the President's Scholarship ($570 per semester for up to four semesters), the Honors Fee Waiver (up to $200 per semester, not to exceed four semesters), the Betty Heiden Elsner Scholarship ($100 per semester for two semesters), Chancellor's Scholarship (full tuition and fees for one year plus $150 per semester for books and supplies), and the Foundation Scholarship ($1000 annually per college to be distributed at the discretion of the college).

Contact: Coordinator: Loman B. Clark Jr., 2411 West 14th Street, Tempe, Arizona 85281-6941; *Telephone:* 602-731-8026; *Fax:* 602-731-8786; *E-mail:* clark@maricopa.edu

Northern Arizona University
Honors Program
Flagstaff, Arizona

The Northern Arizona University (NAU) Honors Program is the oldest in Arizona, having begun in 1955. NAU's Honors Program provides many opportunities for academically motivated students to succeed by offering a challenging set of seminar-style courses that encourage the free exchange of ideas. Classes are small and interactive, and students and faculty members work closely together. Honors students are members of a close, supportive community of scholars and benefit from one-on-one advising with professional academic advisers, priority registration, and specialized scholarship opportunities.

Honors students are encouraged to live in the Cowden Learning Community, a 24-hour, quiet, substance-free residence hall providing a free 24-hour computer lab, on-site tutoring, Honors Program classrooms, and access to honors offices. Because it is close to the Cline Library, the University Union, and other residence halls, Cowden is the ideal location for students dedicated to their studies. There are currently more than 600 students enrolled in the growing program.

Participation Requirements: At the core of the honors program is a formal curriculum aimed at helping students acquire and refine skills while focusing on a range of topics, ideas, and problems. The Liberal Studies Honors curriculum is designed to meet the University's liberal studies requirements without infringing on the opportunity to pursue a major and minor field of course work.

Opportunities and experiences outside the classroom contribute significantly to students' learning. Through service learning activities, study abroad, exchange and immersion experiences, internships, and undergraduate research, program participants are encouraged to apply what they have learned in the classroom and to learn while working with individuals in the many sectors of society. Students are encouraged to participate in these activities as well as the many educational, cultural, and social events coordinated and supported by the Honors Program.

The University honors curriculum is an option for students who have completed the liberal studies honors curriculum and wish to complete a senior thesis during their final year. The thesis involves a two-semester effort of research guided by a faculty adviser.

AP, I.B., and transfer credit is considered on an individual basis, but is generally accepted. To graduate "with liberal studies honors," students must graduate with a cumulative GPA of 3.5 or higher (on a 4.0 scale). The "with liberal studies honors" designation is in addition to the "cum laude" notation.

Admission Process: Through an application process, incoming students who have fewer than 30 transferable credit hours need to meet one of the following: achieve a composite ACT score of 29 or higher, achieve a combined SAT score of 1290 or higher, or graduate in the top 5 percent of their high school class. Students who have participated in honors courses/AP classes in high school but do not meet these requirements may petition to join the Honors Program. To petition, students must include with their completed application a copy of their high school transcript, one letter of recommendation, and a 500-word essay on why being a part of the program is important.

Transfer students (30 or more transferable hours) are admitted if they have a cumulative GPA of 3.5 or higher from their former institution. These students must include a copy of their transcript with their application.

A student who does not meet any of the above entrance criteria can still join the Honors Program after they complete 12 semester hours of course work that leads to an undergraduate degree at NAU. A student who earns a 3.5 or higher cumulative GPA can apply to this program based on their NAU course work.

Scholarship Availability: More than 2,000 scholarships are available; awards range from several hundred to several thousands of dollars. Awards are made on the basis of financial need, academic qualifications, and evidence of student involvement. Applications for scholarships are due in mid-February, with awards announced in mid-March of each year.

Campus Overview

State-supported university, founded 1899, part of Arizona University System • **Coed** 13,333 undergraduate students, 85% full-time, 60% women, 40% men.

Undergraduates 11,358 full-time, 1,975 part-time. Students come from 50 states and territories, 66 other countries, 25% are from out of state, 2% African American, 2% Asian American or Pacific Islander, 11% Hispanic American, 7% Native American, 2% international, 11% transferred in, 38% live on campus.

Faculty *Total:* 1,316, 54% full-time, 59% with terminal degrees. *Student/faculty ratio:* 17:1.

Academic Programs *Special study options:* accelerated degree program, advanced placement credit, cooperative education, distance learning, double majors, English as a second language, freshman honors college, honors programs, independent study, internships, off-campus study, part-time degree program, services for LD students, study abroad, summer session for credit. *ROTC:* Army (b), Air Force (b).

Athletics Member NCAA. All Division I except football (Division I-AA). *Intercollegiate sports:* basketball M(s)/W(s), cross-country running M(s)/W(s), golf W(s), soccer W(s), swimming and diving W(s), tennis M(s)/W(s), track and field M(s)/W(s), volleyball W(s). *Intramural sports:* archery M/W, badminton M/W, baseball M, basketball M/W, bowling M/W, cross-country running M/W, fencing M/W, football M/W, ice hockey M, lacrosse M/W, racquetball M/W, rugby M/W, skiing (cross-country) M/W, skiing (downhill) M/W, soccer M(c), softball M/W, swimming and diving W, table tennis M/W, ultimate Frisbee M/W, volleyball M/W, water polo M/W, weight lifting M/W.

Costs (2004–05) *Tuition:* state resident $3983 full-time, $208 per credit part-time; nonresident $12,503 full-time, $524 per credit part-time. Full-time tuition and fees vary according to program. Part-time tuition and fees vary according to program. *Required fees:*

$90 full-time, $23 per term part-time. *Room and board:* $5785; room only: $3160. Room and board charges vary according to board plan and housing facility.

Financial Aid 588 Federal Work-Study jobs (averaging $1526). 3,041 state and other part-time jobs (averaging $2446). In 2003, 453 non-need-based awards were made. *Average percent of need met:* 70%. *Average financial aid package:* $7943. *Average need-based loan:* $3715. *Average need-based gift aid:* $4501. *Average non-need-based aid:* $1217.

Contact: Director: Professor Bruce Fox, Program Coordinator: Glenn Hansen, P.O. Box 5689, Northern Arizona University, Flagstaff, Arizona 86011-5689; *Telephone:* 928-523-3334; *Fax:* 928-523-6558; *E-mail:* bruce.fox@nau.edu, glenn.hansen@nau.edu; *Web site:* http://www.nau.edu/honors

Paradise Valley Community College
Honors Program
Phoenix, Arizona

*A*t Paradise Valley Community College (PVCC), honors courses are offered as single courses, as concurrent sections with regular sections, and as project courses. With the latter two, honors students are expected to do additional, in-depth work that enhances their classroom experiences.

During the school year, honors students participate in several programs designed to build a learning community among Maricopa Community College District (MCCD) honors students. They may attend special programs, concerts, theater events, and guest lectures each semester. The Maricopa district brings six nationally prominent guest speakers for the honors program each year; they visit with students at several of the campuses during their stay. All honors students from the ten MCCD colleges also have the opportunity to take an annual honors trip to a different site each year. In addition, honors students are recognized each spring at a district-wide Honors Convocation and receive special recognition at graduation. Honors course work receives an honors designation on college transcripts.

The Honors Program is more than fifteen years old and currently enrolls about 150 students.

Participation Requirements: In order to remain eligible for this program, students must enroll in a minimum of 12 hours per semester and maintain a 3.25 GPA or higher. Students must also enroll in and complete at least one honors course each semester.

Admission Process: The Paradise Valley Community College Honors Program is open to all students who graduate in the top 15 percent of a Maricopa County high school class or who have earned a minimum 3.25 GPA in at least 12 credit hours from any of the Maricopa Community Colleges. All students who apply and who qualify are accepted.

Scholarship Availability: The Presidents' Scholarship program is open to all Maricopa County high school graduates who are in the top 15 percent of their high school classes. Students may apply as early as the end of their junior year and remain eligible for two semesters following graduation, provided they do not attend any other college or university during that time. The scholarship is renewable for up to four consecutive semesters, provided students continue to meet the requirements of the Honors Program. This portion of the program is designed to attract top area high school students to Maricopa colleges.

Returning students may be eligible for the fee waiver portion of the program if they have earned a minimum 3.25 GPA in at least 12 credit hours at any of the Maricopa Community Colleges. Fee waivers are awarded depending on the number of credits students are taking. There is no time limit on the number of semesters of eligibility, within

reason, as long as students maintain a minimum 3.25 GPA and take at least one honors course per semester.

Campus Overview

State and locally supported 2-year, founded 1985, part of Maricopa County Community College District System • **Coed** 8,237 undergraduate students, 26% full-time, 60% women, 40% men.

Undergraduates 2,118 full-time, 6,119 part-time. 3% African American, 3% Asian American or Pacific Islander, 10% Hispanic American, 1% Native American.

Faculty *Total:* 344, 24% full-time.

Academic Programs *Special study options:* academic remediation for entering students, adult/continuing education programs, advanced placement credit, cooperative education, distance learning, honors programs, services for LD students, summer session for credit.

Athletics Member NJCAA. *Intercollegiate sports:* cross-country running M/W, golf M/W, soccer M/W, softball W, tennis M/W, track and field M/W.

Costs (2004–05) *Tuition:* area resident $1650 full-time; state resident $55 per hour part-time; nonresident $2400 full-time, $80 per hour part-time.

Financial Aid 50 Federal Work-Study jobs (averaging $2500).

Contact: Director: Dr. Linda Knoblock, 18401 North 32nd Street, Phoenix, Arizona 85032; *Telephone:* 602-787-6571; *Fax:* 602-787-7250; *E-mail:* linda.knoblock@pvmail.maricopa.edu; *Web site:* http://www.pvc.maricopa.edu/

Scottsdale Community College
College Honors Program
Scottsdale, Arizona

*T*he Honors Program at Scottsdale Community College (SCC) provides general education for students who seek challenges in learning, who are curious, who question, and who are eager to test assumptions. The program offers a series of specially designed courses for transfer and two-year students. The purpose of the Honors Program is to foster greater depth of thought in reading, writing, and discussion with faculty members and guest lecturers that will better prepare honors students to complete baccalaureate degrees or begin their careers.

The 17-year-old program enrolls 170 students.

Participation Requirements: Honors students can be enrolled full- or part-time, are expected to enroll in at least one honors course each semester, and must maintain a GPA of 3.25.

Admission Process: Recent high school graduates must rank in the top 15 percent of their graduating class or qualify through placement tests; continuing or transfer students must have completed 12 credit hours of college classes with a 3.5 or better.

Scholarship Availability: Scottsdale Community College offers a variety of stipends for honors students in addition to scholarships that are available to all students. The Chancellor's, Maricopa Foundation, and Betty Elsner Scholarships are Maricopa College District awards for continuing honors students. For recent Maricopa County high school graduates in the upper 15 percent of their graduating class, Presidents' Scholarships are available from the District. Partial fee waivers are awarded to all honors students who do not receive any of the above awards.

Campus Overview

State and locally supported 2-year, founded 1969, part of Maricopa County Community College District System • **Coed** 11,465 undergraduate students, 30% full-time, 56% women, 44% men.

Undergraduates 3,455 full-time, 8,010 part-time. Students come from 49 other countries, 3% are from out of state, 3% African American, 2% Asian American or Pacific Islander, 7% Hispanic American, 4% Native American, 6% international.

Faculty *Total:* 631, 24% full-time, 12% with terminal degrees. *Student/faculty ratio:* 20:1.

Academic Programs *Special study options:* academic remediation for entering students, adult/continuing education programs, advanced placement credit, cooperative education, English as a second language, honors programs, off-campus study, part-time degree program, services for LD students, student-designed majors, summer session for credit.

Athletics Member NJCAA. *Intercollegiate sports:* baseball M, basketball M/W, cross-country running M/W, football M, golf M/W, soccer M/W, softball W, tennis M/W, track and field M/W, volleyball W. *Intramural sports:* archery M/W, badminton M/W, basketball M/W, bowling M/W, racquetball M/W, track and field M/W, volleyball M/W.

Costs (2004–05) *Tuition:* area resident $1650 full-time, $55 per credit hour part-time; state resident $6600 full-time, $214 per credit hour part-time; nonresident $6600 full-time, $220 per credit hour part-time. *Required fees:* $10 full-time.

Financial Aid 75 Federal Work-Study jobs (averaging $2000).

Contact: Neil MacKay, College Honors Program, Scottsdale Community College, 9000 East Chaparral Road, Scottsdale, Arizona 85250; *Telephone:* 480-423-6471; *Fax:* 480-423-6200; *E-mail:* neil.mackay@sccmail.maricopa.edu; *Web site:* http://www.sc.maricopa.edu

South Mountain Community College

Honors Program

Phoenix, Arizona

The philosophy of the Honors Program at South Mountain Community College (SMCC) is consistent with that of the Maricopa Community College District: to provide education for the diverse interests, needs, and capacities of the students it serves. The Honors Program exists to enhance the academic preparation of exceptional students in their initial college years. The aim of the Honors Program is to promote a sense of scholarship and community among its participants.

The Honors Program is designed to enhance students' intellectual growth by offering challenging courses and increased contact with other honors students. The program includes honors sections of general education classes, honors contract options, faculty mentors, special activities, and forum presentations that permit students to hear and talk with prominent lecturers. Each year, the Maricopa District Honors Program presents an Honors Forum Series based on an honors study topic selected in conjunction with Phi Theta Kappa, the international honor society for two-year colleges. The Honors Forum course (HUM 190) is offered to prepare students for concepts discussed at the lectures. Finally, each honors course is designated HONORS on the student's official transcript.

Honors students enjoy a sense of community, an environment of excellence, and greater depth in their academic experience under the guidance of faculty mentors. In addition to honors sections of general education courses, special seminars, and the contract option, students are able to participate in honors-sponsored cultural, social, and educational events, including opportunities for travel to honors conferences and Phi Theta Kappa activities.

The program, which began in 1981, currently enrolls 50 students per academic year.

Participation Requirements: To graduate as a South Mountain Community College Honors Program scholar, a student must complete a total of 15 credits in course work designated as Honors. The course work must include 3 credits of HUM 190 (Honors Forum) and 12 credits selected from at least three different course prefixes. Students who complete the above distribution of courses with grades of A or B and an overall GPA of 3.25 or higher receive special designation as Honors Program Graduates at the annual College award program and on the graduation program. The Honors designation indicates excellence and commitment both to prospective employers and to the admissions offices at other colleges and universities.

Admission Process: Any student may enroll in a specific honors section with the instructor's approval. Recent high school graduates who are in the top 15 percent of their high school class from a Maricopa County high school should apply for the President's Scholarship, which will also give them standing in the Honors Program. Continuing students should submit an Honors Program application to the Honors Coordinator.

Scholarship Availability: Honors Program students have several opportunities for scholarships and fee waivers. Graduates of a Maricopa County high school who have ranked in the top 15 percent at the end of the sixth, seventh, or eighth semester and who have not attended another college or university are eligible for the President's Scholarship. Continuing students who have completed 12 or more credits of college-level work at SMCC or another college or university with a cumulative GPA of at least 3.25 are eligible to apply for fee waiver status. All continuing members of the SMCC Honors Program who plan to return for the following academic year are considered by the Honors Committee for the Chancellor's Scholarship, Honors Foundation Scholarship, and the Betty Hedin Elsner Scholarship. In addition, applications for the All-USA Academic Team and the Guistewhite Scholarship are available through the Honors Office.

Campus Overview

State and locally supported 2-year, founded 1979, part of Maricopa County Community College District System • **Coed** 3,933 undergraduate students.

Undergraduates 2% are from out of state, 14% African American, 2% Asian American or Pacific Islander, 43% Hispanic American, 4% Native American.

Faculty *Total:* 195, 25% full-time, 100% with terminal degrees.

Academic Programs *Special study options:* academic remediation for entering students, adult/continuing education programs, advanced placement credit, cooperative education, English as a second language, honors programs, part-time degree program, services for LD students, summer session for credit. *ROTC:* Air Force (c).

Athletics Member NJCAA. *Intercollegiate sports:* baseball M, basketball M/W, cross-country running M/W, soccer M, softball W, tennis M/W, track and field M/W, volleyball W.

Costs (2005–06) *Tuition:* area resident $1440 full-time; state resident $6192 full-time; nonresident $6192 full-time. *Required fees:* $10 full-time.

Financial Aid 36 Federal Work-Study jobs (averaging $2000).

Contact: Coordinator: Helen Smith, Honors Program, South Mountain Community College, 7050 South 24th Street, Phoenix, Arizona 85042; *Telephone:* 602-243-8122; *E-mail:* helen.smith@smcmail.maricopa.edu; *Web site:* http://www.southmountaincc.edu

The University of Arizona
Honors College
Tucson, Arizona

*T*he mission of the University of Arizona (UA) Honors College is to foster an enduring spirit of inquiry and discovery so that artistically and academically talented students develop the courage to address uncommon challenges and the commitment to promote social responsibility throughout their lives.

The Honors College promotes the growth and development of University of Arizona students by offering challenging honors academic experiences, personalized advising, research opportunities, and social and cultural activities that nourish a student's drive for new knowledge and alliances.

Inquiry is at the heart of university life both in and out of the classroom. The cornerstone of any collegiate honors program is the availability of enriching academic experiences and challenging courses. Because the UA Honors College is University-wide in scope, students in any major have the flexibility to create a unique honors experience by choosing from more than 250 honors courses to satisfy major, minor, general education, or elective credit requirements for the degree. The courses are offered in collaboration with UA's other undergraduate colleges (Engineering, Nursing, Science, Fine Arts, etc.) and are offered in a variety of contexts from independent sections to discussion or lab sections and concurrent sections that require different assignments for honors students. A student's ability to graduate with honors is facilitated by the availability of honors courses, opportunities for research, the integration of an honors thesis or project into capstone experiences in various majors, and the student's drive and initiative to accomplish the goal of graduating with honors.

While the primary benefit of Honors College participation is the opportunity to take challenging academic courses in the company of talented, inquisitive peers, UA Honors College students also enjoy a number of special benefits and privileges. For example, most honors students have more than one adviser; they complement the academic advising available in their major with support from faculty and staff members in the Honors College. This cadre of advisers is eager to work one-on-one with students to support short- and long-term goals through mentoring relationships, research opportunities, classroom experiences, study-abroad opportunities, and exchange programs. In addition, honors students enjoy priority class registration, a computer lab, meeting rooms, extended library book checkout, newsletters, and internship opportunities.

Students seeking to explore research opportunities may access the Honors College's exclusive searchable Web database, obtain advising in the Honors College or through faculty advisers in various departments, and may receive funding through the Honors Undergraduate Research Grant Program (among many other University programs that support undergraduate research).

Outstanding students from across the nation compose the community of scholars. The Honors College seeks to create an environment in which students and faculty members interact with each other in and out of the classroom, exploring ideas and issues of mutual interest. This environment is fostered through designated honors residence halls, topical luncheons, honors-affiliated student organizations, and a variety of social and cultural activities.

Graduates of the University's honors community attain remarkable levels of success. The majority of students immediately enter graduate or professional schools; others immediately enter the workforce. UA Honors College graduates have been highly successful in attaining prestigious graduate fellowships, internships, and scholarships, such as the Fulbright, Udall, Truman, Goldwater, and Rhodes, among others.

Participation Requirements: UA Honors College students have a range of options to craft a unique honors academic experience; these options include taking honors courses listed in the schedule of classes each semester that apply toward major, minor, general education, or elective requirements; contracting for honors credit; an honors internship; honors independent study; an honors undergraduate preceptorship; or, as a senior, taking a graduate-level class. Honors College students must maintain a minimum cumulative 3.5 GPA to stay in the College, and there is a probationary period of at least one semester if the GPA falls below 3.5. Students entering the Honors College as either a freshman or sophomore graduate with honors by completing 24 honors credits, a 6-credit thesis, and earning a cumulative UA GPA of at least 3.5. This requirement is adjusted for students who enter the program as juniors or seniors. Students may graduate with honors in more than one area of study. Students who complete the requirements for graduation with honors earn a notation on the transcript and diploma, receive special recognition and wear a gold medallion at University commencement and/or college-specific awards programs, and receive the academic distinction of cum laude, magna cum laude, or summa cum laude.

Admission Process: New students who apply for admission to the University are automatically considered for Honors College admission and scholarships; no separate application is required. Students are encouraged to apply early in the senior year of high school. Qualified freshmen or transfer students are invited to join the Honors College and receive detailed information about honors at the point of admission to the University or shortly thereafter. Freshmen are considered for Honors College admission based on academic factors, which, in combination, present a profile of students' high school preparation for University course work and their likelihood of academic success at the University. These may include their unweighted GPA, SAT or ACT scores, strength of curriculum, rank in class, and responses to questions on the admission application. Transfer students are considered for Honors College admission based on their cumulative grade point average and number of credit hours completed. Current UA students seeking admission to the Honors College may be admitted via a self- or faculty-nomination process. Students must have completed 12 or more graded units at UA, have a minimum 3.5 GPA, and must submit a personal statement.

Scholarship Availability: The Honors College administers a select number of scholarship and grant programs, primarily for currently enrolled honors students. For more information, students should visit http://www.honors.arizona.edu. Most scholarship awards to new freshmen or transfer students are awarded at the point of admission to the University or soon thereafter. New students who apply for admission to the University are automatically considered for scholarships. Scholarship awards may be made on the basis of scholastic achievement, extracurricular activities, financial need, or other qualifications. More than $21 million in scholarship aid from private donors, corporations, and institutional sources is awarded annually to University of Arizona undergraduates. To be considered for the widest array of aid, students should also file a Free Application for Federal Student Aid (FAFSA) annually.

Campus Overview

State-supported university, founded 1885, part of Arizona Board of Regents • **Coed** 28,368 undergraduate students, 87% full-time, 53% women, 47% men.

Undergraduates 24,595 full-time, 3,773 part-time. Students come from 27 states and territories, 135 other countries, 28% are from out of state, 3% African American, 6% Asian American or Pacific Islander, 15% Hispanic American, 2% Native American, 3% international, 7% transferred in, 18% live on campus.

Faculty *Total:* 1,416, 96% full-time, 98% with terminal degrees. *Student/faculty ratio:* 19:1.

Academic Programs *Special study options:* adult/continuing education programs, advanced placement credit, distance learning, double majors, English as a second language, freshman honors college, honors programs, independent study, internships, part-time degree program, services for LD students, study abroad, summer session for credit. *ROTC:* Army (b), Navy (b), Air Force (b). *Unusual degree* *programs:* 3-2 business administration with American Graduate School of International Management.

Athletics Member NCAA. All Division I except football (Division I-A). *Intercollegiate sports:* baseball M(s), basketball M(s)/W(s), cross-country running M(s)/W(s), golf M(s)/W(s), gymnastics W(s), ice hockey M(c), lacrosse M(c)/W(c), rugby M(c)/W(c), soccer M(c)/W(s), softball W(s), swimming and diving M(s)/W(s), tennis M(s)/W(s), track and field M(s)/W(s), volleyball M(c)/W(s), wrestling M(c). *Intramural sports:* badminton M/W, basketball M/W, bowling M/W, cross-country running M/W, football M/W, golf M/W, racquetball M/W, soccer M/W, softball M/W, swimming and diving M/W, table tennis M/W, tennis M/W, track and field M/W, volleyball M/W, water polo M/W, weight lifting M/W, wrestling M.

Costs (2005–06) *Tuition:* state resident $3998 full-time, $237 per unit part-time; nonresident $12,978 full-time, $566 per unit part-time. *Required fees:* $95 full-time. *Room and board:* $7108; room only: $3820.

Financial Aid *Average financial aid package:* $9993.

Contact: Dean: Dr. Patricia MacCorquodale, The University of Arizona Honors College, P.O. Box 210006, 1027 East Second Street, Tucson, Arizona 85721-0006; *Telephone:* 520-621-6901; *Fax:* 520-621-8655; *E-mail:* honors@honors.arizona.edu; *Web site:* http://www.honors.arizona.edu/

ARKANSAS

Arkansas State University

The Honors College

State University, Arkansas

The Honors College at Arkansas State University (ASU), which evolved from the Honors Program that was established in 1983, aims to transform students over the course of their study of various disciplines to make them active, creative scholars who are fully prepared to contribute their knowledge and skills to the wider world. It offers special opportunities for exceptionally qualified students to develop their abilities to think independently and express their thoughts clearly and forcefully in speech and writing. Students majoring in any department in the University may participate in Honors. Honors work supplements regular course work within the student's major field of concentration. It also encourages work that develops familiarity with the relationships among different academic disciplines.

The Honors curriculum includes honors sections of general education courses, honors options (in which an additional component is added to an upper-division course in the major or minor), special-topic honors seminars, honors independent study, and the honors senior thesis. Students in the University Honors College have additional options for earning honors-caliber credit: they may, with approval, substitute selected upper-level courses for general education courses, claim selected upper-level courses outside the major, and take graduate courses for undergraduate credit as juniors and seniors.

Honors, which begins its third decade, currently enrolls about 400 people.

Participation Requirements: Students join the Honors Program by enrolling in honors courses; there is no formal application procedure. Aside from University Honors Scholars and other students who elect to enroll in the Honors College, which requires two honors-caliber courses each year, honors students are not required to complete a set number of honors courses each year. To graduate with honors, students must complete at least 18 hours of honors course work, 9 or more of them at the upper level, and earn a minimum cumulative 3.5 GPA. Transfer students may graduate in honors by either meeting

these requirements in full or, if entering with 36 or more hours completed, by taking 15 hours of upper-division honors work; they must also have a minimum 3.5 GPA. Those students who are not admitted to Honors can be later nominated by a faculty member. Diplomas of those fulfilling these requirements bear the designation "Honors College." Students in the University Honors College must maintain at least a 3.5 cumulative GPA and complete at least two honors-caliber courses during each academic year, totaling at least 24 credits in all (at least 12 of them at the upper-division level), including an honors senior thesis; diplomas of graduates fulfilling these requirements bear the designation "University Honors College." All honors courses are indicated as such on the student's transcript. Students graduating with honors and University honors are recognized at Commencement by blue honors cords and by special designation in the Commencement booklet, which also records the honors senior theses.

Scholarship Availability: Residents of Arkansas with a composite ACT score of 30 or above who enroll at Arkansas State University in the fall semester immediately following their graduation from an Arkansas high school are eligible to apply for the University Honors Scholarship. This scholarship provides tuition, general fees, room and board, and a stipend of $1200 per year for up to eight consecutive semesters as long as the student completes at least 15 hours of course work in the fall and spring semesters and fulfills the requirements of the University Honors College in which University Honors Scholars are automatically enrolled. Other honors students may be eligible for the Academic Distinction Scholarship, which provides for full tuition in the fall and spring semesters, or the Chancellor's Scholarship, which offers housing, fees, and tuition. In addition, two $500 Hazel Deutsch scholarships are awarded each fall to students who have demonstrated outstanding performance in the Honors College.

Campus Overview

State-supported comprehensive, founded 1909, part of Arkansas State University System • **Coed** 9,262 undergraduate students, 78% full-time, 60% women, 40% men.

Undergraduates 7,263 full-time, 1,999 part-time. Students come from 42 states and territories, 49 other countries, 10% are from out of state, 16% African American, 0.7% Asian American or Pacific Islander, 0.9% Hispanic American, 0.4% Native American, 1% international, 10% transferred in, 18% live on campus.

Faculty *Total:* 621, 73% full-time, 51% with terminal degrees. *Student/faculty ratio:* 18:1.

Academic Programs *Special study options:* academic remediation for entering students, accelerated degree program, advanced placement credit, cooperative education, distance learning, double majors, English as a second language, honors programs, independent study, internships, off-campus study, part-time degree program, services for LD students, study abroad, summer session for credit. *ROTC:* Army (b).

Athletics Member NCAA. All Division I except football (Division I-A). *Intercollegiate sports:* baseball M(s), basketball M(s)/W(s), bowling W(s), cross-country running M(s)/W(s), golf M(s)/W(s), soccer W(s), tennis W(s), track and field M(s)/W(s), volleyball W(s). *Intramural sports:* archery M/W, badminton M/W, basketball M/W, bowling M/W, football M/W, golf M/W, racquetball M/W, soccer M/W, softball M/W, table tennis M/W, tennis M/W, ultimate Frisbee M/W, volleyball M/W.

Costs (2004–05) *Tuition:* state resident $4035 full-time, $135 per credit hour part-time; nonresident $10,395 full-time, $347 per credit hour part-time. Full-time tuition and fees vary according to course load, location, and program. Part-time tuition and fees vary according to course load, location, and program. *Required fees:* $1120 full-time, $35 per credit hour part-time, $25 per term part-time. *Room and board:* $4000. Room and board charges vary according to board plan and housing facility.

Financial Aid 344 Federal Work-Study jobs (averaging $1591). In 2003, 1910 non-need-based awards were made. *Average percent of* *need met: 55%. Average financial aid package: $3900. Average need-based loan: $2100. Average need-based gift aid: $2600. Average non-need-based aid: $2600.*

Contact: Interim Dean: Dr. Gil Fowler, Assistant Dean: Dr. Michael K. Cundall Jr., Post Office Box 2889, State University, Arkansas 72467; *Telephone:* 870-972-2308; *Fax:* 870-972-3884; *E-mail:* honors@astate.edu; *Web site:* http://honors.astate.edu

Arkansas Tech University
University Honors Program
Russellville, Arkansas

The University Honors Program at Arkansas Tech University is designed to enrich the intellectual experience for students who possess exceptional educational talents and potential for leadership. Honors Program students are able to interact with other similarly motivated students along with an outstanding group of professors. This all occurs in the challenging atmosphere of small, innovative honors classes designed to foster rational inquiry, critical thinking, and analytical skills.

Arkansas Tech University was founded in 1909 as a multipurpose, state-supported institution of higher education. While a number of graduate programs are offered at Arkansas Tech, the University's primary mission is teaching.

Curriculum for University Honors works concurrently with any of the majors available at Arkansas Tech University. Honors students are required to take 19 to 23 hours of designated honors courses, including the Freshman Honors Seminar and special honors sections of general education courses in English, history, sciences, economics, philosophy, and literature. Junior honors students serve as mentors to incoming freshmen in the University Honors Program. Each senior completes a Senior Honors Project within his or her major and presents the results at the annual Senior Honors and Undergraduate Research Symposium before graduating.

The University Honors Program enrolls 25 freshmen each year. These students are selected on a competitive basis from among applicants. Applications are mailed to outstanding high school seniors based upon GPA, ACT or SAT scores, and other considerations. The application for University Honors is also available at http://www.atu.edu/acad/honors/. University Honors students who remain in good standing are eligible for renewal up to 9 semesters or 124 semester hours, whichever comes first

Participation Requirements: To remain in good standing within the program, the student in University Honors must maintain a minimum 3.25 cumulative GPA based upon the successful completion of a minimum 12 hours per semester.

Admission Process: To be admitted to the University Honors Program, the applicant must have a minimum 28 ACT composite or SAT equivalent as well as at least a 3.5 cumulative high school GPA. Selected applicants are invited to interview with the Director of University Honors throughout the academic year until all scholarship positions are filled.

Scholarship Availability: Each student admitted to University Honors is granted a scholarship that covers tuition, academic fees, room, and board and provides a stipend each fall and spring semester to defray the costs of books and materials, up to cost of attendance.

Campus Overview

State-supported comprehensive, founded 1909 • **Coed** 6,091 undergraduate students, 86% full-time, 53% women, 47% men.

Undergraduates 5,222 full-time, 869 part-time. Students come from 37 states and territories, 34 other countries, 4% are from out of state, 4% African American, 1% Asian American or Pacific Islander, 2%

Hispanic American, 2% Native American, 1% international, 5% transferred in, 30% live on campus.

Faculty *Total:* 367, 65% full-time. *Student/faculty ratio:* 19:1.

Academic Programs *Special study options:* academic remediation for entering students, adult/continuing education programs, advanced placement credit, distance learning, double majors, external degree program, honors programs, independent study, internships, part-time degree program, services for LD students, summer session for credit. *ROTC:* Army (c).

Athletics Member NCAA. All Division II. *Intercollegiate sports:* baseball M(s), basketball M(s)/W(s), cheerleading M/W, cross-country running W(s), football M(s), golf M(s), tennis W(s), volleyball W(s). *Intramural sports:* basketball M/W, bowling M/W, cross-country running M/W, football M/W, golf M/W, racquetball M/W, soccer M/W, softball M/W, swimming and diving M/W, table tennis M/W, tennis M/W, ultimate Frisbee M/W, volleyball M/W.

Costs (2004–05) *Tuition:* state resident $4158 full-time, $154 per hour part-time; nonresident $8316 full-time, $308 per hour part-time. Full-time tuition and fees vary according to course load and location. Part-time tuition and fees vary according to course load and location. *Required fees:* $310 full-time, $4 per hour part-time, $70 per term part-time. *Room and board:* $3841; room only: $2078. Room and board charges vary according to board plan and housing facility.

Financial Aid 235 Federal Work-Study jobs (averaging $1239). 415 state and other part-time jobs (averaging $1177). In 2003, 1004 non-need-based awards were made. *Average percent of need met:* 47%. *Average financial aid package:* $4840. *Average need-based loan:* $2217. *Average need-based gift aid:* $2535. *Average non-need-based aid:* $4858.

Contact: Dr. Jan Jenkins, Associate Professor of History, 407 West Q Street, WPN 267, Arkansas Tech University, Russellville, Arkansas 72801; *Telephone:* 479-968-0456; *Fax:* 479-964-0218; *Web site:* http://www.atu.edu/acad/honors/

Harding University
Honors Program
Searcy, Arkansas

The Harding University Honors College was established in 1989 to better serve some of the University's many talented students. It provides opportunities for these students to enrich and broaden their academic experiences. Honors courses stimulate and challenge promising students to develop their scholarship and leadership skills as fully as possible. In particular, this program encourages students to develop high intellectual standards, independent thought, logical analysis, and insight into the nature of knowledge while building their faith in God.

Harding University's Honors College features a three-tier approach to honors education. The Honors Scholar tier serves 40 of Harding's top incoming students each year. Recruited from National Merit Finalists and Trustee Scholars in the freshman class, these students earn some of their liberal arts credits in five honors classes that are limited to 20 students each and are based on discussion and student participation rather than lecture. The classes involve more written and oral work from the students, but they also allow exceptionally close relationships with the teachers. Honors 201 deals with communication and critical-thinking skills. Honors 202 replaces the New Testament survey for freshmen. Honors 203 fits in the humanities area of general studies, focusing on the big questions that man has always asked. Honors 204 deals with man and society, covering issues that range from twin studies to chaos theory. Honors 205 addresses the issues of man and his environment.

The Honors Student tier offers students the opportunity to take one or more honors sections of liberal arts classes such as speech,

English, art, music, and Bible. To qualify, students must score 27 or above on the ACT or 1800 or above on the SAT. The courses emphasize student responsibility and participation more than rote memorization. Most classes limit enrollment more than the regular sections do, and all are taught by faculty members selected and trained especially for honors education. Great care is taken that the courses are neither more difficult nor easier than the other general studies offerings; instead, the focus in on different teaching styles and critical thinking. By following an honors track, students are preparing for their future careers in courses geared more to their academic preparation and ability.

The Honors College offers an interdisciplinary Leadership Studies minor intended to provide a strong, broad foundation for Honors students who want to develop a servant leadership lifestyle. The minor requires Honors 204, a leadership practicum developed with a faculty mentor, and a customized selection of courses from toher colleges of the university that encompasses communication, interpersonal relations, conflict management, organizational management, strategies of leadership, and the applied development of leadership skills.

Upper-level students who have completed the liberal arts curriculum in either tier and upper-level and transfer students who qualify can participate in honors contract courses. Individual students and teachers collectively rewrite the syllabus of a course in the student's major, thereby turning it into an honors course. By exchanging some course requirements for other options that fit more with the ideals of honors education, the students can enhance the benefits they receive from courses that they take to complete their majors. The flexible nature of these contracts allows students to go into greater depth in some classes, to explore some supplementary topics in others, and to fine-tune their educational experiences within the limitations of their major and the honors program.

The Honors College is administered by a dean and the Honors Council, which consists of faculty members, administrators, and students. The students elect an executive council that participates on the Honors Council and organizes various activities, including speakers, retreats, picnics, and other social and cultural events. There are currently 750 students enrolled in the Honors College.

Participation Requirements: To remain eligible for the Honors College, students must maintain a minimum 3.25 GPA. Transfers and other students may petition for acceptance by submitting an application. To graduate from the Honors College, students must earn 20 hours of honors credits, including at least four courses in the Honors Scholar tier or the Honors Student tier. Those who earn at least 26 hours of honors credits, including at least four courses in the Honors Scholar tier or the Honors Student tier, four honors contract classes, and an honors capstone project, while maintaining a GPA of at least 3.5 are identified at graduation as Honors College graduates with distinction.

Scholarship Availability: Although most honors students receive University scholarships, the Honors College itself does not award scholarships. Eighty percent of Harding University students receive some type of financial aid.

Campus Overview

Independent comprehensive, founded 1924, affiliated with Church of Christ • **Coed** 4,037 undergraduate students, 96% full-time, 54% women, 46% men.

Undergraduates 3,862 full-time, 175 part-time. Students come from 50 states and territories, 71% are from out of state, 4% African American, 0.7% Asian American or Pacific Islander, 1% Hispanic American, 0.9% Native American, 4% international, 5% transferred in, 73% live on campus.

Faculty *Total:* 316, 67% full-time, 49% with terminal degrees. *Student/faculty ratio:* 18:1.

Academic Programs *Special study options:* academic remediation for entering students, accelerated degree program, adult/continuing education programs, advanced placement credit, cooperative education, distance learning, double majors, English as a second language, freshman honors college, honors programs, independent study,

internships, part-time degree program, services for LD students, student-designed majors, study abroad, summer session for credit. *ROTC:* Army (c). *Unusual degree programs:* 3-2 engineering with University of Arkansas, Georgia Institute of Technology, University of Missouri-Rolla, Louisiana Tech University, University of Southern California.

Athletics Member NCAA. All Division II. *Intercollegiate sports:* baseball M(s), basketball M(s)/W(s), cheerleading M/W, cross-country running M(s)/W(s), football M(s), golf M, lacrosse M(c), soccer M(s)/W(s), tennis M(s)/W(s), track and field M(s)/W(s), ultimate Frisbee M/W, volleyball W(s). *Intramural sports:* basketball M/W, bowling M/W, cross-country running M/W, football M/W, golf M/W, gymnastics W, racquetball M/W, soccer M/W, softball M/W, swimming and diving M/W, table tennis M/W, tennis M/W, track and field M/W, ultimate Frisbee M/W, volleyball M/W, weight lifting M/W.

Costs (2004–05) *Comprehensive fee:* $15,962 includes full-time tuition ($10,380), mandatory fees ($400), and room and board ($5182). Full-time tuition and fees vary according to course load. Part-time tuition: $346 per semester hour. Part-time tuition and fees vary according to course load. *Required fees:* $20 per semester hour part-time. *College room only:* $2572. Room and board charges vary according to board plan and housing facility.

Financial Aid 2,034 Federal Work-Study jobs (averaging $291). 1,629 state and other part-time jobs (averaging $512). In 2003, 1454 non-need-based awards were made. *Average percent of need met:* 64%. *Average financial aid package:* $8673. *Average need-based loan:* $4380. *Average need-based gift aid:* $5444. *Average non-need-based aid:* $7246.

Contact: Dean: Jeffrey T. Hopper, Box 10828, Searcy, Arkansas 72149-0001; *Telephone:* 501-279-4056; *Fax:* 501-279-4184; *E-mail:* honors@harding.edu; *Web site:* http://www.harding.edu/

Henderson State University
Honors Program
Arkadelphia, Arkansas

*T**he Honors College provides special attention, support, and opportunities for those students of the highest academic achievement and potential. The curriculum, which is planned and delivered primarily by a select honors faculty, comprises honors general education courses, upper-level interdisciplinary honors seminars and colloquia, independent- and directed-study opportunities, and honors work in each student's major field of study. The curriculum is arranged so that Honors College students do not need to earn more credits for graduation than their contemporaries who are not in the Honors College.*

As a complement to its academic program, the Honors College promotes a strong sense of community among students through an emphasis on University service, as well as on cultural and social activities. The new Honors College Hall is the hub of community for students. Honors students also have their own organization, the Areté Society, which is administered by the Honors College Council and composed of 12 students, 3 from each academic classification. The Council members are representatives for, and leaders among, their honors classmates. Among its many accomplishments, the Areté Society numbers the establishment and staffing of an award-winning journal, which includes some of the best scholarly and creative work submitted by Henderson students.

The seed of Henderson's Honors College was a single course, the Honors Colloquium, first offered in the spring of 1979. From that course, the honors effort developed into a program by 1982 and a college by 1992.

Currently, 250 students are members of the Honors College.

Participation Requirements: Once admitted to the Honors College, a student remains in good standing by taking at least one honors class each fall and spring, and by maintaining a cumulative GPA of at least 3.25. To graduate as Honors College scholars, students must complete at least 24 hours of honors-designated work and earn a cumulative GPA of at least 3.25. In order to satisfy the 24-hour requirement, each Honors College scholar must complete 12 hours of honors general education courses and 12 hours of upper-division credit, which includes 6 hours designated by the student's major department. At Commencement, Honors College scholars are presented with commemorative medallions. The designation Honors College Scholar is recorded on the diploma and the official transcript of each Honors College graduate, as well as in the Commencement program.

Admission Process: High school students are invited to apply for admission to the Honors College based on their ACT scores. They are selected on the basis of these scores, high school GPA, rank in class, a brief essay, and recommendations.

Scholarship Availability: A limited number of Honors College stipends are available on a competitive basis and are renewable as long as students remain in good standing. Any freshman who is accepted into the Honors College without a stipend may be eligible for one at the beginning of the sophomore year. Freshmen eligible for the Honors College are also eligible to compete for University scholarships, which are awarded on the basis of ACT composite scores at three levels, covering either tuition alone, room and tuition, or room, board, and tuition.

Campus Overview

State-supported comprehensive, founded 1890 • **Coed** 3,036 undergraduate students, 89% full-time, 57% women, 43% men.

Undergraduates 2,698 full-time, 338 part-time. Students come from 24 states and territories, 27 other countries, 12% are from out of state, 17% African American, 0.5% Asian American or Pacific Islander, 1% Hispanic American, 0.7% Native American, 2% international, 9% transferred in.

Faculty *Total:* 218, 72% full-time, 91% with terminal degrees. *Student/faculty ratio:* 17:1.

Academic Programs *Special study options:* academic remediation for entering students, advanced placement credit, distance learning, honors programs, internships, off-campus study, part-time degree program, services for LD students, summer session for credit.

Athletics Member NCAA. All Division II. *Intercollegiate sports:* baseball M(s), basketball M(s)/W(s), cross-country running W(s), football M(s), golf M, softball W(s), swimming and diving M(s)/W(s), tennis M(s)/W(s), volleyball W(s). *Intramural sports:* basketball M/W, football M, golf M/W, soccer M, swimming and diving M/W, tennis M/W, volleyball W.

Costs (2004–05) *Tuition:* state resident $3640 full-time, $130 per credit hour part-time; nonresident $7280 full-time, $260 per credit hour part-time. Full-time tuition and fees vary according to course load. Part-time tuition and fees vary according to course load. *Required fees:* $470 full-time. *Room and board:* $3738. Room and board charges vary according to board plan and housing facility.

Financial Aid 107 state and other part-time jobs (averaging $1648). In 2002, 516 non-need-based awards were made. *Average percent of need met:* 79%. *Average financial aid package:* $5640. *Average need-based loan:* $3820. *Average need-based gift aid:* $4400. *Average non-need-based aid:* $5735.

Contact: Director: Dr. David Thomson, 1100 Henderson Street, Arkadelphia, Arkansas 71999-0001; *Telephone:* 501-230-5129; *Fax:* 501-230-5596; *E-mail:* thomsond@hsu.edu

John Brown University
University Honors Program
Siloam Springs, Arkansas

The John Brown University (JBU) Honors Program, begun in 1987, includes a core of enriched courses that have been developed for gifted, highly motivated students. Participants must complete at least 21 honors hours to receive a University Honors degree. Courses emphasize the development of analytical skills, scholarly growth, and intellectual curiosity. The classes replace regular general education courses. Perhaps more important, the program is the impetus for continued development of JBU as a community of scholars. Many of the courses are experiential, with collaborative and integrative elements that cross disciplinary lines and narrow the gap between school and community by way of projects, field trips, guest speakers, and multimedia experiences. Some courses are modeled on NCHC's Honors Semesters, highlighting Native American and Ozark Mountain cultures, local businesses, and regional arts. The Honors Program emphasizes the exchange of ideas in a variety of settings: in the classroom, in the Honors Center, on field trips, and in the homes of professors.

The Honors Program attempts to recruit successful, innovative professors and serves as a laboratory for the development of pedagogical techniques and courses for the nonhonors curriculum.

JBU honors students are strongly encouraged to model Judeo-Christian principles and good stewardship of their academic gifts through serving in leadership positions on campus and participating in service activities both on and off campus. The Student Honors Organization promotes scholarly presentations and service by the student body as a whole and serves as a peer support group for honors students. The Honors Center, available to honors students 24 hours a day, provides an attractive location for studying, cooking, watching television, and tutoring.

The total program has approximately 160 students.

Participation Requirements: To continue to the junior and senior levels of the program, a student must have an overall GPA of at least 3.6 at the end of the sophomore year. Successful completion of the program is highlighted at an Honors Convocation and by the presentation of a special honors degree diploma at graduation. Courses are designated as "Honors" on the transcript.

Admission Process: Fifty to 60 entering freshmen are selected by application each June from a large and well-qualified pool of applicants. Transfer students and currently enrolled JBU students who have enough general education courses remaining to be taken for the honors degree may also apply. Eligibility for admission is based on high school GPA and class rank, SAT or ACT scores, and an interview by the Admissions Committee.

Scholarship Availability: Each year, JBU awards five 4-year, full-tuition scholarships (Presidentials) to incoming freshmen who have met the following requirements: scored in the 95th national percentile or above on the ACT or SAT, graduated with a 3.9 cumulative high school GPA or above (on 4.0 scale), ranked in the top 5 percent in the high school class, demonstrated leadership abilities, written an outstanding letter of application, and successfully completed an interview process. Presidential scholars may also receive other scholarships to cover room and board. The University also awards thirty Chancellor Scholarships of $6500 each. Recipients must have scored in the 95th national percentile or above on the ACT or SAT, had a GPA of at least 3.8 in high school, and ranked in the top 5 percent of their high school graduating class.

A large number of JBU honors participants come from the remaining scholarship pool. The institution awards ten Engineering Scholarships of $6000 each, numerous academic achievement scholarships ranging from $1000 to $5000 per year, named scholarships donated by individuals and organizations, scholarships in the majors, and various leadership scholarships.

Campus Overview

Independent interdenominational comprehensive, founded 1919 • **Coed** 1,712 undergraduate students, 96% full-time, 49% women, 51% men.

Undergraduates 1,639 full-time, 73 part-time. Students come from 44 states and territories, 37 other countries, 73% are from out of state, 3% African American, 2% Asian American or Pacific Islander, 2% Hispanic American, 2% Native American, 7% international, 4% transferred in, 76% live on campus.

Faculty *Total:* 143, 56% full-time, 57% with terminal degrees. *Student/faculty ratio:* 13:1.

Academic Programs *Special study options:* academic remediation for entering students, adult/continuing education programs, advanced placement credit, distance learning, double majors, English as a second language, external degree program, freshman honors college, honors programs, independent study, internships, services for LD students, study abroad. *ROTC:* Army (c), Air Force (c).

Athletics Member NAIA. *Intercollegiate sports:* basketball M(s)/W(s), soccer M(s)/W(s), swimming and diving M(s)/W(s), tennis M(s)/W(s), volleyball W(s). *Intramural sports:* baseball M, basketball M/W, football M/W, racquetball M/W, rugby M, soccer M/W, softball M/W, tennis M/W, volleyball M/W.

Costs (2004–05) *Comprehensive fee:* $19,758 includes full-time tuition ($13,724), mandatory fees ($710), and room and board ($5324). Full-time tuition and fees vary according to program. Part-time tuition: $572 per semester hour. Part-time tuition and fees vary according to course load and program. *Room and board:* Room and board charges vary according to board plan and housing facility.

Financial Aid 267 Federal Work-Study jobs (averaging $1397). 227 state and other part-time jobs (averaging $1339). In 2004, 287 non-need-based awards were made. *Average percent of need met:* 50%. *Average financial aid package:* $9149. *Average need-based loan:* $4387. *Average need-based gift aid:* $4016. *Average non-need-based aid:* $3763.

Contact: Director: Dr. Brad Gambill, Honors Office JBU Box 3074, 2000 West University, Siloam Springs, Arkansas 72761; *Telephone:* 479-524-7426; *Fax:* 479-238-8580; *E-mail:* bgambill@jbu.edu; *Web site:* http://www.jbu.edu/academics/honors/index.asp

Southern Arkansas University–Magnolia
Honors College Program
Magnolia, Arkansas

The Honors College of Southern Arkansas University–Magnolia is dedicated to the educational and personal enrichment of its students and strives to expand their intellects and talents through curricular and cocurricular learning experiences. The program is an effort to lift, enliven, and stimulate the critical-thinking process and to ensure that students receive the best education possible.

Students in the program find the courses to be both challenging and rewarding. In addition, the Honors College provides students with an opportunity for a quiet living/learning environment in a designated residence hall.

At the completion of the course requirements for graduation, Honors College students receive special recognition at graduation and the distinction as Southern Arkansas University Honors College Scholar on their transcripts and diplomas.

Participation Requirements: As part of their studies, students in the Honors College enroll in 18 hours of general education courses and 6 hours of major-level courses. Students must complete a total of 24

hours of Honors College credit. Classes offered include honors seminars, general education courses, upper-level courses in the student's major field, colloquiums, and independent studies.

For continued participation in the program, students must make satisfactory progress in completing the honors curriculum and maintain a minimum cumulative GPA of 3.25.

Admission Process: Prospective students with ACT scores of 26 or above are invited to apply to the Honors College. Students already attending Southern Arkansas University–Magnolia and who have a GPA of 3.5 or higher may petition the Honors College for admission. Other criteria may also be used to determine eligibility.

Scholarship Availability: Students may apply for a number of scholarships. Students who qualify and participate in the program receive a $250 a year stipend in addition to their academic scholarships. More information is available at Southern Arkansas University–Magnolia's Web site (http://www.saumag.edu).

Campus Overview

State-supported comprehensive, founded 1909, part of Southern Arkansas University System • **Coed** 2,803 undergraduate students, 86% full-time, 57% women, 43% men.

Undergraduates 2,398 full-time, 405 part-time. Students come from 31 states and territories, 37 other countries, 20% are from out of state, 26% African American, 0.8% Asian American or Pacific Islander, 1% Hispanic American, 0.5% Native American, 5% international, 6% transferred in, 36% live on campus.

Faculty *Total:* 184, 77% full-time, 48% with terminal degrees. *Student/faculty ratio:* 15:1.

Academic Programs *Special study options:* academic remediation for entering students, accelerated degree program, adult/continuing education programs, advanced placement credit, distance learning, double majors, freshman honors college, honors programs, independent study, internships, part-time degree program, services for LD students, study abroad, summer session for credit.

Athletics Member NCAA. All Division II. *Intercollegiate sports:* baseball M(s), basketball M(s)/W(s), cross-country running M/W(s), football M(s), golf M, softball W(s), tennis W(s), track and field M/W, volleyball W(s). *Intramural sports:* badminton M/W, basketball M/W, football M, golf M, softball M/W, swimming and diving M/W, table tennis M/W, tennis M/W, volleyball M/W.

Costs (2004–05) *Tuition:* state resident $3528 full-time, $126 per credit hour part-time; nonresident $5348 full-time, $191 per credit hour part-time. Full-time tuition and fees vary according to course load. Part-time tuition and fees vary according to course load. *Required fees:* $330 full-time, $330 per year part-time. *Room and board:* $3600.

Financial Aid 1,129 Federal Work-Study jobs (averaging $2155). 319 state and other part-time jobs (averaging $2278). In 2004, 376 non-need-based awards were made. *Average percent of need met:* 100%. *Average financial aid package:* $6298. *Average need-based loan:* $3062. *Average need-based gift aid:* $3382. *Average non-need-based aid:* $2759.

Contact: Director: Dr. Lynne Belcher, Wilson Hall 325, P.O. Box 9175, Southern Arkansas University–Magnolia, Magnolia, Arkansas 71754; *Telephone:* 870-235-4202; *Fax:* 870-235-5488; *E-mail:* honorscollege@saumag.edu; *Web site:* http://www.saumag.edu/honorscollege

University of Arkansas
Honors College
Fayetteville, Arkansas

In April 2002, the University of Arkansas (U of A) announced the largest gift in the history of American public higher education—a $300-million commitment from the Walton Family Charitable Support Foundation of Bentonville, Arkansas, to establish and endow an undergraduate honors college and graduate school. Of that sum, $190 million is being used to endow Honors College Fellowships and Honors College Academy Scholarships for exceptionally talented students, to establish up to 100 endowed faculty chairs and professorships, and to endow special funds to support study abroad and undergraduate research opportunities.

The Honors College currently enrolls more than 2,000 high-achieving students. In fall 2002, the inaugural freshman class numbered more than 400. Honors College freshmen may live in the newly renovated honors residence hall, the Pomfret honors quarters, or the honors quarters in the quads. Honors College study lounges and the Honors College Dean's Office are located on the fourth floor of the administration building.

The U of A Honors College serves all undergraduate majors. Honors students enjoy small classes, priority registration, special housing, increased interaction with faculty members, and enhanced opportunities for hands-on research. Within the Honors College, the Scholarship Office and the Office of Post-Graduate Fellowships provide additional services.

The Honors College includes honors programs in each of the academic colleges: Bumpers College of Agriculture and Life Sciences, the College of Education and Health Professions, the College of Engineering, the Fulbright College of Arts and Science, the School of Architecture, and the Walton College of Business. Honors education has a long tradition on the campus, dating back to 1956, when Professors Harold Hantz (also a founding member of the National Collegiate Honors Council) and Ben Kimpel created a departmental honors program. The program was later expanded to include the Four-Year Scholars Program, which offers a broad selection of honors core courses and colloquia. A National Endowment for the Humanities–sponsored four-semester humanities course is also available and is designed to combine world literature, world civilization, and fine arts requirements. All students graduating with honors are required to participate in undergraduate research and are encouraged to participate in study abroad.

Participation Requirements: Four-Year Scholars Programs are available in the Fulbright College of Arts and Sciences and in the Walton College of Business. Students complete a specified number of hours in core courses, choosing from a variety of honors classes, and combine that with an undergraduate research project. Department programs exist in all the college and include a minimum of 12 hours of honors course credit and a culminating research project. Students who successfully complete the required course work and research project in their field of study graduate with honors. Cum laude, magna cum laude, or summa cum laude—depending on the quality of work and the number of honors hours taken—are noted on transcripts and diplomas. Students graduate with honors and wear stoles and medals at graduation marking their outstanding achievements.

Admission Process: Students are admitted based on several criteria: high school records, class rank, ACT or SAT scores, academic awards and prizes, and participation in special programs, courses, or institutes. Entering freshmen who participate generally have a 28 or higher ACT and a 3.5 or higher high school GPA. Students wishing to participate in the Walton College of Business Honors Program must have an entering GPA of 3.75. Students who enter the program later in the freshman or sophomore years must have a minimum 3.5 college GPA. These guidelines are flexible. Students who do not meet the basic requirements but are eager to participate should schedule an appointment with the Dean of the Honors College.

Scholarship Availability: The Academic Scholarship Office is part of the Honors College. A variety of scholarships are available, including ninety-five Honors College, Sturgis, and Bodenhamer Distinguished Fellowships ($50,000 for four years), awarded to entering freshmen of all majors. Promising high school seniors are assisted with their applications for the many available fellowships and scholarships. Enrolled honors students are assisted (with a high success rate) with applications for nationally competitive scholarships, including Rhodes, Marshall, Gates Cambridge, Goldwater, Udall, Madison, Fulbright, NSF, Truman, and others. In addition to room, board, and tuition, these fellowships can be used to pay for study abroad, conferences, or for equipment such as computers and musical instruments. A separate application is required.

Campus Overview

State-supported university, founded 1871, part of University of Arkansas System • **Coed** 13,817 undergraduate students, 82% full-time, 50% women, 50% men.

Undergraduates 11,302 full-time, 2,515 part-time. Students come from 50 states and territories, 103 other countries, 14% are from out of state, 5% African American, 3% Asian American or Pacific Islander, 2% Hispanic American, 2% Native American, 2% international, 8% transferred in, 29% live on campus.

Faculty *Total:* 847, 94% full-time, 87% with terminal degrees. *Student/faculty ratio:* 17:1.

Academic Programs *Special study options:* accelerated degree program, advanced placement credit, cooperative education, distance learning, double majors, English as a second language, freshman honors college, honors programs, independent study, internships, part-time degree program, services for LD students, study abroad, summer session for credit. *ROTC:* Army (b), Air Force (b). *Unusual degree programs:* 3-2 law.

Athletics Member NCAA. All Division I except football (Division I-A). *Intercollegiate sports:* baseball M(s), basketball M(s)/W(s), cross-country running M(s)/W(s), golf M(s)/W(s), gymnastics W(s), soccer W(s), softball W(s), swimming and diving W(s), tennis M(s)/W(s), track and field M(s)/W(s), volleyball W(s). *Intramural sports:* badminton M/W, basketball M/W, bowling M(c)/W(c), football M/W, golf M/W, racquetball M/W, rock climbing M/W, rugby M(c)/W(c), soccer M/W, softball M/W, swimming and diving M/W, table tennis M/W, tennis M/W, volleyball M(c)/W(c), water polo M/W.

Costs (2004–05) *Tuition:* state resident $4115 full-time, $137 per credit hour part-time; nonresident $11,405 full-time, $380 per credit hour part-time. *Required fees:* $1020 full-time, $34 per credit part-time, $34 per term part-time. *Room and board:* $5927; room only: $3481. Room and board charges vary according to board plan and housing facility.

Financial Aid 1,898 Federal Work-Study jobs (averaging $2000). In 2003, 2240 non-need-based awards were made. *Average percent of need met:* 74%. *Average financial aid package:* $8260. *Average need-based loan:* $4204. *Average need-based gift aid:* $3650. *Average non-need-based aid:* $5645.

Contact: Dean: Dr. Robert McMath, Administration Building 418, University of Arkansas Honors College, Fayetteville, Arkansas 72701; *Telephone:* 479-575-7678; *Fax:* 479-575-4882; *E-mail:* honors@uark.edu; *Web site:* http://honorscollege.uark.edu/

University of Arkansas at Fort Smith

Honors Program

Fort Smith, Arkansas

The University of Arkansas (UA) at Fort Smith Honors Program provides a variety of activities and options to enrich and broaden the educational experience of highly motivated and talented students. The program provides opportunities for diverse educational activities, such as discussion groups, forums, and mentor relationships that help the students grow both academically and personally. Honors classes at UA Fort Smith present a challenging learning environment where ideas and concepts are examined in seminar formats with small numbers of students. Honors classes explore topics in greater depth and focus on the development of fundamental abilities beyond the basic general education competencies.

The Chancellor's Scholars Program is the UA Fort Smith's premier merit-based award for high school seniors. Chancellor's Scholars are among the top students in their graduating classes, have a proven record of academic and leadership excellence, and show potential for continued growth in an academically challenging environment. The students benefit from honors seminar courses that are exclusive to the Chancellor's Scholars Program and work with distinguished faculty members. Students not accepted into this program may take honors courses and apply for acceptance to the University Honors Program. To receive a bachelor's degree with honors from the UA at Fort Smith, a student must complete a minimum of 24 credit hours of honors courses, including a junior honors seminar and a senior honors project.

The University of Arkansas at Fort Smith honors courses challenge students with a different type of learning experience. The honors courses focus on primary source materials rather than rely on textbook information. Field trips to archeological sites and museums allow honors students to gain firsthand knowledge in subject areas.

Other advantages for honors program students include an honors lounge and media center that is equipped with its own computer, free interlibrary loans at Boreham Library for honors course study, and participation in the community service arm of the UA Fort Smith Honors Program.

Participation Requirements: For a bachelor's degree with honors, students must complete 24 hours of honors credit, achieve mastery in all general education competencies, and maintain a minimum 3.25 GPA in all course work.

Graduating Chancellor's Scholars and University Honors students are given special recognition at the spring honors convocation and receive special medallions to wear at graduation. In addition, an honors seal is placed on the diploma and the honors degree is noted on the student's official transcript.

Admission Process: Applicants for the Chancellor's Scholars Program should demonstrate evidence of high motivation, leadership, and academic skills. An application for the program includes recommendations from high school instructors, an on-campus interview and writing sample, and an ACT composite score of 27 or higher. Applications for the Chancellor's Scholars Program must be submitted by February 15. Annual renewal of the scholarship requires maintenance of a minimum 3.25 GPA and completion of 30 hours or more during the freshman year.

Applicants for the University Honors Program may be submitted at any time and must include recommendations from instructors, a minimum 3.25 GPA in UA Fort Smith classes, or an ACT score of 25 or higher.

Scholarship Availability: The Chancellor's Honors Program awards a full tuition scholarship and $500 toward books and supplies each semester. Other students may qualify for merit-based scholarships and a University Honors book scholarship.

Campus Overview

State and locally supported 4-year, founded 1928, part of University of Arkansas System • **Coed** 6,623 undergraduate students, 57% full-time, 60% women, 40% men.

Undergraduates 3,782 full-time, 2,841 part-time. Students come from 30 states and territories, 10 other countries, 13% are from out of state, 4% African American, 4% Asian American or Pacific Islander, 3% Hispanic American, 4% Native American, 0.2% international, 5% transferred in.

Faculty *Total:* 333, 52% full-time. *Student/faculty ratio:* 21:1.

Academic Programs *Special study options:* academic remediation for entering students, accelerated degree program, adult/continuing education programs, advanced placement credit, cooperative education, distance learning, double majors, English as a second language, external degree program, honors programs, internships, off-campus study, part-time degree program, services for LD students, summer session for credit. *ROTC:* Air Force (c).

Athletics Member NJCAA. *Intercollegiate sports:* baseball M(s), basketball M(s)/W(s), volleyball W(s). *Intramural sports:* basketball M/W, cheerleading M/W, riflery M(c)/W(c), table tennis M/W, volleyball M/W.

Costs (2004–05) *Tuition:* area resident $1740 full-time, $58 per credit hour part-time; state resident $1890 full-time, $63 per credit hour part-time; nonresident $6840 full-time, $228 per credit hour part-time. Full-time tuition and fees vary according to course level. Part-time tuition and fees vary according to course level. *Required fees:* $540 full-time, $17 per credit hour part-time, $15 per term part-time.

Financial Aid 110 Federal Work-Study jobs (averaging $3000). 94 state and other part-time jobs (averaging $3000). In 2004, 350 non-need-based awards were made. *Average percent of need met:* 62%. *Average financial aid package:* $5568. *Average need-based loan:* $3183. *Average need-based gift aid:* $3504. *Average non-need-based aid:* $2643.

Contact: Director: Dr. Henry Q. Rinne, P.O. Box 3649, Fort Smith, Arkansas 72913-3649; *Telephone:* 479-788-7545; *E-mail:* hrinne@uafortsmith.edu; *Web site:* http://www.uafortsmith.edu/Honors/Index

University of Arkansas at Little Rock

Donaghey Scholars Program

Little Rock, Arkansas

The Donaghey Scholars Program, though fairly young and fairly small (20 to 25 new Scholars are admitted each year), has matured into a distinctive and distinguished honors program.

It is distinctive in part because of its smallness (the program's size fosters intimacy and a genuine sense of community). The program's distinctiveness also derives from its curriculum. The Donaghey Scholars Program curriculum is comprehensive and highly structured; it features an interdisciplinary core of team-taught seminar-format courses that replaces the University's general education core. These core courses emphasize primary texts, critical thinking, active debate, and lots of writing (and rewriting). In addition to the core, Donaghey Scholars take seminars on special topics, develop competence in a foreign language, and do a final project. By the time a Scholar graduates, he or she should be both a good generalist and someone ready to contribute to his or her own field.

The Donaghey Scholars Program is also distinctive in linking participation in the program to financial aid. All Donaghey Scholars receive generous scholarships.

The Donaghey Scholars Program began in 1984; currently 80 scholars are enrolled.

Participation Requirements: To complete the program, Donaghey Scholars must complete a core of interdisciplinary courses totaling 35 hours (Colloquium I and II; Rhetoric and Communication I and II; Science and Society I and II; History of Ideas I, II, and III; Individual and Society I and II; and Creative Arts I and II). In addition, scholars must take a math course (3 hours) and a course in American history or American national government (3 hours). Scholars also develop competence in a foreign language and study abroad. They must also take seminars, complete a final project, and do an exit interview. To remain in good standing, scholars must maintain a minimum 3.25 GPA. Upon graduation, scholars receive a certificate indicating they have completed the program, and they wear distinctive maroon robes at commencement.

Admission Process: Since only 20 to 25 new scholars can be admitted each year, admission to the program is highly competitive. The program's admissions committee proceeds holistically. It weighs several factors, including test scores, aptitude for foreign languages, genuine interest in other cultures, letters of recommendation, writing samples, extracurricular and service activities and other evidence of leadership, an interview, and academic record (this last is the most important factor). Highly motivated, broadly curious, articulate, imaginative, and well-organized students who can contribute to and profit from the program (and the University) are sought. Students with previous college work as well as those who have just finished high school are eligible. The students are diverse; they represent a good mix of backgrounds, abilities, and interests. The program has always welcomed nontraditional and international students.

Scholarship Availability: Donaghey Scholars receive the University's most generous academic scholarships. All Donaghey Scholars receive tuition and fees, a generous stipend (currently $4000, $6500, or $9000 each year), and support for study abroad—the Donaghey Scholars Program is one of only a handful of programs in the United States that requires its students to study abroad and subsidizes that study.

Campus Overview

State-supported university, founded 1927, part of University of Arkansas System • **Urban** 150-acre campus • **Coed**

Faculty *Student/faculty ratio:* 16:1.

Athletics Member NCAA. All Division I.

Costs (2004–05) *Tuition:* state resident $4020 full-time, $134 per credit hour part-time; nonresident $10,500 full-time, $350 per credit hour part-time. *Required fees:* $935 full-time, $31 per credit hour part-time. *Room only:* $2850.

Financial Aid *Average financial aid package:* $7190.

Contact: Director: Dr. C. Earl Ramsey, University of Arkansas at Little Rock, 2801 South University, Little Rock, Arkansas 72204; *Telephone:* 501-569-3389; *Fax:* 501-569-3532; *E-mail:* ceramsey@ualr.edu; *Web site:* http://www.ualr.edu/~dsp

University of Arkansas at Pine Bluff

Honors College

Pine Bluff, Arkansas

The Honors College at the University of Arkansas at Pine Bluff (UAPB) is designed for academically oriented and motivated students. Its overall goal is to identify and recruit students of superior academic ability and potential performance and students who have a commitment to challenge, toward the end of developing the Honors College as a standard of excellence and a paradigm for all UAPB students. The program embraces the concept that it is a planned set of arrangements to serve the needs of talented, gifted, and committed students so much so that the general student population will benefit from the leadership of these students and from interaction with them in classes and forums. In addition, the faculty will be challenged to provide for those students the kinds of experiences that will motivate them to work to their potential. Ultimately, the community, state, and nation will receive the benefit of a group of leaders and citizens who will be willing, capable, and able to have a positive impact on the quality of life for all citizens. The program utilizes current faculty members to develop and implement challenging courses; it recruits bright, energetic young people; and it exposes them to activities that increase their probabilities of success in their chosen fields.

The plan of the Honors College corresponds to the mission of the University, part of which is to create a "culturally enriching environment for disadvantaged students" and to provide "specialized research, education, public service, and human resources to the state . . ." One of the University's specific goals is to increase the institution's capability for meeting the needs of both the superior and the inadequately prepared student, and this program targets those superior students.

The Honors College is a participation program that is open to any serious student who wants to respond to the challenge of honors courses and other honors experiences. Admission requirements are not so rigid that a desire to participate is ignored if a student exhibits potential, simply because that student does not meet the established ACT score requirement. This policy is commensurate with the general admission policy adhered to by the University.

The Honors College does not directly offer honors classes; it is an interdisciplinary unit that collaborates with all disciplines in developing either honors sections of existing courses, new honors courses, or contractual honors work in existing courses. Honors sections usually have an average of 15 students; however, students who contract for work in other sections may be in classes of 25 or more. To do this, students must communicate with instructors who agree to assign more challenging course work, and they both sign the contract, which is returned to the Honors College and then submitted to the registrar's office. Honors suites have been established in the dorms for upperclassmen.

Participation Requirements: Members of the Honors College are required to maintain at least a 3.25 GPA. Students who fail to maintain the required GPA are placed on probation and given one semester in which to raise their averages. They are suspended from the program if they fail to comply. Suspended students may apply for readmission, and each case is considered individually.

Honors College students are encouraged to participate in the UAPB Research Forum either individually or collaboratively with faculty members. In order to qualify as an Honors College graduate, students must enroll in and complete a minimum of 15 credit hours and complete each course with at least a B. Having satisfied all Honors College requirements—GPA, community service, maintenance of an acceptable portfolio, accumulation of the required number of hours in honors, and involvement in honors activities—the student has Honors College Graduate indicated on his or her transcript and is so recognized at commencement.

Admission Process: The Honors College administration collaborates with high school counselors and staff members of the University's basic and academic services to recruit incoming freshmen. Though the Honors College caters to freshmen, other students (sophomores, juniors, and transfer students) are accepted. Entering students must apply for formal admission to the Honors College by obtaining an application for admission from the Honors College. Entering freshmen must have an ACT score of 21 or above, must rank in the top 25 percent of their graduating class, and must have a firm commitment. Students already enrolled in the University who can demonstrate that they have made a commitment to the objectives of the Honors College may also apply.

Students admitted into the Honors College are advised to visit with the Dean to discuss desires and expectations and to inquire about scholarships, internships, and other perks of membership. Honors College students form the Honor Student Association, which has scheduled meetings each second and fourth Tuesday. Students are required to attend scheduled meetings and participate in Honor Student Association activities.

Scholarship Availability: The Honors College supervises three scholarship program s per year: the Thurgood Marshall Scholarship, the Rouse Family Scholarship, and the USDA Scholarship. The Thurgood Marshall and the USDA Scholarships are offered to incoming freshmen only. Students applying for these scholarships must obtain a formal application packet, have a cumulative GPA of at least 3.0 on a 4.0 scale and an ACT score of 25 or higher, and submit the completed packet to the Dean of the Honors College, who sits on the scholarship advisory committees.

Thurgood Marshall Scholarship recipients are allowed to enter into any of the academic disciplines; however, the USDA Scholarship recipients must enter into a discipline related to agriculture. Students who receive these scholarships are required to maintain a minimum 3.0 GPA each semester in order to retain their scholarship. Any student who fails to maintain the appropriate GPA automatically loses his or her scholarship privilege.

The Rouse Family Scholarship is available to any upperclassman enrolled at the University. Students interested in receiving the Rouse Family Scholarship must obtain and submit a completed application form and demonstrate financial need. Students applying for this scholarship must be enrolled as full-time students and have a cumulative GPA of at least 3.25. This scholarship is given in the spring semester of each year in amounts ranging from $250 to $1000 and may be used for the purpose of paying the balance of tuition, the purchase of books and/or supplies, or to supplement other educational costs.

Campus Overview

State-supported comprehensive, founded 1873, part of University of Arkansas System • **Coed** 3,200 undergraduate students, 91% full-time, 58% women, 42% men.

Undergraduates 2,897 full-time, 303 part-time. Students come from 30 states and territories, 17 other countries, 30% are from out of state, 95% African American, 0.2% Asian American or Pacific Islander, 0.2% Hispanic American, 0.1% Native American, 0.9% international, 5% transferred in, 43% live on campus.

Faculty *Total:* 236, 71% full-time, 71% with terminal degrees. *Student/faculty ratio:* 16:1.

Academic Programs *Special study options:* academic remediation for entering students, accelerated degree program, adult/continuing education programs, advanced placement credit, cooperative education, distance learning, double majors, external degree program, honors programs, independent study, internships, off-campus study, part-time degree program, services for LD students, summer session for credit. *ROTC:* Army (b). *Unusual degree programs:* 3-2 engineering with University of Arkansas (Fayetteville).

Athletics Member NCAA, NAIA. All NCAA Division I except football (Division I-AA), golf (Division I-AA). *Intercollegiate sports:* baseball M, basketball M(s)/W(s), cross-country running M/W, track and field M/W, volleyball W(s). *Intramural sports:* baseball M, basketball M, bowling M/W, cross-country running M, football M/W, golf M/W, gymnastics M/W, racquetball M/W, softball M/W, swimming and diving M/W, table tennis M/W, tennis M/W, track and field M/W, volleyball M/W, weight lifting M/W.

Costs (2004–05) *Tuition:* state resident $3000 full-time, $100 per credit hour part-time; nonresident $6975 full-time, $233 per credit hour part-time. Full-time tuition and fees vary according to location. Part-time tuition and fees vary according to location. *Required fees:* $1044 full-time. *Room and board:* $5436. Room and board charges vary according to board plan and housing facility.

Financial Aid 375 Federal Work-Study jobs (averaging $1000). *Average percent of need met:* 78%. *Average financial aid package:* $3202. *Average need-based loan:* $4506. *Average need-based gift aid:* $3218.

Contact: Dean: Dr. Carolyn Blakely, 1200 North University Drive, P.O. Box 4931, Pine Bluff, Arkansas 71611; *Telephone:* 870-575-8065; *Fax:* 870-575-8063; *E-mail:* blakely_c@uapb.edu

---

University of Central Arkansas
Honors College
Conway, Arkansas

The University of Central Arkansas (UCA) Honors College has offered a minor in honors interdisciplinary studies for students in all majors since 1982. UCA established the Honors College to heighten the educational experience for intellectually gifted students with demonstrated records of achievement. It provides a structured setting within which the student is encouraged to test varied skills by subjecting them to the give and take of dialogue with other students and faculty members.

The program is divided into two parts: the Honors Program for freshmen and sophomores and the Honors College for juniors and seniors. The Honors Program consists of a two-semester Freshman Honors Seminar and a two-semester Sophomore Honors Seminar. This four-course sequence is entitled The Human Search and is offered for general education credit. The Honors College consists of interdisciplinary seminars, an Oxford tutorial, and the completion of an honors thesis project. This 30-hour curriculum stresses the arts of inquiry, conversation, and collaboration. Dr. Terrel Bell, former U.S. Secretary of Education, called the program "an Ivy League education at a bargain basement price." UCA has been cited by the Carnegie Foundation for having a "creative and innovative program."

Students who graduate from the Honors College receive a hand-crafted medallion worn at commencement, a special certificate that includes printing of the thesis title, and acknowledgment of honors category on the diploma. There are currently about 535 students in the program.

Participation Requirements: Students enrolled in the Honors Program must maintain a minimum 3.25 GPA. To be admitted into the Honors College, the student must have completed at least one course in the Honors Program and must have an overall GPA of at least 3.5. Sophomores deliver a sophomore lecture as part of the College application process, and seniors give an oral presentation of their honors thesis project.

Scholarship Availability: Nearly all students in the program receive University scholarships. Supplemental tuition scholarships are available and are awarded based on merit and need. Funds are also awarded on a competitive basis to students who submit proposals for travel abroad and for undergraduate research or internship programs. Honors scholars have private rooms in residence halls, with a scholarship paying for the private room upgrade.

In 1997, a UCA honors scholar and history major was awarded the prestigious Harry S. Truman Scholarship, a $30,000 award given to only 65 students in the United States each year. That year there were nearly 900 applicants and 175 finalists. In 2001, a UCA Honors Scholar and philosophy major received a Rhodes Scholarship to study classics at Oxford. He was one of only 32 recipients nationwide. More than 85 percent of UCA Honors College graduates go on to postbaccalaureate training.

Campus Overview

State-supported comprehensive, founded 1907 • **Coed** 9,047 undergraduate students, 94% full-time, 60% women, 40% men.

Undergraduates 8,459 full-time, 588 part-time. Students come from 38 states and territories, 55 other countries, 5% are from out of state, 17% African American, 1% Asian American or Pacific Islander, 1% Hispanic American, 0.8% Native American, 2% international, 7% transferred in, 42% live on campus.

Faculty *Total:* 556, 81% full-time. *Student/faculty ratio:* 19:1.

Academic Programs *Special study options:* academic remediation for entering students, accelerated degree program, advanced placement credit, cooperative education, distance learning, double majors, English as a second language, freshman honors college, honors programs, independent study, internships, part-time degree program, study abroad, summer session for credit. *ROTC:* Army (b). *Unusual degree programs:* 3-2 engineering with Arkansas State University.

Athletics Member NCAA. All Division II. *Intercollegiate sports:* baseball M, basketball M(s)/W(s), cheerleading M(s)/W(s), cross-country running W, football M(s)/W, golf M/W, soccer M/W, softball W, tennis W, track and field W, volleyball W(s). *Intramural sports:* badminton M/W, basketball M/W, bowling M/W, cross-country running M/W, football M/W, racquetball M/W, soccer M(c)/W, softball M/W, swimming and diving M/W, table tennis M/W, tennis M/W, track and field M/W, volleyball M/W.

Costs (2004–05) *Tuition:* state resident $4060 full-time, $145 per hour part-time; nonresident $7616 full-time, $272 per hour part-time. Part-time tuition and fees vary according to course load. *Required fees:* $993 full-time, $31 per hour part-time, $61 per term part-time. *Room and board:* $3920; room only: $2200. Room and board charges vary according to board plan and housing facility.

Contact: Director: Dr. Richard I. Scott, P.O. Box 5024/McAlister 306, 201 Donaghey Avenue, Conway, Arkansas 72035; *Telephone:* 501-450-3198; *Fax:* 501-450-3284; *E-mail:* honors@mail.uca.edu; *Web site:* http://www.uca.edu/honors

CALIFORNIA

American River College

Honors Program

Sacramento, California

The American River College (ARC) Honors Program offers small, enriched sections of general education courses to highly motivated, academically talented students. Courses in the ARC Honors Program promote intellectual development and academic achievement at an advanced level. Students in an honors section are more responsible for class presentation and receive a more in-depth sequence of instruction. These course objectives are met through any combination of the following approaches: a more thorough examination of specific topics of inquiry; a more detailed and sophisticated reading list; and a wider variety of assignments requiring greater student input and initiative, such as independent research projects, portfolio submissions, and/or service learning. Successful completion of the honors section results in higher levels of student comprehension and mastery of subject material.

A major element of the program is the series of transfer agreements between American River College and fourteen colleges and universities throughout California, available through the Honors Transfer Council of California (HTCC), a consortium of more than forty California community colleges. These four-year institutions (CSU Fullerton, CSU Long Beach, Chapman University, La Sierra University, Occidental College, Pitzer College, Pomona College, San Diego State University, UC Irvine, UC Riverside, UC San Diego, UC Santa Cruz, Pacific University, and Whitman College) offer priority admission to students who complete the Honors transfer requirements. In addition, priority consideration is available to honors students who wish to transfer to other selective colleges and universities in California through HTCC.

Honors students also have the opportunity to be active in a number of nationally and regionally recognized honor societies: Alpha Gamma Sigma (the California community college honor society), Phi Theta Kappa (the international two-year college honor society), and Beta Psi (the two-year college honor society for psychology majors. Eligibility and membership requirements can be obtained from the College Honors coordinators and society advisers.

The ARC Honors Program began in January 1997. Enrollment in honors sections is limited to 20 students.

Participation Requirements: To graduate from the Honors Program, students must complete a minimum of 15 units in honors with a minimum GPA of 3.25, as well as any special degree requirements for particular majors and/or four-year institutions. Students who complete the Honors Program requirements at ARC have honors designations at graduation and on their transcripts, thus increasing their chances for scholarships.

Admission Process: The requirements for admission to Honors Program courses are unique for each course. In general, students must have at least a 3.0 cumulative GPA and must be eligible for ENGWR 300 College Composition.

Scholarship Availability: At present, there is only one scholarship (for an incoming high school student) specifically designated for the Honors Program.

Campus Overview

Suburban 153-acre campus • **Coed,** 30,000 undergraduate students.

Undergraduates 0.2% are from out of state.

Faculty *Total:* 1,200. *Student/faculty ratio:* 34:1.

Academic Programs *Special study options:* academic remediation for entering students, adult/continuing education programs, advanced placement credit, cooperative education, English as a second language, part-time degree program, services for LD students, summer session for credit.

Athletics *Intercollegiate sports:* basketball M/W, cross-country running M/W, football M, golf M/W, soccer M/W, swimming and diving M/W, tennis M/W, track and field M/W, volleyball M/W. *Intramural sports:* basketball M/W.

Financial Aid 300 Federal Work-Study jobs (averaging $1500). 100 state and other part-time jobs (averaging $2000).

Contact: Dr. Edward Hashima, Faculty Coordinator or Dr. Lee Thiel, Dean of Library Resources and Honors, American River College, 4700 College Oak Drive, Sacramento, California 95841; *Telephone:* 916-484-8166 (Dr. Hashima), 916-484-8408 (Dr. Thiel);; *Fax:* 916-484-8880; *E-mail:* info@arc.losrios.edu

Azusa Pacific University

Honors Program

Azusa, California

The Azusa Pacific University Honors Program consists of enriched courses developed for 40 talented and motivated students selected from among applicants in each incoming freshman class. These general studies courses are distinguished by their greater depth, intensity, intellectual rigor, and close student-faculty collaboration. The class enrollment is limited to 15 to 18 students, and the courses are designed by outstanding professors in their fields. In addition to the honors curriculum, the program offers a variety of extracurricular cultural and social activities and international learning experiences. For qualified students who choose to participate, the Honors Program provides a challenge and opportunity: the challenge to perform at their highest levels of excellence and the opportunity to develop their abilities to the fullest.

Total program enrollment is currently 126. The deadline for applying is April 1.

Participation Requirements: To remain in the program, students must maintain at least a 3.3 cumulative GPA. Those students who complete a minimum of 26 semester units of Honors Program credits receive an honors certificate and a diploma distinguishing them as Honors Scholars.

Admission Process: To be considered for admission, potential participants must represent the top 10 percent of incoming freshmen, based on their high school GPA and SAT or ACT scores. Eligible students are selected for the Honors Program on the basis of academic performance, demonstrated leadership ability, and exemplary character. In addition to completing the usual application and reference forms for admission to Azusa Pacific University, interested students need to complete an Honors Program application and submit one additional reference form from a teacher.

The Honors Program began with the freshman class of 1992. Forty students are selected from each entering freshman class, which limits the enrollment to a maximum of 160 students.

Scholarship Availability: Trustees', President's, and Dean's scholarships are available to honors students but are granted independently through Admissions and Student Financial Services.

Campus Overview

Independent nondenominational comprehensive, founded 1899 • **Coed** 4,441 undergraduate students, 85% full-time, 65% women, 35% men.

Undergraduates 3,770 full-time, 671 part-time. Students come from 44 states and territories, 52 other countries, 21% are from out of state, 3% African American, 5% Asian American or Pacific Islander, 12% Hispanic American, 0.3% Native American, 2% international, 10% transferred in, 69% live on campus.

Faculty *Total:* 356, 97% full-time. *Student/faculty ratio:* 15:1.

Academic Programs *Special study options:* academic remediation for entering students, accelerated degree program, adult/continuing education programs, advanced placement credit, cooperative education, distance learning, double majors, English as a second language, freshman honors college, honors programs, independent study, internships, off-campus study, part-time degree program, services for LD students, study abroad, summer session for credit. *ROTC:* Army (c).

Athletics Member NAIA. *Intercollegiate sports:* baseball M(s), basketball M(s)/W(s), cross-country running M(s)/W(s), football M(s), golf M(s), soccer M(s)/W(s), softball W(s), tennis M(s), track and field M(s)/W(s), volleyball M/W(s). *Intramural sports:* basketball M/W, football M/W, golf M/W, skiing (downhill) M/W, soccer W, volleyball M/W.

Costs (2004–05) *Comprehensive fee:* $26,798 includes full-time tuition ($20,006), mandatory fees ($660), and room and board ($6132). Part-time tuition: $835 per unit. Part-time tuition and fees vary according to course load. *College room only:* $3340. Room and board charges vary according to board plan, housing facility, and student level.

Financial Aid 463 Federal Work-Study jobs (averaging $1430). In 2003, 976 non-need-based awards were made. *Average percent of need met:* 86%. *Average financial aid package:* $15,844. *Average need-based loan:* $10,162. *Average need-based gift aid:* $9450. *Average non-need-based aid:* $8569.

Contact: Director: Dr. Vicky R. Bowden, The Honors Program Office, Azusa Pacific University, Azusa, California 91702-7000; *Telephone:* 626-815-2110; *Fax:* 626-815-2111; *E-mail:* vbowden@apu.edu

California State Polytechnic University, Pomona
Honors Program
Pomona, California

Honors Program students at California State Polytechnic University, Pomona (Cal Poly Pomona) are an interesting group of people. They are future engineers, architects, historians, hotel owners, lawyers, veterinarians, politicians, artists, and many other occupations as well. They will end up as leaders in all walks of life, and they share many things in common. They share a passion for knowledge and an intense motivation to do their best. Many of them are the first in their families to attend university, but few are going to stop at a bachelor's degree. They are aiming for Ph.D.'s, M.B.A.'s, and J.D.'s. They are also very diverse. Applicants to the 2005 freshman class are 29 percent Asian and Pacific Islander, 12 percent Hispanic, 2 percent African American, and 12 percent other. Some of the honors students live on campus, but the commuters also get very involved in campus life, joining clubs in their majors, using the campus fitness center, working with faculty members as research assistants, and even helping care for the University's herd of Arabian horses.

The Honors Program students share the Honors Commons, a suite of rooms in a centrally located building on the main quad. Some students meet in the seminar room or work in the computer lab. Some lay out architectural drawings or math homework on the central table. Some nap on the couches (dubbed the most comfortable on campus by one of their regular denizens). They bring in their lunches and talk about classes, movies, and life. They are a community of friends, as well as being some of the top students on campus.

Many of the honors courses at Cal Poly Pomona are in general education, both lower and upper division (three upper-division general education courses are required of all students on campus). Honors courses are limited to 20 students, whereas regular general education courses can include 50 or more. Some of the most compelling professors on campus teach the honors courses. Students have taken freshman composition from a top Shakespeare scholar and the Universe in Ten Weeks (a physics course) from a professor who does her research in the Antarctic. In these small classes, the honors students get to know one another and their professors very well. Some classes go on field trips together. Others do service-learning projects in the community. Upper-division students may also opt to do honors contracts in courses in their majors, and sometimes a group of honors students work together for honors credit in a course. Each student ultimately pursues a capstone honors course, a one-on-one senior project, with a faculty member. Students are encouraged and assisted in finding internships, summer programs, and scholarships, and the campus has an active study-abroad program.

Each quarter, the Honors Program organizes a field trip for interested students. They hop on a chartered luxury bus and go to downtown Los Angeles for a philharmonic concert or to the Getty Museum for a tour or to a local theater to see a touring company from London. These trips are almost always free to the students. The Honors Club also organizes community service projects, social gatherings, and fund raisers. At the end of the year, they organize a banquet honoring the graduating seniors, the executive board officers, and the high achievers of the year.

The Honors Program at Cal Poly Pomona is relatively new, having started in spring 2003 with just 60 students. About 100 students have joined each year since then as freshmen, continuing sophomores, and transfer students; by fall 2005 it has grown to around 320 and will probably reach 500 in a few years.

Participation Requirements: Continuing honors students must maintain a minimum 3.3 overall Cal Poly Pomona GPA. GPAs are checked by the program once a year, at the end of each spring quarter. If a student's GPA is below 3.3 at that time, there is a two-quarter conditional period to bring it back up to 3.3 (students failing to do so are not permitted to continue in the program). Students must also take and pass honors courses, the number varying depending on the point at which a student joined the program; freshmen must take a total of seven honors courses, sophomores must take five, and incoming transfer students must take four. One of the honors courses must be a capstone course in the student's major. Students must also take and pass at least 36 quarter units of course work per year (this may include the summer). Finally, honors students must complete 20 hours of community service per year, and send the honors program confirmation of the hours. On completion of the program, students receive a medal to wear at graduation, and their transcripts record the fact that they have successfully completed the Honors Program.

Admission Process: In order to qualify for the Honors Program as freshmen, high school seniors must have at least a 3.5 unweighted GPA and must have attained SAT scores of at least 550 in both Verbal and Math or equivalent ACT scores. Students who have a lower GPA but are in the top 5 percent of their graduating class are also eligible to apply. After students have applied to Cal Poly Pomona in November, those who are eligible for the Honors Program are sent invitations to apply in January. Applications are due in February and notification is in April. Transfer students must have GPAs of 3.5 or higher at their previous institutions. They too are invited to apply to the Honors Program after having been accepted to the University, but their application deadline is not until April or May. Continuing sophomores who are not already in the Honors Program but have attained a GPA of 3.5 or higher during their first year at Cal Poly Pomona are invited to apply for admission to the program in the fall. Applications are reviewed by Cal Poly Pomona faculty members.

Scholarship Availability: University scholarships are offered to the top one third of students who are admitted to the Honors Program. These scholarships are merit based and are restricted to students from within California who have achieved unweighted GPAs in high school of 3.75 or higher. Benefits include a four year renewable scholarship for full fees, currently estimated at $2830 per year, reduced room charge for campus housing for four years, currently a reduction of $450 per year, and free preferential parking the first year.

Campus Overview

State-supported comprehensive, founded 1938, part of California State University System • **Coed** 16,955 undergraduate students, 83% full-time, 43% women, 57% men.

Undergraduates 14,126 full-time, 2,829 part-time. Students come from 52 states and territories, 116 other countries, 1% are from out of state, 4% African American, 33% Asian American or Pacific Islander, 25% Hispanic American, 0.4% Native American, 3% international, 9% transferred in, 9% live on campus.

Faculty *Total:* 1,012, 55% full-time, 59% with terminal degrees. *Student/faculty ratio:* 23:1.

Academic Programs *Special study options:* academic remediation for entering students, adult/continuing education programs, advanced placement credit, cooperative education, double majors, English as a second language, honors programs, internships, off-campus study, part-time degree program, services for LD students, study abroad, summer session for credit. *ROTC:* Army (b), Air Force (c).

Athletics Member NCAA. All Division II. *Intercollegiate sports:* baseball M(s), basketball M(s)/W(s), cross-country running M(s)/W(s), soccer M(s)/W(s), tennis M(s)/W(s), track and field M(s)/W(s), volleyball W(s). *Intramural sports:* basketball M/W, bowling M/W, football M/W, softball M/W, tennis M/W, volleyball M/W.

Costs (2005–06) *Tuition:* state resident $0 full-time; nonresident $10,170 full-time, $226 per unit part-time. *Required fees:* $2832 full-time, $682 per term part-time. *Room and board:* $7212. Room and board charges vary according to board plan and housing facility.

Financial Aid 660 Federal Work-Study jobs (averaging $2800). In 2003, 105 non-need-based awards were made. *Average percent of need met:* 85%. *Average financial aid package:* $8258. *Average need-based loan:* $3751. *Average need-based gift aid:* $5277. *Average non-need-based aid:* $1798.

Contact: Honors Program, Cal Poly Pomona, 3801 West Temple Avenue, Pomona, California 91768; *Fax:* 909-869-4246; *Web site:* http://www.csupomona.edu/~honorsprogram. Dr. Amanda Podany, Director of the Honors Program and Professor of History; *Telephone:* 909-869-3875; *E-mail:* ahpodany@csupomona.edu. Dorothy Fleck, Associate Director of the Honors Program; *Telephone:* 909-869-3209; *E-mail:* dmfleck@csupomona.edu. Theola Johnson, Administrative Support Coordinator; *Telephone:* 909-869-3355; *E-mail:* tsjohnson@csupomona.edu

---

California State University, Fullerton
University Honors Program
Fullerton,

The University Honors Program at California State University, Fullerton, provides a select group of students and faculty members with an opportunity to experience a supportive collegiate atmosphere within a large urban public university. The 350 honors students in the program participate in an intellectual and social community featuring small class sizes (15-student maximum in most honors classes), an enriching cocurricular program, and personally meaningful research opportunities. The University Honors Program seeks to expand its students' intellectual horizons and foster a sense of social awareness and responsibility for service to society.

Membership in the University Honors Program provides students with tangible benefits, such as priority registration, recognition at formal University events, close mentoring relationships with faculty and staff members, and honors notation on their official transcript. Perhaps even more important are the intangible benefits that participation in a lively and stimulating community provides. Students gain leadership experience in cocurricular activities and hone their speaking and writing skills in the series of small seminars that are a central feature of the honors curriculum.

Students admitted to the program are expected to be well-rounded individuals who want to make a positive difference in their communities. The program attracts students of diverse backgrounds from a wide range of majors. Students in the Honors Program are among the top 5 to 10 percent of their class and are well prepared for advanced graduate or professional work. The strongest majors on campus are particularly well represented. The program offers students the opportunity to cultivate habits of critical thinking, independent analysis, creativity, collaboration, leadership, and intellectual skills.

Honors Program students work closely with faculty members throughout their undergraduate careers, whether completing general education requirements or working on an individualized senior project or thesis. The Honors Center, located on the first floor of the library, the symbolic center of the University, fosters a strong sense of community among honors students. It provides a place to study, a place to come for academic and other advice, and a place to socialize with fellow honors students. In addition, the center coordinates campus honors societies, which can give students valuable leadership opportunities as well as a chance to participate in meaningful service activities and gain an inside understanding of their academic majors.

Students and faculty members cooperate in assisting the Director of the University Honors Program and the Director of Honors and Scholars Support Services, who have formal responsibility for the program. Students, as well as staff and faculty members, serve on the Honors Board, which establishes basic policy. An Honors Student Advisory Committee provides a direct student voice in the selection and organization of cocurricular activities and valuable advice on the development of the academic curriculum. In these ways, students have the opportunity to become active partners in shaping their honors education and the direction of the University Honors Program.

Participation Requirements: Honors Program students must enroll in an honors course each semester to remain in the program. Students who complete 24 units of honors course work, achieve a cumulative 3.5 grade average for all their University work, and complete an honors thesis or project in their senior year graduate with University Honors. Transfer students may complete up to 12 of their honors units at another institution.

As participants in the campus Honors Program community, students are expected to participate in both curricular and the cocurricular Honors Program activities and pursue a full course of University study (at least 12 units per semester while freshmen and sophomores and at least 9 units per semester while juniors and seniors).

Admission Process: Entering freshmen must have a high school GPA of at least 3.5. Transfer students must have a California State University transferable GPA of at least 3.3 and must have completed a minimum of 9 units of college-level honors credits before transfer to Cal State Fullerton (transfer students with a 3.6 GPA may be eligible for automatic admission). The deadline for freshman applications is March 15. Transfer student applications are reviewed as they are received.

Applicants are evaluated on their academic record, recommendations, and the quality of their personal statement. Transfer applicants must include a writing sample. Successful candidates should be interested in academically enriching course work, have demonstrated leadership and service experience, and seek participation in a community of scholars. Applications are available online or on request.

Scholarship Availability: The University grants substantial academic scholarships. The top award for incoming freshmen is acceptance into the President's Scholars Program. Additional merit and need-based awards are available through the Office of Financial Aid.

The President's Scholars Program recognizes the outstanding achievements of incoming freshmen who have demonstrated excellence in academic work, leadership ability, and community service. Based solely on merit, the program provides a four-year scholarship for California residents that covers CSU enrollment fees, $750 per year for books and supplies, admission into the University Honors Program, a laptop computer for personal use, complimentary parking permits for fall and spring, priority registration, as well as numerous other special benefits. Scholars enjoy opportunities for leadership and participation in numerous campus and community activities. The scholarship is unique in that it provides students with opportunities to get involved and give back to the University and the community. Application forms may be obtained from the President's Scholars Program Screening Committee at 714-278-3458 or online at http://www.fullerton.edu/scholars.

Campus Overview

State-supported comprehensive, founded 1957, part of California State University System • **Coed** 27,228 undergraduate students, 72% full-time, 59% women, 41% men.

Undergraduates 19,526 full-time, 7,702 part-time. Students come from 36 states and territories, 64 other countries, 1% are from out of state, 3% African American, 22% Asian American or Pacific Islander, 26% Hispanic American, 0.6% Native American, 4% international, 14% transferred in, 2% live on campus.

Faculty *Total:* 1,856, 41% full-time. *Student/faculty ratio:* 21:1.

Academic Programs *Special study options:* academic remediation for entering students, adult/continuing education programs, advanced placement credit, cooperative education, distance learning, double majors, English as a second language, honors programs, independent study, internships, off-campus study, part-time degree program, services for LD students, student-designed majors, study abroad, summer session for credit. *ROTC:* Army (b).

Athletics Member NCAA. All Division I. *Intercollegiate sports:* baseball M(s), basketball M(s)/W(s), bowling M(c)/W(c), cross-country running M(s)/W(s), fencing M(s)/W(s), gymnastics W(s), rugby M(c), soccer M(s)/W(s), softball W(s), tennis W(s), track and field M(s)/W(s), volleyball W(s), wrestling M(s). *Intramural sports:* archery M/W, badminton M/W, basketball M/W, bowling M/W, cross-country running M/W, fencing M/W, football M/W, gymnastics M/W, racquetball M/W, skiing (cross-country) M/W, skiing (downhill) M/W, soccer M/W, softball M/W, table tennis M/W, tennis M/W, volleyball M/W, wrestling M.

Costs (2004–05) *Tuition:* state resident $0 full-time; nonresident $10,170 full-time, $339 per unit part-time. Full-time tuition and fees vary according to course load. Part-time tuition and fees vary according to course load. *Required fees:* $2804 full-time, $913 per term part-time. *Room only:* $4356.

Financial Aid 1,424 Federal Work-Study jobs (averaging $2940). In 2004, 1382 non-need-based awards were made. *Average percent of need met:* 61%. *Average financial aid package:* $6689. *Average need-based loan:* $4082. *Average need-based gift aid:* $5648. *Average non-need-based aid:* $4087.

Contact: Program Director: Dr. Susan Jacobsen, 800 North State College Boulevard, Pollak Library 120, Fullerton, California 92834; *Telephone:* 714-278-7440; *Fax:* 714-278-7445; *E-mail:* univhonors@ fullerton.edu; *Web site:* http://www.fullerton.edu/honors

Cerritos College
The Scholars' Honors Program
Norwalk, California

*T*he Scholars' Honors Program (SHP) is Cerritos College's social and academic home for talented and motivated students who plan to transfer to units of the University of California (UC) system, to the California State University (CSU) system, or to private colleges or universities. This is the chief function of honors programs throughout the California Community College system. The SHP offers support and motivation to students through a cohort of like-minded peers and interested faculty members. It organizes social and academic activities to engage students in the life of a nonresidential campus and help them focus their plans for transfer.

The curriculum of the SHP consists, in part, of free-standing, low-enrollment (about 25 students) honors sections of commonly taken general education courses. Most honors work, however, is done on a contract basis with instructors in regular sections of classes. Any transferable course may be taken on an honors basis through the contract process. Students may work on any topic of their choice approved by their instructor. The contract experience develops independent research skills and accustoms students to dealing one-on-one with faculty members.

SHP students participate regularly in national and regional honors conferences. Many students present papers each year at a research conference for community college honors students organized by the Honors Transfer Council of California at the University of California, Irvine.

Major units of the UC and CSU systems, as well as many local private colleges and universities, recognize the value of community college honors programs in preparing students for transfer. A UCLA study in the early 1990s demonstrated that transfer students who had completed a community college honors program significantly outperformed the nonhonors students in their transfer cohort—their GPA was higher, their persistence to graduation was stronger (fewer dropped out), and their time to graduation was shorter.

The SHP participates in the honors transfer programs of UCLA, UC Riverside, and UC Irvine. In recent years, 90 percent of SHP students applying for transfer to UCLA were accepted.

An honors office, conveniently located in the Admissions and Records building, is staffed more than 30 hours a week by experienced and knowledgeable personnel who help students not only with SHP requirements but also with personal advice about navigating the bureaucracy of college policies and procedures.

The program also sponsors the officially recognized Scholars' Honors Club, which meets twice monthly during the semester and provides a meeting place for honors students and faculty members. The SHC organizes mixers at the beginning of each semester, schedules guest speakers, and sponsors an open-mike session during preregistration when students, with no faculty members present, can compare notes on their experience of teachers and classes.

SHP students are prominent in the student government and in other clubs and activities; they are often identified as the most outstanding student of the year in their majors and frequently compete for such distinctions as homecoming queen or Mr. Cerritos.

The SHP was established in 1997 and currently enrolls approximately 350 students.

Participation Requirements: To maintain good standing in the SHP, students are required to maintain a cumulative GPA of 3.0 or above and take at least one honors course or contract per year. Graduates of the program are recognized at commencement with a certificate, a bronze medallion, and a transcript notation. Graduates are also certified as eligible for special priority consideration for admission to UCLA through the Transfer Alliance Program (TAP). Students completing fewer than six honors courses or contracts graduate as participants in the program. Graduates and participants are recognized at a special graduation celebration before commencement each May.

Admission Process: Applications for admission to the program can be filed online through the Web site listed in the contact section. Students entering from high school must have a cumulative high school GPA (unweighted) of 3.25 or above and must provide copies of high school transcripts (unofficial transcripts are acceptable). Current college students may be accepted with a minimum GPA of 3.0

Scholarship Availability: No special scholarships are reserved for SHP students, but many merit scholarships are available to Cerritos College students, and SHP students fare well in these competitions.

Campus Overview

State and locally supported 2-year, founded 1956, part of California Community College System • **Coed** 24,000 undergraduate students.

Undergraduates Students come from 32 other countries.

Faculty *Total:* 690, 36% full-time.

Academic Programs *Special study options:* academic remediation for entering students, adult/continuing education programs, advanced placement credit, English as a second language, part-time degree program, services for LD students, study abroad, summer session for credit.

Athletics Member NJCAA. *Intercollegiate sports:* baseball M, basketball M/W, cross-country running M/W, football M, golf M, soccer M, softball W, swimming and diving M/W, tennis M/W, track and field M/W, volleyball W, water polo M, wrestling M.

Financial Aid 180 Federal Work-Study jobs (averaging $3000). 89 state and other part-time jobs (averaging $2734).

Contact: The Scholars' Honors Program, Cerritos College, 11110 Alondra Boulevard, Norwalk, California 90670; *Telephone:* 562-860-2451 Ext. 2727; *E-mail:* shp-info@cerritos.edu; *Web site:* http://www3.cerritos.edu/shp

Chaffey College
Chaffey College Honors Program
Rancho Cucamonga, California

The Chaffey College Honors Program offers a rich and varied curriculum for honors students in three different modes. One is the stand-alone class, in which one section of a course is designated as honors. All students in these sections who receive a grade of B or better receive honors credit. A second option is the piggyback mode, in which students enroll in any section of a core course, such as English 1, and gather together 1 hour a week for an honors seminar. The third option is the Honors Program contact, in which students may work on a project of their choice in any transfer-level class. All honors classes are limited to 20 students, and every class includes extracurricular activities, such as a visit to the J. Paul Getty Museum, the Museum of Tolerance, or the California Stock Exchange. Honors faculty members take pride in working closely with honors students to enable them to fulfill their potential and transfer to four-year institutions of higher learning. Community service is an integral part of the program. Students participate in tutoring at the elementary, junior high, and high school levels; buy clothing for underprivileged children; raise money to support the American Cancer Society and other charities; show foreign films for free to the public; and honor the faculty with an end-of-the-year faculty reception. The program was founded in 1993 and currently enrolls more than 600 students.

Participation Requirements: Students must complete at least 18 semester units of honors course work with a minimum GPA of 3.0 and 54 hours of community service to graduate from the program. Honors Program graduates receive special certificates and a special gift logo; all honors courses are designated on students' transcripts along with the notation that they are graduates of the Honors Program.

Admission Process: Admission to the Chaffey College Honors Program is based on three criteria: a high school GPA of 3.25 or higher or a college GPA of 3.0 or higher after a minimum of 12 transferable units and one essay. In addition, one of the following criteria must be met: two letters of reference from high school or college faculty members, nomination by a Chaffey College faculty member, combined SAT I scores of 1000 or above or an ACT score of 26 or higher, successful completion of two honors courses at Chaffey College with a grade of B or better or three Advanced Placement classes in high school with grade of B or better, or evidence of special competence or creativity.

Scholarship Availability: Chaffey College is a member of the California Honors Transfer Council, which has developed articulation agreements with UCI, UCLA, UCR, UCSC, Chapman, Occidental, La Siera, CSU San Diego, CSU Fullerton, CSU Stanislaus, Pepperdine, and Pomona. Graduates of the Chaffey College Honors Program not only have guaranteed admission or priority consideration at all these schools but also have the opportunity to access scholarships that range from small prizes to full tuition. In house, many scholarships are available to transferring students that range from $100 to $500. Students may earn more than one scholarship, and many honors students receive $2000 at graduation from various Chaffey scholarships.

Campus Overview

Suburban 200-acre campus with easy access to Los Angeles • **Coed** 17,930 undergraduate students.

Undergraduates 2% are from out of state.

Faculty *Total:* 683, 27% full-time.

Academic Programs *Special study options:* academic remediation for entering students, adult/continuing education programs, advanced placement credit, cooperative education, English as a second language, honors programs, internships, part-time degree program, services for LD students, study abroad, summer session for credit. *ROTC:* Army (c).

Athletics Member NJCAA. *Intercollegiate sports:* baseball M, basketball M/W, football M, soccer M/W, softball W, swimming and diving M/W, tennis M/W, track and field M/W, volleyball W, water polo M/W.

Costs (2004–05) *Tuition:* state resident $0 full-time; nonresident $3576 full-time, $149 per unit part-time. *Required fees:* $470 full-time, $18 per unit part-time.

Financial Aid 1,200 Federal Work-Study jobs (averaging $2000).

Contact: Director of Honors Program: Eva Rose, 5885 Haven Avenue, Rancho Cucamonga, California 91737-3002; *Telephone:* 909-941-2431; *Fax:* 909-466-2865; *E-mail:* honors.program@chaffey.edu; *Web site:* http://www.chaffey.edu/honors

Chapman University
University Honors Program
Orange, California

The University Honors Program at Chapman University is an interdisciplinary academic minor that attracts students from all majors and departments, providing a place to meet a variety of very interesting students from all academic disciplines. It is a supportive, highly active community of fellow students and professors, lending a special excitement to the ongoing quest for knowledge.

The University Honors minor consists of 19 to 23 credits. The curriculum includes core courses, spanning the subjects of the natural sciences, humanities, and the social sciences, in a comprehensive, in-depth mode of learning woven with a degree of self-reflection. These courses meet some of the University's general education requirements. Each student takes four from the following core courses: In Search of Knowledge; In Search of the Meaning of Life; In Search of Self; In Search of Relationships; In Search of Reality: Media, Self and Society in the 20th Century; In Search of People in Nature, and In Search of American Folklife.

In addition, a student must take two satellite courses in varying disciplines that extend the breadth and scope of the honors curriculum. Completion of the program, which is capped by a senior project presentation, enables a student to graduate with a minor in University Honors.

The honors students have helped to design a dynamic and fluid program that is filled with many intellectual, leadership, and social opportunities. Events outside the classroom include mountain retreats, presenting at national and regional honors conferences, and social activities such as attending plays, dining out, and bonfires at the beach.

Space in the program is limited and best serves students who approach their education in a mature and responsible manner.

Participation Requirements: The University Honors Program is an academic minor and is open to qualified students of any major. The program consists of 19 to 23 credits. Each student must take four honors core classes, which are designed as seminar-based, interdisciplinary learning opportunities. These core classes also satisfy general education requirements in specific areas. In addition, students take two satellite courses offered by other departments and must make a senior project presentation to honors faculty members and students. Upon completion of requirements, a student is awarded a minor in University Honors.

Admission Process: The University Honors Program is distinct from "Honors at Entrance," which recognizes a student's high school achievements. Entrance into the University Honors Program requires a short but separate application process. Students who are admitted to the Honors Program ordinarily meet one or more of the following criteria: 1) combined SAT scores of 1250 or above or ACT scores of 28 or above; 2) GPA of 3.7 or above; 3) ranking in the top 10 percent of one's high school class; or 4) outstanding achievement documented by a project, performance, or letters of recommendation. Students can apply for consideration prior to acceptance by Chapman University. The priority deadline for Honors Program applications begins February 15. Application acceptance and admittance continue on a rolling basis after that date.

Scholarship Availability: While the Honors Program administers no scholarships directly, there are a number of generous scholarships available through the Admissions Office to students with high academic performance. Scholarships are awarded on admission.

Campus Overview

Independent comprehensive, founded 1861, affiliated with Christian Church (Disciples of Christ) • **Coed** 3,733 undergraduate students, 94% full-time, 58% women, 42% men.

Undergraduates 3,521 full-time, 212 part-time. Students come from 48 states and territories, 37 other countries, 20% are from out of state, 2% African American, 8% Asian American or Pacific Islander, 10% Hispanic American, 0.6% Native American, 3% international, 9% transferred in, 38% live on campus.

Faculty *Total:* 521, 46% full-time. *Student/faculty ratio:* 16:1.

Academic Programs *Special study options:* academic remediation for entering students, accelerated degree program, adult/continuing education programs, advanced placement credit, cooperative education, distance learning, double majors, English as a second language, honors programs, independent study, internships, part-time degree program, services for LD students, study abroad, summer session for credit. *ROTC:* Army (c), Air Force (c). *Unusual degree programs:* 3-2 engineering with University of California, Irvine.

Athletics Member NCAA. All Division III. *Intercollegiate sports:* baseball M, basketball M/W, cheerleading M/W, crew M(c)/W, cross-country running M/W, football M, golf M/W, lacrosse M(c), soccer M/W, softball W, swimming and diving M(c)/W, tennis M/W, track and field W, volleyball W, water polo M/W. *Intramural sports:* basketball M/W, football M, soccer M/W, softball M/W, tennis M/W, volleyball M/W.

Costs (2004–05) *Comprehensive fee:* $36,150 includes full-time tuition ($25,500), mandatory fees ($650), and room and board ($10,000). Part-time tuition: $795 per credit. Part-time tuition and fees vary according to course load. *Room and board:* Room and board charges vary according to board plan and housing facility.

Financial Aid 750 Federal Work-Study jobs (averaging $1744). In 2003, 741 non-need-based awards were made. *Average percent of need met:* 100%. *Average financial aid package:* $18,900. *Average need-based loan:* $2768. *Average need-based gift aid:* $15,412. *Average non-need-based aid:* $13,364.

Contact: Director: Dr. Patricia W. See, Honors Program, Chapman University, One University Drive, Orange, California 92866; *Telephone:* 714-744-7646; *Fax:* 714-532-6079; *E-mail:* honors@chapman.edu; *Web site:* http://www.chapman.edu/wcls/honors

College of the Redwoods
Honors Program
Eureka, California

College of the Redwoods' Honors Program was created to foster the growth of students who are dedicated, imaginative, and excited about learning. The program nurtures students' self-esteem while encouraging them to stretch to their full potential. It is a selective, challenging program designed for students' successful transfer to competitive four-year schools. Honors classes differ from regular classes in content, creativity, and preparation by both students and faculty members. Each honors course is developed by an experienced, dedicated faculty member and then scrutinized by the college curriculum committee to ensure that it offers an opportunity for active rather than passive learning, significantly different from the mainstream counterpart course. Each honors course has met the transfer general education requirements for full articulation with both the University of California and California State University system. Admission to these courses is limited to honors students, and class size averages fewer than 20. Outstanding members of College of the Redwoods' faculty can work closely with students and incorporate innovative approaches to learning not possible in traditional classrooms. Students are subsidized to participate in out-of-town field trips each semester. Planned to complement the course material, this travel also promotes camaraderie among students and faculty members. Recent trips have ranged from a visit with a Yurok elder in his village at the mouth of the Klamath River to an avant garde play in San Francisco.

Additional benefits also available to honors students include priority registration, a partial fee waiver, special academic advising, and library privileges at nearby Humboldt State University. The College of the Redwoods' Honors Program is seventeen years old and currently has 50 students.

Participation Requirements: The honors curriculum is a program of eleven classes selected from those required to transfer to either a California State University or a University of California. These classes are upgraded to honors-level rigor and are offered in a two-year cycle, three classes each semester. The curriculum has been carefully designed to provide a high-quality, well-integrated program of stimulating classes that satisfy general education transfer requirements. To remain a member of the program, a student takes at least one honors course each semester. Honors students are free to select their remaining general education classes and those that fulfill their major requirements. Each honors course completed is noted on the student's transcript, as is successful completion of the program. To graduate as an Honors Program Scholar, a student must complete 15 honors units and have a minimum 3.0 overall GPA. Each spring, the program acknowledges its incoming students and graduates with a dinner. Students receive certificates of completion, and graduates receive special honors medallions to distinguish them at commencement.

Admission Process: An invitation to apply is sent to college students and to local high school seniors whose GPAs are 3.5 or higher. College students' applications are accepted with a minimum GPA of 3.3. Applicants submit recommendations from two of their teachers as well as an essay, which is evaluated as a writing sample. High school students also submit SAT or ACT scores. A selection committee made up of honors faculty members reviews these materials from high school students in the spring for acceptance the upcoming year and from college applicants both in the fall for spring semester and in spring for the fall semester.

Scholarship Availability: Scholarships of various amounts are awarded through the College Scholarship Office based on academic performance and other criteria. Honors students are among the most frequent recipients of scholarships.

Campus Overview

State and locally supported 2-year, founded 1964, part of California Community College System • **Coed** 7,708 undergraduate students.

Undergraduates Students come from 52 states and territories, 2% live on campus.

Faculty *Total:* 414, 25% full-time. *Student/faculty ratio:* 21:1.

Academic Programs *Special study options:* academic remediation for entering students, adult/continuing education programs, advanced placement credit, cooperative education, distance learning, English as a second language, honors programs, off-campus study, part-time degree program, services for LD students, summer session for credit.

Athletics *Intercollegiate sports:* baseball M, basketball M/W, cross-country running M/W, football M, golf M, soccer W, softball W, track and field M/W, volleyball W.

Financial Aid 50 Federal Work-Study jobs (averaging $4000). 20 state and other part-time jobs (averaging $4000).

Contact: Coordinator: Pat McCutcheon, 7351 Tompkins Hill Road, Eureka, California 95501-9300; *Telephone:* 707-476-4327; *Fax:* 707-476-4422; *E-mail:* pat-mccutcheon@redwoods.edu; *Web site:* http://www.redwoods.cc.ca.us

Dominican University of California
Scholar in the World Honors Program
San Rafael, California

The Honors Program at Dominican University of California, the Scholar in the World program, promotes holistic development of scholars with global perspectives. Through a distinctive and enriched curriculum, students are educated to be creative learners, critical thinkers, writers, and responsible citizens of the world. The program's foundations rest on the four ideals of Dominican education: study, service, community, and reflection. Honors seminars involve students in active learning, challenging them to make the four ideals of Dominican's Honors Program their own. The program emphasizes interdisciplinary seminars, colloquia, and independent study and offers special opportunities for independent study, research under faculty mentors, enrollment in graduate courses, and an honors-sponsored international or multicultural experience.

The program began in 1989 and currently enrolls approximately 110 students.

Participation Requirements: At Dominican University of California, students enroll in seminars and colloquia that fulfill the general education requirements for the Honors Program. To graduate from the Honors Program, an incoming freshman must successfully complete two honors seminars during the first year; two during the sophomore year; three during the junior year; one during the senior year; a portfolio, senior thesis, or project; and a multicultural or international experience. Transfer students are expected to complete a portion of this requirement, depending on their entrance to Dominican University of California. The student projects are guided by faculty mentors; in addition, they must complete an honors thesis and satisfy the multicultural or international experience.

Students must maintain a minimum 3.3 cumulative GPA (including transfer courses) to remain active in the program and a minimum 3.5 GPA to graduate as an Honors Program Scholar. For students who graduate as Honors Program Scholars, the title of the honors thesis or project and the designation of the Scholar in the World appear on the University transcript.

For the nontraditional Pathways students, the Honors Program consists mainly of honors contracts between the student and a faculty mentor but may also include honors seminars. An Honors Contract documents the projects that students propose and construct in lieu of an honors course.

Admission Process: Students are invited into the Honors Program based on SAT or ACT scores (usually a minimum combined SAT score of 1150 or ACT score of 26), a high school GPA of 3.5 or higher, the Honors Program application essay, and honors or AP courses taken in high school (helpful but not required). Following their first semester at Dominican, students with a minimum 3.5 GPA who are not enrolled in the program receive invitations to participate. Highly motivated transfer students with a minimum 3.5 cumulative GPA, including transfer work, are also admitted into the Honors Program

Scholarship Availability: A number of academic scholarships are available at Dominican University of California. Those of interest to honors students include a Presidential Scholarship, Dean's Scholarship, Trustee Scholarship, and Dominican Scholarship. These are available for entering freshmen with a strong academic record.

Campus Overview

Independent comprehensive, founded 1890, affiliated with Roman Catholic Church • **Coed** 1,273 undergraduate students, 78% full-time, 78% women, 22% men.

Undergraduates 996 full-time, 277 part-time. Students come from 20 states and territories, 22 other countries, 6% are from out of state, 8%

African American, 17% Asian American or Pacific Islander, 15% Hispanic American, 1% Native American, 3% international, 22% transferred in, 42% live on campus.

Faculty *Total:* 250, 26% full-time, 37% with terminal degrees. *Student/faculty ratio:* 12:1.

Academic Programs *Special study options:* academic remediation for entering students, adult/continuing education programs, advanced placement credit, double majors, English as a second language, external degree program, honors programs, independent study, internships, off-campus study, part-time degree program, services for LD students, student-designed majors, study abroad, summer session for credit.

Athletics Member NAIA. *Intercollegiate sports:* basketball M(s)/W(s), cheerleading W, soccer M(s)/W(s), softball W(s), tennis M(s)/W(s), volleyball W(s).

Costs (2004–05) *Comprehensive fee:* $34,724 includes full-time tuition ($24,254), mandatory fees ($200), and room and board ($10,270). Full-time tuition and fees vary according to course load, degree level, location, and program. Part-time tuition: $1011 per unit. Part-time tuition and fees vary according to degree level, location, and program. *Required fees:* $100 per term part-time. *Room and board:* Room and board charges vary according to board plan.

Financial Aid 335 Federal Work-Study jobs (averaging $2562). 29 state and other part-time jobs (averaging $5876). In 2004, 148 non-need-based awards were made. *Average percent of need met:* 13%. *Average financial aid package:* $17,436. *Average need-based loan:* $5639. *Average need-based gift aid:* $13,356. *Average non-need-based aid:* $7504.

Contact: Director: Dr. Jayati Ghosh, 50 Acacia Avenue, San Rafael, California 94901; *Telephone:* 415-485-3238; *Fax:* 415-259-3206; *E-mail:* jghosh@dominican.edu

El Camino College
Honors Transfer Program
Torrance, California

The El Camino College (ECC) Honors Transfer Program (HTP) offers highly motivated students the opportunity to participate in an academic community where they interact with outstanding faculty members and other students who have the goals to obtain a quality education, be better prepared to transfer to a four-year university, and pursue a bachelor's degree. The HTP is a College-wide program appropriate for all eligible students taking transferable courses.

About thirty sections of honors courses are offered each semester. These are primarily general education courses in the fields of art, astronomy, economics, English, history, music, philosophy, and political science. The enrollment in honors classes is limited to about 75 percent of the enrollment for other classes. On rare occasions, honors contract courses are allowed to accommodate special academic needs. The HTP, in conjunction with the study-abroad program, allows interested students to do honors work while studying abroad. The College typically runs either two or three study-abroad programs each year.

A cornerstone of the program is the high level of support it receives from several major universities; they offer priority admission guarantees to students who complete the requirements of the HTP. These honors transfer agreements have been established between the HTP and California State University at Dominguez Hills, Fullerton, and Long Beach; Chapman University; Occidental College; Pomona College; and the University of California at Irvine, Los Angeles, Riverside, and Santa Cruz.

The HTP has an excellent track record for transferring students to the university of their choice. Over the past several years, almost 100

percent of students who completed the program and applied to the universities listed above were accepted.

In addition to the priority admission guarantees offered by the universities listed above, students who complete the HTP have graduation with honors designated on their associate degrees and completion of honors designated on their transcripts. These students have increased chances of receiving scholarships. Some universities offer transfer scholarships designated only for students who have completed community college honors programs, while others offer priority consideration for their regular transfer scholarships.

Benefits offered to HTP members prior to their completion of the program include honors membership designated on transcripts each semester and priority registration in all El Camino College classes. Students have opportunities to serve on HTP student committees such as the Newsletter Committee and the Activities Committee. Special privileges are offered by the universities with which ECC has honors transfer agreements. Examples include an organized Honors Transfer Day visit to campuses, use of libraries, priority scholarship consideration, and complimentary opportunities to attend academic, cultural, and athletic events.

The HTP is sixteen years old and has a membership of approximately 350 students. Each academic year begins with a welcome reception for new members and their families.

Participation Requirements: Each semester, students are required to complete at least one honors course, maintain a minimum 3.0 cumulative GPA, and attend at least four honors enrichment seminars. New students must complete English 1A in their first semester in the program.

To complete the HTP, students must complete at least six honors courses, maintain a minimum 3.0 cumulative GPA, be a member of the HTP for a minimum of two semesters, and complete the requirements necessary to transfer as a junior.

A reception at the end of each academic year is held to honor students completing the program and transferring to a university. At this reception, students receive a certificate of completion. Special certificates and plaques are given to selected students to recognize outstanding academic achievement in honors and outstanding contributions to the Honors Program.

Admission Process: The requirements for admission to the HTP are a minimum 3.0 cumulative GPA from high school or from at least 9 academic units in college and eligibility for English 1A Freshman Composition.

Campus Overview

State-supported 2-year, founded 1947, part of California Community College System • **Coed** 27,039 undergraduate students.

Undergraduates 18% African American, 19% Asian American or Pacific Islander, 29% Hispanic American, 0.4% Native American.

Faculty *Total:* 533, 62% full-time.

Academic Programs *Special study options:* academic remediation for entering students, advanced placement credit, cooperative education, English as a second language, honors programs, part-time degree program, services for LD students, student-designed majors, summer session for credit.

Athletics *Intercollegiate sports:* baseball M, basketball M/W, cross-country running M/W, football M, golf M, gymnastics W, soccer M, swimming and diving M/W, tennis M/W, track and field M/W, volleyball M/W, water polo M, wrestling M. *Intramural sports:* archery M/W, badminton M/W, bowling M/W.

Contact: Director: Joseph W. Holliday, 16007 Crenshaw Boulevard, Torrance, California 90506; *Telephone:* 310-660-3815; *Fax:* 310-660-3818; *E-mail:* htp@elcamino.edu; *Web site:* http://www.elcamino.edu

Fullerton College

Honors Program

Fullerton, California

*T*he Fullerton College Honors Program was established to serve
motivated students who want to transfer to highly competitive and
respected four-year public and private universities. Transfer is
strongly supported to partner institutions belonging to the Honors
Transfer Council of California, and these include several campuses of
the University of California as well as Chapman University,
Occidental College, Pepperdine University, Pitzer College, Pomona
College, and the University of Southern California. Honors courses at
Fullerton College are designed to appeal to the imagination and
challenge the intellect. The philosophy of the Honors Program is to
offer an enriched educational experience that challenges first- and
second-year college students to explore their ideas under the
guidance of experienced teachers who are themselves scholars active
in their fields.

The Honors Program offers sixteen courses in the humanities, fine
arts, natural sciences, social sciences, and mathematics that satisfy
the general education requirements of most majors. Class sizes are
small (20–25 students), and many courses incorporate interdisciplinary
activities, off-campus experiences, and service learning projects.
Honors classes are conducted as seminars, and students are
encouraged to participate actively in their own learning through
expanded projects and presentations. While the course work is more
challenging, most students discover that honors classes stimulate
them to do extra work, to be more creative, and to achieve academic
excellence. The Honors Program actively recruits students who are
stimulated by ideas, who tend to be skeptical of easy solutions, and
who are in pursuit of an education, not just a degree.

The Honors Program was established in 1996. Approximately 250
students enroll in ten to twelve honors courses offered each semester,
and 150 students are actively enrolled in the Honors Program
every year.

Participation Requirements: In order to be eligible for transfer
certification by the Honors Program, students must complete at least
17 units in honors course work. Honors students must also enroll in at
least one honors course each semester while fulfilling additional
requirements for transfer or graduation (a one-semester leave of
absence may be granted under special circumstances). Honors
students must maintain a cumulative GPA of at least 3.0 in
transferable courses. All honors classes are noted on transcripts, and
students who complete the Honors Program requirements receive a
special diploma and are recognized at an Honors Program
graduation ceremony.

Admission Process: Honors courses at Fullerton College are open to
all interested students. Admission to the Honors Program can be
achieved in three ways. New students are automatically accepted with
SAT I scores of 1175 or above, ACT scores of 27 or above, or a high
school GPA of 3.25 or above. Continuing students must have a GPA
of 3.25 or above in at least 9 transferable courses. A third way of
gaining admission is for ongoing students to complete one honors
course with a grade of B or above. All students accepted to the Honors
Program must have taken or be eligible to take freshman composition
(ENGL 100). All interested students are encouraged to enroll in
honors courses before seeking admission to the Honors Program.

To apply to the Honors Program, students must complete an
application form, submit transcripts, and write an application essay.
The selection process evaluates the applicant's expressed motivation
and interest in an honors education, the record of achievement, and
the applicant's educational goals. Students may apply to the Honors
Program at any time during the academic year.

Scholarship Availability: Each year two scholarships are made
available to Fullerton College honors students through the Honors
Transfer Council of California. In addition, the Honors Program

works closely with other honors organizations, including Alpha
Gamma Sigma and Phi Theta Kappa, to inform students enrolled in
honors courses about scholarship opportunities available to honors
transfer students through four-year colleges and universities. Although
the Honors Program does not directly award scholarships, many
students enrolled in the Honors Program receive academic recognition
through financial awards.

Campus Overview

State and locally supported 2-year, founded 1913, part of California
Community College System • **Coed** 19,862 undergraduate students.

Undergraduates Students come from 21 other countries.

Faculty *Total:* 835, 39% full-time.

Academic Programs *Special study options:* academic remediation for
entering students, adult/continuing education programs, advanced
placement credit, cooperative education, English as a second
language, honors programs, part-time degree program, services for
LD students, study abroad, summer session for credit. *ROTC:* Army
(c), Navy (c), Air Force (c).

Athletics *Intercollegiate sports:* basketball M/W, cross-country
running M/W, football M, golf M/W, soccer M, swimming and diving
M/W, tennis M/W, track and field M/W, volleyball W, water polo M.

Financial Aid 200 Federal Work-Study jobs (averaging $3000).

Contact: Coordinators: Dr. Lynne Negus and Dr. Bruce Hanson, 321
E. Chapman Avenue, Fullerton, California 92832; *Telephone:*
714-992-7370; *Fax:* 714-447-4097; *E-mail:* anegus@fullcoll.edu,
bhanson@fullcoll.edu, honors@fullcoll.edu

Golden West College

Golden West College Honors Program

Huntington Beach, California

*T*he Golden West College Honors Program offers highly motivated
students an enriched course of study leading them to excel in
scholarship, service, and leadership at the community-college level
and beyond. A curriculum offering six or seven honors classes per
semester brings them to advanced levels of critical thinking, research,
and communication skills. With a course of study fostering
experiential and interactive learning, the program offers enrichment
activities such as field trips to concerts, dramas, and museum
exhibits. Each year, several honors students give presentations at an
academic scholarship conference held at the University of California,
Irvine (UCI), hosted by the University and the Honors Transfer
Council of California (HTCC).

Students taking the Honors Seminar, the honors core course,
donate 18 hours to various organizations within the immediate
community. In addition, the program develops leadership skills
through a system of self-governance involving student representation
for each class and participation in the Honors Council, an advisory
group that helps determine policy and coordinate projects. Students
may also serve as writers or editors for the honors newsletter.

A major goal of the program is to enhance student desirability for
transferring to four-year institutions. Courses involve rigorous
discussions, research, written work, collaborative learning, and
examination of discipline methodologies. With a specially designated
honors counselor and a core cadre of dedicated faculty members
working with students in seminar classes, this program nurtures a
community of high-spirited learners who enjoy working together and
take pride in meeting rigorous standards of academic excellence and
community involvement. Students are both challenged and encouraged by their honors professors, who spend considerable time outside
class engaging in friendly conversations or ad hoc study sessions with
small groups as well as individual students.

All qualified students are welcome to take honors classes without joining the program, and the best students are encouraged to apply for membership. Members earning the designation of Honors Program Graduate receive special consideration when transferring to four-year institutions—and their honors programs—with which the GWC Honors Program has honors agreements, such as Chapman University; the University of California, Irvine; the University of California, Riverside; Occidental College; and others. The program began in 2000 and currently has approximately 110 students enrolled in honors classes.

Participation Requirements: To retain membership in the honors program, students must satisfactorily complete at least one honors course per semester and maintain at least a 3.0 cumulative GPA. They are expected to complete English 100H (Introductory Freshman Composition Honors), and Humanities 190H, the Honors Seminar, preferably in the first year. They are also encouraged to participate in the life of the campus and the community.

To graduate as an Honors Program Graduate, students must earn at least a 3.25 GPA, complete at least 18 hours of community service work, and hold membership in the GWC Honors program for two or more semesters. They must also earn at least a B letter grade in the honors version of Freshman Composition (English 100H), or write an acceptable honors thesis.

Scholarship Availability: In addition to scholarship assistance obtained via the Golden West College financial aid office, including Pell Grants, Federal Supplemental Educational Opportunity Grants (FSEOG), Cal Grants, Board of Governors (BOG) Enrollment Fee Waivers, and Federal Work-Study (FWS) funds and loans, students may compete for cash awards ranging in value from $200 to $500, through the program's relationship with the Honors Transfer Council of California and UCI.

Campus Overview

State and locally supported 2-year, founded 1966, part of Coast Community College District System • **Coed** 13,091 undergraduate students, 32% full-time, 54% women, 46% men.

Undergraduates 4,244 full-time, 8,847 part-time. Students come from 28 other countries.

Faculty *Total:* 440, 44% full-time. *Student/faculty ratio:* 32:1.

Academic Programs *Special study options:* academic remediation for entering students, adult/continuing education programs, advanced placement credit, cooperative education, English as a second language, external degree program, internships, part-time degree program, student-designed majors, study abroad, summer session for credit. *ROTC:* Air Force (c).

Athletics Member NJCAA. *Intercollegiate sports:* baseball M, basketball M/W, cross-country running M/W, football M, golf M/W, soccer M/W, softball W, swimming and diving M/W, tennis M/W, track and field M/W, volleyball M/W, water polo M/W, wrestling M.

Contact: Coordinator: Professor Charles Whitchurch, 15744 Golden West Street, Huntington Beach, California 92647; *Telephone:* 714-892-7711 (Ext. 51156); *E-mail:* cwhitchurch@gwc.cccd.edu

La Sierra University
La Sierra University Honors Program
Riverside, California

The Honors Program at La Sierra University seeks to provide intellectual excellence in the context of a learning community. A community of scholars, involving honors students and faculty members, centers on the series of interdisciplinary courses making up the core curriculum. These courses focus on three themes, drawn from the University's mission: knowing—developing an understanding of the perspectives of different groups (ranging from prophets in the Hebrew Scriptures through twenty-first-century scientists) and how these perspectives interrelate; serving—encouraging students to engage in their communities (civic, professional, religious, cultural, and global) to transform and build them with integrity, courage, openness, and compassion; and seeking—enabling students to contribute to the definition of their own education as they develop excellence in scholarship in a manner and with a subject that is uniquely their own and facilitating the development of students' worldviews as they begin a lifelong process of seeking truth through religious understanding, spiritual contemplation, and moral courage.

Since its inception in 1983, the Honors Program has grown to approximately 100 students. The diversity of the student body, including gender diversity, international diversity, ethnic diversity, and disciplinary diversity (a significant number of students come from the sciences and professional programs, as well as the humanities students typical of almost any honors program), allows for challenging interactions between students as they seek to understand each others' perspectives.

Students travel internationally as part of their first-year core sequence, complementing their on-campus work in understanding global cultures. Many students choose to study abroad later in their programs as well.

During the junior year, students work in groups to apply their skills and understanding to improve their community; these projects are presented at a celebration of service at the beginning of students' senior year.

Under the supervision of a faculty mentor, honors scholars plan and carry out a program of original scholarly or creative work. During the sophomore or junior year each student selects a mentor and develops a project proposal. During the senior year the project is completed and culminates in a paper, production, or exhibition, including a presentation in an on- or off-campus forum. Every spring, honors research presentations are at the heart of the University Research Emphasis Week.

As part of the senior capstone year, students complete a course examining the religious, moral, and social aspects of their disciplines. This gives them a chance to integrate what they have learned in their majors, their theses, and the core curriculum.

As a community of scholars, students participate in cultural activities throughout the year. In addition to this, the Honors Residence Hall, housing approximately 25 students, allows for a deeper level of interaction and support for students as they create a community that values scholarship and study.

Participation Requirements: Students complete a series of interdisciplinary courses focusing on the themes of knowing, serving, and seeking. These courses focus on global cultures, the process of science, religious understandings, rhetoric, the arts, and changing communities. In addition to these courses, students complete an Honors Community Involvement Project, in which they work to meet an identified community need, and an Honors Scholarship project, in which they conduct an original research or creative project that culminates in a written thesis, production, or exhibition, as well as an oral presentation in an on- or off-campus forum. Students must maintain a minimum 3.5 GPA and complete original scholarship and a thesis to graduate with honors, but those who do not complete the thesis requirements may still participate in the program in order to fulfill their general education requirements. Students completing the program receive a University Honors Program designation on their diplomas and on the graduation program; the graduation program also lists the title of the students' theses.

Admission Process: First-year honors scholars are selected based on a separate application process from regular University admissions. To apply to the Honors Program, students must first be accepted into the University. Selection is based on high school GPA, SAT/ACT scores, a letter of recommendation, and an essay. Applicants may appeal negative decisions to a committee consisting of the Honors Director, 2 faculty members, and a senior about to graduate from the program.

Students may apply with a minimum 3.5 cumulative GPA and SAT or ACT verbal and math scores above the 60th percentile.

Applications are accepted at any time, but preference is given to applicants who apply by March 20 (for fall admission).

Transfer students may apply for entry into the Honors Program at any time. These applicants should have a minimum 3.5 cumulative GPA, submit an application essay, and supply a letter of recommendation from a faculty member. Students transferring from an honors program of a member school of the Honors Transfer Council of California (HTCC) receive priority admission; honors students transferring from an HTCC school with a minimum GPA of 3.75 receive guaranteed admission.

Scholarship Availability: Students in the program automatically receive scholarships (currently ranging from $110 to $440 per quarter); the amounts awarded are based on the length of time in the program. The University also gives substantial academic scholarships based on academic merit and need; students in the Honors Program receive many of these scholarships, and the Honors Director sits on the Student Awards and Scholarship Committee.

Campus Overview

Independent Seventh-day Adventist comprehensive, founded 1922 • **Coed** 1,585 undergraduate students, 87% full-time, 57% women, 43% men.

Undergraduates 1,385 full-time, 200 part-time. Students come from 34 states and territories, 51 other countries, 17% are from out of state, 10% African American, 23% Asian American or Pacific Islander, 27% Hispanic American, 1% Native American, 10% international, 11% transferred in.

Faculty *Total:* 186, 49% full-time, 42% with terminal degrees. *Student/faculty ratio:* 13:1.

Academic Programs *Special study options:* academic remediation for entering students, accelerated degree program, adult/continuing education programs, advanced placement credit, double majors, English as a second language, honors programs, independent study, internships, off-campus study, part-time degree program, services for LD students, student-designed majors, study abroad, summer session for credit.

Athletics *Intercollegiate sports:* basketball M/W, soccer M(c), volleyball M(c)/W(c). *Intramural sports:* badminton M/W, baseball M, basketball M/W, football M/W, golf M/W, softball M/W, table tennis M/W, tennis M/W, volleyball M/W, weight lifting M/W.

Costs (2005–06) *Comprehensive fee:* $24,327 includes full-time tuition ($18,432), mandatory fees ($651), and room and board ($5244). Part-time tuition: $512 per unit.

Contact: Director: Paul Mallery, Ph.D., South Hall #100, La Sierra University, 4500 Riverwalk Parkway, Riverside, California 92515; *Telephone:* 951-785-2310; *E-mail:* honors@lasierra.edu; *Web site:* http://www.lasierra.edu/honors

Los Medanos College
Honors Transfer Program
Pittsburg, California

The Los Medanos College (LMC) Honors Transfer Program guarantees a high-quality academic experience and offers excellent transfer and scholarship advantages. By choosing to complete their first two years of university at a community college, students cut the cost of the bachelor's degree almost in half and benefit from advanced honors curriculum, small classes, and one-on-one interaction with professors.

LMC Honors Transfer Program graduates are rewarded with access to priority admission agreements and special scholarships with eleven transfer partners, including the University of California, Los Angeles (UCLA); Mills College; and San Francisco State University. For example, the agreement with UCLA more than doubles students' admission rates to the College of Letters and Sciences from about 40 percent to 85–90 percent. The Mills College agreement guarantees between $10,000 and $12,500 in scholarships to admitted honors students with 3.5 or better GPAs. Many more admission and scholarship benefits are listed on the College Web site.

The partners offer these benefits, because they trust the high-quality education LMC honors students receive. The outstanding honors faculty members have specially designed courses that focus on more advanced topics and are limited to 25 students, guaranteeing personalized attention and stimulating discussions. Honors course work is available in more than sixteen departments, including music, political science, history, astronomy, philosophy, biology, humanities, and mathematics. All honors work is acknowledged with transcript notations and special recognition in graduation ceremonies.

One of the most popular perks of the program is access to the Honors Learning and Research Center, the program's own building, with computers, couches, and study tables. Los Medanos College is located in the beautiful San Francisco Bay Area, with easy access to cultural events, outdoor activities, and prestigious universities, such as the University of California, Berkeley, and Stanford University.

Participation Requirements: Students must complete at least one honors course or contract every academic year to be considered an active honors student. In addition, they must participate in the Honors Club at least one semester per year. To be an Honors Scholar graduate, students must complete five honors courses or contracts (individualized honors projects) with a 3.25 or higher GPA. These five courses must include the Honors Seminar plus at least one from each of the following three areas: humanities and fine arts, social and behavioral sciences, and natural sciences and Mathematics.

Admission Process: There is both an English requirement and an academic requirement for admission to the Honors Transfer Program. Students may fulfill the English requirement by receiving an A or B in the College Composition course or by receiving a 4 or 5 on the AP English exam. The academic requirement may be fulfilled by having a 3.25 or higher cumulative college GPA.

First time freshmen with a 3.25 or higher high school GPA who are assessed at the College Composition level may join the program provisionally and must complete this course with an A or B their first semester at LMC.

Campus Overview

Suburban 120-acre campus with easy access to San Francisco • **Coed,** 7,152 undergraduate students.

Undergraduates Students come from 3 states and territories, 15 other countries, 0.2% are from out of state.

Faculty *Total:* 244, 43% full-time.

Academic Programs *Special study options:* academic remediation for entering students, advanced placement credit, cooperative education, double majors, English as a second language, honors programs, independent study, part-time degree program, services for LD students, study abroad, summer session for credit.

Athletics *Intercollegiate sports:* baseball M, basketball M/W, football M, soccer M, softball W, volleyball W.

Financial Aid 150 Federal Work-Study jobs (averaging $800).

Contact: Director: Jennifer Saito, Counselor: Phil Gottlieb, 2700 East Leland Road, Pittsburg, California 94565-5197; *Telephone:* 925-439-2181 Ext. 3369 (Director), 925-439-2181 Ext. 3382 (Counselor); *E-mail:* jsaito@losmedanos.edu (Director), pgottlieb@losmedanos.edu (Counselor); *Web site:* http://www.losmedanos.edu

Loyola Marymount University
University Honors Program
Los Angeles, California

As a means of creatively challenging the potential of the outstanding student and thereby contributing to the intellectual life of the entire academic community, Loyola Marymount University (LMU) adopted the Honors Program in 1958. By constant experimentation and periodic revision, the program attempts to keep true to its original intent of providing intellectual adventure

The program is interdepartmental and does not involve a separate faculty. It relies on the interest and generosity of the entire University faculty and on the enthusiasm of the truly exceptional students to become mutually involved in an intellectual experience. By not being a separate unit apart from the rest of the University community, the University Honors faculty members and students share with the rest of the school the stimulation of their special academic experience.

Taking advantage of its freedom from some of the restrictions involved in the structure of regular courses, the University Honors Program attempts to challenge as well as to inform; to ask hard questions as well as to examine tested solutions. Its goal is to provide a carefully integrated and demanding curriculum for the exceptional student.

The University Honors Program is open to students from all the undergraduate colleges and the undergraduate school of Loyola Marymount. The program is administered by the Honors Director with the assistance of the Associate Director, the Program Coordinator, and the Honors Advisory Council. Faculty members from all disciplines at Loyola Marymount University (LMU) are invited to participate.

The University Honors core curriculum begins with an intensive undergraduate experience combining interdisciplinary courses in the humanities and sciences with an individualized sequence in writing, critical thinking, and cultural studies. They are HNRS 100: Writing Tutorial, HNRS 101: American Persona, HNRS 115: On the Sublime, HNRS 120: On Human Dignity, HNRS 130: Society and Its Discontents, and HNRS 140: On Motion and Mechanics. A second-year sequence in historiography, theology, and natural philosophy consists of HNRS 215: Imago Dei, HNRS 220: Republic to Prince, HNRS 230: Age of Leviathan, and HNRS 240: On the Nature of Things. The third honors year includes seminars in ethics, interdisciplinary study, and thesis preparation. The courses are HNRS 330: Beyond Good and Evil, HNRS 398: Interdisciplinary Seminar, and the HNRS 495: Thesis Seminar I. Finally, the fourth year requires the completion of HNRS 496: Thesis Seminar II and HNRS 497: Honors Thesis, resulting in the publication of the capstone thesis project, the culmination of independent research under the individual guidance of a professor and the participation in the Senior Thesis Forum before an audience of peers, faculty members, and alumni.

There are many benefits to being in the LMU Honors Program. Honors Program courses are smaller than regular core courses (15 or fewer students in each class). There are dedicated Honors Program advisers and counselors. Students are placed with faculty mentors and directors for help with research, presenting at national conferences, and publishing work. The program also helps students pursue and capture scholarships, graduate school placement, internships, awards, grants, and study-abroad opportunities. Unique housing options and Honors Program facilities include guaranteed en suite housing with honors roommates, a dedicated study room with computers, a conference room, a designated classroom, and an available outdoor courtyard for social gatherings. Honors students receive priority registration every semester and often receive Trustee or Presidential Scholarships in addition to regular financial aid. Because of the intensity of the Honors Program, participants build relationships with students, professors, and advisers that most likely are stronger than would be built without the benefit of the program. The program also hosts frequent events, socials, dinners with professors, guest speakers,

and graduate school information sessions. Students can join Lawton's Literati, a private book group with the President of LMU. Being an honors student builds bridges to leadership opportunities within the University and the Los Angeles community.

Participation Requirements: University Honors students must maintain an average GPA of at least 3.5 and display proficiency in a foreign language. Successful completion of the University Honors Program is announced at the annual commencement ceremonies and noted on the student's permanent transcript. This recognition is of lasting personal, professional, and academic value.

Admission Process: The University Honors Program is open to incoming and current first-year students. First-semester sophomores and transfer students may also apply. More is expected of students in the Honors Program; not everyone is qualified to join. The program looks for students with a sense of academic adventure, high motivation, rigorous educational experience, social awareness, personal responsibility, interesting personal background, a first-rate cumulative GPA (on a 4.0 scale), highly competitive test scores (SAT and/or ACT), and the constant pursuit of excellence. Interested students should complete an application; schedule an interview with the Director, Associate Director, Program Coordinator, or member of the Honors Advisory Council; provide a critical writing sample; and submit a letter of reference. The program currently enrolls 120 students. Each fall, the University Honors Program carefully selects a limited number of incoming students to join the program. Application materials are available at the program's Web site.

Scholarship Availability: Honors students often receive Trustee or Presidential Scholarships in addition to other financial aid. Honors students are also eligible for the prestigious Cahn Scholarship, which supports study both at LMU and abroad. The University Honors Program works closely with the National and International Scholarship Office (NISO) in helping honors students compete for high profile scholarships, such as Rhodes, Gates Cambridge, Marshall, Udall, Fulbright, Truman, and Goldwater.

Campus Overview
Independent Roman Catholic comprehensive, founded 1911 • **Coed** 5,721 undergraduate students, 94% full-time, 60% women, 40% men.

Undergraduates 5,375 full-time, 346 part-time. Students come from 51 states and territories, 32 other countries, 23% are from out of state, 7% African American, 13% Asian American or Pacific Islander, 18% Hispanic American, 0.6% Native American, 2% international, 1% transferred in, 50% live on campus.

Faculty Total: 868, 50% full-time. Student/faculty ratio: 13:1.

Academic Programs Special study options: accelerated degree program, adult/continuing education programs, advanced placement credit, cooperative education, double majors, honors programs, independent study, internships, part-time degree program, services for LD students, student-designed majors, study abroad, summer session for credit. ROTC: Army (c), Air Force (b).

Athletics Member NCAA. All Division I. Intercollegiate sports: baseball M(s), basketball M(s)/W(s), crew M/W(s), cross-country running M(s)/W(s), golf M(s), lacrosse M(c)/W(c), rugby M(c), soccer M(s)/W(s), swimming and diving W(s), tennis M(s)/W(s), volleyball M(c)/W(s), water polo M(s)/W(s). Intramural sports: basketball M/W, football M/W, soccer M/W, softball M/W, tennis M/W, volleyball M/W.

Costs (2004–05) Comprehensive fee: $35,212 includes full-time tuition ($25,266), mandatory fees ($490), and room and board ($9456). Part-time tuition: $1052 per unit. Part-time tuition and fees vary according to course load. College room only: $7206. Room and board charges vary according to board plan and housing facility.

Financial Aid 1,600 Federal Work-Study jobs (averaging $2000). 579 state and other part-time jobs (averaging $2800). In 2004, 130 non-need-based awards were made. Average percent of need met: 76%. Average financial aid package: $17,254. Average need-based loan: $5401. Average need-based gift aid: $9378. Average non-need-based aid: $9577.

Contact: Kelly Younger, Ph.D. Director, Kathleen Harris, Ph.D. Associate Director, Beatrice Henson-O'Neal, M.F.A. Honors Coordinator, University Honors Program, Loyola Marymount University, One LMU Drive, Suite 4820, Los Angeles, California 90045; *Telephone:* 310-338-1780; *Fax:* 310-338-5215; *E-mail:* honors@lmu.edu; *Web site:* http://www.lmu.edu/honors

Mt. San Antonio College

Honors Program

Walnut, California

Mt. San Antonio College's Honors Program provides an enhanced curriculum for highly motivated students. To help students reach their full academic potential and to facilitate transfer to highly competitive universities, the College has developed twenty-eight honors courses from the Humanities and Social Sciences Division, the Natural Sciences Division, and the Business Division. These course are designed to foster not only mastery of content but also advanced critical thinking, analysis, discussion, and writing skills. Classes are designed to maximize student participation through group and individual presentations of course material.

Classes range from 10 to 20 students, offering a full range of courses throughout the disciplines, from biology to art history, from statistics to world religions, from micro economics to literary genres. The Honors Program encourages its participants to join Phi Theta Kappa and take advantage of leadership opportunities and the annual Honors Topic Teleconference. Honors Program students help coordinate and implement the honors topic seminars and related field trips.

The Honors Program includes summer honors study-abroad opportunities. Two honors courses (6 units) are offered each summer in London or Paris for an accelerated four-week semester.

The Mt. San Antonio College Honors Program accepted its first students in 1995 and currently has 386 students actively pursuing honors certification. Approximately 50 to 75 students a year are certified as Honors Program graduates.

Participation Requirements: Students are required to take any six honors courses. They must attend the Honors Topic Teleconferences each fall and maintain a minimum 3.2 GPA for honors certification. Successful completion of the Honors Program is recognized at commencement and is also noted on the official transcript and the graduation diploma.

Admission Process: High school and college students are recruited on the basis of their high school or college GPAs, SAT scores, an application, and a teacher/professor recommendation. Students may apply for admission directly from high school or after having completed 12 transferable college units. In addition, for admission into the program, all students must be eligible for Freshman Composition. Students may major in any discipline. Application to the program is open throughout the year. Students with lower than a 3.5 GPA may be waived into the program based on faculty recommendations and personal interviews.

Scholarship Availability: Scholarships of various amounts are awarded through the Financial Aid Office based on academic performance and financial need. Scholarships are not offered through the Honors Program. Most Honors Program students receive the major scholarships on campus each year.

Campus Overview

Suburban 421-acre campus with easy access to Los Angeles • **Coed** 26,440 undergraduate students, 30% full-time, 57% women, 43% men.

Undergraduates 7,971 full-time, 18,469 part-time. Students come from 51 states and territories, 6% African American, 24% Asian American or Pacific Islander, 39% Hispanic American, 0.5% Native American, 2% international.

Faculty *Total:* 1,114, 33% full-time.

Academic Programs *Special study options:* academic remediation for entering students, adult/continuing education programs, cooperative education, distance learning, English as a second language, honors programs, part-time degree program, services for LD students, study abroad, summer session for credit.

Athletics *Intercollegiate sports:* badminton W, baseball M, basketball M/W, cross-country running M/W, football M, golf M/W, soccer M/W, softball W, swimming and diving M/W, tennis M/W, track and field M/W, volleyball M/W, water polo M/W, wrestling M.

Costs (2004–05) *Tuition:* state resident $0 full-time; nonresident $3386 full-time, $165 per unit part-time. *Required fees:* $672 full-time, $26 per unit part-time, $48 per term part-time.

Financial Aid 250 Federal Work-Study jobs (averaging $2898).

Contact: Contact: Carolyn Inmon, Director of Honors, Mt. San Antonio College, 1100 North Grand Avenue, Walnut, California 91789; *Telephone:* 909-594-5611, Ext. 4665; *Fax:* 909-468-3999; *E-mail:* cinmon@mtsac.edu; *Web site:* http://www.mtsac.edu/

San Diego City College

Honors Program

San Diego, California

In keeping with the mission statement of San Diego City College, the Honors Program was conceived as a means to enhance both the transferability of students to four-year institutions and the employability of students enrolled in occupational/vocational curricula. By employing multiple measures of prior achievement as well as an interview component and an extensive faculty referral system, program coordinators recruit a broad range of motivated and talented students, many who have never recognized their own honors potential. Sixteen years of experience have proven that honors students are not found, but made.

Three distinct program strands can be distinguished in the honors curriculum. The official class schedule for each semester lists twelve departmental honors courses from all across the college, selected through a faculty proposal process. Several of these are linked thematically within a general education core curriculum, A World of Ideas. A flexible, student-driven honors contact component extends the reach of the program into departments and time periods that could not support full honors sections. Contracts are signed agreements between students and professors committing both to an enriched experience of a regular course with additional honors-level objectives specified beyond the regular ones. This is euphemistically called "the people's honors program," since it is predominantly student driven.

Honors offerings are distinguished from their mainstream counterparts by their rigor, depth, intensity, interdisciplinary or cross-disciplinary content, and innovation in the modes of classroom teaching and learning. Students can expect smaller, more interactive classes with an extra measure of faculty member and counselor consultation and much more collaborative work, including research and class presentation. Transfer-level skills in critical thinking, writing, and general communication are emphasized, and development of motivation and self-confidence are of prime importance. Social and cultural events, either planned or purely spontaneous, are an important part of the student and faculty experience.

The City College Honors Program has been recognized by a number of major universities through formal transfer alliances, which prioritize (sometimes even guarantee) acceptance of program graduates into upper-division studies. Among these partners are the

University of California at Irvine, Los Angeles (UCLA), Riverside, San Diego, and Santa Cruz; University of Southern California (USC); San Diego State University; Pomona College; Pitzer College; Whitman College; Chapman University; and Occidental College.

Participation Requirements: Generally speaking, individual City College honors courses are open to all qualified students. However, the thematically linked pairs of courses taught within the honors core curriculum, A World of Ideas, are core requisite and also require that students first indicate their commitment to complete the 15-unit graduation requirement of the Honors Program, generally using core classes to do so. For these core students, the advantage of sharing the challenges and rewards of participation with the same group of peers over several semesters quickly becomes evident. All Honors Program graduates, either core students or those accumulating individual departmental honors courses and honors contracts to total at least 15 units, must maintain an overall GPA of at least 3.25, with no honors grade less than B.

Admission Process: To enroll in individual departmental honors sections or to qualify for an honors contract attached to a regular nonhonors course, students with no previous college work must satisfy at least one of the following criteria. They must have a high school GPA of at least 3.5, a minimum SAT I score of 1100, a minimum ACT score of 25, a City College placement score of R5W5, or permission of the honors course instructor with concurrence of an Honors Program coordinator.

Students with previous college experience must satisfy at least one of the following criteria. They must have a minimum cumulative GPA of at least 3.25 in 12 or more baccalaureate-level units or a minimum GPA of 3.50 in the field of the selected honors class or permission of the honors course instructor with concurrence of an Honors Program coordinator.

For admission to the honors general education core curriculum, A World of Ideas, honors core students must submit a personal essay and a transcript and participate in an orientation interview with program coordinators. Most students apply during the summer months for startup core classes in the fall semester, although it is possible to join the core on a space-available basis at later dates.

To arrange honors contracts: Within the first two weeks of the semester students and professors, in close consultation with an Honors Program coordinator, formulate honors objectives to append to the curriculum of a regular, nonhonors course. Signoffs by the department chair and honors dean then extend authority to the College Records Office to administratively transfer students into newly created honors contract courses, which are noted on the final transcript exactly as honors sections are.

Scholarship Availability: All City College students are eligible for scholarships made available through the college foundation, which distributes nearly half a million dollars every year to deserving students. Honors Program students (those who, like the honors core cohort, have committed to completion of at least 15 units of transferable honors courses) may compete for several City College Presidential Honors Scholarships. The same group is also eligible for the San Diego Scholarship Foundation Book Awards, which pay for all books and supplies for up to four semesters and may be continued after a student transfers to a local university.

Campus Overview

State and locally supported 2-year, founded 1914, part of San Diego Community College District System • **Coed** 13,625 undergraduate students.

Undergraduates 13% African American, 11% Asian American or Pacific Islander, 29% Hispanic American, 1% Native American.

Faculty *Total:* 485, 33% full-time, 26% with terminal degrees. *Student/faculty ratio:* 35:1.

Academic Programs *Special study options:* academic remediation for entering students, adult/continuing education programs, cooperative education, distance learning, English as a second language, external degree program, honors programs, independent study, off-campus

study, part-time degree program, services for LD students, student-designed majors, summer session for credit. *ROTC:* Air Force (c).

Athletics Member NJCAA. *Intercollegiate sports:* baseball M, basketball M/W, cross-country running M/W, football M, golf M/W, soccer M/W, softball W, tennis M/W, track and field M/W, volleyball M/W. *Intramural sports:* archery M/W, badminton M/W, baseball M, basketball M/W, bowling M/W, racquetball M/W, soccer M/W, softball W, swimming and diving M/W, tennis M/W, track and field M/W, volleyball M/W, weight lifting M/W.

Costs (2005–06) *One-time required fee:* $36. *Tuition:* state resident $0 full-time; nonresident $3840 full-time, $160 per unit part-time. Full-time tuition and fees vary according to course load. Part-time tuition and fees vary according to course load. *Required fees:* $650 full-time, $26 per unit part-time, $13 per term part-time.

Financial Aid 100 Federal Work-Study jobs (averaging $4000).

Contact: Coordinators: Dr. Herald Kane, Dr. Kelly Mayhew, or Dr. Candace Waltz, 1313 12th Avenue, San Diego, California 92101; *Telephone:* 619-388-3642 or 619-388-3512; *Fax:* 619-388-3931; *E-mail:* hkane@sdccd.net, kmayhew@sdccd.net or cwaltz@sdccd.net

San Diego Mesa College
Honors Program
San Diego, California

*S*an Diego Mesa College's Honors Program serves self-motivated and qualified students by providing exceptional and intense learning experiences in classes that are usually highly interactive. Topics are explored in depth; typical assignments emphasize critical thinking, extensive reading and writing, and student presentations and critiques. Activities may also include opportunities for individual research projects, close interaction with faculty members and participation in community and cultural events.

The Honors Program is open to all qualifying students (part-time or full-time, day or evening) and can be found in all disciplines (liberal arts, fine arts, sciences, business, vocational, etc.).

Participation Requirements: Mesa College offers a variety of honors courses on a semester-by-semester basis. Students may graduate with honors by completing 15 hours of honors course work with a minimum 3.25 cumulative GPA. Core honors courses currently include English 101 (Reading and Composition), English 205 (Intermediate Composition and Critical Thinking), Music 100 (Introduction to Music), Music 110 (Music), Music 125 (Creativity, Diversity, and Esteem), Art History 110 (Prehistoric to Gothic), and Art History 111 (Renaissance to Modern). The range of core courses is currently under expansion.

Students may create Honors Contracts for all transferable nonhonors sections. The Honors Contract allows a student to enhance the classroom experience and obtain honors credit in the course. The contract requires participation from both the student and the faculty member. The result is a course-within-a-course in which the honors student completes both the regular course material and the agreed upon honors-level work within that course.

Honors students have the opportunity to work closely with honors faculty members both in and out of the classroom. The Honors Campus Coordinators help students choose courses, design Honors Contracts, and pursue transfer to four-year institutions.

Admission Process: Students with no previous college work must satisfy one of the following: high school GPA of at least 3.5 or SAT I minimum score of 1100 or ACT minimum score of 25 or honors instructor recommendation.

Students with previous college work must satisfy one of the following: at least a 3.25 overall GPA in 12 or more units or a minimum 3.5 GPA in the field of the selected honors class or honors instructor recommendation.

Transfer students should note that honors courses at Mesa College may qualify them for early registration at San Diego State University and for its Honors Program. In addition, honors transfer agreements are in effect at Chapman and Pacific Universities; Pitzer, Pomona, Occidental, and Whitman Colleges; University of California campuses Irvine, Los Angeles, Riverside, and Santa Cruz; and California State University campuses Dominguez Hills and Fullerton. University of California, San Diego, and Brigham Young University are pending.

In addition to honors class sections, the Honors Program at Mesa College encompasses Honors Contracts. These are individual agreements between a student and an instructor that enable a student to do honors-level work and receive honors credit within a regular nonhonors section. Contracts are established and processed within the normal drop/add period with all paperwork completed by the fourth week of the semester. San Diego City College and San Diego Miramar College have honors programs with the same participation requirements, admission processes, and scholarship availability.

Scholarship Availability: Mesa College, through the generosity of the San Diego Scholarship Foundation, offers a Book Scholar Award. Criteria include honors participation, financial need, and full-time status. This scholarship, for qualifying honors students, pays for textbooks (250 maximum per semester) for up to four semesters.

The Mesa College Scholarship Foundation offers a host of scholarships, which are available to honors students as well as the general student body.

Campus Overview

State and locally supported 2-year, founded 1964, part of San Diego Community College District System • **Coed** 22,573 undergraduate students, 100% full-time, 55% women, 45% men.

Undergraduates 22,573 full-time. 6% African American, 15% Asian American or Pacific Islander, 15% Hispanic American, 0.9% Native American.

Faculty *Total:* 900, 31% full-time.

Academic Programs *Special study options:* academic remediation for entering students, adult/continuing education programs, English as a second language, external degree program, honors programs, independent study, part-time degree program, services for LD students, summer session for credit.

Athletics *Intercollegiate sports:* baseball M, basketball M/W, cross-country running M/W, football M, soccer M/W, softball W, swimming and diving M/W, tennis M/W, track and field M/W, volleyball M/W, water polo M/W. *Intramural sports:* badminton M/W, basketball M/W, bowling M/W, fencing M/W, football M, golf M/W, gymnastics M/W, racquetball M/W, skiing (downhill) M, soccer M/W, softball M/W, swimming and diving M/W, tennis M/W, volleyball M/W, weight lifting M/W.

Financial Aid 180 Federal Work-Study jobs (averaging $4000).

Contact: Coordinators: Dr. Alison Primoza and Jennifer Cost, 7250 Mesa College Drive, San Diego, California 92111; *Telephone:* 619-388-2341 (Honors Office), 619-388-2351 (Primoza), 619-388-2363 (Cost); *E-mail:* aprimoza@sdccd.edu or jcost@sdccd.edu. Honors Counselor: Anthony Reuss; *Telephone:* 619-388-2674; *E-mail:* areuss@sdccd.edu; *Web site:* http://teachers.sdmesa.sdccd.cc.ca.us/~aprimoza/honors/index.html. City College Coordinators: Kelly Mayhew and Maria Figueroa, 1313 Park Boulevard, San Diego, California 92101; *Telephone:* 619-388-3512 (Honors Office), 619-388-3136 (Mayhew), 619-388-3695 (Figueroa); *E-mail:* kmayhew@sdccd.edu or mfigueroa@sdccd.edu. City College Honors Counselor: Duane Short; *Telephone:* 619-388-3951; *E-mail:* dshort@sdccd.edu; *Web site:* http://www.sccity.edu. Miramar College Coordinators: Carmen Jay and Susan Scott, 1044 Black Mountain Road, San Diego, California 92126; *Telephone:* 619-388-7532 (Honors Office), 619-388-7894 (Jay), 619-388-7534 (Scott); *E-mail:* cjay@sdccd.edu or sscott@sdccd.edu. Miramar College Honors Counselor: Judy Patacsil; *Telephone:* 619-388-7564; *E-mail:* jpatacsil@sdccd.edu; *Web site:* http://www.miramarcollege.net/depts./instructionalprograms/honors/index.asp

San Diego State University
University Honors Program
San Diego, California

The University Honors Program (UHP) at San Diego State University (SDSU) offers well-qualified students an opportunity to enhance their undergraduate years at San Diego State University. This program serves students from all majors who wish to develop and challenge their potential by taking special sections of general education classes. These small classes emphasize rigorous, collegial examinations of course materials and provide individuals the opportunity to be among intellectual peers from various backgrounds and disciplines. The mission of the University Honors Program is to provide opportunities to highly motivated and academically qualified students who strive for intellectual, personal, and professional growth. The University Honors Program serves as a learning community for students who seek creative and innovative ways to inform and engage the University community.

Students are encouraged to contribute and develop in an active way and to get to know the instructors personally. To ensure this, honors classes are limited to 30 students, and the course work is developed to appeal to superior students. Honors classes emphasize uniqueness in organization, method, and approach; they do not simply demand greater quantity of work.

Because of the general nature of the program, students in all majors are encouraged to apply. Students should consider applying to the Honors Program if they are stimulated by ideas, tend to be skeptical of definitive answers or easy solutions, and are pursuing an education, not just a degree. As Honors Program participants, students may satisfy many of the University's general education requirements in stimulating classes that explore the ideas, people, and writings that shape the world. If accepted, Honors Program students will find themselves in an intellectual peer group with a wide variety of backgrounds and perspectives. One of the strengths of the program is the opportunity to be involved in the University Honors Program Student Council. The UHP Student Council exists to give voice to the concerns of the UHP students. In addition to planning social and community service events for all UHP students, the council also acts as an advisory board to the UHP faculty and staff. Membership is open to all UHP students.

In addition to the opportunities in conjunction with the classes, honors students are encouraged to develop original projects and research inspired by their personal interests. The work may culminate in a senior thesis during the final year, and it provides valuable preparation for careers in many fields, both academic and nonacademic. Projects may involve students in off-campus internships if they so desire.

The Honors Director meets personally with each student to help in identifying special interests and talents and in defining the student's future plans. Honors students receive privileges in registration and are given a personal academic adviser and access to a private study space in the Love Library and the Division of Undergraduate Studies as well as conference, scholarship, study-abroad, and independent-study opportunities.

There are currently 250 students enrolled in the program.

Admission Process: Entering freshmen should have an SAT score of 1900 or above (minimum ACT score of 28) or a GPA of 3.7 or above. The selection committee is guided in its decision by the student's motivation and interest in the program and by high school records, test scores, and other evidence of a commitment to learning.

Students may also apply before the start of their third semester in college if their SDSU GPA is 3.5 or above. Upper class students should include a statement of purpose describing in detail their general academic and related interests (including possible choice of major) and their plans, however tentative, for a future career; a writing sample addressing the diversity prompt; two letters of recommendation; and the application form.

Campus Overview

State-supported university, founded 1897, part of California State University System • **Coed** 26,853 undergraduate students, 81% full-time, 58% women, 42% men.

Undergraduates 21,630 full-time, 5,223 part-time. Students come from 50 states and territories, 125 other countries, 5% are from out of state, 4% African American, 15% Asian American or Pacific Islander, 22% Hispanic American, 0.7% Native American, 3% international, 13% transferred in, 11% live on campus.

Faculty *Total:* 1,618, 57% full-time, 49% with terminal degrees. *Student/faculty ratio:* 24:1.

Academic Programs *Special study options:* academic remediation for entering students, advanced placement credit, distance learning, double majors, English as a second language, honors programs, independent study, internships, off-campus study, part-time degree program, services for LD students, student-designed majors, study abroad, summer session for credit. *ROTC:* Army (b), Navy (b), Air Force (b).

Athletics Member NCAA. All Division I except football (Division I-A). *Intercollegiate sports:* baseball M(s), basketball M(s)/W(s), cross-country running W(s), golf M(s)/W(s), soccer M(s)/W(s), softball W(s), swimming and diving W(s), tennis M(s)/W(s), track and field W(s), volleyball M/W(s), water polo W(s). *Intramural sports:* badminton M(c)/W(c), basketball M/W, crew M/W(c), football M/W, golf M/W, ice hockey M(c), lacrosse M(c)/W(c), racquetball M/W, rugby M(c), sailing M(c)/W(c), skiing (downhill) M(c)/W(c), soccer M(c)/W(c), softball M/W, table tennis M/W, tennis M/W, volleyball M(c)/W(c).

Costs (2004–05) *Tuition:* state resident $0 full-time; nonresident $10,170 full-time, $339 per unit part-time. Full-time tuition and fees vary according to degree level. Part-time tuition and fees vary according to course load and degree level. *Required fees:* $2936 full-time, $979 per term part-time. *Room and board:* $9391; room only: $5488. Room and board charges vary according to board plan and housing facility.

Financial Aid In 2003, 280 non-need-based awards were made. *Average percent of need met:* 86%. *Average financial aid package:* $8500. *Average need-based loan:* $2800. *Average need-based gift aid:* $4000. *Average non-need-based aid:* $1400.

Contact: Director: Dr. Jung M. Choi, University Honors Program, San Diego State University, 5500 Campanile Drive, San Diego, California 92182-1623; *Telephone:* 619-594-8071; *Fax:* 619-594-7934; *E-mail:* jchoi@mail.sdsu.edu

Santa Clara University
University Honors Program
Santa Clara, California

Inspired by Santa Clara's Catholic, Jesuit tradition, the University Honors Program (UHP) pursues academic excellence enlightened by ethical reflection and openness to the spiritual dimensions of human experience. It seeks to educate especially talented students for responsible leadership in their professions and communities.

The program gives selected students an opportunity to combine the breadth of liberal learning with the depth achieved through specialization in a major field. Students take part in small, seminar-style classes marked by close faculty-student interaction, student participation, and a focus on written expression. Students may specialize in any of the majors offered in the humanities, natural and social sciences, business, and engineering.

An Honors Program seminar enrolls from 10 to 16 students. Students blend honors courses with regular classes as they pursue undergraduate degrees in their major fields. Most Honors Program classes fulfill core requirements required of every student. These include distinctive, cross-disciplinary Western culture seminars as well as special courses in writing, mathematics, chemistry, and religious studies. Most freshmen reside on campus, where they are placed in residential learning communities that encourage both mutual support and interaction with the general student body. The University Honors Program is divided into two stages. Level I accepts students arriving for their first year of university study. After completing Level I, most students qualify to continue to the University Honors Program, Level II. Level II also accepts students who did not begin at the first level but qualify after starting college.

Special features include a senior thesis in each student's major. A University scholarship annually sponsors one junior honors student for a year of study at the University of Oxford in England. The Santa Clara University School of Law guarantees admission to Honors Program students who meet specific requirements while completing the program.

The University Honors Program was founded in 1963. It accepts 45 to 50 students a year and has a four-year enrollment of about 180.

Participation Requirements: Level I requires that students complete six designated Honors Program courses during their first two years. These courses include the Western culture, religious studies, and writing seminars. For students who start at Level I, Level II requires an additional three courses plus a thesis or capstone project. Those entering at Level II must complete five designated honors courses and a thesis project. Study abroad brings Honors Program credit. The minimal GPA is 3.3. Successful completion of either or both levels is noted on a student's permanent transcript.

Admission Process: High school seniors interested in admission to the University Honors Program should first complete the application process for the University. Admission to the program itself may occur either through invitation or application. Invitations are issued on the basis of scores, grades, and other information in the University admissions file. Freshman students typically present a verbal SAT I above 720, a combined score in the mid-1360s or higher, and a correspondingly high GPA in college-prep courses. In 2004, UHP freshmen showed a median unweighted GPA of 3.94 and a median combined SAT I of 1420. Submitting an application guarantees review of a student's academic record by the program director. An application is available at the program's Web site.

Enrolled students who apply for Level II should have a Santa Clara GPA of at least 3.5 and submit two letters of recommendation from Santa Clara faculty members. Transfer students should complete 32 quarter units at Santa Clara or a similar four-year institution before applying to the program.

Scholarship Availability: Santa Clara bases financial aid primarily on demonstrated need. All candidates are advised to file FAFSA and Financial Aid PROFILE forms as required by the Office of Financial Aid. Students invited to the University Honors Program are automatically considered for available merit grants, that is, Academic Deans' Scholarships and Honors Awards. Merit scholarships usually, but not necessarily, supplement need-based awards.

Campus Overview

Independent Roman Catholic (Jesuit) university, founded 1851 • **Coed** 4,434 undergraduate students, 97% full-time, 56% women, 44% men.

Undergraduates 4,316 full-time, 118 part-time. Students come from 35 states and territories, 11 other countries, 32% are from out of state, 3% African American, 19% Asian American or Pacific Islander, 13% Hispanic American, 0.5% Native American, 4% international, 5% transferred in, 44% live on campus.

Faculty *Total:* 710, 60% full-time, 75% with terminal degrees. *Student/faculty ratio:* 12:1.

Academic Programs *Special study options:* advanced placement credit, cooperative education, double majors, honors programs, independent study, internships, student-designed majors, study abroad, summer session for credit. *ROTC:* Army (b), Air Force (c).

Athletics Member NCAA. All Division I. *Intercollegiate sports:* baseball M(s), basketball M(s)/W(s), crew M/W, cross-country running M(s)/W(s), golf M(s)/W(s), lacrosse M(c)/W(c), rugby M(c)/W(c), soccer M(s)/W(s), softball W(s), tennis M(s)/W(s), volleyball M(c)/W(c), water polo M(s). *Intramural sports:* basketball M/W, football M/W, soccer M/W, softball M/W, swimming and diving M/W, table tennis M/W, tennis M/W, ultimate Frisbee M/W, volleyball M/W.

Costs (2004–05) *Comprehensive fee:* $36,828 includes full-time tuition ($27,135) and room and board ($9693). Part-time tuition and fees vary according to course load. *Room and board:* Room and board charges vary according to board plan and housing facility.

Financial Aid 487 Federal Work-Study jobs (averaging $2201). In 2003, 480 non-need-based awards were made. *Average percent of need met:* 78%. *Average financial aid package:* $18,400. *Average need-based loan:* $4766. *Average need-based gift aid:* $14,308. *Average non-need-based aid:* $5025.

Contact: Director: Dr. Richard H. Osberg, University Honors Program, Santa Clara University, Santa Clara, California 95053-0638; *Telephone:* 408-554-4439; *Fax:* 408-554-4837; *E-mail:* rosberg@scu. edu; *Web site:* http://www.scu.edu/SCU/Programs/Honors/honors.htm

---

Skyline College
Honors Transfer Program
San Bruno, California

*T*he Skyline College Honors Transfer Program (HTP) provides a challenging curriculum to prepare highly motivated, academically talented students for transfer to selective colleges and universities. Typically, honors sections provide small class sizes, freedom to work independently and collaboratively with peers, one-to-one interaction with honors faculty members, and a rigorous learning environment. The program also provides academic enrichment activities, leadership development, personalized academic counseling, recognition of scholarly accomplishments, and support in the transfer process. The HTP is a College-wide program that is open to all qualified students taking transferable courses who seek a challenging academic experience and strong preparation for selective universities.

Honors sections of regular courses offer a stimulating environment and the opportunity to delve into subject matter in greater depth than in traditional classes and to work with other highly motivated students and outstanding faculty members. Honors students are expected to carry out in-depth research, write critical analysis papers, and expand their critical- and creative-thinking skills. The level of in-depth discussion and interaction in the honors classes provides enrichment and enhanced opportunities for intellectual growth. HTP students also have the opportunity to develop honors contracts with their professors, through which they can pursue topics of interest in greater depth and work closely with professors in any transfer-level class. In addition to stand-alone honors courses and honors contracts, honors students may also receive honors credit for any transfer-level biology course by enrolling in a 1-unit honors biology seminar, in which they complete in-depth research projects on a given topic.

The Honors Transfer Program encourages participation from all students in the College's diverse student body by providing open enrollment in honors courses.

Most of the honors courses have met the transfer general education requirements for full articulation with both the University of California and California State University systems, and all are transferable. Honors faculty members and an Honors Advisory Committee meet regularly to ensure the highest-quality education for honors students.

The Honors Transfer Program offers transfer incentives by providing access to priority transfer agreements and special scholarships with the transfer partners of the Honors Transfer Council of California (HTCC), which include the University of California, Los Angeles (UCLA); University of California, Santa Cruz; Chapman University; Pepperdine University; Pitzer College; Pomona College; and others. The program is a member of the Transfer Alliance Program of UCLA. Special privileges are offered by the colleges and universities with which the HTP has honors transfer agreements. Examples are an organized Honors Transfer Day visit; use of libraries; priority scholarship consideration; complimentary opportunities to attend academic, cultural, and athletic events; and guaranteed housing. Honors students have opportunities to participate in transfer seminars, cultural activities, field trips, conferences, and social events.

Skyline College's Honors Transfer Program was established in 2000. To date, 275 students have enrolled in the program.

Participation Requirements: To graduate from the program, students are required to complete successfully at least 15 semester units in honors, with a minimum cumulative and honors GPA of 3.25, and 16 hours of community service. Each course taken in the Honors Program is designated on the student's transcript as honors.

Students who successfully complete the Honors Transfer Program receive a Certificate of Completion and the designation of Honors Transfer Program Graduate on both their degrees and transcripts. They are recognized at a campuswide Student Awards and Recognition Reception at the end of the school year, where they are awarded a specially designed honors medallion to wear as part of their graduation dress. At commencement, students are recognized from the stage as HTP graduates as their names are called to receive their degrees.

Admission Process: Admission to the Honors Transfer Program is based on a minimum high school GPA of 3.5, an SAT score of at least 1200, an enhanced ACT composite score of at least 26, or a minimum college cumulative GPA of at least 3.25 in a minimum of 9 units of college degree–applicable courses and eligibility for first-semester English composition and intermediate algebra. Interested students who do not meet the eligibility criteria may be admitted into the program on a provisional basis.

Scholarship Availability: The Honors Transfer Program awards a $500 scholarship each spring semester to a member who meets the scholarship eligibility criteria. Also, as a member of the Honors Transfer Council of California, Skyline College's Honors Transfer Program not only offers its members guaranteed admission or priority consideration with the transfer partners of the HTCC, it also affords members the opportunity to access scholarships available from these partners.

Campus Overview
State and locally supported 2-year, founded 1969, part of San Mateo County Community College District System • **Coed** 8,573 undergraduate students.

Undergraduates Students come from 9 other countries, 2% are from out of state, 4% African American, 40% Asian American or Pacific Islander, 21% Hispanic American, 0.5% Native American, 2% international.

Faculty *Total:* 300, 29% full-time. *Student/faculty ratio:* 27:1.

Academic Programs *Special study options:* academic remediation for entering students, adult/continuing education programs, advanced placement credit, cooperative education, distance learning, English as a second language, honors programs, part-time degree program, services for LD students, study abroad, summer session for credit.

Athletics Member NJCAA. *Intercollegiate sports:* baseball M, basketball M, cross-country running M/W, soccer M, softball W, track and field M/W, volleyball W, wrestling M.

Financial Aid 125 Federal Work-Study jobs (averaging $4000).

Contact: Honors Coordinator: Connie Beringer, 3300 College Drive, San Bruno, California 94066; *Telephone:* 650-738-4343; *Fax:* 650-738-4210; *E-mail:* beringer@smccd.net; *Web site:* http://www. smccd.net/accounts/skyhon/

University of California, Davis
Integrated Studies Honors Program
Davis, California

Integrated Studies Honors Program (ISHP) is an invitational, residential honors program for 114 first-year students. Its goals are to help students integrate ideas from humanities, natural sciences, and social sciences and correlate information from self-contained disciplines through interdisciplinary or multidisciplinary approaches to learning; to provide excellent teaching for first-year students in small, highly personalized situations; to provide an academic residential community, similar to the best small-college communities, within a large research university; to provide students with challenging, participatory approaches to learning to encourage student-faculty interactions on a more personal level than that realized in the large classroom situation common to public research universities; and to provide effective, personalized advising on academic matters.

Integrated Studies Honors Program faculty members are disciplinary specialists with proven excellence in teaching who have a particular interest in how their research and discipline are related to other disciplines, to contemporary society, and to philosophical issues of the day. The Integrated Studies Honors Program is 36 years old and currently enrolls 114 students.

Participation Requirements: Integrated Studies Honors Program students are required to take three specially designed, 4-unit ISHP courses and two 1-unit ISHP seminars during the academic year. All students who complete the program receive transcript notation.

Scholarship Availability: Regents Scholars, selected by an independent faculty committee, are guaranteed places in the Integrated Studies Honors Program. ISHP does not control any scholarship funding or the scholarship selection process.

Campus Overview

State-supported university, founded 1905, part of University of California System • **Coed** 23,472 undergraduate students, 89% full-time, 56% women, 44% men.

Undergraduates 20,962 full-time, 2,510 part-time. Students come from 48 states and territories, 101 other countries, 4% are from out of state, 3% African American, 39% Asian American or Pacific Islander, 11% Hispanic American, 0.7% Native American, 2% international, 8% transferred in, 25% live on campus.

Faculty Total: 1,950, 83% full-time, 98% with terminal degrees. Student/faculty ratio: 19:1.

Academic Programs Special study options: academic remediation for entering students, adult/continuing education programs, advanced placement credit, double majors, English as a second language, freshman honors college, honors programs, independent study, internships, part-time degree program, services for LD students, student-designed majors, study abroad, summer session for credit. ROTC: Army (b), Navy (c), Air Force (c).

Athletics Member NCAA. All Division II except football (Division I-AA), gymnastics (Division I), wrestling (Division I). Intercollegiate sports: baseball M, basketball M/W, cross-country running M/W, golf M, gymnastics W, soccer M/W, softball W, swimming and diving M/W, tennis M/W, track and field M/W, volleyball W, water polo M, wrestling M. Intramural sports: archery M(c)/W(c), badminton M(c)/W(c), basketball M/W, crew M(c)/W(c), equestrian sports M(c)/W(c), fencing M(c)/W(c), football M/W, golf M/W, gymnastics M(c), ice hockey M(c)/W, lacrosse M(c)/W(c), racquetball M(c)/W(c), riflery M(c)/W(c), rugby M(c), sailing M(c)/W(c), skiing (cross-country) M(c)/W(c), skiing (downhill) M(c)/W(c), soccer M/W, softball M/W, swimming and diving W(c), table tennis M/W, tennis M/W, volleyball M(c)/W, water polo W(c).

Costs (2004–05) Tuition: state resident $0 full-time; nonresident $15,855 full-time, $2746 per term part-time. Required fees: $6936 full-time. Room and board: $10,234. Room and board charges vary according to board plan.

Financial Aid In 2004, 1158 non-need-based awards were made. Average percent of need met: 75%. Average financial aid package: $11,181. Average need-based loan: $4557. Average need-based gift aid: $8544. Average non-need-based aid: $3854.

Contact: Director: James F. Shackelford, 162 Everson Hall, One Shields Avenue, Davis, California 95616-8715; Telephone: 530-752-9906; Fax: 530-752-8643; E-mail: jfshackelford@ucdavis.edu; Web site: http://www.integratedstudies.ucdavis.edu

University of California, Irvine
Campuswide Honors Program
Irvine, California

Located on 1,500 acres of beautiful coastal foothills 5 miles from the Pacific Ocean, the University of California, Irvine (UCI), offers its most talented students the opportunities of its Campuswide Honors Program. UCI, known for research and teaching excellence, has a lively student body with an international background and a casual lifestyle. The Campuswide Honors Program is dedicated to promoting high standards of scholastic excellence and personal growth by combining the best of an excellent liberal arts college with the broad range of opportunities offered by a major research university.

The Campuswide Honors curriculum features interdisciplinary and discipline-based classes designed to challenge and introduce talented students to important topics, issues, and methods of inquiry. Honors students gain from the dynamic and creative spirit that has led to 3 UCI faculty members receiving the Nobel Prize in different disciplines (physics, chemistry, and medicine). All honors students pursue research in their individual academic disciplines under the supervision of faculty members. Research grants, summer research programs, and research symposia are part of the Campuswide Honors Program experience as well.

The Campuswide Honors Program enrolls approximately 615 students from the freshman through senior years (about 3 percent of the undergraduates) and represents every major on campus.

Honors advising by faculty members, professional staff members, and peers provides program participants with assistance in planning their course of study and applying for scholarships, graduate and professional schools, internships, and education-abroad programs.

Two hundred Campuswide Honors students live in honors houses on campus. Honors students also have the privilege of special reading rooms in the UCI libraries; extended library privileges; participation in many social and cultural activities, including weekly coffee hours, beach bonfires, poetry readings, and visits and informal lectures in faculty members' and students' homes; and annual camping retreats.

Participation Requirements: To graduate from the Campuswide Honors Program, students complete sequences of honors classes, finish a research thesis project, and achieve a minimum cumulative GPA of 3.2 (most honors students have GPAs above 3.5). Successful completion of the Campuswide Honors Program is noted at the annual Honors Convocation and appears on the diploma and final transcript.

The majority of Campuswide Honors graduates pursue graduate or professional degrees at excellent schools.

Admission Process: Admission is competitive, with most students invited while in high school. In 2004, the average SAT score of incoming freshmen was 1431, and the average GPA was 4.2 (honors-course weighted). Transfer students and continuing UCI students apply for entry into the program.

Scholarship Availability: A majority of Campuswide Honors Program students are awarded Regents' Scholarships, the most prestigious University of California award. Regents' Scholars are selected for outstanding scholastic achievement and leadership potential and in recent years have received more than full in-state fees for four years plus funding for summer school. A few Distinguished Honors Scholarships that pay all expenses associated with a UCI education are awarded to outstanding honors students who require financial assistance.

Campus Overview

State-supported university, founded 1965, part of University of California System • **Coed** 19,862 undergraduate students, 97% full-time, 50% women, 50% men.

Undergraduates 19,333 full-time, 529 part-time. Students come from 43 states and territories, 36 other countries, 2% are from out of state, 2% African American, 49% Asian American or Pacific Islander, 12% Hispanic American, 0.4% Native American, 3% international, 8% transferred in, 26% live on campus.

Faculty *Total:* 1,290, 77% full-time, 98% with terminal degrees. *Student/faculty ratio:* 18:1.

Academic Programs *Special study options:* academic remediation for entering students, adult/continuing education programs, advanced placement credit, distance learning, double majors, English as a second language, honors programs, independent study, internships, off-campus study, part-time degree program, services for LD students, study abroad, summer session for credit. *ROTC:* Army (c), Air Force (c).

Athletics Member NCAA. All Division I. *Intercollegiate sports:* badminton M/W, baseball M(s), basketball M(s)/W(s), crew M(s)/W(s), cross-country running M(s)/W(s), fencing M/W, golf M(s)/W(s), lacrosse M/W, racquetball M/W, rugby M, sailing M/W, soccer M(s)/W(s), softball M/W, swimming and diving M(s)/W(s), table tennis M/W, tennis M(s)/W(s), track and field M(s)/W(s), volleyball M(s)/W(s), water polo M(s)/W, weight lifting M/W. *Intramural sports:* badminton M(c)/W(c), baseball M, basketball M/W, bowling M(c)/W(c), cheerleading M/W, fencing M(c)/W(c), field hockey M(c)/W(c), golf M/W, ice hockey M(c), lacrosse M(c)/W(c), racquetball M/W, rugby M(c)/W(c), soccer M(c)/W(c), softball M/W, swimming and diving M/W, table tennis M/W, tennis M/W, track and field M/W, ultimate Frisbee M(c)/W(c), volleyball M(c)/W(c), water polo M(c)/W(c), wrestling M(c)/W(c).

Costs (2005–06) *Tuition:* state resident $0 full-time; nonresident $18,277 full-time. *Required fees:* $6313 full-time. *Room and board:* $9176. Room and board charges vary according to board plan.

Financial Aid 3,755 Federal Work-Study jobs (averaging $1117). In 2003, 708 non-need-based awards were made. *Average percent of need met:* 80%. *Average financial aid package:* $10,882. *Average need-based loan:* $4626. *Average need-based gift aid:* $7606. *Average non-need-based aid:* $3535.

Contact: Director: Dr. Roger McWilliams, Division of Undergraduate Education, 1200 Student Services II, Irvine, California 92697-5680; *Telephone:* 949-824-5461; *Fax:* 949-824-2092; *E-mail:* honors@uci. edu; *Web site:* http://www.honors.uci.edu/

University of California, Santa Barbara
College of Letters and Science Honors Program
Santa Barbara, California

*T*he College of Letters and Science Honors Program provides a four-year educational experience designed to challenge the University's most motivated students, encourage them to their finest

efforts, and stimulate them to assume their place in the world of ideas. The Honors Program attracts students who wish to take full advantage of the resources of a research university. Typically, they enter the University already thinking of themselves as scholars. Their aim is to leave the University of California, Santa Barbara (UCSB), with an education, not just a degree. They are not afraid to seek out their professors; they thrive in an intimate collegiate atmosphere where they can participate in a long tradition of intellectual inquiry, working closely with peers and professors in small classes, research laboratories, and special programs. Because the Honors Program is open to qualified students in all majors, it provides a cross-disciplinary meeting place for students with wide-ranging interests.

The College Honors Program is committed to the creation of a vital, richly textured community both on and off campus. In the spirit of shared governance, students in the Honors Program work with the deans, the faculty, and the honors adviser to ensure that the program is responsive to the needs of today's undergraduates. Housing is available to interested students in the Scholars Floors, which are designated floors of University-owned residence halls for high-achieving students, with special interdisciplinary programming that brings students together with their faculty mentors. Juniors and seniors in the Honors Program complete a minimum of 10 hours of community service each year, and lower-division students are encouraged to prepare themselves for the service requirement by exploring the many opportunities for volunteerism at UCSB's Community Affairs Board, one of the largest student volunteer organizations in the nation. Through the Honors Program's Isla Vista Tutoring Program, students mentor sixth graders in the local elementary school, assisting them with math and English and providing academic encouragement and support. Honors students are eligible for numerous internships that supplement their regular course work. They also work as program coordinators, peer advisers, mentors, and proctors in the honors study lounge. Many honors students find positions assisting the faculty members on research teams.

Participation Requirements: To complete the College Honors Program and earn the Academic Excellence Award at commencement, students must take at least 36 honors-designated units during their years of undergraduate study and fulfill the service requirements. At least 20 of these units must be upper division. Transfer students admitted to the College Honors Program upon entrance to UCSB only need to complete the 20 upper-division, honors-designated units. More flexible rules apply to students who participate in the yearlong University of California Education Abroad Program. Students who complete the College Honors Program are acknowledged at commencement by a special reception and are entitled to wear special regalia. Completion of the College Honors Program is noted on the final transcript.

Admission Process: The College Honors Program is open to any student with an overall UCSB GPA of at least 3.5 on a minimum of 12 graded baccalaureate units. Entering first-year students are invited into the College Honors Program based on a comprehensive review of the application for UC admission. In the typical entering freshman class, 10 percent of students are in the College Honors Program. Transfer students with a minimum 3.6 GPA when they enter UCSB are eligible and are encouraged to apply. Once accepted, students may continue as program members as long as they maintain the required GPA and complete honors courses. Eligibility criteria are subject to change at any time.

Scholarship Availability: Many students in the College Honors Program receive Regents Scholarships at the time of admission. Regents Scholarship recipients are selected from among the top student scholars applying for admission to the University. Selection criteria include academic excellence, depth and breadth of academic preparation, and potential for success at UC Santa Barbara. Financial aid is awarded on the basis of financial need as well as scholastic merit. In a typical year, 62 percent of UC Santa Barbara's students receive some form of financial aid.

Campus Overview

State-supported university, founded 1909, part of University of

California System • **Coed** 18,121 undergraduate students, 97% full-time, 55% women, 45% men.

Undergraduates 17,529 full-time, 592 part-time. Students come from 51 states and territories, 110 other countries, 5% are from out of state, 3% African American, 16% Asian American or Pacific Islander, 17% Hispanic American, 0.8% Native American, 1% international, 9% transferred in, 26% live on campus.

Faculty *Total:* 1,033, 87% full-time. *Student/faculty ratio:* 17:1.

Academic Programs *Special study options:* accelerated degree program, advanced placement credit, cooperative education, distance learning, double majors, English as a second language, honors programs, independent study, internships, off-campus study, services for LD students, student-designed majors, study abroad, summer session for credit. *ROTC:* Army (b).

Athletics Member NCAA. All Division I. *Intercollegiate sports:* baseball M(s), basketball M(s)/W(s), bowling M(c)/W(c), crew M(c)/W(c), cross-country running M(s)/W(s), equestrian sports M(c)/W(c), fencing M(c)/W(c), field hockey W(c), golf M(s)/W(s), gymnastics M/W(s), lacrosse M(c)/W(c), rugby M(c), sailing M(c)/W(c), skiing (downhill) M(c)/W(c), soccer M(s)/W(s), softball W(s), swimming and diving M(s)/W(s), tennis M(s)/W(s), track and field M(s)/W(s), ultimate Frisbee M(c)/W(c), volleyball M(s)/W(s), water polo M(s)/W(s). *Intramural sports:* badminton M/W, basketball M/W, bowling M/W, crew M/W, cross-country running M/W, football M/W, golf M/W, gymnastics M/W, racquetball M/W, soccer M/W, softball M/W, squash M/W, tennis M/W, ultimate Frisbee M/W, volleyball M/W, water polo M/W.

Costs (2004–05) *Tuition:* state resident $0 full-time; nonresident $16,476 full-time. *Required fees:* $6495 full-time. *Room and board:* $9897; room only: $7491.

Financial Aid In 2003, 388 non-need-based awards were made. *Average percent of need met:* 81%. *Average financial aid package:* $11,439. *Average need-based loan:* $5407. *Average need-based gift aid:* $6960. *Average non-need-based aid:* $3913.

Contact: Mary J. Nisbet, Associate Dean, Division of Student Academic Affairs; Regina Fletcher, Honors Coordinator; College of Letters and Science, University of California, Santa Barbara, Santa Barbara, California 93106; *Telephone:* 805-893-3109; *Fax:* 805-893-7654; *E-mail:* rfletcher@LTSC.ucsb.edu; *Web site:* http://www.honors.LTSC.ucsb.edu

University of La Verne
University Honors Program
La Verne, California

The University of La Verne (ULV) Honors Program is open to students majoring in all fields of study. For those who demonstrate exceptional academic achievement and motivation, the ULV Honors Program offers increased opportunities for intellectual and personal growth through an interdisciplinary curriculum that emphasizes critical thinking skills and the integration of knowledge from various disciplines. Honors students participate in specially designed seminars and colloquia, receive individualized attention from faculty mentors, and take part in community outreach activities and cultural programs.

There are approximately 75 students in the program.

Participation Requirements: Students receive the designation "Honors Program Graduates" on their diplomas and final transcripts by completing four interdisciplinary seminars (topics vary), a minimum of three colloquia, and a senior capstone seminar that integrates their major field of study with a broadly focused theme. Honors Program participants complete at least 10 semester hours of honors course work, including representative seminars and colloquia.

Honors Program graduates and participants are recognized at the Honors Commencement Breakfast, when their graduation medallions and certificates are presented by the Honors Director, the President, and other academic officers.

Honors Program students are given preferential registration schedules, receive individual academic advisement from the Honors Director, and have access to computers and printing at the Honors Center.

Admission Process: Candidates must have a combined SAT I score of 1100 or above/ACT of 25 and a minimum 3.5 cumulative high school average. Transfer students need a minimum cumulative college GPA of 3.3. Students are encouraged to apply by March 1 for fall admission and by December 1 for spring admission. Candidates for admission after these dates will be considered on a space-available basis. The University of La Verne subscribes to the Candidate's Reply Date of May 1 (for fall semester) and does not require advance payment or confirmation or intent to enroll prior to this date.

Scholarship Availability: The University of La Verne offers Honors Program Scholarships to students who are enrolled in the Honors Program. These renewable annual scholarships of $1000 are offered in addition to the guaranteed scholarships available to all entering students, based on GPA. In 2001–02, entering freshmen with a GPA of 3.5 or higher received a $7500 merit scholarship. Merit scholarships are also available to transfer students. The sum of grant and scholarship funds received by any individual student may not exceed the total cost of tuition.

Campus Overview

Independent university, founded 1891 • **Coed** 1,650 undergraduate students, 94% full-time, 64% women, 36% men.

Undergraduates 1,554 full-time, 96 part-time. Students come from 25 states and territories, 7 other countries, 5% are from out of state, 9% African American, 5% Asian American or Pacific Islander, 38% Hispanic American, 0.7% Native American, 0.7% international, 10% transferred in, 32% live on campus.

Faculty *Total:* 389, 47% full-time, 40% with terminal degrees. *Student/faculty ratio:* 13:1.

Academic Programs *Special study options:* academic remediation for entering students, accelerated degree program, adult/continuing education programs, advanced placement credit, distance learning, double majors, English as a second language, external degree program, freshman honors college, honors programs, independent study, internships, off-campus study, part-time degree program, services for LD students, student-designed majors, study abroad, summer session for credit.

Athletics Member NCAA. All Division III. *Intercollegiate sports:* baseball M, basketball M/W, cross-country running M/W, football M, golf M, soccer M/W, softball W, swimming and diving M/W, tennis M/W, track and field M/W, volleyball W, water polo M/W. *Intramural sports:* basketball M/W, cheerleading W, skiing (downhill) M/W, softball M/W, table tennis M/W, tennis M/W, volleyball M/W.

Costs (2005–06) *One-time required fee:* $110. *Comprehensive fee:* $31,910 includes full-time tuition ($22,800) and room and board ($9110). Full-time tuition and fees vary according to course load, degree level, location, and program. *Part-time tuition:* $650 per unit. Part-time tuition and fees vary according to course load, degree level, location, and program. *College room only:* $4490. Room and board charges vary according to board plan and housing facility.

Financial Aid 752 Federal Work-Study jobs (averaging $1997). In 2004, 202 non-need-based awards were made. *Average financial aid package:* $21,604. *Average need-based loan:* $3442. *Average need-based gift aid:* $10,995. *Average non-need-based aid:* $7716.

Contact: Director: Dr. Andrea Labinger, University of La Verne, 1950 Third Street, La Verne, California 91750; *Telephone:* 909-593-3511 Ext. 4357; *Fax:* 909-392-2714; *E-mail:* labinger@ulv.edu

University of San Diego
University Honors Program
San Diego, California

The University of San Diego Honors Program is designed to provide students of superior ability and accomplishment with challenges and opportunities that allow them to realize their potential more fully. The four-year course of study provides an interdisciplinary curriculum that is integrated with a student's major area of study as well as the University's general education requirements. The program emphasizes teaching excellence, small classes, and a core curriculum of innovative and exciting courses. Honors students have numerous opportunities for individual counseling and discussions with honors faculty members.

In the freshman year, honors students enroll in an honors preceptorial during fall semester and a section of a lower-division general education course in the spring. During their sophomore and junior years, honors students enroll in at least two upper-division, team-taught interdisciplinary courses. These courses, which change yearly, represent the honors core curriculum. In the team-taught courses, students approach traditional topics from a fresh perspective, which cuts across standard disciplinary boundaries. Students come to realize that scholarly work is not restrained or limited by the boundaries of disciplines or areas of study.

The Honors Senior Colloquium, offered each spring, provides honors students with the opportunity to explore a topic that has interested them during their undergraduate work at USD. Students are encouraged to consider topics that have been most engaging and lend themselves to further study. Some students choose to expand work initiated in another class. All projects include original research, primary sources, an oral presentation, and considerable dedication and time. Each student works under the direction of a faculty adviser in his or her major.

The USD Housing Office began Residence Learning Community housing for the Honors Program in 1995, open to freshmen and upperclass students. The suite-style apartments offer amenities not available in the regular freshmen dorms, as well as increased opportunities for honors freshmen to get to know each other.

The USD Honors Program was established in 1979. The program admits approximately 100 students per year, and there are 280 students currently enrolled.

Participation Requirements: Students must complete a minimum of 25 honors units for graduation with the honors diploma. This is an average of one honors course each semester. Of these 25 units, students must take at least two upper-division, team-taught interdisciplinary courses. Students studying abroad for one semester receive 4 honors program units toward the required 25 honors units. Honors students must maintain a GPA of at least 3.4.

The curriculum begins with the Honors Preceptorial, which introduces new students to the University and the Honors Program. It ends with a senior capstone experience, which includes a mandatory independent study, a thesis, and participation in the Honors Senior Colloquium.

Students who complete the 25-unit course of study receive an honors diploma and are the only undergraduate students who wear a gold stole during the spring commencement ceremonies.

Admission Process: Most honors students enter the program at the beginning of their freshman year, although students with excellent academic records may apply for admission at the end of their freshman year. Transfer students are evaluated for admission on an individual basis. In general, students in the program are among those who have the highest high school GPAs and SAT or ACT scores upon entering USD. Invitations to apply to the Honors Program are issued to students on the basis of scores, grades, and personal achievement. In 2004, freshman entering the Honors Program had an average weighted GPA of 4.12 and an average combined SAT I score of 1332.

Applicants answer a set of four questions that ask students to describe their achievements and their experience in completing a difficult project. Students are expected to have an active interest in their own education and an appreciation for academic challenges. In evaluating the records of high school seniors, the Office of Admissions and the Director of the Honors Program seek to choose those students who have the ability and motivation to achieve in the program. Attention is paid to those who will most benefit from the honors curriculum.

Scholarship Availability: University scholarships are awarded through the Office of Undergraduate Admissions in cooperation with the Office of Financial Aid Services, but the Honors Program does not offer separate scholarships. Most honors students, however, are awarded merit-based scholarships.

Campus Overview

Independent Roman Catholic university, founded 1949 • **Coed** 4,908 undergraduate students, 97% full-time, 61% women, 39% men.

Undergraduates 4,770 full-time, 138 part-time. Students come from 50 states and territories, 64 other countries, 38% are from out of state, 2% African American, 7% Asian American or Pacific Islander, 15% Hispanic American, 1% Native American, 2% international, 7% transferred in, 50% live on campus.

Faculty *Total:* 706, 48% full-time, 74% with terminal degrees. *Student/faculty ratio:* 16:1.

Academic Programs *Special study options:* advanced placement credit, double majors, English as a second language, honors programs, independent study, internships, part-time degree program, services for LD students, study abroad, summer session for credit. *ROTC:* Army (c), Navy (b), Air Force (c).

Athletics Member NCAA. All Division I. *Intercollegiate sports:* baseball M(s), basketball M(s)/W(s), crew M/W, cross-country running M(s)/W(s), equestrian sports W(c), football M, golf M(s), ice hockey M(c), lacrosse M(c)/W(c), rugby M(c), soccer M(s)/W(s), softball W, swimming and diving W(s), tennis M(s)/W(s), volleyball M(c)/W(s). *Intramural sports:* basketball M/W, football M/W, golf M/W, sailing M(c)/W(c), skiing (downhill) M(c)/W(c), soccer M/W, softball M/W, tennis M/W, ultimate Frisbee M(c)/W(c), volleyball M/W, water polo M(c)/W(c), wrestling M(c).

Costs (2004–05) *Comprehensive fee:* $37,046 includes full-time tuition ($26,660), mandatory fees ($196), and room and board ($10,190). Part-time tuition: $920 per unit. Part-time tuition and fees vary according to course load. *College room only:* $7670. Room and board charges vary according to board plan and housing facility.

Financial Aid 816 Federal Work-Study jobs (averaging $2557). 117 state and other part-time jobs (averaging $5208). In 2003, 679 non-need-based awards were made. *Average percent of need met:* 100%. *Average financial aid package:* $21,804. *Average need-based loan:* $4347. *Average need-based gift aid:* $16,473. *Average non-need-based aid:* $5241.

Contact: Director: Dr. Noelle Norton, 5998 Alcala Park, San Diego, California 92110; *Telephone:* 619-260-7847; *Fax:* 619-260-7880; *E-mail:* norton@sandiego.edu; *Web site:* http://www.sandiego.edu/honors

University of Southern California
Baccalaureate/M.D. Program
Los Angeles, California

Students who want to attend the University of Southern California (USC) next year as a college freshman and plan to attend medical school after graduation may apply to enter the Baccalaureate/M.D.

Program. Students who earn admission to both the University and the program for the fall of their freshman year also have a space in the entering first-year class at the USC Keck School of Medicine upon completing their undergraduate degree. USC offers the Baccalaureate/ M.D. program to students who want to incorporate a broad understanding of human experience alongside their professional expertise. The program does not offer accelerated study to provide a shortcut for students to become younger doctors. Rather, the year program prepares students to be better doctors. The guaranteed space in medical school allows students freedom to explore many academic subjects and student activities. During their first four years, Baccalaureate/M.D. students engage the widest possible range of ideas, faculties, and the community available at one of the nation's largest private research universities. Many of USC's students volunteer, engage in cutting-edge research, and study abroad. The Keck School of Medicine, where Baccalaureate/M.D. students spend their final four years, has meant better health for people around the globe in all fields of medical care. Through fourteen affiliated hospitals in southern California, USC physicians serve more than 1 million patients each year. USC's Health Sciences campus, located 3 miles northeast of downtown Los Angeles, is a major center for basic and clinical biomedical research, especially in the fields of cancer, gene therapy, the neurosciences, and transplantation biology.

Participation Requirements: Once enrolled at USC, Baccalaureate/ M.D. students are required to complete the sequence of undergraduate courses considered prerequisites for the nation's best medical schools, including two semesters each of calculus, physics, chemistry, organic chemistry, and biological sciences, and one semester each of microbiology and biochemistry. To retain eligibility for admission to the Keck School of Medicine, students must maintain a minimum 3.3 GPA overall and in their science prerequisite courses. Students must take the MCAT exam and score above average on all sections.

Admission Process: USC selects Baccalaureate/M.D. students through a competitive process. Excellent grades and test scores are important but do not guarantee admission. USC also looks for extraordinary credentials of community involvement, preparation for medicine, and enthusiastic recommendation. From the annual group of 500 or more applicants, USC invites only 100 for an interview. While this number seems a bit daunting, applicants should know that USC accepts into the program not only highly qualified students, but students that represent the diversities of a growing and changing world culture. Final enrollment for the program each year is 25–30 students.

Campus Overview

Independent university, founded 1880 • **Coed** 16,474 undergraduate students, 96% full-time, 51% women, 49% men.

Undergraduates 15,776 full-time, 698 part-time. Students come from 52 states and territories, 134 other countries, 32% are from out of state, 6% African American, 21% Asian American or Pacific Islander, 13% Hispanic American, 0.7% Native American, 9% international, 8% transferred in, 36% live on campus.

Faculty *Total:* 2,408, 62% full-time, 76% with terminal degrees. *Student/faculty ratio:* 10:1.

Academic Programs *Special study options:* accelerated degree program, advanced placement credit, cooperative education, distance learning, double majors, English as a second language, freshman honors college, honors programs, independent study, internships, off-campus study, part-time degree program, services for LD students, student-designed majors, study abroad, summer session for credit. *ROTC:* Army (b), Air Force (b). *Unusual degree programs:* 3-2 economics, mathematics, accounting.

Athletics Member NCAA. All Division I except football (Division I-A). *Intercollegiate sports:* baseball M(s), basketball M(s)/W(s), crew W(s), cross-country running M(s)/W(s), golf M(s)/W(s), soccer W(s), swimming and diving M(s)/W(s), tennis M(s)/W(s), track and field M(s)/W(s), volleyball M(s)/W(s), water polo M(s)/W(s). *Intramural sports:* archery M(c)/W(c), badminton M(c)/W(c), basketball

M(c)/W(c), bowling M(c)/W(c), cheerleading M(c)/W(c), crew M(c), cross-country running M(c)/W(c), equestrian sports M(c)/W(c), fencing M(c)/W(c), football M/W, golf M(c)/W(c), ice hockey M(c)/W(c), lacrosse M(c)/W(c), racquetball M(c)/W(c), riflery M(c)/W(c), rugby M(c)/W(c), sailing M(c)/W(c), skiing (cross-country) M(c)/W(c), skiing (downhill) M(c)/W(c), soccer M(c)/W(c), softball W(c), swimming and diving M(c)/W(c), table tennis M(c)/W(c), tennis M(c)/W(c), ultimate Frisbee M(c)/W(c), volleyball M(c)/W(c), water polo M(c)/W(c), weight lifting M(c)/W(c), wrestling M(c)/W(c).

Costs (2004–05) *Comprehensive fee:* $39,500 includes full-time tuition ($29,988), mandatory fees ($524), and room and board ($8988). Full-time tuition and fees vary according to program. Part-time tuition: $1010 per credit hour. Part-time tuition and fees vary according to course load and program. *Required fees:* $524 per term part-time. *College room only:* $4960. Room and board charges vary according to board plan and housing facility.

Financial Aid 4,984 Federal Work-Study jobs (averaging $2764). In 2003, 2808 non-need-based awards were made. *Average percent of need met:* 100%. *Average financial aid package:* $26,812. *Average need-based loan:* $6110. *Average need-based gift aid:* $17,341. *Average non-need-based aid:* $11,494.

Contact: Contact: Director: Jane Armstrong, College Admission Office, CAS 100, University of Southern California, University Park, Los Angeles, California 90089-0152; *Telephone:* 213-740-5930; *Fax:* 213-740-1338; *Web site:* http://college.usc.edu/bamd/

University of Southern California
Thematic Option Honors Program
Los Angeles, California

The Thematic Option Program at the University of Southern California (USC) is for serious students who recognize the value of a liberal arts education. Thematic Option courses eliminate the barriers that separate disciplines, teaching students to appreciate the relationships among literature, history, philosophy, and science. An interdisciplinary core curriculum, intensive writing seminars, individual advisement, and extensive interaction with faculty members are at the heart of the Thematic Option experience. Professors selected for their commitment to students, scholarship, and teaching foster lively discussions in small classes.

Students who enroll in the Thematic Option curriculum explore the diversity of the liberal arts while satisfying the University's general education requirements. The Thematic Option curriculum consists of four core classes taught around distinct themes. In the core classes students ask the big questions: What is human nature? What is justice? How can we know these things? The first two core courses center on broad ethical issues and approaches to historical change. The second two focus on epistemology, representation, and social construction. Linked writing seminars with one-on-one writing tutorials allow students to improve their writing skills through close personal attention. Students round out their general education requirements with two additional courses chosen from a wide array of University offerings—one in either the humanities or the social sciences and the other in the natural sciences.

Thematic Option reaches beyond the classroom, making extracurricular activities an important part of the overall learning experience. The program sponsors films, dinners, seminars, excursions in and around Los Angeles, and weekend retreats. These activities become the context for an enjoyable and stimulating intellectual community. Each year, Thematic Option hosts a two-day Undergraduate Research Conference in which students present their own academic work in a public forum on panels chaired by USC faculty members. Past conference topics include postmodernism, the millennium, the idea of high/low in contemporary culture, and anarchy. The program also sponsors films, dinners, seminars, and excursions in and around Los Angeles. Students can also unite their academic and residential lives by choosing to live in one of the residential colleges, including the deans' halls, where honors students and faculty-in-residence share a supportive and stimulating environment.

Participation Requirements: The program requires completion of the four core classes, two semesters of writing instruction, and two supplemental courses. For most students, a foreign language is also required. Students working toward a B.A. degree usually take two core classes and a writing seminar each semester of the freshman year. Students working toward a B.S. degree in the College of Letters, Arts, and Sciences; the School of Engineering; or the Marshall School of Business usually take one core class and a writing seminar each semester of the first two years. Students working toward bachelor's degrees in architecture, filmic writing, performing arts, public administration, and other selected programs follow course schedules compatible with their major requirements. Thematic Option requirements are typically completed by the end of a student's second year. Upon graduation, students who satisfy all curricular requirements for the program receive a certificate of completion.

Admission Process: Students with a grade average of at least an A- and an SAT score of 1400, with greater weight accorded to the verbal score, are invited to participate in Thematic Option. Those who do not receive an invitation may apply directly to the program after admission to USC is granted. Because the program fills quickly, students interested in securing a place are urged to apply as soon as possible. Students from all majors at the University can participate.

Scholarship Availability: Thematic Option students compete well for all merit scholarships, including Trustee (full-tuition), Presidential (half-tuition), and Deans (quarter-tuition). Students who wish to be considered for Trustee and Presidential Scholarships must apply to USC before the scholarship consideration deadline in early December of each year.

Campus Overview

Independent university, founded 1880 • **Coed** 16,474 undergraduate students, 96% full-time, 51% women, 49% men.

Undergraduates 15,776 full-time, 698 part-time. Students come from 52 states and territories, 134 other countries, 32% are from out of state, 6% African American, 21% Asian American or Pacific Islander, 13% Hispanic American, 0.7% Native American, 9% international, 8% transferred in, 36% live on campus.

Faculty *Total:* 2,408, 62% full-time, 76% with terminal degrees. *Student/faculty ratio:* 10:1.

Academic Programs *Special study options:* accelerated degree program, advanced placement credit, cooperative education, distance learning, double majors, English as a second language, freshman honors college, honors programs, independent study, internships, off-campus study, part-time degree program, services for LD students, student-designed majors, study abroad, summer session for credit. *ROTC:* Army (b), Air Force (b). *Unusual degree programs:* 3-2 economics, mathematics, accounting.

Athletics Member NCAA. All Division I except football (Division I-A). *Intercollegiate sports:* baseball M(s), basketball M(s)/W(s), crew W(s), cross-country running M(s)/W(s), golf M(s)/W(s), soccer W(s), swimming and diving M(s)/W(s), tennis M(s)/W(s), track and field M(s)/W(s), volleyball M(s)/W(s), water polo M(s)/W(s). *Intramural sports:* archery M(c)/W(c), badminton M(c)/W(c), basketball M(c)/W(c), bowling M(c)/W(c), cheerleading M(c)/W(c), crew M(c), cross-country running M(c)/W(c), equestrian sports M(c)/W(c), fencing M(c)/W(c), football M/W, golf M(c)/W(c), ice hockey M(c)/W(c), lacrosse M(c)/W(c), racquetball M(c)/W(c), riflery M(c)/W(c), rugby M(c)/W(c), sailing M(c)/W(c), skiing (cross-country) M(c)/W(c), skiing (downhill) M(c)/W(c), soccer M(c)/W(c),

softball W(c), swimming and diving M(c)/W(c), table tennis M(c)/W(c), tennis M(c)/W(c), ultimate Frisbee M(c)/W(c), volleyball M(c)/W(c), water polo M(c)/W(c), weight lifting M(c)/W(c), wrestling M(c)/W(c).

Costs (2004–05) *Comprehensive fee:* $39,500 includes full-time tuition ($29,988), mandatory fees ($524), and room and board ($8988). Full-time tuition and fees vary according to program. Part-time tuition: $1010 per credit hour. Part-time tuition and fees vary according to course load and program. *Required fees:* $524 per term part-time. *College room only:* $4960. Room and board charges vary according to board plan and housing facility.

Financial Aid 4,984 Federal Work-Study jobs (averaging $2764). In 2003, 2808 non-need-based awards were made. *Average percent of need met:* 100%. *Average financial aid package:* $26,812. *Average need-based loan:* $6110. *Average need-based gift aid:* $17,341. *Average non-need-based aid:* $11,494.

Contact: Robin Romans, Ph.D., Director, Thematic Option Honors Program, CAS 200, University of Southern California, University Park, Los Angeles, California 90089-0153; *Telephone:* 213-740-2961, 800-USC-2961 (toll-free); *Fax:* 213-740-4839; *Web site:* http://www.usc.edu/thematicoption

University of the Pacific
Honors Program
Stockton, California

The Honors Program at the University of the Pacific (Pacific) supports excellence in academic and cocurricular endeavors and encourages Pacific's strongest students to take leadership and service roles during their undergraduate years and beyond. The University supports special academic programs and many extracurricular experiences designed to enrich the social, cultural, and intellectual lives of its students. The Honors Program also supports students who wish to apply for competitive graduate fellowships.

Participation Requirements: Freshman/Sophomore General Education Courses: Honors students begin by taking honors sections of Mentor Seminars I and II, General Education courses required of all University students. These courses expose students to a wide variety of disciplines while developing research and writing skills. In addition, students must take at least one more of their General Education courses in courses restricted to honors students. In the past few years, Pacific has offered honors courses in art history, biology, calculus, chemistry, economics, English, geology, history, music appreciation, political science, and religious studies. Freshmen must also attend eight extracurricular events per year from an extensive list that is published, and regularly updated, online. The list includes lectures, musical and theatrical performances, and museum exhibitions. These events help students see that a university's intellectual and cultural breadth and richness extends far beyond the classroom.

Pacific encourages, but does not require, freshman honors students to live in honors housing. The University attributes much of the success of its Honors Program to the honors residence halls, John Ballantyne and Carter Houses, which have become well known as two of the best places on campus for freshmen to live. Because the students tend to be quite responsible to begin with and because freshmen students live with a number of sophomore honors peers who set the tone, Pacific finds that its freshmen make the transition to college life much more smoothly and quickly than do the residents of most halls. Honors students develop a real community, one that supports not only academics, but also recreation. Students have active social lives, participate in intramural athletics at the highest rate of any residence hall on campus, and still pull down the highest grades of any freshman residences. It is a well-balanced community, exactly the kind of supportive environment that encourages students to do their best work and have fun in the process.

Sophomore/Junior Honors Seminars: Students must take this four-course sequence of 1-unit seminars designed to help students make connections between their General Education courses and their majors. The first, "Creativity and Knowledge," asks students to read a selection of essays on how human beings create and organize knowledge and asks students to consider their education to date in this light. The second, "Knowledge and Human Values," addresses the ethics of knowledge, asking about the rights and responsibilities students acquire as they become experts in particular fields, and how they as nonexperts should relate to the authority of knowledge. The third, "Social Uses of Knowledge," asks students how to apply knowledge to contemporary world affairs The fourth asks students to communicate specialist knowledge to a nonspecialist audience by having each write a proposal for a senior project.

Senior Project: Most senior projects will be research projects arising out of the fourth seminar, although students may choose other kinds of projects appropriate to their majors. Studio art majors, for example, may submit original work instead of a research project.

Admission Process: Students are invited on the strength of their application to the University. On average, students have combined SATs of about 1340, ACT composite scores of 30, and GPAs of 3.8.

Scholarship Availability: To be eligible for scholarships, the student must be a matriculated sophomore or junior pursuing a degree at an accredited institution of higher education at the time of nomination; have a college grade point average of at least B or the equivalent; and be a United States citizen, a permanent resident alien, or a United States national. It should be noted that this is only one of several qualifiers and that applicants are also judged on the basis of other experiences.

In the case of scholarships in the areas of tribal policy and health care, nominees must be Native American or Alaska Native. For the purposes of the Udall Scholarship Program, a Native American or Alaska Native is any individual who is a member of an Indian tribe or band; a descendent, in first or second degree, of a member of an Indian tribe or band; considered by the Secretary of the Interior to be an Indian for any purpose; or an Eskimo, Aleut, or other Alaska Native. Documentation must be provided. To be considered, a student must be nominated by his or her college or university using the official nomination materials provided to each institution.

Campus Overview

Independent university, founded 1851 • **Coed** 3,459 undergraduate students, 97% full-time, 57% women, 43% men.

Undergraduates 3,371 full-time, 88 part-time. Students come from 30 states and territories, 8 other countries, 13% are from out of state, 3% African American, 28% Asian American or Pacific Islander, 10% Hispanic American, 0.6% Native American, 2% international, 7% transferred in, 58% live on campus.

Faculty *Total:* 656, 61% full-time, 84% with terminal degrees. *Student/faculty ratio:* 14:1.

Academic Programs *Special study options:* academic remediation for entering students, accelerated degree program, adult/continuing education programs, advanced placement credit, cooperative education, double majors, English as a second language, honors programs, independent study, internships, part-time degree program, services for LD students, student-designed majors, study abroad, summer session for credit.

Athletics Member NCAA. All Division I. *Intercollegiate sports:* baseball M(s), basketball M(s)/W(s), cross-country running W(s), field hockey W(s), golf M(s), soccer W(s), softball W(s), swimming and diving M(s)/W(s), tennis M(s)/W(s), volleyball M(s)/W(s), water polo M(s)/W(s). *Intramural sports:* badminton M(c)/W(c), basketball M/W, bowling M/W, football M/W, golf M, lacrosse M(c)/W(c), rugby M(c), soccer M(c)/W(c), tennis M/W, volleyball M/W.

Costs (2004–05) *Comprehensive fee:* $32,608 includes full-time tuition ($24,320), mandatory fees ($430), and room and board

($7858). Part-time tuition: $839 per unit. Part-time tuition and fees vary according to course load. *College room only:* $3914. Room and board charges vary according to board plan and housing facility.

Financial Aid 2,123 Federal Work-Study jobs (averaging $1432). In 2004, 399 non-need-based awards were made. *Average financial aid package:* $22,114. *Average need-based loan:* $4955. *Average need-based gift aid:* $17,092. *Average non-need-based aid:* $7784.

Contact: Dr. Gregg Camfield, Honors Program Director, John Ballantyne Hall 115, University of the Pacific, 3601 Pacific Avenue, Stockton, California 95211; *Telephone:* 209-946-2283; *Fax:* 209-946-2378; *E-mail:* gcamfiel@pacific.edu; *Web site:* http://honors.uop.edu

COLORADO

Colorado State University
University Honors Program
Fort Collins, Colorado

*S*ince its founding in 1957, the University Honors Program at Colorado State University has successfully developed students' intellectual capabilities and personal talents through curricular and cocurricular learning experiences. Honors students obtain a public ivy experience where they receive a world-class education, enjoy the personalized attention typically found at a small college, and benefit from the resources and diversity of an outstanding national University.

The academic foundation of the University Honors Program is composed of two curricular tracks. The University Honors Scholar track (Track 1) offers students an enriched program of interdisciplinary studies and promotes active student learning by emphasizing critical reading, writing, and speaking. Track 1 fulfills the majority of Colorado State's general education requirements. It includes four interdisciplinary honors seminars, two honors courses in the major, and a faculty-mentored senior honors thesis. The University Honors Program also provides special honors sections of regular courses that students may take as electives or use to satisfy other academic requirements. Honors seminars and classes range from 15 to 25 students and are taught by the University's best teachers.

A new Department Honors Scholar curricular track (Track 2) has been approved for implementation in fall 2005. Track 2 is designed for students who have completed many general education credits (new freshmen, transfers, and on-campus students). It focuses on upper-division honors experiences in the student's major and a faculty-mentored senior honors thesis. Students may participate in one or both of the honors curricular tracks.

The honors thesis is required in both tracks and guarantees that all honors students have the opportunity for a senior-year creative activity. Students work one-on-one with faculty mentors to complete original research or creative artistry or design projects in an area of their choice. The senior honors thesis is the culminating learning experience of the honors curriculum and is often cited by honors graduates as the most rewarding experience of their academic careers.

A special feature of the University Honors Program is the Honors Living and Learning Community (LLC) located in Newsom residence hall. In addition to housing more than half of the honors first-year students, the Honors LLC is home to the University Honors Program offices, two honors seminar rooms, and the honors study lounge. Honors resident assistants live on each of the honors floors, and honors faculty and peer mentors teach classes in the residence hall. Many special events take place in the Honors LLC, including the Faculty Fireside program, peer advising sessions, social activities, and Honors Student Association meetings.

Participation Requirements: To continue participation in the program, students must make satisfactory progress in completing the curricular requirements of Track 1 and/or Track 2 and maintain at least a 3.25 cumulative GPA. Students who complete Track 1 requirements and achieve at least a 3.5 cumulative GPA are recognized at graduation and receive the designation of University Honors Scholar on their transcripts and diplomas. Students who complete Track 2 requirements and achieve at least a 3.5 cumulative GPA are recognized at graduation and receive the designation of Department Honors Scholar (e.g., History Honors Scholar) on their transcripts and diplomas.

Admission Process: The University Honors Program is open to all majors and enrolls between 250 and 300 students per year who have outstanding records of academic achievement, special talents, and cocurricular accomplishments. Invitations to apply are sent to students admitted to Colorado State who have strong records of academic performance as evidenced by high school grade point average, standardized test scores, and class rank. In addition, any interested student may apply to the program.

Scholarship Availability: Students are automatically considered for the full range of the University's merit scholarships if they are admitted to Colorado State by February 15. More information is available at the University's financial aid Web site at http://sfs.colostate.edu/. Honors students may apply for Honors Enrichment Awards of up to $500 each academic year. Honors Enrichment Awards provide funding for enhanced educational experiences and are available to support groups and individual enrichment opportunities. The University Honors Program also offers scholarships to outstanding junior and senior honors students who uphold the ideals of the program.

Campus Overview

State-supported university, founded 1870, part of Colorado State University System • **Coed** 21,729 undergraduate students, 89% full-time, 51% women, 49% men.

Undergraduates 19,294 full-time, 2,435 part-time. Students come from 50 other countries, 18% are from out of state, 2% African American, 3% Asian American or Pacific Islander, 6% Hispanic American, 1% Native American, 1% international, 7% transferred in, 23% live on campus.

Faculty *Total:* 896, 96% full-time, 99% with terminal degrees. *Student/faculty ratio:* 17:1.

Academic Programs *Special study options:* accelerated degree program, adult/continuing education programs, advanced placement credit, cooperative education, distance learning, double majors, English as a second language, honors programs, independent study, internships, off-campus study, part-time degree program, services for LD students, student-designed majors, study abroad, summer session for credit. *ROTC:* Army (b), Air Force (b).

Athletics Member NCAA. All Division I except football (Division I-A). *Intercollegiate sports:* basketball M(s)/W(s), cross-country running M(s)/W(s), golf M(s)/W(s), softball W(s), swimming and diving W(s), tennis W(s), track and field M(s)/W(s), volleyball W(s), water polo W(s). *Intramural sports:* badminton M(c)/W(c), baseball M(c)/W(c), basketball M/W, equestrian sports M/W, fencing M(c)/W(c), golf M/W, gymnastics M(c)/W(c), ice hockey M(c)/W(c), lacrosse M(c)/W(c), racquetball M(c)/W(c), riflery M(c)/W(c), rugby M(c)/W(c), skiing (downhill) M/W, soccer M/W, softball M/W, tennis M/W, ultimate Frisbee M/W, volleyball M/W, water polo M/W, weight lifting M/W, wrestling M.

Costs (2004–05) *Tuition:* state resident $2940 full-time, $163 per credit part-time; nonresident $13,527 full-time, $751 per credit part-time. Part-time tuition and fees vary according to course load. *Required fees:* $850 full-time, $52 per term part-time. *Room and board:* $5766. Room and board charges vary according to board plan and housing facility.

Financial Aid 623 Federal Work-Study jobs (averaging $1872). 1,156 state and other part-time jobs (averaging $1800). In 2003, 831 non-need-based awards were made. *Average percent of need met:* 82%. *Average financial aid package:* $7948. *Average need-based loan:* $5312. *Average need-based gift aid:* $4288. *Average non-need-based aid:* $1402.

Contact: Director: Dr. Robert Keller, Colorado State University, 1025 Campus Delivery, Fort Collins, Colorado 80523-1025; *Telephone:* 970-491-5679; *Fax:* 970-491-2617; *E-mail:* honors@colostate.edu; *Web site:* http://www.honors.colostate.edu

Mesa State College
Honors Program
Grand Junction, Colorado

The Honors Program at Mesa State College offers promising and motivated students enhanced opportunities for academic growth. All aspects of the program are focused on exciting learning experiences, an emphasis on developing intellectual skills rather than collecting facts, close relationships with the honors faculty members and with other honors students, and the assistance of the Honors Program Director in accessing the academic, administrative, and personal support that will allow students to make the most of their college careers.

Lower-division honors courses consist of specially designed sections of general education courses, taught by faculty members recruited for their expertise and teaching excellence. By varying the offerings from semester to semester, students are able to fulfill the general education requirement in small, discussion-based classes instead of large lecture classes. Upper-division honors courses are interdisciplinary, focused around themes or issues that can be illuminated from various perspectives.

Honors students also have the option of producing an honors thesis on some topic within their major. Under the guidance of an adviser they pursue a line of research/inquiry culminating in a written work that will be bound and included in the College library's holdings. Such projects are especially valuable in preparing students for graduate work, and the successful completion of an honors thesis is cited at graduation and on students' transcripts.

The program is still growing, having begun in 1993. There are currently 175 students enrolled in the program.

Participation Requirements: Students selected for enrollment must maintain a GPA of at least 3.0 and must take at least one honors course a year to be retained in the program. If students accumulate an average of at least 3.0 in 18 hours of honors courses, 6 of which are upper-division, they are cited at graduation as having earned academic honors.

Admission Process: Students must submit an application to the Honors Program separate from the application to the College. For application information, students should contact the Director.

Entering freshmen should apply by May 1. Currently enrolled students may apply each semester.

Scholarship Availability: Mesa State College offers a large number of scholarships for exceptional students.

Campus Overview

State-supported comprehensive, founded 1925, part of State Colleges in Colorado • **Coed** 6,192 undergraduate students, 74% full-time, 58% women, 42% men.

Undergraduates 4,612 full-time, 1,580 part-time. Students come from 46 states and territories, 9% are from out of state, 2% African American, 2% Asian American or Pacific Islander, 8% Hispanic American, 1% Native American, 0.6% international, 6% transferred in, 18% live on campus.

Faculty *Total:* 361, 53% full-time. *Student/faculty ratio:* 20:1.

Academic Programs *Special study options:* academic remediation for entering students, accelerated degree program, adult/continuing education programs, advanced placement credit, cooperative education, distance learning, double majors, honors programs, independent study, internships, off-campus study, part-time degree program, services for LD students, student-designed majors, study abroad, summer session for credit.

Athletics Member NCAA. All Division II. *Intercollegiate sports:* baseball M(s), basketball M(s)/W(s), cross-country running W(s), football M(s), golf W(s), soccer W(s), softball W(s), tennis M(s)/W(s), volleyball W(s). *Intramural sports:* basketball M/W, equestrian sports M/W, football M/W, golf M/W, lacrosse M, racquetball M/W, rock climbing M/W, skiing (cross-country) M/W, skiing (downhill) M/W, soccer M/W, softball M/W, swimming and diving M/W, tennis M/W, track and field M/W, volleyball M/W, water polo M/W, weight lifting M/W.

Costs (2004–05) *Tuition:* state resident $2063 full-time, $94 per hour part-time; nonresident $8349 full-time, $380 per hour part-time. Part-time tuition and fees vary according to course load. *Required fees:* $661 full-time, $34 per hour part-time. *Room and board:* $6501; room only: $3260. Room and board charges vary according to board plan and housing facility.

Financial Aid 189 Federal Work-Study jobs (averaging $1428). 394 state and other part-time jobs (averaging $1669). *Average percent of need met:* 59%. *Average financial aid package:* $6206. *Average need-based loan:* $3212. *Average need-based gift aid:* $2678.

Contact: Director: Dr. Aparna D. Nageswaran Palmer, 1100 North Avenue, Grand Junction, Colorado 81501; *Telephone:* 970-248-1984; *Fax:* 970-248-1700; *E-mail:* aparna@mesastate.edu

Metropolitan State College of Denver
College Honors Program
Denver, Colorado

The Honors Program at Metropolitan State College of Denver is approaching its twentieth anniversary. Its goal is to provide students who enjoy learning with a curriculum that is challenging and promotes critical thinking. One of the most important features of the Honors Program is that the class size is limited to 20 students, ensuring a close relationship between students and faculty members. To complete the Honors Program, students must complete 27 hours in the program. The core of the Honors Program is a 6-hour, two-semester course entitled Legacy of Arts and Letters. After completing this sequence, students are free to take electives in history, arts and letters, the social sciences, and the natural sciences. In their senior year, students register for the honors thesis. This experience gives students an opportunity to engage in original research or a creative writing or arts project. They work closely with a mentor and present their results to students and faculty members.

One of the major accomplishments of the Honors Program is that its students have organized a very successful club. One of the main goals of the club is to provide students with an opportunity to take advantage of the unique cocurricular opportunities available to them. Metropolitan State College is located in the center of Denver and across the street from the Denver Center for the Performing Arts. This gives students easy access to the Colorado Symphony and plays performed by professional actors. The Honors Program also organizes a fall conference devoted to important national and international events. Finally, the Honors Program has a lounge where students congregate for informal discussions and social events. All of these activities combine to produce a unique learning community.

The Honors Program enrolls between 84 and 100 students. Its graduates have been very successful in earning admission to graduate and professional programs.

Participation Requirements: To participate in the Honors Program, students must maintain a minimum 3.0 GPA and make steady progress toward completing the program.

Admission Process: Prospective students are required to provide a writing sample and two letters of recommendation.

Scholarship Availability: Because of a state budget shortfall, there is no money available for scholarships.

Campus Overview
State-supported 4-year, founded 1963 • **Coed** 20,761 undergraduate students, 60% full-time, 56% women, 44% men.

Undergraduates 12,397 full-time, 8,364 part-time. Students come from 40 states and territories, 58 other countries, 2% are from out of state, 6% African American, 4% Asian American or Pacific Islander, 14% Hispanic American, 1% Native American, 0.9% international, 11% transferred in.

Faculty *Total:* 1,141, 35% full-time, 41% with terminal degrees. *Student/faculty ratio:* 23:1.

Academic Programs *Special study options:* accelerated degree program, adult/continuing education programs, advanced placement credit, cooperative education, distance learning, double majors, external degree program, honors programs, independent study, internships, off-campus study, part-time degree program, services for LD students, student-designed majors, study abroad, summer session for credit. *ROTC:* Army (c), Air Force (c).

Athletics Member NCAA. All Division II. *Intercollegiate sports:* baseball M(s), basketball M(s)/W(s), cheerleading M(s)/W(s), soccer M(s)/W(s), swimming and diving M(s)/W(s), tennis M(s)/W(s), volleyball W(s). *Intramural sports:* badminton M(c)/W(c), baseball M/W, basketball M/W, football M/W, golf M/W, lacrosse M(c), racquetball M/W, rugby M(c), soccer M/W, softball M/W(c), swimming and diving M/W, tennis M/W, ultimate Frisbee M(c)/W(c), volleyball M(c)/W(c), water polo M(c)/W(c).

Costs (2005–06) *Tuition:* state resident $2283 full-time; nonresident $9366 full-time. Full-time tuition and fees vary according to course load and location. Part-time tuition and fees vary according to course load and location. *Required fees:* $576 full-time.

Financial Aid 203 Federal Work-Study jobs (averaging $3328). 412 state and other part-time jobs (averaging $3612). In 2003, 454 non-need-based awards were made. *Average percent of need met:* 25%. *Average financial aid package:* $6580. *Average need-based loan:* $3656. *Average need-based gift aid:* $4335. *Average non-need-based aid:* $1802.

Contact: Director: Adolph H. Grundman, Department of History #27, Metropolitan College of Denver, Denver, Colorado 80217; *Telephone:* 303-556-4865; *E-mail:* grundmaa@mscd.edu

Pueblo Community College
Pueblo Community College Academic Honors Program
Pueblo, Colorado

The Pueblo Community College Academic Honors Program provides enhanced educational opportunity to students of exceptional academic potential. The program serves a wide range of students: traditional students who are academic high achievers as well as nontraditional students who may be discovering for the first time that their hard work and motivation are preparing them for greater *academic challenges. The Honors Program enhances the educational experience by providing more challenging academic work, greater opportunities for independent study, guided research under the supervision of honors instructors, opportunities to present the results of honors projects, and participation in honors conferences with other honors students locally and regionally.*

The program operates on the basis of individual Honors Contracts that students fulfill in their regular classes. Honors Contracts allow students to develop and complete special projects under the supervision of course instructors and with the approval of the Honors Adviser. These contracts require academic work of a higher level than that normally offered in the class: independent research in scholarly publications, personally designed scientific experiments, performance pieces demonstrating theoretical concepts, and in-depth study of seminal writers and thinkers. In classes with service-learning components, honors students may take on an expanded service-learning commitment as part of their academic project. The end result of a student's honors project might be a paper written to specified requirements, an oral presentation supported by visuals, a performance of an original composition, the teaching of a class, or any combination of these products. Because the goal is to provide students with higher-level study instead of just greater amounts of work, honors contract projects may be substituted for some portion of the regular curriculum. When students successfully complete the course and the contract, they receive honors credit recorded on their transcripts.

The other major component of the program is the Honors Seminar, which allows honors students from across the campus to collaboratively explore topics of general interest and/or public concern in an atmosphere of critical thinking and debate. The seminar topic may be drawn from the Phi Theta Kappa Honors Society annual honors topic, or it may be chosen based on current issues and events. Plans are underway to institute an annual Honors Day event to celebrate the achievement of honors students and allow them to present their projects to a wider audience. The program is now in its second year, with a projected enrollment of 25 students for 2005–06.

Participation Requirements: Once students are accepted into the program, they must complete Honors Contracts in four different classes and attend the Honors Seminar for two semesters in order to be recognized as graduates of the Honors Program. Students negotiate with individual instructors concerning the nature and scope of the honors projects. For each project, the instructor, the student, and the Honors Adviser sign a contract outlining the requirements for completion. Students must earn at least a B in the classes in which they complete an honors project in order to receive credit for the project. The Honors Seminar meets a minimum of four times per semester. All students who complete the requirements are recognized as graduates of the Honors Program at commencement and receive an honors credit designation on their transcripts.

Admission Process: The program seeks to involve students who have high potential for future growth and success, not necessarily those who have demonstrated exceptional abilities in the past; therefore, students are admitted to the program using a holistic determination of potential based on the following factors: high school or college grade point average, instructor recommendation, written essay, and interview with the Honors Adviser. Generally, those students who have earned the recommendation of their instructors, demonstrate enthusiasm for learning, and possess the ability to express themselves clearly in oral and written form are admitted to the program.

Scholarship Availability: When the College's budget allows, honors scholarships may be available in varying amounts. Scholarships are focused on paying full or partial tuition and fees for the courses in which students successfully complete an honors project. In addition to these scholarships, the Pueblo Community College Foundation offers the Helen Davis Honors Scholarship for honors students who demonstrate severe financial need.

Campus Overview

State-supported 2-year, founded 1933, part of Colorado Community

College and Occupational Education System • **Coed** 5,747 undergraduate students, 38% full-time, 64% women, 36% men.

Undergraduates 2,208 full-time, 3,539 part-time. 1% are from out of state, 2% African American, 1% Asian American or Pacific Islander, 31% Hispanic American, 3% Native American, 0.2% international, 2% transferred in.

Faculty *Total:* 368, 23% full-time, 4% with terminal degrees. *Student/faculty ratio:* 19:1.

Academic Programs *Special study options:* academic remediation for entering students, accelerated degree program, advanced placement credit, cooperative education, distance learning, double majors, independent study, internships, part-time degree program, services for LD students, summer session for credit.

Costs (2004–05) *Tuition:* state resident $2004 full-time, $66 per credit hour part-time; nonresident $10,355 full-time, $345 per credit hour part-time. Full-time tuition and fees vary according to location and program. Part-time tuition and fees vary according to location and program. *Required fees:* $223 full-time, $19 per credit hour part-time, $12 per term part-time.

Financial Aid 116 Federal Work-Study jobs (averaging $1450). 207 state and other part-time jobs (averaging $2235).

Contact: Adviser: Bill Lewis, 900 West Orman Avenue, Pueblo, Colorado 81004; *Telephone:* 719-549-3111; *Fax:* 719-543-7566; *E-mail:* bill.lewis@pueblocc.edu; *Web site:* http://www.pueblocc.edu/clubs/AcademicHonors.htm

---

University of Colorado at Boulder
The Honors Program and the Kittredge Honors Program
Boulder, Colorado

*T*he Honors Program at the University of Colorado at Boulder is designed to provide special educational opportunities for highly motivated students.

Its home in the College of Arts and Sciences reflects its roots in the values and traditions of a liberal arts education. Honors is open to well-prepared freshmen as well as sophomores and upper-division students from all colleges on campus. The program offers a wide-ranging curriculum, thoughtful advising, close contact with faculty members and other honors students, and an opportunity to write an honors thesis. Each year more than eighty honors courses are offered in a wide variety of areas.

Courses are designed for students who actively seek academic and intellectual challenges and who know that the mind expands only with effort. Honors courses encourage students to combine and synthesize concepts and methodologies among courses and disciplines. Many honors courses are explicitly interdisciplinary, and all encourage students to read widely and think critically. The faculty is renowned for excellence in teaching, scholarship, and service. Beyond its curriculum, the Honors Program operates in two forms, departmental and general honors. Currently, thirty-six departments in the College of Arts and Sciences and the College of Business and Administration offer honors degrees through the arts and sciences program. Honors degrees are based on overall and major GPA, specific course work, and the preparation and defense of an honors thesis. Students find the process of graduating with honors (cum laude, magna cum laude, or summa cum laude) to be a most challenging and rewarding capstone to their college careers. Requirements for graduating with honors are among the most rigorous—and most rewarding—in the country.

An exciting option for first-year-honors, qualified students is the residential honors program, the Kittredge Honors Program (KHP).

Qualified first-year students who are invited to participate in the Honors Program may elect to live in an honors part of the Kittredge residence hall complex. Space is limited, so interested students are urged to respond promptly to their invitations. Selection is on a first-come, first-served basis. There is a fee ($725 a year) to participate in this residence program. KHP provides the flavor of a small liberal arts college within the context of the vast resources of a major university. Incoming students have the opportunity to associate with other bright, highly motivated students in the College of Arts and Sciences, becoming part of a special community of peers and faculty members. By sharing a common living space, students more easily find, interact with, and learn from other good students. This relationship is enhanced by the intimate environment of the KHP classroom, located in the dorm building itself, and by the presence of the KHP and director's office.

Participation Requirements: Students who maintain a cumulative GPA of 3.30 or higher are welcome to enroll in honors courses in any semester. However, while there are no minimum honors course requirements for participation in the Honors Program, students desiring to graduate with honors should consult with their major departments and the Honors Program to insure that minimum requirements are met leading to the successful completion of the honors thesis.

Admission Process: There is no application process to the Honors Program. CU-Boulder students may become eligible at any time during their undergraduate experience. The top 10 percent of the incoming freshman class of the College of Arts and Sciences is automatically invited to participate in the Honors Program. The top 10 percent is calculated by the admissions office based upon students' unweighted high school GPAs and SAT or ACT scores on a flexible scale.

Continuing Students: Continuing students do not need to be invited as freshmen to be involved in the Honors Program. Any student in the College of Arts and Sciences with a cumulative GPA of 3.30 or higher is welcome to take an honors course at any time.

Transfer Students: Transfer students' eligibility for their first semester at CU-Boulder is based on a cumulative GPA of at least 3.30 from the school they last attended.

Scholarship Availability: In conjunction with the CU Leadership, Excellence, Achievement, and Diversity Program (CU-LEAD), ten scholarships are offered each year to incoming students. These scholarships may be continued for subsequent years if the student maintains honors eligibility.

Campus Overview

State-supported university, founded 1876, part of University of Colorado System • **Coed** 26,182 undergraduate students, 92% full-time, 47% women, 53% men.

Undergraduates 24,036 full-time, 2,146 part-time. Students come from 52 states and territories, 100 other countries, 32% are from out of state, 2% African American, 6% Asian American or Pacific Islander, 6% Hispanic American, 0.8% Native American, 1% international, 5% transferred in, 22% live on campus.

Faculty *Total:* 1,746, 67% full-time, 71% with terminal degrees. *Student/faculty ratio:* 17:1.

Academic Programs *Special study options:* accelerated degree program, adult/continuing education programs, advanced placement credit, cooperative education, distance learning, double majors, English as a second language, freshman honors college, honors programs, independent study, internships, off-campus study, part-time degree program, services for LD students, student-designed majors, study abroad, summer session for credit. *ROTC:* Army (b), Navy (b), Air Force (b). *Unusual degree programs:* 3-2 nursing with University of Colorado Health Sciences Center; child health associate, dental hygiene, medical technology, pharmacy at University of Colorado Health Sciences Center.

Athletics Member NCAA. All Division I except football (Division I-A). *Intercollegiate sports:* baseball M(c), basketball M(s)/W(s), bowling M(c)/W(c), crew M(c)/W(c), cross-country running M(s)/W(s), equestrian sports M(c)/W(c), fencing M(c)/W(c), field hockey M(c)/W(c), golf M(s)/W(s), ice hockey M(c)/W(c), lacrosse M(c)/W(c), racquetball M(c)/W(c), rugby M(c)/W(c), skiing (cross-country) M(s)/W(s), skiing (downhill) M(s)/W(s), soccer M(c)/W(s), softball W(c), squash M(c)/W(c), swimming and diving M(c)/W(c), tennis M(s)/W(s), track and field M(s)/W(s), ultimate Frisbee M(c)/W(c), volleyball M(c)/W(s), water polo M(c)/W(c), wrestling M(c). *Intramural sports:* badminton M/W, basketball M/W, cross-country running M(c)/W(c), football M/W(c), ice hockey M/W, racquetball M/W, skiing (cross-country) M(c)/W(c), skiing (downhill) M(c)/W(c), soccer M/W(c), softball M/W, squash M/W, table tennis M/W, tennis M/W, ultimate Frisbee M/W, volleyball M/W(c), water polo M/W.

Costs (2004–05) *Tuition:* state resident $3480 full-time; nonresident $20,592 full-time. Full-time tuition and fees vary according to program. Part-time tuition and fees vary according to course load and program. *Required fees:* $861 full-time. *Room and board:* $7564. Room and board charges vary according to board plan, location, and student level.

Financial Aid 1,117 Federal Work-Study jobs (averaging $1599). 875 state and other part-time jobs (averaging $2155). In 2004, 3799 non-need-based awards were made. *Average percent of need met:* 89%. *Average financial aid package:* $9089. *Average need-based loan:* $4989. *Average need-based gift aid:* $5251. *Average non-need-based aid:* $5496.

Contact: The Honors Program at the University of Colorado at Boulder, Professor Dennis Van Gerven, Director, Campus Box 184, Boulder, Colorado 80309; *Telephone:* 303-492-6617; *Fax:* 303-492-3851; *Web site:* http://www.colorado.edu/honors. The Kittredge Honors Program, Dr. Paul R. Strom, Director, Campus Box 33, Boulder, Colorado 80309; *Telephone:* 303-492-3695; *Fax:* 303-735-5100; *Web site:* http://www.colorado.edu/honors

University of Denver
University Honors Program
Denver, Colorado

The University Honors Program combines the individual attention of a small liberal arts college with the resources of a midsized national university. Highly motivated students of proven intellectual ability and curiosity are invited to engage their peers and professors in scholarship and interdisciplinary learning. All majors—arts and humanities, business, natural sciences, social sciences, international studies, and performing arts—are represented. Honors students may take advantage of special opportunities on and off campus to enhance their undergraduate education and prepare for graduate work and professional careers. Most important, the University Honors Program cultivates a standard of intellectual excellence applicable to any walk of life and fosters habits of thought and mind that lead to a lifetime of inquiry and liberal learning. Students leave the program with well-developed minds because they are liberally educated persons.

Challenging and interdisciplinary course work together with enriching extracurricular activities allow honors students to excel in the company of intelligent and energetic peers and in close contact with distinguished faculty members. The four-year program affords students the opportunity to complete their university requirements with specially designed honors classes in the Divisions of Arts, Humanities, and Social Sciences; the Division of Natural Sciences and Mathematics; the School of Engineering and Computer Science; the Graduate School of International Studies; and the Daniels College of Business. First-year honors students elect to take the Coordinated Humanities program, an integrated three-quarter sequence that spans antiquity to the twenty-first century and combines history, literature, religion, art, philosophy, and religious studies.

Many departments offer honors sections of introductory and advanced classes. Honors professors teach a wide variety of interdisciplinary upper-level seminars designed to allow students to pursue their majors while expanding and crossing disciplinary boundaries. In all, more than forty honors courses are offered each quarter. In most cases, honors classes range from 8 to 15 students.

The University Honors Program fosters a community of conversation—a place to meet other bright and energetic students who want to explore the world of ideas. Activities within and outside the classroom aim not only at the acquisition of knowledge but also at learning through conversation—a two-way engagement with the books of the past and the minds of the present in the company of one's peers. Learning through conversation means more than acquiring a facility in self-expression and the capacity for analysis, argumentation, reflection, and investigation. Conservation cultivates habits of thought and personality in which one learns how best to speak, to listen, and to attend to the voice of the creative imagination. Of course, because the best conservations are frequently those punctuated by laughter and light-heartedness, the Honors Program offers times to get away and enjoy each other's company. The Honors House Living and Learning Community (an optional residential environment), mountain retreats, outdoor activities, and cultural events in the city of Denver provide honors students with opportunities for unstructured time to converse and delight in what nature and civilization have to offer. Honors students are leaders on campus and in the Denver community; they are regularly competitive for the major national and postgraduate fellowships, including the Fulbright, Rhodes, and Marshall Scholarships. University of Denver honors students are those who are willing—and have the courage—to contemplate the past so as to understand the present and form intelligent hopes for the future.

The University Honors Program was founded in 1960 and currently has 450 students.

Participation Requirements: Students must take between 12 and 24 credits of honors courses during their first two years and at least two interdisciplinary honors seminars during their second and third years and complete either a senior honors thesis/project or 6 credits of business honors seminars. Students must maintain a GPA of 3.4 or higher to remain in good standing and graduate with University Honors distinction on their transcripts.

Admission Process: Qualified students admitted to the University of Denver are invited to apply to the University Honors Program. High school GPA, class rank, test scores, and the admissions essay are all considered when inviting students to apply. Because numeric records do not always adequately reflect a student's talent and promise, the honors application gives students an opportunity to further demonstrate their intellectual ability and curiosity. Applications are sent directly to the student shortly after the University extends an offer for admission. Most students admitted to the program have at least a 3.85 high school GPA, are in the top 10 percent of their graduating class, and have at least a score of 1290 on the SAT or 28 on the ACT. The fall 2004 entering class had an average SAT score of 1340 and an average ACT score of 30.

Scholarship Availability: Almost all students admitted to the University Honors Program receive merit awards ranging from $4000 to full tuition. Scholarships are renewable, provided that the students meet the academic standards of their respective programs. Sixty-eight percent of undergraduate students receive financial aid; 51 percent of aid distributed to undergraduate students is in the form of scholarships or grants, 36 percent is student loans, and 13 percent of aid is work-study.

Campus Overview

Independent university, founded 1864 • **Coed** 4,669 undergraduate students, 90% full-time, 55% women, 45% men.

Undergraduates 4,206 full-time, 463 part-time. Students come from 52 states and territories, 54 other countries, 50% are from out of state, 3% African American, 5% Asian American or Pacific Islander, 7%

Hispanic American, 1% Native American, 4% international, 4% transferred in, 49% live on campus.

Faculty *Total:* 997, 46% full-time. *Student/faculty ratio:* 9:1.

Academic Programs *Special study options:* accelerated degree program, adult/continuing education programs, advanced placement credit, cooperative education, double majors, English as a second language, freshman honors college, honors programs, independent study, internships, part-time degree program, services for LD students, student-designed majors, study abroad, summer session for credit. *ROTC:* Army (c), Air Force (c).

Athletics Member NCAA. All Division I. *Intercollegiate sports:* basketball M(s)/W(s), golf M(s)/W(s), gymnastics W(s), ice hockey M(s), lacrosse M(s)/W(s), skiing (cross-country) M(s)/W(s), skiing (downhill) M(s)/W(s), soccer M(s)/W(s), swimming and diving M(s)/W(s), tennis M(s)/W(s), volleyball M(c)/W(s). *Intramural sports:* badminton M/W, baseball M(c)/W(c), basketball M/W, cross-country running M(c)/W(c), equestrian sports M(c)/W(c), football M/W, ice hockey M(c)/W(c), racquetball M/W, rugby M(c)/W(c), skiing (downhill) M(c)/W(c), soccer M(c)/W(c), softball M/W, squash M/W, tennis M(c)/W(c), volleyball M(c)/W(c), water polo M(c)/W(c).

Costs (2004–05) *Comprehensive fee:* $34,973 includes full-time tuition ($25,956), mandatory fees ($654), and room and board ($8363). Full-time tuition and fees vary according to class time, course load, and program. Part-time tuition: $721 per quarter hour. Part-time tuition and fees vary according to class time, course load, and program. *College room only:* $5093. Room and board charges vary according to board plan and housing facility.

Financial Aid 306 Federal Work-Study jobs (averaging $1644). 418 state and other part-time jobs (averaging $1768). In 2003, 1161 non-need-based awards were made. *Average percent of need met:* 70%. *Average financial aid package:* $18,539. *Average need-based loan:* $4655. *Average need-based gift aid:* $13,359. *Average non-need-based aid:* $7845.

Contact: Todd Breyfogle (Director) or Cassandra Balent (Assistant Director), University Honors Program, Mary Reed Building 17, 2199 South University Boulevard, Denver, Colorado 80208; *Telephone:* 303-871-2035; *Fax:* 303-871-4783; *E-mail:* tbreyfog@du.edu or cbalent@du.edu; *Web site:* http://www.du.edu/honors

University of Northern Colorado
University Honors Program
Greeley, Colorado

The University Honors Program is designed to offer exceptional students both the resources of a comprehensive University and the individual attention traditionally associated with a small college. It asks that they be alive to the life of the mind and pushes them to raise the expectations they have for themselves and their education. The program seeks to involve students in learning, heighten their critical awareness, and encourage their independent thinking and research.

Students from across the campus are invited and encouraged to participate in honors, and each major program on campus has an honors faculty adviser to assist students wishing to include honors in their studies. Advising is coordinated by honors office staff members and the designated honors faculty advisers. This shared coordination helps ensure that students in the program receive supportive and comprehensive advising for their work in honors.

Honors students annually have opportunities to attend national, regional, and local conferences to present their research and become more familiar with the work that other University students are

engaged in. In addition, students in the program have opportunities to hone their presentation skills through campus-exclusive research conferences, including the annual Works in Progress Symposium and campuswide University Research Day, which is cosponsored by the University Honors Program and the Graduate Student Association during Academic Excellence Week.

An honors-designated residence hall, centrally located in the heart of the campus and designated in the Colorado State Register of Historic Places, is available to students in the program. The well-appointed space includes two lounges and a full kitchen for common use. Students who choose this residence option have the opportunity to participate in in-hall academic advising, study groups, and regular honors pizza seminars with faculty members.

The Honors lounge is located in the honors office suite in the James A. Michener Library. The lounge is open Monday through Friday during regular office hours for student use. It serves as a comfortable meeting place for Student Honors Council meetings and other activities.

Honors students belong to one of the University's most active student organizations, the Student Honors Council. The council plans monthly social gatherings, community service projects, and other events for the honors community. It also sponsors or cosponsors such campuswide events as the International Film Series and Academic Excellence Week.

The University of Northern Colorado (UNC) University Honors Program was established in 1958. Currently, some 150 students actively participate in the program.

Participation Requirements: The curriculum requirements of the University Honors Program have been designed to provide students with enhanced experiences both in course work that serves as part of their undergraduate academic foundation and in major-specific enrichment and application of academic inquiry. Students in the program also have opportunities to take interdisciplinary courses through the campus Life of the Mind and Honors Connections Seminar offerings and participate in study abroad, National Student Exchange, and National Collegiate Honors Council semesters. Depending on the student's major, up to half of the required honors courses may simultaneously satisfy University general education requirements. All students in the program are required to maintain a minimum 3.25 cumulative grade point average and must take 18 semester credits, including 6 credits in honors-related research or thesis. Honors students graduate with Honors Distinction for their participation in the program, which has been the custom since 1968. All completed student research theses are placed in the permanent collection of the James A. Michener Library on campus.

Admission Process: Students are urged to join the University Honors Program as freshmen, but they may enter up to the second semester of their junior year. All applications must be accompanied by two letters of recommendation and a written statement of intent. Entering freshmen should have a minimum 3.5 high school GPA and meet one of the three additional criteria: be in the top 10 percent of their high school graduating class, have a minimum ACT composite score of 27, or have a minimum SAT score of 1170 based on the critical reading and math sections. Prospective students who are already enrolled at the University of Northern Colorado or those transferring from another college or university need a minimum GPA of 3.25 to be considered for the University Honors Program. The annual preferred deadline for admission to honors is April 30. Applications are, however, reviewed on a year-round basis.

Scholarship Availability: The University Honors Program annually awards $2500 in Academic Talent Scholarships. Student grade point average, academic writing, recognition, and involvement in campus and community activities are among the criteria considered in reviewing scholarship applications. The scholarships are awarded to students who are returning to UNC in the following academic year. In addition, the Becky R. Edgerton Award, with a $500 stipend, is given annually to the graduating senior who has completed the honors research thesis requirement and who has demonstrated the greatest breadth of intellectual curiosity among his or her honors peers.

Scholarship and award applications are made available through the University Honors Program office, usually by late March each year.

Campus Overview

State-supported university, founded 1890 • **Coed** 10,664 undergraduate students, 89% full-time, 62% women, 38% men.

Undergraduates 9,488 full-time, 1,176 part-time. Students come from 48 states and territories, 10% are from out of state, 2% African American, 3% Asian American or Pacific Islander, 8% Hispanic American, 0.8% Native American, 0.4% international, 8% transferred in, 31% live on campus.

Faculty *Total:* 581, 71% full-time, 63% with terminal degrees. *Student/faculty ratio:* 23:1.

Academic Programs *Special study options:* academic remediation for entering students, adult/continuing education programs, advanced placement credit, cooperative education, distance learning, double majors, English as a second language, external degree program, honors programs, independent study, internships, off-campus study, part-time degree program, services for LD students, student-designed majors, study abroad, summer session for credit. *ROTC:* Army (b), Air Force (b).

Athletics Member NCAA. All Division I. *Intercollegiate sports:* baseball M(s), basketball M(s)/W(s), cross-country running W(s), football M(s), golf M(s)/W(s), lacrosse M(c), rugby M(c)/W(c), soccer M(c)/W(c), softball W(s), swimming and diving W(s), tennis M(s)/W(s), track and field M(s)/W(s), volleyball W(s), wrestling M(s). *Intramural sports:* basketball M/W, football M/W, soccer M/W, softball M/W, volleyball M/W, water polo M/W.

Costs (2004–05) *Tuition:* state resident $2850 full-time, $143 per credit hour part-time; nonresident $11,740 full-time, $587 per credit hour part-time. *Required fees:* $520 full-time, $26 per credit hour part-time. *Room and board:* $5954; room only: $2876. Room and board charges vary according to board plan and housing facility.

Financial Aid 350 Federal Work-Study jobs (averaging $2259). 734 state and other part-time jobs (averaging $2049). In 2003, 794 non-need-based awards were made. *Average percent of need met:* 100%. *Average financial aid package:* $9109. *Average need-based loan:* $3728. *Average need-based gift aid:* $3503. *Average non-need-based aid:* $2587.

Contact: Director: Dr. Marie Livingston, University Honors Program, University of Northern Colorado, Campus Box 13, Greeley, Colorado 80639; *Telephone:* 970-351-2940; *Fax:* 970-351-2947; *E-mail:* honors@unco.edu; *Web site:* http://www.unco.edu/honors

CONNECTICUT

Albertus Magnus College
Honors Program
New Haven, Connecticut

The Honors Program at Albertus Magnus College is designed to enrich highly motivated students' experiences in the general education program and to provide an opportunity for them to pursue their particular intellectual interests in collaboration with faculty members as they progress through the College. The program is 7 years old and open to approximately 70 students per year. The number of students who participate varies. Students work with an adviser to tailor the program to meet their individual goals. Honors students can choose to take honors courses, develop independent projects, participate in graduate seminars, and pursue honors option work in regular courses. Practica and internships are offered in many areas to *well-prepared and highly motivated students. Credit is given for work done outside the classroom in an environment suited to the student's major interest.*

The program enables students to work closely with faculty members on a one-to-one basis and to take small classes that allow for individualized attention and promote intellectual development through collaboration with faculty members and peers. The program also regularly sponsors cocurricular activities, such as theater trips and honors luncheons.

The College is sponsored by the members of the Congregation of Dominican Sisters of St. Mary of the Springs.

Participation Requirements: Eligible first-year students complete 13 credits in honors humanities and English courses. To successfully complete the program, students must take four additional 3-credit honors courses. Students not completing the courses in the first-year program for honors credit must take six 3-credit honors courses. All honors students must take two upper-level honors courses that satisfy general education requirements. The other honors courses that students take can be general education or non-general education courses. In addition, honors students are eligible to take graduate courses in the Master of Arts in Liberal Studies program, or opt to take independent study, tutorial, or regular courses where honors course work is assigned in order to complete their honors requirements. To participate in the Honors Program, students must maintain a 3.5 GPA. Those who finish the requirements and have a cumulative GPA of at least 3.7 receive a note on their transcript and a certificate of achievement at the Albertus Magnus College awards banquet.

First-year students are admitted to the Honors Program based upon an evaluation of SAT scores, high school ranking, and placement tests administered by the College. Second semester first-year students, sophomores, juniors, and seniors are eligible to participate in the program by maintaining at least a 3.5 cumulative grade point average.

Scholarship Availability: Albertus Magnus College seeks to make it possible for every student accepted for admission to attend the College by providing financial assistance to its students. Assistance for meeting the cost of a private education is available in the form of scholarships, grants, loans, and employment.

Each year, Albertus Magnus College awards a variety of merit and need-based scholarships. These scholarships are not offered directly through the Honors Program. Academic scholarships, based on the academic achievement of the entering student, are awarded automatically to qualifying students upon acceptance to the College. These scholarships are then incorporated with other funding based on the student's eligibility.

In addition, students with financial need may be eligible to participate in the Federal Work-Study Program. This program provides for the employment of students on campus. Students are also eligible to participate in the Federal Community Service Work-Study program. This program provides for the employment of students to work off-campus at nonprofit organizations and primarily benefits the community.

Campus Overview

Independent Roman Catholic comprehensive, founded 1925 • **Coed** 1,906 undergraduate students, 94% full-time, 69% women, 31% men.

Undergraduates 1,795 full-time, 111 part-time. Students come from 9 states and territories, 4 other countries, 3% are from out of state, 23% African American, 0.9% Asian American or Pacific Islander, 9% Hispanic American, 0.2% Native American, 0.3% international, 1% transferred in, 60% live on campus.

Faculty *Total:* 201, 17% full-time, 29% with terminal degrees. *Student/faculty ratio:* 16:1.

Academic Programs *Special study options:* academic remediation for entering students, accelerated degree program, adult/continuing education programs, advanced placement credit, distance learning, double majors, English as a second language, freshman honors

college, honors programs, independent study, internships, part-time degree program, services for LD students, student-designed majors, summer session for credit.

Athletics Member NCAA. All Division III. *Intercollegiate sports:* baseball M, basketball M/W, cross-country running M/W, soccer M/W, softball W, tennis M/W, volleyball W. *Intramural sports:* basketball M/W, racquetball M/W, soccer M/W, squash M/W, table tennis M/W.

Costs (2004–05) *Comprehensive fee:* $24,408 includes full-time tuition ($16,250), mandatory fees ($608), and room and board ($7550). Full-time tuition and fees vary according to class time and program. Part-time tuition and fees vary according to class time and program.

Financial Aid 83 Federal Work-Study jobs (averaging $1310). 46 state and other part-time jobs (averaging $2660). *Average percent of need met:* 87%. *Average financial aid package:* $8500. *Average need-based loan:* $4800. *Average need-based gift aid:* $7500. *Average non-need-based aid:* $7000.

Contact: Director: Kenneth Jorgensen, 700 Prospect Street, New Haven, Connecticut 06511; *Telephone:* 203-773-8551; *Fax:* 203-773-3117; *E-mail:* jorgensen@albertus.edu

---

Eastern Connecticut State University
University Honors Program
Willimantic, Connecticut

The mission of the University Honors Program is to promote undergraduate scholarship by providing academically talented students with opportunities to participate in specially designed courses that prepare them to conduct independent research and/or scholarly activity under the oversight of a faculty mentor. Each of the courses in the honors curriculum satisfies a University general education requirement, and completion of an acceptable honors thesis satisfies all University writing requirements. The honors colloquiums, characterized by small class sizes, interdisciplinary topics, and professors dedicated to teaching, create an atmosphere conducive to the open discussion of ideas and active learning. In short, the honors curriculum is intended to prepare students to conduct independent work, culminating in an acceptable honors thesis. The successful completion of an honors thesis is the focal point of the program and the capstone experience of all honors graduates.

In addition to their academic pursuits, honors scholars become involved in a variety of leadership roles and rewarding activities. Many of these, such as the weekend in April when prospective freshmen are invited to visit the campus and stay over in dorms or apartments, are entirely planned and carried out by students. The Honors Club sponsors trips to cultural and academic events, including the NE-NCHC conference each spring, at which more than a dozen students regularly participate as presenters. Student representatives on the University Honors Council act as liaisons between honors students and the faculty council.

Participation Requirements: Entering freshmen take Honors Expository Writing (HON 200), which emphasizes the role of writing in intellectual and social processes. This course focuses on critical analysis, challenging students to frame complex ideas within relevant contexts and to tailor their writing to more effectively address specific purposes and audiences. In their second semester, freshmen take Reading Across the Curriculum (HON 201), a course involving professors from a variety of disciplines, which provides students with an opportunity to engage a topic from multiple perspectives. Through this experience, students gain an appreciation that different disciplines approach the same subject with different assumptions, methodologies, values, and goals.

During their sophomore and junior years, students take three honors colloquiums (HON 360–362), which are innovative interdisciplinary courses designed specifically for the program by outstanding scholars and respected teachers. Utilizing small class sizes and novel approaches to subject matter, instructors challenge students with open-ended assignments that encourage them to move beyond the goal of instructor satisfaction and define their personal standards of performance. Student performance evaluations reward exceptional effort, but they also recognize originality and disciplined creativity. Most importantly, honors colloquiums provide opportunities for students to demonstrate their attitudes toward learning, their intellectual curiosity, and their capacity for self-education. Topics recently covered include the Anthropology of Violence, Astrobiology, the American Dream, Mass-Mediated Political Rhetoric, and Globalization.

In the spring of their junior year, students take Directed Honors Research (HON 380) with a faculty mentor, ordinarily a professor in their major department, and develop a thesis proposal. During both semesters of their senior year, students register for Honors Thesis (HON 488) and, working with their respective mentors, complete their honors thesis. These courses comprise the capstone experience for honors students at Eastern. The completion of this 7-credit thesis requirement provides an opportunity to utilize many of the skills on which their earlier honors courses focused. Successful students demonstrate their capacity to identify a question or project, understand its relevance within their particular discipline, articulate a strategy for execution of the project, and complete a thesis written in the format appropriate to the discipline. Moreover, this experience provides evidence of the students' capacity to successfully complete a long-term project that reflects higher-order learning and a sense of what constitutes scholarship in their discipline.

Admission Process: Program admission is determined by the University Honors Council on the basis of high school standing, accomplishments, and recommendations only after students have been accepted into the University. Guidelines include graduation in the top 20 percent of the high school class and a minimum combined SAT score of 1150. The Honors Council is particularly interested in students who have participated in educational, social, cultural, or other extracurricular projects or activities and whose applications suggest enthusiasm, a willingness to get involved, and leadership. Honors students are welcomed to campus at a reception held at the beginning of each academic year and are encouraged to be active members of the honors community.

Scholarship Availability: All students accepted into the University Honors Program receive full in-state tuition scholarships, which cover up to 18 credits per semester. These scholarships are renewable for a total of eight semesters for students who maintain good standing in the program. In addition, supplementary scholarships, for either merit or financial need, and jobs on campus are often available through the Financial Aid Office, which works closely with the Honors Program.

Campus Overview

State-supported comprehensive, founded 1889, part of Connecticut State University System • **Coed** 4,720 undergraduate students, 78% full-time, 56% women, 44% men.

Undergraduates 3,700 full-time, 1,020 part-time. Students come from 24 states and territories, 21 other countries, 8% are from out of state, 7% African American, 1% Asian American or Pacific Islander, 4% Hispanic American, 0.8% Native American, 0.8% international, 10% transferred in.

Faculty *Total:* 374, 49% full-time, 60% with terminal degrees. *Student/faculty ratio:* 16:1.

Academic Programs *Special study options:* academic remediation for entering students, adult/continuing education programs, advanced placement credit, cooperative education, distance learning, double

majors, freshman honors college, honors programs, independent study, internships, off-campus study, part-time degree program, services for LD students, student-designed majors, study abroad, summer session for credit. *ROTC:* Army (c), Air Force (c).

Athletics Member NCAA. All Division III. *Intercollegiate sports:* baseball M, basketball M/W, cheerleading W(c), cross-country running M/W, field hockey W, lacrosse M/W, soccer M/W, softball W, swimming and diving W, track and field M/W, volleyball W. *Intramural sports:* badminton M/W, basketball M/W, bowling M(c)/W(c), cross-country running M/W, football M, gymnastics W, racquetball M/W, rugby M/W(c), skiing (cross-country) M/W, skiing (downhill) M/W, soccer M/W, softball M/W, squash M/W, swimming and diving M/W, tennis M/W, track and field M/W, ultimate Frisbee M/W, volleyball M/W, water polo M/W.

Costs (2005–06) *Tuition:* state resident $3034 full-time, $277 per credit part-time; nonresident $9820 full-time, $277 per credit part-time. Full-time tuition and fees vary according to degree level. Part-time tuition and fees vary according to course load, degree level, and reciprocity agreements. *Required fees:* $3438 full-time, $35 per term part-time. *Room and board:* $7580; room only: $4230. Room and board charges vary according to board plan and housing facility.

Financial Aid In 2002, 327 non-need-based awards were made. *Average percent of need met:* 80%.

Contact: Director: Dr. Phillip F. Elliott, Eastern Connecticut State University, Willimantic, Connecticut 06226; *Telephone:* 860-465-4317 or 4496; *Fax:* 860-465-5213; *E-mail:* elliottp@easternct.edu; *Web site:* http://www.easternct.edu/depts/honors/index.html

---

Quinnipiac University
University Honors Program
Hamden, Connecticut

*T*he Quinnipiac University Honors Program fosters the needs and interests of the University's most academically talented and committed students. The program is founded on the core values that guide the campus—excellence in education, sensitivity to students, and a spirit of community. Honors students participate in small seminar courses (20 students or fewer) with instructors who are dedicated to working cooperatively to mold a unique learning environment. This student-centered approach supports increasingly independent learning and also engages students in the larger campus as well as regional, national, and world communities. Honors students are encouraged to actively participate in and contribute to campus culture through lectures, book discussions, and unique events that enhance the distinctive learning opportunities available in the University environment. In addition, honors students have the opportunity for off-campus learning experiences in nearby areas such as Boston, New Haven, and New York City as well as in the local culture and history in Connecticut.

While Quinnipiac for more than ten years has had a less-formal honors program that provides a select group of students with opportunities for enhanced study and experiences in the local community, this more-formal Honors Program is scheduled to begin in fall 2006. Enrollment is 60 students per entering class, with a total of 240 students.

Participation Requirements: Honors students take a minimum of 22 credits in their existing core curriculum or major courses; the University Honors Program preserves freedom to pursue electives and minors. Students are expected to meet high academic standards, including maintaining a minimum GPA of 3.0.

Admission Process: As part of the admissions process, students with strong standardized test scores who have shown excellence in a challenging academic curriculum in high school are identified by the Admissions Committee and invited to participate in the Honors

Program. The Honors Program also considers internal and external applicants who meet the academic standards and wish to apply to join the program as sophomores or juniors.

Scholarship Availability: Applicants to Quinnipiac University are considered for merit awards based on their academic background. Trustee Awards, Deans Scholarships, and Quinnipiac Academic Awards are offered to incoming freshmen based on meeting criteria involving their rank in class in high school and their combined SAT score. The criteria for awarding a merit scholarship for fall 2006 are a rank in the top 15 percent of the high school class and a minimum SAT score of 1150 when using just the critical reading and mathematics scores on the new SAT. If the high school does not provide a rank in class, the Admissions Committee estimates an approximate rank. For fall 2005, scholarships range from $4000 to $15,000 per year. These scholarships are renewable each year, provided the student maintains a minimum 3.0 grade point average and satisfactory academic progress toward their bachelor's degree.

Campus Overview

Independent comprehensive, founded 1929 • **Coed** 5,464 undergraduate students, 93% full-time, 61% women, 39% men.

Undergraduates 5,091 full-time, 373 part-time. Students come from 28 states and territories, 20 other countries, 72% are from out of state, 2% African American, 2% Asian American or Pacific Islander, 4% Hispanic American, 0.2% Native American, 1% international, 3% transferred in, 70% live on campus.

Faculty *Total:* 741, 38% full-time, 29% with terminal degrees. *Student/faculty ratio:* 15:1.

Academic Programs *Special study options:* adult/continuing education programs, advanced placement credit, distance learning, double majors, honors programs, independent study, internships, part-time degree program, services for LD students, student-designed majors, study abroad, summer session for credit. *ROTC:* Army (c), Air Force (c).

Athletics Member NCAA. All Division I. *Intercollegiate sports:* baseball M(s), basketball M(s)/W(s), cross-country running M(s)/W(s), field hockey W(s), golf M(s), ice hockey M(s)/W(s), lacrosse M(s)/W(s), soccer M(s)/W(s), softball W(s), tennis M(s)/W(s), track and field M(s)/W(s), volleyball W(s). *Intramural sports:* baseball M, basketball M/W, bowling M/W, field hockey M/W, soccer M/W, softball W, tennis M/W, volleyball M/W.

Costs (2005–06) *Comprehensive fee:* $34,640 includes full-time tuition ($23,360), mandatory fees ($980), and room and board ($10,300). Part-time tuition: $570 per credit. Part-time tuition and fees vary according to course load. *Required fees:* $30 per credit part-time. *Room and board:* Room and board charges vary according to housing facility.

Financial Aid 1,443 Federal Work-Study jobs (averaging $1978). 41 state and other part-time jobs (averaging $1450). In 2004, 472 non-need-based awards were made. *Average percent of need met:* 66%. *Average financial aid package:* $13,160. *Average need-based loan:* $4087. *Average need-based gift aid:* $8937. *Average non-need-based aid:* $5272.

Contact: Kathy J. Cooke, University Honors Director and Professor of History, CL-AC3, Quinnipiac University, 275 Mt. Carmel Avenue, Hamden, Connecticut 06518; *Telephone:* 203-582-3475; *Fax:* 203-582-3423; *E-mail:* kathy.cooke@quinnipiac.edu

Sacred Heart University
The Thomas More School of Honors Studies
Fairfield, Connecticut

The Honors Program at Sacred Heart University is organized around the ultimate questions about reality and human life, which are an unavoidable part of the human experience and at the core or foundation of the human puzzle. The program is firm in the conviction that the honors experience should offer gifted students the opportunity to raise these questions, explore the answers that have been offered in the history of human thought and reflection, and test those answers in light of their own experience in the historical moment in which they live. Honors students are then given the opportunity to explore in a special way, through a series of unique courses, the mystery that surrounds human existence. The issues on which a liberal arts education is centered; the questions of purpose and orientation; the meaning of suffering; the reality of death; the questions of freedom, responsibility, morality, justice, character, hope, God, and the nature of the physical world; and an appreciation of ourselves as historical beings are the core of the honors academic experience. In providing this opportunity, the Honors Program reflects the fundamental commitment of Sacred Heart University to the liberal arts as the cornerstone of higher education and to an educational experience that is liberated from ignorance, prejudice, and unexamined beliefs and opinions.

The Honors Program at Sacred Heart University is looking for that kind of student—one who sets higher goals in life, one who seeks new challenges every day, one who seeks an educational experience that will, as Aristotle proposed, be truly liberating from ignorance, prejudice, and unexamined opinions. Students who participate in the Honors Program experience some of the greatest cultural and intellectual events in the world—museum exhibitions, theatrical productions, opera, concerts, and a world of intellectual stimulation—thanks to the University's ideal location between New York City and Boston.

Sacred Heart University is committed to exploring and developing the Catholic intellectual tradition. As part of that commitment, it seeks to aid each of its students in the full realization of human personhood. The goal of the Thomas More School of Honors Studies is to allow the quest for that realization to be taken up on a deeper and more rigorous level than occurs in nonhonors courses. Thomas More School of Honors Studies offers the student a challenging and unique educational experience in the course of four years of study. The University offers courses that respect the academic ability demonstrated by the students enrolled as well as a series of cultural experiences that supplement the student's core and major and contribute in a unique way to the University's goal of realization of human personhood. The quest for the full meaning of humanity can usefully be divided into three components: the cognitive, the aesthetic, and the moral or ethical. It is the goal of the Honors Program at Sacred Heart University to provide students with the richest possible resources for exploring these three components of the quest for satisfying and responsible personhood.

Participation Requirements: The curriculum for the Thomas More School of Honors Studies requires that at least 20 percent of the student's degree program be constituted of honors courses. This requirement is fulfilled by 15 credits in the honors core and an additional minimum of 9 credits in upper-level honors electives. Students may also undertake an independent senior project in their major that counts toward the 20 percent requirement. More information can be found on the University's Web site at http://www.sacredheart.edu.

Admission Process: The Honors Program provides an opportunity for academically advanced students to be challenged in an encouraging environment. The admissions process for the Honors

Program is competitive. There are two ways that students are admitted to the program. First, students with the following credentials are automatically invited to participate as a member of the Sacred Heart University Honors Program: minimum 3.7 grade point average, rank in the top 10 percent of the high school graduating class, and minimum SAT score of 1250, with a verbal score of 650 or higher. In addition, students are also welcome to apply to the program. They must meet the following requirements: minimum 3.5 grade point average, rank in the top 10 percent of the high school graduating class, and minimum SAT score of 1200. They must also submit a completed application, including an essay on the topic "What Additional Item Would You Add to the List of Thirty Things You Should Do, See, or Hear Before You Are 30?" and have an interview with the Honors Committee.

For more information, students should contact Karen Guastelle, Dean of Undergraduate Admissions, at 203-371-7880.

Scholarship Availability: Students admitted to the Honors Program beginning with the class of 2009 receive the $2000 Thomas More Scholarship. Students are also eligible for the University's Trustee Scholars or the University Scholars Program awards, which range from $3000 to $10,000, depending upon their high school academic profile. In order to receive these scholarships, the FAFSA and CSS PROFILE forms must be completed and sent to the Office of Student Financial Assistance.

For more information, students should contact the Office of Student Financial Assistance at 203-371-7980.

Campus Overview

Independent Roman Catholic comprehensive, founded 1963 • **Coed** 4,081 undergraduate students, 76% full-time, 61% women, 39% men.

Undergraduates 3,088 full-time, 993 part-time. Students come from 37 other countries, 53% are from out of state, 6% African American, 1% Asian American or Pacific Islander, 6% Hispanic American, 0.2% Native American, 1% international, 2% transferred in, 68% live on campus.

Faculty *Total:* 446, 36% full-time, 45% with terminal degrees. *Student/faculty ratio:* 13:1.

Academic Programs *Special study options:* academic remediation for entering students, accelerated degree program, adult/continuing education programs, advanced placement credit, cooperative education, distance learning, double majors, English as a second language, honors programs, independent study, internships, off-campus study, part-time degree program, services for LD students, student-designed majors, study abroad, summer session for credit. *ROTC:* Army (b). *Unusual degree programs:* 3-2 physical therapy, occupational therapy.

Athletics Member NCAA. All Division I except football (Division I-AA). *Intercollegiate sports:* baseball M(s), basketball M(s)/W(s), bowling M/W(s), cheerleading W, crew W(s), cross-country running M(s)/W(s), equestrian sports W(s), fencing M/W(s), field hockey W(s), golf M(s)/W(s), ice hockey M(s)/W, lacrosse M(s)/W(s), soccer M(s)/W(s), softball W(s), swimming and diving W(s), tennis M(s)/W(s), track and field M(s)/W(s), volleyball M(s)/W(s), wrestling M(s). *Intramural sports:* basketball M/W, bowling M/W, football M/W, golf M/W, gymnastics W, ice hockey M(c), rugby M(c)/W(c), skiing (downhill) M(c)/W(c), soccer M/W, softball M/W, table tennis M/W, tennis M/W, ultimate Frisbee M/W, volleyball M/W, weight lifting M/W.

Costs (2004–05) *Comprehensive fee:* $31,270 includes full-time tuition ($21,990) and room and board ($9280). Full-time tuition and fees vary according to program. Part-time tuition: $370 per credit. Part-time tuition and fees vary according to program. *Required fees:* $72 per term part-time. *College room only:* $6780. Room and board charges vary according to board plan and housing facility.

Financial Aid 439 Federal Work-Study jobs (averaging $1320). 672 state and other part-time jobs (averaging $1109). In 2003, 455 non-need-based awards were made. *Average percent of need met:* 72%. *Average financial aid package:* $13,393. *Average need-based loan:* $5215. *Average need-based gift aid:* $8762. *Average non-need-based aid:* $9864.

Contact: Director: Dr. Walter Brooks, Assistant Director: Dr. Amy VanBuren, The Honors Program, Sacred Heart University, 5151 Park Avenue, Fairfield, Connecticut 06432-1000; *Telephone:* 203-371-7730 or 7721; *Fax:* 203-371-7731; *E-mail:* brooksw@sacredheart.edu or vanburena@sacredheart.edu

Saint Joseph College
Honors Program
West Hartford, Conecticut

The Honors Program at Saint Joseph College offers highly motivated students the opportunity to excel in a challenging academic environment. Students join a community of learners in a sequence of stimulating classes and independent studies that culminate in a capstone team-taught interdisciplinary seminar. They participate in honors courses drawn from a wide array of academic disciplines, as well as broadening their intellectual and cultural horizons through diverse extracurricular activities. Trips to major museums in Boston and New York City are often planned in conjunction with academic topics. The program also provides low-cost tickets that encourage students to sample the rich cultural opportunities of nearby Hartford (e.g., theater at the Hartford Stage Company and intellectual conversations at the Connecticut Forum). The interdisciplinary honors curriculum draws from outstanding faculty members who work closely with students to develop fully their individual talents. In a program that promotes self-reliance and initiative, students work with a faculty mentor to explore an area of academic interest through an in-depth independent study, service learning, or study-abroad project. Honors students present these projects at the College's annual Undergraduate Research Symposium, as well as at regional and national conferences.

Participation Requirements: Honors students complete four honors classes designed to help them meet their general education and liberal arts requirements. These courses include Introduction to Astronomy: Astrophysics and Cosmology; fine arts electives such as Art of Egypt: Ancient to Coptic, History of Greek Art, and French and American Impressionism; Honors Problems of Philosophy; Human Heredity and Birth Defects; and Honors Thematic Approaches to Literature. During their junior year, honors students work with a faculty mentor on an independent study, service-learning course, or study-abroad experience. As their capstone honors experience, seniors participate in a team-taught, interdisciplinary course. Topics include Writing Women's Lives: The Construction of Self; Political Psychology; and Native American Literature and History.

Honors students are expected to maintain a minimum 3.25 GPA, complete the honors course sequence, and participate in the intracurricular and extracurricular enrichment opportunities. Students completing the honors sequence graduate with "In Honors" on their transcript.

Admission Process: Incoming first-year students with strong SAT scores (minimum combined scores of 1100) and excellent high school records are identified by the College's Admissions Office. Students meeting honors criteria are invited into the program by the Honors Director. The Director and an honors student worker provide additional information about the program upon request.

Transfer students with minimum GPA scores of 3.5 and outstanding Saint Joseph College students identified by advisers or faculty members may also be nominated for the program. Interested students write a letter of interest and are interviewed by the Honors Director and a member of the Honors Council.

Scholarship Availability: The College provides numerous merit scholarships. A majority of the incoming honors students benefit from these awards. The program provides stipends to students participating in regional or national academic conferences.

Campus Overview

Independent Roman Catholic comprehensive, founded 1932 • **Suburban** 84-acre campus with easy access to Hartford • **Women only** 1,172 undergraduate students, 73% full-time.

Undergraduates 860 full-time, 312 part-time. Students come from 6 states and territories, 1 other country, 7% are from out of state, 14% African American, 2% Asian American or Pacific Islander, 8% Hispanic American, 0.4% Native American, 0.1% international, 20% transferred in.

Faculty *Total:* 85, 88% full-time, 82% with terminal degrees. *Student/faculty ratio:* 12:1.

Academic Programs *Special study options:* academic remediation for entering students, accelerated degree program, adult/continuing education programs, advanced placement credit, distance learning, double majors, English as a second language, honors programs, internships, off-campus study, part-time degree program, services for LD students, student-designed majors, study abroad, summer session for credit. *Unusual degree programs:* 3-2 psychology, counseling.

Athletics Member NCAA. All Division III. *Intercollegiate sports:* basketball W, cross-country running W, soccer W, softball W, swimming and diving W, tennis W, volleyball W. *Intramural sports:* badminton W, basketball W, lacrosse W, soccer W, softball W, tennis W, volleyball W, water polo W.

Costs (2004–05) *Comprehensive fee:* $31,195 includes full-time tuition ($21,370), mandatory fees ($600), and room and board ($9225). Part-time tuition: $515 per credit. *Required fees:* $60 per course part-time. *College room only:* $4345. Room and board charges vary according to board plan.

Financial Aid 175 Federal Work-Study jobs (averaging $1000). 125 state and other part-time jobs (averaging $1500). In 2003, 74 non-need-based awards were made. *Average percent of need met:* 72%. *Average financial aid package:* $16,273. *Average need-based loan:* $5756. *Average need-based gift aid:* $11,151. *Average non-need-based aid:* $12,346.

Contact: Dr. Susan W. Ahern, Honors Director, Saint Joseph College, 1678 Asylum Avenue, West Hartford, Connecticut 06117; *Telephone:* 860-231-5398; or 860-231-5409 (Honors Lounge); *E-mail:* sahern@sjc.edu

Southern Connecticut State University
Honors College
New Haven, Connecticut

Honors College students at Southern Connecticut State University (SCSU) are independent thinkers, captivated by courses dealing with cross-cultural and intellectual movements and stimulated by creative debate and analytical dialogue. They thrive in an interdisciplinary setting, forming a close-knit community in which professors and students embark on a shared journey toward individual excellence.

The SCSU Honors College is a small, four-year integrated program designed for the academically inquiring, superior student. SCSU structures the Honors College as an interdisciplinary program so that students better understand connections among academic fields. Courses are organized around themes and questions that are common to many disciplines. Honors classes are team-taught, with professors from different departments approaching the honors class from the distinct perspectives of their own training and scholarship. Honors classes are small, limited to an enrollment of 20 students, thus fostering a high level of student involvement in the classroom. The courses are writing intensive, and students receive individualized feedback on their papers and creative work. Through this technique of lively interdisciplinary interchange, honors students are encouraged to analyze, interpret, and think freely, which permits them to discover underlying structures of knowledge across multiple areas of study. From introductory freshman writing and analytical courses through the senior-year honors thesis, honors classes are highly interactive, interesting, in-depth, and intense.

There is a connection among students and faculty members that both fosters individual achievement and promotes group camaraderie. Faculty advisement, which begins at registration and continues throughout the honors student's University career, plays a key role in the program. Honors students receive counsel from the honors coordinator, from other specially chosen honors professors, and from advisers in their major areas of study. Freshman honors students are also assigned a student mentor.

In addition to its academic component, the Honors College offers many special programs during the year, ranging from fun to serious and social to intellectual. As a result, Honors College students form a close-knit community and often become leaders on campus, traditionally involved in such activities as student government, theater, music, literature reviews, and the student newspaper. While Honors College students are interested in local causes, they also look outward to the larger world community. To support these ideals in honors students, the Honors College is strongly and actively committed to community service activities, preprofessional internships, and study abroad.

The Honors College was founded in 1982. There are currently 120 students enrolled in the program.

Participation Requirements: Students in the Honors College may select a major in any department and may be enrolled in any school of the University. They must complete the same requirements set by their major as would students not in the Honors College. During the first two years, honors students enroll in two honors classes each semester, along with three other courses selected from their major or minor fields and free electives. These eight honors courses replace most of the all-University requirements. Four of these honors courses are specifically required; the remaining four courses may be chosen from among a variety of options. Juniors take a research seminar in the Honors College, and seniors complete an honors thesis or creative project, working closely with a faculty adviser. Students are expected to maintain a minimum cumulative GPA of 3.0 during their first two years and must achieve a cumulative GPA of at least 3.3 before beginning their thesis. Honors College students who successfully complete this program are recognized individually at the University Honors Convocation, where they receive certificates in University Honors from their department(s) as well as a certificate from the Honors College.

Admission Process: Students accepted by SCSU must apply separately to the Honors College. Selection is made on the basis of two sets of criteria, the first being SAT scores (most often 1150 or higher), high school achievement (usually graduating in the top quarter of their class), and a letter of recommendation from a high school English teacher. Candidates must also attend an on-campus Essay Day, at which they submit a prepared essay, write a spontaneous essay, and participate in a simulated honors class. Admission is decided by the program director, in consultation with faculty members who have evaluated essays and participated in the on-campus class. First-year Honors College students typically rank in the top 15 percent of their high school classes, and their average SAT score is over 1150. The deadline for applying to the Honors College is February 1. Transfer students are accepted into the program based upon past academic performance.

Scholarship Availability: Each year, the majority of honors freshmen entering in August are awarded a Presidential Merit Scholarship, which covers full in-state tuition and fees. This scholarship is not need-based and therefore does not require a financial aid application. (Other forms of financial assistance are available through the Office of Financial Aid.) The Presidential Merit Scholarship, which is available only to Honors College members, is awarded competitively every year, and it may be renewed for a maximum of eight academic semesters as long as the student remains in good academic standing and meets the minimum GPA requirements of 3.0 at the end of the freshman year, 3.1 at the end of the sophomore year, and 3.3 at the end of the junior year. Transfer students become eligible for scholarships one year after joining the program and receive scholarships as they become available.

Campus Overview

State-supported comprehensive, founded 1893, part of Connecticut State University System • **Coed** 8,314 undergraduate students, 80% full-time, 61% women, 39% men.

Undergraduates 6,617 full-time, 1,697 part-time. Students come from 34 states and territories, 46 other countries, 6% are from out of state, 12% African American, 2% Asian American or Pacific Islander, 6% Hispanic American, 0.3% Native American, 1% international, 11% transferred in, 33% live on campus.

Faculty *Total:* 816, 50% full-time. *Student/faculty ratio:* 18:1.

Academic Programs *Special study options:* academic remediation for entering students, accelerated degree program, adult/continuing education programs, advanced placement credit, cooperative education, distance learning, double majors, freshman honors college, honors programs, independent study, internships, off-campus study, part-time degree program, services for LD students, student-designed majors, study abroad, summer session for credit. *ROTC:* Army (c), Air Force (c).

Athletics Member NCAA. All Division II except gymnastics (Division I). *Intercollegiate sports:* baseball M, basketball M/W, cross-country running M/W, field hockey W, football M, golf M, gymnastics M/W, soccer M/W, softball W, swimming and diving M/W, track and field M/W, volleyball W, wrestling M(s). *Intramural sports:* badminton M/W, basketball M/W, cross-country running M/W, football M, golf M/W, gymnastics M/W, ice hockey M(c), rugby M(c)/W(c), skiing (downhill) M/W, soccer M/W, softball W, volleyball M/W.

Costs (2005–06) *Tuition:* state resident $3034 full-time, $307 per credit part-time; nonresident $9820 full-time, $307 per credit part-time. *Required fees:* $2780 full-time, $63 per term part-time. *Room and board:* $7698; room only: $5558. Room and board charges vary according to housing facility.

Financial Aid 91 Federal Work-Study jobs (averaging $2743). 15 state and other part-time jobs (averaging $3781). In 2003, 468 non-need-based awards were made. *Average percent of need met:* 84%. *Average financial aid package:* $5185. *Average need-based loan:* $3724. *Average non-need-based aid:* $3012.

Contact: Honors College Director: Dr. Terese M. Gemme, 501 Crescent Street, New Haven, Connecticut 06515; *Telephone:* 203-392-5499; *Fax:* 203-392-6637; *E-mail:* gemmet1@southernct.edu

University of Connecticut
Honors Scholar Program
Storrs, Connecticut

The Honors Scholar Program represents the University of Connecticut's (UConn) commitment to providing a superlative educational experience to intellectually able and highly motivated students. The Honors Scholar Program offers the personal attention and community orientation of a liberal arts college along with the research, cultural, and athletic opportunities of a vibrant major

research university. A midsized institution ranked as the top public university in New England, the University of Connecticut is undergoing a dramatic transformation, as a $2.3 billion investment from the State of Connecticut is creating one of the nation's most attractive and technologically advanced campuses. The Honors Program fosters a tight-knit community of scholars and leaders who both enjoy their interactions with fellow honors students and actively engage in the dynamic and diverse opportunities of University life.

The goal of the Honors Program is to enable students who show significant achievement and substantial promise to use their college years to their utmost benefit. The program's vision is to graduate students who are not only well versed in their disciplines but who are also strong communicators, skilled team members, knowledgeable global citizens, and practiced leaders. This vision is furthered through a rich curriculum and a wide range of opportunities for student engagement beyond the classroom.

Challenging academics is the cornerstone of UConn's Honors Scholar Program. Students enroll in honors classes, which are limited in size and designed to spark intellectual curiosity and promote active learning. Students relish the opportunity to share in learning experiences with other high-achieving students under the tutelage of faculty members dedicated to creating involving and exciting learning environments. Honors students also experience the excitement of creation or discovery and the personal mentorship of a dedicated faculty adviser through completing the honors thesis, a requirement for graduation as an Honors Scholar.

During the first two years, students enroll in special honors courses offered across the undergraduate curriculum to fulfill the general education requirements of all University undergraduates. Most also enroll in specially designed Honors First-Year Seminars. Junior/senior-level honors study is specific to each student's major. Typical honors work in the major may involve special projects in major courses, departmental seminars, independent study, and graduate courses. To further students' academic goals, certain privileges are extended to honors students, including priority class registration, graduate-level library lending privileges, and relaxed semester-credit-hour enrollment restrictions. The Honors Program's close ties with the Office of Undergraduate Research facilitates honors students' placement in faculty members' laboratories, funding for summer scholarly projects, and opportunities to present work at the annual Frontiers in Undergraduate Research Exhibition (http://ugradresearch.uconn.edu/).

Being part of the honors community beyond the classroom and research setting dramatically enriches the collegiate experience for honors students at UConn. An active living-learning environment is fostered through the First-Year Honors Residential Community, the honors residence hall in South Campus, and the student-run Honors Council. A full calendar of social, cultural, and intellectual events organized by the Honors Program and Honors Council facilitates socializing, exposure to culture, and keeping up with the latest ideas in students' fields of interest. Honors students are frequently invited to meet in small venues with governmental leaders, noted authors, and acclaimed scientists visiting the campus.

Leadership skills and global perspectives can be gained through special Honors Program–sponsored opportunities. Students may elect a course sequence designed to prepare them to be student facilitators for the first-year honors seminars. Ambitious students aiming to compete for prestigious national scholarships, such as the Marshall or Rhodes, may obtain mentorship through the Office of National Scholarships. Students may earn honors credit on specially designated study-abroad programs, including an internship-based program in Cape Town, South Africa, to begin in spring 2006.

In addition to the Honors Scholar Program, the University of Connecticut offers admission to the prestigious University Scholar Program to no more than 30 juniors each year. This highly selective program offers motivated and academically talented students the flexibility to craft individualized plans of study during their last three semesters, with guidance from a faculty advisory committee. Centered around a major piece of research or creative work, the plan of study enables University Scholars to focus on topics, issues, or concerns of particular relevance to their intellectual interests. Graduation as a University Scholar is the highest academic honor bestowed on undergraduates by the University of Connecticut.

Throughout their enrollment in the Honors Program, honors students can benefit from the guidance of a range of faculty and staff advisers. All honors students are matched to a faculty honors adviser, based on the student's intended major. Students also form valuable relationships with faculty mentors during the process of completing their honors thesis and benefit from the dedication, knowledge, and mentorship of the staff of the Honors Program office.

The Honors Scholar Program, which began its pilot program in 1964, currently enrolls approximately 1100 students.

Participation Requirements: Honors Scholars must be an active participant and earn honors credit in at least one course per academic year to remain in good standing in the Honors Program. Student academic transcripts are also monitored for minimum academic standards for students at different academic levels to remain in good standing.

The Sophomore Honors Certificate is awarded after the second year and upon the fulfillment of honors credit, activity, and grade point average requirements. Recipients are recognized through a notation on their academic transcript as well as the presentation of the award at the Sophomore Honors Certificate Ceremony.

To graduate as an Honors Scholar, students must earn a cumulative GPA of at least 3.2, complete at least 12 approved advanced-level honors credits in their major or related areas, and submit a departmentally approved honors thesis. Honors Scholars must also meet any specific and/or additional honors requirements set by their academic department. Students who graduate as Honors Scholars receive an Honors notation on the diploma and transcript. Medals to wear at University commencement are awarded at the annual Honors Medals Ceremony.

Admission Process: Qualified entering first-year students at Storrs are admitted to the Honors Scholar Program by invitation only. Candidates are expected to have superior academic ability as demonstrated by a rigorous high school curriculum and excellent scores on the College Board Scholastic Aptitude Test. First-year students are notified of their admission to the Honors Program in their letter of admission to the University. Students admitted to the Honors Program as incoming first-year students are typically awarded merit-based University scholarships.

Current and transfer students with excellent academic records may apply for admission to the Honors Program. Rising sophomores and entering transfer students are admitted on a space-available basis. Rising juniors may also apply with the nomination of their major programs.

Scholarship Availability: The University's Undergraduate Admissions Office awards a number of four-year, merit-based scholarships to incoming first-year students. These scholarships are renewable for up to four years, provided that students meet the minimum grade and credit requirements. Further information regarding scholarship for incoming first-year students is available at http://www.admissions.uconn.edu/schlprog.htm.

University of Connecticut undergraduates may be eligible for many of the interdisciplinary honors societies, such as Golden Key, Phi Kappa Phi, Phi Beta Kappa, Alpha Lambda Delta, Lambda Theta Alpha, and Mortar Board. More information is available at http://www.honorsocieties.uconn.edu/.

Campus Overview

State-supported university, founded 1881 • **Coed** 15,751 undergraduate students, 94% full-time, 52% women, 48% men.

Undergraduates 14,843 full-time, 908 part-time. Students come from 50 states and territories, 65 other countries, 24% are from out of state, 5% African American, 7% Asian American or Pacific Islander, 4% Hispanic American, 0.3% Native American, 0.9% international, 4% transferred in, 72% live on campus.

Faculty *Total:* 1,234, 75% full-time, 93% with terminal degrees. *Student/faculty ratio:* 17:1.

Academic Programs *Special study options:* academic remediation for entering students, accelerated degree program, adult/continuing education programs, advanced placement credit, cooperative education, distance learning, double majors, English as a second language, honors programs, independent study, internships, off-campus study, part-time degree program, services for LD students, student-designed majors, study abroad, summer session for credit. *ROTC:* Army (b), Air Force (b). *Unusual degree programs:* 3-2 education, pharmacy.

Athletics Member NCAA. All Division I except football (Division I-A). *Intercollegiate sports:* baseball M(s), basketball M(s)/W(s), crew W, cross-country running M(s)/W(s), field hockey W(s), golf M(s), ice hockey M(s)/W(s), lacrosse W, soccer M(s)/W(s), softball W(s), swimming and diving M(s)/W(s), tennis M(s)/W(s), track and field M(s)/W(s), volleyball W(s). *Intramural sports:* badminton M/W, baseball M, basketball M/W, bowling M(c)/W(c), crew M(c), cross-country running M/W, equestrian sports M(c)/W(c), fencing M(c)/W(c), football M, gymnastics W(c), ice hockey M(c)/W(c), lacrosse M(c)/W(c), racquetball M/W, rugby M(c)/W(c), sailing M(c)/W(c), skiing (downhill) M(c)/W(c), soccer M/W, softball M/W, squash M/W, swimming and diving M/W, table tennis M/W, tennis M/W, track and field M/W, volleyball M/W, water polo W, weight lifting M(c), wrestling M(c).

Costs (2005–06) *Tuition:* state resident $6096 full-time, $254 per credit part-time; nonresident $18,600 full-time, $775 per credit part-time. Part-time tuition and fees vary according to course load. *Required fees:* $1816 full-time, $605 per term part-time. *Room and board:* $7848; room only: $4104. Room and board charges vary according to board plan and housing facility.

Financial Aid 1,412 Federal Work-Study jobs (averaging $1756). 5,502 state and other part-time jobs (averaging $1890). In 2004, 1747 non-need-based awards were made. *Average percent of need met:* 73%. *Average financial aid package:* $8662. *Average need-based loan:* $3276. *Average need-based gift aid:* $5508. *Average non-need-based aid:* $5567.

Contact: Associate Vice Provost and Director of Honors Program: Dr. Lynne Goodstein, 368 Fairfield Road, CUE 419 Unit 2147, Storrs, Connecticut 06269-2147. *Telephone:* 860-486-4223; *Fax:* 860-486-0222; *E-mail:* honors@uconn.edu; *Web site:* http://www.honors.uconn.edu

University of Hartford
University Honors Program
West Hartford, Connecticut

The University Honors Program at the University of Hartford is an academic program designed to offer a stimulating, challenging intellectual environment for highly motivated and talented students across campus. Honors courses are kept small to allow for frequent participation and exchanges among students and faculty members. Moreover, faculty members who teach in the Honors Program are among those who have proved themselves both in scholarship and research and in the classroom. Faculty-student interaction is highly prized and cultivated to encourage students to develop their intellectual abilities and talents and their desire to continue lifelong learning and experience personal fulfillment. Many students work along with their professors in the laboratories and studios, honing their skills and contributing to their field long before graduation.

The curriculum is flexible and not only provides special honors sections of courses and honors seminars but also promotes interdisciplinary acquisition of knowledge through the University's nationally acclaimed All University Curriculum, a program that encourages students not only to cross disciplinary lines but to apply their learning and life's experiences in subjects ranging from Epidemics and AIDS to Literature and Films of Other Cultures, the

Caribbean Mosaic, Creativity, Hunger: Problems of Scarcity and Choice, A Western Heritage: The Humanities, and Sources of Power. There are twenty-five widely recognized national honors societies at the University and numerous undergraduate scholarships as well as the John G. Martin Scholarship to Oxford for one graduating senior each year. Each year, the Honors Program sponsors the Undergraduate Research and Creativity Colloquium, which showcases outstanding student research, creative work, and special projects. Some of these students have also presented at national conferences and have had their work published in journals in their fields.

The University believes that the total honors experience involves life outside the classroom. The Honors Residential College provides an atmosphere supportive and conducive to study as well as a cohesive social and intellectual environment. There is one faculty member in residence there at all times. Participation in the University Honors Program is not a requirement to live in the Honors Resident College. The Honors Student Organization sponsors annual cultural, scientific, and social events. Opportunities also exist for volunteer and community service work as well as internships both on campus and in the greater Hartford area.

Participation Requirements: The usual honors load comprises 3 to 9 credits of general education courses, 6 credits in honors seminars, and 6 credits in either Thesis Research/Honors Research Writing, Humanities Center Seminar work, or a University Scholar Project. Eighteen credits of honors course work are required to complete the program. The honors curriculum has been designed both to encourage student interaction across the colleges in honors sections of required general education courses and to provide opportunities for enriched or accelerated work within the curricula of the individual colleges. Each college has defined a special honors experience for its students. Students matriculated in one college may complete all the requirements for honors in another college and thereby earn the University Honors designation. The students' programs must be approved by the Honors Coordinators of both the college of matriculation and the one in which they are completing the honors requirements. Contract honors courses may be taken when students find a particular course that they would like to pursue in-depth that is not offered as an honors section.

Admission Process: Students in all colleges of the University may participate. Eligibility is determined upon admission to the University on the basis of SAT I or Act scores and class rank. Approximately 150 incoming freshmen qualified for the University Honors Program last year. Subsequently, students can participate in the program once they have fulfilled the eligibility requirements for honors in their college. Students may continue in the program as long as they maintain the GPA required by their college. To graduate with University Honors in most colleges, students must have an overall average of at least 3.25 and at least a 3.0 in their honors course work. The designation of University Honors on the diploma is different from Graduation Honors, which is based purely on GPA (Latin honors).

Scholarship Availability: Scholarships of various amounts up to full tuition are awarded through the Office of Admissions and Financial Aid based on academic performance. Scholarships are not offered directly through the University Honors Program. Most honors students are recipients of academic or talent scholarships. There are other scholarships available through the colleges of the University after matriculation.

Campus Overview

Independent comprehensive, founded 1877 • **Coed** 5,566 undergraduate students, 82% full-time, 52% women, 48% men.

Undergraduates 4,545 full-time, 1,021 part-time. Students come from 46 states and territories, 53 other countries, 60% are from out of state, 10% African American, 2% Asian American or Pacific Islander, 4% Hispanic American, 0.2% Native American, 3% international, 5% transferred in, 74% live on campus.

Faculty Total: 744, 43% full-time. Student/faculty ratio: 14:1.

Academic Programs Special study options: academic remediation for entering students, adult/continuing education programs, advanced

placement credit, cooperative education, distance learning, double majors, English as a second language, honors programs, independent study, internships, off-campus study, part-time degree program, services for LD students, student-designed majors, study abroad, summer session for credit. ROTC: Army (c), Air Force (c).

Athletics Member NCAA. All Division I. Intercollegiate sports: badminton M(c)/W(c), baseball M(s), basketball M(s)/W(s), cross-country running M(s)/W(s), golf M(s)/W(s), lacrosse M(s), racquetball M(c)/W(c), rugby M(c)/W(c), soccer M(s)/W(s), softball W(s), squash M(c)/W(c), tennis M(s)/W(s), track and field M/W, volleyball M(c)/W(s). Intramural sports: basketball M/W, football M/W, racquetball M/W, soccer M/W, softball M/W, tennis M/W, ultimate Frisbee M/W, volleyball M/W, water polo M/W.

Costs (2004–05) Comprehensive fee: $32,476 includes full-time tuition ($22,290), mandatory fees ($1190), and room and board ($8996). Full-time tuition and fees vary according to program. Part-time tuition: $320 per credit. Part-time tuition and fees vary according to course load and program. College room only: $5548. Room and board charges vary according to board plan and housing facility.

Financial Aid 400 Federal Work-Study jobs (averaging $1554). 89 state and other part-time jobs (averaging $8901). In 2003, 381 non-need-based awards were made. Average percent of need met: 74%. Average financial aid package: $19,230. Average need-based loan: $5185. Average need-based gift aid: $10,189. Average non-need-based aid: $8302.

Contact: Director: Dean Catherine B. Stevenson, 327 Gengras Student Union, 200 Bloomfield Avenue, West Hartford, Connecticut 06117; Telephone: 860-768-5101; Fax: 860-768-4726; E-mail: stevenson@hartford.edu; Web site: http://uhaweb.hartford.edu/uhonors

University of New Haven
University of New Haven Honors Program
West Haven, Connecticut

The University of New Haven Honors Program is a comprehensive program designed for highly motivated students who have shown high levels of academic achievement. Students typically apply for admission to the program during the second semester of their first year of college.

Students in the program take one honors seminar each semester for four semesters. These seminars actively involve students in problem solving and inquiry. Topics in the seminars draw from several disciplines and study linkages between disciplines. These courses are nearly always team taught, usually by faculty members from different disciplines. Some typical recent courses are Cultural Entrepreneuralism, Engineering and Society, Contexts and Images–African Americans in Literature and Film, Psycholinguistics and Science Fiction, Arabic and Christian Influences on Western Culture in the Middle Ages, Classical Experiments in Science, The Ethics of Sport, and Politics and American Art.

During the senior year, each student writes an honors thesis in the major department. This thesis is a major research project on a topic of interest to the student. Results of the research are presented orally as well as in polished professional form to members of the student's major department and to members of the Honors Program Committee. Students regularly also present the results of their research at the annual Connecticut State Honors Conference.

Classes are kept small in order to provide an opportunity for participation in a setting where students get to know their instructors and other students. Students in the Honors Program receive priority over all other students in the semester class preregistration process.

Students who have completed two of the required honors seminars are given hooded Honors Program sweatshirts.

The UNH Honors Program has been in existence for more than twenty-five years but was redefined to its present format in 1994. The first class in the present format graduated in 1997. Currently, there are approximately 30 students in the program.

Participation Requirements: Students must take a total of four interdisciplinary honors seminars, each of which satisfies one of the University core curriculum requirements. They must write an honors thesis in their major field of study, for which they may receive up to 6 additional credits. In order to remain in the Honors Program, a student must maintain a cumulative grade point average of at least 3.3. Once all the requirements are completed, students receive the designation Honors Scholar on their transcripts and are presented with a gold medallion at commencement.

Admission Process: Students generally apply for admission to the program during the second semester of their first year at the University of New Haven. They submit their current college grade point average, SAT scores, and high school rank. They submit a "Statement of Goals" and a 250–300 word essay on the topic "Why I Would Like to Enter the UNH Honors Program." Finally, at least two college professors must submit references for them. The application deadline is generally the end of the week after spring break. Students are evaluated on the preceding criteria, but particular attention is paid to writing ability and evaluation by their college professors.

Scholarship Availability: Students who have completed the four required honors seminars, are in their final semester of residence, and who are actively working on their honors thesis receive 50 percent tuition scholarships during their final semester of residence. In addition, students in the Honors Program are eligible to apply for one of six John Hatfield Scholar Program awards. All of these latter awards go to Honors Program students who have a minimum grade point average of 3.5 and who have been active in community and campus life. Three awards go to junior Honors Program students and three to senior Honors Program students. The John Hatfield Scholar Program awards are in the amount of $2000 per year applied toward tuition.

Campus Overview

Independent comprehensive, founded 1920 • **Coed** 2,570 undergraduate students, 80% full-time, 47% women, 53% men.

Undergraduates 2,062 full-time, 508 part-time. Students come from 33 states and territories, 33 other countries, 38% are from out of state, 9% African American, 2% Asian American or Pacific Islander, 6% Hispanic American, 0.7% Native American, 3% international, 9% transferred in, 64% live on campus.

Faculty *Total:* 367, 46% full-time. *Student/faculty ratio:* 14:1.

Academic Programs *Special study options:* academic remediation for entering students, accelerated degree program, adult/continuing education programs, advanced placement credit, cooperative education, double majors, honors programs, independent study, internships, part-time degree program, services for LD students, summer session for credit.

Athletics Member NCAA. All Division II. *Intercollegiate sports:* baseball M(s), basketball M(s)/W(s), cheerleading M/W, cross-country running M(s)/W(s), golf M(s), lacrosse W(s), soccer M(s)/W(s), softball W(s), tennis W(s), track and field M(s)/W(s), volleyball M(s)/W(s). *Intramural sports:* basketball M/W, bowling M/W, cross-country running M/W, football M, lacrosse M, racquetball M/W, soccer M/W, softball M/W, table tennis M/W, tennis M/W, ultimate Frisbee M/W, volleyball M/W, weight lifting M/W.

Costs (2005–06) *Comprehensive fee:* $32,532 includes full-time tuition ($22,380), mandatory fees ($602), and room and board ($9550). Full-time tuition and fees vary according to course load. Part-time tuition: $746 per credit hour. Part-time tuition and fees vary according to class time, course load, and location. *College room only:* $5796. Room and board charges vary according to board plan and housing facility.

Financial Aid In 2002, 223 non-need-based awards were made. *Average percent of need met:* 79%. *Average financial aid package:* $17,042. *Average need-based loan:* $7076. *Average need-based gift aid:* $11,121. *Average non-need-based aid:* $14,673.

Contact: Dr. Thurmon Whitley, Honors Program Director, University of New Haven, 300 Boston Post Road, West Haven, Connecticut 06516; *Telephone:* 203-932-7296; *Fax:* 203-931–6035; *E-mail:* twhitley@newhaven.edu; *Web site:* http://www.newhaven.edu/academics (click on Honors Program)

DELAWARE

University of Delaware
University Honors Program
Newark, Delaware

The University of Delaware (UD) Honors Program, begun in 1976, combines the considerable resources of a major research university with the small class sizes and the personal attention that are typical of the nation's finest small colleges. After nearly a decade of rapid growth, the program now offers honors degrees in more than 100 majors throughout all six of the University's colleges, as well as honors residence hall living (required for first-year students and optional for upperclass students) and extensive cocurricular programming. Historically, the program has also functioned as a laboratory for pedagogical innovation, piloting programs such as undergraduate research, which offers students an opportunity to collaborate on research with faculty mentors; problem-based learning in the sciences; and peer tutoring.

Participation Requirements: First-year honors students are encouraged to enroll in a program of studies that can qualify them for the General Honors Award. Requirements include 18 honors credits in the first two years of University study, with 12 in the first year; a 3.0 or higher cumulative GPA; and residence in first-year honors housing. In addition to honors sections of courses that satisfy departmental, college, and University general education requirements, this course work must include a first-year honors colloquium, a small-enrollment (20 students), writing-intensive interdisciplinary seminar.

Upper-division students work toward various forms of recognition in addition to the General Honors Award, including the Honors Foreign Language Certificate, the Honors Degree, the Honors Degree with Distinction, and the Degree with Distinction. Both versions of an honors degree require 30 credit hours of honors course work; the Honors Degree with Distinction and the Degree with Distinction recognize the successful completion of a 6-credit senior thesis. Honors degree tutorials (4 students per section) and interdisciplinary honors degree seminars complement departmental capstone course offerings and discovery-learning experiences for seniors. Honors Program students participate extensively in the full complement of academic enrichment activities available to UD students, including UD's nationally renowned undergraduate research program, study-abroad programs on all seven continents, community service projects, academic internships, and service-learning experiences.

Two unique opportunities within the Honors Program are also of note. The Writing Fellows Program is a service-learning program that trains approximately 40 advanced Honors Program undergraduates to work as writing tutors with first-year honors colloquium students and in a variety of assignments across the University population at large. The Alison Scholars Program provides exceptional arts, humanities, and social science students with an early introduction to academic enrichment and special-event programming. It also allows some flexibility in meeting University general education requirements so that participants can move more quickly into advanced undergraduate (and even graduate) course work or pursue a more creative combination of studies spanning various general education groups.

The Honors Program enrolls approximately 440 new freshmen each year, creating a University-wide living-learning community for students in all six undergraduate colleges. Extensive cultural, social, recreational, and academic cocurricular programming reinforces the strong sense of community among students living either in first-year honors housing or in one of several centrally located upper-division honors residence areas.

Admission Process: First-year students apply for admission to the Honors Program when they apply for admission to the University. Other UD students may begin participating in honors courses and enrichment opportunities after they have achieved a 3.0 (B) or higher GPA in courses taken at the University. A formal application process for internal transfer is available, once students have obtained an overall GPA of at least 3.4 at UD. At present, there are approximately 2,000 students enrolled in the program (about 13 percent of the University's undergraduate population). All students completing applications by January 15 are automatically considered for merit scholarships.

Scholarship Availability: Honors students compete for and receive the lion's share of the University's general pool of merit scholarships, which range from $1000 to complete coverage of tuition, room and board, a book stipend, and academic enrichment funds.

Campus Overview

State-related university, founded 1743 • **Coed** 17,318 undergraduate students, 87% full-time, 57% women, 43% men.

Undergraduates 15,144 full-time, 2,174 part-time. Students come from 52 states and territories, 100 other countries, 58% are from out of state, 6% African American, 3% Asian American or Pacific Islander, 4% Hispanic American, 0.3% Native American, 1% international, 3% transferred in, 45% live on campus.

Faculty *Total:* 1,379, 81% full-time, 74% with terminal degrees. *Student/faculty ratio:* 13:1.

Academic Programs *Special study options:* academic remediation for entering students, accelerated degree program, adult/continuing education programs, advanced placement credit, cooperative education, distance learning, double majors, English as a second language, honors programs, independent study, internships, part-time degree program, services for LD students, student-designed majors, study abroad, summer session for credit. *ROTC:* Army (b), Air Force (b). *Unusual degree programs:* leadership, public administration.

Athletics Member NCAA. All Division I except football (Division I-AA). *Intercollegiate sports:* baseball M(s), basketball M(s)/W(s), bowling M(c)/W(c), cheerleading M(s)/W(s), crew M(c)/W(s), cross-country running M/W, equestrian sports M(c)/W(c), field hockey W(s), golf M, ice hockey M(c), lacrosse M(s)/W(s), rugby W(c), sailing M(c)/W(c), soccer M(s)/W(s), softball W(s), swimming and diving M/W(s), tennis M/W, track and field M/W(s), volleyball W(s), wrestling M(c). *Intramural sports:* badminton M/W, basketball M/W, field hockey W(c), football M/W, golf M/W, lacrosse M(c)/W(c), racquetball M/W, soccer M/W(c), softball M/W, squash M/W, table tennis M/W, tennis M/W, ultimate Frisbee M/W, volleyball M(c)/W(c), water polo M/W.

Costs (2004–05) *Tuition:* state resident $6304 full-time, $263 per credit part-time; nonresident $15,990 full-time, $667 per credit part-time. *Required fees:* $650 full-time, $15 per term part-time. *Room and board:* $6458; room only: $3668. Room and board charges vary according to housing facility.

Financial Aid In 2004, 3261 non-need-based awards were made. *Average percent of need met:* 78%. *Average financial aid package:* $10,200. *Average need-based loan:* $4750. *Average need-based gift aid:* $5800. *Average non-need-based aid:* $4050.

Contact: Director: Dr. John Courtright, University Honors Program, Elliott Hall, Newark, Delaware 19716; *Telephone:* 302-831-2340; *Fax:* 302-831-4194; *E-mail:* johnc@udel.edu or honorsprogram@udel.edu; *Web site:* http://www.udel.edu/honors/

DISTRICT OF COLUMBIA

American University
University Honors Program
Washington, District of Columbia

The University Honors Program at American University is a community of students and faculty members dedicated to academic excellence, intellectual curiosity, and personal growth. The program offers specialized courses, residence in honors housing, individual honors advisement, preparation and support for national scholarship competitions, and cultural opportunities. Honors students have the opportunity to involve themselves in honors work throughout their college years, culminating in the Senior Honors Capstone. The University Honors Program combines the benefits of a small liberal arts college with opportunities offered by a major university— renowned faculty members, exceptional students, and access to the resources of the nation's capital, from the Library of Congress to Capitol Hill internships.

The honors classroom resembles a forum, a place where students rigorously examine ideas and beliefs and are encouraged to take their scholarship to the next level. Honors classes are consistently small, usually fewer than 20 students, which allows for greater professor-student interaction and learning. Approximately seventy honors classes are offered each semester. The hallmark of the program is the innovative, interdisciplinary Honors colloquia that explore cutting-edge topics. Examples include Oral Histories of the Civil Rights Movement by NAACP chair Julian Bond, Persons and Selves by Oxford's Rom Harre, and Language in the New Millennium by Edinburgh Prize winner Naomi Baron. The program features special honors colloquia and Honors Study/Travel Abroad excursions over spring break to key cities or countries in the world. In recent years, honors students have traveled to Prague, Berlin, and Bolivia for academic credit.

The University Honors Program sponsors special events such as trips to the Kennedy Center to see the Kirov Opera, the American Ballet Theater, and Yo-Yo Ma and the National Symphony Orchestra; concerts featuring major and alternative bands; and Student Honors Board–run evens such as the Brain Bowl. Students can also participate in lively Oxford-style debates with honors faculty members on topics such as U.S. Foreign Policy in Iraq or Gandolf v. Yoda.

The 28-year-old program currently has approximately 1,000 students. Graduates have reached careers in the highest levels of government, business, the arts, medicine, law, and community service.

In the past two years, program participants have won the following scholarships, among others: Truman, Fulbright, Boren, Killiam, Pickering, and Goldwater.

Participation Requirements: Honors students must complete 30 credit hours of their course work (roughly ten courses) for honors credit, of which 12 credits must be upper-level courses. Students must achieve a grade B or better in honors courses to attain honors credit. The four-year program of options draws from courses in the General Education Program and in individual academic departments across the university. Early honors work gives students a broad base of knowledge, skills, and understanding, which serves as a foundation for increasingly specialized and in-depth advanced course work in the major and related areas. Students have the option of completing requirements for either University Honors in the major or General University Honors, depending on the type of upper-level courses pursued in the program. Each student also completes an Honors Capstone, which is a senior thesis or project. Among the hundreds of past capstones are book-length manuscripts, publishable-quality essays, student magazines, mathematical models, cutting-edge computer programs, art portfolios, films and documentaries, fiction, poetry, musical composition, and theatrical performances. Capstones are permanently stored in the University Library Archives.

Admission Process: Students are admitted to the University Honors Program in three ways. Most students are directly admitted to the program upon their acceptance to American University based on their university application, including high school record and standardized test scores. Transfer students who have exceptional college grades may be invited to join the program if their cumulative GPA is higher than 3.75. A third avenue is through self-nomination by freshman and sophomores who are enrolled at American University and have a minimum GPA of 3.6. Self-nominating students must complete an application and personal statements, submit a recommendation from a professor, and be interviewed by the program director. The 30-credit honors credit requirement may be reduced accordingly to an established formula for those students who enter the University Honors Program after their freshman year.

Scholarship Availability: Scholarships are not available through the Honors Program but are available from the Undergraduate Admissions Office to applicants who present excellent academic credentials and leadership skills or creative excellence.

Campus Overview

Independent Methodist university, founded 1893 • **Coed** 5,811 undergraduate students, 95% full-time, 62% women, 38% men.

Undergraduates 5,504 full-time, 307 part-time. Students come from 54 states and territories, 117 other countries, 95% are from out of state, 6% African American, 5% Asian American or Pacific Islander, 5% Hispanic American, 0.4% Native American, 7% international, 7% transferred in, 68% live on campus.

Faculty *Total:* 914, 54% full-time. *Student/faculty ratio:* 15:1.

Academic Programs *Special study options:* accelerated degree program, adult/continuing education programs, advanced placement credit, cooperative education, double majors, honors programs, independent study, internships, off-campus study, part-time degree program, services for LD students, student-designed majors, study abroad, summer session for credit. *ROTC:* Army (c), Air Force (c). *Unusual degree programs:* 3-2 engineering with University of Maryland College Park.

Athletics Member NCAA. All Division I. *Intercollegiate sports:* basketball M(s)/W(s), cross-country running M(s)/W(s), field hockey W(s), golf M(s), lacrosse W(s), soccer M(s)/W(s), swimming and diving M/W, tennis M(s)/W(s), track and field M(s)/W(s), volleyball W(s), wrestling M(s). *Intramural sports:* basketball M/W, bowling M/W, cheerleading W, crew M(c)/W(c), fencing M(c)/W(c), golf M/W, ice hockey M(c)/W(c), lacrosse M(c)/W(c), rugby M(c)/W(c), sailing M(c)/W(c), skiing (downhill) M(c)/W(c), soccer M/W, softball M/W, tennis M/W, ultimate Frisbee M(c)/W(c), volleyball M/W.

Costs (2004–05) *Comprehensive fee:* $36,567 includes full-time tuition ($25,920), mandatory fees ($387), and room and board ($10,260). Part-time tuition: $864 per semester hour. *Required fees:* $130 per year part-time. *Room and board:* Room and board charges vary according to board plan and housing facility.

Financial Aid 2,169 Federal Work-Study jobs (averaging $2016). In 2004, 767 non-need-based awards were made. *Average percent of need met:* 78%. *Average financial aid package:* $25,846. *Average need-based loan:* $7592. *Average need-based gift aid:* $13,304. *Average non-need-based aid:* $14,153.

Contact: Director: Michael Mass, 4400 Massachusetts Avenue, NW, Hurst Hall 206, Washington, D.C. 20016-8119; *Telephone:* 202-885-6194; *Fax:* 202-885-7013; *E-mail:* mmass@american.edu

Gallaudet University
Honors Program
Washington, District of Columbia

The Gallaudet University Honors Program is a learning community for the most academically capable and motivated students. The overall goal is to foster skills, work habits, and attitudes conducive to future achievement and lifelong learning. To this end, the program focuses on linking rigorous, challenging, and innovative curricular offerings with cocurricular activities. It also serves as a leader in and test laboratory of curricular, cocurricular, and extracurricular innovations; successes may then be replicated for all students.

As part of its mission to enhance academic culture, the Honors Program invites well-informed and recognized individuals to lecture on campus. Choices of speakers are based often on honors courses or honors summer readings. In addition to campuswide presentations, speakers meet with honors students in special seminars. In this last year alone, the Honors Program has welcomed Steven Pinker (The Blank Slate), Eric Schlosser (Fast Food Nation) and Christopher Darden (the O. J. Simpson trial).

The Honors Program supports the Student Honors Organization (SHO) to encourage student discussion on academic issues and to socialize. The Honors Student Organization plans activities that may include museum trips; book and film discussions; nature hikes and overnight camping; presentations by faculty members, off-campus individuals, and fellow students; discussions following lectures on or off the campus; and pizza jam sessions.

Honors classes average 10–12 students per class. The Honors Program offers a wide variety of interdisciplinary classes (both general education and upper-level seminars) and honors sections of single-discipline general education courses. New courses have focused on the nature of the self, nutrition and the American diet, globalization, social justice, and stress. To broaden the students' scope of learning, these courses not only invite speakers but also arrange for off-campus excursions. The Honors Program recognizes the extensive variety of interests among the students and has developed the Honors Option to accommodate the individual learning interests of all. Students who exercise this option enroll in a regular course and collaborate with the instructor and the honors director to maximize learning in the course by completing more challenging and in-depth work.

The Honors program was founded in 1981 and currently has approximately 80 students enrolled in the program.

Participation Requirements: The Gallaudet University Honors Program currently has two tiers. The first is General Studies Honors and the second is University Capstone Honors. Students must complete a minimum total of 21 credits to receive General Studies Honors. Fifteen of these credits must be honors sections of general education courses. Six of these credits must be other honors courses such as Honors Option or Honors Seminar courses. Students must complete a total of 15 credits to receive University Capstone Honors. Students must complete 9 credits of upper-level honors courses. These courses can be Honors Option major courses, graduate courses, consortium courses, honors seminar, or independent-study courses. Another six credits must be courses related to completion of the honors capstone project. Honors 487 (Honors Thesis Proposal Development) must be completed in the spring semester of junior year and Honors 488 (Honors Thesis Writing) must be completed in the spring semester of senior year. Students must have a cumulative GPA of at least 3.4 and must receive a B or better in all honors requirements.

Admission Process: Every year a small group of hearing undergraduates are admitted to the university, and some of these students qualify and are welcomed to apply to the Honors Program. The admissions criteria for honors are the same for all incoming students. Besides qualifying test scores, honors provisional admission criteria include an interview (on campus or via videoconferencing), a review of transcript(s), and participation in an online discussion of honors summer reading; full acceptance after the first semester is based on performance on an essay on the summer reading and achievement in first semester honors courses. Students already at Gallaudet must meet the following criteria: a GPA of 3.2 or above, an essay about interest in honors or summer reading, an interview, and three letters of recommendation from professors.

Campus Overview

Independent university, founded 1864 • **Coed** 1,207 undergraduate students, 91% full-time, 52% women, 48% men.

Undergraduates 1,098 full-time, 109 part-time. Students come from 49 states and territories, 28 other countries, 96% are from out of state, 12% African American, 5% Asian American or Pacific Islander, 7% Hispanic American, 4% Native American, 11% international, 6% transferred in, 70% live on campus.

Faculty *Total:* 230, 100% full-time, 76% with terminal degrees. *Student/faculty ratio:* 7:1.

Academic Programs *Special study options:* academic remediation for entering students, accelerated degree program, adult/continuing education programs, advanced placement credit, cooperative education, distance learning, double majors, English as a second language, honors programs, independent study, internships, off-campus study, part-time degree program, services for LD students, student-designed majors, study abroad, summer session for credit.

Athletics Member NCAA. All Division III. *Intercollegiate sports:* baseball M, basketball M/W, cross-country running M/W, football M(c), soccer M/W, softball W, swimming and diving M/W, tennis M, track and field M/W, volleyball W, wrestling M. *Intramural sports:* basketball M/W, football M/W, gymnastics M(c)/W(c), soccer M, softball W.

Costs (2004–05) *Comprehensive fee:* $19,675 includes full-time tuition ($9630), mandatory fees ($1625), and room and board ($8420). Part-time tuition: $482 per credit. *College room only:* $4720. Room and board charges vary according to board plan.

Financial Aid 250 Federal Work-Study jobs (averaging $1800). In 2004, 20 non-need-based awards were made. *Average percent of need met:* 75%. *Average financial aid package:* $13,935. *Average need-based loan:* $2658. *Average need-based gift aid:* $12,375. *Average non-need-based aid:* $6622.

Contact: Director: Dr. Shirley Shultz Myers, 800 Florida Avenue, NE, Washington, D.C. 20002-3695; *Telephone:* 202-651-5555 (V\TTY); *Fax:* 202-651-5896; *E-mail:* shirley.myers@gallaudet.edu

FLORIDA

Brevard Community College

Honors Program

Melbourne, Florida

The Brevard Community College (BCC) Honors Program offers *exceptional students an academic program of study to challenge them beyond the rigors of traditional classes. Honors students enjoy an environment of scholarly inquiry, creative interaction, and intellectual stimulation through special courses and enrichment activities.*

The program offers honors courses across the curriculum and attracts students seeking both Associate of Arts and Associate of Science degrees.

Honors Program students enjoy small classes (generally 8–15 students), priority registration, an Honors Resource Center (Melbourne

Campus), special library privileges, and a special agreement of admission to the University of Central Florida (UCF) Honors College.

Participation Requirements: Students may participate in the Honors Program in two ways: as honors students or as honors affiliates. Honors students work toward an honors diploma by completing 18 credit hours (out of a required 60 hours for an associate degree) of honors courses, participating in at least 20 hours of community service, and completing the Phi Theta Kappa–sponsored leadership course while maintaining a 3.5 GPA. Honors affiliates meet the same admissions requirements as honors students but participate in the program for access to honors classes. Affiliates may take as many or as few honors courses as they like and are not required to perform community service or take the leadership course. They are, however, required to maintain a 3.5 GPA. Honors students are recognized at graduation, and the transcripts of all participants in the Honors Program show the special designation of honors classes.

Admission Process: To be admitted to the Honors Program, students must meet one of the following requirements: have a high school GPA of 3.5 or above on a 4.0 scale; be in the top 10 percent of their high school graduating class; have an SAT I combined score of at least 1100; have an ACT score of at least 26; have a CPT or FELPT score of 100 or higher on sentence skills and 97 or higher in reading; show a 3.5 cumulative GPA from at least 12 credit hours of college-level work at Brevard; show a 3.5 GPA from no more than 6 credit hours in the case of students transferring from another accredited postsecondary school. All applicants must also present a letter of recommendation by a high school teacher and/or guidance counselor, a Brevard adviser or faculty member, or a faculty member from another college, in the case of transfer students.

Scholarship Availability: The Brevard Community College Honors Program offers limited scholarship assistance. Scholarships funded from many other sources are also available to Honors Program students. All scholarships require a separate application and have a variety of criteria.

Campus Overview

State-supported 2-year, founded 1960, part of Florida Community College System • **Coed** 14,616 undergraduate students, 36% full-time, 59% women, 41% men.

Undergraduates 5,332 full-time, 9,284 part-time. Students come from 34 states and territories, 72 other countries, 4% are from out of state, 9% African American, 3% Asian American or Pacific Islander, 6% Hispanic American, 0.6% Native American, 0.9% international.

Faculty *Total:* 1,061, 19% full-time. *Student/faculty ratio:* 18:1.

Academic Programs *Special study options:* academic remediation for entering students, accelerated degree program, adult/continuing education programs, advanced placement credit, cooperative education, distance learning, double majors, English as a second language, external degree program, honors programs, independent study, internships, part-time degree program, services for LD students, study abroad, summer session for credit. *ROTC:* Army (b), Air Force (b).

Athletics Member NJCAA. *Intercollegiate sports:* baseball M(s), basketball M(s)/W(s), golf M(s), softball W(s), volleyball W(s).

Costs (2004–05) *Tuition:* state resident $1428 full-time, $60 per credit hour part-time; nonresident $5400 full-time, $225 per credit hour part-time.

Financial Aid 200 Federal Work-Study jobs (averaging $2244). 200 state and other part-time jobs (averaging $2000).

Contact: Director: Beverly J. Slaughter, Honors Program, 3865 North Wickham Road, Melbourne, Florida 32935; *Telephone:* 321-433-5730; *Fax:* 321-433-5820; *E-mail:* slaughterb@brevardcc.edu; *Web site:* http://www.brevardcc.edu/honors

Broward Community College
Honors Institute
Fort Lauderdale, Florida

The Honors Institute is a comprehensive honors program that offers honors classes and Phi Theta Kappa chapters on three campuses. The students strive toward excellence in the four hallmarks of scholarship, leadership, service, and fellowship that are promoted in all Phi Theta Kappa chapters. In addition to the honors curriculum, there are honors extracurricular programs that enrich the students' college experiences. For example, the Brain Bowl Team and Mathematics Team provide opportunities for academic competition and teamwork among the participants. Both teams have won numerous state and national honors. The Brain Bowl Team has won the regional championship for fourteen years.

Students are encouraged to achieve through a program of recognition, including nominations to the National Dean's List and Who's Who as well as receptions and convocation where university scholarships are awarded.

The Honors Institute is a national leader in the percentage of graduates who receive university scholarships. More than 90 percent of all graduates have continued at universities across the country on scholarship.

The Honors Institute is twenty-three years old. College-wide, there are more than 900 students enrolled in honors classes.

Participation Requirements: Honors students take a minimum of 18 credits in honors classes, small seminar-type classes that emphasize writing, research, and critical and creative thinking.

Admission Process: One hundred top high school graduates from Broward County high schools who meet the Scholar's Award criteria are admitted annually. Students are also admitted with high SAT and ACT scores or if they have completed 12 college-level credits with a 3.5 GPA or higher or if they are home schooled and have an SAT of 1100 or higher or if they have passed the GED in the top 1 to 2 percent with a score of 3500 or higher.

Scholarship Availability: Most high school students who qualify for the Honors Institute receive scholarships based on high school performance that cover the two years at Broward Community College. Full-time and part-time honors students are eligible for semester scholarships Term I and Term II every year. Brain Bowl and Math Team members are eligible for scholarships. Upon graduation from the Honors Institute, students are awarded continuing scholarships to in-state and out-of-state universities.

Campus Overview

State-supported 2-year, founded 1960, part of Florida Community College System • **Coed** 33,141 undergraduate students, 30% full-time, 62% women, 38% men.

Undergraduates 10,029 full-time, 23,112 part-time. Students come from 100 other countries, 28% African American, 3% Asian American or Pacific Islander, 22% Hispanic American, 0.2% Native American, 9% international.

Faculty Total: 1,428, 26% full-time, 19% with terminal degrees.

Academic Programs Special study options: academic remediation for entering students, adult/continuing education programs, advanced placement credit, cooperative education, English as a second language, honors programs, part-time degree program, services for LD students, student-designed majors, study abroad, summer session for credit. ROTC: Army (b).

Athletics Member NJCAA. Intercollegiate sports: baseball M(s), basketball M(s)/W(s), soccer W, softball W(s), swimming and diving M(s)/W(s), tennis W(s), volleyball W(s), wrestling M(s). Intramural sports: baseball M, basketball M/W, tennis W.

Costs (2005–06) Tuition: state resident $1500 full-time, $59 per credit hour part-time; nonresident $6001 full-time, $219 per credit hour part-time. Required fees: $255 full-time.

Contact: Associate Vice President: Dr. Irmgard Bocchino, Honors Institute, Broward Community College, 225 East Las Olas Boulevard, Fort Lauderdale, Florida 33301; Telephone: 954-201-7645; Fax: 954-201-7648; E-mail: ibocchin@broward.edu

Florida Agricultural and Mechanical University
Honors Program
Tallahassee, Florida

The Florida Agricultural and Mechanical University (FAMU) Honors Program, which is now in its fourteenth year of operation, offers a challenging experience for academically talented students in all majors who are pursuing the baccalaureate degree. The approaches to learning in the program are innovative and stimulating. The program's small classes allow for lively and in-depth discussion of topics from which both students and professors benefit. Students in the program also enjoy personalized advisement and, when necessary, scheduling priority that allows them access to appropriate professors and courses. The program stresses four major areas of concentration: scholarship, leadership, community service, and cultural enrichment. There are currently 240 students in the program.

Special sections of the University's required general education sequence courses are offered as honors courses each semester. These special sections allow students to fulfill the honors requirements, as well as fulfill the requirement of their areas of interest.

The program offers a wide variety of experiences for its students. Among these are internship opportunities, participation in experiential learning/outreach programs, presenting and publishing research papers, travel/study-abroad opportunities, and membership in the Honor Student Association. Other not-for-credit experiences that contribute to the development of the students include lectures, forums, and leadership seminars.

Participation Requirements: To graduate from the Honors Program, students must have completed one of three major tracks that are designed to accommodate the honors students' varying degrees of interest. All students are required to have at least a 3.0 cumulative GPA. They must also have accumulated the total number of honors credit as designated by their chosen tract and are required to have completed a community service component. Students are encouraged to complete the Honors in the Major Thesis/Project during their junior and senior years. Students work under the directorship of a major professor on a thesis or project, which commences during the junior year and is completed before graduation.

Admission Process: The Honors Program recruits potential honors students based on a combination of outstanding scholastic ability as indicated by their SAT or ACT scores and their high school GPA. At the beginning of each school year, new honors students are selected from among the freshman class. These students must meet the following qualifications: a 3.5 minimum high school GPA, plus a score of at least 1200 on the SAT I or 27 on the ACT. High school graduates must complete a separate application for admission to the Honors Program and submit their high school transcript along with two letters of recommendation. Currently, enrolled and transfer students may apply for admission to the program, but not later than the first semester of their junior year.

In exceptional circumstances, promising students who may not meet the above criteria are given consideration. The Honors Program welcomes applications from interested students in all disciplines. The common thread linking the students in the program is their desire for an innovative and challenging education.

Scholarship Availability: Florida Agricultural and Mechanical University offers a variety of merit-based academic scholarships, which are administered through the Office of Recruitment and Scholarships. Many of the students in the Honors Program are recipients of the various scholarships the University offers.

Campus Overview

State-supported university, founded 1887, part of State University System of Florida • **Coed** 10,576 undergraduate students, 88% full-time, 56% women, 44% men.

Undergraduates 9,349 full-time, 1,227 part-time. Students come from 47 states and territories, 73 other countries, 20% are from out of state, 97% African American, 0.3% Asian American or Pacific Islander, 0.7% Hispanic American, 3% transferred in.

Faculty *Total:* 621, 100% full-time, 74% with terminal degrees. *Student/faculty ratio:* 21:1.

Academic Programs *Special study options:* academic remediation for entering students, accelerated degree program, adult/continuing education programs, advanced placement credit, cooperative education, honors programs, internships, off-campus study, part-time degree program, services for LD students, summer session for credit. *ROTC:* Army (b), Navy (b), Air Force (c).

Athletics Member NCAA. All Division I except football (Division I-AA). *Intercollegiate sports:* baseball M, basketball M(s)/W(s), cross-country running M(s)/W(s), golf M(s)/W(s), softball W, swimming and diving M(s)/W(s), tennis M(s)/W(s), track and field M(s)/W(s), volleyball W(s). *Intramural sports:* basketball M/W, cross-country running M, football M, soccer M/W, tennis M/W, volleyball M/W.

Costs (2005–06) *Tuition:* state resident $3318 full-time, $111 per credit hour part-time; nonresident $16,662 full-time, $555 per credit hour part-time. Full-time tuition and fees vary according to course load. Part-time tuition and fees vary according to course load. *Room and board:* $5766; room only: $3476. Room and board charges vary according to board plan and housing facility.

Financial Aid 524 Federal Work-Study jobs (averaging $1227). In 2003, 397 non-need-based awards were made. *Average percent of need met:* 60%. *Average financial aid package:* $7926. *Average need-based loan:* $3356. *Average need-based gift aid:* $3047. *Average non-need-based aid:* $6572.

Contact: Director: Dr. Ivy Mitchell, 107 University Honor House, Tallahassee, Florida 32307; *Telephone:* 850-599-3540; *Fax:* 850-561-2125; *E-mail:* ivy.mitchell@famu.edu

Florida Atlantic University
The University Scholars Program/Boca Raton Campus
Boca Raton, Florida

*S*ince 1992, through its University Scholars Program, Florida Atlantic University (FAU) has offered highly motivated and well-prepared students at the Boca Raton Campus a unique educational experience that goes well beyond the normal course requirements for freshmen and sophomores.

There are currently 60 students enrolled in the program.

Participation Requirements: The program consists of a minimum of 16 honors course credits. The core of the program is four 3-credit honors seminars taken during the freshman year. These seminars, developed and taught by highly experienced faculty members, are limited to 18 students. They substitute for required core-curriculum

courses and topics are drawn from the humanities, social sciences, and the sciences. Because of the small size and individual attention, students typically do as well, if not better, academically in these courses as they do in the normal core-curriculum courses.

In addition to the core seminars, students are required to take a 1-credit honors colloquium during the fall semester of the freshman year. This colloquium includes lectures by distinguished faculty members, outside speakers, and performances. Students also take 4 additional credits comprising honors sections of college writing and of the core-curriculum courses, upper-division honors equivalences of core courses, elective honors seminars, and a 2- to 3-credit honors-directed independent study.

To successfully complete the program, a student must fulfill all the course requirements and maintain a minimum overall GPA of 3.5 and an honors GPA of at least 3.0

Admission Process: Minimum requirements for acceptance into the honors program are SAT scores of 1250 or higher or ACT scores of 28 or higher and a GPA of at least 3.5. To apply, students must submit an application, a personal statement, and a letter of recommendation. Because of the limited number of spaces in the program, admission is selective; the application deadline is in mid-May. The program accepts 35 entering freshmen each year.

Scholarship Availability: Although the honors program does not award scholarships, a large number of University scholarships are available; many of them are based solely on academic merit. The FAU Presidential Scholarship, for example, awards $3000 per year for four years to students with a high school average of at least 3.5 on a 4.0 scale and an SAT score of 1270 or higher or ACT score of 28 or higher. It is renewable up to four years based on academic achievement.

Campus Overview

State-supported university, founded 1961, part of State University System of Florida • **Coed** 21,358 undergraduate students, 53% full-time, 61% women, 39% men.

Undergraduates 11,311 full-time, 10,047 part-time. Students come from 50 states and territories, 175 other countries, 5% are from out of state, 18% African American, 5% Asian American or Pacific Islander, 16% Hispanic American, 0.4% Native American, 4% international, 14% transferred in, 9% live on campus.

Faculty *Total:* 1,304, 56% full-time, 76% with terminal degrees. *Student/faculty ratio:* 18:1.

Academic Programs *Special study options:* accelerated degree program, adult/continuing education programs, advanced placement credit, cooperative education, distance learning, double majors, English as a second language, freshman honors college, honors programs, independent study, internships, off-campus study, part-time degree program, services for LD students, study abroad, summer session for credit. *ROTC:* Army (c), Air Force (c).

Athletics Member NCAA. All Division I. *Intercollegiate sports:* baseball M(s), basketball M(s)/W(s), cheerleading W, cross-country running M(s)/W(s), football M(s), golf M(s)/W(s), soccer M(s)/W(s), softball W(s), swimming and diving M(s)/W(s), tennis M(s)/W(s), track and field W(s), volleyball W(s). *Intramural sports:* basketball M/W, bowling M/W, cross-country running M/W, fencing M(c)/W(c), football M/W, golf M/W, ice hockey M(c)/W(c), rock climbing M(c)/W(c), rugby M(c)/W(c), soccer M/W, softball M/W, swimming and diving M/W, table tennis M/W, tennis M/W, track and field M/W, volleyball M/W, water polo M(c), wrestling M(c).

Costs (2004–05) *Tuition:* state resident $3092 full-time, $103 per credit hour part-time; nonresident $15,599 full-time, $520 per credit hour part-time. Full-time tuition and fees vary according to course load. Part-time tuition and fees vary according to course load. *Room and board:* $7100. Room and board charges vary according to board plan and housing facility.

Financial Aid 173 Federal Work-Study jobs (averaging $3387). 8 state and other part-time jobs (averaging $4472). In 2004, 391 non-need-based awards were made. *Average percent of need met: 72%. Average financial aid package: $6845. Average need-based loan: $3687. Average need-based gift aid: $5086. Average non-need-based aid: $2144.*

Contact: Director: Dr. Fred Fejes, University Scholars Program, 240 GCS, Florida Atlantic University, 777 Glades Road, Boca Raton, Florida 33431-0991; *Telephone:* 561-297-3858; *Fax:* 561-297-2615; *E-mail:* fejes@fau.edu; *Web site:* http://honorsboca.fau.edu

Florida Atlantic University
Wilkes Honors College
Jupiter, Florida

The Harriet L. Wilkes Honors College of Florida Atlantic University (FAU) is the first public honors college built from the ground up. Students reside for all four years on the John D. MacArthur campus located in Jupiter, Florida, in northern Palm Beach County. The campus is 10 minutes from the beach.

With 1 faculty member for every 12 students, classes are small, and learning is pursued in formal and informal settings. Unlike the honors options at almost all other universities, at the Wilkes Honors College, students are able to complete all of the 120 credit hours required for graduation in the Honors College, with courses restricted to honors students. The Honors College faculty members do all of their teaching within the Honors College. This allows the students and faculty members to form a living-learning community that lasts throughout the students' undergraduate careers. At the same time, students are able to take advantage of the resources of Florida Atlantic University (FAU), a state university with more than 25,000 students and nearly 1,000 faculty members.

At the Wilkes Honors College, special emphasis is given to interdisciplinary team-taught courses, international and environmental studies, and core courses that emphasize critical thinking and writing. Students may concentrate in the traditional disciplines of the liberal arts and sciences or design their own concentration under the supervision of faculty advisers. Honors College students complete a senior thesis and are required to do either an internship or study-abroad program. Students interested in environmental studies or marine life can take advantage of the Honors College's proximity to several research centers in the area, and with the recent arrival to its campus of the Scripps Research Institute, a world-renowned nonprofit biomedical research center, there are tremendous opportunities for students in the sciences. Though only in its sixth year, graduates of the Honors College have already been admitted into leading graduate and professional programs at institutions such as MIT, Caltech, Georgetown, and the University of Chicago. The Honors College also offers Pathway programs in which students continue with graduate training in either FAU's College of Business (the M.B.A. pathway) or FAU's College of Education (the M.Ed. pathway).

Recognizing that a crucial aspect of student growth and development occurs outside the classroom, the Honors College encourages social interaction with faculty and staff members and other students through a variety of residential-life programs and requires on-campus living for most students. Students have a private bedroom in a four-room suite. Bedrooms are equipped with telephone, cable television, and high-speed Internet connections, and each suite has a shared common living room and split bathroom.

The Wilkes Honors College opened in fall 1999 with 74 students and 16 faculty members. In 2005–06 it has more than 400 students and 37 faculty members. At the completion of its growth phase, the Honors College expects to have 500 students and 50 faculty members.

Participation Requirements: The Wilkes Honors College is a stand-alone college within Florida Atlantic University and is, therefore, distinct from other honors programs. It is best compared to a small, selective liberal arts college. Students complete all of the 120 credit hours required for graduation within the Honors College. In addition to the requirement that each student must complete either an internship or study-abroad program, each student writes a senior-year honors thesis in an area of concentration under the direction of a primary faculty adviser, with another faculty member as second reader. Except for transfer students entering with an A.A. degree, each Honors College student must complete an innovative interdisciplinary core curriculum. In addition, all students take three critical-inquiry seminars that are each team taught by two faculty members from two distinct academic disciplines. For example, a psychologist and a biologist team teach How and Why we Age, a sociologist and a historian team teach History and Practice of Marriage, and an English professor and a political theorist team teach Good and Evil in Film and Literature. Students must maintain a 2.0 GPA or better to remain in good academic standing and should maintain a 3.0 GPA or better to ensure renewal of their Honors College scholarships. All concentrations in the Honors College lead to a Bachelor of Arts degree in the liberal arts and sciences.

Admission Process: The Wilkes Honors College is highly selective. It looks not only for high grade point averages but also for evidence that students have sought out the most challenging high school courses, those that prepare them for the Honors College's curriculum. The Honors College gives extra weight to honors, Advanced Placement, and International Baccalaureate courses when calculating the applicant's GPA. Two letters of evaluation, a graded writing sample, and a resume are required in addition to a completed State University System of Florida application and a $30 application fee. At least one letter should be from a counselor or teacher. The graded writing sample should be a typed analytical paper of 500 to 1,000 words. The resume should cover extracurricular activities, community involvement, and work experience as well as honors and awards. There is no minimum GPA or test score required for admission, however, the mid-50 percent range for weighted GPA for the 2004 entering class was 3.8–4.4, and the mid-50 percent range for SAT scores was 1200–1320.

Scholarship Availability: As a member of the State University System of Florida, the Wilkes Honors College offers a high-quality education at a surprisingly affordable cost; however, many qualified students still need financial aid to attend college. The Honors College awards extensive financial aid to students who desire a college education but cannot pay the full cost. Every student admitted to the Honors College receives an academic scholarship. Among the scholarships provided are the prestigious Henry Morrison Flagler Awards, worth more than $55,000 over four years and given to 5 incoming first-year students each year (Florida residents only). Many other scholarships are available for both Florida and non-Florida residents. In 2004–05 the Honors College awarded more than $1 million in scholarships to 348 students, for an average award of more than $3000. Scholarship awards are renewed for up to four years if the student maintains a minimum 3.0 GPA. Need-based financial aid is also available to those applicants who complete the Free Application for Federal Student Aid (FAFSA).

Campus Overview

Public university founded 1961 • **Coed** 1,662 undergraduate students, 69% women, 31% men.

Undergraduates Student population is 11% African American, 3% Asian American or Pacific Islander, 10% Hispanic American, 1% Native American, 2% international.

Faculty *Total:* 81.

Academic Programs *Special study options:* internships, study abroad.

Athletics Member NCAA. All Division I. *Intercollegiate sports:* baseball (M), basketball (M/W), cross-country (M/W), golf (M/W), soccer (M/W), softball (W), swimming (W), swimming and diving (M), tennis (M/W), track and field (W), and volleyball (W).

Costs (2004–05) *Tuition:* state resident $3100; nonresident $14,900. *Room and board:* room only: $5870; board only: $2926.

Contact: Interim Dean: Dr. Nancy Poulson, Wilkes Honors College, Florida Atlantic University, John D. MacArthur Campus, 5353 Parkside Drive, Jupiter, Florida 33458; Phone: 561-799-8578 or 561-799-8646 or 800-920-8705 (toll-free) *E-mail:* npoulson@fau.edu or hcadmissions@fau.edu; *Web site:* http://www.honorscollege.edu

Florida International University
The Honors College
Miami, Florida

Talented students are often forced to choose between the exciting opportunities and challenges available at large, research-oriented universities and the close, personal environment offered by small liberal arts colleges. Florida International University (FIU) offers the best of both worlds. The Honors College is a small community of outstanding students, committed teachers, and dedicated scholars who work together in an atmosphere usually associated with small private colleges but with all of the resources of a major urban university.

The College provides an important foundation for students who want to get the most out of their undergraduate years. The transition into higher education is made easier by the student's immediate association with a small group of students and teachers with similar capabilities and aspirations. The undergraduate experience is significantly enhanced by the interdisciplinary focus of the curriculum and the opportunity to work closely with experienced faculty members. Opportunities for graduate and professional study or employment are greatly expanded because of the range of activities and experiences made available to students in the College. The Honors College at FIU offers some of the very best experiences in undergraduate education.

The 15-year-old College currently enrolls 900 students from fifty-seven countries and twenty-one states.

Participation Requirements: Students in the College possess dual academic citizenship. They pursue almost any major available in the University and at the same time complete the honors curriculum. In most cases, participation in the College does not increase the number of credits required for graduation. During each term, students enroll in one honors seminar that is designed to stimulate thoughtful discussion and creativity and to develop communications skills. Honors seminars are limited to a student-faculty ratio of 20:1 and are taught by some of the best teachers in the University. All classes are interdisciplinary, and many are team-taught.

The first two years are structured similarly. All students and faculty members at each level meet in a large-group session one day each week for activities such as lectures, panel discussions, case studies, and student presentations; another class meeting each week is spent in small-group preceptorials. Professors meet with the same small groups throughout the year. Third-year seminars meet as independent classes with an emphasis on synthesizing the students' experiences during the previous two years. Many are introduced to graduate-level research activities.

During the senior year, students may choose to continue the sequence of honors seminars, complete a research-based honors thesis, or participate in one of the Honors College study-abroad programs in Italy, Spain, or the Caribbean.

The unique nature of the College extends far beyond the classroom door. The Honors College Society organizes social and community service activities. The faculty and staff members of the Honors College make every effort to ensure that students are aware of the many opportunities available to them, such as fellowships, internships, and summer-study programs. Every year, as the result of this mentoring, many students win national awards and travel throughout the country for funded activities, and teams of students and faculty members travel to regional and national conferences to make presentations.

Students who complete all graduation requirements receive special recognition at commencement, a medallion, and a notation on their transcripts indicating that they graduated through the Honors College.

Admission Process: Admission to the Honors College is selective and limited. Students are admitted only at the beginning of each academic year (fall term). Freshmen with at least a 3.5 overall high school GPA and commensurate scores on the SAT or ACT are eligible for admission to the College. Transfer and continuing FIU students who have maintained a minimum 3.3 GPA in all college-level work and have at least two full academic years remaining in their undergraduate programs are eligible for admission to the College.

Scholarship Availability: Various private and institutional scholarships are available at both the freshman and transfer levels.

Campus Overview

State-supported university, founded 1965, part of State University System of Florida • **Coed** 28,865 undergraduate students, 59% full-time, 56% women, 44% men.

Undergraduates 16,955 full-time, 11,910 part-time. Students come from 52 states and territories, 115 other countries, 5% are from out of state, 13% African American, 4% Asian American or Pacific Islander, 58% Hispanic American, 0.2% Native American, 6% international, 8% transferred in, 7% live on campus.

Faculty *Total:* 1,459, 53% full-time, 54% with terminal degrees. *Student/faculty ratio:* 17:1.

Academic Programs *Special study options:* accelerated degree program, adult/continuing education programs, advanced placement credit, cooperative education, distance learning, double majors, English as a second language, freshman honors college, honors programs, independent study, internships, off-campus study, part-time degree program, services for LD students, study abroad, summer session for credit. *ROTC:* Army (b), Air Force (b).

Athletics Member NCAA. All Division I. *Intercollegiate sports:* baseball M(s), basketball M(s)/W(s), cross-country running M(s)/W(s), football M(s), golf W(s), soccer M(s)/W(s), softball W(s), tennis W(s), track and field M(s)/W(s), volleyball W(s). *Intramural sports:* basketball M/W, bowling M/W, cross-country running M/W, football M, golf M/W, lacrosse M, racquetball M/W, rugby M, sailing M/W, soccer M/W, softball M/W, swimming and diving M/W, table tennis M/W, tennis M/W, volleyball M/W, weight lifting M/W.

Costs (2004–05) *Tuition:* state resident $2914 full-time, $97 per credit hour part-time; nonresident $15,420 full-time, $514 per credit hour part-time. Full-time tuition and fees vary according to course load. Part-time tuition and fees vary according to course load. *Required fees:* $244 full-time, $122 per term part-time. *Room and board:* $8860; room only: $5336. Room and board charges vary according to housing facility.

Financial Aid 660 Federal Work-Study jobs (averaging $2558). In 2002, 515 non-need-based awards were made. *Average percent of need met:* 53%. *Average financial aid package:* $6140. *Average need-based loan:* $3933. *Average need-based gift aid:* $5067. *Average non-need-based aid:* $1919.

Contact: Dean: Dr. Ivelaw L. Griffith, University Park, DM 233, Miami, Florida 33199; *Telephone:* 305-348-4100; *Fax:* 305-348-2118; *E-mail:* griffiti@fiu.edu

Florida State University
University Honors Program
Tallahassee, Florida

The Florida State University (FSU) Honors Program is intended to assist talented and motivated students in taking advantage of the best opportunities at FSU, a Carnegie Research I institution with world-class educational and research programs in a broad range of fields from the sciences to the arts and humanities. The honors experience at FSU begins in the student's first fall semester with the Honors Colloquium, a weekly gathering where students meet some of the University's outstanding researchers and scholars. In addition, the colloquium introduces students to other opportunities available at FSU such as international study. Honors courses feature small class sizes (generally fewer than 30 students), and honors seminars provide in-depth introductions to some of the most exciting research being done on campus directly from the professors performing the research. Approximately eighty honors courses and seminars are available each year.

Students who complete 18 honors credits are awarded the University Honors Medallion. These honors credits can be accumulated in honors classes, in research and creative activities, and in other individual study activities that meet Honors Program standards and are approved by the Director of the Honors Office. Honors Program students are encouraged to complete their Honors Medallion credits by completing an Honors Thesis with a faculty expert in their major area of study.

First-year students in the Honors Program have the opportunity to reside in the Honors Housing Complex. In the fall of 2006, the reopening of the newly renovated Landis Hall and its addition to the Honors Housing Complex is anticipated.

Honors Program students have access to the honors advising staff and are entitled to the priority registration privilege.

Funding to support Honors Program students engaged in research and international study is available on a competitive basis through the Bess Ward Endowment.

FSU has recently opened the Office of National Fellowships (ONF) to assist students in preparing for national scholarship competitions. The Director of ONF works with students on a one-on-one basis and in credit-bearing classroom situations to develop the skills necessary to compete successfully.

The University Honors Program admits approximately 600 students per year.

Participation Requirements: Students must maintain at least a 3.2 cumulative GPA. The Honors Colloquium is required during the student's first fall semester.

Admission Process: Students must have at least a 3.9 weighted high school GPA (as calculated by the FSU Office of Admissions) and either a minimum 1300 SAT I or a minimum 29 ACT score to be invited to apply to the Honors Program.

Scholarship Availability: Academic scholarships are awarded by the FSU Undergraduate Admissions Office.

Campus Overview

State-supported university, founded 1851, part of State University System of Florida • **Coed** 30,373 undergraduate students, 88% full-time, 57% women, 43% men.

Undergraduates 26,608 full-time, 3,765 part-time. Students come from 51 states and territories, 126 other countries, 15% are from out of state, 12% African American, 3% Asian American or Pacific Islander, 10% Hispanic American, 0.4% Native American, 0.5% international, 7% transferred in, 14% live on campus.

Faculty Total: 1,486, 74% full-time, 92% with terminal degrees. Student/faculty ratio: 22:1.

Academic Programs Special study options: accelerated degree program, adult/continuing education programs, advanced placement credit, cooperative education, distance learning, double majors, English as a second language, honors programs, independent study, internships, off-campus study, part-time degree program, services for LD students, study abroad, summer session for credit. ROTC: Army (b), Navy (c), Air Force (b). Unusual degree programs: 3-2 emotional disturbances/learning disabilities.

Athletics Member NCAA. All Division I except football (Division I-A). Intercollegiate sports: baseball M(s), basketball M(s)/W(s), bowling M(c)/W(c), cheerleading M/W, cross-country running M(s)/W(s), golf M(s)/W(s), rugby M(c)/W(c), soccer M(c)/W(s), softball W(s), swimming and diving M(s)/W(s), table tennis M(c)/W(c), tennis M(s)/W(s), track and field M(s)/W(s), volleyball M(c)/W(s), wrestling M(c)/W(c). Intramural sports: badminton M(c)/W(c), basketball M/W, bowling M/W, crew M(c)/W(c), equestrian sports M(c)/W(c), fencing M(c)/W(c), football M/W, golf M/W, ice hockey M(c)/W(c), lacrosse M(c)/W(c), racquetball M/W, sailing M(c)/W(c), soccer M/W, softball M/W, squash M(c)/W(c), swimming and diving M/W, table tennis M/W, tennis M/W, track and field M/W, ultimate Frisbee M(c)/W(c), volleyball M/W, water polo M(c)/W(c), weight lifting M/W, wrestling M/W.

Costs (2004–05) Tuition: state resident $3038 full-time, $101 per credit hour part-time; nonresident $15,544 full-time, $518 per credit hour part-time. Full-time tuition and fees vary according to location. Part-time tuition and fees vary according to location. Room and board: $7208; room only: $4170. Room and board charges vary according to board plan and housing facility.

Financial Aid 710 Federal Work-Study jobs (averaging $1887). In 2004, 3411 non-need-based awards were made. Average percent of need met: 83%. Average financial aid package: $8269. Average need-based loan: $3939. Average need-based gift aid: $3917. Average non-need-based aid: $2302.

Contact: Director: Dr. Paul Cotte, 3600 UCA, Florida State University, Tallahassee, Florida 32306-2380; Telephone: 850-644-1841; Fax: 850-644-2101; Web site: http://honors.fsu.edu

Hillsborough Community College
Honors Institute
Tampa, Florida

Hillsborough Community College's (HCC) Honors Institute is designed to provide an intellectually stimulating academic program for exceptionally talented and motivated students. The overall goal of the program is to provide an academic atmosphere in which students learn to think critically, to grow intellectually, and to mature as responsible citizens and leaders. Academic emphasis is on encouraging students to present scholarly papers and projects, to use primary sources, to participate in alternative learning strategies, and to experience related cultural and social activities.

Known and respected for their excellence in teaching, the honors professors are dedicated to inspiring and challenging the students to make the most of their educational experiences. The majority of the honors professors have designed the honors courses that they teach. Currently, thirty-two honors courses have been developed across the curriculum. As risk takers, the honors professors experiment with alternative learning strategies to foster an environment that results in creative interaction and intellectual flexibility for both professors and students. Cultural excursions and other extracurricular activities within the courses are always encouraged and subsidized by the Honors Institute. Honors courses are offered on all four campuses. All students are required to take the honors leadership course, which includes a service learning component. All honors courses are capped at 15 students.

In addition to enhanced educational opportunities, honors students have other advantages that help them develop individually and as members of the honors group. All four campuses have fully equipped honors study lounges that are accessible only to honors students. These gathering places provide an atmosphere for healthy competition and camaraderie among the students. The rooms provide seclusion for studying and comfortable areas for socializing. With the Honors Institute emphasis on being student driven, all honors students are members of the Arete Club. The students also may apply to serve as honors ambassadors. Each fall, the Honors Institute generously subsidizes a state-side trip. The trip is designed around a particular theme, with an honors professor serving as the expert on the topic and traveling with the students. In February of each year, a select honors delegation travels to Boston to participate in the Harvard National Model United Nations. This activity is fully funded by the Honors Institute. Also funded by the Institute, the Brain Bowl Teams compete with other college Brain Bowl Teams. The Honors Institute sponsors student trips to state, regional, and national honors conferences each year. Every spring, the Honors Institute subsidizes a trip to another country so that the students can experience the world beyond the textbook. Students have traveled to such countries as Russia, China, Ecuador, Greece, and Peru. The program began in 1996 and currently enrolls 220 students.

Participation Requirements: Students must take a minimum of eight honors courses (24 credit hours). The College president hosts a special luncheon for the honors graduates. At the College commencement ceremony, the honors graduates are presented with honors medallions and receive diplomas with the Honors Institute seal. Students who do not fulfill all Honors Institute requirements but complete at least 12 hours of honors credit with a minimum overall GPA of at least 3.0 earn the HCC Honors Institute certificate. Each year, 100 percent of the Honors Institute graduates transfer to the universities of their choice. A majority of the students transfer to prestigious institutions on full or partial scholarships.

Admission Process: Students must complete the HCC application forms for admission and the HCC Honors Institute application forms, which include high school or college transcripts and a written recommendation from a high school or college faculty member. Applicants must meet a least one of the following criteria to qualify for the Honors Institute: a minimum high school GPA of 3.5 on a 4.0 scale; a minimum high school GPA of 3.4 on a 5.0 scale; a minimum SAT I combined score of 1160 or ACT composite score of 26; a minimum SAT I combined score of 1050, ACT composite score of 25, CPT writing score of 90 or higher, or CPT reading score of 92 for students who graduated in the top 10 percent of their class; a minimum GPA of 3.3 for 12 hours of dual enrollment; or a minimum cumulative GPA of 3.3 or higher with a minimum of 6 semester hours of college credit. For the fall term, the application deadline with scholarship consideration is February 15. Students should apply by December 1 for the spring term.

Scholarship Availability: Full tuition and $650 per fall and spring semesters are offered on a competitive basis.

Campus Overview

State-supported 2-year, founded 1968, part of Florida Community College System • **Coed** 22,149 undergraduate students, 32% full-time, 59% women, 41% men.

Undergraduates 7,009 full-time, 15,140 part-time. Students come from 40 states and territories, 100 other countries, 4% are from out of state, 19% African American, 4% Asian American or Pacific Islander, 19% Hispanic American, 0.4% Native American, 0.8% international, 19% transferred in.

Faculty *Total:* 774, 30% full-time, 10% with terminal degrees. *Student/faculty ratio:* 28:1.

Academic Programs *Special study options:* academic remediation for entering students, adult/continuing education programs, advanced placement credit, cooperative education, distance learning, English as a second language, honors programs, off-campus study, part-time degree program, services for LD students, summer session for credit. *ROTC:* Army (c), Air Force (c).

Athletics Member NJCAA. *Intercollegiate sports:* baseball M(s), basketball M(s)/W(s), softball W(s), tennis W(s), volleyball W(s).

Costs (2004–05) *Tuition:* state resident $1833 full-time, $61 per credit hour part-time; nonresident $6835 full-time, $228 per credit hour part-time.

Contact: Director: Dr. Lydia Lyons, HCC Honors Institute, 10414 East Columbus Drive, Tampa, Florida 33619; *Telephone:* 813-253-7894; *Fax:* 813-253-7940; *Web site:* http://www.hccfl.edu/honors

---

Indian River Community College
Honors Program
Ft. Pierce, Florida

The Honors Program at Indian River Community College (IRCC) provides students with the opportunity to expand their academic horizon and enter into a shared inquiry that leads them to develop their intellectual capacities beyond the scope of the standard Associate of Arts degree.

Participation Requirements: A prospective honors student at IRCC must have a cumulative grade point average of 3.5 or higher on a 4-point scale, an ACT composite score of 26 or higher, an SAT combined score of 1100 or higher, or a cumulative college grade point average of 3.3 or higher, with a minimum of 12 credit hours, excluding college preparatory courses, or a combined College Placement Test score of 280 or above.

Students must successfully complete all degree requirements and at least one Honors Interdisciplinary Seminar, at least two intermediate-level course sequences in a foreign language, the service learning project, and a capstone project. They are expected to attend fine arts performances and participate in campus activities such as Brain Bowland CCG and are encouraged to participate in IRCC study abroad.

To receive an honors diploma, in addition to or as part of the degree requirements, students must complete 24 hours of honors-designed credit, 25 hours of documented service learning, and an acceptable honors capstone project and attain an overall GPA of 3.5 or better.

To receive an honors certificate, in addition to or as part of the degree requirements, students must complete 15 hours of honors-designated credit and 10 hours of documented service learning and attain an overall GPA of 3.5 or better.

Honors credit may be earned by completing one honors interdisciplinary seminar, the honors capstone project, and 6 hours of honors English. If an honors student has completed one or more traditional English courses, he or she may substitute the Advanced College Writing and/or World Literature course. Three additional honors credit hours are required for the honors certificate.

Admission Process: Students must apply to the Honors Program and write a proctored essay on a topic of the Honors Committee's choice and interview with the Honors Committee. If accepted to the program, an invitation is issued.

Scholarship Availability: There are five honors scholarships currently available, and students may be eligible for IRCC scholarships as well as multiple scholarships available for transferring students.

Campus Overview

State-supported 2-year, founded 1960, part of Florida Community College System • **Coed** 38,464 undergraduate students.

Undergraduates Students come from 33 states and territories, 2% are from out of state, 17% African American, 1% Asian American or Pacific Islander, 12% Hispanic American, 0.4% Native American.

Faculty *Total:* 1,562, 10% full-time.

Academic Programs *Special study options:* academic remediation for entering students, adult/continuing education programs, advanced placement credit, distance learning, English as a second language, independent study, part-time degree program, services for LD students, summer session for credit.

Athletics Member NJCAA. *Intercollegiate sports:* baseball M(s), basketball M(s)/W(s), softball W(s), swimming and diving M(s)/W(s), volleyball W(s). *Intramural sports:* basketball M/W, racquetball M/W, soccer M, volleyball M/W.

Costs (2004–05) *Tuition:* state resident $1740 full-time, $58 per credit part-time; nonresident $6570 full-time, $219 per credit part-time.

Financial Aid 130 Federal Work-Study jobs (averaging $1500).

Contact: Dean of Arts and Sciences, Dr. Henri Sue Bynum, Indian River Community College Main Campus, 3209 Virginia Avenue, Ft. Pierce, Florida 34981-5596; *Telephone:* 772-462-4722; *Web site:* http://www.ircc.edu

Nova Southeastern University
Undergraduate Honors Program
Ft. Lauderdale, Florida

The Undergraduate Honors Program at Nova Southeastern University serves academically talented students who are committed to personal and professional excellence and have a thirst for knowledge. In addition to creative and diverse honors courses and seminars (capped at 15 students), the program offers cocurricular programs and activities that foster individual growth as well as community spirit. Honors students meet with distinguished speakers and visitors in private seminars. Honors students sponsor and plan unique social events. Honors students enjoy early registration privileges. The Honors Program funds student research and travel to regional and national conferences and provides grants for study abroad. The undergraduate honors program serves approximately 160 students.

The Undergraduate Honors Program includes two distinct programs: General Honors and Divisional Honors. General Honors serves freshman and sophomore students and requires the completion of 15 (or more) credits of honors course work. Students must maintain a minimum 3.4 cumulative grade point average. Successful completion leads to the Citation in General Honors, a notation on the student's transcript, and recognition at graduation. Honors course work includes unique seminars and honors versions of core courses. Honors faculty members are specially selected and spend time with students outside of class in cocurricular programs. Students can also use honors course work to satisfy general education and/or major course requirements.

Divisional Honors serves junior and senior students and requires successful completion of a senior honors thesis. Students complete and defend a comprehensive thesis proposal, which is then funded. With assistance from faculty advisers/mentors, students engage in research and scholarship, culminating in the senior thesis (and, often, published articles and presentations at regional or national or international conferences). Successful completion leads to the Citation in Divisional Honors, a notation on the student's transcript, and recognition at graduation.

Honors students are actively supported to explore distinguished fellowships and scholarships. An honors seminar is offered for students seriously considering national and international fellowships.

A student-directed Honors Student Association sponsors numerous cocurricular activities throughout the year. Additional programs and events are hosted by the Honors Program Office and the dean. The Honors Student Association strives to create a spirit of community and engagement among students and faculty members. Recent events include Dinner and Movie Night, Faculty-Student Trivial Pursuit Challenge, and several Ice Cream and Faculty Socials. Recent distinguished speakers who have conducted small seminars for honors students include such national and international leaders as the Dalai Lama, Paul Bremer, and Bob Woodward.

Honors students are also eligible to participate in dual admissions, securing enrollment in graduate and professional school programs, including medical and dental schools, law school, and graduate programs in business and education.

Participation Requirements: Academic progress of honors students is reviewed regularly. Students who fall below course and grade requirements are invited to petition for continued affiliation. Participation in cocurricular programs supports continued honors program affiliation.

Students seeking the Citation in General Honors must complete a minimum of 15 credits of honors course work and maintain a minimum 3.4 cumulative grade point average. Student seeking the Citation in Divisional Honors must complete a senior honors thesis and maintain a minimum 3.4 cumulative grade point average.

Admission Process: Prospective honors students may apply for affiliation based on previous academic performance (high school or college/transfer). The program seeks to enroll students in the top 10 percent of entering students by academic major (using grades, standardized test scores, and class rank). The application includes three short essays. Applications and essays are reviewed by a Faculty Selection Committee. There are no specific minimum scores or grades required for honors affiliation. The average SAT score for entering honors students this past year was 1220 (composite math and verbal scores). The average high school grade point average for entering honors students this past year was 4.2 (weighted).

Students presently attending Nova Southeastern University may also apply based on their current and recent academic performance and references from current faculty members.

Scholarship Availability: Several scholarships are available to students in the Undergraduate Honors Program. Nearly all honors students qualify for significant merit-based Honor Awards. Additional need-based honor scholarships are also awarded. Honors students are awarded a Residence Hall Scholarship, which supplements partial costs for campus housing. Honors students may apply for scholarships for Leadership, Service, and Involvement. First Week Scholarships are awarded to first-year honors students based on initial contact and engagement with faculty members and student leaders. Distinguished Honors Student Scholarships are awarded to students based on extended records of participation and performance in honors. Additional grants are available to all honors students to supplement costs of study abroad and international travel.

Campus Overview

Independent university, founded 1964 • **Coed** 5,355 undergraduate students, 63% full-time, 74% women, 26% men.

Undergraduates 3,351 full-time, 2,004 part-time. Students come from 53 states and territories, 42 other countries, 37% are from out of state, 27% African American, 4% Asian American or Pacific Islander, 25% Hispanic American, 0.4% Native American, 7% international, 5% transferred in, 9% live on campus.

Faculty *Total:* 1,531, 35% full-time. *Student/faculty ratio:* 12:1.

Academic Programs *Special study options:* academic remediation for entering students, accelerated degree program, adult/continuing education programs, advanced placement credit, cooperative education, distance learning, double majors, honors programs, internships, part-time degree program, services for LD students, study abroad, summer session for credit. *Unusual degree programs:* 3-2 marine biology, occupational therapy, psychology, mental health counseling, speech language pathology, computer science, education, physical therapy.

Athletics Member NCAA, NAIA. All NCAA Division II. *Intercollegiate sports:* baseball M(s), basketball M(s)/W(s), cheerleading W, crew W(s), cross-country running M(s)/W(s), golf M(s)/W(s), soccer M(s)/W(s), softball W(s), tennis W(s), volleyball W(s). *Intramural sports:* basketball M, cross-country running M/W, football M, golf M, soccer M/W, softball W, tennis M/W, volleyball W.

Costs (2004–05) *Comprehensive fee:* $23,946 includes full-time tuition ($15,600), mandatory fees ($220), and room and board ($8126). Full-time tuition and fees vary according to class time and program. Part-time tuition: $520 per credit hour. Part-time tuition and fees vary according to class time, course load, and program. *College room only:* $5662. Room and board charges vary according to board plan and housing facility.

Financial Aid 1,018 Federal Work-Study jobs (averaging $6284). 261 state and other part-time jobs (averaging $3029). In 2004, 276 non-need-based awards were made. *Average percent of need met:* 64%. *Average financial aid package:* $14,653. *Average need-based loan:* $5192. *Average need-based gift aid:* $7551. *Average non-need-based aid:* $3595.

Contact: Dean: Dr. Don Rosenblum, Farquhar College of Arts and Sciences, Office of the Dean, Nova Southeastern University, 3301 College Avenue, Ft. Lauderdale, Florida 33314; *Telephone:* 954-262-8408; *Fax:* 954-262-3930; *E-mail:* honors@nsu.nova.edu; *Web site:* http://www.undergrad.nova.edu/honors/

Palm Beach Atlantic University
Frederick M. Supper Honors Program
West Palm Beach, Florida

The Frederick M. Supper Honors Program at Palm Beach Atlantic University (PBA) provides motivated students from all majors with the opportunity to participate in a community of scholars. Members of this community share a genuine passion for intellectual contemplation and discussion, and they encourage, challenge, and support one another in the endeavor to seek wisdom.

To develop a thoughtful and insightful Christian worldview, honors students take seminar classes based on reading and discussing the great works of human civilization. These works, referred to as the Great Conversation, integrate literature, history, religion, philosophy, art, and science, and they address timeless questions and issues that continue to shape society's worldviews. These works serve as a core curriculum to educate students broadly for any vocation. Because of the focus on character formation, honors courses help students prepare for any career and, more importantly, for life. The program is intended to produce servant leaders who glorify God in word, thought, and deed.

Honors courses are kept small to encourage students to interact with one another and to develop relationships with honors faculty members. Faculty members embrace the opportunity to serve as academic role models who mentor students inside and outside the classroom. Likewise, students in the Honors Program learn a great deal from one another and provide leadership for the greater campus community. The sense of community is enhanced by honors housing and a number of honors travel-study opportunities. Members of the Honors Program form a cohesive group of scholars on campus, and they often establish friendships that last a lifetime.

Located in the heart of downtown West Palm Beach, Florida, PBA affords excellent opportunities for honors students to attend and participate in cultural and social events. These activities are often integrated into the classroom experience. Palm Beach Atlantic also requires its students to give time in service to the community. There are countless ways that students can serve, and these activities often become important social and intellectual experiences for honors students.

Graduates of the program have been very successful in graduate school, law school, medical school, and seminary. They have also had successful careers in business, education, communication, politics, law, and other areas.

Founded in 1989, the program enrolls an average of 100 students.

Participation Requirements: Honors students take worldview courses that integrate various disciplines from the humanities, including history, philosophy, literature, art, and religion. These courses substitute for a significant portion of the University's general core curriculum. Students also take honors versions of core courses, including public speaking and composition. In addition, honors students take seminar courses exploring issues in Christianity, non-Western civilizations, economics, political science, and the philosophy of science. Honors students also complete a senior project in their major or some other area of interest.

To remain in good standing, students must maintain a minimum 3.5 cumulative GPA and may not receive more than one C in honors course work.

Students who successfully complete the program and graduate from the University are recognized by a note on their transcript, a seal on their diploma, and special recognition at commencement. Honors alumni maintain ties to one another and the program through several communication channels, including a newsletter.

Admission Process: Acceptance is based on high performance on the ACT (29 or above) or SAT (1300 or above) and on outstanding high school grades (minimum 3.5 GPA on a 4.0 scale or a ranking in the top 5 percent of their class). Students also write an essay expressing their understanding of and desire to participate in the Frederick M. Supper Honors Program. An interview may also be scheduled with members of the honors committee. Students not meeting these requirements may be considered on a case-by-case basis by the honors committee.

Scholarship Availability: Financial aid is not directly linked to the Honors Program, but other financial assistance, including scholarships, grants, loans, and part-time employment, is available to honors students at Palm Beach Atlantic. Students who live in the honors residence hall receive a significant housing discount.

Campus Overview

Independent nondenominational comprehensive, founded 1968 • **Coed** 2,406 undergraduate students, 92% full-time, 62% women, 38% men.

Undergraduates 2,211 full-time, 195 part-time. Students come from 46 states and territories, 17 other countries, 26% are from out of state, 15% African American, 1% Asian American or Pacific Islander, 8% Hispanic American, 0.4% Native American, 3% international, 12% transferred in, 45% live on campus.

Faculty *Total:* 253, 55% full-time. *Student/faculty ratio:* 12:1.

Academic Programs *Special study options:* academic remediation for entering students, accelerated degree program, adult/continuing education programs, advanced placement credit, cooperative education, double majors, English as a second language, freshman honors college, honors programs, independent study, internships, part-time degree program, study abroad, summer session for credit.

Athletics Member NCAA. All Division II. *Intercollegiate sports:* baseball M, basketball M/W, cross-country running M/W, golf M, soccer M/W, softball W, tennis M/W, volleyball M/W. *Intramural sports:* basketball M/W, bowling M/W, cheerleading M/W, football M/W, lacrosse M, racquetball M/W, soccer M/W, table tennis M/W, ultimate Frisbee M/W, volleyball M/W.

Costs (2005–06) *Comprehensive fee:* $23,648 includes full-time tuition ($17,130), mandatory fees ($212), and room and board

($6306). Full-time tuition and fees vary according to course load, degree level, program, and reciprocity agreements. Part-time tuition: $420 per credit. Part-time tuition and fees vary according to course load, degree level, program, and reciprocity agreements. *Required fees:* $85 per term part-time. *College room only:* $3350. Room and board charges vary according to board plan and housing facility.

Financial Aid 215 Federal Work-Study jobs (averaging $1673). In 2003, 636 non-need-based awards were made. *Average percent of need met:* 63%. *Average financial aid package:* $10,659. *Average need-based loan:* $3256. *Average need-based gift aid:* $2059. *Average non-need-based aid:* $1684.

Contact: Director: Dr. Thomas St.Antoine, Honors Program, Palm Beach Atlantic University, P.O. Box 24708, West Palm Beach, Florida 33416-4708; *Telephone:* 561-803-2279; *Fax:* 561-803-2280; *E-mail:* tom_stantoine@pba.edu; *Web site:* http://www.pba.edu

Palm Beach Community College

Honors Program

Lake Worth, Florida

Honors at Palm Beach Community College (PBCC) pursues a more active and interactive learning environment in which students and faculty members share responsibility for attaining a more creative and comprehensive understanding and deeper analytical interpretation of course concepts and their applications in an interdisciplinary and global context.

PBCC's Honors Program serves approximately 200 students each term. PBCC students can participate in honors by enrolling in honors courses or through the completion of honors project contracts in any credit course.

Honors classes are offered for many general education courses. Honors class sizes at PBCC are smaller, from 6 to 15 students, thus allowing for more discussion, presentations, and in-depth learning. Students develop critical-thinking and research skills in collaborative learning environments that may include field trips, field experiments, and guest speakers. Students learn to use discipline-specific research methodologies and primary resources as they collect, analyze, and evaluate data. If the student chooses to complete an honors project, the student and faculty member sign a contract in which the student agrees to complete a research paper in the course with the guidance of the faculty member.

Participation Requirements: The student is admitted to the Honors Program when the student has a cumulative GPA of at least 3.5 for both PBCC and non-PBCC course work; fewer than 12 PBCC credits but minimum scores of 26 on the ACT, 1170 on the SAT, and 97 CPT Reading and 97 CPT Writing; or a PBCC grade point average of at least 3.5 and 12 hours of PBCC credit. If a student's transcript from another institution is older than 5 years, it is not used in calculating the eligibility for automatic admission into the Honors Program. If it is more recent than 5 years, it is used in calculating eligibility. Should the student's GPA be between 3.4 and 3.5, the student may be granted provisional acceptance into the Honors Program.

Upon completion of 12 credit hours of honors course work while maintaining a minimum 3.5 GPA, students become eligible to apply for honors graduation. Honors graduates receive an honors graduate notation on their transcript and an honors seal on their diploma.

Admission Process: There is no application process for the Honors Program. Students must meet the eligibility requirements to enroll in classes or complete honors projects.

Scholarship Availability: PBCC does not offer honors scholarships; however, transfer scholarships to universities are available.

Campus Overview

State-supported 2-year, founded 1933, part of Florida Community College System • **Coed** 24,024 undergraduate students, 31% full-time, 59% women, 41% men.

Undergraduates 7,403 full-time, 16,621 part-time. Students come from 49 states and territories, 138 other countries, 5% are from out of state, 10% transferred in.

Faculty *Total:* 1,164, 21% full-time, 13% with terminal degrees. *Student/faculty ratio:* 22:1.

Academic Programs *Special study options:* academic remediation for entering students, adult/continuing education programs, advanced placement credit, cooperative education, distance learning, double majors, English as a second language, freshman honors college, honors programs, independent study, internships, off-campus study, part-time degree program, services for LD students, student-designed majors, study abroad, summer session for credit.

Athletics Member NJCAA. *Intercollegiate sports:* baseball M(s), basketball M(s)/W(s), softball W(s), volleyball M(s)/W(s). *Intramural sports:* basketball M/W, bowling M/W, football M/W, racquetball M/W, soccer M, tennis M/W, volleyball M/W.

Costs (2004–05) *Tuition:* state resident $1740 full-time, $58 per credit part-time; nonresident $6540 full-time, $215 per credit part-time. *Required fees:* $300 full-time, $10 per term part-time. *Room and board:* room only: $6000.

Contact: Dr. Steven Konopacki, Director of Honors, Palm Beach Community College, 4200 Congress Avenue, Lake Worth, Florida 33461; *Telephone:* 561-868-3520; *E-mail:* konopacs@pbcc.cc.fl.us; *Web site:* http://www.pbcc.cc.fl.us/honors/

Rollins College

Honors Degree Program

Winter Park, Florida

Rollins College offers a special program in the liberal arts for students with exceptional abilities. The Honors Degree Program provides unusual breadth in the liberal arts and exceptional depth in the student's chosen major. Successful completion of the Honors curriculum leads to a distinct and separate undergraduate degree, Artium Baccalaureus (A.B.) Honoris—the Honors Bachelor of Arts degree.

Honors students complete a core of interdisciplinary courses designed to provide an integrated understanding of the liberal arts. A series of four team-taught seminars during their first and second years introduces students to the various methods of inquiry in the liberal arts. These courses substitute for some of the general education requirements of the regular A.B. program and are designed to teach students to think and write critically across a broad range of disciplines, to encourage a synthetic interdisciplinary understanding of the liberal arts, and to encourage and prepare students to be independent thinkers. Honors seminars in the third and fourth years support significant independent research projects that represent the culmination of students' careers at Rollins.

First-year honors students also live in the same housing unit so that they can easily continue their conversations from class and participate in special programs specifically designed for honors students. These living arrangements significantly enhance the experience of community so unique to the honors program.

Participation Requirements: Honors degree students must take a special team-taught honors seminar in each of their first four semesters at the College. These seminars are designed to encourage students to think across traditional disciplinary boundaries. Adventurous students are encouraged to spend a semester away from the campus (usually during the junior year) pursuing experiential learning, study abroad, or some other exceptional educational opportunity. Seniors engage in a two-term independent research project in their major fields. Honors degree students are expected to maintain a cumulative GPA of at least 3.33 at all times. Successful graduates receive special recognition at Commencement and are awarded a distinctive degree—the Artium Baccalaureus Honoris.

Admission Process: Entering first-year students are invited to join the Honors Degree Program only if their high school records show evidence of a special scholastic aptitude and attitude. Candidates for admission are evaluated by reference to their high school grades, standardized test scores (SAT or ACT), and quality of application essay. Honors students normally constitute the top 10 percent of the Rollins entering class. Invitation to join the program is extended at the time of notice of admission to the College.

Students who transfer to Rollins at or prior to the beginning of their sophomore year may be considered for admission to the Honors Degree Program as well. A few students are invited into the program at the end of the freshman year based on outstanding academic achievement during the first year at Rollins.

Scholarship Availability: There are no scholarships specifically related to the Honors Degree Program, though most honors students receive merit-based and need-based financial aid for attending Rollins.

Campus Overview

Independent comprehensive, founded 1885 • **Coed** 1,759 undergraduate students, 100% full-time, 60% women, 40% men.

Undergraduates 1,759 full-time. Students come from 46 states and territories, 43 other countries, 51% are from out of state, 5% African American, 4% Asian American or Pacific Islander, 8% Hispanic American, 0.5% Native American, 3% international, 3% transferred in, 66% live on campus.

Faculty *Total:* 229, 78% full-time, 79% with terminal degrees. *Student/faculty ratio:* 11:1.

Academic Programs *Special study options:* academic remediation for entering students, accelerated degree program, adult/continuing education programs, advanced placement credit, double majors, honors programs, independent study, internships, off-campus study, part-time degree program, services for LD students, student-designed majors, study abroad. *Unusual degree programs:* 3-2 engineering with Washington University in St. Louis, Columbia University, Georgia Institute of Technology, Case Western Reserve University, Auburn University; forestry with Duke University; nursing with Emory University; medical technology, environmental management with Duke University.

Athletics Member NCAA. All Division II. *Intercollegiate sports:* baseball M(s), basketball M(s)/W(s), cheerleading M/W, crew M/W, cross-country running M/W, golf M(s)/W(s), sailing M(c)/W(c), soccer M(s)/W(s), softball W(s), swimming and diving M/W, tennis M(s)/W(s), volleyball W(s). *Intramural sports:* basketball M/W, bowling M/W, football M/W, soccer M/W, softball M, table tennis M/W, tennis M/W, volleyball M/W.

Costs (2004–05) *Comprehensive fee:* $36,270 includes full-time tuition ($26,910), mandatory fees ($790), and room and board ($8570). *College room only:* $5000.

Financial Aid In 2004, 219 non-need-based awards were made. *Average percent of need met:* 93%. *Average financial aid package:* $26,666. *Average need-based loan:* $4844. *Average need-based gift aid:* $21,699. *Average non-need-based aid:* $8439.

Contact: Director: Professor Barry Levis, Honors Degree Program, Rollins College, Box 2762, 1000 Holt Avenue, Winter Park, Florida 32789-4499; *Telephone:* 407-646-2437; *Fax:* 407-646-2363; *E-mail:* blevis@rollins.edu

Saint Leo University
Honors Program
Saint Leo, Florida

The Saint Leo University Honors Program consists of an integrated sequence of six interdisciplinary courses that are spread over the first three years of college. In addition, there is an extensive senior-year honors project that is carried out under the supervision of a distinguished faculty mentor.

Honors courses focus on the reading, interpretation, and assimilation of great books in the liberal arts and sciences. Informed absorption of great ideas, rather than mere acquaintance with them, is the goal of the program. The Honors Program does not seek to provide a comprehensive treatment of world intellectual achievement or to undertake a survey of Western civilization. Its purpose is to probe in depth the original minds of a few significant thinkers, doers, and dreamers.

Honors courses are small in size and emphasize responsive writing, discussion, and collaborative learning. Each course has its own theme or focus supplied by the instructor, but the entire sequence of honors courses is carefully integrated so that knowledge obtained in one course applies directly to the next one. The Honors Program strives to reinforce the notion that a liberal arts education furnishes a coherent body of knowledge that serves the whole human being.

The Honors Program provides an alternative means of satisfying the general education requirements that all Saint Leo University students must fulfill. Students are therefore encouraged to apply regardless of their major. In the Honors Program, students representing a wide variety of intellectual perspectives meet on common ground, frequently debating controversial subjects and exploring personal concerns and interests.

The Honors Program, which has been in existence since 1982, admits 40 to 50 freshmen each year. There are approximately 100 students enrolled in the program.

All freshmen honors students are provided with free state-of-the-art computers and high-speed access to the Internet. Each honors class uses a Web site to supplement classroom learning and every student is expected to maintain a personal Web site as an academic portfolio. Students are frequently involved in activities that explore the boundaries of computer-enhanced learning.

Participation Requirements: In the freshman year, students take The Classical World View and The Christian Vision. The two freshmen English composition courses are linked to these core courses, so that learning and assignments are frequently shared. In the sophomore year, students take The Humanistic Tradition, which covers the period from the Renaissance to the Enlightenment and scientific revolutions. In the junior year, students take The Human Condition, which details the founding of the social sciences in the eighteenth and nineteenth centuries, and The Modern World View. Junior-year courses are taught in the Oxbridge tutorial style of small groups working quasi-independently. In the spring of the junior year, students take a 1-credit Honors Research Methods course to assist them in developing their senior-year honors project. During the entire senior year, students work independently on a research or creative project of their choice under the supervision of a faculty member. Seniors present the results of their projects in an evening forum open to the University community.

Students arriving from junior college honors programs may elect to join the Saint Leo University Honors Program in its third year. Students wishing to study abroad at the Saint Leo University Madrid campus may substitute a directed study abroad course for either of the junior year core courses.

To graduate from the program, students must complete the honors core requirements (18 credit hours for freshmen, 6 credit hours for transfer students), the research methods course, and the senior research project, 4 credit hours. In addition, students must maintain a minimum 3.0 GPA and have not received less than a B in two honors courses.

Upon graduation from the program, honors students receive a medallion to be worn during graduation ceremonies and an Honors Program Graduate distinction on their transcripts and diplomas.

Admission Process: To be eligible for participation in the Honors Program, freshman students must have at least a 3.25 GPA with a score of 1100 on the SAT I or 24 on the ACT. Transfer students must have 60 to 75 credit hours with a minimum 3.5 GPA or a minimum 3.25 GPA if they have been involved in honors courses at their previous college. All students must also submit a letter of recommendation from a teacher or instructor as well as a letter to the honors program director stating why they wish to participate in the Honors Program and what they feel they will add to the program. All students wishing to participate in the Honors Program must first complete the standard admission process and be admitted to Saint Leo University before applying to the Honors Program.

Scholarship Availability: Academic scholarships are available for both freshmen and transfer students entering the Honors Program. Freshmen receive a $3000 annual, renewable scholarship and a Pentium computer, which is theirs to keep after completing 60 credit hours and two years in the Honors Program. Freshmen who complete the Honors Program with a GPA of at least 3.5 also receive tuition remission worth approximately $6000 for their final semester.

Transfer students entering the Honors Program are awarded either a $3000 or $4000 annual, renewable scholarship that depends on their cumulative college GPA, but do not receive a computer. A $4500 scholarship is awarded to transfer students who are members of the Phi Theta Kappa Honor Society.

Campus Overview

Independent Roman Catholic comprehensive, founded 1889 • **Coed** 1,241 undergraduate students, 96% full-time, 55% women, 45% men.

Undergraduates 1,187 full-time, 54 part-time. Students come from 35 states and territories, 42 other countries, 31% are from out of state, 7% African American, 1% Asian American or Pacific Islander, 7% Hispanic American, 0.6% Native American, 6% international, 9% transferred in, 68% live on campus.

Faculty *Total:* 122, 52% full-time, 56% with terminal degrees. *Student/faculty ratio:* 15:1.

Academic Programs *Special study options:* academic remediation for entering students, adult/continuing education programs, advanced placement credit, distance learning, double majors, English as a second language, honors programs, independent study, internships, part-time degree program, services for LD students, study abroad, summer session for credit. *ROTC:* Army (b), Air Force (c).

Athletics Member NCAA. All Division II except baseball (Division I), men's and women's basketball (Division I), men's and women's cross-country running (Division I), field hockey (Division I). *Intercollegiate sports:* baseball M(s), basketball M(s)/W(s), crew M(s)(c)/W(s)(c), cross-country running M(s)/W(s), field hockey W(s), golf M(s)/W(s), lacrosse M(s), soccer M(s)/W(s), softball W(s), swimming and diving M(s)/W(s), tennis M(s)/W(s), volleyball W(s). *Intramural sports:* basketball M/W, field hockey W(c), football M/W, golf M/W, racquetball M/W, soccer M/W, softball M/W, table tennis M/W, tennis M/W, ultimate Frisbee M/W, volleyball M/W.

Costs (2004–05) *Comprehensive fee:* $21,340 includes full-time tuition ($13,650), mandatory fees ($430), and room and board ($7260). Full-time tuition and fees vary according to location. Part-time tuition and fees vary according to location. *College room only:* $3820. Room and board charges vary according to board plan and housing facility.

Financial Aid In 2002, 183 non-need-based awards were made. *Average percent of need met:* 88%. *Average financial aid package:* $17,695. *Average need-based loan:* $3691. *Average need-based gift aid:* $12,077. *Average non-need-based aid:* $5760.

Contact: Director: Dr. Hudson Reynolds, MC 2127, P.O. Box 6665, Saint Leo, Florida 33574-6665; *Telephone:* 352-588-8340; *E-mail:* reynolds@saintleo.edu; *Web site:* http://www.saintleo.edu/honors

Santa Fe Community College
Honors Program
Gainesville, Florida

*S*anta Fe Community College's (SFCC) Honors Program offers academically talented and motivated students a wide variety of special-topic 3-credit seminars and 1-credit colloquia, most of which are elective. All courses stress creative thinking, and many are interdisciplinary. The twenty-year-old program enrolls about 185 students and has recently been expanded to include honors sections or options for general education courses.

Participation Requirements: Students must take 15 hours of honors courses and maintain a GPA of at least 3.5 to graduate with an Honors Certificate. Students who have completed these requirements receive special recognition at graduation and an Honors Program designation on their transcript.

Admission Process: Students are eligible for honors courses after completing at least 12 hours of college credits at SFCC with a minimum 3.5 GPA, and they are invited into the program. Transfer students and those who do not meet these criteria may be enrolled in specific courses with special permission from the Honors Coordinator.

Scholarship Availability: Honors students can apply for special Honors Program scholarships and can also receive Board of Trustees scholarships available to the top 10 percent of the high school graduates from Bradford and Alachua Counties. Other scholarships for students who meet the criteria are available from the SFCC Endowment Corporation and the Florida Bright Futures Program.

Campus Overview

State and locally supported 2-year, founded 1966, part of Florida Community College System • **Coed** 13,806 undergraduate students, 48% full-time, 53% women, 47% men.

Undergraduates 6,560 full-time, 7,246 part-time. Students come from 46 states and territories, 80 other countries, 3% are from out of state, 12% African American, 3% Asian American or Pacific Islander, 8% Hispanic American, 0.7% Native American, 3% international, 11% transferred in.

Faculty *Total:* 782, 40% full-time.

Academic Programs *Special study options:* academic remediation for entering students, adult/continuing education programs, advanced placement credit, cooperative education, distance learning, English as a second language, honors programs, independent study, part-time degree program, services for LD students, student-designed majors, summer session for credit. *ROTC:* Army (c), Air Force (c).

Athletics Member NJCAA. *Intercollegiate sports:* baseball M(s), basketball M(s)/W(s), softball W(s). *Intramural sports:* basketball M/W, football M, golf M/W, racquetball M/W, soccer M/W, softball M/W, tennis M/W, volleyball M/W, weight lifting M/W.

Costs (2005–06) *Tuition:* state resident $1755 full-time, $59 per credit hour part-time; nonresident $6540 full-time, $218 per credit hour part-time.

Financial Aid 190 Federal Work-Study jobs.

Contact: Coordinator: Dr. Marisa McLeod, 3000 North West 83rd Street, Gainesville, Florida 32606; *Telephone:* 352-395-5010; *Web site:* http://www.sfcc.edu

Seminole Community College
Honors Institute
Sanford, Florida

The Honors Institute at Seminole Community College (SCC) has a 23-credit curriculum that offers all qualifying students a unique academic opportunity to broaden and enrich their college experiences. The primary goal is to provide an atmosphere in which talented students can learn to think critically, grow intellectually, and expand their education beyond the classroom and into the public arena. The Honors Institute offers enriching classes in all areas of the general education requirements. Students are encouraged to attend conferences to present scholarly papers as well as experience and participate in related cultural and social activities offered within the College and the community.

Upon completing a minimum of 23 honors credits, students in the program graduate with an Associate of Arts Honors Diploma. The Honors Institute also offers an Honors Certificate Program. Students who qualify for the Honors Diploma Program may elect to earn a minimum of 13 credit hours in honors classes to receive a certificate upon graduation. This allows students whose majors require a strict course of study to take some of their general education courses, such as English, speech, and humanities, within the Honors Institute.

Respected for their excellence in teaching as well as ability to motivate students, the honors professors are committed to building and expanding the program. They enjoy the challenge and the opportunity to develop courses that include alternative teaching and learning strategies that result in creative interaction for both students and teachers. Moreover, the Honors Coordinator works closely with each student to give personal advisement for classes as well as scholarship and transfer guidance and information.

SCC honors students traditionally excel. Many have earned prestigious scholarships, such as the Woodrow Wilson Scholarship, upon transferring to four-year institutions in Florida, the United States, and abroad. In addition, they earn places on the All-USA Academic Teams sponsored by USA Today and Who's Who in American Colleges and Universities.

Honors classes typically have 16 to 20 students. Consequently, ample opportunity is available for students to bond with each other as well as the professors. Small class size allows for intellectual growth through collaborative and experiential learning, hands-on activities, and intellectual interaction.

The Honors Institute also offers a Science Diploma track. Students in this track must take seven science courses and Calculus I. These courses provide a diverse, strong educational foundation for upper-division work for students who plan to major in science, medicine, or engineering-related disciplines. Students in this track must maintain a minimum 3.3 GPA to graduate with a Science Merit Diploma.

Participation Requirements: The SCC Honors Diploma Program welcomes any student who meets the following qualifications: high school seniors must have an GPA of at least 3.2 and a score of 1050 or higher on the SAT (verbal and math) or 23 or higher on the ACT. Those who take the College Placement Test must have minimum scores of 95 in reading and sentence skills and a minimum of 75 in math skills. Higher scores than minimums are preferred on all entrance tests. In addition, students are required to submit letters of recommendation, come for an interview, and prepare and submit a writing sample on campus. Once admitted to the Honors Diploma Program, students must maintain a minimum 3.2 GPA. Students are required to complete a minimum of 23 credit hours of honors classes to graduate with an Honors Diploma. Those who wish to earn the Honors Certificate must complete a minimum of 13 credit hours in honors classes. Students are expected to volunteer their time and talent for activities sponsored by the College and the campus Phi Theta Kappa chapter.

Because SCC is a community college, many nontraditional students attend. Those who are uncertain of their qualifications as previously explained are still urged to apply or call for more information. Questions and concerns can be discussed in an interview.

Admission Process: Students who wish to apply to the Honors Institute must have an interview with the Honors Coordinator and provide transcripts, submit written work, and provide letters of recommendation. The admission process is further explained in Honors brochures, which are available upon request.

Scholarship Availability: Honors students who have financial needs can receive scholarships funded by the Bright Futures Scholarship Program established by the Florida State Legislature. These merit scholarships were created to provide money for academically talented students and to expand diversity among community college students. In addition, Seminole Community College hosts a Dream Auction and other fund-raising events whose proceeds are matched by the state. Most of the monies go into scholarship funds that qualifying students may be eligible for. All honors students receive some kind of scholarship aid.

Campus Overview

State and locally supported 2-year, founded 1966 • **Coed** 12,202 undergraduate students, 37% full-time, 58% women, 42% men.

Undergraduates 4,461 full-time, 7,741 part-time. Students come from 18 states and territories, 123 other countries, 3% are from out of state, 14% African American, 4% Asian American or Pacific Islander, 14% Hispanic American, 0.4% Native American, 0.1% international, 19% transferred in.

Faculty *Total:* 850, 24% full-time, 12% with terminal degrees. *Student/faculty ratio:* 23:1.

Academic Programs *Special study options:* academic remediation for entering students, accelerated degree program, adult/continuing education programs, advanced placement credit, cooperative education, distance learning, double majors, English as a second language, external degree program, honors programs, independent study, internships, part-time degree program, services for LD students, study abroad, summer session for credit. *ROTC:* Army (b).

Athletics Member NJCAA. *Intercollegiate sports:* baseball M(s), basketball M(s)/W(s), softball W(s). *Intramural sports:* basketball M/W, golf M, tennis M/W, volleyball M/W.

Costs (2004–05) *Tuition:* state resident $1514 full-time, $50 per credit hour part-time; nonresident $5813 full-time, $194 per credit hour part-time. Full-time tuition and fees vary according to course load. Part-time tuition and fees vary according to course load. *Required fees:* $417 full-time, $14 per credit hour part-time.

Contact: Laura Ross, Honors Coordinator, Seminole Community College, 100 Weldon Boulevard, Sanford, Florida 32773; *Telephone:* 407-328-2062 or 2335 (Honors Center); *Fax:* 407-328-2201; *E-mail:* honors@scc-fl.edu or rossl@scc-fl.edu

South Florida Community College
Honors Program
Avon Park, Florida

The Honors Program at South Florida Community College (SFCC) invites academically talented students to engage in a rigorous and self-directed educational experience. Students who complete 15 honors credits receive recognition at graduation. Their classes are smaller with increased student involvement, which makes this program challenging and exciting. Students master and document *such skills as critical thinking and writing, verbal presentations, and rhetorical and logical analysis, and such attributes as leadership and service. Courses are currently provided in the humanities, social/behavioral sciences, and the sciences.*

SFCC instituted its Honors Program in order to offer less expensive and more challenging learning experiences to the best students in the district. The main focus is on transferring students into honors programs at Florida's four-year colleges and universities and on making sure that students can compete for scholarship money that is available only to honors program graduates.

Courses that meet the general education requirements are offered in a variety of formats to fit students' schedules and learning styles. Examples of courses include an honors symposium for groups of speakers or a series of presentations on campus, an honors seminar for an interdisciplinary study of a theme or subject, and an honors section of a course for learning the subject matter via interactive and self-directed teaching methods. In the past, the program has used the honors topics and televised broadcasts produced by the National Collegiate Honors Council.

The Honors Program offers a variety of extracurricular activities, including service learning and several clubs and student organizations dedicated to motivated students. The program requires that students document at least 25 hours of service learning in the communities and offers many opportunities each semester for meaningful volunteer work.

The Honors Program also requires that each student take a capstone course, The Competitive Edge. This course is designed to familiarize students with two subjects: success in a four-year college and success in the business world. The course involves leadership skills and professional standards as well as study skills and academic planning.

Participation Requirements: In order to receive recognition from the Honors Program with a gold seal on the diploma and a pin, students must complete 15 or more honors credit hours with a cumulative GPA of 3.3 or higher; a major research project that indicates critical, independent thinking and the ability to present in-depth, authoritative research, both verbally and in a well-written and well-documented paper; and at least one honors seminar. In addition, students' computerized records must indicate the proper documentation for rhetorical analysis, logical analysis, critical-thinking skills, writing skills, 25 logged hours of service learning, at least one major verbal presentation with visual aids (at least 10 to 15 minutes), and completion of the course, The Competitive Edge.

Admission Process: There are several paths into the Honors Program at South Florida Community College. A student wishing to enter the program must provide proof of one of the following to be accepted automatically: SAT I score of at least 1100, ACT score of at least 25, top 5 percent of high school class or minimum cumulative GPA or 3.65 out of 4.0, minimum cumulative GPA of 3.3 in at least 12 hours of college credit courses, 111 or higher on sentence skills component of Computerized Placement Test (CPT), or at least 111 on sentence structure component of the Florida College Entry-level Placement Test. Should a student wish to be accepted into the Honors Program, he or she is welcome to enroll in honors courses even before joining the program.

Scholarship Availability: There are three ways that graduates of the Honors Program can receive scholarships for their four-year programs. There are scholarships for transfer students with a good academic record, Phi Theta Kappa scholarships, and honors program scholarships to students with an A.A. degree with recognition from the Honors Program. Furthermore, the South Florida Community College Foundation is prepared to provide some level of assistance to each student selected for the SFCC Honors Program as an incentive to participate.

Campus Overview

State-supported 2-year, founded 1965, part of Florida Community College System • **Coed** 2,076 undergraduate students, 39% full-time, 59% women, 41% men.

Undergraduates 813 full-time, 1,263 part-time. Students come from 12 states and territories, 4 other countries.

Faculty *Total:* 203, 23% full-time, 9% with terminal degrees. *Student/faculty ratio:* 15:1.

Academic Programs *Special study options:* academic remediation for entering students, accelerated degree program, adult/continuing education programs, advanced placement credit, cooperative education, English as a second language, internships, part-time degree program, services for LD students, summer session for credit.

Athletics Member NJCAA. *Intercollegiate sports:* baseball M(s), tennis W(s), volleyball W(s).

Contact: Director of the Honors Program, 600 West College Drive, Avon Park, Florida 33825; *Telephone:* 863-453-6661; *Fax:* 863-784-7229; *Web site:* http://www.southflorida.edu

University of Central Florida
The Burnett Honors College
Orlando, Florida

*T*he Burnett Honors College at the University of Central Florida *(UCF) is the center of academic excellence at the University. Its purpose is to enhance and broaden the education of the most talented undergraduate students attending UCF. University Honors is a four-year program that includes intensified course work within the General Education Program (GEP) as well as upper-division interdisciplinary seminars, lectures, and activities beyond the classroom. Honors in the Major typically involves two semesters of study at the junior or senior level, culminating in the preparation and defense of an honors thesis. Students may participate in both programs.*

Honors classes are the main attraction of the University Honors program. Honors GEP classes are limited to 20 students (15 for composition) and are taught by select faculty members. Interdisciplinary seminars, involving innovative, cutting-edge scholarships, are proposed by faculty members and selected on a competitive basis. Because the University Honors program draws students from across the University, it must maintain strong academic course work tailored to the needs of each student. The Burnett Honors College values diversity of education and is as responsive to the demands of the psychology student as it is to the demands of the engineer. To that end, the College offers upper-division honors course work for specific majors, including business, engineering, computer science, and molecular biology and microbiology.

Social acclimation of students to the University is an important priority. For honors students, this process begins in the Honors Freshman Symposium, one of the oldest traditions in honors and the premier First Year Experience class at UCF. This 1-credit class is intended to introduce new students to University life and to celebrate the love of learning. Students are divided into teams of about 20 who are mentored by an upper-division honors student. Students receive individual weekly contact from their team leaders in addition to meeting together for the symposium, in which a different faculty member presents a research topic or other informative lecture each week. These faculty members are among UCF's best—world-class scholars who offer exciting and innovative ways of thinking about a subject. Students then have an opportunity to ask questions and participate in discussions about the evening's topic. In addition, students are kept informed of important University information and local cultural events.

The College staff is dedicated exclusively to the needs of its students, who have the opportunity for personal academic advisement at every stage of their University experience, from freshman to senior year. Also housed in the Burnett Honors College is the Office of Student Scholarship and Fellowship Advisement (OSSFA). OSSFA serves all UCF students who apply for prestigious scholarships such as *Rhodes, Truman, Hertz, and Marshall, providing guidance throughout the application process.*

With the opening of the Burnett Honors College building in spring 2002, students have a state-of-the-art center located in the core of campus. In addition to classroom and meeting space, facilities include an honors reading room, with kitchen facilities for between-class breaks, and an honors computer lab, where students use the latest available computer technology for class assignments or Internet access.

Student participation in the administration of the Burnett Honors College is integral to its success. The College's vital student organization, Honors Congress, participates in seminar selection and discusses program policy as well as sponsoring educational and social activities for honors students. In addition, the College provides support for educational and cultural events, such as offering reduced-price tickets to museums and local cultural events and sponsoring informal lunches where students can hear from internationally known speakers. The College also supports honors students' participation in national and regional meetings of professional organizations, such as the National Collegiate Honors Council.

Graduates of the Burnett Honors College have attended such institutions as Berkeley, Duke, Harvard, UCLA, and the University of Chicago. Since its origin in 1989, the program's enrollment has grown to approximately 1,500 students. In 1998, the Florida Board of Regents conferred college status to the Honors Program. Presently, the Burnett Honors College is a premier program in terms of academic integrity and student support, one that relishes future challenges and changes.

The deadline for applying is March 31.

Participation Requirements: To graduate from the Honors College, students must maintain both a minimum 3.2 UCF GPA and a 3.0 GPA in honors courses and take 12 credit hours of General Education course work in honors, 1 credit hour of Honors Symposium, and a minimum of 9 hours of upper-division honors course work that varies by college, for a total of 22 hours. Honors in the Major students must maintain a minimum 3.2 overall GPA and a 3.5 in the major in addition to successful completion of a thesis or project that is overseen by a 3-member faculty committee. University Honors students may also elect to do Honors in the Major if qualified. All honors course work is undertaken in small classes limited to 20 or fewer students where close student-faculty interaction is essential.

Successful completion of the University Honors and/or Honors in the Major is recorded on the student's transcript and noted at graduation. Graduating honors students receive the Honors Medallion to wear at commencement.

Campus Overview

State-supported university, founded 1963, part of State University System of Florida • **Coed** 35,159 undergraduate students, 77% full-time, 55% women, 45% men.

Undergraduates 26,953 full-time, 8,206 part-time. Students come from 52 states and territories, 131 other countries, 3% are from out of state, 8% African American, 5% Asian American or Pacific Islander, 12% Hispanic American, 0.5% Native American, 1% international, 9% transferred in, 20% live on campus.

Faculty *Total:* 1,628, 71% full-time, 64% with terminal degrees. *Student/faculty ratio:* 25:1.

Academic Programs *Special study options:* adult/continuing education programs, advanced placement credit, cooperative education, distance learning, double majors, English as a second language, external degree program, freshman honors college, honors programs, internships, off-campus study, part-time degree program, services for LD students, study abroad, summer session for credit. *ROTC:* Army (b), Air Force (b). *Unusual degree programs:* 3-2 history.

Athletics Member NCAA. All Division I except football (Division I-A). *Intercollegiate sports:* baseball M(s), basketball M(s)/W(s), cheerleading M(s)/W(s), crew W, cross-country running M(s)/W(s), golf M(s)/W(s), soccer M(s)/W(s), tennis M(s)/W(s), track and field

W(s), volleyball W(s). *Intramural sports:* baseball M(c), basketball M/W, bowling M(c)/W(c), crew M(c), fencing M(c)/W(c), golf M/W, ice hockey M(c)/W(c), lacrosse M(c)/W(c), racquetball M/W, rock climbing M(c)/W(c), rugby M(c)/W(c), sailing M(c)/W(c), soccer M(c)/W(c), softball M/W, table tennis M(c)/W(c), tennis M(c)/W(c), ultimate Frisbee M(c)/W(c), volleyball M(c)/W(c), water polo M(c)/W(c), weight lifting M/W, wrestling M.

Costs (2004–05) *Tuition:* state resident $2982 full-time, $99 per credit part-time; nonresident $15,488 full-time, $516 per credit part-time. Full-time tuition and fees vary according to course load. Part-time tuition and fees vary according to course load. *Required fees:* $198 full-time, $6 per credit part-time. *Room and board:* $7232; room only: $4300. Room and board charges vary according to board plan and housing facility.

Financial Aid In 2003, 1441 non-need-based awards were made. *Average percent of need met:* 71%. *Average financial aid package:* $5397. *Average need-based loan:* $3982. *Average need-based gift aid:* $3709. *Average non-need-based aid:* $1728.

Contact: Director: Dr. Madi Dogariu, The Burnett Honors College, University of Central Florida, P.O. Box 161800, Orlando, Florida 32816-1800; *Telephone:* 407-823-2076; *Fax:* 407-823-6583; *E-mail:* honors@pegasus.cc.ucf.edu; *Web site:* http://honors.ucf.edu

University of Florida
University Honors Program
Gainesville, Florida

*T*he University Honors Program at the University of Florida (UF) is designed to create opportunities. First among these is a selection of exclusive honors courses with limited enrollment to enhance the general education requirements of the University. Honors courses reflect the academic diversity of UF, with faculty members from almost all colleges participating. Honors courses provide the students with an opportunity to work with outstanding faculty members in a small class environment. Some honors courses are limited enrollment sections of regular courses, such as calculus and Spanish, while others are special interest courses designed by their instructors specifically for the honors program, such as Biology and Natural History of Fireflies and Ancient Greek Literature and Medicine.

In addition, the honors program offers students access to other opportunities. Honors students receive individualized academic advising from senior faculty members and have access to a writing coach assigned to the honors program. Honors students may apply for housing in the Honors Residential College at Hume Hall. This is the first residential honors college created from the ground up at a major U.S. university. Located in the central part of the campus, this residential facility features suite-type rooms, large commons areas, classrooms, and office space for honors advisers. UF is proud to be a leader in housing and honors among its peer institutions. Space in the Honors Residential College is limited, and requests are accepted on a first-come, first-served basis. Honors students sponsor a variety of extracurricular events and produce an annual literary and arts review. Honors students are encouraged to study abroad (including the UF Honors in Paris program), work internships, and participate in service activities.

Honors students should consider combined-degree programs offered by many departments that allow students to double count up to 12 to 15 credits for both the bachelor's and master's degrees, thus decreasing the time it takes to get both degrees by at least one semester. In addition, undergraduates may participate in cutting-edge research through the University Scholars Program. Students selected as University Scholars are awarded $2500 stipends for summer research under the direction of a leading faculty member.

The University of Florida is one of the most comprehensive universities in the U.S., with degree programs in almost every field.

The honors program at UF combines the advantages of a large, state university—large libraries, advanced laboratories, big-time athletics, academic diversity, a superior faculty, and low tuition—with the small-class environment of a small college.

The University of Florida is located in Gainesville, Florida, in the north-central part of the state. Known as the "tree city," Gainesville and UF are heavily wooded with majestic oaks and towering longleaf pines. Gainesville is about an hour away from historic fishing villages on the Gulf and endless white beaches on the Atlantic.

The University Honors Program was created in 1989 by expanding a program that had been resident in the College of Liberal Arts and Sciences for many years. There are currently about 1,800 students active in the University Honors Program. They represent students from all colleges that grant the bachelor's degree.

Participation Requirements: In order to remain active in the University Honors Program, students must take at least one honors course during each semester (other than summer) and maintain a GPA of at least 3.0. Participation in the honors program is entirely voluntary and usually lasts for the first two years of a student's program, leading to the completion of the general education requirements. At that time, the successful honors student may apply for the Associate of Arts degree with honors and may request a Certificate of Completion. Individual colleges administer honors in the junior and senior years that can lead to a baccalaureate degree cum laude, magna cum laude, or summa cum laude.

Admission Process: Incoming freshmen are invited to participate in the University Honors Program if they have scored at least 1400 (reading plus quantitative) on the SAT or at least 33 on the ACT and have a high school GPA of 4.0 as computed by the UF admissions office (these criteria are subject to change; current information is available at http://www.honors.ufl.edu.) For additional information concerning admission to UF, students should visit the admission Web site at http://www.reg.ufl.edu.

A student who does not meet the above criteria for invitation into honors may be considered for admission to the program after completion of the first semester at UF if performance indicates potential benefit from the program.

The University of Florida accepts up to 30 semester credits based on Advanced Placement and/or International Baccalaureate examination scores. UF also accepts credit earned during dual enrollment.

Scholarship Availability: The University Honors Program sponsors a number of scholarships, including several to support study abroad for a semester or for a full year. The prestigious Lombardi Scholarships are awarded to 8 outstanding freshmen from Florida high schools. Beckman Scholarships are available to several outstanding students to support research in the fields of biochemistry, biology, chemistry, and medical sciences. Wentworth Scholarships are awarded to very promising students in their second semester at UF; two Wentworth Scholarships support five or six months of study at European universities.

For additional scholarship opportunities, students should contact the Office of Student Financial Affairs and the Dean's office of the college in which enrollment is anticipated. Links to individual colleges are available at http://www.ufl.edu/websites.

Campus Overview

State-supported university, founded 1853, part of Board of Trustees
• **Coed** 33,982 undergraduate students, 92% full-time, 53% women, 47% men.

Undergraduates 31,217 full-time, 2,765 part-time. Students come from 52 states and territories, 114 other countries, 4% are from out of state, 9% African American, 7% Asian American or Pacific Islander, 12% Hispanic American, 0.5% Native American, 0.9% international, 6% transferred in, 21% live on campus.

Faculty *Total:* 1,654, 98% full-time, 90% with terminal degrees. *Student/faculty ratio:* 23:1.

Academic Programs *Special study options:* accelerated degree program, adult/continuing education programs, advanced placement credit, cooperative education, distance learning, double majors, English as a second language, external degree program, honors programs, independent study, internships, off-campus study, part-time degree program, services for LD students, student-designed majors, study abroad, summer session for credit. *ROTC:* Army (b), Air Force (b). *Unusual degree programs:* 3-2 mathematics.

Athletics Member NCAA. All Division I except football (Division I-A). *Intercollegiate sports:* baseball M(s), basketball M(s)/W(s), cross-country running M(s)/W(s), golf M(s)/W(s), gymnastics W(s), soccer W(s), softball W(s), swimming and diving M(s)/W(s), tennis M(s)/W(s), track and field M(s)/W(s), volleyball W(s). *Intramural sports:* archery M/W, badminton M(c)/W(c), baseball M, basketball M/W, bowling M/W, crew M(c)/W(c), cross-country running M/W, equestrian sports M(c)/W(c), fencing M(c)/W(c), field hockey M/W, football M, golf M/W, gymnastics W, ice hockey M(c), lacrosse M(c)/W(c), racquetball M(c)/W(c), rugby M(c)/W(c), sailing M(c)/W(c), soccer M(c)/W, softball W, swimming and diving M/W, table tennis M(c)/W(c), tennis M/W, track and field M/W, ultimate Frisbee W(c), volleyball M(c)/W, water polo M(c)/W(c), weight lifting M, wrestling M(c).

Costs (2004–05) *Tuition:* state resident $2955 full-time, $99 per credit hour part-time; nonresident $15,827 full-time, $528 per credit hour part-time. *Room and board:* $6040; room only: $3780. Room and board charges vary according to board plan and housing facility.

Financial Aid 1,507 Federal Work-Study jobs (averaging $1454). 4,517 state and other part-time jobs (averaging $1696). In 2003, 16126 non-need-based awards were made. *Average percent of need met:* 84%. *Average financial aid package:* $10,004. *Average need-based loan:* $4138. *Average need-based gift aid:* $4368. *Average non-need-based aid:* $3909.

Contact: Director: Dr. Sheila Dickison, Suite 140, Tigert Hall, Box 113260, Gainesville, Florida 32611-3260; *Telephone:* 352-392-1519; *Fax:* 352-392-1888; *E-mail:* honors@ufl.edu; *Web site:* http://www.honors.ufl.edu

---

University of North Florida
University Honors Program
Jacksonville, Florida

The University Honors Program provides students with an interdisciplinary educational experience that is dedicated to developing responsible and creative leaders. Students and faculty members form learning communities that connect the classroom to Jacksonville and beyond as a lab. Both the curriculum and the cocurricular features challenge students to make connections between the University and the world. Student power and responsibility shape every aspect of the program. Freshmen first see this power in action in a three-day student-run orientation, which focuses on goal setting, leadership, and experiential and service learning. The first two years include 14 hours of active seminars designed to help students learn from different points of view, discover how knowledge connects, and assist them in creating their honors portfolio and making connections to their major. Second-, third-, and fourth-year students may serve as facilitators for honors colloquiums; they also benefit from subsidized programs designed to expand their ability to apply their knowledge to the wider world through international travel, Washington internships, and study-abroad options. The program has subsidized group travel to Indonesia, Japan, Ghana, Ecuador, Guatemala, England, the Czech Republic, and the Bahamas. The cultural learning that takes place during these trips is experiential learning in the richest sense. Students and faculty members form a learning community that explores clashing cultures and radically different natural and urban environments. Every honors student interested in a semester's internship in Washington has been funded and accepted by the

Washington Center. Students of every major have been placed in prestigious internships at such places as the National Institutes of Health, the Tribune Company, Newsweek, the Kennedy Center, the National Organization for Women, and the Shakespeare Theatre. Student-facilitated service-learning colloquiums are offered every term in areas such as refugee services, domestic violence, at-risk youth, health issues, and poverty. Because of the strength of student commitment to service, the Jacksonville Jaguars Foundation and Nike Corporation have formed a nationally unique partnership with the University of North Florida (UNF) Honors Program. Honors students created and run the Nike/Jaguars Foundation Community Scholars Mentoring Program, which provides precollege mentoring and full academic scholarships to at-risk youths who are admitted to the University. Students take responsibility, under the guidance of the Honors Service Learning Coordinator, for creating the scholarship process, administering the funds, and designing and running a four-year mentoring program. An honors residence hall and computer and community rooms are available for honors students. The University Honors Program was founded in 1990 and enrolls 500 students.

Participation Requirements: The Honors Program is a four-year program that includes University Honors for the first and second years. Upper-level students have the option to pursue research through Honors in the Major or Interdisciplinary Honors. Students who complete 14 hours of lower-division course work, pass their portfolio requirement, and post a minimum 3.4 GPA earn the distinction of University Honors. Interdisciplinary Honors requires 8 hours of honors work, which consists of two colloquiums to aid students in the thesis writing and presentation processes and 6 hours of thesis and research work. Honors in the Major is the second track at the upper level. A variety of departments throughout the University offer this 8-hour program. GPA requirements for participation vary by department, but all Honors in the Major students enroll in 6 hours of thesis and research work through their department and take two colloquiums to aid them in the thesis writing and presentation processes. At graduation, students who successfully complete University Honors and one of the upper-level tracks earn the highest honors distinction on their diploma, Baccalaureate Honors. Students who enroll only in upper-level honors and who have their thesis or special project approved earn the diploma distinction of Interdisciplinary Honors or Honors in the Major.

Admission Process: The Honors Program is highly selective, admitting fewer than 15 percent of the entering freshman class for participation. The program admits students whose scholastic performance demonstrates an enthusiastic and curious approach to learning. The program looks not only for students who have high grade point averages and test scores but also for students who have sought out the most challenging high school courses, are leaders in their school and community, and give back to the larger community through service. The Honors Program works on a rolling admissions basis. Graduating high school seniors are encouraged to apply to the Honors Program if any of the following criteria are met: are in the top 10 percent of their high school class, have an SAT score of 1250 or above or ACT score of 28 or above, have a recalculated UNF GPA of 3.75 or higher, have International Baccalaureate or Advanced Placement credit, or have outstanding writing and analytical skills. Both Honors in the Major and Interdisciplinary Honors admit students transferring into the program from UNF and other institutions. Requirements vary from a minimum 3.4 GPA to a 3.7 GPA, depending on track and major.

Scholarship Availability: The Honors Program awards scholarships in several different categories: four-year University Honors Scholarships ($1200 per year), Washington Center Scholarships, and out-of-state fee waivers ($5000 per year). Special leadership and cultural scholarships in honor of Alan Ling reward students for their superior leadership in enriching the Honors Program and the University of North Florida (vary depending on experience). Students must maintain a minimum 3.0 GPA for leadership and 3.4 GPA for cultural scholarships and actively participate in honors to receive a scholarship.

Campus Overview

State-supported comprehensive, founded 1965, part of State University System of Florida • **Coed** 12,669 undergraduate students, 72% full-time, 58% women, 42% men.

Undergraduates 9,059 full-time, 3,610 part-time. Students come from 49 states and territories, 54 other countries, 5% are from out of state, 10% African American, 5% Asian American or Pacific Islander, 6% Hispanic American, 0.5% Native American, 0.8% international, 7% transferred in, 17% live on campus.

Faculty Total: 652, 65% full-time, 59% with terminal degrees. Student/faculty ratio: 23:1.

Academic Programs Special study options: accelerated degree program, adult/continuing education programs, advanced placement credit, cooperative education, distance learning, double majors, English as a second language, freshman honors college, honors programs, independent study, internships, off-campus study, part-time degree program, services for LD students, student-designed majors, study abroad, summer session for credit. ROTC: Navy (c).

Athletics Member NCAA. All Division II except golf (Division I), swimming and diving (Division I). Intercollegiate sports: baseball M(s), basketball M(s)/W(s), cheerleading M/W, cross-country running M(s)/W(s), golf M(s), soccer M(s)/W(s), softball W(s), swimming and diving W(s), tennis M(s)/W(s), track and field M(s)/W(s), volleyball W(s). Intramural sports: badminton M/W, basketball M/W, bowling M/W, football M/W, golf M/W, lacrosse M(c)/W(c), racquetball M(c)/W(c), rugby M, sailing M/W, soccer M/W, softball M/W, squash M/W, swimming and diving M/W, table tennis M/W, tennis M/W, track and field M/W, ultimate Frisbee M(c)/W(c), volleyball M(c)/W(c), water polo M/W, weight lifting M/W, wrestling M/W.

Costs (2004–05) Tuition: state resident $3101 full-time, $103 per semester hour part-time; nonresident $14,851 full-time, $495 per semester hour part-time. Room and board: $6278; room only: $3768. Room and board charges vary according to housing facility.

Financial Aid 127 Federal Work-Study jobs (averaging $3210). In 2004, 954 non-need-based awards were made. Average percent of need met: 75%. Average financial aid package: $2286. Average need-based loan: $3768. Average need-based gift aid: $1956. Average non-need-based aid: $3197.

Contact: Director: Dr. Charles R. Paulson, University of North Florida, 4567 St. Johns Bluff Road, South, Jacksonville, Florida 32224; Telephone: 904-620-2649; Fax: 904-620-3896; E-mail: cpaulson@unf.edu; Web site: http://www.unf.edu/dept/honors/

University of South Florida
The Honors College
Tampa, Florida

Honors at the University of South Florida (USF) is designed for the academically superior student who wishes to go the extra mile, who embraces challenge, who wants to enhance the University experience, and who is intrigued by alternative approaches to learning. USF offers a four-year honors track for incoming freshmen and a two-year track for qualified transfer and upper-level students. Honors is for motivated students regardless of major. Honors students develop a strong sense of community.

Honors seeks to attract students of superior academic ability and provide them with intellectual challenges and enrichment. The program assists students in developing and refining critical skills in thinking, reasoning, analysis, and writing. These skills prove invaluable as students pursue graduate or professional school and career choices and challenges. Honors' goals are achieved by providing opportunities for students and faculty members to interact closely in a series of liberal arts–oriented, mainly team-taught, interdisciplinary classes of limited size. Subsequently, students work independently on a senior thesis/project under the close supervision of faculty mentors. Many students also participate in undergraduate research.

Honors students are afforded special services within a highly individualized and nurturing environment. This environment fosters a sense of belonging and provides both an academic and social home throughout the USF years. USF honors is an exciting experience that combines the advantage of a small, highly personalized college with the resources of a major research university. It is a place where students can reach out, learn, and grow. Students in the program receive special recognition at the University's graduation ceremony, and their honors status is noted on the transcript and the diploma.

The program began in 1983 and currently enrolls more than 1,600 students.

Participation Requirements: The Four-Year Track (28 credits that substitute for the University's liberal arts requirements) encompasses a student's entire college career; the Two-Year Track (13 credits that substitute for an equal number of liberal arts requirements) is for the junior and senior years. Small, intimate classes encourage interaction among students and faculty members.

Admission Process: Students in the Four-Year Track typically have weighted high school GPAs of 3.75 and SAT scores of 1300 or ACT scores of 29. Two-Year Track students typically have 3.5 transfer GPAs and SAT scores or ACT scores similar to Four-Year Track students. Students with these credentials are invited to participate in honors. Students earning the International Baccalaureate (I.B.) diploma or graduating in the top 5 percent of their classes are also invited.

Scholarship Availability: Every student who is enrolled in an honors course and maintains the required honors GPA is awarded a scholarship each semester. Scholarships range from $500 to $2000 per year. Non-Florida residents receive scholarships in the form of out-of-state tuition waivers that average about $3000 per year. Students must apply by December 31 to be eligible for other USF scholarships.

Campus Overview

State-supported university, founded 1956, part of State University System of Florida • **Coed** 33,266 undergraduate students, 68% full-time, 59% women, 41% men.

Undergraduates 22,787 full-time, 10,479 part-time. Students come from 52 states and territories, 133 other countries, 4% are from out of state, 13% African American, 6% Asian American or Pacific Islander, 11% Hispanic American, 0.4% Native American, 3% international, 13% transferred in, 13% live on campus.

Faculty Total: 1,802, 91% full-time, 91% with terminal degrees. Student/faculty ratio: 16:1.

Academic Programs Special study options: academic remediation for entering students, accelerated degree program, adult/continuing education programs, advanced placement credit, cooperative education, distance learning, double majors, external degree program, freshman honors college, honors programs, independent study, internships, off-campus study, part-time degree program, services for LD students, student-designed majors, study abroad, summer session for credit. ROTC: Army (b), Navy (b), Air Force (b).

Athletics Member NCAA. All Division I. Intercollegiate sports: baseball M(s), basketball M(s)/W(s), cross-country running M(s)/W(s), football M(s), golf M(s)/W(s), soccer M(s)/W(s), softball W(s), tennis M(s)/W(s), track and field M(s)/W(s), volleyball W(s). Intramural sports: badminton M/W, basketball M/W, bowling M/W, cross-country running M/W, football M, golf M/W, racquetball M/W, soccer M/W, softball M/W, swimming and diving M/W, tennis M/W, track and field M/W, volleyball M/W, wrestling M.

Costs (2004–05) Tuition: state resident $3090 full-time, $103 per credit hour part-time; nonresident $15,960 full-time, $532 per credit hour part-time. Full-time tuition and fees vary according to course

level, course load, and location. Part-time tuition and fees vary according to course level, course load, and location. Required fees: $74 full-time, $37 per term part-time. Room and board: $6730; room only: $3519. Room and board charges vary according to board plan, housing facility, and location.

Financial Aid 880 Federal Work-Study jobs (averaging $3600). In 2003, 1318 non-need-based awards were made. Average percent of need met: 32%. Average financial aid package: $9439. Average need-based loan: $4913. Average need-based gift aid: $3667. Average non-need-based aid: $1626.

Contact: Dean: Dr. Stuart Silverman, 4202 East Fowler Avenue-SVC 1088, Tampa, Florida 33620; Telephone: 813-974-3087; Fax: 813-974-5801; E-mail: silverman@honors.usf.edu

The University of Tampa
Honors Program
Tampa, Florida

*A*cademic achievement, global perspective, critical thinking and leadership are the cornerstones of The University of Tampa (UT) Honors Program. Honors Program courses and activities build upon these as they encourage participants to challenge mindsets and aspire to excellence.

The curriculum of The University of Tampa Honors Program centers on an array of courses that encourage students to question conventional wisdom, pursue excellence, and prepare themselves for graduate studies, successful careers and societal leadership. Each year, the courses and many of the activities relate to a particular theme. Themes include: Conflicting Perspectives, Roots and Context of Ideas, Revolutions, and the Cutting Edge. Beginning with a 2-credit Gateways to Honors class, most of the Honors Program courses fulfill general education requirements as well as Honors Program requirements. Every year, they include courses from the humanities and fine arts, the natural sciences, and the social sciences; but most courses are linked to the common theme. Honors classes bring the best students together with the best faculty members in stimulating, small-group settings.

In addition to its array of special theme courses that link different fields of study in a common endeavor, the Honors Program offers many outstanding learning opportunities and practical experiences. Each year, 6 University of Tampa Honors Program students receive one-term scholarships to Oxford University in England, where they study in a one-on-one tutorial atmosphere with Oxford faculty members. Another special aspect of the program is its nonfiction journal, Respondez, entirely written and edited by Honors Program students. The UT Honors Program also offers a Washington, D.C., Semester; Undergraduate Research Fellowships to undertake research with faculty members; Model United Nations activities (including participation in the Harvard National Model United Nations); College Bowl competition among teams on campus and against other colleges and universities; numerous short-term study-abroad classes; and special Honors Enrichment Tutorials, modeled on the Oxford system, within upper-level classes. The Honors Council gives students an active role in shaping the program and provides extracurricular activities that support program goals. Honors residence hall areas, an Honors lounge, and an Honors study are available and help foster a sense of community.

Founded in 1983, The University of Tampa Honors Program is a University-based honors program that welcomes and includes students from all majors. In the past three years, it has more than doubled in size. Its current enrollment is 750 students.

Participation Requirements: Freshmen enrolling in the program must complete a 2-credit Gateways to Honors course designed to introduce them to The University of Tampa and its Honors Program. To graduate with Honors Program Distinction, they must complete at least five Honors Programs courses and earn a cumulative GPA of at least 3.5. Sophomores entering the program must meet the same requirements, with the exception of the Gateways to Honors course. Juniors entering the program who have had previous honors program experience or have graduated from a recognized community college honors program are required to take three Honors Program courses. Two of these may be Honors Thesis, Honors Independent Study, Oxford Term, Washington Semester, or Honors Enrichment Tutorials.

Graduates with Honors Program Distinction are honored at a special reception and ceremony each term, receive an Honors Graduate medallion and ribbon, and are given special recognition at the graduation ceremony and in the graduation program. In addition, all Honors Program courses are designated as such on students' transcripts (even if they do not graduate with Honors Program Distinction).

Admission Process: Students are automatically considered for admission to the Honors Program when they are admitted to the University. Last year, 93 percent of those invited to join at entry did so. Freshmen should have an academic GPA of at least 3.5 or an SAT I score of 1200 or higher (ACT score of 26). Transfer students should have a minimum 3.5 GPA or very strong recommendations. Students from recognized university, college, or community college honors programs are accepted upon receipt of a letter of recommendation from that institution's Director of Honors.

Scholarship Availability: Full-time Honors Program students who are U.S. citizens or resident aliens receive an academic scholarship: Presidential, Dean's, or Transfer. These vary in amount based on academic qualifications. The Honors Program awards Oxford Term and Study Abroad Scholarships to continuing students on a competitive basis. It also awards Honors Research Fellowships to continuing students on a competitive basis.

Campus Overview

Independent comprehensive, founded 1931 • **Coed** 4,348 undergraduate students, 89% full-time, 62% women, 38% men.

Undergraduates 3,856 full-time, 492 part-time. Students come from 50 states and territories, 100 other countries, 53% are from out of state, 6% African American, 2% Asian American or Pacific Islander, 9% Hispanic American, 0.6% Native American, 5% international, 7% transferred in, 59% live on campus.

Faculty *Total:* 408, 49% full-time, 62% with terminal degrees. *Student/faculty ratio:* 17:1.

Academic Programs *Special study options:* academic remediation for entering students, adult/continuing education programs, advanced placement credit, cooperative education, double majors, English as a second language, honors programs, independent study, internships, off-campus study, part-time degree program, services for LD students, student-designed majors, study abroad, summer session for credit. *ROTC:* Army (b), Air Force (c).

Athletics Member NCAA. All Division II. *Intercollegiate sports:* baseball M(s), basketball M(s)/W(s), crew M/W(s), cross-country running M(s)/W(s), golf M(s), soccer M(s)/W(s), softball W(s), swimming and diving M/W, tennis W(s), volleyball W(s). *Intramural sports:* baseball M/W, basketball M/W, bowling M/W, crew M, equestrian sports W, field hockey W, football M, golf M/W, soccer M/W, softball M/W, swimming and diving M/W, tennis W, volleyball M/W.

Costs (2004–05) *Comprehensive fee:* $24,838 includes full-time tuition ($17,250), mandatory fees ($922), and room and board ($6666). Full-time tuition and fees vary according to class time. Part-time tuition: $368 per hour. Part-time tuition and fees vary according to class time. *Required fees:* $35 per term part-time. *College room only:* $3567. Room and board charges vary according to board plan and housing facility.

Financial Aid In 2004, 309 non-need-based awards were made. *Average percent of need met:* 83%. *Average financial aid package:* $14,398. *Average need-based loan:* $3828. *Average need-based gift aid:* $6810. *Average non-need-based aid:* $6668.

Contact: Director: Dr. Richard Piper, Box 100F, 410 West Kennedy Boulevard, Tampa, Florida 33606-1490; *Telephone:* 813-253-3333 Ext. 3570; *Fax:* 813-258-7404; *E-mail:* rpiper3404@aol.com

University of West Florida
University Honors Program
Pensacola, Florida

At the University of West Florida, the University Honors Program (UHP) is defined by the following words: areté, téchne, and sophía. With a focus on excellence, skill, and wisdom, the UHP engages academically talented students in learning that has breadth, depth, and a richness of texture; provides an expeditious and enriching path to a first degree; and opens the right doors to life beyond the University environment.

Areté, or excellence, is the overarching concept for the University Honors Program. Honors students, as well as the program that serves them, are dedicated to the pursuit of excellence through determination and vitality. Téchne means skill, and it is through pursuing areté in any discipline or art—whether it be computer programming, accounting, marine biology, history, music, psychology, film production, management, or anything else—that one becomes first competent and then expert in that discipline. Sophía means wisdom, which is the knowledge achieved through study, insight attained through experience, satisfaction gained from serving others, understanding that stems from struggling with and then solving a problem, and the sound judgment that comes from being able to see not just two sides, but all sides of an issue.

With students who are enrolled in many different majors, the academic portion of the University Honors Program is centered upon smaller honors sections of general studies courses and special honors seminars. Honors classes are designed to have more depth, not be more difficult. All honors classes are restricted to Honors Program students, and the seminars are usually limited to 15 students. Honors sections of general study courses can be found in everything, ranging from chemistry to religion. Honors seminars are truly unique opportunities. Designed to enrich the academic lives of students with interesting topics, recent seminars have been The Philosophy of Horror Films, Tolkien: Text and Film Text, Cuba at the Crossroads, and Field Studies in Marine Biology. For students with interests beyond the regularly offered general studies courses and seminars, additional courses of study can be arranged with individual professors to fulfill academic requirements. The culmination of the honors student's experience in the program is the honors thesis, which is a focused research project completed in cooperation with the University's best faculty members.

Beyond the classroom, the program, along with the student-composed Honors Council, seeks to provide enriching and meaningful activities. Service events such as Habitat for Humanity and Make-A-Difference-Day, along with student social gatherings are regular occurrences. The program also strives to couple academic classes with domestic and international travel experiences. Recent trips have been to Cuba; Kobe, Japan; and Portsmouth, England. The University Honors Program also publishes an award-winning newsletter, Infinite Wisdom (first place in the nation, 2001), which can afford writing and publishing opportunities.

The University Honors Program houses a study area, student lounge, computers specifically for use by honors students, and administrative offices. The program also has special honors student housing in new dorm facilities. Honors students have registration priority over other students and receive recognition by the University president at the University's commencement exercises.

Founded in 1989, the University Honors Program currently enrolls 450 students.

Participation Requirements: Once admitted, students in the University Honors Program must maintain a GPA of at least 3.0 (B average). To graduate as a University Honors Scholar, which includes a special Honors Graduation Ceremony and recognition at the University's commencement exercises, students entering as freshmen must complete 24 semester hours of honors course work. This includes four lower division honors courses, three upper division honors seminars or electives, and an honors thesis. The honors thesis should be the culmination of a student's experience in the program. Transfer students and students not admitted as freshmen complete a more concentrated version of these requirements. Upon graduation from the University Honors Program, students receive an annotated transcript asserting their status as an Honors Scholar.

Admission Process: Entering freshmen seeking admission to the University Honors Program are asked to submit an Honors Program application. In general, the applicant must have a cumulative, unweighted GPA of 3.5 or higher or rank in the top 10 percent of their graduating high school class, and must have an ACT composite score of 26 or higher, or a combined 1170 or higher on the SAT. Applicants who do not meet these requirements are encouraged to apply, as some students are admitted on probational status each year. Transfer students seeking admission to the program must submit an Honors Program application, have an overall transfer GPA of 3.25, and submit a letter of recommendation from the Honors Director of their previous institution. UWF students seeking admission to the program who were not admitted as freshmen must submit an application, have an overall UWF GPA of 3.25, and submit a letter of recommendation from a UWF faculty member.

Scholarship Availability: In addition to the state-sponsored scholarship programs for Florida students, the University offers a number of different scholarships designed for many different types of students. Both merit-based and need-based scholarships are offered, as are student loans. There are seven different merit-based scholarships offered by the University to qualified students upon admission. Among these are the following: the Pace Scholars Program, $4000 per year for four years; The John C. Pace, Jr. Scholarship, $1000 per year for four years; and the Presidential Scholarship, $1000 per year for four years. The University Honors Program offers financial assistance to students wishing to pursue international or other alternative educational experiences.

Campus Overview

State-supported comprehensive, founded 1963, part of State University System of Florida • **Coed** 7,974 undergraduate students, 72% full-time, 59% women, 41% men.

Undergraduates 5,738 full-time, 2,236 part-time. Students come from 49 states and territories, 13% are from out of state, 10% African American, 4% Asian American or Pacific Islander, 5% Hispanic American, 1% Native American, 0.8% international, 17% transferred in, 18% live on campus.

Faculty *Total:* 547, 47% full-time. *Student/faculty ratio:* 20:1.

Academic Programs *Special study options:* advanced placement credit, cooperative education, distance learning, English as a second language, honors programs, independent study, internships, off-campus study, part-time degree program, services for LD students, study abroad, summer session for credit. *ROTC:* Army (b), Air Force (b).

Athletics Member NCAA. All Division II. *Intercollegiate sports:* baseball M(s), basketball M(s)/W(s), cross-country running M(s)/W(s), golf M(s), soccer M(s)/W(s), softball W(s), tennis M(s)/W(s), volleyball W. *Intramural sports:* basketball M/W, bowling M/W, cheerleading W, fencing M/W, football M/W, sailing M/W, soccer M/W, swimming and diving M/W, tennis M/W, volleyball M/W.

Costs (2004–05) *Tuition:* state resident $2045 full-time, $68 per semester hour part-time; nonresident $14,552 full-time, $485 per semester hour part-time. Full-time tuition and fees vary according to location. Part-time tuition and fees vary according to location.

Required fees: $994 full-time, $33 per semester hour part-time. *Room and board:* $6294. Room and board charges vary according to housing facility.

Financial Aid 178 Federal Work-Study jobs (averaging $2350). 1,545 state and other part-time jobs.

Contact: Director: Dr. Greg Lanier, University Honors Program, 11000 University Parkway, Building 50, Room 224, Pensacola, Florida 32514; *Telephone:* 850-474-2934; *Fax:* 850-473-7256; *E-mail:* glanier@uwf.edu; *Web site:* http://www.uwf.edu/honors

Valencia Community College
Honors Program
Orlando, Florida

*V**alencia Community College inaugurated its Honors Program in January 1990 and now serves more than 1,000 students on four campuses. The program annually attracts dozens of students with SAT I scores in excess of 1400 and ACT scores in excess of 32. Valencia's Honors Program includes many high school valedictorians and salutatorians, as well as students from many other states and countries. In addition, more than 450 of the 1,000 honors students are currently on full-tuition scholarships administered by the Honors Program. The program offers students a choice of more than forty different honors courses across the curriculum. In addition, it offers a four-semester sequence of Interdisciplinary Studies (IDS). Students may choose to take only honors courses or only IDS or to mix and match the two approaches to honors. The Honors Program emphasizes small classes (average size is 15) and participative learning. Most classes are seminar style and seek to help the student become an independent learner. The Honors Program faculty is made up of master teachers, many of whom are noted authors and scholars in their disciplines. There is a close mentoring relationship between honors faculty members and students. Students are advised by 5 special honors counselors and receive preferential early registration for classes.*

For the past twelve years, virtually 100 percent of Honors Program graduates have transferred as full juniors to upper-division colleges and universities, including many of the nation's most prestigious institutions, such as Columbia, Duke, Emory, Georgetown, Harvard, Tulane, and Yale. Currently, two thirds of the graduates are receiving scholarships to these institutions. In addition, the Honors Program office currently has more than seventy transfer scholarships to colleges and universities, which allow Valencia's Honor Program Director to select the scholarship recipients.

One of the hallmarks of the Honors Program is its holistic approach to developing honors students. This approach seeks to develop students' social and leadership skills in addition to intellectual and academic abilities. Toward this end, the program sponsors numerous field trips, a speakers series, social events, leadership training, and trips to state, regional, and national honors conferences (all at program expense). In addition, the program provides an annual spring break trip to a different country. While this trip is not paid for entirely by the program, it is heavily subsidized so that students pay only a fraction of the cost.

In addition to the resources offered by Valencia and the Orlando area, students in the Honors Program have full check-out privileges at the libraries of Rollins College and the University of Central Florida. Each of Valencia's campuses also offers an Honors Resource Center, where honors students have access to computers, group study areas, and other resource materials in addition to a comfortable and well-appointed room in which to just relax or carry on a conversation.

Participation Requirements: Students in the program may elect to take as many or as few honors courses as they wish. Students with 12 hours of honors course work (out of 60 hours required for an Associate of Arts degree) and a minimum 3.25 overall GPA at graduation, receive an Honors Certificate. Students with 24 hours of honors course work and a minimum 3.5 overall GPA at graduation receive an Honors Degree. Both Honors Certificate and Honors Degree graduates and their guests participate in a special buffet dinner/graduation ceremony. In addition, they are distinguished at the regular College commencement ceremony by the wearing of honors stoles and honors medallions as well as having a special section in the commencement program. Honors Degree graduates also have their transcripts marked with the designation Graduated with an Honors Degree.

Admission Process: To be admitted to the Honors Program, students must meet one of the following requirements: be in the top 10 percent of their high school graduating class; have a cumulative high school GPA of at least 3.5 on a 4.0 scale or 4.3 on a 5.0 scale; have a minimum combined SAT I score of 1170 or a minimum composite ACT score of 26; have a CPT score of 100 or higher in writing and 97 or higher in reading or a 92 or higher in elementary algebra and 44 or higher in college-level mathematics; or have a cumulative Valencia GPA of 3.25 or higher with a minimum of 12 hours of college-level course work completed.

Campus Overview

State-supported 2-year, founded 1967, part of Florida Community College System • **Coed** 29,447 undergraduate students.

Undergraduates Students come from 40 states and territories, 92 other countries, 4% are from out of state.

Faculty *Total:* 934, 36% full-time, 14% with terminal degrees. *Student/faculty ratio:* 21:1.

Academic Programs *Special study options:* academic remediation for entering students, accelerated degree program, adult/continuing education programs, advanced placement credit, cooperative education, distance learning, double majors, English as a second language, honors programs, independent study, internships, part-time degree program, services for LD students, student-designed majors, summer session for credit. *ROTC:* Army (c).

Costs (2004–05) *Tuition:* state resident $1451 full-time, $60 per credit hour part-time; nonresident $5452 full-time, $227 per credit hour part-time.

Financial Aid 238 Federal Work-Study jobs (averaging $2400).

Contact: Director: Ronald G. Brandolini, Honors Program, 1800 South Kirkman Road, Orlando, Florida 32811; *Telephone:* 407-582-1729 or 1980; *Fax:* 407-582-1671; *E-mail:* rbrandolini@valenciacc.edu; *Web site:* http://www.valenciacc.edu/honors/

GEORGIA

Albany State University
Dr. Velma Fudge Grant Honors Program
Albany, Georgia

The Velma Fudge Grant Honors Program represents a commitment made by Albany State University (ASU) to broaden and enrich the educational experiences of bright, highly motivated, and creative students. Honors Program students are provided opportunities for scholarships, access to special extracurricular programs, a chance to pursue independent projects and research interests, professional experience through internship programs, and special service options. Through its specially designed curriculum, the University provides the opportunity for faculty members to teach academically talented students in inventive, interdisciplinary, small-class settings designed to fulfill core curriculum requirements as well as in advanced or intensive classes in particular disciplines. The Honors Program is specifically designed for the Presidential Scholars and other academic scholarship recipients and entering freshmen with a proven dedication to academic excellence and scholarship. The Honors Program student must reach beyond good grades for success and have the courage to demonstrate superior ethical leadership in his or her chosen field of study.

There are several primary goals of the Honors Program. The first goal is to encourage academic excellence through special courses and seminars. The second goal is to provide a supportive environment where young scholars can develop their potential. The third goal is to encourage advanced study and research under the guidance of, or in partnership with, selected faculty members and national leaders. The final goal is to expose students to a humanistic perspective as they engage in the various disciplines of academic inquiry and service.

Honors Program courses have limited enrollment and are reserved for successful and motivated students. These courses encourage participatory learning through the interchange of ideas between students and professors and among students themselves. Honors Program courses may be special sections of regularly offered courses or special courses available only to Honors Program students. Some courses are interdisciplinary in nature while others explore topics of current interest.

The honors curriculum may be customized through Honors Contracting and/or Honors Independent Study. With the approval of the instructor and the Honors Program Director, students may receive honors credit by enrolling in nonhonors, advanced-level courses and engaging in a written Honors Contract to undertake work that is more challenging and to meet with the professor for individualized instruction. Students may also undertake personalized study or research with a professor by registering for Honors Independent Study. Honors Contracting and Honors Independent Study are available to Honors Program students after they have completed 9 credit hours of regular Honors Program courses.

Participation Requirements: Velma Fudge Grant Honors Program students at ASU pursue majors in any of the degree programs available to undergraduates through the Colleges of Arts and Sciences, Business, Education, and Health Professions. In fulfilling departmental Honors Program and University requirements, Honors Program students have the opportunity to choose the combination of honors courses and regular course selections that best meet their needs and interests.

Program participants must maintain a minimum 3.0 cumulative grade point average each semester. At least 15 hours each semester must be completed successfully. A minimum of 20 hours in the sequence of Honors Core Curriculum courses and Honors Seminar courses must be completed. Participants must also take part in the social, cultural, and service life of the University.

Scholarship Availability: The Velma Fudge Grant Honors Program is only responsible for the selection of Presidential Scholarship recipients. The Albany State University Foundation, Inc., grants Presidential Scholarships in the amount of $6000 annually. For consideration of the Presidential Scholarship, the applicant must have a minimum combined score of 1140 on the SAT (verbal and math sections), a minimum grade point average of 3.5, rank in the upper 5 percent of the graduating class, and exhibit outstanding leadership abilities through specific activities and events. The selection process is highly individualized. Each applicant must submit three letters of recommendation and complete a 500-word essay. Finalists are interviewed.

Those prospective scholars who are not selected for a Presidential Scholarship are referred to the Office of Financial Aid, which grants other academic scholarships that also allow admission into the Honors Program.

Campus Overview

State-supported comprehensive, founded 1903, part of University System of Georgia • **Coed** 3,212 undergraduate students, 83% full-time, 68% women, 32% men.

Undergraduates 2,658 full-time, 554 part-time. 35% live on campus.

Faculty *Total:* 211, 67% full-time, 79% with terminal degrees. *Student/faculty ratio:* 16:1.

Academic Programs *Special study options:* academic remediation for entering students, adult/continuing education programs, advanced placement credit, cooperative education, distance learning, double majors, honors programs, independent study, internships, off-campus study, part-time degree program, services for LD students, study abroad, summer session for credit. *ROTC:* Army (b). *Unusual degree programs:* 3-2 engineering with Georgia Institute of Technology.

Athletics Member NCAA. All Division II. *Intercollegiate sports:* baseball M(s), basketball M(s)/W(s), cross-country running M(s)/W(s), football M(s), softball W(s), tennis M(s), track and field M(s)/W(s), volleyball W(s). *Intramural sports:* basketball M/W, softball M, swimming and diving M/W.

Costs (2004–05) *Tuition:* state resident $2322 full-time, $97 per credit hour part-time; nonresident $9290 full-time, $388 per credit hour part-time. *Required fees:* $574 full-time, $287 per term part-time. *Room and board:* $3690; room only: $1866. Room and board charges vary according to board plan and housing facility.

Financial Aid 440 Federal Work-Study jobs (averaging $1050). 178 state and other part-time jobs (averaging $1655). In 2003, 164 non-need-based awards were made. *Average percent of need met:* 68%. *Average financial aid package:* $7057.

Contact: Director: Dr. Ontario S. Wooden, Velma Fudge Grant Honors Program, Holley Institute Building, Albany State University, 504 College Drive, Albany, Georgia 31705; *Telephone:* 229-430-1871; *Fax:* 229-420-1111; *E-mail:* ontario.wooden@asurams.edu

---

Augusta State University
University Honors Program
Augusta, Georgia

The Honors Program offers superior full-time and part-time students in all fields the opportunity to pursue a program of study that leads to recognition as an Honors Program Graduate. Balancing breadth and depth, the Honors Program includes sections of core courses specifically designed for able and energetic learners, seminars that cross the boundaries of discipline and/or culture, a thesis, the possibility of additional honors work in the major field, and a synthesizing capstone. The Honors Program is not a separate degree program but is designed to augment the course work required for a degree, providing the best learning experience possible for its students and faculty. It encourages students to take advantage of a range of opportunities, from study abroad to cooperative learning to presentations at student and professional conferences. Honors classes differ in kind from other classes. They are usually smaller, enrolling a maximum of 20 students; they involve more interaction with the instructor; and they encourage independent work and collaboration among students and between students and professors. Often, professors in honors courses, who are chosen for their commitment to and excellence in undergraduate teaching, see themselves more as facilitators than as instructors or lecturers. Students take an active role in program design and curriculum planning. A relatively new program (approved February 1997), the Augusta State University (ASU) Honors Program currently enrolls 100 students.

Participation Requirements: Honors Program students complete at least five honors sections of freshman and sophomore courses, two upper-level honors classes (one of which must be interdisciplinary and/or multicultural), and an Honors Program capstone. In their last terms, Honors Program students work independently to design and produce an acceptable honors thesis. Honors theses are bound and housed in Reese Library. To graduate from the Honors Program, a student must have achieved a minimum GPA of 3.3.

Admission Process: Students may seek entry into the Honors Program by submitting to the Director an application form and either a letter of intent in which the students introduce themselves and tell what they will contribute to the Honors Program through their participation or an essay in which they define their personal and professional goals. Entering freshmen who meet one of the following criteria are invited to join the Honors Program and cleared to sign up for honors classes: combined SAT I scores of 1160 or better and a cumulative high school GPA of 3.2 or better or combined SAT I scores of 1100 or higher and a cumulative high school GPA of 3.5 or better. Students already enrolled at ASU are invited to join the Honors Program and cleared to sign up for honors classes if they have completed at least 10 semester hours of academic work at ASU, have an overall GPA of at least 3.4, and are not simultaneously in Learning Support. Transfer students who bring in an unadjusted minimum GPA of 3.4 on at least 10 semester hours of course work from another institution and have SAT I scores at least equivalent to those required of entering ASU freshmen are eligible to apply for admission to the program after they have completed at least 6 semester hours at ASU with an ASU unadjusted GPA of 3.4 or higher.

Scholarship Availability: Honors Program students compete favorably for a variety of partial and full University and departmental scholarships. Georgia residents who meet Honors Program requirements are eligible for HOPE scholarships. Augusta State awards more than $15 million each year in scholarships, grants, and loans.

Campus Overview

State-supported comprehensive, founded 1925, part of University System of Georgia • **Coed** 5,502 undergraduate students, 66% full-time, 65% women, 35% men.

Undergraduates 3,618 full-time, 1,884 part-time. Students come from 42 states and territories, 57 other countries, 11% are from out of state, 28% African American, 3% Asian American or Pacific Islander, 3% Hispanic American, 0.3% Native American, 0.9% international, 8% transferred in.

Faculty *Total:* 322, 65% full-time, 54% with terminal degrees. *Student/faculty ratio:* 26:1.

Academic Programs *Special study options:* academic remediation for entering students, adult/continuing education programs, advanced placement credit, cooperative education, double majors, English as a second language, honors programs, independent study, internships, off-campus study, part-time degree program, services for LD students, study abroad, summer session for credit. *ROTC:* Army (b).

Athletics Member NCAA, NAIA. All NCAA Division II. *Intercollegiate sports:* baseball M, basketball M(s)/W(s), cross-country running M(s)/W(s), softball W, tennis M(s)/W(s), volleyball W. *Intramural sports:* softball W, volleyball M/W, weight lifting M/W.

Costs (2004–05) *Tuition:* state resident $2322 full-time, $97 per hour part-time; nonresident $9290 full-time, $388 per hour part-time. *Required fees:* $380 full-time, $190 per term part-time.

Financial Aid 100 Federal Work-Study jobs (averaging $2783). 200 state and other part-time jobs (averaging $1713). In 2003, 677 non-need-based awards were made. *Average percent of need met:* 70%. *Average financial aid package:* $1013. *Average need-based loan:* $1573. *Average need-based gift aid:* $1440. *Average non-need-based aid:* $505.

Contact: Director: Dr. J. Andrew Hauger, 2500 Walton Way, Augusta, Georgia 30904-2200; *Telephone:* 706-729-2083; *Fax:* 706-729-2247; *E-mail:* honorsprogram@aug.edu; *Web site:* http://www.aug.edu/honors_program

Berry College
Honors Program
Mt. Berry, Georgia

Berry College Honors Program provides students with an opportunity to learn within an intellectually challenging community of peers and instructors. Honors courses familiarize students with works that have been central to past and contemporary intellectual traditions while encouraging them to examine issues or themes from multiple and conflicting perspectives. All honors courses are taught as seminars, which provides an ideal environment for the development of effective communication and critical-thinking skills. Class size is restricted to 15 students, with primary emphasis placed on student initiative in discussion, research, and presentations. The program sponsors a Speakers Series that enables honors students to interact with eminent scholars, thinkers, and writers.

There are currently 100 students in the program.

Participation Requirements: Lower-division course work requirements include satisfactory completion of two 3-credit hour Honors Colloquia (HONORS 201, 202) and at least two Honors Seminars (HONORS 211, 212, 221, 222, 250), for which a student receives a minimum of 6 credit hours. Honors Seminars vary in content and emphasis and are taught in rotation. Recent offerings include Europe between the Wars, Hindu Religious Texts, Foundations of Modern Biology, and Individual and Society: Economic and Literary Perspectives. Lower-division honors courses may be used to fulfill various general education requirements. Upper-division course work includes the satisfactory completion of at least two 3-credit hour honors-designated courses at the 300 or 400 level in the major or minor, to be determined by the student in consultation with his or her adviser and the director of the Honors Program. In addition, the student must complete two honors thesis courses in the major, each of which carries 3 credit hours, and perform satisfactorily in a defense of their Senior Honors Thesis, scheduled during the last semester of the student's residence at Berry College.

Admission Process: Students who wish to be admitted into the Honors Program simply complete an application and, upon acceptance, undertake the appropriate course work. Criteria for entering freshmen are scores of 1200 or higher on the SAT I or 27 or higher on the ACT, a 3.5 high school GPA or higher, and a writing sample. Criteria for enrolled Berry students are a 3.5 GPA or higher on college work completed, a writing sample, and names of two Berry College faculty members for reference.

Scholarship Availability: Berry College offers full-tuition Presidential Scholarships as well as partial-tuition Merit and Academic Scholarships. Many students who receive these awards participate in the Honors Program.

Campus Overview

Independent interdenominational comprehensive, founded 1902 • **Coed** 1,878 undergraduate students, 97% full-time, 65% women, 35% men.

Undergraduates 1,827 full-time, 51 part-time. Students come from 30 states and territories, 18 other countries, 18% are from out of state, 3% African American, 1% Asian American or Pacific Islander, 1% Hispanic American, 0.1% Native American, 1% international, 4% transferred in, 72% live on campus.

Faculty *Total:* 167, 80% full-time, 80% with terminal degrees. *Student/faculty ratio:* 13:1.

Academic Programs *Special study options:* accelerated degree program, adult/continuing education programs, advanced placement credit, cooperative education, double majors, honors programs, independent study, internships, part-time degree program, student-designed majors, study abroad, summer session for credit. *Unusual*

degree programs: 3-2 engineering with Georgia Institute of Technology, Mercer University; nursing with Emory University.

Athletics Member NAIA. *Intercollegiate sports:* baseball M(s), basketball M(s)/W(s), cheerleading M/W, crew M(c)/W(c), cross-country running M(s)/W(s), equestrian sports M(c)/W(c), golf M(s)/W(s), lacrosse M(c)/W(c), soccer M(s)/W(s), tennis M(s)/W(s), track and field M(s)/W(s), volleyball W. *Intramural sports:* badminton M/W, baseball M, basketball M/W, bowling M/W, cross-country running M/W, football M/W, golf M/W, racquetball M/W, rock climbing M/W, soccer M/W, softball M/W, table tennis M/W, tennis M/W, ultimate Frisbee M/W, volleyball M/W.

Costs (2004–05) *Comprehensive fee:* $22,690 includes full-time tuition ($16,240) and room and board ($6450). Part-time tuition: $540 per credit hour. *College room only:* $3650. Room and board charges vary according to board plan and housing facility.

Financial Aid 400 Federal Work-Study jobs (averaging $1800). 1,200 state and other part-time jobs (averaging $1800). In 2004, 751 non-need-based awards were made. *Average percent of need met:* 86%. *Average financial aid package:* $14,480. *Average need-based loan:* $3271. *Average need-based gift aid:* $10,907. *Average non-need-based aid:* $11,836.

Contact: Director: Dr. Elizabeth Kaufer Busch, P.O. Box 495010, Mt. Berry, Georgia 30149; *Telephone:* 706-238-7896; *Fax:* 706-236-2205; *E-mail:* ekaufer@berry.edu

Brenau University
Women's College Honors Program
Gainesville, Georgia

The Honors Program of Brenau University Women's College provides students of proven academic skills and motivation an opportunity to excel in their studies. Striving to combine a variety of innovative and traditional approaches, the Honors Program is designed to encourage analytical and creative thinking, to foster an awareness of the diversity of opinions in the global community, and, above all, to stimulate a love of learning that will continue throughout a student's lifetime. Grounded in a variety of liberal and professional studies, the program seeks to prepare students for future graduate education and to enrich their professional and personal lives.

Small class size is central to the Women's College Honors Program. Classes of approximately 15 students stimulate interactive student-faculty dialogue that often continues outside the classroom as students develop their thinking and assume leadership roles on campus. Honors students are actively encouraged to explore study abroad, internships, and other opportunities at appropriate junctures in their undergraduate careers. The curriculum includes several research options, honors disciplinary and interdisciplinary courses, and an optional two-semester capstone project or thesis. An honors international-study course, which may be repeated for credit, is offered, and an honors housing option is available.

Founded in 1988, the Honors Program admits approximately 30 to 35 students annually. Currently, about 85 students are enrolled in the program.

Participation Requirements: In their freshman and sophomore years, honors students begin the first phase of their program by taking at least six honors courses to help fulfill their general education requirements. Students are encouraged to take as many honors courses as their interests and schedules allow, and they may extend these courses into their upper-division years, depending on their majors. As many as twelve of these courses may be taken. A special feature of the freshman and sophomore portion of the program, which is open by invitation to selected students, is the opportunity to develop an independent, guided research project on a topic of interest. Up to four independent research courses may be taken by qualified honors students.

In the junior year, students take an interdisciplinary seminar focusing in depth on various topics, such as Literature and the Environment, Women in the Arts, and Exploring Careers in the Postmodern World. Students completing this second phase of the program graduate with Honors in Liberal Studies.

Students then may choose to complete the Honors Program with an extended Senior Honors Thesis or Project. Usually this is related to the student's major. This two-semester course, often begun in the spring of the junior year, culminates with the award of High Honors in Liberal Studies.

To graduate with honors or high honors, students must maintain a minimum 3.3 GPA in both their honors courses and their cumulative GPA. These students receive special recognition, a certificate, and an embossed gold seal on their diploma at graduation. Students who maintain a minimum 3.0 GPA may continue in the Honors Program and will be recognized as a graduate of the Honors Program if they complete the Junior Seminar.

Admission Process: Admission to the Honors Program is based on SAT scores, high school GPA, and other factors. Normally, admission is granted to students with an SAT score of 1800 (SAT I score of 1200) or an equivalent ACT score and a GPA of about 3.5, although students of exceptional promise are considered on a case-by-case basis. No special application to the Honors Program is needed. Currently enrolled students may apply to the Honors Program with a minimum 3.5 GPA, and transfer students are welcomed into the program.

Scholarship Availability: Scholarships are available through the Admissions Office, and many honors students receive generous financial aid packages.

Campus Overview

Independent comprehensive, founded 1878 • **Small-town** 57-acre campus with easy access to Atlanta • **Women only** 680 undergraduate students, 93% full-time.

Undergraduates 634 full-time, 46 part-time. Students come from 16 states and territories, 15 other countries, 8% are from out of state, 16% African American, 2% Asian American or Pacific Islander, 3% Hispanic American, 0.4% Native American, 3% international, 16% transferred in, 55% live on campus.

Faculty *Total:* 113, 62% full-time, 63% with terminal degrees. *Student/faculty ratio:* 10:1.

Academic Programs *Special study options:* academic remediation for entering students, advanced placement credit, cooperative education, distance learning, double majors, honors programs, independent study, internships, off-campus study, part-time degree program, services for LD students, study abroad, summer session for credit.

Athletics Member NAIA. *Intercollegiate sports:* crew W, cross-country running W(s), soccer W(s), softball W(s), tennis W(s), volleyball W(s).

Costs (2004–05) *Comprehensive fee:* $22,770 includes full-time tuition ($14,610), mandatory fees ($100), and room and board ($8060). Full-time tuition and fees vary according to class time, location, and program. Part-time tuition: $487 per semester hour. Part-time tuition and fees vary according to class time, location, and program. *Required fees:* $50 per term part-time. *Room and board:* Room and board charges vary according to board plan and housing facility.

Financial Aid 162 Federal Work-Study jobs (averaging $1286). 6 state and other part-time jobs (averaging $2293). In 2004, 131 non-need-based awards were made. *Average percent of need met:* 81%. *Average financial aid package:* $15,452. *Average need-based loan:* $3482. *Average need-based gift aid:* $12,114. *Average non-need-based aid:* $8127.

Contact: Director: Dr. Jay Gaspar, Women's College Honors Program, Brenau University, 500 Washington Street, Gainesville, Georgia 30501; *Telephone:* 770-534-6196; *Fax:* 770-534-6137; *E-mail:* jgaspar@lib.brenau.edu

Columbus State University
Honors Program
Columbus, Georgia

The Columbus State University (CSU) Honors Program (HP) began in 1998 and now has 70 students in the program. Honors students can major in any department and college at CSU and, in most cases, can do so without incurring additional credit hours for their degree. The HP provides significant challenges and opportunities to enrich an exceptional student's education, taking the educational experience beyond the ordinary. The HP strives to create a community of outstanding scholars and stimulate involvement in campus and community activities. Special funding is provided for select students to study abroad. Special features include a special luncheon with a guest speaker each semester, small classes (15 students maximum), special access to distinguished visitors on campus, waiver of out-of-state tuition for select students, and early registration before all other categories of students.

Participation Requirements: The honors curriculum includes three core curriculum honors courses, three upper-division honors courses in the major, and a thesis. The program also requires participation in four campus events and an off-campus enrichment activity. In most majors, the HP is accomplished in the same number of credit hours as nonhonors programs. To graduate from the HP, students must have a minimum 3.4 overall GPA. At Honors Convocation, the HP awards graduates with an honors cord to wear at graduation. Completion of the HP is noted on the transcript.

Admission Process: Entering freshmen may apply to the HP if they have applied for admission to CSU and have a high school GPA of 3.5 or higher and a combined SAT I score of 1200 or higher (with a 550 minimum in each subscore). Students must also supply two letters of recommendation and transcripts plus an essay. The final selection is made by interview. Transfer and international students are admitted on an individual basis after eligibility has been determined. Students already at CSU may seek admission to the HP if their college GPA is 3.5 or better, they have a combined SAT I score of at least 1200, and if they have taken fewer than 30 semester hours of core curriculum courses.

Scholarship Availability: At least fifteen honors scholarships are available annually, totaling $13,200 each, of which $3200 must be used toward study-abroad programs. Many other scholarships and grants are also available, including the HOPE scholarship for Georgia residents.

Campus Overview

State-supported comprehensive, founded 1958, part of University System of Georgia • **Coed** 6,300 undergraduate students, 67% full-time, 63% women, 37% men.

Undergraduates 4,199 full-time, 2,101 part-time. Students come from 35 states and territories, 40 other countries, 13% are from out of state, 30% African American, 2% Asian American or Pacific Islander, 4% Hispanic American, 0.4% Native American, 1% international, 8% transferred in, 14% live on campus.

Faculty *Total:* 390, 52% full-time, 52% with terminal degrees. *Student/faculty ratio:* 19:1.

Academic Programs *Special study options:* academic remediation for entering students, adult/continuing education programs, advanced placement credit, cooperative education, distance learning, freshman honors college, honors programs, independent study, internships, part-time degree program, services for LD students, study abroad, summer session for credit. *ROTC:* Army (b).

Athletics Member NCAA. All Division II. *Intercollegiate sports:* baseball M(s), basketball M(s)/W(s), cross-country running M(s)/W(s), golf M(s), soccer W(s), softball W(s), tennis M(s)/W(s).

Intramural sports: badminton M/W, basketball M/W, bowling M/W, cross-country running M/W, football M/W, golf M/W, racquetball M/W, skiing (downhill) M/W, soccer M/W, softball M/W, table tennis M/W, tennis M/W, volleyball M/W.

Costs (2004–05) *Tuition:* state resident $2322 full-time, $97 per semester hour part-time; nonresident $9290 full-time, $388 per semester hour part-time. *Required fees:* $486 full-time. *Room and board:* $5550; room only: $3510. Room and board charges vary according to board plan and location.

Financial Aid In 2004, 1174 non-need-based awards were made. *Average percent of need met:* 70%. *Average financial aid package:* $4015. *Average need-based loan:* $3501. *Average need-based gift aid:* $3324. *Average non-need-based aid:* $1749.

Contact: Dr. Barbara Hunt; *Telephone:* 706-568-2054; *E-mail:* hunt_barbara@colstate.edu

Georgia College & State University
Honors and Scholars Program
Milledgeville, Georgia

The mission of the University's Honors Program is to meet the intellectual expectations and aspirations of exceptional and highly motivated students. Small classes with some of the University's most outstanding faculty members are enriched through interdisciplinary classes and colloquia, service learning, and extracurricular events. Intensive writing courses, small group discussion, innovative capstone experiences, and extensive interaction with faculty members beyond the classroom characterize the program.

Honors classes are small and interactive. Professors encourage students to take responsibility for their own learning, think critically, and develop positions on major questions that they are able to defend. Honors options in upper-level courses and a seamless residential living-learning community are available for students who choose to participate in these opportunities. Students who achieve a minimum of 3.5 on 60 semester hours of academic credit are eligible for individualized learning experiences, such as research and thesis, study abroad, and independent study, through the Scholars Program. Sanford Hall houses the Honors Living-Learning Community, which is staffed by honors residential assistants and houses 20 upper-level students who serve as mentors for 50 incoming first-year students. Currently 80 students are selected each year to participate in the Honors and Scholars Program.

Eta Sigma Alpha, the student organization of the Honors and Scholars Program, sponsors community-service opportunities and social events and provides the experiential arm of the program. The officers of this group provide a voice for honors students to the Honors Council, the governing body of the Honors and Scholars Program.

Participation Requirements: Students must complete a minimum of 20 hours of work in the Honors and Scholars Program and must have participated in at least 80 hours of service learning before graduating. The curriculum must contain some honors core classes and one upper-level interdisciplinary honors colloquium. The additional hours may be obtained through honors option courses and work in the Scholars Program. Students must maintain a minimum 3.3 GPA to remain in the program and to graduate with honors recognition. Those who achieve a 3.5 GPA or better are eligible for work in the major or a closely related area through research and thesis, independent study, internships, and study abroad in the Scholars Program. Completion of the Honors and/or Scholars Program is recorded on the student's academic transcript, and they are acknowledged at the graduation ceremony.

Admission Process: All entering students who have a high school GPA of at least 3.3 and SAT of 1200 (ACT 26) or better are eligible to apply to the Honors Program. The application includes an essay and a recommendation from a high school counselor or teacher. Upon receipt of an electronic application, student files are reviewed on an ongoing basis and selections are made until the program is filled. Occasionally, when additional information is needed, students are interviewed.

Scholarship Availability: The University's Presidential Scholars are awarded full four-year scholarships with membership in the Honors and Scholars Program and participation in the honors living-learning community. Small awards are made each year for outstanding work in the Scholars Program. A few honors scholarships are available for incoming first-year students.

Campus Overview
State-supported comprehensive, founded 1889, part of University System of Georgia • **Coed** 4,575 undergraduate students, 87% full-time, 60% women, 40% men.

Undergraduates 3,986 full-time, 589 part-time. Students come from 39 states and territories, 42 other countries, 1% are from out of state, 9% African American, 1% Asian American or Pacific Islander, 1% Hispanic American, 0.3% Native American, 2% international, 9% transferred in, 36% live on campus.

Faculty *Total:* 407, 66% full-time. *Student/faculty ratio:* 14:1.

Academic Programs *Special study options:* academic remediation for entering students, accelerated degree program, advanced placement credit, distance learning, double majors, English as a second language, freshman honors college, honors programs, independent study, internships, part-time degree program, services for LD students, student-designed majors, study abroad, summer session for credit. *ROTC:* Army (c). *Unusual degree programs:* 3-2 engineering with Georgia Institute of Technology.

Athletics Member NCAA. All Division II. *Intercollegiate sports:* baseball M(s), basketball M(s)/W(s), cross-country running M(s)/W(s), fencing M(c)/W(c), golf M(s), soccer W(s), softball W(s), tennis M(s)/W(s). *Intramural sports:* archery M/W, basketball M/W, bowling M/W, football M/W, golf M, racquetball M/W, rugby M(c), soccer M/W, softball M/W, swimming and diving M/W, table tennis M/W, tennis M/W, ultimate Frisbee M/W, volleyball M/W.

Costs (2004–05) *Tuition:* state resident $3152 full-time, $132 per semester hour part-time; nonresident $12,608 full-time, $526 per semester hour part-time. Part-time tuition and fees vary according to course load. *Required fees:* $710 full-time, $355 per term part-time. *Room and board:* $6482. Room and board charges vary according to board plan and housing facility.

Financial Aid In 2003, 240 non-need-based awards were made.

Contact: Director: Doris C. Moody, Honors and Scholars Program, Lanier Hall, Room 129, CBX 29, Georgia College & State University, Milledgeville, Georgia 31061; *Telephone:* 478-445-4463; *E-mail:* doris.moody@gcsu.edu

Georgia Perimeter College
Honors Program
Atlanta, Georgia

The Georgia Perimeter College Honors Program is an academic and student services program for students in any area of study who have demonstrated outstanding achievement and motivation. The Honors Program offers intellectually challenging courses taught by dedicated faculty members, interaction with other students, and opportunities for recognition and service. Courses are offered in the *humanities, social sciences, science, fine arts, and business. The purpose of the Honors Program is to encourage students to achieve excellence in all aspects of their experience at Georgia Perimeter College.*

Enrollment in honors courses is typically 12 to 15 students. Courses often have a seminar format and emphasize communication skills. Some classes, such as honors composition, meet in fully equipped computer classrooms. Interdisciplinary options are available in a number of courses.

Students in the Honors Program enjoy a number of important benefits, including priority registration, membership in the Honors Program Student Association, and opportunities to travel to various honors conferences. Travel by students to attend and present at state, regional, and national honors conferences is funded by the school. The Honors Program and the Honors Program Student Association also sponsor literary, cultural, and academic programs throughout the year.

Students may join the Honors Program at any point in their academic career at Georgia Perimeter College. The Honors Program began in 1983 and currently enrolls 450 students.

Participation Requirements: Open to students majoring in any discipline, the Honors Program welcomes qualified students at any juncture in their tenure at Georgia Perimeter College. To earn an Honors certificate, the student must have completed at least 45 semester hours of college work with a cumulative GPA of at least 3.3. Of these 45 semester hours, 15 semester hours must have been earned in honors courses in which the student received a grade of B or higher. All classes taken through the Honors Program appear on a student's transcript with an honors designation.

Admission Process: The following eligibility requirements are considered for acceptance into the Honors Program: a composite SAT I score of at least 1200, a minimum 650 SAT I verbal score, or at least a 620 SAT I math score; an ACT composite score of at least 26, an ACT English score of at least 29, or an ACT mathematics score of at least 27; National Merit Semi-Finalist status; eligibility for Phi Theta Kappa, the national honorary society for two-year colleges; 9 or more college-transfer credit hours and a minimum 3.5 GPA from another college; at least a 3.5 GPA in academic courses taken at Georgia Perimeter College; and a recommendation from a faculty member and approval of the Honors Program Coordinator.

Scholarship Availability: Each campus of Georgia Perimeter College has several academic scholarships designated for students in the Honors Program; students who have completed at least two honors courses are eligible to apply. Priority is given to those students who have completed the most honors courses and have the highest cumulative GPA.

Campus Overview

State-supported 2-year, founded 1964, part of University System of Georgia • **Coed** 18,986 undergraduate students, 45% full-time, 63% women, 37% men.

Undergraduates 8,548 full-time, 10,438 part-time. Students come from 40 states and territories, 125 other countries, 7% are from out of state, 37% African American, 9% Asian American or Pacific Islander, 4% Hispanic American, 0.3% Native American, 5% international, 5% transferred in.

Faculty *Total:* 1,653, 20% full-time, 20% with terminal degrees. *Student/faculty ratio:* 21:1.

Academic Programs *Special study options:* academic remediation for entering students, adult/continuing education programs, advanced placement credit, distance learning, English as a second language, honors programs, part-time degree program, services for LD students, study abroad, summer session for credit. *ROTC:* Army (c).

Athletics Member NJCAA. *Intercollegiate sports:* baseball M(s), basketball M(s)/W(s), soccer M(s)/W(s), softball W(s), tennis M(s)/W(s).

Costs (2004–05) *Tuition:* state resident $1468 full-time, $62 per credit hour part-time; nonresident $5872 full-time, $245 per credit hour part-time. *Required fees:* $256 full-time, $128 per term part-time.

Financial Aid 218 Federal Work-Study jobs (averaging $3000).

Contact: Director, Clarkston Campus: Dr. Susan McGrath, 555 North Indian Creek Drive, Clarkston, Georgia 30021-2396; *Telephone:* 678-891-3620; *Fax:* 404-298-3957; *E-mail:* smcgrath@gpc.edu. Director, Decatur Campus: Ted Wadley, 3251 Panthersville Road, Decatur, Georgia 30021-2396; *Telephone:* 678-891-2530; *Fax:* 404-244-5799; *E-mail:* twadley@gpc.edu. Director, Dunwoody Campus: Dr. James Engstrom, 2101 Womack Road, Dunwoody, Georgia 30021-2396; *Telephone:* 770-274-5280; *Fax:* 770-604-3798; *E-mail:* jengstro@gpc.edu. Director, Lawrenceville Campus: Dr. Jeffrey A. Portnoy, 1000 University Center Lane, Lawrenceville, Georgia 30043; *Telephone:* 678-407-5324; *Fax:* 678-407-5273; *E-mail:* jportnoy@gpc.edu. Director, Rockdale Center: Dr. Robert Alderson, 115 West Avenue, Conyers, Georgia 30012; *Telephone:* 770-278-1344; *Fax:* 770-785-6867; *E-mail:* ralders@gpc.edu

Georgia Southern University
The University Honors Program and 1906 Scholars
Statesboro, Georgia

The Georgia Southern University Honors Program (UHP) encourages superior students to explore a course of study designed for greater depth. The program creates a learning environment of small classes enriched by inventive, interdisciplinary instruction and extracurricular experiences that connect classroom learning with the larger world. It also happens at a campus that prides itself on a tradition of teaching as its paramount priority. The Honors Program classes are smaller than regular courses and are taught by some of Georgia Southern's best classroom teachers in seminary style.

As a member of the Honors Program, students also benefit from these special opportunities: seal on the diploma, signifying completion of the University Honors Program; honors-oriented freshman- to senior-year mentoring; priority assignment to an Honors Residence Hall; eligibility to apply for scholarships for study abroad; a book loan program, which covers most core honors courses; an honors alcove in the Russell Union and an honors center for study and relaxation; leadership training; independent study; special events, such as guest speakers, musical programs, and socials; and backstage access to selected speakers and performers.

Within the UHP, a select group of 15 to 18 freshmen are selected each year to be 1906 Scholars. These students receive full-tuition scholarships and are encouraged to take a more demanding collection of honors core courses. Their course of study also includes a weekly seminar to emphasize discussion and independent endeavor and to nurture curiosity and the sharing of ideas among students and faculty members. These students also have the full benefits of UHP students, including transcript designation and recognition at graduation, as well as an honors curriculum within their majors. Additional benefits available to the 1906 Scholars include a lecture series emphasizing leadership, social events involving key campus leaders and administrators, and consideration for national and international scholarship recognition.

Participation Requirements: The Georgia Southern University Honors Program is divided into two levels leading to graduation with honors: the Core Curriculum Honors Program for freshmen and sophomores requires a minimum of 12 semester hours of course work and seminars, usually including at least one 3-hour honors course per semester, and at least 25 hours of community service each semester.

The College Honors Program for juniors and seniors includes at least 9 semester hours of course work and seminars, plus a well-defined capstone experience (thesis, performance, project, or exhibit). Graduates are recognized for their achievement by an honors seal on their diplomas and notation on their University transcripts.

Admission Process: General criteria for admission to the Core Curriculum Honors Program include a minimum score of 1200 on the SAT, or equivalent score on the ACT, and a high school academic or college grade point average of at least 3.5. Exceptions may be made for students who demonstrate special abilities, talents, or achievements. Admission to the College Honors Program requires an application and an approved course of study for the junior and senior years as well as a University GPA of 3.5.

Scholarship Availability: New students admitted to the University Core Curriculum Honors Program receive a $500 scholarship, renewable annually through the sophomore year, in addition to any other aid for which they may qualify (such as HOPE Grants). Students admitted to the College Honors Program for the junior and senior years also receive a $500 renewable annual scholarship in addition to any other aid for which they may qualify.

Campus Overview

State-supported comprehensive, founded 1906, part of University System of Georgia • **Coed** 14,092 undergraduate students, 90% full-time, 49% women, 51% men.

Undergraduates 12,658 full-time, 1,434 part-time. Students come from 45 states and territories, 77 other countries, 4% are from out of state, 23% African American, 1% Asian American or Pacific Islander, 1% Hispanic American, 0.2% Native American, 0.9% international, 6% transferred in, 23% live on campus.

Faculty *Total:* 708, 89% full-time, 71% with terminal degrees. *Student/faculty ratio:* 20:1.

Academic Programs *Special study options:* academic remediation for entering students, accelerated degree program, adult/continuing education programs, advanced placement credit, cooperative education, distance learning, double majors, English as a second language, external degree program, honors programs, independent study, internships, off-campus study, part-time degree program, services for LD students, study abroad, summer session for credit. *ROTC:* Army (b). *Unusual degree programs:* 3-2 engineering with Georgia Institute of Technology; forestry with University of Georgia; physics with Georgia Institute of Technology.

Athletics Member NCAA. All Division I except football (Division I-AA). *Intercollegiate sports:* baseball M(s), basketball M(s)/W(s), bowling M(c)/W(c), cheerleading M/W, cross-country running W(s), equestrian sports M(c)/W(c), fencing M(c)/W(c), golf M(s), lacrosse M(c), rugby M(c)/W(c), soccer M(s)/W(s), softball W(s), swimming and diving W(s), tennis M(s)/W(s), track and field W(s), ultimate Frisbee M(c)/W(c), volleyball W(s), wrestling M(c)/W(c). *Intramural sports:* baseball M(c), basketball M/W, bowling M/W, football M/W, golf M/W, soccer M/W, softball M/W, tennis M/W, track and field M(c)/W(c), volleyball M/W.

Costs (2004–05) *Tuition:* state resident $2232 full-time, $97 per semester hour part-time; nonresident $9290 full-time, $388 per semester hour part-time. Full-time tuition and fees vary according to location. Part-time tuition and fees vary according to course load and location. *Required fees:* $830 full-time, $415 per term part-time. *Room and board:* $6000; room only: $3734. Room and board charges vary according to board plan and housing facility.

Financial Aid 350 Federal Work-Study jobs (averaging $1243). In 2003, 321 non-need-based awards were made. *Average percent of need met:* 71%. *Average financial aid package:* $6606. *Average need-based loan:* $3737. *Average need-based gift aid:* $4294. *Average non-need-based aid:* $1404.

Contact: Honors Program Office, Cottage 215, Forest Drive, P.O. Box 8130, Statesboro, Georgia 30460; *Telephone:* 912-871-1465 or 486-7926; *E-mail:* lwrushing@georgiasouthern.edu; *Web site:* http://academics.georgiasouthern.edu/honors/

Georgia State University
Honors Program
Atlanta, Georgia

The Honors Program at Georgia State University (GSU) provides a place for high-achieving students to obtain many of the benefits of a small liberal arts college while also receiving the advantages of attending a comprehensive research university. It provides small discussion-oriented classes at the core level as well as the upper division. The program provides a natural home for both multicultural and interdisciplinary courses, and it offers some of the most innovative courses in the University. Students are given opportunities to propose and complete a senior thesis and to participate in the design and coordination of colloquia.

Students have the option of residence on an honors floor in dormitory housing. A special community assistant provides programming and guidance for these students.

Approximately 500 students are enrolled in the Georgia State University Honors Program, which was founded in 1975.

Participation Requirements: Students must maintain at least a 3.3 GPA to graduate with an Honors Recognition. Although there is no minimum number of courses required to remain enrolled in the Honors Program, students who are in good academic standing in the program and who have taken at least one honors course in the past three semesters are considered active in the program. Active students are eligible for priority registration and Honors Program Scholarships. Each spring, the Honors Program presents medallions to any student who has completed the requirements for general, advanced, or research honors at an awards ceremony. This recognition is also noted on the student's diploma and transcript.

Admission Process: Students may be admitted to the Honors Program at any stage of their academic careers. Freshmen admitted to the University with a high school GPA of 3.3 or higher and an SAT I score of at least 1200 are eligible to apply to the program. Transfer students should have completed 10 hours of transfer credit with a GPA of 3.3 or above. Georgia State University students who are already matriculated may also apply to the program if they have completed 10 hours at GSU and have a GPA of 3.3 or better. Students complete an application that requests basic academic data and a short writing sample. Upon receipt of the application, an interview is held and a decision is made at that time.

Scholarship Availability: The Honors Program awards ten Alumni Association Scholarships once a year. Students need to have completed at least two honors courses to be eligible to apply. Recipients are selected by a faculty committee on the basis of academic achievement. The University awards a number of Presidential Scholarships each year to incoming freshmen. These stipends include a cash allowance of $4000 per year for four years plus a grant of $1500 to be used for a summer study or a research project.

Campus Overview

State-supported university, founded 1913, part of University System of Georgia • **Coed** 19,894 undergraduate students, 69% full-time, 61% women, 39% men.

Undergraduates 13,676 full-time, 6,218 part-time. Students come from 52 states and territories, 142 other countries, 3% are from out of state, 32% African American, 10% Asian American or Pacific Islander, 3% Hispanic American, 0.2% Native American, 3% international, 8% transferred in, 10% live on campus.

Faculty *Total:* 1,428, 72% full-time. *Student/faculty ratio:* 19:1.

Academic Programs *Special study options:* academic remediation for entering students, accelerated degree program, advanced placement credit, cooperative education, distance learning, double majors,

English as a second language, honors programs, independent study, internships, off-campus study, part-time degree program, services for LD students, study abroad, summer session for credit. *ROTC:* Army (b), Navy (c), Air Force (c).

Athletics Member NCAA. All Division I. *Intercollegiate sports:* baseball M(s), basketball M(s)/W(s), cross-country running M(s)/W(s), golf M(s)/W(s), soccer M(s)/W(s), softball W(s), tennis M(s)/W(s), track and field M(s)/W(s), volleyball W(s). *Intramural sports:* badminton M/W, basketball M/W, bowling M/W, cross-country running M/W, football M/W, soccer M/W(c), softball M/W, table tennis M/W, tennis M/W, track and field M/W, volleyball M/W.

Costs (2004–05) *Tuition:* state resident $3529 full-time, $141 per semester hour part-time; nonresident $14,115 full-time, $562 per semester hour part-time. Full-time tuition and fees vary according to course load, degree level, and program. Part-time tuition and fees vary according to course load, degree level, and program. *Required fees:* $783 full-time, $393 per term part-time. *Room and board:* $7118; room only: $5130. Room and board charges vary according to board plan and housing facility.

Financial Aid 292 Federal Work-Study jobs (averaging $2154). In 2002, 1498 non-need-based awards were made. *Average percent of need met:* 70%. *Average financial aid package:* $7780. *Average need-based loan:* $5457. *Average need-based gift aid:* $4538. *Average non-need-based aid:* $4024.

Contact: Director: Dr. Timothy Renick, Honors Program, Georgia State University, University Plaza, P.O. Box 3966, Atlanta, Georgia 30302-3966; *Telephone:* 404-651-2924; *Fax:* 404-651-4890; *Web site:* http://www.gsu.edu/honors

Kennesaw State University
Undergraduate Honors Program and Joint Enrollment Honors Program
Kennesaw, Georgia

The Honors Program at Kennesaw State University (KSU) houses the Undergraduate Honors Program and the Joint Enrollment Honors Program.

The Undergraduate Honors Program is organized around three fundamental principles: Honors Faculty mentorship, formal Honors Experiences, and the Honors Colloquium.

Honors students are provided with Honors Faculty mentors who help them create a balanced and academically rigorous Honors curriculum consistent with their major requirements and engage them in active intellectual exchange. Sharing academic interests and professional objectives, they work together for the duration of the students' participation in the program.

The program's four "Honors Experiences" are designed to stimulate creativity and self-direction, and require work that is qualitatively, not quantitatively, different from traditional assignments. These experiences fall into three basic categories: those based exclusively in course work; those based in applied learning and offered primarily (though not exclusively) outside the traditional classroom; and the senior capstone experience (which, for the majority of Honors students, culminates in the writing of an Honors thesis).

Students can complete experiences based in course work through plenary Honors courses such as the Honors Seminar or through Honors dimension courses—non-Honors courses in which the instructor and student negotiate an Honors contract. The applied learning experience, based in a student's major, can be completed through an internship, research assistantship, teaching assistantship, or other context. The capstone experience can be an original research project growing out of a student's major concentration; a project based in applied research that provides new insights into that

discipline; an original synthesis of information or research already available in the discipline; a substantial service learning project designed and coordinated by the Honors student; or, for fine arts majors, a production or performance. The Senior Capstone Experience is documented in a formal written paper submitted for final review to the Honors Director and Honors Program Council.

The interdisciplinary Honors Seminar and Honors Colloquium are taught exclusively by Honors Faculty, and class sizes are limited to between fifteen and twenty students. Honors housing in the "Honors Wing" of the university's newest residence hall is available to all Honors students, but first-year residential Honors students enroll in an Honors Learning Community with a cohort of their peers.

The Undergraduate Honors Program was founded in 1995 and currently has 235 active members.

KSU's Joint Enrollment Honors Program (JEHP) is a refinement of the state of Georgia's ACCEL Program, which allows rising high school juniors or seniors to attend public colleges of universities, part-time or full-time, and receive dual credit for selected courses. Unlike other Joint Enrollment programs in Georgia, KSU's program offers special Honors sections of the six most popular dual-credit courses: Composition I, Composition II, Pre-calculus, Calculus, Global Economics, and American Government in a Global Perspective. Other Honors perquisites include priority registration, special advising services, and the opportunity to live in the Honors Wing of KSU's University Village, as well as participate in Honors social activities.

The Joint Enrollment Honors Program began in 1996, and 165 students are currently enrolled.

Participation Requirements: Students in the Undergraduate Honors Program must maintain a minimum cumulative GPA of 3.5 in their KSU course work to remain in good standing; they are allowed a probationary period if their average drops below 3.5. To graduate with the designation "Honors Scholar" on their transcript and diploma, they must complete four Honors Experiences—one or two in traditional classroom settings, one or two in applied learning contexts, and one designated as the capstone experience—and two one-hour, pass-fail Honors Colloquia. In addition, they must submit both an Honors thesis (or equivalent artistic product) and an Honors Portfolio documenting the products of their work in the Honors Program; the introduction to this portfolio must be a narrative illuminating the value added to their college experience by their Honors work.

Admission Process: Each year, the Undergraduate Honors Program admits incoming first-year students with an academic GPA of 3.7 or better and a composite SAT score of at least 1100; and currently enrolled students with a GPA of 3.7 or better in 30 to 60 hours of KSU course work. The Honors Director identifies Honors-eligible first-year students from a list provided by KSU's Office of Admissions, and other eligible students from a similar list compiled by KSU's Academic Computing Services. The director interviews students failing to meet the eligibility criteria, admitting them if they present a convincing case for their potential to succeed in Honors.

The Joint Enrollment Honors Program (JEHP) accepts rising high school juniors or seniors with an academic GPA of 3.0 or better and a composite score of at least 1100 on the SAT. The Office of Admissions recruits these students from more than twenty high schools in northwest Georgia and processes their applications, sending their contact information to the Honors Director. Members of the Honors Faculty advise JEHP students twice a year; the director approves the dual-credit courses subsidized by the state's ACCEL Program, which covers tuition and fees and provides a book allowance.

Scholarship Availability: The Undergraduate Honors Program does not offer scholarships for its members, but the Honors Director does provide scholarship counseling and sits on the University Scholarship Committee. The ACCEL Program that subsidizes tuition, fees, and books for Joint Enrollment Honors students taking designated dual-credit courses is not a scholarship *per se*, but functions like one; it is, in fact, an extension of the state's HOPE scholarship program for all public college or university students maintaining a "B" average in their course work.

Campus Overview

State-supported comprehensive, founded 1963, part of University System of Georgia • **Coed** 16,073 undergraduate students, 66% full-time, 62% women, 38% men.

Undergraduates 10,647 full-time, 5,426 part-time. Students come from 40 states and territories, 132 other countries, 4% are from out of state, 10% African American, 3% Asian American or Pacific Islander, 3% Hispanic American, 0.3% Native American, 3% international, 9% transferred in, 9% live on campus.

Faculty *Total:* 858, 63% full-time, 56% with terminal degrees. *Student/faculty ratio:* 19:1.

Academic Programs *Special study options:* academic remediation for entering students, adult/continuing education programs, advanced placement credit, cooperative education, freshman honors college, honors programs, internships, off-campus study, part-time degree program, services for LD students, study abroad, summer session for credit. *ROTC:* Army (b), Air Force (b).

Athletics Member NCAA. All Division II. *Intercollegiate sports:* baseball M(s), basketball M(s)/W(s), cheerleading W, cross-country running M(s)/W(s), golf M(s), softball W(s), tennis W(s). *Intramural sports:* basketball M/W, bowling M/W, football M/W, soccer M/W, softball M/W, swimming and diving M/W, tennis M/W, volleyball M/W, weight lifting M/W.

Costs (2004–05) *Tuition:* state resident $2322 full-time, $97 per credit hour part-time; nonresident $9290 full-time, $388 per credit hour part-time. *Required fees:* $436 full-time, $218 per term part-time. *Room only:* $5376. Room and board charges vary according to housing facility.

Financial Aid In 2003, 654 non-need-based awards were made. *Average percent of need met:* 20%. *Average financial aid package:* $3907. *Average need-based loan:* $1625. *Average need-based gift aid:* $1324. *Average non-need-based aid:* $770.

Contact: Dr. Liza Davis, Director of the Honors Program, Department of University Studies, Mail Drop # 1802, Kennesaw State University, 1000 Chastain Road, Kennesaw, Georgia 30144-5591; *Telephone:* 770-423-6116 or 770-499-3514; *Fax:* 770-423-6748; *E-mail:* ldavis@kennesaw.edu or honors@kennesaw.edu; *Web site:* http://www.kennesaw.edu/university_studies/honors

Mercer University
Honors Program
Macon, Georgia

Mercer University's Honors Program offers an opportunity for academically outstanding students to develop their talents and potential to the fullest through intellectually enriched and stimulating learning experiences. Qualified students may be admitted to the Honors Program in the College of Liberal Arts, the Stetson School of Business and Economics, the Tift College of Education, or the School of Engineering.

The Engineering Honors Program provides a program of study that presents challenges beyond the normal requirements for an undergraduate degree in engineering. The goals of the Engineering Honors Program are to provide a common first-year experience that challenges the students and faculty members both technically and nontechnically and to provide a project experience that demonstrates knowledge and skills that exceed normal undergraduate requirements. A limited number of students are admitted each fall.

The honors experience for first- and second-year students in the three other undergraduate schools is organized by the College of Liberal Arts; business students and students in secondary education complete the last two years of honors in their respective schools. During the first two years, honors students are enrolled in a

thematically organized seminar each semester. The seminars are led by outstanding faculty members and are limited in enrollment; the emphasis is upon student leadership and discussion. Students also participate in community-building activities, such as dinners, other social occasions, and special cultural events and trips. First-year honors students complete Great Books I, which concentrates on the ancient Greeks and includes works by Homer, Aeschylus, Sophocles, Thucydides, and Plato.

In the College of Liberal Arts, sophomores and juniors must complete one honors option course each year. Junior and senior honors colloquiums are provided each fall semester for these students. During the spring semester of the junior year, they participate in a project preparation seminar, which prepares them for the senior project required of all graduates of the program.

Mercer's Honors Program was established in the fall of 2000. Enrollment for 2004–05 was approximately 150 students University-wide.

Participation Requirements: The requirements for honors are set by each undergraduate school or college. Students who complete the requirements and attain an overall GPA of 3.5 or above are awarded the distinction of University Honors, which is noted on diplomas. At the spring Honors Convocation, honors graduates are presented baccalaureate hoods, which they wear as a part of graduation regalia.

Admission Process: Honors participants are recruited each spring from entering students who have a minimum 3.5 high school average and high SAT or ACT scores. Transfers and other students may apply as space is available in the program, up until they have attained 60 hours of credit.

Scholarship Availability: Scholarships are offered to entering students on the basis of high school performance and campus interviews. Continuation of scholarships is contingent upon participation in the Honors Program.

Campus Overview

Independent Baptist comprehensive, founded 1833 • **Coed** 4,628 undergraduate students, 84% full-time, 68% women, 32% men.

Undergraduates 3,890 full-time, 738 part-time. Students come from 39 states and territories, 37 other countries, 22% are from out of state, 29% African American, 3% Asian American or Pacific Islander, 2% Hispanic American, 0.2% Native American, 2% international, 2% transferred in, 65% live on campus.

Faculty *Total:* 577, 59% full-time, 66% with terminal degrees. *Student/faculty ratio:* 14:1.

Academic Programs *Special study options:* accelerated degree program, adult/continuing education programs, advanced placement credit, cooperative education, double majors, English as a second language, honors programs, independent study, internships, off-campus study, part-time degree program, services for LD students, student-designed majors, study abroad, summer session for credit. *ROTC:* Army (b).

Athletics Member NCAA. All Division I. *Intercollegiate sports:* baseball M(s), basketball M(s)/W(s), cross-country running M(s)/W(s), golf M(s)/W(s), riflery M(s)/W(s), soccer M(s)/W(s), softball W(s), tennis M(s)/W(s), volleyball W(s). *Intramural sports:* basketball M/W, bowling M/W, football M/W, golf M/W, racquetball M/W, soccer M/W, softball M/W, tennis M/W, ultimate Frisbee M/W, volleyball M/W, water polo M/W.

Costs (2004–05) *Comprehensive fee:* $29,110 includes full-time tuition ($22,050) and room and board ($7060). Full-time tuition and fees vary according to class time, course load, and location. Part-time tuition: $735 per credit hour. Part-time tuition and fees vary according to class time, course load, and location. *College room only:* $3400. Room and board charges vary according to board plan, housing facility, and location.

Financial Aid In 2004, 694 non-need-based awards were made. *Average percent of need met:* 90%. *Average financial aid package:*

$22,126. *Average need-based loan:* $6580. *Average need-based gift aid:* $13,293. *Average non-need-based aid:* $13,852.

Contact: Vice President for University Admissions: John Cole, Mercer University, 1400 Coleman Avenue, Macon, Georgia 31207; *Telephone:* 478-301-2650, 800-840-8577 (toll-free); *E-mail:* admissions@mercer.edu; *Web site:* http://www2.mercer.edu/HonorsProgram

Morehouse College
Honors Program
Atlanta, Georgia

Morehouse College offers a four-year, comprehensive Honors Program (HP) providing special learning opportunities for students of superior intellectual ability, high motivation, and broad interests. Faculty members in the program nurture the students throughout their college life, in the areas of scholarly inquiry, independent and creative thinking, and exemplary scholarship. Honors Program students take special sections of regular Morehouse courses, taught by honors faculty members who are chosen on the basis of their reputations as outstanding teachers. Course enrollment is limited to 20 students. The program is open to all students in all academic disciplines.

The Honors Program Club (HPC), one of the College's chartered student groups, elects its officers and sponsors activities for HPC members and for the College community. Morehouse is actively involved in the state, regional, and national Honors organizations; Georgia State Honors Council affords students a chance to try out their leadership skills and to be elected to offices.

The Honors Program at Morehouse College was established in 1981 and restructured in 1987. It currently enrolls 200 students, 65 of whom are freshmen.

Participation Requirements: Students in lower-division honors (freshmen and sophomores) are enrolled in special sections of English, foreign languages, world history, mathematics, philosophy, political science, and sociology. Other freshman and sophomore courses are chosen by the student and are taken with members of the student body in the regular program. On the basis of his or her status as an Honors Program freshman and sophomore, a student is expected to earn honors on the departmental level as a junior and senior. In upper-division honors there are no Honors Program courses; rather, the student completes special course-related assignments, makes presentations, participates in seminars, and focuses on departmental research.

The honors senior thesis is a staple of honors programs across the country. Currently under study at Morehouse, the senior thesis (or project) component of the HP degree will provide excellent preparation for students desiring to do graduate or professional study or to enter high-level jobs upon graduation. Also being considered is a community service component that will enable talented, concerned students in the HP to help persons in Atlanta neighborhoods and to receive recognition for this kind of work.

Honors Program students must maintain a GPA of at least 3.2 during the freshman and sophomore years. The minimum for juniors and seniors is 3.25. Any students that fall below the minimum have the next semester to raise their GPA and to resume their good standing in the program. If they do not attain the minimum, they are dropped from the program. Students below the minimum 3.2 have until May to improve their GPAs. No first-semester freshmen below 2.7 are dropped from the program or put on probation unless they fall so low that they cannot reach the minimum cumulative GPA by May.

Admission Process: Admission to the Honors Program is based on SAT I scores and high school GPA. Second-semester freshmen and first-semester sophomores may apply to the program if they are not admitted as incoming freshmen, but the most desirable time to join is at the start of the freshman year. Generally, students with combined SAT I scores of at least 1160 or an ACT composite of 27 or above are eligible for the program. The deadline for applying to the program is April 18.

Scholarship Availability: The Morehouse Honors Program does not award scholarships to its students. More than 90 percent of HP students receive full or partial awards from the College's scholarship pool. Morehouse College Honors Program students have been recipients of the following national competitive scholarships: the Rhodes Scholarship (1994), Marshall Scholarships (1994 and 1996), and the UNCF Mellon Scholarship (1991, 1994, and 1996).

Campus Overview

Independent 4-year, founded 1867 • **Urban** 61-acre campus • **Men only** 2,891 undergraduate students, 94% full-time.

Undergraduates 2,729 full-time, 162 part-time. Students come from 49 states and territories, 15 other countries, 70% are from out of state, 94% African American, 0.2% Hispanic American, 0.1% Native American, 3% international, 2% transferred in, 40% live on campus.

Faculty *Total:* 225, 71% full-time, 57% with terminal degrees. *Student/faculty ratio:* 15:1.

Academic Programs *Special study options:* academic remediation for entering students, advanced placement credit, cooperative education, double majors, honors programs, internships, off-campus study, part-time degree program, services for LD students, study abroad, summer session for credit. *ROTC:* Army (b), Navy (b), Air Force (b). *Unusual degree programs:* 3-2 engineering with Georgia Institute of Technology, Boston University, Auburn University, Rensselaer Polytechnic Institute, Rochester Institute of Technology, Columbia University, Dartmouth College-Thayer School, NC A&T State Univ., Univ. of Florida at Gainesville.

Athletics Member NCAA. All Division II. *Intercollegiate sports:* basketball M(s), cross-country running M(s), football M(s), tennis M(s), track and field M(s). *Intramural sports:* baseball M, basketball M, bowling M, football M, table tennis M, tennis M.

Costs (2004–05) *Comprehensive fee:* $24,488 includes full-time tuition ($14,318), mandatory fees ($1422), and room and board ($8748). Part-time tuition: $597 per semester hour. *College room only:* $4982. Room and board charges vary according to board plan.

Financial Aid In 2003, 1033 non-need-based awards were made. *Average percent of need met:* 25%. *Average financial aid package:* $11,079. *Average need-based loan:* $3864. *Average need-based gift aid:* $3561. *Average non-need-based aid:* $10,593.

Contact: Director: Jocelyn W. Jackson, 830 Westview Drive, SW, P.O. Box 140141, Atlanta, Georgia 30314; *Telephone:* 404-215-2679; *Fax:* 404-215-2679

Reinhardt College
Reinhardt College Honors Program
Waleska, Georgia

The honors experience at Reinhardt College extends beyond course work into building a supportive community for academic achievers. The experience begins in the freshman year, when students choose honors-designated courses from a variety of disciplines, such as biology, sociology, history, or English. Honors scholars also take occasional field trips together. Cultural, business, and recreational events in Atlanta, Georgia, only an hour to the south, offer opportunities for hands-on learning through films, art shows, and plays.

The stimulation and pace of honors classes keep gifted students engaged. The honors courses at Reinhardt College do not necessarily involve more work or more reading; instead, the reading selections and other assignments are more sophisticated. Students in honors history, for example, engage with challenging primary source materials rather than textbook summaries. Some classes might be distinguished with a thematic focus, like recent honors communications classes, Global Cultural Politics in 2002 and Southern Cultures: Beyond the Stereotypes in 2003. Other honors-designated courses address broader, more universal issues and the interrelatedness of seemingly disparate subjects. In 2004, students in a section of honors English 101 studied Jean-Jacques Rousseau's eighteenth-century Discourse on Inequality along with Aung San Suu Kyi's twentieth-century Freedom from Fear. Classes are designed to be more interactive and to utilize creative presentations and in-depth research.

The Honors Program is part of a long history of recognizing excellence in teaching and learning at Reinhardt College. Founded in 1883, the College has been home to national scholastic honor societies for over fifty years. The current Honors Program follows in this tradition. Initially called Freshman Scholars 2001, the Reinhardt College Honors Program now has about 85 students spread throughout all four undergraduate levels. Juniors and seniors in the program may also be tapped for discipline-specific honors societies, such as Beta Beta Beta (Biology) or Sigma Beta Delta (Business). Reinhardt College hosts the Georgia Mu Chapter of Alpha Chi National College Honor Society.

Participation Requirements: Students must maintain a minimum 3.0 GPA to remain in the program. Students who earn an A or B grade in four honors-designated courses may apply to receive an Honors Certificate. Those who earn an A or B in six honors-designated courses and who finish the bachelor's degree with a cumulative GPA of at least 3.5. are recognized as Honors Program graduates, with a seal of the Reinhardt College Honors Program on their diplomas.

Admission Process: Entering freshmen and transfer students are invited to apply on the basis of high school GPA (3.5 minimum), SAT (1050 minimum), or ACT (23 minimum) scores. Returning students may apply with a faculty recommendation and minimum 3.0 GPA. Students who have completed 12 semester hours of Reinhardt College course work with a minimum 3.5 GPA may apply without a faculty recommendation.

Scholarship Availability: Freshmen and sophomores are eligible to apply for an Honors Scholarship, up to $1000 a year, based on participation and achievement in the program. Juniors and seniors may also qualify to apply for an Honors Mentor Scholarship of $500 a year. Reinhardt College also awards merit, leadership, athletic, United Methodist, academic, division, and need-based aid scholarships and grants to eligible students.

Campus Overview

Independent 4-year, founded 1883, affiliated with United Methodist Church • **Coed** 1,096 undergraduate students, 87% full-time, 57% women, 43% men.

Undergraduates 957 full-time, 139 part-time. Students come from 18 states and territories, 21 other countries, 4% are from out of state, 6% African American, 0.7% Asian American or Pacific Islander, 2% Hispanic American, 0.5% Native American, 1% international, 1% transferred in, 39% live on campus.

Faculty Total: 112, 46% full-time, 42% with terminal degrees. Student/faculty ratio: 10:1.

Academic Programs Special study options: academic remediation for entering students, adult/continuing education programs, advanced placement credit, cooperative education, double majors, external degree program, honors programs, independent study, internships, part-time degree program, services for LD students, study abroad, summer session for credit.

Athletics Member NAIA. Intercollegiate sports: baseball M, basketball M(s)/W(s), cross-country running M/W, golf M(s), soccer M(s)/W(s), softball W(s), tennis M(s)/W(s). Intramural sports: basketball M/W, football M/W, soccer M/W, softball M/W, volleyball M/W.

Costs (2004–05) Comprehensive fee: $17,962 includes full-time tuition ($12,000), mandatory fees ($200), and room and board ($5762). Full-time tuition and fees vary according to course load and location. Part-time tuition: $400 per credit hour. Part-time tuition and fees vary according to course load and location. Room and board: Room and board charges vary according to board plan and housing facility.

Financial Aid 68 Federal Work-Study jobs (averaging $1138). 156 state and other part-time jobs (averaging $909). Average financial aid package: $6570.

Contact: Director: Dr. Margaret M. Morlier, Associate Professor of English, Reinhardt College, 7300 Reinhardt College Circle, Waleska, Georgia 30114-2981; Telephone: 770-720-5579; Fax: 770-720-5602; E-mail: MMM@Reinhardt.edu; Web site: http://faculty.reinhardt.edu/honors

Southern Polytechnic State University
University Honors Program
Marietta, Georgia

The University Honors Program at Southern Polytechnic State University provides academically talented students opportunities to develop their talents in an enriched curriculum emphasizing smaller class sizes, experiential learning, intellectual rigor, and research projects. The University Honors Program is based on an interdisciplinary approach that merges the technological mission of the school with the classical training of the arts and sciences. The program reflects this approach by offering several types of enriched honors courses: core courses, interdisciplinary courses, and discipline-specific capstone courses.

The University Honors Program offers a unique opportunity to junior-level students: a project-based, interdisciplinary seminar that focuses on the way knowledge within their major field converges and intersects with other fields. It asks honors students to use their growing understanding of their own discipline to work in teams with students from diverse disciplines to solve problems of an interdisciplinary nature. The senior capstone project follows and compels students to narrow their field of subject as they conduct research, design projects, and report on the results of their findings.

Community is fostered by placing students who wish to live on campus in an honors section of Howell Hall with honors roommates who share the same or similar majors. Community is further enhanced for residential and nonresidential students alike by access to a study lounge adjacent to the University Honors Program Office. Students use the lounge for study, workshops, social activities, and for Student Honors Council meetings.

The University Honors Program is a relatively new program at Southern Polytechnic State University. It was established in the fall of 2003 and has garnered strong support from Southern Polytechnic State University's President Lisa A. Rossbacher, who has helped to raise scholarship funds for the program. The University Honors Program enrolls between 20 and 30 first-year students (approximately 6 to 7 percent of Southern Polytechnic State's first-year class) who have excellent records of academic achievement and extracurricular accomplishments. Letters of invitation and applications are mailed to students who have strong records of academic performance as evidenced by high school GPA and standardized test scores. Students are also recruited through Open Houses and campus visits. Current SPSU students and transfer students with strong records of academic performance are encouraged to apply for the Departmental Honors Program, which asks that they complete 6 hours of upper-division work

Participation Requirements: In order to participate in the University Honors Program, students must maintain grades according to the following scale: freshmen and sophomores must attain a cumulative GPA of at least 3.2, juniors are expected to attain a cumulative GPA of at least 3.3, and seniors must attain a cumulative GPA of at least 3.4.

Students who graduate with 18 hours (with a minimum of 6 upper-division hours), who complete an honors project, and who achieve the minimum 3.4 GPA are recognized at graduation and on the diploma as University Honors Scholars. Students who complete 6 hours of upper-division class work, who complete an Honors Project, and who achieve the minimum 3.4 GPA are recognized at graduation and on the diploma as Departmental Honors Scholars.

Admission Process: Students who apply to the University Honors Program with a minimum GPA of 3.5 and a minimum SAT I score of 1200 are automatically admitted into the University Honors Program. Transfer students and current SPSU students who meet the following requirements may also apply to the program: students with up to 29 semester hours of college work who have a minimum 1200 SAT score or ACT equivalent and a high school minimum GPA of 3.5 as well as a college minimum GPA of 3.5, and students with 30 or more semester hours of college work who have a minimum 3.5 college GPA.

Students who do not meet these guidelines but who have other achievements that show promise of academic excellence are encouraged to apply.

Scholarship Availability: The HOPE Scholarship, which covers tuition, some mandatory fees, and some book costs, is available to all Georgia residents who have earned a minimum 3.0 cumulative GPA in high school. Additional scholarship monies are available to new and current honors students. Scholarship decisions are based upon the quality of the student application and/or the quality of work achieved at Southern Polytechnic State University. Students are also eligible for the full range of scholarships offered through the University. The list of current scholarship offerings as well as an application form can be found on Southern Polytechnic State's Web site: http://www.spsu.edu/home/prospective/financing/index.html. Honors students who are nonresidents of the state of Georgia are eligible for out-of-state tuition fee waivers as well.

Campus Overview

State-supported comprehensive, founded 1948, part of University System of Georgia • **Coed** 3,255 undergraduate students, 64% full-time, 17% women, 83% men.

Undergraduates 2,082 full-time, 1,173 part-time. Students come from 40 states and territories, 5% are from out of state, 21% African American, 6% Asian American or Pacific Islander, 3% Hispanic American, 0.2% Native American, 5% international, 12% transferred in, 12% live on campus.

Faculty *Total:* 226, 61% full-time. *Student/faculty ratio:* 17:1.

Academic Programs *Special study options:* adult/continuing education programs, advanced placement credit, cooperative education, distance learning, double majors, honors programs, independent study, internships, part-time degree program, services for LD students, student-designed majors, study abroad, summer session for credit. *ROTC:* Army (c), Navy (c), Air Force (c).

Athletics Member NAIA. *Intercollegiate sports:* baseball M(s), basketball M(s)/W(s), soccer M. *Intramural sports:* badminton M/W, basketball M/W, cheerleading W, football M/W, golf M/W, racquetball M/W, rock climbing M/W, softball M/W, table tennis M/W, ultimate Frisbee M/W, volleyball M/W.

Costs (2004–05) *Tuition:* state resident $2428 full-time, $102 per credit hour part-time; nonresident $9710 full-time, $405 per credit hour part-time. *Required fees:* $464 full-time. *Room and board:* $4946; room only: $2740. Room and board charges vary according to board plan.

Financial Aid *Average percent of need met:* 93%. *Average financial aid package:* $2406. *Average need-based loan:* $3595. *Average need-based gift aid:* $2539.

Contact: Director: Dr. Nancy Reichert, D103, Southern Polytechnic State University, 1100 South Marietta Parkway, Marietta, Georgia 30060; *Telephone:* 678-915-3928; *E-mail:* honors@spsu.edu; *Web site:* http://www.spsu.edu/honors

Spelman College
Ethel Waddell Githii Honors Program
Atlanta, Georgia

Working with all the academic departments and programs, the Ethel Waddell Githii Honors Program of Spelman College seeks to amplify the intellectual opportunities for the students and faculty members of the entire Spelman community. The program identifies students who have a love of learning and equips them to become lifelong learners by granting them the opportunity to participate actively in their intellectual and personal development from the early stages of their college careers. Students are invited to choose from among the more challenging and innovative courses within a wide variety of disciplines, select courses which have been specially designed for the program, and suggest new courses to meet their intellectual curiosity. The Honors Program also sponsors special events, makes arrangements for the students to attend cultural activities in Atlanta, and promotes community service opportunities in keeping with the student's academic explorations.

Participation Requirements: Honors students may major in any traditional department or develop their own major. Honors students take the same number of credits for graduation as all other Spelman students. Honors students take a core curriculum of honors math, honors freshman composition, honors philosophy, and two honors electives. If a student has received AP credits for one of these courses, she may be exempted from the corresponding course. All of the courses may be used to fulfill the College's core curriculum. In addition, all students in the Honors Program write an honors thesis in their major. The thesis might include—for example, in the case of an art student—a portfolio or performance.

To remain in the program, freshmen and sophomores must maintain a 3.1 GPA. Juniors and seniors must maintain a 3.2 GPA. Successful completion of the Honors Program is noted on the transcript and on the graduation program.

Admission Process: Freshmen are selected from the admissions pool each year for the Honors Program on the basis of their high school average and SAT scores.

Scholarship Availability: There are no scholarships given for participation in the Honors Program; however, Honors Program students are encouraged to apply for regular scholarships given by the College.

Campus Overview

Independent 4-year, founded 1881 • **Urban** 32-acre campus • **Women only** 2,186 undergraduate students, 95% full-time.

Undergraduates 2,082 full-time, 104 part-time. Students come from 42 states and territories, 18 other countries, 70% are from out of state, 94% African American, 0.1% Hispanic American, 0.1% Native American, 2% international, 1% transferred in, 53% live on campus.

Faculty *Total:* 233, 70% full-time, 75% with terminal degrees. *Student/faculty ratio:* 12:1.

Academic Programs *Special study options:* academic remediation for entering students, adult/continuing education programs, advanced placement credit, double majors, honors programs, independent study, internships, off-campus study, part-time degree program, services for LD students, student-designed majors, study abroad. *ROTC:* Army (c), Air Force (c). *Unusual degree programs:* 3-2 engineering with North Carolina Agricultural and Technical State University, Rensselaer Polytechnic Institute, Georgia Institute of Technology, Boston University, The University of Alabama in Huntsville, Auburn University.

Athletics Member NCAA. *Intercollegiate sports:* basketball W, cross-country running W, golf W, soccer W, tennis W, track and field W, volleyball W. *Intramural sports:* softball W, swimming and diving W.

Costs (2005–06) *Comprehensive fee:* $24,400 includes full-time tuition ($13,525), mandatory fees ($2420), and room and board ($8455). Part-time tuition: $565 per credit hour.

Financial Aid *Average percent of need met:* 45%. *Average financial aid package:* $9500. *Average need-based gift aid:* $2000. *Average non-need-based aid:* $2000.

Contact: Director: Dr. Pushpa N. Parekh, 350 Spelman Lane, SW, Box 1395, Atlanta, Georgia 30314; *Telephone:* 404-270-5664; *Fax:* 404-270-5666; *E-mail:* pparekh@spelman.edu

University of Georgia
Honors Program
Athens, Georgia

The Honors Program provides participants with special honors classes in the freshman/sophomore core curriculum, honors courses in a variety of majors, the opportunity to design and pursue interdisciplinary majors, more intensive versions of courses required for departmental majors, and independent study under faculty supervision culminating in an honors thesis or project. In addition to individualized advising throughout their education, the program provides students with special support for graduate and professional school application as well as national fellowship and scholarship competitions. The Honors Program is open to qualified undergraduates in all the schools and colleges of the University.

Most honors classes and seminars have enrollments of 20 students or fewer and are taught by specially selected faculty members. Unlike high school honors or Advanced Placement classes, the University's honors courses do not carry more credit or offer higher grade points than regular classes. Rather, they are smaller, enriched in content, and, sometimes, more specialized. Honors classes provide faculty members with opportunities to introduce their disciplines more deeply, employing innovative and more individualized approaches. Students in the program choose from more than 300 honors classes offered annually. These classes usually fulfill core curriculum requirements. The University of Georgia (UGA) Undergraduate Bulletin lists honors classes under the departments in which they are offered. Honors class course numbers are followed by an H.

Honors students may enroll in upper-division classes in the major with honors option to pursue a subject more deeply within the setting of a regular course. Students arrange additional readings and other assignments with the class instructor and secure honors credit for these classes by filing a form with the Honors Program. Honors students may also enroll in directed-study classes that enable them to work independently on a sustained research project under the guidance of a faculty member. This usually leads to an honors thesis, often comparable to a master's thesis, but the outcomes may take a different form—a recital, exhibition, performance, or internship. Alternatively, honors students may enroll in graduate classes or pursue a joint bachelor's/master's degree program. Honors-directed reading classes and honors theses classes are available in most departments.

Honors students are advised by professional advisers and honors faculty members. In addition, the Honors Program provides graduate and professional school application support and selects and prepares students for national and international fellowships and scholarships. In the past ten years, students at Georgia have secured four Rhodes

Scholarships, four Mellon Humanities awards, and one Udall, twenty-four Goldwater, thirty-six Fulbright, four Gates-Cambridge, three Marshall, and six Truman scholarships.

Students may enter the Honors Program as freshmen or by collegiate entry after at least one semester's enrollment. The Honors Program accepts transfer students as well. Transfer students may petition to count honors classes from their previous institutions toward graduation with honors from UGA. In order to make timely progress toward their degrees while registering for honors classes, students in the program are accorded registration priority ahead of nonhonors undergraduates.

The Honors Program was founded in 1960 and currently enrolls 2,500 students.

Complete information about the University of Georgia Honors Program is available at its Web site, listed below.

Participation Requirements: To graduate with honors, students must complete nine honors classes across a range of subjects with a minimum 3.4 GPA. To graduate with high or highest honors, students must complete the requirements for graduation with honors and an additional capstone experience, with a minimum 3.7 GPA for high honors and a minimum 3.9 GPA for highest honors. Students have three options for the capstone experience: research and a thesis, research and an applied internship, or completion of three graduate-level courses.

Admission Process: Admissions is highly competitive and is based on high school grades, SAT or ACT scores, high school curriculum, and an application that includes an essay and a description of extracurricular and public service activities during high school. In 2004, the median ranges for entering first-year honors students were a 4.0–4.1 high school GPA, 1370–1470 SAT I, and 30–33 ACT composite score. The application for first-year admission is available each fall on the Honors Program Web site.

Students not admitted as first-semester freshmen are eligible to apply for collegiate entry to the Honors Program based on a University GPA of at least 3.75 in 15 semester hours of academic credit. Students must apply for collegiate entry within their first two semesters.

Transfer students are eligible for admission based on their academic records. Transfer students must have a minimum 3.75 GPA on 28 hours of college credit. Both transfer and collegiate entry applications are available at the Honors Program Web site.

Scholarship Availability: Almost all Georgia resident students in the Honors Program receive Georgia HOPE scholarships covering tuition, fees, and book expenses.

The University awards twenty to twenty-five Foundation Fellowships per year. These four-year scholarships pay the full cost of attendance and provide one summer-study opportunity, two independent travel-study opportunities, and two annual spring travel-study programs. The scholarships also offer individual faculty mentorships and a wealth of on-campus academic experiences, cultural and recreational advantages, and public service opportunities. Foundation Fellowships are awarded on the basis of a separate application and an interview process. Successful candidates are required to participate in the Honors Program.

University of Georgia charter scholarships and a number of out-of-state tuition waivers are awarded on several, mainly academic, criteria. All other scholarships are offered through the Office of Student Financial Aid and the Office of Admissions of the University.

Campus Overview
State-supported university, founded 1785, part of University System of Georgia • **Coed** 25,019 undergraduate students, 90% full-time, 57% women, 43% men.

Undergraduates 22,616 full-time, 2,403 part-time. Students come from 54 states and territories, 105 other countries, 15% are from out of state, 5% African American, 5% Asian American or Pacific Islander, 2% Hispanic American, 0.2% Native American, 0.7% international, 3% transferred in, 27% live on campus.

Faculty *Total:* 2,080, 80% full-time, 87% with terminal degrees. *Student/faculty ratio:* 15:1.

Academic Programs *Special study options:* academic remediation for entering students, accelerated degree program, adult/continuing education programs, advanced placement credit, cooperative education, distance learning, double majors, English as a second language, freshman honors college, honors programs, independent study, internships, off-campus study, part-time degree program, services for LD students, student-designed majors, study abroad, summer session for credit. *ROTC:* Army (b), Air Force (b). *Unusual degree programs:* 3-2 engineering with Georgia Institute of Technology.

Athletics Member NCAA. All Division I except football (Division I-A). *Intercollegiate sports:* baseball M(s), basketball M(s)/W(s), cheerleading M/W, cross-country running M(s)/W(s), equestrian sports M(s)/W(s), golf M(s)/W(s), gymnastics W(s), soccer M(c)/W(s), softball W, swimming and diving M(s)/W(s), tennis M(s)/W(s), track and field M(s)/W(s), volleyball M(c)/W(s). *Intramural sports:* badminton M(c)/W(c), baseball M(c), basketball M/W, bowling M/W, crew M(c), cross-country running M/W, equestrian sports M(c)/W(c), fencing M(c), football M/W, golf M/W, ice hockey M(c), lacrosse M(c)/W(c), racquetball M/W, rugby M(c)/W(c), sailing M(c)/W(c), soccer M/W, softball M/W, swimming and diving M/W, tennis M/W, track and field M/W, ultimate Frisbee M(c)/W(c), volleyball M/W, water polo M(c), weight lifting M/W, wrestling M(c).

Costs (2004–05) *Tuition:* state resident $3368 full-time, $141 per credit part-time; nonresident $14,684 full-time, $612 per credit part-time. Full-time tuition and fees vary according to course load, location, program, and reciprocity agreements. Part-time tuition and fees vary according to course load, location, program, and reciprocity agreements. *Required fees:* $904 full-time, $452 per term part-time. *Room and board:* $6006; room only: $3234. Room and board charges vary according to board plan and housing facility.

Financial Aid 406 Federal Work-Study jobs (averaging $2632). In 2004, 1220 non-need-based awards were made. *Average percent of need met:* 74%. *Average financial aid package:* $7058. *Average need-based loan:* $3686. *Average need-based gift aid:* $5392. *Average non-need-based aid:* $1896.

Contact: Director: David S. Williams, Honors Program, University of Georgia, Athens, Georgia 30602-6116; *Telephone:* 706-542-3240; *Fax:* 706-542-6993; *E-mail:* honors@uga.edu; *Web site:* http://www.uga.edu/honors

University of West Georgia
Honors College
Carrollton, Georgia

The Honors College provides participating students with special honors courses in the core curriculum, more extensive versions of courses required for departmental majors, the ability to convert regular courses into honors courses, and independent study opportunities under faculty supervision. Beyond the diverse and stimulating curriculum, students receive individualized academic advising, academic and financial support for undergraduate research, and assistance in applying for graduate and professional school as well as national fellowships and scholarships. The University of West Georgia (UWG) offers honors distinctions in all of its undergraduate degree programs and all qualified individuals are welcome to apply.

Most traditional honors courses and seminars have enrollment of 15 students or fewer and are always taught by full-time faculty members who have a strong commitment to excellence in undergraduate education. Honors courses are taught seminar style and provide faculty members with the opportunity to offer more individualized attention and delve deeper into their discipline. Courses are centered on discussion, with greater opportunities to share opinions and develop ideas, and faculty members are free to delve into specialized areas. More than fifty honors courses per year are offered exclusively to honors students, and the majority of courses satisfy University core curriculum requirements.

Honors students also have the option of converting courses within their major into honors courses. Students are expected to arrange this conversion with their professor by agreeing to complete an additional assignment or project and then completing an Honors Conversion Form in the Honors College office. Students also have the option of completing an independent study, guided by a University faculty member, which typically leads to the completion of an original research project. Undergraduate research is a cornerstone of the Honors College, and students have excelled in research presentations at national, regional, and statewide conferences. In addition, many of these students have gone on to have their research published in academic journals.

Honors College staff members also assist students in applying to graduate and professional programs. In fact, almost 90 percent of those who completed the Honors College curriculum requirements have gone on to graduate or professional school. Via staff assistance and the strong preparation afforded by the Honors College, UWG honors students have been accepted for admission at the following institutions: Cambridge, Columbia, Georgia Tech, Harvard, MIT, Stanford, the University of Georgia, the University of West Georgia, and many others. Students also receive support and guidance in applying for national scholarships and fellowships. Students in the Honors College have received the Goldwater, Truman, Fulbright, Gates, and Marshall scholarships/fellowships, among others.

Honors College administrative offices are located in the Honors House, which also features a computer lab; patio, with outdoor grill and picnic tables; and kitchen facilities for student use. The Honors College residence hall has its own computer lab, music practice room, recreation room, kitchen facilities, Internet access in each room, and extensive residence hall programming provided by Honors College staff members. Honors students receive priority registration ahead of all nonhonors undergraduates and are advised by professional staff members within the Honors College. Students may enter the Honors College as freshmen or by collegiate entry after at least one semester of enrollment. Graduation with honors designation requires the completion of ten honors courses and an honors thesis in the student's major.

The Honors College also houses UWG's nationally recognized debate team. West Georgia has qualified for the National Debate Tournament for thirty-three consecutive years, the fifth-longest streak in the country. While competing against all universities, including Berkeley, Northwestern, Stanford, and the Ivy League schools, they place among the top ten teams in 95 percent of the tournaments in which they participate and have twice been named National Champions by the Cross Examination Debate Association.

The Advanced Academy of Georgia, also a part of the Honors College, is a residential, early-entrance-to-college program for gifted and talented students who would have been high school juniors or seniors had they remained in high school. One of very few such programs in the country, the academy provides a boarding school–type experience for gifted students who earn concurrent high school and college credit through full-time study at the University. As part of their studies, students complete challenging courses, often honors courses, offered through any of the University's 113 programs of study and are encouraged to conduct original research, either with a professor or individually, in any field of interest. Upon completion of the Advanced Academy, students are well prepared to either transfer to their university of choice or complete their degree at the University of West Georgia.

The West Georgia Honors Program was established in 1975. In 1999, the Board of Regents of the University System of Georgia elevated the status of the program to Honors College, thereby creating the first Honors College in the state of Georgia.

Participation Requirements: To graduate with Honors College distinction, students must earn credit for ten or more honors courses, including two seminars at the junior or senior level; complete an honors senior thesis or research project in their major; and maintain a minimum GPA of 3.2 in Honors College courses and in all other academic work. Completion of this distinctive curriculum is a mark of scholarly excellence and is appropriately recognized on all official West Georgia transcripts.

Admission Process: Admission to the Honors College is open to entering freshmen who meet two of the following three criteria: a combined SAT I score of at least 1200 or the ACT equivalent (those who have taken the new SAT should only use the critical reading and math section to determine their composite score), a minimum score of 610 on the verbal/critical reading portion of the SAT I or ACT equivalent, or a minimum high school GPA of 3.5. The Honors College is also open to any student who has completed 15 or more hours at West Georgia with a minimum overall GPA of 3.2.

Scholarship Availability: All Honors College students who are Georgia residents are recipients of HOPE scholarships, which cover all tuition costs and some additional expenses. In addition, the Honors College offers more than forty Presidential Scholarships. Most of these are worth $4000 per year and are good for eight semesters provided that the recipients maintain eligibility for honors and make progress in completing the Honors College curriculum. There are many other scholarships available through the University for which honors students are eligible. Finally, the Honors College also offers a number of out-of-state tuition waivers for non-Georgia Honors College students.

Campus Overview

State-supported comprehensive, founded 1933, part of University System of Georgia • **Coed** 8,279 undergraduate students, 83% full-time, 60% women, 40% men.

Undergraduates 6,899 full-time, 1,380 part-time. Students come from 36 states and territories, 62 other countries, 3% are from out of state, 23% African American, 1% Asian American or Pacific Islander, 1% Hispanic American, 0.2% Native American, 1% international, 8% transferred in, 30% live on campus.

Faculty *Total:* 511, 75% full-time, 68% with terminal degrees. *Student/faculty ratio:* 19:1.

Academic Programs *Special study options:* academic remediation for entering students, accelerated degree program, adult/continuing education programs, advanced placement credit, cooperative education, distance learning, double majors, external degree program, honors programs, independent study, internships, off-campus study, part-time degree program, services for LD students, study abroad, summer session for credit. *ROTC:* Army (b). *Unusual degree programs:* 3-2 engineering with Georgia Institute of Technology, Auburn University, Mercer University, University of Georgia.

Athletics Member NCAA. All Division II. *Intercollegiate sports:* baseball M(s), basketball M(s)/W(s), cheerleading M(s)/W(s), cross-country running M(s)/W(s), football M(s), softball W(s), volleyball W(s). *Intramural sports:* basketball M/W, football M/W, golf M/W, soccer M/W, softball M/W, table tennis M/W, tennis M/W, track and field M/W, ultimate Frisbee M/W, volleyball M/W, water polo M/W, weight lifting M/W.

Costs (2004–05) *Tuition:* state resident $2322 full-time, $97 per semester hour part-time; nonresident $9290 full-time, $388 per semester hour part-time. Part-time tuition and fees vary according to course load. *Required fees:* $584 full-time, $16 per semester hour part-time, $102 per term part-time. *Room and board:* $4550; room only: $2600. Room and board charges vary according to board plan and housing facility.

Financial Aid 538 Federal Work-Study jobs (averaging $2400). In 2004, 143 non-need-based awards were made. *Average percent of need met:* 68%. *Average financial aid package:* $6771. *Average need-based loan:* $2819. *Average need-based gift aid:* $4336. *Average non-need-based aid:* $1532.

Contact: Dean: Dr. Donald R. Wagner, Honors College, University of West Georgia, 1600 Maple Street, Carrollton, Georgia 30118;

Telephone: 678-839-6636; *Fax:* 678-839-0636; *E-mail:* dwagner@westga.edu; *Web site:* http://www.westga.edu/~honors/

Valdosta State University
University Honors Program
Valdosta, Georgia

The Honors Program at Valdosta State University provides special classes and activities for students who have demonstrated their commitment to academic achievement and who are looking for experiences that will enrich them beyond the scope of the average. Honors courses are not more difficult than nonhonors courses, just more enjoyable and rewarding, designed to encourage students to think creatively, foster in them a love of learning, and provide the best possible foundation for their academic careers and personal lives.

The Honors Program offers special sections of classes in a wide variety of disciplines, including the humanities, the sciences, mathematics, fine arts, and the social sciences. Each course satisfies core curriculum requirements while at the same time counting toward completion of the Honors Program. Enrollment is limited to 15 students per section, with each course offering a unique blend of solid content and stimulating format in an enriched environment.

Honors seminars are a special feature of the Honors Program. These seminars are interdisciplinary and discussion based, focused each year on a different timely and interesting topic. Entering students enroll in the Honors Introductory Seminar during their first year. After having completed the requisite number of honors courses, students then finish their honors experience with the Honors Capstone Seminar. These seminars—Myth and Ritual in Modern Society, the Question of Evil, Native American Religions, Cosmology, Modern and Contemporary Views of Human Nature, Society and the Sexes, the Individual and Society, Moving Beyond Hatred, Developing Ethical Decision Making Skills, Geology and Mythology in the Mediterranean, Issues in Science and Religion, the American View of Nature, Women in the Arts, and the Role and Function of a University—are designed to give all students in the Honors Program a shared intellectual experience in order to develop a community of learners and encourage a spirit of collegiality in the pursuit of knowledge, a spirit that is essential for intellectual growth and personal fulfillment.

The Honors Option allows students to continue honors work during their junior and senior years. Through the Honors Option, students may receive honors credit while enrolled in regular course sections by extending class work into new areas or pursuing it in greater depth.

Honors students may also become members of the Honors Student Association and enjoy a variety of special activities and social events. Through participation in the Honors Forum, a series of lectures and discussions led by VSU faculty, visiting scholars, and members of the community, honors students have the opportunity to discuss new ideas and exciting research in a relaxed yet challenging atmosphere. Honors students also engage in public and community service learning projects. Finally, through its membership in the National Collegiate Honors Council, the Southern Regional Honors Council, and the Georgia Collegiate Honors Council, the VSU Honors Program opens the door to numerous conventions, symposia, trips, and study abroad and offers many opportunities to meet and work with other honors students from all parts of the nation and the world.

There are 300 students in the 25-year-old program.

Participation Requirements: To complete the program, students must accrue 24 hours of honors course credit, including two honors seminars, and participate in some form of community service. Students who complete the Honors Program receive an Honors Program diploma, transcript notation, and a gold seal on their University diploma. Students also receive public recognition at the University's annual Honors Day ceremony.

Admission Process: Students with a high school GPA of 3.0 and a verbal or math SAT I score of 550 receive invitations to join the Honors Program. Other students who demonstrate qualities of the superior student are encouraged to apply. Students already enrolled in a university should have at least a 3.0 GPA to seek admittance.

Scholarship Availability: The Honors Program does not offer scholarships itself; however, the University offers a large number of scholarships. Residents of Georgia who have the Hope Scholarship have most of their tuition paid for them.

Campus Overview

State-supported university, founded 1906, part of University System of Georgia • **Coed** 9,013 undergraduate students, 82% full-time, 59% women, 41% men.

Undergraduates 7,403 full-time, 1,610 part-time. Students come from 45 states and territories, 61 other countries, 6% are from out of state, 21% African American, 1% Asian American or Pacific Islander, 2% Hispanic American, 0.3% Native American, 1% international, 7% transferred in, 17% live on campus.

Faculty *Total:* 491, 86% full-time. *Student/faculty ratio:* 21:1.

Academic Programs *Special study options:* academic remediation for entering students, accelerated degree program, advanced placement credit, cooperative education, distance learning, double majors, English as a second language, freshman honors college, honors programs, independent study, internships, off-campus study, part-time degree program, services for LD students, study abroad, summer session for credit. *ROTC:* Air Force (b). *Unusual degree programs:* 3-2 engineering with Georgia Institute of Technology.

Athletics Member NCAA. All Division II. *Intercollegiate sports:* baseball M(s), basketball M(s)/W(s), cross-country running M(s)/W(s), football M(s), golf M(s), softball W(s), tennis M(s)/W(s), volleyball W(s). *Intramural sports:* badminton M/W, basketball M/W, bowling M/W, cross-country running M/W, field hockey M/W, football M/W, golf M/W, racquetball M/W, soccer M/W, softball M/W, swimming and diving M/W, table tennis M/W, tennis M/W, ultimate Frisbee M/W, volleyball M/W, weight lifting M/W.

Costs (2004–05) *Tuition:* state resident $2322 full-time, $97 per semester hour part-time; nonresident $9290 full-time, $388 per semester hour part-time. Part-time tuition and fees vary according to course load. *Required fees:* $670 full-time. *Room and board:* $5208; room only: $2664. Room and board charges vary according to board plan and housing facility.

Financial Aid 185 Federal Work-Study jobs (averaging $2369). In 2003, 175 non-need-based awards were made. *Average percent of need met:* 89%. *Average financial aid package:* $8045. *Average need-based loan:* $3325. *Average need-based gift aid:* $1522. *Average non-need-based aid:* $1411.

Contact: Director: Dr. Brian Adler, VSU Honors House, Valdosta State University, Valdosta, Georgia 31698; *Telephone:* 229-249-4894; *Fax:* 229-219-1396; *E-mail:* honors@valdosta.edu; *Web site:* http://www.valdosta.edu/honors

HAWAII

Brigham Young University–Hawaii

University Honors Program

Laie, Hawaii

*T*he University Honors Program at Brigham Young University–Hawaii is made up of students and faculty members who are committed to an enhanced university experience through the Honors Colloquium, academic activities, service opportunities, and a variety of unique learning experiences. The University Honors Program is divided into four academic areas, creating an educational experience designed to connect rather than isolate different areas of study: the Honors Colloquium, honors classes, honors service, and the Senior Honors Project.

The Honors Colloquium is the heart of the Honors Program and meets once weekly. Speakers are invited from both on and off campus to present a topic they are passionately interested in. These informal academic gatherings encourage invaluable faculty, community, and student interaction.

Honors classes at BYU–Hawaii provide an academic environment that stimulates interaction among the University's best faculty members and students, who welcome the challenge of a more student-driven approach to encountering new ideas. During their freshman year, honors students enroll in Honors 100, Introduction to a University Education, a class designed to introduce students to the resources and opportunities available to assist them in their education. Honors students can choose from a core of twelve to fifteen courses in a variety of University divisions. Honors courses are usually general education courses that range widely across the curriculum and focus on interdisciplinary and multicultural approaches. Distinctive to the University is the Interdisciplinary Studies course in the general education requirements. Each section is on a different topic, and a number are offered as honors seminars. Courses are capped at 20 students.

A key component to the Honors Program is service, which is given throughout the campus and especially in the community. The Honors Service Project requirement, which is completed by each honors student, may be done any time but must be completed within a single semester. The student designs a project that can be completed in approximately 15 hours, has a potentially lasting benefit, and in some way improves the quality of life of the beneficiary. In addition, the Colloquium course has service opportunities built into the curriculum.

The Honors Senior Project is a culminating effort that reflects a student's finest intellectual and creative abilities and is presentation worthy. It can be combined with the Service Project and/or with a major senior thesis.

Most features of the program, including planning the Colloquium speakers and service opportunities, are planned and carried out by a volunteer Student Honors Council. The program was founded in 1979 by Academic Vice President Jay Fox. There are currently 80 students enrolled.

Participation Requirements: Students participate in the program in two ways: either on an occasional basis, registering for an occasional course to enrich their overall general education experience, or as a student committed to meeting all the requirements for the distinction of University Honors Program Graduate, which is received at graduation. Requirements include seven honors courses (five courses for transfer students), which should total 21 semester hours. One religion class is allowed to be part of this total. Also, a student should attend four semesters of Honors Colloquium, complete a Senior Service Project (about 15 hours, junior or senior year), and complete a Senior Honors Thesis or Creative Project. The program is open to all students, but they must have a GPA of at least 3.5 upon completion. Students who successfully complete the program requirements graduate with University Honors Distinction, with a special notation on their transcripts, recognition at graduation, and a certificate from the program.

Admission Process: The program has no application/acceptance process. Students select themselves into the program. The act of registering for an honors class or direct application to the Director puts them into the program. If an honors professor believes a student is not academically prepared, the professor can ask him or her to drop the course and transfer to a nonhonors section.

Scholarship Availability: The program currently has no funding for scholarships.

Campus Overview

Independent Latter-day Saints 4-year, founded 1955, administratively affiliated with Brigham Young University • **Coed** 2,486 undergraduate students, 88% full-time, 57% women, 43% men.

Undergraduates 2,190 full-time, 296 part-time. Students come from 47 states and territories, 67 other countries, 39% are from out of state, 0.4% African American, 22% Asian American or Pacific Islander, 2% Hispanic American, 0.6% Native American, 45% international, 9% transferred in, 52% live on campus.

Faculty *Total:* 224, 50% full-time, 32% with terminal degrees. *Student/faculty ratio:* 15:1.

Academic Programs *Special study options:* academic remediation for entering students, accelerated degree program, adult/continuing education programs, advanced placement credit, cooperative education, double majors, English as a second language, freshman honors college, honors programs, internships, off-campus study, part-time degree program, services for LD students, summer session for credit. *ROTC:* Army (c), Navy (c), Air Force (c).

Athletics Member NCAA. All Division II. *Intercollegiate sports:* basketball M(s), cross-country running M(s)/W(s), softball W(s), tennis M(s)/W(s), volleyball W(s), water polo M(s). *Intramural sports:* badminton M(c)/W(c), basketball M/W, bowling M/W, cross-country running M/W, golf M/W, gymnastics M/W, racquetball M/W, rugby M/W, soccer M(c)/W(c), softball M/W, swimming and diving M/W, table tennis M/W, tennis M/W, volleyball M/W, water polo M, weight lifting M/W, wrestling M/W.

Costs (2004–05) *Comprehensive fee:* $7460 includes full-time tuition ($2660) and room and board ($4800). Full-time tuition and fees vary according to program. Part-time tuition: $181 per credit. Part-time tuition and fees vary according to program. *College room only:* $2164. Room and board charges vary according to board plan and housing facility.

Financial Aid 600 state and other part-time jobs (averaging $4500). In 2003, 500 non-need-based awards were made. *Average percent of need met:* 80%. *Average financial aid package:* $2850. *Average need-based loan:* $1410. *Average need-based gift aid:* $3000. *Average non-need-based aid:* $1300.

Contact: Director: Dr. Randal W. Allred, University Honors, Brigham Young University–Hawaii, 55-220 Kulanui Street, Laie, Hawaii 96762; *Telephone:* 808-293-3633; *Fax:* 808-293-3662; *E-mail:* allredr@byuh.edu; *Web site:* http://w2.byuh.edu/honors/

IDAHO

Boise State University
University Honors College
Boise, Idaho

Featuring small classes, interdisciplinary study, and cocurricular activities focusing on the environment, the Honors College at Boise State is designed to enhance a student's academic experience. Along with motivated classmates, students are challenged by honors courses that require a more thorough and rigorous analysis of the material. In addition, students have the opportunity to work closely with advisers who help to identify internship, fellowship, and scholarship options to support their educational and career goals.

Admission to the Honors College is an invitation to a lifetime committed to the wonders of the human mind, heart, and spirit. Each semester students choose from a variety of honors courses, including honors seminars, departmental courses, and colloquia. The basic purpose of the seminars is to bring students (especially freshmen and sophomores) together for informal small-group discussions about specific topics. Departmental honors courses are offered regularly in several departments and sometimes may be used to fulfill general University requirements. Recommended for juniors and seniors, interdisciplinary honors colloquia feature a team-taught exploration of subject areas.

The College currently enrolls 250 students.

Participation Requirements: A cumulative GPA of at least 3.5 is a fixed requirement for retention. Any student whose GPA falls below 3.5 for two consecutive semesters is automatically dropped from the program. Students who do not complete any honors work for two consecutive semesters are withdrawn from the program unless they can demonstrate, to the satisfaction of the Director, continuing progress toward the completion of honors graduation requirements. Exceptions may be only to Admission and Retention requirements, and these rare exceptions are granted by the Honors College Committee of the Faculty Senate upon express written petition by the student justifying the exceptions on the basis of other evidence of academic potential.

To graduate with honors, a student must have 26 honors credits. To graduate with honors from the program, a student must have a cumulative undergraduate GPA of at least 3.5. Students whose cumulative undergraduate GPA is at least 3.75 and whose records of academic and cocurricular activities indicate outstanding performance in both areas may be considered by the Honors College Committee of the Faculty Senate for graduation with Distinguished Honors. Cocurricular activities may include publication of undergraduate work, presentations at regional or national conferences, and outstanding service in the Honors Student Association.

Admission Process: Students are required to have a cumulative GPA of at least 3.5 and score in at least the ninetieth percentile on the combined portion of the ACT or SAT in order to apply to BSU on the basis of high school graduation. A cumulative GPA of at least 3.5 for a minimum of 15 college credits will be required for all others, including continuing students, transfers, and students whose admission to BSU has not been based upon regular high school graduation and ACT or SAT I scores.

Scholarship Availability: Through the generosity of the estate of Dean and Thelma Brown, BSU offers numerous scholarships. Brown Honors Scholars receive full fees plus room and board worth up to $16,000. Up to ten Brown Honors Residential Scholarships are awarded. Moreover, each of these is renewable for up to a total of four years. Numerous other merit-based scholarships are available.

Campus Overview

State-supported comprehensive, founded 1932, part of Idaho System of Higher Education • **Coed** 16,719 undergraduate students, 63% full-time, 54% women, 46% men.

Undergraduates 10,578 full-time, 6,141 part-time. Students come from 35 states and territories, 47 other countries, 7% are from out of state, 1% African American, 2% Asian American or Pacific Islander, 5% Hispanic American, 1% Native American, 2% international, 6% transferred in, 8% live on campus.

Faculty *Total:* 1,138, 46% full-time, 61% with terminal degrees. *Student/faculty ratio:* 18:1.

Academic Programs *Special study options:* academic remediation for entering students, adult/continuing education programs, advanced placement credit, cooperative education, distance learning, double majors, English as a second language, freshman honors college, honors programs, independent study, internships, off-campus study, part-time degree program, services for LD students, student-designed majors, study abroad, summer session for credit. *ROTC:* Army (b).

Athletics Member NCAA. All Division I except football (Division I-A). *Intercollegiate sports:* basketball M(s)/W(s), cross-country running M(s)/W(s), golf M(s)/W(s), gymnastics W(s), skiing (downhill) W, soccer W, tennis M(s)/W(s), track and field M(s)/W(s), volleyball W(s), wrestling M(s). *Intramural sports:* basketball M/W, bowling M/W, lacrosse W(c), racquetball M/W, skiing (downhill) M(c)/W(c), soccer M/W, softball M/W, tennis M/W, volleyball M/W, weight lifting M/W.

Costs (2004–05) *Tuition:* state resident $3520 full-time, $177 per credit part-time; nonresident $10,567 full-time, $177 per credit part-time. Part-time tuition and fees vary according to course load. *Room and board:* $5384. Room and board charges vary according to board plan and housing facility.

Financial Aid In 2003, 1229 non-need-based awards were made. *Average percent of need met: 75%. Average financial aid package:* $6978. *Average need-based loan:* $3540. *Average need-based gift aid:* $3072. *Average non-need-based aid:* $1306.

Contact: Director: Dr. Gregory A. Raymond, Driscoll Hall, Boise State University, Boise, Idaho 83725-1125; *Telephone:* 208-426-1122; *Fax:* 208-426-1247; *E-mail:* graymon@boisestate.edu; *Web site:* http://www.idbsu.edu/honors/

University of Idaho
University Honors Program
Moscow, Idaho

Established in 1983, the University Honors Program (UHP) at the University of Idaho (UI) offers a stimulating course of study and the benefits of an enriched learning community for exceptional students from all colleges and majors. The program's diverse curriculum serves a variety of student needs and interests. Beyond the classroom, the program's extracurricular opportunities include concerts, plays, films, lectures, and other excursions that foster cultural enrichment, fellowship, and learning. The great majority of the 550 students currently active in the program are able to participate without adding to the total number of credits needed for graduation.

Honors faculty members support students in developing their initiative and their abilities to think critically and creatively. Most honors classes are small, and honors students thus benefit from close intellectual contact and discussion with their instructors and fellow students. The program director, associate director, and program adviser act as supplemental academic advisers to all students who qualify for honors study. The UHP is devoted to enabling each student to achieve his or her potential.

Many honors students are leaders on campus and in their living groups. Elected members of the Honors Student Advisory Board help to determine innovative honors seminar offerings and take the lead in planning UHP trips and social events. As part of a dynamic, broad-based education, members are also encouraged to participate in either domestic or international exchange programs. Honors advisers work with students individually to determine appropriate credit within the honors curriculum.

Participation Requirements: A member in good standing of the University Honors Program must be registered at UI, take an average of one honors course every second semester, and maintain a minimum 3.2 cumulative GPA. Students who complete 19 credits of required honors courses and achieve a cumulative GPA of 3.0 or higher in those courses earn the University Honors Core Award. Students who complete 27 credits of required honors course work and achieve a cumulative GPA of 3.0 or higher in those courses earn the University Honors Program Certificate. Depending on which courses students select, 26 of 27 credits required for an honors certificate also satisfy the general University core requirements in the humanities, social sciences, and sciences that all students must complete to graduate.

Admission Process: Incoming freshmen are invited to apply to the program on the basis of their high school GPA and standardized test score(s). Criteria for admission are based on a correlation between the student's high school GPA and the ACT composite score or SAT combined score. For example, students who have an ACT composite score of 28 or an SAT combined score of 1250 and a 3.7 high school GPA meet the initial minimum criteria. The correlation, however, is

based on a sliding scale so that students with test scores higher than those noted above may have GPAs below 3.7 and still meet the minimum criteria; students with higher GPAs may have test scores lower than the examples offered above and still meet the minimum criteria. Those who do not meet the above criteria but who would like to participate in the honors program are encouraged to apply and may be asked to submit letters of recommendation from two teachers. To be considered for admission, students applying from high school must also submit a two-page essay as part of the application. Students who demonstrate superior performance upon completing their first semester at the University of Idaho (achieving a minimum 3.5 GPA) may also apply for admission. Transfer students are considered for admission on a case-by-case basis; students in good standing in an honors program at their previous school are automatically considered for admission, and their transcripts will be evaluated and appropriate credit given toward the honors certificate.

Scholarship Availability: Each year scholarships are offered to a select number of students entering the program. These non-need-based awards are based on academic merit and are applied to resident fees. No additional application form is required. Likewise, a select number of honors program out-of-state tuition waivers are offered to non-Idaho residents. Both scholarships and tuition waivers are awarded for up to eight semesters for freshmen, six semesters for sophomores, and so on. Renewal of funding is contingent on a student's satisfactory progress toward earning an honors certificate while maintaining an overall GPA of 3.3. In addition, UHP members have been successful in taking advantage of close mentorship and advice regarding prestigious national scholarship opportunities.

Campus Overview
State-supported university, founded 1889 • **Coed** 9,550 undergraduate students, 88% full-time, 45% women, 55% men.

Undergraduates 8,402 full-time, 1,148 part-time. 0.8% African American, 2% Asian American or Pacific Islander, 4% Hispanic American, 1% Native American, 2% international, 55% live on campus.

Faculty *Total:* 557, 96% full-time, 83% with terminal degrees.

Academic Programs *Special study options:* academic remediation for entering students, accelerated degree program, adult/continuing education programs, advanced placement credit, cooperative education, distance learning, double majors, honors programs, independent study, internships, off-campus study, part-time degree program, services for LD students, student-designed majors, study abroad, summer session for credit. *ROTC:* Army (b), Navy (b), Air Force (c).

Athletics Member NCAA. All Division I except football (Division I-A). *Intercollegiate sports:* baseball M(c), basketball M(s)/W(s), cross-country running M(s)/W(s), golf M(s)/W(s), ice hockey M(c), riflery M(c)/W(c), rugby M(c)/W(c), skiing (cross-country) M(c)/W(c), skiing (downhill) M(c)/W(c), soccer M(c)/W(s), tennis M(s)/W(s), track and field M(s)/W(s), volleyball W(s). *Intramural sports:* baseball M, basketball M/W, equestrian sports M/W, fencing M, football M/W, golf M/W, ice hockey M, racquetball M/W, riflery M/W, rugby M/W, skiing (cross-country) M/W, skiing (downhill) M/W, soccer M/W, softball M/W, squash M/W, swimming and diving M/W, table tennis M/W, tennis M/W, track and field M/W, volleyball W, water polo M, weight lifting M/W, wrestling M.

Costs (2004–05) *Tuition:* state resident $0 full-time; nonresident $8020 full-time, $123 per credit part-time. Full-time tuition and fees vary according to degree level and program. Part-time tuition and fees vary according to course load, degree level, and program. *Required fees:* $3632 full-time, $178 per credit part-time. *Room and board:* $5034. Room and board charges vary according to board plan and housing facility.

Financial Aid 498 Federal Work-Study jobs (averaging $1483). 231 state and other part-time jobs (averaging $1757). In 2002, 2174 non-need-based awards were made. *Average percent of need met:*

79%. *Average financial aid package:* $9177. *Average need-based loan:* $5806. *Average need-based gift aid:* $2991. *Average non-need-based aid:* $3697.

Contact: Director: Stephan Flores, Room 315, Idaho Commons, P.O. Box 442533, Moscow, Idaho 83844-2533; *Telephone:* 208-885-6147; *Fax:* 208-885-7722; *E-mail:* honors@uidaho.edu; *Web site:* http://www.uidaho.edu/honors_program

ILLINOIS

Chicago State University
The Honors College
Chicago, Illinois

The Honors College at Chicago State University is devoted to identifying, supporting and nurturing highly motivated, academically talented and inquisitive students, and to instilling in them a love of and commitment to lifelong learning. Membership in the Honors College is open to undergraduate students in any of the university's degree-granting and professional programs.

The academic centerpiece of the Honors College is the Honors Core Curriculum, a thirty-nine credit hour sequence of courses that satisfies the university's general education requirement. Designed and taught by some of Chicago State's finest professors, the courses in the Core Curriculum are all interdisciplinary and team-taught. Since these courses are restricted to Honors students, class sizes range from 11 to 20 students. The organizing theme of the Core Curriculum is Principles of Inquiry. The first year courses introduce students to inquiry in mathematics, the natural and physical sciences, philosophy, the social and behavioral sciences, history and the arts. Subsequent courses give students the opportunity to apply those principles to a wide variety of social, scientific and political issues. Upon completion of the Core Curriculum, students in the Honors College move on to honors-enriched courses in their major fields of study.

The Honors College follows a cohort model in which all students who enter the College at the same time take all of their Core Curriculum courses together. This promotes a sense of community and shared learning and insures that students in the College are one another's first line of support. Honors students also enjoy close and frequent interaction with their professors both inside and outside the classroom. The Honors office provides a student lounge and study carrels with computers and printers. Coffee, tea, snacks and sodas are also available in the Honors office.

Students in the Honors College advise the College and plan social events through the Honors Student Council. Two events have already become Honors College traditions: the Honors Induction Ceremony for new students and their families, and the Dean's Winter Reception for students and faculty. News, views and honors events are disseminated through Word of Honor, *the Honors College student newsletter. Honors students are guided toward a variety of co-curricular and extracurricular service and learning opportunities, including volunteering with local social service agencies, serving as tutors/mentors on campus and in the Chicago Public Schools, and participating in planning and hosting university events.*

The greater Chicago area offers world-class social and cultural attractions. Students in Chicago State's Honors College have many opportunities to broaden their experience and learning through field trips and informal excursions to museums, concerts, sporting events, and more.

Founded in 2004 with an initial enrollment of eleven students, the Chicago State University Honors College will admit between fifteen and twenty new freshmen each fall semester. The College reviews the applications of all freshmen admitted to Chicago State and invites those with the strongest academic and personal credentials to join the College.

Participation Requirements: Students in the Honors College are expected to maintain a minimum cumulative GPA of 3.0 in their first year and at least a 3.25 cumulative GPA in subsequent years. Students who graduate in good standing in the Honors College are recognized with Honors designations on their diplomas and transcripts.

Admission Process: Freshman students admitted to Chicago State University are invited to join the Honors College if they have a high school GPA of 3.5 or above or a composite ACT score of 23 or above, or if they graduated in the top ten per-cent of their high school classes. No separate application is required, but prospective students must be interviewed and recommended for admission by a committee of the students currently in the Honors College.

Scholarship Availability: Students entering the Honors College are eligible to receive a variety of university scholarships and other forms of financial aid. Both need-based and merit-based scholarships are available. Full details can be found on the Chicago State University web site (http://www.csu.edu).

Campus Overview

State-supported comprehensive, founded 1867 • **Coed** 4,867 undergraduate students, 66% full-time, 73% women, 27% men.

Undergraduates 3,236 full-time, 1,631 part-time. Students come from 32 states and territories, 9 other countries, 2% are from out of state, 87% African American, 0.4% Asian American or Pacific Islander, 6% Hispanic American, 0.1% Native American, 0.6% international, 13% transferred in, 7% live on campus.

Faculty *Total:* 431, 71% full-time, 53% with terminal degrees. *Student/faculty ratio:* 13:1.

Academic Programs *Special study options:* academic remediation for entering students, accelerated degree program, adult/continuing education programs, advanced placement credit, cooperative education, distance learning, double majors, external degree program, honors programs, internships, part-time degree program, student-designed majors, study abroad, summer session for credit. *ROTC:* Army (b), Navy (c), Air Force (c).

Athletics Member NCAA, NAIA. All NCAA Division I. *Intercollegiate sports:* baseball M(s), basketball M(s)/W(s), cross-country running M(s)/W(s), golf M(s)/W(s), tennis M(s)/W(s), track and field M(s)/W(s), volleyball W(s).

Costs (2004–05) *Tuition:* state resident $4830 full-time, $161 per credit hour part-time; nonresident $9660 full-time, $322 per credit hour part-time. Full-time tuition and fees vary according to course load, degree level, location, and student level. Part-time tuition and fees vary according to course load, degree level, location, and student level. No tuition increase for student's term of enrollment. *Required fees:* $1313 full-time, $210 per term part-time. *Room and board:* $6032. Room and board charges vary according to board plan.

Contact: Dean: Dr. Richard Milo, Cordell Reed Student Union 231, 9501 S. King Drive, Chicago, Illinois 60628-1598; *Telephone:* 773-995-3801; *Fax:* 773-995-4522; *E-mail:* honors@csu.edu; *Web site:* http://www.csu.edu.

College of DuPage
Honors Program
Glen Ellyn, Illinois

Honors courses at the College of DuPage offer additional challenges and depth to students' college experience and more opportunities to use their minds well. Students who love to learn, are willing to work, and enjoy bringing their imagination and originality to class should consider applying to honors.

Honors courses are enriched versions of regular courses, designed to help academically talented and highly motivated students achieve

their maximum potential. Each year, a range of courses in the liberal arts and sciences is offered, consistent with the emphasis on general education in the first two years of college. Honors classes are characterized by small class sizes and a seminar format, which encourage extensive interaction among students as well as between students and the professor. Many students especially appreciate this opportunity to get to know other students better and to feel more like a part of the academic environment of the College.

Each honors course offers an in-depth treatment of course content; emphasizes the development of such intellectual skills as analysis, synthesis, critical inquiry, application, and discussion; and contains a significant writing component.

Additional program benefits include the opportunity to select an honors mentor among faculty members who teach in the Honors Program, assistance with transfer and scholarship applications, and participation in special honors-related activities.

The program began in 1984 and currently has approximately 1,000 students taking honors courses each term. There are currently more than 1,000 students in the Honors Scholar Program. Three Honors Program students have been awarded Guistwhite Scholarships (ten are awarded nationally each year), and in 1998, 1 graduate was awarded a Rhodes Scholarship.

Participation Requirements: Students may participate in honors in one of two ways: by taking individual honors courses or by participating in the Honors Scholar Program. To participate by way of individual honors courses, students who meet the general eligibility criteria may apply to the honors coordinator for a permit to register for individual honors courses. Entering first-year students may apply after achieving one of these two criteria: a cumulative high school GPA of at least 3.5 (on a 4.0 scale) or a composite ACT score of 25 or higher. Current College of DuPage students must meet these two criteria: completion of 8 or more college-level semester credits or the equivalent and a cumulative GPA of at least 3.2. To participate by way of the Honors Scholar Program, students who meet the eligibility criteria may apply for admission to the Honors Scholar Program at any time, though first-year entrance is preferred. Admissions requirements for entering first-year students are a cumulative high school GPA of at least 3.5 (on a 4.0 scale) or a composite ACT score of 25 or higher. Current College of DuPage students must have a minimum cumulative GPA of 3.5 in addition to having completed 8 semester credits or the equivalent.

Students who complete the Honors Scholar Program receive special recognition at Commencement, at the Celebration of Academic Excellence, and on their transcripts and diplomas.

Scholarship Availability: Those who are admitted to the program are entitled to a waiver of in-district tuition on all honors courses as long as they maintain a minimum cumulative GPA of 3.5 and make satisfactory progress toward completing other program requirements (a minimum of 18 semester credits or the equivalent of honors courses, including an honors seminar). Special transfer programs and scholarships are also available to students seeking a baccalaureate degree.

Campus Overview

State and locally supported 2-year, founded 1967, part of Illinois Community College Board • **Coed** 29,854 undergraduate students, 36% full-time, 57% women, 43% men.

Undergraduates 10,657 full-time, 19,197 part-time. Students come from 19 states and territories, 6% African American, 12% Asian American or Pacific Islander, 8% Hispanic American, 0.3% Native American, 6% transferred in.

Faculty *Total:* 1,651, 19% full-time, 13% with terminal degrees. *Student/faculty ratio:* 22:1.

Academic Programs *Special study options:* academic remediation for entering students, accelerated degree program, adult/continuing education programs, advanced placement credit, cooperative education, distance learning, double majors, English as a second language, external degree program, honors programs, independent study, internships, off-campus study, part-time degree program, services for LD students, student-designed majors, study abroad, summer session for credit.

Athletics Member NJCAA. *Intercollegiate sports:* baseball M, basketball M/W, cheerleading M/W, cross-country running M/W, football M, golf M, soccer M/W, softball W, swimming and diving M/W, tennis M/W, track and field M/W, volleyball W. *Intramural sports:* basketball M/W, bowling M/W, golf M/W, ice hockey M(c), racquetball M/W, soccer M/W, softball M/W, swimming and diving M/W, tennis M/W, volleyball M/W, weight lifting M/W.

Costs (2005–06) *Tuition:* area resident $2251 full-time, $87 per semester hour part-time; state resident $7243 full-time, $243 per semester hour part-time; nonresident $8619 full-time, $226 per semester hour part-time. *Required fees:* $533 full-time.

Contact: Honors Program Office, 425 Fawell Boulevard, Glen Ellyn, Illinois 60137-6599; *Telephone:* 630-942-2749; *Fax:* 630-942-3295; *E-mail:* honorsprogram@cdnet.cod.edu.; *Web site:* http://www.cod.edu/Academic/AcadProg/Hon_Prog/Honors.htm

Concordia University
Honors Program
River Forest, Illinois

*D**esigned to enhance a student's overall college career, the Honors Program offers academically successful students the opportunity to broaden and enrich their undergraduate education at Concordia University in River Forest, Illinois. The current focus of the program is the intentional cultivation, development, and application of critical-thinking skills across the curriculum.*

All honors classes are limited to honors students and have smaller enrollments than general education classes. Taught by talented faculty members who develop courses in their areas of expertise, honors seminars in particular offer professors opportunity to examine cutting-edge scholarship that might otherwise not be covered in standard courses. Alternative approaches to learning and attention to academic excellence are regular features of honors courses, with special emphasis given to student presentations. The introductory courses—one on perceptions and realities of the American West and one on the history and literature of the Holocaust—each semester prepare an exhibit for the campus community as their culminating class project.

Concordia's campus is only 10 miles from the Chicago Loop, which offers a full range of cultural experiences and events. Honors students have attended plays, performances, and sporting events off campus and the program has in turn brought speakers and performers to campus. Plans for a dedicated study/community space for honors students await completion of current campus building projects and reallocation of facilities.

The Honors Program, founded in 1990, has an average participation of 65 students.

Participation Requirements: Students must complete 12 hours or the equivalent of four courses, beginning with an initial honors experience, Introduction to Honors: Critical Thinking (3 hours), an interdisciplinary humanities-based course. Subsequently, students design their own program, choosing from several flexible options including midlevel Honors Seminars in the Disciplines (topics and readings courses in four discipline areas: social and behavioral sciences, humanities and the arts, theology and philosophy, and math and the sciences), study abroad/semester away opportunities, and independent senior honors projects. In addition, honors students contribute 30 service learning hours to church or community. Program expectations add no additional burden to graduation requirements, but students must maintain a minimum 2.75 GPA to remain in the program. Students successfully completing the course work and service requirements are recognized at commencement as Concordia Scholars.

Admission Process: Incoming students meeting the minimum admission profile—26 ACT and 3.7 high school GPA—receive an invitation to apply to the Honors Program following acceptance to the University, and do so by submitting an application form, essay, and teacher recommendation. In addition, freshman students with a minimum 3.5 GPA after their first semester at Concordia are invited to make application under the same process but must be supported by faculty nominations.

Scholarship Availability: All honors students are eligible for presidential scholarships.

Campus Overview

Independent comprehensive, founded 1864, affiliated with Lutheran Church–Missouri Synod, part of Concordia University System • **Coed** 1,134 undergraduate students, 84% full-time, 65% women, 35% men.

Undergraduates 950 full-time, 184 part-time. Students come from 22 states and territories, 1 other country, 36% are from out of state, 7% African American, 1% Asian American or Pacific Islander, 6% Hispanic American, 0.3% Native American, 0.4% international, 10% transferred in, 40% live on campus.

Faculty *Total:* 209, 32% full-time. *Student/faculty ratio:* 11:1.

Academic Programs *Special study options:* academic remediation for entering students, accelerated degree program, adult/continuing education programs, advanced placement credit, distance learning, double majors, honors programs, independent study, internships, off-campus study, part-time degree program, services for LD students, study abroad, summer session for credit.

Athletics Member NCAA. All Division III. *Intercollegiate sports:* baseball M, basketball M/W, cheerleading M/W, cross-country running M/W, football M, golf M, soccer M/W, softball W, tennis M/W, track and field M/W, volleyball W. *Intramural sports:* badminton M/W, basketball M/W, bowling M/W, football W, swimming and diving M/W, table tennis M/W, tennis M/W, volleyball M/W.

Costs (2004–05) *Comprehensive fee:* $24,900 includes full-time tuition ($18,700), mandatory fees ($300), and room and board ($5900). Full-time tuition and fees vary according to program. Part-time tuition: $560 per semester hour. Part-time tuition and fees vary according to program.

Financial Aid 350 Federal Work-Study jobs (averaging $356). In 2003, 185 non-need-based awards were made. *Average percent of need met:* 45%. *Average financial aid package:* $11,333. *Average need-based loan:* $3670. *Average need-based gift aid:* $5179. *Average non-need-based aid:* $6928.

Contact: Director: Dr. Marilyn E. Moehlenkamp, Concordia University, 7400 Augusta, River Forest, Illinois 60305; *Telephone:* 708-209-3129; *Fax:* 708-209-3176; *E-mail:* m.moehlenkamp@curf.edu

DePaul University

University Honors Degree Program

Chicago, Illinois

The DePaul University Honors Degree Program offers challenging courses for well-prepared, serious students majoring in any discipline. The Honors Degree Program seeks to widen students' perspectives beyond their academic majors and foster critical thinking, self-reflection, and an examination of values. In addition, the Honors Degree Program works to foster active participatory learning,

promote interdisciplinary and cross-cultural studies, encourage students to develop facility in a second language and develop the skills necessary for pursuing independent research, help students see themselves as members of larger communities in which they can be leaders through service work and other means, and assist interested students in thinking about and preparing for postgraduate education. The program offers a choice of two capstone experiences, the senior seminar and the senior thesis, both involving dialogue about lifelong learning.

In order to meet these goals, the program offers small classes (about 20 students) organized in seminar format and taught by faculty members committed to realizing the program's goals. All core courses develop students' expertise in critical reading, analysis, writing, and research. In addition, the Honors Degree Program requires proficiency in a second language, encourages self-directed learning through third-year elective courses that include a research project, and supports an honors community of scholars through its lecture and film series, faculty-student dinners, a study-abroad program, an honors student government association, and opportunities for community service. The program provides information and counseling regarding admission to graduate schools and applications for fellowships.

Faculty members teaching in the program are among the most talented and dedicated instructors at DePaul. They teach their areas of expertise to students who are highly motivated and eager to engage in the learning process.

The College of Liberal Arts and Sciences Honors Degree Program was founded in 1986–87, and it became a University-wide Honors Degree Program in 2004–05. There are now 473 students enrolled in all four years.

Participation Requirements: The Honors Degree Program consists of fourteen to twenty courses, representing between 56 and 80 credit hours; hour requirements vary depending on the student's home college within the University. The program includes a six-course foundations core (core courses include world literature; History in a Global Context; Religious Worldviews and Ethical Perspectives; data analysis; States, Markets, and Societies; and an honors Chicago course); a second-language proficiency requirement; second-year courses in the arts, sciences, and cognitive science; junior electives and a junior research seminar; and either a senior thesis or senior seminar. To graduate from the Honors Degree Program, students must have attained a minimum 3.2 GPA by the last quarter of their senior year. Students who successfully complete the program have their transcripts stamped Honors Program Graduate; students who complete the foundations courses receive an Honors Foundations certificate.

Admission Process: Students are invited to join the Honors Degree Program when they apply for admission to DePaul. Invitations are issued on the basis of high school GPA, class rank, or ACT scores. In addition, students submit an essay that is evaluated by an honors committee. Students whose numerical profile does not match the honors profile but who show promise of exceptional contributions to the program may be invited for an interview with the Director and Associate Director. Such promise may be evidenced in extensive travel abroad, a keen interest in a subject, or an intense engagement with the community throughout high school. DePaul students and transfer students may be considered for admission into the Honors Degree Program through the first quarter of their sophomore year.

Scholarship Availability: Scholarships of various amounts are awarded through the Office of Admissions, based on academic performance or financial need. Scholarships are not offered through the Honors Degree Program. Most honors students are recipients of academic scholarships.

Campus Overview

Independent Roman Catholic university, founded 1898 • **Coed** 14,678 undergraduate students, 76% full-time, 58% women, 42% men.

Undergraduates 11,109 full-time, 3,569 part-time. Students come from 50 states and territories, 74 other countries, 13% are from out of state, 10% African American, 9% Asian American or Pacific Islander, 13% Hispanic American, 0.3% Native American, 2% international, 9% transferred in, 18% live on campus.

Faculty *Total:* 1,546, 54% full-time. *Student/faculty ratio:* 18:1.

Academic Programs *Special study options:* academic remediation for entering students, accelerated degree program, adult/continuing education programs, advanced placement credit, cooperative education, distance learning, double majors, English as a second language, freshman honors college, honors programs, independent study, internships, part-time degree program, services for LD students, study abroad, summer session for credit. *ROTC:* Army (c). *Unusual degree programs:* 3-2 engineering with University of Illinois at Urbana-Champaign, University of Illinois at Chicago, University of Detroit Mercy, University of Southern California, Northwestern University, Iowa State University, Ohio State University.

Athletics Member NCAA. All Division I. *Intercollegiate sports:* basketball M(s)/W(s), cross-country running M(s)/W(s), golf M(s)/W, soccer M(s)/W(s), softball W(s), tennis M(s)/W(s), track and field M(s)/W(s), volleyball W(s). *Intramural sports:* badminton M/W, baseball M, basketball M/W, crew M/W, cross-country running M/W, football M/W, golf M, ice hockey M/W, racquetball M/W, rugby M/W, skiing (downhill) M/W, soccer M/W, softball W, swimming and diving M/W, table tennis M/W, tennis M/W, track and field M/W, ultimate Frisbee M/W, volleyball W, weight lifting M/W, wrestling M.

Costs (2004–05) *One-time required fee:* $100. *Comprehensive fee:* $29,072 includes full-time tuition ($19,700), mandatory fees ($65), and room and board ($9307). Full-time tuition and fees vary according to program. *Part-time tuition:* $369 per quarter hour. Part-time tuition and fees vary according to program. *College room only:* $6316. Room and board charges vary according to board plan, housing facility, and location.

Financial Aid 900 Federal Work-Study jobs (averaging $2000). In 2003, 692 non-need-based awards were made. *Average percent of need met:* 70%. *Average financial aid package:* $15,280. *Average need-based loan:* $4457. *Average need-based gift aid:* $10,085. *Average non-need-based aid:* $7194.

Contact: Director: Dr. Helen Marlborough, McGaw Hall 234, 802 West Belden, Chicago, Illinois 60614; *Telephone:* 773-325-7486; *Fax:* 773-325-7328; *E-mail:* hmarlbor@depaul.edu; *Web site:* http://www.depaul.edu/~honors

Eastern Illinois University

Honors Program

Charleston, Illinois

*E*astern Illinois University offers superior students challenging and *rewarding opportunities to develop intellectually, personally, and professionally. The three curricular programs—University Honors, Presidential Scholars, and Departmental Honors—aid students in developing qualities such as independence of mind through an enriched curriculum of in-depth studies.*

The University Honors Program is designed for students who begin as first-year-students at Eastern. It provides enriched and rigorous honors sections of general education courses, each with an enrollment of 18 or fewer students. The Presidential Scholars Program is an enhanced version of university honors with additional curricular and experiential requirements, designed to encourage students to think reflectively, learn actively, and plan their college experiences with a focused view toward career, personal, and educational goals. The Departmental Honors Program encourages students to pursue areas of personal interest by delving deeply and independently into a topic. Students take advantage of departmental

resources to research, explore, investigate, and analyze information on a subject appropriate to the discipline. Course work advances progressively, culminating in a senior thesis.

Honors faculty members are devoted and experienced professors who enjoy their subjects and care about teaching talented students. Their teaching methods foster inquiry with an emphasis on undergraduate research. Honors faculty members grade students against norms established in regular classes. Students are aware that, as a result of this arrangement, they will not be penalized for taking intellectual risks and participating in classes with other superior students. Honors courses emphasize quality over quantity. Assignments are not merely more of the same, but encourage students to think, write, and express themselves with clarity and grace. The excitement of exchanges within smaller classes and the stimulation of intellectual challenge make honors courses among the most popular on campus.

The Honors College also provides students with many co-curricular opportunities, including undergraduate research, national scholarship application, and campus and community service. The Honors College is committed to promoting the highest quality research opportunities for students by advocating faculty mentoring of student research, thereby fostering collegial relationships and supporting enriched teaching-learning experiences. The Honors College sponsors a competitive grant program for undergraduate researchers, many of whom author publications and present their research at professional conferences. Several students each year present their research at the spring conference of the Honors Council of the Illinois Region.

The Honors College, through academic and fellowship advising, also provides students with support and preparation for national scholarship application, study abroad, internship and externship experiences, and graduate school applications. Honors students are actively encouraged to pursue the many opportunities open to them both nationally and internationally.

Locally, honors students participate actively in athletics, music, and student government. The Association of Honors Students (AHS) sponsors trips to cultural events, community service projects, and social activities. AHS students nominate their own representatives to the Honors Advisory Council. These students, along with Honors faculty representatives, advise the Dean on curricular, scholarship, and other matters of import to the Honors College.

Honors at Eastern Illinois University was initiated in 1982, became a college in 2003, and currently enrolls 630 students.

Participation Requirements: University honors students complete a minimum of 25 hours of honors general education course work, primarily at the lower division level. The program also requires a 4-hour interdisciplinary capstone seminar outside of the student's major field. Presidential scholars complete the University Honors Program requirements with the addition of HON 1191, a team-taught, first-year seminar, and a self-initiated Sophomore/ Junior Experience project, which may be research, service, or creative in its orientation. Departmental honors candidates complete a minimum of 12 hours of honors course work within the major, including independent research or creative activity under the direction of a faculty mentor and the writing of an undergraduate honors thesis. Many departmental programs also require a graduate course. All honors classes are designated as such on student transcripts. In addition, all University and departmental honors students receive honors certification on their final transcripts and are recognized at commencement, provided they complete the university and/or departmental programs with a GPA of 3.5 or higher. For all programs, student must meet GPA and continuous enrollment criteria.

Admission Process: Admission to the University Honors Program is open to incoming students who meet at least two of the following criteria: ACT composite score of 26 or higher (SAT I score of at least 1100), upper 10 percent of high school graduating class, high school GPA of 3.5 or better on a four-point scale, and permission of the Dean. Continuing students with a minimum 3.5 GPA for at least 12 hours of course work undertaken at Eastern Illinois University may also be admitted. The Presidential Scholars Program is limited to 20 students per year. Its minimum requirements are an ACT composite score of 30 with a GPA of 3.5 or class rank in the upper 10 percent of high school graduating class. Students with an ACT composite score of 28 with a GPA of 3.75 or class rank in the upper 5 percent of high school graduating class are also considered. The Departmental Honors Program is open to continuing and transfer students with a college or university GPA of 3.5 or better on a four-point scale and permission of the appropriate departmental honors coordinator and the Dean of the Honors College.

Scholarship Availability: The Honors College at Eastern Illinois University offers a variety of merit-based scholarships. Presidential Scholars Awards are eight-semester awards limited to those students accepted into the Presidential Scholars Program. Other freshman awards include the four-year Talented Student Award and the one-year Freshman Honors Scholarship. Students admitted to the University Honors Program are invited to apply for all the above scholarships. The application process includes a letter of recommendation from a high school teacher and the writing of an essay. Continuing students compete annually for one-year Continuing Student, Charles Austin, Rachel Richardson, Dorothy Davis Bunge, KC Summers, and First Neighbor Bank scholarships. To receive and/or maintain eligibility for scholarships, a student must remain in good standing in the University and/or Departmental Honors Programs

Campus Overview

State-supported comprehensive, founded 1895 • **Coed** 9,928 undergraduate students, 90% full-time, 58% women, 42% men.

Undergraduates 8,958 full-time, 970 part-time. Students come from 32 states and territories, 44 other countries, 1% are from out of state, 6% African American, 1% Asian American or Pacific Islander, 2% Hispanic American, 0.2% Native American, 0.6% international, 10% transferred in, 44% live on campus.

Faculty *Total:* 730, 87% full-time, 64% with terminal degrees. *Student/faculty ratio:* 15:1.

Academic Programs *Special study options:* academic remediation for entering students, adult/continuing education programs, advanced placement credit, double majors, external degree program, honors programs, independent study, internships, off-campus study, part-time degree program, services for LD students, study abroad, summer session for credit. *ROTC:* Army (b). *Unusual degree programs:* 3-2 engineering with University of Illinois.

Athletics Member NCAA. All Division I except football (Division I-AA). *Intercollegiate sports:* baseball M(s), basketball M(s)/W(s), cross-country running M(s)/W(s), golf M(s)/W(s), rugby M(c)/W(s), soccer M(s)/W(s), softball W(s), swimming and diving M(s)/W(s), tennis M(s)/W(s), track and field M(s)/W(s), volleyball W(s), wrestling M(s). *Intramural sports:* badminton M/W, basketball M/W, bowling M/W, cross-country running M/W, football M/W, lacrosse M(c), racquetball M/W, soccer M/W, softball M/W, table tennis M/W, tennis M/W, volleyball M/W, wrestling M.

Costs (2004–05) *Tuition:* state resident $4133 full-time, $138 per credit hour part-time; nonresident $12,398 full-time, $413 per credit hour part-time. Full-time tuition and fees vary according to course load and student level. Part-time tuition and fees vary according to course load and student level. No tuition increase for student's term of enrollment. *Required fees:* $1649 full-time, $53 per credit hour part-time. *Room and board:* $7150. Room and board charges vary according to board plan and housing facility.

Financial Aid 391 Federal Work-Study jobs (averaging $1422). In 2003, 380 non-need-based awards were made. *Average percent of need met:* 18%. *Average financial aid package:* $9126. *Average need-based loan:* $3348. *Average need-based gift aid:* $2693. *Average non-need-based aid:* $6712.

Contact: Dean: Dr. Bonnie D. Irwin, The Honors College, Eastern Illinois University, 600 Lincoln Avenue, Charleston, Illinois 61920; *Telephone:* 217-581-2017; *Fax:* 217-581-7222; *E-mail:* bdirwin@eiu. edu; *Web site:* http://www.eiu.edu/~honprog

Elgin Community College
Honors Program
Elgin, Illinois

Elgin Community College's (ECC) Honors Program provides academically talented students a coherent set of challenging, enriched course sections that meet general education core requirements for baccalaureate degrees in the areas of communications, mathematics, physical sciences and life sciences, humanities and fine arts, social science, and behavioral sciences. Emphasis is on small class size and innovative learning experiences, including interdisciplinary approaches to common topics, service learning, and specific real-world applications of classroom concepts.

The emphasis for second-semester students is on building a cohort of adventurous students and teachers who get to know each other and learn with one another better than is possible with regular community college scheduling. Options include dual enrollment in subjects linked across disciplines that meet on and off campus, fine arts appreciation courses focused on live performance and gallery-based experiences, and major-related, faculty-mentored, independent study. The 15-year-old program currently has 75 participating students.

Participation Requirements: All students can sample honors sections of core courses and may later choose to commit to the Honors Program. Program enrollees must complete a minimum of 15 hours of honors course work distributed across at least three of the five categories in the general education core for transfer degrees with an A or B.

In addition to course work, Honors students must meet participation and service requirements in Phi Theta Kappa or one of five major-related honors societies. A minimum 3.5 GPA at graduation leads to the Honors Scholar designation on the transcript and diploma for the Associate in Arts, Associate in Science, or Associate in Fine Arts degrees.

The Honors Program accepts honors course work from other NCHC member schools. The College offers dual admission and enrollment in four-year institutions, which has led to awarding Honors Scholar status on the transcripts of students who complete all program requirements and successfully transfer to an upper-division program without graduating.

Admission Process: New students are identified and counseled at orientation as potential Honors Program students, while continuing students are identified by College faculty members and screening of student records. To participate in the Honors Program, a student must have met at least two of the following criteria: graduation in the top 10 percent of the high school class, a cumulative high school GPA of at least 3.5 on a 4.0 scale, submission of a composite ACT score of 25 or higher or an SAT I combined score of at least 1000, completion of at least 12 credit hours of articulated college-level course work with a cumulative GPA of 3.25 or higher on a 4.0 scale, submission of written recommendations from 3 high school or college faculty members in at least two disciplines, and approval of the Honors Coordinator.

Scholarship Availability: Trustee Scholarships are available in the categories of academic excellence and leadership in one of ten specific areas. Academic scholarships are noncompetitive awards to students graduating in the upper 10 percent of their high school class who present evidence of rank the semester after high school graduation. Leader scholarships are awards available to current students based on excellence in a particular major or activity. All students who earn an A or B in an honors course and maintain a 3.25 or higher GPA receive credit in the number of those credit hours toward in-district tuition in future semesters.

Campus Overview
State and locally supported 2-year, founded 1949, part of Illinois

Community College Board • **Coed** 10,851 undergraduate students, 31% full-time, 55% women, 45% men.

Undergraduates 3,348 full-time, 7,503 part-time. Students come from 4 states and territories, 22 other countries, 1% are from out of state, 5% African American, 6% Asian American or Pacific Islander, 16% Hispanic American, 0.2% Native American, 0.3% international, 29% transferred in.

Faculty *Total:* 512, 24% full-time, 11% with terminal degrees. *Student/faculty ratio:* 23:1.

Academic Programs *Special study options:* academic remediation for entering students, accelerated degree program, adult/continuing education programs, advanced placement credit, cooperative education, distance learning, double majors, English as a second language, honors programs, independent study, internships, off-campus study, part-time degree program, services for LD students, student-designed majors, summer session for credit.

Athletics Member NJCAA. *Intercollegiate sports:* baseball M(s)/W, basketball M(s)/W(s), cross-country running M/W, golf M(s), softball W, tennis W(s), volleyball W(s).

Costs (2005–06) *Tuition:* area resident $2250 full-time, $75 per credit hour part-time; state resident $7666 full-time, $256 per credit hour part-time; nonresident $9947 full-time, $332 per credit hour part-time. *Required fees:* $10 full-time, $5 per term part-time.

Contact: Alice Biggers, Honors Program Coordinator, 1700 Spartan Drive, Elgin, Illinois 60123-7193; *Telephone:* 847-214-7577; *Fax:* 847-888-5570; *E-mail:* abiggers@elgin.edu

Elmhurst College
Elmhurst College Honors Program
Elmhurst, Illinois

The Elmhurst College Honors Program affords a unique, enhanced educational experience for distinguished undergraduates who are committed to the pursuit of academic excellence. Fostering intellectual independence, scholarly achievement, and the integration of liberal learning and professional activity, the interdisciplinary program nurtures a community of learners and contributes to the intellectual vibrancy of the entire college.

Honors Program students are concurrently enrolled in one of the College's undergraduate programs, where they earn their bachelor's degrees. Study in the Honors Program is intended to complement the curricula of all academic programs, providing students the benefits of challenging course work with recognized teacher-scholars and other academically motivated students.

Program participants are expected to contribute to the well-being of the common life of the College and to continue academic achievement consistent with the expectations of the Honors Program.

Providing unique academic, cultural, and social opportunities, the program clearly reflects Elmhurst College's mission and goals to foster critical and creative inquiry and to emphasize socially responsible and ethical citizenship, while focusing on the synergy between the liberal arts and professional preparation. This synergy is reinforced through the housing of the Honors Program within the College's unique Center for Professional Excellence, which also provides opportunities for career exploration, international study, intercultural education, and service learning.

Academic components of the program include challenging courses and opportunities for independent research. Courses provide powerful student-centered learning experiences, featuring intellectually stimulating interactive classroom environments. They frequently rely on primary texts and advanced technological resources and also encourage experiential learning through field trips, on-site participation, and service-learning opportunities. The junior-year independent research project allows students to work closely with a faculty mentor

in designing a significant research project in his or her discipline. All projects are presented and/or published in an appropriate public, scholarly venue, such as the Elmhurst College Research and Performance Showcase and/or off-site professional conferences.

In addition to the formal academic components of the Honors Program, students are provided with a myriad of intellectual, cultural, and social opportunities to further enhance their College experience. These include personal advising by full-time faculty members and the Honors Program Director; skilled guidance in applying for special funding opportunities for research, preprofessional activities, and/or graduate study; and various on-campus and off-campus activities, such as private receptions with distinguished guest speakers, attendance at various Chicago-area cultural events, and social gatherings with other Honors Program participants. The Elmhurst College Honors Program was established in 1965 and currently has approximately 80 members.

Participation Requirements: The Honors Program consists of seven academic components: six courses and an independent research project. Each of these components, which are distributed across a student's years at the College, draws its intentions explicitly from the College's mission statement. The four early seminars, which fulfill general education core requirements, focus on social responsibilities, values, critical and creative inquiry, and lifelong learning. They are offered in a variety of disciplines, affording choices that appeal to a wide range of interests. Two additional courses include a January-term honors elective and the senior Honors Capstone Seminar. The January-term electives are offered at the College as well as abroad. International travel is strongly encouraged, though not required, for all Honors Program participants. The interdisciplinary, team-taught Capstone explores a contemporary issue and affords in-depth research that is relevant for all majors. To complete the junior-year independent research, students work closely with a faculty mentor to design a significant research project that is reflective of their discipline.

Participation in the program becomes a part of the student's permanent academic record. Student transcripts acknowledge Honors Program participation; students completing the entire Honors Program are recognized with the distinction of Honors Program Scholar and honored at the College's Honors Convocation.

Admission Process: To be considered for the Honors Program, students must first be admitted to Elmhurst College. First-year students with excellent academic records who receive Elmhurst College academic merit scholarships (Presidential, with a mean ACT score of approximately 29, and Dean's, with a mean ACT score of approximately 26) are invited by the director to participate in the program. Transfer students with a grade point average of 3.5 or better or who have participated in good standing in an honors program at another institution are eligible to apply to the program as well. Students demonstrating superior academic achievement once at Elmhurst may join the program at the discretion of the program director upon receipt of a strong faculty recommendation.

Scholarship Availability: Academic merit scholarships are offered to traditional and transfer students based upon ACT scores and outstanding high school or previous college performance. These scholarship recipients are invited to participate in the program. In addition, the Swords Scholar Grant is available exclusively to Honors Program students for support of their independent junior research projects.

Campus Overview

Independent comprehensive, founded 1871, affiliated with United Church of Christ • **Coed** 2,484 undergraduate students, 86% full-time, 64% women, 36% men.

Undergraduates 2,129 full-time, 355 part-time. Students come from 26 states and territories, 21 other countries, 8% are from out of state, 5% African American, 3% Asian American or Pacific Islander, 5% Hispanic American, 0.4% Native American, 1% international, 40% live on campus.

Faculty *Total:* 278, 40% full-time, 44% with terminal degrees. *Student/faculty ratio:* 13:1.

Academic Programs *Special study options:* academic remediation for entering students, accelerated degree program, adult/continuing education programs, advanced placement credit, cooperative education, double majors, honors programs, independent study, internships, off-campus study, part-time degree program, services for LD students, study abroad, summer session for credit. *ROTC:* Army (c), Air Force (c). *Unusual degree programs:* 3-2 engineering with Illinois Institute of Technology, Northwestern University, Washington University in St. Louis, University of Illinois at Chicago, University of Southern California.

Athletics Member NCAA. All Division III. *Intercollegiate sports:* baseball M, basketball M/W, cross-country running M/W, football M, golf M/W, soccer W, softball W, tennis M/W, track and field M/W, volleyball W, wrestling M. *Intramural sports:* basketball M/W, football M, golf M/W, racquetball M/W, soccer M, softball M/W, volleyball M/W.

Costs (2004–05) *Comprehensive fee:* $26,394 includes full-time tuition ($20,090) and room and board ($6304). Part-time tuition: $572 per credit hour. *College room only:* $3634. Room and board charges vary according to board plan and housing facility.

Financial Aid 316 Federal Work-Study jobs (averaging $1065). 214 state and other part-time jobs (averaging $2300). In 2004, 314 non-need-based awards were made. *Average percent of need met:* 91%. *Average financial aid package:* $18,079. *Average need-based loan:* $6180. *Average need-based gift aid:* $12,972. *Average non-need-based aid:* $7727.

Contact: Dr. Mary Kay Mulvaney, Director, Honors Program, 190 Prospect Avenue, Elmhurst, Illinois 60126; *Telephone:* 630-617-6479; *E-mail:* marym@elmhurst.edu

Governors State University
University Honors Program
University Park, Illinois

While recognizing academic excellence, the University Honors Program is designed to give students an opportunity to pursue an enriched education while attending Governors State University. In so doing, honors students pursue greater depth within their academic major by completing advanced work within their existing curriculum. In addition, honors students obtain greater breadth by taking an interdisciplinary honors seminar in which guest speakers from across the University's campus address a common integrative theme. Having been exposed to a rich diversity of academic perspectives, students then complete a project relevant to their academic major in cooperation with a faculty mentor.

The curricular components of the University Honors Program include one course in the students' major in which they contract with the instructor to do advanced work, one advanced interdisciplinary Honors Seminar, and an honors thesis/project/internship that is completed under the supervision of a faculty mentor.

The curricula of the University are offered through four colleges: the College of Arts and Sciences, the College of Business and Public Administration, the College of Education, and the College of Health Professions.

Beyond the above enriched academic program, honors students also have the combined benefits of a speakers series, the support and guidance of a faculty mentor, participation in special social events, and membership in a community of scholars and learners. Participation in honors is reflected on the student's transcript and with a letter of commendation from the president of the University.

Participation Requirements: The University Honors Program is open to all students who are interested and who expect to be able to meet the graduation requirements for the program. At the beginning of the students' participation in the program, advisement takes place with the Honors Director. At this time, the student signs a letter of agreement that acknowledges the major curricular requirements of the program. Transfer students and students nominated by faculty members are highly encouraged to register with the program.

Admission Process: Students not yet admitted to the University should contact the Admissions Office. Since Governors State University is an upper-divisional university, students need a minimum of 60 hours of college credit to be admitted.

Scholarship Availability: Governors State University offers an array of different scholarships and work-study opportunities. In particular, there is a community college (transfer) scholarship available to students. Community college honors students who are in the process of successfully completing their program can receive a letter of scholarship recommendation from the director of the Honors Program.

Campus Overview

State-supported upper-level, founded 1969 • **Coed** 2,752 undergraduate students, 31% full-time, 71% women, 29% men.

Undergraduates 844 full-time, 1,908 part-time. Students come from 8 states and territories, 20 other countries, 3% are from out of state, 36% African American, 1% Asian American or Pacific Islander, 6% Hispanic American, 0.2% Native American, 1% international.

Faculty *Total:* 212, 87% full-time, 75% with terminal degrees. *Student/faculty ratio:* 17:1.

Academic Programs *Special study options:* adult/continuing education programs, advanced placement credit, distance learning, external degree program, honors programs, independent study, internships, off-campus study, part-time degree program, services for LD students, student-designed majors, study abroad, summer session for credit. *ROTC:* Army (c), Air Force (c).

Athletics *Intramural sports:* badminton M/W, basketball M/W, racquetball M/W, skiing (cross-country) M/W, softball M/W, table tennis M/W, volleyball M/W.

Costs (2004–05) *Tuition:* state resident $3264 full-time, $136 per credit part-time; nonresident $9792 full-time, $408 per credit part-time. Full-time tuition and fees vary according to course load and location. Part-time tuition and fees vary according to course load and location. *Required fees:* $440 full-time, $10 per credit part-time, $131 per term part-time.

Contact: Director: Dr. Larry Levinson, University Honors Program, Governors State University, University Park, Illinois 60466; *Telephone:* 708-534-4578; *Fax:* 708-534-7895; *E-mail:* l-levinson@govst.edu

Illinois State University
Honors Program
Normal, Illinois

The nationally recognized Honors Program at Illinois State University provides enriching educational opportunities for academically talented students. Excellent students committed to their own personal development and to rewarding careers find that their Illinois State Honors education prepares them well for professional schools, graduate schools, and for satisfying employment after they graduate. Honors students enjoy the benefits of a small college in the rich context of a large multipurpose university. The University offers them, among other benefits, early registration; special courses taught by distinguished teachers and scholars; close, caring personal advisement by Honors Program advisers; unique opportunities for undergraduate research/scholarship with world-class faculty scholars, including monetary support for student research; and special living accommodations that bring them into close acquaintance with other honors students in academic and social programs. Successful graduates of the Honors Program attend law schools, medical schools, and graduate schools. They also obtain outstanding employment with national corporations, both within Illinois and in other states.

Honors students enjoy special sections of regular University courses, including courses in the general education program. They may also enroll in special courses taught by the University's distinguished scholars and faculty members, including advanced colloquia on various topics, independent honor study, and individualized honors projects in the context of regular courses.

The Honors Program sponsors programs designed to help students pursue research and scholarship as undergraduates. This is an especially important opportunity for students aiming for advanced study in graduate or professional schools. Students have used such research opportunities as a basis for publishing articles, networking with professors in their disciplines, and receiving national scholarships and academic prizes, including the Goldwater and Udall awards.

Honors students may, with the advice of select faculty members and Honors Program advisers, participate in the design of their own educational curricula, reflecting their special interests and goals. This option, called the Faculty Colleague Program, includes individualized curricula for academic majors and minors and for general education. It allows outstanding students the ability to shape for themselves curricular options that might not be available in any other university.

All honors course work and honors academic designations are recorded on student transcripts. Students may earn certificates in University honors, may become University honors scholars, and may become departmental honors scholars. Other academic honors at Illinois State include traditional Latin-named honors and special scholarships for outstanding students. The program was established in 1964 to meet the needs of academically talented and motivated students. It currently enrolls 1,200 students, which is 7 percent of the undergraduate student enrollment.

Participation Requirements: Students in the program are expected to complete a minimum of 3 credit hours of honors course work per semester. Students taking more than 3 credits of honors work can have these hours banked against future semesters. Once students have accumulated 24 credit hours, they have met the participation requirements.

Admission Process: The program admits new freshmen, transfer students, and current students eligible for the program. All students must apply for admission to the Honors Program and must complete a personal statement designed to indicate how prepared and motivated an applicant is to pursue academic work. Students admitted usually have at least an ACT composite score of 27 and a GPA of at least 3.5. Applying high school students are usually in the top 10 percent of their graduating class.

Scholarship Availability: Incoming students are eligible to apply for various achievement-based scholarships, including Presidential Scholarships, Dean's Scholarships, and Honors First Year Scholarships. These scholarships are valued from $1000 for one year to $8000 for each of four years. National Merit Finalists may receive additional scholarship funding if they list Illinois State as their university of choice with the NMS Corporation. Current honors students may apply for tuition scholarships, research mentorships, and summer research scholarships.

The Presidential Scholars Program is an exclusive and unique academic program that offers students holding Presidential Scholarships special curricula, both in general education and in their major courses of study; opportunities for study abroad; and select internship and service learning experiences. Presidential scholars in this program enjoy special social activities, such as dinners with the president and special advisement.

Campus Overview

State-supported university, founded 1857 • **Coed** 17,878 undergraduate students, 93% full-time, 57% women, 43% men.

Undergraduates 16,613 full-time, 1,265 part-time. Students come from 43 states and territories, 46 other countries, 1% are from out of state, 6% African American, 2% Asian American or Pacific Islander, 3% Hispanic American, 0.3% Native American, 0.8% international, 10% transferred in, 35% live on campus.

Faculty *Total:* 1,088, 76% full-time, 72% with terminal degrees. *Student/faculty ratio:* 19:1.

Academic Programs *Special study options:* academic remediation for entering students, accelerated degree program, adult/continuing education programs, advanced placement credit, cooperative education, distance learning, double majors, English as a second language, honors programs, independent study, internships, off-campus study, part-time degree program, services for LD students, student-designed majors, study abroad, summer session for credit. *ROTC:* Army (b). *Unusual degree programs:* 3-2 engineering with University of Illinois.

Athletics Member NCAA. All Division I except football (Division I-AA). *Intercollegiate sports:* baseball M(s), basketball M(s)/W(s), cross-country running M(s)/W(s), golf M(s)/W(s), gymnastics W(s), soccer W(s), softball W(s), swimming and diving W(s), tennis M(s)/W(s), track and field M(s)/W(s), volleyball W(s). *Intramural sports:* badminton M/W, baseball M, basketball M/W, bowling M(c)/W(c), field hockey M/W, football M, golf M/W, gymnastics M(c), ice hockey M(c), lacrosse M(c), racquetball M/W, rugby M(c)/W(c), soccer M/W, softball M/W, tennis M/W, ultimate Frisbee M/W, volleyball M(c)/W.

Costs (2004–05) *Tuition:* state resident $4800 full-time, $160 per credit hour part-time; nonresident $10,020 full-time, $334 per credit hour part-time. Full-time tuition and fees vary according to course load. Part-time tuition and fees vary according to course load. No tuition increase for student's term of enrollment. *Required fees:* $1528 full-time, $43 per credit hour part-time, $648 per term part-time. *Room and board:* $5576; room only: $2762. Room and board charges vary according to board plan.

Financial Aid 556 Federal Work-Study jobs (averaging $1889). 39 state and other part-time jobs (averaging $2295). In 2004, 370 non-need-based awards were made. *Average percent of need met:* 81%. *Average financial aid package:* $8717. *Average need-based loan:* $4988. *Average need-based gift aid:* $6372. *Average non-need-based aid:* $4295.

Contact: Director: Dr. Douglas D. Hesse, Normal, Illinois 61790-6100; *Telephone:* 309-438-2559; *Fax:* 309-439-8196; *E-mail:* honors@ilstu.edu; *Web site:* http://www.honors.ilstu.edu

Joliet Junior College
Honors Program
Joliet, Illinois

The Joliet Junior College (JJC) Honors Program, currently in its fourteenth year, is designed to intellectually stimulate and challenge students striving for the utmost in their college education. It consists of a select group of students and faculty members from all disciplines and a core of courses in which the material is covered in greater depth and breadth than in regular courses. Writing and critical thinking are stressed, and because honors classes are small (15 students maximum), many teaching and learning approaches are used.

As their adviser, the coordinator of the Honors Program assists all honors students during their careers at Joliet Junior College and thereafter in, among other things, transferring, seeking scholarships, and gaining employment.

There are currently 74 students in the program.

Participation Requirements: To graduate from the Honors Program students must satisfy all college requirements for graduation, complete 15 credit hours of honors course work, participate in at least one half of all honors colloquia (lecture-discussion sessions run by guest scholars) and honors forums (biweekly discussion sessions run by honors students), and earn a 3.5 or better GPA. All honors courses are designated as such on student transcripts, as is successful completion of the program.

Admission Process: Entering freshmen must satisfy one of the following requirements: graduation in the top 10 percent of the high school class, an ACT composite score of 25 or better, or membership in the National Honor Society. Joliet Junior College students must have a GPA of 3.5 or higher for 15 or more credit hours or two letters of recommendation from college faculty members. An interview with the Honors Program Coordinator is required of all applicants.

Scholarship Availability: Joliet Junior College offers a number of endowed scholarships to qualified applicants. In some cases, participation in the Honors Program may be a factor.

Campus Overview

State and locally supported 2-year, founded 1901, part of Illinois Community College Board • **Coed** 13,245 undergraduate students.

Undergraduates Students come from 12 states and territories, 0.3% are from out of state, 10% African American, 2% Asian American or Pacific Islander, 13% Hispanic American, 0.2% Native American, 0.2% international.

Faculty *Total:* 641, 28% full-time, 7% with terminal degrees. *Student/faculty ratio:* 12:1.

Academic Programs *Special study options:* academic remediation for entering students, adult/continuing education programs, advanced placement credit, distance learning, English as a second language, honors programs, independent study, internships, part-time degree program, services for LD students, summer session for credit.

Athletics Member NJCAA. *Intercollegiate sports:* basketball M/W, football M, golf M, softball W, tennis M/W, volleyball W.

Costs (2004–05) *Tuition:* area resident $2040 full-time, $68 per credit hour part-time; state resident $6190 full-time, $206 per credit hour part-time; nonresident $7273 full-time, $242 per credit hour part-time.

Financial Aid 96 Federal Work-Study jobs (averaging $1168). 254 state and other part-time jobs (averaging $1778).

Contact: Coordinator: John D. Schroeder, 1215 Houbolt Road, Joliet, Illinois 60431-8938; *Telephone:* 815-729-9020 Ext. 2643; *E-mail:* jschroed@jjc.edu

Lake Land College
Honors Program
Mattoon, Illinois

*O*utstanding students desire a challenging and inspiring college experience. These students are eager to take on in-depth projects, engage in discussions, interact with and learn from people with diverse backgrounds, and seek out new and better ways of solving problems. The Lake Land College Honors Program exists for these students.

The purpose of the Honors Program is to provide enriched learning opportunities for exceptional college transfer students through special honors courses and through opportunities to participate in honors independent study in their area of interest. The Honors Program is guided by a program director and committee.

The Honors Program has many advantages. Honors students attend class with other academically talented and motivated students. They may receive special scholarship aid. Monetary awards have been made to approximately 15 students per semester. Academic achievement is the primary criterion for the awards. Students' transcripts show honors designation for each honors course or honors independent study successfully completed. They may also participate in educational field trips and special social activities, such as the honors luncheons (fall and spring) and honors conferences. Honors students who successfully graduate from the Honors Program receive an honors designation on their transcript and honors recognition at the graduation ceremony.

In 1978, Lake Land College began its Honors Program. As of fall 2004, 159 students have completed the requirements and graduated as Lake Land College honors students. There are currently 21 students enrolled in the program.

Participation Requirements: Honors students must successfully complete at least one honors option (honors course or honors independent study) within the first two semesters after being admitted into the Honors Program. Honors students must also maintain a minimum 3.5 cumulative GPA. A student whose cumulative GPA falls below 3.5 is placed on probation and has one semester to raise their GPA to the minimum requirement. Students who do not meet these requirements are removed from the Honors Program.

In order to graduate with full status, honors students must maintain at least a 3.5 overall GPA at Lake Land College, graduate from a college transfer program, and successfully complete at least four honors options (four honors courses or at least two honors courses and two honors independent studies).

In order to graduate with associate status, honors students must maintain at least a 3.5 overall GPA at Lake Land College, graduate from a college transfer program, and successfully complete at least two honors options (honors courses or honors independent studies).

Admission Process: Entering freshmen must enroll in a college transfer program at Lake Land College and submit an application package, including a completed application form for entering freshmen, the applicant's official high school transcript, a copy of the applicant's ACT or SAT record, and two letters of recommendation, to the Honors Program Director. Applicants must meet at least two of the following indices of academic ability and preparedness: an ACT composite score of 25 or above, a high school GPA of at least 3.5 on a 4-point scale (or the equivalent), and graduation in the top 10 percent of their high school class.

Scholarship Availability: The Lake Land College Foundation provides students with scholarships through funds contributed by individuals, agencies, and corporations. Thanks to the many individual and corporate donors to the Lake Land College Foundation, numerous scholarships are available for students attending or planning to attend Lake Land College.

Scholarship eligibility requirements vary. Specific criteria are determined by the donor. Some scholarships are available for students who graduate in the top 10 percent of their high school graduating class, some for students who plan to pursue a degree in a particular curriculum, some for students who need help financially, and others for students who meet the specific criteria of the donor.

Applicants must submit a Scholarship Application Form by 5 p.m. March 1 of each year to be considered for a scholarship for the following academic year. Application forms can be obtained from the Foundation Office, from high school counselors' offices, or via the Internet. Applicants who graduate from a high school within the Lake Land College District and are in the top 10 percent of their class upon completion of their seventh semester are eligible to apply for the Presidential Scholarship.

Campus Overview

State and locally supported 2-year, founded 1966, part of Illinois Community College Board • **Coed** 7,196 undergraduate students, 44% full-time, 48% women, 52% men.

Undergraduates 3,144 full-time, 4,052 part-time. Students come from 23 other countries, 8% African American, 0.4% Asian American or Pacific Islander, 3% Hispanic American, 0.3% Native American, 0.5% international.

Faculty *Total:* 191, 61% full-time, 5% with terminal degrees. *Student/faculty ratio:* 21:1.

Academic Programs *Special study options:* academic remediation for entering students, accelerated degree program, adult/continuing education programs, cooperative education, distance learning, English as a second language, external degree program, honors programs, internships, part-time degree program, services for LD students, summer session for credit.

Athletics Member NJCAA. *Intercollegiate sports:* baseball M(s), basketball M(s)/W(s), cheerleading W, softball W(s), tennis M(s)/W, volleyball W(s). *Intramural sports:* basketball M/W, bowling M/W, golf M/W, softball M/W, volleyball M/W.

Costs (2005–06) *Tuition:* area resident $1545 full-time, $52 per credit hour part-time; state resident $3595 full-time, $120 per credit hour part-time; nonresident $7568 full-time, $252 per credit hour part-time. *Required fees:* $358 full-time, $12 per credit hour part-time.

Financial Aid 120 Federal Work-Study jobs (averaging $1400).

Contact: Director: Travis Sola, Lake Land College Honors Program, 5001 Lake Land Boulevard, Mattoon, Illinois 61938; *Telephone:* 217-234-5292; *E-mail:* honors@lakeland.cc.il.us; *Web site:* http://www.lakelandcollege.edu/honors

Lincoln Land Community College

Honors Program

Springfield, Illinois

The Lincoln Land Community College Honors Program provides unique educational experiences for academically superior students in order to challenge, educate, and reward them at a level consistent with their intellectual needs and abilities. The Honors Program, initiated in fall 1985, offers opportunities for critical thinking, greater student/teacher interaction, in-depth reading and discussion, smaller classes, and contact with other high-ability students.

Each honors student is assigned an administrator or faculty person as a mentor. The mentor advises the student on such matters as Honors Program requirements, scheduling, transferability, and career opportunities.

Students who complete the program are awarded a medallion to wear at graduation. Nominated on the basis of high scholarship, evidence of leadership, and Honors Program participation, one student, upon program completion, is selected as the outstanding honors student. Students who serve on committees are given certificates of appreciation.

There are currently 58 students enrolled in the Honors Program.

Participation Requirements: To successfully complete the program and receive special recognition at commencement, students must have successfully completed 15 credit hours of honors course work maintaining a minimum cumulative GPA of 3.25. Successful course completion is defined as receiving a grade of C or higher in all honors courses. Honors courses are enhanced sections of current courses, interdisciplinary courses designed specifically for the Honors Program, and special honors courses. Honors students must register for Leadership Development (SOC 112). This course is an interdisciplinary course based on the PTK leadership model. Students are also strongly encouraged to attend an orientation program. Monthly student meetings are an integral part of the program.

Admission Process: Students may be admitted to the Honors Program at any time. However, the deadline for scholarship applications is March 1. Transfer students can be admitted to the program; however, as most honors classes offered are general

education courses, the student may have already completed some of these courses. Therefore, it is more difficult for transfer students to complete the program.

Scholarship Availability: The LLCC Foundation has established ten $1200 renewable Honors Program scholarships. Scholarships are available to entering freshmen or LLCC students who have earned fewer than 12 semester hours of college credit. Applications must be sent to the Honors Program Director by March 1. Applicants should return the application form and submit high school and college transcripts, two letters of recommendation, and an essay before the applicant can be considered for a scholarship. The committee meets in mid-March to review applications for scholarships and admission to the program.

Campus Overview

Suburban 441-acre campus with easy access to St. Louis • **Coed** 6,942 undergraduate students, 40% full-time, 59% women, 41% men.

Undergraduates 2,756 full-time, 4,186 part-time. Students come from 4 states and territories, 3 other countries, 0.1% are from out of state, 8% African American, 1% Asian American or Pacific Islander, 1% Hispanic American, 0.4% Native American, 0.3% international, 3% transferred in.

Faculty *Total:* 361, 34% full-time, 34% with terminal degrees. *Student/faculty ratio:* 19:1.

Academic Programs *Special study options:* academic remediation for entering students, accelerated degree program, adult/continuing education programs, advanced placement credit, distance learning, English as a second language, external degree program, honors programs, independent study, internships, off-campus study, part-time degree program, services for LD students, study abroad, summer session for credit.

Athletics Member NJCAA. *Intercollegiate sports:* baseball M(s), basketball M(s)/W(s), soccer M(s), softball W(s), volleyball W(s). *Intramural sports:* basketball M/W, tennis M/W.

Costs (2004–05) *Tuition:* area resident $1620 full-time, $54 per credit hour part-time; state resident $6750 full-time, $225 per credit hour part-time; nonresident $8310 full-time, $277 per credit hour part-time. Full-time tuition and fees vary according to course load. Part-time tuition and fees vary according to course load. *Required fees:* $165 full-time, $6 per credit hour part-time.

Contact: David Laubersheimer, Lincoln Land Community College, P.O. Box 19256, Springfield, Illinois 62794-9256; *Telephone:* 217-786-2270; *E-mail:* david.laubersheimer@llcc.edu

Loyola University Chicago

Honors Program

Chicago, Illinois

Since 1936, the Honors Program has served the most intellectually talented and highly motivated students at Loyola University Chicago. In an atmosphere charged with challenging teaching methods and enthusiastic student participation, professors and students work together in small, stimulating honors classes, exploring critical issues in each discipline.

The intimate, collegial atmosphere helps develop a close working relationship among honors students and faculty members. The most motivated students capitalize on this relationship by becoming involved with independent faculty research projects and by attending a multitude of "brown bag" colloquia by resident and visiting scholars.

While honors students and faculty members come from all across the country and from all walks of life, they share a common bond—the

search for truth and meaning through analysis, discussion, and research. Collaboration and individual attention are the hallmarks of the program. As a result, honors students experience a unique sense of community even within the context of the larger university community.

This sense of community is manifest outside the classroom as well. Honors students enjoy social and intellectual interaction in the honors common rooms. They plan social and cultural events as members of the Honors Student Association. Lively classroom discussion, close faculty-student working relationships, a strong sense of community, and intellectual rigor combine in the Honors Program to create the best atmosphere for students wanting to take full advantage of the educational opportunities at Loyola University Chicago.

Each year, 100 incoming students are admitted, which represents 5 percent of each class.

Participation Requirements: Designed for flexibility, the Honors Program curriculum provides an opportunity for in-depth exploration of critical issues within Loyola's Core Curriculum. No additional courses are required to earn the honors degree. Approximately one third (42 semester hours) of an honors student's courses must carry honors credit. Honors credits can be earned by taking special honors sections in core courses, by contracting with a professor in a regular course, or by taking graduate-level courses. Students who fulfill the course requirements of the Honors Program with a GPA of 3.3 receive the honors degree. This distinction is noted at graduation and is recorded on transcripts.

Admission Process: Students who have a weighted GPA of at least a 3.75 and an ACT score of 29 or higher or an SAT score of 1270 or higher are invited to apply to the Honors Program after they are admitted to the University. The completed Honors Program application includes an essay; a list of extracurricular involvement, leadership experience, and service; one faculty recommendation; and a current high school transcript. Completed applications must be received by February 1.

Scholarship Availability: Students who apply to the Honors Program are automatically considered for one of three full-tuition scholarships. Candidates are selected for a faculty interview on campus in April. In addition, Loyola University Chicago provides scholarships, grants, loans, and work-study jobs for those students who qualify.

Campus Overview

Independent Roman Catholic (Jesuit) university, founded 1870 • **Coed** 8,319 undergraduate students, 87% full-time, 66% women, 34% men.

Undergraduates 7,251 full-time, 1,068 part-time. Students come from 50 states and territories, 60 other countries, 34% are from out of state, 7% African American, 11% Asian American or Pacific Islander, 10% Hispanic American, 0.2% Native American, 2% international, 7% transferred in, 29% live on campus.

Faculty Total: 1,046, 48% full-time. Student/faculty ratio: 13:1.

Academic Programs Special study options: academic remediation for entering students, accelerated degree program, adult/continuing education programs, advanced placement credit, double majors, English as a second language, honors programs, internships, off-campus study, part-time degree program, services for LD students, study abroad, summer session for credit. ROTC: Army (c), Navy (c). Unusual degree programs: 3-2 engineering with University of Illinois at Urbana-Champaign, Washington University in St. Louis.

Athletics Member NCAA. All Division I. Intercollegiate sports: basketball M(s)/W(s), cross-country running M(s)/W(s), golf M(s)/W(s), soccer M(s)/W(s), softball W(s), track and field M(s)/W(s), volleyball M(s)/W(s). Intramural sports: badminton M/W, baseball M(c), basketball M/W, football M, racquetball M/W, rugby M(c), sailing M/W, soccer M/W, softball M/W, table tennis M/W, tennis M/W, volleyball M/W.

Costs (2005–06) Comprehensive fee: $32,896 includes full-time tuition ($23,100), mandatory fees ($736), and room and board ($9060). Part-time tuition: $500 per semester hour. College room only: $6200.

Financial Aid In 2003, 492 non-need-based awards were made. Average percent of need met: 73%. Average financial aid package: $16,465. Average need-based loan: $5514. Average need-based gift aid: $11,975. Average non-need-based aid: $8253.

Contact: Director: Dr. Joyce Wexler, 6525 North Sheridan, Chicago, Illinois 60626; Telephone: 312-508-2780

McHenry County College
Honors Program
Crystal Lake, Illinois

The Honors Program is devised to attract and retain academically talented students. Its curriculum is structured to help students develop a strong foundation in academic skills such as critical thinking, problem solving, reading, and writing within a small-class environment. Students in the program have an opportunity to participate in NCHC activities, including honors semesters. Honors at McHenry provides students with local recognition of their academic achievement and then assists them in making a link to the honors programs at four-year/senior institutions through transcript notation and individual articulation.

Founded in 1987, the program currently enrolls 75 students per semester.

Participation Requirements: Honors Program members must maintain a 3.5 GPA. Students in the program complete 16 to 20 hours of honors courses, which are separate sections of existing courses and are identified on the transcript. At graduation, honors graduates have a special tassel to identify them and a special gold seal on their diplomas.

Admission Process: Students may gain admission to the Honors Program based on any two of the following criteria: a high school GPA of 3.5; a minimum composite ACT score of 24 or minimum combined SAT I score of 1000; college-transfer GPA of 3.5 for a minimum of 12 hours; MCC GPA of 3.5 for a minimum of 12 hours; membership in good standing of Phi Theta Kappa; two academic letters of recommendation; and a personal interview with the Honors Coordinator or appointed representative. Any student with a 3.2 GPA can enroll in an honors course.

Scholarship Availability: The Honors Program offers five scholarships per semester. These generally are for tuition in honors courses, although they can be applied to books if the student already has other tuition scholarships.

Campus Overview

State and locally supported 2-year, founded 1967, part of Illinois Community College Board • **Coed** 5,940 undergraduate students, 34% full-time, 58% women, 42% men.

Undergraduates 2,048 full-time, 3,892 part-time. Students come from 6 states and territories, 17 other countries, 1% are from out of state, 0.6% African American, 2% Asian American or Pacific Islander, 5% Hispanic American, 0.3% Native American, 0.5% international, 6% transferred in.

Faculty Total: 295, 30% full-time, 11% with terminal degrees. Student/faculty ratio: 20:1.

Academic Programs Special study options: academic remediation for entering students, accelerated degree program, adult/continuing education programs, advanced placement credit, cooperative education, distance learning, English as a second language, honors programs, independent study, internships, part-time degree program, services for LD students, study abroad, summer session for credit.

Athletics Member NJCAA. *Intercollegiate sports:* baseball M(s), basketball M(s)/W(s), soccer M(s), softball W(s), tennis M(s)/W(s), volleyball W(s). *Intramural sports:* bowling M/W.

Costs (2004–05) *Tuition:* area resident $1740 full-time, $58 per credit part-time; state resident $7333 full-time, $244 per credit part-time; nonresident $8601 full-time, $287 per credit part-time. Full-time tuition and fees vary according to reciprocity agreements. Part-time tuition and fees vary according to reciprocity agreements. *Required fees:* $284 full-time, $9 per credit part-time, $7 per term part-time.

Financial Aid 200 Federal Work-Study jobs (averaging $3700). 130 state and other part-time jobs (averaging $2000).

Contact: Directors: Kathy Chamberlain and Elaine Whalen-Pedersen, 8900 U.S. Highway 14, Crystal Lake, Illinois 60012-2761; *Telephone:* 815-455-8568, 815-479-7563; *Fax:* 815-455-3762; *E-mail:* kchamber@ mchenry.edu

McKendree College

Honors Program

Lebanon, Illinois

The McKendree College Honors Program is designed to enhance the undergraduate educational experience of exceptionally able students. It is a four-year interdisciplinary program for the talented student—a challenging, unified, but diverse curriculum offering an opportunity to do independent work in one's major field. The program has five main goals. The first is to provide special opportunities to explore the liberal arts in greater depth and variety than is currently available in the core curriculum, to investigate the connections among the various disciplines, and to make the liberal arts an integral part of students' development into thinking, feeling, knowledgeable, and morally aware critical thinkers. The second is to provide an environment that increases the quantity and quality of interaction with intellectual peers and faculty members and to stress the sharing of talents with all peers. The third is to ensure that the atmosphere created ultimately benefits the entire College community through a revitalization of interest in the liberal arts, in learning for its own sake, in infusing knowledge and ideas into the everyday life of the College, and in sponsoring and attending cultural activities that can help enrich the education of all McKendree students. The fourth is to provide the opportunity to engage in independent research to better prepare students for graduate study or employment in their major fields. The fifth is to develop leadership skills that will enhance the campus community and prepare students to assume leadership roles as interested and involved citizens of the local, state, national, and world communities.

Participation Requirements: The McKendree College Honors Program comprises two parts. The first is an integrated, interdisciplinary series of courses organized around a broad theme. The second is a thesis based on research activity or a creative product in the student's major field, completed during the junior and senior years. All students in the program are required to enroll in the honors courses each semester, except in unusual circumstances as approved by the Honors Council. The Honors Council comprises a representative from each of six divisions and 2 student members. The council serves to review curricular matters as well as to assist the Director in matters of policy, planning, recruitment, and retention. Each honors seminar requires extensive outside reading coupled with frequent writing assignments and active discussion participation. Students in the program are expected to maintain a GPA of 3.0 or better to remain in the program. Students who successfully complete all requirements in the program and who meet all other graduation requirements of McKendree

College are identified on their transcripts and diplomas as graduates of the McKendree College Honors Program.

Admission Process: To qualify for admission to the McKendree College Honors Program, applicants must meet three criteria. They must have a cumulative high school GPA of 3.6 or better (on a 4.0 scale), rank in the top 10 percent of their high school graduating class, and have a composite ACT score of 27 or better or a combined SAT I score of 1200 or better.

High school seniors who meet all three of these criteria and who are interested in participating in the program must submit a completed application for admission to the College; the application must include an official high school transcript and official test scores for the ACT or SAT I. Students will then receive an invitation from the program in the spring of their senior year in high school. Included in that invitation will be a response card indicating the student's interest in joining the program as well as the deadline for returning the card, normally by March 31. Only 18 students are admitted per year.

Scholarship Availability: Presidential Scholarships are awarded to qualified freshman students, who must be enrolled full-time. No distinctions are made for those students enrolled in the Honors Program.

Campus Overview

Independent 4-year, founded 1828, affiliated with United Methodist Church • **Coed** 2,156 undergraduate students, 75% full-time, 57% women, 43% men.

Undergraduates 1,615 full-time, 541 part-time. Students come from 23 states and territories, 22 other countries, 28% are from out of state, 12% African American, 0.9% Asian American or Pacific Islander, 2% Hispanic American, 0.1% Native American, 2% international, 15% transferred in, 54% live on campus.

Faculty *Total:* 225, 31% full-time, 36% with terminal degrees. *Student/faculty ratio:* 12:1.

Academic Programs *Special study options:* academic remediation for entering students, accelerated degree program, advanced placement credit, double majors, honors programs, independent study, internships, off-campus study, part-time degree program, services for LD students, student-designed majors, study abroad, summer session for credit. *ROTC:* Army (c), Air Force (c). *Unusual degree programs:* 3-2 occupational therapy with Washington University in St. Louis.

Athletics Member NAIA. *Intercollegiate sports:* baseball M(s), basketball M(s)/W(s), bowling M(s)/W(s), cheerleading M(s)/W(s), cross-country running M(s)/W(s), football M(s), golf M(s)/W(s), ice hockey M, soccer M(s)/W(s), softball W(s), tennis M(s)/W(s), track and field M(s)/W(s), volleyball W(s), wrestling M(s). *Intramural sports:* basketball M/W, football M/W, softball M/W, table tennis M/W, ultimate Frisbee M/W, volleyball M/W.

Costs (2004–05) *Comprehensive fee:* $22,960 includes full-time tuition ($16,400), mandatory fees ($200), and room and board ($6360). Full-time tuition and fees vary according to location. Part-time tuition: $550 per hour. Part-time tuition and fees vary according to course load and location. *College room only:* $3360. Room and board charges vary according to board plan and housing facility.

Financial Aid 441 Federal Work-Study jobs (averaging $1276). 173 state and other part-time jobs (averaging $1164). In 2004, 252 non-need-based awards were made. *Average percent of need met:* 81%. *Average financial aid package:* $13,846. *Average need-based loan:* $3251. *Average need-based gift aid:* $10,940. *Average non-need-based aid:* $9433.

Contact: John Greenfield, Honors Program, 701 College Road, Lebanon, Illinois 62254-1299; *Telephone:* 618-537-6890; *E-mail:* jgreenfi@mckendree.edu; *Web site:* http://www.mckendree.edu

Millikin University
Millikin University Honors Program
Decatur, Illinois

The Millikin University Honors Program is a self-sustaining community dedicated to exploring distinctive approaches to learning. The opportunity for gifted scholars to work together benefits the individual, the Millikin University Honors Program, and the academic community at large. Based on the belief that excellence requires, the Millikin University Honors Program utilizes innovative pedagogies consistent with the goals outlined in the Program of Student Learning; fosters educational excellence worthy of imitation within the University and beyond; attracts and challenges highly motivated and talented students and faculty members committed to an education comprehensive in breadth and depth; develops students' scholarly practices with diverse methods of inquiry and encourages creative pursuits that incorporate risk taking; and provides students with flexibility in their plans of study, support for independent and collaborative learning, and the opportunity to work closely with faculty mentors.

The Millikin University Honors Program has three levels of scholarship. During their freshman and sophomore years, honors scholars are introduced to college-level scholarship, research, critical thinking, and writing. Classes are taught as seminars—sessions that involve intense discussion and require active participation. At the end of the sophomore year, the strongest students are invited to join the next phase of the Millikin University Honors Program and become James Millikin Scholars.

Established in 1974, the James Millikin Scholars (JMS) program offers opportunities for independent study and research to sophomore, junior, and senior students. The selection processes for James Millikin Scholars, while rigorous, is not unreasonable. Selection is based on academic records, an interview with faculty members and several James Millikin Scholars, an essay, and faculty recommendations. A limited number of applicants are chosen each year. James Millikin Scholars must be capable of outstanding academic performance, demonstrate intellectual curiosity, be willing to take academic risks, and be strongly motivated for study at the college level. All students, honors scholars or not, may apply as long as they have a minimum 3.4 grade point average.

James Millikin Scholars develop more research skills, adding statistical and mathematical tools to those learned as freshmen. They are on their way to becoming truly independent scholars as they work on their honors projects during junior and senior years. In addition, James Millikin Scholars regularly present their projects at state, regional, and national honors conferences and professional meetings.

The final level of scholarship is the Presidential Scholarship, which is Millikin's best scholarship. The Presidential Scholars Program was established in 1984 as the University sought to identify students who combine outstanding academic records with service to their communities (broadly defined) and leadership in community and school activities. Each year, 5 to 8 students are selected for Presidential Scholarships out of the hundreds that apply to the Millikin University Honors Program.

Admission Process: Incoming freshmen with a minimum ACT of 27 or SAT I of 1200 and who were graduated in the top 10 percent of their high school class may apply to become members of the Millikin University Honors Program. Any qualified sophomore student may apply for the JMS program during the spring of the sophomore year. Students must maintain a cumulative grade point average of 3.4 out of 4.0 to remain in the JMS program. Presidential Scholars automatically enter the JMS Program at the end of the freshman year; they must maintain a minimum cumulative grade point average of 3.5.

Scholarship Availability: Gift Scholarship Awards: Presidential Scholars, 27 ACT or 1200 SAT I, top 10 percent, full tuition, minimum 3.5 GPA; James Millikin Scholars, 27 ACT or 1200 SAT I, top 10 percent, selection during spring, second year, half tuition, minimum 3.4 GPA; Honors Scholars, 27 ACT or 1200 SAT, top 10 percent, half tuition, minimum 3.4 GPA.

Campus Overview

Independent comprehensive, founded 1901, affiliated with Presbyterian Church (U.S.A.) • **Coed** 2,645 undergraduate students, 96% full-time, 57% women, 43% men.

Undergraduates 2,532 full-time, 113 part-time. Students come from 30 states and territories, 4 other countries, 13% are from out of state, 9% African American, 1% Asian American or Pacific Islander, 2% Hispanic American, 0.1% Native American, 0.6% international, 5% transferred in, 70% live on campus.

Faculty *Total:* 287, 48% full-time, 36% with terminal degrees. *Student/faculty ratio:* 14:1.

Academic Programs *Special study options:* advanced placement credit, double majors, honors programs, independent study, internships, off-campus study, part-time degree program, services for LD students, student-designed majors, study abroad, summer session for credit. *Unusual degree programs:* 3-2 engineering with Washington University in St. Louis; physical therapy, occupational therapy, medical technology, pharmacy with Midwestern University.

Athletics Member NCAA. All Division III. *Intercollegiate sports:* baseball M, basketball M/W, cross-country running M/W, football M, golf M/W, soccer M/W, softball W, swimming and diving M/W, tennis W, track and field M/W, volleyball W, wrestling M. *Intramural sports:* basketball M/W, bowling M/W, softball M/W, table tennis M/W, tennis W, volleyball M/W.

Costs (2004–05) *Comprehensive fee:* $26,810 includes full-time tuition ($19,900), mandatory fees ($400), and room and board ($6510). Full-time tuition and fees vary according to course load. *College room only:* $3618. Room and board charges vary according to board plan and housing facility.

Financial Aid In 2002, 655 non-need-based awards were made. *Average percent of need met:* 88%. *Average financial aid package:* $16,233. *Average need-based loan:* $3748. *Average need-based gift aid:* $9951. *Average non-need-based aid:* $6535.

Contact: Dr. Brian Posler, Director of Millikin Honors, *Telephone:* 217-424-6273 or 217-424-6276; *E-mail:* bposler@millikin.edu. Office of Admission, 1184 West Main Street, Decatur, Illinois 62522; 800-373-7733 press 5 (toll-free) or 217-424-6210

North Central College
College Scholars Program
Naperville, Illinois

The College Scholars Program was created to attract students capable of superior work and to provide them with the opportunity to have a challenging and broadening intellectual experience. Course work emphasizes interdisciplinary study, individualized research, and other special projects. The five-course History of Ideas seminar series is of particular interest to freshmen and sophomores. The seminar format encourages lively discussion of intellectually engaging issues ranging from the classical era through the twentieth century. College Scholars are advised by specially selected honors advisers, usually in their major, and are encouraged to develop independent studies and take designated honors courses. Members of the College Scholars Program are encouraged to become involved in Wingspread Scholars (a regional conference program) and the Richter Fellowship Program (funding for independent study work). Social activities throughout the academic year encourage contact with professors and other students to provide intellectual stimulation and support.

The College Scholars Program at North Central College (NCC) was established in 1982. There are approximately 200 members.

Participation Requirements: To sustain membership in the program, a student must maintain a minimum GPA of 3.0 and earn at least 3 hours of honors work each year.

College Scholar is a title bestowed upon graduating students who have completed 30 hours of honors work, including at least one Honors Seminar at the 300 or 400 level and a Senior Honors Thesis (which is hardcover bound and shelved in the College library). College Scholars Participant is a title bestowed upon graduating students who have completed at least 18 hours of honors credit, including one Honors Seminar at the 300 or 400 level. A grade of A or B must be earned for honors credit to be awarded. All honors course work is noted on the student's transcript.

Admission Process: Admission to the program is by invitation (entering freshmen) and by application (throughout the academic year). Acceptance of entering freshmen is based on the student's ACT/SAT I score, high school record, NCC Admission Counselor's recommendation, and results of a personal interview. Other applicants are selected using demonstrated interest in the program, ACT/SAT I scores, high school and/or college GPA, and a recommendation from an NCC professor.

Transfer students who participated in an honors program at another institution are admitted to the College Scholars Program upon submission of an application. They may bring honors credit to NCC from a similar program, provided they were in good standing at the institution from which they are transferring.

Scholarship Availability: Freshmen applying to North Central College may qualify for Presidential Scholarships (academic) in amounts from $3000 to $16,000; transfer students may qualify for renewable academic scholarships of up to $10,000 and/or one of ten Phi Theta Kappa (a community college honor society) scholarships of $2000 awarded each year. Performing arts scholarships are awarded in amounts up to $4500. Endowed departmental scholarships are available.

Campus Overview

Independent United Methodist comprehensive, founded 1861 • **Coed** 2,036 undergraduate students, 88% full-time, 59% women, 41% men.

Undergraduates 1,788 full-time, 248 part-time. Students come from 26 states and territories, 24 other countries, 9% are from out of state, 3% African American, 3% Asian American or Pacific Islander, 4% Hispanic American, 0.1% Native American, 1% international, 12% transferred in, 58% live on campus.

Faculty *Total:* 209, 60% full-time, 61% with terminal degrees. *Student/faculty ratio:* 13:1.

Academic Programs *Special study options:* academic remediation for entering students, accelerated degree program, adult/continuing education programs, advanced placement credit, cooperative education, double majors, English as a second language, honors programs, independent study, internships, off-campus study, part-time degree program, services for LD students, student-designed majors, study abroad, summer session for credit. *ROTC:* Army (c), Air Force (c). *Unusual degree programs:* 3-2 engineering with Washington University in St. Louis; University of Illinois at Urbana-Champaign; Marquette University; University of Minnesota, Twin Cities Campus; medical technology with Rush University.

Athletics Member NCAA. All Division III. *Intercollegiate sports:* baseball M, basketball M/W, cheerleading W, cross-country running M/W, football M, golf M/W, soccer M/W, softball W, swimming and diving M/W, tennis M/W, track and field M/W, volleyball W, wrestling M. *Intramural sports:* badminton M/W, basketball M/W, bowling M/W, cross-country running M/W, football M/W, golf M/W, racquetball M/W, skiing (cross-country) M/W, skiing (downhill) M/W, soccer M/W, softball M/W, swimming and diving M/W, table tennis M/W, tennis M/W, track and field M/W, volleyball M/W.

Costs (2004–05) *Comprehensive fee:* $27,147 includes full-time tuition ($20,160), mandatory fees ($240), and room and board ($6747). Part-time tuition: $505 per semester hour. *Required fees:* $20 per term part-time. *Room and board:* Room and board charges vary according to housing facility.

Financial Aid 217 Federal Work-Study jobs (averaging $698). In 2004, 375 non-need-based awards were made. *Average percent of need met:* 86%. *Average financial aid package:* $18,447. *Average need-based loan:* $5993. *Average need-based gift aid:* $11,338. *Average non-need-based aid:* $7604.

Contact: Director: Dr. Thomas F. Sawyer, College Scholars Program, 30 North Brainard Street, Naperville, Illinois 60540; *Telephone:* 630-637-5330; *Fax:* 630-637-5121; *E-mail:* tfsawyer@noctrl.edu

Northeastern Illinois University
University Honors Program
Chicago, Illinois

The University Honors Program at Northeastern Illinois University (NEIU) prepares undergraduates for success in graduate and professional schools. The NEIU Honors Program offers an outstanding educational experience for undergraduate students in all colleges and majors who have a commitment to excellence. The program provides a nurturing environment for qualified students to take the long-term view, to look beneath the surface, and to probe issues in depth. The program serves as a laboratory for academic innovation that seeks to improve undergraduate education and provides a place for students to discover the best in themselves. The University Honors Program does not replace a regular program of study but enhances it by encouraging students to build strong relationships with faculty members and their fellow honors students in small, innovative classes emphasizing analytic writing and communication and critical-thinking skills.

The University Honors Program encourages students to enhance their undergraduate experience with out-of-classroom academic experiences. Honors students are active participants in NEIU's Annual Student Research and Creative Activities Symposium. They also present papers at other academic conferences. The University Honors Program is an integral part of the NEIU community, and its students are active campus leaders. It helps students to reach their full potential as undergraduates and prepares them for the challenges of graduate education or employment.

Founded in 1986, the University Honors Program currently enrolls 265 full- and part-time students.

Participation Requirements: The University Honors Program offers an unusual two-tier program that allows transfer students to join the program easily. Freshmen and sophomores (Level I) take seven of their thirteen required general education courses in special honors sections. Juniors and seniors (Level II) take two honors electives in their major or minor, the Honors Seminar, and the Honors Colloquium. Level II culminates with the Honors Thesis, an independent research or creative project.

Students must maintain a cumulative GPA of at least 3.25 in their honors and nonhonors work to remain in good standing. All students completing Level I or Level II receive a certificate at NEIU's annual Student Awards Ceremony. Completion of Level I is noted on the official transcripts. Students completing Level II are designated as Honors Scholars, which is marked on the official transcript and diploma. They receive a gold medallion designating the Honors Scholarship, which is worn at graduation.

Admission Process: To be eligible for the University Honors Program, entering freshmen must have a minimum ACT score of 26 or have an ACT score of 23 to 25 and rank in the top 10 percent of their high school graduating class. Transfer students must have a GPA of 3.25 or above. Students already enrolled at NEIU may seek admission if they have a GPA of 3.25 or above. All applicants must complete an University Honors Program application, which includes an essay. Two letters of recommendation are required.

Scholarship Availability: Students enrolled in the University Honors Program are eligible to apply for Honors Merit Tuition Awards. The program has designated Tuition Awards for transfer students and members of minority groups. In addition, NEIU has merit scholarship programs at the university, college, and departmental levels. Honors students are frequent recipients of these awards.

Campus Overview

State-supported comprehensive, founded 1961 • **Coed** 9,305 undergraduate students, 55% full-time, 63% women, 37% men.

Undergraduates 5,137 full-time, 4,168 part-time. Students come from 18 states and territories, 45 other countries, 1% are from out of state, 12% African American, 11% Asian American or Pacific Islander, 29% Hispanic American, 0.3% Native American, 4% international, 13% transferred in.

Faculty *Total:* 664, 63% full-time, 52% with terminal degrees. *Student/faculty ratio:* 17:1.

Academic Programs *Special study options:* academic remediation for entering students, adult/continuing education programs, advanced placement credit, cooperative education, distance learning, double majors, English as a second language, external degree program, honors programs, independent study, internships, off-campus study, part-time degree program, services for LD students, study abroad, summer session for credit. *ROTC:* Army (c), Air Force (c).

Athletics *Intramural sports:* badminton M/W, baseball M, basketball M/W, cross-country running M/W, ice hockey M(c), racquetball M/W, soccer M/W, softball M/W, swimming and diving M/W, table tennis M/W, tennis M/W, volleyball M/W, water polo M/W, weight lifting M/W.

Costs (2004–05) *Tuition:* state resident $3720 full-time, $124 per credit hour part-time; nonresident $7440 full-time, $248 per credit hour part-time. Full-time tuition and fees vary according to student level. *Required fees:* $515 full-time.

Financial Aid 250 Federal Work-Study jobs (averaging $1928). 448 state and other part-time jobs (averaging $1863). In 2004, 125 non-need-based awards were made. *Average percent of need met:* 62%. *Average financial aid package:* $6043. *Average need-based loan:* $3731. *Average need-based gift aid:* $4462. *Average non-need-based aid:* $1080.

Contact: Coordinator: Kathleen Kardaras, Psy.D., University Honors Program, Northeastern Illinois University, 5500 North St. Louis Avenue, Chicago, Illinois 60625; *Telephone:* 773-442-6044; *E-mail:* k-kardaras@neiu.edu; *Web site:* http://www.neiu.edu/Honors.htm

Northern Illinois University
University Honors Program
DeKalb, Illinois

The University Honors Program at Northern Illinois University (NIU) serves to provide a special educational experience for academically talented students with a commitment to the pursuit of knowledge and understanding. Honors courses provide the opportunity for greater intellectual interaction among faculty members and students and among students themselves. The classes are usually special sections of regular courses with smaller enrollments, taught by faculty members who have demonstrated exceptional ability to teach undergraduate students. The University Honors Program is broad and inclusive enough to provide this opportunity to students

pursuing any undergraduate major. The curriculum of the Honors Program provides students the opportunity to participate in the design of their own educational study and research in their chosen discipline. All honors credit applies toward the University graduation requirements, and therefore the program may be completed without any extra time requirements.

All incoming freshmen honors students are required to attend the Taft Retreat, an overnight orientation program held at NIU's Lorado Taft field campus (35 miles west of DeKalb). It is designed to introduce new honors students to NIU and the Honors Program, and it is conducted by upper-division honors students and honors staff and faculty members.

Honors Residence Floors provide a coed, quiet lifestyle environment for like-minded and academically motivated students. Students participating in the Honors Residence Program are required to participate in educational, cultural, and/or community/campus programs while in residence.

There is no limit placed on the number of honors-eligible students admitted to the program. Approximately 1,200 students are active in the University Honors Program at NIU. These students may represent any major and any class level. All honors students are strongly encouraged to be active on and off campus in educational, cultural, social, and service programs. Honors students may receive personalized academic advising at the Honors Center.

Participation Requirements: Students may be admitted as new freshmen, transfer students, or continuing NIU students. The four-year program is divided into Phase I (primarily freshmen and sophomores) and Phase II (primarily juniors and seniors). Phase I of the program requires students to complete 15 credit hours of honors course work over approximately four semesters. Based on a 4.0 scale, students must maintain a minimum 3.0 cumulative GPA and a minimum 3.2 honors GPA while in Phase I. Students who complete Phase I with the minimum GPAs are awarded Lower Division Honors, which appears only on the transcript. In order to continue to Phase II, students must have at least a 3.2 cumulative GPA and at least a 3.2 honors GPA. Phase II requires 12 credit hours of honors course work over approximately four semesters. All courses in Phase II must be at the 300–400 level and include an Honors Seminar (taken outside the student's major) and a Capstone (senior independent study). Students who complete both phases with a minimum 3.2 cumulative GPA and a minimum 3.2 honors GPA are awarded University Honors, which appears on the transcript and diploma and allows the student to wear a gold cord at graduation. An additional certificate is awarded to graduates with Upper Division Honors or University Honors at the Excellence in Undergraduate Education Ceremony shortly before graduation.

Admission Process: Incoming freshmen graduating in the top 10 percent of their high school class with an ACT composite of 27 or better are encouraged to participate in the University Honors Program. Freshmen applicants are also required to submit an essay and two teacher/counselor evaluations. Students who have already earned college credit, either as a transfer student or as a continuing NIU student, must have at least a 3.2 GPA on a 4.0 scale. A brief essay is also required as part of the transfer/continuing student application. Any applicant who is slightly below the requirements may be admitted on a provisional basis. New honors-eligible freshmen and transfer students who have not applied to the Honors Program prior to summer orientation may be invited to visit the Honors Center on that day. Admission is rolling.

Scholarship Availability: Through the University Scholarships Committee, the Honors Program offers numerous highly competitive, merit-based scholarships for both incoming freshmen and transfer students. The awards are University Scholar/Academic Finalist: freshmen (6–7), transfers (1–2); Faculty Fund Academic Finalist: freshmen (2); Phi Theta Kappa: transfers (1); Academic Finalist: freshmen (10–15), transfers (4–8); and Phi Kappa Scholarship: transfers (4). For continuing honors students, there are six peer adviser, three community leader, and five honors house leader positions, with availability varying depending on current recipient graduation rates. Numerous other scholarships are disseminated through the Honors Program but may be open to any qualified applicants.

Campus Overview

State-supported university, founded 1895 • **Coed** 18,029 undergraduate students, 90% full-time, 53% women, 47% men.

Undergraduates 16,157 full-time, 1,872 part-time. Students come from 50 states and territories, 105 other countries, 3% are from out of state, 12% African American, 6% Asian American or Pacific Islander, 6% Hispanic American, 0.2% Native American, 0.9% international, 12% transferred in, 33% live on campus.

Faculty *Total:* 1,152, 76% full-time. *Student/faculty ratio:* 17:1.

Academic Programs *Special study options:* accelerated degree program, adult/continuing education programs, advanced placement credit, cooperative education, double majors, honors programs, independent study, internships, off-campus study, part-time degree program, services for LD students, student-designed majors, study abroad, summer session for credit. *ROTC:* Army (b), Air Force (c). *Unusual degree programs:* 3-2 engineering with University of Illinois.

Athletics Member NCAA. All Division I except football (Division I-A). *Intercollegiate sports:* baseball M(s), basketball M(s)/W(s), cross-country running W, golf M(s)/W(s), gymnastics W(s), soccer M(s)/W(s), softball W(s), swimming and diving M(s)/W(s), tennis M(s)/W(s), volleyball W(s), wrestling M(s). *Intramural sports:* archery M(c)/W(c), badminton M/W, basketball M/W, bowling M(c)/W(c), cross-country running W, football M/W, golf M/W, ice hockey M(c)/W(c), lacrosse M(c)/W(c), racquetball M/W, rugby M(c)/W(c), skiing (downhill) M(c)/W(c), soccer M/W, softball M/W, table tennis M/W, tennis M/W, track and field M(c)/W(c), volleyball M/W, water polo M(c)/W(c), weight lifting M(c)/W(c).

Costs (2004–05) *Tuition:* state resident $4830 full-time; nonresident $9690 full-time. Full-time tuition and fees vary according to course load. Part-time tuition and fees vary according to course load. *Required fees:* $930 full-time. *Room and board:* $5740. Room and board charges vary according to board plan and housing facility.

Financial Aid 436 Federal Work-Study jobs (averaging $1320). 3,763 state and other part-time jobs (averaging $1579). In 2003, 589 non-need-based awards were made. *Average percent of need met:* 79%. *Average financial aid package:* $9042. *Average need-based loan:* $3852. *Average need-based gift aid:* $5498. *Average non-need-based aid:* $2207.

Contact: Director, University Honors Program, DeKalb, Illinois 60115; *Telephone:* 815-753-0694; *Web site:* http://www.honors.niu.edu

---

Oakton Community College
Honors at Oakton
Des Plaines, Illinois

Honors at Oakton offers academically talented students all the advantages of a traditional liberal arts college education: small classes, distinguished faculty members, and challenging courses. It is a program designed for students who have the ability to succeed anywhere but who choose to remain close to home and obtain a high-quality education at an affordable cost. Through participation in the student-centered, writing-intensive program, students are prepared to face the challenges of further education and competitive career markets.

Honors students themselves are the best advocates of Honors at Oakton. These comments are typical of those found on students' evaluations of their courses: "There is a closeness established among a smaller group, and I felt more at ease." "Honors students were really excited about the class and challenges. They were trying to achieve something extra for themselves, which impressed me." Honors classes feature discussions, student involvement, and independent and collaborative work. One student wrote: "We were guided into an understanding of the whys rather than just bone dry facts."

Honors at Oakton features interdisciplinary, team-taught seminars, honors sections of general education courses, and the opportunity to pursue honors contract work in regular courses. Honors classes are usually composed of about 15 students, and they are taught by the best faculty members in the College. Oakton honors students have won a Truman Fellowship and a place on the Phi Theta Kappa All-American team; they have given papers at the National Undergraduate Research Conference, the annual conference of the National Collegiate Honors Council (NCHC), and the conference of the Society for Ecological Restoration.

Honors at Oakton sponsors a student organization and a variety of out-of-classroom activities, including trips to the theater, symphony, and Chicago area museums; visits from guest speakers, such as Scott Turow, Tim O'Brien, Leon Lederman, and Frances Fitzgerald; an off-campus leadership workshop; and an annual banquet. Personalized counseling assists students at every step with academic choices, and when the time comes to transfer, students are able to attend workshops on choosing a transfer institution, finding and applying for financial aid, and completing the application. An annual luncheon brings transfer admission directors from Northwestern University, the University of Chicago, Loyola University, DePaul University, and other Chicago-area colleges and universities to campus to meet with honors students. Oakton honors students have successfully transferred to these institutions as well as Cornell University, Oberlin College, Grinnell College, the University of Notre Dame, and many other outstanding colleges.

Honors at Oakton enrolls between 150 and 200 students every year.

Participation Requirements: Students must take 18 hours of honors courses to graduate as an Honors Program Scholar, but many students take fewer than 18 hours, and some take many more. All honors courses are specially designated on the transcript. To graduate as an Honors Scholar, students must maintain a minimum 3.25 GPA; honors program graduates are specially noted at graduation.

Admission Process: To be admitted to Honors at Oakton, a student must have an ACT score of at least 25 or an SAT score of at least 1150 and be in the top 20 percent of the high school class. Students are also admitted to Honors at Oakton based on a minimum 3.5 GPA at Oakton or a transfer school or a GED score of at least 300. Students with a bachelor's degree or higher are automatically eligible for Honors at Oakton. Students must maintain a minimum 3.25 GPA to continue in the program.

Campus Overview

Suburban 193-acre campus with easy access to Chicago • **Coed** 9,893 undergraduate students.

Undergraduates Students come from 50 other countries, 7% are from out of state, 5% African American, 17% Asian American or Pacific Islander, 7% Hispanic American, 0.2% Native American, 2% international.

Faculty *Total:* 662, 23% full-time, 16% with terminal degrees. *Student/faculty ratio:* 25:1.

Academic Programs *Special study options:* academic remediation for entering students, adult/continuing education programs, advanced placement credit, distance learning, English as a second language, honors programs, independent study, part-time degree program, services for LD students, study abroad, summer session for credit.

Athletics Member NJCAA. *Intercollegiate sports:* baseball M, basketball M/W, cross-country running M/W, golf M, soccer M/W, softball W, tennis M/W, track and field M/W, volleyball W. *Intramural sports:* basketball M/W, cheerleading W, soccer M, table tennis M/W, volleyball M/W.

Costs (2004–05) *Tuition:* $62 per credit part-time; state resident $183 per credit part-time; nonresident $247 per credit part-time. *Required fees:* $3 per credit part-time, $15 per term part-time.

Financial Aid 15 Federal Work-Study jobs (averaging $3500). 200 state and other part-time jobs (averaging $3200).

Contact: Director: Dr. Richard Stacewicz, 1600 East Golf Road, Des Plaines, Illinois 60016; *Telephone:* 847-635-1914; *Fax:* 847-635-1764; *E-mail:* rstacewi@oakton.edu

---

Parkland College
Parkland College Honors Program
Champaign, Indiana

The Parkland College Honors Program strives to develop excellence in education through the creation and enhancement of opportunities for academically gifted and highly motivated students who need challenges and rewards at a level consistent with their intellectual abilities, as well as to cultivate the unique capabilities of the educators who participate in the program.

There are a few courses designated specifically as honors courses such as English 106. A student needs to earn an A or a B in one of these courses to merit honors credit. Many students earn honors credit through the A with Honors option (or what other colleges call an honors contract). For the A with Honors, a student writes a project proposal to do extra work in a course; after the instructor approves the project and the student completes it, the student's transcript is annotated with an A with Honors. Several departments (Social Sciences and Natural Sciences) and one branch (Literature) of a department (English and Critical Studies) offer discussion series that fulfill the requirements for an A with Honors. Students who are taking a class within the field are allowed to participate in the discussion series run by one or more instructors within that field, so long as their classroom instructors agree. If these students successfully meet the requirements of the discussion series (reading, writing, participation, or group projects), then their classroom instructors give them credit for the A with Honors. For example, one literature discussion series involved reading and discussing a novel by the internationally renowned author Richard Powers, who led one of the discussions.

Perhaps the most unique aspect of the Parkland College Honors Program is the Honors Integrated Studies Community (ISC) offered to eligible incoming freshmen each fall. The ISC offers a different approach to freshmen requirements. Instructors from diverse disciplines (for example, English, Chemistry, and Sociology) forge connections between their subjects, which help the freshmen broaden their horizons and see the patterns in diversity. The ISC also connects people. The same three instructors and group of 20 students will attend all the classes. Thus a community of learners and teachers is formed, creating a one-of-a-kind intellectually challenging experience for all those involved.

The Parkland College Honors Program was established in 2000 and enrolls between 50 and 60 students.

Participation Requirements: Career program students are required to complete two honors courses with an A or B in each. Transfer program students must complete three honors course with an A or B in each, and at least one of those honors courses must be a special honors section (not just an A with Honors grade). Depending on the final GPA, the student may receive Honors (3.4–3.59), High Honors (3.6–3.79), or Highest Honors (3.8–4.0) at graduation; these designations will show up on the student's diploma and transcript. Honors Program students are also specially recognized at the spring Honors Convocation.

Admission Process: To be admitted to the Parkland College Honors Program, a student must have an ACT of 25 or higher, or an SAT of 1100 or higher, or have earned a 3.5 or higher cumulative GPA in high school. Current Parkland students are admitted based on a 3.4 GPA or higher for at least 12 credit hours. All prospective Honors Program participants must also write a brief essay for admission into the program.

Scholarship Availability: There are $150 per annum scholarships available for those who meet the Honors Program scholarship requirements.

Campus Overview

Suburban 233-acre campus • **Coed** 9,536 undergraduate students, 48% full-time, 54% women, 46% men.

Undergraduates 4,614 full-time, 4,922 part-time. Students come from 30 states and territories, 14 other countries, 1% are from out of state, 14% African American, 3% Asian American or Pacific Islander, 3% Hispanic American, 0.5% Native American, 3% international, 6% transferred in.

Faculty *Total:* 527, 32% full-time, 12% with terminal degrees. *Student/faculty ratio:* 17:1.

Academic Programs *Special study options:* academic remediation for entering students, accelerated degree program, adult/continuing education programs, advanced placement credit, cooperative education, distance learning, double majors, English as a second language, honors programs, independent study, internships, off-campus study, part-time degree program, services for LD students, student-designed majors, study abroad, summer session for credit. *ROTC:* Army (c), Navy (c), Air Force (c).

Athletics Member NJCAA. *Intercollegiate sports:* baseball M(s), basketball M(s)/W(s), golf M(s), soccer M(s)/W(s), softball W(s), volleyball W(s). *Intramural sports:* basketball M/W, bowling M/W, softball M/W, volleyball M/W.

Costs (2005–06) *Tuition:* area resident $2070 full-time, $69 per credit hour part-time; state resident $6000 full-time, $200 per credit hour part-time; nonresident $8850 full-time, $295 per credit hour part-time.

Financial Aid 100 Federal Work-Study jobs (averaging $2000).

Contact: Director: Tom Barnard, Champaign, 2400 W. Bradley Avenue, Champaign, Indiana 61821-1899; *Telephone:* 217-353-2349; *Fax:* 217-373-3899; *E-mail:* tbarnard@parkland.edu

---

Prairie State College
Honors Program
Chicago Heights, Illinois

The Prairie State College (PSC) Honors Program offers to good students an opportunity to fulfill standard requirements in a more stimulating and personalized environment than that of regular classes. The program was founded in 1991 and has tripled in size since then. Eligible students may enroll in honors sections of first-year required courses in the areas of art, astronomy, biology, earth science, English, history, humanities, music, philosophy, psychology, social sciences, and speech. Classes are limited to 18 students and are taught by full-time instructors who are interested in complementing or replacing lectures and tests with in-depth, project-oriented activities. Courses include at least one field trip or visiting speaker. Some honors classes have been scheduled to fit together into a single, 6-credit-hour learning community.

Participation Requirements: Students may enter the program at any time that they become eligible; most eligible students are informed by letter. Eligibility is based on at least college-level placement scores in reading, writing, and math or a minimum 3.5 GPA in 12 hours of college-level course work.

Admission Process: Students may enroll in as many or few honors courses as they wish. At least a 3.5 GPA must be maintained. Honors courses are designated on the students' transcripts.

Campus Overview

State and locally supported 2-year, founded 1958, part of Illinois Community College Board • **Coed** 5,342 undergraduate students, 33% full-time, 62% women, 38% men.

Undergraduates 1,745 full-time, 3,597 part-time. Students come from 4 states and territories, 4% are from out of state, 45% African American, 1% Asian American or Pacific Islander, 12% Hispanic American, 0.7% Native American, 0.2% international, 0.4% transferred in.

Faculty *Total:* 363, 21% full-time. *Student/faculty ratio:* 17:1.

Academic Programs *Special study options:* academic remediation for entering students, adult/continuing education programs, advanced placement credit, distance learning, English as a second language, honors programs, internships, part-time degree program, services for LD students, student-designed majors, summer session for credit.

Athletics Member NJCAA. *Intercollegiate sports:* baseball M(s), basketball M(s)/W(s), football M(s), golf M(s)/W(s), soccer M/W, softball M/W(s), tennis W(s). *Intramural sports:* basketball M/W, soccer M/W, softball W, table tennis M/W, volleyball W.

Costs (2005–06) *Tuition:* area resident $1824 full-time, $67 per credit hour part-time; state resident $5280 full-time, $211 per credit hour part-time; nonresident $7200 full-time, $291 per credit hour part-time. Full-time tuition and fees vary according to course load. Part-time tuition and fees vary according to course load. *Required fees:* $236 full-time, $9 per credit hour part-time, $10 per term part-time. *Room and board:* $4500. Room and board charges vary according to location.

Financial Aid 60 Federal Work-Study jobs (averaging $2500).

Contact: Enrollment Advisor for Honors: Wallace Bailey; *Telephone:* 708-709-3641; *E-mail:* wbailey@prairiestate.edu; Honors Coordinator: Maurine Stein; *Telephone:* 708-709-3771; *E-mail:* mstein@prairiestate.edu

Roosevelt University
Roosevelt Scholars Program
Chicago, Illinois

*T*he Roosevelt Scholars Program is designed to train the future leaders of the Chicago metropolitan area. The program attracts some of Roosevelt's most talented undergraduate students who wish to prepare for a career and also to explore the world of ideas. By bringing students and professors together in small classes and individual research settings, the Scholars Program fosters a strong feeling of community.

Students in the Scholars Program participate in one of two tracks: the science concentration, for students pursuing majors in the sciences, or the metropolitan issues concentration, which is open to students of all majors. Faculty mentors help students shape their academic programs. Professional mentors—accomplished Chicago-area leaders—help keep students on the paths to success. There are internships and research opportunities at leading business, cultural, and governmental organizations. Roosevelt Scholars receive generous merit scholarship support (as well as need-based financial aid).

The courses include honors sections of the University General Education curriculum in the humanities, social sciences, and sciences. In addition, students take other honors-level studies in the sciences or in urban and metropolitan issues. The curriculum culminates in an honors thesis.

Besides taking honors courses, students attend lectures, plays, concerts, and other cultural events on and off campus.

The Roosevelt Scholars Program began in 1998. There are 150 students currently enrolled in the program.

Participation Requirements: For students entering the Scholars Program as freshmen, the Scholars Program curriculum is a ten course sequence culminating in an honors thesis, in which students pursue original research under the guidance of a faculty mentor. Students who enroll in the Scholars Program after their freshmen year are not required to take the full ten-course sequence. The program is tailored specifically for each student depending upon their previous academic course work taken at Roosevelt or another institution.

Admission Process: Admission to the Roosevelt Scholars Program is competitive. The program is open to entering freshmen with strong high school academic records, class ranks, and ACT or SAT I scores. Roosevelt students already enrolled or transfer students who have demonstrated outstanding academic achievement are also eligible. To be considered for the program, students must fill out an application form requiring three short essays. Finalists are invited for personal interviews.

Scholarship Availability: All participants in the Roosevelt Scholars Program receive merit scholarship support ranging from partial to full tuition over four years. Need-based financial aid is also available for those who qualify.

Campus Overview

Independent comprehensive, founded 1945 • **Coed** 4,103 undergraduate students, 45% full-time, 68% women, 32% men.

Undergraduates 1,827 full-time, 2,276 part-time. Students come from 44 states and territories, 65 other countries, 6% are from out of state, 25% African American, 5% Asian American or Pacific Islander, 11% Hispanic American, 0.4% Native American, 2% international, 15% transferred in, 9% live on campus.

Faculty *Total:* 662, 32% full-time. *Student/faculty ratio:* 11:1.

Academic Programs *Special study options:* academic remediation for entering students, accelerated degree program, adult/continuing education programs, advanced placement credit, distance learning, double majors, English as a second language, external degree program, honors programs, independent study, internships, off-campus study, part-time degree program, services for LD students, student-designed majors, study abroad, summer session for credit.

Costs (2004–05) *Comprehensive fee:* $24,730 includes full-time tuition ($16,080), mandatory fees ($250), and room and board ($8400). Full-time tuition and fees vary according to program. Part-time tuition: $536 per semester hour. Part-time tuition and fees vary according to program. *Required fees:* $125 per term part-time. *College room only:* $6200. Room and board charges vary according to board plan and housing facility.

Financial Aid *Average percent of need met:* 75%. *Average financial aid package:* $11,600. *Average need-based gift aid:* $6200. *Average non-need-based aid:* $6030.

Contact: Director: Dr. Samuel Rosenberg, School of Policy Studies, 430 South Michigan Avenue, Chicago, Illinois 60605; *Telephone:* 312-341-3697; *Fax:* 312-341-3762; *E-mail:* srosenbe@roosevelt.edu

Saint Xavier University
Undergraduate Honors Program
Chicago, Illinois

*S*aint Xavier University's Undergraduate Honors Program offers an enriched academic experience to talented and highly motivated students. The distinctive feature of the program is collaborative student and faculty member research and creative projects. The program is designed to nurture skills and habits of mind that enable students to become independent thinkers and learners and leaders in their chosen fields.

Honors at Saint Xavier features interdisciplinary seminars designed around themes of compelling interest. Because of the interdisciplinary focus of the seminars, students gain an understanding of the types of questions posed and the methodologies employed in a range of fields in the arts and sciences, preparing them for more independent research. Students also engage in junior-year fieldwork that provides hands-on experience to enrich learning in the students' areas of interest. Fieldwork activities are designed to help generate ambitious proposals for senior-year independent or group research under the direction of faculty mentors. The fruits of these senior projects are presented at University-wide forums, and students are encouraged to submit them to regional and national undergraduate conferences and journals. The program also provides ongoing cultural and social activities to stimulate thinking and to foster community.

Small class sizes encourage student participation and promote close student-faculty relationships. An Honors Student Center centrally located on campus is designed to reinforce a strong sense of intellectual and social community among program participants.

Participation Requirements: In their first two years, students take five Honors Seminars that satisfy 27 semester hours of University core requirements. These seminars include Honors English, Honors Humanities, Honors Social Science, Honors Science, and Honors Philosophy. The interdisciplinary seminars each year are designed around broad themes that also are explored in guest lectures and cultural activities. Upcoming themes include The Idea of America and The Good Life.

In their junior year, honors students engage in 6 semester hours of fieldwork that might include local internships, an apprenticeship at a research laboratory, on-campus research under faculty direction, study abroad, or group creative or research activities. By the end of their junior year, honors students, working in collaboration with faculty mentors, have formulated fairly detailed proposals for senior-year research or creative projects. Throughout their fieldwork year, students continue to meet periodically as a group, sharing their progress and discoveries and critiquing one another's proposals.

Working collaboratively with their faculty mentors, senior-year students receive 6 semester hours of credit for conducting, completing, and presenting their research and creative projects.

Students must maintain at least a 3.2 cumulative GPA to remain in the program. Successful completion of the program is noted on the student's official transcript and diploma.

Admission Process: High school students are invited into the program on the basis of their high school averages, ACT or SAT I scores, and other credentials that they supply in their applications to Saint Xavier. Students may pursue any major offered by the University.

Scholarship Availability: All honors students are considered for Presidential Scholarships. In addition, students are awarded up to $500 in each of their first two years and up to $1000 in their junior and senior years for learning and research technology, supplies, or travel. Students must submit an itemized request for these funds, explaining how they will be used.

Campus Overview

Independent Roman Catholic comprehensive, founded 1847 • **Coed** 3,075 undergraduate students, 75% full-time, 71% women, 29% men.

Undergraduates 2,311 full-time, 764 part-time. Students come from 23 states and territories, 2 other countries, 4% are from out of state, 18% African American, 2% Asian American or Pacific Islander, 12% Hispanic American, 0.3% Native American, 0.3% international, 15% transferred in, 20% live on campus.

Faculty Total: 398, 42% full-time, 43% with terminal degrees. Student/faculty ratio: 15:1.

Academic Programs Special study options: academic remediation for entering students, accelerated degree program, adult/continuing education programs, advanced placement credit, cooperative education, double majors, English as a second language, honors programs, independent study, internships, part-time degree program, services for LD students, student-designed majors, study abroad, summer session for credit. ROTC: Air Force (c).

Athletics Member NAIA. Intercollegiate sports: baseball M(s), basketball M(s), cross-country running W(s), football M(s), golf M(s), soccer M(s)/W(s), softball W(s), volleyball W(s). Intramural sports: basketball M, bowling M/W, volleyball M/W, weight lifting M.

Costs (2004–05) Comprehensive fee: $24,054 includes full-time tuition ($17,150), mandatory fees ($180), and room and board ($6724). Full-time tuition and fees vary according to course load. Part-time tuition: $575 per credit hour. Part-time tuition and fees vary according to course load. College room only: $3836. Room and board charges vary according to board plan.

Financial Aid 1,193 Federal Work-Study jobs (averaging $2424). 42 state and other part-time jobs (averaging $5514). In 2003, 347 non-need-based awards were made. Average percent of need met: 83%. Average financial aid package: $14,910. Average need-based loan: $3930. Average need-based gift aid: $8610. Average non-need-based aid: $4287.

Contact: Director: Dr. Judith R. Hiltner, 3700 West 103rd Street, Chicago, Illinois 60655; Telephone: 773-298-3230; Fax: 773-799-9061; E-mail: hiltner@sxu.edu; Web site: http://www.sxu.edu/honors

Sauk Valley Community College
SVCC Honors Program
Dixon, Illinois

In 1977, a steering committee met to study the feasibility of establishing an honors program. Their planning resulted in the start of the Sauk Valley Community College's SVCC Honors Program in the fall semester of 1978. The infant program experienced the struggles associated with all new programs. Perhaps the most fundamental issue was the selection of the method by which the student would experience honors work. Both separate honors courses and honors work integrated into the regular course structure were used and evaluated. The latter method evolved as the method of choice.

The student and the course teacher establish a contract detailing the honors work that extends beyond the normal course requirements. The experience of working individually with a subject area expert is learning at its best. Beyond the obvious benefit of increased learning, the student's transcript displays the selected course as an honors course, and today more than ever superior transcripts lead to superior opportunities. Membership also provides the student with the opportunity to compete for SVCC Honors Scholarships. The supervision of the honors students often brings renewed professional vitality to the individual teacher.

Providing opportunities for the most talented students to interact with the instructional staff members leads to greater student satisfaction and success. The program provides the College with excellent public relations and generates several news releases each year. The program provides an excellent basis for contact with area high school educators and is an important part of SVCC's overall recruitment effort. Successful students are the best recruiters the College can have.

The program is administered by the honors director with the assistance of the honors committee. The committee is chaired by the honors director and consists of 1 delegate from each of the instructional divisions. The committee provides advice in all areas of program operation with the primary functions of screening candidates for admission and selection of scholarship recipients.

Participation Requirements: To be an honors graduate, the student must complete a minimum of 12 semester hours of honors course work. The student must have a GPA of 3.5 or greater on a 4.0 scale.

Admission Process: Potential members must complete a request for admittance form, which includes an essay detailing their academic goals and how the Honors Program relates to those goals. The essays are reviewed and evaluated by the honors committee. The student must also meet at least one of the following criteria: minimum ACT score of 27, graduation in the upper 10 percent of their high school class, membership in their high school's National Honor Society, or have been named an Illinois State Scholar. Students who do not meet any of the criteria may apply after completion of 12 semester hours of SVCC course work with a GPA of 3.5 or greater. Such students must also obtain a faculty member referral.

Scholarship Availability: The Honors Program provides scholarships based on academic excellence. Each semester Honors Program members compete for the awards, which currently are valued at a total of $2000.

Campus Overview

Rural 165-acre campus • **Coed** 3,161 undergraduate students.

Undergraduates 1% African American, 1% Asian American or Pacific Islander, 7% Hispanic American, 0.4% Native American.

Faculty *Total:* 152, 39% full-time. *Student/faculty ratio:* 18:1.

Academic Programs *Special study options:* academic remediation for entering students, accelerated degree program, adult/continuing education programs, cooperative education, distance learning, English as a second language, honors programs, independent study, internships, off-campus study, part-time degree program, services for LD students, student-designed majors.

Athletics Member NJCAA. *Intercollegiate sports:* baseball M(s), basketball M(s)/W(s), softball W, tennis M(s)/W(s), volleyball W(s). *Intramural sports:* basketball M/W.

Costs (2005–06) *Tuition:* $74 per credit hour part-time; state resident $259 per credit hour part-time; nonresident $293 per credit hour part-time.

Financial Aid 150 Federal Work-Study jobs (averaging $3000).

Contact: Contact: Steven Shaff, Honors Program Co-Director, Sauk Valley Community College, 173 Illinois Route 2, Dixon, Illinois 61021; *Telephone:* 815-288-5511; *E-mail:* shaffs@svcc.edu; *Web site:* http://www.svcc.edu/academics/honors.html

Southern Illinois University Carbondale

University Honors Program

Carbondale, Illinois

The University Honors Program (UHP) was created by Southern Illinois University Carbondale (SIUC) as a reward to its best undergraduates for their high academic achievement. It is a program of options, intended to give the honors student a taste of the private-college experience at a state-university price.

The heart of the program is the honors curriculum: small classes, unique in character and specially designed for University honors students by outstanding SIUC faculty members. Each honors course is limited in size to 15 students and restricted in enrollment to honors students only. The University allows honors students to substitute honors courses for any or all of their 29 semester hours of core curriculum requirements in disciplinary and integrative studies.

Membership in the University Honors Program brings other advantages as well. For example, honors students may check books out at Morris Library for eight weeks at a time (compared to four weeks for other undergraduates). A limited number of study floor spaces are reserved each year for honors students (and other serious students) in various campus residence halls. Honors students are eligible to submit their best creative or scholarly work (essays, term papers, poems, short stories, photography, painting, sculpture, etc.) to be considered for publication in Papyrus, the journal of the University Honors Program. Honors students are eligible for the limited-seating breakfast seminars with visiting lecturers—question-and-answer sessions around the breakfast table the morning after the speaker's public lecture. Speakers in the recent past have included poets, archeologists, anthropologists, musicians, novelists, playwrights, politicians, pundits, astronauts, scientists, journalists, and theologians.

All members of the University Honors Program are recognized publicly at Honors Day and at commencement. Continuing University honors students (those who have completed one semester in the Honors Program at SIUC) are entitled to apply for an Honors Scholarship.

Participation Requirements: Retention in the Honors Program requires maintaining a minimum cumulative 3.25 GPA on all course work and no failing grades in honors courses.

In order to receive the designation University Honors Program on diplomas and transcripts, entering freshmen, continuing students, and transfer students without an associate degree must complete a minimum of 15 hours of honors course work, including at least two University honors courses and a senior honors project or thesis, and have a cumulative 3.25 GPA or higher on all course work at graduation.

Transfer students who enter SIUC with an A.A. or an A.S. degree, capstone students, and two-year students in the College of Applied Sciences and Arts must complete a minimum of 9 hours of honors course work, including at least one University honors course and a senior honors project or thesis, and have a cumulative 3.25 GPA or higher on all course work at graduation.

Admission Process: Continuing students qualify for the UHP on the basis of a cumulative GPA of 3.25 or higher, with at least 12 semester hours completed.

Transfer students with at least 12 semester hours of transfer credit qualify for admission on the basis of a GPA of 3.25 or higher on all non-SIUC college-level work.

Entering freshmen qualify on the basis of an ACT composite score in the 95th percentile or higher.

Scholarship Availability: Continuing University honors students (those who have completed one semester in the Honors Program at SIUC) are entitled to apply for the Charles D. Tenney Academic Scholarship (full in-state tuition waiver), the Albert and Leyla Somit University Honors Scholarship (variable cash award), and the partial tuition waiver Honors Scholarship.

The University Honors Program serves as the clearing house for major scholarships at SIUC.

Campus Overview

State-supported university, founded 1869, part of Southern Illinois University • **Coed** 16,872 undergraduate students, 89% full-time, 43% women, 57% men.

Undergraduates 15,032 full-time, 1,840 part-time. Students come from 57 states and territories, 120 other countries, 12% are from out of state, 15% African American, 2% Asian American or Pacific Islander, 3% Hispanic American, 0.4% Native American, 2% international, 12% transferred in, 27% live on campus.

Faculty *Total:* 1,061, 82% full-time, 78% with terminal degrees. *Student/faculty ratio:* 18:1.

Academic Programs *Special study options:* academic remediation for entering students, accelerated degree program, adult/continuing

education programs, advanced placement credit, cooperative education, distance learning, double majors, English as a second language, honors programs, independent study, internships, off-campus study, part-time degree program, services for LD students, study abroad, summer session for credit. *ROTC:* Army (b), Air Force (b).

Athletics Member NCAA. All Division I except football (Division I-AA). *Intercollegiate sports:* baseball M(s), basketball M(s)/W(s), cheerleading M(s)/W(s), cross-country running M(s)/W(s), golf M(s)/W(s), softball W(s), swimming and diving M(s)/W(s), tennis M(s)/W(s), track and field M(s)/W(s), volleyball W(s). *Intramural sports:* archery M(c)/W(c), badminton M(c)/W(c), baseball M(c), basketball M/W, bowling M(c)/W, cross-country running M/W, equestrian sports M(c)/W(c), fencing M(c)/W(c), football M/W, golf M/W, lacrosse M(c), racquetball M(c)/W(c), riflery M(c)/W(c), rock climbing M(c)/W(c), rugby M(c)/W(c), sailing M(c)/W(c), soccer M(c)/W(c), softball M/W, squash M(c)/W, table tennis M(c)/W, tennis M/W, track and field M(c)/W(c), ultimate Frisbee M(c)/W(c), volleyball M(c)/W(c), water polo M(c)/W, weight lifting M(c)/W(c), wrestling M(c).

Costs (2004–05) *Tuition:* state resident $4920 full-time, $164 per semester hour part-time; nonresident $12,300 full-time, $410 per semester hour part-time. Full-time tuition and fees vary according to course load and student level. Part-time tuition and fees vary according to course load and student level. No tuition increase for student's term of enrollment. *Required fees:* $1421 full-time. *Room and board:* $5200; room only: $2640. Room and board charges vary according to board plan and housing facility.

Financial Aid 1,898 Federal Work-Study jobs (averaging $1205). 4,351 state and other part-time jobs (averaging $1680). In 2003, 1060 non-need-based awards were made. *Average percent of need met:* 95%. *Average financial aid package:* $8117. *Average need-based loan:* $3496. *Average need-based gift aid:* $4420. *Average non-need-based aid:* $3102.

Contact: Director: Dr. Frederick Williams, Faner Hall, Room 3341, Mailcode 4520, Southern Illinois University Carbondale, Carbondale, Illinois 62901; *Telephone:* 618-453-2824; *Fax:* 618-453-2831; *E-mail:* honors@siu.edu; *Web site:* http://www.siu.edu/~honors/

Southwestern Illinois College
Honors Program
Belleville, Illinois

The Honors Program, currently only offered at the Granite City campus of Southwestern Illinois College, seeks to enrich the experiences of intellectually curious students by providing an academically rigorous learning environment that can offer a challenging academic experience. The intent of the program is to provide a stimulating environment that expands critical and creative thinking skills and enhances opportunities for intellectual growth. Students in the program have the opportunity to enroll in specified honors courses or the option of honors contracts in disciplines such as literature, music, business, history, political science, psychology, or sociology. In all honors course work, students and faculty members alike seek and expect excellence.

Students who complete the program are awarded a medallion to wear at graduation. The Honors Program, initiated in fall 2001, currently enrolls approximately 20 students.

Participation Requirements: To successfully complete the course of study and graduate from the Honors Program, students must have successfully completed 12 credit hours of honors course work maintaining a minimum cumulative GPA of 3.5. Successful course completion is defined as receiving a grade of B or higher in all honors courses. Honors course work includes either enhanced sections of regular courses (honors sections) or individual contracts made within

the context of a regular course (honors contracts). Honors sections are kept small and are taught by selected faculty members. Collaborative learning and nontraditional methods of instruction are highly encouraged.

Admission Process: Students may be admitted to the program at any time. Candidates must complete an application, which includes space for students to clarify their reasons for applying to the program, what they hope to accomplish in the program, and what they will contribute to the program. In addition, students must meet one of the following criteria: graduate in the top 10 percent of their high school class and be eligible for placement into ENG 101, graduate from high school with a cumulative GPA of 3.5 or above and be eligible for placement into ENG 101, score 540 on the verbal section of the SAT or have a composite score of 26 on the ACT, earn 12 college credit hours with a minimum cumulative GPA of 3.5 and be eligible for placement into ENG 101, or obtain special permission from the Honors Program Committee.

Scholarship Availability: Any student attending Southwestern Illinois College District 522 public or private high schools and graduating in the top 10 percent of his or her class can apply for the Top 10 Percent Tuition Scholarship. Potential honors students are strongly encouraged to apply for this program, which is awarded for up to six continuous semesters.

Campus Overview

Suburban 150-acre campus with easy access to St. Louis • **Coed** 16,425 undergraduate students.

Undergraduates Students come from 6 states and territories, 19 other countries, 17% African American, 2% Asian American or Pacific Islander, 3% Hispanic American, 0.5% Native American.

Faculty *Total:* 791, 17% full-time. *Student/faculty ratio:* 16:1.

Academic Programs *Special study options:* academic remediation for entering students, accelerated degree program, adult/continuing education programs, advanced placement credit, cooperative education, distance learning, double majors, English as a second language, internships, off-campus study, part-time degree program, services for LD students, study abroad, summer session for credit. *ROTC:* Army (c), Air Force (c).

Athletics Member NJCAA. *Intercollegiate sports:* baseball M(s), basketball M(s)/W(s), soccer M(s), softball W(s), tennis M(s)/W(s), volleyball W(s). *Intramural sports:* basketball M/W, bowling M/W, softball M/W, tennis M/W, volleyball M/W.

Costs (2004–05) *Tuition:* area resident $1650 full-time; state resident $4680 full-time; nonresident $7410 full-time.

Financial Aid 170 Federal Work-Study jobs (averaging $1537). 179 state and other part-time jobs (averaging $1004).

Contact: Honors Program Coordinator: Dianna Shank, 4950 Maryville Road, Granite City, Illinois 62040; *Telephone:* 618-931-0600 Ext. 6685, 800-222-5131 (toll-free in Illinois); *E-mail:* dianna.shank@swic.edu

Trinity Christian College
Honors Program
Palos Heights, Illinois

The Honors Program of Trinity Christian College provides a community of challenge and support for academically gifted students. These students take delight in learning and discovery both inside and outside of the classroom. The program began in 1998 and includes 75 students. Because Trinity's Honors Program is driven by the conviction that effective education must involve learners as whole persons, the program situates its academic, curricular components within a rich context of cocurricular opportunities. These opportunities include exploring and enjoying the cultural resources of Chicago, cultivating friendships with fellow students and faculty members through social interaction, spiritual growth, and service through projects on Trinity's campus and in the surrounding community.

The curriculum of the Honors Program is designed to foster the development of intellectual responsibility, encouraging students to become responsible for their own ideas and intellectual growth. They are also responsible to their fellow students through participating in a collaborative approach to learning. In addition, students are responsible to society through discovering, articulating, and beginning to implement a personal vision for Christian intellectual leadership in their vocations and in public life. This emphasis on the development of intellectual responsibility is evident in the structure and content of honors courses. These courses range in size from 5 to 15 students and are conducted in a seminar style, which offers intensive, personal engagement with faculty members and fellow students. The focus of honors courses is on foundational issues approached through primary texts, with constant attention to the relevance of these texts and issues to life today.

Participation Requirements: During their freshman year, students take an honors writing course, which substitutes for the required writing course in the college core. During their sophomore year, students take an honors philosophy course; this course substitutes for one of the required philosophy courses in the college core. During their sophomore, junior, or senior year, students take at least one interdisciplinary honors seminar course centered on a specific topic. During their junior or senior year, students complete at least 2 semester hours of honors work in their major discipline. In addition, each student in the Honors Program has two of their Interim courses designated for honors credit by arrangement with the Honors Program Director. Interim is a two-week, 2-credit term in January, and all Trinity students are required to take courses in at least two Interim terms.

To remain in the Honors Program, students must have a minimum 3.3 cumulative GPA at the end of each academic year. To graduate from the Honors Program, students must complete the honors curriculum and have at least a 3.5 cumulative GPA upon graduation. Successful completion is recognized at the College's Honors Convocation and is noted on the student's official transcript.

Admission Process: Incoming freshmen are invited to apply for admission to the Honors Program if they have a minimum ACT composite score of 28 and are either in the top 10 percent of their graduating class or have at least a 3.5 GPA on a 4.0 scale. Students who do not meet these criteria or who are not formally part of the program may apply to the Director of the Honors Program for permission to enroll in honors courses.

Trinity students may apply for admission to the Honors Program after the freshman year if they have a cumulative GPA of at least 3.5. Transfer students who transfer fewer than 33 credits and have a minimum ACT composite score of 28 and at least a 3.5 GPA in college-level course work may also apply. The deadline for prospective new students to apply to the program is March 1.

Scholarship Availability: Scholarships of various amounts, based on academic performance, leadership (in athletics, music, journalism, or student organizations), or demonstrated need, are awarded through the Office of Admission and Financial Aid. No scholarships are directly administered by the Honors Program. All entering students are automatically considered for honors scholarships when their applications are reviewed. Most students in the Honors Program are recipients of academic or leadership scholarships.

Campus Overview

Independent Christian Reformed 4-year, founded 1959 • **Coed** 1,234 undergraduate students, 85% full-time, 64% women, 36% men.

Undergraduates 1,050 full-time, 184 part-time. Students come from 38 states and territories, 12 other countries, 55% are from out of state, 7% African American, 2% Asian American or Pacific Islander, 4%

Hispanic American, 0.2% Native American, 2% international, 7% transferred in, 67% live on campus.

Faculty *Total:* 127, 51% full-time, 41% with terminal degrees. *Student/faculty ratio:* 13:1.

Academic Programs *Special study options:* academic remediation for entering students, adult/continuing education programs, advanced placement credit, cooperative education, double majors, honors programs, independent study, internships, off-campus study, part-time degree program, services for LD students, study abroad.

Athletics Member NAIA, NCCAA. *Intercollegiate sports:* baseball M(s), basketball M(s)/W(s), cross-country running M(s)/W(s), soccer M(s)/W(s), softball W(s), track and field M(s)/W(s), volleyball W(s). *Intramural sports:* badminton M/W, basketball M/W, soccer M/W, volleyball M/W.

Costs (2004–05) *Comprehensive fee:* $22,444 includes full-time tuition ($16,250), mandatory fees ($150), and room and board ($6044). Part-time tuition: $545 per semester hour. Part-time tuition and fees vary according to course load. *College room only:* $3224. Room and board charges vary according to board plan.

Financial Aid 91 Federal Work-Study jobs (averaging $1400). In 2002, 120 non-need-based awards were made. *Average percent of need met:* 67%. *Average financial aid package:* $9875. *Average need-based loan:* $3920. *Average need-based gift aid:* $2572. *Average non-need-based aid:* $1908.

Contact: Director: Aron D. Reppmann, 6601 West College Drive, Palos Heights, Illinois 60463; *Telephone:* 708-239-4750; *Fax:* 708-597-5858; *E-mail:* aron.reppmann@trnty.edu; *Web site:* http://www.trnty.edu/depts/honors/

University of Illinois at Chicago
Honors College
Chicago, Illinois

The Honors College at the University of Illinois at Chicago (UIC) offers an enhanced academic experience to approximately 1,200 talented and motivated undergraduates. Freshmen enroll in yearlong interdisciplinary honors core course sequences and may also register for departmental honors offerings. Beyond the freshman year, students choose from a variety of other honors options, including honors seminars in a broad range of disciplines, undergraduate research, and the College peer-tutoring program. All these activities are monitored through a faculty mentoring system that is one of the College's strengths.

At the end of the first year, each student is assigned to an Honors College fellow, a faculty member in the student's major interested in working with honors students. The fellows, who include many of UIC's outstanding scholars, act as advisers for the students' honors work and as resources for information on academic opportunities in the major, courses, graduate school, and careers. The Honors College fellow mentoring process allows students a chance to develop contacts with faculty members at an early stage in their university experience.

In addition, the Honors College offers its students personalized attention and advising, as well as dedicated facilities such as a computer lab, a social lounge, and study rooms and events such as student-faculty luncheons, an annual Honors College Ball, and an honors convocation for graduating seniors. The Honors College sponsors the Ampersand, the College newsletter; Red Shoes Review, a student literary journal; and the Journal of Pre-Health Affiliated Students. Honors College students also receive extended library privileges.

Students who opt to live on campus may take advantage of special honors housing, where residents enjoy a special living/learning environment and a sense of honors community within the residence halls.

Participation Requirements: All members of the Honors College are expected to fulfill two requirements: students must successfully complete an honors activity each fall and spring terms, and students must maintain a minimum cumulative UIC GPA of 3.25 (on a 4.0 scale).

Admission Process: Honors College students are selected on the basis of their academic achievement and promise for university study. Entering freshmen typically have a minimum ACT score of 28 (SAT of 1240) and rank in the upper 15 percent of their high school graduating class. Enrolled students with at least a 3.25 cumulative UIC GPA and transfer students with at least a 3.5 cumulative GPA are also encouraged to apply.

Scholarship Availability: The Honors College offers a variety of scholarship opportunities for beginning freshmen, covering full or half tuition and fees for up to four years. Only Illinois residents are eligible.

The College also grants a limited number of one-semester tuition waivers to its continuing students based on a combination of merit and need, in addition to the Flaherty Awards for Study Abroad and the Sarah Madonna Kabbes Awards for Undergraduate Research. Phi Theta Kappa scholarships are available for transfer students. The UIC Office of Special Scholarship Programs assists students in applying for nationally competitive scholarships.

Campus Overview

State-supported university, founded 1946, part of University of Illinois System • **Coed** 15,457 undergraduate students, 90% full-time, 54% women, 46% men.

Undergraduates 13,929 full-time, 1,528 part-time. Students come from 52 states and territories, 48 other countries, 2% are from out of state, 9% African American, 25% Asian American or Pacific Islander, 16% Hispanic American, 0.2% Native American, 1% international, 9% transferred in, 11% live on campus.

Faculty *Total:* 1,456, 82% full-time, 80% with terminal degrees. *Student/faculty ratio:* 16:1.

Academic Programs *Special study options:* academic remediation for entering students, accelerated degree program, advanced placement credit, cooperative education, distance learning, double majors, English as a second language, honors programs, independent study, internships, off-campus study, part-time degree program, services for LD students, student-designed majors, study abroad, summer session for credit. *ROTC:* Army (b), Navy (c), Air Force (c).

Athletics Member NCAA. All Division I. *Intercollegiate sports:* baseball M(s), basketball M(s)/W(s), cross-country running M(s)/W(s), gymnastics M(s)/W(s), soccer M(s), softball W(s), swimming and diving M(s)/W(s), tennis M(s)/W(s), track and field M(s)/W(s), volleyball W(s). *Intramural sports:* badminton M/W, basketball M/W, bowling M/W, cross-country running M/W, fencing M(c)/W(c), field hockey M/W, football M/W, golf M/W, lacrosse M(c)/W(c), racquetball M/W, rugby M(c)/W(c), soccer M/W, softball M/W, squash M/W, table tennis M/W, tennis M/W, volleyball M(c)/W, water polo M(c)/W(c), wrestling M.

Costs (2005–06) *Tuition:* state resident $6194 full-time; nonresident $18,584 full-time. *Required fees:* $2308 full-time. *Room and board:* $7160.

Financial Aid 514 Federal Work-Study jobs (averaging $1700). 2,635 state and other part-time jobs (averaging $2600). In 2003, 1003 non-need-based awards were made. *Average percent of need met:* 89%. *Average financial aid package:* $11,750. *Average need-based loan:* $4069. *Average need-based gift aid:* $7059. *Average non-need-based aid:* $3060.

Contact: Executive Associate Dean: Janet Madia, UIC Honors College, University of Illinois at Chicago, 828 South Halsted Street

(M/C 204), Chicago, Illinois 60607-7031; *Telephone:* 312-413-2260; *E-mail:* jmadia@uic.edu; *Web site:* http://www.hc.uic.edu

University of Illinois at Urbana–Champaign
Campus Honors Program
Urbana, Illinois

The Campus Honors Program (CHP) offers special challenges and opportunities to a small number of academically talented and highly motivated undergraduate students. It fosters collaborative relationships between students and distinguished faculty members through small intensive classes, a faculty mentor system for introducing students to the intellectual standards and methodologies of academic disciplines, and informal contacts encouraged by cocurricular offerings. CHP sponsors several series of noncredit cocurricular events, including a Scholar Adventurers lecture series on faculty research and a series of dress-rehearsal visits at Krannert Center for the Performing Arts. The aim is to encourage breadth and excellence from the outset of the student's college career and to facilitate interaction with scholars at the cutting edge of their disciplines.

Only 125 new students can be admitted to the CHP each year as first-year students, out of approximately 7,000 entering freshmen. A few additional students, however, may join the program on an off-cycle basis at the beginning of the sophomore year. Designated as Chancellor's Scholars, CHP students may be enrolled in any undergraduate curriculum. Those who meet retention requirements continue as Chancellor's Scholars throughout their undergraduate career. Required CHP course work is concentrated in the freshman and sophomore years, when students take intensive and specialized versions of general education courses. At the junior and senior levels, when students are necessarily involved in their majors, they are required to take only one advanced CHP seminar. In short, the emphasis is on fundamental principles and interdisciplinary connections, because the CHP is for students who desire an undergraduate education that is broad and general as well as professionally specialized.

CHP seeks to combine the advantages of a major public institution with those of a small liberal arts college. Opportunities offered by the program include challenging, limited-enrollment courses; summer research and travel grants; social and intellectual activities beyond the classroom; use of Honors House, with computer facilities and an electronic communications bulletin board; access to the University library stacks; priority registration for classes; and interaction with an outstanding group of peers.

CHP courses represent additional opportunities for academically gifted and adventurous students; they are not an alternative curriculum. They provide an honors-quality way of satisfying general education requirements for graduation and of helping students to discover the interrelations between their own discipline and other disciplines. CHP does not supplant or conflict with the University's departmental honors programs. In consultation with their departmental academic advisers, Chancellor's Scholars develop their own combination of regular and CHP courses. Most important, CHP is a challenge. A Chancellor's Scholar must make a commitment to intellectual life and to the dialogue and community in the Honors House.

This is not a "residential" honors program. In their housing and social life, Chancellor's Scholars are not isolated from the thousands of other excellent students on this "public ivy" University campus. The University Housing Division offers a wide variety of theme-

oriented and special-interest housing options, and honors students are encouraged to choose options that suit their personal needs and open doors into the larger community.

The Campus Honors Program was established in fall 1986. Its steady-state enrollment is 500 students—125 students at each undergraduate (freshman through senior) class level.

On the University of Illinois at Urbana-Champaign (UIUC) campus, many of the colleges also host an honors program called the James Scholar program—named in honor of the fourth president of the University of Illinois, Edmund J. James (1904–20). This honors program, as hosted by individual colleges, recognizes academic excellence, fosters independent study, and encourages research opportunities.

Participation Requirements: Honors students are not required to take specific courses. Students choose from a varied menu of CHP offerings those that suit their personal interests as well as their college and department curricular requirements. The majority of honors courses satisfy general education requirements (directly or by petition) and are taken during the first two years of undergraduate study. In fact, four of the five CHP courses honors students must take can be either honors versions of general education courses or special-topics courses that may be taken as electives.

The fifth course is an interdisciplinary seminar taken during either the junior or senior year, when students are occupied with honors programs at the department level; by formal petition, study abroad may be substituted for this seminar. Most majors can accommodate the five-course/15-credit CHP requirement without difficulty.

Chancellor's Scholars must also attend a total of four Scholar Adventurers faculty lectures and one dress rehearsal at the Krannert Center for the Performing Arts and must maintain a minimum cumulative GPA of 3.3 (on a 4.0 scale). All CHP students receive transcript notation of Chancellor's Scholar status. In addition, those who successfully complete the academic challenges and cocurricular participation required by the program receive a special certificate upon graduation.

Depending on the college of matriculation, students enroll in honors courses, complete honors credit learning agreements, and/or meet additional curriculum and grade point requirements to remain eligible for continuation in the program. James Scholars in all colleges receive early registration privileges and may concurrently be recognized by other University and college honors programs or groups.

Admission Process: Interested students should apply for admission to the University of Illinois at Urbana-Champaign by November 15 of their senior year in high school. To be considered for admission to the Campus Honors Program and the college James Scholar honors programs, students must check the "honors box" on the UIUC application form. The individual programs notify students of acceptance.

Acceptance to the Campus Honors Program is based upon such factors as standardized test scores, high school class rank and GPA, evidence of creative and leadership abilities as displayed in extracurricular interests and activities, the strength of the application essays, and evidence of willingness to accept CHP challenges and contribute to the program. The Campus Honors Program is open to students in all majors offered on the Urbana-Champaign campus, and an effort is made to ensure that each incoming class of Chancellor's Scholars is broadly representative of the curricula of the University as a whole. The Campus Honors Program seeks students who are strongly motivated not only to excel but also to make a difference at Illinois.

Active participants in the college James Scholar programs represent the top 10 to 15 percent of students at the University of Illinois. Admitted first-year students are characterized by outstanding academic records, high general aptitudes for college work, and reputations for seriousness of purpose, persistence, and self-discipline in educational endeavors.

Scholarship Availability: One of the attractions of the University of Illinois is its low cost, compared to many other top-rated American colleges and universities. Beyond that, CHP can offer a limited number of partial tuition waiver scholarships to accepted students who are not Illinois residents. These waivers defray part of the out-of-state portion of tuition for the first year and may be renewed for the second year if the student meets all requirements for continuance in CHP. First-year Chancellor's Scholars from Illinois receive a $200 scholarship to help with educational expenses.

High-achieving students who can demonstrate financial need have an excellent chance of being granted additional financial aid beyond what the CHP is able to provide. To receive University-awarded financial aid, undergraduate students must be enrolled for at least 12 credit hours and must complete a need-analysis document for the Office of Student Financial Aid. The deadline date for first-priority processing and equal consideration of financial aid applications is mid-March prior to the academic year for which aid is desired.

There are no extra costs or additional fees for applying to CHP or being a student in the Campus Honors Program.

A limited number of merit-based scholarships are available to entering James Scholars in specific colleges.

For further information, students should visit the UIUC Web site at http://www.honors.uiuc.edu/honors-at-illinois/index.html.

Campus Overview

State-supported university, founded 1867, part of University of Illinois System • **Coed** 29,639 undergraduate students, 97% full-time, 47% women, 53% men.

Undergraduates 28,697 full-time, 942 part-time. Students come from 52 states and territories, 70 other countries, 8% are from out of state, 7% African American, 13% Asian American or Pacific Islander, 6% Hispanic American, 0.2% Native American, 4% international, 4% transferred in, 39% live on campus.

Faculty *Total:* 2,559, 85% full-time, 82% with terminal degrees. *Student/faculty ratio:* 14:1.

Academic Programs *Special study options:* academic remediation for entering students, advanced placement credit, cooperative education, distance learning, double majors, English as a second language, honors programs, independent study, internships, off-campus study, services for LD students, student-designed majors, study abroad, summer session for credit. *ROTC:* Army (b), Navy (b), Air Force (b). *Unusual degree programs:* 3-2 accounting.

Athletics Member NCAA. All Division I except football (Division I-A). *Intercollegiate sports:* baseball M(s), basketball M(s)/W(s), cheerleading M/W, cross-country running M(s)/W(s), golf M(s)/W(s), gymnastics M(s)/W(s), soccer W(s), swimming and diving W(s), tennis M(s)/W(s), track and field M(s)/W(s), volleyball W(s), wrestling M(s). *Intramural sports:* archery M/W, badminton M/W, basketball M/W, bowling M/W, cross-country running M/W, equestrian sports M(c)/W(c), fencing M(c)/W(c), field hockey W(c), football M/W, golf M/W, gymnastics M(c)/W(c), ice hockey M/W, lacrosse M(c)/W(c), racquetball M/W, riflery M(c)/W(c), rugby M(c)/W(c), sailing M(c)/W(c), skiing (cross-country) M(c)/W(c), skiing (downhill) M(c)/W(c), soccer M/W, softball M/W, squash M(c)/W(c), swimming and diving M/W, table tennis M/W, tennis M/W, volleyball M/W, water polo M/W, weight lifting M(c)/W(c), wrestling M/W.

Costs (2005–06) *Tuition:* state resident $7042 full-time; nonresident $21,128 full-time. Full-time tuition and fees vary according to course load, program, and student level. No tuition increase for student's term of enrollment. *Required fees:* $1511 full-time. *Room and board:* $6710; room only: $2970. Room and board charges vary according to board plan and housing facility.

Financial Aid 1,702 Federal Work-Study jobs (averaging $1421). In 2003, 3657 non-need-based awards were made. *Average percent of need met:* 89%. *Average financial aid package:* $17,612. *Average need-based loan:* $7827. *Average need-based gift aid:* $12,433. *Average non-need-based aid:* $6634.

Contact: Director: Prof. Bruce F. Michelson, Campus Honors Program, 1205 West Oregon, Urbana, Illinois 61801; *Telephone:* 217-244-0922; *Fax:* 217-333-2563; *E-mail:* chp@uiuc.edu; *Web site:* http://www.honors.uiuc.edu

University of St. Francis
The Duns Scotus Fellows and Scholars Program
Joliet, Illinois

The Duns Scotus Fellows and Scholars Program is named after a medieval monk and scholar (John Duns Scotus) as a reminder that the program and University are heirs to the rich Franciscan intellectual tradition and to evoke the sense that scholarship should always be tempered with humility and used in service to humankind. The program aims to help motivated students develop their full academic potential within the context of a caring, supportive community of learners. Through the use of accelerated study, interdisciplinary exchanges, service learning, independent study, and enrichment activities outside of the classroom, the program encourages students to sharpen their skills and academic prowess. The core of the program is research and service.

The Duns Scotus program is flexible and can be tailored to meet students' needs. The program has two tracks: fellows are participants for all four years of their undergraduate career, and scholars are transfer students or entrants in their sophomore or junior years. Students from all campus-based colleges and all majors may participate. The program has a strong interdisciplinary and general education component, but in the junior and senior years, it focuses on the work the student does in his or her chosen major, thereby adding proficiency in that field. Faculty members in the student's major area supervise honors-level research or projects.

Students in the program have close contact with faculty members, and each fellow or scholar has both an honors and a major adviser. The program promotes a variety of cultural and social activities on campus each year and capitalizes on the rich cultural offerings in nearby Chicago as well as further afield.

Participation Requirements: Fellows are required to complete a sequence of core courses in their freshman and sophomore years (16 hours), one general education course (3 hours), three 1-hour seminars, and 9 hours of honors course work in their major area. In addition, students must complete an honors thesis or capstone project. Fellows are also expected to attend at least three cultural experiences each year and to participate in service learning.

Scholars are required to complete 12 hours of honors course work, 9 of which are in their major area and 3 of which are 1-hour seminars. In addition, students must complete an honors thesis or capstone project. Scholars are also expected to attend at least three cultural experiences each year and participate in service learning.

Completion of either program requires a cumulative GPA of 3.25 or higher.

Admission Process: Entering freshmen may apply as fellows until a month before classes begin. Prospective fellows must complete an application, write an essay explaining their desire to be in the program, and be interviewed by the director of the program. Continuing USF students may apply to the scholars program from the time they are second-semester freshmen until midway through their junior year. They must have a recommendation from a faculty member, fill out an application, write an essay, and have an interview. Transfer students may apply to the scholars program upon acceptance to the University. They must demonstrate a cumulative GPA of at least 3.25 at their previous institution, fill out an application, write an essay, and have an interview.

Scholarship Availability: Each fellow and scholar receives $1000 per year toward tuition (with a few exceptions) as well as a 10 percent discount on University housing. Duns Scotus Fellows and Scholars are also eligible for the University Trustee or Presidential Scholarships and may receive awards up to full tuition.

Campus Overview

Independent Roman Catholic comprehensive, founded 1920 • **Coed** 1,249 undergraduate students, 86% full-time, 68% women, 32% men.

Undergraduates 1,076 full-time, 173 part-time. Students come from 8 states and territories, 4 other countries, 2% are from out of state, 8% African American, 3% Asian American or Pacific Islander, 7% Hispanic American, 0.3% Native American, 1% international, 14% transferred in, 22% live on campus.

Faculty *Total:* 208, 35% full-time, 37% with terminal degrees. *Student/faculty ratio:* 13:1.

Academic Programs *Special study options:* academic remediation for entering students, accelerated degree program, adult/continuing education programs, advanced placement credit, distance learning, double majors, external degree program, independent study, internships, off-campus study, part-time degree program, services for LD students, student-designed majors, study abroad, summer session for credit.

Athletics Member NAIA. *Intercollegiate sports:* baseball M(s), basketball M(s)/W(s), cheerleading W, cross-country running W(s), football M(s), golf M(s)/W(s), soccer M(s)/W(s), softball W(s), tennis M(s)/W(s), track and field W(s), volleyball W(s). *Intramural sports:* basketball M/W, bowling M/W, golf M/W, racquetball M/W, skiing (downhill) M/W, table tennis M/W, volleyball M/W.

Costs (2004–05) *Comprehensive fee:* $23,850 includes full-time tuition ($17,310), mandatory fees ($360), and room and board ($6180). Full-time tuition and fees vary according to course load and degree level. Part-time tuition: $500 per semester hour. Part-time tuition and fees vary according to course load and degree level. *Required fees:* $15 per term part-time.

Financial Aid 232 Federal Work-Study jobs (averaging $1600). 286 state and other part-time jobs (averaging $1360). In 2004, 229 non-need-based awards were made. *Average percent of need met:* 83%. *Average financial aid package:* $13,698. *Average need-based loan:* $4172. *Average need-based gift aid:* $8276. *Average non-need-based aid:* $5086.

Contact: Dr. Jeff Chamberlain, University of St. Francis, 500 Wilcox Street, Joliet, Illinois 60435; *Telephone:* 815-740-3603; *Fax:* 815-740-4285; *E-mail:* jchamberlain@stfrancis.edu; *Web site:* http://www.stfrancis.edu/duns-scotus

Western Illinois University
Centennial Honors College
Macomb, Illinois

The Centennial Honors College (CHC) at Western Illinois University (WIU) is a free-standing academic unit committed to providing academically talented and motivated students an enriched academic curriculum and opportunities for leadership, professional growth, and service.

Consistent with its commitment to academic excellence, the Centennial Honors College offers special general honors tutorials and honors seminars and mentored research opportunities within departments and academic areas. The general honors courses are taught by select honors faculty members, who foster opportunities for discussion and debate and who promote critical reasoning, cross-disciplinary thinking, and communication skills. These general honors courses count toward the honors student's general education requirements. The honors courses within disciplines and major/

specialty areas provide opportunities for in-depth study, research, and professional development. These courses fulfill the student's major or minor requirements. Students at the Quad Cities campus complete a program of mentored honors experiences in Upper Division Honors.

The CHC also fosters leadership, professional growth, and service. This is accomplished in part through the honors curriculum and in part through activities and events sponsored by the program. Research and thesis projects afford students opportunities to form mentoring relationships with faculty members. Mentored honors projects promote the development of portfolios to be used at the time of job or graduate school interviews. In addition, the CHC encourages students to participate in its governance through representation on the University Honors Council, the Honors Student Advisory Board, and the Student Honors Association.

Special programs available to Western's honors students include several preprofessional programs. Study in the pre-engineering, prearchitecture, premedicine, prenursing, preoptometry, predentistry, and preveterinary dual programs is available. Of particular interest is the CHC's specially developed interdisciplinary prelaw honors minor, which is open to all majors. This minor provides a valuable background for the study and practice of law and emphasizes writing, effective speaking, and critical-thinking skills.

Western Illinois University's University Honors Program was established in 1983 and currently enrolls approximately 550 students from thirty-four academic departments.

Participation Requirements: Students may graduate from the CHC as Honors Scholars in University Honors, Lower Division Honors, or Upper Division Honors. University Honors requires the completion of a sequence of general honors seminars and discipline-specific honors seminars, research, and internships. Lower Division Honors entails the completion of the general honors sequence; Upper Division Honors is satisfied by the completion of discipline-specific honors seminars, research, and internships. All honors students complete a 1-hour interdisciplinary colloquium. Students must also maintain a GPA of at least 3.4 in all course work. Upon completion of honors requirements, seniors are recognized at a special honors convocation, and the appropriate honors level is indicated on their transcripts.

Admission Process: Admission of first-year students to the CHC is based on a variable standard that includes both ACT or SAT scores and class rank; on-campus and transfer students intending to participate in Upper Division Honors must have an earned GPA of 3.4 or better in all of their college-level work.

Scholarship Availability: The CHC and the Western Illinois University Foundation offer a number of scholarships for first-year students, transfers, and continuing honors students. The program awards four-year WIU Foundation-Honors Scholarships, Sherman Honors Freshman Scholarships, Outstanding New Freshmen Scholars, WIU Transfers Honors Scholarships, and Sophomore, Junior, and Senior Scholarships. The Keith Webb Memorial Scholarship is awarded annually to outstanding students in the prelaw honors minor. The Martin Dupuis Award for Leadership in Historically Under-Represented Communities is awarded annually to an honors student from an underrepresented group. In addition, the CHC awards a number of Research Grants, Study Abroad Honors Scholarships, and a Writing Prize Award.

Campus Overview

State-supported comprehensive, founded 1899 • **Coed** 11,310 undergraduate students, 90% full-time, 49% women, 51% men.

Undergraduates 10,130 full-time, 1,180 part-time. Students come from 37 states and territories, 46 other countries, 6% are from out of state, 7% African American, 1% Asian American or Pacific Islander, 4% Hispanic American, 0.2% Native American, 1% international, 12% transferred in, 51% live on campus.

Faculty *Total:* 704, 87% full-time, 64% with terminal degrees. *Student/faculty ratio:* 17:1.

Academic Programs *Special study options:* academic remediation for entering students, adult/continuing education programs, advanced placement credit, distance learning, double majors, English as a second language, external degree program, freshman honors college, honors programs, independent study, internships, off-campus study, part-time degree program, services for LD students, student-designed majors, study abroad, summer session for credit. *ROTC:* Army (b). *Unusual degree programs:* 3-2 engineering with University of Illinois at Urbana–Champaign, Case Western Reserve University.

Athletics Member NCAA. All Division I except football (Division I-AA). *Intercollegiate sports:* baseball M(s), basketball M(s)/W(s), cross-country running M(s)/W(s), golf M(s)/W, soccer M(s)/W(s), softball W(s), swimming and diving M(s)/W(s), tennis M(s)/W(s), track and field M(s)/W(s), volleyball W(s). *Intramural sports:* badminton M/W, basketball M/W, bowling M/W, cheerleading M/W, cross-country running M/W, football M/W, golf M/W, lacrosse M, racquetball M/W, rugby M/W, soccer M/W, softball M/W, swimming and diving M/W, table tennis M/W, tennis M/W, volleyball M/W, water polo M/W.

Costs (2004–05) *Tuition:* state resident $4537 full-time, $151 per semester hour part-time; nonresident $9075 full-time, $303 per semester hour part-time. Full-time tuition and fees vary according to location. Part-time tuition and fees vary according to location. No tuition increase for student's term of enrollment. *Required fees:* $1646 full-time, $39 per semester hour part-time. *Room and board:* $5768; room only: $3428. Room and board charges vary according to housing facility.

Financial Aid 184 Federal Work-Study jobs (averaging $1865). 1,761 state and other part-time jobs (averaging $834). In 2004, 541 non-need-based awards were made. *Average percent of need met:* 67%. *Average financial aid package:* $7659. *Average need-based loan:* $3540. *Average need-based gift aid:* $4889. *Average non-need-based aid:* $2138.

Contact: Illinois Centennial Honors College, 1 University Circle, Macomb, Illinois 61455-1390; *Telephone:* 309-298-2228; *Fax:* 309-298-2591; *E-mail:* honors@wiu.edu

William Rainey Harper College
Honors Program
Palatine, Illinois

The Harper College Honors Program offers a variety of general education courses to all students who have been accepted into the program. Students choose those courses that fit their academic and career needs. Honors courses differ from traditional courses in ways determined by the instructors in consultation with the institutional Honors Committee; in general, students are given greater responsibility for designing projects, taking on leadership roles in class discussions, and planning classroom activities. On occasion, interdisciplinary courses are offered. Small classes are the norm: they usually have between 8 and 15 students. Honors instructors are selected for their demonstrated excellence in teaching and for expertise in their chosen disciplines. Honors students are advised by the Honors Coordinator, honors faculty members, and college counselors.

English 101, English 102, and Speech 101 (the communications core) are offered every semester during the regular academic year. A journalism independent study is also offered for those students interested in working on the honors newsletter, The Challenger. Other courses in business/social science, the humanities, and mathematics/science are also regularly offered. Summer honors courses are also available.

In addition, honors students at Harper automatically become members of the Honors Society, the social arm of the program. The

Honors Society elects its own officers and meets weekly to discuss program plans and conduct wide-ranging, open discussions on topics of current interest. Cultural, social, and community service events are planned and carried forward by members of the society.

Honors students are encouraged to attend and actively participate in honors conferences and conventions.

The Harper College Honors Program has been active since 1989 and currently enrolls 200 students.

Participation Requirements: Honors students must successfully complete four honors courses, including an Honors Colloquium course (Humanities 105, Great Ideas of World Civilizations), and maintain a minimum 3.25 GPA in order to graduate from the Harper College Honors Program. Students who take three or fewer honors courses will have the honors course designation indicated on transcripts but will not qualify for honors graduation. The number and type of honors courses taken is at discretion of the student. Each Honors Program graduate receives a citation on the diploma as well as an Honors Program pin, which is awarded at the annual Honors Convocation.

Scholarship Availability: Students who qualify with a 3.5 or better GPA are encouraged to join Phi Theta Kappa (PTK). There are a number of scholarships available only to PTK members.

Campus Overview

State and locally supported 2-year, founded 1965, part of Illinois Community College Board • **Coed** 14,991 undergraduate students.

Undergraduates Students come from 13 states and territories, 31 other countries.

Faculty *Total:* 806, 26% full-time. *Student/faculty ratio:* 5:1.

Academic Programs *Special study options:* academic remediation for entering students, adult/continuing education programs, advanced placement credit, cooperative education, distance learning, English as a second language, honors programs, independent study, internships, part-time degree program, services for LD students, study abroad, summer session for credit.

Athletics Member NJCAA. *Intercollegiate sports:* baseball M, basketball M/W, cross-country running M/W, football M, golf M, soccer M/W, softball W, tennis M/W, track and field M/W, volleyball W, wrestling M. *Intramural sports:* baseball M, basketball M/W, bowling M, racquetball M/W, skiing (cross-country) M/W, skiing (downhill) M/W, softball M/W, table tennis M/W, tennis M/W, volleyball M/W.

Costs (2004–05) *Tuition:* area resident $2130 full-time, $71 per credit hour part-time; state resident $8430 full-time, $281 per credit hour part-time; nonresident $10,440 full-time, $348 per credit hour part-time. *Required fees:* $382 full-time.

Financial Aid 85 Federal Work-Study jobs (averaging $1210).

Contact: Coordinator: Dr. Andrew Wilson, Liberal Arts Division, William Rainey Harper College, Palatine, Illinois 60067; *Telephone:* 847-925-6791; *Fax:* 847-925-6039; *E-mail:* awilson@harpercollege.edu; *Web site:* http://www.harpercollege.edu/cluborgs/honors/

INDIANA

Ball State University

Honors College

Muncie, Indiana

. . . to offer distinctive opportunities for students who show promise of outstanding academic achievement, and to do this so well that our graduates are competitive with the best students of any other college or university.

For more than forty years, honors education at Ball State University has tried to accomplish the above-stated purpose. While this purpose guides all that happens in the Honors College, it does not explain the attitude behind its operations. Honors education is intended to be interdisciplinary, assuming the students' abilities to do rote learning and asking them to do more. Concerns with critical and creative thinking and problem-solving tasks form major components of honors education at Ball State.

Classes and other opportunities are not automatically intended to be more difficult than might be experienced in nonhonors situations, but are *expected to be different. Honors College is as much an attitude as an administrative unit—it is truly a college within a larger university. The excellent instruction and individual attention of the honors programs create many opportunities for students to enrich their educational pursuits and realize the benefits of a first-rate, small-college atmosphere within a progressive university setting.*

Honors students take honors courses in classes of 25 or fewer students, restricted to honors only. All Honors College students are granted extended privileges in the University's libraries. They have scheduling privileges that help ensure enrollment in desired classes at the times preferred. In addition, honors students have their own residence hall and have academic advisers assigned to work exclusively with them. All incoming freshman honors students receive a Presidential Scholarship worth 50 percent of tuition for eight semesters. The Honors College sponsors a program of Honors Undergraduate Fellowships. Students work in one-to-one partnerships with faculty mentors on research or creative endeavors. Undergraduate Fellows receive $825 for each semester of a fellowship.

Honors College and Departmental Honors graduates receive special recognition during graduation ceremonies and are awarded special diplomas. The designations are also part of the final transcript.

There are 1,450 students in the program.

Participation Requirements: The Honors College offers two types of academic programs. The first, designated University Honors, is applicable to all majors. Students must take a core curriculum of six specially designed University Core Curriculum courses and at least two upper-level colloquia designed specifically for the Honors College. Furthermore, they must complete senior theses or creative projects and finish their undergraduate work with a cumulative GPA of at least a 3.33 (B+). Students completing this program earn the designation Honors College Graduate on their diplomas.

The second program is called Departmental Honors. Students selecting this option usually begin work in the third year, pursuing specialized study in their majors and completing requirements specifically tailored to those majors. The students must also complete theses or creative projects. Grade point requirements are established individually by each department. A number of students complete both University and Departmental Honors programs.

Admission Process: Students with at least a 3.6 GPA in a college-preparatory curriculum in high school and SAT I scores of at least 1210 (with a 600 verbal) or ACT composites of 27 (with a 26 English) or higher are reviewed for admission into the Honors College. Other interested students are encouraged to apply. Evaluations are made on the basis of SAT or ACT scores, academic background, and personal references. Students interested in the Honors College are expected to have had a thorough college-preparatory sequence, including classes in all the basic disciplines. Transfer students are evaluated individually by the Dean of the College.

Scholarship Availability: Ball State University offers many scholarships. All Honors College students can expect to receive a Presidential Scholarship (half tuition) if their application is submitted in a timely manner. Those with a minimum 3.7 GPA who have at least a 1300 combined score on the SAT I or 29 composite on the ACT are eligible to compete for the Whitinger Scholarship. This competition requires a conversation with a representative of the committee, a spontaneous essay, and a prepared writing sample. In addition, Ball State University sponsors National Merit and National Achievement awards. Information about these and other competitive scholarships can be obtained from the Office of Scholarships and Financial Aid.

Campus Overview

State-supported university, founded 1918 • **Coed** 17,535 undergraduate students, 92% full-time, 53% women, 47% men.

Undergraduates 16,196 full-time, 1,339 part-time. Students come from 49 states and territories, 9% are from out of state, 7% African American, 0.7% Asian American or Pacific Islander, 1% Hispanic American, 0.3% Native American, 5% transferred in, 41% live on campus.

Faculty *Total:* 1,169, 77% full-time, 64% with terminal degrees. *Student/faculty ratio:* 17:1.

Academic Programs *Special study options:* academic remediation for entering students, adult/continuing education programs, advanced placement credit, cooperative education, distance learning, double majors, English as a second language, freshman honors college, honors programs, independent study, internships, part-time degree program, study abroad, summer session for credit. *ROTC:* Army (b). *Unusual degree programs:* 3-2 engineering with Purdue University, Tri-State University.

Athletics Member NCAA. All Division I except football (Division I-A). *Intercollegiate sports:* baseball M(s), basketball M(s)/W(s), cross-country running M(s)/W(s), equestrian sports M(c)/W(c), field hockey W(s), golf M(s), gymnastics W(s), ice hockey M(c), rugby M(c)/W(c), sailing M(c)/W(c), soccer M(c)/W, softball W(s), swimming and diving M(s)/W(s), tennis M(s)/W(s), track and field M(s)/W(s), volleyball M(s)/W(s), water polo M(c), wrestling M(c). *Intramural sports:* archery M/W, badminton M(c)/W(c), basketball M/W, bowling M(c)/W(c), cross-country running M/W, fencing M(c)/W(c), football M, golf M, lacrosse M(c), racquetball M/W, soccer M, softball M/W, squash M/W, swimming and diving M/W, table tennis M(c)/W(c), tennis M/W, track and field M/W, volleyball M/W, weight lifting M(c)/W(c).

Costs (2004–05) *Tuition:* state resident $5752 full-time; nonresident $14,928 full-time. Part-time tuition and fees vary according to course load. *Required fees:* $508 full-time. *Room and board:* $6228. Room and board charges vary according to board plan and housing facility.

Financial Aid 1,268 Federal Work-Study jobs (averaging $2280). 4,141 state and other part-time jobs (averaging $1568). In 2004, 491 non-need-based awards were made. *Average percent of need met:* 68%. *Average financial aid package:* $7263. *Average need-based loan:* $3526. *Average need-based gift aid:* $4355. *Average non-need-based aid:* $3695.

Contact: James S. Ruebel, Dean of the Honors College, Muncie, Indiana 47306; *Telephone:* 765-285-1024; *Fax:* 765-285-2072; *E-mail:* honors@bsu.edu; *Web site:* http://www.bsu.edu/honors

Butler University

Honors Program

Indianapolis, Indiana

Butler's Honors Program is a University-wide program that fosters interdisciplinary as well as discipline-specific learning through course work, the honors thesis, and cultural events. In the first half of their study, students from all five colleges take courses together and complete an honors curriculum that draws from more than sixty engaging fields of study. Regardless of course choices, students can always count on individualized faculty mentoring and small, interactive classes. In the remaining semesters, students concentrate on their honors thesis, which offers them the chance to work one-on-one with a faculty mentor and to complete a major project or performance. Thesis topics reflect the students' diversity and imagination, which are the hallmarks of the University's Honors Program.

The course work and thesis are complemented by cultural events, which include field trips, workshops, lectures, artistic readings, and performances. While attending these events, students enjoy interaction with inspiring authors, scholars, and artists. The program is also complemented by the activities of the Student Honor's Council, which sponsors orientation, volunteer, and social events.

The Honors Program is further enriched by the efforts of the honors faculty advisers, who are trained to aid the students in pursuing their academic, graduate study, and career goals.

The University's highest two Latin honors (summa and magna cum laude) are reserved exclusively for students who complete the Honors Program.

The program is more than 30 years old. There are 350 students in the program; 15 percent of eligible freshmen accept the invitation to participate.

Admission Process: Participation is voluntary. Incoming students who have graduated in the top 7 percent of their high school classes and who have combined SAT I scores of at least 1280 or composite ACT scores of 29 or better are qualified for consideration. The program then issues invitations based on the students' high school academic records, extracurricular/leadership activities, and application essays. Also invited are Butler students who receive a faculty endorsement, achieve a 3.5 GPA or better, and complete 16 credit hours at the end of their first semester (or 32 credit hours at the end of their first year). Transfer students are eligible to apply.

Campus Overview

Independent comprehensive, founded 1855 • **Coed** 3,722 undergraduate students, 98% full-time, 63% women, 37% men.

Undergraduates 3,651 full-time, 71 part-time. Students come from 47 states and territories, 44 other countries, 41% are from out of state, 4% African American, 2% Asian American or Pacific Islander, 2% Hispanic American, 0.2% Native American, 2% international, 3% transferred in, 57% live on campus.

Faculty *Total:* 435, 64% full-time, 63% with terminal degrees. *Student/faculty ratio:* 12:1.

Academic Programs *Special study options:* adult/continuing education programs, advanced placement credit, cooperative education, double majors, English as a second language, honors programs, independent study, internships, off-campus study, part-time degree program, student-designed majors, study abroad, summer session for credit. *ROTC:* Army (b), Air Force (c). *Unusual degree programs:* 3-2 engineering with Indiana University-Purdue University Indianapolis.

Athletics Member NCAA. All Division I except football (Division III). *Intercollegiate sports:* baseball M(s), basketball M(s)/W(s), crew M(c)/W(c), cross-country running M(s)/W(s), football M, golf M(s)/W(s), ice hockey M(c), lacrosse M(s), rugby M(c), soccer M(s)/W(s), softball W(s), swimming and diving M/W, tennis M(s)/W(s), track and field M/W, volleyball W(s). *Intramural sports:* badminton M/W, baseball M, basketball M/W, bowling M/W, football M, soccer M/W, softball M/W, swimming and diving M/W, table tennis M/W, tennis M/W, track and field M/W, volleyball M/W, weight lifting M/W.

Costs (2004–05) *Comprehensive fee:* $30,264 includes full-time tuition ($22,250), mandatory fees ($234), and room and board ($7780). Full-time tuition and fees vary according to program. Part-time tuition: $930 per credit. Part-time tuition and fees vary according to program. *College room only:* $3400. Room and board charges vary according to housing facility.

Financial Aid In 2004, 1010 non-need-based awards were made. *Average financial aid package:* $17,165. *Average need-based loan:* $5320. *Average need-based gift aid:* $12,380. *Average non-need-based aid:* $9080.

Contact: Director: Anne Wilson, 4600 Sunset Avenue, Indianapolis, Indiana 46208; *Telephone:* 317-940-9408 or 9302; *Fax:* 317-940-3232 *E-mail:* honors@butler.edu; *Web site:* http://www.butler.edu/honors

DePauw University
Honor Scholar Program, Management Fellows Program, Media Fellows Program, and Science Research Fellows Program
Greencastle, Indiana

DePauw University offers four challenging and rewarding honors programs so that high-achieving students with specialized interests can benefit even more from their undergraduate education. A student may apply to and enroll in more than one of these programs.

The purpose of the Honor Scholar Program is to provide a rigorous interdisciplinary experience to academically talented students within a liberal arts educational philosophy. Students selected for the program must not only demonstrate a level of academic achievement that predicts their ability to handle academic content, but also have the ability to generalize from specifics and to apply these generalizations to new and seemingly unrelated knowledge. The Honor Scholar Program complements the required academic courses with discussion-based classes containing 10 to 12 students and a senior thesis through a process similar to a master's thesis. The discussion-based seminars are taught by faculty members recruited for expertise in their own discipline and for competence in facilitating participatory learning among students. The Honor Scholar Program was founded in 1979 and presently has 90 students enrolled.

The DePauw Management Fellows Program is an honors program for students interested in business, management, and entrepreneurship. This four-year learning experience integrates the study of management and entrepreneurship with a liberal arts education. Students complete courses in business ethics, quantitative analysis, economics, and accounting. Management Fellows also participate in a semester-long, credit-bearing, paid internship. Students have interned all over the world in the private, public, and not-for-profit sectors. Past internship sites include Eli Lilly and Co., Indianapolis; Goldman Sachs and Co., Chicago; and Ernst & Young International in London. The Management Center Lecture Series relates practice to theory and is an integral part of the program. Students interact and network with business leaders in a wide variety of industries through the lecture series.

The Media Fellows Program combines analytical and critical study with hands-on media experience within the Eugene S. Pulliam Center for Contemporary Media, a state-of-the-art media facility that is unique to a small liberal arts college. It is intended for students who plan careers in media and for students who want to know how media operate to help them perform effectively in other careers. The first year of the Media Fellows Program lays a philosophical base for media study and an introduction to media in their various forms. During the sophomore year, Media Fellows attend a luncheon discussion series with faculty members and senior Media Fellows. During the junior year, students participate in a semester-long, professional internship in a media setting such as a television network, newspaper, public relations office, or entertainment program. In the senior year, Media Fellows take part in a capstone seminar that includes media projects and extensive reading and discussion. Throughout the four years, students are expected to complete four semesters of work in one of the student media and attend special lectures, luncheons, and seminars featuring media experts. The Media Fellows Program was founded in 1992 and currently has 81 students enrolled.

The Science Research Fellows Program is an honors program for science students. Although the program places an emphasis on science, it maintains a liberal arts focus. There are four major components to the program: a first-year seminar, a student-faculty summer research collaboration, a semester internship, and a capstone seminar. Science Research Fellows have the advantage of getting hands-on research experience during their first year. They are given the opportunity to work in small groups to develop their technical and communication skills. They are also granted the unique opportunity to perform summer research with a science faculty member to more fully develop their investigative ability. The program is excellent preparation for graduate and professional schools.

Participation Requirements: Honor Scholars are required to enroll in two full-credit seminars during their first year. Three additional interdisciplinary seminars are required: one each in the social sciences, the humanities, and the sciences. These classes also fulfill certain general education requirements. During the senior year, Honor Scholars may enroll in independent-study classes to generate their thesis. Students must maintain a cumulative GPA of at least 3.2 to graduate from the program.

Management Fellows must complete course requirements in the major of their choice and the Management Fellows core curriculum. To remain a Management Fellow in good standing, a student must attend at least four lectures from the McDermond Center Lecture Series each semester, participate in a paid internship that lasts a minimum of fifteen weeks, and earn at least a 3.2 GPA each semester.

Media Fellows must complete two courses, one emphasizing the process side of media, the other analytical. Media Fellows have a list of courses to choose from, but only one of the two courses can be in their major. Members of the program have three semesters to achieve at least a 3.1 GPA, which they must maintain to remain in good academic standing. By the second semester of the senior year, Media Fellows must complete 7 credits and achieve at least a 3.2 GPA to graduate.

Science Research Fellows are required to enroll in an interdisciplinary, introductory seminar their first year. During the following summer, students participate in a paid, on-campus research project. During their junior or senior year, students have a semester-long internship in a major research setting, such as Harvard Medical School or the National Institutes of Health. The program culminates with a capstone seminar in which students present their off-campus research. Students must achieve a minimum 3.1 GPA by the end of the second year.

Admission Process: Students are invited to join the Honor Scholar Program through a tiered application process. Prospective students submit essay responses to posed questions, which are evaluated by 2 faculty members. Based on the ranking of the essays, a select group of students are invited to interview on campus. During the interview, the student's ability to articulate thoughts, to grapple with indicated inconsistencies in logic, and to incorporate new information is evaluated. From this interviewed pool, a percentage of students are invited to join the program.

Admission to the Management Fellows Program is based on superior academic ability, a high degree of intellectual curiosity, leadership potential, and an interest in a management career. Most students apply to the Management Fellows Program during their high school senior year, although students may be admitted in their first year of college. Admission decisions are based on SAT and/or ACT scores, high school GPA and rank, a written essay, and a formal interview.

Students must complete a special application to the Media Fellows Program in addition to the DePauw University application. Decisions on admission are made based on the quality of the application, which consists of three essay questions, SAT or ACT scores, class rank, and an interview with a member of the faculty governing board for Media Fellows. The program admits approximately 25 students per class.

Students must complete a special application to the Science Research Fellows Program in addition to the regular application to

DePauw. Admission decisions are made on the basis of SAT or ACT scores, class rank, quality of the essays on the application form, and a personal interview. The program admits only 18 to 20 students per class.

Scholarship Availability: Students applying to any of the four programs are eligible for merit scholarships. To be considered a candidate for one of the four merit scholarships available to Management Fellows, a student must demonstrate evidence of superior academic performance, leadership abilities, and other personal characteristics necessary for success both at DePauw and after graduation. Selection is made from among those high school seniors who have been admitted to the Management Fellows Program for the following fall. Scholarships are renewable, provided the recipient remains a member in good standing of the Management Fellows Program.

Campus Overview

Independent 4-year, founded 1837, affiliated with United Methodist Church • **Coed** 2,391 undergraduate students, 99% full-time, 55% women, 45% men.

Undergraduates 2,359 full-time, 32 part-time. Students come from 42 states and territories, 21 other countries, 51% are from out of state, 5% African American, 2% Asian American or Pacific Islander, 3% Hispanic American, 0.4% Native American, 2% international, 0.3% transferred in, 95% live on campus.

Faculty *Total:* 254, 84% full-time, 86% with terminal degrees. *Student/faculty ratio:* 10:1.

Academic Programs *Special study options:* advanced placement credit, double majors, honors programs, independent study, internships, off-campus study, part-time degree program, student-designed majors, study abroad. *ROTC:* Army (c), Air Force (c). *Unusual degree programs:* 3-2 engineering with Columbia University, Washington University in St. Louis, Case Western Reserve University.

Athletics Member NCAA. All Division III. *Intercollegiate sports:* baseball M, basketball M/W, cheerleading M(c)/W(c), crew M(c)/W(c), cross-country running M/W, field hockey W, football M, golf M/W, rugby M(c), soccer M/W, softball W, swimming and diving M/W, tennis M/W, track and field M/W, volleyball W. *Intramural sports:* badminton M/W, basketball M/W, bowling M/W, football M/W, golf M, racquetball M/W, soccer M/W, softball M/W, table tennis M/W, tennis M/W, ultimate Frisbee M/W, volleyball M/W.

Costs (2004–05) *Comprehensive fee:* $32,800 includes full-time tuition ($25,000), mandatory fees ($500), and room and board ($7300). Part-time tuition: $781 per semester hour. *College room only:* $3800. Room and board charges vary according to board plan.

Financial Aid 703 Federal Work-Study jobs (averaging $1579). 26 state and other part-time jobs (averaging $480). *Average percent of need met:* 99%. *Average financial aid package:* $20,208. *Average need-based loan:* $4241. *Average need-based gift aid:* $16,693. *Average non-need-based aid:* $12,135.

Contact: Anne Harris, Honor Scholar Office, DePauw University, 436 Anderson Street, Greencastle, Indiana 46135; *Telephone:* 765-658-4345; *Fax:* 765-658-6262; *E-mail:* aharris@depauw.edu; *Web site:* http://www.depauw.edu/honors/index.asp

Holy Cross College

Honors Program

Notre Dame, Indiana

The Honors Program at Holy Cross College in Notre Dame, Indiana, is a distinctive and flexible program designed to meet the needs of highly motivated students who want a rigorous, intellectually challenging experience in the context of a small Catholic college in the Midwest. The goal of the Honors Program is to challenge students and enrich their educational experience while developing excellence in leadership, character, and service.

Small classes and individual guidance by excellent professors offer outstanding opportunities for academic growth. Courses are selected by the student within a flexible framework, and students may progress at their own pace and concentrate on their own areas of interest. Students may choose a designated honors section of a course or an upper-division course, or they may complete an honors component of a regular class. In keeping with the small size of the college, most honors credits are earned in honors components or contracts in regular courses. Honors contracts are arranged between the student and the professor and reflect the direction and interests of the student.

The Honors Program challenges students to integrate excellence in scholarship, leadership, character, and service. Students are encouraged to participate in an honors service-learning project and have the opportunity to attend cultural events in conjunction with the Honors Program. The director of the Honors Program also serves as the academic adviser of Honors Program participants. Students may decide to join the Honors Program before they enter the College or during their first or second semester.

The Honors Program at Holy Cross College was established in 1999. There were approximately 20 students participating in honors classes in the 2004–05 academic year.

Participation Requirements: The Honors Program requires 18 credit hours of honors courses, with at least one course in each of the four college divisions: Philosophy and Religious Studies, Humanities, Social and Behavioral Studies, and Life and Physical Sciences. A service-learning project is also required. Students must achieve a grade of B or higher in all honors courses and must maintain a minimum 3.3 cumulative GPA in order to remain in the Honors Program. Courses taken for honors have the honors designation on the student's transcript, and students completing the Honors Program have that noted on their transcripts and wear the honors cord at graduation.

Admission Process: Applicants to the College who score at least 1760 on the new SAT or 26 on the ACT are automatically invited to join the Honors Program. Students who have a strong personal motivation to participate are also considered for admission to the program at the discretion of the Honors Program Director and the Honors Council. Students may also apply during the spring semester if they have earned at least a 3.3 GPA on a 4.0 scale and have a faculty member's recommendation. In addition, students desiring to participate in a more challenging experience in an individual course may elect to fulfill an honors learning contract for that course with the permission of the professor and the director of the Honors Program.

Scholarship Availability: Freshmen entering the program are eligible to compete for a variety of academic scholarships. Honors Program participants may be eligible for Holy Cross College merit scholarships. Students should contact the Office of Admissions for more information.

Campus Overview

Independent Roman Catholic primarily 2-year, founded 1966 • **Coed** 492 undergraduate students, 96% full-time, 37% women, 63% men.

Undergraduates 471 full-time, 21 part-time. Students come from 37 states and territories, 12 other countries, 46% are from out of state, 7% transferred in, 54% live on campus.

Faculty *Total:* 38, 68% full-time, 32% with terminal degrees. *Student/faculty ratio:* 12:1.

Academic Programs *Special study options:* academic remediation for entering students, advanced placement credit, English as a second language, freshman honors college, internships, off-campus study, part-time degree program, summer session for credit. *ROTC:* Army (c), Air Force (c).

Athletics *Intercollegiate sports:* basketball M, crew M/W, equestrian sports M/W, ice hockey W, lacrosse M, water polo M/W. *Intramural sports:* basketball M/W, football M/W, golf M/W, lacrosse M, rugby M, skiing (downhill) M, soccer M, softball M/W, table tennis M/W, tennis M/W, ultimate Frisbee M/W, volleyball M/W.

Costs (2004–05) *Comprehensive fee:* $18,300 includes full-time tuition ($10,750), mandatory fees ($450), and room and board ($7100). Part-time tuition: $345 per semester hour. *Room and board:* Room and board charges vary according to housing facility.

Financial Aid 54 Federal Work-Study jobs (averaging $857).

Contact: Honors Program Director: Sandy Ohlund, Associate Professor of Spanish, Holy Cross College, 54515 State Road 933 North, P.O. Box 308, Notre Dame, Indiana 46556-0308; *Telephone:* 574-239-8389; *Fax:* 574-239-8323; *E-mail:* sohlund@hcc-nd.edu; *Web site:* http://www.hcc-nd.edu/Academics/HP/

Indiana University Bloomington
Edward L. Hutton Honors College
Bloomington, Indiana

The Hutton Honors College represents a commitment made by Indiana University (IU) to broaden and enrich the college experience of bright, highly motivated, and creative students. For the University, the Hutton Honors College is a way to coordinate honors programs on campus and provide special services for honors students. For faculty members serving in the Hutton Honors College, the program means the opportunity to teach bright students in inventive, interdisciplinary, and small-class settings and advanced or intensive classes devoted to particular disciplines. For the prospective Honors student, participation in the Hutton Honors College can mean opportunities for scholarships, additional housing options, access to special extracurricular programs, study abroad, opportunities to participate in faculty research projects, or a chance to spend a semester or summer pursuing research interests or gaining teaching or other professional experience through internships.

Begun in 1965, the Hutton Honors College currently accepts approximately 700 incoming freshmen.

Participation Requirements: Hutton Honors students normally take one honors course each semester. It is a challenging experience, but it is also fun. Right from the start, students get to know their fellow students in a small-class environment as they begin the process of expanding each other's minds under the tutelage of an outstanding teacher.

Admission Process: Students interested in the Hutton Honors College should obtain and file the freshman application for admission with the IU Office of Admissions. Freshman applicants with combined SAT scores of 1350 or above (verbal and math scores only) or an ACT score of 31 or above or who rank in the top 5 percent of their graduating class automatically receive an invitation to join the Hutton Honors College.

The program encourages other highly motivated students interested in the academic opportunities provided by the Hutton Honors College to apply directly after they have been accepted to IU. Students who do not meet initial criteria may have a high school teacher send a letter of recommendation attesting to their ability to do honors work. Applicants should also send a copy of their high school transcript and write a brief letter explaining why they wish to join the program. The program is especially interested in candidates who have taken either Advanced Placement, accelerated, or honors courses in high school.

Students who do not enter the Hutton Honors College as incoming freshmen but demonstrate outstanding academic performance in the first semester or year of college may ask to participate in the program at the end of the first or second semester.

Scholarship Availability: The Hutton Honors College gives more than 125 scholarships each year to entering freshmen. Honors College Scholarships are competitive merit scholarships that range in value from $1000 to $10,000 per year and are awarded solely on the basis of high school achievement. The application requires information about test scores (SAT and ACT), class rank, and academic and extracurricular involvement; a short essay; and a brief personal statement. Hutton Honors College faculty members carefully read each application and select the award recipients.

The Wells Scholars Program offers a four-year merit scholarship (tuition, academic fees, and a living stipend) and a unique educational opportunity to approximately 18 to 22 incoming freshmen who have excelled academically and shown exceptional qualities of character and leadership. The program emphasizes close interaction with faculty members and provides special seminars, a grant for an internship or other enriching summer experience, and support for up to an academic year of study abroad. Wells Scholars may pursue any course of undergraduate study offered at Indiana University. To be considered for the award, candidates must be nominated by an eligible high school or, if they do not attend an eligible high school, students must be nominated by the IU Bloomington Office of Admissions. For deadline information and additional details, students should go online to http://www.indiana.edu/~wsp/.

The Kelley Scholars Program also offers full funding (tuition, room, and board) to a select group of outstanding students majoring in business.

Campus Overview

State-supported university, founded 1820, part of Indiana University System • **Coed** 29,549 undergraduate students, 94% full-time, 52% women, 48% men.

Undergraduates 27,743 full-time, 1,806 part-time. Students come from 56 states and territories, 135 other countries, 29% are from out of state, 4% African American, 3% Asian American or Pacific Islander, 2% Hispanic American, 0.2% Native American, 4% international, 3% transferred in, 42% live on campus.

Faculty *Total:* 2,251, 85% full-time, 66% with terminal degrees. *Student/faculty ratio:* 18:1.

Academic Programs *Special study options:* academic remediation for entering students, accelerated degree program, adult/continuing education programs, advanced placement credit, cooperative education, distance learning, double majors, English as a second language, external degree program, freshman honors college, honors programs, independent study, internships, off-campus study, part-time degree program, services for LD students, student-designed majors, study abroad, summer session for credit. *ROTC:* Army (b), Air Force (b). *Unusual degree programs:* 3-2 accounting.

Athletics Member NCAA. All Division I except football (Division I-A). *Intercollegiate sports:* baseball M(s), basketball M(s)/W(s), crew W(s), cross-country running M(s)/W(s), field hockey W, golf M(s)/W(s), soccer M(s)/W(s), softball W(s), swimming and diving M(s)/W(s), tennis M(s)/W(s), track and field M(s)/W(s), volleyball W(s), water polo W(s), wrestling M(s). *Intramural sports:* archery M/W, badminton M(c)/W(c), baseball M/W, basketball M/W, bowling M(c)/W(c), crew M(c)/W(c), cross-country running M/W, equestrian sports M(c)/W(c), fencing M(c)/W(c), field hockey W(c), golf M/W, gymnastics M/W, ice hockey M/W, lacrosse M(c)/W, racquetball M(c)/W(c), riflery M(c)/W(c), rugby M(c)/W(c), sailing M(c)/W(c), skiing (downhill) M(c)/W(c), soccer M/W(c), softball M/W, squash M/W, swimming and diving M/W, table tennis M/W, tennis M(c)/W, track and field M/W, volleyball M/W, water polo M(c)/W, weight lifting M(c)/W(c), wrestling M(c).

Costs (2004–05) *Tuition:* state resident $5986 full-time, $187 per credit hour part-time; nonresident $17,799 full-time, $556 per credit hour part-time. Full-time tuition and fees vary according to location and program. Part-time tuition and fees vary according to course load, location, and program. *Required fees:* $791 full-time. *Room and board:* $6006; room only: $3616. Room and board charges vary according to board plan and housing facility.

Financial Aid 949 Federal Work-Study jobs (averaging $1511). In 2004, 1426 non-need-based awards were made. *Average percent of need met:* 54%. *Average financial aid package:* $6171. *Average need-based loan:* $3904. *Average need-based gift aid:* $4835. *Average non-need-based aid:* $3679.

Contact: Karen Hanson, Dean or Jill Baker, Director of Honors Admissions, Hutton Honors College, Indiana University, 324 North Jordan Avenue, Bloomington, Indiana 47405; *Telephone:* 812-855-3550; *Fax:* 812-855-5416; *E-mail:* hansonk@indiana.edu, babaker@indiana.edu; *Web site:* http://www.indiana.edu/~iubhonor

Indiana University–Purdue University Indianapolis

Honors Program

Indianapolis, Indiana

The Honors Program was developed in 1979 to enhance the evolvement of Indiana University–Purdue University Indianapolis (IUPUI) as a national leader among urban institutions, with its mission to promote excellence in research, teaching, and service. The Honors Program is located in University College, the academic unit that serves all incoming students. In emphasizing honors programming, IUPUI demonstrates its conviction that the creation of knowledge through research, the dissemination of knowledge through teaching, and the cultivation of knowledge through student learning are its principal values. Students are not required to pursue their degree with honors in order to participate in honors courses. To optimize opportunities for academic achievement, the Honors Program offers courses designed specifically for honors students, departmental courses for honors and highly motivated students in their majors, and honors independent research papers or projects. Students are also encouraged to participate in international study, field study, and the National Collegiate Honors Council (NCHC) Honors Semesters. Outstanding undergraduates, with the permission of their department, may earn honors credit by enrolling and successfully completing graduate course work.

In addition to academic enrichment, honors students, through the University College Reading Room, can access their personal e-mail and all of the research opportunities available in the University library. The room is equipped with an electronic scanner and software, enabling honors students to enhance their papers and presentations. It is also the meeting area for members of the Honors Club, who use it as a base for campus/club activities and personal socialization. Because the campus is located only six blocks from downtown Indianapolis, students have excellent opportunities for internships and partnerships with the city. The Honors Club annually cosponsors two campus blood drives with the Central Indiana Regional Blood Bank for the benefit of central Indiana citizens.

Upon completion of the honors requirements, Honors Program participants are awarded the following: mention at graduation, a medallion on a neck ribbon that is worn during graduation ceremonies, honors notations placed on the transcript and diploma, and certificates for outstanding service to Honors Club members.

Participation Requirements: All students graduating with general honors degrees must earn a minimum of 18 honors credit hours, an overall GPA of at least 3.3, and a minimum 3.3 GPA in all honors work. Students earning Departmental Honors must meet the additional requirements prescribed by their department. A third option, graduation with honors from one's school, is available to students in the Schools of Business, Nursing, and Public and Environmental Affairs.

Admission Process: Acceptance into the Honors Program is based on meeting one of the following qualifications: SAT I scores of at least 1200 (ACT scores of at least 26) and rank in the top 10 percent of one's high school class, a 3.0 or higher GPA earned in a minimum of 12 credit hours of course work, or transferring from another university with a 3.3 or higher GPA or from another university's Honors Program. Application to enroll in specific honors courses or independent study is also available to students with a strong interest or demonstrably high ability in a specific area of study. Academically gifted high school students who are admitted to IUPUI through the SPAN Program (based on high SAT I scores and part-time non-degree-student status) may apply to the program for permission to enroll in honors courses.

Scholarship Availability: The Honors Program offers a number of scholarships for incoming freshmen and continuing students. Some of these scholarships are renewable for one or three years, depending upon the student's continuing academic performance. Entering freshmen who score at least 1200 on the SAT I (26 on the ACT) and are in the top 10 percent of their class automatically receive an IUPUI Academic Excellence Scholarship of $1500 that is renewable for three years if the student attends full time and maintains a GPA of at least 3.0. The Honors Program also offers support for competitive student- and faculty-initiated undergraduate research proposals across the campus. Support is also available for students who are invited to present their research at local, state, or national conferences.

Campus Overview

State-supported university, founded 1969, part of Indiana University System • **Coed** 21,172 undergraduate students, 64% full-time, 59% women, 41% men.

Undergraduates 13,637 full-time, 7,535 part-time. Students come from 49 states and territories, 122 other countries, 2% are from out of state, 11% African American, 2% Asian American or Pacific Islander, 2% Hispanic American, 0.3% Native American, 2% international, 10% transferred in, 2% live on campus.

Faculty *Total:* 3,107, 70% full-time, 64% with terminal degrees. *Student/faculty ratio:* 17:1.

Academic Programs *Special study options:* academic remediation for entering students, adult/continuing education programs, advanced placement credit, cooperative education, distance learning, double majors, English as a second language, external degree program, honors programs, independent study, internships, off-campus study, part-time degree program, services for LD students, study abroad, summer session for credit. *ROTC:* Army (b), Navy (c), Air Force (c).

Athletics Member NCAA. All Division I. *Intercollegiate sports:* basketball M(s)/W(s), cross-country running M(s)/W(s), golf M(s)/W, soccer M(s)/W(s), softball W(s), swimming and diving M(s)/W(s), tennis M(s)/W(s), volleyball W(s). *Intramural sports:* badminton M/W, baseball M, basketball M/W, cross-country running M/W, football M, golf M/W, racquetball M/W, soccer M/W, softball M/W, swimming and diving M/W, table tennis M/W, tennis M/W, track and field M/W, volleyball M/W, water polo M/W.

Costs (2004–05) *Tuition:* state resident $5357 full-time, $179 per credit hour part-time; nonresident $15,194 full-time, $506 per credit hour part-time. Full-time tuition and fees vary according to course load and program. Part-time tuition and fees vary according to course load and program. *Required fees:* $573 full-time. *Room only:* $2656. Room and board charges vary according to board plan and housing facility.

Financial Aid 1,018 Federal Work-Study jobs (averaging $3422). In 2004, 395 non-need-based awards were made. *Average percent of need met:* 53%. *Average financial aid package:* $6811. *Average need-based loan:* $3772. *Average need-based gift aid:* $4597. *Average non-need-based aid:* $2622.

Contact: Director: E. Theodore Mullen Jr., UC3140, 815 West Michigan Street, Indianapolis, Indiana 46202-5164; *Telephone:* 317-274-2660; *Fax:* 317-274-2365; *E-mail:* emullen@iupui.edu; *Web site:* http://uc.iupui.edu

Indiana University South Bend
Honors Program
South Bend, Indiana

*T*hrough its Honors Program, Indiana University South Bend (IU South Bend) provides a special intellectual challenge for its keenest and most highly motivated undergraduates. Drawing upon the full range of resources that a large university can offer, this program encompasses a broad variety of classes, tutorials, and independent study opportunities. The program expects its most talented students to respond by engaging in academic pursuits that encourage them to strive for individual excellence in their University course of study.

Augmented by the 45 to 50 new students admitted each year, the program's annual participants number between 150 and 200.

Participation Requirements: Classes in the arts and humanities, business and economics, education, nursing, social and behavioral sciences, and science are offered. An Honors Program certificate is granted to students who have taken a minimum of 18 hours of credit in at least five honors-qualified courses (including the Freshman Honors Colloquium) and have completed an honors-qualified project under the individual mentoring of an IU South Bend faculty member.

Offered for the first time in 1996, the Freshman Honors Colloquium consists of lectures by distinguished faculty members from across the University and a weekend symposium spearheaded by a noted scholar. The faculty members chosen to make these ten presentations include the best teachers and scholars on the campus. Each honors student then prepares a 250–500 word response to the lecture/discussion and turns in a paper at the next lecture. Graduate students grade the papers and return them to the students on a weekly basis.

A weekend symposium led by a well-known scholar serves as the capstone event of the Colloquium. One week before the symposium, each honors student turns in a five-page opinion paper based on materials written by the scholar. After the weekend of presentations by the scholar, each honors student submits a twelve- to twenty-page research paper that examines a topic or issue generated by the symposium. All incoming freshman honors students are required to take this class. Although the 2 credit hours earned count toward the student's completion of the honors certificate, the course ordinarily does not fulfill the requirement that all students who receive an Honors Scholarship take at least one honors class during the year.

Admission Process: Admission to the Honors Program and its classes is open to all qualified students (those with an overall GPA of 3.3 or higher), including part-time students and those who enter the University several years after leaving high school, without restriction with regard to school, major, or class standing.

Scholarship Availability: Several scholarships available only to Honors Program participants are awarded each year. A few particularly promising incoming honors students receive IU South Bend Alumni Association Scholarships, which cover the students' tuition and mandatory fees during the freshman year. These scholarships, as well as the IU South Bend Honors Scholarship, are awarded to entering freshmen who fulfill at least two of the following three criteria: a score of 1200 or above on the SAT, a class rank in the top 10 percent of their high school graduating class, and the attainment of an overall high school GPA of at least 3.5 (on a 4.0 scale). These scholarships also are available to transfer students who enter with a cumulative GPA of 3.5 or higher. Annual continuation of these scholarships is based on students' attaining a cumulative GPA of 3.5 or above and the completion of at least one honors course during the academic year. To remain in the program, nonscholarship recipients must maintain at least a 3.3 cumulative GPA. Because the honors scholarships are tuition specific, the University administration requires the filing of the Free Application for Federal Student Aid (FAFSA) and the IU South Bend Financial Aid forms as a condition precedent for receiving (and then retaining) these scholarships.

Campus Overview

State-supported comprehensive, founded 1922, part of Indiana University System • **Coed** 6,322 undergraduate students, 56% full-time, 63% women, 37% men.

Undergraduates 3,544 full-time, 2,778 part-time. Students come from 13 states and territories, 2% are from out of state, 7% African American, 1% Asian American or Pacific Islander, 3% Hispanic American, 0.5% Native American, 2% international, 9% transferred in.

Faculty *Total:* 551, 53% full-time, 42% with terminal degrees. *Student/faculty ratio:* 14:1.

Academic Programs *Special study options:* accelerated degree program, adult/continuing education programs, distance learning, double majors, English as a second language, external degree program, honors programs, internships, off-campus study, part-time degree program, study abroad, summer session for credit. *ROTC:* Army (c), Navy (c), Air Force (c).

Athletics Member NAIA. *Intercollegiate sports:* basketball M(s)/W(s). *Intramural sports:* badminton M/W, baseball M, basketball M/W, cross-country running M/W, golf M/W, racquetball M/W, soccer M/W, volleyball M/W.

Costs (2004–05) *Tuition:* state resident $4349 full-time, $145 per credit hour part-time; nonresident $11,420 full-time, $381 per credit hour part-time. Full-time tuition and fees vary according to course load. Part-time tuition and fees vary according to course load. *Required fees:* $406 full-time.

Financial Aid 70 Federal Work-Study jobs (averaging $2339). In 2004, 57 non-need-based awards were made. *Average percent of need met:* 57%. *Average financial aid package:* $5636. *Average need-based loan:* $3318. *Average need-based gift aid:* $4013. *Average non-need-based aid:* $1170.

Contact: Director: Dr. Brenda E. Knowles, 1700 Mishawaka Avenue, P.O. Box 7111, Administration Building 206(a), South Bend, Indiana 46634-7111; *Telephone:* 574-520-4355; *Fax:* 574-520-4866; *E-mail:* bknowles@iusb.edu

Indiana Wesleyan University
John Wesley Honors College
Marion, Indiana

*T*he Honors College offers a select group of students a challenging academic environment in which to maximize their intellectual potential and prepare to impact society for Christ as thoughtful and articulate servant leaders. John Wesley Scholars participate in a distinctive curriculum that allows them to satisfy several general education and major requirements by taking special honors courses. These courses have a low student-faculty ratio and emphasize independent thinking and research, in-class discussion, and creative ways of mastering course material. John Wesley Scholars are also permitted to take part in many unique extracurricular activities, including Honors College Forum (a series of stimulating and thought-provoking cultural events that give students access to highly regarded scholars and leaders, as well as the chance to experience a broad spectrum of music and the arts).

Participation Requirements: Upon the completion of 18 credit hours of honors courses, four semesters of Honors College Forum, and a faculty-supervised research thesis or creative project, students are eligible to receive an Honors College degree and special recognition at graduation.

Admission Process: Students are admitted to the Honors College through a competitive application process. In order to apply, one must be accepted into Indiana Wesleyan University, possess a combined score of at least 1250 on the SAT or 28 on the ACT, hold at least a 3.6 high school GPA or class rank in the top 10 percent, and desire to participate in an interdisciplinary community of committed learners.

Scholarship Availability: Eighty-two percent of Indiana Wesleyan students receive financial aid from the University.

Campus Overview

Independent Wesleyan comprehensive, founded 1920 • **Coed** 7,609 undergraduate students, 91% full-time, 64% women, 36% men.

Undergraduates 6,908 full-time, 701 part-time. Students come from 37 states and territories, 1 other country, 30% are from out of state, 13% African American, 0.8% Asian American or Pacific Islander, 2% Hispanic American, 0.4% Native American, 0.3% international.

Faculty *Total:* 148, 100% full-time, 45% with terminal degrees.

Academic Programs *Special study options:* academic remediation for entering students, accelerated degree program, adult/continuing education programs, advanced placement credit, distance learning, double majors, freshman honors college, honors programs, independent study, internships, off-campus study, part-time degree program, services for LD students, student-designed majors, study abroad, summer session for credit.

Athletics Member NAIA, NCCAA. *Intercollegiate sports:* baseball M(s), basketball M(s)/W(s), cheerleading M(s)/W(s), cross-country running M(s)/W(s), golf M(s), soccer M(s)/W(s), softball W(s), tennis M(s)/W(s), track and field M(s)/W(s), volleyball W(s). *Intramural sports:* badminton M/W, basketball M/W, bowling M/W, football M/W, golf M/W, racquetball M/W, soccer M/W, softball M, table tennis M/W, tennis M/W, ultimate Frisbee M/W, volleyball M/W, weight lifting M/W.

Costs (2005–06) *Comprehensive fee:* $22,074 includes full-time tuition ($16,184) and room and board ($5890). Part-time tuition: $515 per credit hour. *College room only:* $2800.

Contact: Director: Dr. David Riggs, Indiana Wesleyan University, 4201 South Washington Street, Marion, Indiana 46953; *Telephone:* 765-677-2808; *Fax:* 765-677-1539; *E-mail:* david.riggs@indwes.edu; *Web site:* http://jwhc.indwes.edu/

Manchester College

Honors Program

North Manchester, Indiana

Manchester College has developed the Honors Program to encourage and stimulate students who are seriously interested in expanding their educational opportunities. Currently, more than 10 percent of the student body participates in the Honors Program. Those involved say they enjoy the freedom to study in their own style. At Manchester College, those who become honors students often share common traits. They are self-disciplined, creative, and organized. They are motivated, with a strong desire to learn. They want to do their best. They know that when they expand their minds and move beyond the norm, they expand their opportunities. Unlike some honors programs at other colleges, Manchester honors students aren't set apart from other students. On Manchester's campus, honors students are involved in many campus activities. One current student participates in the Accounting Club, Hispanos Unidos, Modern Languages Club, and is on the women's golf team. Another is a member of the Student Education Association, the Honors Organization, and the cross-country and track teams. A third student worked with the Manchester College Mediation and Reconciliation Team, Manchester Activities Council, and founded TUNSIS, a residential theme unit in Oakwook Hall for students interested in the relationships between science and society. Participants in the Honors

Program may sign up for honors courses offered each year; convert regular courses for honors credit; choose to write an Honors Thesis, earning 6 credits toward graduation and public recognition at commencement; earn an Honors Diploma; show graduate schools and employers their accomplishments, because all honors courses are marked on their transcripts; and participate in off-campus cultural events sponsored by the Student Honors Organization. In the 2001–02 academic year, 130 students participated in the program.

Participation Requirements: Honors program participants must maintain a GPA of 3.5 or higher and complete at least 5 semester hours of honors work per academic year. Honors status is maintained for up to a full year for students participating in an approved off-campus program. A small percentage of honors students choose to complete the Honors Diploma. This diploma testifies to the student's ability both to do broad-based study and to plan and complete a significant project associated with the student's major. Requirements for the diploma include a distribution of honors courses and an Honors Thesis.

Admission Process: There are two ways to be admitted to the Honors Program. First, students can be admitted as first-year students. Highly qualified students automatically receive an application for the Honors Program. Such students typically have excellent standardized test scores (an SAT I of 1200 or above, for example) and class rank (generally in the top 5 percent) or other qualifications that indicate strong academic potential. Second, students can apply after starting at Manchester College. Current students can qualify once they have accumulated 28 semester hours of Manchester College credit and have a cumulative GPA of at least 3.5. Transfer students with sophomore standing and a cumulative GPA of at least 3.5 after 12 semester hours of Manchester College credit may also apply.

Scholarship Availability: Nearly all Manchester College Honors Program students receive merit-based scholarships that are awarded through the Offices of Admissions and Financial Aid. While participation in the Honors Program is not a condition for these awards, most of the College's top scholars actively pursue honors work.

Campus Overview

Independent comprehensive, founded 1889, affiliated with Church of the Brethren • **Coed** 1,056 undergraduate students, 95% full-time, 55% women, 45% men.

Undergraduates 1,004 full-time, 52 part-time. Students come from 23 states and territories, 29 other countries, 10% are from out of state, 3% African American, 0.8% Asian American or Pacific Islander, 2% Hispanic American, 0.7% Native American, 7% international, 4% transferred in, 74% live on campus.

Faculty *Total:* 73, 77% full-time, 89% with terminal degrees. *Student/faculty ratio:* 14:1.

Academic Programs *Special study options:* adult/continuing education programs, advanced placement credit, double majors, honors programs, independent study, internships, off-campus study, part-time degree program, services for LD students, student-designed majors, study abroad, summer session for credit. *Unusual degree programs:* 3-2 engineering with Washington University in St. Louis; nursing with Goshen College; physical therapy, occupational therapy.

Athletics Member NCAA. All Division III. *Intercollegiate sports:* baseball M, basketball M/W, cheerleading M/W, cross-country running M/W, football M, golf M/W, soccer M/W, softball W, tennis M/W, track and field M/W, volleyball W, wrestling M. *Intramural sports:* badminton M/W, basketball M/W, bowling M/W, football M/W, racquetball M/W, soccer M/W, table tennis M/W, tennis M/W, track and field M/W, ultimate Frisbee M/W, volleyball M/W.

Costs (2005–06) *Comprehensive fee:* $26,270 includes full-time tuition ($18,750), mandatory fees ($610), and room and board ($6910). *College room only:* $4250. Room and board charges vary according to board plan and housing facility.

Financial Aid In 2003, 100 non-need-based awards were made. *Average percent of need met:* 93%. *Average financial aid package:*

$17,269. *Average need-based loan:* $3661. *Average need-based gift aid:* $13,395. *Average non-need-based aid:* $7416.

Contact: Director: Dr. Diane Monaco, Manchester College, 604 East College Avenue, North Manchester, Indiana 46962; *Telephone:* 260-982-5301; *Fax:* 260-982-5043; *E-mail:* dkmonaco@manchester. edu; *Web site:* http://www.manchester.edu/

Purdue University
Honors Program
West Lafayette, Indiana

Purdue University offers a wide range of honors experiences, and its two largest colleges, the College of Engineering and the College of Liberal Arts, offer many varied opportunities for honors work. Many departments throughout the University also have special honors tracks of their own, so that some students at Purdue are able to graduate with departmental, College, and University honors.

The College of Liberal Arts Honors Program is designed to foster excellence and intellectual curiosity and to provide a rich, stimulating, and challenging educational experience for creative and highly motivated students throughout the University. The program offers both Honors Only courses (courses with limited enrollment, stressing close student-faculty interaction) and Honors Option courses, in which students enroll in regular courses but are provided with special honors experiences. Advanced students in the program design their own honors work through Honors by Special Arrangement, through which they arrange individual honors projects with professors and tailor their honors experiences to their particular personal and professional interests. Many students become part of their professors' research teams, refining their skills by participating in major research projects and contributing to their field long before graduation. Each year, the program sponsors an Honors Colloquium, featuring outstanding undergraduate work in the College, and students often go on to present their work at regional and national professional conferences.

Students in the Liberal Arts Honors Program also enjoy a wide range of supplementary activities through the Honors Experience. These include special information sessions, often led by members of the Honors Council; meals with visiting speakers; and reduced-price tickets to a wide variety of concerts, plays, films, lectures, special exhibitions, and other experiences on and off campus. Members of the Honors Council help to determine the program's activities and events each year and sponsor numerous opportunities for community service work in the greater Lafayette area.

Founded in 1979, the College of Liberal Arts Honors Program involves more than 800 students, with approximately 500 students actively taking courses each semester.

The Freshman Engineering Honors Program is designed to provide the highly motivated and academically successful student with a broader and more enriched educational experience during his or her freshman year. The program is intended to cultivate the inquisitive nature of its participants by allowing them to explore, expand, and excel in a curriculum, which promotes both scholastic achievement and breadth of knowledge.

Begun in 1958, the Freshman Engineering Honors Program traditionally enrolls approximately 160 students each year.

Both programs provide students with a small-school environment while enjoying the resources of many of the nation's top programs. Honors students in these programs have the opportunity to enroll in smaller classes, to form relationships with other high-achieving students, and to develop strong, personal relationships with faculty members and advisers. Students in the Freshman Engineering Honors Program are also able to interact with professional engineers in industry, both on campus and during visits to industrial sites. The Freshman Engineering Honors Program stresses team-based learning, an approach that presents students with hands-on projects that allow application and demonstration of knowledge. All courses taken for honors are noted on the students' transcripts.

In fall 2005, Purdue University will inaugurate a University-wide honors program whose students may be enrolled in any undergraduate curriculum. Admission is by invitation, with an initial enrollment of approximately 140 first-year students drawn from across the University. Program requirements may be met by a combination of courses specially developed by the University Honors Program curriculum committee, honors courses in the colleges, and honors-level study-abroad courses. A scholarly activity/project is an integral part of every University Honors student's plan of study. Students who successfully complete the program requirements, as certified by the Director of the UHP, will receive a University honors diploma at graduation.

Participation Requirements: Students in the College of Liberal Arts Honors Program may take as many honors courses as they wish. To maintain honors eligibility, students must maintain a minimum 3.0 GPA. For Full Honors, students must graduate with a 3.3 GPA, take a minimum of 24 hours of honors credit, and fulfill the distribution requirements of the College honors degree.

Students in the College of Engineering Honors Program must successfully complete the following requirements: enroll in and complete 7 credit hours of honors and/or honors-designated courses each semester of the freshman year, earn a 3.4 cumulative GPA at the end of that year, and be active in at least one student organization throughout the year.

Admission Process: To take honors courses in the College of Liberal Arts, entering students must have graduated in the top 10 percent of their high school class or have a composite ACT score of 27 or above or a combined SAT I score of 1150 or above. No special application is required. Students arrange to enroll in honors courses through their counselors.

Students interested in the Freshman Engineering Honors Program must meet one of the following eligibility requirements: be a Merit Scholarship recipient (which includes but is not limited to National Merit Finalist or Scholar Award, Beering Scholar Award, Dean's Engineering Scholar Award, Minority Engineering Program Honors Merit Award, or Women in Engineering Program Honors Merit Award); or have an SAT of 1360 (or an equivalent ACT of 31) or above and be in the top 10 percent of their high school class (or have a GPA of 3.8 or above at schools that do not provide rankings).

Scholarship Availability: Most honors students receive one of the many academic or talent scholarships offered by the Division of Financial Aid. Purdue grants an Academic Success Award, which is based solely on the SAT or ACT score and class rank and is automatically awarded with admission. There are also major scholarships ranging from the Beering Scholars Program for the 80–100 top high school seniors who have been admitted by the first week in December (full financial support through graduate school at Purdue), the Indiana Resident Top Scholar Award (150 awards covering eight semesters of undergraduate study), National Merit Finalist Scholarships, and Valedictorian Scholarships.

Three specific scholarships are dedicated to beginning engineering students: the Dean's Engineering Scholarship, the Women in Engineering Scholarship, and the Minority Engineering Scholarship. These scholarships require a separate application, including essays. All Dean's Engineering Scholarship winners are also automatically eligible for additional merit scholarships, often dependent upon the student's chosen specialty.

In addition, the College of Liberal Arts offers approximately forty merit-based scholarships for entering students in the Clarence E. Dammon Dean's Scholar Program, which offers students the opportunity to work one-on-one with professors in various departments while earning $1000 stipends. These awards require a separate application, including essays and recommendations. The Honors Program also offers limited additional merit-based scholarships for upper-level students in the program.

Campus Overview

State-supported university, founded 1869, part of Purdue University System • **Coed** 30,747 undergraduate students, 94% full-time, 41% women, 59% men.

Undergraduates 28,954 full-time, 1,793 part-time. Students come from 53 states and territories, 98 other countries, 26% are from out of state, 3% African American, 5% Asian American or Pacific Islander, 2% Hispanic American, 0.4% Native American, 6% international, 4% transferred in, 34% live on campus.

Faculty *Total:* 2,224, 86% full-time, 97% with terminal degrees. *Student/faculty ratio:* 15:1.

Academic Programs *Special study options:* accelerated degree program, adult/continuing education programs, advanced placement credit, cooperative education, distance learning, double majors, English as a second language, freshman honors college, honors programs, independent study, internships, part-time degree program, services for LD students, study abroad, summer session for credit. *ROTC:* Army (b), Navy (b), Air Force (b). *Unusual degree programs:* pharmacy.

Athletics Member NCAA. All Division I except football (Division I-A). *Intercollegiate sports:* baseball M(s), basketball M(s)/W(s), cross-country running M(s)/W(s), golf M(s)/W(s), soccer W(s), softball W(s), swimming and diving M(s)/W(s), tennis M(s)/W(s), track and field M(s)/W(s), volleyball W(s), wrestling M(s). *Intramural sports:* badminton M(c)/W(c), basketball M/W, bowling M/W, crew M(c)/W(c), cross-country running M/W, equestrian sports M(c)/W(c), fencing M(c)/W(c), football M/W, golf M/W, gymnastics M(c)/W(c), ice hockey M(c), lacrosse M(c)/W(c), racquetball M(c)/W(c), riflery M(c)/W(c), rock climbing M(c)/W(c), rugby M(c)/W(c), sailing M(c)/W(c), soccer M(c)/W(c), softball M/W, squash M/W, swimming and diving M/W, table tennis M/W, tennis M/W, track and field M/W, ultimate Frisbee M(c)/W(c), volleyball M(c)/W(c), water polo M(c)/W(c), weight lifting M/W.

Costs (2005–06) *Tuition:* state resident $6335 full-time, $227 per credit part-time; nonresident $19,822 full-time, $658 per credit part-time. Full-time tuition and fees vary according to course load and program. Part-time tuition and fees vary according to course load. *Room and board:* $7406. Room and board charges vary according to board plan and housing facility.

Financial Aid 1,290 Federal Work-Study jobs (averaging $1742). In 2004, 3764 non-need-based awards were made. *Average percent of need met:* 90%. *Average financial aid package:* $9426. *Average need-based loan:* $4022. *Average need-based gift aid:* $7630. *Average non-need-based aid:* $10,865.

Contact: Director: Professor James Nairne, College of Liberal Arts, Honors Program, Purdue University, BANG 1175, 100 North University Street, West Lafayette, Indiana 47907-2098; *Telephone:* 765-494-5847, 765-494-3235; *Fax:* 765-494-1910; *E-mail:* nairne@cla.purdue.edu; *Web site:* http://www.cla.purdue.edu/studentserv/honors. Director: Professor Christian Y. Oseto, University Honors Program, Young Hall 144, Purdue University, West Lafayette, Indiana 47907; *Phone:* 765-494-2901. Freshman Engineering Honors Program, 1286 Engineering Administration, Purdue University, West Lafayette, Indiana 47907; *Telephone:* 800-440-9885 (toll-free); *Fax:* 765-494-5819; *E-mail:* frehonor@ecn.purdue.edu; *Web site:* http://engineering.Purdue.edu/ENE/specialprograms/firstyear/honors

University of Evansville

Honors Program

Evansville, Indiana

The University of Evansville Honors Program admits bright, talented students who have the desire to excel scholastically in a stimulating academic environment. The program challenges students to maximize their potential in all areas of study and offers an enhanced curriculum with the opportunity to share ideas and viewpoints with other outstanding students. The program attracts students from all majors and fosters independent thinking. All honors students seek a significant challenge from their professors as well as from each other. Participation in the Honors Program provides students with a rewarding college experience both in and out of the classroom.

Honors classes are interdisciplinary and are taught across the curriculum. Students in the Honors Program are able to enroll in any honors class regardless of major. The student research project is intended to serve as the capstone of the program and is presented at the University of Evansville, at a regional conference, or at the National Undergraduate Conference for Undergraduate Research. Among the many benefits of participating in the program is optional honor student housing and priority class registration.

Currently, 230 students are participating in the program.

Participation Requirements: Honors students are required to earn a minimum of 21 points through taking honors courses, attending honors activities, conducting student research, participating in study abroad, and internships. Students must also maintain a minimum 3.5 overall GPA.

Admission Process: Entering freshman students who have an SAT of 1970 or higher (SAT 1300 or higher if taken prior to March 2005) or an ACT of 30 or higher or a weighted high school GPA of 3.75 or higher are invited to apply to the program, as are incoming transfer students with a college GPA of 3.5 or higher. Students are selected on the basis of an Honors Program application, sample essay, standardized test scores, grade point average, strength of high school or college curriculum, and extracurricular activities. Applications are accepted on a rolling basis until early April or until the honors class is full.

Scholarship Availability: Scholarships ranging from $5000 to full tuition per year are available, although they are not restricted to Honors Program participants. The average merit-based scholarship for Honors Program freshmen enrolling in 2004 was $13,000. (Note: This is only the amount of merit scholarship received and does not include other forms of financial aid.) The average award of aid from all sources for the entire freshman class was $16,000 in 2004.

Campus Overview

Independent comprehensive, founded 1854, affiliated with United Methodist Church • **Coed** 2,632 undergraduate students, 87% full-time, 61% women, 39% men.

Undergraduates 2,293 full-time, 339 part-time. Students come from 42 states and territories, 38 other countries, 35% are from out of state, 2% African American, 1% Asian American or Pacific Islander, 1% Hispanic American, 0.3% Native American, 5% international, 3% transferred in, 67% live on campus.

Faculty *Total:* 229, 74% full-time. *Student/faculty ratio:* 13:1.

Academic Programs *Special study options:* accelerated degree program, adult/continuing education programs, advanced placement credit, cooperative education, distance learning, double majors, English as a second language, external degree program, freshman honors college, honors programs, independent study, internships, part-time degree program, services for LD students, student-designed majors, study abroad, summer session for credit.

Athletics Member NCAA. All Division I. *Intercollegiate sports:* baseball M(s), basketball M(s)/W(s), cross-country running M(s)/W(s), golf M(s), soccer M(s)/W(s), softball W(s), swimming and diving M(s)/W(s), tennis W(s), volleyball W(s). *Intramural sports:* badminton M/W, basketball M/W, bowling M/W, cheerleading M/W, cross-country running M/W, football M/W, golf M/W, racquetball M/W, soccer M/W, softball M/W, swimming and diving M/W, table tennis M/W, tennis M/W, track and field M/W, ultimate Frisbee M/W, volleyball M/W.

Costs (2004–05) *Comprehensive fee:* $26,525 includes full-time tuition ($19,995), mandatory fees ($520), and room and board

($6010). Part-time tuition: $550 per hour. Part-time tuition and fees vary according to course load. *Required fees:* $35 per term part-time. *College room only:* $2820. Room and board charges vary according to board plan and housing facility.

Financial Aid 412 Federal Work-Study jobs (averaging $1288). 80 state and other part-time jobs (averaging $1260). In 2004, 511 non-need-based awards were made. *Average percent of need met:* 90%. *Average financial aid package:* $18,532. *Average need-based loan:* $4595. *Average need-based gift aid:* $13,909. *Average non-need-based aid:* $9203.

Contact: Director of Honors Program: Dr. William Connolly, Director of Scholar Recruitment: Cherie Leonhardt, 1800 Lincoln Avenue, Evansville, Indiana 47722; *Telephone:* 812-488-2468, 800-423-8633 (Ext. 2468) (toll-free); *Fax:* 812-474-4076; *E-mail:* dc25@evansville. edu, cl29@evansville.edu; *Web site:* http://www.evansville.edu

University of Southern Indiana
University Honors Program
Evansville, Indiana

The Honors Program at the University of Southern Indiana (USI) is designed to offer expanded opportunities for those students who show promise of outstanding academic achievement. Participation in the program exposes students to a wider range of intellectual and academic experience, provides enriching extracurricular activities, promotes rewarding interaction between students and honors faculty members, and gives students the opportunity to form lasting friendships with other students who are committed to academic excellence. The Honors Program curriculum serves to supplement and enrich the students' overall experience within any of the University's major fields of study. Honors classes are generally smaller in size, providing increased class participation and discussion. Students in the program grow through special classes that stress the interrelatedness of knowledge, skill in oral and written communication of ideas, and methods and techniques for the analysis, synthesis, and evaluation of information. In addition to priority registration, honors students have the opportunity to live in honors housing and make use of an honors common room, which is used for study, informal meetings, classes, and programs the students themselves plan. Participation in honors housing, especially during the freshman year, also facilitates the very helpful mentoring program sponsored by the Student Honors Council. The designation of University Honors Scholar is awarded to those students who successfully complete the honors curriculum, a distinction that is noted on both the diploma and the official transcript.

Some departments offer students the further opportunity to combine Program Honors with Departmental Honors. The course requirements for Departmental Honors are specific to each major that offers this option. Students may choose to complete both Program and Departmental Honors by arrangement with the Director of Honors, the department chairperson, and the individual professor. These students receive a diploma that documents their accomplishment as a University Honors Scholar and designates their graduation with Distinction in the Major.

Participation Requirements: Typically, honors students enroll in specially designated sections of courses taken either from the University Core Curriculum or from the student's major. Students generally take one or two honors courses in a given semester as part of their normal progress toward the baccalaureate degree. To receive an honors diploma, students must complete their undergraduate work with a cumulative GPA of 3.25 or above and complete a minimum of 21 hours of honors credit with grades of A or B—including a 1-hour freshman colloquium and an honors component to their 3-hour senior synthesis course.

Admission Process: Students who have earned an SAT score of 1200 or an ACT composite of 27 or higher are immediately accepted into the Honors Program. Other interested students are encouraged to apply. Evaluations of these students are made on the basis of cumulative GPA, class rank, academic background, and extracurricular activities. Students who have completed a minimum of 15 semester hours at USI or elsewhere with a minimum cumulative GPA of 3.25 may apply as space permits.

Scholarship Availability: USI has numerous merit scholarships at the departmental, college, and University level. As an ongoing service, honors students are provided with assistance in identifying and applying for these scholarships and awards. Most honors students are recipients of scholarships.

Campus Overview

State-supported comprehensive, founded 1965, part of Indiana Commission for Higher Education • **Coed** 9,217 undergraduate students, 81% full-time, 60% women, 40% men.

Undergraduates 7,426 full-time, 1,791 part-time. Students come from 34 states and territories, 34 other countries, 9% are from out of state, 5% African American, 0.6% Asian American or Pacific Islander, 0.7% Hispanic American, 0.2% Native American, 0.5% international, 7% transferred in, 31% live on campus.

Faculty *Total:* 576, 51% full-time, 41% with terminal degrees. *Student/faculty ratio:* 19:1.

Academic Programs *Special study options:* academic remediation for entering students, adult/continuing education programs, advanced placement credit, cooperative education, distance learning, double majors, English as a second language, honors programs, independent study, internships, part-time degree program, services for LD students, study abroad, summer session for credit. *ROTC:* Army (b).

Athletics Member NCAA. All Division II. *Intercollegiate sports:* baseball M(s), basketball M(s)/W(s), cheerleading M/W, cross-country running M(s)/W(s), golf M(s)/W(s), ice hockey M(c), rugby M(c), soccer M(s)/W(s), softball W(s), tennis M(s)/W(s), ultimate Frisbee M(c)/W(c), volleyball W(s). *Intramural sports:* badminton M/W, basketball M/W, bowling M/W, football M/W, golf M/W, rock climbing M/W, skiing (downhill) M/W, soccer M/W, softball M/W, table tennis M/W, tennis M/W, volleyball M/W.

Costs (2005–06) *Tuition:* state resident $4017 full-time, $132 per semester hour part-time; nonresident $9582 full-time, $319 per semester hour part-time. Full-time tuition and fees vary according to course load and reciprocity agreements. Part-time tuition and fees vary according to course load and reciprocity agreements. *Required fees:* $60 full-time, $23 per term part-time. *Room and board:* $5480; room only: $3000. Room and board charges vary according to board plan and housing facility.

Financial Aid 146 Federal Work-Study jobs (averaging $1574). In 2004, 495 non-need-based awards were made. *Average percent of need met:* 57%. *Average financial aid package:* $5452. *Average need-based loan:* $3108. *Average need-based gift aid:* $4233. *Average non-need-based aid:* $2139.

Contact: Dr. Dane Partridge, Director of Honors, University of Southern Indiana, 8600 University Boulevard, Evansville, Indiana 47712; *Fax:* 812-465-1044; *E-mail:* dpartrid@usi.edu

Valparaiso University
Christ College, the Honors College
Valparaiso, Indiana

Christ College is the Honors College of Valparaiso University (VU). Established in 1967, Christ College celebrates forty years of providing honors-level, interdisciplinary study to academically talented students. The curriculum, taught by master teacher-scholars, emphasizes the liberal arts and the humanities. In the tradition of those colleges, Christ College is dedicated to the cultivation of intellectual, moral, and spiritual virtues. The College's name also suggests its accord with VU's goal of academic excellence in a Christian context.

All Christ College (CC) students are concurrently enrolled in one of VU's other colleges—Arts and Sciences, Business Administration, Engineering, or Nursing—where they earn their bachelor's degrees. Study in Christ College complements all academic programs, and many CC courses fulfill the University's general education requirements. Christ College honors courses invite the more intellectually curious student into the rigors and rewards of the life of the mind by offering an integrated approach to university studies and subtler methods of independent inquiry.

The Honors College is located in Mueller Hall, a modern building at the center of VU's campus, with a state-of-the-art multimedia lecture hall, comfortable classrooms and seminar rooms, faculty offices, presentation space, and a gracious fireside commons/art gallery. The College has its own dean, associate dean/academic adviser, and 10 full-time faculty members. Direct and personal relationships are promoted between students and faculty members as they create together a distinctive learning community in and out of the classroom.

The nationally respected Christ College Freshman Program is a two-semester study of great works of history, literature, philosophy, and religion, from the earliest writings to the present day in both Western and Eastern traditions. Critical reading, writing, and discussion are emphasized. To balance the critical and literary focus of the discussion classes, the program also meets one evening each week for group activities connected with the fine and performing arts. During the fall semester, these sessions culminate in the Christ College Freshman Production, an original dramatic-musical performance, based on ideas and themes discussed in the program, and written and produced entirely by students. Oxford Union–style debates of significant current issues are the focus of the spring semester.

Typical sophomore courses include study of selected classic intellectual and literary texts and their relationships to works of art, an exploration of the nature and purpose of Christian theology, and attention to central theories and issues of interpretation in the humanities, social sciences, or natural sciences. Junior/senior-level students choose from a variety of topical interdisciplinary seminars. A senior capstone course provides an integrative experience in which students give shape to the substance of their lives through autobiographical narrative and reflect upon the character and meaning of their future work. Seniors prepare resumes and are closely advised in applying to professional and graduate schools.

Approximately 80 first-year students are accepted for membership in Christ College as they enter Valparaiso University. Total Christ College enrollment is 310 students.

Participation Requirements: Christ College students are concurrently enrolled in one of Valparaiso University's other colleges: Arts and Sciences, Business Administration, Engineering, or Nursing. The Christ College curriculum, which complements all academic programs and meets many general education requirements, extends from freshman year to graduation. The yearlong 16-credit CC Freshman Program meets the University's core requirements for first-year students. CC sophomores, juniors, and seniors typically earn 3 to 7 additional credits in honors courses each year. Undergraduate research, independent study, and the writing of an honors essay or thesis are encouraged. A student who successfully completes 38 credit hours in a sequence of Christ College courses receives the designation Christ College Scholar upon graduation from Valparaiso University. A graduate with 30 credits is designated Christ College Associate. Students are expected to maintain a 3.3 (B+) or better GPA in all University course work and in CC courses. Successful students receive the transcript designation Christ College Scholar or Christ College Associate upon graduation. Seniors are honored at a banquet at which honors medallions are presented. Christ College also offers a complementary major in humanities, a minor in humanities, and a joint admissions program with the Valparaiso University School of Law.

Admission Process: Students admitted to Valparaiso University who have demonstrated academic excellence in high school, strong SAT or ACT scores, intellectual curiosity and creativity, and leadership in extracurricular activities are identified by the Office of Admission for review by Christ College. A CC faculty committee and the CC Dean review the students' VU applications, giving particular attention to performance in high school AP and honors courses and to the application essay. Qualified students are then invited to apply to Christ College. Decisions on acceptance are made by the CC Dean after reviewing the CC applications. Approximately 80 first-year students are accepted for membership each year. The Christ College freshman class of 2004–05 presented combined average SAT I scores of 1395 and average English ACT scores of 32. Admissions are on a rolling basis. VU upperclass students and transfer students with superior records of academic achievement may be invited to join CC after the freshman year.

Scholarship Availability: Valparaiso University offers merit scholarships and awards for students with special academic talents, interests, abilities, or backgrounds. Christ College does not award regular academic scholarships of its own, though most honors college students are the recipients of academic scholarships. Generous funding for undergraduate research and conference presentations as well as support for special student projects is available to Christ College students.

Campus Overview

Independent comprehensive, founded 1859, affiliated with Lutheran Church • **Coed** 3,067 undergraduate students, 94% full-time, 53% women, 47% men.

Undergraduates 2,897 full-time, 170 part-time. Students come from 49 states and territories, 32 other countries, 65% are from out of state, 4% African American, 2% Asian American or Pacific Islander, 3% Hispanic American, 0.2% Native American, 1% international, 3% transferred in, 65% live on campus.

Faculty *Total:* 362, 65% full-time, 76% with terminal degrees. *Student/faculty ratio:* 13:1.

Academic Programs *Special study options:* accelerated degree program, adult/continuing education programs, advanced placement credit, cooperative education, distance learning, double majors, English as a second language, freshman honors college, honors programs, independent study, internships, off-campus study, part-time degree program, services for LD students, student-designed majors, study abroad, summer session for credit. *ROTC:* Air Force (b).

Athletics Member NCAA. All Division I. *Intercollegiate sports:* baseball M(s), basketball M(s)/W(s), cross-country running M(s)/W(s), football M, soccer M(s)/W(s), softball W(s), swimming and diving M(s)/W(s), tennis M(s)/W(s), volleyball W(s). *Intramural sports:* badminton M/W, baseball M, basketball M/W, bowling M/W, cheerleading M/W, football M/W, golf M/W, ice hockey M(c), racquetball M/W, soccer M/W, softball M/W, swimming and diving M/W, table tennis M/W, tennis M/W, track and field M/W, ultimate Frisbee M(c)/W(c), volleyball M/W, water polo M.

Costs (2004–05) *Comprehensive fee:* $27,540 includes full-time tuition ($21,000), mandatory fees ($700), and room and board ($5840). Part-time tuition: $925 per credit hour. Part-time tuition and fees vary according to course load. *Required fees:* $60 per term part-time. *College room only:* $3690. Room and board charges vary according to housing facility and student level.

Financial Aid 437 Federal Work-Study jobs (averaging $915). 850 state and other part-time jobs (averaging $1294). In 2004, 642 non-need-based awards were made. *Average percent of need met:* 93%. *Average financial aid package:* $18,419. *Average need-based loan:* $5128. *Average need-based gift aid:* $12,778. *Average non-need-based aid:* $8720.

Contact: Dean: Dr. Mel Piehl, Christ College, Valparaiso University, Valparaiso, Indiana 46383-6493; *Telephone:* 219-464-5022; *Fax:* 219-464-5159; *E-mail:* christ.college@valpo.edu; *Web site:* http://www.valpo.edu/christc

IOWA

Clarke College
Honors Program
Dubuque, Iowa

The Clarke College Honors Program offers enriched educational opportunities to Clarke's exceptional students. The Honors Program is designed to invigorate students to deepen the love of learning, build supportive relationships with peers and faculty members, and foster global awareness and social responsibility.

Honors courses are offered each semester on a rotating basis. They are all general education courses drawn from the four liberal arts divisions of the College (humanities, fine arts, social sciences, and natural sciences) and from foundational studies (Honors Cornerstone, philosophy, and religious studies). Honors courses do not add extra hours to general education requirements, and they provide academic rigor suitable to challenge and encourage honors students to excel. Honors contract courses are also available to students.

Each honors course provides opportunities to meet outside the classroom for educationally related activities. Students have attended concerts, film festivals, and public lectures and have participated in service-learning projects. First-year students in the Honors Cornerstone course attend the Upper Midwest Honors Council conference in the spring. All of these activities are fully funded by the Honors Program.

Students in the Honors Program have many hands-on research opportunities, and each spring, the Honors Program sponsors the Clarke Student Research Conference. The conference features student projects that have been presented at national and regional undergraduate honors and research conferences. It also provides a venue for all Clarke students to present their academic work to the Clarke community.

Honors students gather socially throughout the semester. First-semester freshmen are invited to the Honors Brunch in the fall, which highlights the activities of the Honors Program. Students who have completed the first year of honors course work are officially inducted into the Honors Program in the spring, and honors graduates are recognized at the College honors banquet.

Participation Requirements: Clarke honors students must complete 21 hours of honors-designated courses, including Honors Cornerstone, a two-semester course taken in the first year, which emphasizes writing, speaking, and technology skills. In addition, all honors students must make a presentation at the Clarke Student Research Conference and submit some of the work they have done at Clarke for external academic recognition. Honors students must maintain a grade point average (GPA) of 3.5 or higher to remain in the program. Successful completion of the program is recognized at commencement and is noted on the student's official transcript.

Admission Process: Incoming freshmen can apply for admission into the Honors Program any time after being admitted to the College. Selection is based on ACT scores, the high school GPA, and an essay.

Scholarship Availability: Honors students are eligible for academic scholarships that are offered to all Clarke students. Clarke College does not offer a scholarship specifically designated for honors students.

Campus Overview
Independent Roman Catholic comprehensive, founded 1843 • **Coed** 1,053 undergraduate students, 82% full-time, 74% women, 26% men.

Undergraduates 867 full-time, 186 part-time. Students come from 10 states and territories, 8 other countries, 35% are from out of state, 3% African American, 0.4% Asian American or Pacific Islander, 3% Hispanic American, 0.3% Native American, 1% international, 11% transferred in, 47% live on campus.

Faculty *Total:* 92, 88% full-time, 63% with terminal degrees. *Student/faculty ratio:* 12:1.

Academic Programs *Special study options:* adult/continuing education programs, advanced placement credit, cooperative education, distance learning, double majors, English as a second language, honors programs, independent study, internships, off-campus study, part-time degree program, student-designed majors, study abroad, summer session for credit.

Athletics Member NCAA. All Division III. *Intercollegiate sports:* baseball M, basketball M/W, cross-country running M/W, golf M/W, soccer M/W, softball W, tennis M/W, volleyball M/W. *Intramural sports:* badminton M/W, basketball M/W, bowling M/W, football M/W, golf M/W, racquetball M/W, skiing (cross-country) M/W, skiing (downhill) M/W, softball M/W, swimming and diving M/W, table tennis M/W, tennis M/W, track and field M/W, volleyball M/W, water polo M/W, weight lifting M/W.

Costs (2004–05) *Comprehensive fee:* $24,249 includes full-time tuition ($17,410), mandatory fees ($550), and room and board ($6289). Full-time tuition and fees vary according to class time. Part-time tuition: $443 per credit. Part-time tuition and fees vary according to class time. *College room only:* $3059. Room and board charges vary according to board plan and housing facility.

Financial Aid 246 Federal Work-Study jobs (averaging $1349). In 2004, 123 non-need-based awards were made. *Average percent of need met:* 100%. *Average financial aid package:* $15,305. *Average need-based loan:* $4088. *Average need-based gift aid:* $11,445. *Average non-need-based aid:* $10,118.

Contact: Director: Dr. Kent Anderson, 1550 Clarke Drive, Dubuque, Iowa 52001; *Telephone:* 563-588-6562; *Fax:* 563-588-6789; *E-mail:* kent.anderson@clarke.edu

Dordt College
Kuyper Scholars Program
Sioux Center, Iowa

A program in Christian scholarship, the Kuyper Scholars Program emphasizes interdisciplinary and theoretical work with seminar participation and leadership. The program seeks not only to prepare academically gifted students to become leaders in the Christian community and the rest of the world, but also to advance the academic atmosphere for all students and faculty members at Dordt College. Students who enroll in the Kuyper Scholars Program develop their understanding of integral Christian scholarship; increase their ability to do interdisciplinary, theoretical, and collaborative scholarly work; identify and cultivate their scholarly gifts; and develop a Kuyperian sense of scholarly work as calling to a particular kind of service in God's kingdom. The program's first class began in fall 2005; 15–20 new freshmen are expected annually.

Participation Requirements: After a foundational course in rhetoric and Christian scholarship, students participate in four to eight semesters of scholar events and/or seminars in which the scholars community engages a guest lecturer or a scholars presentation. In addition, students lead two scholars seminars in which a scholars presentation is engaged. Students complete scholars contracts in connection with some of their regular courses, in which they pursue a theoretical, interdisciplinary, and Christian-scholarship focus; this gives scholars credit to the regular course as well. Students complete individual and group projects across the disciplines and report on and discuss their work in seminars. (At least one laboratory-based science course and mathematics are also required.) A total of 18 scholars credits are required to graduate with the Kuyper Scholars Program designation on their transcript. To remain in the Kuyper Scholars Program, students must maintain a minimum 3.25 GPA and remain active participants.

Admission Process: Student admission into the Kuyper Scholars Program depends on an entrance essay, letters of recommendation, and demonstrated academic ability. For new freshmen, academic ability is demonstrated by letters of recommendation and a composite ACT score of 28 (1240 on the SAT I) or higher and a cumulative high school GPA of at least 3.5. Applications are accepted from November 15 through February 15, with early admissions possible to those applying by January 1. Applications are reviewed by the Kuyper Scholars Program Committee.

Scholarship Availability: A $1000 Kuyper Scholarship is available for all admitted students, in addition to all other scholarships.

Campus Overview

Independent Christian Reformed comprehensive, founded 1955 • **Coed** 1,285 undergraduate students, 95% full-time, 54% women, 46% men.

Undergraduates 1,222 full-time, 63 part-time. Students come from 31 states and territories, 12 other countries, 59% are from out of state, 0.5% African American, 1% Asian American or Pacific Islander, 0.6% Hispanic American, 0.1% Native American, 10% international, 3% transferred in, 90% live on campus.

Faculty *Total:* 110, 68% full-time, 60% with terminal degrees. *Student/faculty ratio:* 15:1.

Academic Programs *Special study options:* academic remediation for entering students, advanced placement credit, distance learning, double majors, English as a second language, honors programs, independent study, internships, off-campus study, part-time degree program, services for LD students, student-designed majors, study abroad.

Athletics Member NAIA. *Intercollegiate sports:* baseball M(s), basketball M(s)/W(s), cross-country running M(s)/W(s), golf M(s), ice hockey M(s), lacrosse M, soccer M(s)/W(s), softball W(s), tennis M(s)/W(s), track and field M(s)/W(s), volleyball W(s). *Intramural sports:* basketball M/W, bowling M/W, field hockey M/W, gymnastics M/W, ice hockey M, lacrosse M, racquetball M/W, skiing (cross-country) M/W, soccer M/W, softball M/W, swimming and diving M/W, table tennis M/W, tennis M/W, track and field M/W, volleyball M/W, weight lifting M/W.

Costs (2004–05) *Comprehensive fee:* $21,320 includes full-time tuition ($16,450), mandatory fees ($220), and room and board ($4650). Part-time tuition: $650 per credit hour. *Required fees:* $110 per term part-time. *College room only:* $2440. Room and board charges vary according to board plan and housing facility.

Financial Aid 591 Federal Work-Study jobs (averaging $1300). 475 state and other part-time jobs (averaging $1300). In 2004, 205 non-need-based awards were made. *Average percent of need met:* 84%. *Average financial aid package:* $15,583. *Average need-based loan:* $4736. *Average need-based gift aid:* $8231. *Average non-need-based aid:* $7987.

Contact: Dr. Mary Dengler, Associate Professor of English, Co-Director of the Kuyper Scholars Program, 498 4th Avenue NE, Sioux Center, Iowa 51250; *Telephone:* 712-722-6251; *Fax:* 712-722-1185; *E-mail:* dengler@dordt.edu

Drake University
Honors Program
Des Moines, Iowa

*T*he Drake Honors Program is designed for students who want to participate in challenging, discussion-based courses on interdisciplinary and topical issues. The program provides a unique opportunity for intellectual enrichment both in and out of the classroom. Two basic questions—What do we know? How do we know it?—shape the learning experience in the Honors Program.

The Honors Program at Drake allows students to substitute the Honors Program Track for most of the general education requirements needed for graduation. Students choose from a constantly changing variety of classes, most designed specifically for the program. These classes are seminar style, with a focus on discussion and writing, and class sizes are always fewer than 20 students. Senior capstone projects culminate the four-year honors experience.

The Honors Program is a multidisciplinary program and operates under the Office of the Provost rather than under any single college or school. The program is administered by the Honors Director and the Faculty Advisory Board, made up of honors faculty members from each of the University's five Colleges/Schools that enroll undergraduate students and a student representative from the Honors Student Curriculum Committee. The program has its own student governance body, the Honors Student Council. The Student Council is involved in both academic matters and extracurricular activities, including organizing speaking engagements and other programs and social and service activities.

Participation Requirements: Students in the Honors Program complete the Honors Track of the Drake general education program, the Drake Curriculum. This allows students to substitute 15 credits in honors seminars (usually five 3-credit classes) and Paths to Knowledge (a 4-credit, team-taught honors seminar usually taken in the sophomore or junior year) for most of the Drake Curriculum's Areas of Inquiry requirement. (Honors students must still fulfill the Drake Curriculum requirements in "the artistic experience," "quantitative reasoning" and one lab science). Students who wish to go beyond the general education role of the Honors Program and graduate with honors (and have this honors designation listed on their degrees) need to maintain a GPA of at least 3.5 (on a 4.0 scale) and complete a Senior Honors Thesis.

Admission Process: The Drake Honors Program is a general education option that is available to any Drake student. While a minimum ACT of 29 or SAT I of 1270 with a high school GPA of at least 3.75 on a 4.0 scale or class rank in the top 5 percent are recommended, these are only recommendations, and applications from any motivated student are encouraged. Any Drake student who prefers taking a series of small, interdisciplinary honors seminars to the "normal" general education "areas of inquiry" requirement, can participate in the honors program. The application consists of a personal essay. There is a priority deadline of March 1, but later applications are accepted.

Scholarship Availability: There are no particular scholarships available through the Honors Program, but students who meet the recommended requirements are eligible for Drake's Alumni Scholarship Program.

Campus Overview

Independent university, founded 1881 • **Coed** 3,164 undergraduate students, 92% full-time, 58% women, 42% men.

Undergraduates 2,913 full-time, 251 part-time. Students come from 47 states and territories, 53 other countries, 61% are from out of state, 3% African American, 3% Asian American or Pacific Islander, 1% Hispanic American, 0.2% Native American, 5% international, 5% transferred in, 57% live on campus.

Faculty *Total:* 374, 67% full-time. *Student/faculty ratio:* 14:1.

Academic Programs *Special study options:* accelerated degree program, advanced placement credit, cooperative education, distance learning, double majors, English as a second language, honors programs, independent study, internships, off-campus study, services for LD students, student-designed majors, study abroad, summer session for credit. *ROTC:* Army (b), Air Force (c). *Unusual degree programs:* 3-2 engineering with Washington University in St. Louis, Cornell University; journalism and law, arts and sciences and law, accounting.

Athletics Member NCAA. All Division I except football (Division I-AA). *Intercollegiate sports:* basketball M(s)/W(s), cheerleading M(s)/W(s), crew W, cross-country running M(s)/W(s), golf M(s), soccer M(s)/W(s), softball W(s), tennis M(s)/W(s), track and field M(s)/W(s), volleyball W(s). *Intramural sports:* basketball M/W, football M/W, golf M/W, racquetball M/W, soccer M(c)/W, softball M/W, swimming and diving M/W, table tennis M/W, tennis M/W, volleyball M/W(c).

Costs (2004–05) *Comprehensive fee:* $26,470 includes full-time tuition ($20,200), mandatory fees ($350), and room and board ($5920). Full-time tuition and fees vary according to class time, course load, and student level. Part-time tuition: $410 per hour. Part-time tuition and fees vary according to class time. *Required fees:* $8 per hour part-time. *College room only:* $2870. Room and board charges vary according to board plan.

Financial Aid 922 Federal Work-Study jobs (averaging $1532). 38 state and other part-time jobs (averaging $5921). In 2002, 1056 non-need-based awards were made. *Average percent of need met:* 98%. *Average financial aid package:* $16,354. *Average need-based loan:* $5606. *Average need-based gift aid:* $11,441. *Average non-need-based aid:* $8936.

Contact: Program Director: Arthur Sanders; Assistant Director: Charlene Skidmore, Honors Program, Drake University, 209 Medbury Hall, 2730 Forest Avenue, Des Moines, Iowa 50311; *Telephone:* 515-271-2999, 800-44DRAKE (toll-free); *E-mail:* honors.program@drake.edu; *Web site:* http://www.drake.edu/honors/

Iowa State University of Science and Technology
University Honors Program

Ames, Iowa

The Iowa State University (ISU) Honors Program is a University-wide program that provides opportunities for students who want to achieve academic excellence, get ahead of the competition, and have a great time in college. It allows students the option of taking introductory courses with smaller enrollments and top-notch instruction. It also assists honors students in creating their own degree programs and working closely with faculty members through a research mentor program and honors project.

Honors courses offer small class sizes and stress more student interaction than lecture. Most students find that taking honors courses does not hurt their GPAs. In fact, students often do their best work in these classes.

Honors seminars give students the opportunity to explore topics not offered to the larger University population. Seminars are offered for 1–2 credits on a pass/fail basis. Students are encouraged to take seminars outside of their major field. Recent popular seminar topics have included emerging infectious diseases, symbiotic relationship between sports and business, apocalypse now and then, and leadership development and team building.

Honors projects give students the opportunity to choose a topic for in-depth study. Many times, students decide to work on projects completely outside of their major. Research grants are awarded to students to help defray the cost of their projects.

The Freshman Honors Program introduces a limited number of qualified and motivated students to the advantages of an honors education, emphasizes learning in small groups, and fosters a sense of community among students with similar abilities and interests.

An honors English composition class, a special freshman honors seminar, and an honors section of the required University library course form the academic core of the program during the fall semester. During spring semester, students may opt to participate in the Mentor Program, a program that places the freshmen with faculty members in a research environment.

Iowa State has offered University Honors since 1960 and Freshman Honors since 1973. There are approximately 900 students in the seven-college Honors Program and 400 students in the Freshman Honors Program. The notation "Graduated in the University Honors Program" is entered on the permanent record, diploma, and in the Commencement program. A certificate is also awarded at the convocations preceding the University Commencement ceremony.

Participation Requirements: Students must submit a program of study approved by the college's Honors Committee. Graduation in the University Honors Program requires a minimum GPA of 3.35, completion of the required number of honors courses and honors seminars, and completion of the honors project.

Admission Process: For the Freshman Honors Program, invitations are sent to students who meet one of the following categories: they are in the upper 5 percent of their high school class, have an ACT composite score of 30 or above, or are a National Merit or National Achievement finalist. Admission is competitive and the program size is limited to 400 students.

Scholarship Availability: There are five competitive scholarships based on the activity level of Honors Program membership.

Campus Overview

State-supported university, founded 1858 • **Coed** 21,354 undergraduate students, 94% full-time, 44% women, 56% men.

Undergraduates 20,004 full-time, 1,350 part-time. Students come from 54 states and territories, 114 other countries, 20% are from out of state, 3% African American, 3% Asian American or Pacific Islander, 2% Hispanic American, 0.3% Native American, 3% international, 7% transferred in, 31% live on campus.

Faculty *Total:* 1,610, 86% full-time, 88% with terminal degrees. *Student/faculty ratio:* 17:1.

Academic Programs *Special study options:* academic remediation for entering students, accelerated degree program, adult/continuing education programs, advanced placement credit, cooperative education, distance learning, double majors, English as a second language, external degree program, freshman honors college, honors programs, independent study, internships, off-campus study, part-time degree program, services for LD students, student-designed majors, study abroad, summer session for credit. *ROTC:* Army (b), Navy (b), Air Force (b). *Unusual degree programs:* 3-2 engineering with William Penn College.

Athletics Member NCAA. All Division I except football (Division I-A). *Intercollegiate sports:* basketball M(s)/W(s), cross-country running M(s)/W(s), golf M(s)/W(s), gymnastics W(s), soccer W(s), softball W(s), swimming and diving M(s)/W(s), tennis W(s), track and field M(s)/W(s), volleyball W(s), wrestling M(s). *Intramural sports:* archery M(c)/W(c), badminton M(c)/W(c), basketball M/W, bowling M(c)/W(c), cross-country running M/W, equestrian sports M(c)/W(c), fencing M(c)/W(c), football M/W, golf M/W, ice hockey M(c)/W(c), lacrosse M(c)/W(c), racquetball M(c)/W(c), riflery M(c)/W(c), rugby M(c)/W(c), sailing M(c)/W(c), skiing (cross-country) M(c)/W(c), skiing (downhill) M(c)/W(c), soccer M(c)/W(c), softball M/W, squash M/W, swimming and diving M/W, table tennis M(c)/W(c), tennis M/W, volleyball M(c)/W(c), water polo M(c)/W(c), weight lifting M(c)/W(c), wrestling M/W.

Costs (2004–05) *Tuition:* state resident $4702 full-time, $196 per semester hour part-time; nonresident $14,404 full-time, $601 per semester hour part-time. Full-time tuition and fees vary according to class time, degree level, and program. Part-time tuition and fees vary according to class time, course load, degree level, and program. *Required fees:* $724 full-time. *Room and board:* $5958; room only: $3168. Room and board charges vary according to board plan and housing facility.

Financial Aid 779 Federal Work-Study jobs (averaging $2168). 9,458 state and other part-time jobs (averaging $1779). In 2004, 3431 non-need-based awards were made. *Average percent of need met:* 82%. *Average financial aid package:* $7738. *Average need-based loan:* $4489. *Average need-based gift aid:* $3148. *Average non-need-based aid:* $3480.

Contact: Director: Ricki Shine, Martin C. Jischke Honors Building, Ames, Iowa 50011-1150; *Telephone:* 515-294-4371; *Fax:* 515-294-2970; *E-mail:* rshine@iastate.edu; *Web site:* http://www.public.iastate.edu/~honors/homepage.html

Loras College
Honors Degree Program
Dubuque, Iowa

The Loras College Honors Degree Program is designed to offer a coherent sequence of courses to academically superior students who wish to pursue a broadly based, comprehensive liberal arts education. The program emphasizes a humanistic and synoptic approach to the various academic disciplines that comprise the liberal arts. Each semester the Honors Degree Program sponsors two or three intra- or inter-divisional courses that explore themes central to the study of the liberal arts. The courses are interdisciplinary in approach, employ a variety of learning styles, have enrollments of 15 to 20 students, and are offered in a seminar format.

By completing courses sponsored by the Honors Degree Program and also through independent learning opportunities, service activities, and research projects, students become more active learners better able to synthesize information from their various College courses and construct for themselves a complete learning experience. Finally, by integrating its in-class and cocurricular activities within the larger framework of students' lives, the Honors Degree Program underscores the necessary connection between academic experience and the world beyond the academy in the development of principled thinkers. In recognition of their accomplishments in a variety of courses and a senior capstone experience students earn the Honors Degree.

In addition to its purpose to attract and retain highly motivated and academically superior students, the Honors Degree Program serves to attract excellent teachers. The Honors Degree Program enriches the academic experience of all students at Loras by providing an opportunity for innovative course development.

The current version of the Loras College Honors Degree Program was introduced in 1989. Annually 20 first-year students begin the first course in the program. There are approximately 70 students currently enrolled in the program.

Participation Requirements: In their first three semesters, students in the Honors Degree Program complete several foundational courses: a Modes of Inquiry course in which students employ a holistic critical-thinking approach to explore a seminal event in the Western cultural tradition; a Democracy and Global Diversity course in which students use primary texts to explore both Western and non-Western cultures at a movement of historical crisis; a Catholic Traditions course in which students develop an awareness of the religious dimensions of human experience either by exploring the lives of several significant Catholic figures or by contrasting Catholicism and another religious tradition. During the following five semesters,

students complete honors courses in three of the following general education categories: Humanity in the Physical Universe, Foundations for Values and Decisions, Identity and Community, The Aesthetic Dimension of Human Experience, and Cultural Traditions Across Generations. These honors courses are distinguished from their general education counterparts by their strong emphasis on interdisciplinary content and their enhanced opportunities for participation in field trips, conferences, and collaborative research. Representative Advanced Honors courses include Contested Conceptions of Political Economy, Native American Literature, The Vietnam War and American Culture, The Holocaust and Resistance, Great Ideas in Physics, Slavery and Democracy, and Aldo Leopold and the Land Ethic. During their junior year, honors students complete a 1-credit course for the honors dimension of their general education portfolio in which they explore how a liberal arts honors education connects to their major and to their future plans. In the senior year, honors students participate in a 3-credit Service Learning course in which they spend 50 hours at a local community organization developing a project that addresses a significant organizational need.

Students are expected to maintain a minimum GPA (GPA) of 3.35 and complete a total of 22 credits in honors courses or projects. The completion of these requirements results in the awarding of the Honors Degree on the official transcript, presentation of a special plaque, and a notation in the commencement program in addition to the degree(s) in an academic major.

Admission Process: On the basis of ACT scores, high school average, and a review of the college preparatory courses on their high school transcript, students are invited to apply to the Honors Degree Program. Final placement in the program is based on the recommendation of the Honors Director and a personal interview between the student and a faculty member who serves as the student's summer registration counselor. A key factor in admission to the program is the individual student's desire to follow the course of studies. Annually a small number of students may be placed in the program after the first or second semester of the first year. Students may major in any discipline in the College.

Scholarship Availability: Scholarships of various amounts are awarded through the Office of Admissions and Financial Aid. These scholarships are based on academic performance and financial need. Scholarships are not offered through the Honors Degree Program. Almost all honors students are recipients of academic scholarships.

Campus Overview

Independent Roman Catholic comprehensive, founded 1839 • **Coed** 1,618 undergraduate students, 96% full-time, 50% women, 50% men.

Undergraduates 1,551 full-time, 67 part-time. Students come from 23 states and territories, 8 other countries, 44% are from out of state, 1% African American, 0.9% Asian American or Pacific Islander, 1% Hispanic American, 0.1% Native American, 2% international, 18% transferred in, 64% live on campus.

Faculty *Total:* 143, 79% full-time, 84% with terminal degrees. *Student/faculty ratio:* 13:1.

Academic Programs *Special study options:* academic remediation for entering students, adult/continuing education programs, advanced placement credit, cooperative education, double majors, English as a second language, honors programs, independent study, internships, off-campus study, part-time degree program, services for LD students, student-designed majors, study abroad, summer session for credit. *Unusual degree programs:* 3-2 engineering with Iowa State University of Science and Technology, University of Illinois, University of Notre Dame, University of Iowa; nursing with University of Iowa.

Athletics Member NCAA. All Division III. *Intercollegiate sports:* baseball M, basketball M/W, cross-country running M/W, football M, golf M/W, ice hockey M(c), rugby M(c), skiing (downhill) M(c), soccer M/W, softball W, swimming and diving M/W, tennis M/W, track and field M/W, volleyball M(c)/W, wrestling M. *Intramural sports:* badminton M/W, baseball M, basketball M/W, cross-country running M/W, football M, golf M/W, ice hockey M, racquetball M/W, rugby M, skiing (cross-country) M/W, skiing (downhill) M/W, soccer M/W, softball M/W, swimming and diving M/W, table tennis M/W, tennis M/W, track and field M/W, volleyball M/W, water polo M/W, weight lifting M/W, wrestling M.

Costs (2004–05) *Comprehensive fee:* $25,523 includes full-time tuition ($18,670), mandatory fees ($1008), and room and board ($5845). Full-time tuition and fees vary according to course load and degree level. Part-time tuition: $400 per credit. *College room only:* $2950. Room and board charges vary according to board plan and housing facility.

Financial Aid 280 Federal Work-Study jobs (averaging $942). 254 state and other part-time jobs (averaging $2581). In 2004, 498 non-need-based awards were made. *Average percent of need met:* 89%. *Average financial aid package:* $17,723. *Average need-based loan:* $4408. *Average need-based gift aid:* $7203. *Average non-need-based aid:* $8641.

Contact: Director: Dr. Kristin Anderson-Bricker, Loras Mail #105, Dubuque, Iowa 52004-0178; *Telephone:* 563-588-7893; *E-mail:* kristin.andersonbricker@loras.edu. Admissions Office; *Telephone:* 800-245-6727; *Fax:* 563-588-7964; *E-mail:* adms@loras.edu; *Web site:* http://www.loras.edu

Mount Mercy College
Honors Program
Cedar Rapids, Iowa

The Honors Program at Mount Mercy College offers accomplished students unique classes that encourage the exploration of ideas beyond traditional academic boundaries. Open to students from all majors, honors courses stress depth of engagement, creative problem solving, and interdisciplinary approaches. Honors faculty members are drawn from a variety of departments and collaborate to create truly interdisciplinary honors seminars.

Qualified freshman and sophomores are invited to take honors general education classes. These classes feature subjects from the core curriculum, such as composition, literature, science, philosophy, or religious studies, but the designated honors sections are designed to stimulate students to assume high levels of responsibility for their own learning. Small class size and instruction by dedicated professors create a learning environment where students are encouraged to speak out on issues and engage in academic inquiry with their instructors and peers.

Honors students with sophomore standing may enroll in honors seminars, unique interdisciplinary courses. Recent seminar offerings have included courses on the Human Genome Project, the City as Text, Primate Intelligence, and the psychological and philosophical theories of happiness. Students in seminars engage in high-level inquiry, critical thinking, and interdisciplinary collaboration.

An active Student Honors Association supplements the academic curriculum by planning social events, inviting speakers to campus, publishing a newsletter, and providing input to the program director. Honors students enjoy the use of an honors lounge for studying or socializing. Exemplary students are invited to present their work at the College's annual Undergraduate Scholars Day. In addition, students may attend conferences of the National Collegiate Honors Council and the Upper Midwest Honors Council.

Founded in 1989, the program involves an average of 100 students.

Participation Requirements: Students are recognized as graduating with Distinction in the Honors Program if they satisfactorily complete 12 semester hours in designated honors courses (at least 6 semester hours must be honors seminars) and maintain an overall cumulative GPA of at least 3.4. Students must earn a minimum 3.0 GPA in honors courses.

Admission Process: Students who meet the following criteria are eligible to participate in the Honors Program: an ACT composite score of 26, a high school GPA of 3.6, and a rank in the top quartile of their graduating class. First-year students who do not meet the stated criteria but believe they could do well in the Honors Program may petition the honors director for a probationary admittance to the program. Transfer students who have successfully completed honors courses at other colleges and universities may petition for the courses to apply towards honors requirements at Mount Mercy College.

Scholarship Availability: The College gives more than $5 million in financial aid. One-hundred percent of full-time freshmen receive some form of financial aid. Students eligible for the Honors Program are invited to compete for two academic scholarships: the Holland Scholarship (full tuition for four years) and the Presidential Scholarship (up to $9000 per year for four years).

Mount Mercy College hosts a chapter of Kappa Gamma Pi, the National Catholic College Graduate Honor Society.

Campus Overview

Independent Roman Catholic 4-year, founded 1928 • **Coed** 1,486 undergraduate students, 67% full-time, 70% women, 30% men.

Undergraduates 989 full-time, 497 part-time. Students come from 23 states and territories, 13% are from out of state, 2% African American, 0.8% Asian American or Pacific Islander, 1% Hispanic American, 0.4% Native American, 14% transferred in, 28% live on campus.

Faculty *Total:* 142, 51% full-time, 38% with terminal degrees. *Student/faculty ratio:* 13:1.

Academic Programs *Special study options:* academic remediation for entering students, accelerated degree program, adult/continuing education programs, advanced placement credit, double majors, freshman honors college, honors programs, independent study, internships, off-campus study, part-time degree program, services for LD students, student-designed majors, summer session for credit.

Athletics Member NAIA. *Intercollegiate sports:* baseball M, basketball M/W, cheerleading W, cross-country running M/W, golf M/W, soccer M/W, softball W, track and field M/W, volleyball W. *Intramural sports:* baseball M, basketball M/W, football M/W, racquetball M/W, tennis M/W, volleyball M/W, weight lifting M/W.

Costs (2005–06) *Comprehensive fee:* $24,520 includes full-time tuition ($18,030), mandatory fees ($810), and room and board ($5680). Full-time tuition and fees vary according to course load. Part-time tuition: $500 per credit hour. Part-time tuition and fees vary according to course load. *Room and board:* Room and board charges vary according to board plan and housing facility.

Financial Aid 322 Federal Work-Study jobs (averaging $1461). 102 state and other part-time jobs (averaging $1067). In 2003, 114 non-need-based awards were made. *Average percent of need met:* 81%. *Average financial aid package:* $14,145. *Average need-based loan:* $5167. *Average need-based gift aid:* $9081. *Average non-need-based aid:* $9878.

Contact: Director: Dr. Joy Ochs, Mount Mercy College, 1330 Elmhurst Drive NE, Cedar Rapids, Iowa 52402-4797; *Telephone:* 319-363-8213 Ext. 1224; *E-mail:* jochs@mtmercy.edu; *Web site:* http://www.mtmercy.edu/honors/honors1.htm

The University of Iowa
Honors Program
Iowa City, Iowa

The University Honors Program is dedicated to the academic and personal enrichment of outstanding University of Iowa undergraduates of all majors and colleges. The Honors Program recognizes that students have different educational needs and goals. For this reason, the Honors Program offers a curriculum that is flexible, broad, and challenging. Honors course options begin as early as the students' first semester and continue through the last semester of the senior year.

University Honors Program staff members help honors students create their own "personal honors curriculum" and explore interests inside and outside the classroom. Honors students enjoy additional course options in research, writing, teaching, and independent study, as well as opportunities to work closely with professors and other honors students within existing courses. Cocurricular activities in foreign relations, the arts, volunteering, and more provide students with important experience outside the classroom. By offering these academic opportunities and cocurricular programs, the University Honors Program strives to be a "Community of Opportunity."

In January 2004 the University Honors Program moved into the Blank Honors Center. This new facility is dedicated to fostering a sense of community among honors students, offering extended hours, social areas, a kitchenette, quiet study areas, classrooms, a computer lab, office space for honor societies, and administrative staff offices. Attached by a skywalk to the Blank Honors Center are the Honors Learning Communities, located in Daum Residence Hall. Students living on the honors floors are brought together for a variety of cultural, academic, and social events.

The learning communities in both halls offer students the chance to socialize and study with other honors students and to participate in programs such as group outings to arts events, workshops on scholarship and research opportunities, volunteer activities, and dinners with faculty members.

Each semester the program features a variety of honors seminars—introductory courses on exciting topics in the humanities, social sciences, and natural sciences. Honors seminars are small, highly interactive, and cover new topics each semester. Individual departments offer courses in a wide range of subject areas for honors credit, from lab and discussion sections of introductory courses to specialized studies for students within their discipline. Students can also turn any non-honors course into an honors course through honors designation, which allows students to delve more deeply into a topic under the guidance of the instructor by developing a plan of study that goes beyond the course requirements.

Students who complete at least 12 semester hours of honors course work with a grade of B or higher in each graded course before they have completed their second year or their first 59 semester hours (whichever comes last) receive Honors Commendation, which includes a certificate of commendation from the Honors Program and the University president.

Most majors offer upper-level honors courses, honors seminars, independent research, and/or the opportunity to pursue an original senior honors thesis or project under the guidance of a faculty member. Each college and department determines its own requirements for graduation with honors, and faculty members in each department serve as honors advisers

The University Honors Program was founded in 1963 and currently enrolls 5,000 students.

Participation Requirements: While the choices are many, there are no required courses for students to maintain membership in the University Honors Program. Students are free to design a curriculum that best suits their background and interests. Students may select honors options to meet the requirements of the General Education Program, their major department(s), or for elective credit. The Academic Advising Center, departmental honors advisers, and Honors Program staff members are all available to help students develop an appropriate plan of study.

Membership in the University Honors Program is open to undergraduate students enrolled in the Colleges of Education, Engineering, Liberal Arts and Sciences, and Nursing and the Tippie College of Business. First-, second-, or third-year students will be admitted early in the spring semester of each academic year if their University of Iowa (UI) GPA is at a 3.33 (B+) or above. A UI GPA of 3.33 (B+) or above is required to remain in the University Honors Program.

Students who graduate with honors receive special recognition during commencement, and their achievement is noted on their permanent academic record.

Admission Process: Entering first-year students are granted membership in the University Honors Program based on their Admissions Index Score, which is the sum of the class-rank percentage plus double the ACT score (or SAT equivalent). Students with a minimum Index Score of 148 and above are automatically admitted to the University Honors Program.

For example, a student who ranks in the 90th percentile of the graduating class and presents an ACT score of 29 would have an Index Score of 148 [90 + (29 + 29) and would be admitted automatically. Students who attend high schools that do not assign class rank must have a GPA of 3.75 or greater and a minimum ACT composite score of 29 or 1250 on the SAT. If a student has been home schooled, he or she must achieve minimum scores of ACT 29/SAT 1250. Entering students who are not admitted automatically may gain admission via a parallel process, which requires a transcript, a letter of recommendation from a teacher, and a personal letter describing how the student would gain from the Honors Program.

Transfer student may enter the Honors Program if they have 24 credit hours in college courses with a GPA of 3.50 or above. If student has earned fewer than 24 hours of college credit at the time of application, admission is based on the first-year student requirements.

Scholarship Availability: The Honors Program helps students prepare to apply for a variety of scholarship awards and prizes. The program offers its own scholarships of $1000 to $3000 to selected continuing honors students in all colleges as well as research grants for students working to complete senior honors theses or projects. These awards are made possible in part by a bequest from Professor Rhodes Dunlap, the program's founder and director for more than 20 years. Announcements concerning Honors Program scholarships are made through the Honors Program newsletter and listserv. The program does not offer scholarships to incoming first-year or transfer students.

Students from The University of Iowa Honors Program are awarded national and international scholarships each year. Information, advice, and encouragement for potential Rhodes Scholars, Marshall Scholars, Truman Scholars, Goldwater Scholars, and others are available through the Honors Program.

Campus Overview

State-supported university, founded 1847 • **Coed** 20,135 undergraduate students, 89% full-time, 54% women, 46% men.

Undergraduates 17,879 full-time, 2,256 part-time. Students come from 51 states and territories, 68 other countries, 30% are from out of state, 2% African American, 4% Asian American or Pacific Islander, 2% Hispanic American, 0.4% Native American, 1% international, 6% transferred in, 28% live on campus.

Faculty Total: 1,713, 95% full-time, 97% with terminal degrees. Student/faculty ratio: 14:1.

Academic Programs Special study options: academic remediation for entering students, accelerated degree program, adult/continuing education programs, advanced placement credit, cooperative education, distance learning, double majors, English as a second language, external degree program, honors programs, independent study, internships, off-campus study, part-time degree program, services for

LD students, student-designed majors, study abroad, summer session for credit. *ROTC:* Army (b), Air Force (b).

Athletics Member NCAA. All Division I except football (Division I-A). *Intercollegiate sports:* baseball M(s), basketball M(s)/W(s), crew M(c)/W(s), cross-country running M(s)/W(s), field hockey W(s), golf M(s)/W(s), gymnastics M(s)/W(s), ice hockey M(c), lacrosse M(c)/W(c), rugby M(c)/W(c), sailing M(c)/W(c), soccer M(c)/W(s), softball W(s), swimming and diving M(s)/W(s), table tennis M(c)/W(c), tennis M(s)/W(s), track and field M(s)/W(s), ultimate Frisbee M(c)/W(c), volleyball M(c)/W(c), wrestling M(s). *Intramural sports:* badminton M/W, basketball M/W, bowling M/W, fencing M(c)/W(c), football M/W, golf M/W, racquetball M/W, rugby M(c)/W(c), sailing M(c)/W(c), skiing (cross-country) M(c)/W(c), skiing (downhill) M(c)/W(c), soccer M/W, softball M/W, table tennis M/W, tennis M/W, track and field M/W, ultimate Frisbee M/W, volleyball M/W, water polo M(c)/W(c), wrestling M.

Costs (2005–06) *Tuition:* state resident $4890 full-time, $204 per semester hour part-time; nonresident $16,276 full-time, $678 per semester hour part-time. Full-time tuition and fees vary according to course load and program. Part-time tuition and fees vary according to course load and program. *Required fees:* $722 full-time, $361 per term part-time. *Room and board:* $6560. Room and board charges vary according to board plan and housing facility.

Financial Aid 1,200 Federal Work-Study jobs (averaging $2500). In 2003, 3866 non-need-based awards were made. *Average percent of need met:* 88%. *Average financial aid package:* $7386. *Average need-based loan:* $3861. *Average need-based gift aid:* $4497. *Average non-need-based aid:* $4192.

Contact: The University Honors Program, The University of Iowa, 420 Blank Honors Center, Iowa City, Iowa 52242; *Telephone:* 319-335-1681; *Fax:* 319-335-0549; *E-mail:* honors-program@uiowa.edu; *Web site:* http://www.uiowa.edu/~honors

University of Northern Iowa
University Honors Program
Cedar Falls, Iowa

The University Honors Program at the University of Northern Iowa (UNI) is a program that allows motivated and interested students to make the most of their collegiate experience. The program offers challenging classroom experiences, interactions with faculty members, and social connections with other capable students. The program includes all five undergraduate colleges, and membership in the University Honors Program is compatible with any of the University's 120 majors.

The University Honors Program provides unique educational opportunities for motivated students. Honors sections of liberal arts core and University courses are made up entirely of honors students, with a class limit of 20. Students also choose from Honors Seminars, unique courses developed specifically for the program. Students round out their University Honors Program curriculum by selecting honors electives. These hours can be earned in additional honors sections of liberal arts core classes, seminars, or major courses or through independent studies. The culmination of the honors experience comes in the form of the senior thesis/project. This project allows students to independently explore a scholarly area of interest prior to graduation.

Participation in the University Honors Program helps students develop close ties with UNI faculty members. Small honors sections of classes allow for in-depth, one-on-one interaction, and a faculty member guides the honors thesis/project. Small class sizes also allow for considerable interactions with classmates. In addition, honors social events extend the group's connection beyond the walls of the classroom. Out-of-class activities include events like guest speakers, hayrides, and movie nights. Students can also take advantage of group attendance at theater

events at the Gallagher-Bluedorn Performing Arts Center or field trips that offer cultural and practical experience. An Honors Student Advisory Board gives students the opportunity to influence the direction of the program, share their ideas on a variety of programming issues, and help plan academic, social, and outreach events.

The University Honors Program is housed at 2401 College Street, which is affectionately referred to as the Honors Cottage. The Honors Cottage, built in 1890, originally served as the President's Cottage and has the distinction of being the oldest surviving building on campus. The facility consists of a seminar room for honors classes, lounge space for relaxing and studying, a kitchen, a small computer lab, private study rooms, and the program's administrative offices. Honors students are encouraged to make the space their own and use it as a center for their intellectual and social pursuits.

The program began in 2001 with an inaugural class of 65 students. Within four years, enrollment has grown to almost 300, and plans call for an eventual target size of approximately 600 students.

Participation Requirements: The University Honors Program offers two designations for participation, University Honors with Distinction and University Honors. To remain in good standing in the University Honors Program, students are required to maintain a minimum GPA of 3.3. Graduates of the program are honored at commencement and have an honors designation noted on their transcripts.

Students pursuing University Honors with Distinction take 30 hours of honors courses, consisting of 12 hours of liberal arts core courses, 6 seminar hours, 9 hours of honors electives, and a 3-hour senior honors thesis/project. University Honors, designed with transfer students in mind, requires 18 hours of honors courses, made up of 6 seminar hours, 9 hours of honors electives, and a 3-hour senior honors thesis/project.

Admission Process: Entering first-year students with an ACT score of 27 or higher or an SAT score of 1210 or higher and a high school class rank in the top 10 percent are automatically invited to join the University Honors Program upon their admission to the University of Northern Iowa. Letters of invitation are sent to qualifying students shortly after they are admitted to the University. Students are asked to respond to confirm their position in the program. Responses are accepted until the program reaches its capacity, so it is important for students to apply for admission to UNI as early as possible and respond promptly to an honors invitation. Students who do not meet the criteria for an automatic invitation can request that their case be reviewed on an individual basis by sending a copy of their transcript and a one-page letter describing why they would be a good candidate for the University Honors Program.

Current UNI students can apply for admission to the program with a UNI cumulative GPA of 3.3 or better and a professor's recommendation. Transfer students can apply with a GPA of 3.3 or better from their transfer institution and a professor's recommendation.

Scholarship Availability: The University Honors Program awards fifty scholarships per year to high school seniors with a history of outstanding academic performance. Top recipients are those whose strong academic credentials are matched by personal involvement in leadership and service activities. Twenty students are awarded Presidential Scholarships worth $28,000 over four years ($7000 per year). Thirty students are awarded Provost Scholarships worth $8000 over four years ($2000 per year). Application criteria include an ACT composite score of 29 or better and a high school class rank in the top 10 percent (or one of the top 5 students in a class of 50 or fewer).

In addition, the Nadyne Harris Endowed Scholarship makes funding available to current University Honors Program students majoring in the liberal arts. The Nadyne Harris Scholarship for Honors Travel provides funding to students traveling for academic purposes. Travel must result in earned academic credit that is accepted by the University of Northern Iowa and designated for honors credit by the University Honors Program. The maximum award is $500. The Nadyne Harris Scholarship for Honors Research provides funding to students completing the honors thesis/project. Awards offset research costs such as supplies, specialized software, photocopying, printing, mailing, photography, and travel to research sites. The maximum award is $300.

Campus Overview

State-supported comprehensive, founded 1876, part of Board of Regents, State of Iowa • **Coed** 11,266 undergraduate students, 89% full-time, 57% women, 43% men.

Undergraduates 9,989 full-time, 1,277 part-time. Students come from 42 states and territories, 58 other countries, 5% are from out of state, 3% African American, 1% Asian American or Pacific Islander, 2% Hispanic American, 0.3% Native American, 2% international, 10% transferred in, 34% live on campus.

Faculty *Total:* 784, 83% full-time, 74% with terminal degrees. *Student/faculty ratio:* 16:1.

Academic Programs *Special study options:* academic remediation for entering students, accelerated degree program, adult/continuing education programs, advanced placement credit, cooperative education, distance learning, double majors, English as a second language, external degree program, honors programs, independent study, internships, off-campus study, part-time degree program, services for LD students, student-designed majors, study abroad, summer session for credit. *ROTC:* Army (b). *Unusual degree programs:* 3-2 nursing with University of Iowa; medical technology with St. Luke's Hospital/University of Iowa Medical School, cytotechnology with Mayo School of Health-Related Sciences, Wisconsin State Laboratory of Hygiene and Mercy School of Cytotechnology, chiropractic with Logan College of Chiropractic.

Athletics Member NCAA. All Division I except football (Division I-AA). *Intercollegiate sports:* baseball M(s), basketball M(s)/W(s), cross-country running M(s)/W(s), golf M(s)/W(s), soccer W(s), softball W(s), swimming and diving W(s), tennis M/W(s), track and field M(s)/W(s), volleyball W(s), wrestling M(s). *Intramural sports:* badminton M/W, basketball M/W, bowling M(c)/W(c), cheerleading M/W, crew M(c)/W(c), cross-country running M(c)/W(c), football M, golf M/W, ice hockey M(c), lacrosse W(c), racquetball M(c)/W(c), rugby M(c)/W(c), skiing (cross-country) M(c)/W(c), skiing (downhill) M(c)/W(c), soccer M(c)/W(c), softball M(c)/W(c), swimming and diving M(c)/W(c), table tennis M/W, tennis M(c)/W(c), track and field M(c)/W(c), volleyball M(c)/W(c), water polo M/W, wrestling M.

Costs (2004–05) *Tuition:* state resident $4702 full-time, $196 per hour part-time; nonresident $12,020 full-time, $501 per hour part-time. Full-time tuition and fees vary according to course load. Part-time tuition and fees vary according to course load. *Required fees:* $685 full-time. *Room and board:* $5261; room only: $2431. Room and board charges vary according to board plan and housing facility.

Financial Aid 573 Federal Work-Study jobs (averaging $1845). 145 state and other part-time jobs (averaging $1974). In 2004, 783 non-need-based awards were made. *Average percent of need met:* 63%. *Average financial aid package:* $6907. *Average need-based loan:* $4177. *Average need-based gift aid:* $3140. *Average non-need-based aid:* $2964.

Contact: Director: Jessica Moon, 2401 College Street, University of Northern Iowa, Cedar Falls, Iowa 50614-0355; *Telephone:* 319-273-3175; *E-mail:* jessica.moon@uni.edu; *Web site:* http://www.uni.edu/honors

Waldorf College

Honors College

Forest City, Iowa

*T*he Honors College at Waldorf provides a rewarding learning environment for highly capable students. The program is distinguished by its select faculty members, challenging curriculum, interdisciplinary courses and seminars, independent projects, and a culminating world trip.

In addition to special course offerings and the world trip, Honors College students may choose to go on regional cultural trips, usually at no cost, to attend plays, concerts, lectures, and conferences.

The Honors College was established in 1988, and there are 60 students currently enrolled in the program.

Participation Requirements: Honors College students must maintain a GPA of at least 3.25. Each semester students may take honors sections of general education courses, honors courses, and/or independent projects in their majors. Honors College students who complete the honors curriculum with a GPA of 3.5 or higher, undertake a special research project in their major, and present their work at Waldorf's annual academic conference are eligible for Waldorf Scholar status. Waldorf Scholars travel to global destinations to complete their studies. The airfare is paid for by the College as a reward for academic achievement and leadership.

Entering students take a two-semester freshman seminar that replaces the first-year English requirement. Sophomores typically take honors religion and a team-taught philosophy course. Honors colloquia, which focus on controversial issues in a seminar setting, are offered each semester. Students write and present their honors theses during their third or fourth year.

Admission Process: Entering freshman with a GPA of at least 3.5 and an ACT of 26 or higher are granted admission to the Honors College. All students with curious intellects are encouraged to petition the honors director for admission.

Scholarship Availability: The College offers numerous academic scholarships. Students should contact the director of the Honors College for details.

Campus Overview

Independent Lutheran 4-year, founded 1903 • **Coed** 629 undergraduate students, 87% full-time, 54% women, 46% men.

Undergraduates 546 full-time, 83 part-time. Students come from 20 states and territories, 11 other countries, 33% are from out of state, 3% African American, 0.5% Asian American or Pacific Islander, 0.5% Hispanic American, 5% international, 11% transferred in, 93% live on campus.

Faculty *Total:* 53, 68% full-time, 30% with terminal degrees. *Student/faculty ratio:* 17:1.

Academic Programs *Special study options:* academic remediation for entering students, accelerated degree program, adult/continuing education programs, advanced placement credit, cooperative education, double majors, English as a second language, freshman honors college, honors programs, internships, part-time degree program, services for LD students, study abroad, summer session for credit.

Athletics Member NAIA. *Intercollegiate sports:* baseball M(s), basketball M(s)/W(s), football M(s), golf M(s)/W(s), soccer M(s)/W(s), softball W(s), volleyball W(s), wrestling M(s). *Intramural sports:* basketball M/W, football M, racquetball M/W, skiing (cross-country) M/W, skiing (downhill) M/W, soccer M/W, softball M/W, tennis M/W, volleyball M/W.

Costs (2004–05) *Comprehensive fee:* $18,600 includes full-time tuition ($13,500), mandatory fees ($700), and room and board ($4400). Full-time tuition and fees vary according to class time and course load. Part-time tuition: $180 per credit. *Required fees:* $35 per credit part-time. *College room only:* $2200. Room and board charges vary according to board plan and housing facility.

Financial Aid 296 Federal Work-Study jobs (averaging $1527). 97 state and other part-time jobs (averaging $906). In 2003, 66 non-need-based awards were made. *Average percent of need met:* 85%. *Average financial aid package:* $15,752. *Average need-based loan:* $4677. *Average need-based gift aid:* $11,062. *Average non-need-based aid:* $8717.

Contact: Director: Dr. Robert Alsop, 106 South Sixth Street, Forest City, Iowa 50436; *Telephone:* 641-585-8225; *Fax:* 641-585-8194; *E-mail:* alsopb@waldorf.edu; *Web site:* http://www.waldorf.edu/academics/honors/Benefits_waldorfscholar2.html

Wartburg College
Wartburg Scholars Program
Waverly, Iowa

The Wartburg Scholars Program is dedicated to encouraging students to expand their horizons and take an active interest in their education. Scholars students are offered unique opportunities in the areas of convocations, retreats, service projects and travel. With flexibility and a close student-teacher relationship in mind, enrollment is capped at 15 students per class.

First year students are enrolled in the Scholars Program 101 instead of the normal first year requirement, Inquiry Studies 101. Here they have the choice of fall or winter semester: each semester is taught by a different professor and studies a different text. Second year students create their own independent symposium focussing on lectures, plays, sporting events and musical performances and how they apply to the campus or community. Third year scholars create a student designed seminar class involving important world issues and possible service projects. The third year seminar replaces Wartburg College's Interdisciplinary course requirements. Fourth year students spend time researching their own independent, faculty-approved projects based on any subject.

Created in March of 2003, the Wartburg Scholars Program currently has 30 students enrolled with the intention of expansion to just over 100 students in the next four years.

Participation Requirements: Members of the Scholars Program are required to take both SCH 101 and SCH 301. They are also expected to work independently on a second year symposium and a fourth year project.

Members who complete the program successfully graduate with an Honors Diploma. They must maintain a 3.5- 3.699 GPA for Cum Laude, 3.700-3.849 GPA for Magna Cum Laude and 3.85-4.00 GPA for Summa Cum Laude.

Admission Process: Students who have graduated in the top ten percent of their High School class OR received a 26 ACT score or higher OR been nominated for the program by an individual who is familiar with their extended intellectual purpose are eligible to apply for the Scholars program. All students who receive Regent or Presidential scholarships through Wartburg College are specially invited to apply for the Scholars Program. Each potential member must complete the application and a personal or phone interview with the Program Committee. The application deadline for first year students is March 15, with late applications accepted on a rolling basis until the cohort is complete. Continuing and transfer students may apply to the program if space is available in their cohort. Their application process is similar to that of beginning students.

Scholarship Availability: Regent (up to full tuition) and presidential (up to $7,500) scholarships are available through Wartburg College. Students eligible for Regent scholarships must have ranked in the upper 30 percent of their high school graduating class and received a 28 or higher on the ACT (1240 SAT) OR were ranked in the top 10 percent of their class OR received a GPA of at least 3.85. Regent scholarships may be renewed by maintaining at least a 3.0 GPA. Students eligible for Presidential scholarships must have a minimum ACT score of 25 (1140 SAT) OR rank in the top 20 percent of their class OR have a cumulative grade point average of 3.5 or higher. Students must rank in the top 50 percent of their class and have a cumulative grade point average of 3.0. Presidential scholarships may be renewed by maintaining at least a 2.7 GPA. Meistersinger music scholarships (up to $4,00) are also available based on merit and audition but students do not have to be music majors to receive a scholarship. All scholarships are renewed each semester (up to 8 terms).

Campus Overview

Independent Lutheran 4-year, founded 1852 • **Coed** 1,804 undergraduate students, 96% full-time, 55% women, 45% men.

Undergraduates 1,725 full-time, 79 part-time. Students come from 25 states and territories, 36 other countries, 19% are from out of state, 3% African American, 2% Asian American or Pacific Islander, 1% Hispanic American, 0.1% Native American, 5% international, 2% transferred in, 79% live on campus.

Faculty Total: 165, 64% full-time, 62% with terminal degrees. Student/faculty ratio: 13:1.

Academic Programs Special study options: academic remediation for entering students, accelerated degree program, advanced placement credit, double majors, honors programs, independent study, internships, off-campus study, part-time degree program, student-designed majors, study abroad, summer session for credit. Unusual degree programs: 3-2 engineering with Iowa State University of Science and Technology, University of Iowa, University of Illinois at Urbana-Champaign, Washington University in St. Louis; occupational therapy with Washington University in St. Louis.

Athletics Member NCAA. All Division III. Intercollegiate sports: baseball M, basketball M/W, cheerleading W, cross-country running M/W, football M, golf M/W, soccer M/W, softball W, tennis M/W, track and field M/W, volleyball W, wrestling M. Intramural sports: badminton M/W, basketball M/W, golf M/W, racquetball M/W, rugby W, softball M/W, tennis M/W, ultimate Frisbee M/W, volleyball M/W.

Costs (2004–05) Comprehensive fee: $25,215 includes full-time tuition ($19,230), mandatory fees ($470), and room and board ($5515). Part-time tuition: $710 per credit. Part-time tuition and fees vary according to course load. Required fees: $15 per term part-time. College room only: $2715. Room and board charges vary according to board plan and housing facility.

Financial Aid 401 Federal Work-Study jobs (averaging $1489). 631 state and other part-time jobs (averaging $1622). In 2004, 366 non-need-based awards were made. Average percent of need met: 95%. Average financial aid package: $17,996. Average need-based loan: $6680. Average need-based gift aid: $11,749. Average non-need-based aid: $23,078.

Contact: Dr. Mariah Birgen, Wartburg College, 100 Wartburg Boulevard, Waverly, Iowa 50677; Telephone: 319-352-8565; Fax: 319-352-8606; E-mail: scholars@wartburg.edu

KANSAS

Emporia State University
University Honors Program
Emporia, Kansas

The mission of the University Honors Program is to create a community of student scholars who promote academic excellence, develop leadership, and encourage service to others. The Honors Program at Emporia State University (ESU) offers the best students a challenging academic program to achieve their full potential. The program supplements the regular curriculum at Emporia State University and prepares students for success by encouraging broad reading, individual thinking, creative problem solving, intellectual growth, and personal commitment. The courses within the Honors Program seek to provide a common intellectual experience for students from a variety of disciplines and degree programs. The program is very flexible and can accommodate students from a wide variety of majors.

In addition to the honors courses offered, Honors Program students get to meet and work individually with faculty members, participate in several community and University service activities, travel to special lectures, attend special presentations, and attend national and regional honors conventions. Members of the University Honors Program are regularly leaders in campus politics, student organizations, varsity sports, student ambassadors, residential life, theater, and other departmental activities. Members of the University Honors Program can also elect to stay on the Honors Floor.

Established in 1983, the University Honors Program currently has between 50 and 100 students who are active in the program.

Participation Requirements: Students who complete six honors courses or activities, one of which must be the Freshman Honors Seminar, graduate "with honors." Students who complete six honors courses or activities and do a public presentation of a senior thesis graduate "with high honors." To remain in the Honors Program, students must maintain a minimum GPA, which varies by classification, and make good progress toward graduation with honors. With completion of the program, graduates have "with honors" or "with high honors" entered on their diploma and transcript. Students may also graduate with summa, magna, and cum laude recognition, depending upon their GPA.

Admission Process: Students must apply to the program and submit two essays with the application. Admission to the University Honors Program requires a minimum composite ACT score of 26 and a cumulative high school GPA of at least 3.5. Students who do not meet both of these requirements may be admitted to the program after careful review of high school performance and commitment to excellence. Transfer students must have a cumulative GPA of 3.5 or above to apply.

Scholarship Availability: The University Honors Program does not administer its own scholarships. However, the University offers a number of scholarships to academically talented students. Emporia State University also offers Presidential Academic Achievement Awards to outstanding first-year freshmen. These are based on high school GPA and ACT scores.

Campus Overview

State-supported comprehensive, founded 1863, part of Kansas Board of Regents • **Coed** 4,370 undergraduate students, 87% full-time, 62% women, 38% men.

Undergraduates 3,796 full-time, 574 part-time. Students come from 30 states and territories, 30 other countries, 5% are from out of state, 4% African American, 0.8% Asian American or Pacific Islander, 4% Hispanic American, 0.7% Native American, 2% international, 11% transferred in, 25% live on campus.

Faculty *Total:* 273, 92% full-time, 72% with terminal degrees. *Student/faculty ratio:* 18:1.

Academic Programs *Special study options:* academic remediation for entering students, accelerated degree program, adult/continuing education programs, advanced placement credit, distance learning, double majors, English as a second language, honors programs, independent study, internships, off-campus study, part-time degree program, services for LD students, study abroad, summer session for credit. *Unusual degree programs:* 3-2 engineering with Kansas State University, University of Kansas, Wichita State University.

Athletics Member NCAA. All Division II. *Intercollegiate sports:* baseball M(s), basketball M(s)/W(s), cheerleading M(s)/W(s), cross-country running M(s)/W(s), football M(s), soccer W(s), softball W(s), tennis M(s)/W(s), track and field M(s)/W(s), volleyball W(s). *Intramural sports:* badminton M/W, basketball M/W, bowling M(c)/W(c), fencing M(c)/W(c), football M/W, rugby M(c), soccer M(c)/W(c), softball M/W, table tennis M/W, tennis M/W, volleyball M/W.

Costs (2004–05) *Tuition:* state resident $2410 full-time, $80 per credit hour part-time; nonresident $9130 full-time, $304 per credit hour part-time. Full-time tuition and fees vary according to degree level. Part-time tuition and fees vary according to degree level. *Required fees:* $626 full-time, $38 per credit hour part-time. *Room and board:* $4474; room only: $2208. Room and board charges vary according to board plan and housing facility.

Financial Aid 282 Federal Work-Study jobs (averaging $1282). 38 state and other part-time jobs (averaging $1021). In 2003, 371 non-need-based awards were made. *Average percent of need met:*

71%. *Average financial aid package:* $5430. *Average need-based loan:* $2899. *Average need-based gift aid:* $1735. *Average non-need-based aid:* $880.

Contact: Director: Dr. Dwight Moore, University Honors Program, Box 4073, Emporia State University, 1200 Commercial Street, Emporia, Kansas 66801-5087; *Telephone:* 620-341-5899; *Fax:* 620-341-5607; *E-mail:* honors@emporia.edu; *Web site:* http://www.emporia.edu/honors or http://www.emporia.edu

Johnson County Community College
Honors Program
Overland Park, Kansas

*T*he Johnson County Community College Honors Program is designed to stimulate and challenge academically talented students. By enrolling in the honors courses, motivated students can develop their intellectual potential and, at the same time, become active members of their academic and surrounding community.

Proof of academic excellence is the first stop for acceptance into the Honors Program. Students must submit, or have on file, an official transcript and have at least a 3.5 high school or college cumulative GPA. Students who do not have a 3.5 GPA may be considered for admission if they have a composite score of 25 on the ACT, a combined SAT score of 1200, or equivalent scores on other standardized tests taken within the last three years. Students may enter the Honors Program at the beginning of any semester and must maintain a minimum 3.5 GPA to graduate from the program.

Participation Requirements: Students may elect to participate in any part of the Honors Program; however, to graduate from the program, students must complete a minimum 10 hours of honors credit and 20 hours of specified community service. There are courses across the curriculum that combine an emphasis on specific content and skill development in interaction, analysis, synthesis, and conflict resolution. Students are asked to read primary and secondary sources, take initiative in course-related activities, and use analytical and evaluative skills.

Admission Process: Students must meet with one of the two Academic Counselors or the Honors Program Coordinator. The names and locations for these individuals can be found on the Honors Program Web site at http://www.jccc.net/home/depts/5214.

Scholarship Availability: Scholarships are available for students who plan to graduate from the College and the Honors Program. Scholarships are based on a minimum enrollment of 6 credit hours and a maximum enrollment of 15 credit hours. The intent of the scholarships is to cover tuition, books, and fees. Scholarships are awarded on a semester basis and are renewable.

Campus Overview

State and locally supported 2-year, founded 1967, part of Kansas State Board of Education • **Coed** 18,612 undergraduate students, 34% full-time, 55% women, 45% men.

Undergraduates 6,378 full-time, 12,234 part-time. Students come from 26 states and territories, 36 other countries, 5% are from out of state, 4% African American, 4% Asian American or Pacific Islander, 3% Hispanic American, 0.7% Native American, 1% international, 1% transferred in.

Faculty *Total:* 837, 36% full-time. *Student/faculty ratio:* 21:1.

Academic Programs *Special study options:* academic remediation for entering students, adult/continuing education programs, advanced placement credit, cooperative education, distance learning, double majors, English as a second language, honors programs, independent study, internships, off-campus study, part-time degree program, services for LD students, student-designed majors, summer session for credit.

Athletics Member NJCAA. *Intercollegiate sports:* baseball M(s), basketball M(s)/W(s), cross-country running M(s)/W(s), soccer M(s), softball W(s), tennis M(s)/W(s), track and field M(s)/W(s), volleyball W(s). *Intramural sports:* basketball M/W, soccer M, tennis M/W, volleyball M/W.

Costs (2005–06) *Tuition:* area resident $1920 full-time, $64 per credit hour part-time; state resident $2370 full-time, $79 per credit hour part-time; nonresident $4350 full-time, $145 per credit hour part-time. Full-time tuition and fees vary according to course load. Part-time tuition and fees vary according to course load.

Financial Aid 85 Federal Work-Study jobs (averaging $4000).

Contact: Director: Ruth Fox-Randall, 12345 College Boulevard, Overland Park, Kansas 66210-1299; *Telephone:* 913-469-2512; *Fax:* 913-469-2564; *E-mail:* rfox@jccc.edu

Neosho County Community College
Honors Leadership Academy
Chanute, Kansas

The Neosho County Community College (NCCC) Honors Leadership Academy challenges students to take honors level courses, practice leadership skills, and experience being a member of an exciting learning community. The program, started in 2000, offers a unique and challenging learning experience to students with the desire to excel. Members of the Academy have the opportunity to enroll in special sections of select general education courses that provide a stimulating learning experience. Members are also encouraged to realize their full potential and responsibility for leadership by studying leadership skills that use current research and classic examples. They share these experiences as a member of an exciting and committed learning community. The Honors Leadership Academy is a member of the National Collegiate Honors Council and the Great Plains Honors Council.

To be accepted by the Academy, students must have a high school or college cumulative GPA of 3.5 or higher and an ACT score of 25 or above or an SAT score of 700 or above. To begin the admissions process, students must complete the general admissions requirements. Students must then fill out an Honors Leadership Academy application and write an essay that includes a biographical sketch with educational and personal goals, along with what the student feels they offer the Academy. A copy of ACT or SAT scores, high school and/or college transcripts, and three letters of recommendation must accompany the application and essay.

Participation Requirements: Members of the Academy must maintain a 3.5 GPA, enroll full-time in honors core courses, participate in Academy activities, and volunteer 20 hours of community or school service each semester. To graduate from NCCC as an Honors Scholar, students must complete 21 or more hours of honors courses, have a 3.5 GPA, and fulfill all other requirements of the Honors Leadership Academy.

Scholarship Availability: Neosho County Community College offers a variety of scholarships, as well as federal financial assistance. The College awards more than $1 million of assistance each year to help students fund their educational expenses. Students are encouraged to inquire about federal financial aid, academic scholarships, in-district scholarships, and endowment scholarships. Talent and program scholarships are available from one of the following areas: academic excellence challenge team, art, athletic training, baseball,

basketball, coed cheerleading, dance, cross-country/track and field, debate, forensics, golf, Honor's Leadership Academy (Honors Program), music (vocal and instrumental), nursing, senior citizen, soccer, softball, sports information, technical and industrial, theater, volleyball, and wrestling.

Campus Overview
State and locally supported 2-year, founded 1936, part of Kansas State Board of Education • **Coed** 1,826 undergraduate students, 34% full-time, 67% women, 33% men.

Undergraduates 615 full-time, 1,211 part-time. Students come from 15 states and territories, 5% African American, 2% Asian American or Pacific Islander, 3% Hispanic American, 1% Native American, 5% live on campus.

Faculty *Total:* 126, 32% full-time.

Academic Programs *Special study options:* academic remediation for entering students, adult/continuing education programs, advanced placement credit, part-time degree program, services for LD students, student-designed majors, summer session for credit.

Athletics Member NJCAA. *Intercollegiate sports:* baseball M(s), basketball M(s)/W(s), cross-country running M(s)/W(s), softball W(s), track and field M(s), volleyball W(s). *Intramural sports:* basketball M/W, cross-country running M/W, softball M/W, track and field M/W, volleyball M/W.

Financial Aid 73 Federal Work-Study jobs (averaging $800).

Contact: Coordinator: Brad Wilkinson, Honors Leadership Academy, 800 West 14th Street, Chanute, Kansas 66720; *Telephone:* 620-431-2820 Ext. 223; *Fax:* 620-431-0082; *E-mail:* bwilkinson@neosho.edu

Pittsburg State University
Honors College and Departmental Honors Program
Pittsburg, Kansas

Pittsburg State University offers two types of honors programs: the Honors College and the Departmental Honors Program.

The primary mission of the Honors College is to provide a more meaningful educational experience for select superior students. The Honors College curriculum at the freshman-sophomore level offers intellectually stimulating general education courses. The junior-senior level Honors College students become integrated into the Departmental Honors Program.

Established in 1988, the Honors College currently enrolls approximately 125 students.

Participation Requirements: To graduate from the Honors College program, entering freshmen must complete a minimum of 12 hours of general education honors courses and honors orientation. A minimum 3.4 GPA must also be maintained. Presidential and transfer scholars must also complete the Departmental Honors Program with a minimum of 9 credit hours. Departmental Honors offers the opportunity for mentored research above normal requirements for designated upper-level course work. Other Honors College scholars are also encouraged to complete Departmental Honors. A 3.5 GPA is required to enter Departmental Honors course work, which is open to any qualified campus student.

Admission Process: Honors College members are a carefully screened and select group of scholarship recipients. Most enter the program their freshman year after formal application and acceptance. A small number of junior-level transfer students and screened international students are also admitted. To be eligible, freshmen must have a minimum composite ACT score of 28, a minimum high school GPA of 3.5 (on a 4.0 scale), and/or provide proof of adding multicultural diversity to the Honors Program. Transfer scholars must have completed 40 semester hours with a minimum GPA of 3.75 on a 4.0 scale. The application package consists of a transcript verifying class standing and course preparation, a letter of activities and awards, recommendations, and an essay. The deadline for applicants is February 1.

Scholarship Availability: The Honors College has 12 Presidential Scholars, 17 University Scholars, 6 Transfer Scholars, and an additional group of select scholars admitted annually. Presidential Scholars receive fall and spring tuition, room and board, and a book allowance. University and Transfer Scholars receive fall and spring in-state tuition and are eligible for other awards.

Campus Overview

State-supported comprehensive, founded 1903, part of Kansas Board of Regents • **Coed** 5,493 undergraduate students, 92% full-time, 49% women, 51% men.

Undergraduates 5,034 full-time, 459 part-time. Students come from 25 states and territories, 48 other countries, 19% are from out of state, 3% African American, 0.5% Asian American or Pacific Islander, 2% Hispanic American, 2% Native American, 4% international, 10% transferred in, 14% live on campus.

Faculty *Total:* 376, 76% full-time, 68% with terminal degrees. *Student/faculty ratio:* 18:1.

Academic Programs *Special study options:* academic remediation for entering students, adult/continuing education programs, advanced placement credit, cooperative education, distance learning, double majors, English as a second language, external degree program, freshman honors college, honors programs, independent study, internships, off-campus study, part-time degree program, services for LD students, student-designed majors, study abroad, summer session for credit. *ROTC:* Army (b). *Unusual degree programs:* 3-2 engineering with Kansas State University, University of Kansas.

Athletics Member NCAA. All Division II. *Intercollegiate sports:* baseball M(s), basketball M(s)/W(s), cross-country running M(s)/W(s), football M(s), golf M(s), softball W(s), track and field M(s)/W(s), volleyball W(s). *Intramural sports:* basketball M/W, cheerleading M(c)/W(c), football M/W, racquetball M/W, rugby M(c), soccer M(c), softball M/W, table tennis M/W, tennis M/W, volleyball M/W.

Costs (2004–05) *Tuition:* state resident $2632 full-time, $88 per credit hour part-time; nonresident $8990 full-time, $300 per credit hour part-time. *Required fees:* $662 full-time, $30 per credit hour part-time. *Room and board:* $4234. Room and board charges vary according to board plan.

Financial Aid 246 Federal Work-Study jobs (averaging $1309). 1,019 state and other part-time jobs (averaging $1457). In 2004, 414 non-need-based awards were made. *Average percent of need met:* 87%. *Average financial aid package:* $6785. *Average need-based loan:* $3762. *Average need-based gift aid:* $3165. *Average non-need-based aid:* $1745.

Contact: Director: Dr. Becky Brannock, 1701 South Broadway, Pittsburg, Kansas 66762; *Telephone:* 620-235-4569

University of Kansas
University Honors Program

Lawrence, Kansas

The University of Kansas (KU) has one of the oldest honors programs in the nation and was one of a core group of institutions that helped shape the early honors movement. KU also hosted the first annual National Collegiate Honors Council conference in 1966. The University Honors Program (UHP) exists to help provide its students with the intellectually challenging and stimulating courses, the out-of-class experiences, and the personalized advising they need to gain the most from their undergraduate years and to be well prepared for the future. Honors courses emphasize critical thinking and skill in self-expression and are taught by outstanding faculty members. The UHP encourages students to take advantage of study-abroad programs, internships, scholarships, and fellowships. Honors students have several options for on-campus housing. They can choose from nine scholarship halls or from two honors floors in suite style or traditional residence-hall setting.

Participation Requirements: The UHP is a four-year program that does not add extra course hours to degree requirements. Students take a Freshman Honors Seminar and 8 honors units, consisting of at least six honors courses plus at least one of the following approved projects: research, creative arts project, service, internship, or study abroad. The eighth unit may be a course or other approved project to fulfill the program. Students must also maintain a minimum grade-point average of 3.25. Completion of the UHP is noted on students' transcripts.

Admission Process: Honors staff members consider several aspects in admitting students into the program, including high school curriculum and GPA, standardized test scores, extracurricular activities, and an essay. Most students are accepted to begin their freshman year. Students not accepted before the beginning of their first year may reapply after completing at least one semester.

Scholarship Availability: KU offers nearly $5 million in scholarships to incoming students. Some scholarships are awarded based solely on merit and others on both merit and need. Returning students may compete for approximately eighty Undergraduate Research Awards and twenty University Scholars Program Awards. There are also the Sara and Mary Paretsky Award for Creativity, the J. Michael Young Opportunity Award, the College Scholarships, and several other awards and scholarships for graduating seniors. The UHP coordinates the local nomination of several national scholarships and coordinates the selection process for the Rhodes, Marshall, Mitchell, Gates, Churchill, Soros, Jack Kent Cooke, Truman, Udall, and Goldwater scholarships. The UHP also provides assistance to applicants of the National Science Foundation, the Fulbright, and the Mellon Fellowships.

The UHP awards nearly $80,000 annually to students in support of undergraduate research. The UHP administers the Undergraduate Research Awards and the annual Undergraduate Research Symposium. Students are encouraged to present their research at professional conferences and seek publication when applicable.

Campus Overview

State-supported university, founded 1866 • **Coed** 21,343 undergraduate students, 88% full-time, 51% women, 49% men.

Undergraduates 18,687 full-time, 2,656 part-time. Students come from 52 states and territories, 113 other countries, 24% are from out of state, 3% African American, 4% Asian American or Pacific Islander, 3% Hispanic American, 1% Native American, 3% international, 7% transferred in, 23% live on campus.

Faculty *Total:* 1,336, 89% full-time, 89% with terminal degrees. *Student/faculty ratio:* 19:1.

Academic Programs *Special study options:* academic remediation for entering students, accelerated degree program, advanced placement credit, cooperative education, distance learning, double majors, English as a second language, honors programs, independent study, internships, part-time degree program, services for LD students, study abroad, summer session for credit. *ROTC:* Army (b), Navy (b), Air Force (b).

Athletics Member NCAA. All Division I except football (Division I-A). *Intercollegiate sports:* baseball M(s), basketball M(s)/W(s), crew M(c)/W(s), cross-country running M(s)/W(s), fencing M(c)/W(c), golf M(s)/W(s), rugby M(c)/W(c), soccer W(s), softball W(s), swimming and diving W(s), tennis W(s), track and field M(s)/W(s), volleyball W(s). *Intramural sports:* basketball M/W, bowling M(c)/W(c), crew M(c)/W(c), football M/W, golf M/W, gymnastics M(c)/W(c), ice hockey M(c)/W(c), lacrosse M(c)/W(c), racquetball M/W, rock climbing M(c)/W(c), sailing M(c)/W(c), soccer M(c)/W(c), softball M/W, table tennis M/W, tennis M/W, ultimate Frisbee M(c)/W(c), volleyball M(c), water polo M(c)/W(c), wrestling M.

Costs (2004–05) *Tuition:* state resident $4163 full-time, $139 per credit hour part-time; nonresident $12,117 full-time, $404 per credit hour part-time. Full-time tuition and fees vary according to program and reciprocity agreements. Part-time tuition and fees vary according to program and reciprocity agreements. *Required fees:* $574 full-time, $48 per credit hour part-time. *Room and board:* $5216; room only: $2576. Room and board charges vary according to board plan and housing facility.

Financial Aid 393 Federal Work-Study jobs (averaging $2148). 106 state and other part-time jobs (averaging $4412). In 2003, 1922 non-need-based awards were made. *Average percent of need met:* 70%. *Average financial aid package:* $6610. *Average need-based loan:* $3602. *Average need-based gift aid:* $3353. *Average non-need-based aid:* $4054.

Contact: Professor Stanley Lombardo, University Honors Program, University of Kansas, 1506 Engel Road, Lawrence, Kansas 66045-3854; *Telephone:* 785-864-4225; *Fax:* 785-864-5178; *E-mail:* honors@ku.edu; *Web site:* http://www.ku.edu/~honors/

Wichita State University
Emory Lindquist Honors Program
Wichita, Kansas

The Emory Lindquist Honors Program serves students in all six degree-granting colleges of the University. The honors curriculum includes honors tracks through the University's general education requirements and the major. Additional nonrequired honors courses are also available.

The Honors Program provides academic advising services and faculty mentoring, actively supports students seeking national postgraduate scholarships and fellowships, and encourages participation in regional and national honors organizations.

The program maintains a popular student lounge, computer room, and an honors residence facility. The student-led Honors Society sponsors a continuing series of lectures, discussions, field trips, and social occasions. The annual freshman retreat orients students to college life and academics.

In addition to recognition awarded by the University to all students achieving outstanding academic records, Honors Program graduates receive the notation Honors Program Graduate on their transcripts and are recognized at Commencement. Most also earn departmental honors at graduation.

The program is more than 40 years old and currently enrolls 600 students.

Participation Requirements: The honors track in general education is a sequence of three freshman/sophomore seminars. Enrollment in these seminars is limited to 15 students. Seminar topics range widely but are consistent with the general education program's focus on the traditional liberal arts and sciences. Honors seminars are also designed to develop a student's learning skills by emphasizing writing, oral communication, library research, and mathematics. At the upper division, students complete a 12-hour honors track in their major department, including a senior thesis or project.

Admission Process: Generally, freshmen are admitted to the program if their composite score on the ACT is 26 or higher or if their high school GPA is 3.5 or higher, as certified by the University. Transfer and continuing students may enter the program if they have

achieved a minimum GPA of 3.25 in university-level studies and if they satisfy the minimum GPA requirements. Those who are not members of the program may enroll in honors courses if they have the permission of the honors director.

Scholarship Availability: Many participants hold major University scholarships, most of which are awarded through the annual Distinguished Scholarship Invitational.

Campus Overview
State-supported university, founded 1895, part of Kansas Board of Regents • **Coed** 11,199 undergraduate students, 64% full-time, 57% women, 43% men.

Undergraduates 7,217 full-time, 3,982 part-time. Students come from 45 states and territories, 77 other countries, 3% are from out of state, 7% African American, 7% Asian American or Pacific Islander, 5% Hispanic American, 1% Native American, 5% international, 11% transferred in, 7% live on campus.

Faculty *Total:* 522, 90% full-time, 76% with terminal degrees. *Student/faculty ratio:* 18:1.

Academic Programs *Special study options:* academic remediation for entering students, accelerated degree program, advanced placement credit, cooperative education, distance learning, double majors, English as a second language, freshman honors college, honors programs, independent study, internships, off-campus study, part-time degree program, services for LD students, student-designed majors, study abroad, summer session for credit. *Unusual degree programs:* 3-2 accounting.

Athletics Member NCAA. All Division I. *Intercollegiate sports:* baseball M(s), basketball M(s)/W(s), bowling M(c)/W(c), cheerleading M/W, crew M(c)/W(c), cross-country running M(s)/W(s), golf M(s)/W(s), ice hockey M(c)/W(c), racquetball M(c)/W(c), rugby M(c), soccer M(c)/W(c), softball W(s), swimming and diving M(c)/W(c), tennis M(s)/W(s), track and field M(s)/W(s), volleyball M(c)/W(s), wrestling M(c). *Intramural sports:* badminton M/W, basketball M/W, bowling M/W, football M/W, golf M/W, racquetball M/W, soccer M/W, softball M/W, swimming and diving M/W, table tennis M/W, tennis M/W, ultimate Frisbee M/W, volleyball M/W, weight lifting M/W.

Costs (2004–05) *Tuition:* state resident $3150 full-time, $105 per credit hour part-time; nonresident $11,362 full-time, $353 per credit hour part-time. Full-time tuition and fees vary according to course load. *Required fees:* $759 full-time, $24 per credit hour part-time, $17 per credit hour part-time. *Room and board:* $4900. Room and board charges vary according to board plan and housing facility.

Financial Aid 195 Federal Work-Study jobs (averaging $2576). In 2003, 675 non-need-based awards were made. *Average percent of need met:* 51%. *Average financial aid package:* $5207. *Average need-based loan:* $4224. *Average need-based gift aid:* $3453. *Average non-need-based aid:* $1419.

Contact: Director: Almer J. Mandt III, 1845 Fairmount, Wichita, Kansas 67260-0102; *Telephone:* 316-978-3375; *Fax:* 316-978-3351; *E-mail:* honors@wichita.edu

KENTUCKY

Bellarmine University
Honors Program
Louisville, Kentucky

The Bellarmine University Honors Program provides opportunities for academic excellence and for meaningful learning in and outside the classroom. It features an enhanced track of courses allowing for advanced study in a wide variety of areas and provides in-depth

research opportunities across the disciplines. The program is open to qualified, motivated students of all majors.

Honors students take specially designated interdisciplinary seminars through their four years (at least five seminars total). These innovative seminars offer an honors-quality track for satisfying general education courses required of all students. For instance, while all Bellarmine students take a freshman seminar, Honors students choose a specially designated honors section of the freshman seminar. The sequence of core courses continues with the U.S. Experience course, the Transcultural Experience course, and a Senior Seminar. Other general education requirements may also be earned through honors. Honors seminars offer small, discussion-oriented sections. A significant benefit of the seminar sequence is the experience of moving through a series of classes with a group of academically motivated peers and the intellectual and social relationships that develop. We aim to encourage participatory learning through the interchange of ideas between students and professors and among students themselves. Outside the classroom, Honors students have distinguished themselves through their involvement in student government, Mock Trial (recent National Champions), the Model Arab League, campus theater, various campus publications, and service outreach programs. We also encourage Honors Program participants to engage with the world outside of Bellarmine: most spend a semester or a summer in a study abroad program.

During the junior year, Honors students begin designing independent studies under the guidance of a committee of three mentors/professors; these projects continue with in-depth study through the senior year, culminating in a Senior Honors Thesis. Senior honors students present the results of their work at a formal event each spring.

On the social front, throughout the four years Honors students are invited to a number of formal and informal cultural and social events; we have had picnics, receptions, ice cream parties, trips to the zoo, canoe trips, and more. At least once a semester students are invited on a guided tour of exhibits at Louisville's Speed Museum. In addition, tickets to plays, concerts, ballets, and operas are frequently made available to Honors students at little or no cost. Honors students are invited to meet distinguished visitors to the campus in small group discussions; recently this has meant Honors students have been able to engage in discussions with such figures as recent-Poet Laureate Billy Collins, internationally acclaimed novelist Isabel Allende, journalists Andrea Mitchell and Seymour Hersh, and Pulitzer-Prize winning scientist Jared Diamond, among others.

Honors students also have the opportunity to take advantage of Specialty Housing. Bonaventure Hall has been designated for Honors program participants, providing the opportunity for more out-of-class interaction and a quieter study environment, along with an Honors lounge and meeting room. Educational and social programming beyond that typical to Residence Life is part of the package.

Over 120 students currently participate in the Honors Program.

Participation Requirements: Honors Program participants take at least five honors seminars and complete a senior honors thesis. Twenty-two credit hours are required to complete the program, fifteen through seminars and seven for the senior thesis. The seminar hours, however, also fulfill general education requirements.

Students are asked to maintain a 3.25 to continue in the program; a grace period to rebuild is typically provided to those who slip below that mark. At graduation, Honors graduates wear special regalia, receive a certificate at an awards banquet, and have their achievement recorded on their permanent transcript. The Honors Thesis is listed in the graduation program and housed in the campus library.

Admission Process: The Honors Council reviews files of qualified incoming students and issues invitations in the spring before matriculation. An ACT of 27+ and a high GPA are typical. Looking beyond such numbers, however, the program seeks students who demonstrate a love of learning and a desire to pursue advanced education. Motivated students are encouraged to contact the director

with a letter of interest. Transfer students and current students with a strong academic profile may join the program through the sophomore year.

Scholarship Availability: The Bellarmine Scholar Award provides full-tuition for four years and a stipend of $4,000 for study abroad. Bellarmine Scholars must maintain a 3.5 GPA and remain active in the Honors Program.

Campus Overview

Independent Roman Catholic comprehensive, founded 1950 • **Coed** 2,561 undergraduate students, 62% full-time, 60% women, 40% men.

Undergraduates 1,586 full-time, 975 part-time. Students come from 39 states and territories, 31% are from out of state, 4% African American, 2% Asian American or Pacific Islander, 0.8% Hispanic American, 0.3% Native American, 0.3% international, 4% transferred in, 37% live on campus.

Faculty *Total:* 251, 46% full-time. *Student/faculty ratio:* 13:1.

Academic Programs *Special study options:* accelerated degree program, adult/continuing education programs, advanced placement credit, double majors, honors programs, independent study, internships, off-campus study, part-time degree program, services for LD students, student-designed majors, study abroad, summer session for credit. *ROTC:* Army (c), Air Force (c).

Athletics Member NCAA. All Division II except lacrosse (Division I). *Intercollegiate sports:* baseball M(s), basketball M(s)/W(s), cross-country running M(s)/W(s), field hockey W(s), golf M(s)/W(s), lacrosse M(s), soccer M(s)/W(s), softball W(s), tennis M(s)/W(s), track and field M(s)/W(s), volleyball W(s). *Intramural sports:* basketball M/W, football M/W, golf M/W, soccer M/W, table tennis M/W, tennis M/W, volleyball M/W, weight lifting M/W.

Costs (2005–06) *Comprehensive fee:* $27,910 includes full-time tuition ($20,800), mandatory fees ($730), and room and board ($6380). *College room only:* $3480.

Financial Aid In 2002, 390 non-need-based awards were made. *Average percent of need met:* 89%. *Average financial aid package:* $13,762.

Contact: Director: Dr. Kathryn West, Bellarmine University, 2001 Newburg Road, Louisville, Kentucky 40205; *Telephone:* 502-452-8210; *E-mail:* kwest@bellarmine.edu

Eastern Kentucky University
Honors Program
Richmond, Kentucky

T he Eastern Kentucky University (EKU) Honors Program has been designed especially for those intellectually promising students who seek a strong grounding in the liberal arts along with their more specialized major. Such students may be most at home in an intellectually intense, small-college atmosphere within the context of the larger University. Small class sizes of no more than 20 students per class allow for individualized attention and for one-on-one dialogue with the instructors. A distinctive feature of the Honors Program is that many courses are team-taught by professors from different disciplines. Such an approach contributes to the integration of knowledge, and the program as a whole provides students with a necessary model of civilized intellectual interaction and allows students to see how ideas become enriched when approached from two different perspectives.

Students share with one another and with the faculty the pleasure and stimulation of outside speakers, films, suppers, trips to historical sites and cultural events, retreats, and state, regional, and national conferences. They have the opportunity of living in an honors hall and making use of an honors common room for study, informal meetings, classes, and programs they plan themselves.

The 31-credit-hour program offers courses that emphasize the development of skills in effective communication, critical thinking, and the integration of knowledge from various disciplines. All course work in the EKU Honors Program meets University general education requirements. Therefore, regardless of major, any qualified student can participate in the program.

Fourth-year Honors Scholars complete a senior-level thesis and seminar. This thesis project can take whatever form suits the subject (e.g., a research paper, a creative composition or art work, a performance or recital). Each student works with a faculty mentor, who offers guidance and support throughout the development of the thesis project.

Students who successfully complete the EKU Honors Program curriculum are designated Honors Scholars when they graduate, and the phrase appears on their diplomas and on their official transcripts from the University.

There are currently 420 students in the program.

Admission Process: Students with strong academic backgrounds are invited to apply to the Honors Program. National Merit Finalists and Semifinalists are automatically accepted. Beyond these, students with high school GPAs of 3.5 or better on a 4.0 scale and with a score of at least 26 on the ACT are given priority. Other students who demonstrate the potential for outstanding academic performance are considered.

Scholarship Availability: Abundant opportunities for scholarships exist under Eastern's academic scholarship program, and students interested in scholarship aid should apply directly to that program. All students in the Honors Program receive at least a Presidential-level scholarship as well as a Books-on-Loan Award for eight semesters.

Campus Overview

State-supported comprehensive, founded 1906, part of Kentucky Council on Post Secondary Education • **Coed** 13,837 undergraduate students, 78% full-time, 61% women, 39% men.

Undergraduates 10,833 full-time, 3,004 part-time. Students come from 41 states and territories, 42 other countries, 11% are from out of state, 4% African American, 1% Asian American or Pacific Islander, 0.7% Hispanic American, 0.4% Native American, 0.6% international, 7% transferred in, 33% live on campus.

Faculty Total: 956, 58% full-time. Student/faculty ratio: 17:1.

Academic Programs Special study options: academic remediation for entering students, accelerated degree program, adult/continuing education programs, advanced placement credit, cooperative education, distance learning, double majors, English as a second language, external degree program, honors programs, independent study, internships, part-time degree program, services for LD students, student-designed majors, study abroad, summer session for credit. ROTC: Army (b), Air Force (c). Unusual degree programs: 3-2 engineering with Georgia Institute of Technology, University of Kentucky, Auburn University.

Athletics Member NCAA. All Division I. Intercollegiate sports: baseball M(s), basketball M(s)/W(s), cheerleading M/W, cross-country running M(s)/W(s), football M(s), golf M(s)/W(s), softball W(s), tennis M(s)/W(s), track and field M(s)/W(s), volleyball W(s). Intramural sports: badminton M/W, basketball M/W, fencing M(c)/W(c), football M/W, golf M/W, ice hockey M(c), racquetball M/W, rugby M(c)/W(c), soccer M(c)/W(c), softball M/W, tennis M/W, track and field M/W, ultimate Frisbee M/W, volleyball M/W, weight lifting M/W.

Costs (2004–05) Tuition: state resident $3332 full-time, $158 per credit hour part-time; nonresident $10,004 full-time, $436 per credit hour part-time. Part-time tuition and fees vary according to course load. Required fees: $460 full-time. Room and board: $4658; room only: $2208. Room and board charges vary according to board plan and housing facility.

Financial Aid 1,573 Federal Work-Study jobs (averaging $1712). 1,288 state and other part-time jobs (averaging $1749). In 2003, 2618 non-need-based awards were made. Average percent of need met: 87%. Average financial aid package: $6183. Average need-based loan: $2547. Average need-based gift aid: $3877. Average non-need-based aid: $1835.

Contact: Director: Dr. Bonnie J. Gray, 168 Case Annex, Richmond, Kentucky 40475; Telephone: 859-622-1403; Fax: 859-622-5089; E-mail: bonnie.gray@eku.edu; Web site: http://www.honors.eku.edu

---

Georgetown College
Honors Program
Georgetown, Kentucky

The Honors Program at Georgetown College offers talented students a variety of opportunities to make the most of their intellectual abilities. Honors students enjoy challenging course work and engaging discussions as they interact with each other and select faculty members in honors activities. The program seeks to propel students to higher academic achievement even as it introduces them to an array of new viewpoints. At the same time, the program prepares students to complete an honors thesis in the senior year by fostering students' capacity for independent thought and research in a series of class experiences.

Students have three options for earning honors credit. Honors courses are available only to honors students, so usually they contain 10–15 students. In these classes, the course material and assignments are adjusted to be more suitable for honors students, so the pace is appropriate, work is meaningful, and discussions are lively and engaging. Another credit option is honors increments, which are standard classes (open to anyone) with an enriching honors component added for honors students. In an increment, honors students often interact with each other and the professor to examine an extra topic, discuss original source material, or undertake a project. Finally, students may create an honors contract to convert any class into an honors experience, tailoring the additional expectations to the student's interests and abilities. Most honors credit is earned in the general education classes. For the increments and contracts, the full class usually has no more than 25 students, and the honors component usually has fewer than 8 students.

The breadth of credit options enables students to earn honors credit in a variety of disciplines. As a result, a cross-section of the faculty is actively engaged in the Honors Program. The program also includes informal opportunities for honors students and faculty members to interact. Each year, there are dinner meetings at which students and faculty members discuss a variety of topics. Students are actively involved in the planning, in an effort to select topics that interest current participants in the program.

Since Georgetown College has a partnership with Regents Park College at Oxford, honors students may study for a semester or year at Oxford and count some of those classes for honors credit. In addition, select students may participate in an accelerated program and earn degrees from both Georgetown College and Oxford University in only five years.

Seniors develop an independent research project (or artistic project) for an honors thesis. This study enables the student, under the guidance of faculty members, to complete an independent, original investigation of a question that interests the student (or produce an artistic work of comparable achievement). At this point, the student becomes the scholar and teacher, presenting the work to the campus community at an open poster session in the spring.

There are approximately 80 students in this program, which was founded in 2002.

Participation Requirements: Students in the Honors Program must complete 15 hours of honors credit in honors classes, increments, or contracts. In addition, they must take an interdisciplinary honors seminar in the junior year. To complete the program, they must take a class dedicated to producing an honors thesis, and 2 faculty readers (from different disciplines) must approve the thesis. Students must maintain a minimum 3.3 GPA to remain in the program.

Students who successfully complete the Honors Program are recognized at commencement, and their transcript includes an Honors Program designation to indicate the student's accomplishment.

Admission Process: Georgetown College encourages talented students who delight in learning to apply to the program. Students applying directly from high school must report both standardized test scores (ACT or SAT) and high school GPA, and submit three brief essays. If students do not join the program as incoming freshmen, they may still apply at any time prior to the end of the sophomore year. Georgetown students who wish to apply must report their college GPA and submit the three essays. The Honors Committee reviews applications and decides whom to admit to the program. There is a rolling admission process, but space is limited to 30 students per class year.

Scholarship Availability: Almost all of Georgetown's honors students receive merit-based scholarships from the college when they enroll. These scholarships are available regardless of whether the student joins the Honors Program. There are no scholarships restricted to honors students at this time.

Campus Overview

Independent comprehensive, founded 1829, affiliated with Baptist Church • **Coed** 1,334 undergraduate students, 94% full-time, 54% women, 46% men.

Undergraduates 1,259 full-time, 75 part-time. Students come from 22 states and territories, 11 other countries, 17% are from out of state, 4% African American, 0.8% Asian American or Pacific Islander, 0.7% Hispanic American, 0.2% Native American, 1% international, 2% transferred in, 88% live on campus.

Faculty *Total:* 160, 63% full-time, 55% with terminal degrees. *Student/faculty ratio:* 11:1.

Academic Programs *Special study options:* advanced placement credit, cooperative education, double majors, honors programs, independent study, internships, off-campus study, part-time degree program, student-designed majors, study abroad, summer session for credit. *ROTC:* Army (c), Air Force (c). *Unusual degree programs:* 3-2 engineering with University of Kentucky, Washington University in St. Louis; nursing with University of Kentucky.

Athletics Member NAIA. *Intercollegiate sports:* baseball M(s), basketball M(s)/W(s), cheerleading W(s), cross-country running M(s)/W(s), football M(s), golf M(s)/W(s), soccer M(s)/W(s), softball W(s), tennis M(s)/W(s), track and field M(s)/W(s), volleyball W(s). *Intramural sports:* basketball M/W, football M/W, golf M/W, racquetball M/W, soccer M/W, softball M/W, table tennis M/W, tennis M/W, ultimate Frisbee M/W, volleyball M/W.

Costs (2005–06) *Comprehensive fee:* $24,950 includes full-time tuition ($19,170) and room and board ($5780). Part-time tuition: $800 per hour. *College room only:* $2790.

Financial Aid 472 Federal Work-Study jobs (averaging $1117). In 2004, 341 non-need-based awards were made. *Average percent of need met:* 88%. *Average financial aid package:* $15,594. *Average need-based loan:* $3916. *Average need-based gift aid:* $7544. *Average non-need-based aid:* $8029.

Contact: Dr. Thomas E. Cooper, Honors Committee Chair, Box 204, Georgetown College, 400 East College Street, Georgetown, Kentucky 40324; *Telephone:* 502-863-7957; *Fax:* 502-868-8886; *E-mail:* tcooper2@georgetowncollege.edu; Web site: http://spider.georgetown college.edu/english/thehonorsprogram.htm

Kentucky State University
The Whitney Young School of Honors and Liberal Studies
Frankfort, Kentucky

The Whitney Young School of Honors and Liberal Studies (WYS) is named after the late Whitney M. Young Jr., Executive Director of the National Urban League from 1961 to 1971. He was one of the most distinguished leaders of the American civil rights movement and a graduate of Kentucky State University (KSU). The mission of the School is to develop in students the qualities of leadership that were demonstrated by Mr. Young. Such leadership qualities and skills include the development of intellectual skills that help students deal with fundamental questions of human existence and make them better able to guide their own lives. WYS is an integrated liberal arts program. It emphasizes student participation in classroom discussion, small classes of 15 or fewer students, a challenging interdisciplinary curriculum with multicultural components, a faculty devoted to undergraduate education, and a community spirit among faculty members and students. WYS has its own faculty.

The WYS program is an integrated sequence of seminar, math/science, and language courses. It is a great-books program in which students develop the precision and power of their minds by reading and discussing some of the world's best books.

In addition, WYS also administers the Institute for Liberal Studies, the Integrative Studies courses of the University's liberal studies requirements, and the newly designed international studies program minor.

Several options are available for honors students at WYS. Most honors students fulfill all University general education requirements by taking an integrated sequence of honors core courses. Students who complete the honors core may also elect to receive an Associate of Arts degree in liberal studies. WYS also offers a bachelor's degree in liberal studies, with a liberal studies curriculum flexible enough to allow most students to double-major in liberal studies and a traditional discipline.

WYS offers opportunities for study abroad as well as paid summer internships in Washington, D.C. Students gain automatic membership in the National Collegiate Honors Council, with opportunities to attend regional and national conferences. The Whitney Young School Student Council organizes social activities, engages in public service, and participates in field trips. Approximately 70 students are enrolled in WYS. Honor students major in every department and college at KSU.

Participation Requirements: To fulfill the honors core requirements, students ordinarily complete 48 credit hours of an integrated sequence of freshman and sophomore courses. Science majors, nursing majors, and math majors have special honors packages of less than 48 credit hours. To earn a Bachelor of Arts in liberal studies, students must complete at least 30 credit hours in the major, take a minor, and complete a minimum of 128 credit hours overall. To earn an Associate of Arts degree in liberal studies, students must complete the honors core and 67 credit hours overall. To earn a minor in liberal studies, students must complete 18 credit hours.

Admission Process: Admission of first-year students to WYS is by special application. After students have applied and been admitted to KSU, prospective students must apply to WYS. Students applying for admission to WYS must possess a strong academic background in high school, a minimum ACT composite score of 21 or the SAT equivalent, and a strong desire to learn. Transfer students are also considered and may pursue a major or minor in liberal studies.

Scholarship Availability: WYS administers its own scholarship program. Applications must be made to the Director of the School. In addition, KSU has a merit-based institutional scholarship program.

Campus Overview

State-related comprehensive, founded 1886 • **Coed** 2,183 undergraduate students, 74% full-time, 59% women, 41% men.

Undergraduates 1,617 full-time, 566 part-time. Students come from 29 states and territories, 24 other countries, 37% are from out of state, 64% African American, 1% Asian American or Pacific Islander, 0.7% Hispanic American, 0.1% Native American, 0.2% international, 5% transferred in, 26% live on campus.

Faculty *Total:* 162, 94% full-time. *Student/faculty ratio:* 15:1.

Academic Programs *Special study options:* academic remediation for entering students, accelerated degree program, adult/continuing education programs, advanced placement credit, cooperative education, English as a second language, honors programs, independent study, internships, off-campus study, part-time degree program, services for LD students, student-designed majors, study abroad, summer session for credit. *ROTC:* Air Force (c). *Unusual degree programs:* 3-2 engineering with University of Kentucky, University of Maryland College Park.

Athletics Member NCAA. All Division II. *Intercollegiate sports:* baseball M, basketball M(s)/W(s), cross-country running M(s)/W(s), football M(s), golf M(s), softball W, tennis M(s)/W(s), track and field M(s)/W(s), volleyball W(s). *Intramural sports:* archery M/W, basketball M/W, bowling M/W, football M/W, soccer M/W, swimming and diving M/W, tennis M/W, track and field M/W, volleyball M/W.

Costs (2004–05) *Tuition:* state resident $3172 full-time, $130 per credit part-time; nonresident $8929 full-time, $367 per credit part-time. Full-time tuition and fees vary according to class time, course level, course load, location, program, reciprocity agreements, and student level. Part-time tuition and fees vary according to class time, course level, course load, location, program, reciprocity agreements, and student level. *Required fees:* $608 full-time, $19 per credit part-time, $43 per term part-time. *Room and board:* $5658; room only: $2630. Room and board charges vary according to board plan, housing facility, location, and student level.

Financial Aid 500 Federal Work-Study jobs. In 2003, 381 non-need-based awards were made. *Average percent of need met:* 85%. *Average financial aid package:* $11,500. *Average non-need-based aid:* $4000.

Contact: Dean: Dr. Thomas McPartland, Carver Hall, Room 133, Frankfort, Kentucky 40601; *Telephone:* 502-597-6411; *Fax:* 502-597-6041; *E-mail:* tmcpartland@gwmail.kysu.edu

Murray State University
Honors Program
Murray, Kentucky

The Murray State University Honors Program is designed to enrich the educational experience of highly motivated students by increasing the opportunity for interacting with outstanding research faculty members, both in small class settings such as honors seminars and in ongoing research experiences.

The Honors Program seminars are courses specially designed to meet the needs of the most able students. Instruction takes various forms, but interactive learning is stressed. The honors seminars are distributed among the social sciences, fine arts, humanities, literature, natural sciences, and international affairs. Students typically enroll in one of these seminars throughout their college experience or until the honors sequence is completed.

There are approximately 210 students in the Honors Program out of a campus population of 9,100 students.

Participation Requirements: Honors students may be enrolled in any undergraduate curriculum. To remain in good standing in the Honors Program, a student must maintain a GPA of at least 3.2 (on a 4.0 scale). A student who successfully completes all the requirements of the Honors Program (course sequence, language and mathematics competencies, travel abroad, senior thesis) is awarded the honors medallion, which is worn at Commencement. The honors diploma is also awarded at graduation and a citation on the academic transcript indicates successful matriculation in the Honors Program.

Admission Process: The program accepts entering first-year students who are National Merit Semifinalists or have a composite ACT score of 28 or above and rank in the top 10 percent of their high school class.

Scholarship Availability: Ten Presidential Scholarships are awarded annually to entering freshmen who generally have a composite ACT score of 28 or above and rank in the top 7 percent of their high school class. The award covers in-state tuition, fifteen meals per week, and a semiprivate dormitory room. Numerous departmental scholarships are also available.

Campus Overview

State-supported comprehensive, founded 1922, part of Kentucky Council on Postsecondary Education • **Coed** 8,363 undergraduate students, 84% full-time, 58% women, 42% men.

Undergraduates 6,988 full-time, 1,375 part-time. Students come from 49 states and territories, 56 other countries, 29% are from out of state, 6% African American, 0.8% Asian American or Pacific Islander, 0.8% Hispanic American, 0.5% Native American, 2% international, 8% transferred in, 40% live on campus.

Faculty *Total:* 539, 71% full-time, 64% with terminal degrees. *Student/faculty ratio:* 17:1.

Academic Programs *Special study options:* academic remediation for entering students, accelerated degree program, adult/continuing education programs, advanced placement credit, cooperative education, distance learning, double majors, English as a second language, external degree program, honors programs, independent study, internships, off-campus study, part-time degree program, services for LD students, study abroad, summer session for credit. *ROTC:* Army (c).

Athletics Member NCAA. All Division I. *Intercollegiate sports:* baseball M(s), basketball M(s)/W(s), bowling M/W, cheerleading M/W, crew M(s)/W(s), cross-country running M(s)/W(s), equestrian sports M(s)/W(s), football M(s), golf M(s)/W(s), riflery M(s)/W(s), soccer W(s), tennis M(s)/W(s), track and field M(s)/W(s), volleyball W(s). *Intramural sports:* basketball M/W, bowling M/W, fencing M/W, field hockey M/W, football M/W, golf M/W, racquetball M/W, rugby M, sailing M/W, soccer M/W, softball M/W, swimming and diving M/W, track and field M/W, volleyball M/W, weight lifting M/W.

Costs (2004–05) *Tuition:* state resident $3420 full-time, $143 per hour part-time; nonresident $5600 full-time, $272 per hour part-time. Full-time tuition and fees vary according to reciprocity agreements. Part-time tuition and fees vary according to reciprocity agreements. *Required fees:* $564 full-time, $23 per hour part-time. *Room and board:* $4510; room only: $2256. Room and board charges vary according to board plan.

Financial Aid 455 Federal Work-Study jobs (averaging $1295). 1,905 state and other part-time jobs (averaging $1638). In 2003, 2306 non-need-based awards were made. *Average percent of need met:* 89%. *Average financial aid package:* $4612. *Average need-based loan:* $1950. *Average need-based gift aid:* $2181. *Average non-need-based aid:* $2553.

Contact: Administrative Assistant: Lori Rogers, 324 Wells Hall, Murray, Kentucky 42071; *Telephone:* 502-762-3166; *Fax:* 502-762-3405; *E-mail:* lori.rogers@murraystate.edu

Northern Kentucky University

Honors Program

Highland Heights, Kentucky

The Honors Program offers interdisciplinary seminars in its own campus building, which includes student facilities, such as a lounge, reading room, and computer room. At the core of the honors experience, the seminars emphasize discussion and discovery of ideas, almost always with an interdisciplinary emphasis. Seminars are organized on a topical basis, fulfilling the overall framework of four general areas: Humanity and Nature, Humanity and Society, Humanity and the Imagination, and Humanity and the Machine. In addition to an interdisciplinary focus, seminars are also available in a World Cities/World Cultures series, designating specific cities and regions for intensive study. Students may also substitute or use designated international study opportunities for honors credit. A number of seminars are cross-listed with disciplines when appropriate (e.g., a World Cities course about the Caribbean is cross-listed with the French major). Faculty members noted for their excellence in teaching are recruited from all University departments to participate in the program. An annual Visiting Professorship in Honors offers additional opportunities for student course work and projects.

All students must complete a Senior Honors Thesis (often but not necessarily in their majors), which gives them the opportunity to research and write about topics of significance, conduct original research, or develop creative projects. The thesis may be completed in written form or it may document a creative project (such as a photography exhibition).

In addition, cocurricular activities sponsored by both the program and the student Honors Club are available. These include campus events, lecture series, field trips, and other activities that integrate learning and experience. Students may choose to be active in state or national associations of honors students.

The 20-year-old program currently enrolls 350 students.

Participation Requirements: The Northern Kentucky University Honors Program provides qualified students with 15 semester hours of seminars, each having a maximum enrollment of 15 students, and 6 hours of Senior Honors Thesis credit. Those students who successfully complete the 21 hours become designated "University Honors Scholars" and fulfill the requirement of a minor toward graduation.

Admission Process: Entering freshmen with a composite ACT score of at least 26 or an SAT score of at least 1180 (or significant achievement in high school), already-enrolled students with a minimum GPA of 3.25, and transfer students from other honors programs are eligible for the program.

Scholarship Availability: Scholarships are offered for outstanding junior honors students and outstanding honors students majoring in business; students who do individual research projects or international study are eligible for Zalla Fellowship monies.

Campus Overview

State-supported comprehensive, founded 1968 • **Coed** 12,057 undergraduate students, 75% full-time, 59% women, 41% men.

Undergraduates 8,989 full-time, 3,068 part-time. Students come from 32 states and territories, 11 other countries, 30% are from out of state, 6% transferred in, 9% live on campus.

Faculty *Total:* 788, 62% full-time, 42% with terminal degrees. *Student/faculty ratio:* 18:1.

Academic Programs *Special study options:* academic remediation for entering students, adult/continuing education programs, advanced placement credit, cooperative education, distance learning, double majors, honors programs, independent study, internships, off-campus study, part-time degree program, services for LD students, study

abroad, summer session for credit. *ROTC:* Army (b), Air Force (c). *Unusual degree programs:* 3-2 engineering with University of Kentucky, University of Louisville, University of Cincinnati.

Athletics Member NCAA. All Division II. *Intercollegiate sports:* baseball M(s), basketball M(s)/W(s), cheerleading M(s)/W(s), cross-country running M(s)/W(s), golf M(s)/W(s), soccer M(s)/W(s), softball W(s), tennis M(s)/W(s), volleyball W(s). *Intramural sports:* basketball M/W, football M/W, racquetball M/W, rugby M(c), soccer M/W, softball M/W, swimming and diving M/W, table tennis M/W, tennis M/W, volleyball M/W.

Costs (2004–05) *Tuition:* state resident $4368 full-time, $182 per credit hour part-time; nonresident $9096 full-time, $379 per credit hour part-time. Full-time tuition and fees vary according to location. Part-time tuition and fees vary according to location. *Room and board:* $4660; room only: $2580. Room and board charges vary according to board plan, housing facility, and location.

Financial Aid 283 Federal Work-Study jobs (averaging $1622). 782 state and other part-time jobs (averaging $1749). In 2003, 1321 non-need-based awards were made. *Average percent of need met:* 85%. *Average financial aid package:* $7079. *Average need-based loan:* $5306. *Average need-based gift aid:* $4368. *Average non-need-based aid:* $3766.

Contact: Director: Tom Zaniello, Honors House, Highland Heights, Kentucky 41099; *Telephone:* 859-572-5400; *Fax:* 859-572-6093; *E-mail:* tzaniello@nku.edu; *Web site:* http://www.nku.edu/~honorsprgm

University of Louisville

University Honors Program

Louisville, Kentucky

The University of Louisville has a comprehensive University Honors Program for students who have shown promise of sustained, advanced intellectual achievement. Established in 1982, the University Honors Program provides the opportunity for students to study in small classes and engage in an intensive and challenging educational experience. Honors classes promote discussion, in-depth research and writing, and close relationships with faculty members and peers.

Eligible freshmen are invited to participate in an introduction to campus life for honors students presented before the fall new student welcome weekend. Honors sections of general education courses are offered each semester. These classes provide a strong foundation for upper-level study and meet requirements across colleges. Sophomores, juniors, and seniors may enroll in Honors Scholar seminars, interdisciplinary courses that tend to focus on topics of immediate interest to students. Some recent courses include Medical Ethics; Existentialism and Freedom Across the World; The Past and Culture in African-American Literature; Postmodernism and Film; Globalization and Cities; and Intellectuals and Anti-Intellectualism in the Modern World. In addition, the Overseers International Seminars combine semester-long, in-depth study with substantially subsidized travel to locations outside the United States. Recent seminars have included Exploration of Britain and the Transition to the Modern Age, The Traditional and the Modern in Japanese Society, Royalty in Indian History, and The Examination of Post-apartheid South Africa. Seminar topics change annually; specific descriptions are posted online each semester.

The University Honors Program is based in the Etscorn Honors Center and the Overseers Honors House. The Etscorn Center, located on the ground floor of Threlkeld Hall, the Honors residence, houses the new administrative offices of the University Honors Program, a high-tech classroom, advising offices, and a study area. The Overseers Honors House, a renovated c.1870 town house typical of

Victorian Louisville, is home to a classroom, library, computer center, and the National Scholarship and Fellowship Office. Threlkeld and the nearby Honors House are conveniently located at the center of campus. Situated close to commuter parking, residence halls, the Student Activity Center, and many classroom buildings, the Etscorn Center and the Honors House are convenient, informal places for honors students to study, relax, and meet for meals. Throughout the year, honors facilities are also the site of many presentations, receptions, and social events that are open to honors students.

Redefined in 2001, the Honors Program has been enrolling and tracking increasing numbers of students. Approximately 1,100 students are currently involved in honors work at the University of Louisville.

Participation Requirements: Honors students may major in any undergraduate program at the University and fulfill the same requirements as all students. Although there are no required honors courses, eligible students are advised by the Honors Program staff and are encouraged to take at least 24 hours of honors-designated course work during their academic career to graduate as a University Honors Scholar. In addition, active honors students choose to be involved in many of the extracurricular offerings of the University Honors Program, such as peer mentoring, community service projects, career mentoring with experienced professionals in the local area, attendance at regional and national honors conferences, and undergraduate research related to senior honors projects.

All honors course work is noted on a student's transcript, and college honors are awarded on the basis of GPA and other factors that are determined by each undergraduate unit. Graduation as a University Honors Scholar is noted on a student's transcript and diploma.

Admission Process: New students are eligible to take courses in the University Honors Program if they have an ACT composite score of 27 or higher or the equivalent SAT score of 1210 or higher (composite math and verbal scores) and a minimum high school GPA of 3.35. Belated admission to or continuation in the program requires a GPA of 3.35 or higher. Transfer students are eligible to participate if their transferred GPA is at least 3.35. Registration in the University Honors Program courses requires permission acquired during advising with an Honors Program staff member.

Scholarship Availability: While no admission scholarships are awarded through the University Honors Program, full-tuition scholarships are awarded to most honors-eligible students through the Office of Admissions. Continuing students may apply for annual scholarships that are awarded solely on the basis of academic performance.

Campus Overview

State-supported university, founded 1798 • **Coed** 14,872 undergraduate students, 75% full-time, 53% women, 47% men.

Undergraduates 11,085 full-time, 3,787 part-time. Students come from 51 states and territories, 65 other countries, 11% are from out of state, 14% African American, 3% Asian American or Pacific Islander, 1% Hispanic American, 0.2% Native American, 1% international, 6% transferred in, 15% live on campus.

Faculty Total: 1,294, 62% full-time, 58% with terminal degrees. Student/faculty ratio: 17:1.

Academic Programs Special study options: academic remediation for entering students, accelerated degree program, adult/continuing education programs, advanced placement credit, cooperative education, distance learning, double majors, English as a second language, external degree program, honors programs, independent study, internships, off-campus study, part-time degree program, services for LD students, student-designed majors, study abroad, summer session for credit. ROTC: Army (b), Air Force (b).

Athletics Member NCAA. All Division I except football (Division I-A). Intercollegiate sports: baseball M(s), basketball M(s)/W(s), cheerleading M(s)/W(s), crew W(s), cross-country running M(s)/ W(s), field hockey W(s), golf M(s)/W(s), soccer M(s)/W(s), softball W(s), swimming and diving M(s)/W(s), tennis M(s)/W(s), track and field M(s)/W(s), volleyball W(s). Intramural sports: badminton M/W, basketball M/W, bowling M/W, cross-country running M/W, fencing M/W, football M/W, golf M/W, ice hockey M, racquetball M/W, soccer M/W, softball M/W, swimming and diving M/W, table tennis M/W, tennis M/W, track and field M/W, ultimate Frisbee M/W, volleyball M/W.

Costs (2004–05) Tuition: state resident $5040 full-time, $210 per hour part-time; nonresident $13,752 full-time, $573 per hour part-time. Full-time tuition and fees vary according to reciprocity agreements. Part-time tuition and fees vary according to course load and reciprocity agreements. Room and board: $4640; room only: $2940. Room and board charges vary according to board plan and housing facility.

Financial Aid In 2004, 1633 non-need-based awards were made. Average percent of need met: 58%. Average financial aid package: $8173. Average need-based loan: $4230. Average need-based gift aid: $5350. Average non-need-based aid: $4927.

Contact: Director: Dr. John Richardson, Etscorn Honors Center, University of Louisville, Louisville, Kentucky 40292; Telephone: 502-852-6293; Fax: 502-852-3919; E-mail: john.richardson@louisville. edu; Web site: http://www.louisville.edu/a-s/honors

Western Kentucky University
University Honors Program
Bowling Green, Kentucky

The University Honors Program challenges Western's most outstanding students to achieve intellectual and personal excellence and to take an active role in their professional training and personal growth. By marrying a community of highly motivated students with the most dedicated and active scholars on campus, the University Honors Program creates an environment centered on self-determined, interdisciplinary, and participatory learning. Honors students and faculty members interact with and learn from one another as peers; as a result, students are contributors to, rather than simply assimilators of, their educational experience. The program also sees community service as an educational benefit, and students participate in (among other things) adult literacy programs and in mentoring at-risk children to enhance student growth and the well-being of the community.

Honors courses stress independent and critical thinking, development of writing and speaking skills, and a broad world view. There is a greater focus on original source material and research methodology than exists in nonhonors courses. Most classes incorporate classroom debates, student-led discussion, and group research projects. This approach facilitates a deeper presentation of course material and freer, more wide-ranging discussion than is possible in nonhonors courses.

The 24-credit honors curriculum includes enriched sections of general education courses as well as interdisciplinary honors colloquia and an honors thesis. Class size in honors courses is limited, and enrollment is restricted to honors-eligible students. With the exception of two 1½-credit colloquia, all honors work can be used to simultaneously fulfill general education or major/minor requirements; as such, the honors program can be completed without increasing the total number of hours required for graduation.

Currently, general education courses are available to be taken for honors credit, representing the areas of written and spoken communication, humanities, social and behavioral sciences, natural sciences and mathematics, and cultural diversity. Upper-division honors credit may be earned through either advanced honors courses or honors augmentation of upper-division courses in students' major or minor disciplines. Students find the flexibility of honors *augmentation particularly appealing, as it allows them to expand their knowledge and skills in areas of particular relevance to their professional development.*

Honors colloquia are offered each semester, organized around specific topics selected by each instructor within the broad theme of culture, science, and the self. Many focus on contemporary social or ethical issues, while others are devoted to reading and discussing the works of important thinkers. All emphasize self-directed learning, analytical writing, and free discussion of ideas.

The honors experience culminates in the honors thesis, which is a work of sustained original research or creative activity completed under the guidance of one of Western's best scholars. Thesis projects vary widely in both nature and content; students in the humanities, business, and social or natural sciences develop their research skills, while those in creative disciplines enhance their craft. All bring new insight or a novel perspective to the topic at hand. Thesis work requires students to put into practice the analytical and communication skills emphasized throughout the honors curriculum, resulting in concrete evidence of their ability to undertake and complete meaningful scholarly activity.

Students receive a number of tangible benefits from participation in the honors program, including the opportunity to live in honors housing, priority registration, and funding to support thesis research and travel to professional conferences. Honors graduates have their achievement noted on their official transcript and are presented with a bronze medallion carried on a red-and-white–striped ribbon to be worn at commencement. While these features are significant, the greatest benefit of honors participation is the chance to interact on a daily basis with others who are equally committed to learning, inquiry, reflection, and action.

There are currently more than 550 students and 50 participating faculty members in the honors program; approximately 150 first-year students join the program each year.

Participation Requirements: Participants must maintain a college GPA of at least 3.2. However, a one-semester grace period is usually provided for those whose GPA falls below 3.2.

Students recognized as Honors Program graduates must have a final GPA of 3.4 or higher. The designation Graduate of the University Honors Program is added to each graduate's final transcript, as is the title of the student's senior honors thesis. Graduates also receive an Honors Program certificate and medallion in recognition of completion of the program.

Admission Process: Students starting the Honors Program as entering freshmen should have a minimum 3.5 high school GPA and a score of at least 25 on the ACT or 1150 on the recentered SAT I. Those with very strong grades or aptitude scores who do not meet the other standards are considered individually. Students with at least 16 hours of college work are admitted with a minimum 3.2 college GPA.

Scholarship Availability: The Honors Program awards about sixty-five $400 scholarships each year to upperclass students in good standing with and making regular progress toward completing the honors program. These scholarships may be added to any other scholarship a student receives. Applications for scholarships are submitted online. Students currently receiving honors scholarships are required to apply for renewal each year. The deadline for submission of both types of applications is April 1.

Honors scholarships are awarded on a competitive basis, and students must be in good standing with the program in order to be considered. To be in good standing, students must have an overall GPA of 3.2 or higher, a minimum of 6 hours of honors credits within the first 30 credit hours after joining the program, a minimum of 12 hours of honors credits within the first 60 hours after joining the program, and have filed a degree program (with honors courses approved by the Honors Director) by the end of the fall semester of the junior year. The criteria apply as applicable at the time of the application.

Campus Overview

State-supported comprehensive, founded 1906 • **Coed** 15,818 undergraduate students, 82% full-time, 59% women, 41% men.

Undergraduates 12,944 full-time, 2,874 part-time. Students come from 45 states and territories, 51 other countries, 17% are from out of state, 9% African American, 1% Asian American or Pacific Islander, 0.9% Hispanic American, 0.3% Native American, 1% international, 5% transferred in, 31% live on campus.

Faculty *Total:* 1,143, 60% full-time, 49% with terminal degrees. *Student/faculty ratio:* 18:1.

Academic Programs *Special study options:* academic remediation for entering students, accelerated degree program, adult/continuing education programs, advanced placement credit, cooperative education, distance learning, double majors, English as a second language, honors programs, independent study, internships, part-time degree program, services for LD students, student-designed majors, study abroad, summer session for credit. *ROTC:* Army (b), Air Force (c).

Athletics Member NCAA. All Division I except football (Division I-AA). *Intercollegiate sports:* baseball M(s), basketball M(s)/W(s), cheerleading M/W, cross-country running M(s)/W(s), golf M(s)/W(s), riflery M(c)/W(c), soccer M(s), softball W(s), swimming and diving M(s)/W(s), tennis M(s)/W(s), track and field M(s)/W(s), volleyball W(s). *Intramural sports:* archery M/W, badminton M/W, basketball M/W, bowling M/W, equestrian sports M/W, fencing M(c)/W(c), golf M/W, lacrosse M(c)/W(c), racquetball M/W, rugby M(c)/W(c), soccer M/W, softball M/W(c), swimming and diving M(c)/W(c), table tennis M/W, volleyball M(c)/W(c), water polo M/W, wrestling M.

Costs (2005–06) *Tuition:* state resident $5391 full-time, $217 per hour part-time; nonresident $13,167 full-time, $529 per hour part-time. Full-time tuition and fees vary according to course load, location, program, and reciprocity agreements. Part-time tuition and fees vary according to course load, location, program, and reciprocity agreements. *Room and board:* $4778; room only: $2600. Room and board charges vary according to board plan and housing facility.

Financial Aid 729 Federal Work-Study jobs (averaging $1453). 1,469 state and other part-time jobs (averaging $1728). In 2003, 3955 non-need-based awards were made. *Average percent of need met:* 36%. *Average financial aid package:* $6955. *Average need-based loan:* $3127. *Average need-based gift aid:* $3555. *Average non-need-based aid:* $3025.

Contact: WKU Honors Program, Honors Center, 1 Big Red Way, Bowling Green, Kentucky 42101-3576; *Telephone:* 270-745-2081; *Fax:* 270-745-2081; *E-mail:* honors@wku.edu; *Web site:* http://www.wku.edu/Honors/

LOUISIANA

Louisiana State University at Alexandria
Honors Program
Alexandria, Louisiana

The Louisiana State University at Alexandria (LSUA) Honors Program is a dynamic, evolving program, which enhances the quality of an LSUA education through curricular and extracurricular learning experiences, through enhanced interactions between students and faculty members, and through experimentation with new courses and pedagogies. The mission of the Honors Program at LSUA is to make available to qualified and willing students both a broad education in the liberal arts core and specific preparation in a chosen discipline. The Honors Program and its courses emphasize the use of primary materials and hands-on investigations rather than secondary sources and textbooks; promote clarity of thought and expression in both writing and speaking, critical thinking skills, and an appropriate degree of information literacy; foster a sense of communal achievement through seminars, discussion groups, or colloquiums;

promote a sense of collegiality in learning through a high degree of access to faculty members; and provide opportunities for participation in field trips, travel, lectures, conferences, community service, and international elements.

Honors courses include interdisciplinary courses in the humanities which draw on history, philosophy, arts, and sciences to study important periods of Western civilization including the ancient, medieval, and Renaissance worlds; the enlightenment; the American experiment; and the modern world. These interdisciplinary courses form the basis of the honors experience and lend a unity and cohesiveness to the Honors Program; therefore, all honors students are required to take at least two of these courses. The remaining courses within the Honors Program focus on the individual student's major with each honors student enrolling in courses appropriate for the academic major selected. Discussions between the honors student and LSUA faculty members lead to the development of individualized enhancements of the major's courses. Enhancement options include tutorials, lectures, seminars, research projects, and participation in professional meetings.

Enhancement options must be approved by the academic department chairman, the appropriate dean, and the Honors Committee. Honors-level courses are designated as such on student transcripts. Students who complete 20 hours of honors-level courses receive recognition, such as University Honors, on transcripts and during graduation ceremonies.

Participation Requirements: Admission into the LSUA Honors Program at the freshman level requires regular admission into LSUA, a composite ACT score of at least 25 (or the equivalent SAT score), and completion of an honors application packet.

Admission into the LSUA Honors Program at other levels is contingent upon a recommendation by an LSUA faculty member and at the discretion of the Director of the Honors Program and members of the Honors Committee. All students admitted into the Honors Program may take honors courses; however, only candidates for the baccalaureate degree may receive University Honors. Honors students must maintain a total GPA of 3.5 (with a minimum of 3.0 in their honors courses) to remain in good standing in the Honors Program.

The presentation of a capstone project in the student's senior year is required to ensure that the honors experience carries through all four years. The capstone project represents a substantial undertaking in the student's chosen field (an original critical essay, investigative study, thesis, public lecture or presentation, artwork, or similar approved project) and represents the culmination of the student's tenure at LSUA.

The international element may include foreign language proficiency, area specialization, study abroad, or two or more classes whose primary content is international in nature, such as travel courses.

Scholarship Availability: Honors students have the same opportunities for financial aid as any other LSUA student and may compete for additional scholarships dedicated to the Honors Program. Because the Honors Program emphasizes a community of learners whose education extends beyond the classroom, students in the Honors Program may compete for development funds to defray costs for travel to regional cultural events, performances, museums, historical sites, lectures, and professional meetings. Additional support may be available by application to the Student Government Association.

Contact: Dr. Thomas Armstrong, Vice Chancellor for Academic Affairs, LSUA, 8100 Highway 71 South, Alexandria, Louisiana 71302; *Telephone:* 318-473-6446; *Fax:* 318-473-6480; *E-mail:* tarmstrong@lsua.edu; *Web site:* http://www.lsua.edu

Loyola University New Orleans
Honors Program
New Orleans, Louisiana

The Loyola University Honors Program offers the opportunity for academically superior, highly motivated students to take challenging honors courses and to participate in special cultural and intellectual enrichment activities.

Honors students also participate together in such cultural activities as trips to the opera, theater, and art museums, and they attend special seminars and lectures. These supplemental activities are optional but are usually very popular and well-attended. Honors students also have the use of a University honors center as a place to study, relax, and discuss. In addition, students in the full University Honors Program have priority registration with seniors. An active student University Honors Association plans social activities and programming and works with the Honors Director and the University Honors Advisory Board on developing curriculum and policy for the program.

In addition to the University Honors Program and Honors Certificate Program, several departments at Loyola have departmental honors programs, which usually consist of special research projects in the senior year and require GPAs of 3.5 in the major. Students can participate in both the University Honors Program and the honors program of their major.

University Honors graduates wear a white stole at graduation, and their achievement is noted in the graduation program and on their diploma and transcript. Honors Certificate Students are so designated in the graduation program and on their transcripts. A University Honors Program Outstanding Student Award is presented annually to the graduating senior with the highest GPA in honors classes, and a University Honors Association Award is presented to the graduating senior who has the most outstanding record of community service to the Honors Program, Loyola University, and the larger community.

The 25-year-old program currently has an enrollment of 175. About 8 percent of the entering first-year students are in the Honors Program.

Participation Requirements: The Honors Program is open to qualified students of all undergraduate colleges and majors. Students in the University Honors Program take a total of 27 credit hours of honors courses throughout the four undergraduate years. These honors courses replace the required common-curriculum courses and therefore do not add to the number of requirements for graduation. In addition to the full University Honors Program, qualified students may choose to participate in the Honors Certificate Program, which consists of 24 credit hours of honors courses, omitting the senior project. Students in the University Honors Program and the Honors Certificate Program are required to maintain a 3.3 overall GPA.

The Honors curriculum includes courses in literature, philosophy, history, religious studies, art, economics, political science, math, and sciences. In their senior year, honors students do a senior project based on original research. The honors classes, which are taught by the most outstanding faculty members, are usually smaller than the regular classes, and emphasize active student participation, extensive readings in primary sources, and challenging writing assignments.

Admission Process: Incoming freshmen with high standardized test scores (prospective students should check the Honors Program Web page at http://www.loyno.edu/honors/ for current criteria) and high school GPAs of 3.5 or better are invited to apply to the University Honors Program. The application consists of an essay and a teacher recommendation. The University Honors Advisory Board, consisting of faculty members and Honors students, evaluates the applications and selects the participants. In addition, students with outstanding academic records (3.5 GPA or higher) in their freshman year at Loyola, as well as qualified transfer students, are invited to apply to the Honors Program. If accepted, they are given Honors credit for previous work that was equivalent to the Loyola freshman honors courses.

The deadline for applying to the program is mid-March.

Scholarship Availability: Although many students in the University Honors Program receive full or partial University scholarships, the scholarships are not tied to participation in the University Honors Program.

Campus Overview

Independent Roman Catholic (Jesuit) comprehensive, founded 1912
• **Coed** 3,688 undergraduate students, 87% full-time, 61% women, 39% men.

Undergraduates 3,220 full-time, 468 part-time. Students come from 52 states and territories, 56 other countries, 56% are from out of state, 10% African American, 4% Asian American or Pacific Islander, 11% Hispanic American, 0.5% Native American, 3% international, 6% transferred in, 40% live on campus.

Faculty *Total:* 483, 63% full-time, 64% with terminal degrees. *Student/faculty ratio:* 11:1.

Academic Programs *Special study options:* academic remediation for entering students, accelerated degree program, adult/continuing education programs, advanced placement credit, distance learning, double majors, English as a second language, honors programs, independent study, internships, off-campus study, part-time degree program, services for LD students, student-designed majors, study abroad, summer session for credit. *ROTC:* Army (c), Navy (c), Air Force (c). *Unusual degree programs:* 3-2 engineering with Tulane University.

Athletics Member NAIA. *Intercollegiate sports:* baseball M, basketball M(s)/W(s), bowling M(c)/W(c), cheerleading M(c)/W(c), crew M(c)/W(c), cross-country running M/W, golf M(c)/W(c), rugby M(c), soccer M(c)/W, swimming and diving M(c)/W(c), tennis M(c)/W(c), track and field M/W, ultimate Frisbee M(c)/W(c), volleyball W, wrestling M(c). *Intramural sports:* basketball M/W, racquetball M/W, soccer M/W, softball M/W, swimming and diving M/W, tennis M/W, volleyball M/W, water polo M/W, weight lifting M/W.

Costs (2005–06) *Comprehensive fee:* $33,558 includes full-time tuition ($24,410), mandatory fees ($836), and room and board ($8312). Part-time tuition: $696 per credit hour. *College room only:* $5166.

Financial Aid 764 Federal Work-Study jobs (averaging $1858). In 2003, 1092 non-need-based awards were made. *Average percent of need met:* 85%. *Average financial aid package:* $18,013. *Average need-based loan:* $5831. *Average need-based gift aid:* $12,927. *Average non-need-based aid:* $9669.

Contact: Director: Lynn Vogel Koplitz, Monroe 568, Box 75, 6363 St. Charles Avenue, New Orleans, Louisiana 70118; *Telephone:* 504-865-2708; *Fax:* 504-865-2709; *E-mail:* honors@loyno.edu or koplitz@loyno.edu

---

McNeese State University

Honors Program

Lake Charles, Louisiana

The establishment of the Honors College at McNeese strengthens the University's commitment to "Excellence with a Personal Touch" in undergraduate education. The program is designed for outstanding students with strong academic records who desire an alternative course of instruction at the college level. Twenty-five students are selected by the Honors College Admission Committee for entrance into the Honors College for the fall semester each year. The Honors College provides unique courses taught by exemplary professors, providing intellectual stimulation, opportunities for interdisciplinary experiences, and enhanced probability for success in a career or in graduate and professional schools.

The elements of McNeese's honors program include unique core courses that satisfy general education requirements. Communications, humanities, natural sciences, and applied sciences courses are designed to stimulate thinking, improve written and oral communication skills, and promote classroom discussion. The average class size of a core honors course is 25. Students are required to earn 12 hours of credit in freshman and sophomore core honors courses. During the junior year, students can investigate a special topic through independent reading and writing, in-depth scholarly research, or completion of a creative project under the guidance of an honors professor. They may also choose an honors option contract for traditional courses by adding independent elements (e.g., a research paper/project, a presentation at a regional or national meeting, and a volunteer service project) as decided by the professor of the course, the department head, and the director of the Honors College. Seniors are required to conduct undergraduate research and present their findings in a seminar and write a Senior Honors Thesis. Students must complete 25 hours of honors courses as well as service and leadership requirements in order to earn the Honors College Distinction on their diplomas and official transcripts.

The high-quality of the teaching in core honors courses is superb, and the professors are highly acclaimed for their teaching styles. These professors have been selected for their expertise in their academic fields, excellence in the classroom, and enthusiasm for teaching. All honors professors and academic advisers of Honors College students are committed to the academic and personal development of students and work diligently to encourage their growth.

The four-room Honors Suite is conveniently located on the first floor of Drew Hall. The Honors Student Center, adjacent to the Director's office, provides a spacious room for honors students to study, discuss issues, and exchange ideas as well as to socialize. Students gather there for the initial meeting for honors seminars, a 1-hour required course for freshman- and sophomore-level honors students. Students also conduct some of the work and planning for service activities in the Honors Student Center. The Honors College Office and a small reading room are also located in the Honors Suite.

Students participate in various leadership positions, and honors officers have attended the NCHC national conferences in Chicago and Washington, D.C. They are actively involved in service projects, including tutoring at the women's shelter, painting ceramic butterflies, bowling for the homeless, and participating in science shows at local elementary schools and CHEM EXPO. They fraternize at the honors' socials, such as honors picnics, pizza parties, barbecue by the lake, and supper with professors. The Honors College sponsors 3 guest lecturers annually, including prestigious speakers from the Welch Foundation and Fortune 500 companies. The Honors College at McNeese was founded in fall 2000 and currently has 46 students enrolled.

Participation Requirements: Students enrolled in the Honors College at McNeese must earn at least 24 credit hours each year with an overall 3.0 average and volunteer 50 hours of service during their freshman and sophomore years in order to renew their Honors College Scholarships. They must earn 25 credit hours in honors courses, including the core honors courses; maintain an overall 3.0 average; and complete the service and leadership requirements in order to graduate with the Honors College Distinction.

Admission Process: High school seniors and early admission students having excellent academic records and college preparatory backgrounds, as well as a desire to excel, are encouraged to apply for the Honors College Scholarship at McNeese. The minimum scores for consideration are an ACT of 27 or an SAT of 1210 and a cumulative GPA of 3.4 on a 4.0 scale. Other considerations are leadership and service activities during high school and a personal or telephone interview with the Honors College Admissions Committee. Students must send an application packet that includes a completed application, two copies of their high school transcript, a written essay, and three letters of recommendation to the admissions committee before the priority deadline of February 1, 2002. (The second deadline is April 1, 2002.)

Scholarship Availability: The Honors College Scholarship pays for all tuition and other required fees for registration. It pays for a dormitory room and provides $1000 in Cowboy Cash toward meals and $1000 for purchasing books and other instructional items per year. All students accepted into the Honors College are given a full scholarship that is renewable for three years, providing the student earns at least 24 credit hours each year and meets the service and leadership requirements for the Honors College Scholarship.

Campus Overview

State-supported comprehensive, founded 1939, part of University of Louisiana System • **Coed** 7,726 undergraduate students, 83% full-time, 60% women, 40% men.

Undergraduates 6,399 full-time, 1,327 part-time. Students come from 33 states and territories, 37 other countries, 6% are from out of state, 20% African American, 0.8% Asian American or Pacific Islander, 1% Hispanic American, 0.8% Native American, 2% international, 5% transferred in, 12% live on campus.

Faculty *Total:* 413, 73% full-time, 50% with terminal degrees. *Student/faculty ratio:* 22:1.

Academic Programs *Special study options:* academic remediation for entering students, accelerated degree program, adult/continuing education programs, advanced placement credit, cooperative education, distance learning, double majors, English as a second language, freshman honors college, honors programs, independent study, internships, off-campus study, part-time degree program, services for LD students, study abroad, summer session for credit.

Athletics Member NCAA. All Division I except football (Division I-AA). *Intercollegiate sports:* baseball M(s), basketball M(s)/W(s), cross-country running M(s)/W(s), golf M(s)/W(s), riflery M/W, soccer W(s), softball W(s), tennis W(s), track and field M(s)/W(s), volleyball W(s), weight lifting M(c)/W(c). *Intramural sports:* badminton M/W, baseball M, basketball M/W, football M/W, golf M/W, racquetball M/W, soccer M/W, softball W, swimming and diving M/W, table tennis M/W, tennis M/W, volleyball M/W, water polo M/W, weight lifting M/W.

Costs (2005–06) *Tuition:* state resident $2226 full-time, $572 per term part-time; nonresident $8292 full-time, $572 per term part-time. *Required fees:* $933 full-time, $293 per term part-time. *Room and board:* $4637.

Financial Aid In 2002, 2610 non-need-based awards were made. *Average percent of need met:* 58%.

Contact: Director: Dr. Scott Goins, McNeese State University, Box 93430, Lake Charles, Louisiana 70609; *Telephone:* 337-475-5456, 800-622-3352 Ext. 5456 (toll-free); *Fax:* 337-475-5526; *E-mail:* sgoins@mcneese.edu; *Web site:* http://www.mcneese.edu

Northwestern State University of Louisiana
Louisiana Scholars' College
Natchitoches, Louisiana

Reflecting growing public recognition that a liberal arts education constitutes the best possible preparation for intelligent and responsible citizenship, for a successful professional career, and for a fulfilling life, the Louisiana Scholars' College was established in 1987 by the Louisiana Board of Regents for Higher Education. In its early years, the College was cited by outside reviewers as "a model for the state and the nation." In 1997, the Regents recognized the value of the Bachelor of Arts degree in the liberal arts at the College, saying, "The broad, multidisciplinary nature of the program will provide superior students with a greater opportunity to develop an individualized degree program of enhanced academic rigor."

The Scholars' College serves as Louisiana's sole four-year, selective admissions, state Honors College in the liberal arts and sciences, providing highly motivated students with a rigorous, innovative, and individualized curriculum; extensive access to a high-quality faculty; and a one-to-one mentor relationship during the senior thesis experience. In seminars and small classes, in tutorials and laboratories, and in independent research, undergraduates develop close, collaborative relationships with the College faculty members. Freshmen and select upperclassmen live together in an honors residence and attend classes together in Morrison Hall; students form a distinctive community within the larger University—a community emphasizing shared inquiry and vigorous debate and wholly dedicated to undergraduate learning.

Since its inception nearly two decades ago, the Honors College has changed in many ways. Through the years, faculty members have been added, broadening the representation of disciplines within the Scholars' College and providing students with intellectual role models who have been trained in the interdisciplinary and multidisciplinary modes of inquiry inherent in the Common Curriculum. Several years ago, in response to student interest, the College began offering traditional majors in addition to its four interdisciplinary concentrations within the major in liberal arts.

Over the years, numerous courses have been added to the Scholars' College's offerings—many due to input from students. Recent student-initiated additions include a philosophy course in existentialism, an interdisciplinary course on law and economics, and courses on such major writers as Toni Morrison and Edgar Allen Poe. In these and many other ways, the College has evolved to meet the needs of its exceptional students and will continue to do so. The Louisiana Scholars' College is especially proud of its graduates, who now include the state's first Goldwater and Marshall Scholar, currently studying medicine at Oxford University.

Approximately 150 students are enrolled in the Louisiana Scholars' College. In recent years, the recruitment and admissions procedures have been moved from the College to a newly restructured University Recruitment office, although faculty and staff members and students of the College remain highly engaged in the admissions process. On one day in each of the fall and spring semesters, the College hosts Scholars' Day, an opportunity for prospective students and parents to visit the College, sit in on parent and student panels, and attend sample seminars.

Participation Requirements: All those who satisfactorily complete the Common Curriculum (no grade lower than a C may be used to satisfy this requirement), their major or concentration requirements, their other senior course work, and their thesis, while earning a cumulative GPA of 3.0 or higher, are awarded the Bachelor of Arts, Bachelor of Fine Arts, Bachelor of Music, Bachelor of Music Education, or Bachelor of Science degree in the Louisiana Scholars' College at Northwestern State University. The major or concentration and thesis title are recorded on each graduate's transcript. Those whose academic record and thesis reflect unusual intellectual accomplishment and who have been active in the life of the College and University are chosen each year by the faculty to be awarded degrees "with distinction" or "with highest distinction." Scholars' College students are also eligible to receive the scholastic honors cum laude, magna cum laude, and summa cum laude from the University.

Admission Process: The College seeks highly motivated students interested in an exciting liberal arts education. Candidates begin by submitting the College's application for admission and scholarships, together with teacher or guidance counselor recommendations, and an essay. An interview, either in person or by telephone, is required, and a campus visit is strongly encouraged. Requirements include an ACT composite score of at least 25 or an SAT of at least 1130 (composite math and verbal scores), with no ACT subscore below 20 or SAT subscore below 480; an unweighted high school GPA in the Regent's Curriculum of at least 3.0 on a 4.0 scale; a satisfactory evaluation of the strength of the high school program; counselor and/or teacher recommendations; an essay; a list of honors and other activities; and an interview by the Scholars' College Admissions Committee.

Students who fail to meet one of the items above may be considered for provisional admission for one semester, after which their performance is reevaluated and admission to the College is either offered or denied. Students already at Northwestern State University may seek admission to the Scholars' College depending on their GPA.

Scholarship Availability: The College's application for admission serves as an application for all academic scholarships offered by the University, including the prestigious Louisiana Scholars' College Scholarship. Undergraduate work-assistantships are also available for helping out in the library, in the computer center or scientific laboratories, in the office of the College, or in some other area of particular interest to the student. In addition to academic awards, students in the College may also qualify for Pell grants, PLUS loans, ROTC scholarships, and other forms of financial assistance. Students who are not Louisiana residents may qualify for out-of-state fee waivers.

Campus Overview

State-supported comprehensive, founded 1884, part of University of Louisiana System • **Coed** 9,414 undergraduate students, 74% full-time, 66% women, 34% men.

Undergraduates 6,950 full-time, 2,464 part-time. Students come from 40 states and territories, 25 other countries, 6% are from out of state, 32% African American, 0.9% Asian American or Pacific Islander, 2% Hispanic American, 2% Native American, 0.4% international, 7% transferred in, 21% live on campus.

Faculty *Total:* 578, 52% full-time. *Student/faculty ratio:* 21:1.

Academic Programs *Special study options:* academic remediation for entering students, adult/continuing education programs, advanced placement credit, cooperative education, distance learning, double majors, freshman honors college, honors programs, independent study, internships, part-time degree program, summer session for credit. *ROTC:* Army (b).

Athletics Member NCAA. All Division I except football (Division I-AA). *Intercollegiate sports:* baseball M(s), basketball M(s)/W(s), cross-country running M(s)/W(s), soccer W(s), softball W(s), tennis W(s), track and field M(s)/W(s), volleyball W(s). *Intramural sports:* badminton M/W, basketball M/W, bowling M/W, cheerleading M(c)/W(c), crew M(c)/W, football M/W, golf M/W, racquetball M/W, riflery M/W, soccer M/W, softball M/W, table tennis M/W, tennis M/W, track and field M/W, ultimate Frisbee M/W, volleyball M/W, water polo M/W, weight lifting M/W, wrestling M/W.

Costs (2004–05) *Tuition:* state resident $2144 full-time, $227 per credit part-time; nonresident $8222 full-time, $480 per credit part-time. Full-time tuition and fees vary according to course load. Part-time tuition and fees vary according to course load. *Required fees:* $1097 full-time. *Room and board:* $3426; room only: $1850. Room and board charges vary according to board plan, housing facility, and location.

Financial Aid 375 Federal Work-Study jobs (averaging $715). 859 state and other part-time jobs (averaging $1130). In 2003, 1587 non-need-based awards were made. *Average percent of need met:* 38%. *Average financial aid package:* $5200. *Average need-based loan:* $3075. *Average need-based gift aid:* $3983. *Average non-need-based aid:* $3366.

Contact: Director, Louisiana Scholars' College, 110 Morrison Hall, Northwestern State University, Natchitoches, Louisiana 71497; *Telephone:* 318-357-4577; *Fax:* 318-357-5908; *Web site:* http://www.nsula.edu/scholars/

Southeastern Louisiana University
University Honors Program
Hammond, Louisiana

*T*he University Honors Program (UHP) at Southeastern Louisiana University is designed to prepare students to recognize and be conversant with significant ideas, deeds, and events that have shaped the world and will shape the future; to have confidence in their abilities to think for themselves, write clearly, and speak effectively; and to be leaders in their communities and professions. It aims to prepare responsible individuals to be perpetual learners who realize their potential for a fully human, ethical, and prosperous life.

The University Honors Program offers integrated sequences of courses that provide highly motivated students a strong foundation in liberal education and career preparation. In small classes (the average class has 15 students), honors students enjoy conditions for learning at the peak of their abilities. Five honors curriculum options, distinguished by comprehensive and in-depth coverage of the material in a learning community environment, facilitate discussion, debate, and intellectual friendship among students and with professors. Special scholarships, travel opportunities, extracurricular events and lectures, designated honors housing, and achievement awards round out the benefits of honors education at Southeastern.

The honors learning-community experience is centered in two sequences of four courses, taught by professors recognized for their excellence in the classroom. The Freshman Honors Seminar, a constellation of two English and two history honors courses, provides an excellent foundation of knowledge through study of some of the most influential books written and the major historical events that have shaped Western civilization. In English, students read and discuss the culture-creating epics of Homer, Virgil, Dante, Milton, and selected modern authors. In history, with the aid of primary sources, they learn about the intellectual, political, religious, artistic, social, scientific, and technological changes that have made the present world possible. A sequence of four Ideas in Conflict courses familiarizes advanced students with great books written by thinkers whose ideas have sharpened human understanding of such central issues as the nature of justice, claims of truth, the structure of nature, the meaning of political right and obligation, and the forces of modern social, psychological, and cultural development.

Honors courses are also available in math, biology, economics, interdisciplinary arts, U.S. history, dramatic literature, and modern fiction as well as in the curricula of the different majors that Southeastern offers.

In addition to foundational courses in the core of the University Honors Program, Southeastern also offers upper-division honors tracks in its six colleges of Arts, Humanities, and Social Sciences; Education and Human Development, Business; Nursing and Health Sciences; Science and Technology; and General Studies. A standard of participation in the UHP must be met to qualify for entry into one of the college honors tracks, which are designed to provide the most dedicated students special course and research opportunities for enhancing their preparation for success in their professions and careers.

Many alumni have reported that their Honors Program experience at Southeastern made a transformative difference in their undergraduate education and strengthened their credentials for graduate, law, and medical schools and for careers in education, government, business, research, and the health fields.

Participation Requirements: Five alternative curriculum paths leading to different graduation awards are available to students. The Honors Diploma in a Major requires 15 hours in UHP courses, 9–15 hours in honors courses in a major, 6 hours of foreign language, and a senior thesis. The Honors Diploma in UHP requires 24 hours in UHP courses, 3 honors hours in a major, 12 hours of foreign language, and a senior thesis. The Honors Diploma in UHP and in a Major entails the same requirements as the Honors Diploma in UHP, plus 9–15 hours in honors courses in a major. The Honors Diploma in Liberal Studies requires 36 hours of UHP courses, including four Ideas in Conflict courses; 3 honors hours in a major; 12 hours of foreign language; and a senior thesis. The Honors Diploma in Liberal Studies and in a Major entails the same requirements as the Honors Diploma in Liberal Studies, plus 9–15 hours in honors courses in a major. Students should note that many honors curricula requirements overlap with requirements in nonhonors curricula, and many honors courses substitute for required nonhonors electives and courses.

Admission Process: A composite score of 21 on the ACT and a 3.0 high school GPA qualify an entering freshman to join; a cumulative GPA of 3.0 in 12 or more hours of University credit qualifies an advanced student to join. Traditional and nontraditional students in every major are encouraged to participate. Each college may have special criteria for accepting students into its upper-division honors track. To earn awards, transfer students must meet minimum participation requirements proportioned to their point of entering Southeastern.

Scholarship Availability: Honors students compete for generous academic scholarships based on ACT scores, high school GPA, and other criteria. Information regarding many other available scholarships may be obtained by calling the Financial Aid Office (985-549-2244 Ext. 2245).

Campus Overview

State-supported comprehensive, founded 1925, part of University of Louisiana System • **Coed** 13,664 undergraduate students, 82% full-time, 62% women, 38% men.

Undergraduates 11,157 full-time, 2,507 part-time. Students come from 42 states and territories, 39 other countries, 3% are from out of state, 16% African American, 0.6% Asian American or Pacific Islander, 1% Hispanic American, 0.4% Native American, 0.7% international, 5% transferred in, 11% live on campus.

Faculty *Total:* 730, 68% full-time, 47% with terminal degrees. *Student/faculty ratio:* 27:1.

Academic Programs *Special study options:* academic remediation for entering students, adult/continuing education programs, advanced placement credit, distance learning, double majors, honors programs, independent study, internships, off-campus study, part-time degree program, services for LD students, study abroad, summer session for credit. *ROTC:* Army (c).

Athletics Member NCAA. All Division I except football (Division I-AA). *Intercollegiate sports:* baseball M(s), basketball M(s)/W(s), cheerleading M(s)/W(s), cross-country running M(s)/W(s), golf M(s), soccer W(s), softball W(s), tennis M(s)/W(s), track and field M(s)/W(s), volleyball W(s). *Intramural sports:* badminton M/W, basketball M/W, football M/W, racquetball M/W, rugby M(c), soccer M(c)/W, softball M/W, table tennis M/W, tennis M/W, volleyball M/W, weight lifting M/W.

Costs (2004–05) *Tuition:* state resident $3191 full-time, $133 per credit hour part-time; nonresident $8519 full-time, $355 per credit hour part-time. Full-time tuition and fees vary according to course load. Part-time tuition and fees vary according to course load. *Room and board:* $4290; room only: $2300. Room and board charges vary according to board plan and housing facility.

Financial Aid 477 Federal Work-Study jobs (averaging $1461). 1,159 state and other part-time jobs (averaging $1596). In 2003, 3605 non-need-based awards were made. *Average financial aid package:* $6033. *Average need-based loan:* $3132. *Average need-based gift aid:* $3011. *Average non-need-based aid:* $2307.

Contact: Director: Dr. Jim Walter, SLU Honors Program, 611 North Pine Street, SLU Box 10489, Hammond, Louisiana 70402; *Telephone:* 985-549-2135; *E-mail:* jwalter@selu.edu; *Web site:* http://www.selu.edu/Academics/Honors/

Southern University and Agricultural and Mechanical College
Southern University Honors College
Baton Rouge, Louisiana

*T*he Honors College at Southern University in Baton Rouge provides an enhanced educational experience for students who have a history of strong academic achievement and motivation and who have shown exceptional creativity or talent. Innovative pedagogy, flexible and competitive curricula, and mentoring relationships with distinguished faculty members and scholars are focal points of the program. The College also provides cultural and intellectual opportunities designed to motivate students to perform at the highest level of excellence that they are capable of and through which they may become knowledgeable and effective leaders. The core curriculum consists of honors colloquiums, designated honors courses in the general education curriculum, and honors courses in the student's major area of study. Students pursue Honors Option Contracts from the general education curriculum and the student's major area of study to complete the requirements for the honors degree.

Honors core courses are taught in a newly constructed honors building. This complex houses the main office, instructors' offices, classrooms, a media laboratory, a conference room, and a student activity center. Honors housing, equipped with computer laboratories and study rooms, is available for freshmen and upperclass students. Program enhancements include an Annual Pinning Ceremony; Scholar-in-Residence/Visiting Scholars Program; study-abroad opportunities in Orizaba, Mexico, and Accra, Ghana; scholarship opportunities; co-ops and internships; membership in professional organizations; and service-learning opportunities, sometimes associated with the study-abroad programs. In 1987, the Southern University Board of Supervisors designated the Honors Program as the Southern University Honors College. The current membership is 602 students.

Participation Requirements: Participation in the Honors College is voluntary. However, students must maintain a minimum 3.0 cumulative GPA within a two-semester period. Students who complete the honors curriculum have special designations of honors included on their transcripts and diplomas. In order to achieve this recognition, the following requirements must be met: a minimum cumulative 3.0 GPA in all course work pursued; a minimum cumulative 3.3 GPA in all honors work pursued; at least 32 honors credit hours, including 6 hours of honors colloquiums, 2 hours of honors thesis or independent study, and 9 hours in a junior- or senior-level course in the student's major area; and the recommendation of the College Dean that Honors College distinction can be awarded.

In addition to the honors diploma, a bronze medallion containing an engraved replica of the Honors College logo attached to a ceremonial ribbon is presented to all students completing the program.

Admission Process: Students must apply for admission to the program. Membership in the College is based on two classification types, General Honors and University Scholars. Requirements for entering freshmen in the General Honors classification include a minimum ACT composite score of 23 or SAT combined score of 1060; a minimum high school GPA of 3.3; assessment of cocurricular activities; two letters of recommendation from a high school principal, counselor, or instructor; and submission of an essay on a designated topic or a recently corrected writing activity, three to five pages in length.

Requirements for the University Scholars classification include a minimum ACT composite score of 27 or SAT combined score of

1210; a minimum high school GPA of 3.5; assessment of cocurricular activities; two letters of recommendation from a high school principal, counselor, or instructor; and submission of an essay on a designated topic or a recently corrected writing activity, three to five pages in length.

Other areas evaluated for admission are class rank, interviews, and college-preparatory courses. Application deadlines, determined by the Office of the Registrar, are July 1 for the fall semester, November 1 for the spring semester, and April 1 for the summer term. Admission to the College for continuing and transfer students is based on a minimum cumulative GPA of 3.5, two letters of recommendation, full-time status, and an interview. Transfer students must have full-time status at the time of their transfer or the last semester of college matriculation.

Scholarship Availability: Scholarships are available in two categories. Tier I, a maximum full scholarship that is available to incoming freshmen, includes tuition with out-of-state fees, room and board, and books and supplies in variable amounts. Applicants must have a minimum cumulative GPA of 3.5, a minimum ACT score of 28 or SAT score of 1270, thirteen college-preparatory courses, and 12 credit hours pursued. Students may also be eligible if they rank first in their graduating class, are National Achievers or National Merit Scholars, and have a GPA of less than 3.4 but an ACT score of 29 or higher or an SAT score of 1300 or higher. Tier I scholarship retention is based on a minimum cumulative GPA of 3.3 and 12 credit hours earned the previous semester. Transfer students must have a minimum cumulative GPA of 3.5 and full-time status the previous semester and may not include any developmental education courses.

Tier II partial scholarships offering tuition or room and board are available to incoming freshmen who have a minimum cumulative GPA of 3.2 and a minimum ACT score of 23 or minimum SAT score of 1060 with thirteen college-preparatory classes and 12 credit hours pursued. Students may also be eligible if they rank first or second in their graduating class or are National Achievers or National Merit Scholars. Tier II scholarship retention is based on a cumulative GPA of 3.0 with 12 credit hours earned the previous semester. Transfer students with a minimum cumulative GPA of 3.5 and 30 credit hours, which may not include developmental education courses, are also eligible.

The following awards, certificates, citations, etc., are also available: graduating senior with the highest average award, student with the highest average in the College award, Straight "A" Student Awards, Chancellor's Scholars/Circle of Excellence, ADTRAN Corporation Scholarships, Georgia Pacific Scholarships, Thurgood Marshall Scholarships, and Honors Medallion Awards.

Campus Overview

State-supported comprehensive, founded 1880, part of Southern University System • **Coed** 8,023 undergraduate students, 91% full-time, 61% women, 39% men.

Undergraduates 7,305 full-time, 718 part-time. Students come from 41 states and territories, 28 other countries, 17% are from out of state, 97% African American, 0.4% Asian American or Pacific Islander, 0.1% Hispanic American, 0.1% Native American, 1% international, 3% transferred in, 35% live on campus.

Faculty *Total:* 561, 75% full-time, 58% with terminal degrees. *Student/faculty ratio:* 17:1.

Academic Programs *Special study options:* academic remediation for entering students, adult/continuing education programs, advanced placement credit, cooperative education, distance learning, honors programs, internships, off-campus study, part-time degree program, services for LD students, study abroad, summer session for credit. *ROTC:* Army (b), Navy (b), Air Force (c).

Athletics Member NCAA. All Division I except football (Division I-AA). *Intercollegiate sports:* baseball M, basketball M(s)/W(s), bowling W(s), cross-country running M(s), golf M(s)/W(s), softball W(s), tennis M(s)/W(s), track and field M(s)/W(s), volleyball W(s). *Intramural sports:* archery M/W, basketball M/W, football M/W, track and field M/W, volleyball M/W, weight lifting M/W.

Costs (2004–05) *Tuition:* state resident $3440 full-time; nonresident $9232 full-time. Full-time tuition and fees vary according to course load and location. Part-time tuition and fees vary according to course load and location. *Room and board:* $4310. Room and board charges vary according to board plan and housing facility.

Financial Aid 900 Federal Work-Study jobs (averaging $1800). 300 state and other part-time jobs (averaging $2500). In 2003, 193 non-need-based awards were made. *Average percent of need met:* 61%. *Average financial aid package:* $7098. *Average need-based loan:* $4280. *Average need-based gift aid:* $3680. *Average non-need-based aid:* $4280.

Contact: Dean: Dr. Beverly D. Wade, Honors College, Southern University and Agricultural and Mechanical College, P.O. Box 9413, Baton Rouge, Louisiana 70813; *Telephone:* 225-771-4845; *Fax:* 225-771-4848; *Web site:* http://www.suhsa.homestead.com

Tulane University
The Honors Program at Tulane University
New Orleans, Louisiana

*T*he Honors Program offers superior students an enhanced educational experience to broaden and enrich their undergraduate education and intensify their preparation for graduate work. Established in 1982, the Honors Program offers exceptional students a unique resource to enhance the educational opportunities already available at Tulane University.

Members of the Honors Program usually enroll in at least one honors course each semester during their freshman, sophomore, and junior years. Honors courses, which are taught only by full-time faculty members or distinguished visitors, have a maximum enrollment of 20 students. The emphasis in these courses is on class discussion, and, in most cases, course material is studied in greater depth than might be possible in a regular course. Honors students may also enhance their regular course offerings by requesting to add an "Honors Option" to a course they are currently taking. With the instructor's approval, the student will then engage in additional work that merits honors credit that also appears on their transcript. The H-Option allows honors students to craft a unique honors curriculum that fits their own interests and talents. Each semester, Tulane offers a limited number of honors colloquia. These colloquia, which are interdisciplinary in subject and approach, may be initiated by students or by faculty members and are designed around some integrating factor: a theme, a period, a creative work, or a problem. Usually, the colloquium meets once a week in a seminar format, with emphasis upon class discussion. The Honors Program scholar may receive individual academic advising and career planning from the director of the program and from members of the honors faculty. The scholarship adviser works under the auspices of the Honors Program to help identify promising candidates for fellowships and scholarships such as the Rhodes, Marshall, Churchill, Truman, and Goldwater and to assist them in preparing their applications, supporting materials, and interview strategies.

Butler Hall is the designated honors residence hall. This residence hall has freshmen as well as a few upperclassmen that help develop an even greater sense of community for the Honors Program. Butler Hall houses 256 students and is equipped with study lounges, kitchen access, and relaxation areas containing pool and Ping-Pong tables. Weekly round-table discussions are held with faculty members and distinguished visitors. Approximately 10 percent of Tulane students participate in the Honors Program.

Participation Requirements: Students not admitted as incoming freshmen may apply after completing one or more semesters at Tulane. After the first semester of residence, the criterion for admission and retention is a minimum cumulative 3.45 for freshmen and sophomores and 3.6 for juniors and seniors. Four honors courses, two of which must be upper-level courses (300 or higher), are required along with an honors thesis or an equivalent honors project completed by the senior year. As the culminating achievement of the scholar's undergraduate career, this thesis or project involves substantial independent research and study under the direction of a professor in the scholar's major department.

Students graduate as Summa or Magna Cum Laude as dictated by their GPA as well as with department honors.

Admission Process: The top 10 to 12 percent of the incoming freshmen are admitted to the program by the Office of Admissions. While scores vary from year to year, the most recent scores have been 1450 on the SAT I and a high school GPA of 3.8. Transfer students must complete one semester at Tulane before they may apply to the Honors Program. Students may apply to enter the Honors Program at any time after their first semester.

Scholarship Availability: While no admission scholarships are awarded through the Honors Program, many full and partial scholarships are awarded to honors-eligible students through the Office of Admissions.

Campus Overview

Independent university, founded 1834 • **Coed** 7,976 undergraduate students, 77% full-time, 53% women, 47% men.

Undergraduates 6,151 full-time, 1,825 part-time. 70% are from out of state, 9% African American, 4% Asian American or Pacific Islander, 3% Hispanic American, 0.5% Native American, 2% international, 3% transferred in, 65% live on campus.

Faculty *Total:* 1,371, 80% full-time, 88% with terminal degrees.

Academic Programs *Special study options:* accelerated degree program, adult/continuing education programs, advanced placement credit, cooperative education, double majors, English as a second language, freshman honors college, honors programs, independent study, internships, off-campus study, part-time degree program, services for LD students, student-designed majors, study abroad, summer session for credit. *ROTC:* Army (b), Navy (b), Air Force (b). *Unusual degree programs:* 3-2 public health, tropical medicine.

Athletics Member NCAA. All Division I except football (Division I-A). *Intercollegiate sports:* baseball M(s), basketball M(s)/W(s), crew M(c)/W(c), cross-country running M(s)/W(s), golf M(s)/W(s), gymnastics M(c)/W(c), ice hockey M(c)/W(c), lacrosse M(c)/W(c), rugby M(c), sailing M(c)/W(c), soccer M(c)/W(s), swimming and diving M(c)/W(s), tennis M(s)/W(s), track and field M(c)/W(s), volleyball M(c)/W(s), water polo M(c)/W(c). *Intramural sports:* baseball M(c), cheerleading M(c)/W(c), crew M(c)/W(c), cross-country running M(c), fencing M(c)/W(c), field hockey M(c)/W(c), gymnastics M(c)/W(c), ice hockey M(c), lacrosse M(c)/W(c), racquetball M(c)/W(c), rock climbing M(c)/W(c), rugby M(c), sailing M(c)/W(c), soccer M(c)/W(c), swimming and diving M(c)/W(c), tennis M(c)/W(c), track and field M(c)/W, ultimate Frisbee M(c)/W(c), volleyball M(c)/W(c), water polo M(c)/W(c).

Costs (2004–05) *Comprehensive fee:* $39,135 includes full-time tuition ($28,900), mandatory fees ($2310), and room and board ($7925). Part-time tuition: $1204 per credit hour. *College room only:* $4700. Room and board charges vary according to board plan and housing facility.

Financial Aid In 1999, 1303 non-need-based awards were made. *Average percent of need met:* 94%. *Average financial aid package:* $22,948. *Average need-based loan:* $5217. *Average need-based gift aid:* $16,286. *Average non-need-based aid:* $13,797.

Contact: Director: Dr. Chris Brady, 105 Hébert Hall, Tulane University, New Orleans, Louisiana 70118; *Telephone:* 504-865-5517; *E-mail:* honors@tulane.edu; *Web site:* http://www.tulane.edu/~honors

MAINE

University of Maine
Honors College
Orono, Maine

Honors at the University of Maine (UMaine) originated in 1935 and today provides a unique opportunity for a community of more than 600 motivated students to investigate diverse academic areas of the University, to be challenged in a supportive intellectual environment, and to critically engage fellow students and enthusiastic, distinguished faculty members in thoughtful, provocative discussions. The benefits and rewards are substantial, and the program is flexible enough to be tailored precisely to the individual student's needs and interests. Students enrolled in the Honors College simultaneously complete their degree requirements in one of the five degree-granting colleges at the University.

The Honors College at UMaine is founded on the belief that genuine excellence in college-level studies means substantial understanding and informed appreciation of areas outside a major field of specialization as well as focused excellence within it. With an emphasis on learning that both broadens and deepens, the College serves to expand students' perspectives by exploring areas of thought not closely related to their disciplines and to allow them to work in their majors with greater intensity than would be possible within a conventional course pattern. Honors study begins with interdisciplinary broadness and concludes with an in-depth thesis project in the major field.

Honors College classes are small, typically no more than a dozen students. The interdisciplinary core Civilizations sequence, four courses that satisfy most of the University's general education requirements, engages students in a trajectory of great works from Sumerian times to the present, from Plato to Rachel Carson, and from the Roman Forum to quantum mechanics. The honors curriculum also includes outside-the-classroom educational experiences focused on the arts and citizenship and third-year tutorials in which 8 students and a faculty member explore a topic in great depth.

The senior-year thesis provides students with an opportunity to bring to bear the tools of critical engagement developed in their honors work on an exploration in their major informed by disciplinary studies and mentored by a member of the faculty. The thesis is the capstone of the curriculum, and, whether it is primarily accomplished in a laboratory, library, neighboring community, or studio, it ensures that Honors College students engage in research or creative activity in an appropriate and rewarding manner.

Two dedicated honors residence halls provide living-learning experiences as they also house the Thomson Honors Center, the honors library, three honors classrooms, and other student-centered spaces. Additional opportunities for honors students include funding for research and travel, annual trips to the NCHC conference, and study-abroad scholarships. Honors students play an important role in the governance of the Honors College. The Student Advisory Board meets biweekly with the Dean to provide input on questions of policy and curriculum, and 4 of the 12 voting members on the University's Honors Council are students in the Honors College. Groups of honors students independently select each year's Honors Read, distributed to the incoming first-year honors class, and the Visiting Scholar on Ethics, who is brought to campus for a public lecture and several student interactions.

Participation Requirements: Students are considered to be in good-standing in the Honors College as long as their cumulative GPAs remain above a 3.0. In order to graduate with honors, students must complete the honors curriculum through the senior thesis and graduate with a cumulative GPA of at least 3.3. Honors distinction is recorded on the diplomas and transcripts of these students, their thesis titles are noted on their transcripts, and they are recognized by the President and via their honors medallions at commencement.

Admission Process: Students who are accepted to the University as first-year students are invited to join the Honors College based on a profile incorporating high school and standardized test performance in a sliding scale. The Honors College works with the Admissions Office to identify appropriate candidates; no special application is necessary. The College works with the Office of Admissions and the Office of International Programs to identify transfer and international students who would be good candidates for honors. Students who perform very well during their first and second semesters at the University are invited to join the Honors College in their second semester or their second year, and students who are motivated and interested in the Honors College are always encouraged to contact the Dean.

Scholarship Availability: Students in the Honors College are awarded scholarships, both merit- and need-based, along with all other students at UMaine. The Honors College awards a small number of scholarships to outstanding students who are recognized for their high achievement and potential.

Campus Overview

State-supported university, founded 1865, part of University of Maine System • **Coed** 9,085 undergraduate students, 82% full-time, 52% women, 48% men.

Undergraduates 7,467 full-time, 1,618 part-time. Students come from 41 states and territories, 47 other countries, 12% are from out of state, 1% African American, 1% Asian American or Pacific Islander, 0.8% Hispanic American, 2% Native American, 2% international, 5% transferred in, 30% live on campus.

Faculty *Total:* 740, 68% full-time, 68% with terminal degrees. *Student/faculty ratio:* 15:1.

Academic Programs *Special study options:* accelerated degree program, adult/continuing education programs, advanced placement credit, cooperative education, distance learning, double majors, English as a second language, external degree program, freshman honors college, honors programs, independent study, internships, off-campus study, part-time degree program, services for LD students, student-designed majors, study abroad, summer session for credit. *ROTC:* Army (b), Navy (b).

Athletics Member NCAA. All Division I except football (Division I-A). *Intercollegiate sports:* baseball M(s), basketball M(s)/W(s), cross-country running M(s)/W(s), field hockey W(s), ice hockey M(s)/W(s), soccer M(s)/W(s), softball W(s), swimming and diving M/W(s), track and field M(s)/W(s), volleyball W(s). *Intramural sports:* badminton M/W, basketball M/W, cross-country running M/W, equestrian sports M(c)/W(c), fencing M(c)/W(c), field hockey M(c)/W(c), golf M/W, lacrosse M(c)/W(c), racquetball M/W, rock climbing M(c)/W(c), rugby M(c)/W(c), skiing (cross-country) M/W, skiing (downhill) M(c)/W(c), soccer M/W, softball M/W, swimming and diving M/W, table tennis M/W, tennis M/W, track and field M/W, ultimate Frisbee M(c)/W(c), volleyball M(c)/W(c), water polo M/W, weight lifting M(c)/W(c), wrestling M(c).

Costs (2004–05) *Tuition:* state resident $5040 full-time, $168 per credit hour part-time; nonresident $14,370 full-time, $479 per credit hour part-time. Full-time tuition and fees vary according to reciprocity agreements. Part-time tuition and fees vary according to reciprocity agreements. *Required fees:* $1288 full-time. *Room and board:* $6412; room only: $3238. Room and board charges vary according to board plan and housing facility.

Financial Aid 1,916 Federal Work-Study jobs (averaging $1755). In 2003, 1304 non-need-based awards were made. *Average percent of need met:* 85%. *Average financial aid package:* $9238. *Average need-based loan:* $4290. *Average need-based gift aid:* $4963. *Average non-need-based aid:* $5374.

Contact: Dean: Charlie Slavin, 5716 Robert B. Thomson Honors Center, Orono, Maine 04469-5716; *Telephone:* 207-581-3262; *Fax:* 207-581-3265; *E-mail:* slavin@honors.umaine.edu; *Web site:* http://www.honors.umaine.edu

The University of Maine at Augusta
Honors Program
Augusta, Maine

*T*he Honors Program at the University of Maine at Augusta (UMA) offers those students who have demonstrated intellectual potential and personal commitment an enriched academic experience. Not only are studies at UMA enhanced socially and intellectually, but the honors student is better prepared to continue his or her advanced studies and bring academic talents and abilities to the attention of prospective employers.

The Honors Program is not a separate degree program, but is designed to augment the course work required for a degree. In most cases, honors courses can be substituted for required or elective credits.

Any student, upon the recommendation of the Director of the Honors Program, may register for an honors course without being formally admitted into the program. However, to graduate from the program with honors designation, a student must meet the specific requirements of the Honors Program. There are currently 80 students enrolled in the program.

Participation Requirements: The requirements of the Honors Program are flexible to meet the needs of students—part-time, full-time, traditional, and nontraditional.

UMA offers two honors options, one for associate degree students and another for bachelor's degree students. For those students in the Associate Degree Honors Program, 15 credit hours of honors courses are required, and for those in the Bachelor's Degree Honors Program, 21 to 24 hours are required. All Honors Program participants are required to take a foundation course in critical thinking and writing, an interdisciplinary topical seminar (honors colloquium), and a capstone seminar with thesis. The remaining credits may include other topical seminar courses, honors independent studies, or nonhonors courses contracted for honors credit.

In addition, an Honors Program student has the option of completing 45 hours of community service in lieu of an honors elective. Also, upon completion of the associate degree honors requirements, a student may continue in the bachelor's degree honors program. In addition to the requirements for the associate degree program, the continuing student is required to complete 6 additional hours of honors electives and a senior honors thesis.

It is also possible for students at a distance to participate in the UMA Honors Program, since at least one honors course per year is offered over the University of Maine interactive television system.

The UMA Honors Program began offering courses in the spring semester of 1986, with 24 students. All students admitted to the program automatically become members of the Honors Program Student Association. Upon completion of the Honors Program requirements, the student receives a Certificate of Completion and a medallion to be worn at graduation.

Admission Process: To enter the Honors Program, an interview with the Program Director is scheduled, and the student must submit an application form and three letters of recommendation for consideration by the Honors Council. To continue in the program, the student must maintain a minimum GPA of 3.2 and earn a minimum grade of B in honors courses.

Scholarship Availability: The Honors Program administers two scholarships of its own, which are awarded annually to active participants in the program. There are also eight UMA Presidential Scholarships that are dedicated to program participants. All entering students are eligible for general Presidential Scholarships based on merit.

Campus Overview

State-supported 4-year, founded 1965, part of University of Maine

System • **Coed** 5,538 undergraduate students, 30% full-time, 74% women, 26% men.

Undergraduates 1,640 full-time, 3,898 part-time. Students come from 16 states and territories, 4 other countries, 1% are from out of state, 0.8% African American, 0.2% Asian American or Pacific Islander, 0.6% Hispanic American, 2% Native American, 4% transferred in.

Faculty *Total:* 288, 34% full-time, 14% with terminal degrees. *Student/faculty ratio:* 19:1.

Academic Programs *Special study options:* academic remediation for entering students, adult/continuing education programs, advanced placement credit, distance learning, double majors, honors programs, independent study, internships, off-campus study, part-time degree program, services for LD students, student-designed majors, study abroad, summer session for credit.

Athletics Member NSCAA. *Intercollegiate sports:* basketball M(s)/W(s), soccer W(s). *Intramural sports:* racquetball M/W, soccer M, softball M/W, tennis M/W, volleyball M/W.

Costs (2004–05) *Tuition:* state resident $3960 full-time, $132 per credit part-time; nonresident $9600 full-time, $320 per credit part-time. Full-time tuition and fees vary according to reciprocity agreements. Part-time tuition and fees vary according to reciprocity agreements. *Required fees:* $735 full-time, $25 per credit hour part-time.

Financial Aid 241 Federal Work-Study jobs (averaging $1507). In 2004, 108 non-need-based awards were made. *Average percent of need met:* 68%. *Average financial aid package:* $7474. *Average need-based loan:* $3512. *Average need-based gift aid:* $4667. *Average non-need-based aid:* $3959.

Contact: Director: Jon A. Schlenker, 46 University Drive, Augusta, Maine 04330; *Telephone:* 207-621-3262; *Fax:* 207-621-3232; *E-mail:* jons@maine.edu; *Web site:* http://www.uma.maine.edu

---

University of Southern Maine
University Honors Program
Portland, Maine

Honors at USM is a community-style program in which all students take the same series of courses. These begin with four 4-credit colloquia, taken one per semester, and include Wisdom Stories From Antiquity, which investigates justice and the relationship of the individual to social institutions in ancient Greece, Rome, the Judaic world, and early Christianity; Truth(s), Lie(s), and Legacy(ies) in a Medieval Mindscape, which focuses on the relationship of religion and political power and the development of the mystical tradition in Christianity and Islam into the later Catholic Church and the Islamic Empire; Scientific Revolutions and Critiques, which traces the structure of science from Aristotle to the modern genomic movement, through seminar and lab work. Progress, Process, or Permanence deals with alienation and uncertainty, particularly as exemplified in nineteenth- and twentieth-century literature and philosophy. All of the colloquia emphasize readings from original materials, extensive writing, and a discussion format. Classes are limited to 15 students.

Honors faculty members are from departments in various colleges and schools at USM. They are chosen for their excellent teaching records and their desire to teach in an interdisciplinary environment.

The University of Southern Maine enrolls many nontraditional students, and this diversity is reflected in those taking honors courses. An honors class usually includes traditional students just out of high school, part-time students who also work, and older students who are returning to school. Students with many different majors are found in the program.

All honors courses are taught at the Honors House, a converted residential building within the Portland campus. The building contains offices, seminar rooms, a kitchen, and a reading room. It is also the editorial headquarters for The Southern Maine Review, a refereed journal supported by the Provost's Office of the University of Southern Maine. The Review accepts works from students, faculty, and independent writers that are directed academic exploration, creative fiction, non-fication, and poetry.

There is an active Honors Student Organization that sponsors social and cultural events on campus and coordinates volunteer work by members of the program. Two student representatives are voting members of the Honors Faculty Council, which governs program operations.

The program was developed in the early 1980s with the help of funding from the National Endowment for the Humanities and accepted its first students in 1986. About 40 students each year are now accepted. The total enrollment is approximately 100 or roughly 1 percent of the USM undergraduate student body.

Participation Requirements: Besides the four 4-credit colloquia, honors students take an optional 3-credit Thinking and Writing in Honors course plus one required 3-credit honors seminar offered each semester on a different topic. Under the direction of a faculty committee, all students also do a senior thesis project to complete their honors work, beginning with a thesis workshop. Elective honors courses are available in writing and in directed research or reading. Completion of the colloquium sequence and writing course, which satisfies 22 credits of USM general education requirements, plus the seminar and thesis allows students to graduate with university honors.

Admission Process: Students must apply by April 1 to start the program the following fall. There is no GPA requirement for applicants. The application portfolio includes a completed application form, two letters of recommendation, a personal essay, and academic transcripts. Students and families can talk to current honors students and faculty and staff members anytime during the year. Applications are accepted from individuals entering the University for the first time, those who are currently attending or have previously attended USM, and those who are transfers. Completion of program requirements normally requires three years, although it is possible to complete them in two.

Scholarship Availability: Honors currently awards eight $1000 renewable scholarships per year to students entering honors and two to continuing honors students. Academic performance, civic engagement, and financial need are considered in scholarship awards. Small grants are also available to assist with thesis expenses. Honors students are usually very successful at competing for University-wide scholarships as well.

Campus Overview

State-supported comprehensive, founded 1878, part of University of Maine System • **Coed** 8,736 undergraduate students, 55% full-time, 61% women, 39% men.

Undergraduates 4,762 full-time, 3,974 part-time. Students come from 33 other countries, 8% are from out of state, 1% African American, 1% Asian American or Pacific Islander, 0.8% Hispanic American, 1% Native American, 0.1% international, 9% transferred in, 40% live on campus.

Faculty *Total:* 597, 57% full-time, 50% with terminal degrees. *Student/faculty ratio:* 13:1.

Academic Programs *Special study options:* academic remediation for entering students, accelerated degree program, adult/continuing education programs, advanced placement credit, cooperative education, distance learning, double majors, English as a second language, external degree program, honors programs, independent study, internships, off-campus study, part-time degree program, services for LD students, student-designed majors, study abroad, summer session for credit. *ROTC:* Army (c), Air Force (c). *Unusual degree programs:* 3-2 education.

Athletics Member NCAA. All Division III. *Intercollegiate sports:* baseball M, basketball M/W, cheerleading M/W, cross-country running M/W, field hockey W, golf M/W, ice hockey M/W, lacrosse M/W, sailing M/W, soccer M/W, softball W, tennis M/W, track and field M/W, volleyball W, wrestling M. *Intramural sports:* basketball M/W, cheerleading W, football M/W, ice hockey M/W, lacrosse M(c)/W(c), racquetball M/W, rugby M(c)/W(c), skiing (downhill) M(c)/W(c), soccer M/W, softball M/W, squash M/W, table tennis M/W, tennis M/W, ultimate Frisbee M/W, volleyball M/W, weight lifting M/W.

Costs (2004–05) *Tuition:* state resident $4620 full-time, $154 per credit hour part-time; nonresident $12,780 full-time, $426 per credit hour part-time. Full-time tuition and fees vary according to course load, degree level, and reciprocity agreements. Part-time tuition and fees vary according to course load, degree level, and reciprocity agreements. *Required fees:* $890 full-time. *Room and board:* $6908; room only: $3978. Room and board charges vary according to board plan, housing facility, and location.

Financial Aid In 2004, 441 non-need-based awards were made. *Average percent of need met:* 78%. *Average financial aid package:* $8907. *Average need-based loan:* $4355. *Average need-based gift aid:* $3857. *Average non-need-based aid:* $4360.

Contact: Director: Janice L. Thompson, or Coordinator of Student and Alumni Affairs: Bethany Round, 96 Falmouth Street, P.O. Box 9300, Portland, Maine 04104-9300; *Telephone:* 207-780-4330; *Fax:* 207-780-4333; *E-mail:* jthomp@usm.maine.edu or bround@usm.maine.edu; *Web site:* http://www.usm.maine.edu/honors

MARYLAND

Allegany College of Maryland
Honors Program
Cumberland, Maryland

Allegany College of Maryland's Honors Program allows academically talented students to take a minimum of 12 hours of honors courses by contract either in their major subjects or in their general electives. The honors contract provides an opportunity for students to participate in the Honors Program who otherwise would not be able to complete the requirements of the Honors Program. Members of the Honors Program are eligible to participate in special activities such as receptions, conferences, cultural affairs, and travel, which are planned by and for the Honors Program students. The students have an Honors Lounge. The 11-year-old program currently enrolls 60 students.

Participation Requirements: Honors students are required to complete a minimum of 12 credit hours of honors course work by contract, with a minimum GPA of 3.0 in the contracted honors courses, to receive an honors diploma. The students in the Honors Program have the opportunity to work closely with their faculty mentors in the completion of their contracts and gain an enhanced appreciation and knowledge of the course material.

Admission Process: Students are identified at registration as potential honors students. Freshmen are selected each summer for the Honors Program on the basis of their high school GPA or demonstration of special talents or abilities and an interview with the Honors Director and/or members of the Honors Committee. Students currently enrolled at Allegany College of Maryland can apply at any time during the academic year, but the applicants must have at least a 3.5 GPA at Allegany College of Maryland in order to be eligible.

Scholarship Availability: All members of the Honors Program enrolled in one or more honors courses by contract have half of their in-county tuition for the honors course(s) paid by the Allegany College of Maryland Foundation.

Campus Overview

State and locally supported 2-year, founded 1961, part of Maryland State Community Colleges System • **Coed** 3,705 undergraduate students, 57% full-time, 68% women, 32% men.

Undergraduates 2,102 full-time, 1,603 part-time. Students come from 21 states and territories, 49% are from out of state, 7% African American, 0.5% Asian American or Pacific Islander, 0.8% Hispanic American, 0.4% Native American.

Faculty Total: 245, 42% full-time. *Student/faculty ratio:* 17:1.

Academic Programs *Special study options:* academic remediation for entering students, adult/continuing education programs, advanced placement credit, distance learning, double majors, honors programs, independent study, internships, part-time degree program, summer session for credit. *ROTC:* Army (c).

Athletics Member NJCAA. *Intercollegiate sports:* baseball M, basketball M/W, soccer M/W, softball W, tennis M/W, volleyball W.

Costs (2004–05) *Tuition:* area resident $2550 full-time, $85 per credit part-time; state resident $5010 full-time, $167 per credit part-time; nonresident $5910 full-time, $197 per credit part-time. Full-time tuition and fees vary according to course load and location. Part-time tuition and fees vary according to course load and location. *Required fees:* $184 full-time, $7 per credit part-time, $39 per term part-time.

Contact: Director: Dr. James D. Stickler, 12401 Willowbrook Road, SE, Cumberland, Maryland 21502-2596; *Telephone:* 301-784-5256; *Fax:* 301-784-5070; *E-mail:* jstickler@allegany.edu; *Web site:* http://www.allegany.edu

Bowie State University
Honors College
Bowie, Maryland

The Bowie State University (BSU) Honors Program is designed to both challenge and foster intellectual growth of academically talented students. The program has provided a diverse and stimulating educational experience for its honors students. Drawing from the rich cultural resources that Bowie State University offers, students are encouraged to confront contemporary issues facing society. BSU has well-motivated and skilled faculty members who constitute the core faculty. Honors faculty members are accomplished authorities in their field, proficient at teaching and motivating students to expand their knowledge across disciplines. Students are advised by faculty members in the student's field of interest. The relatively small size of Bowie State University offers the students close personal attention in their studies.

Students in the Honors Program have access to all BSU facilities. They have the benefits of a challenging program and the support of a major university within the Maryland University system. This includes a fully equipped computer laboratory, a fully accredited staff, and a library with nearly a quarter million volumes of information and services.

Honors students must complete 24 honors credits in order to have Honors Scholar on the transcript at graduation. All majors are accepted and honors classes are incorporated into the schedule. Eighteen to twenty honors classes are offered each semester and center on a wide range of studies and disciplines. Students are encouraged to use the honors contract for honors credit in major courses. If an Advanced Placement course covers the same material as an honors course, the AP test score, which meets University standards, can be accepted as a substitute.

The Honors Program currently has 177 members.

Participation Requirements: Honors members must have a 3.3 GPA in order to graduate, 24 honors credits, and 150 hours of community service.

Admission Process: Freshmen and transfer students are selected each fall based upon high school performance and SAT scores. A 3.3 GPA and a minimum 1100 SAT score are required of freshmen members. Transfer students must have a 3.5 GPA or higher, 15 completed credit hours, and recommendations from at least 2 instructors.

Campus Overview

State-supported comprehensive, founded 1865, part of University System of Maryland • **Coed** 4,027 undergraduate students, 80% full-time, 64% women, 36% men.

Undergraduates 3,216 full-time, 811 part-time. Students come from 33 states and territories, 47 other countries, 8% are from out of state, 89% African American, 1% Asian American or Pacific Islander, 1% Hispanic American, 0.3% Native American, 1% international, 9% transferred in, 34% live on campus.

Faculty *Total:* 351, 54% full-time, 55% with terminal degrees. *Student/faculty ratio:* 20:1.

Academic Programs *Special study options:* academic remediation for entering students, adult/continuing education programs, advanced placement credit, cooperative education, distance learning, double majors, external degree program, honors programs, independent study, internships, off-campus study, part-time degree program, services for LD students, study abroad, summer session for credit. *ROTC:* Army (b). *Unusual degree programs:* 3-2 engineering with George Washington University, University of Maryland College Park, Howard University.

Athletics Member NCAA. All Division II. *Intercollegiate sports:* basketball M(s)/W(s), bowling W, cross-country running M(s)/W(s), football M(s), softball W(s), tennis W(s), track and field M(s)/W(s), volleyball W(s).

Costs (2005–06) *Tuition:* state resident $5096 full-time; nonresident $13,088 full-time. *Required fees:* $1750 full-time. *Room and board:* $8674; room only: $6513.

Financial Aid 121 Federal Work-Study jobs (averaging $1865). In 2003, 364 non-need-based awards were made. *Average percent of need met:* 65%. *Average financial aid package:* $9311. *Average need-based loan:* $357. *Average need-based gift aid:* $5601. *Average non-need-based aid:* $3305.

Contact: Director: Dr. Monika E. Gross, Thurgood Marshall Library, Suite 279D 2nd Floor, 14000 Jericho Park Road, Bowie, Maryland 20715; *Telephone:* 301-860-4090, 301-860-4091; *Fax:* 301-860-4089; *E-mail:* mgross@bowiestate.edu

Carroll Community College
Honors Program
Westminster, Maryland

The Honors Program at Carroll Community College offers all students opportunities for enriched learning experiences during their term of study. The intent of the Honors Program is to foster intellectual inquiry, critical-thinking skills, and a passion for lifelong learning. The program emphasizes an active learning community of students and faculty members working together. Each term, a variety of honors opportunities is offered across the disciplines. Honors credit can be earned in honors courses, seminars, and individual contracts and is recorded on the student's transcript with the honors designation. These small classes and seminars are taught by full-time faculty members and emphasize active student participation. Upon

graduation, students who earn a combination of 13 honors credits receive a Certificate in Honors Study.

The program was founded in 1989, revised in 1994, and updated again in 2002. On average, 25 students are enrolled in the Honors Program each semester. An Honors Program Web page is available through the Carroll Community College Web site.

Participation Requirements: Students must complete 13 credits at the honors level with a grade of B or better to successfully complete the program. At least 3 of these credits must be from an honors seminar. Remaining credits may be earned through honors contracts (individually designed projects in other classes), through independent study, or by completing additional honors seminars. Honors Program students must maintain a GPA of 3.25 or higher.

Admission Process: A GPA of at least 3.25, a teacher recommendation, and a completed application (including application essay) are required for admission of students with 12 or more completed credits at Carroll. Students seeking admission directly from high school need two recommendations, a completed application, and evidence of strong verbal skills. There is rolling admission.

Scholarship Availability: There are currently no dedicated Honors Program scholarships; however, a merit-based scholarship cohort program is in development. Program graduates have received scholarships to Western Maryland College, University of Baltimore, and Hood College.

Campus Overview

State and locally supported 2-year, founded 1993, part of Maryland Higher Education Commission • **Coed** 3,073 undergraduate students, 44% full-time, 65% women, 35% men.

Undergraduates 1,359 full-time, 1,714 part-time. Students come from 3 states and territories, 4 other countries, 1% are from out of state, 3% African American, 1% Asian American or Pacific Islander, 2% Hispanic American, 0.4% Native American, 0.2% international.

Faculty *Total:* 227, 22% full-time, 3% with terminal degrees. *Student/faculty ratio:* 17:1.

Academic Programs *Special study options:* academic remediation for entering students, advanced placement credit, distance learning, English as a second language, honors programs, independent study, internships, part-time degree program, services for LD students, summer session for credit.

Costs (2005–06) *Tuition:* area resident $3234 full-time, $92 per credit part-time; state resident $4476 full-time, $128 per credit part-time; nonresident $6788 full-time, $195 per credit part-time.

Financial Aid 22 Federal Work-Study jobs (averaging $1772).

Contact: Director: Kristie Crumley, 1601 Washington Road, Westminster, Maryland 21157; *Telephone:* 410-386-8572; *Fax:* 410-876-8563; *E-mail:* kcrumley@carrollcc.edu; *Web site:* http://www.carrollcc.edu

College of Notre Dame of Maryland
The Elizabeth Morrissy Honors Program
Baltimore, Maryland

Founded in 1981, the Elizabeth Morrissy Honors Program, named to honor the memory of an outstanding Notre Dame professor, meets the needs and interests of students with high ability and motivation. Several honors seminars are offered each semester. There are currently 100 students in the program.

Participation Requirements: Students in the Morrissy Honors Program may major in any area that the College offers and take the same number of credits for graduation as every other student. A student must take at least one Morrissy seminar a year and complete a minimum of 18 credits of honors course work to receive an honors diploma. They must maintain a minimum 3.3 cumulative GPA and 3.0 GPA in honors courses. They must also attend honors events during the year.

Scholarship Availability: Morrissy students hold several kinds of scholarships offered by the College as well as outside scholarships.

Campus Overview

Independent Roman Catholic comprehensive, founded 1873 • **Suburban** 58-acre campus • **Women only** 1,686 undergraduate students, 36% full-time.

Undergraduates 607 full-time, 1,079 part-time. Students come from 26 states and territories, 15 other countries, 8% are from out of state, 26% African American, 3% Asian American or Pacific Islander, 3% Hispanic American, 0.5% Native American, 2% international, 3% transferred in, 57% live on campus.

Faculty *Total:* 88, 90% full-time, 78% with terminal degrees. *Student/faculty ratio:* 13:1.

Academic Programs *Special study options:* accelerated degree program, adult/continuing education programs, advanced placement credit, double majors, English as a second language, honors programs, independent study, internships, off-campus study, part-time degree program, services for LD students, student-designed majors, study abroad, summer session for credit. *ROTC:* Army (c). *Unusual degree programs:* 3-2 engineering with University of Maryland, College Park; Johns Hopkins University; nursing with Johns Hopkins University; radiological science with Johns Hopkins University.

Athletics Member NCAA. All Division III. *Intercollegiate sports:* basketball W, field hockey W, lacrosse W, soccer W, swimming and diving W, tennis W, volleyball W. *Intramural sports:* cross-country running W, softball W.

Costs (2005–06) *Comprehensive fee:* $29,600 includes full-time tuition ($21,100), mandatory fees ($500), and room and board ($8000). Part-time tuition: $345 per credit. *Required fees:* $60 per term part-time.

Financial Aid 168 Federal Work-Study jobs (averaging $1368). In 2003, 98 non-need-based awards were made. *Average percent of need met:* 100%. *Average financial aid package:* $19,127. *Average need-based loan:* $4749. *Average need-based gift aid:* $14,417. *Average non-need-based aid:* $9640.

Contact: Director: Charles F. Ritter, 4701 North Charles Street, Baltimore, Maryland 21210-2476; *Telephone:* 410-532-5738; *Fax:* 410-532-5798; *E-mail:* critter@ndm.edu

The Community College of Baltimore County–Essex Campus

Honors Program

Baltimore, Maryland

The Community College of Baltimore County (CCBC) Essex Honors Program is intended to promote academic excellence in students who are both intellectually gifted and highly motivated. The program aims to enrich the educational experience of the exceptional student and seeks to admit students who have the ability, interest, and initiative to be successful in such a program. Honors students are distinguished by their pursuit of challenge and their willingness to question, and the Honors Program is designed to meet the special needs of these students.

The Honors Program seeks students with outstanding academic records. However, students who are highly capable but who have not previously performed up to their potential are encouraged to apply as well, provided they can demonstrate that they have now found the motivation to excel. Any full- or part-time Essex student may apply for admission to the Honors Program.

Honors courses are designed to foster collaboration and inquiry through an emphasis on student involvement. Honors courses are not designed simply to require more work; rather, they require work at a more sophisticated level. Students are encouraged to think analytically and creatively and are taught to communicate their thoughts effectively in both oral and written projects. Honors courses at Essex can take several forms. There are honors sections of existing courses as well as specially designed honors seminars that examine a wide variety of topics, often from an interdisciplinary perspective. Enrollment in honors courses is limited to 15, and as a result, students have a greater opportunity for interaction with their instructors and with each other.

Regardless of the format, honors courses have in common their emphasis on originality and critical thinking. There is extensive opportunity for open discussion, and collaborative learning rather than individual competition is encouraged. The common focus of all honors courses is on the expansion of the students' ability to learn and the students' ability to use that learning to make discriminating, intellectual choices.

The program is seventeen years old, and current enrollment is 204.

Participation Requirements: Once students are admitted to the program, they are members literally forever. But in order to complete the program and earn an honors certificate, honors students must maintain a minimum overall 3.5 GPA and must complete a minimum of 15 honors credits. When members of the Honors Program graduate, they are recognized at commencement.

In addition, those students who complete the program are guaranteed admission to the College of Notre Dame, Coppin State College, Goucher College, Johns Hopkins School of Continuing Studies, Loyola College, McDaniel College, Morgan State University, Towson University, University of Baltimore, University of Maryland Baltimore County, and University of Maryland College Park.

Admission Process: In order to apply to the Honors Program, students must complete an application form, submit three letters of recommendation, and write two brief essays. Students who are interested in honors are interviewed by three members of the Honors Committee, generally 2 faculty members and a student. The Honors Committee meets eight times a year to review applications. While the committee reads transcripts and acknowledges SAT I scores, emphasis is placed less on past grades and test scores than on current performance and level of motivation. The committee has decided that it is generally not interested in the students' past but rather in their present and future; students who are able to demonstrate academic ability and enthusiasm for learning are likely to succeed in honors and will be accepted.

Scholarship Availability: Each member of the Honors Program receives a scholarship for one honors course per semester, provided that the student has earned an A or a B in the honors course and a minimum overall GPA of 3.0 for the semester. Some full scholarships are available.

Campus Overview

County-supported 2-year, founded 1957 • **Coed** 20,025 undergraduate students.

Undergraduates 28% African American, 4% Asian American or Pacific Islander, 2% Hispanic American, 0.4% Native American, 2% international.

Faculty *Total:* 1,006, 35% full-time, 10% with terminal degrees. *Student/faculty ratio:* 20:1.

Costs (2004–05) *Tuition:* area resident $2610 full-time, $87 per hour part-time; state resident $4500 full-time, $150 per hour part-time; nonresident $6150 full-time, $205 per hour part-time. *Required fees:* $340 full-time.

Contact: Director: Rae Rosenthal, 7201 Rossville Boulevard, Baltimore, Maryland 21237; *Telephone:* 410-780-6880; *Fax:* 410-918-4220; *E-mail:* essexhonors@ccbcmd.edu

Coppin State University
Honors Program
Baltimore, Maryland

Coppin State University offers an Honors Program for outstanding students who have demonstrated exceptional ability. The primary focus of the Honors Program is preparation for the graduate school experience. The program accomplishes this task through the offering of general education honors courses, a series of research courses, graduate school workshops, and graduate school entrance exam preparatory seminars. In addition, the Honors Program provides students with unique opportunities to participate in community service programs, cultural activities, and paid summer internships.

There are two categories within the Honors Program to accommodate high-ability students in all majors who desire an honors experience and are at various stages of their university careers. The Four-Year Honors Program is designed for incoming freshmen, and the Upper-Division Honors Program is for transfer students.

The first student began in honors in 1981–82. On average, 65 students are enrolled in the program yearly.

Participation Requirements: Students entering the Four-Year Honors Program are required to complete the following courses to earn an honors citation: five honors versions of General Education Requirement courses, HONS 150 (Honors Community-Service Seminar), HONS 380 (Honors Introduction to Research I), HONS 381 (Honors Introduction to Research II), and HONS 490 (Honors Thesis). In addition, students must complete one of the following courses: HONS 470 (Honors Field Practicum I), HONS 480 (Honors Research Assistantship), EDUC 460 (Teaching Assistantship Seminar), and MNSC 150 (Computer Literacy). Students who complete the required honors courses, maintain full-time status, and earn a GPA of at least 3.0 overall and in their honors courses receive honors citations on their academic records and honors program graduation medallions.

Students participating in the Upper-Division Honors Program complete HONS 380 (Honors Introduction to Research I), HONS 381 (Honors Introduction to Research II), and HONS 490 (Honors Thesis). In addition, they are required to complete two of the following courses: HONS 470 (Honors Field Practicum I), HONS 480 (Honors Research Assistantship), EDUC 460 (Teaching Assistant Seminar), and MNSC 150 (Computer Literacy). Participants in the Upper-Division Honors Program who complete the required honors courses, maintain full-time status, and earn a GPA of at least 3.0 overall and in their honors courses receive honors citations on their academic records. Prior to graduation, these students receive completion certificates from the Upper-Division Honors Program.

Admission Process: The Four-Year Honors Program offers three scholarships to high school seniors: the Golden Eagle Scholarship, the Eagle Scholarship, and the Opportunity Scholarship. The minimum admission criteria for the Golden Eagle Scholarship are a minimum high school GPA of 3.2 and a combined SAT score of 1820 or 27 ACT; for the Eagle Scholarship, a GPA of at least 3.0 and SAT score of 1600 or ACT of 24 or greater; and for the Opportunity Scholarship, a minimum GPA of 2.0 and SAT score of at least 1700 or ACT of at least 25. The Upper-Division Honors Program applicant must have completed at least 45 graduation credits, including English Composition I and II, and obtained a transfer GPA of 3.5 or greater.

Scholarship Availability: The Golden Eagle Scholarship provides tuition, fees, and room and board for a maximum of eight semesters. The Eagle Scholarship provides tuition and fees for a maximum of eight semesters. The Opportunity Scholarship provides one-half of tuition and fees for one semester. The Opportunity Scholarship recipient who obtains a minimum 3.0 GPA and maintains full-time status is converted to an Eagle Scholarship recipient. Each scholarship recipient is required to maintain a GPA of at least 3.0 overall and in their honors courses and to earn at least 12 graduation credits each semester they receive scholarship support. The Upper-Division Scholarship provides $500 each semester for a maximum of four semesters. All Upper-Division Scholarship recipients are required to maintain a minimum GPA of 3.3 overall and in their honors courses and to earn at least 12 graduation credits each semester they receive scholarship support.

Campus Overview

State-supported comprehensive, founded 1900, part of University System of Maryland • **Coed** 3,092 undergraduate students.

Undergraduates Students come from 20 states and territories, 19 other countries, 95% African American, 0.2% Asian American or Pacific Islander, 0.6% Hispanic American, 0.4% Native American, 2% international, 10% live on campus.

Faculty *Total:* 202, 54% full-time. *Student/faculty ratio:* 17:1.

Academic Programs *Special study options:* academic remediation for entering students, adult/continuing education programs, advanced placement credit, cooperative education, double majors, English as a second language, external degree program, freshman honors college, honors programs, internships, off-campus study, part-time degree program, services for LD students, summer session for credit. *ROTC:* Army (b). *Unusual degree programs:* 3-2 engineering with University of Maryland College Park.

Athletics Member NCAA. All Division I. *Intercollegiate sports:* baseball M(s), basketball M(s)/W(s), bowling M/W, cross-country running M(s)/W(s), rugby M(c), softball W, tennis M(s)/W(s), track and field M(s)/W(s), volleyball W(s), weight lifting M(s)/W(s), wrestling M(s). *Intramural sports:* basketball M/W, bowling M/W, softball W, tennis M/W, track and field M/W, volleyball W, weight lifting M/W, wrestling M.

Costs (2005–06) *Tuition:* state resident $3527 full-time, $151 per credit hour part-time; nonresident $10,048 full-time, $347 per credit hour part-time. *Required fees:* $1352 full-time, $22 per credit hour part-time, $150 per term part-time. *Room and board:* $6239; room only: $3881.

Financial Aid 126 Federal Work-Study jobs (averaging $1687). In 2004, 10 non-need-based awards were made. *Average percent of need met:* 69%. *Average financial aid package:* $7050. *Average need-based loan:* $3530. *Average need-based gift aid:* $5258. *Average non-need-based aid:* $3025.

Contact: Dean: Ron L. Collins Sr., Assistant Dean: DeChelle Forbes, Coppin State University, 2500 West North Avenue, Baltimore, Maryland 21216; *Telephone:* 410-951-3388; *Fax:* 410-951-3389; *E-mail:* rcollins@coppin.edu or dforbes@wye.coppin.edu

Frederick Community College
Honors Program
Frederick, Maryland

The Honors Program at Frederick Community College (FCC) started in 1982 and has earned state and national recognitions. It is designed for students who want more out of their college learning experience. Small classes (10–15 students), close interaction with superb faculty members, and academic activities (e.g., research *projects, field trips, and guest speakers) inside and outside the classroom create such opportunities.*

Honors classes offer an exciting small-group setting, in-depth study, and an environment that encourages individual participation. Each course emphasizes higher-level reading, essay writing, critical thinking, group processing skills, and unique research projects. Every semester, the Honors Program at FCC schedules a variety of general education and elective courses.

Linked courses are a special feature of the Honors Program. Linked courses focus on the relations between two subjects. FCC traditionally offers a combined English composition and speech fundamentals course as well as an American literature and U.S. history course. Other linked courses are offered periodically.

ID 200H (Honors Seminar: Special Topics in Interdisciplinary Studies) is a new offering in the FCC Honors Program. This course is designed for honors students and is open to other qualified students with permission of the instructor. Topics vary from semester to semester but synthesize work from at least two different academic content areas and focus on issues of importance to society and enhance each student's ability to think critically and draw conclusions based on multiple points of view. It gives honors students an academically challenging way to fulfill 3 credits of their general education core requirement.

Independent study with a faculty mentor allows for in-depth research of a topic selected by the student. A corequisite for the independent study is the 1-credit Honors Forum taught by the Honors Coordinator. Students in the Honors Forum share their progress and act as peer evaluators for each other. Students present their work to the campus community at the end of the spring semester with a reception that follows.

Cocurricular learning activities are another special feature of the Honors Program at FCC. Each year the Honors Advisory Board selects an annual theme for the upcoming academic year. Honors faculty members integrate the theme and cocurricular activities, such as speakers and field trips, into their courses as appropriate. This allows students to explore a topic across multiple disciplines and enhance their learning.

FCC is developing an Honors Scholars Program that will provide highly qualified students with an enriched degree program. Students will be matched with a faculty mentor in experiential learning activities in the areas of leadership, civic engagement, character development, and the disciplines of mind that lead to scholarly excellence in the chosen field. The mentor will assist the student with research design and processes and help the student develop a portfolio of academic achievements, leadership and civic engagement activities, and extracurricular and cocurricular work and support the student's transfer goals to highly selective colleges and universities. Selection criteria for this program include class standing, extracurricular activities, student essay, teacher recommendations, and student transfer goals. Students who enter FCC as FCC Honors Scholars must remain in good academic standing (minimum 3.5 GPA.) and take at least 12 hours of honors-designated courses over the two year program of study.

The Honors Program at FCC provides students the opportunity to explore their potential. The resulting personal and academic growth frequently gives students a competitive advantage when applying to four-year universities and colleges.

Participation Requirements: Once admitted to the Honors Program, there are no requirements per se. Poor academic performance can lead to restriction from taking future honors courses. Students are encouraged to become involved in the honors activities. There is an Honors Student Association that meets regularly; organizes student activities, such as an annual talent show; and sponsors community service projects. Honors students also have their own study lounge with access to a computer/printer.

Students who complete 12 honors credits with a minimum 3.5 GPA receive an honors certificate and are recognized at commencement.

Admission Process: Membership in the Honors Program is by invitation. Students with high scores on SAT/ACT or FCC placement tests automatically qualify. Applicants with strong academic records (3.5 GPA) or faculty recommendations are also encouraged to contact the Honors Coordinator or the FCC Counseling Department to schedule an interview.

Scholarship Availability: FCC Honors Scholars receive tuition and fee waivers for two consecutive years of full-time study, sufficient to complete an associate degree in an FCC transfer program. In addition, the student can receive financial support to conduct and present original research on a scholarly topic related to the discipline. This support includes travel, research expenses incurred for access to and copying of documents, faculty mentorship, and conference fees.

Campus Overview

State and locally supported 2-year, founded 1957 • **Coed** 4,736 undergraduate students, 38% full-time, 63% women, 37% men.

Undergraduates 1,791 full-time, 2,945 part-time. Students come from 9 states and territories, 1% are from out of state, 7% African American, 2% Asian American or Pacific Islander, 2% Hispanic American, 0.5% Native American.

Faculty *Total:* 326, 24% full-time.

Academic Programs *Special study options:* academic remediation for entering students, adult/continuing education programs, advanced placement credit, cooperative education, distance learning, external degree program, honors programs, independent study, off-campus study, part-time degree program, services for LD students, study abroad, summer session for credit. *ROTC:* Army (c).

Athletics Member NJCAA. *Intercollegiate sports:* baseball M, basketball M/W, golf M/W, soccer M/W, softball W, volleyball W.

Costs (2005–06) *Tuition:* area resident $2040 full-time, $85 per credit hour part-time; state resident $4368 full-time, $187 per credit hour part-time; nonresident $6096 full-time, $254 per credit hour part-time. *Required fees:* $292 full-time, $11 per credit hour part-time, $18 per term part-time.

Financial Aid 25 Federal Work-Study jobs (averaging $1368). 14 state and other part-time jobs (averaging $2715).

Contact: Honors Coordinator: Dr. Bruce A. Thompson, Frederick Community College, 7932 Opossumtown Pike, Frederick, Maryland 21702; *Telephone:* 301-846-2535; *Fax:* 301-846-2498; *E-mail:* bthompson@frederick.edu

Frostburg State University
University Honors Program
Frostburg, Maryland

The Honors Program at Frostburg State University (FSU) prides itself upon blurring boundaries traditionally found in academia. These boundaries include the authority divide between faculty members, students, and administrators; the boundaries between academic disciplines; and the boundaries between the classroom and the other arenas.

In FSU's Honors Program, students cofacilitate the freshman orientation course, participate in faculty development workshops, serve on the Honors Program governing committee, and function as equal partners in the redesign of the program's curriculum and requirements. Administrators from diverse sectors of the University routinely teach honors courses and seminars. An Undergraduate Research Opportunity Program pairs honors students with faculty mentors. There are social activities, such as picnics, film discussions, and field trips. Throughout the program, students, faculty members, and administrators operate as collaborators in the learning process.

Honors courses, even if they are housed in a particular discipline, are expected to incorporate material from multiple disciplines and

encourage critical thinking. Specially designed interdisciplinary seminars are offered each semester. These seminars are often team taught. Recent topics have included Women, Science, and Society; The Sixties in America; Myths of America and the Ecological Dilemma; Political Psychology; The American South; Native Peoples of North America; Asian Culture; Physics and Metaphysics; The Literature of the Other; The African-American Experience; Self and Other; and The Holocaust. Some of the seminars, such as The Holocaust, are intense, 6-credit experiences.

The Honors Program at Frostburg State offers more than merely a set of traditional courses. Travel/study experiences are offered as honors seminars. Since May 1995, the following Honors-sponsored travel/study experiences have been offered: International Politics in Ireland, Mythology as Sacred Geography in Greece, Art and the Social World in New York City, and Environmental Issues in Ecuador. Honors/international housing in Cambridge and Westminster Halls offers students the opportunity to live in a learning community with special programming to complement their honors courses. An Honors Learning Community (Culture, Communication, and Community) offer integrated courses and cocurricular activities. Students and faculty members are active participants in state, regional, and national collegiate honors councils. FSU's Honors Program students are campus leaders active in student government, campus publications, Greek life, and other cocurricular organizations.

The FSU Honors Program is 25 years old and currently enrolls 353 students.

Participation Requirements: Most of the students in the Honors Program are pursuing the distinction of graduating with honors in general education. This requires completion of 24 credits of honors course work, including liberal arts courses and interdisciplinary seminars. Courses taken for honors credit at a community college or another university may be used to complete these requirements.

Students who complete the 24-credit requirement for graduating with honors in general education receive a certificate and recognition at the University's Honors Convocation. In addition, they are recognized at Commencement and their transcript notes the distinction of graduated with honors in general education.

Admission Process: Incoming first semester students are invited to join FSU's Honors Program on the basis of their high school GPA and SAT scores. Transfer students and others joining the program after their first semester are expected to have a 3.5 college GPA or above.

Scholarship Availability: The Nelson P. Guild Scholarship is available for juniors participating in the Honors Program. Students are nominated by the Honors Program director based upon their GPA, their involvement in the Honors Program, and their leadership activities.

Meritorious Achievement Awards are available for entering first-year students and transfer students. In addition, more than 137 departmental and interest-related scholarships are available for first-year and continuing students.

Campus Overview

State-supported comprehensive, founded 1898, part of University System of Maryland • **Coed** 4,522 undergraduate students, 93% full-time, 49% women, 51% men.

Undergraduates 4,227 full-time, 295 part-time. Students come from 23 states and territories, 27 other countries, 11% are from out of state, 13% African American, 2% Asian American or Pacific Islander, 2% Hispanic American, 0.5% Native American, 0.7% international, 7% transferred in, 35% live on campus.

Faculty Total: 346, 66% full-time. Student/faculty ratio: 18:1.

Academic Programs Special study options: adult/continuing education programs, advanced placement credit, distance learning, double majors, freshman honors college, honors programs, independent study, internships, off-campus study, part-time degree program, services for LD students, study abroad, summer session for credit. Unusual degree programs: 3-2 engineering with University of Maryland, College Park.

Athletics Member NCAA. All Division III. Intercollegiate sports: baseball M, basketball M/W, cross-country running M/W, field hockey W, football M, golf M, lacrosse W, soccer M/W, softball W, swimming and diving M/W, tennis M/W, track and field M/W, volleyball W. Intramural sports: badminton M/W, basketball M/W, field hockey M/W, football M/W, golf M/W, lacrosse M(c)/W, racquetball M/W, rugby M(c), soccer M/W, softball M/W, squash M/W, table tennis M/W, tennis M/W, volleyball M(c)/W, water polo M/W, weight lifting M/W, wrestling M.

Costs (2005–06) Tuition: state resident $5000 full-time, $207 per credit hour part-time; nonresident $13,250 full-time, $374 per credit hour part-time. Full-time tuition and fees vary according to course load and program. Part-time tuition and fees vary according to course load and program. Required fees: $1230 full-time, $59 per credit hour part-time, $9 per term part-time. Room and board: $6148; room only: $3072. Room and board charges vary according to board plan and housing facility.

Financial Aid 196 Federal Work-Study jobs (averaging $958). 535 state and other part-time jobs (averaging $360). In 2004, 416 non-need-based awards were made. Average percent of need met: 71%. Average financial aid package: $6689. Average need-based loan: $3271. Average need-based gift aid: $4229. Average non-need-based aid: $2788.

Contact: Director: Maureen Connelly, 101 Braddock Road, Frostburg, Maryland 21532; Telephone: 301-687-4998; Fax: 301-687-1069; E-mail: mconnelly@frostburg.edu

Prince George's Community College
Honors Program
Largo, Maryland

The mission of the Honors Program at Prince George's Community College (PGCC) is to promote the intellectual growth and enrichment of academically outstanding students. Founded in 1981 as a single seminar course with a few students, the program now offers an average of twenty-four honors sections each semester to approximately 225 students. In addition, the Honors Program offers an interdisciplinary honors colloquium each year in a variety of areas.

The Honors Program emphasizes small classes (usually 10 to 15 students) that offer unique opportunities in participatory learning, interaction, and faculty mentoring. Most honors classes are seminar-style and seek to help the student become an independent learner and critical thinker. The honors faculty consists of more than 40 senior faculty members and master teachers, many of whom are actively involved in professional development in their fields.

Members of the College's Honors Program enjoy many unique opportunities. Some of the benefits include access to the honors student center, which houses computers, desks, a phone, a study area, and meeting space in which to socialize. In addition to a full-time Honors Coordinator, the Honors Program employs 2 part-time Assistant Faculty Coordinators in Marketing and Recruitment and in Advising to work with honors students. The honors society provides many cocurricular activities for students, including the College Bowl, the Model United Nations club, and Tau Pi, the College's chapter of Phi Theta Kappa. Honors students also can earn credit for internships related to their majors through the College co-op education program.

Students who graduate from the honors program transfer to many top four-year institutions locally and nationally, including Georgetown, Johns Hopkins, American, Catholic, George Washington, and Howard Universities; the University of Maryland; and Goucher and Washington Colleges, to name a few.

In 2000, the Honors Academy was introduced into the Honors Program. The Honors Academy is designed for academically outstanding students who are interested in a rigorous program of academic excellence, intellectual development, leadership, and community service. Benefits of the academy include dual admission to selected four-year academic institutions; full tuition while at PGCC and scholarship upon transfer through completion of the B.A. degree; and seamless transfer from Prince George's Community College to the partnering institutions. Eligibility for the academy is competitive; students must have and maintain a GPA of 3.5 or above, have a combined SAT score of 1050 or higher, complete at least seven honors courses, perform 15 hours of community service each semester, and assume a leadership role within the honors program.

Participation Requirements: Students in the honors program must take a minimum of two honors courses. However, to graduate with a Citation in Honors, students must complete a minimum of five honors courses with a cumulative GPA of 3.25 or higher. Each May, students are recognized for high academic achievement and excellence in research, writing, or a particular discipline or for overall merit at the Honors Convocation, which is followed by a reception for the students, faculty, and family members.

Admission Process: To be admitted into the Honors Program, incoming and currently enrolled students must meet the following criteria: a high school GPA of 3.0 or higher and scores of 550 or higher on the SAT verbal and math tests or scores of 95 or higher on the Accuplacer Reading test administered by the College testing center. Students must be eligible for college-level math. To remain eligible for the Honors Program, students must maintain a 3.0 cumulative GPA in the College.

Campus Overview

County-supported 2-year, founded 1958 • **Coed** 12,564 undergraduate students, 27% full-time, 66% women, 34% men.

Undergraduates 3,352 full-time, 9,212 part-time. Students come from 20 states and territories, 98 other countries, 4% are from out of state, 76% African American, 4% Asian American or Pacific Islander, 3% Hispanic American, 0.5% Native American, 3% international, 13% transferred in.

Faculty *Total:* 639, 39% full-time, 23% with terminal degrees. *Student/faculty ratio:* 18:1.

Academic Programs *Special study options:* academic remediation for entering students, adult/continuing education programs, advanced placement credit, cooperative education, distance learning, English as a second language, external degree program, honors programs, part-time degree program, services for LD students, summer session for credit. *ROTC:* Army (c).

Athletics Member NJCAA. *Intercollegiate sports:* baseball M, basketball M/W, bowling M/W, golf M, soccer M/W, softball W, tennis M/W, volleyball W. *Intramural sports:* basketball M/W, tennis M/W, volleyball W.

Costs (2004–05) *Tuition:* area resident $2808 full-time, $90 per credit part-time; state resident $4464 full-time, $159 per credit part-time; nonresident $6528 full-time, $245 per credit part-time. Full-time tuition and fees vary according to program and reciprocity agreements. Part-time tuition and fees vary according to program and reciprocity agreements. *Required fees:* $74 full-time, $1 per credit part-time, $25 per semester part-time.

Financial Aid 99 Federal Work-Study jobs (averaging $2000).

Contact: Contact Dr. Melinda Frederick, Coordinator, Honors Program and Honors Academy, Marlboro 1087, 301 Largo Road, Largo, Maryland 20774; *Telephone:* 301-322-0433; *Fax:* 301-808-0960; *E-mail:* mfrederick@pgcc.edu; *Web site:* http://academic.pg.cc.md.us/honorsprogram/

St. Mary's College of Maryland
Scholars Program
St. Mary's City, Maryland

The St. Mary's College of Maryland Scholars Program was created in 1998. The program is designed to provide exceptional opportunities for students who have demonstrated their commitment to the liberal arts and sciences through their outstanding academic success and their commitment to the improvement of society, especially through leadership and service roles. By combining academic excellence with a leadership and service orientation, the Scholars Program aims to develop in students an understanding of leadership and leaders, especially those individuals who can inspire others to subordinate narrow self-interest for a greater good.

Scholars Program participants are exempt from some of the requirements for the general education program. Instead, they complete an alternative curriculum that is designed as an enriching and challenging means of attaining a liberal arts education of high quality, combining academic rigor and scholarship with an understanding of the importance of leadership and service.

Students take interdisciplinary seminars and a tutorial that focus on the themes of leadership and service in the first two years of the program. In addition to the seminars, students must obtain advanced proficiency in two of three proficiency areas (writing, mathematics, and a foreign language) and complete a leadership/service portfolio. Moreover, in the senior year, each Scholars Program student completes an 8-credit original project, guided by a faculty mentor with expertise in the subject matter of the project.

In addition to the special curriculum and individualized attention from scholars administrators and faculty members, the Scholars Program also sponsors extracurricular events, both on and off campus, for Scholars students. These events frequently take advantage of the College's proximity to Washington, D.C., and Baltimore and the extraordinary cultural events that these cities offer.

Participation Requirements: Students are required to attain and maintain a minimum 3.5 cumulative GPA to be eligible for graduation with Latin honors. Furthermore, all required courses must be completed with a grade of C or better.

Admission Process: About half of the students in the Scholars Program are selected directly from high school based on their cumulative GPA, the rigor of their course work, their combined SAT I scores, an application essay, and special talents and activities related to leadership and service. The other half of the students in the program are selected after they have completed at least a semester of college work, either at St. Mary's or elsewhere. Most of those students join the program at the beginning of their sophomore year. Around 20 students join the program each year.

Campus Overview

State-supported 4-year, founded 1840, part of Maryland State Colleges and Universities System • **Coed** 1,935 undergraduate students, 95% full-time, 58% women, 42% men.

Undergraduates 1,830 full-time, 105 part-time. Students come from 36 states and territories, 18% are from out of state, 7% African American, 4% Asian American or Pacific Islander, 3% Hispanic American, 0.1% Native American, 0.6% international, 4% transferred in, 84% live on campus.

Faculty *Total:* 199, 60% full-time, 78% with terminal degrees. *Student/faculty ratio:* 13:1.

Academic Programs *Special study options:* advanced placement credit, cooperative education, double majors, freshman honors college, honors programs, independent study, internships, off-campus study, part-time degree program, services for LD students, student-designed majors, study abroad, summer session for credit. *Unusual degree programs:* 3-2 engineering with University of Maryland, College Park.

Athletics Member NCAA. All Division III. *Intercollegiate sports:* baseball M, basketball M/W, crew M(c)/W(c), fencing M(c)/W(c), field hockey W, golf M(c)/W(c), lacrosse M/W, rugby M(c)/W(c), sailing M/W, soccer M/W, swimming and diving M/W, tennis M/W, ultimate Frisbee M(c)/W(c), volleyball M(c)/W. *Intramural sports:* basketball M/W, bowling M/W, cross-country running M(c)/W(c), equestrian sports M(c)/W(c), football M/W, lacrosse M/W, sailing M/W, soccer M/W, softball M/W, swimming and diving M/W, tennis M/W, track and field M(c)/W(c), volleyball M/W, water polo M/W.

Costs (2004–05) *Tuition:* state resident $8092 full-time, $150 per credit part-time; nonresident $15,572 full-time, $150 per credit part-time. Part-time tuition and fees vary according to course load. *Required fees:* $1588 full-time. *Room and board:* $7400; room only: $4165. Room and board charges vary according to board plan, housing facility, and student level.

Financial Aid 105 Federal Work-Study jobs (averaging $794). In 2004, 429 non-need-based awards were made. *Average percent of need met:* 62%. *Average financial aid package:* $6250. *Average need-based loan:* $5500. *Average need-based gift aid:* $4000. *Average non-need-based aid:* $4000.

Contact: Director: Dr. Michael Taber, Academic Services, St. Mary's College of Maryland, 18952 East Fisher Road, St. Mary's City, Maryland 20686; *Telephone:* 240-895-4900; *E-mail:* mstaber@smcm.edu

Salisbury University
Thomas E. Bellavance Honors Program
Salisbury, Maryland

The Thomas E. Bellavance Honors Program at Salisbury University (SU) is designed to bring together superior students and dedicated faculty members in a small University environment within the diversity of opportunity of the larger University community. It offers motivated students who are serious about their intellectual growth a variety of special classes enhanced by many cultural events and activities. The program fosters close individual contact between students and faculty members and brings together talented students with many interests.

Honors courses and extracurricular activities are intended to enrich and complement other educational opportunities and programs available to Salisbury students. The overarching goal of the Honors Program is to give high-achieving students intense and exciting educational experiences to enhance their development as independent thinkers and learners who are able and eager to take an active role in their own intellectual development. Real learning involves exploration and discovery, and the Honors Program gives students the opportunity and encouragement to be Columbuses of the intellectual life. There are currently 205 students enrolled in the program.

Participation Requirements: To begin their intellectual journey, Honors Program students are required to take a sequence of four honors core courses: Critical Thinking and Writing, Issues in Social Science, Issues in Humanities, and Issues in Natural Sciences. These are designed to give students in the Honors Program a shared intellectual experience in the arts and sciences in order to develop a community of learners and to encourage a spirit of collegiality in pursuit of knowledge, a spirit that is essential for intellectual growth and personal fulfillment.

Core courses and honors electives satisfy both general education and honors requirements so that students need not take these courses in addition to those required for graduation in their majors.

Those students who finish the four-course sequence with a 3.0 GPA in the core and in their courses overall are also invited to graduate with honors by taking two additional honors courses and writing an honors thesis in their major or by taking three additional honors courses. The additional honors courses are in a variety of disciplines that are designed to augment the core experience, covering topics such as non-Western cultures, mathematical reasoning, art and music histories, and others.

The honors thesis is the capstone intellectual experience for students in the Honors Program and is a valuable opportunity to do independent research with a faculty mentor on a topic of personal interest in one's major field. Clearly, the thesis experience is excellent preparation for graduate or professional school. Students who fulfill these requirements and receive an overall GPA of 3.35 are recognized on their transcript and diploma as having graduated with "Bellavance Honors—With Distinction." Students who take three additional courses in lieu of two courses and a thesis graduate with "Bellavance Honors."

Tangible benefits of the Honors Program include small, stimulating classes taught by creative, supportive faculty members; recognition on transcripts and diplomas of participation in the Honors Program; use of the Honors Center, a lovely nine-room house adjacent to campus with lounges, a computer room, study areas, a kitchen, and a recreation room; participation in a variety of cultural, social, and public-service activities; and scholarships and small monetary awards to recognize outstanding scholars in the program. But even more important are the intangible benefits the students have received. As one honors graduate stated, "The Honors Program provided me with a nurturing environment in which to develop a higher level of thinking skills which I will use throughout college and throughout my life."

Admission Process: Incoming freshmen with superior academic records (minimum 3.25 GPA/combined SAT I scores of 1250) are invited to join the program prior to arriving at Salisbury. Current undergraduates with a University GPA of 3.25 or better are also invited to apply for admission.

Campus Overview

State-supported comprehensive, founded 1925, part of University System of Maryland • **Coed** 6,366 undergraduate students, 89% full-time, 56% women, 44% men.

Undergraduates 5,648 full-time, 718 part-time. Students come from 30 states and territories, 23 other countries, 14% are from out of state, 8% African American, 3% Asian American or Pacific Islander, 2% Hispanic American, 0.3% Native American, 0.8% international, 11% transferred in, 46% live on campus.

Faculty *Total:* 494, 64% full-time, 54% with terminal degrees. *Student/faculty ratio:* 16:1.

Academic Programs *Special study options:* academic remediation for entering students, adult/continuing education programs, advanced placement credit, double majors, English as a second language, honors programs, independent study, internships, off-campus study, part-time degree program, services for LD students, student-designed majors, study abroad, summer session for credit. *ROTC:* Army (c). *Unusual degree programs:* 3-2 engineering with University of Maryland College Park, Old Dominion University, Widener University; social work with University of Maryland Eastern Shore; environmental marine science with University of Maryland Eastern Shore.

Athletics Member NCAA, NAIA. All NCAA Division III. *Intercollegiate sports:* baseball M, basketball M/W, cross-country running M/W, field hockey W, football M, lacrosse M/W, soccer M/W, softball W, swimming and diving M/W, tennis M/W, track and field M/W, volleyball W. *Intramural sports:* basketball M/W, cross-country running M/W, fencing M(c)/W(c), field hockey W(c), football M/W, golf M(c)/W(c), ice hockey M(c), lacrosse M(c)/W, racquetball M/W, rugby M(c)/W(c), sailing M(c)/W(c), soccer M(c)/W(c), softball W, swimming and diving M/W, tennis M/W, track and field M/W, volleyball W, water polo M/W.

Costs (2004–05) *Tuition:* state resident $4546 full-time, $188 per credit hour part-time; nonresident $12,124 full-time, $487 per credit hour part-time. *Required fees:* $1430 full-time, $8 per credit hour part-time. *Room and board:* $7050; room only: $3450. Room and board charges vary according to board plan and housing facility.

Financial Aid 81 Federal Work-Study jobs (averaging $1887). In 2003, 332 non-need-based awards were made. *Average percent of need met:* 58%. *Average financial aid package:* $5839. *Average need-based loan:* $3587. *Average need-based gift aid:* $5418. *Average non-need-based aid:* $8128.

Contact: Director: Dr. Tony Whall, Bellavance Honors Center, Salisbury University, Salisbury, Maryland 21802; *Telephone:* 410-546-6902; *Fax:* 410-677-5019; *E-mail:* rawhall@salisbury.edu; Assistant Director: Dr. Richard England; *Telephone:* 410-546-6943; *E-mail:* rengland@salisbury.edu; *Web site:* http://www.salisbury.edu/schools/honors/

Towson University
Honors Programs
Towson, Maryland

Honors programs at Towson University include the Honors College and the Departmental Honors Program.

The Honors College at Towson University is a community of scholars interested in intellectual interaction, academic achievement, and leadership opportunities. Students may major in any field at Towson and be part of the Honors College. Established in 1969, the Honors College includes more than 800 students who take exclusive honors classes, live in honors residence halls, conduct research with faculty members, and participate in special honors study-abroad programs. Honors College classes are small (usually enrolling 18 or fewer students) to facilitate discussion and collaborative learning.

Honors College courses are offered in a variety of disciplines and the majority of them satisfy the University's general education requirements. Honors seminar courses on various topics are offered as well. In addition, leadership courses in Community Service and Community Building provide an opportunity for honors students to integrate service-learning into their class schedules.

Getting involved and connecting with the campus are also part of the Honors College experience. Honors students are invited to join Excelsior, the Honors Student Association, which organizes activities such as barbecues, trips to Baltimore theaters, and volunteer opportunities with groups like Habitat for Humanity. The Honors College also offers guidance and support to students applying for fellowships and grants for advanced academic work, such as the Fulbright or Marshall Scholar awards.

The Honors College is headquartered on the fifth floor of Cook Library. The Honors College Lounge is a convenient place to study or relax, with computers available for e-mail, research, and word processing. Another center of Honors College activities is the Lieberman Room in the Lecture Hall, which houses an extraordinary collection of contemporary paintings, drawings, and sculptures. The Richmond Hall Commons Room is a fully equipped, high-tech classroom used for a number of honors courses. It also serves as a meeting place for special Honors College functions and as a study lounge for honors students.

The Departmental Honors Program is distinct from the Honors College. It represents intensive, individualized, and directed education beyond the normal course of instruction. The program includes 6 to 9 credits in seminars, directed readings, and research projects in the major. A senior thesis is required, as is an oral defense of the thesis.

To be admitted to the program, students must present a cumulative GPA of at least 3.25 and a minimum GPA of 3.5 in their major, or have the consent of their faculty adviser. Students who complete an approved program receive a diploma and transcript with the designation Bachelor of Science or Bachelor of Arts with honors. Currently, the departments of art; biological sciences; computer and information sciences; economics; electronic media and film; English; history; mass communication and communication studies; mathematics; modern languages; kinesiology; physics, astronomy, and geosciences; political science; psychology; and sociology, anthropology, and criminal justice offer Departmental Honors Programs.

Students interested in Departmental Honors should meet with their faculty adviser and the chairperson or honors coordinator of their major department to discuss their plans at the beginning of their sophomore year.

Participation Requirements: There will be new requirements for students entering in fall 2006. Students should contact the Honors College for current details.

To be eligible for Departmental Honors, students must have a minimum GPA of 3.25 and a GPA of at least 3.5 in those courses. To graduate with departmental honors, the student must complete and successfully defend a research thesis or a creative project (depending on the major) and maintain at least a 3.25 overall average and a minimum 3.5 average in required courses in the major.

Admission Process: New students apply to the Honors College when they apply to the University. The Honors College requests a separate essay and additional information beyond the regular application, so students interested in the Honors College must be sure to complete the optional Honors College portion of the application. Current Towson students may apply to the Honors College if they have completed 2 semesters with a 3.5 minimum GPA. The Honors College application deadline is in early February (check the current application for the exact date). Students are strongly encouraged to apply by December 1 to qualify for merit scholarships in addition to the Honors College Scholarship. Admission to the Honors College is very competitive. Students admitted for fall 2005 had an average SAT I of 1260 and an average GPA of 3.9 on a 4.0 scale. The middle 50 percent of accepted students had an SAT I range of 1200 to 1310 and GPA range of 3.8 to 4.0. Students below one or both of these ranges are admitted if their application demonstrates strong writing skills and outstanding leadership, artistic, and creative achievements.

Scholarship Availability: All students admitted to the Honors College as a first year student receive an Honors College Scholarship of between $1000 and $3000 annually. Honors College Scholarships are renewable for four years as long as the student remains in good standing in the Honors College. In addition, Towson University offers a variety of other merit scholarships that can be combined with the Honors College scholarship. These other scholarships do not require a separate application, but student's must apply to Towson University by December 1 to guarantee best consideration for these awards. Need-based financial aid is also available from Towson University.

Campus Overview

State-supported university, founded 1866, part of University System of Maryland • **Coed** 14,311 undergraduate students, 87% full-time, 61% women, 39% men.

Undergraduates 12,405 full-time, 1,906 part-time. Students come from 45 states and territories, 106 other countries, 19% are from out of state, 10% African American, 3% Asian American or Pacific Islander, 2% Hispanic American, 0.2% Native American, 2% international, 10% transferred in, 24% live on campus.

Faculty *Total:* 1,259, 50% full-time, 52% with terminal degrees. *Student/faculty ratio:* 18:1.

Academic Programs *Special study options:* academic remediation for entering students, accelerated degree program, adult/continuing education programs, advanced placement credit, cooperative education, distance learning, double majors, English as a second language, freshman honors college, honors programs, independent study, internships, off-campus study, part-time degree program, services for LD students, student-designed majors, study abroad, summer session for credit. *ROTC:* Army (c), Air Force (c). *Unusual degree programs:* 3-2 engineering with University of Maryland College Park; law with University of Baltimore.

Athletics Member NCAA. All Division I. *Intercollegiate sports:* baseball M(s), basketball M(s)/W(s), cheerleading M/W, cross-country running M(s)/W(s), field hockey W(s), football M(s), golf M(s), gymnastics W(s), lacrosse M(s)/W(s), soccer M(s)/W(s), softball W(s), swimming and diving M(s)/W(s), tennis M(s)/W(s), track and field M(s)/W(s), volleyball M/W(s). *Intramural sports:* badminton M(c)/W(c), basketball M/W, bowling M(c)/W(c), crew M(c)/W(c), equestrian sports M(c)/W(c), fencing M(c)/W(c), football M/W, golf M(c)/W(c), ice hockey M, lacrosse M/W, racquetball M(c)/W(c), rugby M, sailing M(c)/W(c), soccer M/W, softball M/W, table tennis M/W, tennis M/W, ultimate Frisbee M(c)/W(c), volleyball M/W, wrestling M.

Costs (2004–05) *Tuition:* state resident $4890 full-time, $212 per credit part-time; nonresident $13,570 full-time, $508 per credit part-time. Full-time tuition and fees vary according to course load. *Required fees:* $1782 full-time, $69 per credit part-time. *Room and board:* $6468; room only: $3816. Room and board charges vary according to board plan and housing facility.

Financial Aid In 2004, 1475 non-need-based awards were made. *Average percent of need met: 66%. Average financial aid package:* $7508. *Average need-based loan: $3938. Average need-based gift aid:* $4895. *Average non-need-based aid: $4353.*

Contact: Jeffrey A. Michael, Associate Dean, Honors College, Towson University, 8000 York Road, Towson, Maryland 21252-0001; *Telephone:* 410-704-4865; *Fax:* 410-704-4916; *E-mail:* jmichael@towson.edu; *Web site:* http://www.towson.edu/honors

University of Baltimore
Helen P. Denit Honors Program
Baltimore, Maryland

The University of Baltimore's Helen P. Denit Honors Program was developed in 1978 with a unique mandate to serve the last two years of undergraduate education to a broad mix of students majoring in business and the liberal arts.

Known as the "career-minded university," the University of Baltimore (UB) provides professionally oriented students an opportunity to continue their education with an array of flexible programs and schedules.

UB's Honors Program emphasizes the notion that "career" involves the lifelong pursuit of learning, excellence, and intellectual satisfaction. The academic curriculum, taught by faculty members from all areas of the University, is designed to engage, challenge, and enrich students' professional study by offering innovative honors classes and interdisciplinary seminars. Students are encouraged to become involved in independent study and research opportunities with faculty members who share their same interests. There are also opportunities for students to present their ideas at local, regional, and national conferences and to travel and study abroad.

Because of the University's downtown location, the Honors Program is able to take advantage of the cosmopolitan nature of Baltimore by offering an array of enrichment opportunities at no cost to students. These opportunities include enjoying opera next door at the Lyric Theatre, listening to the Baltimore Symphony Orchestra at the nearby Meyerhoff Symphony Hall, and viewing exciting theater at Center Stage. Because of its location close to Annapolis and Washington, D.C., there are numerous museums and other attractions of historical and cultural interest within a short driving distance.

The Honors Program has a lounge in the Merrick School of Business on the fourth floor, room 425. There, students find an excellent place for hanging out, with comfortable chairs, computers, printers, snacks, a refrigerator, and a microwave. Students should visit http://www.ubalt.edu/honors to learn more about the Honors Program and staff members.

Participation Requirements: Students are expected to achieve and maintain at least a 3.5 GPA to be eligible for participation in the Helen P. Denit Honors Program. Students are expected to take a minimum of four honors courses (12 credit hours), one of which should be a capstone project. These capstone projects are archived at the Langsdale Library and may be displayed, with permission of the student, on the Honors Program's Web site.

Students in good standing are eligible to participate in the cultural and social activities that the Honors Program has to offer. Limited funds are available to carry out research toward the completion of the capstone project, field trips, and attendance at conferences.

Successful completion of the program is noted on the diploma as graduating cum laude, magna cum laude, or summa cum laude and on the transcript as graduating from the University of Baltimore's Helen P. Denit Honors Program.

Admission Process: Students transferring to UB with a GPA of 3.5 or higher are invited to participate in the Honors Program. Students who complete their A.A. degree with honors at a community college with which UB has an articulation agreement are automatically admitted into the Honors Program. Current undergraduate students in both the Yale Gordon College of Liberal Arts and the Merrick School of Business whose GPA is 3.5 or above or who have been nominated by a professor are encouraged to participate.

Given the complexity and diversity of the student body and the large number of older students returning to school, students not meeting the GPA requirement may petition for provisional acceptance into the Honors Program. Decisions are made on a case-by-case basis.

UB has a rolling admissions policy, and applications are accepted until the last day of registration each semester, space permitting. However, the earlier an application and credentials are received, the earlier an admission decision can be made. It is recommended that students file an application by July 1 for the fall semester, November 1 for the spring semester, and April 1 for the summer session. A nonrefundable $35 paper application fee is required at the time of application. The online application is $20 and is available at http://www.ubalt.edu/admissions, or students may request an application by calling or writing to Admissions Office, University of Baltimore, 1420 North Charles Street, Baltimore, Maryland 21201-5779; Telephone: 410-837-4777 or 877-ApplyUB (toll-free).

Scholarship Availability: Although the Honors Program does not offer scholarships, UB funds a number of merit scholarships for outstanding transfer students. For example, the Wilson Scholarship offers Maryland residents 100 percent of in-state tuition; for nonresidents, it offers 100 percent of in-state tuition plus an additional award of $1500 per year. To qualify for this scholarship, the student must have an entering cross-institutional GPA of at least 3.5, be enrolled full-time, be nominated by a community college, qualify for the Maryland State Distinguished Scholarship, or have an application to UB.

The Dean's Scholarship covers 50 percent of in-state tuition for Maryland residents; for nonresidents, it covers 50 percent of in-state tuition plus an additional award of $1500 per year. To qualify for this scholarship, the student must have an entering cross-institutional GPA of at least 3.25 and be enrolled full-time.

The Phi Theta Kappa Scholarship is available for Phi Theta Kappa members designated by community colleges. The scholarship covers 75 percent of in-state tuition for Maryland residents; for nonresidents, it covers 75 percent of in-state tuition plus an additional award of $1500 per year. To qualify for this scholarship, the student must have an entering GPA of at least 3.5 and be enrolled full-time.

Part-Time Scholars Program Scholarships covers 50 percent of in-state tuition (6 to 11 credits per semester) for Maryland residents; for nonresidents, it covers 50 percent of in-state tuition (6 to 11 credits per semester), plus an additional award of $750 per year. To qualify for this scholarship, the student must have an entering GPA of at least 3.5.

Campus Overview

State-supported upper-level, founded 1925, part of University

System of Maryland • **Coed** 2,117 undergraduate students, 50% full-time, 60% women, 40% men.

Undergraduates 1,051 full-time, 1,066 part-time. Students come from 26 states and territories, 62 other countries, 7% are from out of state, 33% African American, 3% Asian American or Pacific Islander, 2% Hispanic American, 0.8% Native American, 0.6% international, 98% transferred in.

Faculty *Total:* 331, 48% full-time, 70% with terminal degrees. *Student/faculty ratio:* 15:1.

Academic Programs *Special study options:* academic remediation for entering students, accelerated degree program, adult/continuing education programs, advanced placement credit, cooperative education, distance learning, honors programs, independent study, internships, off-campus study, part-time degree program, services for LD students, student-designed majors, summer session for credit. *ROTC:* Army (c), Air Force (c). *Unusual degree programs:* 3-2 law.

Athletics *Intramural sports:* basketball M/W, golf M/W, racquetball M/W, soccer M, table tennis M/W, volleyball M/W, weight lifting M/W.

Costs (2005–06) *Tuition:* $243 per credit part-time; state resident $5324 full-time, $243 per credit part-time; nonresident $16,904 full-time, $704 per credit part-time. Full-time tuition and fees vary according to class time, course load, and degree level. Part-time tuition and fees vary according to class time, course load, and degree level. *Required fees:* $1469 full-time, $27 per credit part-time.

Financial Aid *Average financial aid package:* $11,210.

Contact: Ronald Legon, Ph.D., Director of the Helen P. Denit Honors Program, Professor of Classics, 1420 North Charles Street, Baltimore, Maryland 21201-5779; *Telephone:* 410-837-6583; *Fax:* 410-837-5722; *E-mail:* emateronarum@ubalt.edu

University of Maryland, Baltimore County

Honors College

Baltimore, Maryland

The Honors College at the University of Maryland, Baltimore County (UMBC), is a community where honors students quickly discover how learning is a lifelong pursuit that spills into every area of their lives. Members have the opportunity to obtain a rich liberal arts experience through honors classes, interactions with scholars, internships, international programs, and cocurricular activities.

Membership in the Honors College is intentionally kept small to enhance the quality of the educational experience. Limited to an enrollment of 500, the College seeks to matriculate 125 new freshmen each fall. Honors students declare majors in virtually all the disciplines at UMBC, from engineering, visual arts, and biochemistry to dance, physics, and English. Many also choose to take a double major or minor program.

One of the hallmarks of the Honors College is specialized attention. Each semester, students receive individual, formal advising from Honors College faculty and staff members, who are also available for one-on-one academic or personal consultation throughout the year. First-year honors students also meet with a peer adviser, a specially trained upper-level honors student.

The Honors College encourages its students to participate in international educational experiences such as study abroad. Students may also participate in the annual Honors College Study-Travel Program; recent trips have included visits to Italy, France, Ireland, Greece, and Turkey.

Honors College students explore the cultural resources on the UMBC campus, in the Baltimore-Washington area, and beyond.

Students may attend a musical theater production in New York; the opera, symphony, or ballet in Baltimore or Washington; or a Shakespearean drama in Washington. Students may visit museums, parks, festivals, and historical sites worldwide.

The Honors College works closely with the Shriver Center at UMBC to place students in credit-bearing community service or applied learning experiences. Honors College students work on an array of projects, from volunteering with a Chesapeake Bay cleanup program to tutoring disadvantaged youth or enrolling in internships with the Maryland governor's office.

Honors College students have the option to live in the Honors College living-learning community in one of the UMBC residence halls. The community allows students to continue their collaborative learning experiences in a unique residential setting with like-minded, academically motivated peers. These students share an important venue in which they can make lifelong friends through common classes, conversations, and fun activities.

The Honors College at UMBC seeks to develop the talented and curious student's faculties of analysis and exposition through an enhanced liberal arts experience, to foster a sense of membership in an intellectual community, and to instill learning as a way of life. The College provides the atmosphere of a small community of learning and energetically sponsors a variety of programs and activities that often intentionally blur the distinction between the curricular and the extracurricular. The motto of the College is "Learning for living."

Participation Requirements: Honors students follow a curriculum designed to augment the UMBC general requirements and to enrich their liberal arts experience. Honors students are required to take a minimum of one honors course each semester. They choose from more than fifty classes and seminars, which generally enroll between 10 and 25 students. Upon completion of the honors curriculum and the University graduation requirements, students receive a Certificate of General Honors, which is noted on their transcripts.

Admission Process: Admission to the Honors College is highly selective. In reviewing applications, the College places a special emphasis on the written material submitted. The strength of the high school curriculum, grade point average, and standardized test scores are also very important. Critical criteria for admission to the College are an abiding curiosity and a will and energy during the university years to learn how to satisfy that curiosity. Generally, a minimum combined SAT I score of 1350 and a minimum cumulative high school GPA of 3.5 are expected for consideration for admission as a freshman to the Honors College. In fall 2004, the profile of the Honors College freshmen consisted of an average SAT I score of 1440 and high school GPA of 4.0.

Transfer students or current UMBC students are expected to have established a minimum cumulative college GPA of 3.25 to be considered for membership. Members maintain their eligibility by taking at least one honors course per academic semester and maintaining at least a 3.25 cumulative GPA.

Fall semester application deadlines for freshmen are January 15 for Honors College scholarship consideration; March 15 is the final deadline. Application deadlines for transfer and current UMBC students are May 31 for the fall semester and December 1 for the spring semester.

Scholarship Availability: The Honors College offers scholarships for both the regular academic year and special sessions. All prospective freshmen who submit applications by January 15 are considered for academic-year scholarships that are highly competitive. Approximately 15 percent of the freshmen entering the College receive such scholarships, which range from $1000 per year to full tuition, room, and board. Each year, all members of the College are invited to apply for summer- and winter-session scholarships; proposals involving independent research and/or study abroad are particularly encouraged for these awards.

Campus Overview

State-supported university, founded 1963, part of University System of Maryland • **Coed** 9,668 undergraduate students, 84% full-time, 47% women, 53% men.

Undergraduates 8,162 full-time, 1,506 part-time. Students come from 43 states and territories, 91 other countries, 9% are from out of state, 15% African American, 20% Asian American or Pacific Islander, 3% Hispanic American, 0.4% Native American, 4% international, 11% transferred in, 33% live on campus.

Faculty *Total:* 731, 62% full-time, 68% with terminal degrees. *Student/faculty ratio:* 19:1.

Academic Programs *Special study options:* academic remediation for entering students, adult/continuing education programs, advanced placement credit, cooperative education, distance learning, double majors, English as a second language, external degree program, freshman honors college, honors programs, independent study, internships, off-campus study, part-time degree program, services for LD students, student-designed majors, study abroad, summer session for credit. *ROTC:* Army (c).

Athletics Member NCAA. All Division I. *Intercollegiate sports:* baseball M(s), basketball M(s)/W(s), bowling M(c)/W(c), crew M(c)/W(c), cross-country running M(s)/W(s), fencing M(c)/W(c), field hockey W(s), ice hockey M(c), lacrosse M(s)/W(s), rugby M(c)/W(c), sailing M(c)/W(c), skiing (downhill) M(c)/W(c), soccer M(s)/W(s), softball W(s), swimming and diving M(s)/W(s), tennis M(s)/W(s), track and field M(s)/W(s), ultimate Frisbee M(c)/W(c), volleyball M(c)/W(s), wrestling M(c). *Intramural sports:* badminton M/W, basketball M/W, cross-country running M/W, football M/W, lacrosse M(c)/W(c), soccer M(c)/W(c), softball M/W, swimming and diving M/W, tennis M/W, track and field M/W, volleyball M/W(c).

Costs (2004–05) *Tuition:* state resident $6120 full-time, $255 per credit hour part-time; nonresident $13,720 full-time, $571 per credit hour part-time. *Required fees:* $1900 full-time, $80 per credit hour part-time. *Room and board:* $7620; room only: $4650. Room and board charges vary according to board plan and housing facility.

Financial Aid In 2004, 1369 non-need-based awards were made. *Average percent of need met:* 60%. *Average financial aid package:* $7090. *Average need-based loan:* $4564. *Average need-based gift aid:* $4294. *Average non-need-based aid:* $6445.

Contact: The Honors College, University of Maryland, Baltimore County, 1000 Hilltop Circle, Baltimore, Maryland 21250; *Telephone:* 410-455-3720; *Fax:* 410-455-1063; *E-mail:* honors@umbc.edu; *Web site:* http://www.umbc.edu/honors

University of Maryland, College Park
University Honors Program
College Park, Maryland

The University Honors Program (http://www.honors.umd.edu) is the University of Maryland's distinguished and prestigious program *offering special educational and enrichment programming and opportunities to students with exceptional academic talents. Its distinctive reputation for academic excellence and experiences attracts intellectually gifted students and offers them an outstanding living and learning environment.*

Honors students combine Honors (HONR) Seminars and honors versions of departmental courses with studies in their major and electives. Honors Seminars, sponsored by the University Honors Program, offer small classes (no more than 20 students) taught by outstanding faculty members and characterized by exciting topics (often interdisciplinary), active participation and discussion, critical thinking, intensive writing, and creativity. Most Honors Seminars fulfill CORE (general education; distribution) requirements. Students

may earn an Honors Citation by taking 15 credits of honors courses (at least nine of which must be HONR courses) and a 1-credit colloquium, along with maintaining a minimum overall 3.2 GPA. Most students earn their Honors Citation by the end of five semesters, although there is no time limit, and completion of the Citation is optional. Continued activity in the program, even post-Citation, is welcomed. Research, scholarship, internship, study abroad, service, and other experiential opportunities are encouraged.

University Honors is a living/learning program seeking to create a smaller, friendly, supportive academic community nested within the extensive resources and opportunities of the broader campus. Honors residence halls, classrooms, and offices are located in Anne Arundel Hall, Denton Hall, Easton Hall (Honors Humanities), Ellicott Hall (Gemstone), and Queen Anne's Hall. Many honors upperclass students enjoy apartment-style housing in South Campus Commons.

High school students apply to the University through a single application process. Students with exceptionally strong academic records are thoroughly reviewed, and outstanding candidates are invited into the University Honors Program (target number of first-year students is typically 700 per year). Transfer students with between 12 and 30 credits (excluding AP or IB credits) and excellent academic records may also apply for admission to Honors. As of fall 2005, there were 3005 University Honors students enrolled at UMCP.

The Gemstone (http://www.gemstone.umd.edu) and Honors Humanities (http://www.honorshumanities.umd.edu) programs are smaller, more structured programs within University Honors (although administered independently). All Gemstone and Honors Humanities students are admitted to University Honors and, in addition, are invited to participate in one of those more focused programs. Gemstone (a four-year program involving approximately 180 first-year students doing team research) and Honors Humanities (a two-year program with approximately 50 students entering each year) have all of the rights, privileges, and resources available to University Honors students, including access to Honors courses, residence halls, facilities, programming and events, advising, academic support, scholarships, grants, and awards.

Participation Requirements: An incoming class of approximately 700 students with exceptional academic talents enters Honors each year by invitation after applying to the University through the standard admissions process. Students may earn an Honors Citation by taking five honors courses plus a 1-credit colloquium; most students complete their Citation after four or five semesters, but they are welcome to remain active in Honors until they graduate. The average combined SAT score of admitted students is 1410; the average GPA (weighted) is 4.25.

Scholarship Availability: Merit scholarships, some of which offer four-year support, are available for some incoming students. There are some smaller honors scholarships for upperclass students.

Campus Overview

State-supported university, founded 1856, part of University System of Maryland • **Coed** 25,379 undergraduate students, 91% full-time, 49% women, 51% men.

Undergraduates 22,979 full-time, 2,400 part-time. Students come from 54 states and territories, 159 other countries, 24% are from out of state, 12% African American, 14% Asian American or Pacific Islander, 6% Hispanic American, 0.3% Native American, 2% international, 8% transferred in, 39% live on campus.

Faculty *Total:* 2,097, 75% full-time, 85% with terminal degrees. *Student/faculty ratio:* 18:1.

Academic Programs *Special study options:* academic remediation for entering students, accelerated degree program, adult/continuing education programs, advanced placement credit, cooperative education, distance learning, double majors, English as a second language, external degree program, honors programs, independent study, internships, off-campus study, part-time degree program, services for LD students, student-designed majors, study abroad, summer session for credit. *ROTC:* Army (b), Navy (c), Air Force (b).

Athletics Member NCAA. All Division I except football (Division I-A). *Intercollegiate sports:* baseball M(s), basketball M(s)/W(s), cheerleading W(s), cross-country running M(s)/W(s), field hockey W(s), golf M(s)/W(s), gymnastics W(s), lacrosse M(s)/W(s), soccer M(s)/W(s), softball W(s), swimming and diving M(s)/W(s), tennis M(s)/W(s), track and field M(s)/W(s), volleyball W(s), water polo W(s), wrestling M(s). *Intramural sports:* badminton M(c)/W(c), baseball M(c), basketball M/W, bowling M(c)/W(c), crew M(c)/W(c), cross-country running M/W, equestrian sports M(c)/W(c), fencing M(c)/W(c), field hockey W(c), football M/W, golf M/W, ice hockey M(c)/W(c), lacrosse M(c)/W(c), racquetball M(c)/W(c), rugby M(c)/W(c), sailing M(c)/W(c), soccer M(c)/W(c), softball W, swimming and diving M(c)/W(c), table tennis M/W, tennis M/W, track and field M/W, ultimate Frisbee M/W, volleyball M(c)/W, water polo M(c)/W(c), weight lifting M/W, wrestling M.

Costs (2004–05) *Tuition:* state resident $6200 full-time, $258 per credit hour part-time; nonresident $17,500 full-time, $729 per credit hour part-time. Part-time tuition and fees vary according to course load. *Required fees:* $1210 full-time, $276 per term part-time. *Room and board:* $7931; room only: $4796. Room and board charges vary according to board plan.

Financial Aid 801 Federal Work-Study jobs (averaging $1436). In 2003, 3363 non-need-based awards were made. *Average percent of need met:* 68%. *Average financial aid package:* $12,132. *Average need-based loan:* $3845. *Average need-based gift aid:* $4722. *Average non-need-based aid:* $5889.

Contact: University Honors Program, Anne Arundel Hall, University of Maryland, College Park, Maryland 20742; *Telephone:* 301-405-6771; *Fax:* 301-405-6723; *E-mail:* dhebert@umd.edu; *Web site:* http://www.honors.umd.edu

MASSACHUSETTS

Bridgewater State College
Honors Program
Bridgewater, Massachusetts

The Honors Program at Bridgewater encourages gifted and highly motivated students to reach their highest potential through critical thinking and research. Small classes and close student-faculty relations provide for the vigorous and thorough exchange of ideas, while the program as a whole attempts to create an atmosphere fostering intellectual, artistic, and academic achievement.

Students earn honors credits by taking specially designed honors sections of regular courses and/or unique honors colloquia during their first two years, and by completing honors research projects and the student-generated thesis in the junior and senior years. Honors sections are capped at fifteen students, and all honors research projects, including the thesis, are mentored by faculty members individually.

Students in the program have access throughout the year to the Honors Center on the first floor of Maxwell Library, in the Academic Achievement Center. Designed for study, online research and relaxation, the center has student art, computers, printers, refrigerator, coffee maker and comfortable furniture, and receives The New York Times *daily. The Center is open 9 a.m. to 5 p.m. Monday through Friday throughout the academic year, and has slightly reduced hours during the summer and during breaks.*

Each term the program hosts the Honors Dinner, featuring presentations by Honors Outstanding Faculty Award recipients. Each year the program holds pre-thesis workshops, an Honors Book Club, and other social events. In addition, many Honors students every year publish their research in The Undergraduate Review, *a journal of undergraduate research, and give presentations at the National*

Conference on Undergraduate Research, the American Chemical Society annual meeting, and other academic conferences.

The honors experience at Bridgewater may be approached either through Commonwealth Honors, encompassing all four years of study, or Departmental Honors, encompassing only the last two years of study. Students transferring in as juniors or seniors should consider Departmental Honors. Current enrollment for both programs is 300. The Honors Program has been approved by the Commonwealth Honors Council of the state of Massachusetts, which means that it meets rigorous criteria and has articulation agreements with honors programs at other approved Massachusetts state universities, state colleges and community colleges.

Participation Requirements: Each semester, the program offers a wide range of 3-credit honors classes and 1-credit honors colloquia. During their freshman and sophomore years, students in Commonwealth Honors are free to chose whatever they please from these offerings provided they accumulate at least 12 honors credits by the end of their sophomore year. The 3-credit honors courses usually satisfy general education requirements; the colloquia, which tend to be more specialized, do not. Students must maintain a minimum 3.3 GPA.

As juniors, All-College Honors students may either enter a departmental honors program or, in consultation with the Honors Director, develop an individualized interdisciplinary honors program. During the junior year, students must complete two upper-division courses on an honors-credit basis by engaging in special advanced work under the instructor's direction. During the senior year, students research and write their honors theses under individual faculty member's supervision. Whether the thesis qualifies the student to graduate with honors is determined by either the relevant departmental honors committee or the student's interdisciplinary honors committee. A minimum of 21 credits is required for Commonwealth Honors: 12 in Honors sections and/or colloquia, and 9 in Honors research projects including the thesis.

Emphasizing independent study and research in the major, Departmental Honors programs are currently offered in accounting and finance; anthropology; art; biology; chemistry; communication studies and theater arts; English; foreign languages; history; management; mathematics and computer science; movement arts, health promotion, and leisure studies; philosophy; physics; political science; psychology; and sociology and criminal justice. Although GPA requirements vary, most departments require either an overall GPA of at least 3.0 or a minimum 3.3 in the major. Admission to Departmental Honors programs does not require completion of honors courses or honors colloquia at the freshman and sophomore levels.

A minimum of 6 credits of honors course work is required for Departmental Honors as well as a thesis or research project for an additional 3 credits.

All honors work is recorded on students' transcripts, and at commencement distinctive sashes are worn by students graduating with Commonwealth or Departmental Honors.

Admission Process: Incoming freshmen who have SAT I scores of at least 580V and 530M and who graduated in the top 30 percent of their high school class are invited to enter the program as are matriculated students with GPAs of 3.3 or better. In special cases, students who do not meet these criteria are also admitted. Admission is rolling.

Scholarship Availability: Each year the College awards five renewable merit scholarships, covering tuition and fees, to entering freshmen, and these scholarships are linked to ongoing participation in the Honors Program.

Campus Overview

State-supported comprehensive, founded 1840, part of Massachusetts Public Higher Education System • **Coed** 7,597 undergraduate students, 82% full-time, 61% women, 39% men.

Undergraduates 6,247 full-time, 1,350 part-time. Students come from 32 states and territories, 28 other countries, 3% are from out of

state, 5% African American, 1% Asian American or Pacific Islander, 2% Hispanic American, 0.3% Native American, 2% international, 9% transferred in, 31% live on campus.

Faculty *Total:* 494, 53% full-time, 51% with terminal degrees. *Student/faculty ratio:* 20:1.

Academic Programs *Special study options:* academic remediation for entering students, accelerated degree program, adult/continuing education programs, advanced placement credit, distance learning, double majors, English as a second language, honors programs, independent study, internships, off-campus study, part-time degree program, services for LD students, study abroad, summer session for credit. *ROTC:* Army (c), Air Force (c).

Athletics Member NCAA. All Division III. *Intercollegiate sports:* baseball M, basketball M/W, cross-country running M/W, field hockey W, football M, lacrosse M(c)/W, soccer M/W, softball W, swimming and diving M/W, tennis M/W, track and field M/W, volleyball W, water polo M(c)/W(c), wrestling M. *Intramural sports:* basketball M/W, football M/W, soccer M/W, softball M/W, tennis M/W, volleyball M/W.

Costs (2004–05) *Tuition:* state resident $910 full-time, $38 per credit hour part-time; nonresident $7050 full-time, $294 per credit hour part-time. *Required fees:* $4386 full-time, $181 per credit hour part-time. *Room and board:* $6512; room only: $4048. Room and board charges vary according to board plan and housing facility.

Financial Aid 517 Federal Work-Study jobs (averaging $1250). In 2003, 658 non-need-based awards were made. *Average percent of need met:* 72%. *Average financial aid package:* $7777. *Average need-based loan:* $3438. *Average need-based gift aid:* $3336. *Average non-need-based aid:* $5453.

Contact: Director: Dr. Charles C. Nickerson, Honors Center, Harrington Hall, Bridgewater, Massachusetts 02325; *Telephone:* 508-697-1378; *Fax:* 508-697-1336; *E-mail:* cnickerson@bridgew.edu

Emerson College
Honors Program
Boston, Massachusetts

The Emerson College Honors Program is a community of undergraduate scholars who pursue interdisciplinary study in the liberal arts and in the fields of communication and the performing arts. The four-year Honors Program is available to 50 entering students a year and a small number of transfers with outstanding academic ability. All students in the program receive a Trustee Scholarship. Honors Program students enjoy early registration privileges. Honors Program faculty members excel in teaching and are active researchers, artists, and professionals across the disciplines.

Three first-year honors courses fulfill general education requirements and are team-taught in small discussion-based classes comprising 17 students and 2 professors. The First-Year Honors Seminars and Writing Symposia introduce Emerson students to the interdisciplinary study of literature of the Americas, with an emphasis on writing and research skills. The seminars address the relationship between language, power, and social action in various multicultural contexts and from various theoretical perspectives. The Sophomore Honors Seminar acquaints students with the methods of scientific reasoning and the philosophy of science and addresses issues of ethics and values in an interdisciplinary manner.

The Junior Seminar consists of an upper-division course in interdisciplinary studies. The Junior Honors Colloquia encourages students to work closely with a professor in their field in preparation for the senior thesis/project. The Honors Program Director and each student's faculty adviser work with seniors in the completion of their year-long concentrated research or creative project. Seniors meet in colloquia where they critique each other's work. Just before

graduation, they present their completed work in a Senior Thesis/Project Showcase before the entire community. Each year, one student is granted the Outstanding Honors Thesis/Project Award.

Participation Requirements: Honors work includes the year-long first-year and sophomore seminars, a one-semester junior seminar, and a senior thesis/project. Students fulfill six general education requirements upon the completion of four semesters of interdisciplinary work. To graduate from the Honors Program, students must have at least a 3.3 GPA overall, at least a 3.0 GPA in honors seminars, and must complete the senior thesis/project. Successful completion of the Honors Program requirements is noted at graduation and is recorded on the student's transcript.

Admission Process: High school seniors who maintain outstanding academic records and achievement in school and/or community affairs and seek an additional intellectual challenge at the college level may be invited to participate in the Emerson College Honors Program. To be considered, applicants must complete the regular application procedures listed for first-year students by February 1, including the honors essay. Transfer students may enter the program no later than the first term of their sophomore year.

Campus Overview

Independent comprehensive, founded 1880 • **Coed** 3,418 undergraduate students, 88% full-time, 59% women, 41% men.

Undergraduates 3,020 full-time, 398 part-time. Students come from 47 states and territories, 43 other countries, 63% are from out of state, 2% African American, 4% Asian American or Pacific Islander, 5% Hispanic American, 0.4% Native American, 3% international, 7% transferred in, 45% live on campus.

Faculty *Total:* 340, 41% full-time, 54% with terminal degrees. *Student/faculty ratio:* 15:1.

Academic Programs *Special study options:* adult/continuing education programs, advanced placement credit, double majors, honors programs, independent study, internships, off-campus study, part-time degree program, services for LD students, student-designed majors, study abroad, summer session for credit.

Athletics Member NCAA. All Division III. *Intercollegiate sports:* baseball M(c), basketball M/W, cross-country running M/W, lacrosse M/W, soccer M/W, softball W, tennis M/W, volleyball W. *Intramural sports:* weight lifting M/W.

Costs (2005–06) *Tuition:* $718 per credit hour part-time.

Financial Aid 357 Federal Work-Study jobs (averaging $2000). 40 state and other part-time jobs (averaging $10,156). In 2002, 458 non-need-based awards were made. *Average percent of need met:* 80%. *Average financial aid package:* $11,820. *Average need-based loan:* $4208. *Average need-based gift aid:* $10,497. *Average non-need-based aid:* $12,958.

Contact: Director: Dr. Nigel C. Gibson, 120 Boylston Street, Boston, Massachusetts 02116; *Telephone:* 617-824-8769; *Fax:* 617-824-7857; *E-mail:* Nigel_Gibson@emerson.edu; *Web site:* http://www.emerson.edu/undergraduate_admission.cfm

Endicott College
Endicott College Honors Program
Beverly, Massachusetts

The Endicott College Honors Program provides the opportunity for the most highly motivated student to seek a deeper intellectual experience. The Program creates an environment in which students challenge themselves to pursue an advanced level of intellectual inquiry and independent thought.

In the intimate setting of the small seminar (honors seminars are capped at 20 students, but more usually run with from six to fifteen students) our most intellectually adventurous students read, write, question, discuss, ponder, claim, and critique. Past seminars have looked closely at Race in American Society and Culture, The Business of Books, Swedish Media and Culture (with a trip to Sweden), and Art and Identity in America. Our goal is to create an environment in which students thrive intellectually, learn to ask discerning questions, and think boldly across disciplinary boundaries. The Endicott Honors Program was founded in 1997, and currently numbers 102 students.

Participation Requirements: Honors students take two three-credit interdisciplinary seminars, one in each of their sophomore and junior years, then complete an honors Senior Thesis. Seminars count as core requirements and/or electives. Students must maintain a 3.5 GPA in order to remain in the Program.

Admission Process: Second semester freshmen with distinguished records of academic performance and leadership are invited to participate in two three-credit seminars to be undertaken in the second and third years, and to complete, in their final year, an Honors Senior Thesis, the substantial piece of independent research all Endicott Seniors undertake as the capstone to their Endicott experience. Many of our seniors are also members of our Triumph chapter of Mortar Board, the senior honor society.

Scholarship Availability: Each year, the Endicott College Honors Program awards up to 25 scholarships in the amount of $2,500 each, to be posted toward tuition, room, and board. Selection for the scholarship is based on academic performance, recommendations, leadership, service, and a topical essay determined each year.

Campus Overview

Independent comprehensive, founded 1939 • **Coed** 1,973 undergraduate students, 89% full-time, 59% women, 41% men.

Undergraduates 1,758 full-time, 215 part-time. Students come from 28 states and territories, 33 other countries, 50% are from out of state, 1% African American, 0.8% Asian American or Pacific Islander, 2% Hispanic American, 0.3% Native American, 5% international, 3% transferred in, 84% live on campus.

Faculty Total: 131, 48% full-time, 42% with terminal degrees. Student/faculty ratio: 15:1.

Academic Programs Special study options: academic remediation for entering students, accelerated degree program, adult/continuing education programs, advanced placement credit, distance learning, English as a second language, honors programs, independent study, internships, off-campus study, part-time degree program, student-designed majors, study abroad, summer session for credit. ROTC: Army (c).

Athletics Member NCAA. All Division III. Intercollegiate sports: baseball M, basketball M/W, cross-country running M/W, equestrian sports M/W, field hockey W, football M, golf M/W, lacrosse M/W, soccer M/W, softball W, tennis M/W, volleyball M/W. Intramural sports: basketball M/W, cheerleading M(c)/W(c), crew M(c)/W(c), football M/W, ice hockey M(c), racquetball M/W, sailing M(c)/W(c), soccer M/W, softball M/W, tennis M/W, ultimate Frisbee M/W, volleyball M/W.

Costs (2004–05) Comprehensive fee: $28,732 includes full-time tuition ($18,752), mandatory fees ($680), and room and board ($9300). Full-time tuition and fees vary according to program and student level. Part-time tuition: $576 per credit. Part-time tuition and fees vary according to program and student level. Required fees: $180 per term part-time. College room only: $6520. Room and board charges vary according to board plan and housing facility.

Financial Aid 338 Federal Work-Study jobs (averaging $1500). In 2004, 219 non-need-based awards were made. Average percent of need met: 59%. Average financial aid package: $12,120. Average need-based loan: $4071. Average need-based gift aid: $5363. Average non-need-based aid: $4827.

Contact: Eloise Knowlton, Ph.D., Director of the Endicott College Honors Program and Associate Dean of the College, Endicott College,

376 Hale Street, Beverly, Massachusetts 01915; Telephone: 978-232-2292; Fax: 978-232-2150; E-mail: eknowlto@endicott.edu

Framingham State College
Honors Program
Framingham, Massachusetts

The Framingham State College Honors Program is designed to provide academically talented students with the opportunity to enrich their college experience. Courses bearing the honors designation are designed to be intensive experiences that are intellectually challenging and emphasize creativity and analytical thinking.

Honors courses are designed for a maximum enrollment of 15 to 20 students to foster in-depth class discussion and a close student-instructor relationship. All honors courses may be applied to the general education requirements specified by the College. Honors courses may be taken by students who are not participating in the program on a space-available basis with the permission of the instructor.

Upon their arrival on campus, honors students receive a special orientation to the College and its Honors Program. Thereafter, these students convene regularly to share information, exchange ideas, and discuss topics of interest. Each honors student has a special Honors Program adviser who assists in course selection. Residents may choose to live in a special residence hall reserved for honors students. Because the program is available to majors from every department on campus, the Academic Vice-President, the Director of the Honors Program, the Honors Program Advisory Committee, and the department chairs make a special effort to develop and offer a wide variety of challenging courses.

Founded in 1990, the program currently enrolls approximately 95 students.

Participation Requirements: Freshmen entering the Framingham State College Honors Program must take the honors section of the freshman writing course. During the remaining three years, participants are required to complete a minimum of four more courses bearing the honors designation, including the honors senior seminar, completed as an independent study.

Course topics and information about honors courses to be offered can be found in the Schedule of Classes bulletin or through the program administrator's office. During their senior year, participating students must complete an honors thesis. As a condition of continued enrollment in the Honors Program, freshmen and sophomores must maintain a GPA of at least 3.0 overall and in honors courses. Students falling below these requirements are allowed to continue in the program for a probationary period of one semester. Subsequent continuance is at the discretion of the Honors Program Committee.

Honors students have priority in course registration, special advising, and a customized program of extracurricular enrichment activities. Participation in the Framingham State College Honors Program is noted on the students' transcripts. The notation of honors student is made on the transcript and the diploma, and students are recognized at graduation.

Admission Process: Entering freshmen are invited to participate in the Framingham State College Honors Program based on a weighted composite of their combined SAT scores, class rank, and demonstrated potential for superior work at the college level. Any student admitted to the College who was not initially invited to participate in the program may apply directly to the Honors Program Committee for admission. Students may also apply for admission to the Framingham State College Honors Program as sophomores. A minimum GPA of 3.25 together with two letters of recommendation from faculty members and a brief statement of intent should be submitted to the Honors Program Committee for evaluation before October 1 of the student's sophomore year.

Scholarship Availability: Scholarships are awarded annually to the top 10 honors students who have taken at least three honors courses and are in good standing. Scholarship recipients are recognized at the annual awards assembly of the College.

Campus Overview

State-supported comprehensive, founded 1839, part of Massachusetts Public Higher Education System • **Coed** 3,873 undergraduate students, 79% full-time, 67% women, 33% men.

Undergraduates 3,062 full-time, 811 part-time. Students come from 15 states and territories, 20 other countries, 8% are from out of state, 3% African American, 3% Asian American or Pacific Islander, 3% Hispanic American, 0.5% Native American, 2% international, 8% transferred in, 45% live on campus.

Faculty *Total:* 296, 54% full-time, 49% with terminal degrees. *Student/faculty ratio:* 16:1.

Academic Programs *Special study options:* adult/continuing education programs, advanced placement credit, distance learning, double majors, English as a second language, honors programs, independent study, internships, off-campus study, part-time degree program, study abroad, summer session for credit. *ROTC:* Army (b).

Athletics Member NCAA. All Division III. *Intercollegiate sports:* baseball M, basketball M/W, cross-country running M/W, field hockey W, football M, ice hockey M, soccer M/W, softball W, volleyball W. *Intramural sports:* basketball M/W, cheerleading W, equestrian sports M/W, football M, rugby M/W, softball M/W, volleyball W.

Costs (2004–05) *Tuition:* state resident $970 full-time, $210 per credit part-time; nonresident $7050 full-time, $463 per credit part-time. Full-time tuition and fees vary according to class time. Part-time tuition and fees vary according to class time and course load. *Required fees:* $3770 full-time, $156 per credit part-time. *Room and board:* $5539. Room and board charges vary according to board plan and housing facility.

Financial Aid In 2001, 100 non-need-based awards were made. *Average percent of need met:* 89%. *Average financial aid package:* $6558. *Average need-based loan:* $2080. *Average need-based gift aid:* $3020. *Average non-need-based aid:* $1454.

Contact: Director: Susanne H. Conley, Dean of Academic and Student Affairs, P.O. Box 9101, Framingham, Massachusetts 01701-9101; *Telephone:* 508-626-4596; *Fax:* 508-626-4087; *E-mail:* sconley@frc.mass.edu; *Web site:* http://www.framingham.edu

Holyoke Community College
Honors Program
Holyoke, Massachusetts

The Honors Program at Holyoke Community College (HCC) offers a challenging and rigorous program of study that can be individually designed to fit a student's interests and curriculum. The Honors Program provides a chance to obtain an excellent education at a very low cost with unequaled opportunities for transfer.

The Honors Program consists of a variety of components. During the first year, the program offers an honors learning community that is team taught, integrating the arts and sciences. Students have the opportunity to work closely with faculty members, a reference librarian, and with each other. The Honors Learning Community is limited to 20 students per semester. Learning communities promote multidisciplinary learning experiences that emphasize student seminars, collaborative research projects, and an introduction to scientific and humanistic intellectual history while completing required courses (English 101 and 102 and two lab sciences). Learning communities at HCC have been supported by grants from the National Endowment for the Humanities, the National Science Foundation, the Fund for the Improvement of Post-Secondary Education, and the National Collegiate Honors Council.

Honors students may generally take one honors colloquium during the second year. Honors colloquia are designed to bring students from all academic disciplines together to confront a theme or issue of current concern from the variety of perspectives that the different disciplines represent. Honors colloquia are multidisciplinary seminars (e.g. Infinity, Monsters, Mind, Reality, Gaia, Holocaust: Paradigm of Genocide) that are competitively enrolled and limited to 15 students who are selected each semester by the Honors Committee. The Honors Program awards a colloquium textbook scholarship to all colloquium students. Colloquia generally offer field trips and a series of expert guest speakers. An Honors Colloquium is strongly recommended to those students who wish to transfer to more selective colleges and universities. A colloquium is offered each semester during the day and in the fall semester at night through continuing education. A letter of invitation to apply is mailed to all eligible students.

Students may also complete an honors project (sometimes called a component), which consists of additional, independent work that a student chooses to undertake in conjunction with a professor in most HCC courses. Such work may consist of an extra paper, a paper of greater length or complexity, a research project in a practical setting such as a lab or darkroom, or creative work such as painting, sculpture, writing, or performance. An honors project may be suggested by either the student or a professor. Project topics are limited only by the student's imagination or ability, the professor's course guidelines, and a regard for the degree of academic rigor that is expected by the HCC Honors Program. Upon successful completion of an honors project, the student receives an additional credit for the course, and the student's transcript shows that the course was taken with honors. Projects must receive initial and final approval from the Honors Committee.

Students may also elect to fulfill the honors curriculum option, which amounts to choosing honors as a major. This option is similar to the arts and sciences transfer option but requires the completion of four semesters (or the equivalent) of a foreign language, an honors project, an honors colloquium, and a graduating GPA of 3.5 or better. Students who do not meet these criteria can still graduate in the arts and sciences transfer option. In the near future, students who complete the honors curriculum option will be granted Commonwealth Scholar distinction upon graduation.

The Honors Program was founded in 1984 by Dr. Marion Copeland. The program averages about 100 students per year who are generally expected to maintain a GPA of at least 3.5.

Participation Requirements: Entrance into the program is flexible. Usually, a student must either enter the College as an honors student or achieve a GPA of at least 3.5 after earning 12 credit hours. All courses within the program emphasize writing, critical and creative thinking across disciplines, and analysis.

Students may elect to fulfill the honors curriculum option, which amounts to choosing honors as a major. This option is similar to the arts and science transfer option, but requires completion of an honors learning community, an honors colloquium, and a foreign language.

Students who achieve a GPA of at least 3.5 after 30 hours earned at HCC are invited to be inducted into the international honor society of Phi Theta Kappa. Members are eligible for scholarships and other benefits. They may also wear the society's gold stole and tassel at commencement.

Scholarship Availability: Several scholarships are awarded each year to entering students. Four Honors Program scholarships (one for a Continuing Education student) of $500 each are given annually to graduating or returning students, and the College offers several larger scholarships that are frequently awarded to Honors Program students. Additional scholarship opportunities are also available.

Campus Overview

State-supported 2-year, founded 1946, part of Massachusetts Public Higher Education System • **Coed** 6,298 undergraduate students, 51% full-time, 65% women, 35% men.

Undergraduates 3,215 full-time, 3,083 part-time. Students come from 18 states and territories, 11 other countries, 1% are from out of state, 6% African American, 2% Asian American or Pacific Islander, 13% Hispanic American, 0.5% Native American, 0.2% international, 5% transferred in.

Faculty *Total:* 498, 22% full-time. *Student/faculty ratio:* 18:1.

Academic Programs *Special study options:* academic remediation for entering students, adult/continuing education programs, advanced placement credit, cooperative education, English as a second language, honors programs, independent study, internships, off-campus study, part-time degree program, services for LD students, student-designed majors, study abroad, summer session for credit. *ROTC:* Army (c), Air Force (c).

Athletics Member NJCAA. *Intercollegiate sports:* baseball M, basketball M/W, golf M/W, skiing (downhill) M(c)/W(c), soccer M/W, softball W, tennis M/W, volleyball W.

Costs (2005–06) *Tuition:* area resident $2498 full-time, $100 per credit part-time; nonresident $7442 full-time, $230 per credit part-time.

Contact: Kim Hicks, Holyoke Community College, 303 Homestead Avenue, Holyoke, Massachusetts 01040; *Telephone:* 413-552-2197; *E-mail:* khicks@hcc.mass.edu; *Web site:* http://www.hcc.mass.edu

---

Lasell College

Honors Program

Newton, Massachusetts

The Honors Program emphasizes the Lasell hallmarks of student-centered teaching, connected learning, and social responsibility in an academic environment that meets the needs of highly motivated, enthusiastic students. The program encourages students to explore broadly across disciplines and probe deeply in their chosen fields of study. Students gain facility with synthesis of complex ideas, application of knowledge to problems in the professional world, and collaboration with peers and faculty members. Students participate in community service to build leadership skills and social responsibility. Through a mix of discussions, field explorations, independent and collaborative projects, and personal attention, the program strives to foster a life-long love of learning and independent thinking. Designation as a Lasell Honor Student represents a high level of academic achievement and unique accomplishments that demonstrate initiative and responsibility.

The objectives of the Honors Program are consistent with the educational objectives of the college but are designed for highly motivated students to work more intensively and creatively to achieve the following: improvement of writing skills, improvement of oral communication and presentation skills, learning to work collaboratively with peers, learning to approach issues from an interdisciplinary perspective, connecting theory to practice through community-based projects, and demonstration of leadership skills through community service.

Participation Requirements: Students are required to complete eight courses in the Honors Program to be awarded the Honors Program designation on their transcript. The eight courses include four required courses and four honors electives. Required honors courses include: Honors Colloquium (1c) 100 level, first year; Honors Seminar I: Leadership (3c) 200 level, second year; Honors Seminar II:

Interdisciplinary special topic (3c) 300 level, third year; Honors Capstone Course/Electronic Portfolio Reflection (1c) 400 level, fourth year.

Students also must choose four elective honors courses, two of which must be at the 200 level or higher. Possible options for honors-level courses include Honors Writing I and II (students place into honors writing classes independently of admission into the Honors Program), special topics seminars, and Honors Components. Each semester, specified courses across the college curriculum are identified as Honors Component courses. Honors students who enroll for the Honors Components of these courses work closely with their instructors on projects that enable them to explore the subject matter of these courses in alternative ways and in greater depth than is required within the regular course syllabi. Honors students are notified each semester of Honors Component options through the College Registrar and the Honors Program Director. Students do not receive additional credit for an Honors Component, but the Honors Component is designated as such on their transcripts.

In addition, students in the Honors Program create their own electronic portfolios in which they showcase their academic and cocurricular accomplishments. The electronic portfolios also aid students in reflecting upon their academic goals and accomplishments and are an important element of the Honors Capstone Seminar in the senior year, when students write a major reflective piece on their educational experiences and development at Lasell. Students must complete the indicated requirements of the electronic portfolio each academic year.

Students in the Honors Program must maintain at least a 3.0 cumulative GPA and pass all honors courses (HON designation and Honors Components) on the first attempt with a grade of C or better.

Students who graduate having completed the Honors Program are acknowledged at an Academic Recognition Ceremony at which they receive an Honors Program completion certificate and a gold cord to wear at commencement. They are also recognized as Honors Program graduates in the printed commencement program and when called up to receive their diplomas, and completion of the Honors Program is indicated on their transcripts.

Admission Process: During the College admissions process, students are named Presidential Scholars based on high school GPA and SAT scores. Those Presidential Scholars who accept the Presidential Scholarship are admitted to the Honors Program. Renewal of the scholarship each year is contingent upon remaining in good standing in the Honors Program. Students who are not admitted to the program upon admission to the College are eligible to apply at the end of their first semester. Students who are recommended by a faculty member and have a 3.0 GPA in the first semester of their first year may be admitted to the Honors Program in the second semester; these students must submit a written statement and demonstrate the desire and ability to engage in challenging learning experiences. There is no scholarship associated with second-semester admission to the Honors Program. Admission requirements for transfer students include a minimum 3.0 GPA from another accredited postsecondary institution, a maximum of 15 transfer credits upon admission, a written statement, and demonstrated ability to engage in challenging learning experiences. There is no scholarship associated with transfer admissions to the Honors Program. Returning sophomores, juniors, and seniors are not eligible for entry into the Honors Program, but all students may petition to the Honors Program Director to take an individual honors course or component.

Campus Overview

Independent comprehensive, founded 1851 • **Coed** 1,155 undergraduate students, 99% full-time, 71% women, 29% men.

Undergraduates 1,139 full-time, 16 part-time. Students come from 16 states and territories, 15 other countries, 45% are from out of state, 6% African American, 4% Asian American or Pacific Islander, 6% Hispanic American, 0.4% Native American, 4% international, 6% transferred in, 80% live on campus.

Faculty *Total:* 150, 37% full-time, 20% with terminal degrees. *Student/faculty ratio:* 13:1.

Academic Programs *Special study options:* advanced placement credit, cooperative education, double majors, English as a second language, honors programs, independent study, internships, part-time degree program, student-designed majors, study abroad.

Athletics Member NCAA. All Division III. *Intercollegiate sports:* basketball M/W, cross-country running M/W, field hockey W, lacrosse M/W, soccer M/W, softball W, volleyball M/W. *Intramural sports:* basketball M/W, cheerleading M/W, crew M/W, soccer M/W, volleyball M/W.

Costs (2005–06) *Comprehensive fee:* $28,500 includes full-time tuition ($18,700), mandatory fees ($1000), and room and board ($8800). Part-time tuition: $620 per credit hour. *Required fees:* $250 per term part-time. *Room and board:* Room and board charges vary according to housing facility.

Financial Aid 718 Federal Work-Study jobs (averaging $2000). In 2003, 123 non-need-based awards were made. *Average percent of need met:* 70%. *Average financial aid package:* $15,500. *Average need-based loan:* $3500. *Average need-based gift aid:* $11,500. *Average non-need-based aid:* $13,400.

Contact: Director: Steven F. Bloom, Dean, School of Arts and Sciences and Director of General Education and the Honors Program, Lasell College, 1844 Commonwealth Avenue, Newton, Massachusetts 02466; *Telephone:* 617-243-2440; *Fax:* 617-243-2480; *E-mail:* sbloom@lasell.edu; *Web site:* http://www.lasell.edu/html/honors.html

Massachusetts College of Liberal Arts
Honors Program
North Adams, Massachusetts

The Honors Program at Massachusetts College of Liberal Arts (Mass. College) concentrates on two primary goals: offering courses that meet the demands of talented students and fostering a supportive community that places a high value on scholarly and creative achievement. The courses all explore interdisciplinary questions that bring into common focus several different dimensions of life, such as ethical standards, scientific exploration, social policy, personal beliefs, and the natural environment. Recent offerings have included such courses as Professional Ethics, Math and Social Justice, The Romantic Movement, The Holocaust and the Nature of Prejudice, and Art and Society. A complete list is available on the program's Web site. The courses are all taught in small sections with a discussion format by the most stimulating faculty members at the College. Groups of students are encouraged to engage the faculty in discussions about developing fresh course topics.

To promote a community of inquiry, honors students are invited to meet regularly together for informal discussions on subjects of current interest, and they hold discussions with visiting scholars over meals. The Honors Center is stocked with a reference library, computers, artistic supplies, and study spaces that are all reserved for use by honors students. The Honors Program promotes a spirit of intellectual adventure for the entire campus and not just for a select group of students, and everyone who takes an interest in honors events is encouraged to participate in them.

There are currently more than 140 students in the program.

Participation Requirements: To remain in the program, students need a minimum 3.2 overall GPA. To earn the All College Honors notation on the diploma and the transcript, students must complete six honors courses with an overall GPA of at least 3.4. By completing a

thesis or capstone project, students can graduate as a Commonwealth Scholar, a recognition granted by the statewide Commonwealth Honors Program.

Admission Process: Entering students with at least a 3.2 GPA are invited to become honors students, and currently enrolled students receive similar invitations every term. Students may also join on their own initiative or be recommended by faculty members.

Scholarship Availability: While the Honors Program administers no scholarships directly, there are a number of generous scholarships available through the Admissions Office to students with high academic performance. Scholarships are awarded on admission.

Campus Overview
State-supported comprehensive, founded 1894, part of Massachusetts Public Higher Education System • **Small-town** 80-acre campus • **Coed**

Faculty *Student/faculty ratio:* 14:1.

Athletics Member NCAA. All Division III.

Financial Aid In 2003, 198 non-need-based awards were made. *Average percent of need met:* 73. *Average financial aid package:* $6865. *Average need-based loan:* $3452. *Average need-based gift aid:* $4167. *Average non-need-based aid:* $3620.

Contact: Director: David J. Langston, 375 Church Street, North Adams, Massachusetts 01247; *Telephone:* 413-662-5371; *Fax:* 413-662-5010; *E-mail:* dlangsto@mcla.edu; *Web site:* http://www.mcla.mass.edu/honr/

Mount Wachusett Community College
Honors Program
Gardner, Massachusetts

The Honors Program at Mount Wachusett Community College provides an intellectually challenging academic experience, emphasizing stimulating courses, a high degree of student-faculty interaction, and an interdisciplinary perspective. Consequently, students who have demonstrated substantial potential in prior high school or college-level study are exposed to a highly individualized experience. As a result of the program, honors graduates are better prepared to continue their advanced studies at colleges and universities throughout the country and to bring their academic talents to the attention of future employers.

The College's Honors Program is 14 years old, has an enrollment of about 50 to 60 students, graduates 8 to 16 students per year, and has been designated Commonwealth Honors Program status by the Massachusetts Board of Higher Education.

Participation Requirements: Participation in the program requires a minimum 3.3 GPA. Honors students whose GPA drops below the required 3.3 are allowed on probationary semester to continue the program and raise their cumulative average. All honors students are required to participate in certain classes, including an honors college–level English course, an honors college–level math course, and a lab science as well as two honors courses. These may be component courses based upon courses already required by a student's degree program or specially designed honors courses. A component course is any course already required by a student's degree program that has been deemed suitable as an honors component by the respective division. A component course is designed to require such additional activities as independent research, one-on-one tutorials, and/or a special project such as service-learning. Any particular component course is the result of a written agreement between a faculty member and a student that receives approval by the respective Division Dean. An Honors Colloquium is also required. Interdisciplinary in nature and team taught, past titles of these classes have been Gender Issues in American Society, Literature and Culture, Perspectives on Leadership, Critical Thinking, Emerging Issues in Justice, and How Cancer Works.

Students completing the Honors Program receive special recognition at graduation, and the title of Commonwealth Honors Scholar is designated on their official transcripts.

Scholarship Availability: Mount Wachusett Community College provides a tuition waiver to all honors students during their final semester, when they are completing both their honors and degree requirements with a minimum 3.3 average.

Campus Overview

State-supported 2-year, founded 1963, part of Massachusetts Public Higher Education System • **Coed** 4,165 undergraduate students, 44% full-time, 65% women, 35% men.

Undergraduates 1,821 full-time, 2,344 part-time. Students come from 6 states and territories, 8 other countries, 5% are from out of state, 4% African American, 2% Asian American or Pacific Islander, 8% Hispanic American, 0.3% Native American, 0.9% international, 8% transferred in.

Faculty *Total:* 205, 34% full-time. *Student/faculty ratio:* 15:1.

Academic Programs *Special study options:* academic remediation for entering students, adult/continuing education programs, advanced placement credit, cooperative education, distance learning, double majors, English as a second language, honors programs, independent study, internships, part-time degree program, services for LD students, study abroad, summer session for credit.

Costs (2004–05) *Tuition:* state resident $750 full-time, $25 per credit part-time; nonresident $6900 full-time, $230 per credit part-time. Full-time tuition and fees vary according to program and reciprocity agreements. Part-time tuition and fees vary according to program and reciprocity agreements. *Required fees:* $3330 full-time, $106 per credit part-time, $55 per term part-time.

Financial Aid 60 Federal Work-Study jobs (averaging $1870).

Contact: Coordinator: Professor Sheila M. Murphy, 444 Green Street, Gardner, Massachusetts 01440-1000; *Telephone:* 978-630-9331; *Fax:* 978-630-9561; *E-mail:* smurphy@mwcc.mass.edu; *Web site:* http://www.mwcc.mass.edu

---

Northeastern University
University Honors Program
Boston, Massachusetts

*T*he University Honors Program at Northeastern University offers outstanding students academic, career service, and extracurricular opportunities to enhance their academic experience. Honors students complete the requirements of their major and college, but they also participate in honors courses as part of their curriculum.

The honors curriculum consists of separate honors offerings of selected courses as well as honors seminars that are designed specifically for sophomore and middler (third year) honors students. Separate honors courses are 4 credits and feature small class sizes with extensive faculty-student interaction. Honors seminars are thematic and interdisciplinary, and some of the topics chosen change each academic year. In addition, many honors students complete a two-course junior/senior honors project as the capstone experience of their undergraduate career.

Offices of the Honors Program include a student lounge and computer lab. Many freshmen students live in Kennedy Residence

Hall, which features suite living arrangements and various activities for honors students. A limited number of spaces in West Village C are available for upperclass honors students via the housing lottery. All honors students can participate in social activities sponsored by the Honors Program, including discounted tickets to cultural and sports events in Boston.

The University Honors Program began in 1986 and currently includes 1,450 students. Each year, approximately 280 students enter the program as freshmen, and a number of other students may join after one semester of the first year or at the beginning of the second year.

Participation Requirements: Honors students who begin during their first year complete three or four honors courses that year, one course in each of their sophomore and middler years (one of which must be an honors seminar), and the junior/senior honors project. Honors Course Distinction is earned after completing six honors courses, including one honors seminar. College Honors Project Distinction is earned after completing the junior/senior honors project. University Honors Program Distinction is earned after completing requirements for both of the other distinctions. Students must maintain a minimum 3.4 GPA to remain in the Honors Program.

Admission Process: Incoming freshman are admitted to the Honors Program based upon their high school GPA and SAT/ACT scores. Students at Northeastern may enter at the end of the first semester of the first year, the beginning of the sophomore year, or the beginning of the junior/senior year if they intend to complete the junior/senior honors project with a cumulative GPA of 3.4 or higher.

Scholarship Availability: Scholarships are available specifically for honors students. In the spring semester of each year, honors students are eligible to apply for a scholarship if they have completed or registered for the requisite number of honors courses during that year. The amount of the award depends upon a student's financial need and GPA. In addition, honors students are eligible for a number of other scholarships available to all students at the University.

Campus Overview

Independent university, founded 1898 • **Coed** 14,618 undergraduate students, 100% full-time, 51% women, 49% men.

Undergraduates 14,618 full-time. Students come from 50 states and territories, 123 other countries, 65% are from out of state, 6% African American, 7% Asian American or Pacific Islander, 5% Hispanic American, 0.4% Native American, 5% international, 23% transferred in.

Faculty *Total:* 1,174, 71% full-time, 67% with terminal degrees. *Student/faculty ratio:* 16:1.

Academic Programs *Special study options:* academic remediation for entering students, accelerated degree program, adult/continuing education programs, advanced placement credit, cooperative education, distance learning, double majors, English as a second language, honors programs, independent study, internships, off-campus study, part-time degree program, services for LD students, student-designed majors, study abroad, summer session for credit. *ROTC:* Army (b), Navy (c), Air Force (c).

Athletics Member NCAA. All Division I except football (Division I-AA). *Intercollegiate sports:* baseball M(s), basketball M(s)/W(s), crew M(s)/W(s), cross-country running M(s)/W(s), field hockey W(s), ice hockey M(s)/W(s), soccer M(s)/W(s), swimming and diving W(s), tennis M(s), track and field M(s)/W(s), volleyball W(s). *Intramural sports:* basketball M/W, cheerleading M(c)/W(c), fencing M(c)/W(c), field hockey M(c)/W(c), football M/W, ice hockey M/W, lacrosse M(c)/W(c), racquetball M/W, rugby M(c)/W(c), sailing M(c)/W(c), skiing (cross-country) M(c)/W(c), skiing (downhill) M(c)/W(c), soccer M/W, softball M/W, squash M/W, swimming and diving M(c)/W(c), table tennis M(c)/W(c), tennis M(c)/W(c), ultimate Frisbee M(c)/W(c), volleyball M(c)/W, water polo M/W, wrestling M(c).

Costs (2004–05) *Comprehensive fee:* $37,260 includes full-time tuition ($26,750), mandatory fees ($330), and room and board

($10,180). *College room only:* $5440. Room and board charges vary according to board plan and housing facility.

Financial Aid 3,479 Federal Work-Study jobs (averaging $1448). In 2004, 2233 non-need-based awards were made. *Average percent of need met: 61%. Average financial aid package: $15,974. Average need-based loan: $4763. Average need-based gift aid: $11,737. Average non-need-based aid: $12,932.*

Contact: Director: Maureen Kelleher, Associate Director: Faith Crisley, Assistant Director: Lauren Pouchak, Staff Assistant: Carol Dicecca, 1 Nightingale Hall, Northeastern University, Boston, Massachusetts 02115; *Telephone:* 617-373-2333; *Fax:* 617-373-5300; *E-mail:* m.kelleher@neu.edu, f.crisley@neu.edu, l.pouchak@neu.edu, c.dicecca@neu.edu; *Web site:* http://www.honors.neu.edu.

Salem State College
Honors Program
Salem, Massachusetts

The Honors Program of this state-supported College provides motivated and talented students with the stimulating and challenging educational opportunities typically found at name-brand private campuses. The academic program features small-sized, discussion-based classes that fulfill core and distribution requirements. Interdisciplinary honors seminars orient students toward a senior-year capstone project, typically a research project or academic thesis conducted in close affiliation with a faculty mentor. The program enables students to present research at a variety of conferences, to undertake internships, and to study and travel abroad.

The Honors Program at Salem functions as a community within the College, and events include large and small dinners, speakers, social events, and outings (e.g., whale watches, apple picking, etc.). Students have access to an Honors Center in the library and to honors housing. Honors students run their own undergraduate organization.

Founded in 1983, the Salem State College Honors Program is an active participant in Massachusetts' Commonwealth Honors Program as well as in the National Collegiate Honors Council. Of 4,800 students at the College, 140 are in the Honors Program.

Participation Requirements: The Honors Program is appropriate for students in all majors. Students satisfy all College core requirements by taking required a 3-credit honors freshman writing class, a 6-credit honors literature sequence, a 6-credit honors history sequence, and a 3-credit honors speech course.

Honors Program students may also elect to satisfy all College distribution requirements through honors electives in biology, philosophy, political science, psychology, and sociology. As juniors and seniors, students in the program participate in 2 one-semester interdisciplinary seminars. Senior honors projects are generally conducted through departmental honors courses. Students maintain a 3.2 or higher cumulative average.

Participation in the Honors Program is highlighted in the Commencement program and indicated on students' permanent transcripts.

Admission Process: Applicants to the program are evaluated on the quality of their responses to a prompt that asks the student: to attach a statement about himself or herself and the student's outlook on college; what makes the Honors Program a good fit for the student; and assuming that the student is more than his or her GPA and SAT scores, what can the student tell Salem to fill in the picture. While applicants are expected to score above 600 on either the verbal or the quantitative scales of the SAT and to have high school GPAs at or above 3.3, the program coordinator may take other factors into account in deciding admissions. Currently enrolled students and transfer applicants should have an overall college GPA of 3.5 or better and fewer than 35 college credits.

Scholarship Availability: The great majority of students receive scholarships from funding sources that are restricted to members of the Honors Program. The Senator Paul Tsongas Scholarship, for qualified in-state students, covers tuition and fees for four years. Presidential Honors Scholarships cover the cost of tuition for four years. Charlotte Forten Scholarships provide tuition and fees for students from underrepresented groups. Salem State College Foundation Grants provide grants of varying amounts. Students also may receive stipends for study abroad and Washington internships.

Campus Overview
State-supported comprehensive, founded 1854, part of Massachusetts Public Higher Education System • **Coed** 6,771 undergraduate students, 74% full-time, 63% women, 37% men.

Undergraduates 4,998 full-time, 1,773 part-time. Students come from 18 states and territories, 5% African American, 2% Asian American or Pacific Islander, 5% Hispanic American, 0.4% Native American, 4% international, 12% transferred in, 22% live on campus.

Faculty *Total:* 562, 49% full-time. *Student/faculty ratio:* 17:1.

Academic Programs *Special study options:* academic remediation for entering students, adult/continuing education programs, advanced placement credit, double majors, English as a second language, honors programs, independent study, internships, off-campus study, part-time degree program, services for LD students, student-designed majors, study abroad, summer session for credit.

Athletics Member NCAA. All Division III. *Intercollegiate sports:* baseball M, basketball M/W, cross-country running M/W, field hockey W, golf M, ice hockey M, soccer M/W, softball W, swimming and diving M/W, tennis M/W, track and field M/W, volleyball W. *Intramural sports:* archery M/W, badminton M/W, basketball M/W, cross-country running M/W, fencing M/W, field hockey W, football M, golf M/W, gymnastics M/W, ice hockey M/W, lacrosse M/W, racquetball M/W, skiing (cross-country) M/W, skiing (downhill) M/W, soccer M/W, squash M/W, swimming and diving M/W, tennis M/W, volleyball M/W, water polo M/W, weight lifting M/W, wrestling M.

Costs (2004–05) *Tuition:* state resident $910 full-time, $38 per credit part-time; nonresident $7050 full-time, $294 per credit part-time. Full-time tuition and fees vary according to class time. Part-time tuition and fees vary according to class time. *Required fees:* $4374 full-time, $182 per credit part-time, $14 per credit part-time. *Room and board:* $7350. Room and board charges vary according to board plan and housing facility.

Financial Aid 726 Federal Work-Study jobs (averaging $2000). *Average percent of need met: 66%. Average financial aid package: $6512. Average need-based loan: $8855. Average need-based gift aid: $8568.*

Contact: Coordinator: Professor Rod Kessler, Honors Program, Salem State College, 352 Lafayette Street, Salem, Massachusetts 01970; *Telephone:* 978-542-6247; *Fax:* 978-542-6753; *E-mail:* rod-kessler-ab71@post.harvard.edu; *Web site:* http://www.salem.mass.edu/honorsprogram/index.html

Simmons College
Simmons College Honors Program
Boston, Massachusetts

Located in the Fenway neighborhood of Boston, Simmons College is within walking distance of world-renowned museums, libraries, theaters, hospitals and research facilities. Its Honors Program provides outstanding undergraduate students with the opportunity to participate in an enriched four-year curriculum, a four-year co-curricular Career Exploration Program as well as social events that take advantage of the exciting cultural life of a world-class city.

The Honors curriculum emphasizes the values and goals of a Simmons education: multicultural awareness, international perspectives, and interdisciplinary approaches to knowledge as well as depth in a major discipline. Honors students take a minimum of one Honors seminar per year but may take more if they so choose; the Honors Program is compatible with all majors. The Honors seminars are small, usually with fewer than 15 students, in order to foster class discussion, oral presentations, and independent learning projects.

Honors students take part in the development of the Program thorough an active Liaison that meets monthly with the Director. The Liaison sponsors a yearly Liaison Lecture, inviting a faculty member to share his or her current research with all members of the Simmons community. The Liaison also plans and hosts a number of informal events in he residence halls. Students volunteer to become peer advisors of first-year Honors students, introducing them to Boston as well as to the social and academic life of the campus.

Participation Requirements: All first-year Honors students participate in an eight-credit Learning Community in the fall semester. The Learning Community, comprised of two distinct courses as well as a common integrative seminar, explores topics that bring to light the challenges and opportunities of a multicultural society. Recent Learning Communities include: Democracy and Difference, Seeing and Hearing: A Critical Look at Communication, Revisioning the Past.

Second-year students take one or more Honors seminars that look at cultures and contemporary issues outside of the United States and Western Europe. International Perspectives courses include: The Colonial Legacy in Africa, Islam and the West, Political Upheaval and Its Expression in Twentieth-Century Latin America, Islam in Africa. Second-year students are encouraged to travel abroad on a Simmons short-term course during their sophomore year.

Third-year students choose one or more courses that examine intellectual and social debates. Many of these seminars are either team-taught or have considerable participation by guest speakers. Interdisciplinary Approaches courses offer: Sustainable Development and Green Chemistry, Disability and Society: Private Lives, Public Debates and HIV/AIDS: Intersections of Science and Society.

Seniors undertake an eight-credit independent project in their major. This can include an Honors thesis, an internship, or any other project that is specific to the student's discipline. Each senior also enrolls in an Honors senior seminar that meets "face-to-face" for monthly workshops as well as on-line in order to develop the skills necessary for career development and planning.

All Honors students must maintain a 3.2 cumulative GPA to remain in the Program. Students receive a Certificate of Participation and Honors cords to wear at graduation.

Their membership in Honors is recognized at the graduation ceremony as well as on their transcripts.

Admission Process: High school seniors complete an Honors application in addition to their electronic or paper application to Simmons. The Honors Director and Steering Committee select a small group of students based on official transcripts from all schools attended, teacher recommendations, guidance counselor recommendation, official SAT or ACT scores, and the essays included in the Honors application. Approximately 8% of students accepted to Simmons are invited to join the Honors Program.

High-achieving first-year students are invited to apply to the Honors Program for entry in their sophomore year. A very rigorous selection process, based entirely on faculty recommendations and submission of work done in college courses, brings 10-12 new students into Honors.

Scholarship Availability: In addition to any need-based aid, Simmons offers a number of Dean's merit scholarships to incoming students upon admission to the College. These provide from $10,000 to $12,000 of financial support per year. No special financial aid application is required. Although many Honors students do receive merit scholarships, these are not tied to the Honors Program. Students who join the Honors Program receive a $500 Book Award per year.

They are also eligible to apply for the Dolores Amidon D'Angelo Award, a scholarship of $2,500 for Honors students who wish to study abroad.

Campus Overview

Independent university, founded 1899 • **Urban** 12-acre campus • **Women only** 1,812 undergraduate students, 90% full-time.

Undergraduates 1,627 full-time, 185 part-time. Students come from 38 states and territories, 26 other countries, 40% are from out of state, 6% African American, 6% Asian American or Pacific Islander, 2% Hispanic American, 0.2% Native American, 2% international, 2% transferred in, 70% live on campus.

Faculty *Total:* 456, 40% full-time. *Student/faculty ratio:* 12:1.

Academic Programs *Special study options:* academic remediation for entering students, accelerated degree program, adult/continuing education programs, advanced placement credit, double majors, English as a second language, freshman honors college, honors programs, independent study, internships, off-campus study, part-time degree program, services for LD students, student-designed majors, study abroad, summer session for credit. *ROTC:* Army (c), Navy (c), Air Force (c). *Unusual degree programs:* 3-2 physician assistant, pharmacy with Massachusetts College of Pharmacy and Allied Health Sciences, nutrition with Boston University.

Athletics Member NCAA. All Division III. *Intercollegiate sports:* basketball W, crew W, field hockey W, sailing W, soccer W, softball W, swimming and diving W, tennis W, track and field W, volleyball W. *Intramural sports:* basketball W, golf W, racquetball W, skiing (cross-country) W, skiing (downhill) W, soccer W, softball W, tennis W, volleyball W.

Costs (2005–06) *Comprehensive fee:* $35,640 includes full-time tuition ($24,680), mandatory fees ($760), and room and board ($10,200). Full-time tuition and fees vary according to course load. Part-time tuition: $770 per semester hour. Part-time tuition and fees vary according to course load.

Financial Aid In 2004, 24 non-need-based awards were made. *Average percent of need met:* 56%. *Average financial aid package:* $15,854. *Average need-based loan:* $3040. *Average need-based gift aid:* $11,574. *Average non-need-based aid:* $12,785.

Contact: Director: Professor Mary Jane Treacy, Simmons College, 300 The Fenway, Boston, Massachusetts 02115; *Telephone:* 617-521-2233; *E-mail:* treacy@simmons.edu; *Web site:* http://www.simmons.edu/academics/special-programs/honors.shtml

Springfield Technical Community College
The Honors Program at STCC
Springfield, Massachusetts

The Honors Certificate Program at Springfield Technical Community College (STCC) offers a challenging academic experience for qualified students who wish unique study and research opportunities in their major field of study. Working individually with selected professors, participants receive increased scholarship and transfer opportunities, a special notation of distinguished academic work on diploma and transcripts, use of the Honors Center, and numerous opportunities to present their work.

The Honors Colloquia, small interdisciplinary seminars, promote original scholarship and active learning. These 3-credit colloquia include Library Research Methods, American Biographies, The Comic Spirit, and Literature and the City. While these courses are

primarily intended for students enrolled in the Honors Certificate Program, exceptional students may be admitted occasionally with the permission of the instructor.

Students wishing to undertake honors work in any college-level course can do an honors add-on project in that course. With the professor's permission and guidance, the student and the professor design a project based on the topics covered in the course. The project should be relevant to the student and the course. A written component and a presentation before a public audience are required for all projects. Projects must be completed in an academic year. Once the project is completed, a special notation appears on the student's transcript explaining that honors work was done for that course.

Students who are interested in studying a topic or issue not covered in a course taught at STCC can develop an Honors Independent Study (HIS). Once a sponsoring professor has agreed to participate, the student and the professor design the course description, assignments, methodology, grading policy, meetings dates, and other details relevant to the course (all subject to approval by those who sign the HIS contract). The HIS runs the length of a semester and is noted on a student's transcript as honors work.

The Annual Honors Forum, held each April, provides one of several opportunities for students to display their work. Other outlets include national and regional conferences, as well as the annual undergraduate research conference in Boston.

In order to accommodate and recognize all students, levels within the honors program were developed. The Honors Certificate and Scholarship recipient is a student who has completed the 15 credits outlined in the curriculum. The Commonwealth Honors Program scholar is a student who has a minimum cumulative GPA of 3.2 (on a 4.0 scale), completed 9 credit hours in honors courses, and completed on honors seminar or colloquium. The Springfield Technical Community College scholar is a student who has completed 9 credits worth of honors work. Upon graduation, students completing are awarded special certificates at Honors Convocation.

The Massachusetts Board of Higher Education has recognized the program as a Commonwealth Honors Program, providing smoother transfer processes and more scholarship opportunities for students as well as statewide recognition of STCC honors students. Students have access to an honors center equipped with Internet-access computer systems, a reference library, study desks, and meeting space. The Honors Program at STCC was founded in 1989. Currently, 65 students are enrolled.

Participation Requirements: In order to provide honors opportunities to students in all majors, designations within the program have been developed. All requirements and designations require students to earn at least a B in their courses.

The requirements of the Honors Certificate and Scholarship—totaling 15 credits—are two colloquia (6 credits), a library research colloquium (3 credits), and add-on components/honors dependent study (6 or more credits).

To become a Commonwealth Honors Program scholar, a student must have a minimum cumulative GPA of 3.2; completed three honors courses (9 credit hours) with a grade of B or better; completed one honors seminar or colloquium, which is interdisciplinary, for honors-level students only and preferably, team-taught. The program provides students an option to substitute an honors thesis or project involving independent research for one of the three required honors courses.

The requirements for a Springfield Technical Community College scholar are 9 credits worth of honors work, such as add-on projects in three college-level courses or two honors add-ons and one colloquium or two colloquia and one honors add-on.

Admission Process: Honors Program participants are selected on the basis of their academic potential and motivation. Entering freshmen with a minimum 3.5 QPA from high school, or a minimum 3.0 QPA from a high school honors program (or its equivalent), or a 1000 combined SAT score are eligible to apply for admission.

Students currently enrolled at STCC are eligible after completing 12 college-level credits, if their QPA is 3.5 or better.

Students whose QPA's do not meet these standards, but who feel they have the ability and interest necessary to participate in the Honors Certificate Program may apply for admission by submitting a letter of recommendation from a recent teacher and an original piece of writing demonstrating academic competence (for example, a paper for a recent course).

Scholarship Availability: All Honors Certificate recipients are awarded a $500 scholarship upon graduation. In addition, many students are awarded collegewide scholarships and transfer scholarships, including the Frances Perkins Scholars Program at Mount Holyoke College and the Ada Comstock Scholars Program at Smith College.

Campus Overview

State-supported 2-year, founded 1967 • **Coed** 6,114 undergraduate students, 45% full-time, 56% women, 44% men.

Undergraduates 2,760 full-time, 3,354 part-time. Students come from 10 states and territories, 4% are from out of state, 15% African American, 2% Asian American or Pacific Islander, 14% Hispanic American, 0.5% Native American, 0.8% international.

Faculty *Total:* 524, 29% full-time. *Student/faculty ratio:* 22:1.

Academic Programs *Special study options:* academic remediation for entering students, adult/continuing education programs, advanced placement credit, cooperative education, distance learning, English as a second language, honors programs, independent study, internships, off-campus study, part-time degree program, services for LD students, summer session for credit.

Athletics Member NJCAA. *Intercollegiate sports:* basketball M/W, golf M/W, soccer M/W, tennis M/W, wrestling M/W. *Intramural sports:* basketball M/W, cross-country running M/W, golf M/W, skiing (cross-country) M/W, volleyball M/W, weight lifting M/W.

Costs (2005–06) *Tuition:* state resident $750 full-time, $25 per credit hour part-time; nonresident $7260 full-time, $242 per credit hour part-time. Full-time tuition and fees vary according to course load. Part-time tuition and fees vary according to course load. No tuition increase for student's term of enrollment. *Required fees:* $2454 full-time, $75 per credit hour part-time, $116 per term part-time.

Financial Aid 124 Federal Work-Study jobs (averaging $2400).

Contact: Dr. Arlene Rodriguez, Honors Program Coordinator, Springfield Technical Community College, P.O. Box 9000, Suite 1, Springfield, Massachusetts 01102-9000; *Telephone:* 413-755-4244; *Fax:* 413-755-6022; *E-mail:* arodriguez@stcc.edu; *Web site:* http://www.stcc.edu/honors

Stonehill College
Honors Program
Easton, Massachusetts

*T*he Stonehill College Honors Program is designed to enhance and enrich the educational experience of many of the talented and highly motivated students at the College. The program promotes independent learning and thinking, thoughtful and creative expression in writing, collaborative work with fellow students and faculty members, and vigorous discussion and debate about the issues central to the human experience.

Honors courses are limited to 20 students but are frequently smaller. Honors courses are offered in the humanities, the social sciences, and the natural sciences. In the senior year, honors students write a thesis in capstone courses within their majors. Honors students who fulfill all the requirements of the program graduate with a special designation.

Throughout the academic year, the Honors Program sponsors a wide variety of cocurricular programs, including lectures, dramatic

presentations, and trips to Boston, Providence, and New York City. The program also provides students with a strong social and academic bond during all four years. Honors students are not separated from the rest of the student body, and there is no exclusive honors housing; therefore, program participants interact with the entire campus community. In addition, the Honors Program is compatible with all majors and courses of study and with study-abroad programs.

The Honors Program was founded in 1994. Each year, approximately 60 freshman students are enrolled as honors students; the total enrollment in the program is about 250 students.

Participation Requirements: Honors courses, except the electives and the Senior Capstone course, meet general studies requirements at the College. In the freshman year, honors students take two honors courses in the fall semester in philosophy and religious studies or in literature and history. In the sophomore and junior years, students take honors courses in the social and natural sciences. In the senior year, honors students take the Senior Capstone course and write a thesis. In all, honors students must take a minimum of six honors courses over four years, but they may take more if they wish.

Honors students who fulfill all the requirements of the program graduate from the College with the special designation Stonehill Scholar and receive recognition and a distinctive medallion at commencement.

Admission Process: Admission to the Stonehill Honors Program is competitive. The committee carefully reviews each student's high school course profile, academic performance, weighted rank, and standardized test scores (SAT or ACT). The College looks for contributors both in the classroom as well as in the high school community. On average, invited students rank in the top 4 percent of their high school class with combined SAT I scores of 1250 or higher. No separate application is required. Students may petition for admission after the first semester of freshman year.

Scholarship Availability: Talented and financially needy students can receive honors scholarships from $7500 to full tuition. Stonehill also awards merit-based scholarships to outstanding students who do not demonstrate financial need. No special application is required other than the PROFILE and FAFSA forms.

Campus Overview

Independent Roman Catholic comprehensive, founded 1948 • **Coed** 2,466 undergraduate students, 90% full-time, 60% women, 40% men.

Undergraduates 2,228 full-time, 238 part-time. Students come from 27 states and territories, 8 other countries, 40% are from out of state, 3% African American, 3% Asian American or Pacific Islander, 3% Hispanic American, 0.3% Native American, 0.6% international, 1% transferred in, 82% live on campus.

Faculty *Total:* 250, 53% full-time, 61% with terminal degrees. *Student/faculty ratio:* 14:1.

Academic Programs *Special study options:* adult/continuing education programs, advanced placement credit, double majors, honors programs, independent study, internships, off-campus study, part-time degree program, services for LD students, student-designed majors, study abroad, summer session for credit. *ROTC:* Army (b). *Unusual degree programs:* 3-2 computer engineering with University of Notre Dame.

Athletics Member NCAA. All Division II. *Intercollegiate sports:* baseball M(s), basketball M(s)/W(s), cheerleading M(c)/W(c), cross-country running M(s)/W(s), equestrian sports W, field hockey W(s), football M(s), golf M(c)/W(c), ice hockey M, lacrosse M(c)/W(s), rugby M(c)/W(c), soccer M(s)/W(s), softball W(s), tennis M(s)/W(s), track and field M(s)/W(s), ultimate Frisbee M(c)/W(c), volleyball M(c)/W(s). *Intramural sports:* basketball M/W, field hockey M/W, football M/W, racquetball M/W, soccer M/W, softball M/W, tennis M/W, volleyball M/W.

Costs (2004–05) *Comprehensive fee:* $33,214 includes full-time tuition ($22,068), mandatory fees ($940), and room and board ($10,206). Part-time tuition: $800 per course. *Required fees:* $25 per term part-time.

Financial Aid 910 Federal Work-Study jobs (averaging $1728). 218 state and other part-time jobs (averaging $1118). In 2004, 490 non-need-based awards were made. *Average percent of need met:* 81%. *Average financial aid package:* $17,306. *Average need-based loan:* $5164. *Average need-based gift aid:* $12,518. *Average non-need-based aid:* $16,406.

Contact: Director: Professor Gregory Shaw, Department of Religious Studies, 320 Washington Street, Easton, Massachusetts 02357; *Telephone:* 508-565-1355; *E-mail:* gshaw@stonehill.edu

University of Massachusetts Amherst
Commonwealth College
Amherst, Massachusetts

Commonwealth College is the honors college at the University of Massachusetts Amherst. Commonwealth College offers academically talented students the advantages of a small honors college and the wide-ranging opportunities of a nationally recognized major research institution. Honors students participate in small classes and colloquia, receive individual counseling, and have outstanding opportunities to conduct significant research while working closely with faculty members. The honors college is a campuswide, comprehensive, four-year program; students from all majors in every college are eligible to join the honors college.

Love of learning lies at the heart of Commonwealth College. The curriculum of the College emphasizes inquiry and facilitates critical analysis, independent research, collaborative work, and effective communication skills. Consistent with the land-grant mission of the University, Commonwealth College also promotes engagement with society. The College affords its students many opportunities for engagement through a variety of academically based opportunities, including internships, co-ops, experiential learning courses, leadership training, and community service learning courses. The College also promotes student leadership through specific leadership courses, through its speaker series and alumni mentoring/shadowing programs, and by encouraging student participation in College activities, including peer mentoring, committee work, and activity planning. The honors curriculum includes entirely enriched honors courses, colloquia, interdisciplinary seminars, service learning, and a culminating experience requirement. The culminating experience is a 6-credit activity that may range in scope from the more traditional thesis to approved capstone courses integrating academic study, guided reflection, and experience gained through community service, study abroad, or internship. In addition, many junior and senior honors students take graduate-level courses and obtain honors credit. Courses taken through the Five College consortium (Amherst College, Hampshire College, Mount Holyoke College, and Smith College in cooperation with the University of Massachusetts Amherst) may be petitioned for substitution as honors courses.

Commonwealth College offers a variety of special programs. The College sponsors a lecture series that brings distinguished visitors to campus to speak on selected national issues. Through the Pizza & Prof Night seminar series, students meet outstanding faculty members from across the campus. The Citizen Scholars Program, named a model program by the Carnegie Foundation for the Advancement of Teaching, offers scholarships and leadership training for students who engage in challenging work linking academics to community outreach. The International Scholars Program prepares students for study abroad and provides limited scholarship assistance. The Office of National Scholarship Advisement assists eligible students who are applying for national fellowships, such as the Rhodes, Marshall, Fulbright, and Truman Scholarships.

All incoming first-year students arrive on campus two days early in the fall to participate in a special Labor Day Orientation. First-year honors students may select from several residential options, such as theme-based honors learning communities in the Orchard Hill Residential Area, the Talent Advancement Programs (TAP) in the Southwest Residential Area, and Thatcher Language House.

Commonwealth College encourages students to undertake research and supports their efforts by helping to identify faculty mentors, teaching thesis workshops, offering research fellowships for financial assistance, and sponsoring a statewide conference on undergraduate research.

A variety of resources and services are available to students through Commonwealth College. The advising component is both comprehensive and integrative, with individual counseling from faculty, professional, and peer advisers. The College also publishes a newsletter, sponsors service projects and student gatherings, and administers a competitive awards program. Graduating honors students may request a dean's letter of recommendation for prospective employers and graduate schools.

The University Honors Program was established in 1961 and was replaced by the honors college, Commonwealth College, in 1999; it now has a total membership of more than 2,700.

Participation Requirements: All students who complete Commonwealth College requirements graduate as Commonwealth College Scholars. These requirements include a GPA of 3.2 or better, foundation skills, honors courses, and a culminating experience. To graduate with higher Latin honors, students must complete all Commonwealth College requirements and attain a minimum GPA of 3.5 for magna cum laude or 3.8 for summa cum laude. Cum laude is determined by GPA and residency requirements alone. To graduate with any level of honors, a student must complete 45 graded credits in residence. Departmental or Interdisciplinary honors are awarded in addition to Commonwealth College and Latin honors. Specific requirements vary depending on a student's major. Foundation requirements include writing and oral communications. Honors courses must be completed with grades of B or better. Required courses include Honors College Writing; a minimum number of general education honors courses, one of which must have an interdisciplinary designation; and the Dean's Book series (students must complete three 1-credit seminars; the 3 credits count as meeting the Commonwealth College requirement for a second interdisciplinary honors course). Three of the required honors courses must be at the 300 level or above, of which two must comprise a 6-credit culminating experience. Accommodations may be made for those entering the College after the freshman year. Under no circumstance is the Dean's Book requirement or the culminating experience waived. Students who complete a minimum of 45 graded credits in residence and graduate from the Commonwealth College receive one or more of the following types of honors noted on their diplomas and transcripts, depending on their honors track and GPA: Commonwealth College Scholar; Departmental Honors or Interdisciplinary Honors; and cum laude, magna cum laude, or summa cum laude.

Admission Process: Entering first-year students are admitted to the College by invitation. Each student's application to the University is evaluated on the basis of academic achievement in high school, test scores, and an essay by the student. Average first-year honors students who entered in fall 2004 ranked in the top 7 percent of their high school class, attained a weighted high school GPA of 4.0 in their academic course work, and scored 1326 on the SAT I. Entering transfer students may be admitted either by invitation or by applying to the College during the first month of their entering semester if they have a 3.2 GPA or higher from their previous institution. Others may apply based on their academic record at the University if they have a 3.2 GPA or higher.

Scholarship Availability: The University of Massachusetts Amherst has a variety of merit scholarships available for incoming first-year and transfer students. Selections, which are administered by the Admissions Office, are made during the admission process.

In addition, Commonwealth College has an endowed scholarship fund and several research fellowships. Selection criteria for the endowed scholarships are listed on the College Web site. Sophomore and junior honors students may apply for research assistant fellowships of up to $1000 per semester for work done under the direct supervision of a faculty mentor. The Citizen Scholars Program awards scholarships of $1000 per year for two years to a select group of students who wish to serve their community and become active leaders in the commonwealth. Other endowed scholarships support students engaged in community service projects. The scholarships for the International Scholars Program and the Oxford Summer Seminar support students in study-abroad programs. Fifty honors research grants of up to $1000 each are awarded to senior and junior honors students through a competitive application process. Students must submit a proposal outlining their project accompanied by a letter of endorsement from their faculty sponsor.

Commonwealth College also administers a competitive awards program. The deadline for applications is in the spring, generally mid-March. Recipients are announced at the honors graduation and awards ceremony, where they receive a special certificate. These senior awards carry cash prizes of $500 to $1000. While all recognize academic achievement, many are based on excellence of research and others acknowledge public service.

Campus Overview

State-supported university, founded 1863, part of University of Massachusetts • **Coed** 18,966 undergraduate students, 93% full-time, 50% women, 50% men.

Undergraduates 17,563 full-time, 1,403 part-time. Students come from 59 states and territories, 97 other countries, 15% are from out of state, 4% African American, 7% Asian American or Pacific Islander, 3% Hispanic American, 0.3% Native American, 1% international, 6% transferred in, 61% live on campus.

Faculty *Total:* 1,316, 84% full-time, 86% with terminal degrees. *Student/faculty ratio:* 17:1.

Academic Programs *Special study options:* academic remediation for entering students, adult/continuing education programs, advanced placement credit, cooperative education, distance learning, double majors, English as a second language, freshman honors college, honors programs, independent study, internships, off-campus study, part-time degree program, services for LD students, student-designed majors, study abroad, summer session for credit. *ROTC:* Army (b), Air Force (b).

Athletics Member NCAA. All Division I except football (Division I-AA). *Intercollegiate sports:* baseball M(s), basketball M(s)/W(s), cheerleading M/W, crew W(s), cross-country running M(s)/W(s), field hockey W(s), ice hockey M(s), lacrosse M(s)/W(s), skiing (downhill) M(s)/W(s), soccer M(s)/W(s), softball W(s), swimming and diving M(s)/W(s), tennis M(s), track and field M(s)/W(s), volleyball W(s). *Intramural sports:* basketball M/W, crew M(c)/W(c), cross-country running M/W, equestrian sports M(c)/W(c), fencing M(c)/W(c), field hockey W, football M/W, ice hockey M/W, lacrosse M(c)/W, rugby M(c)/W(c), soccer M/W, softball M/W, swimming and diving M/W, tennis M/W, ultimate Frisbee M/W, volleyball M/W, wrestling M/W.

Costs (2004–05) *Tuition:* state resident $1714 full-time, $72 per credit part-time; nonresident $9937 full-time, $414 per credit part-time. Full-time tuition and fees vary according to course load, reciprocity agreements, and student level. Part-time tuition and fees vary according to course load. *Required fees:* $7294 full-time, $1564 per term part-time. *Room and board:* $6189; room only: $3428. Room and board charges vary according to board plan and housing facility.

Financial Aid 4,940 Federal Work-Study jobs (averaging $1684). In 2003, 353 non-need-based awards were made. *Average percent of need met:* 88%. *Average financial aid package:* $10,347. *Average need-based loan:* $3952. *Average need-based gift aid:* $5537. *Average non-need-based aid:* $5049.

Contact: Dean: Dr. Linda L. Slakey, 504 Goodell Building, 140 Hicks Way, Amherst, Massachusetts 01003-9272; *Telephone:* 413-545-2483; *Fax:* 413-545-4469; *E-mail:* comcol@comcol.umass.edu; *Web site:* http://www.comcol.umass.edu

University of Massachusetts Boston
University Honors Program
Boston, Massachusetts

The University Honors Program has been designated a Commonwealth Honors Program within the state system. It is open to students from the Colleges of Liberal Arts, Science and Mathematics, Nursing, Management, and Public and Community Service.

The Honors Program offers, in part, an accelerated, enhanced, and more rigorous version of the campus's general education program. At its heart is an array of 100- and 200-level courses, of which students select five. These courses—unique to the program and not honors sections of standard courses—are multidisciplinary and involve special enrichments, such as assignments at Boston's Museum of Fine Arts, computerized experiments, and presentations by visiting scholars. Recent offerings include Shapers of the 17th Century, Imagining Mars, Melancholia, and the History of Eugenics. Honors students are also required to study math and foreign language and must meet a higher standard in these fields than students in general.

The emphasis at the advanced levels of the four-year program falls on independent projects and research. All honors students take a semester of Junior Colloquium, a unique course in the college that attempts to socialize them to the role of the researcher. Under a faculty leader and with the assistance of visiting scholars, the group explores a common topic while each student defines an individual research project. Recent topics include Media and Cultural Change, Green Chemistry, Imagined Selves, and Humor: Its Many Meanings. All program students are required to complete a senior-year thesis or project. Honors students are also urged to participate in the annual Conference on Undergraduate Research of the Massachusetts Public Higher Education System and in the National Conference on Undergraduate Research.

Since 1999, honors students have won three Fulbright fellowships and one Marshall Scholarship; 1 student has qualified as a semifinalist for the Rhodes Scholarship.

Honors students enjoy priority registration and a study area and seminar room that are equipped with computers and printers. New students are welcomed at special events: an Honors Orientation in the fall, which centers on an Outward Bound experience, and a Family Night in the spring, which features a lecture by a faculty member.

The 25-year-old program currently enrolls 200 students.

Participation Requirements: A student who takes the full program completes 21 credits in honors sections, in addition to the requirements in math and language and the senior thesis. Transfer students and late-admitted students take a modified version of the program. Enrollment in honors classes is limited to 20 students; the Junior Colloquium is limited to 12. Students in the program must maintain a minimum 3.2 GPA. The program awards the Robert H. Spaethling Prize to the 1 or 2 seniors who have outstanding academic records. Successful completion of the entire program is recognized at the spring honors convocations and is recorded on the student's transcript.

Admission Process: Freshmen and new transfer students for fall term are selected mainly during the summer orientation periods. For spring term, these students are selected during the January orientation periods. Continuing students are selected during preregistration periods in November and April. The program chooses students according to ability, motivation, and excellence of preparation, as evidenced by high school and college records, test scores, and special accomplishments. A personal statement and an interview with the Director are required.

Scholarship Availability: For freshmen, admission to the Honors Program is often accompanied by a Chancellor's Scholarship, which covers tuition and fees, or a tuition-only scholarship. In addition, the campus offers thirty Chancellor's Scholarships and four Commonwealth Scholarships to incoming students each year; many of these full-tuition grants are awarded to members of the Honors Program. Continuing students with 30 graduation credits may apply for a variety of merit scholarships.

Campus Overview

State-supported university, founded 1964, part of University of Massachusetts • **Coed** 8,832 undergraduate students, 62% full-time, 57% women, 43% men.

Undergraduates 5,502 full-time, 3,330 part-time. Students come from 35 states and territories, 64 other countries, 5% are from out of state, 15% African American, 12% Asian American or Pacific Islander, 6% Hispanic American, 0.4% Native American, 4% international, 14% transferred in.

Faculty *Total:* 821, 53% full-time, 66% with terminal degrees. *Student/faculty ratio:* 19:1.

Academic Programs *Special study options:* academic remediation for entering students, accelerated degree program, adult/continuing education programs, advanced placement credit, cooperative education, distance learning, double majors, English as a second language, freshman honors college, honors programs, independent study, internships, off-campus study, part-time degree program, services for LD students, student-designed majors, study abroad, summer session for credit. *Unusual degree programs:* 3-2 engineering with University of Massachusetts Lowell, University of Massachusetts Amherst, Northeastern University.

Athletics Member NCAA. All Division III. *Intercollegiate sports:* baseball M, basketball M/W, cross-country running M/W, ice hockey M, lacrosse M, soccer M/W, softball W, tennis M/W, track and field M/W, volleyball W. *Intramural sports:* basketball M/W, ice hockey M, racquetball M/W, sailing M/W, soccer M/W, softball M/W, squash M/W, swimming and diving M/W, tennis M/W, volleyball M/W, weight lifting M/W.

Costs (2004–05) *Tuition:* $72 per credit hour part-time; state resident $8034 full-time, $107 per credit hour part-time; nonresident $18,767 full-time, $407 per credit hour part-time. Full-time tuition and fees vary according to class time, course load, program, reciprocity agreements, and student level. Part-time tuition and fees vary according to class time, course load, program, reciprocity agreements, and student level. *Required fees:* $263 per credit hour part-time.

Financial Aid In 2003, 29 non-need-based awards were made. *Average percent of need met:* 89%. *Average financial aid package:* $8292. *Average need-based loan:* $3274. *Average need-based gift aid:* $5145. *Average non-need-based aid:* $2588.

Contact: Director: Dr. Rajini Srikanth, Campus Center, 100 Morrissey Boulevard, Boston, Massachusetts 02125-3393; *Telephone:* 617-287-5520; *Fax:* 617-287-3858; *E-mail:* rajini.srikanth@umb.edu

University of Massachusetts Dartmouth
University Honors Program
North Dartmouth, Massachusetts

*T*he University Honors Program reflects the goals of an institution that places emphasis on the quality of its undergraduate teaching, dedicates itself to cultivating excellence across the board, and aspires to make enrichment opportunities available to all its students. It does so by offering opportunities for outstanding and highly motivated students to participate in challenging courses and programs. It promotes close interactions between talented faculty members and students in all disciplines, encourages and supports student growth and development through independent and collaborative thinking and research, fosters a public conscience and service, and provides the support and atmosphere for full development of student potential.

Limited-enrollment honors courses encourage active student participation in learning and close faculty-student interaction. These courses offer enrichment features, such as distance learning settings that allow interaction among students on different campuses, access to specially designed information sources and databases, individualized lab experiments, field trips, attendance at performances and social events, and research support. Committed faculty members in a variety of fields also foster honors students' growth by agreeing to sponsor honors contracts, student research, creative and public service projects, and participation in professional conferences and by encouraging students to seek challenges within their majors (such as undergraduate TA programs, scholarships, and summer research opportunities). Honors credit is also available for study abroad and independent research and public service projects.

In addition to a core academic program, the program sponsors a colloquium series and the Margaret Mullaney Panos honors essay contest, an annual honors convocation, and honors undergraduate research grants. Honors students enjoy priority registration, field trips, special library privileges during the senior thesis/project year, and public recognition. The Honors Program offers housing in the Honors Residence area, where the program maintains an office. The University of Massachusetts Dartmouth (UMD) program participates in an annual statewide undergraduate research conference that is sponsored by the Massachusetts public system of higher education and the Commonwealth College at the University of Massachusetts Amherst.

The program is 20 years old and currently enrolls approximately 300 students.

Participation Requirements: The four-year academic honors program requires completion of 30 credits in honors courses. In fulfilling program requirements, students may combine honors courses and contracts with credits from special honors semesters, summer programs, and study abroad. Courses taken outside the major (12–15 credits) generally fulfill distribution and/or general education requirements. Among their honors credits, students must complete a multidisciplinary research seminar and a 3- to 6-credit capstone project (a thesis or a creative or public service project). A GPA of at least 3.2 is required for continuation in the program; successful completion is recognized at the annual University-wide Honors Convocation, at Commencement, and on the official transcript and diploma.

Admission Process: Entering first-year students receive invitations to join the program based on high school grades and rank and performance on standardized tests (SAT I). Recommendations of high school teachers and guidance counselors are also considered. Both UMD students and transfer students with a GPA of 3.2 or higher are accepted into the program as long as they have a reasonable possibility of completing it. Honors credits earned at other schools in the Massachusetts system of public higher education and from other four-year institutions are accepted in fulfillment of program requirements as appropriate.

Scholarship Availability: Recipients of UMass System Commonwealth Scholarships are expected to participate in the honors programs on their respective campuses. These scholarships are awarded to entering freshmen who have a combined SAT I score of at least 1400 and a top 5 percent ranking in their high school graduating classes (or a high school GPA of at least 3.85). As many as eight of these scholarships have been awarded to members of an entering class at UMass Dartmouth. Many University Scholarship winners and recipients of Chancellor's Merit Scholarships receive invitations and participate in the University Honors Program. The Director sits on the University's Merit Scholarship Committee, which awards merit scholarships to upperclass students.

Campus Overview

State-supported university, founded 1895, part of University of Massachusetts • **Coed** 7,290 undergraduate students, 84% full-time, 52% women, 48% men.

Undergraduates 6,151 full-time, 1,139 part-time. Students come from 29 states and territories, 29 other countries, 5% are from out of state, 6% African American, 3% Asian American or Pacific Islander, 2% Hispanic American, 0.5% Native American, 0.7% international, 7% transferred in, 48% live on campus.

Faculty *Total:* 543, 63% full-time. *Student/faculty ratio:* 17:1.

Academic Programs *Special study options:* academic remediation for entering students, adult/continuing education programs, advanced placement credit, cooperative education, distance learning, double majors, honors programs, independent study, internships, off-campus study, part-time degree program, services for LD students, student-designed majors, study abroad, summer session for credit. *ROTC:* Army (c). *Unusual degree programs:* 3-2 chemistry.

Athletics Member NCAA. All Division III. *Intercollegiate sports:* baseball M, basketball M/W, cheerleading W, cross-country running M/W, equestrian sports M(c)/W(c), field hockey W, football M, golf M/W, ice hockey M, lacrosse M/W, soccer M/W, softball W, swimming and diving M/W, tennis M/W, track and field M/W, volleyball W. *Intramural sports:* badminton M/W, basketball M/W, sailing M/W, soccer M/W, softball M/W, table tennis M/W, tennis M/W, ultimate Frisbee M/W, volleyball M/W.

Costs (2004–05) *Tuition:* state resident $1417 full-time, $59 per credit part-time; nonresident $10,917 full-time, $455 per credit part-time. Full-time tuition and fees vary according to reciprocity agreements. Part-time tuition and fees vary according to course load and reciprocity agreements. *Required fees:* $6385 full-time, $266 per credit part-time. *Room and board:* $7471; room only: $4297. Room and board charges vary according to board plan and housing facility.

Financial Aid 718 Federal Work-Study jobs (averaging $1072). 950 state and other part-time jobs (averaging $2842). In 2003, 241 non-need-based awards were made. *Average percent of need met:* 86%. *Average financial aid package:* $7604. *Average need-based loan:* $3800. *Average need-based gift aid:* $4410. *Average non-need-based aid:* $2323.

Contact: Director: Dr. Janet E. Gardner, 285 Old Westport Road, North Dartmouth, Massachusetts 02747; *Telephone:* 508-999-9189 or 999-8820; *Fax:* 508-999-9235; *E-mail:* jgardner@umassd.edu; *Web site:* http://www.umassd.edu/specialprograms/honors/

University of Massachusetts Lowell

Honors Program

Lowell, Massachusetts

The University of Massachusetts Lowell Honors Program is a University-wide, comprehensive enrichment program of undergraduate studies, including research as a basic component, for outstanding students in all majors. Although departmental honors programs have existed since the start of the 1970s, the consolidation into a full-fledged University Honors Program (which still allows purely departmental honors projects) was undertaken in 1995 with the establishment of a 24-member Honors Council under the aegis of the Provost.

The mission of the Honors Program is "to provide enriched academic opportunities to meet the educational needs of exceptionally talented students and to foster the pursuit of scholarly excellence in undergraduate higher education. By fostering interactions among outstanding, motivated students and outstanding, dedicated faculty, the Honors Program is directed toward the recruitment, development, guidance, retention and professional growth of gifted students in activities designed to enhance their critical, cognitive and creative potential."

Normally, all freshman honors students are placed in special sections of the College Writing two-semester course taught by the English department, and all sophomore honors students are enrolled in the two-semester Honors Colloquium conducted by the Honors Director. Over and above this, they are also free to take additional departmental courses, including core and general education courses, for honors credit as either designated honors courses or "Contract Honors" courses. Many of these are given in seminar format; thus honors students enjoy the benefits of small class size and individualized attention. Any student who attains a GPA of at least 3.5 after the first semester is eligible for initiation into the Freshman Honors Society, the Lowell Chapter of Alpha Lambda Delta.

In general, the program emphasizes personalized advising and guidance, encourages students to use the excellent library and multimedia facilities, and offers a wide range of special services, including an honors residence accommodation for students who wish to live on campus. For all participants, field trips, distinguished guest speakers, cultural events, and undergraduate research opportunities are central features of the honors experience. Trips, conferences, receptions, and informal pizza parties promote close contact with honors faculty members and with the Honors Council.

Among the students, there is a strong sense of community; study groups and peer counseling are encouraged as elements of daily life in the "Honors family." Honors students feature prominently in community service projects and are often approached specifically by local employers or institutions as exemplifying the best of the University's undergraduate scholar resources.

Participation Requirements: Students enrolled in the Honors Program in must complete at least 18 honors credits. All Honors Program credits must be completed with a grade of B or better. At least 3 of the total required credits must be obtained from satisfactory completion of an honors thesis or project entailing original research or scholarly activity. This is normally undertaken in one or both semesters of the senior year.

All students' academic transcripts show the honors courses taken by that student for honors credits, regardless of whether the above requirements have been met. Students who graduate with a cumulative GPA of at least 3.25 and the requisite number of honors credits will, in addition to the conventional baccalaureate degree (which may be awarded, where appropriate, at the cum laude, magna cum laude, or summa cum laude level) in their major discipline, have an Honors Diploma conferred upon them at Commencement.

Admission Process: To be eligible for admission to the Honors Program, applicants must have achieved a score of at least 1200 combined on the SAT I scale or at least 26 on the ACT; and have met one of the following: graduated in the top 10 percent of their high school class or have a recalculated GPA of 3.25 or better. Transfer students must have an overall cumulative GPA of at least 3.25 from an acceptable accredited academic institution of higher learning.

Scholarship Availability: Membership in the Honors Program does not entail any additional fees. On the contrary, many of the available Commonwealth of Massachusetts or University scholarships (as well as those from business, industry, and private donations) are awarded to Honors scholars.

Campus Overview

State-supported university, founded 1894, part of University of Massachusetts • **Coed** 8,662 undergraduate students, 67% full-time, 40% women, 60% men.

Undergraduates 5,805 full-time, 2,857 part-time. Students come from 30 states and territories, 12 other countries, 10% are from out of state, 4% African American, 8% Asian American or Pacific Islander, 5% Hispanic American, 0.3% Native American, 2% international, 9% transferred in, 40% live on campus.

Faculty Total: 361. Student/faculty ratio: 15:1.

Academic Programs Special study options: accelerated degree program, adult/continuing education programs, advanced placement credit, cooperative education, distance learning, double majors, honors programs, internships, off-campus study, part-time degree program, services for LD students, study abroad, summer session for credit. ROTC: Air Force (b). Unusual degree programs: 3-2 psychology, radiological science, mathematics, clinical laboratory science, biological science.

Athletics Member NCAA. All Division II except ice hockey (Division I). Intercollegiate sports: basketball M(s)/W(s), crew M/W, cross-country running M(s)/W(s), field hockey W(s), football M, golf M, ice hockey M(s), soccer M, swimming and diving M(s), tennis M(s)/W(s), track and field M(s)/W(s), volleyball W(s), wrestling M(s). Intramural sports: badminton M/W, basketball M/W, bowling M/W, golf M/W, ice hockey M/W, racquetball M/W, soccer M/W, squash M/W, table tennis M/W, tennis M/W, volleyball M/W, water polo M/W.

Costs (2004–05) Tuition: state resident $1454 full-time, $61 per credit part-time; nonresident $8567 full-time, $357 per credit part-time. Full-time required fee for out of state students: $8084. Required fees: $6437 full-time, $280 per credit part-time. Room and board: $6011; room only: $3567. Room and board charges vary according to board plan and housing facility.

Financial Aid 159 Federal Work-Study jobs (averaging $2801). 582 state and other part-time jobs (averaging $3092). In 2003, 253 non-need-based awards were made. Average percent of need met: 96%. Average financial aid package: $8084. Average need-based loan: $3258. Average need-based gift aid: $3922. Average non-need-based aid: $3473.

Contact: Director: Dr. Noëlle McAfee, University of Massachusetts Lowell, 1 University Avenue, Lowell, Massachusetts 01854-2881; Telephone: 978-934-2798; Web site: http://www.uml.edu/honors

Worcester State College

Commonwealth Honors Program at Worcester State College

Worcester, Massachusetts

The mission of the Commonwealth Honors Program at Worcester State College is to offer all qualified students an outstanding undergraduate experience through courses that emphasize innovative pedagogy and the values of liberal learning. Honors classes are small (often fewer than 20 students) and are designed to encourage active and lifelong learning. Small classes and extracurricular programs provide honors students with greater interaction between their peers and a select core of dedicated faculty members. In addition to stimulating classes, honors students also enjoy campus speakers, field trips to cultural centers, occasional luncheons with faculty members, and an annual dinner with the college president. Founded in 1996, the program currently enrolls 150 students and recently earned accreditation as a Commonwealth Honors Program from the Massachusetts Board of Higher Education.

Participation Requirements: The core program requires completion of seven honors courses (21 credits) normally taken during the student's freshman and sophomore years (or two courses per semester). Each course is designed to help fulfill the College's general education requirements and must be passed with a grade of B or better. Students cannot take an honors class on a pass/fail basis. Students can elect to become a Commonwealth Honors Scholar once they fulfill the core requirements of the college-wide program, maintain a minimum GPA of 3.2, and complete a 3-credit capstone course in the junior or senior year. Special accommodations can be made for transfer students and others who have difficulty coordinating Honors Program requirements with those of their academic major.

Admission Process: Students are invited to join the Honors Program in one of two ways. The Office of Admissions selects an initial group of roughly 50 students for each fall term based on a series of indicators (primarily SAT scores and high school GPA) that predict a high likelihood of academic success at the College. A second group is selected at the completion of the fall term based on academic performance while at the College. Students interested in becoming an honors student should contact the admissions office directly.

Scholarship Availability: The College awards approximately fifty scholarships for each incoming class of honors students. Scholarships are intended to support a student for four years and must be maintained with a minimum GPA that varies for each type of award.

Campus Overview

State-supported comprehensive, founded 1874, part of Massachusetts Public Higher Education System • **Coed** 4,554 undergraduate students, 68% full-time, 60% women, 40% men.

Undergraduates 3,109 full-time, 1,445 part-time. Students come from 18 states and territories, 46 other countries, 2% are from out of state, 3% African American, 3% Asian American or Pacific Islander, 3% Hispanic American, 0.3% Native American, 5% international, 10% transferred in, 35% live on campus.

Faculty Total: 270, 63% full-time. Student/faculty ratio: 18:1.

Academic Programs Special study options: accelerated degree program, adult/continuing education programs, advanced placement credit, double majors, honors programs, independent study, internships, off-campus study, part-time degree program, study abroad, summer session for credit. ROTC: Army (c), Navy (c), Air Force (c).

Athletics Member NCAA, NAIA. All NCAA Division III. Intercollegiate sports: baseball M, basketball M/W, cheerleading M/W, crew M(c)/W(c), cross-country running M/W, equestrian sports M(c)/W(c), field hockey W, football M, golf M, ice hockey M, lacrosse W, soccer M/W, softball W, tennis M/W, track and field M/W, volleyball M/W.

Intramural sports: baseball M, basketball M/W, cheerleading M/W, crew M/W, cross-country running M/W, field hockey W, football M, golf M, ice hockey M, lacrosse W, soccer M/W, softball W, tennis M/W, track and field M/W, volleyball M/W.

Costs (2004–05) Tuition: state resident $970 full-time, $40 per credit part-time; nonresident $7050 full-time, $294 per credit part-time. Full-time tuition and fees vary according to class time, course load, and reciprocity agreements. Part-time tuition and fees vary according to class time, course load, and reciprocity agreements. Required fees: $3609 full-time, $146 per credit part-time. Room and board: $6896; room only: $4596. Room and board charges vary according to board plan and housing facility.

Financial Aid In 2003, 40 non-need-based awards were made. Average percent of need met: 79%. Average financial aid package: $6868. Average need-based loan: $1532. Average need-based gift aid: $1836. Average non-need-based aid: $1541.

Contact: Director: Dr. Lisa Boehm, Commonwealth Honors Program, Worcester State College, 486 Chandler Street, Worcester, Massachusetts 01602; Telephone: 508-929-8669; E-mail: lboehm@worcester.edu; Web site: http://wwwfac.worcester.edu/honors/

MICHIGAN

Albion College

Prentiss M. Brown Honors Institute

Albion, Michigan

The Albion College Prentiss M. Brown Honors Institute has been designed to provide an exciting and distinctive variety of academic experiences for highly motivated and talented students. The Institute's mix of discussion-oriented classes, field trips, independent research, and personal attention provides honors students with special challenges and opportunities for growth.

Most students join the Honors Institute right out of high school, although later admission is also possible. Students admitted to the program are high achievers who also possess broad intellectual interests and a strong desire to begin the exciting and challenging process of developing their own independent thinking and research skills.

In each semester of their first two years, honors students take a specially designed, interdisciplinary class. Class size is limited to 15 students, and each seminar emphasizes independent reading, open discussion, and extensive writing. Further, each honors seminar counts toward the College's general education requirements. First- and second-year honors students are also eligible to become Student Research Partners, which allows them to participate in research with an Albion faculty member from the moment they arrive on campus.

In their junior year, honors students begin their own original research or creative project, which culminates in the writing of an honors thesis. Normally, the process starts with participation in a thesis development workshop designed to help students identify a thesis topic, select an adviser, and begin their preliminary research. Research and writing then continue under the close supervision of a faculty thesis adviser, and the thesis is completed during the student's senior year. The Jenkins Prize, awarded at Albion's annual Honors Convocation, recognizes the best senior theses. Albion also provides extensive support for student research and creative projects through its Foundation for Undergraduate Research, Scholarship and Creative Activity (FURSCA). FURSCA helps pay for such things as student research expenses, student travel to specialized libraries and to present their research results at scholarly meetings, and student summer research on campus.

The Prentiss M. Brown Honors Institute occupies the recently renovated Honors Center, located in Old Observatory in the heart of the campus. The center has wireless network access and contains a *seminar room for honors classes, a study lounge with computers, a thesis library, and social space. Honors students have access to this facility on a 24-hours-a-day basis. Honors students also have unique opportunities to meet in small groups with distinguished speakers when they come to the campus, informally socialize with the honors instructors and students, attend an overnight retreat, and go on field trips to concerts, plays, and museums.*

The Prentiss M. Brown Honors Honors Institute, which has been in existence for more than twenty-five years, has been expanding its program in recent years. Currently, it admits approximately 80 first-year students each year and has an overall enrollment of about 270 students.

Participation Requirements: Once admitted to the Honors Institute, students complete four specially designed interdisciplinary seminars drawn from the four divisions of the College during their first two years. These classes count toward the College's general education requirements. As juniors, honors students begin an original research or creative project for their honors thesis under the close supervision of their thesis adviser. These projects are completed no later than April 1 of the student's senior year. To graduate with Albion College honors, students must have at least a 3.5 cumulative GPA. Successful completion of the program is recognized at commencement and is also noted on the student's official transcript and diploma.

Admission Process: High school students are recruited on the basis of their high school average, ACT or SAT I scores, an application and an essay, and a personal interview. Most students apply for admission to the Honors Institute during their senior year of high school. The deadline for application is March 1. A limited number of additional students who miss the March 1 deadline are admitted to the Institute at the end of their first or second semester at Albion.

Scholarship Availability: Academic scholarships of various amounts are awarded through the Office of Admissions based on high school academic performance and leadership and service activities. Scholarships are not offered through the Honors Institute. Last year, all incoming honors students were recipients of academic scholarships.

Campus Overview

Independent Methodist 4-year, founded 1835 • **Coed** 1,867 undergraduate students, 99% full-time, 55% women, 45% men.

Undergraduates 1,852 full-time, 15 part-time. Students come from 32 states and territories, 19 other countries, 9% are from out of state, 4% African American, 2% Asian American or Pacific Islander, 1% Hispanic American, 0.4% Native American, 1% international, 2% transferred in, 93% live on campus.

Faculty *Total:* 169, 78% full-time, 76% with terminal degrees. *Student/faculty ratio:* 13:1.

Academic Programs *Special study options:* advanced placement credit, double majors, honors programs, independent study, internships, off-campus study, part-time degree program, services for LD students, student-designed majors, study abroad, summer session for credit. *Unusual degree programs:* 3-2 engineering with Columbia University, University of Michigan, Case Western Reserve University, Michigan Technological University, Washington University in St. Louis; forestry with Duke University, Washington University in St. Louis; nursing with Case Western Reserve University; public policy studies with University of Michigan, fine arts with Bank Street College of Education.

Athletics Member NCAA. All Division III. *Intercollegiate sports:* baseball M, basketball M/W, cheerleading M/W, cross-country running M/W, football M, golf M/W, soccer M/W, softball W, swimming and diving M/W, tennis M/W, track and field M/W, volleyball M(c)/W. *Intramural sports:* badminton M/W, basketball M/W, bowling M/W, equestrian sports M/W, field hockey W, football M, golf M/W, ice hockey M(c), lacrosse M/W, rugby M(c)/W(c), sailing M(c)/W(c), soccer M/W, softball M/W, swimming and diving M/W, table tennis M/W, tennis M/W, track and field M/W, volleyball M/W, water polo M(c)/W(c).

Costs (2004–05) *Comprehensive fee:* $29,454 includes full-time tuition ($22,650), mandatory fees ($268), and room and board ($6536). Part-time tuition: $962 per quarter hour. *College room only:* $3196. Room and board charges vary according to housing facility.

Financial Aid 542 Federal Work-Study jobs (averaging $1265). In 2003, 638 non-need-based awards were made. *Average percent of need met:* 95%. *Average financial aid package:* $19,544. *Average need-based loan:* $4462. *Average need-based gift aid:* $15,512. *Average non-need-based aid:* $10,462.

Contact: Honors Director, Albion College, KC #4762, Albion, Michigan 49224-5011; *Telephone:* 517-629-0614; *Fax:* 517-629-0659; *E-mail:* honors@albion.edu; *Web site:* http://www.albion.edu/honors

Calvin College
Honors Program
Grand Rapids, Michigan

The Calvin College Honors Program, first introduced in 1969 and greatly expanded since 1993, is a four-year program of special courses and opportunities intended to help students of outstanding academic ability and motivation develop their gifts so that they will be equipped for leadership in service to God, their communities, and the world at large.

The curriculum of Calvin's Honors Program annually includes special sections of ten to fifteen core courses, which are generally taken in the students' first two years at Calvin. In these honors courses, students are encouraged to develop greater than average initiative and independent study skills while working in greater than usual depth and closer collaboration with their professors. At the junior and senior levels, honors work is generally done by contract in each student's major discipline. Honors students receive special advising, orientation, and assistance in scheduling their classes; may contract to take regular courses for honors credit; are offered special opportunities for research and subsidies for participating in academic conferences; and they are invited to various cocurricular activities for honors students, including the McGregor Sophomore Scholars Program.

In recent years, approximately 500 students (about 12 percent of the student body) have been involved in the program annually, along with about 20 faculty members in eleven disciplines.

Participation Requirements: To remain in the Honors Program, students must maintain a GPA of at least 3.5 and take at least one honors course per year. To graduate with honors from Calvin College, students must complete at least six honors courses overall (at least two of these in their major), maintain a GPA of at least 3.5, and fulfill any other departmental requirements for honors in their major discipline, which generally means at least a senior-level research project and a thesis or public presentation. Honors graduates are presented with commemorative medallions at the annual Honors Convocation, and they wear their awards at Commencement. Their achievement is also noted on their transcript and diploma.

Admission Process: Calvin's Honors Program is open to students of all majors and class levels. Incoming students are invited to participate in the Honors Program if they have an ACT composite score of 29 or higher or an SAT I combined score of 1290 or higher.

Scholarship Availability: Virtually all of Calvin's honors students receive merit-based scholarships awarded by the College for academic performance in the highest 15–20 percent of their cohorts. While participation in the Honors Program is not a condition for these awards, a high percentage of the top scholarship groups are active in honors work.

Campus Overview

Independent comprehensive, founded 1876, affiliated with Christian Reformed Church • **Coed** 4,127 undergraduate students, 96% full-time, 54% women, 46% men.

Undergraduates 3,952 full-time, 175 part-time. Students come from 50 states and territories, 45 other countries, 39% are from out of state, 1% African American, 3% Asian American or Pacific Islander, 1% Hispanic American, 0.3% Native American, 8% international, 2% transferred in, 56% live on campus.

Faculty *Total:* 397, 77% full-time, 67% with terminal degrees. *Student/faculty ratio:* 12:1.

Academic Programs *Special study options:* academic remediation for entering students, accelerated degree program, adult/continuing education programs, advanced placement credit, double majors, honors programs, independent study, internships, off-campus study, part-time degree program, services for LD students, student-designed majors, study abroad, summer session for credit. *ROTC:* Army (c). *Unusual degree programs:* 3-2 occupational therapy with Washington University in St. Louis.

Athletics Member NCAA. All Division III. *Intercollegiate sports:* baseball M, basketball M/W, cross-country running M/W, golf M/W, ice hockey M(c), lacrosse M(c)/W(c), soccer M/W, softball W, swimming and diving M/W, tennis M/W, track and field M/W, volleyball W. *Intramural sports:* badminton M/W, basketball M/W, cross-country running M/W, football M/W, golf M/W, racquetball M/W, soccer M/W, softball M/W, swimming and diving M/W, tennis M/W, track and field M/W, volleyball M/W, water polo M/W.

Costs (2004–05) *Comprehensive fee:* $23,955 includes full-time tuition ($17,770) and room and board ($6185). Full-time tuition and fees vary according to program. Part-time tuition: $430 per credit hour. Part-time tuition and fees vary according to course load. *College room only:* $3360. Room and board charges vary according to board plan.

Financial Aid 660 Federal Work-Study jobs (averaging $1140). 1,250 state and other part-time jobs (averaging $1150). In 2003, 1061 non-need-based awards were made. *Average percent of need met:* 84%. *Average financial aid package:* $12,963. *Average need-based loan:* $6283. *Average need-based gift aid:* $7500. *Average non-need-based aid:* $3304.

Contact: Director: Dr. Kenneth Bratt, 365 Hiemenga Hall, 3201 Burton SE, Grand Rapids, Michigan 49546; *Telephone:* 616-526-6296; *Fax:* 616-526-8505; *E-mail:* kbratt@calvin.edu; *Web site:* http://www.calvin.edu/academic/honors

---

Central Michigan University
University Honors Program
Mt. Pleasant, Michigan

Graduates of the Central Michigan University (CMU) Honors Program are found in every walk of professional life. Since its founding in 1961, the program has produced a growing community of leaders who serve in important positions around the state and country.

The CMU honors program promotes development of the important skills of inquiry, analysis, synthesis, and critical evaluation. Honors students are encouraged to reach beyond the classroom into the realm of research, self-direction, creative innovation, and discovery.

Honors professors provide broad yet personalized instruction in the classroom and act as advisers for students' individualized study and research projects.

The Honors Program offers many benefits, including small classes with enrollment limited to 20 students; University Program (general education) honors course selections each semester; eligibility to reside in a designated honors residence community in either Larzelere or Trout Hall; one-on-one faculty-student research project opportunities; a four-year academic planning document; priority registration; access to specialized academic counseling and mentoring by honors program staff members; recognition as an honors program graduate on the official transcript; membership and involvement in the Honors Outreach Network (HON), the student organization for honors program members; involvement in honors activities such as an annual trip to Stratford, Ontario, for the Shakespeare Festival; an annual honors program talent show; and the annual Claude S. Larzelere Trivia Challenge.

Participation Requirements: Honors program requirements are specified in the honors protocol and include 18 credit hours of honors course work, one year of a single foreign language taken at the university level or an approved alternative, completion of 120 hours of community/volunteer service per year, and completion of a senior research project or creative endeavor approved by the Honors Program Director. Note: Protocol is subject to change.

Admission Process: Any incoming freshman with a cumulative high school GPA of 3.6 or higher and an ACT composite score of 25 or higher is invited to apply to the Central Michigan University Honors Program. A graded writing sample must also accompany the honors application. Current CMU undergraduate students and transfer students who have earned a cumulative GPA of 3.5 or higher are also invited to apply. To remain active and graduate from the Honors Program, students must fulfill all protocol requirements and maintain a minimum cumulative GPA of 3.25.

Scholarship Availability: At least forty Centralis Scholarships are awarded each year to high school seniors who have been accepted for admission to Central Michigan University. The Centralis Scholar Award covers the full cost of tuition, fees, room, and board and provides $500 for general expenses. The award pays for up to 36 credit hours per academic year, including summer sessions. The 2005–06 value for four years is $52,000, or $13,000 per academic year. At least twenty of these scholarships are awarded annually. The Centralis Gold Award covers the full cost of tuition, up to 36 credit hours per academic year, including summer sessions. The 2005–06 value for four years is $22,126, or $5531 per academic year. At least twenty of these scholarships are awarded each year. Students are invited to compete for the Centralis Scholarship in the fall of their senior year, provided they have at least a 3.5 cumulative high school GPA. Scholarship information may be obtained by calling 989-774-3076 or 888-292-5366 (toll-free).

In addition to the Centralis Scholarship, honors students with 56 credit hours or more are eligible to compete for an annual $500 scholarship sponsored by the CMU Honors Alumni Board. The scholarship is based on academic achievement in college, community service, and extracurricular accomplishments.

Campus Overview

State-supported university, founded 1892 • **Coed** 19,916 undergraduate students, 88% full-time, 58% women, 42% men.

Undergraduates 17,500 full-time, 2,416 part-time. Students come from 42 states and territories, 39 other countries, 2% are from out of state, 6% African American, 1% Asian American or Pacific Islander, 2% Hispanic American, 0.8% Native American, 0.8% international, 6% transferred in, 35% live on campus.

Faculty *Total:* 1,062, 65% full-time, 62% with terminal degrees. *Student/faculty ratio:* 22:1.

Academic Programs *Special study options:* academic remediation for entering students, accelerated degree program, adult/continuing education programs, advanced placement credit, distance learning, double majors, English as a second language, external degree program, freshman honors college, honors programs, independent study, internships, part-time degree program, student-designed majors, study abroad, summer session for credit. *ROTC:* Army (b).

Athletics Member NCAA. All Division I except football (Division I-A). *Intercollegiate sports:* baseball M(s), basketball M(s)/W(s),

cross-country running M(s)/W(s), field hockey W(s), gymnastics W(s), soccer W(s), softball W(s), track and field M(s)/W(s), volleyball W(s), wrestling M(s). *Intramural sports:* baseball M(c), basketball M/W, bowling M/W, cross-country running M/W, football M/W, golf M/W, ice hockey M(c), lacrosse M(c)/W(c), racquetball M/W, rock climbing M(c)/W(c), rugby M(c)/W(c), skiing (downhill) M(c)/W(c), soccer M/W, softball M/W, table tennis M/W, tennis M/W, track and field M(c)/W(c), ultimate Frisbee M(c)/W(c), volleyball M(c)/W(c), wrestling M.

Costs (2004–05) *Tuition:* state resident $4610 full-time, $154 per credit part-time; nonresident $11,712 full-time, $390 per credit part-time. *Required fees:* $755 full-time, $213 per term part-time. *Room and board:* $6160; room only: $3080. Room and board charges vary according to board plan, housing facility, and location.

Financial Aid 939 Federal Work-Study jobs (averaging $1841). 3,659 state and other part-time jobs (averaging $1854). In 2004, 1962 non-need-based awards were made. *Average percent of need met:* 90%. *Average financial aid package:* $8404. *Average need-based loan:* $4520. *Average need-based gift aid:* $3097. *Average non-need-based aid:* $2620.

Contact: Contact: Director: James P. Hill, University Honors Program, Central Michigan University, 112 Larzelere Hall, Mt. Pleasant, Michigan 48858; *Telephone:* 989-774-3902; *Fax:* 989-774-2335; *E-mail:* hill1jp@cmich.edu; *Web site:* http://www.cmich.edu/honors

Delta College
Honors Program
University Center, Michigan

*T**he Honors Program at Delta College seeks to provide challenging learning opportunities for highly motivated and academically skilled students. The program offers students an opportunity to enhance and enrich their college learning experience. Delta College's specially designed interactive honors courses emphasize creative and critical thinking, which provides a unique experience. The curriculum of the Delta College Honors Program includes fifteen to eighteen honors courses, which range from a variety of divisions. These are general education courses, which usually transfer to other two- or four-year colleges. Students may contract to take regular courses for honors credit through the Honors Option. Some special features of Delta's honors courses include service learning, learning communities, and Internet courses.*

Many students in Delta College Honors Program show leadership within the College and the community. Once a year, the Honors Program recognizes the significant leadership of one student by awarding the Caroline Gruenberg Wirtz Honors Leadership Award. The recipient's name is added to the Wirtz Leadership plaque that is displayed in the Honors Office, and he or she receives a plaque and a cash prize.

Delta's Honors Program was founded in 1987. In the last couple of years, the total number of students enrolled in honors courses has been 230 to 275 students per semester. The Honors Program consists of 20 honors faculty members.

Participation Requirements: Delta's Honors Program is a highly flexible program, and students can participate as much or as little as they like.

To receive an Honors Program Certificate, students are required to complete 12 honors credits, including the Honors Colloquy, with a minimum cumulative GPA of 3.2 and a grade of C or higher in each honors course and Honors Option course. The President's Award for Excellence in Honors is awarded to students who have completed 18 honors credits, including Honors Colloquy, with a minimum cumulative GPA of 3.3, a grade of C or higher in each honors course

and Honors Option course, and a specific learning experience. The Honors Program Certificate and the President's Award for Excellence in Honors are noted on the student's transcript. Students who achieve one or both of these awards are recognized for their academic achievement at the annual Honors Program ceremony held in April.

Admission Process: Eligibility factors include the following: COMPASS Writing Skills score of at least 93 and Reading Skills score of at least 81 or Reading Skills score of at least 92 and Writing Skills score of at least 70; ACT Writing score of 25 or higher; minimum high school GPA of 3.5; top 10 percent of high school graduating class; and 12 Delta College credits, with an overall GPA of 3.2 or higher. Provisional Status may be granted to students who do not meet the eligibility factors but exhibit academic and leadership potential.

Students are required to fill out an Honors Program application, along with a one-to-two-page, typed personal statement.

Scholarship Availability: The Honors Program awards Program Scholarships to several students each year. These are merit scholarships; no financial need is required. Applications are available in February. In addition, there are opportunities for other scholarships available to Honors Program students.

Campus Overview

Rural 640-acre campus • **Coed,** 10,343 undergraduate students, 38% full-time, 58% women, 42% men.

Undergraduates 3,915 full-time, 6,428 part-time. Students come from 22 other countries, 7% African American, 1% Asian American or Pacific Islander, 4% Hispanic American, 0.8% Native American, 0.9% international, 4% transferred in.

Faculty *Total:* 502, 44% full-time. *Student/faculty ratio:* 21:1.

Academic Programs *Special study options:* academic remediation for entering students, adult/continuing education programs, advanced placement credit, cooperative education, distance learning, double majors, external degree program, freshman honors college, honors programs, independent study, internships, off-campus study, part-time degree program, services for LD students, student-designed majors, summer session for credit.

Athletics Member NJCAA. *Intercollegiate sports:* basketball M(s)/W(s), golf M(s), soccer M(s), softball W(s), volleyball W(s). *Intramural sports:* baseball M, basketball M/W, football M, golf M/W, racquetball M/W, soccer M/W, softball M/W, volleyball M/W.

Costs (2004–05) *Tuition:* area resident $2484 full-time, $69 per credit part-time; state resident $3564 full-time, $99 per credit part-time; nonresident $5087 full-time, $141 per credit part-time. *Required fees:* $60 full-time, $30 per term part-time.

Financial Aid 156 Federal Work-Study jobs (averaging $1640). 386 state and other part-time jobs (averaging $1722).

Contact: Director: Marie Faulk, Honors Program, Delta College, University Center, Michigan 48710; *Telephone:* 989-686-9617; *E-mail:* mfaulk@delta.edu

Eastern Michigan University
Honors College
Ypsilanti, Michigan

*S**tudents with special academic ability and ambition for excellence have the opportunity to match their talents with the high standards of the Honors College. They find the small classes, select faculty members, supportive atmosphere, and special programming that make for a distinct scholarly community in a large-campus setting. Those arriving as freshmen can qualify for general education honors. Students at upper levels, including transfers, may complete departmental honors in a specific major or minor.*

Honors students enjoy various advantages, including class sections with enrollment limited to 20 of their academic peers and specially chosen faculty members, priority registration each semester, the possibility of tailoring honors work to their goals through contracts, opportunities for research and conference attendance, excursions and other special programming, and, eventually, the distinction of an honors designation on the official record.

The honors residence hall provides a center for honors activities. It accommodates one third of the program members; furnishes space for meetings, special lectures, receptions, and some classes; and houses the Honors Office.

The program, founded in 1984, enrolls about 900 students.

Participation Requirements: First- and second-year students work on honors in general education, which requires that they complete 24 semester credit hours in honors sections. These sections have limited enrollment; professors selected are among the best in the University and are evaluated each semester. Student recommendations are often used to identify new honors faculty members. Juniors and seniors pursue honors in a major or minor, for which they need to complete 12 semester credit hours, including a 3-credit capstone thesis or project. At all levels, honors students must enroll regularly in honors sections and maintain a GPA of at least 3.3. They must also complete a total of 24 hours of community service.

Admission Process: To be eligible (with some flexibility) from high school, students need a minimum GPA of 3.5, a minimum ACT score of 25 or SAT score of 1250, and excellent recommendations. To be eligible from a community college, students need a minimum GPA of 3.3 (a minimum of 15 credit hours) and excellent recommendations; from a four-year institution, they need a minimum 3.3 GPA. Students must submit a completed application form, including a 500-word essay, transcripts, and recommendations. Applications are received on a rolling admission basis, and replies are made promptly.

Scholarship Availability: Fifteen Presidential Scholarships (tuition, fees, room, and board; eight consecutive semesters), thirty Regents' Plus Scholarships ($3600 per year, eight consecutive semesters), fifteen Regents' Scholarships ($2600 per year, eight consecutive semesters), and several hundred Recognition of Excellence Scholarships ($500) are offered to prospective freshmen based on a competition held in December. Twenty Honors Undergraduate Fellowships ($1200) are offered each semester to juniors and seniors for research/creative activity in their major or minor.

Campus Overview

State-supported comprehensive, founded 1849 • **Coed** 18,868 undergraduate students, 69% full-time, 60% women, 40% men.

Undergraduates 12,994 full-time, 5,874 part-time. Students come from 43 states and territories, 68 other countries, 6% are from out of state, 17% African American, 2% Asian American or Pacific Islander, 2% Hispanic American, 0.5% Native American, 1% international, 9% transferred in, 20% live on campus.

Faculty Total: 1,111, 66% full-time, 46% with terminal degrees. Student/faculty ratio: 20:1.

Academic Programs Special study options: academic remediation for entering students, accelerated degree program, adult/continuing education programs, advanced placement credit, cooperative education, distance learning, double majors, English as a second language, honors programs, independent study, internships, part-time degree program, services for LD students, student-designed majors, study abroad, summer session for credit. ROTC: Army (b), Navy (c), Air Force (c).

Athletics Member NCAA. All Division I except football (Division I-A). Intercollegiate sports: baseball M(s), basketball M(s)/W(s), crew W(s), cross-country running M(s)/W(s), golf M(s)/W(s), gymnastics W(s), soccer W(s), softball W(s), swimming and diving M(s)/W(s), tennis W(s), track and field M(s)/W(s), volleyball W(s), wrestling M(s). Intramural sports: badminton M/W, basketball M/W, bowling M/W, cross-country running M/W, fencing M(c)/W(c), golf

M/W, gymnastics M(c)/W(c), ice hockey M(c), lacrosse M(c)/W(c), racquetball M/W, skiing (cross-country) M/W, soccer M/W, softball M/W, swimming and diving M/W, table tennis M/W, tennis M/W, track and field M/W, ultimate Frisbee M(c)/W(c), volleyball M/W, water polo W(c), weight lifting M/W.

Costs (2004–05) Tuition: state resident $4707 full-time, $157 per credit hour part-time; nonresident $14,714 full-time, $490 per credit hour part-time. Full-time tuition and fees vary according to reciprocity agreements. Part-time tuition and fees vary according to reciprocity agreements. Required fees: $1055 full-time, $33 per credit hour part-time, $40 per term part-time. Room and board: $6082; room only: $2856. Room and board charges vary according to housing facility and location.

Financial Aid 626 Federal Work-Study jobs (averaging $1601). 170 state and other part-time jobs (averaging $1808). In 2003, 1427 non-need-based awards were made. Average percent of need met: 62%. Average financial aid package: $8207. Average need-based loan: $3826. Average need-based gift aid: $3314. Average non-need-based aid: $2050.

Contact: Director: Dr. James Knapp, Margaret E. Wise Honors Residence, Eastern Michigan University, Ypsilanti, Michigan 48197; Telephone: 734-487-0341; Fax: 734-487-0793; E-mail: emuhonors@emich.edu; Web site: http://www.emich.edu/honors/

Ferris State University
Honors Program
Big Rapids, Michigan

The Honors Program at Ferris State University provides intellectual challenges, resources, and support to the University's most able and highly motivated students, while encouraging them to serve and lead in local and global communities. To support this mission, stipends are available for national and international travel, and a strong community service component impacts this college town.

In addition to the honors classes, peer advisers, faculty mentors, symposia, study groups, and excellent residence hall computer labs support the educational process. Many of those in honors form strong ties to the honors community for their entire college career. One student remarked, "In honors you're with a group of people who all want to succeed and do their very best. You never know how it may help you. My employer was impressed that I was in honors and on the Dean's list, and that prompted him to call me and offer me an internship."

The Honors Program at Ferris State features three general education courses plus courses that provide specific support for law, medical, and dental school prospects; opportunities to do research with professors; and an orientation to an honors class in which the students attend plays, concerts, ballets, symphonies, and gallery openings, compliments of the Honors Program. The Honors Senior Symposium, held each spring for the graduating seniors, caps off the honors experience.

The honors halls offer premier living space in the heart of the campus. The upscale, carpeted private rooms with ceiling fans are wired for Internet access and voice mail. Lounges and meeting rooms in the halls are used for study sessions, student gatherings, and seminars.

Founded in 1997, the Honors Program has 500 members in eighty-six different majors. During its short history, it has produced a Bread Loaf Scholar and a Udall Scholar and won second prize in a national contest for honors newsletters.

Participation Requirements: Students are required to maintain a minimum 3.25 GPA, take 10–11 honors credits in general education classes (4 credits freshman year and 6–7 credits sophomore year), commit to 15 hours of community service per semester, attend three cultural events per semester (tickets are provided by the Honors Program), join an organization or group on campus and assume a leadership position in it by junior or senior year, and submit a poster for the Honors Senior Symposium in senior year.

Admission Process: Honors Program students are selected through a special application process. Minimum entrance requirements are a 3.4 high school GPA and 24 on the ACT. However, since the program's inception in 1997, the average high school GPA of entering honors freshmen has been 3.8, and the average ACT score has been 28.

Selection is fairly competitive, since the number of freshman places is set at 180. The factors that affect selection are three recommendation forms, ACT score, GPA, and a writing sample that is produced on campus at the Honors Invitational Competition during the last Saturday in February each year. (For those students who are unable to attend this competition due to circumstances beyond their control, other arrangements are made.)

Applications received by the priority deadline of the first Friday in February are given first consideration. After that date, applications are considered on a space-available basis until March 30. All applicants must also file the standard Ferris State University application by the February deadline.

Internal and external transfer students may also qualify for honors, but only if they have freshman or sophomore standing and apply by the February deadline. For these candidates, the criteria for selection are a minimum 3.25 college GPA and three recommendation forms.

Scholarship Availability: All students who are admitted to honors receive a $2000 Honors Residential Life Scholarship, which can only be used to defray costs of living in an honors residence hall. This scholarship is renewable for four years and can be added to other existing scholarships, with some awards totaling more than $9000 annually. Also, there are stipends awarded annually for national and international travel.

Campus Overview

State-supported comprehensive, founded 1884 • **Coed** 10,711 undergraduate students, 79% full-time, 47% women, 53% men.

Undergraduates 8,470 full-time, 2,241 part-time. Students come from 43 states and territories, 46 other countries, 7% are from out of state, 7% African American, 2% Asian American or Pacific Islander, 1% Hispanic American, 0.8% Native American, 2% international, 12% transferred in, 38% live on campus.

Faculty *Total:* 818, 64% full-time, 31% with terminal degrees. *Student/faculty ratio:* 15:1.

Academic Programs *Special study options:* academic remediation for entering students, accelerated degree program, adult/continuing education programs, advanced placement credit, cooperative education, distance learning, double majors, English as a second language, freshman honors college, honors programs, independent study, internships, off-campus study, part-time degree program, services for LD students, study abroad, summer session for credit. *ROTC:* Army (c).

Athletics Member NCAA. All Division II. *Intercollegiate sports:* basketball M(s)/W(s), cheerleading M/W, cross-country running M(s)/W(s), football M(s), golf M(s)/W(s), ice hockey M(s), softball W(s), tennis M(s)/W(s), track and field M(s)/W(s), volleyball W(s). *Intramural sports:* badminton M/W, baseball M, basketball M/W, bowling M/W, football M, golf M/W, ice hockey M, lacrosse M/W, racquetball M/W, rugby M/W, skiing (downhill) M/W, soccer M/W, softball M/W, swimming and diving M/W, tennis M/W, track and field M/W, volleyball M/W, water polo M, weight lifting M.

Costs (2004–05) *Tuition:* state resident $6190 full-time, $256 per credit hour part-time; nonresident $12,380 full-time, $512 per credit hour part-time. Full-time tuition and fees vary according to reciprocity agreements. *Required fees:* $142 full-time. *Room and board:* $6522; room only: $3312. Room and board charges vary according to board plan and housing facility.

Financial Aid 581 Federal Work-Study jobs (averaging $1026). 126 state and other part-time jobs (averaging $1810). In 2004, 249

non-need-based awards were made. *Average percent of need met:* 80%. *Average financial aid package:* $8000. *Average need-based loan:* $3400. *Average need-based gift aid:* $3500. *Average non-need-based aid:* $2000.

Contact: Coordinator: Maude Bigford, HFE 129, Ferris State University, 809 Campus Drive, Big Rapids, Michigan 49307; *Telephone:* 231-591-2216; *Fax:* 231-591-5948; *E-mail:* bigfordm@ ferris.edu; *Web site:* http://www.ferris.edu/htmls/academics/honored

Grand Valley State University
Grand Valley State University Honors College
Allendale, Michigan

*G*rand Valley State University (GVSU) offers academically talented students an opportunity to participate in an exclusive community of scholars exemplifying intellectual achievement. The GVSU Honors College is an alternative form of general education that integrates courses and disciplines, offers a variety of team-taught courses, and maintains small class size. Professors give individual attention to each student and expend extra time and energy to help students progress. The Honors College chooses faculty members who are experts in their fields and who are excited about working with undergraduates. The Honors College prepares students to be competitive nationally for graduate and professional programs. Honors students develop high levels of proficiency in research, writing, and critical thinking, synthesizing material from multiple disciplines and often applying analytical skills to primary sources.

All students enrolled in the Honors College are required to take an integrated arts and humanities sequence consisting of four 3-credit courses. This arts and humanities experience serves as a gateway for all subsequent honors education and comprises the honors core. Good performance in these classes satisfies all University writing requirements. The Honors College is flexible in permitting course selection in the sciences and social sciences to accommodate requirements of specific majors or programs. The required Honors Senior Project ensures that all students engage in original work; many students choose to join faculty research projects.

Honors students may live in the same building where they attend their honors classes, the Glenn A. Niemeyer Living Center, which incorporates state-of-the-art thinking in communal living and classroom instruction. The Niemeyer Living Center fosters a close-knit community that shares goals and experiences specially designed to foster academic excellence and the joy of learning. The Honors Office and faculty offices located in the Living Center provide maximum opportunity for faculty-student interaction.

An honors education extends beyond the classroom. Students can take advantage of travel opportunities, entertainment offerings, social events, and service projects. Participating in student organizations helps honors students develop leadership skills to complement their academic skills.

Students share in the governance of the Living Center. The Honors Society, the student governance organization, provides all honors students a voice in their honors experience, not just those residing in the Living Center. Through Honors Society, students attend faculty meetings, make recommendations to the College Director, and assume responsibility for the Honors Code.

Honors College students may establish a cocurricular transcript to document their extracurricular activities, which are designed to promote development of leadership skills and appreciation of the richness and diversity of university life.

Participation Requirements: All students who are admitted to GVSU and who have a high school GPA of 3.5 or better and an ACTE composite score of 28 or better are invited to join the Honors College.

The decision about admission depends on the review of the applicant's file by a committee of faculty members. In order to continue in the program, students must maintain a minimum GPA of 3.2 and make adequate progress toward the degree requirements. Students who earn a GPA of less than 3.2 but above 2.8 are placed on probation for a period of one year, after which they either return to good standing or are dropped from the program.

Admission Process: All applicants for admission to GVSU who meet the honors criteria of a GPA of 3.5 or better and an ACTE composite of 28 or better receive a mailing with information about the Honors College and instructions about how to apply. Participants in the scholarship competition are also presented with information about the Honors College from faculty members and students. Prospective students who qualify for the Honors College may use the online application process. Qualified applicants are admitted directly into the College and receive information about orientation/registration sessions held during the summer and the special fall honors orientation. Students may wait until they arrive at the summer orientation/registration to apply. Once students apply and are admitted to the Honors College, the honors staff members work closely with housing staff members to facilitate placement in honors housing, the Glenn A. Niemeyer Living Center.

Scholarship Availability: GVSU offers renewable Faculty Scholarships (up to $4000 per year) and renewable Presidential Scholarships (up to $7000 per year) to incoming first-year students as part of an on-campus scholarship competition. To be considered for a Faculty Scholarship, a student needs an ACTE score of at least 29 and a high school GPA of at least 3.5; for the Presidential Scholarship, the minimum ACTE score needed is 32, and the minimum high school GPA is 3.8. These scholarships are not based on need. National Merit Finalists are awarded up to $2000 in additional funds. The Arend D. and Nancy Lubbers Endowment provides additional funding for students in the Honors College.

Campus Overview

State-supported comprehensive, founded 1960 • **Coed** 18,393 undergraduate students, 86% full-time, 61% women, 39% men.

Undergraduates 15,737 full-time, 2,656 part-time. Students come from 55 states and territories, 51 other countries, 4% are from out of state, 5% African American, 2% Asian American or Pacific Islander, 3% Hispanic American, 0.6% Native American, 0.5% international, 8% transferred in, 29% live on campus.

Faculty *Total:* 1,321, 66% full-time, 47% with terminal degrees. *Student/faculty ratio:* 18:1.

Academic Programs *Special study options:* academic remediation for entering students, accelerated degree program, adult/continuing education programs, advanced placement credit, cooperative education, distance learning, double majors, English as a second language, freshman honors college, honors programs, independent study, internships, part-time degree program, services for LD students, study abroad, summer session for credit.

Athletics Member NCAA. All Division II. *Intercollegiate sports:* baseball M(s), basketball M(s)/W(s), cheerleading M(c)/W(c), crew M(c)/W(c), cross-country running M(s)/W(s), football M(s), golf M(s)/W(s), ice hockey M(c), rugby M(c)/W(c), sailing M(c)/W(c), skiing (downhill) M(c)/W(c), soccer M(c)/W(s), softball W(s), swimming and diving M(s)/W(s), tennis M(s)/W(s), track and field M(s)/W(s), volleyball M(c)/W(s), water polo M(c)/W(c), wrestling M(c). *Intramural sports:* archery M/W, badminton M/W, basketball M/W, bowling M/W, cheerleading M/W, crew M/W, cross-country running M/W, fencing M/W, field hockey M/W, football M/W, golf M/W, gymnastics M/W, racquetball M/W, skiing (cross-country) M/W, skiing (downhill) M/W, soccer M/W, softball M/W, squash M/W, swimming and diving M/W, tennis M/W, volleyball M/W, water polo M/W, weight lifting M/W, wrestling M.

Costs (2004–05) *Tuition:* state resident $5782 full-time, $252 per semester hour part-time; nonresident $12,510 full-time, $532 per

semester hour part-time. Full-time tuition and fees vary according to course level, program, and student level. Part-time tuition and fees vary according to course level, course load, program, and student level. *Room and board:* $6160. Room and board charges vary according to board plan, housing facility, and location.

Financial Aid 865 Federal Work-Study jobs (averaging $1200). 261 state and other part-time jobs (averaging $1340). In 2004, 2038 non-need-based awards were made. *Average percent of need met:* 88%. *Average financial aid package:* $7058. *Average need-based loan:* $3414. *Average need-based gift aid:* $3020. *Average non-need-based aid:* $1988.

Contact: Director: Dr. Guiyou Huang, 181 Niemeyer Living Center, One Campus Drive, Allendale, Michigan 49401; *Telephone:* 616-895-3219; *Fax:* 616-895-3413; *E-mail:* honors@gvsu.edu; *Web site:* http://www.gvsu.edu/honors

Lake Superior State University
University Honors Program
Sault Sainte Marie, Michigan

The Lake Superior State University (LSSU) University Honors Program provides an important dimension of the University's commitment to excellence in teaching and learning. The Honors Program seeks to create a community of scholars characterized by strong student and faculty interaction. This community fosters an approach to education that incorporates the qualities of self-directed learning, a positive response to demanding work, and an appreciation of knowledge for its own sake.

Classes are limited to 15–18 students, and active participation of students is considered essential to the development of a scholarly community. In addition, an interdisciplinary focus is promoted by the inclusion of students and faculty members from all majors as well as in the course design of the honors core curriculum. Excellence in teaching is emphasized in the selection of faculty members, as is a commitment to working with students in and out of the classroom setting.

Honors students are advised by the Honors Director and by faculty members in their major course of study. They are eligible for advanced scheduling, honors retreats, conferences, and extracurricular activities; supportive living and learning arrangements; and an enriched educational experience.

Participation Requirements: The Honors Program student completes 21 credit hours of honors-designated courses. About half of these designated credits may satisfy requirements for General Education and the student's major. The remaining 10 credits meet core requirements for the Honors Program, namely a sophomore- and junior-year seminar as well as the completion of a senior project for honors credit. To remain eligible for participation in the Honors Program, students must achieve a 3.5 overall GPA and be actively enrolled in honors courses.

Admission Process: Students are invited to become honors candidates as freshmen, based on a combination of ACT scores, high school GPA, essay, and/or an interview. Other full-time students who achieve a GPA of 3.5 for their first two semesters at LSSU are also invited to apply for full admission to the Honors Program.

Campus Overview

State-supported 4-year, founded 1946 • **Coed** 2,889 undergraduate students, 80% full-time, 51% women, 49% men.

Undergraduates 2,316 full-time, 573 part-time. Students come from 20 states and territories, 12 other countries, 4% are from out of state, 0.7% African American, 0.5% Asian American or Pacific Islander, 0.9% Hispanic American, 9% Native American, 11% international, 9% transferred in, 29% live on campus.

Faculty *Total:* 211, 53% full-time. *Student/faculty ratio:* 22:1.

Academic Programs *Special study options:* adult/continuing education programs, advanced placement credit, cooperative education, distance learning, double majors, freshman honors college, honors programs, independent study, internships, part-time degree program, services for LD students, student-designed majors, summer session for credit.

Athletics Member NCAA. All Division II except ice hockey (Division I). *Intercollegiate sports:* basketball M(s)/W(s), cross-country running M(s)/W(s), golf M, ice hockey M(s), softball W, tennis M(s)/W(s), track and field M(s)/W(s), volleyball W(s). *Intramural sports:* basketball M/W, football M/W, ice hockey M, racquetball M/W, riflery M/W, tennis M/W, track and field M/W, volleyball M/W, water polo M/W, wrestling M.

Costs (2004–05) *Tuition:* state resident $6054 full-time, $226 per credit hour part-time; nonresident $11,472 full-time, $452 per credit hour part-time. Full-time tuition and fees vary according to reciprocity agreements. Part-time tuition and fees vary according to reciprocity agreements. Residents of Ontario, Canada full-time tuition: $6,054, and Midwest Consortium students' tuition: $8,760. *Required fees:* $318 full-time. *Room and board:* $6165; room only: $5494. Room and board charges vary according to board plan and housing facility.

Financial Aid In 2004, 174 non-need-based awards were made. *Average percent of need met:* 81%. *Average financial aid package:* $8594. *Average need-based loan:* $4528. *Average need-based gift aid:* $3160. *Average non-need-based aid:* $2475.

Contact: Director: Dr. John D. Lenters, School of Environmental and Physical Sciences, Lake Superior State University, 650 West Easterday Avenue, Sault Ste. Marie, Michigan 49783; *Telephone:* 906-635-2156; *Fax:* 906-635-2266; *E-mail:* jlenters@lssu.edu; *Web site:* http://www.lssu.edu

Michigan State University
Honors College
East Lansing, Michigan

*T*he Honors College (HC) serves academically talented, committed students who wish to pursue and achieve academic excellence. The College strives to ensure an enriched academic and social experience for its members and create an environment that fosters active, innovative learning.

Members of the Honors College design their own individualized programs of study in the fields of their choice, enroll in dynamic honors classes and seminars, participate in faculty-led research projects, and join other Honors College students who share curiosity, concern, and enthusiasm in an environment brimming with outstanding social and community activities. Honors College members are not constrained by standard curricular requirements; they are committed instead to academic work enriched by honors courses, research experiences, and graduate course substitutions.

Honors College members can choose to live with other honors students on one of the honors floors in Bryan, Case, Gilchrist, Holmes, or Mason Halls. Students seek advising and can use the computer lab and honors lounge in the recently renovated Honors College facility, Eustace-Cole Hall. The Honors College also supports honors student organizations, including the Honors College Programming Board, the Honors College Student Advisory Committee, the Honors College Service Corps, and MOSAIC (the HC's minority student association).

As one of the first and most distinctive Honors Programs, the Honors College at Michigan State University (MSU) was founded in 1956. Approximately 2,600 students are currently enrolled in the Honors College.

Participation Requirements: In fulfilling the requirements for an enriched program of study, a student may use a combination of the various types of honors opportunities available. Honors College members are not required to take a specific set of classes, freeing them to select from among the University's vast advanced course offerings. Members major in any area; honors experiences are a way to enhance all components of their college education.

Members are required to complete eight honors experiences by the time of graduation, averaging one honors course, section, or option every semester. Honors courses, honors sections of regular courses, honors work in nonhonors classes, graduate courses, honors research, and honors theses are considered appropriate honors experiences.

To remain a member in good standing, an Honors College student must establish a cumulative GPA of at least 3.2 during the freshman year and maintain a GPA of at least 3.2 until graduation. At graduation, the distinction of membership in the Honors College is noted on a student's diploma and transcript. It is also reflected in the commencement gown, which includes the respected honors stole.

Admission Process: Students interested in becoming members of the Honors College should first apply for admission to Michigan State University. A completed application serves as an application for Honors College membership; there is no separate application process.

Membership in the Honors College is by invitation only. Invitations are extended to high school students who rank in the top 5 percent of their high school graduating class and have an ACT composite score of at least 30 or an SAT score of at least 1360 (critical reading and math sections only). While required by MSU for admissions, writing scores are considered as supplemental information. For those students who have outstanding records and are close to the criteria, the Honors College may request additional information before extending an invitation for membership.

Freshmen who establish excellent records at MSU (normally a 3.5 cumulative GPA or higher) may apply for membership after their first semester. Students are also asked to write an essay outlining their interests and aspirations and propose a detailed program of honors study for the sophomore year.

Scholarship Availability: The Honors College sponsors several scholarships for its incoming students. Professional Assistantships, Honors College Tuition Grants, Honors College STATE Scholarships, and Honors College National Scholarships are available for exceptional in- and out-of-state students invited to join the HC. Honors College invitees are candidates for the University's largest merit awards and National Merit Scholarships.

Continuing students enjoy access to other significant HC scholarships, including study-abroad scholarships, academic excellence scholarships, and independent research awards. MSU Honors College members also have an exceptional record of achievement in attaining major national and international scholarships and fellowships, including Rhodes, Marshall, and Truman Scholarships and National Science Foundation graduate fellowships.

Campus Overview

State-supported university, founded 1855 • **Coed** 35,408 undergraduate students, 90% full-time, 53% women, 47% men.

Undergraduates 31,698 full-time, 3,710 part-time. Students come from 54 states and territories, 125 other countries, 7% are from out of state, 8% African American, 5% Asian American or Pacific Islander, 3% Hispanic American, 0.7% Native American, 3% international, 5% transferred in, 42% live on campus.

Faculty *Total:* 2,671, 87% full-time, 90% with terminal degrees. *Student/faculty ratio:* 18:1.

Academic Programs *Special study options:* academic remediation for entering students, accelerated degree program, adult/continuing education programs, advanced placement credit, cooperative education, distance learning, double majors, English as a second language, freshman honors college, honors programs, independent study, internships, off-campus study, part-time degree program, services for LD students, student-designed majors, study abroad, summer session for credit. *ROTC:* Army (b), Air Force (b).

Athletics Member NCAA. All Division I except football (Division I-A). *Intercollegiate sports:* baseball M, basketball M(s)/W(s), cheerleading M/W, crew W(s), cross-country running M(s)/W(s), equestrian sports M(c)/W(c), field hockey W(s), golf M(s)/W(s), gymnastics M/W(s), ice hockey M(s)/W(c), lacrosse M(c), rugby M(c)/W(c), sailing M(c)/W(c), skiing (cross-country) M(c)/W(c), skiing (downhill) M(c), soccer M(s)/W(s), softball W, swimming and diving M(s)/W(s), tennis M(s)/W(s), track and field M(s)/W(s), volleyball M(c)/W(s), water polo M(c)/W(c), wrestling M(s). *Intramural sports:* archery M/W, badminton M/W, baseball M, basketball M/W, crew M/W, cross-country running M/W, fencing M/W, football M/W, golf M/W, gymnastics W, ice hockey M/W, lacrosse M, racquetball M/W, rugby M/W, sailing M/W, skiing (cross-country) M/W, skiing (downhill) M/W, soccer M/W, softball W, squash M/W, swimming and diving M/W, table tennis M/W, tennis M/W, track and field M/W, volleyball M/W, water polo M/W, weight lifting M/W, wrestling M.

Costs (2004–05) *Tuition:* state resident $6188 full-time, $206 per credit part-time; nonresident $17,033 full-time, $568 per credit part-time. Full-time tuition and fees vary according to course load, degree level, program, and student level. Part-time tuition and fees vary according to course load, degree level, program, and student level. *Required fees:* $812 full-time, $812 per year part-time. *Room and board:* $5458; room only: $2364. Room and board charges vary according to board plan and housing facility.

Financial Aid 1,634 Federal Work-Study jobs (averaging $1545). 393 state and other part-time jobs (averaging $1968). In 2004, 2615 non-need-based awards were made. *Average percent of need met:* 75%. *Average financial aid package:* $8022. *Average need-based loan:* $3726. *Average need-based gift aid:* $3562. *Average non-need-based aid:* $2990.

Contact: Dean: Professor Ronald C. Fisher, Eustace-Cole Hall, Michigan State University, East Lansing, Michigan 48824; *Telephone:* 517-355-2326; *Fax:* 517-353-4721; *E-mail:* honors@msu.edu; *Web site:* http://www.msu.edu/unit/honcoll/

Mott Community College
Honors Program
Flint, Michigan

The Mott Community College (MCC) Honors Program is designed to provide a more stimulating and rigorous option for academically talented and motivated students in all majors. Although the emphasis lies in enhancing scholarship opportunities for students whose goals include transferring to a four-year institution, the program also provides a competitive edge to students seeking immediate employment. Honors Program participants have garnered transfer scholarships from prestigious colleges and universities across the nation. A Transfer Alliance Agreement with the University of Michigan–Flint (UM–F) ensures that MCC Honors Program graduates are given first priority for the UM–F Junior/Senior Honors Program.

Two of the program's hallmarks are diversity and flexibility. Because MCC serves a wide range of traditional and nontraditional students, the College offers participation in an honors experience to some students who would otherwise not have such an opportunity. The College serves dually enrolled high school students, traditional high school graduates, those who have a lapse in attendance between high school and college, and those retraining for a second career. This brings a rich blend of experience and interests to the honors discourse. Students select from a rotating schedule of honors courses that either meet a general education requirement or are electives recommended for several majors. The capstone experience is the Honors Colloquium, which focuses on an interdisciplinary topic. The honors topic, selected annually by the Honors Steering Committee, becomes a catalyst for all the honors courses each year and provides

opportunities for guest lectures and extracurricular activities. Honors classes are intimate (usually 15–25 students), stress participative learning, and provide opportunities for research, publication, oral presentations, and community service.

Biannual honors retreats provide leadership training and transfer scholarship preparation. A special honors adviser, in conjunction with an adviser in a student's major, helps coordinate the student's long-range goals. Dedicated honors faculty members have a strong mentoring relationship with students as well. Students are expected to prepare an honors portfolio that demonstrates measurable outcomes to meet stated Honors Program objectives. Honors students have produced College and regional award-winning essays and have placed on All-Michigan and All-America Academic Teams.

Participation in the Honors Program is rewarded with a partial tuition scholarship and special recognition, such as the honors diploma and medallion at graduation. Academic enrichment, such as participation in local, regional, and national conferences, and cultural experiences, such as trips abroad, also prepare MCC honors students for transfer to a four-year institution. Currently, 120 students participate in the Honors Program, which was established in 1988.

Participation Requirements: Students must be enrolled in at least 6 credit hours to qualify for the Honors Program Scholarship. To receive an Honors Program diploma upon graduation, a student must complete at least 12 credit hours in honors course work. At least 3 of these credits must be from the course designated as the Honors Colloquium. In addition, a student must have a minimum cumulative GPA of 3.5 at the time of graduation and must meet all the requirements for an established associate degree at MCC (Associate of Arts, Science, Applied Science, or General Studies). Honors Program participants who choose to transfer early, but who have maintained a minimum GPA of 3.5 or higher and have completed at least 9 credit hours in honors courses, receive an Honors Certificate of Achievement. Both honors diploma and honors certificate recipients and their guests participate in an honors graduation dinner and medallion ceremony. In addition, honors diploma recipients are distinguished at commencement by the wearing of medallions and being the first to receive their degrees. Honors designations for all honors courses are noted on the students' transcripts.

Admission Process: Invitations to apply to the Honors Program are sent to all MCC students who are enrolled in a minimum of 6 credit hours and who have a cumulative GPA of 3.5 or higher after completion of 12 MCC credit hours in 100- or 200-level courses. Transfer students with the same academic profile from other accredited colleges may apply. High school students with a cumulative GPA of 3.5 or higher at graduation are also encouraged to apply. Dual-enrolled high school students with a GPA of 3.5 or higher may be provisionally admitted to the Honors Program, with full admission after one semester at MCC if they meet the standard criteria for all applicants. Dual-enrolled students must have permission from their high school administrator. The Honors Program Coordinator (or, for unusual circumstances, the Steering Committee) determines membership acceptance from the pool of minimally qualified applicants on the basis of high school or college transcripts, evaluation of an original essay, evaluation of two letters of recommendation, and an interview. This is a rolling admissions process.

Scholarship Availability: Students admitted to the MCC Honors Program are eligible for the Honors Program Scholarship, which is awarded purely on academic merit. This scholarship can only be applied to honors-designated sections for a maximum of two courses per semester and up to 32 credit hours total. The scholarship amount is based on in-district tuition and fees and must be used for the semester of application. Other financial assistance, including scholarships, grants, loans, and work-study employment, is available to qualified students who are admitted to MCC.

Campus Overview

Urban 20-acre campus with easy access to Detroit • **Coed** 10,328 undergraduate students, 34% full-time, 61% women, 39% men.

Undergraduates 3,538 full-time, 6,790 part-time. Students come from 10 states and territories, 33 other countries, 0.1% are from out of state, 18% African American, 0.9% Asian American or Pacific Islander, 3% Hispanic American, 1% Native American, 0.3% international, 3% transferred in.

Faculty *Total:* 474, 31% full-time, 10% with terminal degrees. *Student/faculty ratio:* 23:1.

Academic Programs *Special study options:* academic remediation for entering students, accelerated degree program, adult/continuing education programs, advanced placement credit, cooperative education, distance learning, double majors, English as a second language, honors programs, independent study, internships, part-time degree program, services for LD students, summer session for credit.

Athletics Member NJCAA. *Intercollegiate sports:* baseball M(s), basketball M(s)/W(s), cross-country running M(s)/W(s), golf M(s), softball W(s), volleyball W(s).

Costs (2005–06) *Tuition:* area resident $2117 full-time, $71 per contact hour part-time; state resident $3167 full-time, $106 per contact hour part-time; nonresident $4226 full-time, $141 per contact hour part-time. *Required fees:* $95 full-time, $48 per term part-time.

Financial Aid 300 Federal Work-Study jobs (averaging $1000). 300 state and other part-time jobs (averaging $1000).

Contact: Heather S. Sisto, Honors Program Coordinator, PCC-218, Mott Community College, 1401 East Court Street, Flint, Michigan 48503-2089; *Telephone:* 810-232-3058; *E-mail:* Heather.Sisto@mcc.edu; *Web site:* http://www.mcc.edu/honors

Northern Michigan University
Honors Program
Marquette, Michigan

*O*pening in 1998, the Honors Program at Northern Michigan University provides academically motivated students with the opportunity to work toward their undergraduate degrees by taking specially designed departmental and interdisciplinary courses taught by highly skilled faculty members who are eager to work with talented students. The Honors Program exists to encourage excellence for undergraduate students of exceptional academic promise by providing enhanced opportunities for individual learning, collaborative innovation, and close cooperation with faculty members. In addition to taking honors courses, students complete University graduation requirements, including those of their selected majors, and finish as honors seniors completing a senior capstone directed study.

Participation Requirements: The Honors Program offers academically talented students an alternative curriculum to the required liberal studies program. To graduate from the Honors Program, students must complete 24 credits of core courses, 12 credits of honors contract courses, and 4 credits of honors capstone; demonstrate proficiency in precalculus or a higher level and the fourth semester of a foreign language; and maintain a minimum 3.0 overall GPA. Completion of the Honors Program is noted on students' transcripts and by recognition at campus ceremonies.

Admission Process: Admission of first-year students to the Honors Program is by invitation. After students have applied and been admitted to NMU, the Honors Program sends applications, reviews those submitted, and admits students to the program based on their high school GPA (3.5 minimum), test scores (27 ACT or SAT equivalent minimum), applicants' personal essays, and letters of recommendation from high school teachers, counselors, and principals. Students already at NMU and transfer students are admitted on an individual basis after eligibility has been determined.

Within NMU and Honors Program guidelines, the program accepts Advanced Placement credits.

Scholarship Availability: The Honors Program recommends qualified students for the Mary L. Campbell Scholarships each year. In addition, Honors Program students often qualify for other merit-based scholarships.

Campus Overview

State-supported comprehensive, founded 1899 • **Coed** 9,118 undergraduate students, 89% full-time, 55% women, 45% men.

Undergraduates 8,156 full-time, 962 part-time. 19% are from out of state, 2% African American, 0.7% Asian American or Pacific Islander, 0.9% Hispanic American, 2% Native American, 6% transferred in, 32% live on campus.

Faculty *Total:* 428, 73% full-time, 64% with terminal degrees.

Academic Programs *Special study options:* academic remediation for entering students, accelerated degree program, adult/continuing education programs, advanced placement credit, distance learning, double majors, honors programs, independent study, internships, off-campus study, part-time degree program, services for LD students, student-designed majors, study abroad, summer session for credit. *ROTC:* Army (b).

Athletics Member NCAA. All Division II. *Intercollegiate sports:* basketball M/W, cheerleading M/W, crew M(c)/W(c), cross-country running W, equestrian sports M(c)/W(c), football M, golf M, ice hockey M/W(c), lacrosse M(c), rugby M(c)/W(c), skiing (cross-country) M/W, skiing (downhill) M(c)/W(c), soccer W, softball W(c), swimming and diving W, track and field W, volleyball W. *Intramural sports:* basketball M/W, field hockey W, football M/W, ice hockey M/W, lacrosse M, racquetball M/W, soccer M/W, softball M/W, table tennis M/W, ultimate Frisbee M/W, volleyball M/W, water polo M(c)/W(c).

Costs (2004–05) *One-time required fee:* $100. *Tuition:* state resident $4776 full-time, $199 per credit hour part-time; nonresident $8184 full-time, $341 per credit hour part-time. Part-time tuition and fees vary according to location. *Required fees:* $658 full-time, $30 per term part-time. *Room and board:* $6182. Room and board charges vary according to board plan and housing facility.

Financial Aid In 2004, 12 non-need-based awards were made. *Average percent of need met:* 74%. *Average financial aid package:* $7466. *Average need-based loan:* $3788. *Average need-based gift aid:* $3888. *Average non-need-based aid:* $21,548.

Contact: Dr. Robert Goodrich, 401 Cohadas, 1401 Presque Isle Avenue, Marquette, Michigan 49855; *Telephone:* 906-227-2418; *Fax:* 906-227-2315; *E-mail:* honors@nmu.edu

Northwood University
Honors Program
Midland, Michigan

*T*he Northwood University Honors Program began shortly after the University was founded in 1959, but it went through major restructuring in 2004 when additional honors courses were added to the program, allowing students to earn an Honors Certificate and an Honors Diploma. Its general academic mission is to emphasize critical analysis, synthesis, and evaluation of course content. This is accomplished through innovative teaching and assessment methods, greater breadth and depth of content, and higher standards of rigor. Its professional mission is to provide a more comprehensive exploration of disciplines used within various professions. The Honors Program enhances personal growth by creating a community of likeminded students dedicated to maximizing the value of their education

Being limited in size—20 students maximum—honors courses place more emphasis on class participation and discussion-based learning. *They encourage students to direct their own learning and emphasize development of social and leadership skills. By offering a variety of learning experiences, honors courses encourage collaborative learning, offer experiences outside the classroom, seek frequent faculty-student interaction, and accelerate students' intellectual growth. In addition, by developing discipline-appropriate research skills, honors courses stress independent research and learning, present primary sources and original documents, offer access to updated literature from the field, and urge originality in writing and analysis. Honors courses offer an enhanced range and depth of study through increased quality of work, not quantity of work.*

Participation Requirements: Honors students at Northwood University may participate in the program at three different levels. All students who qualify and complete any honors course are considered to be Honors Program participants, and their honors courses are identified on their transcripts. Students who complete 20 term credit hours in specified groups of honors courses earn an Honors Certificate. Those who complete 40 term credit hours earn an Honors Diploma. That a student has earned the Certificate or Diploma is prominently noted on the honor student's transcript, thus indicating that the student has opted for an enhanced and challenging undergraduate education. Successful completion of either the Honors Certificate or Diploma requires a minimum cumulative GPA of 3.25 and a minimum cumulative GPA in honors courses of 3.0.

Admission Process: Admission to the Honors Program from high school requires two of the following three conditions: (1) a 3.25 or better high school GPA, (2) top 10 percent of high school class, or (3) a minimum ACT score of 25 or SAT score of 1150. Any student with at least a 3.25 Northwood University cumulative GPA or transfer student with a minimum 3.25 GPA may join the Honors Program.

Scholarship Availability: Northwood University offers a Presidential Scholarship Award of $9000 per year for students with a minimum 28 ACT or 1240 SAT and at least a 3.8 GPA and who maintain a 3.5 GPA. Also offered is a Freedom Scholarship Award of $7500 per year for students with a minimum 25 ACT or 1150 SAT and at least a 3.0 GPA and who maintain a 3.0 GPA. Students who complete 16 term credit hours of honors courses qualify for significant price reductions on the University's term-long study-abroad programs in Europe, Northern Europe, and Asia.

Campus Overview

Independent comprehensive, founded 1959 • **Coed** 3,432 undergraduate students, 71% full-time, 44% women, 56% men.

Undergraduates 2,435 full-time, 997 part-time. Students come from 38 states and territories, 29 other countries, 14% are from out of state, 13% African American, 1% Asian American or Pacific Islander, 2% Hispanic American, 8% international, 6% transferred in, 39% live on campus.

Faculty *Total:* 84, 61% full-time. *Student/faculty ratio:* 31:1.

Academic Programs *Special study options:* academic remediation for entering students, accelerated degree program, adult/continuing education programs, advanced placement credit, cooperative education, distance learning, double majors, English as a second language, external degree program, honors programs, independent study, internships, off-campus study, part-time degree program, study abroad, summer session for credit.

Athletics Member NCAA. All Division II. *Intercollegiate sports:* baseball M(s), basketball M(s)/W(s), cheerleading M(s)/W(s), cross-country running M(s)/W(s), football M(s), golf M(s)/W(s), soccer M(s)/W(s), softball W(s), tennis M(s)/W(s), track and field M(s)/W(s), volleyball W(s). *Intramural sports:* badminton M/W, baseball M(c), basketball M/W, field hockey M/W, football M, ice hockey M(c), lacrosse M(c), soccer M(c)/W, softball M/W, table tennis M/W, tennis M/W, volleyball M/W.

Costs (2005–06) *Comprehensive fee:* $21,879 includes full-time tuition ($14,625), mandatory fees ($558), and room and board ($6696). Part-time tuition: $304 per credit. *College room only:* $3405. Room and board charges vary according to board plan.

Financial Aid 266 Federal Work-Study jobs (averaging $1709). 269 state and other part-time jobs (averaging $1705). In 2004, 472 non-need-based awards were made. *Average percent of need met:* 79%. *Average financial aid package:* $12,779. *Average need-based loan:* $3729. *Average need-based gift aid:* $5147. *Average non-need-based aid:* $3959.

Contact: Co-Directors: Dr. Jamie H. Burns and Dr. Margaret Colarelli, Northwood University, 4000 Whiting Drive, Midland, Michigan 48640-2398; *Telephone:* 989-837-4828 or 989-837-4259; *E-mail:* burns_j@northwood.edu, colarell@northwood.edu;

Wayne State University
Honors Program
Detroit, Michigan

The Honors Program at Wayne State University (WSU) is designed for highly motivated students with superior abilities who learn in the intimate atmosphere associated with small selective colleges, yet who thrive on being in a leading urban research university with outstanding physical and cultural facilities. Undergraduates in any college or department may, if eligible, take honors courses. There are two honors tracks: students may choose departmental or University honors or do both. Transfer students can complete all requirements in their junior and senior years.

The program is located in the Undergraduate Library, which features a quiet-study space with new computer equipment. A new dormitory facility allots special space to honors students. Currently, approximately 1,000 students are enrolled.

Participation Requirements: Students take 15–20 percent of their course work in honors in a variety of settings: exclusive honors classes, honors sections of regular classes, and Honors–Option, which turns a regular course into honors for individual students. Honors classes are limited to no more than 20 students. Each honors student must take an upper-division interdisciplinary seminar offered by the program and complete an honors thesis or project. The Honors Program designation is attached to both the transcript and the diploma upon successful completion of the program.

Admission Process: Entering freshmen must have a GPA of at least 3.5 to be invited to an annual scholarship event. Transfer students are required to have a GPA of at least 3.3. All Presidential Scholarship recipients are automatically eligible. Current students must have a GPA of at least 3.3.

Scholarship Availability: Research grants of up to $2300 are available. In addition, the University has a Presidential Scholarship Program available to selected Michigan high school students who have demonstrated scholastic ability as they graduate. The award provides tuition for a maximum of eight semesters (32 credits per academic year). Eligibility requirements for high school graduates include a minimum 3.5 GPA. For more information, students should contact the University Admissions Office, Welcome Center, 42 West Warren Avenue; Telephone: 313-577-3577.

Campus Overview

State-supported university, founded 1868 • **Coed** 20,712 undergraduate students, 56% full-time, 60% women, 40% men.

Undergraduates 11,608 full-time, 9,104 part-time. Students come from 34 states and territories, 57 other countries, 1% are from out of state, 32% African American, 5% Asian American or Pacific Islander, 3% Hispanic American, 0.5% Native American, 4% international, 11% transferred in, 7% live on campus.

Faculty *Total:* 1,925, 52% full-time, 39% with terminal degrees. *Student/faculty ratio:* 17:1.

Academic Programs *Special study options:* academic remediation for entering students, accelerated degree program, adult/continuing education programs, advanced placement credit, cooperative education, distance learning, double majors, English as a second language, honors programs, independent study, internships, off-campus study, part-time degree program, services for LD students, student-designed majors, study abroad, summer session for credit. *ROTC:* Air Force (c).

Athletics Member NCAA. All Division II except men's and women's ice hockey (Division I). *Intercollegiate sports:* baseball M(s), basketball M(s)/W(s), cross-country running M(s)/W(s), fencing M(s)/W(s), football M(s), golf M(s), ice hockey M(s)/W(s), softball W(s), swimming and diving M(s)/W(s), tennis M(s)/W(s), volleyball W(s). *Intramural sports:* badminton M/W, basketball M/W, bowling M/W, football M/W, racquetball M/W, soccer M/W, softball M/W, tennis M/W, volleyball M/W.

Costs (2004–05) *Tuition:* state resident $4773 full-time, $159 per semester hour part-time; nonresident $10,941 full-time, $365 per semester hour part-time. Full-time tuition and fees vary according to student level. Part-time tuition and fees vary according to student level. *Required fees:* $626 full-time, $14 per semester hour part-time, $99 per term part-time. *Room and board:* $6700. Room and board charges vary according to housing facility.

Financial Aid 375 Federal Work-Study jobs (averaging $2954). 189 state and other part-time jobs (averaging $1754). In 2003, 253 non-need-based awards were made. *Average percent of need met:* 58%. *Average financial aid package:* $7254. *Average need-based loan:* $4148. *Average need-based gift aid:* $3631. *Average non-need-based aid:* $3626.

Contact: Administrative Assistant: Stuart May, 2100 Undergraduate Library, Detroit, Michigan 48202; *Telephone:* 313-577-3030; *E-mail:* ab1508@wayne.edu

Western Michigan University
Lee Honors College
Kalamazoo, Michigan

The Lee Honors College at Western Michigan University was created more than four decades ago for academically talented students and has become an integral part of the University community. Honors students study in every discipline and take advantage of the diverse and rich array of courses to deepen and develop their major and minor fields of study. The goal is to provide an environment where each student will grow through personal relationships with other students and faculty members while engaging in academic challenges with opportunities for leadership.

When students enter the Lee Honors College, they have all of the resources a large, comprehensive university can offer, with the attention and personal care of a small college of 1,000 students. The academic experience is enhanced by opportunities to live in a residence hall with other honors students, pursue international study, set up rewarding internships, and apply for research grants. The honors experience is an inclusionary one.

Participation Requirements: The program consists of two learning communities, or clusters, of honors classes at the freshman/sophomore level (normally 6 to 9 credit hours at the freshman and at the sophomore level), two single courses at the junior/senior level (for a total of 6-8 credit hours), and a senior-level capstone, Thesis Project.

Students must maintain a 3.25 GPA or higher to remain in good standing. The number of credit hours is variable. Students graduate with a transcript notation and diploma that they are graduates of the Lee Honors College. The notation includes the title of their thesis.

Admission Process: Students may be admitted at various stages of their academic career. They may enter as freshmen, as currently enrolled students at WMU, or as transfer students through the junior year. Chief criteria for freshman admission to the Honors College are high school or university academic achievements and aptitude as measured by GPA (in the range of 3.6 or better) and ACT composite scores (in the range of 26 or better). College transfer students should present a cumulative GPA of 3.5 or better. Students are also evaluated by the quality of an academic essay, cocurricular and community activities, and two recommendations from teachers or counselors.

Scholarship Availability: There is a Dean's Summer Research Grant, which is open to students between the junior and senior year who are researching their Thesis Project. The college also administers the Undergraduate Research and Creative Activities Award for junior- and senior-level students.

Campus Overview

State-supported university, founded 1903 • **Coed** 22,502 undergraduate students, 87% full-time, 51% women, 49% men.

Undergraduates 19,555 full-time, 2,947 part-time. Students come from 53 states and territories, 109 other countries, 6% are from out of state, 5% African American, 1% Asian American or Pacific Islander, 2% Hispanic American, 0.4% Native American, 3% international, 7% transferred in, 24% live on campus.

Faculty *Total:* 1,488, 66% full-time, 58% with terminal degrees.

Academic Programs *Special study options:* academic remediation for entering students, accelerated degree program, adult/continuing education programs, advanced placement credit, cooperative education, distance learning, double majors, English as a second language, freshman honors college, honors programs, independent study, internships, off-campus study, part-time degree program, services for LD students, student-designed majors, study abroad, summer session for credit. *ROTC:* Army (b).

Athletics Member NCAA. All Division I except football (Division I-A). *Intercollegiate sports:* baseball M(s), basketball M(s)/W(s), cross-country running W(s), golf W(s), gymnastics W(s), ice hockey M(s), soccer M(s)/W(s), softball W(s), tennis M(s)/W(s), track and field W(s), volleyball W(s). *Intramural sports:* badminton M/W, basketball M/W, bowling M/W, equestrian sports M(c)/W(c), fencing M(c)/W(c), football M/W, golf M, ice hockey M(c)/W(c), lacrosse M(c)/W(c), racquetball M/W, rugby M(c)/W, sailing M(c)/W(c), soccer M/W, softball M/W, swimming and diving M/W, table tennis M/W, tennis M/W, volleyball M/W.

Costs (2004–05) *Tuition:* state resident $5066 full-time, $169 per credit hour part-time; nonresident $13,221 full-time, $441 per credit hour part-time. Full-time tuition and fees vary according to course load, location, and student level. Part-time tuition and fees vary according to course load, location, and student level. *Required fees:* $602 full-time, $162 per term part-time. *Room and board:* $6496; room only: $3350. Room and board charges vary according to board plan.

Financial Aid In 2003, 2600 non-need-based awards were made. *Average percent of need met:* 69%. *Average financial aid package:* $7300. *Average need-based loan:* $3800. *Average need-based gift aid:* $4100. *Average non-need-based aid:* $2400.

Contact: Dean: Larry Tenharmsel, Western Michigan University, Kalamazoo, Michigan 49008-5244; *Telephone:* 269-387-3230; *Fax:* 269-387-3903; *E-mail:* larry.tenharmsel@wmich.edu; *Web site:* http://www.wmich.edu/honors

MINNESOTA

College of Saint Benedict (Coordinate with Saint John's University)
Honors Degree Program
St. Joseph, Minnesota

The Honors Program at the College of Saint Benedict and Saint John's University comprises a group of students exploring the world of ideas together. These honors students pride themselves on their shared love of learning and an exciting exchange of ideas that rarely ends when the class period is over. The honors program is integrated into the common liberal arts core curriculum, enabling honors students to take honors core curriculum classes in place of classes in the general core curriculum. These courses focus on an interdisciplinary approach to ways of knowing and feature small class sizes (20 to 25 students maximum) built around lively discussion. In this way, completing the honors program does not interfere with either study-abroad opportunities or the pursuit of single or even double majors.

The program features small out-of-class reading and film discussion groups with professors, service opportunities, and cultural enrichment activities.

The program admits approximately 130 students each year.

Participation Requirements: In the first year, students take either the honors first-year symposium or great issues in philosophy. The honors symposium is centered on a variety of topics in natural sciences, fine arts, social sciences, and humanities. Great issues in philosophy examines some of the most challenging questions surrounding the human condition. In the sophomore year, students take either one or two honors courses that serve as lower-division requirements in the core curriculum: natural science, social science, theology, or general humanities. In the junior year, students have the opportunity to take a yearlong course entitled Great Books. This course features the reading and discussion of a large corpus of the world's finest learning and literature. In the senior year, students may research and write the honors thesis. For their thesis, students work closely with faculty members from their major field of study to produce high-quality independent undergraduate research.

To remain in good standing, students must maintain at least a 3.0 cumulative GPA in their first year of study and garner a minimum 3.4 cumulative GPA upon graduation. Students who complete the program receive special recognition at graduation along with final transcripts marked All College Honors.

Admission Process: High school students are offered admission to the Honors Program on the basis of college board scores, high school rank, and GPA. Students not admitted in the first term of freshman year may apply for admission to the Honors Program upon the completion of one full term of study. Transfer students may also apply based upon previous academic work.

Scholarship Availability: Saint John's University and the College of Saint Benedict have Regents and Trustees merit scholarships not explicitly linked to admission in the honors program. All Regents and Trustees scholarship holders are offered admission to the honors program.

Campus Overview
Independent Roman Catholic 4-year, founded 1887 • **Small-town** 315-acre campus with easy access to Minneapolis–St. Paul • **Coed primarily women** 2,033 undergraduate students, 97% full-time, 100% women.

Undergraduates 1,973 full-time, 60 part-time. Students come from 27 states and territories, 29 other countries, 14% are from out of state, 0.5% African American, 2% Asian American or Pacific Islander, 1% Hispanic American, 3% international, 2% transferred in, 84% live on campus.

Faculty *Total:* 174, 85% full-time, 66% with terminal degrees. *Student/faculty ratio:* 13:1.

Academic Programs *Special study options:* accelerated degree program, advanced placement credit, double majors, English as a second language, honors programs, independent study, internships, off-campus study, services for LD students, student-designed majors, study abroad. *ROTC:* Army (c). *Unusual degree programs:* 3-2 engineering with University of Minnesota, Twin Cities Campus.

Athletics Member NCAA. All Division III. *Intercollegiate sports:* basketball W, crew W(c), cross-country running W, golf W, ice hockey W, lacrosse W(c), riflery W(c), rugby W(c), skiing (cross-country) W, soccer W, softball W, swimming and diving W, tennis W, track and field W, ultimate Frisbee W(c), volleyball W. *Intramural sports:* basketball W, football W, racquetball W, rock climbing W(c), skiing (cross-country) W(c), skiing (downhill) W(c), soccer W, softball W, volleyball W, water polo W(c).

Costs (2004–05) *Comprehensive fee:* $28,356 includes full-time tuition ($21,758), mandatory fees ($390), and room and board ($6208). Part-time tuition: $907 per credit. Part-time tuition and fees vary according to course load. *Required fees:* $195 per term part-time. *College room only:* $3292. Room and board charges vary according to board plan and housing facility.

Financial Aid 600 Federal Work-Study jobs (averaging $2000). 300 state and other part-time jobs (averaging $2000). In 2003, 556 non-need-based awards were made. *Average percent of need met:* 88%. *Average financial aid package:* $17,223. *Average need-based loan:* $5009. *Average need-based gift aid:* $11,093. *Average non-need-based aid:* $5790.

Contact: Director: Dr. Richard M. White, Department of Chemistry, CSB/SJU, St. Joseph, Minnesota 56374; *Telephone:* 320-363-5994; *Fax:* 320-363-5582; *E-mail:* rwhite@csbsju.edu; *Web site:* http://www.csbsju.edu/honors

College of St. Catherine
Antonian Scholars Honors Program
St. Paul, Minnesota

The objectives of the Antonian Scholars Honors Program are to attract and provide a challenge for women of superior ability; to provide an opportunity for these women to interact with each other and build intellectually supportive relationships with peers and faculty members; to deepen their love of learning, understanding of great issues, and independent scholarship; and to clarify and emphasize the College's commitment to the liberal arts and academic excellence.

A student will have completed the Honors Program provided she maintains a minimum 3.5 GPA overall and in her major, and completes the six components of the program, including a Senior Honors Project. Each student must complete a minimum of two Honors Seminars, which may be team taught, are interdisciplinary, and focus on the liberal arts; a minimum of two Honors Contracts, work that is broader in scope and/or showing greater depth than that required in a course; and a third Honors Seminar, Honors Contract, or foreign study during the regular academic year (not including January term or summer). As a senior, the student undertakes a major piece of research or creative work under the guidance of a faculty member, which is publicly presented.

The privileges of membership include the opportunity to travel to regional and national conferences and the opportunity to register on the first day of registration.

The Honors Program began in 1986 and currently has 65 members.

Participation Requirements: To maintain eligibility, a student must be registered in the Honors Program each year, unless she is away from campus (e.g., abroad). A student must complete at least one Honors Seminar or Honors Contract within the first two semesters after being admitted to the program. She may complete at most three components in her senior year, one of which is the Senior Project. A student must earn a grade of B or higher in the honors courses. Successful completion of the Honors Program is noted at graduation and is recorded on the student's transcript. A special diploma is awarded.

Admission Process: Any student who has completed at least three courses at the College but no more than fifteen courses while enrolled at the College may apply. Admission is determined by student interest as reflected in the application, a faculty member recommendation, and a minimum 3.5 GPA. In addition, a limited number of entering first-year and transfer students are offered membership.

There is early admission for qualified first-year students and rolling admission for other qualified students.

Scholarship Availability: The College of St. Catherine offers the Presidential Scholarships to students of exceptional ability. Many students receiving these scholarships are also in the Honors Program.

Campus Overview

Independent Roman Catholic comprehensive, founded 1905 • **Urban** 110-acre campus with easy access to Minneapolis • **Women only** 3,582 undergraduate students, 66% full-time.

Undergraduates 2,362 full-time, 1,220 part-time. Students come from 31 states and territories, 30 other countries, 10% are from out of state, 7% African American, 6% Asian American or Pacific Islander, 2% Hispanic American, 0.6% Native American, 2% international, 38% live on campus.

Faculty *Total:* 528, 42% full-time, 42% with terminal degrees. *Student/faculty ratio:* 11:1.

Academic Programs *Special study options:* academic remediation for entering students, adult/continuing education programs, advanced placement credit, distance learning, double majors, English as a second language, external degree program, honors programs, independent study, internships, off-campus study, part-time degree program, services for LD students, student-designed majors, study abroad, summer session for credit. *ROTC:* Air Force (c). *Unusual degree programs:* 3-2 engineering with Washington University in St. Louis, University of Minnesota, Twin Cities Campus; optometry with Illinois College of Optometry.

Athletics Member NCAA. All Division III. *Intercollegiate sports:* basketball W, cross-country running W, ice hockey W, soccer W, softball W, swimming and diving W, tennis W, track and field W, volleyball W. *Intramural sports:* basketball W, cross-country running W, football W, golf W, racquetball W, soccer W, softball W, swimming and diving W, tennis W, track and field W, volleyball W.

Costs (2004–05) *Comprehensive fee:* $24,010 includes full-time tuition ($18,550) and room and board ($5460). Full-time tuition and fees vary according to class time. Part-time tuition: $610 per credit. Part-time tuition and fees vary according to class time. *College room only:* $3060. Room and board charges vary according to board plan and housing facility.

Financial Aid 500 Federal Work-Study jobs. In 2003, 410 non-need-based awards were made. *Average percent of need met:* 77%. *Average financial aid package:* $18,319. *Average need-based loan:* $4752. *Average need-based gift aid:* $6954. *Average non-need-based aid:* $14,651.

Contact: Director: Dr. Diane Heacox, 2004 Randolph Avenue, St. Paul, Minnesota 55105; *Telephone:* 651-690-6614; *Fax:* 651-690-8651; *Web site:* http://www.stkate.edu/Scholars

The College of St. Scholastica
Honors Program
Duluth, Minnesota

Begun in 1995, the Honors Program at the College of St. Scholastica was created to provide an environment for honors students to have enriched learning experiences and to provide a community of support for learners devoted to a vigorous life of the mind. Students who become involved in the Honors Program should strive to love ideas and the discussion of them, not fearing intellectual debate; be able to listen to the ideas of others with respect, no matter how much those ideas might conflict with personal sentiments; be willing to risk the analysis of an idea for its improvement and for the individual's greater understanding; and desire a life of learning.

Approximately 110 students participate in the program each year.

Participation Requirements: Students are required to complete five honors courses (20 credits), at least two of which are upper level. The Honors Colloquium is strongly recommended for freshmen honors students. Transfer students may satisfy the requirements of the Honors Program by completing three honors courses (12 credits), at least two of which are upper level, with the permission of the Honors Director.

Admission Process: To be accepted into the program, students must first meet two of the following three guidelines: be in the top 15 percent of their high school class, have a minimum ACT score of 26 or minimum SAT I score of 1100 (PSAT score of approximately 105 is sufficient to apply), and/or a GPA of 3.5 on a 4.0 scale. All applicants must interview with the Honors Director prior to admission to the program. Students must earn a minimum grade of B in all honors courses and have an overall GPA of at least 3.5 to graduate from the Honors Program.

Scholarship Availability: Exceptional students may apply for a Benedictine scholarship through the Admissions Office.

Campus Overview

Independent comprehensive, founded 1912, affiliated with Roman Catholic Church • **Coed** 2,441 undergraduate students, 90% full-time, 70% women, 30% men.

Undergraduates 2,185 full-time, 256 part-time. Students come from 38 states and territories, 19 other countries, 10% are from out of state, 1% African American, 2% Asian American or Pacific Islander, 0.7% Hispanic American, 2% Native American, 2% international, 7% transferred in, 44% live on campus.

Faculty *Total:* 222, 61% full-time, 66% with terminal degrees. *Student/faculty ratio:* 13:1.

Academic Programs *Special study options:* academic remediation for entering students, accelerated degree program, adult/continuing education programs, advanced placement credit, distance learning, double majors, external degree program, honors programs, independent study, internships, off-campus study, part-time degree program, services for LD students, student-designed majors, study abroad, summer session for credit. *ROTC:* Air Force (c). *Unusual degree programs:* 3-2 occupational therapy.

Athletics Member NCAA, NAIA. All NCAA Division III. *Intercollegiate sports:* baseball M, basketball M/W, cross-country running M/W, ice hockey M, soccer M/W, softball W, tennis M/W, track and field M/W, volleyball W. *Intramural sports:* basketball M/W, football M/W, ice hockey W(c), soccer M/W, tennis M/W, volleyball M/W.

Costs (2004–05) *Comprehensive fee:* $26,676 includes full-time tuition ($20,630), mandatory fees ($130), and room and board

($5916). Full-time tuition and fees vary according to class time. Part-time tuition: $646 per credit hour. Part-time tuition and fees vary according to class time and course load. *College room only:* $3356. Room and board charges vary according to board plan and housing facility.

Financial Aid 221 Federal Work-Study jobs (averaging $1787). 204 state and other part-time jobs (averaging $1934). In 2004, 266 non-need-based awards were made. *Average percent of need met: 85%. Average financial aid package: $16,496. Average need-based loan: $4750. Average need-based gift aid: $5796. Average non-need-based aid: $7366.*

Contact: Director: Dr. Tammy Ostrander, 1200 Kenwood Avenue, Duluth, Minnesota 55811; *Telephone:* 218-723-6046 (Admissions); 800-447-5444 (toll-free) *Fax:* 218-723-5991; *E-mail:* tostrand@css.edu; *Web site:* http://www.ccs.edu/admiss/honors.html

Minnesota State University Mankato

Honors Program

Mankato, Minnesota

The mission of the Honors Program at Minnesota State University is to provide a challenging interdisciplinary program of study for a highly motivated group of undergraduates and to function as an alternative to the traditional general education curriculum. By providing opportunities for students to meet weekly with professors in small, personalized classroom settings, the Honors Program allows participants to become part of a community of scholars that includes experienced faculty members who share a commitment to the program's goals. Honors Program participants have opportunities to attend special lectures, go on field trips, and work at one's own pace in a setting that encourages goal setting, perspective taking, and independence. The Honors Program is designed to help ensure a successful undergraduate experience, to foster creativity and self-direction, and to prepare students for future professional and postgraduate work.

The program consists of three main components. The first is seminars, meeting once weekly. These seminars are taken each semester, with varied topics. Honors sections of general education courses are another component. These are sections of regular general education courses that are taken only by honors students. These classes are often much smaller than regular sections and offer students a chance to work more closely with faculty members. Topics courses are the third component. These consist of classes taught in a discussion/seminar format, offered through different disciplines. The topics courses are taken by upper-level students. The final requirement is a senior project, completed in the student's major discipline with a faculty member as adviser.

A new and exciting feature of the Honors Program is the Honors Learning Community, in which 15 entering honors students are enrolled. This honors cohort takes a group of courses together during the first year on campus and is housed on the same floor of a University residence hall. The Honors Club plans activities such as trips to the Twin Cities area for plays, pizza parties, and discussions on courses to be offered.

The flexible course requirements of the Honors Program at Minnesota State University allow many students to graduate with a double major or to graduate early. The combination of small classes and top students and faculty members allows students to actively learn and interact. The Honors Club provides for social interaction for honors students. The combination of these features makes the Honors Program at Minnesota State University a unique opportunity for students to get all that they can out of their college experience.

Upon graduation from the University, the Honors Program student is designated a University Scholar. This distinction is noted upon the transcript and in a certificate presented to the student. Honors stoles are worn by graduates at the graduation ceremonies.

Students in the program number approximately 250.

Participation Requirements: In order to graduate as part of the Honors Program, a student must maintain a minimum 3.3 GPA and manifest high competency in communication skills. Those students pursuing a B.A. degree are also required to complete at least one year of a foreign language.

Admission Process: Students must first apply and be admitted to Minnesota State University. If they meet the requirements, they may then apply for admission to the Honors Program. Qualifications for entering the program are graduation in the upper 10 percent of the high school class and a minimum composite score of 25 on the ACT test or its equivalent.

Scholarship Availability: No scholarships are offered strictly to Honors students. However, Minnesota State University offers a variety of scholarships to both incoming freshmen and transfer students and students in their major disciplines. Students are urged to contact either their major department or the Admissions Office for further details on these scholarships.

Campus Overview

State-supported comprehensive, founded 1868, part of Minnesota State Colleges and Universities System • **Coed** 12,466 undergraduate students, 90% full-time, 53% women, 47% men.

Undergraduates 11,231 full-time, 1,235 part-time. Students come from 44 states and territories, 68 other countries, 12% are from out of state, 2% African American, 2% Asian American or Pacific Islander, 0.6% Hispanic American, 0.3% Native American, 3% international, 8% transferred in, 22% live on campus.

Faculty *Total:* 696, 70% full-time, 54% with terminal degrees. *Student/faculty ratio:* 23:1.

Academic Programs *Special study options:* academic remediation for entering students, adult/continuing education programs, advanced placement credit, distance learning, double majors, English as a second language, honors programs, independent study, internships, off-campus study, part-time degree program, services for LD students, student-designed majors, study abroad, summer session for credit. *ROTC:* Army (b).

Athletics Member NCAA. All Division II except men's and women's ice hockey (Division I). *Intercollegiate sports:* baseball M(s), basketball M(s)/W(s), cheerleading M/W, cross-country running M(s)/W(s), football M(s), golf M(s)/W(s), ice hockey M(s)/W(s), soccer W(s), softball W(s), swimming and diving M(s)/W(s), tennis M(s)/W(s), track and field M(s)/W(s), volleyball W(s), wrestling M(s). *Intramural sports:* archery M/W, basketball M/W, bowling M/W, fencing M/W, football M, ice hockey M/W, lacrosse M/W, racquetball M/W, rugby M/W, sailing M/W, skiing (cross-country) M/W, skiing (downhill) M/W, soccer M/W, softball M/W, swimming and diving M/W, table tennis M/W, tennis M/W, track and field M/W, volleyball M/W, wrestling M.

Costs (2004–05) *Tuition:* state resident $4376 full-time, $175 per credit part-time; nonresident $9286 full-time, $370 per credit part-time. Full-time tuition and fees vary according to course load and reciprocity agreements. Part-time tuition and fees vary according to course load and reciprocity agreements. *Required fees:* $712 full-time, $30 per credit part-time. *Room and board:* $4716. Room and board charges vary according to board plan.

Financial Aid 367 Federal Work-Study jobs (averaging $3084). 337 state and other part-time jobs (averaging $3057). In 2004, 556 non-need-based awards were made. *Average percent of need met: 79%. Average financial aid package: $6836. Average need-based loan: $3918. Average need-based gift aid: $3475. Average non-need-based aid: $1732.*

Contact: Director: Dr. Rajiv Kapadia, 134 Carkoski Commons, Minnesota State University, Mankato, Minnesota 56001; *Telephone:* 507-389-1314; *E-mail:* rajiv.kapadia@mnsu.edu

North Hennepin Community College

Honors Program

Brooklyn Park, Minnesota

The North Hennepin Community College (NHCC) Honors Program is designed to give the College's top students a way to increase their academic abilities. Two honors seminars, limited to 20 participants, offer students the opportunity to hear and interact with speakers from the community and from the College. The seminars also provide students the opportunity to get to know and work with other students in the program. While the College does not have specific honors courses, students are able to work one-on-one with faculty members who offer Honors Option contracts in their courses. Individual scholarship advising and help is offered to students through the Honors Coordinator and through a special scholarship seminar. At the end of spring semester, a special reception, attended by members of the faculty and administration, friends, and family, is held for those who have completed the program. Since its beginning in 1989, more than 60 students have completed the program. Each year, 25 to 50 students contract to take Honors Option credits. Of those students, an average of 8 to 10 enroll in the program annually.

Participation Requirements: Students take two 1-credit seminars taught by the Honors Coordinator and successfully complete three Honors Contracts offered by Honors Program faculty members. They must maintain at least a 3.3 GPA in order to complete the program. The notation "Honors Program" appears at the top of their transcripts. At graduation they lead the procession of graduates. Their names appear first on the graduation program, designating that they are graduates of the Honors Program, and they are called up to the podium, where the Vice President presents them as the school's premier students and awards each a special certificate.

Admission Process: Students must complete 15 credits and obtain at least a 3.3 GPA. They must also be recommended by an instructor, write a 500-word essay explaining why they wish to be a part of the Honors Program, and have an interview with the Honors Coordinator.

Scholarship Availability: The Presidential Scholarship ($3000) is for high school seniors who graduate in the top 15 percent of their high school class. Selection criteria include academic achievement, extracurricular activities, a written statement describing the importance of the scholarship to the applicant and the importance of higher education to the applicant's goals, and academic need.

The Barbara Mantini Phi Theta Kappa Scholarship ($1000) is awarded to an outstanding student (cumulative GPA of 3.5 or better) who is a PTK member and has given exceptional service to PTK, either as an officer or as an active member. Selection criteria (in order of importance) include 40 PTK or more service points or equivalent academic performance, a written statement describing the importance of the scholarship to the applicant in meeting academic or career goals, an NHCC faculty member's written reference, and financial need.

The Baccalaureate Scholarship ($5000) is given annually to encourage and support an NHCC student who continues to pursue higher education after graduation or transfer from North Hennepin Community College. Application is open only to students currently enrolled at the College who complete their studies in the academic year the scholarship is offered. Eligibility requirements include earning at least 30 credits with a minimum GPA of 3.0 at North Hennepin through the spring semester in which the student plans to graduate. Selection criteria include academic achievement, a demonstrated strong belief in the value of a liberal arts education,

qualities of thoughtfulness and creativity demonstrated through the essay and an interview, and a demonstrated concern for the future, which extends beyond oneself.

Campus Overview

State-supported 2-year, founded 1966, part of Minnesota State Colleges and Universities System • **Coed** 6,602 undergraduate students, 37% full-time, 62% women, 38% men.

Undergraduates 2,461 full-time, 4,141 part-time. Students come from 4 states and territories, 96 other countries, 0.3% are from out of state, 14% African American, 7% Asian American or Pacific Islander, 2% Hispanic American, 0.5% Native American, 1% international, 29% transferred in.

Faculty *Total:* 194, 45% full-time, 100% with terminal degrees. *Student/faculty ratio:* 28:1.

Academic Programs *Special study options:* academic remediation for entering students, accelerated degree program, adult/continuing education programs, advanced placement credit, distance learning, English as a second language, honors programs, independent study, internships, off-campus study, part-time degree program, services for LD students, study abroad, summer session for credit.

Athletics Member NJCAA. *Intramural sports:* basketball M/W, bowling M/W, football M, golf M/W, soccer M, tennis M/W, volleyball M/W.

Costs (2004–05) *Tuition:* state resident $2892 full-time, $121 per credit part-time; nonresident $5355 full-time, $223 per credit part-time. *Required fees:* $247 full-time, $10 per credit part-time.

Contact: Honors Coordinator: Sandra Hofsommer, Honors Program, North Hennepin Community College, 7411 85th Avenue, North, Brooklyn Park, Minnesota 55445; *Telephone:* 763-424-0856; *Fax:* 763-493-0531; *E-mail:* sandra.hofsommer@nhcc.mnscu.edu

Rochester Community and Technical College

Honors Program

Rochester, Minnesota

Honors at Rochester Community and Technical College (RCTC) offers challenge, recognition, and a myriad of other opportunities through several avenues.

First, the Honors Program curriculum offers special honors courses to provide students with a strong grounding in primary texts and critical thinking.

Second, the Honors Program offers mentoring and help in transferring. Students work closely with the RCTC Honors Program Coordinator, who serves as a personal academic mentor, often with the help of a faculty member in the major field. Working with the Coordinator on schedule set-up also earns them the right to priority registration. In addition, to help take the mystique out of the transfer process, Honors Program students are able to participate in "Bridging the Transfer Gap," a workshop designed specifically to address the transfer needs of highly motivated Honors Program students. The Coordinator also writes recommendations and calls transfer institutions.

Third, the RCTC Honors Program offers camaraderie and activities meant to stimulate the intellect. Students can attend special Honors Program SALON sessions throughout the year, have the option of working with GATE (Gifted and Talented) children in the Rochester Public Schools, develop special events for the University Center-Rochester (UC–R) campus, have a "big brother" or "big sister" to help them with various aspects of college life, and have the opportunity to attend conferences with other honors program students from the state, Midwest, and/or nation.

Fourth, students who qualify can also become a member of Phi Theta Kappa (PTK), an international two-year college academic honor society that provides educational and cultural programs and scholarships. The 3-year-old program currently enrolls 60 students (PTK membership is not included in that number).

Participation Requirements: To earn an Honors Diploma, students must apply to the program, be accepted, take honors credits as listed below, and maintain a GPA of 3.3 or above. At graduation, students who have at least a 3.3 GPA and who have completed the appropriate number of honors credits receive a certificate, receive and wear a golden medallion at the graduation ceremony, are identified on the graduation program, and are named as Honors Program graduates as they walk across the stage. The transcript also clearly identifies honors credits. The Honors Diploma necessitates 18 credits, with a minimum of three disciplines, for the A.A. degree; 15 credits, with a minimum of two disciplines, for the A.S. degree; and 12 credits, with a minimum of two disciplines, for the A.A.S. degree.

Admission Process: Interested individuals may apply anytime during the year by filling out an application form. Honors Program students are selected on the basis of GPA, school and/or community experiences, and other life experiences. For the English Honors sequence, the students must also score above 90 percent on the college writing placement test.

Scholarship Availability: Presidential Scholarships are available to all entering freshmen in the top 5 percent of their high school graduating class. RCTC offers a number of other scholarships for both incoming, returning, and outgoing students, and many students who receive scholarships are also in the Honors Program.

Campus Overview

State-supported primarily 2-year, founded 1915, part of Minnesota State Colleges and Universities System • **Small-town** 460-acre campus • **Coed**

Athletics Member NJCAA.

Financial Aid 500 Federal Work-Study jobs (averaging $3000). 300 state and other part-time jobs (averaging $3000).

Contact: Robert Sanborn, 851 30th Avenue SE, Rochester, Minnesota 55904-4999; *Telephone:* 507-285-7244; *Fax:* 507-285-7496; *E-mail:* robert.sanborn@roch.edu; *Web site:* http://www.acd.roch.edu/honors/

Saint John's University (Coordinate with College of Saint Benedict)
Honors Degree Program
St. Joseph, Minnesota

The Honors Program at the College of Saint Benedict and Saint John's University comprises a group of students exploring the world of ideas together. These honors students pride themselves on their shared love of learning and an exciting exchange of ideas that rarely ends when the class period is over. The honors program is integrated into the common liberal arts core curriculum, enabling honors students to take honors core curriculum classes in place of classes in the general core curriculum. These courses focus on an interdisciplinary approach to ways of knowing and feature small class sizes (20 to 25 students maximum) built around lively discussion. In this way, completing the honors program does not interfere with either study-abroad opportunities or the pursuit of single or even double majors.

The program features small out-of-class reading and film discussion groups with professors, service opportunities, and cultural enrichment activities.

The program admits approximately 130 students each year.

Participation Requirements: In the first year, students take either the honors first-year symposium or great issues in philosophy. The honors symposium is centered on a variety of topics in natural sciences, fine arts, social sciences, and humanities. Great issues in philosophy examines some of the most challenging questions surrounding the human condition. In the sophomore year, students take either one or two honors courses that serve as lower-division requirements in the core curriculum: natural science, social science, theology, or general humanities. In the junior year, students have the opportunity to take a yearlong course entitled Great Books. This course features the reading and discussion of a large corpus of the world's finest learning and literature. In the senior year, students may research and write the honors thesis. For their thesis, students work closely with faculty members from their major field of study to produce high-quality independent undergraduate research.

To remain in good standing, students must maintain at least a 3.0 cumulative GPA in their first year of study and garner a minimum 3.4 cumulative GPA upon graduation. Students who complete the program receive special recognition at graduation along with final transcripts marked All College Honors.

Admission Process: High school students are offered admission to the Honors Program on the basis of college board scores, high school rank, and GPA. Students not admitted in the first term of freshman year may apply for admission to the Honors Program upon the completion of one full term of study. Transfer students may also apply based upon previous academic work.

Scholarship Availability: Saint John's University and the College of Saint Benedict have Regents and Trustees merit scholarships not explicitly linked to admission in the honors program. All Regents and Trustees scholarship holders are offered admission to the honors program.

Campus Overview

Independent Roman Catholic comprehensive, founded 1857 • **Rural** 2400-acre campus with easy access to Minneapolis–St. Paul • **Coed primarily men** 1,895 undergraduate students, 98% full-time, 100% men.

Undergraduates 1,865 full-time, 30 part-time. Students come from 32 states and territories, 27 other countries, 15% are from out of state, 0.8% African American, 2% Asian American or Pacific Islander, 1% Hispanic American, 0.3% Native American, 3% international, 2% transferred in, 83% live on campus.

Faculty *Total:* 167, 89% full-time, 83% with terminal degrees. *Student/faculty ratio:* 12:1.

Academic Programs *Special study options:* accelerated degree program, advanced placement credit, double majors, English as a second language, honors programs, independent study, internships, off-campus study, services for LD students, student-designed majors, study abroad. *ROTC:* Army (b). *Unusual degree programs:* 3-2 engineering with University of Minnesota, Twin Cities Campus.

Athletics Member NCAA. All Division III. *Intercollegiate sports:* baseball M, basketball M, crew M(c), cross-country running M, football M, golf M, ice hockey M, lacrosse M(c), riflery M(c), rugby M(c), skiing (cross-country) M, soccer M, swimming and diving M, tennis M, track and field M, ultimate Frisbee M(c), volleyball M(c), water polo M(c), wrestling M. *Intramural sports:* basketball M, racquetball M, rock climbing M(c), skiing (cross-country) M(c), skiing (downhill) M(c), soccer M, softball M, ultimate Frisbee M, volleyball M.

Costs (2004–05) *Comprehensive fee:* $28,266 includes full-time tuition ($21,758), mandatory fees ($390), and room and board ($6118). Part-time tuition: $907 per credit. Part-time tuition and fees vary according to course load. *Required fees:* $195 per term part-time. *College room only:* $3008. Room and board charges vary according to board plan and housing facility.

Financial Aid 157 Federal Work-Study jobs (averaging $2263). 1,007 state and other part-time jobs (averaging $1977). In 2004, 560 non-need-based awards were made. *Average percent of need met:* 84%. *Average financial aid package:* $18,845. *Average need-based loan:* $4489. *Average need-based gift aid:* $8927. *Average non-need-based aid:* $6143.

Contact: Director: Dr. Richard M. White, Department of Chemistry, CSB/SJU, St. Joseph, Minnesota 56374; *Telephone:* 320-363-5994; *Fax:* 320-363-5582; *E-mail:* rwhite@csbsju.edu; *Web site:* http://www.csbsju.edu/honors

Southwest Minnesota State University
Honors Program
Marshall, Minnesota

The Honors Program provides a way for qualified students to design their own general studies requirements by selecting specific courses from the catalog and/or designing specific projects that complement their particular strengths. Honors students are allowed to enroll in classes that are full at the time of registration and may take any class for an extra honors credit. Upon completion of their work, honors students are given special recognition at Commencement and acknowledgment on their transcripts. The program sponsors an Honors Club, which sanctions social events and trips.

Participation Requirements: The Honors Program was initiated in 1971 and currently enrolls 130 students.

Admission Process: Students wishing to enter the program should have achieved a composite ACT score of at least 27 and must provide a letter of reference from a high school teacher, counselor, or principal.

Scholarship Availability: Scholarships are awarded on a competitive basis to currently enrolled honors students. Incoming and transfer students are awarded scholarships, when qualified, by the Admissions Office working in conjunction with the President's Office.

Campus Overview

State-supported comprehensive, founded 1963, part of Minnesota State Colleges and Universities System • **Coed** 5,167 undergraduate students, 45% full-time, 60% women, 40% men.

Undergraduates 2,310 full-time, 2,857 part-time. Students come from 27 states and territories, 29 other countries, 12% are from out of state, 1% African American, 0.6% Asian American or Pacific Islander, 0.4% Hispanic American, 0.2% Native American, 3% international, 4% transferred in, 53% live on campus.

Faculty *Total:* 159, 77% full-time, 58% with terminal degrees. *Student/faculty ratio:* 18:1.

Academic Programs *Special study options:* academic remediation for entering students, accelerated degree program, adult/continuing education programs, advanced placement credit, distance learning, double majors, external degree program, freshman honors college, honors programs, independent study, internships, off-campus study, part-time degree program, services for LD students, student-designed majors, study abroad, summer session for credit.

Athletics Member NCAA. All Division II. *Intercollegiate sports:* baseball M(s), basketball M(s)/W(s), football M(s), golf W(s), soccer W(s), softball W(s), tennis W(s), volleyball W(s), wrestling M(s).

Intramural sports: badminton M/W, basketball M/W, football M, ice hockey M, racquetball M/W, softball M/W, tennis M/W, volleyball M/W.

Costs (2004–05) *Tuition:* state resident $4538 full-time; nonresident $4538 full-time. *Required fees:* $756 full-time. *Room and board:* $4806.

Financial Aid 120 Federal Work-Study jobs (averaging $2078). 212 state and other part-time jobs (averaging $2100). In 2003, 307 non-need-based awards were made. *Average percent of need met:* 57%. *Average financial aid package:* $6424. *Average need-based loan:* $3237. *Average need-based gift aid:* $3330. *Average non-need-based aid:* $1624.

Contact: Director: Dr. Steve Kramer, Marshall, Minnesota 56258; *Telephone:* 507-537-6240; *Fax:* 507-537-6322; *E-mail:* kramer@southwestmsu.edu.

University of Minnesota, Morris
Honors Program
Morris, Minnesota

The Honors Program at the University of Minnesota, Morris (UMM), is at the core of the University's mission as a public liberal arts college. Its purpose is to provide a distinctive, academically challenging, intellectual experience that inspires students to pursue learning for its own sake and to create their own interdisciplinary links between fields of study. It does this by relying upon an interdisciplinary curriculum that is team taught by UMM faculty members from different academic divisions and disciplines. Successful completion of the Honors Program provides the student a UMM degree With Honors as a recognition of their achievement and willingness to explore ideas beyond disciplinary confines.

All honors students must enroll in a team-taught core course that explores significant works from history, literature, philosophy, and science from an interdisciplinary perspective. The students may then choose from several interdisciplinary elective offerings each semester. Honors courses are team taught by faculty members from different academic divisions, who encourage active learning as the students examine a topic of special interest to the faculty members that design them. Course offerings are quite diverse and typically enroll 15 to 20 students. Among other topics, courses have focused on the enlightenment, networks and innovation, utopia(s), ecological health and sustainability, the medieval mind, the apocalypse, and the tension between notions of a republic and an empire. As seniors, honors students complete an Honors Project: a substantial scholarly or creative interdisciplinary work designed by the student working cooperatively with a project adviser. Upon completion, the project is defended before a panel of faculty members from different disciplines. Many students complete their honors projects in conjunction with the Undergraduate Research Opportunities Program (UROP), which includes a $1700 stipend to support the research and travel to present their work at national conferences.

In addition to these requirements, Honors Program students often volunteer for service initiatives, attend public presentations and music and theatric performances, enjoy occasional field trips and outings, and mentor those just starting in the program.

The UMM Honors Program began in 1989. It admits approximately 30 students per year and currently has an enrollment of 75.

Participation Requirements: Students in UMM's Honors Program must complete a core course, Traditions in Human Thought, in the fall of their sophomore year and complete at least four other honors courses while at UMM. In addition, students must complete a multidisciplinary senior honors project and successfully defend it to a panel of faculty members from different disciplines. Successful completion of these Honors Program requirements and earning a UMM GPA of at least 3.5 entitles a student to special recognition at commencement. Moreover, official transcripts and diplomas bear the designation Honors.

Admission Process: All UMM students are eligible to participate in the Honors Program. Students normally apply to the program by March 15 of their freshman year and begin course work in the fall of their sophomore year. While everyone may apply, academic success in the fall semester, faculty recommendations, and a short essay describing the interdisciplinary interests of the applicant may be used to limit the number of students to those with the proven motivation to likely succeed in the program. Transfer students should contact the Honors Program Director for special instructions.

Scholarship Availability: Campuswide scholarships of varying amounts, awarded through the Office of Admissions, are based on academic performance, leadership, and talent. Automatic awards are given to those students who rank in the top 20 percent of their high school class, in addition to automatic awards for National Merit Finalists, Semifinalists, and Commended Scholars. Students may also apply for competitive scholarships that range in amount from $500 to $3000 per year. Qualified American Indians receive a full tuition waiver in honor of the campus' origins as the Morris Indian School founded in the 1800s. The Honors Program does not offer scholarships; however most honors students are recipients of the academic and talent awards given by the Office of Admissions

Campus Overview

State-supported 4-year, founded 1959, part of University of Minnesota System • **Coed** 1,836 undergraduate students, 91% full-time, 61% women, 39% men.

Undergraduates 1,666 full-time, 170 part-time. Students come from 26 states and territories, 18 other countries, 15% are from out of state, 2% African American, 3% Asian American or Pacific Islander, 1% Hispanic American, 8% Native American, 1% international, 3% transferred in, 51% live on campus.

Faculty *Total:* 161, 75% full-time, 76% with terminal degrees. *Student/faculty ratio:* 13:1.

Academic Programs *Special study options:* accelerated degree program, adult/continuing education programs, advanced placement credit, distance learning, double majors, external degree program, freshman honors college, honors programs, independent study, internships, off-campus study, part-time degree program, services for LD students, student-designed majors, study abroad, summer session for credit. *Unusual degree programs:* 3-2 engineering with University of Minnesota, Twin Cities Campus.

Athletics Member NCAA. All Division III. *Intercollegiate sports:* baseball M, basketball M/W, cross-country running W, football M, golf M/W, soccer W, softball W, swimming and diving W, tennis M/W, track and field M/W, volleyball W. *Intramural sports:* baseball M, basketball M/W, bowling M/W, cheerleading M(c)/W(c), equestrian sports M(c)/W(c), fencing M(c)/W(c), football M/W, ice hockey M/W, racquetball M/W, rock climbing M(c)/W(c), rugby M(c)/W(c), skiing (cross-country) M/W, soccer M(c)/W(c), softball M/W, swimming and diving M/W, table tennis M/W, ultimate Frisbee M(c)/W(c), volleyball M(c)/W(c).

Costs (2004–05) *Tuition:* state resident $7668 full-time, $256 per credit part-time; nonresident $7668 full-time, $256 per credit part-time. Full-time tuition and fees vary according to reciprocity agreements. Part-time tuition and fees vary according to course load and reciprocity agreements. *Required fees:* $1388 full-time, $10 per credit part-time. *Room and board:* $5250; room only: $2510. Room and board charges vary according to board plan and housing facility.

Financial Aid 487 Federal Work-Study jobs (averaging $734). 531 state and other part-time jobs (averaging $900). In 2004, 287 non-need-based awards were made. *Average percent of need met:*

83%. *Average financial aid package:* $12,065. *Average need-based loan:* $6989. *Average need-based gift aid:* $5669. *Average non-need-based aid:* $3374.

Contact: Director: Dr. Bart D. Finzel, 231 Community Services Building, University of Minnesota, Morris, Morris, Minnesota 56267; *Telephone:* 320-589-6464; *Fax:* 320-589-1661; *E-mail:* ummhonor@mrs.umn.edu; *Web site:* http://www.morris.edu/academic/honors/

University of Minnesota, Twin Cities Campus
Honors Programs
Minneapolis, Minnesota

Honors programs at the University of Minnesota are designed to give special recognition to the talents, achievements, and potential of talented and highly motivated students. Honors students enjoy the best of two worlds: the uncommon depth and breadth of study at one of the nation's finest public research universities plus the extra challenge, personal attention, and sense of community often associated with small, highly selective private colleges.

The College of Agricultural, Food, and Environmental Sciences; College of Biological Sciences; College of Human Ecology; College of Liberal Arts; Carlson School of Management; College of Natural Resources; and Institute of Technology admit freshmen to their honors programs. Programs vary, but all share a commitment to scholarship, academic excellence, and personalized learning. Opportunities include research apprenticeships, workshops, and colloquia with outstanding University scholar-teachers; special limited-enrollment courses and seminars; advanced-study opportunities, including internships and independent study; honors housing; study abroad; one-on-one honors advising by professional honors advisers, peer advisers, and honors faculty members; undergraduate teaching and research assistantships; retreats, field trips, and other informal group activities with other honors students and faculty members; social and cultural activities that promote friendship and community among honors students; and honors recognition at special events, culminating in graduation with honors.

Participation Requirements: Honors students who take at least four honors courses and maintain at least a 3.5 GPA during their first two years of study may earn the freshman-sophomore Honors Certificate, which is noted on their transcript. Upperclass students who take at least four more honors courses, maintain at least a 3.5 GPA in their advanced classes, and meet departmental honors requirements may graduate with an honors degree.

Admission Process: New freshmen are admitted by application in the year prior to their arrival on campus. Admissions standards vary by college, but these new freshmen are typically in the 90th percentile of their high school class and have a composite score of at least 28 on the ACT or 1260 (verbal and math combined) on the SAT I. All interested students should visit the Admissions Web site at http://admissions.tc.umn.edu and click on Honors. Transfer students may apply directly to one of the college honors programs.

Scholarship Availability: Merit scholarships are available to students from the University, from colleges, and from departments. The University awards about $4 million in scholarships each year to incoming freshmen, and colleges and departments award several hundred thousand dollars a year in scholarships both to incoming and continuing students.

Campus Overview

State-supported university, founded 1851, part of University of Minnesota System • **Coed** 32,716 undergraduate students, 81% full-time, 53% women, 47% men.

Undergraduates 26,479 full-time, 6,237 part-time. Students come from 55 states and territories, 85 other countries, 27% are from out of state, 4% African American, 9% Asian American or Pacific Islander, 2% Hispanic American, 0.7% Native American, 2% international, 5% transferred in, 22% live on campus.

Faculty *Total:* 3,079, 88% full-time, 95% with terminal degrees. *Student/faculty ratio:* 22:1.

Academic Programs *Special study options:* academic remediation for entering students, accelerated degree program, adult/continuing education programs, advanced placement credit, cooperative education, distance learning, double majors, English as a second language, external degree program, freshman honors college, honors programs, independent study, internships, off-campus study, part-time degree program, services for LD students, student-designed majors, study abroad, summer session for credit. *ROTC:* Army (b), Air Force (b).

Athletics Member NCAA. All Division I except football (Division I-A). *Intercollegiate sports:* baseball M(s), basketball M(s)/W(s), cross-country running M(s)/W(s), golf M(s)/W(s), gymnastics M(s)/W(s), ice hockey M(s)/W(s), soccer W(s), softball W(s), swimming and diving M(s)/W(s), tennis M(s)/W(s), track and field M(s)/W(s), volleyball W(s), wrestling M(s). *Intramural sports:* baseball M/W, basketball M/W, bowling M/W, crew M/W, football M/W, golf M/W, ice hockey M/W, rugby M/W, skiing (cross-country) M/W, skiing (downhill) M/W, soccer M/W, softball M/W, tennis M/W, volleyball M/W, water polo M/W, wrestling M/W.

Costs (2004–05) *Tuition:* state resident $6678 full-time, $257 per credit part-time; nonresident $18,308 full-time, $704 per credit part-time. Full-time tuition and fees vary according to program and reciprocity agreements. Part-time tuition and fees vary according to course load, program, and reciprocity agreements. No tuition increase for student's term of enrollment. *Required fees:* $1352 full-time. *Room and board:* $6458; room only: $3730. Room and board charges vary according to board plan, housing facility, and location.

Financial Aid In 2003, 2638 non-need-based awards were made. *Average percent of need met:* 76%. *Average financial aid package:* $9027. *Average need-based loan:* $5720. *Average need-based gift aid:* $6074. *Average non-need-based aid:* $4238.

Contact: Director: Professor Richard W. McCormick, 115 Johnston Hall, University of Minnesota, Twin Cities Campus, Minneapolis, Minnesota 55455; *Telephone:* 612-624-5522; *Fax:* 612-626-7314; *E-mail:* mccor001@umn.edu; *Web site:* http://cla.umn.edu//honors

MISSISSIPPI

Alcorn State University

Honors Curriculum Program

Lorman, Mississippi

The Honors Curriculum Program at Alcorn State University, established in 1961, is designed to provide unique study and learning experiences for highly motivated students. The program aims to strengthen and encourage students' intellectual curiosity through a broad liberal arts core, critical analysis colloquia, and independent research. Courses are taught by senior-level faculty members, and individual class enrollment is generally 25 or fewer. The program offers students special assistance in identifying and applying for scholarships, internships, student exchange, and study-abroad opportunities. Program participants are assigned to an honors academic adviser for the first two years of study. Thereafter, students are advised by a departmental adviser. The Honors Student Organization (HSO) provides a forum for students-initiated academic, social, and extracurricular activities. A special honors work center, which includes a computer laboratory and reference materials, is provided for students. There are 150 students enrolled in the program.

Participation Requirements: During the freshman year, students may enroll in honors sections of general education courses. A colloquium series, which emphasizes critical thinking and lively communication, grows out of enriched reading experiences for sophomore students. Sophomore students may also enroll in special honors sections of multi-section courses, which are offered in response to student interest. An interdisciplinary honors research-based seminar is provided for juniors. At the senior level, students engage in independent research in their discipline.

Students in the program must enroll in at least 3 hours of honors work each semester. Participants must maintain a cumulative GPA of at least 3.25. Upon graduation, students who complete at least 24 hours of honors course work are recognized as Honors Curriculum Program Scholars. Honors Curriculum Program Scholars are awarded a special honor cord and recognized with appropriate citation on the Commencement program.

Admission Process: Freshmen are selected on the basis of scores on admissions and placement examinations. Students applying after the first semester of the freshman year are selected on the basis of their cumulative average, the recommendation of a faculty member, and an interview with the Director of Honors

Scholarship Availability: Scholarships are provided to participants through the Admissions Office. Full academic scholarships for incoming freshman (tuition and room and board) are available on a first-come, first served basis. More than 90 percent of participants hold a full academic scholarship. The scholarship is renewable, up to four years, provided the student maintains at least a 3.5 cumulative GPA and remains in good standing with the University.

Campus Overview

State-supported comprehensive, founded 1871, part of Mississippi Institutions of Higher Learning • **Coed** 2,834 undergraduate students, 89% full-time, 63% women, 37% men.

Undergraduates 2,516 full-time, 318 part-time. Students come from 31 states and territories, 13 other countries, 14% are from out of state, 91% African American, 0.2% Asian American or Pacific Islander, 0.3% Hispanic American, 2% international, 10% transferred in, 52% live on campus.

Faculty *Total:* 224, 83% full-time, 58% with terminal degrees. *Student/faculty ratio:* 14:1.

Academic Programs *Special study options:* academic remediation for entering students, advanced placement credit, cooperative education, distance learning, double majors, honors programs, independent study, internships, part-time degree program. *ROTC:* Army (b).

Athletics Member NCAA. All Division I. *Intercollegiate sports:* baseball M(s), basketball M(s)/W(s), cross-country running M(s)/W(s), football M(s), golf M(s)/W(s), soccer W(s), softball W(s), tennis M(s)/W(s), track and field M(s)/W(s), volleyball W(s). *Intramural sports:* basketball M/W, football M, gymnastics M/W, softball W, swimming and diving M/W, table tennis M/W, tennis M/W, track and field M/W, volleyball M/W, wrestling M/W.

Costs (2004–05) *Tuition:* state resident $3732 full-time, $156 per hour part-time; nonresident $8463 full-time, $353 per hour part-time. *Required fees:* $733 full-time. *Room and board:* $4012; room only: $2272.

Financial Aid 244 Federal Work-Study jobs (averaging $2060). In 2003, 450 non-need-based awards were made. *Average percent of need met:* 79%. *Average financial aid package:* $10,500. *Average need-based loan:* $5500. *Average need-based gift aid:* $4500. *Average non-need-based aid:* $4900.

Contact: Director: Dr. Donzell Lee, 1000 ASU Drive #175, Alcorn State University, Alcorn State, Mississippi 39096; *Telephone:* 601-877-6138; *Fax:* 601-877-6256; *E-mail:* dlee@alcorn.edu; *Web site:* http://www.alcorn.edu

Delta State University
Honors Program
Cleveland, Mississippi

*T*he Honors Program, designed to enhance the already excellent *educational opportunities at Delta State University, offers a distinctive and singular educational experience for highly motivated, independent students who accept the challenge of a program that stresses intellectual rigor and fosters critical thinking. The Honors Fellows are provided with many opportunities for cocurricular and extracurricular activities, including, but not limited to, cross-cultural experiences, civic engagement, lectures, travel, symposia, and performances. The program also provides additional mentoring and advising opportunities for the Fellows in both formal and casual settings and seeks to create a community of invigorated and thoughtful scholar citizens. A maximum of 16 students are invited to join the program every year.*

The Honors Program is in its second year and currently enrolls 32 students.

Participation Requirements: In addition to their participation in the Honors Program extracurricular and cocurricular activities, Honors Fellows must successfully complete 15 credit hours each semester, maintaining a minimum GPA of 3.5 to maintain scholarships and graduation recognition, which consists of an acknowledgment at commencement and a notation on their transcript.

Admission Process: Guidelines for consideration for the Honors Program include a composite ACT score of 26 or higher (no sub-score may be below 17), a minimum high school GPA of 3.5 (4.0 scale), and documented evidence of leadership and community engagement. A special application packet consists of the application form, a page listing extracurricular activities, two letters of reference from nonfamily members, and a 250- to 500-word essay. Applicants who may not meet all the ACT and/or GPA qualifications are considered for admission on the basis of their exceptional achievements in other areas. The deadline for completed applications is April 1 for fall admission.

Scholarship Availability: The Honors Program offers up to $1000 per semester in scholarship funding to supplement the financial support that most Honors Fellows apply for and receive through the wide range of scholarships Delta State University offers for academic excellence. This award is subject to the University's scholarship policy, which states that institutional, foundation, and state-funded scholarships are all held to a maximum yearly amount that must not exceed the actual cost of tuition, room, board, and a $300-per-semester book allowance.

Campus Overview

State-supported comprehensive, founded 1924, part of Mississippi Institutions of Higher Learning • **Coed** 3,148 undergraduate students, 85% full-time, 61% women, 39% men.

Undergraduates 2,670 full-time, 478 part-time. Students come from 26 states and territories, 21 other countries, 9% are from out of state, 37% African American, 0.3% Asian American or Pacific Islander, 0.7% Hispanic American, 0.2% Native American, 18% transferred in, 35% live on campus.

Faculty *Total:* 281, 58% full-time, 58% with terminal degrees. *Student/faculty ratio:* 14:1.

Academic Programs *Special study options:* academic remediation for entering students, advanced placement credit, cooperative education, distance learning, double majors, honors programs, independent study, internships, part-time degree program, services for LD students, summer session for credit. *ROTC:* Air Force (b).

Athletics Member NCAA. All Division II. *Intercollegiate sports:* baseball M(s), basketball M(s)/W(s), cheerleading M/W, cross-

country running W(s), football M(s), golf M(s), softball W, swimming and diving M(s)/W(s), tennis M(s)/W(s). *Intramural sports:* archery M/W, badminton M/W, basketball M/W, bowling M/W, cross-country running M/W, football M/W, golf M/W, racquetball M/W, riflery M/W, soccer M/W, softball M/W, swimming and diving M/W, table tennis M/W, tennis M/W, track and field M/W, volleyball M/W.

Costs (2004–05) *Tuition:* state resident $3582 full-time, $127 per semester hour part-time; nonresident $8522 full-time, $333 per semester hour part-time. *Required fees:* $490 full-time. *Room and board:* $3734.

Financial Aid 318 Federal Work-Study jobs (averaging $1650).

Contact: Director: Dr. Beverly Moon, Honors Program, Box 3215, Kethley 220A, Delta State University, Cleveland, Mississippi 38733; *Telephone:* 662-846-4091; *Fax:* 662-846-4099; *E-mail:* bmoon@deltastate.edu

Hinds Community College
Honors Program
Raymond, Mississippi

*T*he mission of Hinds Community College Honors Program (HCCH) *is to provide an enhanced and supportive learning environment for outstanding students. The Honors Program curriculum features designated core-curriculum honors course sections, seminars, interdisciplinary studies, independent study, research opportunities, international study, and leadership development. Special cocurricular activities and field trips are also part of the Honors Program. Individual and group counseling are provided through the College Counseling Offices and the HCCH Center. HCCH students are given priority in scheduling courses at HCC. The program also helps honors students locate and apply for scholarships at four-year institutions and schedules campus visits and introductions to honors programs at four-year institutions. The HCCH program works closely with Phi Theta Kappa and other honorary scholastic societies with HCC chapters to encourage and reward academic excellence.*

Honors courses are offered in the core-curriculum areas of art, biology, education, English, history, humanities, math, psychology, and speech. In addition, courses are offered in career exploration, leadership development, and improvement of study. Classes typically have 15–20 students. This allows for collaborative and experiential learning, an assortment of hands-on activities, and more opportunities to read and write at advanced levels. Students are encouraged to become outstanding, independent learners capable of critical thinking and self-expression. Honors courses are taught by experienced members of the Hinds teaching faculty who are known for excellence in the classroom as well as in their academic fields. Students have frequent interaction with other honors students, and faculty members help to build a community spirit. The HCCH Center provides a location for students to gather and visit or study. The center has a library, computer lab, group-study area, and lounge for both faculty member and student use. The Honors Forum, a weekly seminar for all honors students, provides an opportunity for intellectual discussion on the issues facing society today. Honors advisers in the HCC counseling offices and HCCH Center provide students with personalized attention. Students' individual needs and interests are given priority in all advising.

Students also enjoy picnics, lectures, special presentations, workshops, and field trips. Special events are also scheduled for those students living in Main Hall and Virden Hall on the Raymond Campus.

The first year of a comprehensive program was 1995. Courses have been taught on the Raymond Campus for twenty years. There are now 150 students enrolled in the program.

Participation Requirements: Students are eligible to receive all of the HCCH benefits and fringe benefits as long as they are registered participants. Honors scholarship students must undertake at least 3 hours of honors work during a semester and must enroll in the Honors Humanities Forum each semester (1 semester hour credit). To graduate from Hinds Community College Honors Program as a Distinguished Honors Scholar, the HCCH student must complete 18 hours of honors study and the Leadership Program and maintain a minimum overall GPA of 3.5. Students who accomplish this receive an Honors Program medallion and honors cord at the Honors Awards Ceremony in the spring. Students who complete 12 hours of honors study with a minimum cumulative GPA of 3.5 are given honors cords during the Honors Awards Ceremony. Both groups of honors graduates receive a gold seal on their diploma and recognition on their transcripts.

Scholarship Availability: The following scholarships are contingent on criteria in parenthesis: Faculty Scholarships (ACT 21–24), Dean's Scholarships (ACT 25–28), Presidential Scholarship (ACT 29+), and Development Foundation Scholarships (criteria vary). HCCH scholarships are available for a maximum of four consecutive fall and spring semesters. Applicants must be enrolled in 12 or more semester hours, 4 of which must be in honors studies. Scholarship recipients must maintain full-time student status and a minimum 3.25 GPA. Applicants must complete an HCC Financial Aid/Scholarship Application and an HCCH Application and must submit both forms to the HCCH Center. Recipients must be registered with the HCCH Program.

Campus Overview

State and locally supported 2-year, founded 1917, part of Mississippi State Board for Community and Junior Colleges • **Coed** 9,961 undergraduate students, 72% full-time, 65% women, 35% men.

Undergraduates 7,145 full-time, 2,816 part-time. Students come from 16 states and territories, 1 other country, 3% are from out of state, 52% African American, 0.5% Asian American or Pacific Islander, 0.6% Hispanic American, 0.2% Native American, 15% live on campus.

Faculty *Total:* 656, 54% full-time, 13% with terminal degrees. *Student/faculty ratio:* 17:1.

Academic Programs *Special study options:* academic remediation for entering students, accelerated degree program, adult/continuing education programs, advanced placement credit, cooperative education, distance learning, double majors, freshman honors college, honors programs, independent study, part-time degree program, services for LD students, summer session for credit. *ROTC:* Army (c).

Athletics Member NJCAA. *Intercollegiate sports:* baseball M(s), basketball M(s)/W(s), cross-country running M(s), football M(s), golf M(s), soccer M(s), softball W(s), tennis M(s)/W(s), track and field M(s). *Intramural sports:* basketball M/W, football M/W, softball M/W, volleyball M/W.

Costs (2004–05) *Tuition:* state resident $1660 full-time, $85 per semester hour part-time; nonresident $3866 full-time, $170 per semester hour part-time. *Room and board:* $2310; room only: $1010.

Financial Aid 300 Federal Work-Study jobs (averaging $1250). 200 state and other part-time jobs (averaging $1000).

Contact: Director: Kristi Sather-Smith, P.O. Box 1100, HCCH, 212 Administration Building, Raymond, Mississippi 39154; *Telephone:* 601-857-3531 or 800-HINDSCC Ext. 3531 (toll-free); *Fax:* 601-857-1221; *E-mail:* kasather-smith@hindscc.edu

Holmes Community College
Holmes Honors Program
Goodman, Mississippi

*T*he mission of the honors program at Holmes Community College is to encourage excellence in the classroom and to provide faculty members a laboratory for innovation in teaching and learning. The object is to keep intellectually gifted and highly motivated students challenged not only in their studies but in their personal lives. Holmes wishes to continue to stimulate the curious, questioning minds of its honors participants as well as provide ample opportunities for them to exercise their initiative and innovational skills. Qualities necessary for honors students are honesty, character, and motivation. They are characteristically more mature than the average college student and are more goal-oriented. They thrive on class participation and are typically more competitive.

Creative and innovative teaching is encouraged in the Holmes Honors Program. Alternative approaches to testing, the use of resources in addition to the text, and inclusion of current events are all part of honors instruction. There are presently honors courses in English Composition, English Literature, History, and Music Appreciation. Also included is a 1-hour forum in which personal finance, etiquette, genealogy, and tort reform are studied, and interesting people from the surrounding area speak on various subjects. This course also brings together students from different majors. Forum students are offered the opportunity to work with faculty members in research projects and to attend NCHC conferences. Since Holmes is located in a rural area, an appreciation of the arts is fostered by providing opportunities to see plays, attend concerts, and take tours to the nearby capital city, Jackson, funded by the honors budget. The Holmes Honors Program has adopted a portion of the recycling effort on campus, with the proceeds going to scholarships or community service.

The honors program at Holmes Community College was established in 2001. Generously supported by the administration, the program continues to grow and influence the lives of young people. The current enrollment is 98.

Participation Requirements: To be a graduate of the Holmes Honors Program, each student must successfully complete 12 hours of honors credits within four semesters and maintain a minimum 3.5 cumulative GPA. Honors graduates are designated in the graduation program and receive an additional honors diploma. Honors students who continue their education at one of the major universities in Mississippi are accepted into its honors program.

Admission Process: Honors applicants must fulfill general admission requirements of the College. For entering freshmen, full- or part-time, the requirements are a current and complete application for admission (available online at the Web site listed in the Contact section), an official high school transcript, and an ACT score of 24 or above or a letter of recommendation from an academic faculty member at their high school. The College is aware, however, that the ACT is not a definitive evaluation. There are students who, for whatever reason, have not performed up to their potential in prior educational experiences. They may enter the Holmes Honors Program with a letter of recommendation from an academic instructor from their high school, with one-semester probation. They may continue in the program with a minimum cumulative 3.5 GPA.

Scholarship Availability: Students who register for and complete a 3-hour honors course along with the honors forum are awarded a $200 book voucher per semester.

Campus Overview

State and locally supported 2-year, founded 1928, part of Mississippi State Board for Community and Junior Colleges • **Coed** 4,494 undergraduate students, 72% full-time, 66% women, 34% men.

Undergraduates 3,251 full-time, 1,243 part-time. Students come from 11 states and territories, 1% are from out of state, 45% African American, 0.3% Hispanic American, 0.1% Native American, 12% live on campus.

Faculty *Total:* 351, 36% full-time, 3% with terminal degrees. *Student/faculty ratio:* 19:1.

Academic Programs *Special study options:* academic remediation for entering students, adult/continuing education programs, advanced placement credit, cooperative education, distance learning, services for LD students, summer session for credit.

Athletics Member NJCAA. *Intercollegiate sports:* baseball M(s), basketball M(s)/W, football M(s), golf M(s)/W(s), soccer M(s)/W(s), softball W(s), tennis M(s)/W(s). *Intramural sports:* basketball M/W, football M/W, softball M/W, volleyball M/W.

Costs (2004–05) *Tuition:* state resident $1430 full-time, $65 per semester hour part-time. Part-time tuition and fees vary according to course load. *Required fees:* $330 full-time, $10 per term part-time. *Room and board:* $3800. Room and board charges vary according to housing facility.

Financial Aid 160 Federal Work-Study jobs (averaging $700).

Contact: Director: Janet E. Simpson, P.O. Box 369, Goodman, Mississippi 39079; *Telephone:* 662-472-9030; *Fax:* 662-472-9156; *E-mail:* jsimpson@holmescc.edu; *Web site:* http://www.holmescc.edu

Jackson State University
W.E.B. Du Bois Honors College
Jackson, Mississippi

*T*he W.E.B. Du Bois Honors College at Jackson State University has graduated more than 2,000 students since its inception in 1980. Graduates of the Honors College have a 100 percent admission rate to graduate and professional schools and an equally successful record of employment.

Designed to provide its participants with an enriched, rigorous, and challenging curriculum, the W.E.B. Du Bois Honors College aims to foster the intellectual development of students; to encourage creative and analytical thinking, critical inquiry, and scholarship; to nurture intellectual independence; and to prepare students well for graduate and professional schools.

Assistance in securing admission to research programs and graduate and professional schools is available. Smaller classes, honors floors for freshmen in two of the dorms, and honors dorms for upperclassmen are offered. Scholarships are available.

Current enrollment is 500 students. All majors at the University are represented in the enrollment.

Participation Requirements: Honors sections of the University's general education core curriculum constitute the basis of the Honors College requirements at Jackson State University. In addition, students may take honors courses offered by their departments or by other departments. Weekly meetings for freshmen, special lectures, and individualized advice and guidance throughout the students' tenure are aspects of the program.

Certificates of participation are awarded to students after graduation, and all honors classes taken are recorded on student transcripts as such.

Admission Process: Selection of incoming freshmen to the Honors College is based on ACT/SAT I scores, high school GPA, and rank in class. Transfer students may join the Honors College during their freshman or sophomore year.

Campus Overview

State-supported university, founded 1877, part of Mississippi

Institutions of Higher Learning • **Coed** 6,605 undergraduate students, 87% full-time, 62% women, 38% men.

Undergraduates 5,714 full-time, 891 part-time. Students come from 40 states and territories, 38 other countries, 21% are from out of state, 97% African American, 0.3% Asian American or Pacific Islander, 0.2% Hispanic American, 0.1% Native American, 1% international, 5% transferred in, 34% live on campus.

Faculty *Total:* 465, 78% full-time, 64% with terminal degrees. *Student/faculty ratio:* 18:1.

Academic Programs *Special study options:* academic remediation for entering students, adult/continuing education programs, advanced placement credit, cooperative education, distance learning, honors programs, internships, off-campus study, part-time degree program, services for LD students, study abroad, summer session for credit. *ROTC:* Army (b). *Unusual degree programs:* 3-2 engineering with Mississippi State University, Auburn University, Tuskegee University, University of Mississippi, Georgia Institute of Technology, Southern University and Agricultural and Mechanical College, University of Minnesota.

Athletics Member NCAA. All Division I except football (Division I-AA). *Intercollegiate sports:* baseball M(s), basketball M(s)/W(s), bowling W(s), cross-country running M/W, golf M(s)/W(s), soccer W(s), softball W(s), tennis M(s)/W(s), track and field M(s)/W(s), volleyball W(s). *Intramural sports:* archery M/W, badminton M/W, baseball M, basketball M/W, bowling M/W, football M, soccer W, tennis M/W, volleyball M/W.

Costs (2004–05) *Tuition:* state resident $3842 full-time, $160 per credit hour part-time; nonresident $8572 full-time, $357 per credit hour part-time. *Room and board:* $4974; room only: $2928. Room and board charges vary according to board plan.

Contact: Dean: Maria Luisa Alvarez Harvey, P.O. Box 17004, Jackson, Mississippi 39217-0104; *Telephone:* 601-979-2107; *Fax:* 601-979-2299

Mississippi State University
University Honors Program
Mississippi State, Mississippi

*T*he University Honors Program is a challenging variation of the standard curriculum, through which students in all academic majors enrich their undergraduate study. The University-wide program that relies on the Giles Distinguished Professors and the elected Honors Council as its faculty and student advisory groups serves departmental majors in all colleges and schools by tailoring programs for talented students.

Freshmen and sophomores meet institutional core curriculum requirements by choosing from among forty departmental courses in five colleges; juniors and seniors earn elective credits, conduct independent research, formulate special projects, adapt advanced courses for honors credit, or utilize internships, study-abroad, honors seminars, or thesis options. Credits offered through the Honors Program support a unique honors design sequence in the School of Architecture; programs for Presidential Endowed, Schillig, Hearin-Hess, and Stennis scholars; and the early admissions program of the College of Veterinary Medicine.

Individual small-enrollment courses taught by carefully selected outstanding members of the professorial teaching faculty are enhanced by field trips, guest lecturers, and innovative experimentation as expansions of challenging and interesting study that students elect to pursue without adding to degree requirements.

Honors Forum is an emblem of the focus of the program on expanded exposure and experience. The weekly session has consistently relied on cosponsorship with such units as the Cultural Diversity Center, the Women's Study Program, the Center for

International Security and Strategic Studies, and colleges, schools, and departments to host participants of international reputation in diverse fields. Forum also coordinates instructive and analytical programming with the University performing arts and lecture series to ensure students' insight into formal presentations, performances, and exhibitions.

The UHP also provides access to experiential study programs, including a summer archaeological dig in LaHav, Israel, open to students in all disciplines; geology/geography study on San Salvador Island in the Caribbean; and core-level courses and internships through study abroad.

Confidence in the ability of capable students to select options that reflect their interests and concerns is central to the philosophy of a program that presents diverse options for an undergraduate experience. The MSU Honors Program does not impose requirements for particular courses; instead it attempts to present both breadth and depth of options for study and experience that will contribute equally to academic and personal development.

The University Honors Program celebrated its thirty-seventh anniversary in 2005. The liberal arts Stephen D. Lee Honors Program, established in 1968, was expanded into a University-wide program in 1982 and has grown to a 2005 enrollment of 1,168 students who have an average ACT composite of 28 and an average GPA of 3.76. Annual enrollments of 1,000 to 1,200 in fifty rotated honors courses in five colleges/schools reflect a breadth of institutional commitment to the Honors Program as a named MSU priority for undergraduate education.

Participation Requirements: UHP students who complete 12 hours of graded honors course work and 2 pass/fail credits for Forum receive Phase I certification; those who complete a total of 24 hours of graded course work, including internship, independent research, and/or study-abroad credits, and 4 Forum credits receive Phase II certification and distinction as an Honors Scholar. The distinctions are noted on the official transcript and are recognized at an annual awards ceremony, at which students with 4.0 averages, selected outstanding students from each class, and elected outstanding honors faculty members are also identified.

Admission Process: Admission for entering freshmen is determined by two categories: unconditional admission with a minimum composite score of 28 on the ACT and/or a minimum combined score of 1240 on the SAT I, a ranking in the upper 20 percent of one's class, and correlative high school grades; and conditional admission for those who do not meet the primary standard directs advisement for specific courses based on standardized test subscores and evidence of academic strength in a subject matter area. After earning a minimum of 15 hours, at MSU or elsewhere, any student with a 3.4 cumulative average has full privileges, including priority preregistration. Transfer students may apply honors credits earned elsewhere to UHP requirements.

Scholarship Availability: University Freshman Academic Scholarships range from $2000 (minimum composite score of 26 on the ACT or minimum combined score of 1160 on the SAT I) to $10,000 (minimum ACT composite score of 32 or minimum combined SAT I score of 1390). National Merit awards may be added with an MSU award for another $20,000. Recipients of the Schillig Leadership Scholarships ($30,000) and Hearin-Hess ($20,000) engineering awards are named Honors Scholars without additional MSU funding other than National Merit awards. All of these awards carry a waiver of out-of-state tuition; Eminent Scholar awards from the Mississippi Legislature may add from $4000 to $10,000 for Mississippi residents. College and departmental scholarships may be added after the freshman year.

Campus Overview

State-supported university, founded 1878, part of Mississippi Board of Trustees of State Institutions of Higher Learning • **Coed** 12,495 undergraduate students, 88% full-time, 47% women, 53% men.

Undergraduates 10,984 full-time, 1,511 part-time. Students come from 51 states and territories, 39 other countries, 19% are from out of state, 20% African American, 1% Asian American or Pacific Islander, 0.8% Hispanic American, 0.6% Native American, 0.9% international, 12% transferred in, 21% live on campus.

Faculty *Total:* 1,139, 88% full-time, 85% with terminal degrees. *Student/faculty ratio:* 13:1.

Academic Programs *Special study options:* academic remediation for entering students, accelerated degree program, adult/continuing education programs, advanced placement credit, cooperative education, distance learning, double majors, English as a second language, freshman honors college, honors programs, independent study, internships, off-campus study, part-time degree program, services for LD students, student-designed majors, study abroad, summer session for credit. *ROTC:* Army (b), Air Force (b).

Athletics Member NCAA. All Division I except football (Division I-A). *Intercollegiate sports:* baseball M(s), basketball M(s)/W(s), cross-country running M(s)/W(s), golf M(s)/W(s), soccer W(s), softball W(s), tennis M(s)/W(s), track and field M(s)/W(s), volleyball W(s). *Intramural sports:* badminton M/W, basketball M/W, cross-country running M(c)/W(c), fencing M(c)/W(c), football M/W, golf M/W, lacrosse M(c), racquetball M/W, rugby M(c)/W(c), soccer M(c)/W(c), softball M/W, swimming and diving M(c)/W(c), table tennis M/W, tennis M/W, ultimate Frisbee M/W, volleyball M/W, water polo M/W.

Costs (2004–05) *Tuition:* state resident $4106 full-time, $171 per hour part-time; nonresident $9306 full-time, $388 per hour part-time. Part-time tuition and fees vary according to course load. *Room and board:* $5994; room only: $2454. Room and board charges vary according to board plan and housing facility.

Financial Aid 879 Federal Work-Study jobs (averaging $2674). In 2003, 1516 non-need-based awards were made. *Average percent of need met:* 70%. *Average financial aid package:* $8565. *Average need-based loan:* $3827. *Average need-based gift aid:* $3358. *Average non-need-based aid:* $2358.

Contact: Director: Dr. Nancy McCarley, P.O. Box EH, Mississippi State, Mississippi 39762; *Telephone:* 662-325-2522; *Fax:* 662-325-0086; *E-mail:* nmccarley@honors.msstate.edu; *Web site:* http://www.msstate.edu/dept/uhp/

Mississippi University for Women
Honors College
Columbus, Mississippi

The Honors College at Mississippi University for Women (MUW) provides opportunities for academically advanced and motivated students to participate in a learning experience that is intensive and innovative. The Honors College encourages and nurtures intellectual curiosity and advanced scholarship. The college meets the unique learning needs of academically capable students by offering advanced sections of core requirements, interdisciplinary studies, independent research, and training in leadership. The ultimate purpose of the Honors College is to produce students who are exceptionally well educated, who serve as intellectual catalysts on campus, and who, through their success, help ensure the continuing legacy at MUW.

Participation Requirements: Honors students enroll in one of two honors core sequences or at least three honors courses within the core curriculum: Humanities Sequence: English Composition and History of Civilization I and II; Science and Mathematics Sequence: Biology with Lab I and II and a mathematics course more advanced than college algebra. In addition, honors students complete the following courses during the first two years: two semesters of a foreign language and four semesters of Honors Forum (HO 101), a bimonthly lecture series. A special program is scheduled for each session, and at least once a month, students are addressed by a guest speaker. Honors students enroll in Honors Forum for each semester of their freshman and sophomore years.

During their junior year, honors students enroll in two Special Topics Seminars (HO 303), which are interdisciplinary and sometimes team-taught. As one of the unique features of the Honors College, the seminar offers educational opportunities in a nontraditional, undergraduate instruction format modeled on the graduate seminar. The students contribute substantially to the course material and the instructional process. Often, grades are assessed on the basis of participation and a single substantial research project. The seminar is intended to make the most academically advanced students comfortable with the structure of graduate courses in order to encourage them to continue their studies beyond the undergraduate level. Some examples of interdisciplinary topics have included Socio-Biology; Post-Modernism in Art, Film, and Literature; Seminal Texts; and Hitchcock and Freud.

Two semesters of Independent Study (HO 401/402) are required during the senior year. The Independent Study program gives students the opportunity to work closely with faculty advisers on a two-semester project that is modeled on the master's thesis.

Admission Process: The recipients of Centennial, University, and McDevitt scholarships are automatically members of the Honors College. Other students with excellent high school records or proven success in college courses are encouraged to apply and may request an application from the Director of the Honors College.

Scholarship Availability: The University offers substantial academic scholarships, but not through the Honors College, although participation in honors may be a requirement for the scholarship.

Campus Context: MUW has a total enrollment of around 2,300 students and a student-faculty ratio of approximately 16:1. Columbus-Lowndes County has a combined population of approximately 75,000 and is home to the state's third-busiest airport. The community is conveniently located 2 hours from Birmingham, 3 hours from Memphis, and 4–5 hours from New Orleans and Atlanta.

Campus Overview

State-supported comprehensive, founded 1884, part of Mississippi Institutions of Higher Learning • **Small-town** 110-acre campus • **Coed primarily women** 2,166 undergraduate students, 68% full-time, 83% women, 17% men.

Undergraduates 1,483 full-time, 683 part-time. Students come from 26 states and territories, 11% are from out of state, 28% African American, 1% Asian American or Pacific Islander, 0.7% Hispanic American, 0.4% Native American, 2% international, 21% live on campus.

Faculty Total: 214, 63% full-time, 43% with terminal degrees. Student/faculty ratio: 13:1.

Academic Programs Special study options: academic remediation for entering students, accelerated degree program, adult/continuing education programs, advanced placement credit, cooperative education, distance learning, double majors, English as a second language, freshman honors college, honors programs, internships, off-campus study, part-time degree program, services for LD students, study abroad, summer session for credit. ROTC: Army (c), Air Force (c). Unusual degree programs: 3-2 engineering with Auburn University, Mississippi State University.

Athletics Member NCAA. All Division II. Intercollegiate sports: basketball W(s), softball W(s), tennis W(s), volleyball W(s). Intramural sports: basketball M/W, football M/W, golf M/W, racquetball M/W, softball M/W, swimming and diving M/W, table tennis M/W, tennis M/W, volleyball M/W.

Costs (2004–05) Tuition: state resident $3495 full-time, $146 per semester hour part-time; nonresident $8442 full-time, $352 per semester hour part-time. Room and board: $3778. Room and board charges vary according to housing facility.

Financial Aid 120 Federal Work-Study jobs (averaging $3000). 210 state and other part-time jobs (averaging $3000). In 2003, 306 non-need-based awards were made. Average percent of need met: 78%. Average financial aid package: $8925. Average need-based loan: $3700. Average need-based gift aid: $2475. Average non-need-based aid: $2350.

Contact: Eric Daffron, Ph.D., Director of the Honors College and the Study Abroad Program, Professor of English, Mississippi University for Women, 1100 College Street, Box W-1634, Painter 211A, Columbus, Mississippi 39701; Telephone: 662-329-7174; E-mail: edaffron@muw.edu; Web site: www.muw.edu/honors.

University of Mississippi
The Sally McDonnell Barksdale Honors College
University, Mississippi

The Sally McDonnell Barksdale Honors College offers an enriched program of study designed to stimulate the intellectual growth of undergraduate students from all majors while providing them with an entire honors college experience. Originating in 1953 as the University Scholars Program and existing as an Honors Program until 1997, the College was established through an endowment from two Ole Miss alumni: former Netscape Corporation President James L. Barksdale and his wife, Sally McDonnell Barksdale. Through additional gifts, they have provided even more opportunities for honors students. The Honors College brings together select students and distinguished faculty members in an atmosphere of exploration and inquiry.

The honors curriculum begins with two core freshman seminars, interdisciplinary courses divided into units such as Self and Cosmos and Self and Society. These courses develop students' critical-reading and writing skills, and they can count toward freshman composition or humanities/social science hours. Students also take honors sections of departmental courses, which are taught by the University's most outstanding faculty members. Most honors courses are limited to 15 students. The core and departmental courses usually work to fulfill general education requirements. In the junior and senior years, students complete an exploratory research project and senior thesis in their majors. A minimum of 29 hours of honors courses (which includes the research and thesis) is required to graduate as an honors student. Honors students also are expected to engage in community action and attend honors forums each semester.

Honors College students benefit from small classes in which they can develop a camaraderie with other exceptional students and their professors, 24-hour access to the Honors College, study-abroad and internship opportunities, honors floors in residence halls, early registration for classes, and special activities, such as lunch with visiting VIPs. In addition to housing four classrooms and a computer lab, the Honors College offers a lounge, kitchen, study rooms, and a wireless Internet connection. A large deck behind the building and a courtyard in front offer different environments for class, study, or socializing.

Participation Requirements: To graduate from the Honors College, students must achieve a cumulative GPA of at least 3.5 by their senior year (freshmen must achieve a 3.2) and meet the minimum requirements for community action and the forum series. Students who take honors courses receive a special "H" designation on their transcripts for each course that is satisfactorily completed. All students who successfully fulfill all Honors College requirements graduate with special recognition and receive a special distinction on their transcripts.

Admission Process: The Honors College selects its students based on evidence of distinguished academic performance, significant achievement in scholastic and extracurricular activities, and the potential to make a substantial contribution to the University community throughout their college careers. Each incoming class is limited to approximately 135 students, and, in general, the minimum requirements are at least an ACT score of 28 (SAT I combined math and critical reading score of 1230) and a 3.5 minimum high school GPA. Students with less than a 28 ACT score may still apply.

Students in incoming classes have an average ACT score of 30 (SAT I score of 1350) and high school GPA of 3.85. Each class has included, on average, 29 National Merit and National Achievement Semifinalists. Students entering the Honors College have had a history of involvement in extracurricular activities, such as student government, the creative and performing arts, academic competitions, athletics, and community service.

Transfer students may also apply for the junior-entry program. To enter as a junior, a student must have at least a 3.5 GPA and the permission of his or her department to do the research and thesis requirements. Junior-entry students also take at least one additional honors course and fulfill the community action and forum requirements.

Interested students should request an admission packet from the Honors College and submit it by February 1. Students should also submit the University application to the admissions office.

Scholarship Availability: The Honors College awards a total of fourteen scholarships of $6000 to $8000 annually. In addition, the University of Mississippi offers a number of scholarships to students of exceptional ability, including generous awards for National Merit and National Achievement Finalists. The University also participates in a full range of federal and state financial aid programs. Financial aid is available to 80 percent of students through scholarships, grants, loans, and University funds.

Campus Overview

State-supported university, founded 1844, part of Mississippi Institutions of Higher Learning • **Coed** 11,820 undergraduate students, 92% full-time, 53% women, 47% men.

Undergraduates 10,865 full-time, 955 part-time. Students come from 47 states and territories, 67 other countries, 34% are from out of state, 13% African American, 1% Asian American or Pacific Islander, 0.8% Hispanic American, 0.2% Native American, 0.8% international, 11% transferred in, 33% live on campus.

Faculty *Total:* 469. *Student/faculty ratio:* 22:1.

Academic Programs *Special study options:* academic remediation for entering students, accelerated degree program, adult/continuing education programs, advanced placement credit, double majors, English as a second language, freshman honors college, honors programs, independent study, internships, part-time degree program, services for LD students, study abroad, summer session for credit. *ROTC:* Army (b), Air Force (b).

Athletics Member NCAA. All Division I except football (Division I-A). *Intercollegiate sports:* baseball M(s), basketball M(s)/W(s), cheerleading M(s)/W(s), cross-country running M(s)/W(s), fencing M(c)/W(c), golf M(s)/W(s), lacrosse M(c), riflery W(s), rugby M(c), soccer M(c)/W(s), softball W(s), tennis M(s)/W(s), track and field M(s)/W(s), volleyball M(c)/W(s). *Intramural sports:* badminton M/W, basketball M/W, bowling M/W, football M/W, golf M/W, racquetball M/W, riflery M(c), soccer M/W, softball M/W, swimming and diving M/W, table tennis M(c)/W(c), tennis M/W, track and field M/W, ultimate Frisbee M/W, volleyball M/W, water polo M/W.

Costs (2004–05) *Tuition:* state resident $4110 full-time; nonresident $9264 full-time. *Room and board:* $5610; room only: $2800.

Financial Aid 506 Federal Work-Study jobs (averaging $1230). In 2003, 989 non-need-based awards were made. *Average percent of need met:* 64%. *Average financial aid package:* $7532. *Average need-based loan:* $3704. *Average need-based gift aid:* $3779. *Average non-need-based aid:* $3623.

Contact: The Sally McDonnell Barksdale Honors College, P.O. Box 1848, University of Mississippi, University, Mississippi 38677;

Telephone: 662-915-7294; *Fax:* 662-915-7739; *E-mail:* honors@olemiss.edu; *Web site:* http://www.honors.olemiss.edu

University of Southern Mississippi
The University Honors College
Hattiesburg, Mississippi

The University of Southern Mississippi Honors College has its roots in an honors program founded in 1965. It was organized as a separate college in 1976, making it one of the oldest in the nation, and now has approximately 350 students in the program.

The honors curriculum is designed to enhance the education of high-ability students. At the freshman and sophomore levels, undergraduates have the same general education curriculum as other students but are taught in small classes, getting individual attention from experienced professors. In addition to learning from books, lectures, and discussions, they are taught how knowledge is applied. For example, the political science class visits Washington to talk to policy makers, lobbyists, and researchers, and the theater class watches live performances by professional actors in New Orleans. Students are taught how to create knowledge, working with research teams in polymer science and other disciplines. Also, they are encouraged to participate in study-abroad programs that expand their horizons in Australia, Canada, France, Mexico, Spain, the United Kingdom, and other countries. And in their final year, they work with an adviser to prepare a thesis that demonstrates their ability to design and implement a research program.

Most students, when they complete their undergraduate studies, seek further educational opportunities at graduate or professional schools, then pursue careers in law, medicine, veterinary science, business, or academia.

Participation Requirements: The Honors Program has two parts. In General Honors, freshmen and sophomores take the general education curriculum in small classes that encourage discussion, reading, and writing. In Senior Honors, students are required to take a class in research methodology and to complete a thesis on a topic relevant to their major discipline. The General Honors students must complete 22 hours of honors classes before proceeding to Senior Honors. All students must maintain a minimum GPA of 3.25.

Admission Process: Students are admitted as freshmen if they have an ACT score of 24 or higher or an SAT score of 1310 or higher. They must also supply a transcript and an example of their written work. Admission is competitive; preference is given to students with outstanding academic achievement and a record of community work or experience as an officer in a school or club. Transfer students and rising juniors are also accepted if they have a minimum 3.25 GPA and 40 hours or more of course work. All applications must be received by March 15. Honors housing is available but is not required (except for holders of the Presidential Scholarships, described below).

Scholarship Availability: The University offers at least ten Presidential Scholarships each year on a competitive basis. Recipients receive funding to cover the cost of tuition, room, board, and fees. Olliphant Scholarships are also awarded exclusively to distinguished Honors College students. All Honors College students receive a minimum $1200 scholarship.

Campus Overview

State-supported university, founded 1910 • **Coed** 12,520 undergraduate students, 80% full-time, 60% women, 40% men.

Undergraduates 9,965 full-time, 2,555 part-time. Students come from 42 states and territories, 40 other countries, 10% are from out of

state, 28% African American, 1% Asian American or Pacific Islander, 1% Hispanic American, 0.4% Native American, 1% international, 14% transferred in, 31% live on campus.

Faculty *Total:* 808, 82% full-time, 66% with terminal degrees. *Student/faculty ratio:* 17:1.

Academic Programs *Special study options:* academic remediation for entering students, accelerated degree program, adult/continuing education programs, advanced placement credit, cooperative education, distance learning, double majors, English as a second language, honors programs, off-campus study, part-time degree program, services for LD students, study abroad, summer session for credit. *ROTC:* Army (b), Air Force (b).

Athletics Member NCAA. All Division I except football (Division I-A). *Intercollegiate sports:* baseball M(s), basketball M(s)/W(s), cross-country running M(s)/W(s), golf M(s)/W(s), tennis M(s)/W(s), track and field M(s)/W(s), volleyball W(s). *Intramural sports:* badminton M/W, basketball M/W, bowling M/W, cross-country running M/W, fencing M/W, football M/W, golf M/W, racquetball M/W, rugby M, soccer M/W, softball M/W, squash M/W, swimming and diving M/W, table tennis M/W, tennis M/W, track and field M/W, volleyball M/W, weight lifting M/W.

Costs (2004–05) *Tuition:* state resident $4106 full-time, $172 per credit hour part-time; nonresident $9276 full-time, $388 per credit hour part-time. Part-time tuition and fees vary according to course load. *Room and board:* $5010; room only: $3010. Room and board charges vary according to housing facility.

Financial Aid 366 Federal Work-Study jobs (averaging $1226). In 2003, 831 non-need-based awards were made. *Average percent of need met:* 87%. *Average financial aid package:* $7177. *Average need-based loan:* $4264. *Average need-based gift aid:* $3196. *Average non-need-based aid:* $2290.

Contact: Dean: Dr. Ken Panton, 118 College Drive, #5162, Hattiesburg, Mississippi 39406-0001; *Telephone:* 601-266-4533; *Fax:* 601-266-4534; *E-mail:* honors@usm.edu; *Web site:* http://www.usm.edu/honors

MISSOURI

Columbia College
Honors Program
Columbia, Missouri

The Honors Program at Columbia College is designed to enhance the educational opportunities of academically gifted students who seek to participate in analytical, synthetic, and creative study. The program welcomes students who are eager to accept academic challenges and to become creatively involved in their own pursuit of educational excellence. Honors students explore classical works and contemporary thought across the academic disciplines.

Through multidisciplinary and collaborative course work, honors students respond to the significant challenges confronting the next generation of scholars. The honors courses, both within the General Education curriculum and beyond it, are consistent with the students' academic abilities, preparation, and goals. The courses resonate with any academic major or minor and provide opportunities for students to discover their intellectual curiosities, to engage in community service, to develop critical-thinking skills, and to excel in oral and written expression.

The program was created through faculty governance in 1997. Although faculty members may propose to teach a special topic course or to designate a General Education course, favorable consideration is given to courses that cohere to one or more of the following descriptions: multidisciplinary, collaborative teaching; travel/cocurricular activities; and reading and writing intensive. The

classes range in size from 10 to 20 students. Under the direction of a faculty mentor, honors students are encouraged to complete an honors distinction project during their final year. During fall 2004, approximately 50 students enrolled in the various honors courses, seminars, and colloquia.

Participation Requirements: To graduate with honors, a student completes at least 21 academic hours in the Honors Program. Entering freshmen who qualify for the Honors Program are strongly encouraged to enroll in HNRS 110 Introduction to Honors and HNRS 111 Introduction to Honors II. These courses, worth 1 and 2 academic credits, respectively, are intended to foster a sense of community within the group of honors students and to prepare those students for success as honors students during their next three years. A 1-credit-hour community service project for Honors 310 must be completed prior to graduation. Students may enroll in a maximum of 9 hours of honors credits designated for General Education and may be eligible to enroll in a maximum of 3 hours of honors credits for an honors distinction project. An honors student may apply no more than 6 hours of honors credits transferred from accredited institutions toward the completion of the Honors Program. No honors courses may be taken with the pass/fail option. A minimum 3.25 GPA overall and a 3.0 GPA in honors courses is required to remain qualified for graduation from the Honors Program. Graduation from the Honors Program is recognized during the graduation ceremony and indicated on the final transcript.

Admission Process: Eligible students must demonstrate academic achievement meeting at least two of the following minimum standards: a high school GPA of 3.5; 78th or higher percentile on ACT or SAT; or a Columbia College GPA of 3.5.

Eligible students are entered into the Honors Program automatically. Home-schooled or other nontraditionally schooled students are eligible for admission to the Honors Program upon presentation of an ACT, SAT, or GED score at or above the 78th percentile and demonstration of scholarship in high school–level academic course work. Any student may petition for admission to the Honors Program if he or she has completed a minimum of 30 hours of academic credit at Columbia College with a cumulative GPA of at least 3.6. Transfer students with prior college experience must have 30 semester hours of credit with a minimum GPA of 3.6 or higher on a 4.0 scale and submit a petition to the Honors Program Director for admission. To petition for admission, a student must complete a petition form and write a letter to the Honors Program Director that includes the reasons for desiring admission and the anticipated benefits to the student. The student must also have two Columbia College faculty members submit letters to the Director supporting the petition. The Director grants admission to the program.

Scholarship Availability: Columbia College offers competitive scholarships to honors students of high academic ability. Five freshman students are selected at Scholarship Day to receive the Columbia College Scholarship, which includes full tuition, room, and board. In addition, 5 freshman students are selected at Scholarship Day to receive the Presidential Scholarship, which includes a full-tuition award. To participate in Scholarship Day, applicants must complete the admission process and submit two letters of recommendation and a resume of school/community activities. Scholarship Day activities include a written essay and an interview with Columbia College faculty members and administrators. The deadline to apply for the Columbia College and Presidential Scholarships is February 1. Additional scholarships are available for honors students with high academic ability and are awarded based on specific criteria of academic performance.

Interdisciplinary Honorary Societies include Alpha Chi, Alpha Lambda Delta, Psi Chi, and Who's Who Among Students in American Universities and Colleges.

Campus Overview
Independent comprehensive, founded 1851, affiliated with Christian Church (Disciples of Christ) • **Coed** 953 undergraduate students, 78% full-time, 62% women, 38% men.

Undergraduates 742 full-time, 211 part-time. Students come from 22 states and territories, 34 other countries, 7% are from out of state, 5% African American, 1% Asian American or Pacific Islander, 2% Hispanic American, 0.4% Native American, 6% international, 12% transferred in, 36% live on campus.

Faculty *Total:* 94, 60% full-time, 54% with terminal degrees. *Student/faculty ratio:* 12:1.

Academic Programs *Special study options:* academic remediation for entering students, accelerated degree program, adult/continuing education programs, advanced placement credit, cooperative education, distance learning, double majors, English as a second language, honors programs, independent study, internships, off-campus study, part-time degree program, student-designed majors, study abroad, summer session for credit. *ROTC:* Army (c), Air Force (c). *Unusual degree programs:* 3-2 education.

Athletics Member NAIA. *Intercollegiate sports:* basketball M(s)/W(s), cheerleading W, soccer M(s), softball W(s), volleyball W(s). *Intramural sports:* basketball M/W, softball M/W, table tennis M/W, volleyball M/W.

Costs (2004–05) *Comprehensive fee:* $16,502 includes full-time tuition ($11,589) and room and board ($4913). Full-time tuition and fees vary according to class time and course load. Part-time tuition: $248 per credit hour. Part-time tuition and fees vary according to class time, course load, and location. *College room only:* $3090. Room and board charges vary according to board plan.

Financial Aid 92 Federal Work-Study jobs (averaging $555). In 2004, 147 non-need-based awards were made. *Average percent of need met:* 71%. *Average financial aid package:* $12,096. *Average need-based loan:* $4291. *Average need-based gift aid:* $3364. *Average non-need-based aid:* $8759.

Contact: Thomas J. Stauder, CPA, Business Administration Instructor and Honors Program Director, Columbia College, 1001 Rogers Street, Columbia, Missouri 65216; *Telephone:* 573-875-7552; *E-mail:* tjstauder@ccis.edu

Maryville University of Saint Louis

Bascom Honors Program

St. Louis, Missouri

The Bascom Honors Program is named for Marion R. Bascom, a professor who was instrumental in establishing the Honors Program at Maryville University in 1939. Intellectually vital and dynamic, the program has evolved from its original format, modeled after England's Oxford University tutorial system. Today it is a core honors program that recognizes the individual gifts and talents of each student in the program and encourages their maximum development.

Core Honors Program classes are small, usually fewer than 20 students, and are conducted in a seminar-like atmosphere of intellectual sharing. Students' perspectives on the subject help shape and enhance those of their classmates. As a core program, the Bascom Honors Program allows participants to interact with students in all majors offered at Maryville.

Designed for talented students who are capable of independent study, the Honors Program maintains small and challenging classes that encourage discussion, exploration of ideas, and interaction with outstanding faculty members known for their excellence in teaching. Because classes are small and are based mostly on discussion, faculty members almost always know honors students in multiple dimensions rather than just the academic. This makes a real difference when it comes to recommendations to employers or graduate schools.

In Honors Program classes, students take an in-depth approach to the subject matter. For instance, instead of the broad survey of American government, honors students might study the Atomic Age. Rather than the traditional historical chronology of art, a recent Honors Art Seminar sought to design a museum exhibit.

In addition to the core seminars, another highlight of the Bascom Honors Program is the monthly Honors Colloquium. These Sunday evening gatherings provide an opportunity for a social gathering and for stimulating discussions among students and faculty members on a range of important issues. Recent colloquia titles have included Trade and Culture; Gender in the Developing World; and Spiritual Dimensions of the Natural World. The colloquia expose students to totally new ideas not necessarily related to their major. Choosing the Bascom Honors Program adds a depth of experience and involvement to students' Maryville experience.

The Bascom Honors Program currently registers 200 honors students.

Participation Requirements: Bascom Honors Program graduates are required to have completed seven Honors Seminars, two semesters of the Honors Colloquium, and 8 to 15 core elective credits. These requirements produce a total of 52 credit hours, identical to the standard core credit hour requirements for any Maryville graduate.

Upon completion of the requirements for graduation, students receive bachelor's degrees as Bascom Honors graduates in their respective majors and have this noted on their diplomas and in the graduation program.

Admission Process: Freshmen entering Maryville with an ACT of 27 or above and a GPA of 3.5 or higher are invited to join the Bascom Honors Program. Transfer students with fewer than 60 credits and GPAs of 3.5 or higher, as well as currently enrolled Maryville students with GPAs of 3.5 or higher, may apply to join the program. The Director of the Bascom Honors Program accepts students into the program.

Scholarship Availability: The University Scholars Program provides recognition and financial support for outstanding undergraduate students who enter Maryville directly from high school. University Scholars are invited to participate in Maryville's Bascom Honors Program, although all academically eligible prospective undergraduate students are encouraged to apply. Applicants with at least a 3.5 (on a 4.0 scale) high school GPA and at least a 28 ACT composite score (or comparable SAT I combined score) will be considered for these scholarships. Final candidates are selected on the basis of their academic credentials (high school grades and recommendations from high school teachers, counselors, or administrators). Finalists are invited to participate in Scholarship Day Competition, during which each candidate completes an essay based on one of several selected topics, and an interview with a Maryville faculty member. In addition, the Scholarship Day program includes a general information session and a campus tour. The selection committee considers the results of the essays, interviews, academic credentials, and recommendations in selecting scholarship recipients. Applicants should contact Maryville's admissions office for deadlines and other specific information.

Campus Overview

Independent comprehensive, founded 1872 • **Coed** 2,584 undergraduate students, 59% full-time, 76% women, 24% men.

Undergraduates 1,530 full-time, 1,054 part-time. Students come from 18 states and territories, 21 other countries, 11% are from out of state, 6% African American, 2% Asian American or Pacific Islander, 1% Hispanic American, 0.3% Native American, 1% international, 14% transferred in, 32% live on campus.

Faculty *Total:* 342, 28% full-time, 57% with terminal degrees. *Student/faculty ratio:* 12:1.

Academic Programs *Special study options:* accelerated degree program, adult/continuing education programs, advanced placement credit, cooperative education, distance learning, double majors, English as a second language, freshman honors college, honors programs, independent study, internships, off-campus study, part-time degree program, services for LD students, student-designed majors, study abroad, summer session for credit. *ROTC:* Army (c). *Unusual degree programs:* 3-2 engineering with Washington University in St. Louis; social work with Saint Louis University; education.

Athletics Member NCAA. All Division III. *Intercollegiate sports:* baseball M, basketball M/W, cross-country running M/W, golf M/W, soccer M/W, softball W, tennis M/W, volleyball W. *Intramural sports:* basketball M/W, bowling M/W, football M/W, soccer M/W, softball M/W, table tennis M/W, volleyball M/W.

Costs (2004–05) *Comprehensive fee:* $23,300 includes full-time tuition ($16,000), mandatory fees ($300), and room and board ($7000). Full-time tuition and fees vary according to course load. Part-time tuition: $485 per credit hour. Part-time tuition and fees vary according to class time. *Required fees:* $75 per term part-time. *College room only:* $6030. Room and board charges vary according to housing facility.

Financial Aid 283 Federal Work-Study jobs (averaging $914). 102 state and other part-time jobs (averaging $2950). In 2003, 230 non-need-based awards were made. *Average percent of need met:* 42%. *Average financial aid package:* $10,822. *Average need-based loan:* $4591. *Average need-based gift aid:* $5999. *Average non-need-based aid:* $6687.

Contact: Director: Dr. Linda Pitelka, 13550 Conway Road, St. Louis, Missouri 63141-7299; *Telephone:* 314-529-9621; *Fax:* 314-529-9925; *E-mail:* pitelka@maryville.edu

Missouri Southern State University
Honors Program
Joplin, Missouri

The Honors Program at Missouri Southern State University is intended to encourage academic excellence by providing special opportunities and challenges for exceptional students.

Entrance into the program is by invitation. Because admission is selective and competitive, classes normally are smaller than regular classes, with no more than 25 students, permitting honors students to enjoy interaction with other outstanding students in an informal atmosphere conducive to exciting and challenging discussions.

Honors courses put the University's best students in small classes with its best teaching professors from the freshman year onward. Working together, distinguished professors and honors students have opportunities to expand the educational experience beyond that available in regular courses. Students receive personal attention and special guidance and the program is flexible to permit students to pursue particular scholarly interests and to engage in innovative and creative approaches to learning in depth.

The core of the Honors Program experience at Missouri Southern State University is the Developing Scholars Program. In addition to providing specific challenges and opportunities, the Honors Program is designed to help the brightest and best students mature as scholars. The features of the program address specific areas of intellectualism and scholarship, developing self-, cognitive, and cultural awareness from the first year onward.

Students in the Honors Program are required to complete an international study experience, highlighting their further development as scholars by observing or studying a culture other than their own. Following the experience, the students will be guided through a reflective analysis.

Honors students have many opportunities for extracurricular and cocurricular activities, including Epsilon Mu Sigma, the Honors Program student organization, as well as many discipline-specific organizations. In addition, upperclass honors students mentor

first-year students in the program. The Honors Program at Missouri Southern also encourages academic learning outside the classroom, through service-learning and study abroad.

The Honors Program at Missouri Southern was founded in 1986 and currently enrolls approximately 160 students.

Participation Requirements: Honors students at Missouri Southern are required to complete 26 semester credit hours in honors courses, including Honors Forum, a discussion-based course; Service-Learning, a course that emphasizes hands-on experience in the community; international study or travel, with an eye toward developing an appreciation of other cultures; and a senior thesis, in which the student develops an original idea, using primary research in their discipline. In addition to taking other honors courses in their disciplines, students can enhance existing upper-division courses for honors credit.

To maintain honors eligibility, students must have a minimum of a 3.0 GPA their first semester, a 3.25 GPA their second semester, and a 3.5 GPA for the remainder of their time at Missouri Southern. Students successfully completing the requirements of the Honors Program will have a special notation appear both on their diploma and on their transcripts.

Admission Process: All students who wish to participate in the Honors Program must be admitted to Missouri Southern. Incoming freshmen with a composite score on the ACT of at least 28 or with a GPA of at least 3.5 on a 4.0 scale in high school course work are invited to apply for admission to the program. Two letters of recommendation, one from the student's high school principal and one from a high school teacher, are required. In addition, an essay assigned by the Honors Program directors may be required. International students must also score a minimum of 535 on the paper-based TOEFL or a minimum of 200 on the computer-based TOEFL. The Honors Program office evaluates all student applications, and selected students are invited to complete a personal interview with one of the honors directors.

As part of the admissions process, the Honors Committee evaluates all application materials and the results of the personal interview. The deadline for completing all formalities is March 1 of the year prior to fall admission.

Students who have already completed between 15 and 30 hours of course work with a GPA of at least 3.5 at Southern, or any other accredited college or university, are also invited to apply for admission into the program.

Scholarship Availability: Once admitted to the Honors Program at Missouri Southern, students receive the Walter and Fredrica Evans Scholarship. The Evans is a four-year renewable scholarship that covers tuition, book rental fees, and student activity fees for fall and spring semesters. Additional scholarship funds to cover on-campus room and board are available for Evans Scholars who are National Merit Semifinalists or who have an ACT composite score of 31 or better. This scholarship is the finest Southern offers.

The Honors Program offers special admission to Missouri's associate degree graduates who hold the CBHE Bright Flight Scholarship. Those with at least a 3.5 GPA are eligible for a scholarship that covers the full cost of tuition, room and board, activity fees, and textbook rental. Other financial aid is available to students through the Office of Financial Aid.

Campus Overview

State-supported 4-year, founded 1937 • **Coed** 5,256 undergraduate students, 69% full-time, 60% women, 40% men.

Undergraduates 3,621 full-time, 1,635 part-time. Students come from 27 states and territories, 34 other countries, 14% are from out of state, 2% African American, 1% Asian American or Pacific Islander, 2% Hispanic American, 2% Native American, 3% international, 10% live on campus.

Faculty *Total:* 284, 70% full-time, 49% with terminal degrees. *Student/faculty ratio:* 18:1.

Academic Programs *Special study options:* academic remediation for entering students, accelerated degree program, adult/continuing education programs, advanced placement credit, cooperative education, distance learning, double majors, English as a second language, external degree program, honors programs, independent study, internships, off-campus study, part-time degree program, services for LD students, study abroad, summer session for credit.

Athletics Member NCAA. All Division II. *Intercollegiate sports:* baseball M(s), basketball M(s)/W(s), cross-country running M(s)/W(s), football M(s), golf M(s), soccer M(s)/W(s), softball W(s), tennis W(s), track and field M(s)/W(s), volleyball W(s). *Intramural sports:* baseball M/W, basketball M/W, football M/W, golf M/W, racquetball M/W, soccer M/W, softball M/W, swimming and diving M/W, table tennis M/W, tennis M/W, ultimate Frisbee M/W, volleyball M/W.

Costs (2004–05) *Tuition:* state resident $3810 full-time, $127 per credit part-time; nonresident $7620 full-time, $254 per credit part-time. Full-time tuition and fees vary according to course load. *Required fees:* $166 full-time, $83 per term part-time. *Room and board:* $4770. Room and board charges vary according to board plan and housing facility.

Financial Aid 149 Federal Work-Study jobs (averaging $1575). 438 state and other part-time jobs (averaging $1401). In 2003, 602 non-need-based awards were made. *Average percent of need met:* 69%. *Average financial aid package:* $6722. *Average need-based loan:* $3249. *Average need-based gift aid:* $4636. *Average non-need-based aid:* $2560.

Contact: Dr. Patricia P. Kluthe, Director, Honors Program, Missouri Southern State University, 3950 East Newman Road, Joplin, Missouri 64801-1595; *Telephone:* 417-625-3005; *Fax:* 417-625-3168; *E-mail:* kluthe-p@mssu.edu; *Web site:* http://www.mssu.edu/honors

---

Missouri State University

Honors College

Springfield, Missouri

The Honors College provides a program of enhanced, advanced study, and recognition for students of unusually strong academic achievement and motivation and offers these students intellectual opportunities beyond those generally found in the more traditional programs: smaller and enriched classes, direct contact with outstanding faculty members, and the option to pursue their own intellectual, research and creative interests. Approximately forty sections of honors courses representing approximately twenty disciplines are offered in general education each semester, excluding the Freshman Honors Seminar. Honors classes are small (average class size of 16), are reading and writing intensive, and encourage interaction among students and between the students and the professor. Members of the honors faculty are full faculty members with the terminal degree and must go through an application process to teach in the Honors College. They must have a sustained record of research, scholarship, and publication and outstanding teaching evaluations. They are dedicated to the program and to the students.

Honors students enjoy early registration and the same, extended library privileges offered to graduate students. Once a student has decided upon a major, most have a member of the honors faculty within that discipline assigned as an adviser. Working closely with these faculty members gives students a rewarding and enriching academic experience and can be especially valuable as they prepare to go on to graduate studies or to enter the highly competitive workforce.

Honors students who have received the Presidential Scholarship may choose to live in Scholars House, a state-of-the-art facility which houses 130 students. All honors students are members of the Honors

Council which offers opportunities for leadership and service. Traditionally, many honors students have held positions of leadership in many campus organizations, including the University-wide Student Government Association.

The Honors College was formed in 1987 and has an enrollment of 800 students and is a member of the National Collegiate Honors Council.

Participation Requirements: There are two tiers to the Honors program; the first, in general education, is required and the second, in the department of major, is elective. Honors courses in general education substitute for other, required general education courses. All students entering the Honors College must take the Freshman Honors Seminar, a 1-hour course offered each fall. This course introduces the student to the University and to research methods through a seminar revolving around a topic of intellectual significance. During the first two years in the program, all honors students are required to schedule at least five additional honors courses. Prior to graduation, each honors student must complete an honors section of the Capstone Course required of all students. Honors students who complete the general education requirements in honors with a Missouri State University (MSU) cumulative GPA of at least 3.25 qualifies for graduation in the Honors College and this is noted on the transcript and the diploma. Those honors students who have completed the general honors requirement and who wish to pursue advanced studies in their major may continue with Departmental Distinction, which requires a cumulative GPA of at least 3.5 and an additional 12 hours of upper-division honors course work, including a senior project, within their major. Upon completion of these requirements, the notation of Distinction in (major) is added to the transcript and diploma.

Admission Process: Membership in the Honors College is automatically offered in the fall semester to all first-time freshman University applicants with an ACT of 27 or above (or SAT of at least 1220) and who also place in the upper 10 percent of their high school class. Second semester admission is available to all other freshmen based on an MSU cumulative GPA of 3.4 or higher. Those students, as well as those who apply to the University after March 1 or as transfer students or who wish to appeal for first-semester admission, should contact the Dean.

Scholarship Availability: There are no scholarships specifically for the Honors College; however, given the requirements for membership, almost all honors students are eligible for University scholarships.

Campus Overview

State-supported comprehensive, founded 1905 • **Coed** 16,269 undergraduate students, 78% full-time, 57% women, 43% men.

Undergraduates 12,763 full-time, 3,506 part-time. Students come from 49 states and territories, 82 other countries, 7% are from out of state, 3% African American, 1% Asian American or Pacific Islander, 1% Hispanic American, 0.9% Native American, 2% international, 7% transferred in, 24% live on campus.

Faculty *Total:* 978, 74% full-time, 65% with terminal degrees. *Student/faculty ratio:* 18:1.

Academic Programs *Special study options:* accelerated degree program, adult/continuing education programs, advanced placement credit, cooperative education, distance learning, double majors, English as a second language, freshman honors college, honors programs, independent study, internships, off-campus study, part-time degree program, services for LD students, student-designed majors, study abroad, summer session for credit. *ROTC:* Army (b).

Athletics Member NCAA. All Division I except football (Division I-AA). *Intercollegiate sports:* baseball M(s), basketball M(s)/W(s), bowling M(c)/W(c), cross-country running M(s)/W(s), equestrian sports M(c)/W(c), field hockey W(s), golf M(s)/W(s), ice hockey M(c), lacrosse M(c), racquetball M(c)/W(c), riflery M(c)/W(c), soccer M(s)/W(s), softball W(s), swimming and diving M(s)/W(s), tennis M(s)/W(s), track and field M(s)/W(s), ultimate Frisbee M(c)/W(c), volleyball M(c)/W(s), wrestling M(c). *Intramural sports:* badminton M/W, basketball M/W, bowling M/W, fencing M/W, football M/W, golf M/W, racquetball M/W, rock climbing M/W, soccer M/W, softball M/W, table tennis M/W, tennis M/W, track and field M/W, ultimate Frisbee M/W, volleyball M/W, weight lifting M/W, wrestling M.

Costs (2004–05) *Tuition:* state resident $4620 full-time, $154 per credit hour part-time; nonresident $9240 full-time, $308 per credit hour part-time. Full-time tuition and fees vary according to course load and degree level. Part-time tuition and fees vary according to course load and degree level. *Required fees:* $508 full-time. *Room and board:* $4660; room only: $3249. Room and board charges vary according to board plan and housing facility.

Financial Aid 449 Federal Work-Study jobs (averaging $1748). 1,336 state and other part-time jobs (averaging $2924). In 2004, 3420 non-need-based awards were made. *Average percent of need met:* 62%. *Average financial aid package:* $5959. *Average need-based loan:* $3637. *Average need-based gift aid:* $4115. *Average non-need-based aid:* $6989.

Contact: Curtis P. Lawrence, Ph.D., Dean, University College, Missouri State University, 901 South National Avenue, Springfield, Missouri 65804; *Telephone:* 417-836-6370; *Fax:* 417-836-6372; *E-mail:* cpl142f@smsu.edu; *Web site:* http://www.smsu.edu/honors/

Missouri Western State University
Honors Program
St. Joseph, Missouri

The Honors Program at Missouri Western State University provides enhanced educational opportunities for qualified students through special experiences designed to enrich classroom learning, help set personal goals, and develop individual talents. The program fosters students' intellectual growth, independence, and initiative through an array of learning experiences, including colloquia and seminars, general studies honors, and major honors. Founded in 1988, the program receives strong faculty and administrative support and figures prominently in the University's current strategic plan.

Honors Colloquium is a theme-based, interdisciplinary seminar involving in-class discussion, guest speakers, readings, films, field excursions, and student-faculty panel presentations. Several different themed colloquia are offered every semester. Recent offerings have included The Ritual of Food in the World, America's Role in the World, and Finding the Science in Science Fiction. Other colloquia have included excursions to New York City, St. Louis, and New Orleans.

Departments across the campus offer approximately ten different general studies courses every semester. These special sections are designed for 10 to 20 students and provide many opportunities for discussion and interaction between students and professors. Students receive special attention and often experience innovative teaching methods.

Students who want to receive Major Honors work under the direction of professors in their major areas and have the opportunity to conduct investigative research. A special colloquium is offered to help students prepare presentations for their departments that outline their proposed honors projects. Upon completion of the honors project, students make public presentations and are encouraged to submit their papers to appropriate conferences and journals for publication.

Students in the Honors Program are particularly enthusiastic about the availability of honors housing, early registration, and extracurricular opportunities. The Student Honors Organization

(SHO) plays an active role in campus life and in the St. Joseph community through service learning experiences. SHO plans social events such as game nights, movies, barbecues, and other activities designed to get students together. The Honors Center provides students with a comfortable setting for studying and socializing. Students in the Honors Program also have the opportunity to participate in field trips to museums, cultural attractions, and athletic events in nearby urban areas.

Participation Requirements: To continue participation in the Honors Program, students must maintain a minimum 3.0 GPA their freshman year and a 3.25 GPA every year thereafter. Students need to take six general studies courses as honors sections and three colloquia to complete the General Studies Honors program. The requirements for Major Honors are set by individual departments and usually involve a public presentation of the honors research/creative project. Students who complete the requirements for General Studies Honors or Major Honors are recognized at the spring Honors Convocation, and the achievement is noted on their transcript.

Admission Process: Incoming freshmen are invited to join the program if they have a minimum ACT score of 26 and a high school GPA of 3.5 or higher. Currently enrolled students and transfer students are eligible to join the program if they have a cumulative GPA of 3.5 or higher from Missouri Western or any other accredited college or university.

Scholarship Availability: Students entering the Honors Program with a 27 or higher ACT are eligible to apply for the Golden Griffon Scholarship, worth $9500 annually. The Golden Griffon Scholarship has a February 1 deadline and can be accessed at the financial aid Web site: http://www.mwsc.edu/finaid/. All students in the Honors Program are eligible to apply for all academic scholarships provided by Missouri Western State University, including the President's Scholarship, valued at $3500 annually. Many other departmental and service scholarships are also available.

Campus Overview

State-supported 4-year, founded 1915 • **Coed** 5,065 undergraduate students, 74% full-time, 60% women, 40% men.

Undergraduates 3,759 full-time, 1,306 part-time. Students come from 31 states and territories, 7 other countries, 7% are from out of state, 11% African American, 0.8% Asian American or Pacific Islander, 2% Hispanic American, 0.9% Native American, 0.2% international, 6% transferred in, 28% live on campus.

Faculty *Total:* 313, 58% full-time, 49% with terminal degrees. *Student/faculty ratio:* 18:1.

Academic Programs *Special study options:* academic remediation for entering students, accelerated degree program, advanced placement credit, distance learning, double majors, freshman honors college, honors programs, internships, part-time degree program, summer session for credit. *ROTC:* Army (b).

Athletics Member NCAA. All Division II. *Intercollegiate sports:* baseball M(s), basketball M(s)/W(s), football M(s), golf M(s)/W, softball W(s), tennis W(s), volleyball W(s). *Intramural sports:* basketball M/W, bowling M/W, football M, golf M/W, ice hockey M, racquetball M/W, rugby M, soccer M, swimming and diving M/W, table tennis M/W, tennis M/W, volleyball M/W.

Costs (2004–05) *Tuition:* state resident $4380 full-time, $146 per credit part-time; nonresident $8010 full-time, $267 per credit part-time. *Required fees:* $398 full-time, $12 per credit part-time, $35 per term part-time. *Room and board:* $4396. Room and board charges vary according to board plan and housing facility.

Contact: Director: Dr. Elizabeth Latosi-Sawin, Spratt Hall 202, 4525 Downs Drive,, St. Joseph, Missouri 64507; *Telephone:* 816-271-4535; *Fax:* 816-271-5610; *E-mail:* sawin@mwsc.edu; *Web site:* http://www.mwsc.edu/honors/

Southeast Missouri State University

Honors Program

Cape Girardeau, Missouri

The Honors Program at Southeast Missouri State affords its students a great deal of flexibility in determining how to best make use of program resources and fulfill program requirements. Students select from a variety of honors sections of courses in the University's nationally recognized University Studies liberal education curriculum. In addition, students can design their own projects to earn honors credit by contract in nonhonors sections of courses. The Senior Honors Project can also be tailored to their individual interests and needs. Given this freedom, former honors students have created senior projects as diverse as original laboratory and/or literature research in a wide variety of disciplines, comparisons of American and Welsh educational practices based on a study-abroad experience, musical and literary analyses based on a senior voice recital, preparation of a one-women exhibition by an fine arts major, and development of an elaborate program for educating junior high students about Shakespeare.

The creativity and exuberance of the honors students is matched by the skill and love of teaching of the honors faculty members. Most honors faculty members are recruited on the basis of student recommendation as one of the best teaching faculty members on campus. The honors faculty members enjoy working closely with students in the classroom as well as on extracurricular projects. Most honors classes are kept to between 15 and 25 students to facilitate the type of interactive learning environment the honors faculty members consider most appropriate for achieving a true honors educational experience. In addition to being successfully involved in their individual disciplines, honors faculty members demonstrate their creativity in the original courses they design. Honors sections have been offered in courses as diverse as Victorian Studies, Science and Religion, North American Indians, and The History of the Future.

Service learning is an integral part of the Honors Program at Southeast. Freshmen are encouraged to participate in modest service activities. Opportunities for much more extensive service involvement are available for all students in the program. All service activity is coordinated by the Learning in Volunteerism committee that is composed of honors students exclusively.

The Honors Program offices are located in a comfortable house situated on one corner of the campus. In addition to work space, the house contains a nice living room for informal gatherings and a handy kitchen, making the honors house a relaxing home-like gathering place for the members of the honors community.

The Southeast Honors Program was established in 1984. It currently has about 500 students.

Participation Requirements: To remain in the Honors Program, students must maintain a minimum GPA of 3.25 and maintain active involvement in the program. A minimum of 24 hours of honors credit must be accumulated to complete the program. Students are also required to complete a senior honors project. Students who complete the Honors Program requirements are designated Honors Scholars and receive highest recognition at both the Honors Convocation and the Commencement Ceremony. They receive a certificate of completion and a medallion to be worn at the commencement exercises. Notification of completion of the Honors Program requirement is added to their academic transcript.

Admission Process: Admission to the Honors Program requires a cumulative high school GPA of at least 3.4 on a 4.0 scale and an ACT composite score of at least 25. Students who do not meet these standards may be admitted to the program by petition if, at the end of 12 semester hours of college work, they have earned a cumulative GPA of at least 3.25.

Scholarship Availability: The Honors Program does not administer its own scholarships. However, the University has a generous merit scholarship program, and the vast majority of honors students hold one of the four top merit scholarships: the Governor's, Regents', University, and President's Scholarships. For the 2001–02 academic year, these scholarships held values as follows. The Governor's scholarship covers incidental fees (tuition), general fees, and textbook rental for the equivalent of up to 32 hours per academic year at Southeast and residence hall fees in a standard, double-occupancy room with fifteen meals per week. National Merit/Achievement Finalists may receive additional allocations. The Regents' scholarship covers incidental fees (tuition) for the equivalent of up to 32 hours per academic year. The University Scholarship provides $2500 per academic year for out-of-state students. The President's Scholarship provides $1500 per academic year for in-state students. For further information on scholarships, students should contact the Admissions Office at 573-651-2590.

Campus Overview

State-supported comprehensive, founded 1873, part of Missouri Coordinating Board for Higher Education • **Coed** 8,460 undergraduate students.

Undergraduates Students come from 39 states and territories, 35 other countries, 10% are from out of state, 8% African American, 0.6% Asian American or Pacific Islander, 1% Hispanic American, 0.5% Native American, 2% international, 28% live on campus.

Faculty Total: 516, 75% full-time, 65% with terminal degrees. Student/faculty ratio: 18:1.

Academic Programs Special study options: academic remediation for entering students, accelerated degree program, adult/continuing education programs, advanced placement credit, cooperative education, distance learning, double majors, English as a second language, honors programs, independent study, internships, part-time degree program, services for LD students, student-designed majors, study abroad, summer session for credit. ROTC: Air Force (b).

Athletics Member NCAA. All Division I except football (Division I-AA). Intercollegiate sports: baseball M(s), basketball M(s)/W(s), cheerleading M(s)/W(s), cross-country running M(s)/W(s), golf M(s), gymnastics W(s), soccer W(s), softball W(s), tennis W(s), track and field M(s)/W(s), volleyball W(s). Intramural sports: basketball M/W, cross-country running M/W, football M/W, golf M/W, lacrosse M(c)/W(c), racquetball M/W, rock climbing M(c)/W(c), soccer M(c)/W(c), softball M/W, swimming and diving M/W, tennis M/W, track and field M/W, ultimate Frisbee M/W, volleyball M/W, wrestling M/W.

Costs (2004–05) Tuition: state resident $4554 full-time, $152 per credit part-time; nonresident $8139 full-time, $267 per credit part-time. Full-time tuition and fees vary according to course load and location. Part-time tuition and fees vary according to course load and location. Required fees: $321 full-time, $11 per credit part-time. Room and board: $5317; room only: $3335. Room and board charges vary according to board plan and housing facility.

Financial Aid 221 Federal Work-Study jobs (averaging $1339). 1,613 state and other part-time jobs (averaging $1425). In 2003, 787 non-need-based awards were made. Average percent of need met: 67%. Average financial aid package: $6175. Average need-based loan: $3493. Average need-based gift aid: $4040. Average non-need-based aid: $3417.

Contact: Director: Dr. Craig Roberts, MS 2050, Cape Girardeau, Missouri 63701; Telephone: 573-651-2513; E-mail: croberts@semo.edu

Truman State University
General Honors in Arts and Sciences
Kirksville, Missouri

Truman State University's General Honors Program is not the usual honors program. With its outstanding student body (Truman is a highly selective institution), highly qualified faculty and staff members, small class sizes, interdisciplinary seminars, and Residential College Program, Truman already gives every student the benefits many universities can only give to their honors students. All Truman State University students are eligible to pursue general honors by taking the courses designated by the respective disciplines as being those courses whose successful completion by a nonmajor is especially noteworthy. These courses explore in-depth topics or encourage a more sophisticated viewpoint than the general requirements.

Participation Requirements: General Honors in Arts and Sciences is awarded to graduating seniors who have completed five approved courses, with at least one course from each of the areas of mathematics, science, humanities, and social science and with a cumulative GPA of at least 3.5. Only grades of A and B count toward the general honors GPA requirement of at least 3.5 in those five courses. Only courses with 3 or more hours of credit count toward general honors. Students who complete a single undergraduate major may not satisfy general honors requirements with any course in their major field. Students who complete two or more majors may use any approved courses to satisfy general honors requirements.

Admission Process: There is no formal admissions process for Truman's General Honors Program. Students are encouraged to attend information sessions and other general honors events and declare their intention to pursue general honors. All students who meet Truman's highly selective admission standards qualify for participation in this program.

Scholarship Availability: Truman State University has a nationwide reputation for providing a high-quality education at an affordable price. In fact, 95 percent of the incoming freshmen receive some form of financial assistance. Currently, there are no scholarships available through the General Honors Program.

Campus Overview

State-supported comprehensive, founded 1867 • **Coed** 5,616 undergraduate students, 98% full-time, 59% women, 41% men.

Undergraduates 5,486 full-time, 130 part-time. Students come from 44 states and territories, 51 other countries, 26% are from out of state, 4% African American, 2% Asian American or Pacific Islander, 2% Hispanic American, 0.5% Native American, 4% international, 2% transferred in, 48% live on campus.

Faculty Total: 377, 92% full-time, 81% with terminal degrees. Student/faculty ratio: 15:1.

Academic Programs Special study options: accelerated degree program, advanced placement credit, double majors, English as a second language, honors programs, internships, off-campus study, part-time degree program, services for LD students, student-designed majors, study abroad, summer session for credit. ROTC: Army (b). Unusual degree programs: 3-2 engineering with University of Missouri-Rolla.

Athletics Member NCAA. All Division II. Intercollegiate sports: baseball M(s), basketball M(s)/W(s), cheerleading M(c)/W(c), cross-country running M(s)/W(s), equestrian sports M(c)/W(c), football M(s), golf M(s)/W(s), lacrosse M(c)/W(c), rugby M(c)/W(c), soccer M(s)/W(s), softball W(s), swimming and diving M(s)/W(s), tennis M(s)/W(s), track and field M(s)/W(s), volleyball M(c)/W(s), wrestling M(s). Intramural sports: badminton M/W, basketball M/W, bowling M/W, cross-country running M/W, football M/W, golf M/W, racquetball M/W, soccer M/W, softball M/W, swimming and diving M/W, table tennis M/W, tennis M/W, track and field M/W, ultimate Frisbee M/W, volleyball M/W, weight lifting M/W.

Costs (2004–05) Tuition: state resident $5410 full-time, $226 per credit hour part-time; nonresident $9510 full-time, $396 per credit hour part-time. Part-time tuition and fees vary according to course load. Required fees: $72 full-time. Room and board: $5175. Room and board charges vary according to housing facility.

Financial Aid 291 Federal Work-Study jobs (averaging $842). 1,914 state and other part-time jobs (averaging $1028). In 2003, 2239 non-need-based awards were made. Average percent of need met: 80%. Average financial aid package: $5842. Average need-based loan: $3868. Average need-based gift aid: $3063. Average non-need-based aid: $3902.

Contact: Maria Di Stefano, Truman State University, 100 East Normal Street, Kirksville, Missouri 63501; Telephone: 660-785-4109; E-mail: mdistefa@truman.edu; Web site: http://honors.truman.edu

University of Missouri–Columbia
Honors College
Columbia, Missouri

The University of Missouri–Columbia (MU) Honors College is a campuswide program designed to provide talented students with appropriate academic challenges and special opportunities. The Honors College does not offer academic degrees; rather, it serves outstanding students from all of MU's undergraduate colleges by providing a more personalized education and individual attention and support. Honors courses are of two types: honors sections of regularly offered courses and special honors colloquia that are limited to 20 honors students (e.g., Medical Ethics, Multicultural Literature, and Paradigms and Paradoxes: A Brief History of Science).

The academic centerpiece of the Honors College, the four-semester Humanities Sequence, provides an interdisciplinary introduction to Western culture and intellectual history from ancient to contemporary times. A staff of outstanding instructors combines lectures and small discussion groups in this study of the artistic, literary, religious, and philosophical expressions of Western civilization. The Humanities Sequence follows a great books tradition. Students are asked to read original works, in translation, from Plato to Sartre in philosophy and from Homer to Arundhati Roy in literature. The Humanities Sequence includes the following courses: the Ancient World, the Middle Ages and the Renaissance, the Early Modern World, and the Modern Era.

The Honors College also offers a Social Science Sequence and a Science Sequence for nonscience majors. As companions to the Humanities Sequence, Asian Humanities and the Emerging Canons of the Americas broaden the curriculum. One-hour Career Explorations in ten different professions are reserved for first-year students.

Entering freshmen with an ACT of 33 or better are eligible for the new Honors College Discovery Fellowship Program. These fellowships, which carry a stipend of $1700, give freshmen the opportunity to work with a faculty member on a research project or other scholarly activity appropriate to their major.

The Honors College Community Involvement Program (HCCIP) is a nationally recognized outreach program that pairs honors students with at-risk youth from local secondary schools. HCCIP encourages MU's brightest and most energetic students to improve the lives of those around them. As mentors, pals, and tutors, the honors students not only make a difference in the lives of the young people, they also develop leadership and public service skills for themselves as well as a sense of social responsibility.

Primarily designed for first- and second-year students, the Honors College accepts approximately 850 new students each year or about 15 percent of the incoming freshman class.

Participation Requirements: Honors College students must complete two honors courses per year for their first two years and maintain a 3.0 or higher GPA to remain honors eligible. Honors classes receive an "H" (Honors) designation on their transcript. If a student completes 20 hours of honors course work and graduates with a 3.3 cumulative GPA or better, he or she can earn an Honors Certificate, which is also noted on the transcript.

Admission Process: Currently, students are automatically eligible for the program out of high school if they have a minimum ACT score of 29 (or its equivalent on the SAT I) and rank among the top 10 percent of their graduating class. Intellectually curious students who are not automatically eligible but who believe they would profit from enrolling in honors courses are encouraged to petition the College by including an essay with their applications. Honors-eligible students are sent an application to the College shortly after being accepted to MU. Other students may apply online or write to the Honors College and request an application. Transfer students and students already attending MU are eligible if they have a 3.5 cumulative GPA and at least 30 college credit hours.

Campus Overview

State-supported university, founded 1839, part of University of Missouri System • **Coed** 22,137 undergraduate students, 94% full-time, 51% women, 49% men.

Undergraduates 20,723 full-time, 1,414 part-time. Students come from 52 states and territories, 85 other countries, 14% are from out of state, 6% African American, 3% Asian American or Pacific Islander, 2% Hispanic American, 0.6% Native American, 1% international, 6% transferred in, 39% live on campus.

Faculty *Total:* 1,364, 92% full-time, 91% with terminal degrees. *Student/faculty ratio:* 18:1.

Academic Programs *Special study options:* accelerated degree program, adult/continuing education programs, advanced placement credit, cooperative education, distance learning, double majors, English as a second language, external degree program, freshman honors college, honors programs, independent study, internships, off-campus study, part-time degree program, services for LD students, student-designed majors, study abroad, summer session for credit. *ROTC:* Army (b), Navy (b), Air Force (b). *Unusual degree programs:* 3-2 accountancy.

Athletics Member NCAA. All Division I except football (Division I-A). *Intercollegiate sports:* baseball M(s), basketball M(s)/W(s), cross-country running M(s)/W(s), golf M(s)/W(s), gymnastics W(s), soccer W(s), softball W(s), swimming and diving M(s)/W(s), tennis W(s), track and field M(s)/W(s), volleyball W(s), wrestling M(s). *Intramural sports:* basketball M/W, cheerleading M(c)/W(c), fencing M(c)/W(c), football M/W, golf M/W, ice hockey M(c)/W(c), lacrosse M(c)/W(c), racquetball M(c)/W(c), riflery M(c)/W(c), rugby M(c)/W(c), soccer W(c), softball M/W, ultimate Frisbee M(c)/W(c), volleyball M(c)/W(c), water polo M(c)/W(c).

Costs (2004–05) *Tuition:* state resident $6276 full-time, $209 per credit hour part-time; nonresident $15,723 full-time, $524 per credit hour part-time. Full-time tuition and fees vary according to course load and program. Part-time tuition and fees vary according to course load and program. *Required fees:* $824 full-time, $32 per credit hour part-time. *Room and board:* $6220. Room and board charges vary according to board plan and housing facility.

Financial Aid 1,276 Federal Work-Study jobs (averaging $1460). In 2003, 4597 non-need-based awards were made. *Average percent of need met:* 84%. *Average financial aid package:* $10,048. *Average need-based loan:* $4078. *Average need-based gift aid:* $5295. *Average non-need-based aid:* $4203.

Contact: Director: Dr. Stuart B. Palonsky, 211 Lowry Hall, Columbia, Missouri 65211; *Telephone:* 573-882-3893; *Fax:* 573-884-5700; *E-mail:* palonskys@missouri.edu; *Web site:* http://honors.missouri.edu/

University of Missouri–Kansas City
UMKC Honors Program
Kansas City, Missouri

*T*he Honors Program at UMKC combines the curricular, cultural, and research opportunities of a large, urban research university in a major metropolitan area with the personalized advising, close-knit community, and small classes of a liberal arts college. These experiences, along with a specially designed curriculum, help to prepare UMKC's best students to become the future leaders of Kansas City, the nation, and, ultimately, the world. The Honors Program seeks exceptionally motivated and academically talented undergraduates from all of UMKC's colleges and schools to study in an environment that challenges students to realize their greatest potential.

The Honors Program offers several ways to achieve these goals. Top professors, many of whom are nationally and even internationally known, teach small, honors-only seminars in their fields. Students enroll in a weekly interdisciplinary colloquium, intended to create a shared intellectual community among the students and introduce them to a wide variety of thinkers from UMKC and the region in general. Advanced honors students are encouraged to design and lead their own discussion sections for general education courses. Leadership is addressed through special institutes and unique courses, wherein students study, theorize, and reflect on the nature of community and community leadership. In addition, all honors students are asked to participate in the innovative Honors-University Academy Partnership, working within their disciplines with high school students at an inner-city college-prep school.

UMKC honors students are actively encouraged to participate in study-abroad programs. Furthermore, the program offers a supportive atmosphere to encourage integrative thinking through an exciting Living/Learning Community (L/LC) in Oak Street Residence Hall and specialized advising with Honors Faculty Fellows. All honors students have open access to the Honors House, where they can find space for quiet individual study or gather for study groups and discussion sections. Honors students get priority class enrollment every semester, a pass that provides one free ticket to all UMKC and Kansas Repertory Theatre productions, and graduate-level borrowing privileges at Miller Nichols Library. With an eye toward giving students a leg up on their graduate school and career goals, honors students are strongly encouraged to work with a UMKC professor to conduct innovative individual and collaborative research or artistic activity in the form of the Senior Honors Thesis. Finally, students in the program can benefit from personalized guidance when applying for national scholarship competitions, such as the Rhodes, Fulbright, Goldwater, Truman, Soros, and Udall.

Approximately 120 students participate in the UMKC Honors Program, which was founded in 1973, and 40–50 students live together in the Honors L/LC. UMKC welcomes transfer students and nontraditional students into its program as well. More information on the program can be found online at http://www.umkc.edu/honors.

Participation Requirements: To graduate with honors, first-year students must complete 28 units of honors credit. Transfer and continuing students, depending on the number of credits they have when they enter the program, must complete either 25 or 21 honors credits. All students are expected to maintain a minimum 3.2 cumulative GPA throughout their tenure in the program and attend the 1-unit Honors Colloquium three fourths of the time they are in the Honors Program. Students may also choose to complete the two-semester Senior Honors Thesis (worth 6 more honors credits) to graduate as an Honors College Scholar. The Honors designation is noted on the student's diploma, while both Honors and Honors College Scholar status are noted on the transcripts.

Admission Process: Prospective students should score in the top 10 percent on the ACT or SAT and be in the top 10 percent of their graduating class. Transfer students may either fulfill the above criteria, have a GPA of at least 3.7, or have participated in the honors program at their previous college or university. The application also includes a personal essay and one letter of recommendation from an instructor or adviser. Admission is competitive and spots are limited, so even students who fulfill these basic criteria may be asked to apply again after a semester or two at UMKC. The priority application deadline is March 15; however, admission is rolling.

Scholarship Availability: There are no honors-only scholarships; however, the majority of honors students receive UMKC scholarships and financial aid. There are a number of employment possibilities within the Honors Program for students after their first year in the program.

Campus Overview

State-supported university, founded 1929, part of University of Missouri System • **Coed** 9,393 undergraduate students, 58% full-time, 60% women, 40% men.

Undergraduates 5,421 full-time, 3,972 part-time. Students come from 45 states and territories, 46 other countries, 24% are from out of state, 14% African American, 5% Asian American or Pacific Islander, 4% Hispanic American, 0.8% Native American, 3% international, 12% transferred in, 13% live on campus.

Faculty *Total:* 993, 61% full-time, 60% with terminal degrees. *Student/faculty ratio:* 13:1.

Academic Programs *Special study options:* accelerated degree program, adult/continuing education programs, advanced placement credit, cooperative education, distance learning, double majors, English as a second language, honors programs, independent study, internships, off-campus study, part-time degree program, services for LD students, study abroad, summer session for credit. *ROTC:* Army (b), Air Force (c). *Unusual degree programs:* 3-2 education.

Athletics Member NCAA. All Division I. *Intercollegiate sports:* basketball M(s)/W(s), cheerleading W, cross-country running M(s)/W(s), golf M(s)/W(s), riflery M(s)/W(s), soccer M(s), softball W(s), tennis M(s)/W(s), track and field M(s)/W(s), volleyball W(s). *Intramural sports:* badminton M/W, basketball M/W, football M/W, golf M/W, racquetball M/W, soccer M/W, softball M/W, squash M/W, swimming and diving M/W, table tennis M/W, track and field M/W, ultimate Frisbee M/W, volleyball M/W, water polo M/W, weight lifting M/W.

Costs (2004–05) *Tuition:* state resident $6276 full-time, $209 per credit hour part-time; nonresident $15,723 full-time, $524 per credit hour part-time. Full-time tuition and fees vary according to course load, program, and student level. Part-time tuition and fees vary according to course load, program, and student level. *Required fees:* $746 full-time, $899 per semester part-time. *Room and board:* $7180; room only: $4385. Room and board charges vary according to board plan and housing facility.

Financial Aid In 2004, 655 non-need-based awards were made. *Average percent of need met:* 58%. *Average financial aid package:* $10,682. *Average need-based loan:* $6507. *Average need-based gift aid:* $4602. *Average non-need-based aid:* $4122.

Contact: Director: Professor Gayle A. Levy, 204 Haag Hall, 5100 Rockhill Road, Kansas City, Missouri 64110-2499; *Telephone:* 816-235-2820; *Fax:* 816-235-5542; *E-mail:* umkchonors@umkc.edu; *Web site:* http://www.umkc.edu/honors

University of Missouri– St. Louis
Pierre Laclede Honors College
St. Louis, Missouri

*F*ounded in 1989 and named after the founder of the city of St. Louis, *Pierre Laclede Honors College (PLHC) is an academic division of the University of Missouri–St. Louis. It is housed in Provincial House, a former ecclesiastical property adjacent to the main campus, where it has its own classroom and residential space as well as faculty, student, and administrative offices. The primary mission of the college is to enrich the intellectual lives of its students by providing a challenging general education curriculum based on the traditional disciplines of the arts and sciences. With this goal in mind, PLHC admits highly motivated undergraduates who have the potential to act as producers, rather than consumers, of their own education. Honors students cultivate their creative capacities through a seminar-based pedagogy where written and spoken arguments are judged not on the status of the producer but on the quality of his or her ideas and the firmness of their foundation in academic study, critical thought, clear expression, and personal and cultural experience. PLHC fosters an intellectual climate in which democracy, diversity, excellence, and civility are fundamental, coequal values and produces graduates whose liberal education readies them for a lifetime of learning in and from a professedly civil, democratic, diverse, and meritocratic society.*

Other than a Freshman Symposium on Western and non-Western cultural traditions, honors seminars range in size from 7 to 15 students. An Honors Writing Program based on individual consultation runs in tandem with the honors seminar curriculum and aims at the production of a personal Writer's Portfolio at graduation. PLHC students are also encouraged to undertake supervised academic research (normally in their major), and all approved research projects carry special scholarship funding. Additional scholarship support is also normally available for those students who wish to pursue an exchange program at another university, whether abroad or in the United States or Canada. Qualified students may enter a special program with the University's College of Optometry that leads to the Doctor of Optometry degree in seven years, and all students are encouraged to take part in internships that include partnerships with leading St. Louis civic and cultural organizations.

The Pierre Laclede Honors College is expanding in size and now enrolls more than 500 students, who major in every division and most departments of the University.

Participation Requirements: Most honors students use their honors seminars principally to meet the University's general education requirements, although a number of honors courses may be used to meet major requirements in a variety of departments. Four-year students must take a minimum of 40 credit hours in honors courses, while two-year (transfer) students must take 22 credit hours in honors courses. Both four-year and transfer honors programs include six credit hours of independent study and/or supervised research. Graduation from the honors program requires maintenance of a minimum 3.2 GPA, and honors graduates are recognized at University commencement exercises, on their final transcripts, and by issuance of a special Honors College graduation certificate.

Admission Process: Students must apply for admission to the University and submit a free supplemental application to the Honors College. Applicants are assessed by previous educational records, test scores (ACT or SAT), two references from teachers, and writing samples (normally, two essays recently submitted in school or college). Applicants are also invited to the Honors College for a tour and an interview with the dean, associate dean, or faculty member.

PLHC follows University of Missouri system guidelines on acceptance of advanced-placement credits and, for transfer applicants, adheres to Missouri state (CBHE) guidelines on transfer and articulation.

Scholarship Availability: PLHC scholarships are based principally on academic merit (some endowed need scholarships are available). The average annual academic scholarship support from the Honors College is about $1000 per student. Most students are also offered residential scholarships (also averaging about $1000), which may be used in any University hall of residence (including the Honors College). Most Honors College students also receive additional scholarships from the University of Missouri–St. Louis and/or from other sources, and National Access awards are available for out-of-state honors college students. In 2005, the University is also instituting need scholarships (FAFSA-based: for information, applicants should contact University Financial Aid at 314-516-5526). Most scholarships are renewable; Honors College scholarships themselves require maintaining of minimum 3.2 GPA.

Students with appropriate musical interests and abilities should also be aware of a range of music performance scholarships available from the Department of Music.

Campus Overview

State-supported university, founded 1963, part of University of Missouri System • **Coed** 12,586 undergraduate students, 44% full-time, 61% women, 39% men.

Undergraduates 5,569 full-time, 7,017 part-time. Students come from 40 states and territories, 60 other countries, 5% are from out of state, 16% African American, 3% Asian American or Pacific Islander, 2% Hispanic American, 0.3% Native American, 2% international, 14% transferred in, 7% live on campus.

Faculty *Total:* 739, 48% full-time, 52% with terminal degrees. *Student/faculty ratio:* 19:1.

Academic Programs *Special study options:* accelerated degree program, adult/continuing education programs, advanced placement credit, cooperative education, distance learning, double majors, English as a second language, freshman honors college, honors programs, independent study, internships, off-campus study, part-time degree program, services for LD students, student-designed majors, study abroad, summer session for credit. *ROTC:* Army (c), Air Force (c).

Athletics Member NCAA. All Division II. *Intercollegiate sports:* baseball M(s), basketball M(s)/W(s), golf M(s)/W(s), ice hockey M(c), soccer M(s)/W(s), softball W(s), tennis M(s)/W(s), volleyball W(s). *Intramural sports:* badminton M/W, basketball M/W, bowling M/W, cheerleading M/W, cross-country running M/W, football M/W, golf M/W, ice hockey M, racquetball M/W, soccer M/W, softball M/W, swimming and diving M/W, table tennis M/W, tennis M/W, volleyball M/W, weight lifting M/W.

Costs (2004–05) *Tuition:* state resident $6276 full-time, $209 per credit hour part-time; nonresident $15,723 full-time, $524 per credit hour part-time. Full-time tuition and fees vary according to course load, program, and reciprocity agreements. Part-time tuition and fees vary according to course load, program, and reciprocity agreements. *Required fees:* $1102 full-time, $42 per credit hour part-time. *Room and board:* $6194; room only: $4430. Room and board charges vary according to board plan and housing facility.

Financial Aid 97 Federal Work-Study jobs (averaging $3242). In 2003, 441 non-need-based awards were made. *Average percent of need met:* 64%. *Average financial aid package:* $9207. *Average need-based loan:* $4247. *Average need-based gift aid:* $3955. *Average non-need-based aid:* $4702.

Contact: Dean: Dr. Robert M. Bliss, Pierre Laclede Honors College, University of Missouri–St. Louis, 1 University Boulevard, St. Louis, Missouri 63121; *E-mail:* rmbliss@umsl.edu

William Woods University
Honors Program
Fulton, Missouri

The Honors Program at William Woods University is dedicated to what we call the "life of the mind." Gathering the best of our students and placing them in a rigorous and stimulating academic environment, the Honors Program affords an opportunity for students of exceptional promise and high motivation to work closely with individual faculty members in ways that challenge their abilities and develop their potential.

The program is committed to two main ideals: the importance of the liberal arts and the value of community. Reflecting the University's commitment to both ideals and its belief in the importance of the freshman year, honors students during their freshman year are enrolled in the honors learning community. Each semester the Honors Program offers three thematically linked Common Studies courses. The students and faculty members in these courses make up the honors learning community. Together, they explore the connections between disciplines as well as develop a deep sense of community.

The Honors Colloquium moves the spirit of the honors learning community outside of the classroom. Once a month, the honors students meet outside of class in the Honors Colloquium. The colloquium is a student-led forum where issues are examined in depth and students engage one another in serious conversations on the major issues affecting the world.

Subsequent honors study builds upon this firm foundation. Two second-year courses are offered: a service learning course and a special interdisciplinary course. Toward a Life of Service explores the interaction between philosophy and practice in the realm of community service. The interdisciplinary courses vary in content, but each course explores a theme or issue from many different academic perspectives, again seeking to break down the somewhat artificial barriers between fields of inquiry.

During their junior and senior years, honors students rightly turn their attention to their majors. They still are honors students, however. In addition to helping with the Honors Colloquium, they may elect to take a course in their major for honors credit. In addition, all honors students are expected in their junior or senior year to write a thesis or do a project that represents high-level work in their field. This work is to be presented to the campus community at either the Undergraduate Research Conference each spring or a similar forum. Honors students may also meet this requirement by participating in the Mentor-Mentee Program.

The Honors Program was established in 2001 and serves approximately 80 students.

Participation Requirements: Students are expected to complete 24 hours of honors credit. Most courses are Common Studies courses developed to challenge very talented students. Major-specific courses are also offered in some majors. With its focus on the first two years of college, the program is designed so that most students are able to complete their course work by the end of their sophomore year. Study-abroad credit can be counted as honors credit. Seniors are also expected to complete a thesis or senior project. To remain in good standing, students should maintain at least a 3.4 GPA and have regular attendance at the Honors Colloquia. Students who complete the program receive recognition at graduation as well as a transcript notation.

Admission Process: Admission to the program is open to students who have a minimum ACT score of 27 (1220 on the SAT) and a high school GPA of 3.5 or above. Applicants are interviewed in the spring by the Honors Committee, a group of faculty members who teach in the program. For details on the application process, students should visit http://www.williamwoods.edu/Attachments/HonorsScholarAward.doc.

Scholarship Availability: William Woods has designed a financial aid program intended to make the University more affordable and, at the same time, to encourage and reward campus and community involvement that makes a complete, well-rounded liberal arts environment. Approximately 90 percent of the University's students receive some form of financial assistance.

Campus Overview

Independent comprehensive, founded 1870, affiliated with Christian Church (Disciples of Christ) • **Coed** 1,012 undergraduate students, 76% full-time, 75% women, 25% men.

Undergraduates 774 full-time, 238 part-time. Students come from 37 states and territories, 13 other countries, 26% are from out of state, 3% African American, 0.4% Asian American or Pacific Islander, 1% Hispanic American, 0.4% Native American, 4% international, 7% transferred in, 80% live on campus.

Faculty *Total:* 79, 71% full-time, 33% with terminal degrees. *Student/faculty ratio:* 13:1.

Academic Programs *Special study options:* academic remediation for entering students, accelerated degree program, adult/continuing education programs, advanced placement credit, double majors, honors programs, independent study, internships, off-campus study, part-time degree program, student-designed majors, study abroad, summer session for credit. *ROTC:* Army (c), Navy (c), Air Force (c).

Athletics Member NAIA. *Intercollegiate sports:* baseball M(s), basketball W(s), cross-country running M(s)/W(s), equestrian sports M/W, golf M(s)/W(s), soccer M(s)/W(s), softball W(s), track and field M/W, volleyball M(s)/W(s). *Intramural sports:* badminton M/W, baseball M, basketball M/W, football M/W, rock climbing M/W, softball M/W, table tennis M/W, tennis M/W, volleyball M/W, weight lifting M/W.

Costs (2004–05) *Comprehensive fee:* $20,420 includes full-time tuition ($14,300), mandatory fees ($420), and room and board ($5700). Full-time tuition and fees vary according to program. Part-time tuition: $465 per credit hour. *Required fees:* $15 per term part-time. *Room and board:* Room and board charges vary according to board plan.

Financial Aid 282 Federal Work-Study jobs (averaging $1177). 170 state and other part-time jobs (averaging $974). In 2004, 257 non-need-based awards were made. *Average percent of need met:* 89%. *Average financial aid package:* $14,783. *Average need-based loan:* $3191. *Average need-based gift aid:* $1967. *Average non-need-based aid:* $3946.

Contact: Director: Professor Shawn Hull, Academic Building, William Woods University, 1 University Avenue, Fulton, Missouri 65251-1098; *Telephone:* 800-995-3159 Ext. 4389 (toll-free); *Fax:* 573-592-1180; *E-mail:* shull@williamwoods.edu; *Web site:* http://www.williamwoods.edu/honors

MONTANA

Montana State University
University Honors Program
Bozeman, Montana

*T*he University Honors Program provides academically motivated students with outstanding opportunities to undertake interdisciplinary course work and undergraduate research leading to a University honors degree. Such studies, in addition to disciplinary course work, provide extraordinary preparation for professional careers or graduate and advanced studies. Honors Seminars constitute the heart of the program and are characterized by individualized instruction and class interaction. Faculty members and students together engage in critical discussions of issues that cut across the diverse range of traditional departmental subjects. Teaching is primarily Socratic: emphasis is placed upon informed class discussion rather than lectures. Considerable attention is given to the development of analytic and critical skills and expression of them through speaking and writing. Texts and Critics is a two-semester course taught by faculty members representing every college at the University. Serving as a University Seminar and Humanities core, the course addresses fundamental issues through critical reading and analysis of seminal books that are the foundation texts of advanced studies in all major discipline fields.

The Honors Program annually offers a variety of seminars for sophomores and upperclass students. These upper-division seminars may also earn University core credit in each of the major discipline categories. The seminars are interdisciplinary and are typically taught by the most respected and stimulating faculty members on campus. Honors sections of chemistry, physics, math, English, music, and economics are also offered. Limited enrollments in seminars and sections permit intensive study and discussion. Opportunities for independent study are available through honors contracts that are taken only at the upper-division level. Contracts permit students to work with a specific faculty member on Oxford-style reading tutorials or research projects.

Extracurricular, outdoor, and social activities are an important feature of the daily life of the program. In order to provide an ideal blend of living and learning, special on-campus housing is also available to honors students.

The Honors Program was founded in 1983. Nearly 600 students are currently enrolled.

Participation Requirements: Graduates of the program receive an Honors Degree in addition to their departmental degree. Graduation in honors requires 16 to 28 credits in honors courses, most of which can be core curriculum honors courses; a minimum overall GPA of 3.5; and one year or its equivalent of a foreign language. To graduate with highest distinction, a thesis and a minimum overall GPA of 3.7 are required. Students with energy, self-reliance, and imagination are encouraged to discuss their interests with the director or assistant director. To maintain good standing in the program, students must demonstrate significant and continuing progress toward their specific degree in addition to satisfying the particular standards of honors course work and research.

Admission Process: Admission to the program is determined by its director according to guidelines approved by the University Honors Program Advisory Committee. Admission is by application and includes an essay along with supporting letters and evidence of standing in the upper percentile of the applicant's high school class. Applicants are expected to have high ACT or SAT scores. Transfer students or those already enrolled in the University are expected to have demonstrated high academic achievement and personal initiative.

Scholarship Availability: Twenty Presidential Scholarships are awarded to first-year students. Presidential Scholars are recipients of the University's most prestigious award. Scholarships provide annual tuition fee waivers for four years as well as a financial merit grant for each of the same four years. Numerous merit-based departmental and outside scholarships are also available to qualified applicants.

Campus Overview

State-supported university, founded 1893, part of Montana University System • **Coed** 10,668 undergraduate students, 86% full-time, 46% women, 54% men.

Undergraduates 9,167 full-time, 1,501 part-time. Students come from 50 states and territories, 59 other countries, 30% are from out of state, 0.5% African American, 1% Asian American or Pacific Islander, 1% Hispanic American, 2% Native American, 1% international, 7% transferred in, 25% live on campus.

Faculty *Total:* 816, 65% full-time, 68% with terminal degrees. *Student/faculty ratio:* 17:1.

Academic Programs *Special study options:* academic remediation for entering students, adult/continuing education programs, advanced placement credit, distance learning, double majors, English as a second language, honors programs, independent study, internships, off-campus study, part-time degree program, services for LD students, student-designed majors, study abroad, summer session for credit. *ROTC:* Army (b), Air Force (b).

Athletics Member NCAA. All Division I except football (Division I-AA). *Intercollegiate sports:* basketball M(s)/W(s), cheerleading M(s)/W(s), cross-country running M(s)/W(s), golf W(s), skiing (cross-country) M(s)/W(s), skiing (downhill) M(s)/W(s), tennis M(s)/W(s), track and field M(s)/W(s), volleyball W(s). *Intramural sports:* archery M/W, badminton M/W, baseball M, basketball M/W, bowling M/W, cross-country running M/W, fencing M/W, football M, golf M/W, gymnastics M/W, racquetball M/W, rugby M/W, skiing (cross-country) M/W, skiing (downhill) M/W, soccer M/W, softball M/W, swimming and diving M/W, table tennis M/W, tennis M/W, track and field M/W, ultimate Frisbee M/W, volleyball M/W, water polo M/W, weight lifting M/W, wrestling M.

Costs (2004–05) *Tuition:* state resident $4577 full-time; nonresident $14,177 full-time. Full-time tuition and fees vary according to course load. Part-time tuition and fees vary according to course load. *Room and board:* $5500. Room and board charges vary according to board plan and housing facility.

Financial Aid 390 Federal Work-Study jobs (averaging $1057). 316 state and other part-time jobs (averaging $1101). In 2003, 700 non-need-based awards were made. *Average percent of need met:* 67%. *Average financial aid package:* $7307. *Average need-based loan:* $4220. *Average need-based gift aid:* $3817. *Average non-need-based aid:* $4336.

Contact: Director: Michael Miles, P.O. Box 172140-MSU, Bozeman, Montana 59717-2140; *Telephone:* 406-994-4110; *Fax:* 406-994-6747; *E-mail:* honors@montana.edu; *Web site:* http://www.montana.edu/honors

The University of Montana–Missoula
The Davidson Honors College
Missoula, Montana

The Davidson Honors College is a campuswide association of faculty and students united by a common concern for academic and personal excellence. Its mission is to foster intellectual and civic values and to support the best possible teaching and learning circumstances for participating faculty and students.

The College offers an academic and social home to motivated and talented students as they pursue their undergraduate education. Students from all major areas in the College of Arts and Sciences and the professional schools are welcome, as are students undecided about a major. Honors is not a major in itself but an enhanced approach to fulfilling General Education requirements. It is compatible with all undergraduate majors.

The Davidson Honors College building is located at the center of the University of Montana–Missoula (UM Missoula) campus. It provides honors students with a large, comfortable lounge area; kitchen space; a multimedia computer lab; and quiet study rooms in addition to classrooms and office space.

The Honors Students' Association sponsors a variety of social activities and community service projects throughout the year. Special honors dormitory floors are available. The Davidson Honors College also sponsors the University of Montana Office for Civic Engagement, which supports the integration of community service experience into the academic curriculum.

There are 550 students in the College.

Participation Requirements: Davidson Honors College students are required to complete a minimum of seven honors courses, including one cluster of lower-division courses, one honors seminar, and an honors thesis or project.

Graduation through the Davidson Honors College requires a cumulative GPA of 3.0 or higher and 3.4 or higher in the major field. Upon completion of the requirements, students receive their bachelor's degrees as University Scholars in their respective majors and have this noted on their diplomas.

Admission Process: Students must apply separately to the Davidson Honors College. Selection is made by the faculty adviser. The priority deadline is December 31.

Scholarship Availability: The Davidson Honors College administers the Presidential Leadership Scholarships, UM's premier academic scholarship program for incoming freshmen. The Davidson Honors College also administers other campus-based scholarship programs for juniors and seniors, as well as several national competitions.

Campus Overview

State-supported university, founded 1893, part of Montana University System • **Coed** 11,431 undergraduate students, 84% full-time, 53% women, 47% men.

Undergraduates 9,628 full-time, 1,803 part-time. Students come from 52 states and territories, 61 other countries, 26% are from out of state, 0.5% African American, 1% Asian American or Pacific Islander, 2% Hispanic American, 4% Native American, 2% international, 26% transferred in, 23% live on campus.

Faculty *Total:* 705, 75% full-time, 68% with terminal degrees. *Student/faculty ratio:* 20:1.

Academic Programs *Special study options:* academic remediation for entering students, adult/continuing education programs, advanced placement credit, cooperative education, distance learning, double majors, English as a second language, freshman honors college, honors programs, independent study, internships, off-campus study, part-time degree program, services for LD students, study abroad, summer session for credit. *ROTC:* Army (b).

Athletics Member NCAA. All Division I except football (Division I-AA). *Intercollegiate sports:* baseball M(c), basketball M(s)/W(s), crew M(c)/W(c), cross-country running M(s)/W(s), equestrian sports M(c)/W(c), fencing M(c)/W(c), field hockey W(c), golf M/W, ice hockey M(c)/W(c), lacrosse M(c)/W(c), rugby M(c)/W(c), skiing (downhill) M(c)/W(c), soccer M/W, tennis M(s)/W(s), track and field M(s)/W(s), ultimate Frisbee M(c)/W(c), volleyball M/W(s). *Intramural sports:* archery M/W, badminton M/W, baseball M, basketball M/W, bowling M/W, cross-country running M/W, football M/W, ice hockey M, racquetball M/W, rugby M/W, skiing (cross-country) M/W, soccer W, softball M/W, swimming and diving M/W, table tennis M/W, tennis M/W, track and field M/W, volleyball M/W, water polo M/W, weight lifting M/W.

Costs (2005–06) *Tuition:* state resident $3470 full-time, $145 per credit part-time; nonresident $12,186 full-time, $508 per credit part-time. Full-time tuition and fees vary according to degree level, program, and reciprocity agreements. Part-time tuition and fees vary according to course load and degree level. *Required fees:* $1229 full-time, $39 per credit part-time. *Room and board:* $5646; room only: $2546. Room and board charges vary according to board plan and housing facility.

Financial Aid 1,098 Federal Work-Study jobs (averaging $1977). In 2002, 1489 non-need-based awards were made. *Average percent of need met:* 79%. *Average financial aid package:* $8034. *Average need-based loan:* $4766. *Average need-based gift aid:* $3742. *Average non-need-based aid:* $3502.

Contact: Dean: James C. McKusick, Ph.D., Davidson Honors College, University of Montana–Missoula, Missoula, Montana 59812; *Telephone:* 406-243-2541; *E-mail:* dhc@mso.umt.edu

NEBRASKA

Union College
Union Scholars

Lincoln, Nebraska

Within the community of learning and holistic growth at Union College, Union Scholars is available for students who have demonstrated superior scholastic ability. By working together, faculty members and students create an atmosphere within which students may discover, organize, and disseminate knowledge and apply value judgments to human thought and activity within the framework of Christian faith and service. The College commits itself to the belief that service and work are the active expressions of knowledge.

The program consists of three main components: core classes, service to humanity, and excellence in the student's chosen field of study. In the core class component of the Honors Program, students are required to take a set of interdisciplinary classes that replace the general baccalaureate core requirements. These classes bring together professors from a variety of disciplines to create a learning experience of broad scope, high intensity, and exceptional creativity.

Through the service to humanity component, a spiritually mature student understands the Bible-based obligation to return to society the time and resources God has freely given. By volunteering, students join with others to be part of the solution to some of the social and spiritual needs in the Lincoln community, as well as on the Union College campus.

In the excellence in the student's chosen field of study component, the junior and senior years at Union College provide an opportunity for intense exploration within the chosen field of study. A senior research thesis supplies the basis for creative investigation in conjunction with a mentoring professor from the chosen area.

Founded in 1996, the program currently has 61 students. Union Scholars graduates are signified by student regalia at graduation. In addition, the designation Union Scholars is noted on the students' transcripts.

Participation Requirements: The Union Scholars general education requirements consist of 23 hours of honors concentration, 3 hours for a senior research project, and 75 hours of community and campus volunteer work. Students must maintain a minimum 3.33 cumulative GPA to remain in the program.

Admission Process: Students must complete a Union Scholars application and should have a minimum cumulative high school GPA of 3.5 or a minimum 3.33 cumulative GPA in previous college work.

Scholarship Availability: There are specific Union Scholars scholarships available.

Campus Overview

Independent Seventh-day Adventist 4-year, founded 1891 • **Coed** 912 undergraduate students, 87% full-time, 56% women, 44% men.

Undergraduates 796 full-time, 116 part-time. Students come from 42 states and territories, 29 other countries, 89% are from out of state, 2% African American, 2% Asian American or Pacific Islander, 6% Hispanic American, 1% Native American, 10% international, 9% transferred in, 13% live on campus.

Faculty *Total:* 105, 50% full-time, 30% with terminal degrees. *Student/faculty ratio:* 14:1.

Academic Programs *Special study options:* accelerated degree program, adult/continuing education programs, advanced placement credit, cooperative education, double majors, English as a second language, honors programs, independent study, internships, off-campus study, part-time degree program, services for LD students, student-designed majors, study abroad, summer session for credit.

Athletics *Intercollegiate sports:* basketball M/W, volleyball W. *Intramural sports:* badminton M/W, baseball M/W, basketball M/W, field hockey M/W, football M/W, golf M/W, gymnastics M/W, racquetball M/W, sailing M/W, soccer M/W, softball M/W, swimming and diving M/W, tennis M/W, volleyball M/W.

Costs (2005–06) *Comprehensive fee:* $18,360 includes full-time tuition ($13,990), mandatory fees ($420), and room and board ($3950). Part-time tuition: $580 per semester hour. *College room only:* $2680.

Financial Aid 172 Federal Work-Study jobs (averaging $1663). In 2003, 323 non-need-based awards were made. *Average percent of need met:* 44%. *Average financial aid package:* $8376. *Average need-based loan:* $4807. *Average need-based gift aid:* $5334. *Average non-need-based aid:* $3162.

Contact: Union Scholars, Union College, 3800 South 48th Street, Lincoln, Nebraska 68516

University of Nebraska at Kearney
Honors Program

Kearney, Nebraska

The Honors Program at the University of Nebraska at Kearney (UNK) is a central academic priority within an undergraduate curriculum noted for integrating liberal arts education and disciplinary specialties that is executed by a faculty known for individualized work with students in the classroom and lab. Designed for students of high academic abilities, the UNK Honors Program offers an exciting experience in the liberal arts tradition. Small general studies classes of 22 students or less enhance student-faculty interaction, encourage active engagement in discussion, and increase opportunities for in-depth intellectual exploration. At the same time, this four-year program enriches and supplements all academic majors in the University by including requirements in both general studies and a student's chosen discipline.

Each semester, approximately twelve to fifteen different general studies classes in a wide variety of departments are offered as honors classes. These classes fulfill University general studies requirements as well as honors requirements. The program also offers interdisciplinary seminars that are designed to reveal the relationships between the disciplines. One example is the Human Genome, a class students may take for political science or biology general studies credit. This class explores the scientific, legal, ethical, economic, and social implications and consequences of the mapping of human DNA. Another example is the Search for Myth, which can fulfill psychology or English literature general studies credit. This class explores a wide variety of cultural and historical mythologies and their current significance through readings of literature and nonfiction. The UNK Honors Program also provides an excellent opportunity for independent study at the major level. Students complete 9 hours in their respective majors through Honors Options, through which a major course is chosen and an honors project is created within the confines of the course requirements. The student works side by side with a professor to complete the honors-level work. Through this personal attention, students gain much more knowledge of their disciplines.

An honors residence hall provides both living and social opportunities. Students may live in the Honors Hall to experience the academically oriented atmosphere. Many service and social activities take place during each semester and often originate in the Honors Hall. Students are not isolated; they mix with the larger community and reap the benefits of social and professional variety.

Participation Requirements: Participation in the Honors Program requires a student in the freshman or sophomore year to enroll in one honors class per semester until 15 honors credits have accumulated. In the junior and senior years, students are required to complete 9 hours of Honors Option courses within their chosen discipline. Honors Option courses are usually taken 3 hours at a time and are culminated by a senior study. Honors participation is designated by an honors notation on the student's transcript as well as an honors designation at graduation.

Admission Process: First-time freshmen must normally have a minimum ACT score of 26 or above, rank in the top 25 percent of their high school class, complete a written essay for admission to the program, and submit two letters of recommendation. Currently enrolled freshman and sophomore students with a cumulative GPA of 3.5 or better are encouraged to apply to the honors program.

Scholarship Availability: The Honors Program offers a room waiver to its students. The Honors Room Waiver Scholarships provide a room in a UNK residence hall for four years. This scholarship is awarded based upon the criteria for acceptance into the program. Two students in each incoming freshman class receive the Omaha World Herald/Kearney Hub Scholarship. This scholarship provides tuition, books, fees, and room and board for four years. To apply for this scholarship, students must have an ACT score of 28 or higher, rank in the top 10 percent of the graduating class, and write an essay. Honors scholarship recipients may hold other scholarships, and students may participate in the program without a scholarship.

Campus Overview

State-supported comprehensive, founded 1903, part of University of Nebraska System • **Coed** 5,380 undergraduate students, 91% full-time, 54% women, 46% men.

Undergraduates 4,881 full-time, 499 part-time. Students come from 38 states and territories, 46 other countries, 6% are from out of state, 0.8% African American, 0.7% Asian American or Pacific Islander, 3% Hispanic American, 0.2% Native American, 7% international, 6% transferred in, 33% live on campus.

Faculty *Total:* 392, 76% full-time. *Student/faculty ratio:* 17:1.

Academic Programs *Special study options:* academic remediation for entering students, advanced placement credit, cooperative education, distance learning, double majors, English as a second language, honors programs, independent study, internships, off-campus study, part-time degree program, services for LD students, study abroad, summer session for credit.

Athletics Member NCAA. All Division II except softball (Division III). *Intercollegiate sports:* baseball M(s), basketball M(s)/W(s), cross-country running M(s)/W(s), football M(s), golf M(s)/W(s), softball W(s), swimming and diving W(s), tennis M(s)/W(s), track and field M(s)/W(s), volleyball W(s), wrestling M(s). *Intramural sports:* badminton M/W, basketball M/W, cross-country running M/W, football M/W, golf M/W, racquetball M/W, soccer M/W, softball M/W, tennis M/W, volleyball M/W, water polo M/W, wrestling M/W.

Costs (2004–05) *Tuition:* state resident $3495 full-time, $117 per hour part-time; nonresident $7148 full-time, $238 per hour part-time. *Required fees:* $765 full-time, $14 per hour part-time. *Room and board:* $4990. Room and board charges vary according to board plan and housing facility.

Financial Aid 325 Federal Work-Study jobs (averaging $1088). In 2002, 120 non-need-based awards were made. *Average percent of need met:* 79%. *Average financial aid package:* $6490. *Average need-based loan:* $3429. *Average need-based gift aid:* $3361. *Average non-need-based aid:* $1920.

Contact: Professor and Honors Director: Dr. Gary Davis, MSAB 112, University of Nebraska at Kearney, Kearney, Nebraska 68849; *Telephone:* 308-865-8497, 800-865-8526 (admissions–toll free); *Fax:* 308-865-8987; *E-mail:* davisg@unk.edu or admissionsug@unk.edu; *Web site:* http://www.unk.edu/acad/honors/

University of Nebraska at Omaha
University Honors Program
Omaha, Nebraska

*T*he Honors Program at the University of Nebraska at Omaha (UNO) is for students who want to get the most out of their efforts and who enjoy stimulating experiences. The Honors Program consists of the University's most talented, involved, and exciting students, along with highly qualified and dedicated faculty members.

Honors students participate in special limited enrollment sections of core requirement courses, taught at a level and pace appropriate for honors students. Interdisciplinary colloquia are the core of the Honors curriculum and allow students to see the interaction between disciplines while offering an alternative way of fulfilling University requirements. An important advantage of honors classes is the stimulation able, motivated students offer each other.

Outside of the classroom, the Honors Program Student Advisory Board provides social and cultural activities, including guest speakers, tours, weekend trips, and an annual banquet. During Honors Week, senior honors students offer colloquia for the entire University community on their senior theses/projects. Honors students have their own lounge and study room in the Honors Office where they can visit, share ideas with friends, study, or just relax. A real sense of community exists.

There are many opportunities available to Honors Program participants. Internships and experiential learning opportunities are also available for students. UNO honors students have been recipients of Truman Scholarships and Rotary Scholarships.

All honors courses are noted on the student's transcript. If a student completes the Honors Program and meets all of the criteria, he or she is recognized at graduation, receives recognition in the Commencement Program, has an appropriate notation made on the diploma, and receives a personal letter of recommendation from the Chancellor.

The 25-year-old program currently enrolls more than 500 students.

Participation Requirements: Students meet the requirements of the University Honors Program by successfully completing 30 hours of credit in honors courses and by meeting their college's GPA requirements of 3.25 to 3.50 for the Honors Program. The 30 hours are part of a student's overall program, not additional hours. The 30 hours of honors credit are usually met in the following manner: 12–15 hours of honors sections of general education requirements; 6 hours of interdisciplinary colloquia; 3–6 hours of senior thesis or project; and 3–6 hours of special seminars, internships, electives, or experiential classes.

Admission Process: Students are admitted to the Honors Program as entering freshmen if they have minimum ACT scores of 26 or minimum SAT I scores of 1200 or by special recommendation from high school principals or counselors. Students already enrolled are admitted to the Honors Program if their overall GPA ranges from 3.25 to 3.5, depending upon their respective colleges. Transfer students from other honors programs are eligible if they were members in good standing in their previous programs and complete the Honors Program requirements.

Scholarship Availability: The Honors Program offers scholarships designed specifically for honors students. They are the Distinguished Scholarship, World Herald Scholarship, and Scottish Rite Scholarship. In order to receive any of these scholarships a student must participate in the Distinguished Scholarship Competition.

Campus Overview

State-supported university, founded 1908, part of University of

Nebraska System • **Coed** 11,041 undergraduate students, 74% full-time, 53% women, 47% men.

Undergraduates 8,172 full-time, 2,869 part-time. Students come from 32 states and territories, 68 other countries, 8% are from out of state, 5% African American, 3% Asian American or Pacific Islander, 3% Hispanic American, 0.5% Native American, 2% international, 9% transferred in, 9% live on campus.

Faculty *Total:* 812, 58% full-time, 61% with terminal degrees. *Student/faculty ratio:* 18:1.

Academic Programs *Special study options:* adult/continuing education programs, advanced placement credit, cooperative education, distance learning, double majors, English as a second language, honors programs, internships, off-campus study, part-time degree program, services for LD students, student-designed majors, study abroad, summer session for credit. *ROTC:* Army (c), Air Force (b).

Athletics Member NCAA. All Division II except ice hockey (Division I). *Intercollegiate sports:* baseball M(s), basketball M(s)/W(s), cross-country running W(s), football M(s), golf W, ice hockey M(s), soccer W, softball W(s), swimming and diving W, tennis W, volleyball W(s), wrestling M(s). *Intramural sports:* basketball M/W, bowling M/W, football M, golf M/W, racquetball M/W, soccer M/W, softball M/W, squash M/W, swimming and diving M/W, tennis M/W, volleyball M/W, wrestling M.

Costs (2004–05) *Tuition:* state resident $3938 full-time, $131 per semester hour part-time; nonresident $11,602 full-time, $387 per semester hour part-time. Full-time tuition and fees vary according to course load and student level. Part-time tuition and fees vary according to course load and student level. *Required fees:* $595 full-time, $16 per semester hour part-time, $72 per term part-time. *Room and board:* $5960; room only: $3570. Room and board charges vary according to board plan.

Financial Aid 359 Federal Work-Study jobs (averaging $1703).

Contact: Rosalie C. Saltzman, Omaha, Nebraska 68182-0218; *Telephone:* 402-554-2598; *Fax:* 402-554-4963; *E-mail:* rosalie_saltzman@mail.unomaha.edu

---

University of Nebraska–Lincoln

University Honors Program

Lincoln, Nebraska

The University Honors Program provides students of proven ability and distinguished high school record with a challenging academic experience in college. The Honors Program is a community of scholars—an intense intellectual experience for the most talented and committed students in a major research university setting. The program gives students who strive for academic excellence an opportunity to explore new knowledge through research, active participation in a process of discovery, and appreciation and respect for diversity of opinions.

In honors classes, special seminars, and research opportunities, students enrich their curriculum regardless of the academic major they have chosen. Honors classes are small, generally limited to 20 students but often with as few as 10 participants, and are taught by faculty members noted for both their teaching and research accomplishments. These classes stress critical-thinking and communication skills and involve the students in an active learning environment. The honors course work prepares students for the program's capstone research or creative project, which is undertaken in the senior year under the supervision of a faculty mentor. Many students have considered the senior project the most rewarding intellectual experience in their academic lives. Many program students present

their research at scholarly conferences and the annual Undergraduate Research Conference, which is held on campus.

Honors Program students are invited to live in a community of scholars in the Neihardt honors residence. Intense discussions and debates spill out of classrooms and into hallways, student rooms, and lounges. Faculty members and campus administrators often stop by to talk with students at fireside chats and in more formal settings. Special events and social activities for honors students take place in Neihardt's common areas and courtyards. The residence also houses the Honors Program office, several classrooms that are used for honors classes, a 24-hour computer lab, study rooms, and student lounge areas.

The honors community is shaped by its students. The Honors Board, 21 elected student representatives, makes a vital contribution to the community by helping develop Honors Program policies and planning social and cultural events for program members.

Students in the program are encouraged to participate in study-abroad opportunities offered by the University, as well as in internship and cooperative education programs.

Participation Requirements: The program consists of a minimum of 24 hours of honors course work. Students enroll in a section of the required freshman honors seminar and complete at least 6 honors hours per year and a total of 15 honors hours in the first two years. Juniors and seniors in the program complete at least 3 honors hours per year and a total of 9 honors hours in the final two years, including the required upper-level honors seminar and an honors research or creative project (e.g., thesis).

To ensure that students make proper progress toward completing Honors Program requirements, they file a Statement of Academic Interest that outlines their educational and professional goals prior to completing 64 hours of college work and a Memorandum of Study in their junior year that identifies the research or creative activity they intend to complete in their senior year. Students must have a minimum 3.5 cumulative GPA at the time of graduation. Completion of the program is recorded on the student's academic transcript and a special notation is made on the diploma and in the University's Commencement Program.

Admission Process: The program is available by application only. A faculty committee reviews applications twice a year, first after the November 18 early notification deadline and again after the March 1 final deadline for application. A total of 500 students, approximately 13 percent of the University's freshman class, are admitted annually.

The application requests information about the student's academic performance in high school, including a transcript and letters of recommendation from teachers and counselors, scores earned on the ACT and SAT, and essays on assigned topics. Most students admitted to the program are in the top 10 percent of their high school graduating class, have ACT composite scores of 29 or higher, and have taken full advantage of honors or AP courses, if offered, in their schools.

Scholarship Availability: All honors students benefit from a book scholarship that pays for all their required textbooks in honors and nonhonors classes. Retention of the scholarship requires that students fulfill program participation requirements outlined above and maintain a minimum 3.5 cumulative GPA. The scholarship may be held for up to four years.

Campus Overview

State-supported university, founded 1869, part of University of Nebraska System • **Coed** 17,137 undergraduate students, 92% full-time, 47% women, 53% men.

Undergraduates 15,684 full-time, 1,453 part-time. Students come from 52 states and territories, 110 other countries, 20% are from out of state, 2% African American, 2% Asian American or Pacific Islander, 2% Hispanic American, 0.5% Native American, 3% international, 5% transferred in, 24% live on campus.

Faculty *Total:* 1,043, 98% full-time, 97% with terminal degrees. *Student/faculty ratio:* 19:1.

Academic Programs *Special study options:* accelerated degree program, adult/continuing education programs, advanced placement credit, cooperative education, distance learning, double majors, English as a second language, honors programs, independent study, internships, off-campus study, part-time degree program, services for LD students, student-designed majors, study abroad, summer session for credit. *ROTC:* Army (b), Navy (b), Air Force (b).

Athletics Member NCAA. All Division I except football (Division I-A). *Intercollegiate sports:* baseball M(s), basketball M(s)/W(s), bowling M, crew M(c)/W(c), cross-country running M(s)/W(s), fencing M(c)/W(c), golf M(s)/W(s), gymnastics M(s)/W(s), riflery W(s), soccer W(s), softball W(s), swimming and diving W(s), tennis M(s)/W(s), track and field M(s)/W(s), volleyball W(s), wrestling M(s). *Intramural sports:* archery M/W, badminton M/W, basketball M/W, bowling M/W, crew M/W, cross-country running M/W, fencing M/W, football M/W, golf M/W, ice hockey M(c)/W(c), racquetball M/W, riflery M/W, rugby M(c)/W(c), soccer M/W, softball M/W, squash M/W, swimming and diving W, table tennis M/W, tennis M/W, track and field M/W, volleyball M/W, water polo M/W, weight lifting M/W, wrestling M/W.

Costs (2004–05) *Tuition:* state resident $4313 full-time, $144 per credit hour part-time; nonresident $12,803 full-time, $427 per credit hour part-time. Full-time tuition and fees vary according to course load. Part-time tuition and fees vary according to course load. *Required fees:* $955 full-time, $6 per credit hour part-time, $187 per term part-time. *Room and board:* $6008; room only: $3239. Room and board charges vary according to board plan and housing facility.

Financial Aid 1,364 Federal Work-Study jobs (averaging $2121). In 2003, 1008 non-need-based awards were made. *Average percent of need met:* 87%. *Average financial aid package:* $7647. *Average need-based loan:* $3809. *Average need-based gift aid:* $4488. *Average non-need-based aid:* $4295.

Contact: Director: Dr. Patrice Berger, 118 Neihardt Residence Center, 540 North 16th Street, Lincoln, Nebraska 68588-0659; *Telephone:* 402-472-5425; *Fax:* 402-472-8204; *E-mail:* pberger1@unl.edu; *Web site:* http://honors.unl.edu

NEVADA

Community College of Southern Nevada

Honors Program

North Las Vegas, Nevada

The Honors Program at Community College of Southern Nevada (CCSN) seeks to encourage enriched scholarly pursuits. The program's aim is to provide students a variety of opportunities to develop enhanced research, critical thinking, and communication skills. At the beginning of each semester, students with a GPA of 3.4 or higher may ask the instructor of a college-level course if that class may be taken for honors credit. If the instructor agrees, the student must submit an honors project proposal to the Honors Advisory Committee by the end of the third week of class. The students are encouraged to be creative; the Honors Advisory Committee does not want a typical term paper. The Honors Advisory Committee reviews all proposals and then invites those students whose proposals are accepted to continue under the guidance of their faculty mentors. The students must complete all of the course work with a minimum grade of B by the end of the semester. The honors project is given either a pass or a fail designation; it is not calculated as part of the course grade. The students may not create more than two honors projects in a given semester, and all honors projects must be completed in the semester in which they were started. At the end of the semester,

students exhibit their honors projects for fellow students and other faculty members at an honors reception. The Honors Advisory Committee reviews all of the honors projects. Those honors projects accepted as meritorious earn the Honors Credit on the student's transcript.

The Honors Program began in January 2004. In 2004, 10 students satisfactorily completed honors projects.

Participation Requirements: Students who complete five honors projects (two at the 100-level and three at the 200-level) and who maintain a cumulative GPA between 3.4 and 3.59 graduate with an Academic Excellence Diploma. Those who complete seven honors projects (three at the 100-level and four at 200-level) and who maintain a cumulative GPA between 3.6 and 4.0 graduate with an Academic Honors Diploma.

Admission Process: The Honors Program brochures are mailed to all eligible students in August and January, prior to the beginning of each semester. Students participate with the approval of a course instructor.

Scholarship Availability: If students are receiving financial aid, completion of an honors project may increase that aid. Currently, the College is looking for other avenues for scholarships for students who complete honors projects.

Within CCSN's Phi Theta Kappa chapter, scholarship money is available for students needing financial assistance in order to join Phi Theta Kappa, the International Honor Society of the Two-Year College. Sigma Kappa Delta, the national English honor society for students in two-year colleges, does not provide scholarships or financial aid.

Campus Overview

State-supported 2-year, founded 1971, part of University and Community College System of Nevada • **Coed** 34,204 undergraduate students, 23% full-time, 57% women, 43% men.

Undergraduates 7,850 full-time, 26,354 part-time. Students come from 55 states and territories, 13 other countries, 2% are from out of state, 0.8% transferred in.

Faculty *Total:* 2,280, 17% full-time.

Academic Programs *Special study options:* academic remediation for entering students, accelerated degree program, adult/continuing education programs, advanced placement credit, cooperative education, distance learning, double majors, English as a second language, honors programs, independent study, internships, part-time degree program, services for LD students, summer session for credit. *ROTC:* Army (b).

Athletics Member NJCAA. *Intercollegiate sports:* baseball M. *Intramural sports:* basketball M/W, bowling M/W, racquetball M/W, tennis M/W, weight lifting M/W.

Costs (2005–06) *Tuition:* state resident $1523 full-time, $51 per credit part-time; nonresident $6557 full-time, $107 per credit part-time. *Required fees:* $120 full-time, $4 per credit part-time.

Financial Aid 355 Federal Work-Study jobs (averaging $2000).

Contact: Dorothy D. Chase, Ph.D., Honors Program, N2B, Community College of Southern Nevada, 3200 East Cheyenne Avenue, North Las Vegas, Nevada 89030; *Telephone:* 702-651-4229; *Fax:* 702-651-4286; *E-mail:* dorothy_chase@ccsn.edu; *Web site:* http://www.ccsn.edu/honors

University of Nevada, Las Vegas

Honors College

Las Vegas, Nevada

The Honors College is a highly selective small liberal arts college embedded within UNLV, an increasingly widely respected metropolitan research university with a wide diversity of major programs in which College students can participate. The College offers students its own interdisciplinary core curriculum designed to stimulate students and enhance their knowledge, their powers of analysis and synthesis, their understanding, and their wisdom. With small classes and select faculty members, as well as other advantages common to other outstanding universities and small colleges, the Honors College offers students the kind of undergraduate preparation that enables them to compete strongly for satisfying employment or admission to top graduate and professional schools.

The best university and college education brings talented peers together, so as to engender conversation and learning with a highly accomplished faculty. The College's dynamic faculty members, who have studied at top academic institutions across the world, recognize that College students can compete with the best students in the United States. Faculty members greatly enjoy and highly value teaching courses in the College.

Bright peers and outstanding, caring faculty members in the College form the central core of a community of learners who share ideas and value cultural differences. Serious students find that they grow and develop personally in a diverse, small-college environment. The College supports close personal advisement with its own advisers, finds wonderful opportunities for its students, and helps them develop their aspirations and achieve their goals. The College offers the kinds of other opportunities that are accessible at fine universities: special residential arrangements and accompanying programs, study abroad, service-learning opportunities, competitive national scholarship preparation, early registration, and its own scholarships.

The College is attractive to students not just because of its unique curriculum and affiliation with special UNLV programs but also because of its Southwestern location in developing, vibrant Las Vegas. Abundant recreational opportunities in numerous nearby national parks and conservation areas surprise and delight students, especially those unfamiliar with the rich natural and cultural resources of southern Nevada.

Participation Requirements: Six hundred students who participate in the Honors College work toward one or both of two different special College designations in addition to their majors and minors in more than 150 undergraduate degree programs on campus.

Honors students become University Honors Scholars or Department Honors Scholars, or both, and these designations are on their transcripts and diplomas. University Honors Scholars study a special liberal arts core curriculum in addition to their majors and minors. This curriculum enhances basic skills of writing, public speaking, creativity, and critical thinking and also gives students a broad knowledge of language, culture, history, science, math, literature, and the arts.

Department Honors Scholars usually have completed their core curriculum and study largely in their majors. Transfer students and native students who enter the College after the completion of their general education core pursue research in their majors, write a thesis, and take special interdisciplinary seminars to broaden their perspectives.

All College students take unique interdisciplinary seminars taught by distinguished professors, and they usually end up taking more such seminars than required. These seminars include such courses as Lincoln and the American Experience, Wine and Ritual, Development of Moral Ideals, Japanese Culture, Politics of Food and Nutrition, Psychopharmacology of Abused Drugs, Rhetoric of Presidential Campaigns, World Architectural Heritage, Justice and Social Policy, Evolution of Medical Thinking, and numerous others. These seminars, taken during a student's final two years in the College, are widely regarded by students as the culminating benefit of an Honors College education.

Admission Process: Students interested in attending the Honors College need to submit an application both to UNLV and to the College. Available on the College Web site, the application for admission to the College constitutes also an application for scholarships awarded by the College.

The Honors College seeks excellent students to participate in and contribute to its stimulating academic community. Students admitted to the College should have demonstrated outstanding academic talent and have strong academic motivation. Because various factors help identify such students, the College has an admissions process designed to reveal those factors and take them into account in admissions decisions.

The selection of Honors College students is not solely determined by the use of objective grades, scores, and formulas. Because students, parents, and counselors are often misled by the expression of quantitative criteria and because quantitative criteria are just one factor in an admissions decision, the College does not express quantitative criteria for its admissions decisions. The College is looking for excellent students devoted to education, wisdom, and personal growth with honor. Excellence demonstrated by objective scores or grades is important, but not sufficient, for admission. The College evaluates each individual applicant in light of his or her overall background. Applicants differ from one another, each showing different strengths of writing ability, test performance, grades, leadership, and extracurricular involvement, and the College, in admissions decisions, evaluates each applicant's strengths individually

The College considers the following in deciding whether to admit about 130 to 140 new freshman applicants: writing ability, as shown in an essay and personal statements; kinds of courses taken; grades and pattern of grades; ACT or SAT scores; letters of reference; and personal interviews (in appropriate cases).

The College aims for insight into a student's academic abilities, writing skills, critical intellect, commitment to excellence, leadership potential, and educational values and uses these criteria to make an informed admissions decision. The College Admissions Committee advises students that it takes application essays and personal statements very seriously because focused writing reveals much about a person's educational background and academic values.

Students who do not enter the College as freshmen may apply as continuing native students or transfer students.

Scholarship Availability: A variety of scholarships and grants based on academic merit are all available to students in the Honors College. These scholarships come from three sources: Honors College endowments, administered by the College; the UNLV Office of Student Financial Services, which, in cooperation with the Honors College, manages numerous scholarships for talented students; and various UNLV departments and colleges, which, in consultation with the Honors College, award to honors students their own scholarships.

Honors College admissions applications constitute also applications for Honors College scholarships. Because students in the College often have scholarships from the College, other UNLV departments and colleges, and the Office of Student Financial Services, College staff members facilitate and coordinate the award process for applicants and help them identify and obtain substantial scholarships. The staff helps students combine scholarship offers for complete scholarship packages. To ensure maximum scholarship awards, students should on their own submit scholarship applications to the Office of Student Financial Services. Prospective students should see the Honors College Web site for details.

Most new freshman students in the Honors College, from both Nevada and out of state, receive scholarships in varying amounts, up to the full four-year cost of attendance in the Honors College, including tuition, fees, room, and board. The College has special scholarships for students recognized by the National Merit Scholarship Corporation and encourages applications from National Merit Semifinalists and Finalists.

Transfer students and native continuing students who have not been awarded full four-year scholarships to study in the College are invited annually to apply for scholarships during each year they study in the College.

The Honors College also awards competitive scholarships to help its students study abroad during their years at UNLV.

Campus Overview

State-supported university, founded 1957, part of University and Community College System of Nevada • **Coed** 21,783 undergraduate students, 71% full-time, 56% women, 44% men.

Undergraduates 15,570 full-time, 6,213 part-time. Students come from 51 states and territories, 65 other countries, 22% are from out of state, 8% African American, 14% Asian American or Pacific Islander, 11% Hispanic American, 1% Native American, 4% international, 13% transferred in, 4% live on campus.

Faculty *Total:* 1,435, 54% full-time. *Student/faculty ratio:* 20:1.

Academic Programs *Special study options:* academic remediation for entering students, accelerated degree program, adult/continuing education programs, advanced placement credit, cooperative education, distance learning, double majors, English as a second language, honors programs, independent study, internships, off-campus study, part-time degree program, services for LD students, student-designed majors, study abroad, summer session for credit.

Athletics Member NCAA. All Division I except football (Division I-A). *Intercollegiate sports:* baseball M(s), basketball M(s)/W(s), cheerleading M(s)/W(s), cross-country running W(s), equestrian sports W, golf M(s), soccer M(s)/W(s), softball W(s), swimming and diving M(s)/W(s), tennis M(s)/W(s), track and field W(s), volleyball W(s). *Intramural sports:* badminton M/W, basketball M/W, bowling M/W, cross-country running M/W, football M/W, golf M/W, racquetball M/W, soccer M/W, softball M/W, swimming and diving M/W, tennis M/W, track and field M/W, volleyball M/W.

Costs (2005–06) *Tuition:* state resident $3060 full-time, $102 per credit hour part-time; nonresident $12,527 full-time, $209 per credit hour part-time. Full-time tuition and fees vary according to course load. Part-time tuition and fees vary according to course load. *Required fees:* $472 full-time. *Room and board:* $8326; room only: $5278. Room and board charges vary according to board plan.

Financial Aid 300 Federal Work-Study jobs (averaging $3100). 300 state and other part-time jobs (averaging $3000). In 2003, 3907 non-need-based awards were made. *Average percent of need met:* 74%. *Average financial aid package:* $6911. *Average need-based loan:* $3993. *Average need-based gift aid:* $3030. *Average non-need-based aid:* $2094.

Contact: Dean, Dr Stephen Rosenbaum; Associate Dean, Dr. Dolores Tanno, Honors College, Box 457003, University of Nevada, Las Vegas, 4505 Maryland Parkway, Las Vegas, Nevada 89154-7003; *Telephone:* 702-895-2263; *Fax:* 702-895-2289; *E-mail:* honunlv@unlv. nevada.edu; *Web site:* http://honors.unlv.edu

University of Nevada, Reno

Honors Program

Reno, Nevada

The Honors Program at the University of Nevada, Reno, seeks to provide students who are both academically talented and highly motivated with an undergraduate education that nurtures and promotes their capacities to think competently, understand deeply, and

act ethically. The Honors Program is committed to providing strong support for the development of these qualities among a select group of students who have demonstrated exceptional promise. The Honors Program is University-wide and compatible with all academic majors. Successful participation in the Honors Program gives highly qualified students the ability to become skilled in their specific disciplines and the personal satisfaction of having met and accomplished the most innovative and challenging program the University offers.

In accomplishing this challenge, students have opportunities to enroll in small, interactive honors classes taught by outstanding professors; develop mentoring relationships with faculty members; attend honors academic and social functions; participate in programs for national and international study; take part in scholarly and professional activities; and graduate with Latin distinctions. The active Honors Student Association helps build a spirit of community among the members of the Honors Program.

The Honors Program offers students a rewarding curriculum of study. Honors classes are available in the University's core curriculum, in the student's major, and as electives. Students have a wide choice of courses, and they have latitude in choosing courses to fulfill honors credit. All honors students must complete the Honors Senior Thesis/Project, an independent, original scholarly or creative work in a topic of interest to the student in the major; the thesis/project is directed by a faculty mentor for two semesters. Students are required to orally defend their theses/projects. The program is designed to fit within a student's educational program without the need for additional time or credits. In addition, students may earn honors points by attending activities that provide enriching experiences.

A unique feature of the Honors Program is the Honors Living and Learning Community, which is available to incoming first-year honors students who choose to live on campus. Students enroll in a common core of honors classes, participate in scheduled interactive activities with faculty members outside of the classroom, and take part in programs designed to enhance academic and personal success. Honors faculty members join students for seminars, monthly dinners, intellectual discussions, and other activities such as attendance at the University Performance Arts Series and the Nevada Museum of Art. The current Honors Program began in 1989 and now enrolls 400 honors students.

Participation Requirements: In order to complete the Honors Program, students are required to complete 30 honors credits and complete an honors thesis/project and an oral defense. Students must maintain a minimum GPA of 3.25 each semester and achieve a cumulative GPA of at least 3.25 at the time of graduation. In addition, throughout the students' college careers, students must complete a minimum of two honors courses for the first two years, demonstrate significant contributions to honors academic and social activities, and meet with an honors adviser once a year.

Completion of the Honors Program is the only way for students to graduate with Latin distinction at the University of Nevada, Reno. Distinctions are summa cum laude, a 3.9 GPA or higher; magna cum laude, a GPA of 3.7 to 3.89; and cum laude, a GPA of 3.5 to 3.69. All honors students who complete the Honors Program receive special notation on their transcripts and in cursu honorum on their diplomas.

Admission Process: Admission to the Honors Program is selective and competitive. Qualified students must submit an online application to the Honors Program; the Honors Admissions Committee reviews each application carefully. The application contains the student's academic record, extracurricular activities, work experience, teacher recommendations, and an admissions essay. Prospective students are eligible to apply to the Honors Program if the student meets one of the following criteria: minimum 3.65 GPA (unweighted), ACT score of 28 or higher, top 10 percent of graduation class, or evidence of motivation and commitment to academic excellence. Achievement of one or more of these numerical criteria does not guarantee admission. Continuing University of Nevada, Reno, students and transfer students are eligible to apply to the Honors Program if the student has a cumulative GPA of 3.65 or higher. The deadlines for applications are February 1 and November 1.

Scholarship Availability: Scholarships are available by application to the Scholarship Office. Scholarships are primarily based on academic merit. Many students who receive these scholarships are members of the Honors Program. Honors Undergraduate Research Awards are available to fund Honors Senior Theses through the Office of Undergraduate Research.

Campus Overview

State-supported university, founded 1874, part of University and Community College System of Nevada • **Coed** 12,524 undergraduate students, 79% full-time, 55% women, 45% men.

Undergraduates 9,838 full-time, 2,686 part-time. Students come from 52 states and territories, 70 other countries, 18% are from out of state, 2% African American, 7% Asian American or Pacific Islander, 7% Hispanic American, 1% Native American, 3% international, 9% transferred in, 14% live on campus.

Faculty *Total:* 1,144, 61% full-time, 68% with terminal degrees. *Student/faculty ratio:* 15:1.

Academic Programs *Special study options:* academic remediation for entering students, adult/continuing education programs, advanced placement credit, distance learning, double majors, English as a second language, honors programs, independent study, internships, off-campus study, part-time degree program, services for LD students, study abroad, summer session for credit. *ROTC:* Army (b). *Unusual degree programs:* 3-2 biotechnology.

Athletics Member NCAA. All Division I except football (Division I-A). *Intercollegiate sports:* baseball M(s), basketball M(s)/W(s), cheerleading M/W, cross-country running W(s), golf M(s)/W(s), riflery M(s)/W(s), skiing (cross-country) M(s)/W(s), skiing (downhill) M(s)/W(s), soccer W(s), softball W(s), swimming and diving W(s), tennis M(s)/W(s), track and field W(s), volleyball W(s). *Intramural sports:* basketball M/W, bowling M/W, cross-country running M/W, equestrian sports M/W, football M, golf M/W, racquetball M/W, rock climbing M/W, rugby M/W, skiing (cross-country) M/W, skiing (downhill) M/W, soccer M/W, softball M/W, swimming and diving M/W, table tennis M/W, tennis M/W, track and field M/W, ultimate Frisbee M/W, volleyball M/W, water polo M/W.

Costs (2004–05) *Tuition:* state resident $2850 full-time, $95 per credit part-time; nonresident $11,524 full-time, $195 per credit part-time. Full-time tuition and fees vary according to course load. Part-time tuition and fees vary according to course load. *Required fees:* $160 full-time. *Room and board:* $7385; room only: $3990. Room and board charges vary according to board plan and housing facility.

Financial Aid 210 Federal Work-Study jobs (averaging $2464). 16 state and other part-time jobs (averaging $2115). In 2003, 4063 non-need-based awards were made. *Average percent of need met:* 62%. *Average financial aid package:* $7563. *Average need-based loan:* $4171. *Average need-based gift aid:* $3138. *Average non-need-based aid:* $2815.

Contact: Director: Dr. Tamara Valentine, Honors Program, 101 Lincoln Hall, Reno, Nevada 89557; *Telephone:* 775-784-1455; *Fax:* 775-784-1756; *E-mail:* honors@unr.edu; *Web site:* http://www.honors.unr.edu

NEW HAMPSHIRE

Colby-Sawyer College
Wesson Honors Program
New London, New Hampshire

The Colby-Sawyer College Wesson Honors Program is designed to provide highly motivated students with an optional intensive experience in the liberal arts. By creating academic, cultural, and social opportunities for integrative and interdisciplinary intellectual discovery, the program challenges students to not only widen their own avenues of intellectual exploration but to take leadership in a community of scholars and participate as catalysts for inquiry and discussion across the College. The academic courses in the program introduce students to a rich body of interdisciplinary knowledge and the process of interdisciplinary thinking. Small seminar class meetings encourage lively exchanges between students and professors. A four-year program of courses, honors contracts, honors research, and honors internships, begins with an introductory honors seminar or "pathway" to be supplemented with related courses from the regular curriculum and culminates in the second year with a concluding seminar. The College recognizes honors students by permitting them to study in the reading room of the Cleveland, Colby, and Colgate Archives; by providing the Wesson Honors Room in Danforth Hall; by sponsoring monthly out-of-class discussion groups often involving meeting visiting speakers and scholars; and by the award at the time of graduation of an honors certificate. The Honors Program is also a valuable source of information and advice for students wishing to pursue graduate study and graduate fellowships.

Faculty members who teach honors courses are drawn from across the College and represent a broad range of academic disciplines. Founded in the 1994–95 academic year, the Honors Program has offered such courses as History of East Asian Art, Environmental Ethics, Native American Literature and Culture, Myth and Folklore, Gender and Science, Voices of Islam, Leadership Without Leaders, The Science of Science Fiction, The City and Town in American Culture, Many Mansions: Religion in the Americas, Society and Disease, and Performing Shakespeare.

Participation Requirements: The honors curriculum is based on the completion of elective courses with an honors designation, beginning with the honors "pathway" that initiates the general liberal arts program sequence at the College. Each semester, faculty members across the College offer at least two interdisciplinary courses for students in the Wesson Honors Program. These courses may be offered for 1 to 3 credits.

Students participate in the Honors Program in addition to their work in the College's Liberal Education Program and their chosen majors, although some honors courses may satisfy part of the College's Liberal Education requirements. On completion of the honors sequence, graduating students receive an Honors Certificate, and an Honors designation is added to their diploma and transcript.

Admission Process: Incoming students are invited into the Wesson Honors Program based on a minimum cumulative GPA of 3.5 or an SAT score of at least 1150 (composite math and verbal scores). Once at the College, a student may apply for application to enter the program after having achieved Dean's List status and submitting a letter of application to the Coordinator of the Honors Program.

Campus Overview

Independent 4-year, founded 1837 • **Coed** 964 undergraduate students, 97% full-time, 65% women, 35% men.

Undergraduates 939 full-time, 25 part-time. Students come from 23 states and territories, 5 other countries, 71% are from out of state, 0.5% African American, 1% Asian American or Pacific Islander, 0.2% Hispanic American, 0.1% Native American, 1% international, 4% transferred in, 87% live on campus.

Faculty *Total:* 114, 52% full-time, 55% with terminal degrees. *Student/faculty ratio:* 12:1.

Academic Programs *Special study options:* accelerated degree program, advanced placement credit, double majors, English as a second language, honors programs, independent study, internships, off-campus study, part-time degree program, services for LD students, student-designed majors, study abroad. *ROTC:* Army (c), Air Force (c).

Athletics Member NCAA. All Division III. *Intercollegiate sports:* baseball M, basketball M/W, cross-country running M(c)/W(c), equestrian sports M/W, field hockey W(c), ice hockey M(c)/W(c), lacrosse M(c)/W, rugby M(c)/W(c), skiing (cross-country) M(c)/W(c), skiing (downhill) M/W, soccer M/W, softball W(c), swimming and diving M/W, tennis M/W, track and field M/W, volleyball W. *Intramural sports:* basketball M/W, football M/W, golf M/W, soccer M/W, volleyball M/W.

Costs (2005–06) *Comprehensive fee:* $34,190 includes full-time tuition ($24,700) and room and board ($9490). Part-time tuition: $825 per credit hour. Part-time tuition and fees vary according to course load. *College room only:* $5280.

Financial Aid In 2002, 103 non-need-based awards were made. *Average percent of need met: 80%. Average financial aid package: $14,086. Average need-based loan: $4105. Average need-based gift aid: $10,778. Average non-need-based aid: $3432.*

Contact: Coordinator: Professor Ann Page Stecker, Wesson Honors Program, Colby-Sawyer College, 100 Main Street, New London, New Hampshire 03257; *Telephone:* 603-526-3644; *Fax:* 603-526-3452; *E-mail:* astecker@colby-sawyer.edu; *Web site:* http://www.colby-sawyer.edu/academic/admin/honors.html

Saint Anselm College

Honors Program

Manchester, New Hampshire

The Saint Anselm College Honors Program offers outstanding students a challenging and exciting blend of enhanced core courses, honors electives, independent research projects, thesis development, and enriched interaction with faculty members and fellow honors students. Grounded firmly in the belief that a truly liberal education combines breadth and depth, the Honors Program draws highly motivated students and faculty members from all disciplines to work closely together in intensive critical thinking, research, and cultural experiences. The Honors Program enables students to derive the most from their college education, deepen their mastery of the liberal arts, and distinguish themselves as they pursue graduate and professional schools and employment.

The Honors Program encourages students to shape their research and course selection around their interests. The College makes every effort to be flexible regarding study abroad, internships, and independent study requests. Honors classes are typically capped at 15 students. They tend to be interactive seminars, emphasizing individual initiative in research and reading.

As part of their honors experience, students enjoy social and cultural events, such as the yearlong series of honors suppers with faculty members, trips to theaters and museums in nearby Boston, and film discussions with faculty members. The Honors Student Advisory Council provides a forum for student planning and communication. The Honors Room is a place to congregate, study, and meet with faculty members. Founded in 1995, the program involves an average of 175 students.

Participation Requirements: Requirements for the Honors Program include enhanced core courses, honors electives, advanced foreign language/literature, and an honors thesis. Students take four semesters of honors humanities courses during their freshman and sophomore years, honors ethics, and two additional honors core courses selected from theology, philosophy, and English. Two semesters of advanced-level foreign language or literature and four honors electives complete the curricular requirements. Students may substitute an honors contract for one of the honors electives. All Honors Program participants write an honors thesis under the direction of a faculty adviser. The language requirement often serves as the basis for a language certificate; the requirement can be fulfilled abroad or through independent study. Students choose to follow one of two honors tracks: arts and sciences or nursing. Students who complete the program receive an Honors Bachelor of Arts degree or an Honors Bachelor of Science in Nursing.

Admission Process: Admission to the Honors Program is obtained either by invitation or by application. Invitations to participate in the Honors Program are sent to incoming students whose high school records and SAT or ACT scores demonstrate superior academic ability. Highly motivated students who have demonstrated academic success may also apply to the Honors Program. Students must maintain a GPA of 2.8 or better to remain in the program. Application is made to the Director of the Honors Program. Admission to the College is rolling, with an early decision deadline of December 1.

Scholarship Availability: Saint Anselm College offers a merit aid program, awarding Presidential Scholarships on the basis of a student's high school record and ACT or SAT scores. All Presidential Scholars are invited to join the Honors Program, although no financial aid is attached to the program itself.

Campus Overview

Independent Roman Catholic 4-year, founded 1889 • **Coed** 1,987 undergraduate students, 98% full-time, 58% women, 42% men.

Undergraduates 1,946 full-time, 41 part-time. Students come from 28 states and territories, 15 other countries, 77% are from out of state, 0.5% African American, 0.8% Asian American or Pacific Islander, 1% Hispanic American, 0.1% Native American, 1% international, 1% transferred in, 95% live on campus.

Faculty *Total:* 176, 73% full-time, 77% with terminal degrees. *Student/faculty ratio:* 14:1.

Academic Programs *Special study options:* advanced placement credit, honors programs, independent study, internships, off-campus study, part-time degree program, services for LD students, study abroad, summer session for credit. *ROTC:* Army (c), Air Force (c). *Unusual degree programs:* 3-2 engineering with University of Massachusetts Lowell, Catholic University of America, University of Notre Dame, Manhattan College.

Athletics Member NCAA. All Division II. *Intercollegiate sports:* baseball M, basketball M(s)/W(s), cheerleading W(c), field hockey W, football M, golf M, ice hockey M, lacrosse M/W, skiing (downhill) M/W, soccer M/W, softball W, tennis M/W, volleyball W. *Intramural sports:* basketball M/W, football M/W, ice hockey M/W, racquetball M/W, skiing (cross-country) M/W, soccer M/W, softball M/W, tennis M/W, ultimate Frisbee M/W, volleyball M/W, weight lifting M/W.

Costs (2005–06) *Comprehensive fee:* $33,730 includes full-time tuition ($23,990), mandatory fees ($670), and room and board ($9070). Part-time tuition: $2400 per course.

Financial Aid 1,173 Federal Work-Study jobs (averaging $987). 17 state and other part-time jobs (averaging $1941). In 2004, 317 non-need-based awards were made. *Average percent of need met: 83%. Average financial aid package: $18,215. Average need-based loan: $5200. Average need-based gift aid: $12,712. Average non-need-based aid: $11,951.*

Contact: Director: Dr. Mark W. Cronin, Saint Anselm College, P.O. Box 1730, Manchester, New Hampshire 03102-1310; *Telephone:* 603-641-7250; *E-mail:* mwcronin@anselm.edu; *Web site:* http://www.anselm.edu/academics/academic+departments+and+programs/Honors+Program

Southern New Hampshire University

Honors Program

Manchester, New Hampshire

The Southern New Hampshire University Honors Program, founded in 1992, is dedicated to creating an environment in which unusually motivated students are offered an atmosphere in which excellence is expected and a challenging curriculum that fosters independent thinking in the company of like-minded individuals. Participants are encouraged to be actively involved in their own education.

The honors curriculum, comprising a minimum of 20 percent of the students' course work, consists of three kinds of experiences: Honors Sections that are taught in a seminar environment, with approximately 15 students; Honors Labs and Modules that are attached to regular college courses; and four program courses, Honors Freshman Experience, Honors 201, Honors 202, and Honors 401.

The Honors Sections are specifically designated courses that are taught by honors faculty members. Intended to satisfy the disciplinary requirements of the University core or a specific major, they are designed to offer greater challenge, with experiential learning and either more material or a higher level of material than in regular courses.

An Honors Lab or Module is an extra component that is added to a regular college course. The honors student, in consultation with the professor, enters into an agreement to extend the work in the course in order to receive honors credit.

Honors 201/202 is a yearlong interdisciplinary seminar for honors students in their sophomore year. Each year, the focus of the course changes. Past Honors 201/202 topics have included such diverse subjects as business leadership; birth, death, and immortality; sacred violence; the politics of food; and the beginning and ending of the world. Honors 401, or the Honors Thesis, is the culminating experience of the Honors Program. It is a yearlong project undertaken with the guidance of a faculty member chosen by the student. The student and the faculty mentor design a course of study during the spring semester of the junior year and spend the entire senior year completing it.

The SNHU Honors Program encourages a dynamic peer learning environment by maintaining a comfortable honors lounge and regular honors social events. The academic achievement of Honors Program members is facilitated by early registration and other academic privileges and documented on their transcripts and diploma. Students in the Honors Program are required to offer service to the program and the College as a whole by participating in various honors committee and campus organizations.

Honors students are actively involved in running their own program. The Honors Board, which is responsible for maintaining the quality of the program, is made up of 2 senior representatives and 1 representative from each of the other classes. These members invite 2 faculty members to join them. There are additional committees that are charged with responsibilities that include facilities maintenance and planning activities. Students are active in every aspect of the program.

The Honors Program curriculum is thus adaptable to each student's individual needs and interests and works with virtually any undergraduate program offered at Southern New Hampshire University. Honors students are also offered opportunities for trips, conferences, participation in the Model United Nations in New York, special programs, volunteerism, retreats, and other enriching activities.

There are 42 students in the program as of February 1, 2005. Fifteen entering freshmen are accepted each year. The maximum number of program members is 60.

Participation Requirements: Once accepted to the program, students must maintain a minimum 3.0 GPA in every semester, as well as grades of B or higher in all honors experiences. Currently, students in all majors are eligible, with the exception of the two-year culinary program and the three-year accelerated program.

A graduating Honors Program student is recognized at the graduation honors ceremonies by receiving an Honors Program Medal and a special honors certificate, having their names listed in the graduation program, and receiving special notation on their transcripts.

Admission Process: Generally, applicants should have combined SAT I scores of at least 1000 (new scaling), high school GPAs of 3.2 or better, outstanding entrance essays, and evidence of interest in learning, character development, and service. Students usually enter the program at the beginning of their freshman year, but transfer students may also be accepted if they offer fewer than 60 transfer credits. Current Southern New Hampshire University freshmen and sophomores are also accepted for entrance into the next year's honors class on a space-available basis.

Campus Overview

Independent comprehensive, founded 1932 • **Coed** 1,844 undergraduate students, 97% full-time, 55% women, 45% men.

Undergraduates 1,784 full-time, 60 part-time. Students come from 23 states and territories, 63 other countries, 52% are from out of state, 0.9% African American, 2% Asian American or Pacific Islander, 1% Hispanic American, 0.2% Native American, 2% international, 5% transferred in, 78% live on campus.

Faculty *Total:* 389, 29% full-time. *Student/faculty ratio:* 9:1.

Academic Programs *Special study options:* academic remediation for entering students, accelerated degree program, adult/continuing education programs, advanced placement credit, cooperative education, distance learning, double majors, English as a second language, honors programs, independent study, internships, off-campus study, part-time degree program, services for LD students, study abroad, summer session for credit. *ROTC:* Army (c), Air Force (c).

Athletics Member NCAA. All Division II. *Intercollegiate sports:* baseball M(s), basketball M(s)/W(s), cheerleading M/W, cross-country running M(s)/W(s), golf M, ice hockey M, lacrosse M(s)/W(s), soccer M(s)/W(s), softball W(s), tennis M(s)/W(s), volleyball W(s). *Intramural sports:* basketball M/W, crew M(c)/W(c), football M, ice hockey M, racquetball M/W, skiing (downhill) M(c)/W(c), soccer M(c)/W(c), track and field M(c)/W(c), volleyball M/W.

Costs (2004–05) *Comprehensive fee:* $27,180 includes full-time tuition ($18,984), mandatory fees ($330), and room and board ($7866). Full-time tuition and fees vary according to class time. Part-time tuition: $791 per credit. Part-time tuition and fees vary according to class time. *College room only:* $5626. Room and board charges vary according to board plan and housing facility.

Financial Aid 363 Federal Work-Study jobs (averaging $1090).

Contact: Director: Dr. Nicholas Hunt-Bull, 2500 North River Road, Manchester, New Hampshire 03106-1045; *Telephone:* 603-645-9798; *Fax:* 603-645-9610; *E-mail:* n.hunt-bull@snhu.edu; *Web site:* http://www.snhu.edu

University of New Hampshire

The Honors Program

Durham, New Hampshire

Established in 1984, the University Honors Program at the University of New Hampshire is dedicated to providing outstanding students with an individualized undergraduate academic experience

at one of New England's loveliest universities. In 2004, the University's Academic Plan recognized the University Honors Program as central to the mission of "combining the living and learning environment of a small New England liberal arts college with the breadth, spirit of discovery, and civic commitment of a land-grant research institution." That recognition and support have inaugurated new initiatives in the program: an increased emphasis on studying abroad, on independent research, on faculty mentoring, on campus leadership, and on postbaccalaureate opportunities.

The University Honors Program requires excellence in both foundational courses (general education requirements) and in upper-level courses in the student's area of specialization. Students therefore take a minimum of eight 4-credit honors courses: at least four are at the general education level and include a freshman honors seminar, and at least four are in the student's major field and include a senior honors thesis. The honors seminar is a multidisciplinary, discussion-oriented class, enrolling between 15 and 20 students and taught by the finest undergraduate teachers at the University. Honors students enjoy a wide range of lively, sometimes offbeat, seminars; topics include explorations of animal rights, laughter in theater, the origins of the universe, the impact of global climate change on Arctic society, and popular culture and ethnic identity. The senior honors thesis provides a synthesizing and individualized capstone to the student's program of study and results in substantive original work, often of publishable quality. Students also present their work at an annual, University-wide undergraduate research conference. Graduating students report that completing an honors thesis is a powerful personal and professional opportunity—one that translates well to the world outside the University.

Students say that participating in the University Honors Program allows them to benefit from the academic opportunities of a major research university while enjoying a smaller, collegial academic community. Honors students are involved in leadership positions across the campus in a wide range of athletic and extracurricular activities; they also participate in the governance of the program. Many serve in the Admissions Representative Program; others are members of the Honors Program Student Advisory Board, and still others represent the program and the University in a variety of public venues. The Honors Program has especially close programmatic ties with the Center for International Education and the Undergraduate Research Opportunity Program. Students also have the option to reside in an academically oriented dormitory. University Honors Program events are often held there, including an annual freshman meeting, faculty-student get-togethers, and preregistration receptions, where honors faculty members describe upcoming courses in an informal forum.

The University Honors Program enrolls approximately 300 first-year students (approximately 10 percent of the first-year class) with outstanding high school or first-year records. All first-year students entering the University as members of the Honors Program receive a partial tuition, merit-based scholarship. High-achieving upperclass students take advantage of Honors-in-Major programs in individual departments.

Participation Requirements: In order to maintain membership in the program, students must earn a B- or better in all honors courses and a minimum 2.8 cumulative GPA in their freshman year and at least a 3.2 cumulative GPA in their sophomore, junior, and senior years. Students who fulfill graduation requirements and achieve a minimum 3.2 cumulative GPA are awarded an honors designation on their diploma and transcript upon graduation.

Admission Process: Prospective students are admitted to the program based on their overall high school record, with particular attention paid to GPA, SAT or ACT scores, class standing, and leadership qualities. Students enrolled at the University who excel in their first-year studies are invited to apply to the program.

Scholarship Availability: Students admitted to the University Honors Program receive merit-based scholarships for four years, provided they maintain the required minimum GPA. In addition, the University Honors Program offers merit-based scholarships to highly

qualified continuing students. Other scholarships may be available through the financial aid office or through the individual colleges within the University.

Campus Overview

State-supported university, founded 1866, part of University System of New Hampshire • **Coed** 11,394 undergraduate students, 95% full-time, 56% women, 44% men.

Undergraduates 10,769 full-time, 625 part-time. Students come from 44 states and territories, 28 other countries, 41% are from out of state, 1% African American, 2% Asian American or Pacific Islander, 1% Hispanic American, 0.3% Native American, 0.8% international, 4% transferred in, 56% live on campus.

Faculty Total: 689, 88% full-time, 85% with terminal degrees. Student/faculty ratio: 14:1.

Academic Programs Special study options: adult/continuing education programs, advanced placement credit, double majors, English as a second language, external degree program, honors programs, independent study, internships, off-campus study, part-time degree program, services for LD students, student-designed majors, study abroad, summer session for credit. ROTC: Army (b), Air Force (b). Unusual degree programs: 3-2 accounting.

Athletics Member NCAA. All Division I except football (Division I-AA). Intercollegiate sports: archery M(c)/W(c), badminton M(c)/W(c), baseball M(c), basketball M(s)/W(s), crew M(c)/W, cross-country running M(s)/W(s), fencing M(c)/W(c), field hockey W(s), golf M(c), gymnastics W(s), ice hockey M(s)/W(s), lacrosse M(c)/W(s), rugby M(c)/W(c), sailing M(c)/W(c), skiing (cross-country) M(s)/W(s), skiing (downhill) M(s)/W(s), soccer M(s)/W(s), softball W(c), swimming and diving M/W(s), tennis M/W(s), track and field M(s)/W(s), volleyball M(c)/W(s), wrestling M(c). Intramural sports: badminton M(c)/W(c), basketball M/W, field hockey W, football M/W, ice hockey M/W, racquetball M/W, riflery M(c)/W(c), soccer M/W, softball M/W, table tennis M/W, tennis M/W, ultimate Frisbee M/W, volleyball M/W.

Costs (2004–05) Tuition: state resident $7210 full-time, $300 per credit part-time; nonresident $18,240 full-time, $760 per credit part-time. Full-time tuition and fees vary according to program and reciprocity agreements. Part-time tuition and fees vary according to course load, program, and reciprocity agreements. Required fees: $2016 full-time, $15 per term part-time. Room and board: $6612; room only: $3858. Room and board charges vary according to board plan and housing facility.

Financial Aid 3,216 Federal Work-Study jobs (averaging $1818). 2,835 state and other part-time jobs (averaging $1744). In 2004, 2032 non-need-based awards were made. Average percent of need met: 78%. Average financial aid package: $14,867. Average need-based loan: $3453. Average need-based gift aid: $2466. Average non-need-based aid: $5660.

Contact: Director: Dr. Lisa MacFarlane, 211 Hood House, Durham, New Hampshire 03824; Telephone: 603-862-3928; Fax: 603-862-4837; E-mail: honors@unh.edu; Web site: http://www.unh.edu/honors-program/

NEW JERSEY

Bergen Community College
Honors Program
Paramus, New Jersey

The purpose of the Honors Program at Bergen Community College (BCC) is to challenge and prepare students of superior intellectual ability and academic accomplishment in small classes taught by excellent faculty members who provide enriched versions of traditional syllabi. Honors courses encourage greater student participation in classroom discussion, interdisciplinary approaches to learning, and individual initiative. Students benefit from a close relationship with honors faculty members and with each other. They also receive recognition from the College and a network of support in seeking transfer to baccalaureate programs. Honors graduates regularly transfer to some of the finest universities in the region, often with scholarships.

The Honors Program offers a variety of honors courses in the humanities, social sciences, sciences, and other academic areas. In recent semesters, courses have been offered in literature, composition, history, math, sociology, psychology, anthropology, philosophy, religion, marketing, biology, and cinema studies. BCC continues to add courses in other disciplines as well.

In the spring 2005 semester, there were close to 200 students in the Honors Program.

Participation Requirements: Students who complete at least 18 credits in the Honors Program are awarded a special certificate upon graduation, the designation H appears on their transcripts (enabling them more easily to secure admission to more advanced programs and scholarship aid), and public recognition is accorded them at Commencement.

Admission Process: Students are identified after their first semester upon attainment of at least a 3.4 GPA. Future plans are to recruit students directly from high school based upon their grades and an interview with an honors officer during their senior year.

Campus Overview

County-supported 2-year, founded 1965 • **Coed** 14,325 undergraduate students, 51% full-time, 56% women, 44% men.

Undergraduates 7,258 full-time, 7,067 part-time. Students come from 120 other countries, 6% African American, 10% Asian American or Pacific Islander, 24% Hispanic American, 0.2% Native American, 7% international.

Faculty Total: 749, 40% full-time, 20% with terminal degrees. Student/faculty ratio: 20:1.

Academic Programs Special study options: academic remediation for entering students, adult/continuing education programs, cooperative education, distance learning, English as a second language, honors programs, internships, part-time degree program, services for LD students, study abroad, summer session for credit.

Athletics Member NJCAA. Intercollegiate sports: baseball M, basketball M/W, cross-country running M/W, golf M, soccer M/W, softball W, tennis M/W, track and field M/W, volleyball W, wrestling M. Intramural sports: basketball M, soccer M, tennis M/W, volleyball M/W.

Costs (2004–05) Tuition: area resident $1982 full-time, $83 per credit part-time; state resident $4104 full-time, $171 per credit part-time; nonresident $4344 full-time, $181 per credit part-time. Required fees: $403 full-time, $17 per credit part-time.

Financial Aid 159 Federal Work-Study jobs (averaging $1575).

Contact: Director: Dr. Alan Kaufman, English Department, 400 Paramus Road, Paramus, New Jersey 07652; Telephone: 201-493-3550; E-mail: akaufman@bergen.edu; Web site: http://bergen.edu

College of Saint Elizabeth
Honors Program
Morristown, New Jersey

The Honors Program is an integral part of the College of Saint Elizabeth, whose mission is to be a community of learning in the Catholic liberal arts tradition for students of diverse backgrounds and cultures. The Honors Program is offered to the full-time students of the women's college and seeks to promote an intellectual and social environment that challenges students to strive for the highest success academically and culturally. The program encourages leadership that is self-motivated and cooperative. The Honors Program, through its three-pronged goal of scholarship, leadership, and service, endeavors to challenge students to become more responsible, productive, and well-rounded members of society.

Students displaying superior scholarship, leadership, and service are accepted into the program and offered their own curriculum that supplants the general education requirements of the College. Students in the Honors Program are offered two seminars as well as honors sections of already-existing courses and special-topics courses in order to provide them with a broad base of knowledge in the liberal arts and to challenge and enhance their special interests and abilities. The honors curriculum has fewer requirements than those of general education for the College at large, allowing for greater flexibility in curriculum design for the Honors Program student.

In addition, each student in the Honors Program prepares a faculty-mentored honors independent research project that is presented publicly to the College community. This experience, which offers students the opportunity to plan, execute, and present a substantive research or creative project, increases students' ability to organize their work, expand their problem-solving abilities, and practice a variety of leadership skills.

To complement their academic scholarship, Honors Program students exercise their leadership qualities and give service through the various clubs and organizations and in their local communities. Students in the Honors Program are a highly visible and vital presence on campus, where they participate in special workshops, panels, and lectures as well as volunteer work in conjunction with the Volunteer Center. Honors Program students are encouraged to develop their whole person through a responsible giving and sharing of their talents and gifts.

Students are initiated into the program and awarded an honors pin after the successful completion of one honors seminar or two honors sections of courses, usually in October of the sophomore year. All honors courses are labeled as such on the transcripts, and successful completion of the program is also noted on the final transcript. At graduation, honors students who have successfully completed the program wear an honors medallion.

The Honors Program at the College of Saint Elizabeth was initiated in 1961 and has grown steadily to incorporate 100 full-time students at present.

Participation Requirements: Students are expected to complete an honors curriculum of 18 credits, made up of two honors seminars and an additional four honors sections of courses across the liberal arts. These courses are capped at 20 students. In addition, honors students must fulfill the requirements of their major(s) as well as First Year Seminar, English composition I and II, fitness/wellness, and foreign language. Generally during the senior year, students in the program take an honors independent study for 1 to 4 credits in order to work with their mentors on the independent research project, a presentation of which is given at the end of the spring semester of the student's last year of study. The student must maintain at least a 3.5 average and participate in a variety of leadership/service activities in order to remain in the Honors Program.

Admission Process: All students entering the College who have combined SAT scores of 1000 or more (or the equivalent on the new SAT) are invited into the Honors Program on a provisional basis. After a student fills out an Admittance Request that chronicles the leadership and service activities as well as scholarly awards, the director of the program evaluates the content listed and accepts or denies the applicant. At the end of each semester, the director of the program evaluates the cumulative averages of the Honors Program students to ensure that a minimum 3.5 average is being maintained. If it is not, a student is given one semester in which to reestablish that average. There is rolling admission into the Honors Program. Transfer students are welcome.

Scholarship Availability: While there is no particular scholarship offered by the Honors Program itself for entering students, the College at large offers a number of scholarships based on academic excellence, including Presidential Scholarships (full tuition), Elizabethan Scholarships ($7000–$11,000), Seton Scholarships ($5000), International Student Scholarships (full tuition), and a host of endowed scholarships. Many of the students who are awarded scholarships become members of the Honors Program.

Campus Overview

Independent Roman Catholic comprehensive, founded 1899 • **Suburban** 188-acre campus with easy access to New York City • **Women only** 1,327 undergraduate students, 56% full-time.

Undergraduates 741 full-time, 586 part-time. Students come from 13 states and territories, 40 other countries, 4% are from out of state, 16% African American, 5% Asian American or Pacific Islander, 14% Hispanic American, 0.1% Native American, 3% international, 7% transferred in, 68% live on campus.

Faculty *Total:* 196, 32% full-time, 51% with terminal degrees. *Student/faculty ratio:* 11:1.

Academic Programs *Special study options:* academic remediation for entering students, accelerated degree program, advanced placement credit, distance learning, double majors, English as a second language, honors programs, independent study, internships, off-campus study, part-time degree program, services for LD students, student-designed majors, study abroad, summer session for credit.

Athletics Member NCAA. All Division III. *Intercollegiate sports:* basketball W, equestrian sports W, soccer W, softball W, swimming and diving W, tennis W, volleyball W. *Intramural sports:* volleyball W.

Costs (2004–05) *Comprehensive fee:* $27,055 includes full-time tuition ($17,437), mandatory fees ($1000), and room and board ($8618). Full-time tuition and fees vary according to program. Part-time tuition: $549 per credit hour. Part-time tuition and fees vary according to course load, location, and program. *Required fees:* $120 per course part-time.

Financial Aid 74 Federal Work-Study jobs (averaging $289). In 2002, 124 non-need-based awards were made. *Average percent of need met:* 80%. *Average financial aid package:* $15,553. *Average need-based loan:* $3668. *Average need-based gift aid:* $13,069. *Average non-need-based aid:* $10,240.

Contact: Dr. Margaret Roman, Honors Program Director, College of Saint Elizabeth, 2 Convent Road, Morristown, New Jersey 07960; *Telephone:* 973-290-4313; *Fax:* 973-290-4312; *E-mail:* mroman@cse.edu; *Web site:* http://www.cse.edu/honorsprogram.htm

Fairleigh Dickinson University, College at Florham
University Honors Program
Madison, New Jersey

*T*he College at Florham of Fairleigh Dickinson University established its Honors Program in 1975 as part of the University Honors Program. The program provides outstanding students with an enriched curriculum, active interaction with and mentoring by faculty, experiential learning experiences, research seminars, and theses in the major. It offers students opportunities for learning beyond the classroom to develop intellectual curiosity, cultural enrichment, and a sense of community. Honors students take one honors course each semester for a minimum of four consecutive semesters. These courses include honors sections of freshman courses and the four sequential courses in the University Core curriculum. Each course in the University Core Program emphasizes the University's mission to provide students with a global education by providing an interdisciplinary approach and the cultivation of a global perspective. Students also may take additional honors courses in a variety of subjects or course honors in regular classes. All students write junior theses that bring an interdisciplinary focus to research projects; they write senior theses that are year-long capstone projects in students' majors, written under the close direction of faculty mentors. University Honors students are invited to social gatherings, special lectures, events, and exhibits on campus and in the surrounding area, including New York City. The program supports students who present at regional and national honors conferences, and many students also present at disciplinary conferences for undergraduates. The Honors Student Advisory Board actively engages students in running social events, fundraising activities, and focus groups on program issues. Honors housing is available for most honors students, including freshmen. Freshman honors students also may apply to seminar-based Freshman Honors Programs, called the Florham Scholars Programs, in global studies, legal studies, science, or business. The program currently enrolls 190 students.

Participation Requirements: Students must complete four consecutive semesters of honors courses (12 credits), including junior and senior theses, and have an overall GPA of at least 3.5 at graduation. Freshmen must maintain a 3.0 GPA in the first semester. Students must have a minimum 3.2 GPA entering the sophomore year, 3.4 entering the junior year, and 3.5 entering the senior year and upon graduation. The awarding of University Honors is noted on student transcripts and in the graduation program and is reflected in student regalia.

Admission Process: Applicants from the incoming freshman class are admitted in the fall and spring prior to registration. Freshman must have at least 1150 SATs, with a VSAT of 600, and at least a 3.0 high school GPA. Transfer and other eligible students may apply during the freshman or sophomore year prior to each semester if they meet the GPA requirement for their year.

Scholarship Availability: The Honors Program does not offer scholarships to participants; however, many honors students receive Col. Fairleigh S. Dickinson Scholarship (up to $12,000 a year) and Deans Scholarships (up to $9,000 a year) based on their prior academic records. All freshmen are automatically considered for these scholarships. Transfer students are eligible for Phi Theta Kappa Scholarships.

Campus Overview

Independent comprehensive, founded 1942 • **Coed** 2,633 undergraduate students, 85% full-time, 52% women, 48% men.

Undergraduates 2,250 full-time, 383 part-time. Students come from 28 states and territories, 21 other countries, 15% are from out of state, 7% African American, 3% Asian American or Pacific Islander, 7% Hispanic American, 0.2% Native American, 2% international, 6% transferred in, 56% live on campus.

Faculty *Total:* 331, 34% full-time. *Student/faculty ratio:* 16:1.

Academic Programs *Special study options:* academic remediation for entering students, accelerated degree program, adult/continuing education programs, advanced placement credit, cooperative education, distance learning, double majors, honors programs, independent study, internships, off-campus study, part-time degree program, services for LD students, study abroad, summer session for credit. *ROTC:* Army (c). *Unusual degree programs:* 3-2 psychology, communications.

Athletics Member NCAA. All Division III. *Intercollegiate sports:* baseball M, basketball M/W, cross-country running M/W, field hockey W, football M, golf M, lacrosse M/W, soccer M/W, softball W, swimming and diving M/W, tennis M/W, volleyball W. *Intramural sports:* basketball M/W, bowling M/W, cross-country running M/W, football M/W, golf M, racquetball M/W, soccer M/W, softball M/W, table tennis M/W, tennis M/W, volleyball M/W.

Costs (2004–05) *Comprehensive fee:* $31,994 includes full-time tuition ($22,876), mandatory fees ($510), and room and board ($8608). Part-time tuition: $681 per credit. Part-time tuition and fees vary according to course load. *Required fees:* $122 per term part-time. *College room only:* $5098. Room and board charges vary according to board plan and housing facility.

Financial Aid In 2003, 681 non-need-based awards were made. *Average financial aid package:* $15,806. *Average need-based loan:* $3653. *Average need-based gift aid:* $8290. *Average non-need-based aid:* $6952.

Contact: Director: Marilyn Rye, Fairleigh Dickinson University, College at Florham, 285 Madison Avenue, Madison, New Jersey 07940; *Telephone:* 616-417-3297; *Fax:* 973-443-8087; *E-mail:* mrye@fdu.edu

Fairleigh Dickinson University, Metropolitan Campus
University Honors Program
Teaneck, New Jersey

The University Honors Program of the Fairleigh Dickinson University, (FDU) Metropolitan Campus, is a living/learning community that fosters an environment conducive to academic and personal growth. Established in 1960, the program has been designed to provide an intellectually stimulating experience to FDU's most accomplished undergraduates through honors courses and a senior research project completed in collaboration with a faculty mentor.

The curriculum of the program features advanced honors sections of the interdisciplinary University core, including The Global Challenge, Perspectives on the Individual, Cross-Cultural Perspectives, and The American Experience. These courses, in addition to English Composition, Masterpieces of World Literature, and The Life of the Mind, demand additional reading, extensive writing, and in-depth discussions.

University honors students are encouraged to participate in professional conferences, such as those sponsored by the National Collegiate Honors Council (NCHC) and routinely present poster sessions and roundtable discussions at the northeast regional conference of NCHC. They are offered opportunities to participate in social, cultural, and academic events, including receptions hosted by the campus provost. The United Nations Pathways Program brings United Nations ambassadors to the campus, and honors students attend lectures and dinners with the ambassadors. Senior honors students participate in the University Honors Program's annual Research Day, featuring presentations of student theses and dialogue among students, faculty members, and University administrators.

In order to ensure that Honors students are good citizens as well, all members of the program are encouraged to identify and participate in a service activity on campus. Honors students fill many roles on the Metropolitan Campus, from staff members of the campus newspaper and yearbook to leadership roles in student government to participation on athletic teams.

In fall 2003, the University Honors Program opened a unique, new housing opportunity on the Metropolitan Campus. Located in the University Courts, the Honors House offers honors students the opportunity to participate in a close-knit community of scholars who live and learn together.

Special programming and opportunities for interaction with peers and faculty members from different disciplines and cultures enhance the on-campus experience of the honors scholars.

Participation Requirements: To maintain membership in the University Honors Program, all students must meet the following minimum cumulative grade point ratios: end of the first semester, 3.0;

entering sophomore year, 3.2; entering junior year, 3.4; entering senior year, 3.5; and graduating students, 3.5.

In order to graduate in the University Honors Program on the Metropolitan Campus, students must have at least a 3.5 GPA overall and must complete all honors courses, including Junior Honors Seminar. They must also submit an approved senior honors thesis/project, which must be presented to the University community on Research Day. Students who meet these criteria receive a special diploma with the Honors Program designation, recognition on the commencement program, and special commencement regalia.

Admission Process: Admission to the University Honors Program requires a minimum 3.0 grade point average in high school and a combined SAT score of at least 1150 (or an equivalent ACT score.) There is rolling admission of qualified students following the submission of an application form, personal essay, interview, and faculty recommendations. Formal induction occurs each spring at the University Honors Program Research Day dinner.

Scholarship Availability: Colonel Fairleigh S. Dickinson Scholarships and other financial awards are available on the basis of academic merit. Although most honors students receive these scholarships, the awards are not specifically for honors students.

Campus Overview
Independent comprehensive, founded 1942 • **Coed** 5,417 undergraduate students, 39% full-time, 57% women, 43% men.

Undergraduates 2,120 full-time, 3,297 part-time. Students come from 25 states and territories, 52 other countries, 13% are from out of state, 21% African American, 5% Asian American or Pacific Islander, 17% Hispanic American, 0.3% Native American, 8% international, 9% transferred in, 26% live on campus.

Faculty *Total:* 549, 32% full-time. *Student/faculty ratio:* 15:1.

Academic Programs *Special study options:* academic remediation for entering students, accelerated degree program, adult/continuing education programs, advanced placement credit, cooperative education, distance learning, double majors, English as a second language, honors programs, independent study, internships, off-campus study, part-time degree program, services for LD students, student-designed majors, study abroad, summer session for credit. *ROTC:* Army (c). *Unusual degree programs:* 3-2 psychology.

Athletics Member NCAA. All Division I. *Intercollegiate sports:* baseball M(s), basketball M(s)/W(s), bowling W(s), cross-country running M(s)/W(s), fencing W(s), golf M(s), soccer M(s)/W(s), softball W(s), tennis M(s)/W(s), track and field M(s)/W(s), volleyball W(s). *Intramural sports:* basketball M/W, bowling M/W, cross-country running M/W, football M/W, racquetball M/W, skiing (downhill) M/W, softball M/W, table tennis M/W, tennis M/W, track and field M/W, volleyball M/W, weight lifting M/W.

Costs (2004–05) *Comprehensive fee:* $30,790 includes full-time tuition ($21,224), mandatory fees ($510), and room and board ($9056). Part-time tuition: $681 per credit. Part-time tuition and fees vary according to course load. *Required fees:* $122 per semester part-time. *College room only:* $5546. Room and board charges vary according to board plan and housing facility.

Financial Aid In 2003, 272 non-need-based awards were made. *Average financial aid package:* $16,556. *Average need-based loan:* $3666. *Average need-based gift aid:* $7279. *Average non-need-based aid:* $3658.

Contact: M. Patricia Warunek, Ph.D., Director of the University Honors Program, Fairleigh Dickinson University, Metropolitan Campus, Robison Hall 37, 1000 River Road, Teaneck, New Jersey 07666; *Telephone:* 201-692-2407; *Fax:* 201-692-2407; *E-mail:* warunek@fdu.edu; *Web site:* http://ucoll.fdu.edu/honorsprogram

Felician College

Honors Program

Lodi, New Jersey

The Felician College Honors Program is open to all academically superior students in all majors who are pursuing associate or baccalaureate degrees. The Honors Program began in January 1991 and is currently in its fourteenth year. There are 60 students in the program.

Participation Requirements: Students take the honors sections of the required English courses Rhetoric and Composition I and II, honors sections of core courses, and honors courses within the discipline. All of the core courses focus on the mission of the College and the competencies of critical thinking, written and verbal communication, and social interaction. The honors sections emphasize an extensive use of primary sources and the study of specialized topics.

Community-based learning, consisting of 15 hours of volunteering each semester, is required for honors graduation.

A student organization, the Honors Students Association, sponsors many on- and off-campus cocurricular and extracurricular activities, including plays, trips to New York City, and College model U.N.

All graduating seniors in the Arts and Sciences Division complete a senior research project and present it orally before the College community. Honors students may opt to work with a professor and produce an original work of research of honors quality, which is read before presentation by a faculty member in two disciplines outside of the major.

Each spring, honors students receive certificates at the annual Honors and Service Learning Dinner. All graduating seniors who complete the program are designated as honors scholars and receive a trophy and certificate at the Graduation Dinner, which is held the evening before commencement. They wear a gold medallion inscribed with the word honor and attached to a ribbon with the College's colors. The words "honors scholar" appear in calligraphy on the diploma near a specially embossed gold College seal.

Admission Process: Newly admitted students to the College are eligible to enter the Honors Program based on their high school averages, SAT scores, and their ranks in their graduating classes. Transfer students with 36 or fewer credits from other institutions of higher learning may enter the program using the same criteria as well as an evaluation of their other college grades. Current freshmen and first-semester sophomores may be accepted into the program upon application and interview or if placed on the Dean's List for two semesters. Students in the Honors Program are expected to maintain a 3.2 GPA or higher each semester and achieve at least a "B" in all honors courses.

Scholarship Availability: A variety of scholarships are available for students who meet the criteria for each award. Many of the recipients of scholarships offered by the College are in the College's Honors Program.

Campus Overview

Independent Roman Catholic comprehensive, founded 1942 • **Coed** 1,451 undergraduate students, 76% full-time, 76% women, 24% men.

Undergraduates 1,102 full-time, 349 part-time. Students come from 10 states and territories, 7% are from out of state, 13% African American, 5% Asian American or Pacific Islander, 14% Hispanic American, 0.4% Native American, 3% international, 15% transferred in.

Faculty *Total:* 162, 39% full-time. *Student/faculty ratio:* 12:1.

Academic Programs *Special study options:* academic remediation for entering students, accelerated degree program, adult/continuing education programs, advanced placement credit, cooperative educa-tion, distance learning, double majors, English as a second language, external degree program, honors programs, independent study, internships, off-campus study, part-time degree program, services for LD students, student-designed majors, study abroad, summer session for credit. *Unusual degree programs:* 3-2 clinical lab sciences with University of Medicine and Dentistry of New Jersey.

Athletics Member NCAA, NAIA. All NCAA Division II. *Intercollegiate sports:* baseball M(s), basketball M(s)/W(s), cross-country running M(s)/W(s), soccer M(s)/W(s), softball W(s), track and field M(s)/W(s). *Intramural sports:* soccer M/W, softball W, volleyball M/W, weight lifting M/W.

Costs (2005–06) *Comprehensive fee:* $24,600 includes full-time tuition ($15,900), mandatory fees ($1200), and room and board ($7500). Full-time tuition and fees vary according to course level, course load, degree level, and program. Part-time tuition: $530 per credit. Part-time tuition and fees vary according to course level, course load, degree level, and program.

Financial Aid 108 Federal Work-Study jobs (averaging $1300). *Average percent of need met:* 85%. *Average financial aid package:* $11,130. *Average need-based loan:* $6625.

Contact: Director: Dr. Maria Vecchio, 262 South Main Street, Lodi, New Jersey 07644; *Telephone:* 201-559-6017

Georgian Court University

Georgian Court Honors Program

Lakewood, New Jersey

The Honors Program at Georgian Court University (GCU) challenges highly motivated students to set their own educational goals and achieve the very highest levels of academic success. The Honors Program recognizes students with strong academic aptitudes and provides enrichment opportunities for achievement of their highest intellectual potential; empowers students to design challenging and holistic learning plans under the guidance of an honors faculty member; encourages students to gain a deeper understanding of the contemporary and historical issues shaping their major disciplines; invites students to make meaningful connections between courses in different disciplines; promotes insight into values, attitudes, and assumptions and how these factors interact with academic and professional choices; and provides students with enriched opportunities for cocurricular and cultural experiences.

The Honors Program at Georgian Court is highly individualized; it allows students to work with peers and dedicated faculty mentors to design their own honors experience based on their own interests, providing them with a broad range of academic options. The program is unique in that it does not have specific, honors-only courses; instead, it integrates dozens of existing courses with a special honors component. The program culminates in each student's individualized senior capstone project, which cultivates and rewards intellectual curiosity, creativity, and initiative; builds scholarly discipline; and opens avenues for future academic and professional success.

The goals of the Honors Program are not just academic. The program also provides cultural and social opportunities for members of the program and the wider University community. The Honors Program, which begins in fall 2005, empowers, inspires, and rewards students who are committed to making the most of their educational opportunities at Georgian Court University.

Participation Requirements: The program requires completion of a minimum of 21 credits earned for honors-designated courses, distributed as follows:

For Incoming Freshmen: *First-Year Seminar: 3 credits.* Freshmen participate in an honors section of the Freshman Seminar.

General Education Courses: 6–7 credits. Students choose two 3-credit honors courses (or one 3- and one 4-credit course) in two of the following three areas: humanities (or an interdisciplinary course having a humanities focus), social science (or an interdisciplinary course having a social science focus), or natural science or mathematics (or an interdisciplinary course having a natural science or mathematics focus).

Major Course: 6 credits. Students choose two courses with an honors option in their major.

Junior/Senior Capstone Project with an Interdisciplinary Discussion Group: 6 credits. Students work with faculty mentors to develop plans for their honors projects and meet with colleagues in an interdisciplinary discussion group to discuss their work. During their senior year, students present their projects at an Honors Colloquium and submit their work for publication in the honors journal.

For Transfer Students or Those Entering the Honors Program after the Freshman Year: Students take a 3-credit Honors Seminar and follow the preceding requirements.

Admission Process: Admission to the Honors Program is by formal application only. Applications include a written response to an essay question. The Honors Program director and the Advisory Council make the final selections.

Freshmen who score in the top 10 percent of the Accuplacer tests given to all first-year students are invited to submit a completed application along with a letter of recommendation from a high school teacher or guidance counselor.

Current Georgian Court students with a cumulative grade point average of 3.5 or higher after taking a minimum of 12 college-level credits at GCU may apply to the program.

Transfer students with at least 12 college-level credits and a cumulative grade point average of 3.5 or higher are also eligible to apply.

Scholarship Availability: No specific scholarships are available for members of the Honors Program, but merit scholarships are available at Georgian Court.

Campus Overview

Independent Roman Catholic comprehensive, founded 1908 • **Suburban** 150-acre campus with easy access to New York City and Philadelphia • **Women only** 2,046 undergraduate students, 67% full-time.

Undergraduates 1,367 full-time, 679 part-time. Students come from 9 states and territories, 11 other countries, 1% are from out of state, 5% African American, 2% Asian American or Pacific Islander, 6% Hispanic American, 0.2% Native American, 0.7% international, 13% transferred in, 15% live on campus.

Faculty *Total:* 282, 35% full-time, 44% with terminal degrees. *Student/faculty ratio:* 14:1.

Academic Programs *Special study options:* academic remediation for entering students, accelerated degree program, adult/continuing education programs, advanced placement credit, distance learning, double majors, English as a second language, honors programs, independent study, internships, off-campus study, part-time degree program, services for LD students, study abroad, summer session for credit.

Athletics Member NCAA. All Division II. *Intercollegiate sports:* basketball W(s), cross-country running W(s), soccer W(s), softball W(s), tennis W(s), volleyball W(s).

Costs (2004–05) *Comprehensive fee:* $25,124 includes full-time tuition ($17,224), mandatory fees ($700), and room and board ($7200). Full-time tuition and fees vary according to program. Part-time tuition: $464 per credit. Part-time tuition and fees vary according to course load and program. *Required fees:* $175 per term part-time. *Room and board:* Room and board charges vary according to board plan.

Financial Aid 95 Federal Work-Study jobs (averaging $813). 162 state and other part-time jobs (averaging $709). In 2003, 134 non-need-based awards were made. *Average percent of need met:*

60%. *Average financial aid package:* $11,350. *Average need-based loan:* $4537. *Average need-based gift aid:* $8604. *Average non-need-based aid:* $10,761.

Contact: Edward P. Witman, Ph.D., Director, Honors Program, Georgian Court University, 900 Lakewood Avenue, Lakewood, New Jersey 08701-2697; *Telephone:* 732-987-2346; *Fax:* 732-987-2010; *E-mail:* witman@georgian.edu; *Web site:* http://www.georgian.edu/honors_program/index.html

Monmouth University
Honors School
West Long Branch, New Jersey

In 2005, Monmouth University's Board of Trustees voted unanimously to elevate the Honors Program to Honors School status. The University took this step after many years of building the program in order to conform to the National Collegiate Honors Council's "Characteristics of Fully Developed Honors School." The difference between Honors Program and Honors School is the improved resources available to serve student needs at all levels. Monmouth University's Honors School takes a holistic approach to servicing students at all levels. The University has a more than ample budget, which is a combination of funds from a private donor and substantial funds from the institution's commitment to honors education. The Honors School enhances the undergraduate experience for honors students at all levels, not only in the excellence of instruction in the classroom but also the enrichment of social and cultural experiences as well. Recently, the University has centralized the Honors School so that the honors residence hall for freshmen is now equipped with an elaborate student lounge and a separate academic lounge as well as honors offices with computer facilities, conference tables, free copying, and a food station.

The goal of the Honors School at Monmouth University is to present a curriculum with courses that provide a unique learning experience. Group identity materializes among those participating. From the outset of the freshman experience, students see themselves as contributors to an especially dynamic community. A sense of freedom of expression develops inside the classroom and is often carried on outside of class.

Courses in the freshman Honors School are clustered together, with faculty members developing common themes and assignments, enhancing the opportunity for students to make connections and to see issues from different points of view. Every course in each cluster is limited to 20 students, fostering a classroom environment of diversity, discussion, and debate. Honors students annually produce a journal, Crossroads, whose purpose is not only to involve the students in the creative process of a journal, but also to help them gain professional experience publishing their honors theses and projects.

Many of Monmouth's honors students go on to pursue advanced degrees (more than 50 percent) and publish their research in professional journals and present their findings at national, professional conferences, such as the Society of Space and Gravitational Research, the American Psychological Association, and the Bulletin of the New Jersey Academy of Sciences. The University also sends its students on to some of the best graduate and corporate placements in the country. In recent years alone, Monmouth has sent students on scholarship to the University of Medicine and Dentistry of New Jersey, Columbia School of Medicine, the Ph.D. program in psychology at Columbia, a Ph.D. program at Chestnut Hill, a Ph.D. program at Drexel University, and law schools at Rutgers and Seton Hall.

Faculty members are selected for their breadth of learning and multidisciplinary expertise and are distinguished contributors in their respective fields. Students in the honors community are encouraged to develop a special rapport with their professors. Such rapport is

important not only in the classroom, but also during extracurricular activities scheduled to enhance the material and theme of the program. These activities include free trips to some of the great Broadway shows, visits to New York museums, a film series, three annual honors parties, and a series of guest lectures.

The Honors School at Monmouth was established in 1979 and was reconceptualized ten years later, with the cornerstone of the program being the Freshman Honors Cluster. Enrollment in the Honors School is currently about 250 students, including 75 new freshmen.

Participation Requirements: All students in the Honors School must complete the requirements of their major, and they need to maintain a GPA of at least 3.3. In addition, to graduate from the school and have the diploma so noted, the student must successfully complete 25 credits. A total of 12 credits must be completed at the lower (freshman/sophomore) level. These can be fulfilled by taking honors sections of general education course requirements, including freshman English I and II, Western Civilization I and II, Literature I and II, Anthropology, Political Science, Psychology, and Sociology. Next, 13 credits must be earned at the upper (junior/senior) level, which are fulfilled by successfully completing a junior honors seminar, an honors tutorial in the major, a contract course in the major, a senior honors thesis proposal, and a senior honors thesis. (A study-abroad experience may be substituted for some of the upper-level requirements except for the thesis proposal, the thesis, and the tutorial in the major.)

Admission Process: Students eligible for taking courses in the Honors School are those who satisfy at least one of the following requirements: enter the University on academic scholarship; are admitted to the University with an SAT score of 1150, with a grade point average (GPA) no lower than 3.25 or a minimum GPA of 3.5, with an SAT no lower than 1120 (including a verbal SAT of at least 510); have a cumulative GPA of at least 3.5 after taking 12 credits at Monmouth University; or transfer to Monmouth University with at least 30 credits from an acceptable program and a cumulative GPA of at least 3.5 in all previous college-level work.

Scholarship Availability: Many students in the program hold academic scholarships from the University. The Honors School promotes the Truman, Rhodes, Carnegie, Mellon, and Roosevelt scholarships and fellowships. The Honors School also awards five $1000 scholarships to the best senior honors thesis proposal students as well as monetary prizes for the best scholarly paper, best scholarly group project, best nonpaper project, and for the highest GPA. Graduates of the Honors School have their transcripts and diplomas duly noted.

The University utilizes institutional resources (academic grants and scholarship programs) and is a participant in all major state and federal aid programs.

Campus Overview

Independent comprehensive, founded 1933 • **Coed** 4,501 undergraduate students, 90% full-time, 59% women, 41% men.

Undergraduates 4,034 full-time, 467 part-time. Students come from 28 states and territories, 12 other countries, 8% are from out of state, 5% African American, 2% Asian American or Pacific Islander, 4% Hispanic American, 0.2% Native American, 0.3% international, 8% transferred in, 43% live on campus.

Faculty *Total:* 534, 44% full-time, 46% with terminal degrees. *Student/faculty ratio:* 14:1.

Academic Programs *Special study options:* academic remediation for entering students, accelerated degree program, advanced placement credit, cooperative education, distance learning, double majors, honors programs, independent study, internships, part-time degree program, services for LD students, student-designed majors, study abroad, summer session for credit. *ROTC:* Air Force (c).

Athletics Member NCAA. All Division I except football (Division I-AA). *Intercollegiate sports:* baseball M(s), basketball M(s)/W(s), cross-country running M(s)/W(s), field hockey W(s), golf M(s)/W(s), ice hockey M(c), lacrosse W(s), soccer M(s)/W(s), softball W(s), tennis M(s)/W(s), track and field M(s)/W(s). *Intramural sports:* badminton M/W, basketball M/W, cheerleading M/W, field hockey W(c), football M/W, soccer M/W, softball M/W, volleyball M/W.

Costs (2004–05) *Comprehensive fee:* $27,615 includes full-time tuition ($19,108), mandatory fees ($596), and room and board ($7911). Part-time tuition: $553 per credit hour. *Required fees:* $149 per term part-time. *College room only:* $4229. Room and board charges vary according to board plan and housing facility.

Financial Aid In 2004, 1093 non-need-based awards were made. *Average percent of need met:* 74%. *Average financial aid package:* $17,835. *Average need-based loan:* $4580. *Average need-based gift aid:* $7951. *Average non-need-based aid:* $4722.

Contact: Director: Dr. Brian T. Garvey, Honors School, Monmouth University, West Long Branch, New Jersey 07764-1898; *Telephone:* 732-571-3620; *Fax:* 732-263-5293; *E-mail:* garvey@mondec.monmouth.edu; *Web site:* http://www.monmouth.edu/monmouth/academic/honors.html

New Jersey Institute of Technology
Albert Dorman Honors College
Newark, New Jersey

*T*he *Albert Dorman Honors College at the New Jersey Institute of Technology (NJIT) prepares exceptional students to become leaders in the fields of engineering, computing sciences, architecture, management, the sciences, government, law, and medicine. Students are offered special honors classes and seminars taught by dedicated faculty members, a wide array of research opportunities, a special lounge, separate study and computing areas, guaranteed on-campus housing, and a series of honors colloquia at which speakers and panels discuss current scientific and social issues of the day. All students, from both in and out of the state, receive merit-based scholarship packages, which are often supplemented by university, corporate, or endowed grants. Classes are small (generally 20 to 30 students) and are taught by professors chosen for their ability to work especially well with the most talented students.*

In the first year, each student creates an individual education plan in a freshman seminar and meets with an honors adviser. Each student is also advised by a professor from his or her major department. Honors courses, approximately one fourth of each student's degree program, are offered both in the specific curricula required by each of the majors and in the courses required university-wide. The Dorman Honors College offers one of the broadest Honors Programs available, with honors courses spanning the whole curriculum and offered at every level. Another important component of many students' development is provided by research conducted with professors at NJIT or the University of Medicine and Dentistry; by hands-on internships at major corporations or at smaller important specialized firms; or by student-designed and implemented grants. In addition to conventional programs, students may be admitted to accelerated programs in medicine, dentistry, optometry, and law or to a special five-year bachelor's/master's program that includes up to two summers of paid internship experience.

Growing from the Honors Program founded in 1985, the Honors College (1994) now numbers more than 500 students. More than 140 first-year students and 50 transfer or second-/third-year students are enrolled each year. Approximately 1 in 5 first-year students at NJIT is a member of the Albert Dorman Honors College.

Participation Requirements: Each student takes a total of eleven honors courses. Eight honors courses are chosen from offerings across the curriculum, in mathematics, sciences, engineering, computer and information science, and the liberal arts. The remaining three are special upper-division honors courses, including an honors humanities seminar; an honors course in either management, STS (science, technology, and society), or history; and an honors capstone design or research course in the student's major. Architecture students and all who enter after the first year take a slightly modified program. All students are required to maintain at least a 3.2 GPA (3.4 for the accelerated medical program), to attend sixteen colloquia, and to be engaged in campus or community service.

Each student's membership in the Honors College is recognized at graduation and noted on his or her diploma.

Admission Process: In addition to completing the NJIT application, students must submit a one-page honors application. All qualified candidates are interviewed by the Honors College. Applicants should have a minimum combined SAT I score of 1250 (1400 for the accelerated medical program), rank approximately in the top 15 percent of their class (top 10 percent for accelerated programs in medicine, dentistry, optometry, and law), and have participated in activities in or out of school. Exceptions to the required rank and SAT I scores are sometimes made for students who have attended exceptional high schools or have participated in especially noteworthy activities. Admission is not automatically granted to those who meet the minimum requirements. First-year students on average have combined SAT I scores of around 1315 and are ranked in the top 7 percent in their high schools. Transfer students who have been members of honors programs/colleges or who have a GPA of at least 3.4 and have engaged in extracurricular/leadership activities are encouraged to apply. For such students, college performance outweighs SAT scores and high school class rank.

Scholarship Availability: All Honors College students receive a supplementary merit scholarship package. Awards depend on SAT scores and class rank and may include a partial room grant. The average total award for honors students covers tuition and part of the living expenses and usually includes an out-of-state tuition waiver.

Campus Overview

State-supported university, founded 1881 • **Coed** 5,366 undergraduate students, 76% full-time, 20% women, 80% men.

Undergraduates 4,069 full-time, 1,297 part-time. Students come from 24 states and territories, 65 other countries, 4% are from out of state, 10% African American, 22% Asian American or Pacific Islander, 13% Hispanic American, 0.2% Native American, 6% international, 8% transferred in, 28% live on campus.

Faculty *Total:* 643, 65% full-time. *Student/faculty ratio:* 13:1.

Academic Programs *Special study options:* academic remediation for entering students, accelerated degree program, adult/continuing education programs, advanced placement credit, cooperative education, distance learning, double majors, English as a second language, freshman honors college, honors programs, independent study, internships, off-campus study, part-time degree program, services for LD students, study abroad, summer session for credit. *ROTC:* Air Force (b).

Athletics Member NCAA. All Division II. *Intercollegiate sports:* baseball M, basketball M/W, cross-country running M/W, fencing M, golf M, soccer M, softball W, swimming and diving W, tennis M/W, track and field W, volleyball M/W. *Intramural sports:* archery M/W, badminton M/W, basketball M/W, bowling M/W, football M, golf M/W, racquetball M/W, soccer M/W, softball M/W, swimming and diving M/W, tennis M/W, track and field M/W, volleyball M/W, water polo M/W, weight lifting M/W.

Costs (2004–05) *Tuition:* state resident $7918 full-time, $300 per credit part-time; nonresident $13,716 full-time, $587 per credit part-time. Full-time tuition and fees vary according to course load and degree level. Part-time tuition and fees vary according to course load and degree level. *Required fees:* $1262 full-time, $61 per credit part-time, $82 per term part-time. *Room and board:* $8242; room only: $5744. Room and board charges vary according to board plan and housing facility.

Financial Aid In 2004, 731 non-need-based awards were made. *Average percent of need met:* 82%. *Average financial aid package:* $12,676. *Average need-based loan:* $4071. *Average need-based gift aid:* $2262. *Average non-need-based aid:* $4210.

Contact: Director: Dr. David Reibstein, Associate Dean, New Jersey Institute of Technology, University Heights, Newark, New Jersey 07102-1982; *Telephone:* 973-642-4448; *E-mail:* honors@njit.edu; *Web site:* http://honors.njit.edu

Ramapo College of New Jersey
College Honors Program
Mahwah, New Jersey

*T*he Ramapo College Honors Program is designed for students who desire an especially scholarly environment and an opportunity to interact with like-minded faculty members and students. The Honors Program provides expanded opportunities for learning and reflection.
  Approximately 80 students are enrolled in the program.

Participation Requirements: Subsequent to being accepted, students participate in the College Honors Program by completing three H-option courses and receiving an honors certificate or by completing three H-option courses and completing a senior project and receiving full college honors indicated on the diploma. Students may also have the option of enrolling in honors designated courses.

H-option courses are those in which students, in consultation with their instructors, do additional in-depth work. The H-option is not simply an add-on to the given course requirements, it requires students to perform more extensively and more intensively. The number of H-option courses required for graduation with College honors varies from two (for students who transfer into the College Honors Program) to three (for all other students). Each H-option course must be at the 200, 300, or 400 level. Students are encouraged to make experiential education (co-op, service-learning, or fieldwork) a component of one of their H-option courses.

During the first four weeks of the semester, the student designates a course in which he or she is registered as an "H-option" course. This designation is accomplished by completing the H-option contract form with the course instructor and filing that form with the Office of the Provost. At the end of the semester, if the student successfully completes the honors work and attains a grade of A- or A in the course, he or she is awarded an H or an H+ grade. In the event that the student does not successfully complete the honors work or does not earn a grade of at least A- in the course, he or she receives only a letter grade but no honors credit. One course at the 200 level and two courses at the 300 or 400 level can be taken for an H-option as long as the faculty member and the student are in agreement about the contract. Students are encouraged to take their first H-option course during their second or third semester at the College.

The H-option contract provides explicit provision for periodic consultation between the student and instructor for project design and implementation, the description of work to be completed, and the description of the evaluation procedure.

The Honors Project is the culmination of the student's honors work at the College for those who opt for full College honors. The project is proposed and approved in the junior year and undertaken in the senior year as an independent study under the guidance of a faculty member. Students earn a unit for the completion of the proposal and an additional unit for the completion of the project. Projects may result in research monographs, screenplays, performances, and installations. Students must receive a grade of A- or better for the proposal and the project in order to earn honors credits. The benefits of the College Honors Program are numerous. Graduate and professional schools regard enrollment in honors as one indicator of excellence. Students are encouraged to take part in nationwide conferences and are eligible for financial support so that they may attend. Students are recognized for their accomplishments at the annual Honors Convocation. Honors students are invited to participate in a wide range of activities, including special lectures, trips, and regular meetings on campus. Incoming honors students are housed in the same residence hall. There is a student-run Honors Council which helps the Honors Director plan special events, including a reception with the President early in the fall semester.

Admission Process: The Director of the Honors Program, along with the Office of Admissions, invites applications from incoming freshman students who are especially well prepared. Students may also apply on their own if they feel they are qualified. Admission is based on the following criteria: grade point index, SAT scores, extracurricular/leadership activities, and recommendations. Transfer students are also invited to seek admission to the program. Students who were enrolled in an honors program at another institution may transfer credits equivalent to one H-option course. Evaluation is made on a case-by-case basis.

Campus Overview

State-supported comprehensive, founded 1969, part of New Jersey State College System • **Coed** 5,278 undergraduate students, 79% full-time, 59% women, 41% men.

Undergraduates 4,146 full-time, 1,132 part-time. Students come from 24 states and territories, 60 other countries, 9% are from out of state, 7% African American, 4% Asian American or Pacific Islander, 8% Hispanic American, 0.3% Native American, 4% international, 10% transferred in, 51% live on campus.

Faculty *Total:* 388, 46% full-time. *Student/faculty ratio:* 17:1.

Academic Programs *Special study options:* academic remediation for entering students, accelerated degree program, adult/continuing education programs, advanced placement credit, cooperative education, double majors, English as a second language, external degree program, freshman honors college, honors programs, independent study, internships, off-campus study, part-time degree program, services for LD students, student-designed majors, study abroad, summer session for credit. *ROTC:* Air Force (c). *Unusual degree programs:* 3-2 nursing with The University of Medicine and Dentistry of New Jersey (for Dentistry and for Osteopathic Medicine); biology, chemistry with Rutgers, The State University of New Jersey; NY University College of Dentistry; SUNY State College of Optometry.

Athletics Member NCAA. All Division III. *Intercollegiate sports:* baseball M, basketball M/W, cheerleading W, cross-country running M/W, field hockey W, soccer M/W, softball W, tennis M/W, track and field M/W, volleyball M/W. *Intramural sports:* basketball M/W, bowling M/W, softball M/W, swimming and diving M/W, volleyball M/W.

Costs (2004–05) *Tuition:* state resident $5640 full-time, $176 per credit part-time; nonresident $10,192 full-time, $319 per credit part-time. Part-time tuition and fees vary according to course load. *Required fees:* $2441 full-time, $76 per credit part-time, $1220 per term part-time. *Room and board:* $8208; room only: $5628. Room and board charges vary according to board plan and housing facility.

Financial Aid 137 Federal Work-Study jobs (averaging $1703). 501 state and other part-time jobs (averaging $2105). In 2003, 517 non-need-based awards were made. *Average percent of need met:* 81%. *Average financial aid package:* $8928. *Average need-based loan:* $3896. *Average need-based gift aid:* $6387. *Average non-need-based aid:* $6899.

Contact: Director: Dr. Edward Saiff, 505 Ramapo Valley Road, Mahwah, New Jersey 07430; *Telephone:* 201-684-7723; *E-mail:* esaiff@ramapo.edu; *Web site:* http://www.ramapo.edu/academics/specialprograms/honorsprogram.html

The Richard Stockton College of New Jersey
Richard Stockton College Honors Program
Pomona, New Jersey

*T*he Richard Stockton College Honors Program is a coherent sequence of courses designed to accelerate the development of honors students as scholars, creative individuals, and engaged citizens. The program is open to students in all majors and provides each honors student with a distinctive, fully integrated educational experience involving curricular and cocurricular elements. Students are actively engaged in college life, take honors general studies courses, and finish with an enriched capstone experience, usually in their majors.

Entering students take the honors freshman seminar entitled A Life of the Mind. This course sets the stage for the remainder of the Honors Program by exploring what it means to be a scholar or creative artist. Students read books and articles written by scholars and artists, describing the development of their ideas. Scholars and creative artists from Stockton and selected guests are invited to talk to the students about their own intellectual development and how they conduct their scholarship or engage in their creative endeavors. As part of this course, students also begin their own research projects, leading to public presentations at the end of the semester.

Building on Stockton's nationally recognized general studies curriculum, additional honors courses that meet many of the student's graduation requirements make up the core of the honors curriculum. During their junior and senior years, students working for College Honors take a series of seminars and develop an internship or engage in a research or creative project, typically in close collaboration with a faculty member. Either of these leads to a public presentation.

Honors students have opportunities to attend special honors events and travel on special honors trips. Selected honors students receive support to make presentations at national and regional conferences.

Honors classes are restricted in size. Freshman seminars are limited to 15 students and upper-level courses, to 20. Honors students have a space in which to study, access to the College computer network and the Internet, and interaction with other honors students. Honors students have an honors preceptor (adviser) in addition to their regular preceptor and many opportunities to interact with faculty members in individual and small-group settings, such as seminars, dinners, trips, and social settings.

Perhaps the most distinctive feature of Stockton's Honors Program is its newness. The program enrolled its first class in the fall of 2005, with 25 students. The program will ultimately grow to approximately 200 students. Students admitted to the program over the next five years will have a chance to build and shape the program in ways that are impossible in older, more established programs.

Participation Requirements: The Stockton College Honors Program is designed with three options for students. First Year Excellence, General Studies Honors, and College Honors. Throughout their years at Stockton, honors students have a range of opportunities to fulfill the 2-hour-per-week requirement of the Honors Program.

First Year Excellence is for those students who complete two required honors courses (8 credits), contribute 2 hours per week of service to the program, and maintain a minimum 3.3 GPA during their first year at Stockton.

Students can complete requirements for General Studies Honors by completing the five required honors general studies courses (20 credits), meeting the service requirement, and maintaining a minimum 3.3 GPA during their first two years at Stockton. Students who continue in the Honors Program during their junior and senior years, ultimately completing a project or internship (4 credits), taking additional honors courses (4 credits, minimum), continuing to meet the service requirement, and maintaining at least a 3.3 GPA, can earn College Honors.

Students earning College Honors typically present the results of their senior projects or internships at a public forum. Students graduating with one of the categories of honors have that achievement noted on their transcript and receive special recognition at commencement. Honors students are encouraged to build honors portfolios documenting their Honors Program, academic program, and NCHC activities.

Admission Process: Academic scholarship recipients whose records demonstrate the potential for college academic excellence and leadership potential are selected by the admissions staff and invited to apply. Applicants must submit an application including a personal essay and two letters of reference. From that pool, the Honors Advisory Committee invites students to enroll in the Honors Program. As the program grows, the College plans to develop procedures to permit transfer students and students in their sophomore year to apply.

Scholarship Availability: Merit scholarships are readily available at Richard Stockton College. The awards are based upon the student's class rank and SAT scores. Awards range from $500 to full tuition and fees. Students who are eligible for the Honors Program do not necessarily receive a merit award from Stockton. More information about scholarships can be found at http://admissions.stockton.edu/scholarships.html.

Campus Overview

State-supported comprehensive, founded 1969, part of New Jersey State College System • **Coed** 6,580 undergraduate students, 84% full-time, 58% women, 42% men.

Undergraduates 5,533 full-time, 1,047 part-time. Students come from 10 states and territories, 30 other countries, 3% are from out of state, 7% African American, 4% Asian American or Pacific Islander, 6% Hispanic American, 0.4% Native American, 0.7% international, 13% transferred in, 38% live on campus.

Faculty *Total:* 461, 49% full-time, 84% with terminal degrees. *Student/faculty ratio:* 19:1.

Academic Programs *Special study options:* academic remediation for entering students, adult/continuing education programs, advanced placement credit, distance learning, double majors, freshman honors college, honors programs, independent study, internships, off-campus study, part-time degree program, services for LD students, student-designed majors, study abroad, summer session for credit. *Unusual degree programs:* 3-2 engineering with New Jersey Institute of Technology; Rutgers, The State University of New Jersey; criminal justice with Rutgers, The State University of New Jersey.

Athletics Member NCAA. All Division III. *Intercollegiate sports:* baseball M, basketball M/W, cheerleading M/W, crew W, cross-country running M/W, field hockey W, lacrosse M, soccer M/W, softball W, tennis W, track and field M/W, volleyball W. *Intramural sports:* basketball M/W, bowling M(c)/W(c), crew M(c), fencing M(c)/W(c), football M/W, golf M(c)/W(c), skiing (downhill) M(c)/W(c), softball M/W, swimming and diving M/W, tennis M/W, volleyball M/W.

Costs (2004–05) *Tuition:* state resident $5091 full-time, $159 per credit part-time; nonresident $8256 full-time, $258 per credit part-time. *Required fees:* $2112 full-time, $66 per credit part-time. *Room and board:* $7252; room only: $4750. Room and board charges vary according to board plan and housing facility.

Financial Aid 313 Federal Work-Study jobs (averaging $1608). 703 state and other part-time jobs (averaging $1260). In 2004, 350 non-need-based awards were made. *Average percent of need met:* 61%. *Average financial aid package:* $10,764. *Average need-based loan:* $3787. *Average need-based gift aid:* $5780. *Average non-need-based aid:* $2202.

Contact: Director: Dr. Michael J. Hozik, The Honors Program, The Richard Stockton College of New Jersey, P.O. Box 195, Pomona,

New Jersey 08240-0195; *Telephone:* 609-652-4277; *Fax:* 609-626-5515; *E-mail:* hozikm@stockton.edu

Rowan University
Thomas N. Bantivoglio Honors Program
Glassboro, New Jersey

The Rowan University Thomas N. Bantivoglio Honors Program is open to students in every academic major. Emphasis is placed on interdisciplinary study and active learning. The program's smaller classes nurture development of student writing, speaking, and critical-thinking skills. Connections among ideas and disciplines are enriched by encouraging students to question, study, and analyze primary texts.

Students take the initiative in their own learning and work in collaboration with peers. They may join in selecting texts, nominating faculty members for the program, and creating curriculum. The concentration provides the space for students to take up different points of view outside any single discipline. Students think critically about the interplay between liberal learning and career preparation within and beyond academic fields.

The program was the recipient of a $1-million gift from Thomas N. Bantivoglio of Haddonfield, New Jersey, in November 2004. The funds are dedicated to enhance both the curricular and extracurricular involvements of students in the program.

Participation Requirements: Students must complete three lower-level and three upper-level courses in the concentration. An independent honors project may be substituted for one upper-level course. All honors courses fulfill general education requirements. They may also be applicable to writing intensive and multicultural-global requirements. A minimum of 18 credit hours in interdisciplinary studies and a 3.5 GPA are required for completion of the concentration.

Admission Process: Applications for admission are reviewed by the Honors Program Coordinator. Criteria for freshman acceptance rests on a combination of scores on standardized tests (AP exam scores and 1200 on the SAT I), letters of recommendation, and high school rank. Students with a minimum 3.5 GPA at the end of their first year are invited to apply for admission to the program.

Scholarship Availability: More than 70 percent of Rowan University students receive financial aid through an assortment of grants, scholarships, loans, and part-time employment. Last year's grant and loan programs totaled more than $8 million. Each year, alumni, private groups, and individuals also provide more than $120,000 in scholarships to incoming students.

Campus Overview

State-supported comprehensive, founded 1923, part of New Jersey State College System • **Coed** 8,383 undergraduate students, 85% full-time, 56% women, 44% men.

Undergraduates 7,087 full-time, 1,296 part-time. Students come from 20 states and territories, 29 other countries, 3% are from out of state, 9% African American, 3% Asian American or Pacific Islander, 6% Hispanic American, 0.3% Native American, 10% transferred in, 36% live on campus.

Faculty *Total:* 788, 53% full-time, 52% with terminal degrees. *Student/faculty ratio:* 15:1.

Academic Programs *Special study options:* academic remediation for entering students, adult/continuing education programs, advanced placement credit, double majors, English as a second language, freshman honors college, honors programs, independent study, internships, part-time degree program, services for LD students, study abroad, summer session for credit. *ROTC:* Army (c). *Unusual degree programs:* 3-2 optometry with Pennsylvania College of Optometry, podiatry with Pennsylvania College of Podiatric Medicine, pharmacy with Philadelphia College of Pharmacy and Science.

Athletics Member NCAA. All Division III. *Intercollegiate sports:* baseball M, basketball M/W, cross-country running M/W, field hockey W, football M, lacrosse W, soccer M/W, softball W, swimming and diving M/W, tennis M/W, track and field M/W, volleyball W. *Intramural sports:* baseball M, basketball M/W, bowling M/W, golf M/W, ice hockey M, lacrosse M, racquetball M/W, soccer M/W, table tennis M/W, ultimate Frisbee M/W, volleyball M, wrestling M.

Costs (2004–05) *Tuition:* state resident $5828 full-time, $224 per semester hour part-time; nonresident $11,656 full-time, $448 per semester hour part-time. *Required fees:* $2142 full-time, $86 per semester hour part-time. *Room and board:* $7642. Room and board charges vary according to board plan and housing facility.

Financial Aid 617 Federal Work-Study jobs (averaging $899). 537 state and other part-time jobs (averaging $1638). In 2003, 21 non-need-based awards were made. *Average percent of need met:* 50%. *Average financial aid package:* $6213. *Average need-based loan:* $3400. *Average need-based gift aid:* $5000. *Average non-need-based aid:* $1933.

Contact: Director: Mark Hutter, Ph.D., Savitz Hall, Third Floor, Glassboro, New Jersey 08028-1701; *Telephone:* 856-256-4775 or 856-256-4643; *E-mail:* hutter@rowan.edu; *Web site:* http://www.rowan.edu/honors

Rutgers, The State University of New Jersey, Camden College of Arts and Sciences

Honors College

Camden, New Jersey

*T*he Honors College at Rutgers University–Camden offers outstanding students a high-quality education with the top faculty members of the Schools of Arts and Sciences, Business, and Law. Freshmen and sophomores are offered small seminar classes with full-time faculty members in a wide variety of disciplines. Seminars emphasize the latest trends in scholarly study as professors concentrate on the cutting edge of their current research. Recent courses have included Remembering Vietnam; Friday Night Lights: Sports in American Popular Culture; Archaic Greece; Passion in Poetry, Prose, and Play; Genius in Music; Approaches to Leadership; The Comic Tradition; and Inventing America.*

The Honors College is located in the Paul Robeson Library where students are offered separate lounge and study areas, extra computer facilities, and an honors librarian to assist them in their research efforts.

Students may live at home or in the special honors wing of the residence halls. The honors wing has a quiet-study lounge and a 24-hour computer lab to allow students to continue their research in the dormitory setting. Students also participate in a wide variety of extracurricular activities both in Camden, New Jersey, and nearby Philadelphia. Students have toured art and historical museums, attended theatrical productions and movies, and attended lectures by internationally known scholars and film directors. Students prepare their own newsletter and literary magazine for the Honors College and also enjoy social and charitable events sponsored by the Honors Student Organization.

While the first two years of the Honors College focus on the classroom experience and close contact with professors, the third year

of the program encourages honors students to understand "The City and the World." Honors students may participate in international study via the Study-Abroad Program, which has campuses in nineteen different countries, or the International Studies Program, which includes two-week trips in conjunction with classroom study. Recent trips have included study in Greece, Turkey, Mexico, France, China, and Italy as well as many trips to Southern Africa (where Rutgers–Camden is involved in many joint educational and scientific ventures). Students may also participate in the many service-learning courses, which offer close contact with educational and social service agencies in the surrounding area.*

Students complete the Honors College in their senior year by participating in one of the following: a departmental honors program, an honors senior thesis, the completion of a minor, a double major, or two graduate courses from among Rutgers' many graduate programs. This allows students to specialize in their major field of interest and prepare for entrance to graduate or professional school.

Students joining the Honors College enjoy the advantages of a "college within a college." There is considerable contact with professors and fellow students during the four-year program. Furthermore, honors students are offered a "blue ribbon advising service," supervised by Senior Program Coordinator Robert A. Emmons Jr., which helps them with the stressful demands of college life. Honors College administrators are always willing and able to assist students, whatever their problem or concern.

Participation Requirements: Students take honors sections of English and World Masterpieces as well as three honors seminars during the first two years. The third year of the Honors College features an emphasis on "The City and the World." The fourth year includes a senior thesis, departmental honors programs, or the completion of a minor, double major, or two graduate courses. These are not additional courses for honors students; they fulfill the general college curricular requirements. Students must maintain a minimum 3.0 grade point average to remain in the Honors College. Students who graduate in the Honors College receive a designation of general honors on their college transcript.

Admission Process: Freshmen are admitted to the Honors College on their admission to Rutgers–Camden based on their SAT scores, high school class rank, and/or distinctive performance in the creative arts. Students who wish to join the Honors College after their first semester must apply to the Honors College having achieved a minimum 3.7 average during their Rutgers experience. Transfer students and graduates of community colleges are encouraged to join the Honors College, but their course requirements may differ depending on the courses they have taken earlier. The Honors College currently admits approximately 80 students each year.

Scholarship Availability: All freshmen admitted to the Honors College also receive either a Provost Fellowship or a Carr Fellowship.

Campus Overview

State-supported university, founded 1927, part of Rutgers, The State University of New Jersey • **Coed** 4,007 undergraduate students, 76% full-time, 59% women, 41% men.

Undergraduates 3,060 full-time, 947 part-time. 3% are from out of state, 15% African American, 9% Asian American or Pacific Islander, 6% Hispanic American, 0.4% Native American, 0.8% international, 11% transferred in, 13% live on campus.

Faculty *Total:* 419, 54% full-time, 99% with terminal degrees. *Student/faculty ratio:* 12:1.

Academic Programs *Special study options:* academic remediation for entering students, accelerated degree program, advanced placement credit, cooperative education, distance learning, double majors, English as a second language, freshman honors college, honors programs, independent study, internships, part-time degree program, services for LD students, student-designed majors, study abroad, summer session for credit. *ROTC:* Army (c), Air Force (c).

Costs (2004–05) *Tuition:* state resident $6793 full-time, $219 per credit hour part-time; nonresident $13,828 full-time, $448 per credit hour part-time. *Required fees:* $1596 full-time, $316 per term part-time. *Room and board:* $7862; room only: $5452.

Financial Aid 330 Federal Work-Study jobs (averaging $1780). In 2003, 90 non-need-based awards were made. *Average percent of need met:* 85%. *Average financial aid package:* $9516. *Average need-based loan:* $3680. *Average need-based gift aid:* $6611. *Average non-need-based aid:* $4428.

Contact: Director: Dr. Allen Woll, Honors College, Room 298, Paul Robeson Library, Rutgers, The State University of New Jersey, Camden, New Jersey 08102; *Telephone:* 856-225-6670 or 6671; *Fax:* 856-225-6428; *E-mail:* awoll@camden.rutgers.edu; *Web site:* http://honors.camden.rutgers.edu

Rutgers, The State University of New Jersey, New Brunswick/Piscataway
Rutgers College Honors Program
New Brunswick, New Jersey

The Rutgers College Honors Program (RCHP) provides an environment for academically talented undergraduates that combines the best resources of a nationally recognized major public research institution with the advantages of a smaller college environment. Members of the Honors Program have a wide variety of intellectual and cocurricular interests but also belong to a community of scholars—faculty and staff members and peers—who share an enthusiasm for the life of the mind. The Program fosters that enthusiasm by inviting students to take part in the development of an individualized honors experience. The Rutgers College Honors Program challenges students to explore the intellectual and social diversity of the campus and seek ways to put theory into practice beyond the campus.

Members of the Honors Program choose not only from the many undergraduate and graduate course offerings at the University but also from a wide variety of special honors courses, including small interdisciplinary colloquia on nontraditional topics, enhanced sections of traditional courses where the University's best faculty members explore disciplines with students with greater depth and rigor, and nontraditional departmentally based seminars that provide a rich perspective on traditional disciplines. Enrollment in most honors courses is limited to between 15 and 20 students, and the environment of these courses is one in which both faculty members and students consider themselves learners. Many students incorporate internship opportunities and study abroad through Global Programs into their honors experiences.

Honors Program students are invited to take advantage of an extensive mentoring and advising support network. A peer mentoring program helps ease the transition between high school and college by matching each incoming student with an Honors Program member in advanced standing. The Faculty Mentor Program puts students in close and continuing contact with an experienced faculty member in their discipline of choice at the start of the first year; students often develop lasting friendships with faculty mentors and often pursue research projects with their guidance during the course of their college careers. Dedicated Honors Program staff members provide academic and personal advising to students throughout the four years, in addition to running workshops on getting involved in the research life of the University, on admission to graduate school, on securing major fellowships, and on choosing a career path.

Students in the Honors Program actually create new knowledge: faculty members actively seek out Program members for participation in research, and students are encouraged to design their own research projects, for which funding is provided through an application and

proposal process. Students who take advantage of this opportunity have commented on the fact that it prepares them well to do graduate work and to enter the professional world. Many students go on to write senior theses or take graduate courses as an outgrowth of their research.

A shared residential community is also an important aspect of the Rutgers College Honors Program. In two honors residence halls, students participate in a wide variety of cocurricular and social experiences. Incoming students may elect honors housing before matriculation. The Program also often sponsors cultural outings to New York and Philadelphia and purchases tickets for members at performances and screenings in the area.

Created in 1980, the Rutgers College Honors Program now consists of 800 of the most talented undergraduate scholars at a college of 11,000 students.

Participation Requirements: Because the College believes that each student should take an active role in defining his or her own academic experience, RCHP members are not required to fulfill a set of requirements other than the Rutgers College degree requirements. To continue to be a member of the Rutgers College Honors Program in good academic standing, students must maintain a semester grade point average of at least 3.250 during the first year and 3.500 each semester thereafter. If a student's semester average is below the requirement in any one semester, that student is placed on honors probation; if it is below the requirement for two semesters in a row, that student is placed on continued honors probation. Students are dismissed from the RCHP if their semester average is below the required minimum for three consecutive semesters. Advising is available to students who have been placed on honors probation or continued probation, or who have been dismissed from the program. Students who choose to complete the Interdisciplinary Honors Option have that distinction noted on their transcript.

Admission Process: Students who have applied and been admitted to Rutgers College through an application submitted to the Office of Undergraduate Admissions are considered for the Rutgers College Honors Program. Students are encouraged to apply to Rutgers College by the priority application date of December 1 to ensure full consideration for the Honors Program and for Rutgers scholarships. Beginning in early January, letters are sent to students who meet the Program's criteria. Admission to the Rutgers College Honors Program is based upon two components: SAT I score and rank in class (RIC). Both of these components must fall within the following eligibility guidelines in order for a student to be admitted to the Program: SAT I 1500–1600/RIC 85–100; SAT I 1400–1490/RIC 90–100; or SAT I 1350–1390/RIC 95–100. (These criteria are on the basis of the current SAT. Students should check the programs Web site for updated admissions information as a result of the changes in the SAT). Information about eligibility for admission to the RCHP and information about the special nomination process for students who do not fit the automatic admissions profile is sent to guidance counselors in September.

Scholarship Availability: Students who are offered admission to the Rutgers College Honors Program are invited to apply for a Rutgers College Academic Excellence Award. These awards range in value from $1000 to $5000 and are renewable for four years. The Rutgers College Academic Excellence Award is in addition to any other scholarships awarded through the University. More information on scholarships for incoming students is available at http://admissions.rutgers.edu. Rutgers College also has scholarships available for continuing students who maintain a cumulative GPA of 3.75 or better at the end of the first year and 3.500 or better at the end of subsequent years and who complete the appropriate application.

Campus Overview

State-supported university, founded 1766, part of Rutgers, The State University of New Jersey • **Coed** 26,813 undergraduate students, 91% full-time, 52% women, 48% men.

Undergraduates 24,416 full-time, 2,397 part-time. Students come from 9 other countries, 8% are from out of state, 9% African

American, 22% Asian American or Pacific Islander, 8% Hispanic American, 0.2% Native American, 2% international, 5% transferred in, 46% live on campus.

Faculty *Total:* 2,330, 65% full-time, 65% with terminal degrees. *Student/faculty ratio:* 14:1.

Academic Programs *Special study options:* academic remediation for entering students, accelerated degree program, advanced placement credit, cooperative education, distance learning, double majors, English as a second language, honors programs, independent study, student-designed majors, study abroad. *ROTC:* Army (b), Air Force (b). *Unusual degree programs:* 3-2 planning and public policy, education, criminal justice.

Athletics Member NCAA. All Division I except football (Division I-A). *Intercollegiate sports:* baseball M, basketball M/W, crew M/W, cross-country running M/W, fencing M/W, golf M/W, gymnastics W, lacrosse M/W, soccer M/W, softball W, swimming and diving M/W, tennis M/W, track and field M/W, volleyball W, wrestling M. *Intramural sports:* badminton M/W, baseball M(c), basketball M/W, bowling M/W, cross-country running M/W, equestrian sports M(c)/W(c), field hockey W(c), football M, golf M/W, ice hockey M(c), lacrosse M/W, racquetball M/W, rugby M(c)/W(c), sailing M(c)/W(c), skiing (cross-country) M(c)/W(c), skiing (downhill) M(c)/W(c), soccer M/W, softball M/W, squash M(c)/W(c), swimming and diving M/W, table tennis M(c)/W(c), tennis M/W, track and field M/W, volleyball M/W, water polo M/W, wrestling M.

Costs (2004–05) *Tuition:* state resident $6793 full-time, $219 per credit hour part-time; nonresident $13,828 full-time, $448 per credit hour part-time. Part-time tuition and fees vary according to course level. *Required fees:* $1771 full-time. *Room and board:* $8357; room only: $5107. Room and board charges vary according to board plan and housing facility.

Financial Aid 2,646 Federal Work-Study jobs (averaging $1903). In 2003, 2562 non-need-based awards were made. *Average percent of need met:* 83%. *Average financial aid package:* $10,745. *Average need-based loan:* $4101. *Average need-based gift aid:* $7247. *Average non-need-based aid:* $5202.

Contact: Dr. Muffin Lord, 210 Milledoler Hall, 520 George Street, New Brunswick, New Jersey 08901; *Telephone:* 732-932-7964; *Fax:* 732-932-8418; *E-mail:* rcghp@rci.rutgers.edu; *Web site:* http://rchonors.rutgers.edu

William Paterson University of New Jersey

Honors College

Wayne, New Jersey

*T*he William Paterson University of New Jersey Honors College offers in-depth and cross-disciplinary course work at both the general education and advanced levels. For their first semester, high-achieving freshmen are placed into honors sections of required general education courses. After their first semester, all students with at least a 3.0 GPA may select honors general education sections. These courses enroll 20 or fewer students and are taught by faculty members who have designed the course specifically for highly motivated students. Students in these courses benefit from rigorous course work, smaller class sizes, and significant contact with faculty members and peers.

At the advanced level, the Honors College offers eight distinctive tracks: biopsychology, cognitive science, humanities, life science and environmental ethics, music, nursing, performing and literary arts, and social sciences. These tracks operate like a minor, and most are interdisciplinary and open to students of all majors. The music and nursing tracks are intended for majors in their area but share a broader perspective with the other tracks. While the goals of the individual tracks may vary, the overall aim of the Honors College is to enrich student's experiences and provide unique educational opportunities which enhance the student's success in graduate or professional school, strengthen career prospects, and foster a lifelong commitment to learning.

Honors courses are designed to fit into the student's regular curriculum. Students benefit from smaller classes, more individualized instruction and advisement, increased opportunities for faculty-student research, closer interaction with faculty members and other honors students, and the opportunity to participate in regularly scheduled interdisciplinary events. The capstone experience of each track is a public performance. It may take the form of a recital, the presentation of research results or an internship experience, or the production of a play or musical. Honors track graduates are honored at an awards ceremony and receive an honors designation on their diploma and transcript. There are no additional fees for enrolling in the Honors College.

The original Honors Program began in 1976 with offerings in biopsychology and humanities. The remaining five tracks were added in 1999, and the seven tracks were then designated the University Honors Program. In 2004, the social sciences track was added and, in 2005, the University Honors Program became the Honors College with a full-time director. The program currently enrolls 150 students in tracks and an additional 200 in honors sections of general education courses.

Participation Requirements: The tracks vary in required credits but range from 15 to 19 credits plus an additional three-course honors general education requirement. Each track is a vertical progression of courses and experiences: an introductory seminar, courses in advanced techniques and applications, and a senior research and thesis project. This one-on-one intensive interaction with a faculty member is the culmination of the honors experience, providing a practical representation of the student's educational accomplishments. As a public institution that is committed to enrolling a cross section of students in the region, the Honors College strives to balance access and excellence. All students with a minimum 3.0 GPA may enroll in a track and must maintain this GPA to remain in the Honors College.

Admission Process: In order to enter an honors section of a general education course, incoming freshmen need at least a 1200 SAT I score and must rank in the 90th percentile (or its equivalent) in their high school class. Continuing students desiring to take honors general education courses or to enter an honors track should have a minimum 3.0 GPA. Track applications must be completed and are available from the Honors College Office.

Scholarship Availability: Both the University and the Alumni Association award competitive scholarships based on academic merit to entering freshmen and continuing students. These are available through a number of federal and state grants, loan, scholarship, and work-study programs. In addition, the Honors College has the highly selective Rummel Scholars Program, providing support for entering freshmen and Rubin Scholarships for continuing students.

Campus Overview

State-supported comprehensive, founded 1855, part of New Jersey State College System • **Coed** 9,418 undergraduate students, 81% full-time, 59% women, 41% men.

Undergraduates 7,589 full-time, 1,829 part-time. Students come from 39 states and territories, 55 other countries, 2% are from out of state, 12% African American, 5% Asian American or Pacific Islander, 16% Hispanic American, 0.3% Native American, 2% international, 9% transferred in, 24% live on campus.

Faculty *Total:* 1,048, 35% full-time. *Student/faculty ratio:* 15:1.

Academic Programs *Special study options:* academic remediation for entering students, accelerated degree program, adult/continuing education programs, advanced placement credit, distance learning, double majors, English as a second language, honors programs, independent study, internships, off-campus study, part-time degree program, services for LD students, study abroad, summer session for credit. *ROTC:* Air Force (c).

Athletics Member NCAA. All Division III. *Intercollegiate sports:* baseball M, basketball M/W, bowling M(c)/W(c), cheerleading M/W, cross-country running M/W, fencing M/W, field hockey W, football M, golf M, ice hockey M(c), skiing (downhill) M(c)/W(c), soccer M/W, softball W, swimming and diving M/W, track and field M/W, volleyball W. *Intramural sports:* basketball M, equestrian sports M/W, football M, golf M, lacrosse M, racquetball M/W, softball M/W, tennis M(c)/W(c), volleyball M/W, wrestling M.

Costs (2004–05) *Tuition:* state resident $7952 full-time, $255 per credit part-time; nonresident $12,690 full-time, $410 per credit part-time. *Room and board:* $8340; room only: $5490. Room and board charges vary according to board plan and housing facility.

Financial Aid 220 Federal Work-Study jobs (averaging $1136). 192 state and other part-time jobs (averaging $1300). In 2003, 181 non-need-based awards were made. *Average percent of need met:* 83%. *Average financial aid package:* $9511. *Average need-based loan:* $3805. *Average need-based gift aid:* $5745. *Average non-need-based aid:* $4191.

Contact: Director: Dr. Susan Dinan, Program Assistant: Jan Pinkston, Honors College, William Paterson University of New Jersey, 300 Pompton Road, Wayne, New Jersey 07470; *Telephone:* 973-720-3657; *Fax:* 973-720-3693; *E-mail:* dinans@wpunj.edu, pinkstonj@wpunj.edu; *Web site:* http://www.wpunj.edu/icip/honors/

NEW MEXICO

New Mexico State University
University Honors College
Las Cruces, New Mexico

The University Honors College provides motivated undergraduate students with opportunities to broaden and enrich their academic programs. In small classes taught by master teachers, honors students engage in lively discussion and collaborative investigation of interdisciplinary topics. By taking honors courses, students also work toward completing general education requirements and disciplinary requirements in their majors. Honors courses are challenging, but the individual attention students receive makes the honors experience worthwhile.

NMSU's Honors College is the only honors college in the state of New Mexico. Approximately 1,000 students are enrolled in the program each year.

The Honors College offers an honors residence hall option for students interested in living among a community of excellent students. The hall provides numerous educational, social, and cultural activities for honors students.

Participation Requirements: After completing the 18 required credits of honors work (including an honors thesis or creative arts project) with an overall GPA between 3.5 and 3.74, students earn the right to graduate with University Honors. If students attain an overall average of 3.75 or better, including the required honors credits, students are eligible to graduate with Distinction in University Honors. Both forms of recognition are noted on diplomas and transcripts, as well as in Commencement programs. Each student is also awarded a certificate of distinction and a medallion to wear at graduation. Upon completion of two upper-division courses, students receive recognition on the Commencement program along with a certificate of distinction.

Admission Process: An entering freshman must have a minimum composite ACT score of 26 to qualify; other students need a composite ACT score of at least 24 and a minimum high school GPA

of 3.75 to enroll. For new freshmen, continued participation is contingent on maintaining a GPA of 3.3; sophomores, juniors, and seniors must maintain a GPA of at least 3.5. Students who do not meet minimum eligibility requirements may petition the Honors Director for admission to the program. A student may enter the program from the first semester of freshman year until the beginning of the second semester of the sophomore year.

Scholarship Availability: New Mexico State University administers an extensive program of grants, scholarships, and loans. The awarding of grants and loans is based on need, while the awarding of scholarships is based mainly on academic ability and, in some cases, need. Special awards are available for National Merit Semifinalists and Finalists.

Campus Overview

State-supported university, founded 1888, part of New Mexico State University System • **Coed** 12,975 undergraduate students, 82% full-time, 55% women, 45% men.

Undergraduates 10,648 full-time, 2,327 part-time. Students come from 52 states and territories, 44 other countries, 17% are from out of state, 3% African American, 1% Asian American or Pacific Islander, 45% Hispanic American, 3% Native American, 0.7% international, 4% transferred in, 16% live on campus.

Faculty *Total:* 982, 71% full-time, 70% with terminal degrees. *Student/faculty ratio:* 19:1.

Academic Programs *Special study options:* academic remediation for entering students, accelerated degree program, adult/continuing education programs, advanced placement credit, cooperative education, distance learning, double majors, honors programs, independent study, internships, off-campus study, part-time degree program, services for LD students, student-designed majors, study abroad, summer session for credit. *ROTC:* Army (b), Air Force (b).

Athletics Member NCAA. All Division I except football (Division I-A). *Intercollegiate sports:* baseball M(s), basketball M(s)/W(s), cross-country running M(s)/W(s), equestrian sports M/W, golf M(s)/W(s), softball W(s), swimming and diving W(s), tennis M(s)/W(s), track and field W(s), volleyball W(s). *Intramural sports:* archery M/W, badminton M/W, baseball M, basketball M/W, bowling M(c)/W(c), cheerleading M/W, football M/W, golf M/W, racquetball M/W, rock climbing M(c)/W(c), rugby M(c)/W(c), skiing (downhill) M(c)/W(c), soccer M(c)/W(c), softball M/W, tennis M/W, ultimate Frisbee M(c)/W(c), volleyball M(c)/W(c), water polo M/W, weight lifting M(c)/W(c), wrestling M.

Costs (2004–05) *Tuition:* state resident $2628 full-time, $153 per credit part-time; nonresident $11,172 full-time, $509 per credit part-time. *Required fees:* $1038 full-time. *Room and board:* $5046; room only: $2926. Room and board charges vary according to board plan and gender.

Financial Aid 409 Federal Work-Study jobs, 420 state and other part-time jobs. In 2004, 2239 non-need-based awards were made. *Average percent of need met:* 71%. *Average financial aid package:* $8555. *Average need-based loan:* $3907. *Average need-based gift aid:* $5952. *Average non-need-based aid:* $3027.

Contact: Director: Dr. William Eamon, Las Cruces, New Mexico 88003; *Telephone:* 505-646-2005; *Fax:* 505-646-1755; *E-mail:* weamon@nmsu.edu; *Web site:* http://honors.nmsu.edu

University of New Mexico
The University Honors Program
Albuquerque, New Mexico

The mission of the University Honors Program (UHP) at the University of New Mexico is to provide challenging opportunities for intensive interdisciplinary and cross-cultural education to highly motivated, talented, and creative undergraduates in all majors. Founded in 1957 with a group of 30 students, the UHP continues to offer high-achieving students many of the personal advantages of a small liberal arts college within the diversity of a large research university. Through its seminars, field-based courses, extracurricular activities, and individualized research projects, the University Honors Program helps build a community of scholars in a supportive intellectual environment. The small interdisciplinary seminars are taught by selected faculty members who are committed to exploring significant ideas while encouraging active student participation. The UHP promotes world citizenship and involvement with the communities beyond the University through the UHP programs, NCHC Honors Semesters, and other study-abroad programs as well as through service-learning projects in the community.

The UHP is housed in Dudley Wynn Honors Center, named after its founder. In addition to housing five classrooms, the center provides a place for informal discussions, student activities, and various group projects. In a warm, friendly atmosphere, UHP students meet to study together, continue seminar discussions, or just relax between classes. The large central area, affectionately known as the Forum, is also used for more formal lectures and receptions.

The Honors Program is not a separate degree program, but is designed to augment the course work required for a degree in all colleges. With a maximum enrollment of 16 students, honors seminars allow a greater access to faculty members inside and outside the classroom.

There are currently 1,400 students participating in the University Honors Program.

Participation Requirements: Admission is by application only, and students must take a minimum of 24 credit hours (eight seminars) in the UHP, with a minimum of one seminar at each level (100–400). They are required to maintain a minimum cumulative GPA of 3.2. Students may enter the UHP at any point, provided they can complete the requirements. Transfer students may be able to transfer up to 9 hours of comparable work.

The 100-level seminars deal with the development of ideas rather than definitive historical time and are based on legacies that have affected the culture and society of the United States. The 200-level seminars examine other legacies and world views: women, Africa, the Far East, the Americas, the Near East, and the origins of mathematics, science, and technology. The 300-level seminars are interdisciplinary explorations of specific topics designed to demonstrate the interconnectedness of academic disciplines. Recent seminars have focused on the significance of biomedical ethics, arts across cultures, globalization, biodiversity, and the U.S. Constitution. The 400-level seminars deal with inquiry and investigation of intellectual currents. These seminars are more in-depth study than that of the lower-level seminars, and students have greater roles and responsibilities. The end result is a publishable paper or a collaborative mini-conference.

Seniors must complete one of the following options in order to graduate with honors: honors thesis/project; student-teaching; colloquium, with a service-learning component; or departmental thesis/project. Each of these options carries 6 credit hours.

In addition to the curriculum, the UHP affords students a variety of other learning opportunities, including field-based language and cultural programs, international and national exchange opportunities, leadership in student organizations, and the opportunity to staff *Scribendi: The Western Regional Honors Review,* an outstanding literary and arts magazine publishing works from honors students from honors programs and honors colleges in the Western region.

Students who fulfill the requirements of the program become candidates for graduation with an honors designation. Honors distinctions used at UNM are cum laude, magna cum laude, and summa cum laude. Graduation with an honors designation is not automatic. Aside from the minimum requirements of the UHP, students are expected to have a reasonably broad liberal arts education. Students should attempt to take course work in the humanities, languages, social sciences, mathematics, physical sciences, and life sciences insofar as it is possible to do so within the restrictions of their majors and minors.

Admission Process: Students interested in participating in the University Honors Program must apply. They must have a minimum cumulative high school GPA of 3.5, and at least a 29 ACT or 1250 SAT. Students who do not meet these requirements may be accepted for special circumstances with a probationary status. Students must submit a completed application form that can be found on the UHP Web site, an essay, and a copy of their high school or college transcripts.

Campus Overview

State-supported university, founded 1889 • **Coed** 17,932 undergraduate students, 79% full-time, 57% women, 43% men.

Undergraduates 14,130 full-time, 3,802 part-time. Students come from 51 states and territories, 56 other countries, 11% are from out of state, 3% African American, 3% Asian American or Pacific Islander, 34% Hispanic American, 7% Native American, 0.7% international, 6% transferred in, 11% live on campus.

Faculty *Total:* 1,400, 62% full-time, 70% with terminal degrees. *Student/faculty ratio:* 18:1.

Academic Programs *Special study options:* academic remediation for entering students, accelerated degree program, adult/continuing education programs, advanced placement credit, cooperative education, distance learning, double majors, English as a second language, honors programs, independent study, internships, off-campus study, part-time degree program, services for LD students, student-designed majors, study abroad, summer session for credit. *ROTC:* Army (b), Navy (b), Air Force (b). *Unusual degree programs:* 3-2 Latin American studies, business.

Athletics Member NCAA. All Division I except football (Division I-A). *Intercollegiate sports:* baseball M, basketball M(s)/W(s), cross-country running M(s)/W(s), golf M(s)/W(s), skiing (cross-country) M(s)/W(s), skiing (downhill) M(s)/W(s), soccer M(s)/W(s), softball W(s), swimming and diving W(s), tennis M(s)/W(s), track and field M(s)/W(s), volleyball W(s). *Intramural sports:* archery M/W, badminton M/W, basketball M/W, bowling M/W, cross-country running M/W, fencing M/W, football M/W, golf M/W, ice hockey M(c), racquetball M/W, rugby M(c), skiing (downhill) M/W, soccer M/W, softball M/W, swimming and diving W, table tennis M/W, tennis M/W, volleyball M/W, water polo M/W.

Costs (2004–05) *Tuition:* $156 per credit hour part-time; state resident $3738 full-time; nonresident $12,500 full-time. Part-time tuition and fees vary according to course load. *Required fees:* $626 full-time. *Room and board:* $6180; room only: $3580. Room and board charges vary according to board plan and housing facility.

Financial Aid 1,521 Federal Work-Study jobs, 865 state and other part-time jobs. In 2001, 4124 non-need-based awards were made. *Average percent of need met:* 75%. *Average financial aid package:* $7829. *Average need-based loan:* $3261. *Average need-based gift aid:* $4796. *Average non-need-based aid:* $3173.

Contact: Director: Dr. Rosalie C. Otero, University Honors Program, MSC06 3890, University of New Mexico, Albuquerque, New Mexico 87131-0001; *Telephone:* 505-277-4211; *Fax:* 505-277-4271; *E-mail:* otero@unm.edu or honors@unm.edu; *Web site:* http://www.unm.edu/~honors

Western New Mexico University
Millennium III Honors Program
Silver City, New Mexico

*T*he Millennium III Honors Program at Western New Mexico *University is aimed at bright, motivated students in all majors. Most honors courses are enhanced versions of general education courses. The advantages of taking the honors version of general education courses include smaller enrollments (all honors courses are limited to 20 students) and more challenging course work. Another component of the program is that a 1-credit-hour Honors Seminar is offered every semester. These seminars generally include travel, offering trips to such varied locations as Casas Grandes in Mexico, and the Chaco Canyon National Historic Park in New Mexico. Other features of the Honors Program include an annual camping trip in September and regular social events. An honors lounge/study area is available for use by students in the Honors Program.*

Founded in 2000, the program admits no more than 20 new students each year. There are currently 49 students enrolled in the Honors Program.

Participation Requirements: The curriculum allows students to choose at least 24 hours of honors course work to apply toward the 128 hours required for a baccalaureate degree. (Associate degree students complete at least 21 hours of honors course work.) General education courses comprise 18 to 19 credit hours. A minimum of three Honors Seminars must be completed. Baccalaureate students must complete 3 hours of upper-division honors course work. There are three options for meeting this requirement. In the first option, the student can take three Honors Colloquia, which are upper-division versions of the Honors Seminars. Similar to the seminars, the Honors Colloquia can include field trips, the opportunity to attend performances, working on a group project, or other types of nontraditional learning activities. A second option is to complete a contract honors course. This option allows students to sign a contract to do additional work in a course in their major. In the third option, students may complete a project or thesis in those majors that have provided for this as an approved alternative.

First-year students must maintain a minimum 3.3 GPA to remain in the program. Beyond the first year, honors students must maintain a GPA of at least 3.5.

Honors courses are designated as such on students' transcripts, and students who complete the full curriculum have a notation on their transcript indicating they are Millennium III Honors Program graduates. Honors Program graduates are also recognized in the University's commencement program.

Admission Process: Interested students must apply to the director of the Honors Program. An online application is available on the Honors Program Web site. The application includes writing an essay on why the student wants to participate in the program and what qualities he or she will contribute to the program.

To be admitted to the program, an applicant must have an ACT score of 24 or better; or have a combined SAT Verbal and Math score of 1110 or higher; or be in the top 15 percent of their high school class; or have a minimum high school cumulative GPA of 3.8; or have at least 15 hours of college-level credit with a cumulative GPA of 3.5 or higher.

Admission to the Honors Program is rolling, which means that decisions concerning acceptance into the program are made as applications are received. Students accepted into the program are sent a written acceptance letter that must be returned within thirty days confirming that they do intend to participate in the program.

Scholarship Availability: There are no scholarships dedicated only for honors students.

Campus Overview

State-supported comprehensive, founded 1893 • **Coed** 2,555 undergraduate students.

Undergraduates Students come from 33 states and territories, 6 other countries.

Faculty *Total:* 145, 62% full-time. *Student/faculty ratio:* 17:1.

Academic Programs *Special study options:* academic remediation for entering students, accelerated degree program, adult/continuing education programs, advanced placement credit, cooperative education, internships, part-time degree program, services for LD students, student-designed majors, summer session for credit.

Athletics *Intercollegiate sports:* basketball M(s)/W(s), cheerleading M/W, football M(s), golf M(s)/W(s), rock climbing M/W, softball W(s), tennis M(s)/W(s), volleyball W(s). *Intramural sports:* basketball M/W, golf M/W, racquetball M/W, soccer M/W, softball W, swimming and diving M/W, tennis M/W, volleyball M/W.

Financial Aid 134 Federal Work-Study jobs (averaging $1825). 82 state and other part-time jobs (averaging $1937). In 2003, 121 non-need-based awards were made. *Average percent of need met:* 68%. *Average financial aid package:* $5915. *Average need-based loan:* $2980. *Average need-based gift aid:* $2434. *Average non-need-based aid:* $2457.

Contact: Director: Curtis G. Hayes, Millennium III Honors Program, Western New Mexico University, P.O. Box 680, Silver City, New Mexico 88062-0680; *Telephone:* 505-538-6325; *E-mail:* honors@ wnmu.edu; *Web site:* http://www.wnmu.edu/honorsprog.htm

NEW YORK

Adelphi University
Honors College
Garden City, New York

*T*he Honors College at Adelphi University provides a community, a *curriculum, and a wide array of cocurricular activities for students who are passionate about learning, ambitious in their goals, and committed to the hard work and discipline required for superb achievement. Honors classes have an average size of 18 students. In addition to the regular classes, the Dean and Academic Director offer tutorials for single students or very small groups. Honors students may choose any of the majors in the various departments and schools of the University or may craft an interdisciplinary major of their own.*

Honors classes are offered in the honors facility, a building that includes administrative offices, study areas, computer and graphics facilities, and dormitory rooms for those students who wish to reside there. From the first semester, honors classes are taught discussion- or seminar-style, calling upon the students for active participation rather than passive note-taking. Courses are designed by professors to provide significant intellectual challenge and the excitement of interdisciplinary exploration.

Students are encouraged to take advantage of opportunities for research and internships as soon as possible. Individual efforts culminate in the senior thesis, a yearlong project guided by a departmental adviser and the College's Academic Director.

The cocurricular program of the Honors College makes extensive use of the cultural resources offered by New York City. Several times each semester, honors students have the opportunity to attend the opera, plays on and off Broadway, museums, dance, and orchestra at little or no cost. Other honors activities include an on-campus film series with discussions and regular dinners at the Dean's residence (next to the campus), followed by book discussions. The Honors College Foreign Policy Symposium Series provides students with the chance to have lunch with experts in various areas of current interest and to hear presentations on timely topics.

The rigor and range of an honors education provide excellent preparation for graduate and professional study. Recent graduates have been admitted to graduate and professional study at Boston University, Brown, Chicago, Columbia, Cornell, Georgetown, NYU, Pennsylvania, Yale, and a number of major state universities throughout the country.

The Honors College, formally founded in 1995 as an expansion of an honors program begun in 1978, currently includes 280 students.

Participation Requirements: Students who fulfill all the requirements receive an Honors College diploma upon graduation. These requirements include 34 to 46 credits in honors courses that fulfill the University's general education requirements, a senior thesis, and regular attendance at cultural events on or off campus. Students must have a minimum GPA of 3.3 upon graduation.

Admission Process: In the initial screening of applications, a number of criteria are considered: cumulative GPA, class rank (usually top 10 percent), SAT (typically a minimum of 1250, with at least 650 verbal) or ACT (minimum score of 26), evidence of desire to attain an excellent education, and an essay representative of the student's best high school work. No single factor is decisive. Promising applicants are asked to come for an interview with the Dean, the Associate Dean, or one of the professors who teaches in the Honors College. (Applicants unable to visit the campus are interviewed by telephone.)

Scholarship Availability: Honors Scholarships are merit-based. Three levels of scholarship are awarded to honors students. Trustee Scholarships for students with SAT scores above 1350 can cover up to full tuition. Presidential Scholarships for students with SAT scores above 1300 can cover as much as $17,000 a year. Provost awards for students with SAT scores of 1250 or above can cover up to approximately $14,000. Honors students can receive increased scholarships if they qualify for other awards offered at Adelphi, including Service Scholarships and awards for talent and athletics. Other financial assistance, including grants, loans, and part-time employment, is available to qualified students.

Campus Overview

Independent university, founded 1896 • **Coed** 4,425 undergraduate students, 85% full-time, 71% women, 29% men.

Undergraduates 3,747 full-time, 678 part-time. Students come from 38 states and territories, 47 other countries, 8% are from out of state, 12% African American, 5% Asian American or Pacific Islander, 9% Hispanic American, 0.1% Native American, 3% international, 13% transferred in, 24% live on campus.

Faculty *Total:* 751, 32% full-time. *Student/faculty ratio:* 14:1.

Academic Programs *Special study options:* accelerated degree program, advanced placement credit, distance learning, double majors, freshman honors college, honors programs, independent study, internships, part-time degree program, services for LD students, student-designed majors, study abroad, summer session for credit. *ROTC:* Army (c), Air Force (c). *Unusual degree programs:* 3-2 engineering with Columbia University, Polytechnic University, Rensselaer Polytechnic Institute, Stevens Institute of Technology; physical therapy with New York Medical College; dentistry with Tufts; law with NYU; optometry with SUNY College of Optometry; environmental studies with Columbia.

Athletics Member NCAA. All Division II except soccer (Division I). *Intercollegiate sports:* baseball M(s), basketball M(s)/W(s), cross-country running M(s)/W(s), golf M(s), lacrosse M(s)/W(s), soccer M(s)/W(s), softball W(s), swimming and diving M(s)/W(s), tennis M(s)/W(s), track and field M(s)/W(s), volleyball W(s). *Intramural sports:* badminton M/W, basketball M/W, football M/W, racquetball M/W, soccer M/W, softball M/W, volleyball M/W, water polo M/W.

Costs (2004–05) *Comprehensive fee:* $27,200 includes full-time tuition ($17,700), mandatory fees ($1000), and room and board

($8500). Full-time tuition and fees vary according to course level, location, and program. Part-time tuition: $570 per credit. Part-time tuition and fees vary according to course level, location, and program. *Required fees:* $520 per year part-time. *Room and board:* Room and board charges vary according to board plan and housing facility.

Financial Aid 558 Federal Work-Study jobs (averaging $2686). 729 state and other part-time jobs (averaging $1506). In 2004, 821 non-need-based awards were made. *Average percent of need met:* 30%. *Average financial aid package:* $13,450. *Average need-based loan:* $4121. *Average need-based gift aid:* $3889. *Average non-need-based aid:* $7379.

Contact: Dean: Richard Garner, Honors College, 100 Earle Hall, Adelphi University, Garden City, New York 11530; *Telephone:* 516-877-3800; *Fax:* 516-877-3803; *E-mail:* garner@adelphi.edu; *Web site:* http://academics.adelphi.edu/honcol/

Alfred University
University Honors Program
Alfred, New York

It is the Honors Program's mission to enrich Alfred's best undergraduate students' education by providing seminars—all electives—to add a dimension to their lives. In recent years, these courses have considered things of the spirit. Students have studied T'ai Chi, alternative healing, spirituality and the counterculture, and Zen, and one group even attempted a vision quest. Others have focused on music: the evolution of jazz, the blues, opera, Mozart, musical theater, and music video. There have been seminars on superconductivity and lasers, dream theory, the Old Order Amish, Claudius Caesar, fairy tales, biotechnology and bioethics, the beauty of chess, and the World Wide Web. There have also been many seminars on film, including film noir, Shakespeare and Hollywood, horror films, fiction into film, and the silent screen.

There are currently 120 students in honors, comprising about 6 percent of the student body. In most years there are 40–55 applicants, and two thirds are usually admitted. Ten to 15 percent are National Merit Scholars, and Alfred has a very generous scholarship offer for them.

Nonacademic activities include the traditional Death by Chocolate reception in the fall; a banquet in the spring, featuring rock Cornish game hens and student entertainment; and each April seniors have dinner at the president's house. There are road trips to Rochester four or five times a year: first, dinner out at a Greek, Thai, Chinese, or Indian restaurant, then, to the theater or a symphony.

Being in honors also opens doors to other things. When trustees visit, for example, and want to have lunch with students, or when admissions is looking for tour guides, or when public relations wants student stringers for the New York Times, the expectation is that honors provides them. Two honors students have had their articles printed in the Times.

The Honors Program has a motto: Time flies like an arrow; fruit flies like a banana. It is a reminder not to take things too seriously.

Participation Requirements: Honors students are required to take four seminars in their first five semesters. These courses are not a substitute for anything else—the idea is to take these classes just for the fun of it. Because they are fun, most students choose to take more than four. The seminars are small (class limit is 15 students), informal (some meet at the Honors House with its comfortable couches and rocking chairs), and, in many cases, student led. Some are the result of student suggestions. Others, like the vision quest seminar, are experimental.

To graduate in honors, a student must complete four seminars, write a senior thesis, and finish with a 3.2 GPA. Theses vary widely. Students have studied barns, cryptology, vigilantes, and graph theory, among other things. While some theses are essentially research papers, many are not. One student studied traditional quilting techniques and then made a quilt. Other students have built a unicycling robot, created a stained glass window, and written and illustrated a children's book. Some have given public performances. A few years ago a premed student wrote and performed his own piano concerto. The common thread is a chance to work closely with 3 faculty member mentors on a project that really matters. Theses are bound and become a permanent part of Herrick Library's Special Collections. Honors Program graduates have Alfred University Scholar printed on their transcript and hand printed on their diploma.

Admission Process: The single most important consideration for admission is the high school transcript. SAT I scores are taken seriously, but they only measure performance on one day's test. A high school transcript shows what was achieved over four years, so it is a major consideration. Students who have done well taking a demanding schedule, including AP or college-level courses, are the norm in this program. In fact, the majority of those accepted into honors graduate in the top 5 percent of their class, and virtually all are in the top 10 percent. An academic recommendation is a must, as is an essay. The early notification application deadline is March 15; the deadline for traditional notification applications is June 1.

Scholarship Availability: University-funded aid provides more than $13 million to undergraduates. Scholarships include the National Merit Scholarship, Presidential Scholarship, Southern Tier Scholarship, the Jonathan Allen Award for Leadership, and department competition scholarships. Approximately 90 percent of undergraduates received some form of financial aid.

Campus Overview

Independent university, founded 1836 • **Coed** 2,057 undergraduate students, 94% full-time, 50% women, 50% men.

Undergraduates 1,943 full-time, 114 part-time. Students come from 38 states and territories, 32 other countries, 30% are from out of state, 6% African American, 2% Asian American or Pacific Islander, 4% Hispanic American, 0.5% Native American, 2% international, 4% transferred in, 67% live on campus.

Faculty *Total:* 212, 81% full-time, 73% with terminal degrees. *Student/faculty ratio:* 12:1.

Academic Programs *Special study options:* academic remediation for entering students, accelerated degree program, advanced placement credit, cooperative education, double majors, honors programs, independent study, internships, off-campus study, part-time degree program, services for LD students, student-designed majors, study abroad, summer session for credit. *ROTC:* Army (c). *Unusual degree programs:* 3-2 engineering with Columbia University; forestry with Duke University; dentistry with New York University.

Athletics Member NCAA. All Division III. *Intercollegiate sports:* basketball M/W, cross-country running M/W, equestrian sports M/W, football M, lacrosse M/W, skiing (cross-country) M(c)/W(c), skiing (downhill) M/W, soccer M/W, softball W, swimming and diving M/W, tennis M/W, track and field M/W, volleyball W. *Intramural sports:* baseball M(c), basketball M/W, cheerleading W(c), football M/W, ice hockey M(c), lacrosse M/W, racquetball M/W, rugby M(c)/W(c), soccer M/W, softball M/W, squash M/W, tennis M/W, ultimate Frisbee M(c)/W(c), volleyball M/W.

Costs (2004–05) *Comprehensive fee:* $29,434 includes full-time tuition ($19,250), mandatory fees ($810), and room and board ($9374). Full-time tuition and fees vary according to program and student level. Part-time tuition: $630 per credit hour. Part-time tuition and fees vary according to course load and program. *College room only:* $4884. Room and board charges vary according to board plan and housing facility.

Financial Aid 1,064 Federal Work-Study jobs (averaging $1328). In 2004, 261 non-need-based awards were made. *Average percent of need met:* 90%. *Average financial aid package:* $19,364. *Average need-based loan:* $4904. *Average need-based gift aid:* $14,364. *Average non-need-based aid:* $6680.

Contact: Director: Dr. Paul Strong, Seidlin Hall, Alfred University, Alfred, New York 14802; *Telephone:* 607-871-2924 Ext. 2257; *Fax:* 609-871-2831; *E-mail:* fstrongp@alfred.edu; *Web site:* http://www.alfred.edu/

Bernard M. Baruch College of the City University of New York
Baruch College Honors Program
New York, New York

*T*he Baruch College Honors Program offers students a stimulating and enriching intellectual experience during their undergraduate years. It stresses academic rigor, participation in the cultural life of the campus and city, and the importance of community and social responsibility.

The Honors Program offers a wide array of honors classes, including sections of courses in the College's core curriculum, advanced electives, and interdisciplinary courses specially designed for honors students. There is an emphasis on reading great works and on assignments that develop communication and critical-thinking abilities.

Students are introduced to the rich array of cultural programming that is supported by the College. This includes artists- and writers-in-residence, visiting performers, Baruch's Mishkin Gallery, and a broad range of lecture and panel presentations. Given Baruch's educational mission, students have access to expertise in the fields of business and finance, the arts and sciences, and public affairs. Students are also exposed to the cultural and scientific resources of the city-at-large.

The Honors Program requires students to engage in community service, either at the College or in the outside community. Via service, students develop leadership skills and an awareness of the essential relationship between privilege and responsibility.

Students are encouraged to think about life beyond Baruch through internships, networking with alumni, and preprofessional and graduate school workshops.

All students in the Honors Program enjoy a number of additional privileges, including first-day registration, an honors lounge, a study room with desktop computers and wireless capacity, and academic advisement provided by the Honors Office, faculty members who coordinate honors education in their respective departments, and a research librarian. In addition to Latin Honors, students who elect to write an honors thesis graduate with honors in the discipline.

Baruch College is one of seven senior colleges of the City University of New York (CUNY) participating in CUNY's University Scholars Program. Each year, the CUNY University Scholars Program admits approximately 80 entering freshmen via the Honors College. The approximate mean high school GPA of admitted freshmen is 93. The mean verbal and quantitative SAT scores are approximately 660 and 700, respectively.

For the first two years of their program, University Scholars enroll in interdisciplinary seminars especially designed for the Honors College. Limited in size to approximately 20 students, these seminars focus on the arts, history, scientific and technical initiatives, and the economic life of New York City. Participation in the CUNY Honors College also confers many additional benefits, including full tuition and fee remission; a $7500 study grant; special honors study-abroad programs; prestigious internships at some of the city's top financial, business, media, and cultural institutions; a Cultural Passport that provides free or discounted access to the cultural resources of New York City, including concerts, the opera, theater, and museums; a free Apple laptop computer; and a subscription to the

New York Times. *University Scholars also participate in all of the curricular and cultural activities offered by the Baruch College Honors Program.*

Each year, the College admits approximately 40 entering freshmen into the Baruch Scholars Program. Continuing students may apply to the program once they have taken at least one honors course and have met other entrance requirements. Transfer students are also considered as long as they are able to fulfill all of the program's requirements.

Similar to University Scholars, the Baruch Scholars participate in a fully articulated Honors Program, including a freshman learning community, a broad array of honors courses, and cultural and intellectual enrichment opportunities. The campus has very active chapters of the Golden Key International Honor Society and Phi Eta Sigma Honor Society, through which Scholars engage in numerous community-service activities. Study-abroad opportunities and international internships are made available through the Weissman Center for International Business. The Honors Office works with the Career Development Center and with academic departments to provide career and academic program planning.

Participation Requirements: To maintain good standing in the Baruch College Honors Program, students are required to complete at least ten honors courses and maintain a minimum cumulative GPA of 3.3 up to their 59th credit and a minimum 3.5 GPA thereafter. Participation in service and cultural activities is also expected. University Scholars must also comply with the Honors College good-standing policies. For further details, students should visit the Baruch College Honors Program Web site.

Admission Process: The CUNY Honors College accepts applications for freshman admission in the fall term. Applications are widely available at high school advisement offices or via CUNY's Office of Admission Services (800-CUNY-YES or inquireCUNY@ mail.cuny.edu). To be considered for admission at Baruch, applicants should have a minimum cumulative high school GPA of 90 and a minimum SAT score of 1200 (combined math and verbal scores).

Entering freshmen with strong academic credentials may be offered a place in the Baruch Scholars Program. Full or partial tuition remission is available. Continuing students may also apply to the program once they have enrolled in at least one honors course. For further information, students should contact the Baruch College Honors Program Office.

Scholarship Availability: University Scholars are offered full tuition and fee remission for four years of study. Baruch Scholars may receive full or partial tuition remission.

Campus Overview

State and locally supported comprehensive, founded 1919, part of City University of New York System • **Coed** 12,734 undergraduate students, 74% full-time, 56% women, 44% men.

Undergraduates 9,364 full-time, 3,370 part-time. Students come from 14 states and territories, 120 other countries, 3% are from out of state, 14% African American, 27% Asian American or Pacific Islander, 18% Hispanic American, 0.1% Native American, 10% international, 10% transferred in.

Faculty *Total:* 921, 53% full-time, 65% with terminal degrees. *Student/faculty ratio:* 17:1.

Academic Programs *Special study options:* accelerated degree program, adult/continuing education programs, advanced placement credit, distance learning, double majors, English as a second language, honors programs, independent study, internships, part-time degree program, services for LD students, student-designed majors, study abroad, summer session for credit.

Athletics Member NCAA. All Division III. *Intercollegiate sports:* baseball M, basketball M/W, cheerleading W, cross-country running W, soccer M, softball W, tennis M/W, volleyball M/W. *Intramural sports:* archery M/W, badminton M/W, basketball M/W, table tennis M/W, volleyball M/W, weight lifting M/W.

Costs (2005–06) *Tuition:* state resident $4000 full-time, $170 per credit part-time; nonresident $8640 full-time, $360 per credit part-time. Full-time tuition and fees vary according to class time and course load. Part-time tuition and fees vary according to class time and course load. *Required fees:* $300 full-time, $150 per term part-time, $75 per term part-time.

Financial Aid 520 Federal Work-Study jobs. In 2004, 610 non-need-based awards were made. *Average percent of need met:* 63%. *Average financial aid package:* $4930. *Average need-based loan:* $2910. *Average need-based gift aid:* $4300. *Average non-need-based aid:* $1800.

Contact: Director: Dr. Susan Locke, Honors Program, Box J-306, Bernard M. Baruch College of the City University of New York, One Bernard Baruch Way, New York, New York 10010-5585; *Telephone:* 646-312-2122; *Fax:* 646-312-2121; *E-mail:* baruch_honors@baruch. cuny.edu; *Web site:* http://www.baruch.cuny.edu

Brooklyn College of the City University of New York
Honors Academy
Brooklyn, New York

The Brooklyn College Honors Academy, the most comprehensive honors enterprise in the City University of New York (CUNY), federates nine honors-level programs, ranging from 10 to 150 students in size, each with its own faculty director, goals, curriculum, and funding. The total enrollment is about 450 students. The Honors Academy provides an intellectual community for its members, with study facilities, faculty access, computers, and a collegial setting that is conducive to friendly interaction among ambitious, academically talented students. Honors Academy students reflect the ethnic and cultural diversity of Brooklyn. Graduates of the programs enter professional study in medicine and law and Ph.D. programs in classics, history, cultural studies, scientific research, and other fields at such universities as Berkeley, Columbia, Michigan, Princeton, and Yale. Entering students interested in the sciences may take the Honors Academy's four-week summer Science Enrichment Program, which has proven to be superior preparation for the College's basic science courses.

Coordinated B.A.-M.D.: Students committed to a medical career take seminars and colloquia led by medical school faculty members, spend a summer volunteering in direct clinical patient care, and complete three years of community service. Students who complete the program satisfactorily enter SUNY Downstate College of Medicine.

Coordinated Engineering Honors: This program prepares students for upper-division study at any engineering school. Students have been admitted to Brooklyn Polytechnic University, Cooper Union, University of Wisconsin, SUNY Stony Brook, University of Michigan, and MIT.

City University of New York Honors College: Students in this four-year university-wide liberal arts program offered at seven CUNY colleges regularly attend artistic, cultural, and scientific venues throughout the city; complete an internship, a senior colloquium, or honors-level study abroad; and undertake a minimum of 30 hours of community service.

Dean's List Honors Research Program: "Late blooming" students enter this program at end of their sophomore year, signing a contract for rigorous two-year study.

Mellon Mays Undergraduate Fellowship: Open to students intending to pursue graduate study, this program has sent fellows for graduate study to Penn, Princeton, and Yale.

Minority Access to Research Careers: Open to science majors who intend to pursue biomedical research and hold minority status as defined by NIH, the program provides a course on research ethics, paid summer research work at universities and in industry, and mentoring by well-known scientists.

Honors Academy Research Colloquium: The capstone program of the Honors Academy is designed for students who hope to pursue graduate or professional studies leading to research careers in medicine, accountancy, law, college and university teaching, and other research-oriented professions.

Scholars Program: Open to high school applicants and matriculated students until the end of the sophomore year, this program is the only CUNY honors program available to lower-division students based on their college record alone.

Special Baccalaureate Degree Program: A pioneering, highly selective program for adults who have succeeded in the workplace without benefit of a college degree, this is the only honors program for adults and nontraditional students in the CUNY system.

Participation Requirements: Honors Academy members take honors sections of core studies courses and interdisciplinary honors seminars. Entering freshmen take two semesters of honors-level instruction in writing and research. The Honors Academy precisely coordinates B.A.-M.D. and engineering honors courses with medical school and engineering school requirements. The curricula of two upper-division programs have been designed in cooperation with the foundations that established or sustain them, Ford and Mellon. Dean's List–Honors Research students contract with their major departments for individually tailored programs. Special Baccalaureate students pursue intensive liberal studies in seminars designed to accommodate constraints imposed by work and home.

Graduation from all Honors Academy programs requires at least a 3.5 GPA. Graduation from the Scholars Program and Mellon Fellowship requires a senior thesis.

Admission Process: Students apply to the CUNY Honors College, B.A.-M.D., Engineering Honors, and the Scholars Program from high school using the CUNY university honors application form. Application includes SAT scores, a personal essay, and letters of recommendation. The median combined SAT score (math and verbal) of entering students is currently 1260. Transfer and matriculated students may also enter the Scholars Program with up to 48 credits with faculty recommendation and a minimum 3.5 GPA. Entrance to upper-division programs (Mellon, Dean's List–Honors Research, and Senior Colloquium) requires at least a 3.5 GPA. Acceptance by the Special Baccalaureate Degree Program requires demonstration of exceptional accomplishment without benefit of a college diploma and other indications of academic potential.

Scholarship Availability: The Honors Academy does not make scholarship awards. Brooklyn College currently awards most freshman-entry Honors Academy students a four-year, full-tuition Presidential Scholarship.

Campus Overview

State and locally supported comprehensive, founded 1930, part of City University of New York System • **Coed** 11,172 undergraduate students, 71% full-time, 60% women, 40% men.

Undergraduates 7,909 full-time, 3,263 part-time. Students come from 25 states and territories, 75 other countries, 1% are from out of state, 29% African American, 10% Asian American or Pacific Islander, 11% Hispanic American, 0.1% Native American, 6% international, 13% transferred in.

Faculty Total: 1,066, 48% full-time, 63% with terminal degrees. Student/faculty ratio: 15:1.

Academic Programs Special study options: adult/continuing education programs, advanced placement credit, distance learning, double majors, English as a second language, freshman honors college, honors programs, independent study, internships, off-campus study, part-time degree program, services for LD students, study abroad, summer session for credit.

Athletics Member NCAA. All Division III. Intercollegiate sports: basketball M/W, cross-country running M/W, soccer M, softball W,

swimming and diving M/W, tennis M/W, track and field M/W, volleyball M/W. Intramural sports: badminton M/W, basketball M/W, bowling M/W, football M/W, racquetball M/W, soccer M/W, softball M/W, swimming and diving M/W, table tennis M/W, tennis M/W, track and field M/W, volleyball M/W.

Costs (2004–05) Tuition: state resident $4000 full-time, $170 per credit part-time; nonresident $8640 full-time, $360 per credit part-time. Required fees: $353 full-time, $139 per term part-time.

Financial Aid 1,100 Federal Work-Study jobs (averaging $1200). In 2003, 750 non-need-based awards were made. Average percent of need met: 99%. Average financial aid package: $5400. Average need-based loan: $2850. Average need-based gift aid: $3300. Average non-need-based aid: $4000.

Contact: Director: Kenneth A. Bruffee, Honors Academy, Brooklyn, New York 11210; Telephone: 718-951-4114; Fax: 718-951-5249; E-mail: kbruffee@brooklyn.cuny.edu

Broome Community College
Honors Program
Binghamton, New York

The Honors Program at Broome Community College (BCC) is designed for students whose academic ability and personal motivation are so high that existing College programs may not fully challenge them. The BCC Honors Program provides academic opportunities that enrich the traditional educational experience. These opportunities may include working closely with honors faculty members in both regular and seminar classes, studying with other highly motivated students, conducting advanced research projects, participating in conferences and cultural events, qualifying for study-abroad programs and intercollegiate scholarship opportunities, and receiving assistance in securing internships in research and employment. This year, the program began offering a five-day "exploration" in Washington, D.C.

The Honors Program is open to any student across the campus, but so far primarily students in the liberal arts and sciences division have utilized the program. Other students in programs that emphasize transfer to a four-year institution have also entered the program.

BCC Honors Program courses are known for their smaller class size, emphasis on participatory learning styles and learning community methods, stimulating and dedicated faculty members, and an interdisciplinary focus. The program includes regular courses with an enrichment option, advanced-level seminars, honors-level independent study courses, and honors sections of regular courses. However offered, extensive writing and participation by the student are expected components of any course.

To complete the entire honors curriculum, students must acquire college credits holding an honors designation. These are arranged among two general education honors courses, one honors course in the matriculated major field, one interdisciplinary honors seminar, and one honors-level independent study. The heart of the program is the interdisciplinary honors seminar. In this 4-credit course, a small number of students and 2 honors faculty members engage in intensive study of a designated theme. The theme varies each semester; recent investigations have looked at war and peace in American history and literature, leadership development, and the family as myth, metaphor, and reality. Honors faculty members are presently planning two new seminars centering on the underside of the American dream and on local history and architecture. Another important element of the Honors Program is the enriched option. This creates a negotiated honors level to a regular course and involves close and sustained engagement between the instructor and the individual student.

Participation Requirements: In order to complete the entire Honors Program, students must acquire 14 honors-designated credits with a minimum grade of B. An overall GPA of at least 3.5 is the norm for admission and continuation. In enriched courses, students are expected to solicit the agreement of each professor with whom they wish to work.

Honors Program scholarship recipients receive special recognition at a campuswide awards ceremony each spring. Transcripts are annotated for each successfully completed honors course, and each honors graduate receives a certificate of recognition.

Admission Process: Students apply to the program during the first week of the semester or during the advisement process in the previous semester. High school test scores and current GPA are examined as are two recommendations. Each student must meet with the Honors Director.

Scholarship Availability: Small scholarships may be available, depending on the continuing generosity of donors, the number of students enrolled in the program, and successful progress toward completion of the program.

Campus Overview

State and locally supported 2-year, founded 1946, part of State University of New York System • **Coed** 6,590 undergraduate students, 63% full-time, 58% women, 42% men.

Undergraduates 4,132 full-time, 2,458 part-time. Students come from 36 states and territories, 30 other countries, 5% are from out of state.

Faculty *Total:* 399, 36% full-time. *Student/faculty ratio:* 21:1.

Academic Programs *Special study options:* academic remediation for entering students, adult/continuing education programs, advanced placement credit, distance learning, English as a second language, external degree program, honors programs, independent study, internships, off-campus study, part-time degree program, services for LD students, student-designed majors, study abroad, summer session for credit.

Athletics Member NJCAA. *Intercollegiate sports:* baseball M, basketball M/W, cross-country running M/W, golf M, ice hockey M, lacrosse M, soccer M/W, softball W, tennis M/W, volleyball W. *Intramural sports:* basketball M/W, volleyball M/W.

Costs (2004–05) *One-time required fee:* $45. *Tuition:* state resident $2690 full-time, $113 per credit hour part-time; nonresident $5380 full-time, $226 per credit hour part-time. Full-time tuition and fees vary according to course load and location. Part-time tuition and fees vary according to course load and location. *Required fees:* $242 full-time, $5 per credit hour part-time, $29 per term part-time.

Contact: Director: Professor Margaret Wingate, Department of History, P.O. Box 1017, Binghamton, New York 13902; *Telephone:* 607-778-5098; *Fax:* 607-778-5394; *E-mail:* wingate_g@sunybroome. edu; *Web site:* http://www.sunybroome.edu

City College of the City University of New York

Honors Program

New York, New York

The City College Honors Program offers selected high-achieving students in all disciplines a particularly challenging academic program. Small classes are designed and taught by an outstanding faculty. The centerpiece of the program is the honors liberal arts core, an enhanced and enriched curriculum that includes interdisciplinary courses in the humanities, sciences, and social sciences and provides an excellent academic base, regardless of a student's eventual specialization. Most students enter the program as freshmen, but transfer and continuing students are welcome at the discretion of the director.

City College is a home campus for the University-wide CUNY Honors College: University Scholars Program, which accepts new first-year students with outstanding academic records. CUNY Honors College students at City are enrolled in the liberal arts honors core and take special interdisciplinary seminars using New York City as a resource and text. They receive a "cultural passport" that provides entrance to concerts, theater, art, science, and history museums and galleries. (Prospective students should see the separate entry for CUNY Honors College: University Scholars Program.)

Honors students take a special section of new student orientation and have access to early registration and special advising. The Honors Center, a suite including a conference room where students have access to computers and current newspapers, provides a place for honors students to study and meet in a supportive atmosphere. The honors staff is also available in the center to advise and assist students.

Depending on their academic interests, honors students may also apply to join a variety of honors-level programs that provide curricular, advising, and/or scholarship enhancement. Among these programs are the Engineering Leadership Program, the City College Fellows Program (for students pursuing the Ph.D. degree), Isaacs Scholars Program (English and languages), Irani-Summerfield Fellows Program (humanities or arts), Minority Access to Research Careers (MARC) Program (biomedical research), and the Rosenberg-Humphrey Program in Public Policy.

Upperclass students with acceptable GPAs may choose to pursue honors in a particular department. Departmental honors is usually research-oriented, with a sequence of courses or independent study that culminates in research such as a thesis or laboratory research project.

Founded more than thirty years ago, City College's College-wide Honors Program includes approximately 300 students.

Participation Requirements: All students in the City College Honors Program take five prescribed core courses. Additional required courses vary depending on the student's degree objective. The total number of credits in the program varies from 21 to 34. Retention in the program requires a cumulative 3.0 GPA or better. Upon completion of the Honors Program, the designation "Liberal Arts Honors" is entered on the student's record. To remain in the CUNY Honors College: University Scholars Program, students must have a minimum 3.5 GPA by the time they have completed 60 credits. Successful completion of departmental honors is noted on the student's record.

Admission Process: To be admitted to the City College Honors Program as an entering freshman, students must have a high school average of at least 85 percent and the appropriate performance on standardized tests. Continuing and transfer students are also eligible at the discretion of the Director and must present similar academic records. The CUNY Honors College: University Scholars Program admits only new freshmen, who must submit a special application, an essay, and recommendations. (Prospective students should see the separate entry for CUNY Honors College: University Scholars Program.)

Scholarship Availability: The City College Honors Program is not a scholarship program, but many honors students receive merit awards. CUNY Honors College: University Scholars students receive full tuition and fees for four years and a study grant to use for educationally enriching experiences such as study abroad. Information about merit scholarships for honors eligible students is available from the Honors Center.

Campus Overview

State and locally supported university, founded 1847, part of City University of New York System • **Coed** 9,117 undergraduate students, 70% full-time, 49% women, 51% men.

Undergraduates 6,359 full-time, 2,758 part-time. Students come from 130 other countries, 4% are from out of state, 26% African American, 17% Asian American or Pacific Islander, 33% Hispanic American, 0.1% Native American, 12% international, 13% transferred in.

Faculty *Total:* 1,109, 49% full-time. *Student/faculty ratio:* 11:1.

Academic Programs *Special study options:* academic remediation for entering students, accelerated degree program, adult/continuing education programs, advanced placement credit, cooperative education, English as a second language, freshman honors college, honors programs, independent study, internships, off-campus study, part-time degree program, services for LD students, student-designed majors, study abroad, summer session for credit. *ROTC:* Army (c), Air Force (c).

Athletics Member NCAA. All Division III. *Intercollegiate sports:* baseball M, basketball M/W, cross-country running M/W, fencing W, lacrosse M, soccer M, softball W, tennis M/W, track and field M/W, volleyball W. *Intramural sports:* basketball M/W, fencing W, soccer M, softball W, tennis M/W, track and field M/W, volleyball M/W.

Costs (2004–05) *Tuition:* state resident $4080 full-time, $170 per credit part-time; nonresident $8640 full-time, $360 per credit part-time. Full-time tuition and fees vary according to class time and program. Part-time tuition and fees vary according to class time, course load, and program. *Required fees:* $259 full-time.

Financial Aid 1,704 Federal Work-Study jobs (averaging $1343). In 2004, 405 non-need-based awards were made. *Average percent of need met:* 68%. *Average financial aid package:* $5771. *Average need-based loan:* $2234. *Average need-based gift aid:* $5005. *Average non-need-based aid:* $3000.

Contact: Director: Robin Villa, Honors Center, City College of the City University of New York, New York, New York 10031-9160; *Telephone:* 212-650-6917; *Fax:* 212-650-7337; *E-mail:* cityhonors@ccny.cuny.edu; *Web site:* http://www.ccny.cuny.edu/honorscenter

City University of New York
Honors College
New York, New York

The City University of New York Honors College (CUNY Honors College) offers academically gifted students, called University scholars, an extraordinary and tuition-free undergraduate education integrating the vast resources of the City University and New York's cultural, scientific, government, and business communities. Established in 2001, the CUNY Honors College cultivates the experience of a small, supportive college within a great research university. University scholars benefit from individualized mentoring from faculty members and dedicated honors advisers and from interdisciplinary courses that offer exceptional intellectual challenges. Internships, study abroad, senior honors projects, and a Cultural Passport provide opportunities far beyond the traditional classroom.

The CUNY Honors College operates in partnership with seven campuses within the CUNY system: Baruch College, Brooklyn College, the City College, College of Staten Island, Hunter College, Lehman College, and Queens College. University scholars choose one campus as "home" and may cross-register and use the facilities at all others as well as CUNY's outstanding Graduate School and University Center and professional schools for law, business, health care, architecture and engineering, education, public administration, and social work. Early registration privileges enable University Scholars to select courses before other students.

The CUNY Honors College curriculum is centered on traditional scholarly activity with hands-on experiences designed to stimulate interest in and deepen understanding of the institutions and people of New York City. Through the use of instructional technology and intensive reading and writing, students sharpen their analytical, writing, and research skills. The curriculum is enhanced by special events, by visits to New York City cultural institutions, and by the opportunity to meet and work with artists, scientists, and other distinguished professionals.

The center of Honors College life is at CUNY's Graduate School and University Center, located in a landmarked structure in the heart of Manhattan, steps away from the Empire State Building, Broadway, 42nd Street, Madison Avenue, the United Nations, and the world's preeminent arts, science, financial, and media institutions. New York's excellent transportation network makes for easy travel across the city and, quite literally, across the globe. Scholars stay closely connected to the Honors College and one another through a virtual community supported by an intranet and discussion boards organized by Honors College Instructional Technology Fellows.

Each year, the CUNY Honors College enrolls a new cohort of approximately 320 freshmen drawn from public, independent, and parochial schools in the New York City metropolitan area. Other University Scholars hail from states as far away as Alaska and Hawaii, and a few come from other countries.

Participation Requirements: In the first two years, each University scholar participates in a sequence of four interdisciplinary seminar courses that offers exceptional intellectual challenges and rewards. Each seminar emphasizes original research or creative work that University scholars present to the Honors College community at the end of the semester. Each University scholar must also take at least four honors-level courses, which may include electives, courses in the major, and upper-division, interdisciplinary Honors College seminars. In addition, each University scholar must perform at least 30 hours of community service.

To remain in the CUNY Honors College, scholars must meet or exceed a minimum grade point average: 3.3 at the end of freshman year, 3.5 at the end of sophomore year, and in each semester of the junior and senior years.

At graduation, University scholars earn a diploma from their home campus with certification of their special status and accomplishments in the CUNY Honors College.

Admission Process: The CUNY Honors College welcomes applications from outstanding candidates seeking admission as first-time freshmen. Candidates may apply to the Honors College at only one partner campus. All applications receive a thorough review by admissions professionals.

Candidates must submit a complete application, which includes a personal and high school data form, an essay, a transcript of high school grades, two recommendations, and standardized test scores on either the SAT Reasoning Test or the ACT Assessment Test. Candidates who are home schooled or attend a secondary education program that does not give out conventional grades must take the GED test in addition to the SAT or ACT. Overseas candidates are not exempt from testing.

Successful applicants score high on standardized tests and have very strong high school GPAs, extracurricular activities, and recommendations from teachers/counselors. Students admitted to the class of 2009 had an average high school GPA of 93.4 and total SAT score of 1364.

Given the high volume of applications, postmark deadlines are strict: November 1 for early decision applications and December 15 for regular applications.

Scholarship Availability: All University Scholars receive full scholarships for tuition and college and course fees, a free state-of-the-art laptop computer, and access to study grants to fund enriching experiences, such as study abroad, research projects, or living expenses during an unpaid internship (up to a total of $7500 over four years).

Contact: Laura S. Schor, CUNY Honors College, CUNY Graduate Center, 365 Fifth Avenue, New York, New York 10016-4309; *Telephone:* 212-817-1811; *E-mail:* lschor@honorscollege.cuny.edu

Clarkson University
Honors Program
Potsdam, New York

The Honors Program focuses on current and emerging problems in science, technology, and society. It offers special academic challenges and opportunities for Clarkson University's most promising students. The program enables students to take full advantage of their intellectual gifts by providing a first-rate, problem-based curriculum; develops creative problem-solving and leadership abilities; strengthens communication skills, including those required by the new information technologies; and explores the connections between students' engineering, science, liberal arts, or business majors and American society.

The core of the program is its thematic sequence of problem-based courses: first year, The Computer and the Age of Information; second year, The Contemporary World: Its Problems and Their Origins; third year, Science: Problems and Possibilities; and fourth year, Research and Modernity. While the topics for these courses change every year, the goal of the sequence is to bring the viewpoints of different disciplines to bear on current problems. Recent problem-based classes have included a sophomore course in which the students investigated General Motors' claim that the company will launch full-scale commercial sales of hydrogen vehicles by 2010 and a junior seminar, Chaos and Coherency, in which students studied the mathematics of chaos theory and its implications for the stock market.

The program admits 30 first-year students annually and adds approximately 5 students to each class via internal admission or external transfer. Class size is small, typically 13 to 18 students per section, and total honors membership varies between 120 and 140 students.

Participation Requirements: Students take one honors course and perform community service each semester. First-year students take The Computer as an Intellectual Tool I and II. The first course helps to prepare them for using the computer at a technological university like Clarkson and in their careers; the second explores the social impact and ethical issues associated with new information technologies. Second-year students take a contemporary problem sequence. Their first-semester course focuses on a contemporary problem or issue, then in the second semester they investigate the intellectual or historical roots of that same problem. As currently projected, the fall 2005 course will examine biometric analysis for homeland security. (Biometrics is the science of using biological properties to identify individuals.) Third-year students take a science seminar with a different topic each year and begin their honors thesis. The 2005 seminar will investigate cryptography and quantum computing. Fourth-year students complete their thesis and close the Honors Program with a seminar on modernity. The 2005 seminar will use Renaissance breakthroughs in the technology of exploration and communication to examine how mankind's world view may change in the 21st century as a result of contemporary technical discoveries.

To remain in the program, students, except for those in their first year, must maintain at least a 3.25 cumulative GPA. Successful completion of the program is recognized at commencement and is also noted on the official transcript and diploma.

Admission Process: The Honors Program invites applications from students who have 1350 and above SAT I scores and graduate in the top 10 percent of their class or who have outstanding academic or leadership achievements. An honors application consists of an essay, letter(s) of recommendation, and an interview as well as the student's completed Clarkson application form. In evaluating candidates, the admissions committee looks at the applicant's love of learning, intellectual curiosity, initiative, degree of motivation, ability to handle uncertainty, work ethic, and ability to work with others. Admission to the program is by rolling admission; qualified students who apply after the thirty slots in the entering class are filled are placed on a wait list.

Scholarship Availability: All students accepted into the Honors Program receive an Honors Scholarship as part of their Clarkson University financial assistance package.

Campus Overview

Independent university, founded 1896 • **Coed** 2,736 undergraduate students, 99% full-time, 23% women, 77% men.

Undergraduates 2,719 full-time, 17 part-time. Students come from 35 states and territories, 23 other countries, 25% are from out of state, 2% African American, 2% Asian American or Pacific Islander, 2% Hispanic American, 0.4% Native American, 3% international, 4% transferred in, 83% live on campus.

Faculty *Total:* 189, 91% full-time, 83% with terminal degrees. *Student/faculty ratio:* 16:1.

Academic Programs *Special study options:* accelerated degree program, advanced placement credit, cooperative education, double majors, English as a second language, honors programs, independent study, internships, off-campus study, part-time degree program, services for LD students, student-designed majors, study abroad, summer session for credit. *ROTC:* Army (b), Air Force (b).

Athletics Member NCAA. All Division III except men's and women's ice hockey (Division I). *Intercollegiate sports:* baseball M, basketball M/W, bowling M(c)/W(c), cross-country running M/W, golf M, ice hockey M(s)/W(s), lacrosse M/W, skiing (cross-country) M/W, skiing (downhill) M/W, soccer M/W, swimming and diving M/W, tennis M/W, volleyball M(c)/W. *Intramural sports:* archery M(c)/W(c), basketball M/W, bowling M(c)/W(c), crew M(c), football M, ice hockey M/W, racquetball M(c)/W(c), rugby M(c)/W(c), soccer M/W, softball M/W, ultimate Frisbee M(c)/W(c), volleyball M/W.

Costs (2005–06) *Comprehensive fee:* $34,930 includes full-time tuition ($25,185), mandatory fees ($400), and room and board ($9345). Full-time tuition and fees vary according to course load. Part-time tuition: $840 per credit. Part-time tuition and fees vary according to course load. *College room only:* $4896. Room and board charges vary according to housing facility.

Financial Aid 725 Federal Work-Study jobs (averaging $1411). 126 state and other part-time jobs (averaging $965). In 2004, 213 non-need-based awards were made. *Average percent of need met:* 87%. *Average financial aid package:* $17,163. *Average need-based loan:* $7352. *Average need-based gift aid:* $11,709. *Average non-need-based aid:* $9748.

Contact: Director: David Craig, P.O. Box 5755, Potsdam, New York 13699-5755; *Telephone:* 315-268-2320; *Fax:* 315-268-2344; *E-mail:* dcraig@clarkson.edu; *Web site:* http://www.clarkson.edu/honors/

The College of New Rochelle
School of Arts and Sciences Honors Program
New Rochelle, New York

The School of Arts and Sciences Honors Program is designed to foster intellectual independence and initiative, leadership abilities, and appreciation of the value of collaboration and community involvement in talented motivated students. To that end, it offers a variety of challenging interdisciplinary seminars, an annual Honors Colloquium, independent study through contract, and opportunities for leadership and community activity.

Freshmen are enrolled in honors sections of the freshman requirements Self in Context and Critical Research Essay, where they explore self, texts, and contexts through group and individual projects that interrelate individual and community. Seniors conclude their course of study with Senior Symposium, a semester of student-led, *issue-based seminars emanating from a disciplinary perspective but set in an interdisciplinary forum. Honors students are closely advised in the selection of appropriate honors learning options, seminars, colloquia, and contract learning, all of which are open to students above the freshman level. Honors faculty members are selected on the basis of their creative, student-centered teaching.*

Seminars are expressly designed for nonmajors as core alternatives or electives. They are interdisciplinary and issue-based and involve primary-source readings, discussion, projects, experiential learning environments, and extensive writing. Class size is limited to 15 students.

Honors Colloquia are one-year, 6-credit experiences offered annually to all students above the freshman level and consist of a fall seminar and a spring independent study. Cycled according to student choice, the topics are New York City: Anatomy of a Metropolis; Democracy in America; Twentieth-Century Global Issues; Science, Technology, and Values; and the Human Drive for Community.

Students above the freshman level are free to develop an independent study contract with a faculty mentor as either a research project or an internship. On Honors Conference Day students present the results of their research to the College community.

There are approximately 45 active full-time student members.

Founded in 1974, the program marked its twenty-fifth anniversary with a series of lectures, readings, films, and forums that examined the perception of women and their role in society and diverse cultures.

Participation Requirements: Students are required to engage in a minimum of two honors academic studies a year and are strongly encouraged to build honors portfolios that reflect program, College, and NCHC activities.

The Honors Diploma is awarded to graduating seniors who have a minimum 3.5 GPA; eight honors options, including one Colloquium and Senior Symposium; and a consistent record of leadership. The Honors Certificate is awarded to graduating seniors who have achieved at least a 3.5 GPA in the honors program, completed five honors options, and participated in honors activities.

Admission Process: Academic scholarship recipients who exhibit both promise for academic achievement and leadership potential are invited into the program directly from high school. Enrolled and transfer students below the junior level who have a 3.3 GPA or higher are also invited into the program. Juniors and seniors are required to maintain a minimum 3.5 GPA.

Scholarship Availability: Presidential Scholarships (full tuition), Honors Scholarships ($7500), and Academic Scholarships ($5000) are awarded to academically qualified applicants during the admission process. Students selected for scholarships generally rank in the top 20 percent of their high school graduating class, have SAT scores above 1000, and have high school scores above 90 percent. Applicants must file the Free Application for Federal Student Aid (FAFSA). There is no application deadline for entering freshman and transfer students; all financial aid is renewed annually.

Campus Overview

Independent comprehensive, founded 1904 • **Suburban** 20-acre campus with easy access to New York City • **Coed, primarily women,** 1,080 undergraduate students, 62% full-time, 94% women, 6% men.

Undergraduates 670 full-time, 410 part-time. Students come from 16 states and territories, 10 other countries, 10% are from out of state, 31% African American, 5% Asian American or Pacific Islander, 10% Hispanic American, 0.2% Native American, 1% international, 17% transferred in, 37% live on campus.

Faculty *Total:* 162, 45% full-time. *Student/faculty ratio:* 7:1.

Academic Programs *Special study options:* academic remediation for entering students, accelerated degree program, adult/continuing education programs, advanced placement credit, cooperative education, double majors, honors programs, independent study, internships, off-campus study, part-time degree program, services for LD students, student-designed majors, study abroad, summer session for credit.

Athletics Member NCAA. All Division III. *Intercollegiate sports:* basketball W, cross-country running W, softball W, swimming and diving W, tennis W, volleyball W.

Costs (2005–06) *Comprehensive fee:* $28,476 includes full-time tuition ($20,246), mandatory fees ($350), and room and board ($7880). Full-time tuition and fees vary according to course load and program. Part-time tuition: $682 per credit. Part-time tuition and fees vary according to course load. *Required fees:* $60 per term part-time. *Room and board:* Room and board charges vary according to housing facility.

Financial Aid 484 Federal Work-Study jobs (averaging $2012). 10 state and other part-time jobs (averaging $4500). In 2003, 32 non-need-based awards were made. *Average percent of need met:* 100%. *Average financial aid package:* $18,052. *Average need-based loan:* $8325. *Average need-based gift aid:* $7715. *Average non-need-based aid:* $5552.

Contact: Honors Program Director: Dr. Amy Bass, 29 Castle Place, The College of New Rochelle, New Rochelle, New York 10805; *Telephone:* 914-654-5987; *Fax:* 914-654-5259; *Web site:* http://www.cnr.edu/home/honors/

College of Staten Island of the City University of New York

Honors College

Staten Island, New York

*T*he CUNY Honors College (CHC) University Scholars Program at the College of Staten Island (CSI) provides a select group of highly motivated students with a special curriculum of innovative and challenging courses during the first two years of study. These courses, taught in small class settings by select faculty members, provide a broad but coherent foundation for the baccalaureate degree. Included in this curriculum is a series of four seminars investigating New York City from a variety of viewpoints and using the city itself as a classroom. Class work involves field study, independent and collaborative research, and participation in cross-campus events involving students from all CUNY Honors College campuses. Third- and fourth-year University Scholars pursue study in a wide range of majors in which they satisfy departmental honors requirements.

Students accepted into the program receive a cultural passport providing free or reduced-cost admission to New York City's diverse cultural offerings. The program's staff includes a full-time academic adviser and a professional counselor. University Scholars benefit from personalized and individualized attention ranging from priority course registration to ongoing academic and career advisement. Local and CUNY-wide initiatives provide University Scholars with opportunities to successfully compete for prestigious internships, fellowships, and admission to postgraduate programs. The CHC at CSI also houses a student lounge and a designated computer lab for student use.

Participation Requirements: The CUNY Honors College at CSI is a four-year degree program. Its curriculum follows two main plans: one for students intending to pursue a Bachelor of Arts (B.A.) degree and one for those intending to pursue a Bachelor of Science (B.S.) degree. All University Scholars at CSI enroll as cohorts in a sequence of four humanities and social sciences seminars, which use New York City as a "laboratory for learning." These seminars study the arts, people, science and technology, and the future of New York City. Students pursuing a B.A. degree take a one-year sequence of biology, chemistry, or physics; one semester each of math and computer science; and two semesters of humanities and social sciences, focusing on the contemporary world. Students pursuing a B.S. degree enroll in a one-year sequence of biology, chemistry, or physics; two semesters of math; one semester of computer science; and one semester of a humanities and social sciences seminar, focusing on the contemporary world. These requirements range from 40 to 50 credits.

In addition to the Honors College courses, B.A. students must fulfill a foreign language requirement and B.S. students must take a second year of science. Third- and fourth-year students engage in study in a wide range of disciplines, where they pursue honors in their majors through undergraduate research projects and thesis writing. University Scholars are required to maintain a 3.3 or better GPA by the end of their freshman year and a 3.5 or better GPA by the end of their sophomore year and beyond. University Scholars graduate with the designation of honors on their transcripts and diplomas.

Admission Process: The CUNY Honors College accepts applications only for freshman admissions for the fall term. Midterm and transfer applications are not accepted. In September of the senior year, applicants should work with their college advisers to complete the CHC application. Applicants are required to submit this application to the University Application Processing Center (UAPC). This application serves as both the freshman admission application to CUNY and to the CHC. No other application is required. The CHC application is designed to provide information about each applicant's academic record and preparation for a rigorous intellectual experience in college. Admission to the CHC depends on high school grades, SAT/ACT scores, an essay, two letters of recommendation and an interview.

Scholarship Availability: Students accepted into the program receive a comprehensive package of financial assistance, including full tuition for four years and an academic stipend to defray travel, internship, and study-abroad expenses. In addition to the tuition-free package and academic study grant, all University Scholars who have attended New York City high schools are eligible for a Vallone Merit Scholarship of $1000 per year. When eligible, students receive assistance in applying for other external CSI scholarships and awards.

Campus Overview

State and locally supported comprehensive, founded 1955, part of City University of New York System • **Coed** 11,130 undergraduate students, 67% full-time, 59% women, 41% men.

Undergraduates 7,423 full-time, 3,707 part-time. Students come from 5 states and territories, 111 other countries, 1% are from out of state, 9% African American, 7% Asian American or Pacific Islander, 9% Hispanic American, 0.2% Native American, 3% international, 3% transferred in.

Faculty *Total:* 823, 42% full-time, 53% with terminal degrees. *Student/faculty ratio:* 18:1.

Academic Programs *Special study options:* academic remediation for entering students, accelerated degree program, adult/continuing education programs, advanced placement credit, cooperative education, distance learning, double majors, English as a second language, freshman honors college, honors programs, independent study, internships, off-campus study, part-time degree program, services for LD students, study abroad, summer session for credit. *Unusual degree programs:* 3-2 physical therapy, physicians assistant, medical technology.

Athletics Member NCAA. All Division III. *Intercollegiate sports:* baseball M, basketball M/W, soccer M/W, softball W, swimming and diving M/W, tennis M/W, volleyball W. *Intramural sports:* badminton M/W, basketball M/W, football M/W, racquetball M/W, soccer M/W, softball M/W, table tennis M/W, tennis M/W, track and field M/W, volleyball M/W.

Costs (2004–05) *Tuition:* state resident $4000 full-time, $170 per credit part-time; nonresident $8640 full-time, $360 per credit part-time. Full-time tuition and fees vary according to course load. Part-time tuition and fees vary according to course load. *Required fees:* $308 full-time, $91 per term part-time.

Financial Aid 332 Federal Work-Study jobs (averaging $1256). In 2004, 288 non-need-based awards were made. *Average percent of*

need met: 50%. *Average financial aid package:* $5132. *Average need-based loan:* $3438. *Average need-based gift aid:* $4962. *Average non-need-based aid:* $1773.

Contact: Director: Dr. Susan L. Holak, Building 1A, Room 206E, College of Staten Island, 2800 Victory Boulevard, Staten Island, New York 10314; *Telephone:* 718-982-2222; *Fax:* 718-982-2675; *E-mail:* holak@mail.csi.cuny.edu

---

Corning Community College
Honors Program
Corning, New York

In 1976, the Council of Full Professors of Corning Community College, under the aegis of the Faculty Association, developed an honors program that would attract and provide an enriched academic experience for high-ability and curious students in all academic programs, both technical and transfer, offered by the College. The faculty members, however, were concerned that the honors students should not be segregated from the general student body.

In order to achieve these primary goals, Corning Community College established a unique Honors Program; there is not a separate honors curriculum or a series of honors courses that a student must take to earn an honors degree. There are no special honors sections that segregate honors students from the general student body. Rather, all academic courses the College offers may be taken at an advanced or honors level by any qualified student in any academic program offered by the College. The program was designed to be interdisciplinary and give honors students control and responsibility for their own learning and discovery, which very seldom occurs in traditional courses.

An integral part of Corning Community College's Honors Program is the Honors Forum, which is a 3-credit-hour interdisciplinary seminar. The forum is similar to a graduate seminar. The average size of the forum is 12 students and 3 faculty members representing the social sciences, humanities, and the sciences. The forum faculty members function as guides as well as participants, learning along with the students. The Honors Forum serves several vital functions. It provides honors students with a venue for the exchange and testing of ideas and theories derived from their honors projects, provides students with the opportunity to analyze and synthesize information from students representing a wide variety of disciplines, and allows students to develop critical-thinking, argumentative, and oral presentation skills usually reserved for upperclassmen or even graduate students.

There are 15–20 students involved in the Honors Program working either in the Honors Forum or independently with their mentor and not enrolled in the forum.

Corning Community College Honors Program celebrated its twentieth anniversary in 1996, making it the oldest continuous Honors Program in the SUNY College system.

Participation Requirements: A student who has a GPA of 3.5 or better and who is curious as well as highly motivated may take any course at an advanced or honors level by developing an honors project for that course. The honors project or topic to be explored is mutually agreed upon by the student and his or her mentor, who is usually the instructor of that course. The mentor serves as a guide for the honors student, who bears complete responsibility for his or her honors project. The faculty member mentor awards an H (honors designation) for the relevant course.

Honors projects have included the writing of short stories and poems, the building and repair of robots, and the offering of music recitals as well as the more traditional research projects. Several students have had their honors projects published in professional journals of their chosen field.

Upon successful completion of 12 credit hours of honors-level work, which usually entails two or three honors projects as well as Honors Forum and a cumulative GPA of at least 3.5, the student qualifies for an honors diploma. Students who successfully complete honors projects also receive individualized letters from faculty member mentors, as well as honors faculty members describing their projects and indicating the skills and abilities each student demonstrated throughout the semester. These letters are attached to the student's transcripts and are sent out to potential transfer colleges and/or employers.

Campus Overview

State and locally supported 2-year, founded 1956, part of State University of New York System • **Coed** 4,443 undergraduate students, 53% full-time, 59% women, 41% men.

Undergraduates 2,356 full-time, 2,087 part-time. Students come from 13 states and territories, 4% are from out of state, 3% African American, 0.7% Asian American or Pacific Islander, 0.7% Hispanic American, 0.2% Native American, 0.1% international, 4% transferred in.

Faculty *Total:* 243, 39% full-time, 8% with terminal degrees. *Student/faculty ratio:* 19:1.

Academic Programs *Special study options:* academic remediation for entering students, accelerated degree program, advanced placement credit, distance learning, double majors, honors programs, independent study, internships, part-time degree program, services for LD students, student-designed majors, summer session for credit. *ROTC:* Army (c), Navy (c), Air Force (c).

Athletics Member NJCAA. *Intercollegiate sports:* basketball M/W, cheerleading W, soccer M/W, softball W, volleyball W. *Intramural sports:* archery M/W, badminton M/W, basketball M/W, bowling M/W, golf M/W, soccer M/W, softball M/W, table tennis M/W, volleyball M/W, weight lifting M/W.

Costs (2004–05) *Tuition:* state resident $3064 full-time, $128 per credit hour part-time; nonresident $6128 full-time, $256 per credit hour part-time. Part-time tuition and fees vary according to course load. *Required fees:* $400 full-time.

Financial Aid 264 Federal Work-Study jobs (averaging $1128).

Contact: Director: Mr. Joselph J. Hanak, 1 Academic Drive, Corning, New York 14830; *Telephone:* 607-962-9208; *Fax:* 607-962-9456; *E-mail:* hanak@sccvc.corning-cc.edu

Dowling College
Honors Program
Oakdale, New York

The Honors Program at Dowling College, established in the year 2000, is for highly motivated, academically superior, and creative students. The small, intimate-size classes are specifically developed cohort sections of the general education core courses offered by selected faculty members in the Schools of Arts and Humanities, Physical Sciences, and Social Sciences. Currently, there are approximately 40 students enrolled in the Honors Program.

The educational experience of Honors Program students is enhanced with intellectual and cultural opportunities that extend beyond the classroom. These may include lectures, debates, films, and excursions to New York City for theater productions, museum visits, and dance and musical performances. Most recently, these activities have consisted of a Presidential Breakfast, an overnight stay at a Vanderbilt Mansion on the Upper East Side, a tour of The Cloisters, attendance at an Off-Broadway drama, and the viewing of the Space Show projected from the planetarium in the sky dome of the Rose Center for Earth and Space Science. In addition, Honors Program students are instilled with the charitable responsibilities of giving back to the College community and the community at large. Community service projects are developed by the students in concert with the program's director.

Other highlights of the Honors Program include a supportive, enriched academic environment; an annual Honors Forum, where students present summaries of their most outstanding research projects; a special liaison with college librarians and faculty members; festive social gatherings and meals; Freshman and Senior Seminars; and scholarship opportunities.

Participation Requirements: To remain in the Honors Program, students must maintain a cumulative GPA of at least 3.5 and complete 30 credits each year. Students who fall below this minimum are placed on probation for one semester so that they may be given the chance to restore their GPA to Honors Program standards. All honors courses completed by students in the program are designated as such on their transcripts. Four-year honors students are expected to complete 36 credits of honors courses, while transfer students entering in their junior year are expected to complete 9 credits.

Admission Process: Dowling College maintains a rolling admission process as opposed to specific deadlines. Students are invited by letter to participate in the Honors Program if they meet any of the following criteria: a minimum 3.6 GPA or a 96 average at the high school level; placement in the upper 5 percent of their graduating class; a minimum score of 1200 on the SAT or an equivalent score on the ACT; or demonstration of exceptional promise as determined by the Honors Advisory Council.

Scholarship Availability: Each honors student is awarded $1000 in the autumn and spring semesters. Moreover, there are many other scholarship and grant opportunities available through the Office of Financial Aid. In fact, most students in the Honors Program are recipients of these additional awards.

Campus Overview

Independent comprehensive, founded 1955 • **Coed** 3,357 undergraduate students, 67% full-time, 59% women, 41% men.

Undergraduates 2,235 full-time, 1,122 part-time. Students come from 28 states and territories, 56 other countries, 9% are from out of state, 10% African American, 2% Asian American or Pacific Islander, 10% Hispanic American, 0.3% Native American, 4% international, 10% transferred in, 17% live on campus.

Faculty *Total:* 416, 31% full-time, 42% with terminal degrees. *Student/faculty ratio:* 15:1.

Academic Programs *Special study options:* academic remediation for entering students, accelerated degree program, advanced placement credit, cooperative education, double majors, English as a second language, honors programs, independent study, internships, off-campus study, part-time degree program, services for LD students, student-designed majors, summer session for credit. *ROTC:* Air Force (c).

Athletics Member NCAA. All Division II. *Intercollegiate sports:* baseball M(s), basketball M(s)/W(s), crew M(c)/W(c), equestrian sports W, lacrosse M, soccer M(s), softball W(s), tennis M(s)/W(s), volleyball W(s). *Intramural sports:* bowling M/W, cross-country running M/W, track and field M/W, weight lifting M/W.

Costs (2004–05) *Tuition:* $15,210 full-time, $507 per credit part-time. Part-time tuition and fees vary according to course load and degree level. *Required fees:* $840 full-time, $275 per term part-time. *Room only:* $5512. Room and board charges vary according to housing facility and location.

Financial Aid 256 Federal Work-Study jobs (averaging $1300). In 2004, 324 non-need-based awards were made. *Average percent of need met:* 90%. *Average financial aid package:* $13,671. *Average need-based loan:* $3545. *Average need-based gift aid:* $2671. *Average non-need-based aid:* $5006.

Contact: Honors Program Director: Dr. Stephen Lamia, Associate Professor of Visual Arts, Department of Visual Arts, Dowling College, 150 Idle Hour Boulevard, Oakdale, New York 11769; *Telephone:* 631-244-3099; *Fax:* 631-589-6644; *E-mail:* LamiaS@dowling.edu

Dutchess Community College

Honors Advisement Sequence in Liberal Arts and Humanities

Poughkeepsie, New York

The Dutchess Community College (DCC) Honors Advisement Sequence in Liberal Arts and Humanities provides academically able students an enriched liberal arts education by means of correlated courses and an upper-level interdisciplinary seminar. The sequence is designed for students, who, upon completing the program, intend to continue to work toward a bachelor's degree.

The honors experience features small classes, including a freshman seminar that familiarizes students with campus life and provides a forum for questions and answers.

Each semester's course offerings emphasize a central theme. The first semester focuses on global intellectual and cultural traditions; later semesters emphasize American political, historical, and literary development and the complexities and richness of the contemporary world.

Thirty-five students currently participate fully in the Honors Advisement Sequence, which was established thirty years ago, and 40 more students have been admitted into individual honors courses.

Participation Requirements: Students in the Honors Advisement Sequence pursue the Associate in Arts degree in liberal arts and sciences: humanities and social sciences. In order to complete the program, students have to take a minimum of 24 honors credits (out of a total of 64), complete an upper-level interdisciplinary seminar, and maintain a grade point average of 3.2 or higher.

Honors students have the opportunity to participate in out-of-the-classroom activities, such as attending lectures, films, and plays and visiting the campuses of four-year colleges. They are also made aware of off-campus study opportunities, internships, and academic competitions.

Admission Process: Students are selected for the Honors Advisement Sequence on the basis of high school achievement, a grade point average of 3.2 or higher, and an individual interview. High-ability students identified during the registration process are invited to apply for admission to honors.

Scholarship Availability: President's Scholarships offer free Dutchess Community College tuition to any student in the top 10 percent of their high school class. Students must file for financial aid through the traditional channels in order to be eligible for the Presidential Scholarship.

Campus Overview

State and locally supported 2-year, founded 1957, part of State University of New York System • **Coed** 7,810 undergraduate students

Faculty *Total:* 396.

Academic Programs *Special study options:* academic remediation for entering students, adult/continuing education programs, advanced placement credit, English as a second language, freshman honors college, honors programs, internships, off-campus study, part-time degree program, summer session for credit.

Athletics Member NJCAA. *Intercollegiate sports:* baseball M, basketball M/W, bowling M/W, golf M, soccer M/W, softball W, tennis M/W, volleyball W. *Intramural sports:* badminton M/W, basketball M/W, football M, soccer M/W, tennis M/W, volleyball M/W.

Costs (2005–06) *Tuition:* state resident $2600 full-time, $105 per credit part-time; nonresident $5200 full-time, $210 per credit part-time. *Required fees:* $387 full-time, $8 per credit part-time, $25 per term part-time.

Financial Aid 500 Federal Work-Study jobs (averaging $1500).

Contact: Honors Coordinator: Dr. Werner Steger, Dutchess Community College, 53 Pendell Road, Poughkeepsie, New York 12601; *Telephone:* 845-431-8522; *E-mail:* steger@sunydutchess.edu

Erie Community College

Honors Program

Buffalo, New York

Erie Community College (ECC) is a three-campus State University of New York (SUNY) community college. The Honors Program, which has members on each campus, is designed to enhance the education of students showing particular academic ability and interest. It is open to students in all majors but is most accessible to students in the liberal arts and sciences and other programs that are specifically designed for transfer to four-year institutions, because honors courses are liberal arts and science electives.

Honors courses are either selected from general course offerings or represent a special interest topic of a faculty member. Four interdisciplinary honors seminar courses have been developed and are offered on a rotating basis. The Honors Colloquium, which is a 1-credit course and must be taken for three semesters, is really the central focus of the program. Each semester, a theme is selected and lectures, tours, and other activities related to the theme are planned. Since there is an honors group at each of the three college campuses, activities that bring the groups together are planned each semester. These include a talent show and the Honors Great Debates, where the campuses debate each other. As part of the colloquium, students are committed to 10 hours of community service per semester.

While all classes at ECC are small, honors courses are limited to 25 students. Faculty members attempt to make the courses more student-oriented. Students are asked to do more writing and be more self-directed in their studies. Students in the program are required to take a minimum of six honors courses during their time at the College, plus three semesters of honors colloquium. The honors coordinator at a student's campus acts as that student's adviser, ensuring that the requirements are met for honors, the student's degree, and transfer. The relationship among the students in the program and between the students and the coordinator is very close. The students feel very much a part of a learning community and report that, rather than a sense of competition, there is a sense of cooperation that helps them succeed.

Graduates receive special recognition at an awards banquet, wear gold braids at Commencement, and have annotated transcripts.

Instituted in 1987, there are currently nearly 100 students in the program. The Honors Program maintains a maximum of only 35 students per campus.

Participation Requirements: In order to graduate from the Honors Program, students must complete six honors courses, three semesters of colloquium, maintain a minimum 3.25 overall GPA and at least a 3.0 GPA in honors courses, and complete 10 hours of community service per semester.

Admission Process: Students may apply to the program at the time of admission. Placement test scores are used to invite students to apply at admission, and faculty recommendations are used to invite students in their first or second semester. An interview is required.

Scholarship Availability: There are no scholarships specifically designated as honors scholarships.

Campus Overview

State and locally supported 2-year, founded 1971, part of State University of New York System • **Coed** 2,870 undergraduate students, 74% full-time, 63% women, 37% men.

Undergraduates 2,110 full-time, 760 part-time. Students come from 12 states and territories, 3 other countries, 1% are from out of state, 41% African American, 1% Asian American or Pacific Islander, 8% Hispanic American, 1% Native American, 0.1% international, 6% transferred in.

Faculty *Total:* 1,191, 31% full-time. *Student/faculty ratio:* 17:1.

Academic Programs *Special study options:* academic remediation for entering students, adult/continuing education programs, advanced placement credit, cooperative education, distance learning, double majors, English as a second language, honors programs, independent study, internships, part-time degree program, services for LD students, student-designed majors, study abroad, summer session for credit. *ROTC:* Army (c).

Athletics Member NJCAA. *Intercollegiate sports:* baseball M, basketball M/W, bowling M/W, cheerleading W, cross-country running M/W, football M, golf M/W, ice hockey M, soccer M/W, softball W, swimming and diving M/W, track and field M/W, volleyball W.

Costs (2004–05) *Tuition:* area resident $2900 full-time, $121 per credit hour part-time; state resident $5800 full-time, $242 per credit hour part-time; nonresident $5800 full-time, $242 per credit hour part-time. *Required fees:* $300 full-time, $5 per credit hour part-time, $30 per term part-time.

Financial Aid 300 Federal Work-Study jobs (averaging $2000).

Contact: Coordinator, City Campus: Mr. Willard Flynt, Erie Community College–City Campus, 121 Ellicott Street, Buffalo, New York 14203; *Telephone:* 716-270-5149; *Fax:* 716-851-1129. Coordinator, North Campus: Mr. Rene Rojas, Erie Community College–North Campus, 6205 Main Street, Buffalo, New York 14221; *Telephone:* 716-851-1259; *Fax:* 716-851-1429. Coordinator, South Campus: Mr. Christopher Pulinski, Erie Community College–South Campus, 4041 Southwestern Boulevard, Orchard Park, New York 14127; *Telephone:* 716-270-2892; *Fax:* 716-851-1003

Fashion Institute of Technology
Presidential Scholars Program
New York, New York

The Presidential Scholars Program at the Fashion Institute of Technology (FIT) provides academically gifted students an opportunity to have a dialogue with exceptional students from all majors in the college and to discuss ideas and theories in the liberal arts. While pursuing their chosen majors, students participate in challenging liberal arts courses and stimulating colloquia and experience the entire landscape of New York City as their campus as they visit cultural institutions and attend arts performances. The program enrolls approximately 150 students per semester.

Participation Requirements: Each semester students choose from more than a dozen honors liberal arts courses, ranging from Greek mythology to the Bauhaus. Students also participate in four semesters of honors colloquia addressing ideas relating to contemporary cultural, social, political, and economic thought. Students undertake two honors contracts in their major, participate in special projects designed by students and selected faculty members, and engage in cultural outings in New York City. Students must maintain an overall GPA of at least 3.5 to graduate with honors. Benefits include a merit

stipend of $500 annually, recognition as a Presidential Scholar on college transcripts and diplomas, priority registration for honors and nonhonors courses, guarantee of a dormitory room, and the ability to substitute honors classes for required introductory liberal arts courses.

Admission Process: Students admitted to FIT are eligible to apply to the Presidential Scholars Program. For the associate degree Presidential Scholars Program, competitive admission is based on SAT scores, class rank, and high school GPA. For the bachelor's degree Presidential Scholars Program, students need a GPA of at least 3.5 in their A.A.S. program.

Campus Overview

State and locally supported comprehensive, founded 1944, part of State University of New York System • **Urban** 5-acre campus • **Coed primarily women** 10,378 undergraduate students, 63% full-time, 83% women, 17% men.

Undergraduates 6,537 full-time, 3,841 part-time. Students come from 51 states and territories, 60 other countries, 30% are from out of state, 7% African American, 10% Asian American or Pacific Islander, 9% Hispanic American, 0.2% Native American, 11% international, 8% transferred in, 16% live on campus.

Faculty *Total:* 939, 23% full-time. *Student/faculty ratio:* 17:1.

Academic Programs *Special study options:* academic remediation for entering students, adult/continuing education programs, advanced placement credit, cooperative education, distance learning, English as a second language, honors programs, internships, part-time degree program, services for LD students, study abroad, summer session for credit.

Athletics Member NJCAA. *Intercollegiate sports:* basketball M/W, bowling M/W, cross-country running M/W, table tennis M/W, tennis M/W, volleyball W. *Intramural sports:* basketball M/W, bowling M/W, table tennis M/W, tennis M/W, volleyball M/W.

Costs (2004–05) *Tuition:* state resident $4350 full-time, $181 per credit part-time; nonresident $10,300 full-time, $429 per credit part-time. Full-time tuition and fees vary according to degree level and program. Part-time tuition and fees vary according to degree level and program. *Required fees:* $370 full-time, $5 per term part-time. *Room and board:* $7066; room only: $6870. Room and board charges vary according to board plan and housing facility.

Financial Aid 453 Federal Work-Study jobs (averaging $2000). In 2004, 145 non-need-based awards were made. *Average percent of need met:* 72%. *Average financial aid package:* $7288. *Average need-based loan:* $3726. *Average need-based gift aid:* $4002. *Average non-need-based aid:* $1681.

Contact: Director: Dr. Irene Buchman, Seventh Avenue at 27th Street, New York, New York 10001-5992; *Telephone:* 212-217-8660; *Fax:* 212-217-7192; *E-mail:* buchmani@fitsuny.edu; *Web site:* http://www.fitnyc.suny.edu

Fordham University
Fordham College at Rose Hill Honors Program
Bronx, New York

The Fordham College at Rose Hill Honors Program is distinguished by its comprehensive and integrated approach to learning. The heart of the program is a sequence of courses taken during the freshman and sophomore years. These courses work together to provide a comprehensive overview of the intellectual and social forces that have shaped the modern world. Each semester in this sequence is devoted to an integrated study of the art, history, literature, music, philosophy, and religion of a particular period.

In addition, special courses in mathematics and the sciences for nonscience majors help to bring out these disciplines' important role in contemporary society. This sequence is followed by two courses in the junior year that focus on different social and ethical problems of the modern world. The capstone of the honors curriculum is the senior thesis, an extended research project prepared under the individual guidance of a faculty mentor in one's major field.

The Honors Program is not intended for passive students who are satisfied simply to accept and give back the contents of their professors' lectures. Instead, the program offers an environment where students are able to take the initiative in their own education. In order to foster such active learning, most honors classes are seminars of 12 to 14 students that take place around the long wooden table in Alpha House, the program's own building on campus.

A distinctive curriculum and an ideal learning environment are obviously important elements of the Fordham College Honors Program. What really makes the program special, however, is the community of exceptional students who are its members. Such students come from a wide variety of backgrounds and have a number of different majors and career goals. Recent graduates are indicative of this diversity and include students who went on to attend the Johns Hopkins Medical School, the University of Chicago Law School, and Yale Law School. Another recent graduate had to defer her acceptance to Harvard's graduate program in biology in order to study at Oxford on a Fulbright Scholarship. The Honors Program regularly includes among its membership campus leaders in journalism, politics, drama, sports, and community service.

The Honors Program provides an opportunity for such diverse students to get to know each other outside, as well as inside, the classroom. A number of extracurricular activities bring honors students together throughout the year, and these often give students the chance to meet informally with the honors faculty as well. Every honors student has his or her own key to Alpha House, a facility that is available for either private study or meetings with other students 24 hours a day.

Now more than fifty years old, the Fordham College Honors Program currently enrolls approximately 100 students.

Participation Requirements: The honors curriculum takes the place of the regular Fordham College core curriculum, with the exception of the language requirement. Credit is, of course, granted for Advanced Placement courses taken in high school and for college courses taken elsewhere. Successful completion of the program entitles the student to the designation *in cursu honorum* on the diploma and the transcript.

Admission Process: Admission into the program is quite competitive, with usually no more than 25 to 28 incoming students entering the program each year. A limited number of first-year students with strong academic records are invited to join the program during their freshman year.

Scholarship Availability: Honors students usually receive Presidential or Dean's Scholarships in addition to their regular financial aid.

Campus Overview

Independent Roman Catholic (Jesuit) university, founded 1841 • **Coed** 7,394 undergraduate students, 91% full-time, 60% women, 40% men.

Undergraduates 6,725 full-time, 669 part-time. Students come from 53 states and territories, 44 other countries, 43% are from out of state, 5% African American, 6% Asian American or Pacific Islander, 11% Hispanic American, 0.1% Native American, 1% international, 3% transferred in, 60% live on campus.

Faculty *Total:* 1,326, 49% full-time, 46% with terminal degrees. *Student/faculty ratio:* 11:1.

Academic Programs *Special study options:* accelerated degree program, adult/continuing education programs, advanced placement credit, double majors, English as a second language, honors programs, independent study, internships, off-campus study, part-time degree program, services for LD students, student-designed majors, study

abroad, summer session for credit. *ROTC:* Army (b), Navy (c), Air Force (c). *Unusual degree programs:* 3-2 engineering with Columbia University, Case Western Reserve University; education, law, religion.

Athletics Member NCAA. All Division I except football (Division I-AA). *Intercollegiate sports:* baseball M(s), basketball M(s)/W(s), cheerleading M(c)/W(c), crew M(c)/W(s), cross-country running M(s)/W(s), golf M, ice hockey M(c), lacrosse M(c)/W(c), rugby M(c)/W(c), sailing M(c)/W(c), soccer M(s)/W(s), softball W(s), squash M, swimming and diving M(s)/W(s), tennis M(s)/W(s), track and field M(s)/W(s), ultimate Frisbee M(c)/W(c), volleyball W(s), water polo M(s). *Intramural sports:* badminton M/W, baseball M, basketball M/W, cross-country running M/W, fencing M/W, field hockey M/W, football M/W, golf W, racquetball M/W, skiing (cross-country) M/W, skiing (downhill) M/W, soccer M/W, softball M/W, squash M/W, swimming and diving M/W, tennis M/W, volleyball M/W.

Costs (2004–05) *Comprehensive fee:* $37,295 includes full-time tuition ($26,200), mandatory fees ($847), and room and board ($10,248). *Part-time tuition:* $875 per credit. *Required fees:* $40 per term part-time. *College room only:* $6615. Room and board charges vary according to board plan, housing facility, and location.

Financial Aid In 2003, 554 non-need-based awards were made. *Average percent of need met:* 76%. *Average financial aid package:* $18,363. *Average need-based loan:* $4262. *Average need-based gift aid:* $13,771. *Average non-need-based aid:* $8276.

Contact: Director: Dr. Harry P. Nasuti, Fordham University, Bronx, New York 10458; *Telephone:* 718-817-3212; *Fax:* 718-817-4002; *E-mail:* nasuti@fordham.edu

Hartwick College
Hartwick College Honors Program
Oneonta, New York

Hartwick College Honors Program *provides outstanding students diverse opportunities to broaden and deepen their liberal arts and sciences education, enhance the intellectual rigor of their curriculum, and participate in a community of scholars within the greater College community. The Honors Program encourages students from all majors to set high standards for themselves that reflect their commitment to academic excellence. The program is flexible enough so that each participant experiences a broad range of academic projects. The privilege of becoming an honors student is matched by the responsibility the student assumes in designing and carrying out a demanding and coherent program of study.*

Key components of the program are the four student-designed Honors Challenges (scholarly or creative projects pursued in regularly offered courses or through independent collaboration with faculty members or other honors students) and an optional, interdisciplinary Honors Seminar that brings honors students together during the junior or senior year to explore an issue of contemporary significance. Students who successfully complete these elements of the program and maintain a cumulative GPA of at least 3.5 (out of 4.0) graduate with College Honors.

Honors Challenges encourage students to connect their intellectual passions with other academic disciplines to make greater sense of their liberal arts education. Working closely with a professor on traditional or research Honors Challenges, an honors student learns how to propose an individualized intellectual project, see the project through to completion, and summarize it in an abstract. These abstracts, which record the student's achievements in the program, can be valuable additions to a student's college portfolio.

Honors students may have the opportunity to live in an honors floor and to participate in various honors activities, such as pizza parties and trips to Boston or New York City. Honors students also

enjoy early preregistration for courses and discounts on books (other than required) ordered through the College bookstore. They are eligible to participate in National Collegiate Honors Council conventions and Honors Semesters Abroad. Students who complete the program are recognized on their transcripts and at commencement as graduating with College Honors. Founded in 1982, the program currently has 100 honors students.

Participation Requirements: The Honors Program Co-Directors monitor each student's progress toward meeting the standards for graduating with College Honors and advise any student who is falling behind in meeting those requirements. Students admitted to the program at any time prior to their sophomore year are expected to show progress by completing at least one Honors Challenge during the sophomore year. The Honors Program Committee recommends to the faculty members that those honors students who have completed the Honors Program be awarded College Honors upon graduation. To earn that special recognition of achievement, honors students must successfully complete four Honors Challenges, distributed across the three academic divisions of Hartwick College, and earn a GPA of at least 3.5. Students who graduate with College Honors are entitled to wear an honors gold cord and an honors pin at commencement.

The Honors Program Committee consists of 4 elected members of the faculty, with at least 1 member representing each division of the College. The Honors Committee also includes, as voting members, the Honors Program Co-Directors (appointed by the Vice President for Academic Affairs) and 4 honors students. The committee, with the assistance of the Honors Program Co-Directors, is responsible for programmatic changes, reviewing Honors Proposals, and monitoring all elements of the program.

Admission Process: Incoming students who have been awarded Oyaron, Charlotte Miller, Cooper, or Abraham L. Kellogg Scholarships are, upon admission, invited to apply to the Honors Program. The Hartwick College Admissions Office may also nominate exceptional transfer students to the Honors Program Committee. Matriculated students are invited to apply to the Honors Program if they have completed a minimum of five college-level courses with a cumulative GPA of 3.5 or better. Advanced Placement courses prior to matriculation at Hartwick do not count toward the five college-level courses.

Scholarship Availability: The College awards several academic scholarships.

Campus Overview

Independent 4-year, founded 1797 • **Coed** 1,479 undergraduate students, 96% full-time, 57% women, 43% men.

Undergraduates 1,421 full-time, 58 part-time. Students come from 30 states and territories, 34 other countries, 36% are from out of state, 5% African American, 1% Asian American or Pacific Islander, 4% Hispanic American, 0.8% Native American, 3% international, 3% transferred in, 86% live on campus.

Faculty *Total:* 154, 68% full-time, 68% with terminal degrees. *Student/faculty ratio:* 12:1.

Academic Programs *Special study options:* accelerated degree program, advanced placement credit, double majors, honors programs, independent study, internships, off-campus study, part-time degree program, services for LD students, student-designed majors, study abroad. *ROTC:* Army (c), Air Force (c). *Unusual degree programs:* 3-2 engineering with Clarkson University, Columbia University.

Athletics Member NCAA. All Division III except soccer (Division I), water polo (Division I). *Intercollegiate sports:* baseball M, basketball M/W, cross-country running M/W, equestrian sports W, field hockey W, football M, golf M/W, ice hockey M(c), lacrosse M/W, rugby M(c), soccer M(s)/W, softball W, swimming and diving M/W, tennis M/W, track and field M/W, volleyball W, water polo M(c)/W(s). *Intramural sports:* archery M/W, badminton M/W, basketball M/W, cross-country running M/W, equestrian sports M/W, football M/W, golf M/W, racquetball M/W, soccer M/W, squash M/W, swimming and diving M/W, table tennis M/W, tennis M/W, track and field M/W, volleyball M/W, water polo M/W.

Costs (2005–06) *Comprehensive fee:* $33,960 includes full-time tuition ($26,480) and room and board ($7480). *College room only:* $3940. Room and board charges vary according to board plan and housing facility.

Financial Aid In 2002, 298 non-need-based awards were made. *Average percent of need met:* 82%. *Average financial aid package:* $20,000. *Average need-based loan:* $4110. *Average need-based gift aid:* $10,718. *Average non-need-based aid:* $12,440.

Contact: Hartwick Honors Program Co-Directors: Dr. Margaret Schramm and Dr. Gary E. Stevens, 5th Floor, Yager Hall, Hartwick College, Oneonta, New York 13820; *E-mail:* schrammm@hartwick.edu or stevensg@hartwick.edu; *Web site:* http://www.hartwick.edu/honors/

Hilbert College
Honors Program
Hamburg, New York

The Honors Program at Hilbert College, which is contract-based, offers students an opportunity for academic enrichment and personal development. The program allows students to enroll in regular classes and fulfill honors credit requirements by completing advanced work—called in lieu of projects—that is designed by the faculty members teaching those classes. These special projects allow students to have the experience of working one-on-one with the highly credentialed honors faculty members, both within and outside the student's major, from the first semester that the student enrolls.

In addition to the special attention honors students receive at Hilbert College, participants in the program have senior student mentors for the first semester and personal advisement by members of the honors faculty and by faculty members within the student's major.

Started in 2000, the program currently enrolls approximately 20 students, with plans to expand.

Participation Requirements: Students are required to complete 24 credit hours of honors-related course work over four years. (Requirements for transfer students are adjusted accordingly.) These courses are divided equally between lower- and upper-level courses within the major and between lower- and upper-level liberal arts elective courses.

In their first year in the program, students enroll in an Honors Colloquium. The course content is multidisciplinary, and the course structure is discussion-oriented. Each semester, the course focuses on the examination of three important and sometimes volatile issues within the contemporary intellectual community. Through the examination of these issues, the course introduces students to the nature and rigors of intellectual investigation and debate both between and within disciplines.

In their senior year, students participate in a Capstone Colloquium, a culmination of their honors experience, in which they present a version of one of their in lieu of projects to an audience composed of the Honors Council and other interested members of the College community.

Students must also complete 20 hours of community service per academic year and maintain a minimum GPA to remain in good standing in the program.

Students who complete all of the requirements for the program are recognized at the annual academic honors banquet and at commencement and with an indication of honors status on their transcripts.

Admission Process: Eligible students for the program must have the equivalent of at least a 3.5 cumulative average, must be enrolled as full-time day students, and must apply before the first semester of their junior year. The application, which is reviewed by the Honors Council, includes a personal essay and a letter of recommendation. There is a rolling admission process.

Scholarship Availability: Various private benefactors and Hilbert College provide funding for grants and scholarships that are need-based or merit-based. Merit-based aid is given to students in recognition of special skills, talent, or academic ability. Non-need-based aid may also be awarded based on other criteria, such as field of study, ethnicity, or class level.

Campus Overview

Independent 4-year, founded 1957 • **Coed** 1,108 undergraduate students, 72% full-time, 63% women, 37% men.

Undergraduates 799 full-time, 309 part-time. Students come from 6 states and territories, 2 other countries, 0.7% are from out of state, 4% African American, 0.7% Asian American or Pacific Islander, 2% Hispanic American, 1% Native American, 0.2% international, 14% transferred in, 10% live on campus.

Faculty *Total:* 101, 43% full-time, 36% with terminal degrees. *Student/faculty ratio:* 16:1.

Academic Programs *Special study options:* academic remediation for entering students, advanced placement credit, cooperative education, honors programs, independent study, internships, part-time degree program, services for LD students, summer session for credit.

Athletics Member NCAA. All Division III. *Intercollegiate sports:* baseball M, basketball M/W, cross-country running M/W, golf M/W, soccer M/W, softball W, volleyball M/W. *Intramural sports:* baseball M, basketball M/W, bowling M/W, cheerleading W, football M/W, golf M, ice hockey M(c), lacrosse M(c), skiing (downhill) M(c)/W(c), soccer M/W, softball W, table tennis M/W, volleyball M/W.

Costs (2005–06) *Comprehensive fee:* $19,680 includes full-time tuition ($13,750), mandatory fees ($550), and room and board ($5380). Full-time tuition and fees vary according to course load. Part-time tuition: $322 per credit hour. Part-time tuition and fees vary according to course load. *Required fees:* $13 per credit hour part-time, $30 per term part-time. *College room only:* $2350. Room and board charges vary according to board plan and housing facility.

Financial Aid 55 Federal Work-Study jobs (averaging $1718). In 2004, 82 non-need-based awards were made. *Average percent of need met:* 76%. *Average financial aid package:* $9603. *Average need-based loan:* $4116. *Average need-based gift aid:* $6012. *Average non-need-based aid:* $8983.

Contact: Director: Dr. Amy Smith, Honors Program, Hilbert College, 5200 South Park Avenue, Hamburg, New York 14075; *Telephone:* 716-649-7900 Ext. 354; *Fax:* 716-649-0702; *E-mail:* asmith@hilbert.edu; *Web site:* http://www.hilbert.edu/academics/honors.asp

Hofstra University
Hofstra University Honors College
Hempstead, New York

Hofstra University Honors College (HUHC) provides a rich academic and social experience for students who show both the potential and the desire to excel. Each year, HUHC invites more than one hundred new students to join our growing scholarly community. HUHC students can elect to study in any of the University's more than 100 major programs; students are involved in all fields of advanced study, including premedical, prelaw, engineering, business, communications and media, arts, humanities, and social sciences.

HUHC takes full advantage of the uniqueness of Hofstra University, the wealth of opportunity associated with large universities combined with the personality and individual attention one seeks

in a small college. The Honors College curriculum begins with a carefully coordinated sequence of courses, Culture and Expression, that introduces students to college-level intellectual inquiry and provides an arena where the humanities and social science disciplines interact and illuminate one another. Taught by some of Hofstra's most distinguished teacher-scholars, Culture and Expression is the common focal point of the first-year student's experience in HUHC. In addition to Culture and Expression, first-year students may choose to do honors work in science, mathematics, and other areas.

After the first year, students pursue honors work via honors seminars, honors-only sections of departmental courses, and honors options. The honors seminars and sections are deliberately small, consisting of 15 to 20 students, and designed to maximize student involvement. Honors-options are tutorial-based enhancements to regular Hofstra classes. As they progress in their fields of specialization, students are encouraged to work one-on-one with faculty members to create an individualized honors curriculum. This structure encourages motivated and talented students to do honors-level work in the fields of study to which they are most deeply committed.

Outside the classroom, HUHC has built a welcoming and supportive social structure for its students, both those who choose to reside on the Hofstra campus and those who commute. Resident students may live in Honors House, a residential complex with social and community-building programs specifically designed for high-achieving students. Each year, specially chosen Hofstra faculty members serve as Honors College mentors. These mentors maintain regular hours both in the residence hall and elsewhere on campus and are dedicated to helping individual students make a satisfying transition to college life.

With Manhattan only a half hour away by train, Hofstra's honors students do not need to choose between the comforts of campus life and the vibrancy of New York City. HUHC sponsors regular trips to museums, concerts, plays, professional sports, and other events in Manhattan and elsewhere, usually with discounted or free tickets. Even closer to home, the Hofstra campus hosts more than five hundred cultural events each year, including professional quality theater and music events, master classes, lectures by prominent scholars and cultural figures, parties, movies, and other fun events.

Participation Requirements: The 30-credit HUHC curriculum is fully compatible with all Hofstra majors. The first 15 credits consist of the 12-credit, first-year course Culture and Expression, and one 3-credit HUHC seminar. All Culture and Expression credits are counted toward fulfillment of the University's core curriculum requirements. The remaining 15 honors credits can be earned through any combination of HUHC seminars, sections, and honors-option courses that are consistent with the student's own academic objectives. All HUHC students are encouraged to undertake a senior honors thesis/project as a capstone to their honors experience at Hofstra.

Students must maintain a GPA of 3.4 and make timely progress toward completing both their major and honors requirements to remain in good standing in HUHC. Those who fall below these standards are given time and mentoring to help them return to good standing.

The designation Honors College Graduate is awarded to graduating students who complete the 30-credit curriculum and have a cumulative GPA of 3.4 or higher at graduation. The designation Honors College Graduate with Distinction is awarded to graduating students who complete the 30-credit curriculum, are awarded departmental honors in their major, and have a cumulative GPA of 3.6 or higher at graduation. An 18-credit designation Honors College Associate is available for matriculating Hofstra students and for transfer students. It is awarded to graduating students who have completed at least 18 credits of honors, including one HUHC seminar, and have a GPA of 3.4 or higher at graduation.

Admission Process: The entering first-year class of Honors College students is chosen from among students already accepted to Hofstra University. Because Honor's College's aim is to identify the top candidates, there are no hard and fast entrance criteria. In considering candidates, the Office of Admission and the Honors College Office review high school GPA (and rank, if available), standardized test scores (SAT or ACT), the rigor of the student's high school program, extracurricular and service activities, recommendations, and the candidate's expressed interest in joining HUHC (as indicated on the Hofstra application or otherwise).

The average HUHC student in the fall 2004 entering class had a 1306 combined SAT score. Seventy-eight percent graduated in the top 10 percent of their high school class. Seventy-eight percent were members of the National Honors Society; 94 percent were members of other honor societies, such as math, Latin, and French; 30 percent were varsity athletes; and 62 percent have substantial community or volunteer work.

Scholarship Availability: Every student invited to join HUHC is offered a competitive financial aid package by the University Office of Financial Aid. To retain the Honors College component of this award, students must meet published financial aid eligibility requirements and complete the Culture and Expression course in their first two years.

Campus Overview

Independent university, founded 1935 • **Coed** 9,053 undergraduate students, 89% full-time, 54% women, 46% men.

Undergraduates 8,067 full-time, 986 part-time. Students come from 48 states and territories, 51 other countries, 27% are from out of state, 10% African American, 4% Asian American or Pacific Islander, 8% Hispanic American, 0.1% Native American, 2% international, 8% transferred in, 44% live on campus.

Faculty *Total:* 1,256, 41% full-time, 57% with terminal degrees. *Student/faculty ratio:* 14:1.

Academic Programs *Special study options:* accelerated degree program, adult/continuing education programs, advanced placement credit, double majors, English as a second language, external degree program, freshman honors college, honors programs, independent study, internships, part-time degree program, services for LD students, student-designed majors, study abroad, summer session for credit. *ROTC:* Army (b).

Athletics Member NCAA. All Division I except football (Division I-AA). *Intercollegiate sports:* baseball M(s), basketball M(s)/W(s), cross-country running M(s)/W(s), field hockey W(s), golf M(s)/W(s), lacrosse M(s)/W(s), soccer M(s)/W(s), softball W(s), tennis M(s)/W(s), volleyball W(s), wrestling M(s). *Intramural sports:* badminton M/W, basketball M/W, cheerleading M(c)/W(c), crew M(c)/W(c), equestrian sports M(c)/W(c), football M/W, ice hockey M(c)/W(c), lacrosse M(c)/W(c), rugby M(c)/W(c), soccer M/W, softball M/W, table tennis M/W, tennis M/W, ultimate Frisbee M(c)/W(c), volleyball M/W, weight lifting M/W.

Costs (2004–05) *Comprehensive fee:* $29,012 includes full-time tuition ($19,010), mandatory fees ($1002), and room and board ($9000). Full-time tuition and fees vary according to course load and program. Part-time tuition: $615 per semester hour. Part-time tuition and fees vary according to course load and program. *Required fees:* $155 per term part-time. *College room only:* $5900. Room and board charges vary according to board plan and housing facility.

Financial Aid 510 Federal Work-Study jobs (averaging $1965). 2,900 state and other part-time jobs (averaging $1800). In 2004, 1079 non-need-based awards were made. *Average financial aid package:* $11,400. *Average need-based loan:* $6600. *Average need-based gift aid:* $11,100. *Average non-need-based aid:* $6400.

Contact: Dean J. Stephen Russell, Honors College, Hofstra University, Hempstead, New York 11549-1000; *Telephone:* 516-463-4842; *E-mail:* honors@hofstra.edu; *Web site:* http://www.hofstra.edu

Hunter College
CUNY Honors College at Hunter College
New York, New York

*T*he CUNY Honors College at Hunter College (CHC at Hunter) nurtures and supports outstanding students. Open to students of high intellectual ability with a proven record of excellence in high school, it affords students an Honors education that includes a full tuition scholarship, study grant support, and the opportunity to take part in courses and activities at all the member institutions of the City University of New York. It also offers its participants the opportunity to study with faculty members who have indicated an interest in working with exceptional undergraduate students. Membership in the CHC at Hunter is compatible with and complementary to membership in the Thomas Hunter Honors Program (THHP), described elsewhere in this volume, but those students participating in both programs are expected to meet the requirements imposed by each of them.

Fostering critical and integrative thinking and developing the students' capacity for analytic writing are primary goals of the CUNY Honors College. The Honors College also encourages students to be intellectually creative, to become producers of knowledge, and to search for new solutions to seemingly intractable problems. In support of these goals, the Honors College provides students with a laptop computer and broadband access to help with their research, in addition to the full resources of Hunter College and the City University of New York.

Regular and frequent advising and the development of personal knowledge of the students are crucial to the success of the CHC at Hunter. This support follows the students through their careers at Hunter and includes mentoring for those who decide to pursue advanced or professional degrees. Students are expected to take advantage of opportunities for travel, original research, and professional internships. Faculty advisers help students to select appropriate postgraduate institutions, search out fellowship support, and prepare applications. Participation in the Honors College increases the chances of admission to the graduate and professional schools of its students' choice, and also leads to productive careers in the arts, the sciences, and in other professions. The CHC at Hunter began with the fall 2001 semester and currently enrolls 220 students.

Participation Requirements: Students in the Honors College work within an honors system, which requires compliance with both the letter and the spirit of the Good Standing Policy. During their stay in the Honors College, students are required to take four interdisciplinary honors seminars in sequence, one during each semester of their first two years in the program; a passing grade in each of these four seminars is required for retention in the program. The seminar topics are organized around the institutions and people of New York City. Students choose a minimum of four additional honors courses during their four years of study. Students are expected to achieve a minimum overall 3.3 GPA by the end of their freshman year and a GPA of at least 3.5 by the end of their sophomore year; the minimum GPA must be maintained until graduation. They are required to attend a number of cross-campus City University events. Students must also fulfill Hunter College general education and graduation requirements. All student programs must be approved every semester by an adviser. Students who maintain good standing graduate with a B.A. or B.S. from Hunter College and with "City University Honors College" and "University Scholar" on their transcripts and on their diplomas.

Scholarship Availability: All students accepted to the CUNY Honors College receive full tuition scholarships. Students accepted to CHC at Hunter are also offered a dormitory room free of charge.

Admission Process: Admission to the CHC at Hunter College is by application to the University Application Processing Center. The Honors College accepts applications only for freshman admissions in the fall term. Midterm and transfer applications are not accepted.

Students may apply to the Honors College at only one participating CUNY college. The application includes an essay, recommendations, high school transcripts, and SAT or ACT scores; all parts of the application are considered by the Hunter College Admissions Committee. In 2004, the mean CAA (Cumulative High School Academic Average) of applicants was 93.5, and the mean SAT I total was 1365. Application deadlines are November 1 for early decision and December 15 for regular decision.

Campus Overview

State and locally supported comprehensive, founded 1870, part of City University of New York System • **Coed** 15,361 undergraduate students, 67% full-time, 69% women, 31% men.

Undergraduates 10,318 full-time, 5,043 part-time. Students come from 35 states and territories, 153 other countries, 3% are from out of state, 15% African American, 16% Asian American or Pacific Islander, 21% Hispanic American, 0.2% Native American, 7% international, 9% transferred in, 1% live on campus.

Faculty *Total:* 1,358, 47% full-time. *Student/faculty ratio:* 17:1.

Academic Programs *Special study options:* advanced placement credit, distance learning, double majors, English as a second language, freshman honors college, honors programs, independent study, internships, off-campus study, part-time degree program, services for LD students, student-designed majors, study abroad, summer session for credit. *Unusual degree programs:* 3-2 anthropology, economics, English, history, mathematics, music, physics, sociology.

Athletics Member NCAA. All Division III. *Intercollegiate sports:* basketball M/W, cross-country running M/W, fencing M/W, gymnastics W, soccer M, swimming and diving W, tennis M/W, track and field M/W, volleyball M/W, wrestling M. *Intramural sports:* basketball M/W, cross-country running M/W, gymnastics M/W, racquetball M/W, rugby M, soccer M/W, swimming and diving M/W, tennis M/W, volleyball M/W.

Costs (2004–05) *Tuition:* state resident $4000 full-time, $170 per credit part-time; nonresident $360 per credit part-time. *Required fees:* $329 full-time, $96 per term part-time. *Room only:* $2600. Room and board charges vary according to housing facility.

Financial Aid *Average financial aid package:* $4809.

Contact: Coordinator: Ms. Sandra Pryor, Room 140 North, Hunter College, CUNY, 695 Park Avenue, New York, New York 10021; *Telephone:* 212-650-3556; *Fax:* 212-650-3846; *E-mail:* honorscollege@hunter.cuny.edu

Hunter College
Thomas Hunter Honors Program
New York, New York

*T*he Thomas Hunter Honors Program (THHP) nurtures and supports outstanding students who wish to challenge themselves through interdisciplinary study. The program may be combined with, or replace, a formal departmental major or minor. Open to students of high intellectual ability and interdisciplinary interests who are pursuing a B.A. degree and have a proven record of excellence at Hunter, the program permits the students to replace some of the College's general education requirements with a special honors curriculum under the supervision of the Council on Honors, the faculty body that governs the program. The program also offers its participants the opportunity to study with faculty members who have indicated an interest in working with exceptional undergraduate students who have interdisciplinary interests. Membership in the THHP is compatible with and complementary to membership in the Hunter Chapter of the CUNY Honors College, described elsewhere in this volume; but those students participating in both programs are expected to meet the requirements imposed by each of these.

Students selected for the THHP must show evidence of high academic potential, diversified interests and intellectual energy, and sufficient maturity to plan and complete an individualized program of study in consultation with an appropriate faculty adviser. Students in the program are of a wide range of ages and come from diverse ethnic, national, and educational backgrounds. The Program provides a focus for the students, offering the chance to interact with other students whose scholarly interests may be different from theirs but who share their commitment to intellectual endeavor. During their stay in the program, students are required to take three interdisciplinary or multidisciplinary colloquia, the topics of which change every semester. Students choose from among the five or six colloquia that are offered every semester and are reserved for them. These courses offer breadth of exposure and demonstrate how knowledge gained from a variety of disciplines can be related and integrated in an effort to understand complex processes and phenomena. Fostering critical and integrative thinking and developing students' capacity for analytic writing are primary goals of the program. The program also encourages students to be intellectually creative, to become producers of knowledge, and to search for new solutions to seemingly intractable problems.

Regular and frequent advising and the development of personal knowledge of the students are crucial to the success of the program. This support follows the students through their careers at Hunter and includes mentoring for those who decide to pursue advanced or professional degrees. Council members encourage students to find and take advantage of opportunities for travel, original research, and professional internships. Faculty advisers also help students to select appropriate postgraduate institutions, search out fellowship support, and prepare applications. Participation in the program increases the chances of admission to the graduate and professional schools of its students' choice and also leads to productive careers in the arts, the sciences, and in other professions.

Participation Requirements: The THHP requires that students maintain breadth in their programs, create a significant pattern of courses in at least two academic areas (humanities and arts, social sciences, sciences, and mathematics), and take at least one laboratory science course. Students must also successfully complete three special interdisciplinary honors colloquia and maintain a 3.5 minimum cumulative average until their final certification to the program. Certification occurs when the Council decides that the student's continuing academic distinction and promise warrant permanent membership in the THHP. Students must also fulfill certain College graduation requirements, including English composition, foreign language, and Pluralism and Diversity. All student programs must be approved every semester by a Council adviser. Students wishing to design their own interdisciplinary major may do so in consultation with the appropriate Council adviser. Most students in the program, however, elect to fulfill the requirements for a specific departmental major. These students abide by the departmental criteria for their major and minor and are expected to do honors work in their major. All students in the THHP graduate with a B.A. and with "Special Honors Curriculum" listed as their major. Those who also have a departmental major graduate with "Special Honors Curriculum/Specific Department" on their transcript.

Scholarship Availability: In recent years, the THHP has been able to offer a small number of substantial scholarships to students certified in the program. The program also offers several small endowed prizes to its graduating seniors: the Class of '44 Prize, the John Potter Memorial Prize, and the Anne Blatt Prize. In addition, many THHP students also participate in the MMUF (Mellon-Mays Undergraduate Fellowship), the MBRS (Minority Biomedical Research Support), MARC (Minority Access to Research Careers), and COR (Career Opportunities in Research and Education) programs.

Admission Process: The THHP is open only to students pursuing a first B.A. degree (or, in some instances, a first combined B.A./M.A. or B.A./M.S. degree). Premed and prelaw students are eligible, but those students pursuing a professional degree or narrowly concentrating in studio/performance/applied work, are not. To be eligible to be considered for the THHP, students must have achieved a minimum 3.65 cumulative average over a significant number of Hunter credits. Students are invited to a one-hour interview in groups of 2 or 3 with 2 Council interviewers. Students are admitted to the program on the basis of this interview, their transcript, a graded academic writing sample, and answers to a questionnaire. The transcript and interview must show commitment to a broad, interdisciplinary approach to learning. The writing sample must demonstrate, in terms of both form and content, that the student would be able to fare well in the honors colloquia, all of which are graded primarily on papers rather than on exams. Some students with relatively few credits or with a narrow record may be asked to "come back" for another interview when the student has a fuller or more varied record or can present a more convincing paper as a writing sample.

Campus Overview

State and locally supported comprehensive, founded 1870, part of City University of New York System • **Coed** 15,361 undergraduate students, 67% full-time, 69% women, 31% men.

Undergraduates 10,318 full-time, 5,043 part-time. Students come from 35 states and territories, 153 other countries, 3% are from out of state, 15% African American, 16% Asian American or Pacific Islander, 21% Hispanic American, 0.2% Native American, 7% international, 9% transferred in, 1% live on campus.

Faculty *Total:* 1,358, 47% full-time. *Student/faculty ratio:* 17:1.

Academic Programs *Special study options:* advanced placement credit, distance learning, double majors, English as a second language, freshman honors college, honors programs, independent study, internships, off-campus study, part-time degree program, services for LD students, student-designed majors, study abroad, summer session for credit. *Unusual degree programs:* 3-2 anthropology, economics, English, history, mathematics, music, physics, sociology.

Athletics Member NCAA. All Division III. *Intercollegiate sports:* basketball M/W, cross-country running M/W, fencing M/W, gymnastics W, soccer M, swimming and diving W, tennis M/W, track and field M/W, volleyball M/W, wrestling M. *Intramural sports:* basketball M/W, cross-country running M/W, gymnastics M/W, racquetball M/W, rugby M, soccer M/W, swimming and diving M/W, tennis M/W, volleyball M/W.

Costs (2004–05) *Tuition:* state resident $4000 full-time, $170 per credit part-time; nonresident $360 per credit part-time. *Required fees:* $329 full-time, $96 per term part-time. *Room only:* $2600. Room and board charges vary according to housing facility.

Financial Aid *Average financial aid package:* $4809.

Contact: Coordinator: Ms. Sarah Jeninsky, Thomas Hunter Honors Program, Room 1421 West, Hunter College, 695 Park Avenue, New York, New York 10021; *Telephone:* 212-772-4127; *Fax:* 212-650-3490; *E-mail:* thhp@hunter.cuny.edu; *Web site:* http://www.hunter.cuny.edu/honors

Iona College
Honors Degree Program
New Rochelle, New York

The Iona College Honors Degree Program is designed to meet the educational needs of the most able and highly motivated students at Iona. Grounded in a challenging curriculum, the program offers gifted students the resources and opportunities to develop their talents and to perform at the peak of their capabilities. The course of study is designed to develop intellectual curiosity, analytical abilities, and awareness of ethical and civic responsibilities. The program encourages the development of a small nucleus of independent learners able to inspire each other academically and fosters a sense of self-respect in students, encouraging them to stretch their abilities in pursuit of lifelong learning, independent thinking, and personal fulfillment.

The curriculum promotes an appreciation and understanding of the interrelatedness of knowledge and culture by providing a wide range of interdisciplinary courses and opportunities to study abroad. Students in the program take specially designed honors course offerings, advanced courses, and engage in independent research under the guidance of faculty mentors. Small class sizes of approximately 15 encourage student participation and promote a close student-faculty relationship. Students are offered close individual guidance, both academically and in terms of career preparation. There is a faculty committee that works with students who are interested in applying for competitive grants and fellowships. The committee also advises them regarding graduate and professional studies. A career mentoring program affords students a unique chance to explore career opportunities by matching them with appropriate alumni/alumnae or corporate liaison. Students may major in any discipline in the School of Arts and Science or the Hagan School of Business.

Participants in the Honors Degree Program enjoy other significant privileges. Students receive two tuition-free courses per academic year that may be taken in the winter of summer sessions or as sixth courses during the fall and spring semesters. These free courses can facilitate double majors, accelerate graduation, or broaden the educational experience with no financial burden. Honors students have priority registration, thereby assuring their ability to receive class preferences. A student representative from each year is elected to serve, along with faculty members and administrators, on the Honors Council, which is the policy-making body for the Honors Degree Program.

Honors students have the use of an honors study house on campus that is equipped with computers with Internet access. The facility is a comfortable place that can be used for individual work, group study, or socializing with honors students and faculty members. Students are responsible for running the house and elect representatives to serve on a house governance committee. The Honors Degree Program publishes its own newsletter, which is edited by students and contains articles of interest authored by contributing members of the program.

The program has been in existence for more than twenty years, and admits 30 freshmen each year. There are approximately 100 students currently enrolled in the program.

Participation Requirements: During freshman and sophomore years, students are required to take the Honors Humanities Seminar. Offered as four 3-credit courses, the seminar introduces students to the central concepts of philosophy, history, literature, and religious studies in an interdisciplinary fashion. In the first year, students also take Honors English Composition and Honors Logic and Critical Thinking; in the sophomore year, they also take Honors Speech. The Honors Lecture and Seminar course is required for juniors in the program. The junior seminar focuses on developing senior research topics and on advanced writing strategies. The culmination of the program is the completion of a senior thesis undertaken with a faculty mentor. Seniors present the results of their research in a conference setting open to the College community. Students complete the humanities core curriculum by taking upper level courses in philosophy, literature, history, and religious studies. To fulfill the science and mathematics core, honors students are expected to take calculus and a lab science (biology, chemistry, or physics).

To remain in the program, students must maintain at least a 3.5 cumulative GPA. Students who complete the Honors Degree Program are awarded honors medals at the end of senior year. Honors students receive special recognition during commencement exercises, and an honors seal is affixed to their diplomas. Completion of the program is noted on official transcripts.

Admission Process: High school students are recruited for the Honors Degree Program, and those admitted must have completed an Iona College admissions application. Specific requirements for the program include a minimum high school GPA of 90, minimum combined SAT I scores of 1300 or higher (or a comparable ACT score), a completed Honors Degree Program application and essay, and a personal interview. Students may apply for admission after the first or second semester of freshman year. The deadline for applying to the honors program is February 1; interviews are held in March.

Scholarship Availability: The Honors Degree Program does not directly award scholarships, but scholarships of various amounts are awarded through the Office of Admissions. Because of their high academic achievements, candidates for the Honors Degree Program qualify for Iona College scholarship assistance, which may extend to full tuition Dean's Scholarships.

Campus Overview

Independent comprehensive, founded 1940, affiliated with Roman Catholic Church • **Coed** 3,425 undergraduate students, 92% full-time, 54% women, 46% men.

Undergraduates 3,144 full-time, 281 part-time. Students come from 37 states and territories, 51 other countries, 18% are from out of state, 7% African American, 1% Asian American or Pacific Islander, 11% Hispanic American, 0.2% Native American, 2% international, 5% transferred in, 30% live on campus.

Faculty *Total:* 370, 48% full-time. *Student/faculty ratio:* 15:1.

Academic Programs *Special study options:* accelerated degree program, adult/continuing education programs, advanced placement credit, distance learning, double majors, honors programs, internships, off-campus study, part-time degree program, services for LD students, study abroad, summer session for credit. *ROTC:* Army (c). *Unusual degree programs:* 3-2 psychology.

Athletics Member NCAA. All Division I except football (Division I-AA). *Intercollegiate sports:* baseball M(s), basketball M(s)/W(s), crew M/W, cross-country running M(s)/W(s), golf M(s), lacrosse W(s), rugby M(c)/W(c), soccer M(s)/W(s), softball W(s), swimming and diving M(s)/W(s), track and field M(s)/W(s), volleyball W(s), water polo M/W(s). *Intramural sports:* basketball M/W, cheerleading M(c)/W(c), football M, softball M/W, ultimate Frisbee M/W, volleyball M/W.

Costs (2004–05) *Comprehensive fee:* $29,228 includes full-time tuition ($18,990), mandatory fees ($540), and room and board ($9698). Full-time tuition and fees vary according to class time. Part-time tuition: $630 per credit. Part-time tuition and fees vary according to class time and course load. *Required fees:* $185 per term part-time. *Room and board:* Room and board charges vary according to housing facility.

Financial Aid 438 Federal Work-Study jobs (averaging $1474). 254 state and other part-time jobs (averaging $1373). In 2004, 526 non-need-based awards were made. *Average percent of need met:* 24%. *Average financial aid package:* $13,197. *Average need-based loan:* $2983. *Average need-based gift aid:* $3160. *Average non-need-based aid:* $9704.

Contact: Director of Honors: Dr. Deborah Williams, Iona College, New Rochelle, New York 10801; *Telephone:* 914-633-2056; *Fax:* 914-637-2722; *E-mail:* dwilliams@iona.edu

Ithaca College
Humanities and Sciences Honors Program
Ithaca, New York

Based upon a spirit of inquiry, the Ithaca College Honors Program in Humanities and Sciences seeks to build an interdisciplinary academic community both in and out of the classroom. Each year,

exceptionally qualified applicants to the College's School of Humanities and Sciences are invited to apply to the Honors Program. Accepted students are eligible for a series of special seminar courses and an array of program-financed, out-of-class activities.

Honors courses are imaginative, intensive seminars, in which students accept a great degree of responsibility for their own learning. The courses center on a problem or theme that can be looked at from multiple or even conflicting perspectives. Recent topics include the American frontier, the "cultural brain," and the concept of nationhood in the twenty-first century. In the process of exploring this subject, honors students read important and original texts, test time-honored theories, and engage in an active and ongoing exchange of ideas. Dedicated to interdisciplinary education and designed to help students fulfill the School's general education requirements, the Honors Program provides the Ithaca College student with the very best the campus has to offer.

Coordinated with the required honors seminars are various out-of-class activities, including a presemester honors orientation, honors-financed trips to cultural events, and informal get-togethers with fellow students and faculty members. Incoming students are sent a book over the summer, compliments of the program, and they are encouraged to read it before the first honors gathering in the fall.

All honors students are encouraged to partake in the administration of the Honors Program itself. A student advisory committee provides crucial input on the current needs of the program, and students are invited to play a major role in matters of publicity, recruitment, and cocurricular activities.

Participation Requirements: An entering student takes an honors first-year seminar in the fall semester. Before graduation, the student will take a total of seven other honors courses: five intermediate seminars, a junior-year cultural themes seminar, and a senior-year contemporary issues seminar.

Honors students of nearly any major in humanities and sciences can complete the program. Honors requirements are designed to complement departmental requirements, including departmental honors requirements. Qualified students can complete both the schoolwide Honors Program as well as honors within a specific major.

Students successfully completing the full sequence of course work graduate with Honors in Humanities and Sciences on the official college transcript.

Admission Process: Launched in fall 1996, the Humanities and Sciences Honors Program now has a full complement of 150 students. Based on information from the Admissions Office, the Honors Program invites exceptional applicants to the School of Humanities and Sciences to apply to the program. The application process involves two writing samples, such as graded high school essays and a letter of recommendation from a high school teacher. Qualified students not originally invited into the program may apply after they have completed a semester of work at Ithaca College. Transfer students may apply and are considered on a case-by-case basis. If admitted, transfer students with associate honors degrees have a slightly different set of requirements to complete.

Scholarship Availability: Ithaca College offers different levels of merit-based scholarships to qualified applicants. Most students in the Honors Program are recipients of these merit scholarships.

Campus Overview

Independent comprehensive, founded 1892 • **Coed** 6,107 undergraduate students, 98% full-time, 57% women, 43% men.

Undergraduates 5,966 full-time, 141 part-time. Students come from 51 states and territories, 67 other countries, 52% are from out of state, 2% African American, 3% Asian American or Pacific Islander, 3% Hispanic American, 0.3% Native American, 3% international, 2% transferred in, 70% live on campus.

Faculty *Total:* 616, 72% full-time, 81% with terminal degrees. *Student/faculty ratio:* 12:1.

Academic Programs *Special study options:* accelerated degree program, adult/continuing education programs, advanced placement credit, double majors, freshman honors college, honors programs, independent study, internships, off-campus study, part-time degree program, services for LD students, student-designed majors, study abroad, summer session for credit. *ROTC:* Army (c), Air Force (c). *Unusual degree programs:* 3-2 engineering with Cornell University, Rensselaer Polytechnic Institute, Clarkson University, State University of New York at Binghamton.

Athletics Member NCAA. All Division III. *Intercollegiate sports:* baseball M, basketball M/W, crew M/W, cross-country running M/W, field hockey W, football M, gymnastics W, lacrosse M/W, soccer M/W, softball W, swimming and diving M/W, tennis M/W, track and field M/W, volleyball W, wrestling M. *Intramural sports:* basketball M/W, bowling M(c)/W(c), crew M(c)/W(c), football M, golf M/W, ice hockey M(c), rugby W(c), skiing (downhill) M(c)/W(c), soccer M/W, softball M/W, tennis M/W, volleyball M/W.

Costs (2004–05) *Comprehensive fee:* $33,394 includes full-time tuition ($23,690) and room and board ($9704). Part-time tuition: $790 per credit hour. *College room only:* $4946. Room and board charges vary according to board plan and housing facility.

Financial Aid In 2003, 541 non-need-based awards were made. *Average percent of need met:* 88%. *Average financial aid package:* $20,902. *Average need-based loan:* $5407. *Average need-based gift aid:* $13,497. *Average non-need-based aid:* $8802.

Contact: Director: James Swafford, School of Humanities and Sciences, Ithaca, New York 14850-7270; *Telephone:* 607-274-3540; *Fax:* 607-274-1876; *E-mail:* swafford@ithaca.edu; *Web site:* http://www.ithaca.edu/hs/honors

Lehman College of the City University of New York

CUNY Honors College: University Scholars Program

Bronx, New York

The City University of New York (CUNY) Honors College (CHC) began at Lehman College in 2002, and Lehman is one of CHC's seven members. CHC is administered centrally by a University Dean; each branch has a director. There a close curricular relationship with the Lehman Scholars Program (LSP), Lehman's local honors program, which began in 1980. Students are exempt from all undergraduate degree requirements but are subject to the program's requirements. Highly accomplished, curious, and high-achieving students find themselves challenged by CHC and encouraged by fellow students and faculty members to continue to grow.

CHC has New York City as the focus of its intellectual investigation. Over their initial two years, students take four seminars—open only to them. New York City offers the best laboratory in the world for the study of artistic creativity, social science, and science/technology. Individual seminars have covered such topics as the arts in New York City, the peopling (immigration) of New York City, science and technology in New York City, and New York City in the twenty-first century.

Students in CHC have New York City at their fingertips. They receive a "cultural passport," which gives them free or discounted admission to most cultural institutions, theaters, music venues, and lectures for their four years. Scholars also receive state-of-the-art laptop computers, which are considered vital for their honors communications and creativity. Students work on cross-campus projects that allow scholars from the six other colleges to conference and benefit from what everyone is working on. Scholars are grouped by staff members, and topics are drawn from the seminars. This feature makes CHC unique among all honors programs across the

nation. The cross-campus project is similar to the hub of a wheel, and it is essential to the student's journey through the Honors College. The concept is extraordinary and its execution challenging—bringing together curious, talented, and creative CHC students and helping them form networks and establish a transurban student community centered on New York City.

At Lehman, the CHC seminars average 12 students. Lehman is allotted twenty places for an entering class. Currently, there are 31 CHC scholars at Lehman. Faculty members are carefully selected; successful teaching, accessibility, student friendliness, and depth of knowledge in their field are the requisites for service in the program. Students may take courses at the other senior colleges within the University. CHC students are provided with an Honors Space, which they share with Lehman Scholars students; five computer desks are available in a separate laboratory adjacent to the Honors Space. Both rooms afford a spectacular view of the heart of the campus with its greenswards and remarkable foliage. The Honors Space is located on the top floor of the Lehman Library.

Participation Requirements: Scholars must take 12 credits of CHC honors seminars, 12 credits of additional honors seminar/courses chosen from the Lehman Scholars Program or elsewhere in the College, and 15 credits or two years of one language other than English, totaling 39 credits; depending what language level a student tests into, the number of years required is often less than two.

CHC scholars must participate either in an internship (paid or unpaid) or study abroad, or they must complete a senior essay under the tutelage of a faculty member; the senior essay may be submitted for a CHC-wide competition. This is a graduation requirement.

Admission Process: All students are required to have a GPA of at least 3.5 to be admitted to the CHC. In order to remain in the College, students must attain a minimum 3.3 GPA at the end of their first year and a minimum 3.5 GPA thereafter.

Scholarship Availability: Each scholar has access to a Study Grant program award of $7500 that may be used after their first years of study for nonpaid internships or study abroad.

Campus Overview

State and locally supported comprehensive, founded 1931, part of City University of New York System • **Coed** 8,108 undergraduate students, 62% full-time, 72% women, 28% men.

Undergraduates 5,038 full-time, 3,070 part-time. Students come from 5 states and territories, 110 other countries, 0.1% are from out of state, 35% African American, 4% Asian American or Pacific Islander, 49% Hispanic American, 0.1% Native American, 0.3% international, 13% transferred in.

Faculty *Total:* 780, 43% full-time, 53% with terminal degrees. *Student/faculty ratio:* 14:1.

Academic Programs *Special study options:* adult/continuing education programs, advanced placement credit, cooperative education, distance learning, double majors, English as a second language, freshman honors college, honors programs, independent study, internships, off-campus study, part-time degree program, services for LD students, student-designed majors, study abroad, summer session for credit. *ROTC:* Army (c). *Unusual degree programs:* 3-2 mathematics.

Athletics Member NCAA. All Division III. *Intercollegiate sports:* baseball M, basketball M/W, cross-country running M/W, soccer M, softball W, swimming and diving M/W, tennis M/W, track and field M/W, volleyball M/W, water polo M, wrestling M. *Intramural sports:* baseball M/W, basketball M, racquetball M/W, soccer M, softball M/W, tennis M/W, volleyball M/W, wrestling M.

Costs (2005–06) *Tuition:* area resident $4000 full-time, $170 per year part-time; state resident $170 per year part-time; nonresident $8640 full-time, $360 per year part-time. Full-time tuition and fees vary according to course load and program. Part-time tuition and fees vary according to course load and program. *Required fees:* $270 full-time, $270 per year part-time.

Financial Aid 437 Federal Work-Study jobs (averaging $975). In 2003, 113 non-need-based awards were made. *Average percent of need met: 65%. Average financial aid package: $3531. Average need-based loan: $1525. Average need-based gift aid: $1313. Average non-need-based aid: $1352.*

Contact: Director of Honors Programs: Gary Schwartz, Professor of Classics, 316 Library, Lehman College of the City University of New York, 250 Bedford Park Boulevard West, Bronx, New York 10468-1589; *Telephone:* 718-960-6093 or 6094; *Fax:* 718-960-6727; *E-mail:* gary.schwartz@lehman.cuny.edu or florence.aliberti@lehman.cuny.edu; *Web site:* http://www.lehman.cuny.edu

Le Moyne College
Integral Honors Program
Syracuse, New York

The Integral Honors Program at Le Moyne College offers the exceptional student an outstanding educational opportunity. While all students are required to balance courses in a major area with core humanities requirements, the Integral Honors Program student participates in an interdisciplinary sequence designed to encourage learning at an advanced level. The students enjoy the challenge presented by their peers in these honors classes. Both current students and alumni cite the atmosphere of warmth, support, collegiality, and intellectual excitement among participants as one of the chief benefits of the Integral Honors Program. All honors courses are team-taught by faculty members from different disciplines, so that students develop an appreciation for the complexity of the issues and texts studied. The capstone experience of the Integral Honors Program is the senior project, which each student initiates and pursues under the direction of a faculty mentor. A public defense of each project in the spring of senior year is a suitable finale to the student's distinguished undergraduate career.

Le Moyne College recognizes Integral Honors students by according them distinctive privileges. For example, although participants in the Integral Honors Program pay regular tuition, they have the privilege of taking extra courses without charge. (These added hours, however, may not be applied to early graduation.) From the spring of junior year through senior year, Integral Honors students enjoy extended borrowing privileges at the Noreen Reale Falcone Library. An Honors House reserved for the use of participants in the Integral Honors Program offers students a place to study, meet, or just relax.

The program serves all majors, and all are represented in its enrollment. Although the program is challenging, members find time to participate in such campus activities as student government, the performing arts, journalism, varsity and intramural athletics, campus ministry, and community service. In addition, the Integral Honors student has opportunities to participate in special curricular and cocurricular activities. In recent years, Integral Honors students have traveled to New York and Boston to visit museums and to participate in conferences, planned trips to the theater, and sponsored major lectures as well as informal discussions. Each Integral Honors class elects representatives to serve on the Student Honors Council, which has primary responsibility for initiating and planning activities for the program. The Student Honors Council also serves as an advisory body to the Director of the Integral Honors Program for the governance of the program.

A number of departments at Le Moyne offer departmental honors to qualified students, usually through the submission of a senior thesis. The departmental honors option is designed for the student who excels chiefly in the major or for the transfer student who enters Le Moyne too late to participate in the Integral Honors Program. The Integral Honors degree remains the highest distinction conferred by Le Moyne, and includes departmental honors.

The Integral Honors Program was founded in 1982, although a version of an honors program had existed since 1961. The current enrollment is 55 students.

Participation Requirements: In the freshman, sophomore, and senior years, the Integral Honors student enrolls in the honors humanities sequence, which covers developments, ideas, controversies, and classic works from antiquity to the present. This 21-hour series of courses replaces as many hours of general education (core) requirements in the humanities. Along with some lectures, the honors humanities sequence builds on discussions and student presentations, so that students become increasingly responsible for their own learning. In the junior year, the Integral Honors student takes Interdisciplinary Approaches to Knowing: Theory and Applications. One of the goals of this course is to prepare the student for the challenges of the senior project. The senior project, completed under the guidance of a professor-mentor, is the capstone of the Integral Honors Program and allows the student to demonstrate his or her scholarly or creative abilities. The program offers a music elective in alternate years that takes advantage of the rich variety of live performances of music in the area. A student must earn a grade of at least B in each Integral Honors course to maintain Integral Honors status. Although Integral Honors students typically place on the Dean's List (minimum GPA 3.5), a GPA of at least 3.25 is required for graduation with the Integral Honors degree.

Admission Process: The honors humanities sequence does not begin until spring of freshman year, so that students have an opportunity to adjust to campus life before entering the program. In October, all first-year students are invited to a meeting to learn more about the Integral Honors Program and to pick up an application for the program. Outstanding students nominated by the faculty, along with recipients of academic scholarships, receive special invitations and encouragement to apply. Recipients of Presidential scholarships, the most prestigious academic scholarships at Le Moyne, are guaranteed placement in the program should they choose to participate; many of them do. A Faculty Honors Committee comprising representatives from all academic divisions reviews the applications, including high school records, SAT and other standardized test scores, AP and other college-level work, past and current activities, midsemester grades, a writing sample, a brief statement explaining the candidate's interest in the program, and any other material the candidate may wish to supply. Although the majority of each class begins the program in the spring of freshman year, qualified students, including transfer students, are considered for admission to the sophomore class. Students who enroll at Le Moyne after completing the sophomore year are not eligible for participation in the Integral Honors Program but may be eligible for departmental honors.

Scholarship Availability: Le Moyne offers a generous array of merit-based academic scholarships, along with other forms of financial aid, through the Admissions Office. Although most students admitted to the Integral Honors Program are recipients of merit-based scholarships, Le Moyne does not require those who hold such scholarships to participate in the program.

Campus Overview

Independent Roman Catholic (Jesuit) comprehensive, founded 1946 • **Coed** 2,787 undergraduate students, 82% full-time, 63% women, 37% men.

Undergraduates 2,281 full-time, 506 part-time. Students come from 27 states and territories, 6 other countries, 6% are from out of state, 5% African American, 3% Asian American or Pacific Islander, 3% Hispanic American, 0.7% Native American, 0.9% international, 6% transferred in, 60% live on campus.

Faculty *Total:* 300, 51% full-time, 64% with terminal degrees. *Student/faculty ratio:* 13:1.

Academic Programs *Special study options:* academic remediation for entering students, accelerated degree program, adult/continuing education programs, advanced placement credit, double majors, honors programs, independent study, internships, off-campus study, part-time degree program, services for LD students, study abroad, summer session for credit. *ROTC:* Army (c), Air Force (c). *Unusual degree programs:* 3-2 engineering with Manhattan College, Clarkson University, University of Detroit Mercy; forestry with State University of New York College of Environmental Science and Forestry; physician assistant with LeMoyne College.

Athletics Member NCAA. All Division II except baseball (Division I), lacrosse (Division I). *Intercollegiate sports:* baseball M(s), basketball M(s)/W(s), cross-country running M(s)/W(s), golf M(s), lacrosse M(s)/W(s), soccer M(s)/W(s), softball W(s), swimming and diving M/W, tennis M(s)/W(s), volleyball W(s). *Intramural sports:* basketball M/W, cross-country running M/W, field hockey W(c), football M, ice hockey M(c), racquetball M/W, rugby M(c)/W(c), soccer M/W, softball M/W, volleyball M/W.

Costs (2004–05) *Comprehensive fee:* $28,040 includes full-time tuition ($19,640), mandatory fees ($510), and room and board ($7890). Part-time tuition: $417 per credit hour. Part-time tuition and fees vary according to class time. *College room only:* $4990. Room and board charges vary according to board plan and housing facility.

Financial Aid 356 Federal Work-Study jobs (averaging $1096). In 2003, 198 non-need-based awards were made. *Average percent of need met:* 85%. *Average financial aid package:* $17,840. *Average need-based loan:* $4358. *Average need-based gift aid:* $13,980. *Average non-need-based aid:* $8411.

Contact: Director: Sherilyn G. F. Smith, Le Moyne College, 1419 Salt Springs Road, Syracuse, New York 13214-1399; *Telephone:* 315-445-4470; *Fax:* 315-445-4602 or 6017; *E-mail:* smithsg@lemoyne.edu

---

Long Island University, Brooklyn Campus
University Honors Program
Brooklyn, New York

The University Honors Program at the Brooklyn Campus is a liberal arts program for students in all disciplines at the University, designed to assist them to become critical and independent thinkers. This is accomplished through an enriched core curriculum in the liberal arts, with courses usually interdisciplinary in nature, limited to 16 students, stressing student participation and independent study. The Honors Program also gives students freedom to design their own majors. The honors student body reflects the rich cultural and ethnic diversity of New York City, and the cultural advantages offered by New York are incorporated both formally and informally into every facet of the honors experience. Within the University, the Honors Program develops an active community of learners, providing opportunities for intellectual support and social interaction. Most University Honors Program students go on to graduate school or take advanced professional degrees.

The honors curriculum is divided into three components: the freshman sequence, the sophomore sequence, and advanced electives. The freshman sequence is taken by all freshmen and newcomers to honors who have not fulfilled their core requirements. It is a year-long course cluster of history, English, and philosophy in which students study a selected theme that allows the work of each discipline to be interrelated. The sophomore sequence enables students to complete their requirements in speech, psychology, social science, fine arts, and foreign languages in an honors environment. The advanced electives are interdisciplinary courses designed specifically for honors students. Offered in seminar format, the electives encourage student involvement through an emphasis on field experience, the development of original research or arts projects, and other experiential activities. In order to graduate with honors, students must complete the core courses and three advanced electives.

Transfer students who have completed their core requirements can graduate with honors by completing four advanced electives.

Distinction in honors is granted to students who complete an advanced project expanded from a paper or project originally written for an advanced honors elective. These expanded projects are developed under the guidance of a faculty mentor and a 2-member committee. Distinction in honors projects that meet with the approval of the committee and faculty mentor are presented prior to graduation in the annual distinction in honors forum, which is open to the campus community.

The Honors Program stresses experiential education by drawing on the wealth of opportunities provided by resources throughout New York City. Students are assisted in gaining internships and volunteer placements in major corporations and conduct original research projects in which the city is used as a laboratory for testing theory against practice. The Honors Program also encourages students to participate in NCHC international and national honors semesters and offers funding to support students in these semesters.

Participation in the Honors Program gives students membership in two governance boards: the Honors Advisory Board and the Student Activities Board. The Honors Advisory Board determines the Honors Program curriculum, its instructors, electives, and other honors activities. It draws its members from the faculty and students in all disciplines across the University. The Student Activities Board, a student club, sponsors activities such as poetry readings and faculty and student presentations and sponsors honors students' attendance at the National Collegiate Honors Council national and regional conferences and other NCHC events.

Students in the Honors Program can also participate in Spectrum, the literary journal of the Honors Program. Edited by honors students, it accepts fiction, poetry, essays, photographs, and art work from students, faculty members, and administrators across the campus.

There are 350 students in the program.

Participation Requirements: Students are required to have a minimum high school average of 88 percent and a minimum combined score of 1100 on the SAT. Students meeting these criteria may apply for admission and are interviewed after submitting an application. A minimum GPA of 3.0 is required for participation and graduation.

Scholarship Availability: The University Honors Scholar Award is granted, in addition to any University or departmental scholarships, to new honors students who have exhibited extraordinary merit. Honors also grants some book voucher awards for incoming freshmen and some residence hall awards for those who wish to live on campus. Long Island University offers generous academic scholarships to incoming students who have already distinguished themselves in the classroom—in high school or at another college. There is also a competitive Continuing Student Study Grant for students who have exhibited extraordinary academic performance while at the University. Campus Activity Program Grants are available for those with outstanding records who wish to work on campus to earn $2500 for each semester of the award. Generous alumni donations to the program help support student participation in NCHC honors semesters, provide additional assistance for students interested in study abroad, and support independent projects.

Campus Overview
Independent university, founded 1926, part of Long Island University • **Coed** 5,363 undergraduate students, 82% full-time, 72% women, 28% men.

Undergraduates 4,406 full-time, 957 part-time. Students come from 36 states and territories, 8% are from out of state, 42% African American, 14% Asian American or Pacific Islander, 13% Hispanic American, 0.2% Native American, 2% international, 10% transferred in.

Faculty *Total:* 320. *Student/faculty ratio:* 17:1.

Academic Programs *Special study options:* academic remediation for entering students, adult/continuing education programs, advanced placement credit, cooperative education, double majors, English as a second language, honors programs, independent study, internships, part-time degree program, services for LD students, student-designed majors, summer session for credit. *Unusual degree programs:* 3-2 physical therapy, pharmacy.

Athletics Member NCAA. All Division I. *Intercollegiate sports:* baseball M(s), basketball M(s)/W(s), cross-country running M(s)/W(s), golf M(s)/W(s), lacrosse W(s), soccer M(s)/W(s), softball W(s), tennis W(s), track and field M(s)/W(s), volleyball W(s). *Intramural sports:* baseball M, basketball M, cheerleading W, softball W, tennis M/W.

Costs (2004–05) *Comprehensive fee:* $29,272 includes full-time tuition ($20,832), mandatory fees ($1090), and room and board ($7350). Full-time tuition and fees vary according to program. Part-time tuition: $651 per credit. Part-time tuition and fees vary according to course load and program. *Required fees:* $264 per term part-time. *College room only:* $4420. Room and board charges vary according to board plan.

Financial Aid 355 Federal Work-Study jobs (averaging $4143). In 2003, 106 non-need-based awards were made. *Average percent of need met:* 48%. *Average financial aid package:* $13,159. *Average need-based loan:* $4105. *Average need-based gift aid:* $8213. *Average non-need-based aid:* $14,105.

Contact: Co-Directors: Dr. James P. Clarke and Ms. Cris Gleicher, University Honors Program, Long Island University, Brooklyn Campus, 1 University Plaza, Pratt 310, Brooklyn, New York 11201; *Telephone:* 718-780-4023; *Fax:* 718-488-1370; *E-mail:* james.clarke@liu.edu or cris.gleicher@liu.edu; *Web site:* http://www.brooklyn.liu.edu/honors/index.htm

Long Island University, C.W. Post Campus
Honors Program and Merit Fellowship
Brookville, New York

The C.W. Post Honors Program is open to highly motivated students of every major. They may enter the program as freshmen and take 30–32 total honors credits; they may enter as sophomores and take 18–20 honors credits; or they may enter as juniors for a 12- to 14-credit honors component. At every level, the course of study is designed to probe issues, deepen creativity, challenge the status quo, and open up a world of ideas and adventure. Honors courses are limited to 20 students and mingle lectures with discussion-based seminars. The curriculum includes challenging core courses (emphasizing historical and ethical perspectives in traditional disciplines that satisfy campuswide requirements) and advanced electives (reflecting current issues and faculty research or particular expertise). The Politics of Lord of the Rings, The Portrait, The Future of Global Water, Comics and The Graphic Novel, and The Selling of News are some of the most recent advanced seminar topics. Students also have the opportunity to study abroad through Long Island University's Friends World Program, SEAmester, or other academic institutions and apply some of their overseas course work toward the degree with honors. Finally, for one full year, all students in the program do research leading to a thesis in their major on a subject of their choice. They are guided in their work by an experienced faculty member and report their progress and findings in an informal colloquium. In addition to faculty mentoring, the program director serves as a general adviser to all students in the program, reviewing thesis projects as well as their academic progress toward the degree with honors. Students who complete the program receive a diploma with honors designation and wear the honors medal at commencement.

Although all honors students are recognized at commencement, several are also recognized at the annual awards ceremony. The top graduating scholars in the program receive the prestigious Charles Garrett Award and the Junior/Senior Participant's Award; the Nancy Jane Meyer Award is given to the student who has done the most distinguished thesis research. An award for service to honors may also be presented at that ceremony

Students in the Honors Program are members of the Merit Fellowship, providing a broad variety of extracurricular enrichments. During the fall semester, everyone comes together for a one-day conference on campus, with presentations by faculty members, local experts, and honors students. During the spring semester, students have a choice of attending five events drawn from a series of lectures, performances, and neighborhood explorations of New York City or undertaking 20 hours of community service.

Student government in honors is by a self-appointed Student Team that is open to all program members. The team is responsible for social and cultural events. They also play a critical academic role, serving with faculty members from every school on campus on the Honors Advisory Board, which oversees curriculum and chooses honors elective courses. Athena, the honors newsletter, is a team publication. In addition to the newsletter, students and faculty members in the program communicate through a listserv, which publishes important cultural events, deadlines, and job opportunities.

The Honors Program and Merit Fellowship members share a comfortable lounge with couches, computers, and conference space. Students gather there to study, rest, have lunch, and meet friends throughout the day. Honors artists are welcome to display their work in this area. The lounge is also used for special honors sections of College 101, a course that introduces students to college life and work.

Founded in 1963, there are currently 552 students in the program (9 percent of the undergraduate student population). The program has been an NCHC member since 1978, and many students have participated in the national organization as well as NE–NCHC regional meetings.

Participation Requirements: Students generally complete their Honors Program commitment within the 128-credit bachelor's degree program. Four-year participants must complete 30–32 credits in honors as follows: 18–20 credits in honors core classes, 6 credits in honors advanced electives, 3 credits in tutorial, and 3 credits in thesis. Three-year participants must complete 18–20 credits as follows: 6–8 credits in honors core courses, 6 credits in honors advanced electives, 3 credits in tutorial, and 3 credits in thesis. Two-year participants may take 6 credits from either core or advanced electives and then complete the 3-credit tutorial and 3-credit thesis.

Freshmen in the program must maintain a minimum 3.2 GPA; thereafter, a minimum 3.4 GPA is required for all students. Some scholarships linked to honors require a minimum 3.5 GPA. Any student who falls below the required GPA has one semester on probation in the program to recover grades

Students must maintain their specified GPA, take at least one honors component each semester, and fulfill Merit Fellowship obligations to remain in the program and continue receiving scholarships linked to honors.

Admission Process: Although there is no separate application for admission to the Honors Program and Merit Fellowship, prospective participants meet in an informal interview with the director as part of the admissions process. Admission of freshmen to honors is based on high school credentials, including academic average, program of study, SAT or ACT scores, diverse experience such as taking college or AP courses, the IB diploma, extracurricular activities, and other evidence of particular talents or interests. These all become part of the interview discussion. The program is designed for strong academic students—typically those with a 90 or higher high school average and 27+ ACT or 1200+ SAT (1800 new exam) scores. Minimum eligibility for freshman applicants is an 88 high school average and 1100 SAT, with a 550 verbal score. Students entering the program should have strong verbal skills, since the seminars require much writing, and every student in the program completes a thesis. The director is willing to consider students who fall below suggested numerical criteria on standardized tests, provided that the student has a high school average above 90. The program encourages exceptional students and recognizes that statistics do not always present an accurate picture of an individual's capability. Highly motivated students may be admitted to the program on probation at the discretion of the director.

Transfer students and continuing C.W. Post students with a GPA of at least 3.4 (freshmen 3.2) are also eligible to apply and request an interview.

Scholarship Availability: There are many categories of merit-based scholarships for students enrolled at the C.W. Post Campus. Several are contingent upon participation in the Honors Program; some carry with them an invitation to join. Freshmen are offered a range of honors-linked scholarships based on their high school credentials: National Merit Finalists (full tuition); University Scholars Award ($15,000); Academic Excellence Award ($10,000–$12,000); and Post Outstanding Scholars Award ($5000 per year based on an essay contest). An award may be held in conjunction with other awards, but the total may not exceed full tuition. Qualified students offered the Academic Incentive Award ($9000) are invited to join the program. Transfer student scholarships contingent upon participation in the Honors Program are Nassau Community College Scholarship (full tuition), Transfer Scholars Award ($12,000), and the Transfer Excellence Award ($10,000). Transfer students may also enter the essay contest to compete for the Post Outstanding Scholars Award. Qualified students offered the Transfer Achievement Award ($7000) are invited to join the program. Small study-abroad grants are also available from the Honors Program for individual students or as assistance to honors classes going abroad as part of their course.

Students receiving other University aid or currently attending C.W. Post without aid may apply for admission to the Honors Program and be considered for scholarships up to $2000 a year from the Honors Program and Merit Fellowship. Students must file a Free Application for Federal Student Aid (FAFSA) by March 15. Scholarships are renewed for the length of participation in the Honors Program/Merit Fellowship (up to four years). Scholarships from the Honors Program and Merit Fellowship are available to international students.

Students who do not wish scholarship consideration are also eligible for the Honors Program based on a qualifying high school record or minimum 3.2 GPA freshman year.

Campus Overview

Independent comprehensive, founded 1954, part of Long Island University • **Coed** 4,897 undergraduate students, 84% full-time, 63% women, 37% men.

Undergraduates 4,136 full-time, 761 part-time. Students come from 30 states and territories, 8% are from out of state, 9% African American, 2% Asian American or Pacific Islander, 7% Hispanic American, 0.3% Native American, 3% international, 11% transferred in, 30% live on campus.

Faculty *Total:* 1,018, 32% full-time. *Student/faculty ratio:* 15:1.

Academic Programs *Special study options:* academic remediation for entering students, accelerated degree program, adult/continuing education programs, advanced placement credit, cooperative education, double majors, English as a second language, honors programs, independent study, internships, off-campus study, part-time degree program, services for LD students, student-designed majors, study abroad, summer session for credit. *ROTC:* Army (c), Air Force (c). *Unusual degree programs:* 3-2 engineering with Polytechnic University, Arizona State University, Stevens Institute of Technology; respiratory therapy and pharmacy with Long Island University, Brooklyn Campus.

Athletics Member NCAA. All Division II. *Intercollegiate sports:* baseball M(s), basketball M(s)/W(s), crew M(c)/W(c), cross-country running M(s)/W(s), equestrian sports M(c)/W(c), field hockey W(s),

football M, lacrosse M(s)/W(s), soccer M(s)/W(s), softball W(s), swimming and diving W(s), tennis W(s), track and field M(s)/W(s), volleyball W(s).

Costs (2004–05) *Comprehensive fee:* $30,200 includes full-time tuition ($20,870), mandatory fees ($1090), and room and board ($8240). Full-time tuition and fees vary according to program. Part-time tuition: $651 per credit. Part-time tuition and fees vary according to course load and program. *College room only:* $5460. Room and board charges vary according to board plan.

Financial Aid 823 Federal Work-Study jobs (averaging $1620). In 2002, 960 non-need-based awards were made. *Average percent of need met:* 75%. *Average financial aid package:* $8500. *Average need-based loan:* $4000. *Average need-based gift aid:* $4500. *Average non-need-based aid:* $7000.

Contact: Director: Dr. Joan Digby, Long Island University, C.W. Post Campus, 201 Humanities Hall, 720 Northern Boulevard, Brookville, New York 11548-1300; *Telephone:* 516-299-2840; *Fax:* 516-299-2997; *E-mail:* jdigby@liu.edu; *Web site:* http://www.cwpost.liu.edu/cwis/cwp/honors/

Marist College
Honors Program
Poughkeepsie, New York

*T*he Honors Program at Marist College has a three-part mission: to encourage academic excellence, provide opportunities for cultural enrichment, and promote social and ethical responsibilities. The program offers outstanding students in all majors a variety of learning experiences in and outside the academic setting. Honors Seminars and cocurricular activities, such as field trips and lectures, bring together talented students who seek a more intensive and extensive educational experience. Promoting the adventure of intellectual pursuits, the program challenges students to achieve their academic potential as they develop into responsible citizens and leaders in an increasingly culturally complex world

The Marist College Honors Program brings together talented students in classes that often coordinate with cocurricular activities. This cultural enrichment exchange is a highlight of the program. It encourages students to move beyond standard curricula and engage in a broader range of experiences consonant with their interests. Field trips expose students to the cultural life of New York City and other sites of interest in the Northeast. The Honors Lecture, scheduled each semester, brings students into direct contact with scholars in various fields.

Participation Requirements: Honors students complete six courses—five Honors Seminars and the Honors Ethics class— over the course of four years, each with an enrollment of 15 students per seminar. The honors experience culminates in a senior honors project, which may be a product of an honors course (the student's choice and with the consent of the faculty member), an independent study taken within the confines of the honors requirements, or a capping project undertaken with the permission of the capping instructor. The project does not have to be a written essay but rather takes the form of each individual's interest and discipline requirements. The senior honors project may be a research essay, laboratory experiment/project, multimedia presentation, advertising campaign, or a portfolio of work drawn from honors courses. This project is submitted to the Honors Council six weeks before graduation and is part of an Honors Symposium held at the end of each academic year.

Participating students who successfully complete 18 honors credits and an honors project receive an honors certificate, a medallion to be worn at commencement, and special recognition on their college transcript. Once admitted to the program, a student must maintain a cumulative 3.5 GPA or better, with all honors work at the B or higher level to remain in the program. If a student's GPA drops below 3.5, the student is allowed to continue in the program on probationary status for one semester. If the cumulative GPA continues to fall below the minimum 3.5 requirement after one semester, the student must withdraw from the program. There is no reinstatement after an official withdrawal.

The Honors Seminars focus on five different but contiguous points: the self in relation to others (Versions of the Self); culture, including popular culture, fashion, and art in its various forms (The Art of Culture); the world of science, mathematics, computer science, and technology (Science, Technology, and Society); the examined life, considering issues of freedom, spirituality, human dignity, and personal responsibility within a global context (Global Engagement); and the area's own unique literary, historical, artistic, social, environmental, and political position in the Hudson River Valley (Hudson River Valley Studies). Although the content of each seminar may vary from semester to semester, the focus of the seminar remains the same.

Admission Process: Marist recruits high school students for its Honors Program at the time of their application to the College. Approximately 7 percent of each entering class is invited to join the program. Specific requirements include a minimum high school grade average of 90; minimum combined SAT scores of 1300 or comparable ACT scores; a personal essay, which is part of the application process; and a record of involvement in extracurricular activities. Students admitted to the Honors Program are eligible for the College's most competitive scholarships.

Students may also apply for admission to the program during the second semester of their freshman year or first semester of their sophomore year. Students who enter the program after their initial enrollment at the College are not eligible for any additional scholarship funding. The requirements for admission are as follows: minimum GPA of 3.5, a letter of support from a Marist faculty member, an interview with the Director of Honors, and approval of the Honors Council.

Transfer students who were enrolled in an honors program at their previous institution must present a letter of support from a faculty member at their previous institution and a transcript indicating the honors courses taken. In addition, the student must interview with the Director of Honors to assess academic standing and determine which Marist honors courses have been satisfied by those taken at the previous institution.

Scholarship Availability: Approximately 70 percent of the College's full-time students receive aid from Marist and outside sources. Marist also has merit awards for outstanding students, which are not based on financial need. Overall, the College annually awards more than $10 million in grants and scholarships from its own funds.

Campus Overview

Independent comprehensive, founded 1929 • **Coed** 4,800 undergraduate students, 89% full-time, 57% women, 43% men.

Undergraduates 4,273 full-time, 527 part-time. Students come from 37 states and territories, 19 other countries, 39% are from out of state, 4% African American, 2% Asian American or Pacific Islander, 6% Hispanic American, 0.1% Native American, 0.2% international, 75% live on campus.

Faculty *Total:* 596, 33% full-time. *Student/faculty ratio:* 15:1.

Academic Programs *Special study options:* academic remediation for entering students, accelerated degree program, adult/continuing education programs, advanced placement credit, cooperative education, distance learning, double majors, English as a second language, honors programs, independent study, internships, off-campus study, part-time degree program, services for LD students, study abroad, summer session for credit. *ROTC:* Army (b). *Unusual degree programs:* 3-2 psychology, computer science.

Athletics Member NCAA. All Division I except football (Division I-AA). *Intercollegiate sports:* baseball M(s), basketball M(s)/W(s), bowling M(c)/W(c), cheerleading M(c)/W(c), crew M/W, cross-country running M(s)/W(s), equestrian sports M(c)/W(c), fencing M(c)/W(c), ice hockey M(c), lacrosse M(s)/W(s), rugby M(c)/W(c), skiing (downhill) M(c)/W(c), soccer M(s)/W(s), softball W(s), swimming and diving M(s)/W(s), tennis M(s)/W(s), track and field M(s)/W(s), volleyball M(c)/W(c), water polo W(s). *Intramural sports:* basketball M/W, field hockey M/W, soccer M/W, softball M/W, ultimate Frisbee M/W, volleyball M/W.

Costs (2005–06) *One-time required fee:* $25. *Comprehensive fee:* $30,233 includes full-time tuition ($20,535), mandatory fees ($480), and room and board ($9218). Part-time tuition: $463 per credit. *Required fees:* $65 per term part-time. *College room only:* $5890. Room and board charges vary according to board plan and housing facility.

Financial Aid 744 Federal Work-Study jobs (averaging $2232). 506 state and other part-time jobs. In 2004, 636 non-need-based awards were made. *Average percent of need met:* 67%. *Average financial aid package:* $12,685. *Average need-based loan:* $4612. *Average need-based gift aid:* $8520. *Average non-need-based aid:* $5588.

Contact: Dr. Rose De Angelis, Marist College, School of Liberal Arts, Poughkeepsie, New York 12601; *Telephone:* 845-575-3000; *Fax:* 845-575-3560; *E-mail:* rose.deangelis@marist.edu; *Web site:* http://www.marist.edu/academics/honors/

Marymount College of Fordham University
Butler Scholars
Tarrytown, New York

The Butler Scholars program of Marymount College offers breadth, depth, and diversity. Designated sections of required core courses, specially designed seminars, and unique research studies in any discipline give academically strong students the opportunity to challenge themselves, to work closely with professors and peers, and to gain special recognition for their talents. The program is named for Mother Marie Joseph Butler, R.S.H.M., founder of the college.

The program offers sections designated as honors in core courses, which are required from each of the four programs of English, history, philosophy, and theology (two courses are available each semester); courses designated as honors from among other courses required for the core (these are available on a rotating basis); courses designated as honors designed specifically for the Butler Scholars; and the honors thesis, or other suitable culminating project, which is supervised by each academic program for each of its Butler Scholar majors. Each thesis or project is followed by an oral defense of approximately one hour, conducted by 3 faculty members in the same (or a closely related) field as the subject matter, who have read the thesis and determine if it has been successfully defended. It is recommended that students begin the thesis in the second semester of junior year (to allow for research over the summer) and complete it in the first semester of senior year.

Other benefits include: a Faculty Moderator who serves as academic adviser to the Butler Scholars (until they declare their majors) and who supervises the cocurricular and extracurricular activities that are integral to the program; a personal recommendation from the College Dean for a job or graduate study; early registration for all courses each semester; distinctive cords of Marymount Blue to be awarded at convocation and thereafter worn at Convocation and Commencement; a Dean's Dinner in Senior Week for all Butler Scholars (with seniors allowed two guests) at which Butler Scholar medals are distributed to seniors; an Honors Lounge in Butler Hall, to which all Butler Scholars receive a key, equipped with computers, study carrels, and comfortable furniture; individual (in addition to College) membership in the National Collegiate

Honors Council, with funding to attend the annual National Conference to present research; a workshop of approximately three sessions for first-semester honors juniors to prepare the student to begin the thesis in the following semester; and an annual Academic Symposium focusing on the research of all honors seniors and their mentors.

The program enrolls approximately new 20 students each year and will grow each year to reach a maximum of about 80 participants.

Participation Requirements: The program requires eight courses plus an honors thesis. Six of the courses are College core requirements. For the other core requirements students may, but are not required to, select honors sections. To continue as a Butler Scholar, each student must maintain at least a 3.5 cumulative GPA, with at least a B in each honors course. Honors courses for which a grade of B is not achieved may not be counted toward the eight required honors courses but continue to satisfy other requirements. At the end of her freshman year each student must have completed successfully at least three honors courses; at the end of Sophomore year, at least five; and at the end of Junior year, at least seven, to maintain her status as a Butler Scholar. Those students who complete all the requirements with a grade of B or better, while maintaining a minimum cumulative grade point average of 3.5, graduate with the notation *in cursu honorum* on the diploma and transcript.

Admission Process: Approximately 20 incoming freshmen are admitted to the Butler Scholars program each September, based on their GPA and SAT scores.

Scholarship Availability: Butler Scholars are awarded annual scholarships ranging from $12,000 to full tuition, as long as they maintain eligibility.

Campus Overview

Independent 4-year, founded 1907, part of Fordham University •
Suburban 25-acre campus with easy access to New York City •
Women only 1,036 undergraduate students, 88% full-time.

Undergraduates 913 full-time, 123 part-time. Students come from 33 states and territories, 12 other countries, 26% are from out of state, 17% African American, 5% Asian American or Pacific Islander, 14% Hispanic American, 0.1% Native American, 2% international, 8% transferred in, 63% live on campus.

Faculty *Total:* 170, 31% full-time, 46% with terminal degrees. *Student/faculty ratio:* 9:1.

Academic Programs *Special study options:* academic remediation for entering students, adult/continuing education programs, advanced placement credit, double majors, English as a second language, honors programs, independent study, internships, off-campus study, part-time degree program, services for LD students, student-designed majors, study abroad, summer session for credit. *Unusual degree programs:* 3-2 business administration with Fordham University, Pace University, St. Thomas Aquinas College, Richmond University in London; social work with Fordham University; education with Fordham University, optometry with State University of New York State College of Optometry, physical therapy, occupational therapy, physician assistant with Touro College, physical therapy with New York Medical College.

Athletics *Intercollegiate sports:* basketball W, equestrian sports W, soccer W, softball W, swimming and diving W, tennis W, volleyball W. *Intramural sports:* badminton W, basketball W, soccer W, table tennis W, tennis W.

Costs (2004–05) *Comprehensive fee:* $29,462 includes full-time tuition ($19,100), mandatory fees ($602), and room and board ($9760). Full-time tuition and fees vary according to student level. Part-time tuition: $635 per credit hour. Part-time tuition and fees vary according to class time. *Required fees:* $301 per term part-time. *Room and board:* Room and board charges vary according to board plan and housing facility.

Financial Aid 162 Federal Work-Study jobs (averaging $1301). In 2003, 235 non-need-based awards were made. *Average percent of*

need met: 71%. *Average financial aid package:* $15,968. *Average need-based loan:* $5752. *Average need-based gift aid:* $10,406. *Average non-need-based aid:* $7242.

Contact: Faculty Moderator (to be named), Butler Scholars, Marymount College of Fordham University, 100 Marymount Avenue, Tarrytown, New York 10591

Medaille College
Medaille College Scholars Program
Buffalo, New York

The Medaille College Scholars Program is an innovative honors program in which students with strong academic credentials and high school records of active extracurricular participation can develop the skills needed to engage challenging issues. The program combines an honors-level General Education Core curriculum with a suite of mentoring opportunities that seek to encourage vigorous intellectual inquiry, effective leadership ability, and solid social and moral commitment.

The heart of the College Scholars Program is a sequence of nine honors-level liberal arts and sciences courses developed and taught by the program's dedicated and enthusiastic faculty. Honors courses at Medaille are, of course, rigorous, but they are also designed to fit together in a unique and richly integrated sequence; in the College Scholars Program, important skills and ideas are not just introduced once and then left behind, but are reinforced in multiple courses. Thus, the close collaboration among the program's faculty members has produced a distinctive curriculum that aims to develop a deep understanding of the General Education Core's leading ideas. Students seeking entry into competitive professional fields or graduate study programs find these critical thinking tools and communication skills crucial to their success.

Medaille College is proud of its reputation for having small classes and a low student-faculty ratio; so, it is natural for students participating in the College Scholars Program to maintain close contact with their professors. The program also encourages mentoring relationships by sponsoring a variety of special events that bring honors students, faculty members, administrators, and staff members together outside of the classroom. For instance, students participating in the College Scholars Program complete a unique leadership development sequence incorporating seminars, conferences, and service, and they are expected to participate in receptions, presentations, and other cocurricular activities throughout the academic year.

Besides these classroom and mentoring opportunities, students participating in the College Scholars Program are eligible for special honors scholarships in addition to whatever other scholarship aid they may qualify for. They also benefit from a flexible registration procedure that ensures their enrollment in honors courses on schedule and in sequence, and they earn official recognition of their achievements at graduation.

The College Scholars Program builds upon the foundation of the Theodore Roosevelt Scholars Program (established in 2001) and currently enrolls approximately 60 students.

Participation Requirements: To remain in good standing with the College Scholars Program and maintain eligibility for honors scholarship support, students must register for their honors courses in a prescribed sequence as part of a full-time schedule and maintain a minimum 3.0 per semester honors GPA. In addition, Scholars students must complete the Leadership Seminar and participate in receptions, presentations, and other cocurricular mentoring activities.

To graduate with official honors recognition, students must also defend a capstone thesis (typically written for GEN 411 -

---

Baccalaureate Capstone II) and achieve an overall cumulative GPA of at least 3.0, with a 3.0 cumulative GPA in honors courses, at commencement.

Admission Process: Presently, incoming first-year day baccalaureate students who have strong academic credentials and high school records of active extracurricular participation receive automatic consideration for the program by the Medaille College Admissions Office.

Scholarship Availability: As first-time freshmen, students participating in the College Scholars Program are eligible for special honors scholarships in addition to whatever other scholarship aid they may qualify for. Many also receive Trustee, Presidential, or Dean's Scholarships.

Campus Overview

Independent comprehensive, founded 1875 • **Coed** 1,708 undergraduate students, 89% full-time, 63% women, 37% men.

Undergraduates 1,514 full-time, 194 part-time. Students come from 1 other state, 2 other countries, 17% African American, 0.2% Asian American or Pacific Islander, 3% Hispanic American, 0.6% Native American, 0.4% international, 10% transferred in, 21% live on campus.

Faculty *Total:* 297, 26% full-time, 22% with terminal degrees. *Student/faculty ratio:* 15:1.

Academic Programs *Special study options:* academic remediation for entering students, accelerated degree program, adult/continuing education programs, advanced placement credit, double majors, honors programs, independent study, internships, off-campus study, part-time degree program, services for LD students, student-designed majors, summer session for credit. *ROTC:* Army (c). *Unusual degree programs:* 3-2 sports management.

Athletics Member NCAA, NSCAA. All NCAA Division III. *Intercollegiate sports:* baseball M, basketball M/W, cheerleading M/W, cross-country running W, lacrosse M/W, soccer M/W, softball W, volleyball M/W. *Intramural sports:* basketball M/W, skiing (downhill) M/W, soccer M/W, softball M/W, table tennis M/W, tennis M/W, volleyball M/W, weight lifting M/W.

Costs (2004–05) *Comprehensive fee:* $21,120 includes full-time tuition ($14,010), mandatory fees ($310), and room and board ($6800). Full-time tuition and fees vary according to location. Part-time tuition: $467 per credit hour. Part-time tuition and fees vary according to course load. *Required fees:* $90 per term part-time. *Room and board:* Room and board charges vary according to housing facility.

Financial Aid 140 Federal Work-Study jobs (averaging $1500). In 2003, 29 non-need-based awards were made. *Average percent of need met:* 75%. *Average financial aid package:* $10,000. *Average need-based loan:* $4100. *Average need-based gift aid:* $4200. *Average non-need-based aid:* $1000.

Contact: Admissions Office, Medaille College, Buffalo, New York 14214; *Telephone:* 716-884-3281 Ext. 203. Scholars Program Faculty Director; *Telephone:* 716-884-3281; *E-mail:* scholars@medaille.edu

Mercy College
Honors Program
Dobbs Ferry, New York

T he Honors Program at Mercy College is open to all motivated day students who have General Education requirements to fulfill or room in their programs for electives. Some major courses may also be taken as an honors option.

Honors classes are conducted as seminars that emphasize a spirit of inquiry in an atmosphere of collegiality between students and faculty members. The stimulating environment encourages students to raise their academic expectations while the supportive community offers opportunities to develop new leadership capacities. Trips, special events, and service projects provide cultural experiences outside of the classroom.

Students who have taken three or more honors courses and have maintained a GPA of 3.2 or greater receive a Certificate of Membership. Students who have taken nine of more honors classes receive the Christie Scholar Award. Awards are given for scholarship, academic development, and leadership. Outstanding student papers are presented in an annual symposium to which the entire campus is invited.

The twenty-four-year-old program currently enrolls 75 students.

Participation Requirements: To be an official member of the Honors Program, a student must have taken at least three honors courses and must maintain a GPA of 3.2 or above. Members of the Honors Program are also expected to be active in the community life of the honors club.

Scholarship Availability: Mercy College offers scholarships to exceptional students. Many students in the Honors Program take advantage of these scholarships.

Campus Overview

Independent comprehensive, founded 1951 • **Coed** 6,208 undergraduate students, 29% full-time, 35% women, 65% men.

Undergraduates 1,787 full-time, 4,421 part-time. Students come from 6 states and territories, 49 other countries, 27% African American, 3% Asian American or Pacific Islander, 30% Hispanic American, 0.3% Native American, 2% international, 19% transferred in.

Faculty *Total:* 989, 24% full-time. *Student/faculty ratio:* 17:1.

Academic Programs *Special study options:* academic remediation for entering students, accelerated degree program, adult/continuing education programs, advanced placement credit, cooperative education, distance learning, double majors, English as a second language, honors programs, independent study, internships, off-campus study, part-time degree program, services for LD students, student-designed majors, study abroad, summer session for credit. *ROTC:* Air Force (c). *Unusual degree programs:* 3-2 pharmacy.

Athletics Member NCAA. All Division II. *Intercollegiate sports:* badminton M(s), baseball M(s), basketball M(s)/W(s), cross-country running M(s)/W(s), equestrian sports M(c)/W(c), golf M(s), soccer M(s)/W(s), softball W(s), tennis M(s), volleyball W(s). *Intramural sports:* basketball M/W, volleyball M/W.

Costs (2004–05) *Comprehensive fee:* $19,800 includes full-time tuition ($11,230), mandatory fees ($144), and room and board ($8426). Part-time tuition: $472 per credit. *Required fees:* $6 per credit part-time.

Contact: Director: Dr. Nancy A. Benson, Mercy College, 555 Broadway, Dobbs Ferry, New York 10522-1189; *Telephone:* 914-674-7567; *Fax:* 914-674-7433; *E-mail:* nbenson@mercy.edu

Monroe College
Honors Program
New Rochelle, New York

T he Monroe College Honors Program was established in fall 2004 to provide opportunities to the College's most academically accomplished students to engage in advanced academic work and participate in an enhanced shared intellectual experience with Monroe's most distinguished professors and guest lecturers.

In addition, the Monroe College Honors Program sponsors lectures, seminars, and workshops for Honors Program students, the entire College community, and the College's off-campus neighbors. Honors students who reside on campus may opt for assignment to the honors housing unit. Members of the Honors Program enjoy extended borrowing privileges from the campus library, use of the Honors Center for private small-group study, extended hours for research, and utilization of state-of-the-art technology.

Each semester, the Honors Program sponsors the Honors Colloquium, a scholarly and celebratory program where honors students present their projects and papers to the college community. The honors students publish an edition of the honors newsletter, The Student Examiner, twice each semester.

Participation Requirements: To earn distinction as an Honors Program graduate, students must maintain a minimum 3.5 cumulative grade point average and earn 12 honors units while pursuing their first 60 credits, usually while earning their associate degree, and an additional 12 honors units while pursuing the next 60 credits for their bachelor's degree. A student earns 3 honors units for completing a 3-credit honors-designated course with a grade of B or better. Honors units may also be earned by students completing honors work through honors contracts that are approved and monitored by the Honors Board. Honors contracts may be submitted for course enhancements, honors-level internships, and, in some cases, honors cocurricular activities.

All students entering the Honors Program must take a course entitled The Honors Experience as their first honors course. This interdisciplinary course, embedded in the social sciences, introduces students to the rigors of the Honors Program. The course uses New York City as a backdrop to study political, demographic, economic, technological, cultural, scientific, and labor issues specific to major events or time periods in the history of this remarkable metropolis. The specific themes studied vary each academic year. Faculty members with expertise in particular fields of study lecture during the semester and offer the perspective of their fields of specialization. Students are expected to complete reading assignments, participate in classroom discussions, take part in site visits, and conduct extensive research, including the use of primary source material. As a culminating assignment, students present a final project that reflects the information they have learned, both in the classroom and through their own investigation, as well as their own critical thinking and analysis. This course fosters the development of a community of scholars among the students in the program.

Students who successfully meet all the requirements of the Honors Program have a notation on their transcript and are recognized as Honors Program graduates at commencement.

Admission Process: Upon the recommendation of the Director of Admissions or the Director of the International Student Program, prospective students are considered for acceptance to the Honors Program. Students who are selected have a strong record of achievement in their high school or previous college, a recommendation from a guidance counselor or faculty member, an outstanding admissions essay and interview, strong results on the Monroe College placement exams in English and mathematics, and a record of leadership and involvement in extracurricular and cocurricular activities.

Scholarship Availability: Monroe College offers a generous array of merit scholarships, and most students who qualify for the Honors Program are scholarship recipients. Monroe does not currently offer scholarships to students solely on the basis of being accepted into the Honors Program.

Campus Overview

Proprietary primarily 2-year, founded 1983 • **Coed** 1,570 undergraduate students, 85% full-time, 69% women, 31% men.

Undergraduates 1,334 full-time, 236 part-time. Students come from 9 states and territories, 10 other countries, 2% are from out of state, 64% African American, 0.7% Asian American or Pacific Islander, 14% Hispanic American, 0.1% Native American, 13% international, 9% transferred in, 20% live on campus.

Faculty *Total:* 201, 33% full-time, 18% with terminal degrees. *Student/faculty ratio:* 20:1.

Academic Programs *Special study options:* academic remediation for entering students, adult/continuing education programs, cooperative education, English as a second language, external degree program, internships, part-time degree program, summer session for credit.

Athletics Member NJCAA. *Intercollegiate sports:* baseball M, basketball M/W, soccer M, softball W, volleyball W. *Intramural sports:* basketball M/W, bowling M/W, cheerleading W, soccer M, volleyball M/W.

Costs (2004–05) *Comprehensive fee:* $23,370 includes full-time tuition ($8760), mandatory fees ($600), and room and board ($14,010). Part-time tuition: $1095 per course. *Required fees:* $150 per term part-time. *Room and board:* Room and board charges vary according to board plan.

Financial Aid 50 Federal Work-Study jobs (averaging $4000).

Contact: Associate Academic Dean: Karenann Carty, Honors Program, Monroe College, 434 Main Street, New Rochelle, New York 10801-6410; *Telephone:* 914-632-5400; *Fax:* 914-813-1224; *E-mail:* kcarty@monroecollege.edu; *Web site:* http://www.monroecollege.edu

---

Nassau Community College
Honors Program
Garden City, New York

Nassau's rigorous Honors Program, now in its twenty-fifth year, has about 250 students in the program. Students at the College who have a GPA of 3.4 or better are also invited to take some honors classes if seats are available, bringing the number of students taking honors to about 500. The program appeals to the many talented and highly motivated students who want to develop their potential more fully as they study for the associate degree. The transfer-oriented curriculum features at its core enriched work in English, history, calculus, foreign language, philosophy, computers, and the humanities and social sciences.

More than fifty sections of challenging honors classes are offered each term in addition to several special seminars of an interdisciplinary and/or multicultural nature. This umbrella program accommodates all majors at the College and enhances transferability. All students in the program are personally advised by the Coordinator of the Program, who also writes all their letters of recommendation. In addition to the excellent honors faculty, consisting of almost all award-winning instructors for Excellence in Teaching, honors classes, because of their small size (no more than 22 students per class), allow for a great deal of personal interaction and discussion.

Over the years, as the program has continually grown and expanded, participants have the opportunity to supplement their academic work with honors-sponsored extracurricular activities, such as the Adopt-A-Class Program, the Writing Literacy Project, the Selected Scholars Program, and the Honors Club and Journal, which provide creative outlets.

Another special feature of Nassau's Honors Program is its Honors Connection Program, an outreach vehicle to the high schools. The Connection Program provides a unique opportunity to highly motivated high school juniors and seniors to take college courses for credit on campus.

Participation Requirements: To maintain membership in the program, students must keep up a 3.3 GPA each semester. The average GPA of each graduating class has been 3.6 or above. Students usually graduate with a minimum of 35 to 55 honors credits out of the mandatory 64 to 66 credits necessary for a degree. An H designation is noted on the transcript next to each honors course taken.

Admission Process: Freshmen are selected for the program based on their high school transcripts, which must reflect a minimum 90

average in English, social studies, math, and science. Students already in attendance at Nassau can enter the program after their first semester if they have achieved a GPA of 3.4 or better and have been recommended by an instructor.

Scholarship Availability: For 4 graduating Honors Program participants, a scholarship based on academic abilities and service to the program and community is available. A special Honors and Awards Ceremony to honor graduates is held each May. At this time, all honors graduates receive special certificates, and the winners of the two Honors Program Scholarships are announced. Two scholarships are also available for incoming freshmen.

Campus Overview

State and locally supported 2-year, founded 1959, part of State University of New York System • **Coed** 21,446 undergraduate students, 64% full-time, 54% women, 46% men.

Undergraduates 13,788 full-time, 7,658 part-time. 18% African American, 5% Asian American or Pacific Islander, 12% Hispanic American, 0.3% Native American, 5% international, 9% transferred in.

Faculty *Total:* 1,407, 75% with terminal degrees. *Student/faculty ratio:* 18:1.

Academic Programs *Special study options:* academic remediation for entering students, adult/continuing education programs, advanced placement credit, cooperative education, distance learning, English as a second language, honors programs, internships, off-campus study, part-time degree program, services for LD students, summer session for credit. *ROTC:* Army (c).

Athletics Member NJCAA. *Intercollegiate sports:* baseball M, basketball M/W, bowling M/W, cheerleading W, cross-country running M/W, equestrian sports M/W, football M, golf M/W, lacrosse M, soccer M/W, softball W, tennis M/W, track and field M/W, volleyball M/W, wrestling M. *Intramural sports:* badminton M/W, basketball M/W, cross-country running M/W, football M, ice hockey M, lacrosse M/W, racquetball M/W, soccer M/W, softball M/W, table tennis M/W, tennis M/W, volleyball M/W.

Costs (2004–05) *Tuition:* state resident $2900 full-time, $121 per credit part-time; nonresident $5800 full-time, $242 per credit part-time. *Required fees:* $242 full-time.

Financial Aid 400 Federal Work-Study jobs (averaging $3300).

Contact: Coordinator: Dean Carol Farber, 1 Education Drive, Garden City, New York 11530; *Telephone:* 516-572-7194

Orange County Community College

Honors Program

Middletown, New York

Orange County Community College's Honors Program is designed to offer highly motivated and talented students opportunities to more fully develop their potential by challenging them to assume control of their own intellectual development, allowing opportunities for cross-curricular learning and providing more in-depth experience with issues and topics of global and societal importance. Exceptional students have increased opportunities for personal growth in the areas of interdisciplinary academic inquiry, cultural awareness, community responsibility, and transformational leadership.

The College's administration is committed to the program as a means to enliven and enrich the undergraduate experience. Just recently, space in Morrison Hall, a historically registered mansion and campus cornerstone, was dedicated as an honors lounge and study area with computers plus the coordinator's office. This adds to the development of a learning and social community. The program offers peer tutoring, an expanding list of social and cultural activities, and dedicated academic advising.

Faculty members are drawn from many academic disciplines and possess shared qualities: intellectual curiosity; enthusiasm to experiment with alternative learning strategies, including Socratic dialogue, to foster an atmosphere of creative and intellectual exchange; a desire to facilitate student-centered learning; and flexibility to move beyond the confines of a standard syllabus to encompass student interests and challenge everyone to higher levels of academic pursuit. Cross-disciplinary exchanges and team teaching are common.

The curriculum encourages students to prepare and present scholarly research using primary sources and to participate in student-centered, alternative learning strategies. Honors sections of regular courses, taken primarily from the humanities, math, and sciences areas, satisfy both the program and general education requirements in A.A., A.S., and A.A.S. degrees. A minimum of 15 honors credits is mandated, though many students take more. In addition, students complete three 1-credit cross-disciplinary honors seminars and, beginning in fall 2005, a Capstone Project and service-learning course. A leadership course begins in spring 2006. All of these culminate in a portfolio of students' work. Seminars and courses are limited to 15 students.

Courses, including 1-credit seminars or 3-credit options, are drawn from areas such as the basic College curricula, student suggestions, and faculty development. The Golden Ratio was added to the math department's offerings, while new seminar topics have included From Gothic to Goth, Latin American Culture, Frontiers in Biology, and the History of the Future. Many of these include trips, such as to New York's MOMA or DIA Beacon, or special projects.

The new Capstone Project guarantees that all Honors Program students have an opportunity to perform undergraduate research, thereby better preparing them for transfer to four-year institutions. Students work one-on-one with faculty mentors to complete original research, artwork, or other projects in there area of interest. This project, the culminating learning experience, ends with a videotaped presentation to the community.

Each year, the program adds more activities and events to enrich the students' learning experiences. Honors Orientation, including R.O.P.E.S. (team building/leadership) activities, begins the students' experience. Every year, the College president hosts a breakfast for the students to discuss changes, hear suggestions, and honor all achievements, particularly by those graduating.

Participation Requirements: The program requires a total of 15 honors credits. To continue in the program, students must maintain a minimum 3.0 GPA each semester. Students who fulfill the course requirements and achieve a cumulative GPA of at least 3.5 are recognized at graduation and are designated Honors Program graduates on their diplomas.

All students take honors sections of freshman English I and II and three honors seminars. In addition, students in the A.A. program complete 3 credits each of honors social sciences and honors humanities, while A.S. and A.A.S. students take 6 credits of honors social sciences. All students meet a math/science requirement—either calculus or a lower-level math and science with lab combination (nonhonors sections at this point). Beginning in fall 2005, students complete the Honors Capstone Project as well as a service-learning course.

Admission Process: Entering prospective freshmen are eligible to apply for entrance into the Honors Program based on having one of the following: a cumulative GPA of 90 or above, a rank in the top 10 percent of their class, or an SAT score of at least 1200. They must also place into freshman English I. The process includes completing an institution application as well as an Honors Program Supplemental Application and submitting two letters of recommendation. Transfer and current Orange County Community College students may seek admission with a GPA of at least 3.5; they complete an application, provide two letters of recommendation, and complete an essay.

Scholarship Availability: Students are eligible for a range of College scholarships, including Presidential Scholarships. These cover full tuition costs for four semesters' worth of work. The eligibility requirements are very similar to those of the Honors Program.

Campus Overview

State and locally supported 2-year, founded 1950, part of State University of New York System • **Coed** 6,269 undergraduate students, 51% full-time, 61% women, 39% men.

Undergraduates 3,222 full-time, 3,047 part-time. Students come from 22 states and territories, 20 other countries, 1% are from out of state, 10% African American, 2% Asian American or Pacific Islander, 12% Hispanic American, 0.4% Native American, 3% transferred in.

Faculty *Total:* 382, 36% full-time. *Student/faculty ratio:* 15:1.

Academic Programs *Special study options:* academic remediation for entering students, accelerated degree program, adult/continuing education programs, English as a second language, external degree program, honors programs, internships, part-time degree program, services for LD students, summer session for credit.

Athletics Member NJCAA. *Intercollegiate sports:* baseball M(s), basketball M(s)/W(s), golf M/W, soccer M(s)/W(s), softball W(s), tennis M(s)/W(s), volleyball W. *Intramural sports:* basketball M/W, field hockey M, football M, racquetball M/W, soccer M/W, tennis M/W, volleyball M/W.

Costs (2005–06) *Tuition:* state resident $2900 full-time, $118 per credit part-time; nonresident $5800 full-time, $236 per credit part-time. *Required fees:* $315 full-time.

Financial Aid 70 Federal Work-Study jobs (averaging $2000). 25 state and other part-time jobs (averaging $2000).

Contact: Elaine Torda, Honors Program Coordinator, 115 South Street, Middletown, New York 10940; *Telephone:* 845-341-4004; *Fax:* 845-341-4999; *E-mail:* etorda@sunyorange.edu

---

Pace University
Pforzheimer Honors College
New York City and Pleasantville, New York

*T*he Pace University Honors College promotes the intellectual growth of outstanding students in all majors. The program consists of a sequence of honors courses as well as lectures, social events, and cultural activities, drawing on the varied resources of New York City and Westchester, including the Metropolitan Museum of Art, theater performances, and Ellis Island. Students are also involved in completing a senior honors project related to their major field of inquiry. The goals of the Pace Honors College are to deepen the intellectual experience of highly motivated, gifted students, encouraging them to enlarge their scope of knowledge on several levels, and to continue to build a vibrant, close-knit community of students and faculty members who are engaged in the process of learning and teaching.

Through specialized course work, extracurricular activities, and research, students develop relationships with professors and their contemporaries in a stimulating, challenging environment over four years of college. Students have the opportunity to work independently while shaping their own education. Honors courses are offered in a variety of fields, including literature, history, philosophy, business, religion, mathematics, theater, fine arts, language, science, and computer science. These courses are taught by a distinguished faculty and are offered at core and advanced levels. The College is a model within the University community and is dedicated to nurturing and challenging students. First-year students may choose to live together

in special honors sections of the dorms and have special honors study rooms on campus. Pace honors students win awards and grants both within and outside of the University, and alumni often go on to pursue graduate degrees in a variety of fields, such as business, law, and the humanities.

The program has been in existence for more than twenty years and admits approximately 130 first-year students on the New York City campus and 70 on the Pleasantville campus each year. There are more than 800 students currently enrolled in the programs on both campuses.

Participation Requirements: Entering first-year students are required to take a total of eight honors courses. These usually include a sequence of courses in the humanities and sciences. Students who enter the Honors College at the beginning of the sophomore year must take six honors courses. Those who enter at the beginning of the junior year must take four honors courses. One or two of these may be honors option courses, in which honors students develop an agreement with a professor that involves completion of an extra project (such as a significant additional paper or report) to earn honors credit. Honors credit may also be given for supervised internships that are discussed with and approved by the Director. Students are also required to attend various honors-related lectures and events. A minimum GPA of 3.3 must be maintained to remain in the program and receive the honors certificate and medallion upon graduation. Students' transcripts indicate all honors course work and completion of the honors thesis.

Admission Process: To be eligible for membership in the Honors College, entering first-year students must have a minimum high school average of at least 90 or the equivalent and a minimum combined math and verbal SAT I score of 1200, with a minimum score of 550 on the math section and 550 on the verbal section of the SAT I. Students who transfer to Pace and enter in the sophomore or junior year must have achieved a minimum GPA of 3.5 at their prior college or university. Current Pace students in their sophomore or junior year who have achieved a minimum GPA of 3.5 are also eligible.

Scholarship Availability: Honors College students receive scholarship packages from $9000 to $13,000 per year and receive a laptop computer. In addition, a stipend of $1000 is available during the junior or senior year to be used in an approved honors project on or off campus, including research and study abroad. Further, Pace University's financial aid policy is to provide the maximum financial aid available to qualified students to make their attendance at Pace a reality. To this end, the University administers a wide range of scholarship and financial aid programs designed to enable students to pursue their studies to graduation. The basis of selection is ability and/or need. Most financial aid is renewable on a yearly basis, provided there is adequate funding and the student remains eligible. Financial aid offered through Pace University includes President's and Deans' Scholarships, the Trustee Recognition Award, Pace Incentive Awards, the Pace Grant, athletic scholarships, and student employment.

Campus Overview

Independent university, founded 1906 • **Coed** 8,668 undergraduate students, 77% full-time, 61% women, 39% men.

Undergraduates 6,685 full-time, 1,983 part-time. Students come from 41 states and territories, 28 other countries, 23% are from out of state, 10% African American, 12% Asian American or Pacific Islander, 12% Hispanic American, 0.2% Native American, 4% international, 8% transferred in, 34% live on campus.

Faculty *Total:* 1,219, 38% full-time, 53% with terminal degrees. *Student/faculty ratio:* 15:1.

Academic Programs *Special study options:* academic remediation for entering students, accelerated degree program, adult/continuing education programs, advanced placement credit, cooperative education, distance learning, double majors, English as a second language, freshman honors college, honors programs, independent study, internships, part-time degree program, study abroad, summer session for credit. *ROTC:* Army (c). *Unusual degree programs:* 3-2 engineering with Manhattan College, Rensselaer Polytechnic Institute; occupational therapy with Columbia University College of Physicians and Surgeons.

Athletics Member NCAA. All Division II except baseball (Division I). *Intercollegiate sports:* baseball M(s), basketball M(s)/W(s), cross-country running M(s)/W(s), equestrian sports M/W, football M, golf M(s)/W(s), lacrosse M(s), soccer W(s), softball W(s), swimming and diving M/W, tennis M(s)/W(s), track and field M(s)/W(s), volleyball W(s). *Intramural sports:* basketball M/W, football M, soccer M/W, volleyball M/W.

Costs (2004–05) *Comprehensive fee:* $31,112 includes full-time tuition ($22,100), mandatory fees ($612), and room and board ($8400). Full-time tuition and fees vary according to student level. Part-time tuition: $634 per credit. Part-time tuition and fees vary according to course load. No tuition increase for student's term of enrollment. *Required fees:* $160 per term part-time. *Room and board:* Room and board charges vary according to board plan and housing facility.

Financial Aid 1,018 Federal Work-Study jobs (averaging $3585). In 2003, 345 non-need-based awards were made. *Average percent of need met:* 87%. *Average financial aid package:* $12,919. *Average need-based loan:* $4120. *Average need-based gift aid:* $4780. *Average non-need-based aid:* $5644.

Contact: New York City campus: Dr. William Offutt, Honors College, Pace University, One Pace Plaza, New York, New York 10038; *Telephone:* 212-346-1697; *Fax:* 212-346-1948; *E-mail:* woffutt@pace.edu.; Pleasantville campus: Dr. Janetta Rebold Benton, Honors College, Pace University, Mortola Library, 861 Bedford Road, Pleasantville, New York 10570; *Telephone:* 914-773-3848; *Fax:* 914-773-3896; *E-mail:* jbenton@pace.edu.

Polytechnic University, Brooklyn Campus
Polytechnic University Honors College
Brooklyn, New York

The Polytechnic University (Poly) Honors College, established by a vote of the faculty in 2003, is part of Polytechnic's initiative to position itself as a leader in twenty-first-century education in engineering, technology, entrepreneurship, and science-related fields. The Honors College was developed under the auspices of the Othmer Institute for Interdisciplinary Studies, whose mission includes a commitment to educational innovation and is overseen by the Honors College Faculty Board, which has representation from all academic departments at the University.

The Honors College accepts students of exceptional and unique talent from a variety of backgrounds. While most students enter the program as freshmen, transfer students–both internal and external–to Poly are accepted into the sophomore class. Honors College students receive a broad-based education highlighted by close faculty mentoring and interdisciplinary research, resulting in collaborative and independent research and active learning.

All Honors College students are assigned a faculty mentor as entering freshmen. The faculty mentor program is flexible so as to expose students to a variety of faculty members representing different research interests. Ultimately, the student picks a faculty mentor who is responsible for supervising the required Honors College senior thesis.

Honors College students have a special academic adviser for their freshman year and attend honors sections for all common courses, including the freshman Student Life course. Honors classes are intentionally kept small in size. The Honors College offers students of exceptional talent the opportunity to earn both a B.S. and an M.S.

degree in as few as four years (including summers). The bachelor's degree and the master's degree may be in the same or different disciplines chosen from within the University.

Honors College students are required to attend special seminars during their junior and senior years that are interdisciplinary. These seminars are offered by the Othmer Faculty Fellows, who are among the most notable at Poly, through the Othmer Institute for Interdisciplinary Studies.

The Honors College strongly encourages students to study abroad as part of its philosophy to prepare students for participation in the global community.

The Honors College offers a strong peer community. Students have their own lounge that functions as both a social and an academic space and is at the core of the Honors College community. Honors College students form an intellectual and social community that is augmented by off-campus activities. For example, Honors College students learned about team building through cooking at a New York City restaurant, attended Broadway plays, and visited various art galleries in Manhattan.

Rigorous intellectual development through active learning and faculty mentoring combine with the interdisciplinary focus and a global awareness to prepare students to become leaders in their chosen fields.

Established in April, 2003, there are currently 61 students enrolled in the Honors College as it enters its second year of operation.

Participation Requirements: Graduation as an Honors College Scholar is noted on the diploma. Its requirements include a minimum 3.5 GPA overall, completion of Honors College seminars, and completion of a senior thesis.

Admission Process: Members are admitted each fall semester. Criteria for admission to the Honors College includes an SAT score of at least 1350, a high school diploma with a minimum GPA of 90 (or the equivalent), submission of two letters of recommendation, and a personal interview. Transfer students during their freshman year are eligible to apply for admission to the Polytechnic University Honors College. They must have a GPA of 3.5 or greater. Two letters of recommendation, an essay, and a personal interview are also required. Continuation in the Honors College requires a minimum 3.0 GPA freshman year, a minimum 3.2 GPA sophomore year, and a minimum 3.5 GPA junior and senior years.

Scholarship Availability: There are University scholarships available with an Honors College differential of between $1500 and $4000.

Campus Overview

Independent university, founded 1854 • **Coed** 1,543 undergraduate students, 95% full-time, 19% women, 81% men.

Undergraduates 1,471 full-time, 72 part-time. Students come from 18 states and territories, 44 other countries, 5% are from out of state, 11% African American, 35% Asian American or Pacific Islander, 9% Hispanic American, 0.3% Native American, 8% international, 4% transferred in, 13% live on campus.

Faculty *Total:* 277, 47% full-time, 49% with terminal degrees. *Student/faculty ratio:* 12:1.

Academic Programs *Special study options:* academic remediation for entering students, accelerated degree program, advanced placement credit, cooperative education, double majors, English as a second language, honors programs, internships, part-time degree program, summer session for credit. *ROTC:* Air Force (c).

Athletics Member NCAA. All Division III. *Intercollegiate sports:* baseball M, basketball M/W, cross-country running M/W, soccer M/W, softball W, tennis M/W, track and field M/W, volleyball M/W. *Intramural sports:* badminton M/W, basketball M/W, bowling M/W, football M/W, golf M(c)/W(c), soccer M/W, table tennis M(c)/W(c), track and field M(c)/W(c), volleyball M/W, weight lifting M(c)/W(c).

Costs (2004–05) *Comprehensive fee:* $35,170 includes full-time tuition ($26,200), mandatory fees ($970), and room and board

($8000). Full-time tuition and fees vary according to course load. Part-time tuition: $835 per credit. Part-time tuition and fees vary according to course load. *Required fees:* $300 per term part-time. *College room only:* $6500. Room and board charges vary according to housing facility.

Financial Aid 100 Federal Work-Study jobs (averaging $3281). In 2004, 229 non-need-based awards were made. *Average percent of need met:* 89%. *Average financial aid package:* $20,475. *Average need-based loan:* $5485. *Average need-based gift aid:* $6829. *Average non-need-based aid:* $15,515.

Contact: Director: Ann Lubrano, Ph.D., Polytechnic University, 6 MetroTech Center, RH216, Brooklyn, New York 11201; *Telephone:* 718-260-3587; *Fax:* 718-260-3986; *E-mail:* alubrano@poly.edu; *Web site:* http://www.honorscollege.poly.edu

---

Queens College of the City University of New York
Honors Programs
Flushing, New York

Queens College of the City University of New York (CUNY) has a long tradition in honors education, offering programs rich in academic challenge and reward. Queens Honors Programs provide opportunities for advanced research, faculty mentorship, and special individualized advisement. The programs also provide interdisciplinary studies, which encourage students to forge connections among the concepts and ideas introduced in various disciplines and which help students broaden their perspectives on their education and the world.

High-achieving students selected to join the Honors College University Scholars Program participate in a unique and challenging program. They take eight honors courses, including four specially designed seminars that focus on the arts, people, politics, and scientific challenges of New York City. All the seminars combine traditional scholarly activity with hands-on research or creative experiences that deepen learning. Honors College students receive a laptop and a cultural passport, which provides access to the great cultural institutions of New York, including museums, theater, and concerts. University Scholars participate in a wide range of activities with Honors College students from other CUNY campuses and have numerous funded study-abroad and internship opportunities.

The Freshman Honors Program provides a specially designed liberal arts curriculum of interrelated classes that are intended to help students develop critical-thinking and writing skills. The program incorporates experiences, such as visits to cultural events and institutions and interactive student-centered pedagogies, which help students to integrate the work they complete in their honors classes. Students from all majors participate in the Freshman Honors Program; it therefore creates an interactive community where students share ideas across disciplines. On completing the Freshman Honors Program, students are encouraged to enter one of the other honors opportunities on campus.

Honors in the Humanities (HTH) is an 18- to 24-credit honors minor with a sequence of courses in literature and thought. Most courses in the sequence are small seminars. The lively, far-ranging discussion is centered on great works of drama, fiction, history, philosophy, poetry, and religion. The program encourages students to think critically, to read carefully and analytically, and to articulate and defend ideas both orally and in writing. To participate in HTH is to be challenged toward self-realization by professors, books, and other students. HTH has its own reference library with more than 4,000 volumes.

Honors in the Mathematical and Natural Sciences is designed to enhance research skills and opportunities for students interested in a career in the mathematical and natural sciences. An initial interdisciplinary Science Honors Seminar is followed by research courses and opportunities for mentoring, fellowships, and assistantships. Science honors students become participating members of a community of scientific scholars that includes students and faculty members.

Honors in the Social Sciences is a 21-credit program that encourages students to pursue intensive study across the social sciences. Students take an initial interdisciplinary seminar that introduces them to the critical methods and traditions of the social sciences. They then define an area of concentration, based on an area of personal interest, and examine this interest by taking four seminars from at least three social science disciplines. The program culminates in a capstone experience that includes preparing and conducting an original research project, then formulating the results of the research into a senior honors thesis.

The Business in the Liberal Arts (BLA) program is a rigorous, interdisciplinary 24-credit minor that connects liberal arts students to the world of business. The program was designed in consultation with leaders of the corporate world who said their greatest need in applicants for managerial positions was for thinking, writing, and speaking skills. BLA reaffirms the importance of the liberal arts while offering a series of courses designed to bridge traditional liberal arts study with career success in a broad range of disciplines. The program features exciting internships in New York's business community and mentoring by leaders in many fields.

The Mellon Mays Undergraduate Fellowship Program (MMUF) is designed to increase the number of highly qualified candidates for Ph.D.'s in core fields within the arts and sciences. Students from underrepresented minority groups, as well as other students with a demonstrated commitment to the goals of MMUF, are eligible to apply. Mellon Mays scholars receive faculty mentoring; modest term-time compensation for projects related to their academic interest; stipends for summer research; and repayment of undergraduate loans if students pursue doctoral study in a Mellon Mays–designated arts or science discipline.

All of these Honors Programs promote cohesive academic and social communities within the larger Queens College community. Most have their own student lounges. Most have program completion noted on transcripts. Students may participate in more than one program. Approximately 40 incoming first-year students are accepted into the Honors College University Scholars Program.

Admission Process: Applications for these programs may be made through the Office of Undergraduate Admissions, in conjunction with completion of the Queens College Scholars Application. Students may also apply directly to these programs, preferably before the start of their freshman year.

Scholarship Availability: Scholarships are awarded on the basis of a student's high school record, letters of recommendation, SAT scores, and a personal essay. University Scholars receive a special funding package that includes full tuition scholarships, stipends, an academic expense account to pay for enriching experiences such as study abroad, living expenses during unpaid internships, and a free laptop computer. The University Scholars Program awards full tuition and partial two-year scholarships to academically outstanding incoming freshmen. The College awards scholarships to academically strong incoming transfer students who hold an A.A. or A.S. degree. Renewal of scholarships is contingent on a student's maintenance of a high standard of academic performance.

The Mellon Minority Undergraduate Fellowship offers financial support, opportunities for summer research, and close faculty mentoring to highly qualified students in core fields of the arts and sciences. Designed to address the underrepresentation of black, Latino, and Native American people in higher education, it is open to juniors and seniors who have a commitment to attending graduate school and attaining a Ph.D. Students in the program normally receive two years of support, including a tuition fellowship, a stipend during the academic year (offered in compensation for research assistance the student undertakes), and a grant each summer for study or academic travel.

Campus Overview

State and locally supported comprehensive, founded 1937, part of City University of New York System • **Coed** 12,628 undergraduate students, 67% full-time, 62% women, 38% men.

Undergraduates 8,469 full-time, 4,159 part-time. Students come from 15 states and territories, 130 other countries, 1% are from out of state, 10% African American, 19% Asian American or Pacific Islander, 16% Hispanic American, 0.1% Native American, 6% international, 13% transferred in.

Faculty *Total:* 1,180, 46% full-time, 59% with terminal degrees. *Student/faculty ratio:* 17:1.

Academic Programs *Special study options:* accelerated degree program, adult/continuing education programs, advanced placement credit, cooperative education, double majors, English as a second language, freshman honors college, honors programs, independent study, internships, off-campus study, part-time degree program, services for LD students, student-designed majors, study abroad, summer session for credit. *ROTC:* Army (c), Navy (c). *Unusual degree programs:* 3-2 BA/MA degrees in chemistry, biochemistry, computer science, physics, political science, music, philosophy.

Athletics Member NCAA. All Division II. *Intercollegiate sports:* baseball M(s), basketball M(s)/W(s), fencing W(s), golf M(s), soccer W(s), softball M(s), swimming and diving M(s)/W(s), tennis M(s)/W(s), volleyball M(s)/W(s), water polo M(s)/W(s). *Intramural sports:* basketball M/W, fencing M, ice hockey M, racquetball M/W, soccer M/W, softball M/W, tennis M/W, volleyball M/W, water polo M/W.

Costs (2004–05) *Tuition:* state resident $4000 full-time, $170 per credit part-time; nonresident $8640 full-time, $360 per credit part-time. Full-time tuition and fees vary according to program. Part-time tuition and fees vary according to course load and program. *Required fees:* $361 full-time, $112 per term part-time.

Financial Aid 1,253 Federal Work-Study jobs (averaging $1300). In 2003, 292 non-need-based awards were made. *Average percent of need met:* 90%. *Average financial aid package:* $5000. *Average need-based gift aid:* $3400.

Contact: Director: Dr. Ross Wheeler, Office of Honors and Scholarships, Honors Center, Room 129, 65-30 Kissena Boulevard, Flushing, New York 11372; *Telephone:* 718-997-5502; *Fax:* 718-997-5498; *E-mail:* honors@qc.edu; *Web site:* http://www.qc.cuny.edu

Rochester Institute of Technology

Rochester Institute of Technology Honors Program

Rochester, New York

*T*he Rochester Institute of Technology (RIT) Honors Program features seminar-style classes and individualized research and study options and provides a supportive and encouraging environment for students with intellectual curiosity and academic distinction. Students benefit by working closely and sharing academic experiences both in and out of the classroom with other honors students and faculty members.

The Honors Program is designed for students who seek to challenge themselves in exemplary learning experiences such as undergraduate research projects, honors seminars, and study abroad; who wish to extend and share their knowledge through participation in professional associations and conferences; and who hope to join other outstanding students and faculty members in a wide range of special activities throughout the year, including field trips, social events, and community-service projects.

One of the distinguishing features of the RIT Honors Program is its career-oriented focus. Honors activities and courses are designed to enhance the professional dimension of the collegiate experience. The major components of the Honors Program include professional opportunities within the student's college, enhanced general education courses, and specially designed experiential education activities.

Honors students have access to special courses, seminars, projects, and advising in their home college. The honors-level general education curriculum, which provides extracurricular opportunities for learning outside the classroom, brings all honors students together. Capitalizing on RIT's assets as one of the nation's foremost career-oriented universities, the Honors Program offers opportunities for students to work with faculty members on applied and interdisciplinary research projects as well as enhanced cooperative education experiences and internships. Each college has designated an experienced faculty member to serve as its Honors Program advocate. Advocates work with students one-on-one to develop educational and career plans and professional and experiential learning opportunities such as research placements, co-ops, internships, and study abroad. Honors students are encouraged to pursue study abroad to add an international perspective to their education. Whether a first-year or upper-class student, honors students can choose to live in honors housing within the residence halls. This option increases the chances for interaction with other honors students outside the classroom.

Participation Requirements: Students in the Honors Program are expected to participate in honors courses and cocurricular activities in their college and replace approximately half of their liberal arts requirements with honors courses. Honors students are also required to participate in experiential learning experiences each year. All students who wish to continue in the program are subject to an annual review by the Honors Committee. Program continuation is subject to GPA and other requirements.

Admission Process: Applicants who submit the RIT Application for Undergraduate Admission by February 1 are invited to apply for Honors Program admission if their high school grades, rank, and test scores place them among the top five percent of the applicants to the University. This normally requires a high school grade point average and class rank of 95 percent or higher along with excellent SAT or ACT scores. Students who are invited to apply for admission to the Honors Program are asked to submit supplemental application materials, including a teacher recommendation, two admission essays, and a listing of academic awards, college-level courses, and special enrichment programs they have participated in.

Scholarship Availability: All students accepted into the RIT Honors Program receive an Honors Program Scholarship. In addition, RIT has a generous merit scholarship program for all qualified students regardless of financial need (Presidential Scholarships). Renewal criteria are provided with award notification.

Campus Overview

Independent comprehensive, founded 1829 • **Coed** 12,304 undergraduate students, 87% full-time, 29% women, 71% men.

Undergraduates 10,723 full-time, 1,581 part-time. Students come from 50 states and territories, 90 other countries, 45% are from out of state, 5% African American, 7% Asian American or Pacific Islander, 3% Hispanic American, 0.5% Native American, 4% international, 7% transferred in, 60% live on campus.

Faculty *Total:* 1,218, 60% full-time, 81% with terminal degrees. *Student/faculty ratio:* 14:1.

Academic Programs *Special study options:* accelerated degree program, adult/continuing education programs, advanced placement credit, cooperative education, distance learning, English as a second language, honors programs, independent study, internships, off-campus study, part-time degree program, services for LD students, student-designed majors, study abroad, summer session for credit. *ROTC:* Army (b), Navy (c), Air Force (b).

Athletics Member NCAA. All Division III except ice hockey (Division I). *Intercollegiate sports:* baseball M, basketball M/W, bowling M(c)/W(c), cheerleading M(c)/W(c), crew M/W, cross-country running M/W, equestrian sports M(c)/W(c), fencing M(c)/W(c), field hockey W(c), ice hockey M/W, lacrosse M/W, rugby M(c)/W(c), skiing (downhill) M(c)/W(c), soccer M/W, softball W, swimming and diving M/W, tennis M/W, track and field M/W, ultimate Frisbee M(c)/W(c), volleyball M(c)/W, water polo M(c)/W(c), wrestling M. *Intramural sports:* badminton M/W, basketball M/W, bowling M/W, football M, golf M/W, ice hockey M/W, lacrosse M(c), racquetball M/W, rock climbing M(c)/W(c), soccer M/W, softball M/W, table tennis M/W, tennis M/W, volleyball M/W.

Costs (2004–05) *Comprehensive fee:* $30,549 includes full-time tuition ($22,056), mandatory fees ($357), and room and board ($8136). Full-time tuition and fees vary according to course load, program, and student level. Part-time tuition: $491 per credit hour. Part-time tuition and fees vary according to course load, program, and student level. *Required fees:* $29 per term part-time. *College room only:* $4653. Room and board charges vary according to board plan and housing facility.

Financial Aid 2,060 Federal Work-Study jobs (averaging $1330). 4,700 state and other part-time jobs (averaging $1780). In 2003, 920 non-need-based awards were made. *Average percent of need met:* 90%. *Average financial aid package:* $16,300. *Average need-based loan:* $4700. *Average need-based gift aid:* $9900. *Average non-need-based aid:* $5800.

Contact: Director: Dr. Catherine Hutchison Winnie, 21 Lomb Memorial Drive, Rochester, New York 14623-5603; *Telephone:* 585-475-7629; *Fax:* 585-475-7633; *E-mail:* honors@mail.rit.edu; *Web site:* http://www.rit.edu/honors/

Russell Sage College
Honors Program
Troy, New York

*T*he Honors Program at Russell Sage College (RSC) honors women's voices in all fields and endeavors, offers sustained opportunities for cross-disciplinary study through multidisciplinary approaches, and supports students in directing their own learning. Three options are available to students: General Honors, Advanced Honors, and Honors Affiliate. Students in General Honors enroll in a 12-credit program of honors courses and graduate with distinction as Honors Scholars. With the exception of Founder's Seminar, all credits "double count" as general education courses. Students must earn a B or better in each honors course for it to count toward their overall honors credits. Junior and/or senior students may enroll in Advanced Honors where they work in a one-to-one relationship with a faculty member on an Advanced Honor Project (6 credits). Students may design and carry out their own research projects in their majors or in other areas of interest (such as a project related to ITD 420). Finally, students may enroll in one or more honors courses in areas of particular interest without having to complete the 12-credit requirement. Students who choose to be Honors Affiliates receive honors designation on their official transcript. These courses are open to affiliates on a space-available basis.

Class size is limited to 18, and all classes are taught by full-time faculty members. Faculty members address both the content and pedagogical issues that are indicated by the theme of the honors seminar, and each provides an out-of-class experience. Faculty members are encouraged to conduct their courses in such a way as to promote self-discovery.

Admission Process: Admission to the program is automatic for interested students who have a high school average of 92 or better or who have maintained a college GPA of at least 3.4. Transfer students who meet the GPA requirements and who are currently enrolled in an honors program are accepted into the program. The director of the honors program may also admit motivated students who do not yet meet those standards but show special ability or promise.

Scholarship Availability: There are no honors scholarships at this time.

Campus Overview
Independent 4-year, founded 1916, part of The Sage Colleges • **Urban** 8-acre campus • **Women only** 837 undergraduate students, 95% full-time.

Undergraduates 792 full-time, 45 part-time. Students come from 15 states and territories, 3 other countries, 9% are from out of state, 4% African American, 2% Asian American or Pacific Islander, 3% Hispanic American, 0.4% international, 13% transferred in, 47% live on campus.

Faculty *Total:* 121, 52% full-time, 56% with terminal degrees. *Student/faculty ratio:* 11:1.

Academic Programs *Special study options:* academic remediation for entering students, accelerated degree program, adult/continuing education programs, advanced placement credit, cooperative education, double majors, English as a second language, freshman honors college, honors programs, independent study, internships, off-campus study, part-time degree program, services for LD students, student-designed majors, study abroad, summer session for credit. *ROTC:* Army (c), Air Force (c). *Unusual degree programs:* 3-2 business administration with Sage Graduate School; engineering with Rensselaer Polytechnic Institute; nursing with Sage Graduate School; occupational therapy, physical therapy, public administration with Sage Graduate School.

Athletics Member NCAA. All Division III. *Intercollegiate sports:* basketball W, soccer W, softball W, tennis W, volleyball W. *Intramural sports:* badminton W, basketball W, cheerleading W(c), crew W(c), equestrian sports W(c), field hockey W(c), ice hockey W(c), lacrosse W(c), skiing (cross-country) W(c), skiing (downhill) W(c), soccer W, softball W, tennis W, track and field W(c), volleyball W, water polo W.

Costs (2004–05) *Comprehensive fee:* $29,320 includes full-time tuition ($21,500), mandatory fees ($770), and room and board ($7050). Part-time tuition: $715 per credit hour. *College room only:* $3350.

Financial Aid 274 Federal Work-Study jobs (averaging $1500). 124 state and other part-time jobs (averaging $1200). In 2002, 43 non-need-based awards were made. *Average non-need-based aid:* $9600.

Contact: Director: Dr. Julie Ann McIntyre, 405 Gurley Hall, Russell Sage College, Troy, New York 12180; *Telephone:* 518-244-2255; *Fax:* 518-244-4545; *E-mail:* mcintj@sage.edu

Sage College of Albany
Honors Program
Albany, New York

*T*he Sage College of Albany (SCA) Honors Program offers challenging, liberal arts honors courses in which students exercise personal creativity and initiative. Maximum class size is 15. Interdisciplinary and team-taught seminars and honors contract courses provide opportunities for both collaborative study and independent inquiry. Recent course offerings have included American

Ethnic History, Environmental Science, Abstract Expressionism and the Beat Generation, American Romanticism in Literature and Art, the study of Extraordinary Groups, the Psychology of Peace and Violence, and the Humanities Cornerstone Seminar. The Cornerstone Seminar is an investigation into the impact of technology on such disciplines as biology, mathematics, communications, literature, philosophy, art, and music, and students work on a term project with a personal faculty mentor, learning to seek out contacts and resources in the larger community. Projects are presented at a year-end Honors Symposium.

Founded in 1993, the Honors Program has grown from an initial 10 scholars to a current enrollment of 55.

Participation Requirements: Honors Scholars can participate at the Associate and/or at the Baccalaureate levels. Associate Honors Scholars complete at least 12 credit hours in honors courses. The two required courses are Honors Humanities Seminar III and the Honors Cornerstone Seminar: Technology and the Humanities. The remaining 6 credits are taken in other honors courses or by completing honors contracts. Baccalaureate Honors Scholars must complete 13 credits of honors courses or honors contracts. At least 9 credits of these must be in courses numbered at 300 or higher, and 1 credit must be from enrolling in the Honors Thesis Workshop. The Honors Thesis Workshop provides a forum for sharing the problems and results of senior research in the student's major within the interdisciplinary honors environment. Honors Affiliates, students who do not choose to complete the Honors Scholar program but who have demonstrated a high degree of academic achievement and creative ability, may enroll in one or more honors courses.

Admission Process: Entering students will be invited to enroll as Honors Scholars on the basis of their college preparatory courses and SAT scores. Transfer students will be invited to participate during their first semester at the Sage College of Albany.

Scholarship Availability: The Presidential Honors Scholarship is an academic merit scholarship awarded to full-time students who have met Honors Program admission requirements. An interview is required. The award is renewable for students who have maintained at least a 3.0 GPA.

Campus Overview

Independent 4-year, founded 1957, part of The Sage Colleges • **Coed** 1,051 undergraduate students, 59% full-time, 71% women, 29% men.

Undergraduates 621 full-time, 430 part-time. Students come from 9 states and territories, 2 other countries, 2% are from out of state, 10% African American, 2% Asian American or Pacific Islander, 3% Hispanic American, 0.4% Native American, 0.2% international, 16% transferred in, 29% live on campus.

Faculty *Total:* 77, 53% full-time, 49% with terminal degrees. *Student/faculty ratio:* 11:1.

Academic Programs *Special study options:* academic remediation for entering students, adult/continuing education programs, advanced placement credit, cooperative education, English as a second language, external degree program, freshman honors college, honors programs, independent study, internships, off-campus study, part-time degree program, services for LD students, student-designed majors, summer session for credit. *Unusual degree programs:* 3-2 business administration with Albany Law School.

Athletics *Intramural sports:* badminton M/W, basketball M/W, field hockey M(c)/W(c), football M/W, ice hockey M(c)/W(c), lacrosse M(c)/W(c), skiing (downhill) M(c)/W(c), soccer M/W, volleyball W, water polo M/W.

Costs (2004–05) *Comprehensive fee:* $23,170 includes full-time tuition ($15,250), mandatory fees ($770), and room and board ($7150). Part-time tuition: $510 per credit hour. *College room only:* $3450. Room and board charges vary according to board plan and location.

Financial Aid 220 Federal Work-Study jobs (averaging $1500). 86 state and other part-time jobs (averaging $1200). In 2002, 24 non-need-based awards were made. *Average non-need-based aid:* $3600.

Contact: Coordinator: Esther Tornai Thyssen, Sage College of Albany, 140 New Scotland Avenue, Albany, New York 12208; *Telephone:* 518-292-8604; *Fax:* 518-292-1903; *E-mail:* thysse@sage.edu

State University of New York at Binghamton
The Binghamton Scholars Program
Binghamton, New York

Designed for entering students of exceptional merit, the Binghamton Scholars Program consists of a four-year honors curriculum that provides high-achieving students with an intellectually challenging learning experience. The curriculum emphasizes the development of high-level research and computer skills, communication skills in both spoken and written languages, collaborative learning experiences in project-centered courses, and opportunities to work closely with faculty members from across the disciplines and throughout the professional schools. Students also participate in a variety of experiential learning venues and internships, both on and off the Binghamton campus. As Binghamton Scholars, they have many occasions to showcase their best academic work and forge links between education and career.

Students enrolled in the Binghamton Scholars Program enjoy the following benefits: renewable merit scholarships, travel subsidies and research grants, access to reserved study areas and computer work areas, early registration for classes, a guaranteed double room in a residential college of the student's choice in the first year, and special counseling for postgraduate study. Upon graduation and successful completion of the program, students may earn recognition for All-University Honors and/or as Binghamton Scholars.

The Binghamton Scholars Program admitted its first class in fall 2000; the program currently enrolls 230 students and expects to enroll a total of 400 students by fall 2006.

Participation Requirements: Required scholars courses include one course in each of the first two years, one internship or experiential learning activity in the junior year, and one capstone or departmental honors project in the senior year. These are not additional required courses; they typically fulfill general education requirements and may count toward the student's major.

In addition to their scholars courses, students participate in semester-long Scholars Leadership Forums. The forums meet once each week during the semester with a faculty mentor. They have a budget and the freedom to invent, design, and implement a project that will enrich the life of the University or benefit the greater Binghamton community.

In order to graduate with the designation Binghamton Scholar, students must achieve a cumulative GPA of at least 3.25. In order to graduate with the designation All-University Honors, students must achieve a cumulative GPA of at least 3.5. In order to receive either designation and remain in the program, students must demonstrate steady progress toward a degree, including timely completion of Scholars Program credit and noncredit requirements; maintain a cumulative GPA of at least 3.25; and abide by the Rules of Student Conduct, the student conduct code of Binghamton University.

Admission Process: The Binghamton Scholars Program is highly selective. Students invited to participate in the program typically have SAT scores in the high 1300 range or better (30+ on the ACT) and average high school grades in the mid- to high 90s. The selection process is designed to ensure representation of students from each school within the University. Selection criteria may vary slightly among candidates from each school. Special attention is paid to students who have overcome adverse circumstances and achieved academic success.

The program requires no special application. Application to the University includes an initial application, a transcript of secondary school course work and grades, a Supplementary Admissions Form (which asks candidates to write an essay and to present information about honors awards earned, work experiences, extracurricular activities, and community service), and SAT or ACT scores. Scores on standardized tests must be received directly from the testing agency. As the Admissions Office reviews applications, it identifies candidates for the Binghamton Scholars Program and invites them to participate. Competition for spaces in the program runs high.

Binghamton makes admissions decisions on a rolling basis. Admission to the Binghamton Scholars Program is limited to 110 students each year. The University considers those who complete their applications for admission early. Therefore, in order to receive full consideration for this program, prospective students should be sure that the University has received their Supplementary Admissions Form and SAT/ACT scores by January 15.

Scholarship Availability: Students accepted to the Binghamton Scholars Program receive either full or partial tuition scholarships.

Campus Overview

State-supported university, founded 1946, part of State University of New York System • **Coed** 11,034 undergraduate students, 98% full-time, 49% women, 51% men.

Undergraduates 10,779 full-time, 255 part-time. Students come from 39 states and territories, 67 other countries, 6% are from out of state, 5% African American, 17% Asian American or Pacific Islander, 6% Hispanic American, 0.2% Native American, 4% international, 7% transferred in, 58% live on campus.

Faculty *Total:* 719, 71% full-time. *Student/faculty ratio:* 22:1.

Academic Programs *Special study options:* academic remediation for entering students, accelerated degree program, adult/continuing education programs, advanced placement credit, distance learning, double majors, English as a second language, honors programs, independent study, internships, off-campus study, part-time degree program, services for LD students, student-designed majors, study abroad, summer session for credit. *ROTC:* Air Force (c). *Unusual degree programs:* 3-2 business administration with Harpur College, SUNY Oneonta, SUNY Fredonia; management, engineering and physics with Columbia University, Clarkson University, Rochester Institute of Technology, State University of New York at Buffalo, State University of New York at Stony Brook, University of Rochester, chemistry and materials science, biology, computer science.

Athletics Member NCAA. All Division I. *Intercollegiate sports:* badminton M(c)/W(c), baseball M(s), basketball M(s)/W(s), bowling M(c)/W(c), crew M(c)/W(c), cross-country running M(s)/W(s), equestrian sports M(c)/W(c), fencing M(c)/W(c), golf M(s), ice hockey M(c), lacrosse M(s)/W(s), racquetball M(c)/W(c), rugby M(c)/W(c), skiing (downhill) M(c)/W(c), soccer M(s)/W(s), softball W(s), swimming and diving M(s)/W(s), table tennis M(c)/W(c), tennis M(s)/W(s), track and field M(s)/W(s), volleyball M(c)/W(c), wrestling M(s). *Intramural sports:* badminton M/W, basketball M/W, bowling M/W, cross-country running M/W, football M/W, golf M/W, racquetball M/W, soccer M/W, squash M/W, table tennis M/W, tennis M/W, volleyball M/W, water polo M/W.

Costs (2004–05) *Tuition:* state resident $4350 full-time, $181 per credit hour part-time; nonresident $10,610 full-time, $442 per credit hour part-time. *Required fees:* $1406 full-time. *Room and board:* $7710; room only: $4736. Room and board charges vary according to board plan and housing facility.

Financial Aid 988 Federal Work-Study jobs (averaging $1287). In 2004, 340 non-need-based awards were made. *Average percent of*

need met: 81%. *Average financial aid package:* $11,089. *Average need-based loan:* $4296. *Average need-based gift aid:* $4798. *Average non-need-based aid:* $3479.

Contact: Director: Dr. George Catalano, Binghamton Scholars Program, College-in-the-Woods Library, Box 6000, Binghamton University, Binghamton, New York 13902-6000; *Telephone:* 607-777-3583; *E-mail:* scholars@binghamton.edu; *Web site:* http://scholars.binghamton.edu

State University of New York at Buffalo
University Honors Program
Buffalo, New York

*T*he University Honors Program at the State University of New York at Buffalo (UB) provides academically talented students with the opportunity to pursue a rigorous and challenging intellectual experience within their undergraduate studies. The honors program creates a small-college atmosphere within a large-university setting, giving each honors scholar the opportunity to create a program of study that fits his or her unique interests and talents. UB has had a long history of honors programs, and the first was established in 1923. The current University Honors Program was initiated in 1981 and now enrolls more than 900 students.

The honors program encompasses all undergraduate majors and schools. Approximately 250 freshmen are admitted each year. Honors Scholars receive merit-based scholarships, participate in small honors seminars and the honors colloquium, are provided with a faculty mentor in their freshman year, attend Evening with Faculty programs, and work on major research projects early in their college careers. Supplemental scholarships are available for international study, and funding is provided to support student research projects. An honors liberal arts special major is also available for those students seeking a broad undergraduate education. Special early admissions programs are available to Honors Scholars interested in pursuing careers in medicine, dentistry, law, pharmacy, and physical therapy.

The Advanced Honors Program gives Honors Scholars and highly qualified current UB students the opportunity to pursue an individualized honors experience in their junior and senior years. Students conduct advanced scholarship within their major field of study. Once they have completed 60 credit hours and have a minimum overall GPA of 3.5, they are invited to apply for this program. Transfer students are eligible to apply and should contact the Honors Program office for transfer student admissions criteria.

Participation Requirements: To maintain their status in the University Honors Program, entering freshman Honors Scholars participate in the Freshman Honors Colloquium during their first semester. This course has an extensive community service component, with students working in small groups to research, design, and implement a community service project. They also complete four honors seminars within their first two years of study at UB. Freshmen must maintain a minimum GPA of 3.2. Sophomore, junior, and senior Honors Scholars must maintain a 3.5 cumulative GPA to graduate as Honors Scholars. Advanced Honors Scholars must maintain a minimum 3.5 GPA, complete three honors courses (contract honors courses, departmental honors courses, and/or graduate courses), complete a breadth requirement (second major, minor, study abroad, co-op/internship, or community service), and undertake a research project that culminates in a thesis.

Admission Process: The University Honors Program is highly selective. Freshmen are selected on the basis of their high school average and SAT scores. A minimum unweighted high school average of 93 is required along with a minimum SAT score of 1300

(mathematics and critical reading) or ACT score of at least 29. Applications to the University should be received by the end of December, as offers are made in February. Advanced Honors Program applications are available from the Honors Program office, with deadlines of October 1 and March 1.

Scholarship Availability: Students admitted as freshmen to the University Honors Program receive four-year, merit based scholarships. The minimum scholarship is $3000 per year. A smaller number of scholarships are available at the $4500 level or as Distinguished Honors Scholarships, which cover the full cost of the student's undergraduate education at UB.

Campus Overview

State-supported university, founded 1846, part of State University of New York System • **Coed** 17,838 undergraduate students, 93% full-time, 46% women, 54% men.

Undergraduates 16,509 full-time, 1,329 part-time. Students come from 40 states and territories, 78 other countries, 2% are from out of state, 7% African American, 9% Asian American or Pacific Islander, 4% Hispanic American, 0.4% Native American, 6% international, 9% transferred in, 38% live on campus.

Faculty *Total:* 1,746, 65% full-time. *Student/faculty ratio:* 15:1.

Academic Programs *Special study options:* academic remediation for entering students, accelerated degree program, adult/continuing education programs, advanced placement credit, cooperative education, distance learning, double majors, English as a second language, freshman honors college, honors programs, independent study, internships, off-campus study, part-time degree program, services for LD students, student-designed majors, study abroad, summer session for credit. *ROTC:* Army (c). *Unusual degree programs:* 3-2 law.

Athletics Member NCAA. All Division I except football (Division I-A). *Intercollegiate sports:* baseball M(s), basketball M(s)/W(s), crew W(s), cross-country running M(s)/W(s), soccer M(s)/W(s), softball W(s), swimming and diving M(s)/W(s), tennis M(s)/W(s), track and field M(s)/W(s), volleyball W(s), wrestling M(s). *Intramural sports:* badminton M/W, baseball M(c), basketball M/W, crew M(c), cross-country running W, field hockey W(c), gymnastics M(c)/W(c), ice hockey M(c)/W(c), lacrosse M(c)/W(c), rugby M(c)/W(c), skiing (downhill) M(c)/W(c), soccer M/W, softball M/W, squash M/W, tennis M(c)/W(c), ultimate Frisbee M(c)/W(c), volleyball M(c)/W.

Costs (2004–05) *Tuition:* state resident $4350 full-time, $181 per credit hour part-time; nonresident $10,610 full-time, $442 per credit hour part-time. Part-time tuition and fees vary according to course load. *Required fees:* $1616 full-time, $72 per credit hour part-time. *Room and board:* $7226; room only: $4336. Room and board charges vary according to board plan and housing facility.

Financial Aid 2,185 Federal Work-Study jobs (averaging $1076). 913 state and other part-time jobs (averaging $5428). In 2004, 1790 non-need-based awards were made. *Average percent of need met:* 71%. *Average financial aid package:* $7132. *Average need-based loan:* $3143. *Average need-based gift aid:* $3109. *Average non-need-based aid:* $2631.

Contact: Administrative Director: Dr. Josephine Capuana or Academic Director: Dr. Clyde Herreid, Distinguished Teaching Professor of Biology, State University of New York at Buffalo, 214 Talbert Hall, Buffalo, New York 14260; *Telephone:* 716-645-3020; *Fax:* 716-645-3368; *E-mail:* capuana@buffalo.edu; *Web site:* http://buffalo.edu/honors/

State University of New York at New Paltz
SUNY New Paltz Honors Program
New Paltz, New York

*T*he SUNY New Paltz Honors Program exists to challenge New Paltz students beyond what is normally expected of them. It was designed around the philosophy that intense and rigorous courses taught by outstanding instructors (who offer much encouragement) and filled with motivated, focused students would create the optimal learning environment. The SUNY New Paltz Honors Program is small (around 100 students), so selectivity in acceptance is required. Once students are admitted into the program, they take special honors seminars that are cross-disciplinary and in-depth in scope. The honors seminars emphasize discussion and nonlecture-based learning; students are expected to come to class with something to say and to actively participate in debate and discussion.

Beyond the academic requirements, the SUNY New Paltz Honors Program provides students with the opportunity to meet and work with other like-minded students on class-related projects or extracurricular creative endeavors. These projects can take the form of anything from organizing an academic conference or discussion, to painting a mural, working on the newsletter, running a workshop on yoga, or any other skill, talent, or interest. The Honors Center also organizes several trips per semester, including the very popular biannual weekend retreat to the Ashokan Reservoir in the Catskill Mountains.

The SUNY New Paltz Honors Program is centered in the Honors Center, a building designed especially for honors students. It includes study space, a lounge area, a kitchen, seminar rooms, and a computer center complete with photocopiers, scanners, and other equipment. Best of all, it is open 24 hours a day, seven days a week to honors students.

Ultimately, the honors experience is what the student makes of it. The term itself is inclusive of both the academic and extracurricular aspects of the SUNY New Paltz Honors Program. Basically, it refers to life as a member of the program.

Participation Requirements: Academically speaking, honors students are required to take and actively participate in four honors seminars. Seminars focus on a wide variety of topics and students can begin taking them the second semester of their freshman year. Ideally, a student should only take one seminar per semester and should complete them by the end of the junior year.

An honors student is also required to complete a senior thesis project. The senior thesis allows honors students to explore an area of interest in great detail. The student discusses his or her topic with both the Program Director and another professor who works closely with the student throughout the duration the project. A thesis may be based on a topic within the student's major or on a completely unrelated subject. A thesis written as a requirement for the student's major may also be acceptable. In order to complete the thesis, the student should register for an independent study with his or her advising professor on the topic of the thesis. This should be done the first semester of the senior year. If the student chooses to, he or she may present the thesis in a ceremony held prior to commencement.

One requirement that exists outside of the classroom is the completion of 30 hours of community service. Community service (also known as service learning) allows students to help others while learning about themselves and the world around them.

Admission Process: Prospective freshmen are invited to apply to the SUNY New Paltz Honors Program in the course of the admission process to the University. The following criteria are considered minimal qualifications for acceptance into the program: SAT scores of 1250 or higher; high school average of 93 or higher; two writing samples; and two letters of recommendation.

Students who transfer into New Paltz as sophomores of juniors can apply to the SUNY New Paltz Honors Program in the course of the admission process to the University. The following criteria are considered for acceptance into the program: an overall college GPA of 3.5 or higher; a portfolio, i.e., two or more examples of writing from the past year and/or project or project description (for students in the arts and sciences); and recommendations from at least 2 previous college professors.

All honors students must maintain a minimum semester GPA of 3.5. If two consecutive semesters pass without a student enrolling in a seminar (except in the case of Study Abroad), an assumption is made that the student is no longer interested in being a part of the SUNY New Paltz Honors Program, and his or her name is removed from its roster.

Scholarship Availability: A limited number of merit-based scholarships are offered to entering freshmen each year. Participation in the SUNY New Paltz Honors Program is not a requirement for receipt of any of these scholarships.

Campus Overview

State-supported comprehensive, founded 1828, part of State University of New York System • **Coed** 6,191 undergraduate students, 88% full-time, 67% women, 33% men.

Undergraduates 5,430 full-time, 761 part-time. Students come from 23 states and territories, 40 other countries, 3% are from out of state, 7% African American, 4% Asian American or Pacific Islander, 10% Hispanic American, 0.2% Native American, 2% international, 12% transferred in, 52% live on campus.

Faculty *Total:* 686, 43% full-time, 36% with terminal degrees. *Student/faculty ratio:* 16:1.

Academic Programs *Special study options:* academic remediation for entering students, adult/continuing education programs, advanced placement credit, cooperative education, distance learning, double majors, English as a second language, honors programs, independent study, internships, part-time degree program, services for LD students, student-designed majors, study abroad, summer session for credit. *Unusual degree programs:* 3-2 forestry with State University of New York College of Environmental Science and Forestry.

Athletics Member NCAA. All Division III. *Intercollegiate sports:* baseball M, basketball M/W, cross-country running M/W, equestrian sports W(c), field hockey W, ice hockey M(c), lacrosse M(c)/W, rugby M(c)/W(c), soccer M/W, softball W, swimming and diving M/W, tennis M/W, track and field M/W, volleyball M/W. *Intramural sports:* badminton M/W, basketball M/W, football M, golf M/W, racquetball M/W, softball M/W, track and field M/W, volleyball M/W.

Costs (2004–05) *Tuition:* state resident $4350 full-time, $181 per credit part-time; nonresident $10,300 full-time, $429 per credit part-time. *Required fees:* $870 full-time, $26 per credit part-time, $125 per term part-time. *Room and board:* $6860; room only: $4240. Room and board charges vary according to board plan.

Financial Aid 986 Federal Work-Study jobs (averaging $852). 478 state and other part-time jobs (averaging $1053). In 2003, 159 non-need-based awards were made. *Average percent of need met:* 74%. *Average financial aid package:* $2446. *Average need-based loan:* $859. *Average need-based gift aid:* $2229. *Average non-need-based aid:* $1525.

Contact: Director: Jeff Miller, Honors Program, SUNY New Paltz, 75 South Manheim Boulevard, New Paltz, New York 12561; *Telephone:* 845-257-3934; *Fax:* 845-257-3937; *E-mail:* millerj@newpaltz.edu; *Web site:* http://www.newpaltz.edu/honors

State University of New York at Oswego
College Honors Program
Oswego, New York

The SUNY Oswego Honors Program consists of a core of courses designed to stimulate students' intellectual growth and develop their analytical abilities. Unlike traditional courses, which present material from a single field of study, Honors Program courses draw ideas and information from many fields, addressing concerns common to all disciplines and recognizing that there are no boundaries to thought and inquiry. Honors Program courses examine the historical and intellectual origins, growth, and development of today's issues, the connections among them, and their consequences for tomorrow. The program emphasizes small classes—about 20 students—and the lively exchange of ideas in the classroom. The Honors Program seeks out faculty members who have demonstrated excellence in teaching, who are especially skilled in their fields, who are interested in thinking across disciplines, and who are committed to working with students in a variety of formal and informal settings. Honors Program students are advised by the Honors Director and Associate Director and by faculty members in the student's major field of study. Students enjoy a close relationship with honors faculty members and with each other in a network of academic and personal support.

Honors Program students have access to all of SUNY Oswego's facilities. This is one of the great benefits of the Honors Program; while students enjoy the advantages of a small, challenging program, they have access to all the resources of a major university, including an internationally respected faculty, a library with more than 1 million holdings, fully equipped computer labs, and a wide range of student services.

Participation Requirements: Students in the Honors Program can major in any area the College offers and take the same number of credits for graduation as every other SUNY Oswego student. Honors Program students take 18 hours in the Honors Core (Intellectual Traditions I and II, The Social Sciences, Literature and the Arts, Science in the Human Context, and The Search for Meaning), as well as courses in a language, lab science, English, and math. (If an Advanced Placement course covers the same material as an Honors Program course, the AP course will fulfill the honors requirement. For example, a student with AP credit in calculus or a lab science already will have met those particular requirements.) In addition, students in the Honors Program explore a subject of their choice in depth with a faculty adviser—usually within their major—by writing an honors thesis.

To graduate from the Honors Program, students must have a minimum 3.0 GPA overall, a minimum 3.3 GPA in their major, and a minimum 3.3 in the Honors Core. Successful completion of the Honors Program requirements is noted at graduation and is recorded on the student's transcript. There are about 250 students in Oswego's Honors Program.

Admission Process: Freshmen are selected each May for the Honors Program on the basis of their high school average and their SAT scores. Sophomores and first-year students who are not selected may also apply for admission.

Campus Overview

State-supported comprehensive, founded 1861, part of State University of New York System • **Coed** 7,059 undergraduate students, 93% full-time, 54% women, 46% men.

Undergraduates 6,531 full-time, 528 part-time. Students come from 28 states and territories, 19 other countries, 2% are from out of state, 4% African American, 2% Asian American or Pacific Islander, 4% Hispanic American, 0.4% Native American, 0.9% international, 10% transferred in, 57% live on campus.

Faculty *Total:* 467, 67% full-time, 59% with terminal degrees. *Student/faculty ratio:* 19:1.

Academic Programs *Special study options:* accelerated degree program, adult/continuing education programs, advanced placement credit, cooperative education, distance learning, double majors, English as a second language, freshman honors college, honors programs, independent study, internships, off-campus study, part-time degree program, services for LD students, student-designed majors, study abroad, summer session for credit. *ROTC:* Army (c). *Unusual degree programs:* 3-2 engineering with Clarkson University, Case Western Reserve University, State University of New York at Binghamton.

Athletics Member NCAA. All Division III. *Intercollegiate sports:* baseball M, basketball M/W, crew M(c)/W(c), cross-country running M/W, field hockey W, golf M, ice hockey M, lacrosse M/W, soccer M/W, softball W, swimming and diving M/W, tennis M/W, track and field M/W, volleyball W, wrestling M. *Intramural sports:* basketball M/W, cheerleading W(c), equestrian sports M(c)/W(c), fencing M(c)/W(c), field hockey W(c), football M/W, golf M/W, ice hockey M(c)/W(c), lacrosse M/W, racquetball M/W, rugby M(c)/W(c), sailing M(c)/W(c), skiing (cross-country) M(c)/W(c), skiing (downhill) M(c)/W(c), soccer M/W, softball M/W, swimming and diving M/W, tennis M/W, volleyball M(c)/W, weight lifting M, wrestling M.

Costs (2004–05) *Tuition:* state resident $4350 full-time, $181 per credit hour part-time; nonresident $10,160 full-time, $429 per credit hour part-time. Part-time tuition and fees vary according to class time and location. *Required fees:* $888 full-time, $34 per credit hour part-time. *Room and board:* $7890; room only: $4790. Room and board charges vary according to board plan, housing facility, and location.

Financial Aid 574 Federal Work-Study jobs (averaging $1083). 1,260 state and other part-time jobs (averaging $1113). In 2004, 1046 non-need-based awards were made. *Average percent of need met:* 84%. *Average financial aid package:* $8625. *Average need-based loan:* $4831. *Average need-based gift aid:* $3737. *Average non-need-based aid:* $5350.

Contact: Director: Dr. Norman L. Weiner, 105A Mahar Hall, Oswego, New York 13126; *Telephone:* 315-312-2190; *Fax:* 315-312-6790; *E-mail:* weiner@oswego.edu; *Web site:* http://www.oswego.edu/honors

---

State University of New York at Plattsburgh

Honors Program

Plattsburgh, New York

Honors Seminars, Learning Communities, Honors Tutorials, mentoring programs, and research opportunities are just a few of the special teaching/learning opportunities that distinguish SUNY Plattsburgh's Honors Program. All of these relationships are energized by interactions between bright, active, and motivated students and committed teacher/scholars. Intellectual and academic challenges in a supportive and developmental context encourage students to self-discovery and accomplishment beyond what they may believe they can do.

The organization of the Honors Program is fairly simple. It is a four-year program divided between General Honors (primarily for freshmen and sophomores) and Advanced Honors (for juniors and seniors). In the General Honors portion of the Honors Program, students are expected to complete four Honors Seminars. Honors Seminars are highly interactive classes limited to 15 students. Seminar topics change every semester, though all seminars satisfy part of the College's General Education Program. At least one

Learning Community is also offered each semester to General Honors students. The Advanced Honors part of the program allows students to undertake research projects of their own design under the guidance of a faculty mentor. Students are expected to make a public presentation of the honors thesis, which is the normal outcome of the research project. Advanced honors students also can pursue Honors Tutorials dealing with a wide range of topics.

The Honors Program at SUNY Plattsburgh is housed in the Redcay Honors Center. Facilities include a large study/lounge, two specially designed seminar rooms, a library, a computer lab, and a kitchenette. On the administrative side of the Honors Center are a reception/secretarial space, the director's office, and an office for visiting scholars. Students in the Honors Program have direct access to visiting scholars. The distinguished roster of visiting scholars includes a number of Nobel laureates, such as Joseph Brodsky, Eugene Wigner, and Derek Walcott.

The success rate of students who complete the Honors Program and apply to graduate and professional schools is nearly 100 percent. Honors Program alumni have distinguished themselves in many fields and maintain close contact with currently enrolled students.

The Honors Program is fully integrated into the rest of the College. Virtually every academic program at the College is represented among students in the Honors Program. The Honors Program is a supplement to rather than a substitute for other high-quality academic programs on campus.

The Honors Program was established in 1984. There are currently about 300 students in the program.

Admission Process: Entering freshmen whose high school average is 92 or above and whose SAT I scores are 1200 or above are automatically admitted into the Honors Program. Others may be admitted on the basis of an interview. Currently enrolled students with a 3.5 or higher GPA are automatically admitted.

Scholarship Availability: The College awards a number of full-tuition, four-year renewable Presidential Scholarships through the Honors Program each year to incoming freshmen. Additional Sophomore Presidential Scholarships are usually awarded. The Honors Program itself also awards a number of Redcay Honors Scholarships and Redcay Advanced Honors Scholarships.

Campus Overview

State-supported comprehensive, founded 1889, part of State University of New York System • **Coed** 5,275 undergraduate students, 93% full-time, 58% women, 42% men.

Undergraduates 4,908 full-time, 367 part-time. Students come from 26 states and territories, 49 other countries, 4% are from out of state, 5% African American, 2% Asian American or Pacific Islander, 4% Hispanic American, 0.4% Native American, 6% international, 11% transferred in, 48% live on campus.

Faculty *Total:* 446, 57% full-time, 54% with terminal degrees. *Student/faculty ratio:* 17:1.

Academic Programs *Special study options:* academic remediation for entering students, accelerated degree program, adult/continuing education programs, advanced placement credit, cooperative education, distance learning, double majors, English as a second language, honors programs, independent study, internships, off-campus study, part-time degree program, services for LD students, student-designed majors, study abroad, summer session for credit. *Unusual degree programs:* 3-2 engineering with Clarkson University, State University of New York at Stony Brook, Syracuse University, University of Vermont, McGill University, State University of New York at Binghamton; international policy studies with Monterey Institute of International Studies in French and Spanish.

Athletics Member NCAA. All Division III. *Intercollegiate sports:* baseball M, basketball M/W, cross-country running M/W, golf M/W, ice hockey M/W, lacrosse M, soccer M/W, softball W, swimming and diving M/W, tennis W, track and field M/W, volleyball W. *Intramural sports:* basketball M/W, football M, golf M/W, ice hockey M(c)/W(c), lacrosse M, racquetball M(c)/W(c), rugby M(c)/W(c), soccer M/W, softball W, tennis W, volleyball M/W, weight lifting M(c)/W(c).

Costs (2004–05) *Tuition:* state resident $4350 full-time, $181 per credit hour part-time; nonresident $10,610 full-time, $442 per credit hour part-time. Part-time tuition and fees vary according to course load. *Required fees:* $918 full-time, $38 per credit hour part-time. *Room and board:* $6712; room only: $4200. Room and board charges vary according to board plan.

Financial Aid 464 Federal Work-Study jobs (averaging $1564). In 2004, 1209 non-need-based awards were made. *Average percent of need met:* 89%. *Average financial aid package:* $9139. *Average need-based loan:* $5440. *Average need-based gift aid:* $3997. *Average non-need-based aid:* $4741.

Contact: Director: Dr. David N. Mowry, 121-123 Hawkins Hall, Plattsburgh, New York 12901; *Telephone:* 518-564-3075; *Fax:* 518-564-3071; *E-mail:* david.mowry@plattsburgh.edu

State University of New York College at Brockport
College Honors and Upper-Division Honors Program
Brockport, New York

Brockport's Honors Program sponsors two unique programs, the College Honors Program and the Senior Honors Program, for students with strong academic records. These programs allow students to enrich their college experience, maximizing both the breadth and the depth of their academic study. Honors students select courses from the College's wide variety of course offerings and also undertake in-depth research in a specific area of their academic major. Both programs allow students to satisfy the College's general education requirements, enroll in special honors seminars of approximately 15 students taught by SUNY Brockport's most distinguished faculty members, and to complete an honors thesis or project under the personal supervision of a faculty member in their major.

College Honors is designed for students entering the Honors Program in their freshman year. Students in College Honors complete their general education breadth requirements with a flexible mixture of honors seminars and conventional courses. Students take four honors courses in their first two years and they may select these courses on the basis of their academic strengths, personal interests, academic major, or even create their own courses. In the last two years of college, students in the College Honors Program take three honors courses, including the Junior Research Colloquium and an independent research course for the senior honors thesis.

Senior Honors is designed especially for transfer students and SUNY Brockport students who have shown significant academic achievements during their first two years of college courses. Students in this program complete the three upper-division honors courses required in the College Honors Program. SUNY Brockport's 20 year-old Honors Program admits 120 new students each year, and approximately 400 students are enrolled in the program.

Participation Requirements: Honors students must maintain a 3.25 GPA and take at least one honors course each year to participate in the programs. College Honors students must complete seven honors courses, including the honors thesis. Upper-Division honors students complete three Upper-Division honors courses, including the honors thesis. The completion of College Honors or Upper-Division Honors is noted on the students' transcripts.

Admission Process: Students must apply and be accepted in order to enroll in honors seminars and participate in Honors Program

activities. Entering freshmen should have a high school GPA of at least 91 and SAT I total scores of at least 1150 or the equivalent. Transfer students and current SUNY Brockport students should have a GPA of at least 3.5.

Scholarship Availability: SUNY Brockport's wide-ranging program of scholarships make it possible for all entering students in the Honors Program to qualify for financial assistance. In addition, the Honors Program has supplemental scholarships for eligible entering freshmen.

Campus Overview

State-supported comprehensive, founded 1867, part of State University of New York System • **Coed** 6,980 undergraduate students, 89% full-time, 57% women, 43% men.

Undergraduates 6,187 full-time, 793 part-time. Students come from 35 states and territories, 26 other countries, 2% are from out of state, 5% African American, 1% Asian American or Pacific Islander, 3% Hispanic American, 0.4% Native American, 1% international, 13% transferred in, 35% live on campus.

Faculty *Total:* 565, 53% full-time, 90% with terminal degrees. *Student/faculty ratio:* 18:1.

Academic Programs *Special study options:* academic remediation for entering students, accelerated degree program, advanced placement credit, cooperative education, distance learning, double majors, freshman honors college, honors programs, independent study, internships, off-campus study, part-time degree program, services for LD students, student-designed majors, study abroad, summer session for credit. *ROTC:* Army (b), Navy (c), Air Force (c). *Unusual degree programs:* 3-2 environmental science with State University of New York College of Environmental Science and Forestry.

Athletics Member NCAA. All Division III. *Intercollegiate sports:* baseball M, basketball M/W, cross-country running M/W, field hockey W, football M, gymnastics W, ice hockey M, lacrosse M/W, soccer M/W, softball W, swimming and diving M/W, tennis W, track and field M/W, volleyball W, wrestling M. *Intramural sports:* badminton M/W, basketball M/W, bowling M/W, cheerleading M/W, football M/W, racquetball M/W, rugby M/W, soccer M/W, softball M/W, table tennis M/W, tennis M/W, ultimate Frisbee M/W, volleyball M/W.

Costs (2004–05) *Tuition:* state resident $4350 full-time, $181 per credit hour part-time; nonresident $10,300 full-time, $429 per credit hour part-time. Part-time tuition and fees vary according to course load. *Required fees:* $913 full-time, $38 per credit hour part-time. *Room and board:* $7226; room only: $4500. Room and board charges vary according to board plan and housing facility.

Financial Aid 539 Federal Work-Study jobs (averaging $1381). 1,440 state and other part-time jobs (averaging $1422). In 2003, 205 non-need-based awards were made. *Average percent of need met:* 75%. *Average financial aid package:* $7019. *Average need-based loan:* $4162. *Average need-based gift aid:* $3222. *Average non-need-based aid:* $5099.

Contact: Director: Dr. Kenneth P. O'Brien, 219 Holmes Hall, SUNY College at Brockport, 350 New Campus Drive, Brockport, New York 14420; *Telephone:* 585-395-5400 Ext. 5054; *Fax:* 585-395-5046; *E-mail:* honors@brockport.edu

State University of New York College at Cortland

SUNY Cortland All-College Honors Program

Cortland, New York

The State University of New York College at Cortland (SUNY Cortland) All-College Honors Program provides students with demonstrated academic excellence the opportunity for continued intellectual challenge in a rigorous, coherent, and integrative program. Honors students participate in courses with an emphasis on student-faculty interchange and community building. The program provides a mechanism for students to distinguish themselves and also enhances the general learning environment for all students and faculty members, the College, and the community.

Honors classes are small, generally no more than 20 students, providing an opportunity for greater interaction among students and faculty members. Most honors courses are taken in conjunction with the College's general education program, but there are some opportunities to take honors courses in the student's major.

Honors Program students are encouraged to participate in a variety of programs, including an annual retreat at the College's outdoor recreation facility in Raquette Lake, New York, and trips to various cultural events in the region. The Honors Program also sponsors student participation in the annual conference of the Northeast Regional Honors Council.

The Honors Program is staffed by a coordinator, who functions as an unofficial adviser for Honors Program students, and an assistant. The Honors Program office, centrally located in the College's main academic building, includes a meeting room/study lounge for students and a small computer lab in addition to the coordinator's office. The SUNY Cortland All-College Honors Program is affiliated with the National Collegiate Honors Council (NCHC) and is a member of the Northeast Regional Honors Council. The program was founded in 1982, and there are 140 students currently enrolled. Since 2002, all Honors Program freshmen have been housed in the same residence hall.

Participation Requirements: To complete the Honors Program, students must take at least 24 credit hours of honors-level courses. Students fulfill this requirement by taking a combination of specially designated honors courses, contract courses, and a course in which they complete the required honors thesis. Students may also use a maximum of two writing-intensive (WI) courses beyond the All-College requirements toward the completion of the Honors Program. Specially designated honors courses are offered in a variety of general education categories. In addition, a few majors offer honors sections of their courses. Some of the courses offered through the general education program and in the majors are unique to the Honors Program, and others are special honors sections of courses offered to the general student population. All Honors Program students are required to complete an honors thesis for credit in their junior or senior year. In addition, all Honors Program students must complete 40 hours of community service.

Students in the Honors Program are expected to maintain a 3.2 cumulative GPA. Honors Program students who are in the top 5 percent of their respective classes and those seniors who have completed the program are recognized each year at the Honors Convocation. Students who complete the Honors Program requirements earn an honors designation on their diplomas and their transcripts, and they are recognized in the commencement program.

Admission Process: Students seeking to be admitted to the Honors Program as freshmen must indicate upon admission to the University that they would like to be considered for the program. The Honors Program Coordinator then reviews their admissions files and takes into consideration their high school GPAs (unweighted), SAT and/or ACT scores, class rank, extracurricular activities, and admissions essays in making decisions about accepting students for the program. Students are also admitted to the program as second-semester freshmen. Students who are applying to be admitted as second-semester freshmen must be in the top 5 percent of the freshman class in order to be considered. About 40 students are admitted each year as freshmen, and about 10 are admitted as second-semester freshmen.

Scholarship Availability: There are no scholarships tied to admission to the Honors Program. However, SUNY Cortland does offer a number of scholarships that are based on academic merit, and many students who receive these scholarships also participate in the Honors Program. Examples of these scholarships include the SUNY Cortland Presidential Scholarships, the SUNY Cortland Leadership Scholarships, and the Residential Service Scholarships. For more information about SUNY Cortland's many scholarship opportunities (and other sources of financial aid), students should visit the Admissions Office Web site at http://www.cortland.edu/finaid/scholarships.html.

Campus Overview

State-supported comprehensive, founded 1868, part of State University of New York System • **Coed** 5,950 undergraduate students, 96% full-time, 58% women, 42% men.

Undergraduates 5,733 full-time, 217 part-time. Students come from 26 states and territories, 2% are from out of state, 3% African American, 1% Asian American or Pacific Islander, 4% Hispanic American, 0.3% Native American, 0.3% international, 11% transferred in, 50% live on campus.

Faculty Total: 512, 52% full-time, 50% with terminal degrees. Student/faculty ratio: 16:1.

Academic Programs Special study options: academic remediation for entering students, adult/continuing education programs, advanced placement credit, cooperative education, distance learning, double majors, honors programs, independent study, internships, off-campus study, part-time degree program, services for LD students, student-designed majors, study abroad, summer session for credit. ROTC: Army (c), Air Force (c). Unusual degree programs: 3-2 engineering with State University of New York at Buffalo, State University of New York at Stony Brook, Alfred University, Clarkson University, State University of New York at Binghamton, Case Western Reserve University; forestry with Duke University, State University of New York College of Environmental Science and Forestry.

Athletics Member NCAA. All Division III. Intercollegiate sports: baseball M, basketball M/W, cross-country running M/W, field hockey W, football M/W(c), golf W, gymnastics W, ice hockey M/W(c), lacrosse M/W, racquetball M(c)/W(c), rugby M(c)/W(c), soccer M/W, softball W, swimming and diving M/W, tennis W, track and field M/W, volleyball M(c)/W, wrestling M. Intramural sports: archery M/W, badminton M/W, baseball M, basketball M/W, bowling M/W, cross-country running M/W, fencing M/W, field hockey W, football M/W, golf M/W, gymnastics W, ice hockey M, lacrosse M/W, racquetball M/W, rugby M/W, skiing (cross-country) M/W, skiing (downhill) M/W, soccer M/W, softball M/W, squash M/W, swimming and diving M/W, table tennis M/W, tennis M/W, track and field M/W, volleyball M/W, weight lifting M/W, wrestling M.

Costs (2004–05) Tuition: state resident $4350 full-time, $181 per credit part-time; nonresident $10,300 full-time, $442 per credit part-time. Required fees: $950 full-time. Room and board: $7290; room only: $4228. Room and board charges vary according to board plan and housing facility.

Financial Aid In 2002, 942 non-need-based awards were made. Average percent of need met: 79%. Average financial aid package: $8091. Average need-based loan: $3709. Average need-based gift aid: $3234. Average non-need-based aid: $5760.

Contact: Contact: Coordinator: Dr. Arnold Talentino, B-13 Old Main, SUNY Cortland, P.O. Box 2000, Cortland, New York 13045-0900; Telephone: 607-753-4827; Fax: 607-753-5989; E-mail: honors@cortland.edu; Web site: http://www.cortland.edu/honors

State University of New York College at Oneonta
Oneonta Scholars Program
Oneonta, New York

The Oneonta Scholars Program is a four-year, 18-credit program designed for students who wish to seek out challenging academic experiences and want to contribute to the intellectual and cultural life of the academic community. Freshman and sophomore course work emphasizes skill development and interdisciplinary perspectives while junior and senior course work emphasizes discipline-based experiences. The courses are designed to fit into the student's program of study. Scholars take the same number of credits as other students and courses taken during the freshman and sophomore years satisfy general education requirements.

The Oneonta Scholars Program is designed to develop and foster the qualities found in an Oneonta Scholar: inquisitive, creative, independent, and critical thinking; strong academic ability; and a high capacity for independent work. Students who participate in the Scholars Program have the opportunity to enjoy exciting and challenging course work in a small-class setting, to develop close working relationships with Oneonta's best faculty members, and to become part of a network of similarly motivated students.

The four-year Oneonta Scholars Program was implemented in the fall of 1996. It is a direct outgrowth of the pilot Freshmen Scholars Program, which was initiated in 1994. There are currently 94 students involved in the new program.

Participation Requirements: During the freshman year, students take the Freshman Scholars Seminar. The Freshmen Scholars Seminar is designed to build critical-thinking, reading, writing, speaking, and listening skills. In addition, freshmen may take general education courses from a selection of courses offered for scholars.

The junior and senior year course work allows the student to specialize in his or her major. Students may contract with a course instructor and the Oneonta Scholars Program office to take any course for scholars credit. Students must complete at least 3 credits of independent work in their major with a faculty mentor. The independent work can take the form of an internship, field experience, a thesis, a research project, or creative work.

Once accepted into the program, the student must maintain a minimum overall GPA of 3.3 and receive no less than a grade of B in any Scholars course in order to maintain eligibility. Successful completion of the program is noted on the student's transcript.

Admission Process: The eligibility process is flexible to ensure that all qualified students have the opportunity to apply. Students may enter the program up to the first semester of their junior year. Entering freshmen are invited to participate based on SAT I scores, high school class rank, and high school GPA. Returning students and transfer students may initiate the application process.

Scholarship Availability: The College at Oneonta has recently established the Mildred Haight Memorial Scholarships. Beginning in 1997, 20 incoming freshmen receive $500 grants each to purchase books and other educational supplies at the College Bookstore. The awards are being made to accepted students early in the admission cycle, and the primary criterion is high school GPA.

Campus Overview

State-supported comprehensive, founded 1889, part of State University of New York System • **Coed** 5,605 undergraduate students, 97% full-time, 58% women, 42% men.

Undergraduates 5,431 full-time, 174 part-time. Students come from 18 states and territories, 17 other countries, 2% are from out of state, 2% African American, 2% Asian American or Pacific Islander, 4% Hispanic American, 0.2% Native American, 1% international, 9% transferred in, 57% live on campus.

Faculty *Total:* 440, 57% full-time, 52% with terminal degrees. *Student/faculty ratio:* 18:1.

Academic Programs *Special study options:* academic remediation for entering students, adult/continuing education programs, advanced placement credit, distance learning, double majors, English as a second language, honors programs, independent study, internships, off-campus study, part-time degree program, services for LD students, study abroad, summer session for credit. *Unusual degree programs:* 3-2 business administration with State University of New York at Binghamton, Rochester Institute of Technology, University of Rochester; engineering with Georgia Institute of Technology, State University of New York at Buffalo, Clarkson University; forestry with State University of New York College of Environmental Science and Forestry; nursing with Johns Hopkins University; accounting with State University of New York at Binghamton, fashion with American Intercontinental University in London.

Athletics Member NCAA. All Division III except soccer (Division I). *Intercollegiate sports:* baseball M, basketball M/W, cheerleading W(c), cross-country running M/W, field hockey W, ice hockey M(c), lacrosse M/W, rugby M(c)/W(c), soccer M(s)/W, softball W, swimming and diving M/W, tennis M/W, track and field M/W, volleyball M(c)/W, wrestling M. *Intramural sports:* basketball M/W, football M, lacrosse M, skiing (downhill) M/W, soccer M/W, softball M/W, ultimate Frisbee M/W, volleyball M/W.

Costs (2005–06) *Tuition:* Part-time tuition and fees vary according to course load. *Required fees:* $997 full-time. *Room and board:* $7230; room only: $4230. Room and board charges vary according to board plan and housing facility.

Financial Aid 395 Federal Work-Study jobs (averaging $1200). In 2004, 1003 non-need-based awards were made. *Average percent of need met:* 66%. *Average financial aid package:* $9068. *Average need-based loan:* $4226. *Average need-based gift aid:* $3759. *Average non-need-based aid:* $4750.

Contact: Dr. Michael Merilan, 332C Netzer Administration Building, Oneonta, New York 13820-4015; *Telephone:* 607-436-2125; *Fax:* 607-436-2689; *E-mail:* merilamp@oneonta.edu

State University of New York College at Potsdam
Honors Program
Potsdam, New York

The SUNY Potsdam Honors Program has three goals. The first is to recognize, reward, and provide enhanced educational opportunities for the College's best students. The second is to prepare students who, upon graduation from SUNY Potsdam, are ready to become highly successful in their pursuits, whether they include graduate school, full-time employment, or other service, research, or creative endeavors. The third is to provide intellectual enrichment for the entire campus community. The program seeks to develop students' scholarship, leadership, and service capabilities, and students with similar inclinations are sought. The program has approximately 300 honors students in all (roughly the top academic 7 or 8 percent of the College's total undergraduate student population). The program provides honors students with a strong and distinctive academic experience, which includes qualitatively different and academically strengthening interaction with members of the SUNY Potsdam faculty and staff as well as enriched opportunities for interaction with other honors students. There are tangible benefits as well, which are designed to help honors students meet the program's goals. For example, honors students have access to an honors lounge, an honors computer lab, and a nearby study room that were recently opened. Honors students are also offered priority registration, small-enrollment honors sections of courses (average class size of about 15 to 20 students), diverse honors course offerings, other programming of special interest to honors students, an Honors Student Organization, the opportunity to travel to Northeast Regional and National NCHC conventions, and special mentoring and advising relationships with select members of the SUNY Potsdam faculty, staff, and student body. The program was founded in 1998.

Participation Requirements: The Honors Program curriculum is broken into two parts: General Honors, which is intended for freshmen and sophomores, and Advanced Honors, which is intended for juniors and seniors. General Honors students must take at least three honors-level courses, which are offered in a variety of areas, during their careers as students at Potsdam. In addition, a required General Honors Colloquium is offered for first-semester freshmen as well as other SUNY Potsdam students who have not yet taken the colloquium. Later in the program, Advanced Honors students take a colloquium on the topic Scholar as Citizen during their junior year and also complete an Advanced Honors thesis or project as they work in close collaboration with an advising team, a personal librarian mentor, and other members of the College's teaching faculty. There are numerous options available through which Advanced Honors students can complete their thesis or project requirement. Students must maintain a minimum cumulative GPA of 3.0 (for all course work) to remain in good standing within the program. Students who complete either General Honors or Advanced Honors are so recognized at commencement and on their transcripts; anyone completing both the General and Advanced Honors curricula graduates as a SUNY Potsdam Distinguished Scholar.

Admission Process: In order to qualify for application to the Honors Program, incoming first-year students must have a minimum 93 percent high school GPA. (Exceptions to these qualification guidelines can be made at the discretion of the Honors Program Director on a student-by-student basis.) In addition, certain incoming first-year students automatically qualify for admission to the program. These include high school class valedictorians or salutatorians as well as National Merit Finalists or Semifinalists. Transfer students who have completed an honors program at a two-year college are eligible for automatic acceptance into the SUNY Potsdam Honors Program. In addition, transfer or current students who have at least a 3.25 cumulative GPA are eligible to apply for program admission through the Honors Program Director. Interested students from off campus can obtain program and application information by contacting the Honors Program Office at 315-267-2900.

Scholarship Availability: Virtually all incoming first-year honors students qualify for four-year renewable scholarship funds ranging upward from $2000 per year. Renewability of this award is contingent on maintenance of at least a 3.25 GPA each year. Students should contact the SUNY Potsdam Office of Admission at 315-267-2180 for more details. Consideration for these scholarships requires no additional application.

Campus Overview

State-supported comprehensive, founded 1816, part of State University of New York System • **Coed** 3,539 undergraduate students, 96% full-time, 59% women, 41% men.

Undergraduates 3,402 full-time, 137 part-time. Students come from 23 states and territories, 25 other countries, 2% are from out of state, 2% African American, 1% Asian American or Pacific Islander, 2% Hispanic American, 2% Native American, 3% international, 10% transferred in, 52% live on campus.

Faculty Total: 327, 72% full-time, 69% with terminal degrees. Student/faculty ratio: 15:1.

Academic Programs Special study options: adult/continuing education programs, advanced placement credit, distance learning, double majors, honors programs, independent study, internships, off-campus

study, part-time degree program, services for LD students, student-designed majors, study abroad, summer session for credit. ROTC: Army (c), Air Force (c). Unusual degree programs: 3-2 engineering with Clarkson University, State University of New York at Binghamton; management, accounting with State University of New York Institute of Technology at Utica/Rome, applied science with State University of New York College of Technology at Canton.

Athletics Member NCAA. All Division III. Intercollegiate sports: basketball M/W, cross-country running M/W, equestrian sports W(c), golf M, ice hockey M, lacrosse M/W, rugby W(c), soccer M/W, softball W, swimming and diving M/W, tennis W, track and field M(c)/W(c), volleyball W. Intramural sports: badminton M/W, basketball M/W, equestrian sports M/W, racquetball M/W, skiing (cross-country) M/W, skiing (downhill) M/W, squash M/W, tennis M/W, volleyball M/W, water polo M/W.

Costs (2004–05) Tuition: state resident $4350 full-time, $181 per credit hour part-time; nonresident $10,610 full-time, $442 per credit hour part-time. Required fees: $900 full-time, $42 per credit hour part-time. Room and board: $7270; room only: $4220. Room and board charges vary according to board plan and housing facility.

Financial Aid 386 Federal Work-Study jobs (averaging $1000). In 2004, 161 non-need-based awards were made. Average percent of need met: 79%. Average financial aid package: $11,330. Average need-based loan: $4170. Average need-based gift aid: $4396. Average non-need-based aid: $7137.

Contact: Director: Dr. David A. Smith, 149 Morey Hall, Potsdam, New York 13676; Telephone: 315-267-2900; Fax: 315-267-2677; E-mail: smithda@potsdam.edu; Web site: http://www.potsdam.edu/content.php?contentID=9F7C8E2BA7C8D375D5D1966472CBD2DA

Stony Brook University, State University of New York
Honors College
Stony Brook, New York

The Honors College at Stony Brook University is an innovative academic program that promises to challenge, stimulate, and enrich superior students. Each year, a small group of high-achieving students is invited to join the Honors College and take advantage of an exciting curriculum, extraordinary career guidance, an array of cultural activities, and a supportive social environment.

The Honors College has its own interdisciplinary core curriculum, especially tailored to high-achieving students. Students are taught by faculty members with a strong commitment to undergraduate teaching. In 1997, the University at Stony Brook was rated second among all public research universities. Taking advantage of that strength, honors students are engaged in research and other creative activities during their years at Stony Brook. The Honors College also sponsors a range of 1-credit courses that engage students in a range of cultural and community activities.

Honors College students receive priority housing in a renovated residence hall reserved for honors students. The hall has its own computer laboratory, lounges, and access to a nearby fitness center. The College sponsors student social and cultural events throughout the year.

Each year, several incoming Honors College students are accepted into the Scholars for Medicine (B.A./M.D.) program, which reserves them a seat in Stony Brook's School of Medicine upon successful completion of the four-year undergraduate program.

The Honors College at Stony Brook was founded in 1988. There are approximately 250 students enrolled in the College.

Participation Requirements: The Honors College curriculum consists of a four-year program that requires the same number of credits as the general education program. Students take 19 credits of courses designed specially for the program as well as 6 credits of departmental honors courses. Students can major in any field.

To graduate from the Honors College, students must maintain a minimum cumulative GPA of 3.0. Honors College members also complete a senior project that represents the culmination of their honors experience at Stony Brook.

Admission Process: Students must file a general application for the University at Stony Brook as well as the online supplemental application. Students applying for freshmen admission are expected to have minimum SAT I scores of 1300 as well as an unweighted high school average of 93 percent. Transfer students must have compiled a minimum GPA of 3.5 in their college-level work. Special attention is also paid to students' writing ability, as demonstrated through their personal essay and other application materials. Applications from students who have demonstrated leadership in extracurricular activities and/or excellence in visual, performing, or literary arts are particularly encouraged. Students who wish to apply for the Scholars for Medicine program must have minimum SAT I scores of 1350. They also write a second essay as part of the supplemental application.

Admissions folders are initially read by members of the Honors College Advisory Board. The board consists of faculty members from the College of Arts and Sciences, the College of Engineering and Applied Sciences, and the Marine Sciences Research Center as well as members of the Honors College administration. Final decisions are made by the Chair and Assistant to the Chair of the Honors College. The Dean of Admissions for the Medical School chooses candidates for Scholars for Medicine from a group recommended by the Honors College.

The deadline for freshmen admissions is January 15. The deadline for transfer admissions is May 1.

Scholarship Availability: All members of the Honors College receive at least a $2000 scholarship in their first year. Many four-year scholarships are also available. To retain four-year scholarships, students must remain members of the Honors College.

Campus Overview

State-supported university, founded 1957, part of State University of New York System • **Coed** 13,858 undergraduate students, 91% full-time, 49% women, 51% men.

Undergraduates 12,620 full-time, 1,238 part-time. Students come from 42 states and territories, 72 other countries, 2% are from out of state, 10% African American, 23% Asian American or Pacific Islander, 8% Hispanic American, 0.2% Native American, 5% international, 12% transferred in, 63% live on campus.

Faculty *Total:* 1,338, 65% full-time, 95% with terminal degrees. *Student/faculty ratio:* 14:1.

Academic Programs *Special study options:* academic remediation for entering students, adult/continuing education programs, advanced placement credit, distance learning, double majors, English as a second language, freshman honors college, honors programs, independent study, internships, off-campus study, part-time degree program, services for LD students, student-designed majors, study abroad, summer session for credit. *ROTC:* Army (c), Air Force (c).

Athletics Member NCAA, NAIA. All NCAA Division I. *Intercollegiate sports:* baseball M(s), basketball M(s)/W(s), cross-country running M(s)/W(s), football M(s), lacrosse M(s)/W(s), soccer M(s)/W(s), softball W(s), swimming and diving M(s)/W(s), tennis M(s)/W(s), track and field M(s)/W(s), volleyball W(s). *Intramural sports:* badminton M/W, basketball M/W, bowling M/W, cheerleading W, crew M(c)/W(c), equestrian sports M(c)/W(c), golf M, ice hockey M(c), racquetball M/W, rugby M(c)/W(c), soccer M/W, softball M/W, table tennis M/W, tennis M/W, ultimate Frisbee M(c)/W(c), volleyball M/W.

Costs (2004–05) *Tuition:* state resident $4350 full-time, $181 per credit part-time; nonresident $10,610 full-time, $442 per credit part-time. *Required fees:* $1039 full-time, $50 per credit part-time. *Room and board:* $7730. Room and board charges vary according to board plan and housing facility.

Financial Aid 607 Federal Work-Study jobs (averaging $1972). 1,590 state and other part-time jobs (averaging $2070). In 2003, 1029 non-need-based awards were made. *Average percent of need met:* 71%. *Average financial aid package:* $8555. *Average need-based loan:* $3970. *Average need-based gift aid:* $5123. *Average non-need-based aid:* $2746.

Contact: Director: Honors College, Ward Melville Library N3071, Stony Brook, New York 11794-3357; *Telephone:* 631-632-4378; *Fax:* 631-632-4525; *E-mail:* honorscollege@notes.cc.sunysb.edu

---

Sullivan County Community College
SCCC Honors Program
Loch Sheldrake, New York

*T*he Honors Program at Sullivan County Community College (SCCC) is designed for talented students who are interested in a rigorous and rewarding academic experience. The SCCC Honors Program stresses academic excellence and personal achievement so that, after two years at Sullivan, students are well prepared to transfer with full junior status to highly regarded four-year institutions. SCCC's honors students have been accepted into Cornell, Harvard, Ithaca, MIT, NYU, Rensselaer, RIT, Vassar, and SUNY at Albany, Binghamton, Buffalo, and New Paltz, as well as many other prestigious schools in and out of the SUNY system. Sullivan honors students have followed their college careers with success as lawyers, teachers, writers, researchers, and even film directors—people who have impact on the world around them.

Unlike many four-year institutions where freshmen have to scramble for seats in large lecture halls, honors students at Sullivan receive one-on-one attention from professors who excel at teaching and who care about their students. Honors courses stress breadth of knowledge, independent research, and critical-thinking and writing skills.

Honors students at Sullivan enjoy rich experiences inside and outside of the classroom. In addition to academics, honors students take trips to museums in New York City, attend regional and national honors conferences, participate in honors-sponsored campus events, and get together informally for good conversation among friends.

Those accepted into the Honors Program become eligible for a substantial scholarship for their two years at Sullivan. Along with the distinction honors adds to one's academic record, this scholarship could save the student thousands of dollars in tuition and fees over the course of his or her college career.

The Honors Program is designed for those who want to be challenged and who want to make a difference, not simply in their own lives, but also in the lives of others.

Participation Requirements: Honors students are required to take Honors Legacy of Western Society I and II and the Honors Forum. The legacy courses focus on classic texts, such as Dante's *Inferno* and Mary Shelley's *Frankenstein*, and trace the intellectual evolution of Western thought. The Honors Forum meets once a week and brings first- and second-year honors students together to develop service-learning projects and to work on such activities as the Sullivan Honors Annual Writers' Conference (SHAWC) and the College lecture series. In addition, students are required to take four other honors courses, with particular emphasis given to honors composition I and honors ethics. Sullivan also offers honors general psychology, honors sociology, and more specialized courses focusing on various topics, from women's literature to terrorism.

Admission Process: Sullivan welcomes all applicants; however, enrollment in the Honors Program is limited. The College invites prospective students to join the program based on a number of factors. Exceptional performance in one area may offset average performance in another area. Evidence of the following requirements should be included with the student's honors application (distinct from the SUNY-Sullivan application): Above-average academic performance as shown by grade point average, class rank, and scores on the SAT or ACT; a letter indicating interest in the program, which serves as a writing sample (the letter should discuss leadership positions held and any other evidence deemed relevant to qualification for the program); a portfolio (if applicable); and a SUNY application for undergraduate admission to Sullivan County Community College.

Scholarship Availability: An honors scholarship is awarded to all students accepted into the Honors Program. Any student who graduates in the top 10 percent of his or her class in Sullivan County and is accepted into the Honors Program receives the cost of tuition and fees, less PELL, TAP, and any SCCC scholarships, for the fall and spring semesters. International students receive $700 per semester, for a total of $1400 per year. Early admission students are awarded $500 per semester, for a total of $1000 per year. All other students (not in the above categories) receive a minimum award of $500 per semester over and above any PELL and TAP awards and a maximum of $1400 per semester over and above any PELL and TAP awards.

Renewal of the scholarship for the second year is based on the student's having achieved an overall cumulative grade point average of 3.25 or higher at the end of the first year.

Campus Overview

State and locally supported 2-year, founded 1962, part of State University of New York System • **Coed** 1,902 undergraduate students, 62% full-time, 64% women, 36% men.

Undergraduates 1,178 full-time, 724 part-time. Students come from 6 states and territories, 9 other countries, 1% are from out of state, 21% African American, 0.9% Asian American or Pacific Islander, 9% Hispanic American, 0.3% Native American, 0.9% international, 5% transferred in.

Faculty *Total:* 134, 37% full-time. *Student/faculty ratio:* 16:1.

Academic Programs *Special study options:* academic remediation for entering students, adult/continuing education programs, advanced placement credit, distance learning, double majors, honors programs, internships, part-time degree program, services for LD students, summer session for credit.

Athletics Member NJCAA. *Intercollegiate sports:* basketball M/W, cheerleading W, cross-country running M/W, golf M, softball W, volleyball W. *Intramural sports:* basketball M/W, bowling M/W, cross-country running M/W, football M, golf M/W, racquetball M/W, skiing (downhill) M/W, soccer M/W, softball M/W, table tennis M/W, tennis M/W, volleyball M/W, weight lifting M/W.

Costs (2004–05) *Tuition:* state resident $2900 full-time, $115 per credit part-time; nonresident $5800 full-time, $149 per credit part-time. *Required fees:* $301 full-time. *Room and board:* $6050; room only: $3800.

Financial Aid 105 Federal Work-Study jobs (averaging $800). 57 state and other part-time jobs (averaging $841).

Contact: Director: Dr. Timothy M. Russell, Liberal Arts, 112 College Road, Loch Sheldrake, New York 12759-5151; *Telephone:* 845-434-5750 Ext. 4236; *Fax:* 845-434-4806; *E-mail:* trussell@sullivan.suny.edu

Syracuse University
The Renée Crown University Honors Program
Syracuse, New York

The Renée Crown University Honors Program is a selective, demanding, and rewarding program for outstanding students who seek intense intellectual challenge and are prepared to invest the extra effort it takes to meet that challenge. It is marked by heightened expectations, participation in a vibrant learning community, greater intensity of intellectual experience, and special intellectual opportunities.

While students pursue their chosen academic course of study in their individual departments, schools, and colleges, the Honors Program offers intellectual challenge and curricular enrichment through seminars, honors courses, special cultural events, and close contact with faculty members and other honors students. The program is open to qualified students in all of the University's undergraduate schools and colleges.

For students accepting the challenge of Syracuse University's Renée Crown University Honors Program, the completion of courses and seminars is just the beginning of an extraordinary college experience. They engage the resources of a major research university while finding an intellectual and personal home in a congenially sized program dedicated to their success. Their efforts are supported by an inviting honors suite that offers seminar rooms, a student lounge, an honors library, and a computer cluster, many of which are accessible 24 hours a day.

Participation Requirements: Success in the program depends on the development and demonstration of a challenging list of attributes: depth, as marked by significant original accomplishment in a focused area of study; breadth, as marked by a range of challenging courses beyond one's primary area of specialization and the ability to investigate issues best understood through interdisciplinary work; command of language, as marked by a refined ability to read and assess texts in a variety of communications media, to understand the meanings and implications of quantitative information, and to speak and write with a polished and compelling command of language; global awareness, as marked by international sophistication and fruitful reflection on the interconnectedness of the world; collaborative capacity, as marked by the ability to work constructively with others on sustained and challenging projects; and civic engagement, as marked by sustained active involvement in addressing the interests of others.

There are many paths to demonstrating these attributes. To demonstrate depth, a student might write an academic thesis or produce a play—and perhaps perform in it. To demonstrate global awareness, a student might participate in a sustained experience abroad—perhaps in a resource-poor country. To demonstrate a capacity for collaboration, a student might produce an instructional video for a local medical office as part of a team of student writers, filmmakers, and premedical biology majors. To demonstrate civic engagement, a student might play a sustained role in tutoring refugees or in constructing homes for families needing such assistance. To demonstrate superior command of language, students must excel in specific courses demanding high levels of competence in written and oral communication and in understanding, analyzing, and manipulating quantitative information.

Honors students exhibit not only intellectual accomplishment but also a passion for integrating academic work with an evident awareness and consideration of others. They take a series of courses and seminars, designed specifically for them, to satisfy University and college curricular requirements. However, completion of the Honors Program demands engagement in activities and demonstration of qualities beyond course work. Students begin with an honors seminar in the first semester of the first year. They then choose from a set of innovative and interdisciplinary honors courses in the humanities, social sciences, natural sciences, and professional schools, such as public communications and management, many of which are co-taught by 2 or more professors. Some of these courses may incorporate travel during the semester or during semester breaks to foster global awareness; others may be offered in conjunction with the campus visits of distinguished speakers.

A student must also achieve cum laude distinction in his or her home college to be awarded honors.

Admission Process: The average total SAT score of entering first-year students is 1360, and they rank in the top 5 percent of their graduating high school classes. Most incoming students are preselected, but applications received by April 25 are considered. First-year students may apply for admission after their first semester on campus. Second-semester sophomores with a minimum cumulative GPA of 3.5 on a 4.0 scale are invited to apply to Thesis Project Honors.

Scholarship Availability: Syracuse University provides a generous merit scholarship program for all qualified students regardless of financial need. There are no scholarships associated directly with the Honors Program.

Campus Overview

Independent university, founded 1870 • **Coed** 10,750 undergraduate students, 99% full-time, 56% women, 44% men.

Undergraduates 10,665 full-time, 85 part-time. Students come from 52 states and territories, 59 other countries, 60% are from out of state, 6% African American, 6% Asian American or Pacific Islander, 4% Hispanic American, 0.3% Native American, 3% international, 3% transferred in, 73% live on campus.

Faculty *Total:* 1,406, 63% full-time. *Student/faculty ratio:* 12:1.

Academic Programs *Special study options:* accelerated degree program, adult/continuing education programs, advanced placement credit, cooperative education, distance learning, double majors, English as a second language, external degree program, honors programs, independent study, internships, off-campus study, part-time degree program, services for LD students, student-designed majors, study abroad, summer session for credit. *ROTC:* Army (b), Air Force (b).

Athletics Member NCAA. All Division I except football (Division I-A). *Intercollegiate sports:* archery M(c)/W(c), badminton M(c)/W(c), baseball M(c), basketball M(s)/W(s), bowling M(c)/W(c), cheerleading M/W, crew M(s)/W(s), cross-country running M(s)/W(s), equestrian sports M(c)/W(c), fencing M(c)/W(c), field hockey W(s), gymnastics M(c)/W(c), ice hockey M(c)/W(c), lacrosse M(s)/W(s), racquetball M(c)/W(c), riflery M(c)/W(c), rugby M(c)/W(c), sailing M(c)/W(c), skiing (downhill) M(c)/W(c), soccer M(s)/W(s), softball M(c)/W(s), squash M(c)/W(c), swimming and diving M(s)/W(s), table tennis M(c)/W(c), tennis M(c)/W(s), track and field M(s)/W(s), volleyball M(c)/W(s), water polo M(c)/W(c), weight lifting M(c)/W(c). *Intramural sports:* badminton M/W, basketball M/W, cross-country running M/W, football M/W, golf M/W, lacrosse M(c)/W(c), racquetball M/W, soccer M/W, softball M/W, squash M/W, swimming and diving M/W, table tennis M/W, tennis M/W, track and field M/W, ultimate Frisbee M/W, volleyball M/W.

Costs (2004–05) *Comprehensive fee:* $36,704 includes full-time tuition ($25,720), mandatory fees ($1014), and room and board ($9970). Part-time tuition: $1120 per credit hour. *College room only:* $5400. Room and board charges vary according to board plan and housing facility.

Financial Aid In 2004, 1701 non-need-based awards were made. *Average percent of need met:* 80%. *Average financial aid package:* $18,822. *Average need-based loan:* $5300. *Average need-based gift aid:* $13,661. *Average non-need-based aid:* $8140.

Contact: Director: Professor Samuel Gorovitz, 306 Bowne Hall, Syracuse, New York 13244-1200; *Telephone:* 315-443-2759; *Fax:* 315-443-3235; *E-mail:* eholzwar@syr.edu; *Web site:* http://www.honors.syr.edu

Trocaire College
Honors Program
Buffalo, New York

*T*he Honors Program at Trocaire College embodies, encourages, and facilitates the authentic pursuit of excellence academically, socially, culturally, and personally. Participation in honors studies at Trocaire College stimulates students to aspire to their fullest potential; fosters interdisciplinary, multicultural educational experiences; enriches the curriculum with innovative educational projects; challenges students to pursue higher standards; encourages students to become good citizens by contributing to the good of society; cultivates open-mindedness, scholarship, and community in the activity of learning; establishes a community that values excellence; enables students to develop aspects of themselves that previously remained dormant; and sparks interest in lifelong learning through exposure to shared academic, cultural, and social endeavors.

The following benefits are granted to Trocaire College students who participate in the Honors Program: honors designation for all honors courses that are successfully completed and appear on official transcripts; special recognition at College events, namely Honors Convocation, Honors Day, and graduation; honors designation on the Trocaire graduation diploma; special presentation and recognition at Honors Day events; opportunity to work closely with honors faculty members; transferable honors courses and credits; and exposure to and participation in cultural, intellectual, and social events within the local community. In addition, participation in the Honors Program distinguishes a student as a dedicated, highly motivated, and talented individual—as a person who is willing to go above and beyond, both academically and professionally. Honors courses transfer readily to four-year institutions for students who desire to continue on to pursue further educational goals. In the professional world, those who participate in honors studies possess an honors degree, which differentiates them from competing job candidates.

The Honors Program at Trocaire College involves taking In Course Honors Option (ICHO) courses and an Honors Seminar. In Course Honors Options are offered in the following areas: English, sciences, psychology, history, theology, philosophy, and sociology. Each Honors Seminar concentrates on a given honors theme. Invited guests are considered experts on the Honors Seminar theme, and speakers include local celebrities, professionals, public figures, social activists, and specialists who kindly agree to come to Trocaire College to present and to participate in a discussion with those students enrolled in the Honors Program.

Participation Requirements: Each student who desires to graduate with an honors degree is required to take five ICHO courses (and to successfully complete them with a grade of B or higher) before graduation. The In Course Honors Option involves the ability of students to convert any existing liberal arts course into an honors course by completing additional requirements; these supplementary requirements are designated and overseen by the Honors Program Coordinator and by the faculty member teaching the course.

The Honors Seminar meets monthly throughout the semester, and each student who wishes to graduate with honors distinction is required to attend monthly Honors Seminar meetings. Each Honors Seminar concentrates on a given theme, which carries over throughout the semester in both Honors Option courses and the Honors Seminar. The Honors Seminar provides a forum for discussion of community service related to the honors theme, voluntary and supplemental potential for participation in outside related cultural activities, and discussion of readings on the honors theme.

Admission Process: The requirements for admission into the Honors Program are as follows: Accuplacer test scores of at least 90 on Reading and at least 100 on Sentence Skills, a cumulative high school GPA of 3.0 or above, a successful interview with the Honors Program Coordinator, and completion of a 500-word essay explaining why the student desires to be an honors student at Trocaire College. Students who already attend the College could apply for acceptance in the Honors Program if they have a GPA of 3.0 or above in liberal arts, have a GPA of 3.3 or higher in their specific program, complete a 500-word essay explaining why they desire to be an honors student at Trocaire College, and have a successful interview with the Honors Program Coordinator. Students may also be interviewed by the Honors Program Coordinator based on faculty recommendation. Applicants must complete an interview with the Honors Program Coordinator prior to acceptance into the program by January 10 (for admission during the spring semester) or by August 15 (for admission during the fall semester).

Scholarship Availability: A wide variety of scholarship opportunities are available at Trocaire College. The McAuley Scholarship is a full-tuition scholarship that is awarded annually to 2 high school seniors who have been accepted to Trocaire College. Candidates must have a minimum cumulative average of 92 and a minimum score of 1200 on the SAT and be recommended by their high school guidance counselor or principal. This scholarship is renewable, provided a GPA of 3.2 or higher is maintained. Two Presidential Scholarships per high school are awarded annually. The $2000 scholarships are awarded to high school seniors attending Trocaire College. Selection of these scholarships is made based on a recommendation of the high school principal or guidance counselor. The Non-Traditional Scholarship Award is a need-based scholarship awarded to a nontraditional college-bound student. Twenty individually sponsored scholarships are awarded through the Student Affairs Office.

Campus Overview

Independent 2-year, founded 1958 • **Urban** 1-acre campus • **Coed primarily women** 780 undergraduate students.

Undergraduates Students come from 3 states and territories, 4 other countries, 1% are from out of state, 23% African American, 0.8% Asian American or Pacific Islander, 2% Hispanic American, 0.4% Native American, 0.8% international.

Faculty *Total:* 113, 34% full-time. *Student/faculty ratio:* 15:1.

Academic Programs *Special study options:* academic remediation for entering students, adult/continuing education programs, advanced placement credit, external degree program, independent study, internships, off-campus study, part-time degree program, services for LD students, summer session for credit.

Costs (2004–05) *Tuition:* $9560 full-time, $370 per credit hour part-time. Full-time tuition and fees vary according to course load and program. Part-time tuition and fees vary according to course load and program. *Required fees:* $50 per term part-time.

Financial Aid 33 Federal Work-Study jobs (averaging $1500).

Contact: Honors Program Coordinator: Dr. Amy DiMaio, Liberals Arts Division, Trocaire College, 360 Choate Avenue, Buffalo, New York 14220; *Telephone:* 716-827-2455; *E-mail:* dimaioa@trocaire.edu

---

Wagner College

Honors Program

Staten Island, New York

The Wagner College Honors Program offers students in all majors an opportunity for academic enrichment, both inside the classroom and in cocurricular activities.

All honors courses at Wagner fulfill the College-wide distribution requirements, and they are designed to provide the College's best students with a challenging, interactive learning environment that will enhance their overall academic experience at the College. The classes are small and taught by Wagner's finest faculty members.

The honors experience at Wagner extends beyond the classroom to a variety of cocurricular activities organized for honors students, ranging from a speaker series, a foreign film series, and other events on campus to trips to Manhattan to visit galleries and museums and attend plays and concerts. This creates a close-knit learning community for honors students that provides them with stimulation, friendship, and support. Many of Wagner's finest honors students also play important leadership roles on campus in student government, athletics, music, and theater. The Honors Program at Wagner is now in its twelfth year and has become an important feature of the College's academic program.

There are 150 students in the program.

Participation Requirements: Students must complete five honors courses (out of a total of 36 units required for graduation), usually to meet the College distribution requirements. The final honors course is a Senior Honors Project, which is taken in the first semester of the senior year and gives advanced students an opportunity to work independently with a faculty mentor. Students who complete the program and maintain a minimum GPA of 3.5 receive an Honors Certificate upon graduation.

Admission Process: Students first apply to Wagner, and the Admissions Office decides who will be invited to join the Honors Program. Transfer students who wish to join may apply to the program director at the end of the freshman year or the beginning of the sophomore year. February 15 is the priority deadline.

Scholarship Availability: Wagner awards Presidential or Founders' Merit Scholarships to the best incoming freshmen, who are also invited to join the Honors Program. Scholarship recipients are not required to join the program, however, and students who have not received these prestigious scholarships are also encouraged to apply for admission to the Honors Program.

Campus Overview

Independent comprehensive, founded 1883 • **Coed** 1,929 undergraduate students, 97% full-time, 61% women, 39% men.

Undergraduates 1,873 full-time, 56 part-time. Students come from 38 states and territories, 14 other countries, 51% are from out of state, 5% African American, 3% Asian American or Pacific Islander, 5% Hispanic American, 0.3% Native American, 0.2% international, 5% transferred in, 70% live on campus.

Faculty *Total:* 209, 43% full-time. *Student/faculty ratio:* 17:1.

Academic Programs *Special study options:* double majors, honors programs, internships, off-campus study, part-time degree program, services for LD students, study abroad, summer session for credit.

Athletics Member NCAA. All Division I except football (Division I-AA). *Intercollegiate sports:* baseball M(s), basketball M(s)/W(s), cross-country running M(s)/W(s), golf M(s)/W(s), ice hockey M(c), lacrosse M(s)/W(s), soccer W(s), softball W(s), swimming and diving W(s), tennis M(s)/W(s), track and field M(s)/W(s), volleyball W(s), water polo W(s), wrestling M(s). *Intramural sports:* basketball M/W, bowling M/W, football M, soccer M/W, softball M/W, table tennis M/W, tennis M/W, volleyball M/W.

Costs (2004–05) *Comprehensive fee:* $31,400 includes full-time tuition ($23,900) and room and board ($7500). Part-time tuition: $800 per credit hour.

Financial Aid 670 Federal Work-Study jobs (averaging $1176). In 2003, 471 non-need-based awards were made. *Average percent of need met:* 73%. *Average financial aid package:* $14,768. *Average need-based loan:* $4542. *Average need-based gift aid:* $10,955. *Average non-need-based aid:* $7439.

Contact: Director: Dr. Miles Groth, Staten Island, New York 10301; *Telephone:* 718-390-3482; *Fax:* 718-420-4158; *E-mail:* mgroth@wagner.edu; *Web site:* http://www.wagner.edu/prosstud/ugradstud/honors.html

NORTH CAROLINA

Appalachian State University
Heltzer Honors Program
Boone, North Carolina

Honors at Appalachian is more than a collection of courses; it is an approach to learning designed to stimulate active involvement by students in their own education. Critical thinking and analysis are stimulated by free and structured discussions in and outside the classroom. Honors classrooms are lively; honors students are encouraged to excel both by their professors and by their gifted peers. Independent projects frequently allow the student to probe the depths of a topic, with individual professorial encouragement and direction. In honors, faculty members and students work together to uncover the challenging questions that the academy pursues. With certain restrictions, some regular courses can be taken on honors contract.

Approximately 350–375 students enroll in twenty-three to twenty-five honors courses offered each semester. About 40 to 50 students graduate each year from departmental, college, or General Honors programs.

Participation Requirements: Honors courses are available in several departments. Most freshman-sophomore departmental honors courses substitute for core curriculum requirements or for popular electives. At the upper-division level, departmental courses permit students to pursue graduation with departmental honors recognition. General Honors offers an elective interdisciplinary program featuring team-taught topical courses for core curriculum credit in the social sciences and humanities. An exceptional cross-disciplinary program is available for qualified juniors and seniors majoring in the College of Business. Most programs require that a student maintain at least a 3.2 GPA (on a 4.0 scale). A generic University Honors Program Graduate designation is awarded to students who take 18 hours of honors classes (at least 6 of which are outside their major), complete a senior honors project, and maintain at least a 3.4 GPA in honors classes.

Beyond the classroom, the Honors Program at Appalachian seeks to maintain a stimulating and supportive atmosphere for serious students by housing honors students in two different living-learning communities. The Appalachian Honors Association (AHA), a student-led organization, provides social and community service activities for honors students. Honors students often take field trips, sometimes to the facilities the University maintains in New York or Washington, D.C. Some attend regional, state, or national honors conferences or study abroad for honors credit.

Admission Process: Approximately the top 10 percent of the incoming freshman class (about 250 students) get an automatic invitation into honors upon admission or before summer orientation on the basis of their class rank, high school grades, and SAT I or ACT scores. Others may request in writing to be considered. Students already enrolled are recommended for honors work by faculty members or academic advisers. The number of students admitted is determined in part by the number of available seats.

Scholarship Availability: Appalachian's most prestigious merit-based scholarships are the Chancellor's Scholarships. Each year, 25 incoming freshmen are selected for these awards (2004–05 stipend: $4500 per year), which are renewable for four years if a minimum 3.4 GPA is maintained. Chancellor's Scholars must take at least one honors course each semester for their first two years. Many scholars go on to graduate from departmental, college, or General Honors programs.

Campus Overview

State-supported comprehensive, founded 1899, part of University of North Carolina System • **Coed** 13,146 undergraduate students, 91% full-time, 50% women, 50% men.

Undergraduates 11,983 full-time, 1,163 part-time. Students come from 48 states and territories, 23 other countries, 10% are from out of state, 4% African American, 1% Asian American or Pacific Islander, 1% Hispanic American, 0.3% Native American, 0.4% international, 6% transferred in, 42% live on campus.

Faculty Total: 946, 71% full-time, 86% with terminal degrees. Student/faculty ratio: 19:1.

Academic Programs Special study options: academic remediation for entering students, accelerated degree program, adult/continuing education programs, advanced placement credit, distance learning, double majors, English as a second language, honors programs, independent study, internships, off-campus study, part-time degree program, services for LD students, student-designed majors, study abroad, summer session for credit. ROTC: Army (b). Unusual degree programs: 3-2 engineering with Auburn University, Clemson University.

Athletics Member NCAA, NAIA. All NCAA Division I except football (Division I-AA). Intercollegiate sports: baseball M(s), basketball M(s)/W(s), cross-country running M(s)/W(s), field hockey W(s), golf M(s)/W(s), soccer M(s)/W(s), tennis M(s)/W(s), track and field M(s)/W(s), volleyball W(s), wrestling M(s). Intramural sports: archery M/W, badminton M/W, basketball M/W, bowling M/W, cross-country running M/W, fencing M/W, field hockey W, football M/W, golf M/W, gymnastics M/W, racquetball M/W, rugby M, skiing (cross-country) M/W, skiing (downhill) M/W, soccer M/W, squash M/W, swimming and diving M/W, table tennis M/W, tennis M/W, track and field M/W, volleyball M/W, water polo M/W, weight lifting M/W, wrestling M.

Costs (2004–05) Tuition: state resident $1821 full-time; nonresident $11,188 full-time. Part-time tuition and fees vary according to course load. Required fees: $1530 full-time. Room and board: $5270; room only: $2770. Room and board charges vary according to board plan and housing facility.

Financial Aid 431 Federal Work-Study jobs (averaging $1800). 1,687 state and other part-time jobs (averaging $673). In 2004, 687 non-need-based awards were made. Average percent of need met: 78%. Average financial aid package: $6091. Average need-based loan: $3381. Average need-based gift aid: $3893. Average non-need-based aid: $3036.

Contact: Dr. Lynn Moss Sanders, Heltzer Honors Program Coordinator, East Hall, Appalachian State University, Boone, North Carolina 28608; Telephone: 828-262-2083; Fax: 828-262-2734; E-mail: ostwaltce@appstate.edu

Catawba College
Honors Program
Salisbury, North Carolina

The Catawba College Honors Program cultivates a community of academically gifted students who pursue challenging educational experiences with outstanding faculty members. Through interdisciplinary, provocative, and intellectually demanding courses, the Honors Program piques the curiosity of students, encouraging them to become lifelong learners who will enrich their own lives as well as the lives of those in their communities.

Honors students take a series of classes, distinctive in content and quality and often team-taught, along with other honors students. They finish their honors studies with a thesis or capstone experience that is either individualized or a part of their major course of study. These experiences allow students to study in an atmosphere that promotes creativity and critical thinking. Honors courses also contribute to the broader educational program of Catawba College in that they may carry core-area credit and/or departmental major credit. Off-campus study experiences and cocurricular honors experiences at the College complement the curriculum.

The College's Honors Program encourages students to become actively involved in the College and the community through out-of-classroom activities such as lectures, outings, films, and trips to state and regional honors conferences. Some students may choose to reside in a campus Living/Learning Community with other honors students.

The College's Honors Program also seeks to foster a broader worldview in its students, and honors students are required to complete at least one College-sanctioned travel experience endorsed by the Faculty Honors Board. The experience may be an honors seminar with a corequisite trip after or during the semester. Examples include postsemester course-related travel, such as a tour of Ireland after a course on travel writing or a visit to the Galapagos Islands after studying birds from a biological and literary perspective. Also included are domestic trips taken during fall or spring break, such as a trip to Memphis, Tennessee, taken during a class on the Delta blues or travel to New Orleans to further study the language and culture of the region. Other international study opportunities (such as the College-sponsored May trip to Costa Rica) or study-abroad programs also meet this requirement.

Participation Requirements: Students in the College's Honors Program begin their studies with a special First-Year Seminar, which provides a transition into college study and the Honors Program. Those who finish their first semester with a GPA of at least 3.0 are then admitted fully into the program and are eligible to continue taking honors courses. Honors students are expected to take a variety of challenging courses in different disciplines, exploring topics such as Literary New Orleans, Civil Wrongs and Rights, Native American Religion and Literature, the Biogeography and Literature of Islands, Renaissance Florence, Science and Religion, Birds in Evolution and the Imagination, and Mississippi Delta Blues.

Students in the program complete their honors study (which totals 21 semester hours of credit) by providing samples of their work in a portfolio and with an approved Honors Senior Experience (either a senior thesis or capstone course in their major). The senior experience can either be a regular part of a major course of study or it can be an individualized, multidisciplinary project.

Admission Process: The program invites high school students with high standardized test scores and grades and who have demonstrated interest and active participation in their community to submit a brief application essay. Qualified students may then enroll in a section of the Honors First-Year Seminar.

Transfer students with a minimum 3.2 GPA may apply for admission to the program by completing the application and essay and submitting them to the Honors Board. Continuing students with a minimum 3.0 GPA (a minimum 3.2 GPA after the first semester of the sophomore year) may also apply by means of an application and essay. Interested students should contact the Director of the Honors Program for more information.

Campus Overview

Independent comprehensive, founded 1851, affiliated with United Church of Christ • **Coed** 1,375 undergraduate students, 96% full-time, 53% women, 47% men.

Undergraduates 1,319 full-time, 56 part-time. Students come from 33 states and territories, 16 other countries, 30% are from out of state, 15% African American, 0.7% Asian American or Pacific Islander, 2% Hispanic American, 0.6% Native American, 2% international, 9% transferred in, 67% live on campus.

Faculty Total: 109, 70% full-time, 54% with terminal degrees. Student/faculty ratio: 15:1.

Academic Programs Special study options: adult/continuing education programs, advanced placement credit, double majors, honors programs, independent study, internships, part-time degree program, services for LD students, student-designed majors, study abroad, summer session for credit. ROTC: Army (c).

Athletics Member NCAA. All Division II. Intercollegiate sports: baseball M(s), basketball M(s)/W(s), cross-country running M(s)/W(s), field hockey W(s), football M(s), golf M(s), lacrosse M, soccer M(s)/W(s), softball W(s), swimming and diving W(s), tennis M(s)/W(s), volleyball W(s). Intramural sports: archery M/W, basketball M/W, football M/W, golf M, ice hockey M, lacrosse M, racquetball M/W, soccer M/W, swimming and diving M/W, table tennis M/W, tennis M/W, volleyball M/W, weight lifting M/W, wrestling M.

Costs (2004–05) Comprehensive fee: $23,500 includes full-time tuition ($17,600) and room and board ($5900). Full-time tuition and fees vary according to class time. Part-time tuition: $475 per semester hour. Part-time tuition and fees vary according to class time, course load, and degree level.

Financial Aid 214 Federal Work-Study jobs (averaging $1221). 179 state and other part-time jobs (averaging $1231). In 2003, 100 non-need-based awards were made. Average percent of need met: 67%. Average financial aid package: $12,311. Average need-based loan: $4179. Average need-based gift aid: $4062. Average non-need-based aid: $5896.

Contact: Director: Dr. Sheila Brownlow, Catawba College, 2300 West Innes Street, Salisbury, North Carolina 28144-2488; Telephone: 704 637-4102; Fax: 704-637-4444; E-mail: honors@catawba.edu; Web site: http://www.catawba.edu

East Carolina University
Honors Program
Greenville, North Carolina

The University Honors Program at East Carolina University (ECU) provides special classes with an average size of 18 students and a sense of community for academically superior students. Each semester the program offers four or five honors seminars on different, often interdisciplinary, and frequently controversial topics and some forty honors sections of regular departmental courses. Most of these meet general education requirements, and all seminars help satisfy the University requirement for writing-intensive courses. Seminars have covered a wide range of topics in the humanities, fine arts, sciences, and social sciences. Some of these seminars include "The Voices of Generation X," "Gay Literature," "Writing Poems and Making Drawings," "The Music of Latin America," "The Geology of the National Parks," "Chemistry Behind the Headlines," and "Poverty, Discrimination, and Public Policy." Classes emphasize discussion rather than lecture, essay rather than short-answer exams, and active involvement in the education process.

Students who complete 24 semester hours of honors courses with A's or B's and a GPA of 3.3 or higher earn General Education honors. Upperclass students with at least a 3.5 GPA are invited to complete a 6-semester-hour senior project, which may take the form of a thesis, field experience, public service, portfolio, coteaching, or creative work, and earn University honors in their major or minor.

To foster a sense of community of scholars on the larger campus, the program offers students an honors residence hall, a library study room, their own state-of-the-art computer lab, an active student group, a student newsletter, a fall picnic, a spring Honors Recognition Day, representation on the Honors Program Committee, special lectures and trips, occasional teleconferences and seminars, special honors advising and registration assistance, opportunities for exchange and study abroad, and financial assistance in making presentations at regional and national conferences.

Each semester the program sponsors an Honors Recognition Day, at which students make presentations before the honors student body, graduating seniors are presented certificates, and awards are made. The meeting is followed by a reception at the chancellor's house. The names of graduating students are listed in the honors newsletter, the campus newspaper, and the commencement program. The honors notation becomes a permanent part of the student's transcript as soon as it is earned.

The program is more than thirty years old. In the mid-sixties, the University began offering seminars for selected students by request. In 1978, the current Honors Program was created on a two-year, university-wide format. In 1993, it became a four-year program, with all senior-level departmental honors work being coordinated through the Honors Program. Approximately 750 students are currently enrolled in the program. Fifty-five students graduated from the program in spring 2000. Invitations to participate in the program are issued from October to April.

Participation Requirements: Entering freshmen who present SAT I scores of 1200 or higher, at least a 3.5 GPA, and a top 10 percent high school ranking are invited into the program during their senior year in high school; some freshmen who meet two of these criteria receive provisional invitations. During freshman orientation, students are given academic counseling and are registered for courses. Current ECU students and transfer students with a 3.3 GPA or better also qualify to take honors courses. Students who drop below a 3.0 at the end of the school year are not eligible for courses until they again have a minimum 3.3 GPA.

Scholarship Availability: All merit scholarships are handled by the Office of Admissions, not by the Honors Office, but a large number of honors students hold scholarships. Chancellor's Scholars receive $20,000, University Scholars $12,000, and Alumni Honors Scholars $6000 for the four years. Many special scholarships for in-state, out-of-state, minority, transfer, and other distinct groups of students are available.

Campus Overview

State-supported university, founded 1907, part of The University of North Carolina • **Coed** 17,510 undergraduate students, 90% full-time, 59% women, 41% men.

Undergraduates 15,736 full-time, 1,774 part-time. Students come from 42 states and territories, 28 other countries, 15% are from out of state, 15% African American, 2% Asian American or Pacific Islander, 2% Hispanic American, 0.7% Native American, 0.5% international, 8% transferred in, 28% live on campus.

Faculty *Total:* 1,284, 84% full-time, 68% with terminal degrees. *Student/faculty ratio:* 17:1.

Academic Programs *Special study options:* academic remediation for entering students, accelerated degree program, adult/continuing education programs, advanced placement credit, cooperative education, distance learning, double majors, honors programs, independent study, internships, off-campus study, part-time degree program, services for LD students, student-designed majors, study abroad, summer session for credit. *ROTC:* Army (b), Air Force (b). *Unusual degree programs:* 3-2 accounting.

Athletics Member NCAA. All Division I except football (Division I-A). *Intercollegiate sports:* baseball M(s), basketball M(s)/W(s), cross-country running M(s)/W(s), golf M(s)/W(s), soccer M(s)/W(s), softball W(s), swimming and diving M(s)/W(s), tennis M(s)/W(s), track and field M(s)/W(s), volleyball W(s). *Intramural sports:* baseball M(c), basketball M/W(c), bowling M(c)/W(c), cross-country running M/W, equestrian sports M(c)/W(c), fencing M(c)/W(c), field hockey W(c), football M/W, golf M(c)/W(c), lacrosse M(c)/W(c), racquetball M/W, rugby M(c)/W(c), skiing (downhill) M(c)/W(c), soccer M(c)/W(c), softball M(c)/W(c), swimming and diving M(c)/W(c), table tennis M/W, tennis M/W(c), ultimate Frisbee M(c), volleyball W(c), water polo M(c)/W(c), wrestling M(c).

Costs (2004–05) *Tuition:* state resident $2135 full-time; nonresident $12,349 full-time. Part-time tuition and fees vary according to course load. *Required fees:* $1319 full-time. *Room and board:* $6640; room only: $3690. Room and board charges vary according to board plan and housing facility.

Financial Aid 316 Federal Work-Study jobs (averaging $1745). 126 state and other part-time jobs (averaging $5655). In 2003, 3747

non-need-based awards were made. *Average need-based loan:* $3511. *Average need-based gift aid:* $3072. *Average non-need-based aid:* $5659.

Contact: Director: Dr. Michael Bassman, Assistant Vice Chancellor and Director, Brewster D-107, Greenville, North Carolina 27858-4353; *Telephone:* 252-328-6373; *Fax:* 252-328-0474; *E-mail:* bassmanm@mail.ecu.edu; *Web site:* http://www.ecu.edu/honors

---

Elon University
Honors Fellows Program
Elon, North Carolina

The Honors Fellows Program at Elon University is an academic community of exceptional students from any major. It offers all the best features of an Elon education—challenging courses with outstanding faculty mentoring, serious and exciting research opportunities, exposure to international perspectives through study abroad, and a community of kindred spirits, faculty members, and student inquirers who want to be fully engaged in a rewarding academic experience.

The honors program seeks to help students expand their minds by encountering new ideas in small, discussion-based, innovative, liberal arts courses; most of the required courses are interdisciplinary, and two of them are team taught. Honors courses are intended to build upon one another so students improve their critical thinking, research, and communication skills. Studies culminate in an individual capstone, the senior thesis, which is a yearlong project that students complete working closely with a faculty mentor.

Elon University is nationally recognized as a leader in engaged learning. Students participate actively in their learning, with experiences such as study abroad, internships, research, service learning, and leadership. Resources include a study-abroad travel grant, and research funds for independent research are available to support Honors Fellows in such learning outside the classroom. In order to help support Honors Fellows achieve the highest possible academic achievements, Fellows participate in an Elon 101 course with an honors faculty adviser, have an honors peer mentor, and have access to a national fellowship adviser.

The Honors Fellows Program helps prepare students for the world after college—whether in graduate or professional school, a career, or any other pursuit—as independent, hard-working, open-minded, lifelong learners and honorable community members. In an effort to provide an intellectual community that extends beyond the classroom walls, Honors Fellows have the opportunity to live in one of two honors learning communities; Fellows attend speaking and cultural events together and engage in service.

Participation Requirements: Students receive a certificate and are recognized at graduation on the commencement program and on their transcript as Honors Fellow, if they have fulfilled all the requirements of the program. Requirements include having completed the five honors seminar courses, completed a satisfactory senior thesis, abided by the Honor Code and modeled academic citizenship, written a thoughtful annual report each year, completed six semesters of participation in the colloquium program, performed two elements of service, and maintained a minimum 3.2 overall grade point average and a 3.0 in honors courses, while taking a minimum of 30 semester hours per academic year.

Admission Process: Incoming freshmen may apply to the Honors Fellows Program if they have taken a demanding high school curriculum, rank near the top of their class, and have composite math and verbal SAT scores of 1300 (ACT 28) or higher. Each year the best applicants are selected to compete for 40 places in the program, and that competition is based on high school records, standardized test scores, essays, an interview, and teacher recommendation. Lateral entry into the program is sometimes possible. Honors Fellows may pursue any major at the university except for engineering.

Scholarship Availability: All 40 incoming Honors Fellows receive a $6000 scholarship renewable annually, based on meeting program requirements, in addition to a Presidential Scholarship of $3500, bringing the total scholarship funding to $9500 each year. All Honors Fellows also receive a $750 study-abroad grant and may submit proposals for research grants. There is one full tuition Kenan Scholarship awarded each year.

Campus Overview

Independent comprehensive, founded 1889, affiliated with United Church of Christ • **Coed** 4,622 undergraduate students, 97% full-time, 61% women, 39% men.

Undergraduates 4,496 full-time, 126 part-time. Students come from 48 states and territories, 40 other countries, 70% are from out of state, 7% African American, 0.8% Asian American or Pacific Islander, 1% Hispanic American, 0.2% Native American, 1% international, 2% transferred in, 59% live on campus.

Faculty *Total:* 338, 77% full-time, 72% with terminal degrees. *Student/faculty ratio:* 15:1.

Academic Programs *Special study options:* accelerated degree program, advanced placement credit, double majors, English as a second language, honors programs, independent study, internships, off-campus study, part-time degree program, services for LD students, student-designed majors, study abroad, summer session for credit. *ROTC:* Army (b), Air Force (c). *Unusual degree programs:* 3-2 engineering with North Carolina State University, North Carolina Agricultural and Technical State University, Virginia Polytechnic Institute and State University, Washington University, Columbia University.

Athletics Member NCAA. All Division I except football (Division I-AA). *Intercollegiate sports:* baseball M(s), basketball M(s)/W(s), cheerleading M/W, cross-country running M(s)/W(s), golf M(s)/W(s), lacrosse M(c)/W(c), rugby M(c), soccer M(s)/W(s), softball W(s), swimming and diving M(c)/W(c), tennis M(s)/W(s), track and field W(s), volleyball W(s). *Intramural sports:* basketball M/W, bowling M/W, equestrian sports M/W, field hockey W(c), football M/W, golf M/W, racquetball M/W, soccer M/W, softball M/W, table tennis M/W, tennis M/W, ultimate Frisbee M(c)/W(c), volleyball M/W, weight lifting M/W.

Costs (2004–05) *Comprehensive fee:* $23,565 includes full-time tuition ($17,310), mandatory fees ($245), and room and board ($6010). Part-time tuition: $544 per hour. Part-time tuition and fees vary according to course load. *Required fees:* $123 per term part-time. *College room only:* $2936. Room and board charges vary according to board plan and housing facility.

Financial Aid 826 Federal Work-Study jobs (averaging $2271). In 2004, 906 non-need-based awards were made. *Average percent of need met:* 71%. *Average financial aid package:* $11,364. *Average need-based loan:* $3614. *Average need-based gift aid:* $6351. *Average non-need-based aid:* $3713.

Contact: Dr. Mary Jo Festle, Director, Honors Fellows Program, Elon University, Campus Box 2154, Elon, North Carolina 27244; *Telephone:* 336-278-6423; *E-mail:* festle@elon.edu; *Web site:* http://www.elon.edu/honors

Fayetteville State University
Honors Program
Fayetteville, North Carolina

The primary goal of the Honors Program at Fayetteville State University (FSU) is to prepare the University's high-ability students for the graduate-school and professional-school experience through courses and activities that focus on academic preparation, character development, cultural enrichment, and leadership development.

Central to the honors academic experience are honors classes, which are limited usually to 15–20 students to facilitate dialogue among and between students as well as between students and faculty members. Students are required to take responsibility for their learning. Collaboration, rather than competition, is encouraged. The ultimate goal in the honors classroom is to provide students with opportunities to take risks in a "safe" environment and to encourage them to develop to their fullest potential. In addition to small class size, emphasis on collaboration, and incorporation of a discussion format, the honors academic experience includes the frequent use of primary sources, the offering of interdisciplinary courses, and the integration of experiential learning with theoretical and applied experiences in the classroom.

The character development of honors students is addressed in part through the Honors Service-Learning Seminar course, which is designed to increase students' awareness of the needs of their communities. The goal is to heighten social awareness that can stimulate students to "give back." In addition, the service component allows students to take the knowledge and skills they have acquired in the classroom and apply them outside the boundaries of academia.

Honors courses, colloquia, and seminars emphasize the importance of critical thinking, writing, and sharing. They are for students who embrace the chance to work hard, read more, take risks, defend a belief, and challenge received wisdom. Students do not earn extra credit, additional quality points, or an easy A by taking honors courses. Students just participate in the most challenging and enriching educational experience they can find anywhere. Fayetteville State University regards the honors curriculum as a learning laboratory, where new ideas and new ways of teaching constantly stimulate teachers and students.

Participation Requirements: During the freshman and sophomore years, students enroll normally in the 45-credit University College Core Curriculum. Of these 45 credits, honors students complete almost one-third (fourteen credits) of the Core Curriculum by enrolling in honors versions of four courses designated by an "H" in the FSU course schedule.

In addition, honors students are enrolled in the Honors Freshman Seminar (2 credits) and the Honors Service-Learning Seminar course (2 credits).

During their junior year, honors students complete multidisciplinary research and thesis-writing courses.

During the senior year, the honors student completes the honors thesis and presents it in public during the annual Honors Student Conference, to which family, friends, faculty members, and classmates are invited.

In order to meet an Honors Program objective of having 100 percent of the students participate in undergraduate research during their years at FSU, honors students are encouraged to participate in summer-research experiences that prepare them for graduate or professional school.

Finally, honors students engage in service learning throughout all of their undergraduate years at Fayetteville State University.

Admission Process: Incoming freshmen who fit into certain categories are automatically invited to join the Honors Program. These categories include public high school valedictorians and salutatorians, National Merit Achievement Scholarship finalists, and graduates of the North Carolina School of Science and Mathematics.

Other incoming freshmen—including those from charter, private, and home schools—must meet the following criteria to be invited to join the Honors Program: a cumulative, unweighted high school GPA of 3.3 on a 4.0 scale and an SAT score of at least 1000 (math and verbal scores) or ACT score of at least 22.

Freshmen with a minimum combined SAT score of 950 (math and verbal) and an outstanding record of extracurricular activities, community service, and/or leadership experience may also apply. Students in this category who apply for admission to the Honors Program are invited to interviews, and decisions are made about participation on a case-by-case basis.

Transfer students must have earned at least 30 graduation credits and must possess a minimum GPA of 3.3 on a 4.0 scale. Interested transfer students should contact the Honors Program Office for further information about their admission to the FSU Honors Program (telephone: 910-672-1625 or e-mail: carnold@uncfsu.edu).

Scholarship Availability: Each Honors Program student receives an Honors Scholarship that covers tuition, fees, room, and board. Incoming freshmen receive an Honors Scholarship award for four years; incoming Transfer students receive an award for two years. As part of the awards process, all honors students must complete the Federal Application for Federal Student Aid (FAFSA) each year. The FAFSA is a requirement for all incoming and returning FSU students, and it must be completed and on file in the Financial Aid Office each year prior to receiving the Honors Scholarship.

Students are informed through an award letter, which is accompanied by an acceptance of the FSU Honors Scholarship and Acknowledgment of Terms form and a Personal Data Sheet. These forms are completed by the student and returned to the Honors Program Office, where the records are maintained in the students' scholarship files. At the end of the spring semester, when grades have been posted to the transcripts, each continuing honors student receives a scholarship renewal letter and the Acknowledgment of Terms for Continuing Students form as well as the Personal Data Sheet.

Campus Overview

State-supported comprehensive, founded 1867, part of University of North Carolina System • **Coed** 4,410 undergraduate students, 84% full-time, 64% women, 36% men.

Undergraduates 3,715 full-time, 695 part-time. Students come from 41 states and territories, 8 other countries, 11% are from out of state, 80% African American, 1% Asian American or Pacific Islander, 4% Hispanic American, 1% Native American, 0.3% international, 10% transferred in.

Faculty *Total:* 237, 75% full-time, 81% with terminal degrees. *Student/faculty ratio:* 22:1.

Academic Programs *Special study options:* academic remediation for entering students, accelerated degree program, adult/continuing education programs, cooperative education, distance learning, double majors, honors programs, independent study, internships, part-time degree program, summer session for credit. *ROTC:* Army (c), Air Force (b). *Unusual degree programs:* 3-2 engineering with North Carolina State University.

Athletics Member NCAA. All Division II. *Intercollegiate sports:* basketball M(s)/W, bowling M/W, cheerleading M/W, cross-country running M/W, football M(s), golf M/W, tennis M/W, track and field M/W, volleyball W. *Intramural sports:* basketball M/W, golf M/W, gymnastics M/W, tennis M/W, volleyball M/W.

Costs (2005–06) *One-time required fee:* $50. *Tuition:* state resident $1546 full-time; nonresident $11,282 full-time. Full-time tuition and fees vary according to location. Part-time tuition and fees vary according to course load and location. *Required fees:* $1286 full-time. *Room and board:* $4120; room only: $2320. Room and board charges vary according to board plan and housing facility.

Financial Aid In 2001, 247 non-need-based awards were made. *Average percent of need met:* 69%. *Average financial aid package:* $6690. *Average need-based loan:* $9341. *Average need-based gift aid:* $7976. *Average non-need-based aid:* $4106.

Contact: Dr. Carrol Arnold, Assistant Vice Chancellor of Academic Affairs and Honors, Room 114, W. R. Collins Administration Building, Fayetteville State University, 1200 Murchison Road, Fayetteville, North Carolina 28301-4298; *Telephone:* 910-672-1625; *Fax:* 910-672-1485; *E-mail:* carnold@uncfsu.edu; *Web site:* http://www.uncfsu.edu/honors/

Gardner-Webb University
Honors Program
Boiling Springs, North Carolina

The Gardner-Webb University (GWU) Honors Program seeks to nurture academically qualified students in all majors by providing a program of enriched learning experiences in courses taught by an honors faculty. Honors students are inquisitive people, excited by the challenge of scholarship and comfortable in an environment that demands the acquisition of knowledge and the need to think critically about what is learned. Regardless of their majors, honors students are interdisciplinary in their approach. They are able to synthesize their studies and learn from varied cultures and from each other. The Honors Program encourages the highest standards in its students who should exert leadership through their academic and cocurricular accomplishments.

GWU provides an Honors House residence hall for honors students who choose to reside there. The house maintains online capabilities in each room, a computer lab, classroom space, a lobby, and a kitchen. Approximately 30 students may reside in GWU's Honors House.

The GWU Honors Program has been in existence for seventeen years. There are 100 to 130 students in the program each year.

Participation Requirements: The Honors Program requires the completion of a minimum of 24 hours of course work designated as honors. A minimum of 15 hours of course work should be completed in the first two years of study. Honors courses in the first two years may be selected from honors sections (restricted to honors students) of core curriculum offerings or through honors contracts with faculty members teaching regular sections of the University's overall curriculum.

To receive Honors Program recognition during commencement exercises, a student must meet the following requirements: maintain at least a 3.0 GPA; successfully complete a minimum of 24 hours in honors courses, including HONR 395, 400, and 401; initiate, prepare, present, and defend a senior honors thesis of at least 40 pages in length; complete a minimum of 80 hours of community service that contributes to the welfare of the community; and receive the recommendation of the Honors Committee.

Admission Process: Fifty to 80 students are selected to receive Honors Program application materials each year. This initial selection is based on SAT scores and class ranking. Applications are reviewed by the Honors Committee. Selection is based on academic achievement, potential for leadership, extracurricular activities, and a written statement of personal goals.

Scholarship Availability: Gardner-Webb offers several scholarships, which are available to students in the Honors Program. These include Academic Fellows, University Fellows, and Presidential Scholarships. Some of these provide for full-tuition assistance.

Campus Overview

Independent Baptist comprehensive, founded 1905 • **Coed** 2,575 undergraduate students, 84% full-time, 65% women, 35% men.

Undergraduates 2,160 full-time, 415 part-time. Students come from 36 states and territories, 31 other countries, 23% are from out of state, 16% African American, 0.5% Asian American or Pacific Islander, 1% Hispanic American, 0.6% Native American, 20% transferred in, 71% live on campus.

Faculty *Total:* 126, 76% with terminal degrees. *Student/faculty ratio:* 15:1.

Academic Programs *Special study options:* academic remediation for entering students, accelerated degree program, adult/continuing education programs, advanced placement credit, cooperative education, distance learning, double majors, English as a second language, honors programs, internships, off-campus study, part-time degree program, services for LD students, study abroad, summer session for credit. *ROTC:* Army (b). *Unusual degree programs:* 3-2 engineering with Auburn University, University of North Carolina at Charlotte; music business 5 year program at Gardner-Webb University.

Athletics Member NCAA. All Division I except football (Division I-AA). *Intercollegiate sports:* baseball M(s), basketball M(s)/W(s), cheerleading M(s)/W(s), cross-country running M(s)/W(s), golf M(s)/W(s), soccer M(s)/W(s), softball W(s), swimming and diving W(s), tennis M(s)/W(s), track and field M(s)/W(s), volleyball W(s), wrestling M(s). *Intramural sports:* basketball M/W, football M/W, racquetball M/W, soccer M/W, softball M/W, table tennis M/W, tennis M/W, ultimate Frisbee M/W, volleyball M/W.

Costs (2004–05) *Comprehensive fee:* $20,490 includes full-time tuition ($14,960), mandatory fees ($190), and room and board ($5340). Part-time tuition: $285 per credit hour. Part-time tuition and fees vary according to course load. *College room only:* $2730. Room and board charges vary according to board plan and housing facility.

Financial Aid 235 Federal Work-Study jobs (averaging $1113). 611 state and other part-time jobs (averaging $1061). In 2001, 590 non-need-based awards were made. *Average percent of need met:* 85%. *Average financial aid package:* $9921. *Average need-based loan:* $3936. *Average need-based gift aid:* $5467. *Average non-need-based aid:* $4848.

Contact: Director: Dr. Tom Jones, Box 7264, Boiling Springs, North Carolina 28017-7264; *Telephone:* 704-406-4369; *Fax:* 704-406-3917; *E-mail:* tjones@gardner-webb.edu; *Web site:* http://www.gardner-webb.edu

---

Greensboro College
George Center for Honors Studies
Greensboro, North Carolina

The George Center for Honors Studies, the honors degree program at Greensboro College, is designed to challenge and reward students who have a high level of intellectual ability and motivation. One of the program's goals is to build a community of scholars on campus. The program begins developing community among honors students in the freshman year, with a common freshman block composed of two linked honors courses. There are also several extracurricular activities for honors students, such as dinner at the dean's house and pizza with profs—an informal monthly gathering of honors students and professors.

The program is not inward-looking by any means. It offers students significant opportunities to integrate scholarship and service through its Collaborative Service Learning Program (CSLP). The CSLP invites honors students to spend four weeks in a different culture where they engage in community service and a variety of other learning experiences. The George Center has sponsored CSLP projects in Trinidad, Alaska, and England.

The George Center believes that the ability to view issues from multiple disciplinary perspectives is crucial to intellectual development. Interdisciplinary thinking starts in the freshman year, when professors coordinate the material so that honors students have an opportunity to study the same work or theme in two linked courses (e.g., English and history). Later in the curriculum, honors students take special topics seminars that are team-taught by professors from different disciplines. The topics for the interdisciplinary seminars vary from year to year and are based on professors' interests and suggestions from incoming honors students. Recent seminar topics have included Advertising as Art, and Vietnam and the Media.

Greensboro College has had an honors program for more than fifteen years. The program became the George Center for Honors Studies in 1996 when it was endowed by a gift from alumna Eleanor George. There are approximately 70 students enrolled in the program.

Participation Requirements: Freshman honors students take a 6-hour honors block each semester. The block consists of honors English and one other general education course (e.g., history or religion). Sophomores take two honors seminars that are team-taught by professors from different disciplines. The topics for these interdisciplinary seminars vary from year to year and are chosen based on student requests and faculty interests. Honors juniors enroll in a research methods seminar and an independent study. The seminar covers research models, methods, and skills. The independent study is taken under the guidance of a faculty member in the student's major in order to prepare the research plan for the senior honors thesis. Senior honors students enroll in another independent study to carry out the research plan and complete the thesis. Honors students present the results of their senior theses to the campus at the end of the fall or spring semester.

To remain in the program, students must maintain a 3.0 cumulative GPA. Successful completion of the program is recognized at commencement and is also noted on the official transcript and diploma.

Admission Process: Entering freshmen who have an SAT I score of 1100 or higher and a high school GPA of 3.0 or higher are invited to participate in the program. Students transferring into Greensboro College with fewer than 30 hours of college credit who meet the preceding criteria for freshmen and have a college GPA of 3.25 or higher may participate in the program by contacting the program director. Students transferring in with 30 or more hours who have a college GPA of 3.25 or higher may participate in the program by contacting the program director. All students who enter the program without the benefit of the freshman honors block must demonstrate writing proficiency.

Scholarship Availability: Scholarships of various amounts are awarded through the Office of Admissions based on academic performance. Most honors students are recipients of academic scholarships. In addition, students who successfully complete the honors requirements each year are given a $500 participation scholarship for the next academic year. Honors students may enroll in more than 18 hours per semester without paying an overload fee.

Campus Overview
Independent United Methodist comprehensive, founded 1838 • **Coed** 1,165 undergraduate students, 79% full-time, 54% women, 46% men.

Undergraduates 923 full-time, 242 part-time. Students come from 25 states and territories, 9 other countries, 26% are from out of state, 19% African American, 1% Asian American or Pacific Islander, 1% Hispanic American, 0.3% Native American, 0.5% international, 11% transferred in, 48% live on campus.

Faculty *Total:* 125, 49% full-time, 59% with terminal degrees. *Student/faculty ratio:* 13:1.

Academic Programs *Special study options:* academic remediation for entering students, accelerated degree program, adult/continuing education programs, advanced placement credit, double majors, English as a second language, freshman honors college, honors programs, independent study, internships, off-campus study, part-time degree program, services for LD students, student-designed majors, study abroad, summer session for credit. *ROTC:* Army (c), Air Force (c).

Athletics Member NCAA. All Division III. *Intercollegiate sports:* baseball M, basketball M/W, cheerleading M/W, cross-country running M/W, football M, golf M, lacrosse M/W, soccer M/W, softball

W, swimming and diving W, tennis M/W, volleyball W. *Intramural sports:* basketball M/W, bowling M/W, football M/W, racquetball M/W, skiing (downhill) M/W, ultimate Frisbee M/W.

Costs (2004–05) *Comprehensive fee:* $23,280 includes full-time tuition ($16,600), mandatory fees ($220), and room and board ($6460). Full-time tuition and fees vary according to course load. Part-time tuition: $445 per hour. Part-time tuition and fees vary according to course load. *Room and board:* Room and board charges vary according to board plan and housing facility.

Financial Aid 162 Federal Work-Study jobs (averaging $1100). 23 state and other part-time jobs (averaging $1100). In 2002, 238 non-need-based awards were made. *Average percent of need met:* 71%. *Average financial aid package:* $9395. *Average need-based loan:* $4011. *Average need-based gift aid:* $3824. *Average non-need-based aid:* $4473.

Contact: Director: Dr. George Cheatham, Greensboro College, 815 West Market Street, Greensboro, North Carolina 27401-1875; *Telephone:* 336-272-7102 Ext. 303; *E-mail:* cheathamg@gborocollege.edu; Web site: http://www.gborocollege.edu/academics_new/honors.php

Guilford College
Honors Program
Greensboro, North Carolina

The Guilford College Honors Program provides a sequence of classes and independent study options designed to reward and intellectually challenge students seeking superior educational opportunities. Honors classes are small and usually taught as discussion-style seminars, which allow intensive learning in a close and supportive instructional relationship.

Students must take a minimum of five honors courses during their academic career. Students choose from a variety of courses, including codisciplinary and specially designed departmental offerings. Under the individual supervision of a faculty adviser, each student completes a senior thesis or project. The program is open to students majoring in all departments of the College. Successful completion of the Honors Program requirements is noted at graduation and on the student's transcript.

In addition to classwork and independent study, students in the Honors Program are encouraged to attend professional and undergraduate research conferences. The Honors Program offers generous travel support to students who present papers, research, or creative projects.

In keeping with the College's Quaker heritage, honors students at Guilford participate fully in the larger campus community. They live in residence halls and take most of their courses with the full student body. Honors students are active in a full range of campus activities, including athletics, student government, campus publications, choir, theater, community-service projects, and special-interest clubs.

Guilford College, a founding member of the North Carolina Honors Association, participates in the National Collegiate Honors Council and Southern Regional Honors Council. Students, faculty members, and administrators from the College attend the conferences of all three organizations.

There are currently 150 students in the Honors Program.

Admission Process: Most students are admitted to the Honors Program as entering first-year students, and approximately 8–10 percent of the freshman class are accepted into honors. Based on standardized test scores, high school achievement, writing samples, and recommendations, students are invited to apply to the program. In addition, first-year and sophomore students who have earned a cumulative GPA of 3.5 or higher are invited to join the program.

Scholarship Availability: Guilford College has allocated funds for honors scholarships, which are awarded without regard to financial

need and are currently held by two thirds of the students in the program. Scholarships are normally awarded when students are admitted to the College.

Campus Overview

Independent 4-year, founded 1837, affiliated with Society of Friends • **Coed** 2,511 undergraduate students, 83% full-time, 62% women, 38% men.

Undergraduates 2,073 full-time, 438 part-time. Students come from 45 states and territories, 18 other countries, 31% are from out of state, 22% African American, 2% Asian American or Pacific Islander, 2% Hispanic American, 1% Native American, 1% international, 16% transferred in, 80% live on campus.

Faculty *Total:* 173, 56% full-time, 64% with terminal degrees. *Student/faculty ratio:* 16:1.

Academic Programs *Special study options:* academic remediation for entering students, accelerated degree program, adult/continuing education programs, advanced placement credit, cooperative education, double majors, English as a second language, honors programs, independent study, internships, off-campus study, part-time degree program, services for LD students, student-designed majors, study abroad, summer session for credit. *Unusual degree programs:* 3-2 forestry with Duke University.

Athletics Member NCAA. All Division III. *Intercollegiate sports:* baseball M, basketball M/W, cross-country running M/W, football M, golf M, lacrosse M/W, soccer M/W, softball W, swimming and diving W, tennis M/W, volleyball W. *Intramural sports:* cheerleading W(c).

Costs (2005–06) *Comprehensive fee:* $28,170 includes full-time tuition ($21,310), mandatory fees ($330), and room and board ($6530). Part-time tuition: $655 per credit hour. Part-time tuition and fees vary according to course load. *Required fees:* $330 per year part-time. *Room and board:* Room and board charges vary according to board plan, housing facility, and location.

Financial Aid 208 Federal Work-Study jobs (averaging $1325). 70 state and other part-time jobs (averaging $1158). In 2003, 476 non-need-based awards were made. *Average percent of need met:* 85%. *Average financial aid package:* $13,249. *Average need-based loan:* $4928. *Average need-based gift aid:* $9100. *Average non-need-based aid:* $7191.

Contact: Director: Dr. Vance A. Ricks, 5800 West Friendly Avenue, Greensboro, North Carolina 27410; *Telephone:* 336-316-2229; *Fax:* 336-316-2940; *E-mail:* vricks@guilford.edu; *Web site:* http://www.guilford.edu

Lenoir-Rhyne College
Honors Academy
Hickory, North Carolina

Honors Academy students have the opportunity to fulfill some of the core curriculum course requirements by taking classes with other highly motivated, creative honors students. These seminar-like classes have a limited enrollment, which is substantially less than that of other courses in the core curriculum. They are student centered and encourage individual and group learning through close interaction with instructors. Honors Academy professors are selected for their teaching ability and commitment to the intellectual and personal development of students.

Honors students have the opportunity to travel to Europe during spring break as part of the Broyhill International Honors Leadership Program. Participating honors students receive free airfare to Europe and special instruction in cultural interaction and leadership. Selected students receive scholarships to the Hickory Humanities

Forum, a Great Books seminar that meets in the spring at the beautiful Wildacres Conference Center in the North Carolina mountains.

The Honors Academy offers social, recreational, and cultural activities as part of the Lenoir-Rhyne College Honors experience. Honors students attend receptions at the home of the College president, take day hikes in the mountains, attend plays, and talk to world-famous writers and scholars in intimate classroom settings throughout the academic year.

Currently there are approximately 150 students in the program.

Participation Requirements: Students are required to take a minimum of four honors courses in the core curriculum and two Great Books seminars. In addition, they are expected to complete 10 hours of community work each year and maintain a minimum overall GPA of 3.25. Upon graduation, the student is recognized as a graduate of the Honors Academy.

Admission Process: Students are invited to compete for Honors Scholarships on Honors Day. These invitations are extended to applicants on the basis of their SAT scores, high school GPA, and interview at Honors Day. Other criteria include, but are not limited to, high school class rank, a personal essay, and community service. Students wishing to compete for these scholarships should apply by December 31 of the year prior to admission. Students who receive honors financial awards are required to participate in the Honors Academy for the first year. They may, if they choose, withdraw from the Honors Academy without penalty, although they must continue to maintain the minimum GPA. Any student currently enrolled at the College who has an overall GPA of at least 3.25 is eligible to participate in the Honors Academy.

Scholarship Availability: In addition to the financial awards and scholarships indicated above, there are some funds available to support student research and some awards to recognize outstanding honor theses and overall achievement.

Campus Overview

Independent Lutheran comprehensive, founded 1891 • **Coed** 1,407 undergraduate students, 90% full-time, 63% women, 37% men.

Undergraduates 1,273 full-time, 134 part-time. Students come from 28 states and territories, 4 other countries, 26% are from out of state, 8% African American, 2% Asian American or Pacific Islander, 1% Hispanic American, 0.4% Native American, 0.4% international, 9% transferred in, 60% live on campus.

Faculty *Total:* 146, 62% full-time. *Student/faculty ratio:* 13:1.

Academic Programs *Special study options:* academic remediation for entering students, accelerated degree program, adult/continuing education programs, advanced placement credit, cooperative education, distance learning, double majors, English as a second language, honors programs, independent study, internships, part-time degree program, services for LD students, student-designed majors, study abroad, summer session for credit. *ROTC:* Army (c). *Unusual degree programs:* 3-2 engineering with North Carolina State University, University of North Carolina at Charlotte, Clemson University, North Carolina Agricultural and Technical State University; forestry with Duke University.

Athletics Member NCAA. All Division II. *Intercollegiate sports:* baseball M(s), basketball M(s)/W(s), cross-country running M(s)/W(s), football M(s), golf M(s)/W(s), soccer M(s)/W(s), softball W(s), volleyball W(s). *Intramural sports:* basketball M/W, football M/W, soccer M/W, softball M/W, ultimate Frisbee M/W.

Costs (2005–06) *One-time required fee:* $200. *Comprehensive fee:* $25,600 includes full-time tuition ($18,150), mandatory fees ($770), and room and board ($6680). Part-time tuition: $455 per credit. Part-time tuition and fees vary according to class time. *Required fees:* $10 per term part-time. *Room and board:* Room and board charges vary according to board plan and housing facility.

Financial Aid 170 Federal Work-Study jobs (averaging $745). 142 state and other part-time jobs (averaging $823). In 2002, 212 non-need-based awards were made. *Average percent of need met:* 75%. *Average financial aid package:* $11,829. *Average need-based loan:* $3823. *Average need-based gift aid:* $8943. *Average non-need-based aid:* $13,874.

Contact: Honors Directors: Dr. Karen Dill and David C. Ratke, Lenoir-Rhyne College, Hickory, North Carolina 28601; *Telephone:* 828-328-7209 (Dr. Karen Dill), 828-328-7183 (David C. Ratke); *Fax:* 828-328-7372; *E-mail:* dillk@lrc.edu, ratked@lrc.edu; *Web site:* http://www.lrc.edu/honors/index.htm

Meredith College
Honors Program
Raleigh, North Carolina

The Honors Program at Meredith College offers the intellectually gifted and ambitious student rich learning experiences both in and out of the classroom, with a close-knit community of active and motivated women. Individual advising and flexible requirements ensure that each student has the opportunity to develop to her full potential. The program enhances the academic experience of its members through a combination of small, interactive classes; individual student-faculty collaboration; off-campus cultural and travel enrichment programs; and fellowship with other highly motivated students. Each semester, certain courses are designated just for honors students. In addition, students have the ability to designate any course of their choice for honors credit through independent work with faculty members. Students generally complete a quarter of their total course work in honors, including general education, electives, and interdisciplinary colloquia, as well as courses in the major. Honors courses are designed for intellectual stimulation, critical inquiry, and collaborative exploration in areas of most interest to the student. During the senior year, in collaboration with a faculty mentor, each student completes a senior thesis or project. Students are actively encouraged to pursue independent study, undergraduate research, and study-abroad opportunities; they may earn honors credit for such participation.

Students receive individual advising by an Honors Advisor during their freshman and sophomore years and by a faculty adviser within their major, as well as the Honors Director, during their junior and senior years. In addition, new students are assigned a Student Honors Advisor, who provides a peer perspective on academic issues during the first two years.

Each semester, students are given opportunities to participate in a variety of cultural activities in the Research Triangle area through the Focus on Excellence series. In addition, students take weekend trips with other honors students and faculty members. Travel opportunities available to all honors students during 2004–05 included Annapolis, Maryland; Washington, D.C.; and Hilton Head, South Carolina. Smaller groups of students also traveled with the program to New Orleans and New York City. Students receive an annual allowance to use toward cultural events and travel. Honors students also receive additional benefits, including priority registration, the option for housing with other honors students, exclusive use of the Honors Lounge, and preferential access to visiting campus scholars and dignitaries.

Successful completion of the program requirements results in recognition for the student at graduation for completing her undergraduate academic career with distinction. Honors courses and program completion are clearly noted in the transcript. The Meredith College Honors Program was established in 1984 and currently has an enrollment of 118 students.

Participation Requirements: Students complete about a quarter of their course work in honors, including a minimum of eight honors courses and an honors thesis. Course requirements include an honors writing course and an honors lab science course, two honors electives in areas of interest, a minimum of two interdisciplinary honors colloquia, and two additional honors courses completed in the major by collaborative contract with the instructor. Typically, the courses taken for honors credit simultaneously fulfill general education requirements or requirements within the major. Finally, each student completes an honors thesis during her senior year. The thesis may take the form of a research or creative endeavor and is usually the end product of working collaboratively one-on-one with a professor, often as the culmination of a project begun as an honors contract course. Most students can and do choose to take more than the required number of honors courses. Beyond completing the required courses and partaking actively in honors activities, each student must maintain an overall GPA of at least 3.25. Upon completion of the program, students receive recognition of academic distinction at graduation, and honors courses are noted on the student's transcript.

Admission Process: Students interested in the Honors Program should first apply for admission to the College. Students meeting baseline criteria for Honors Program admission are then invited to apply to the Honors Program through an application essay and interview process. Selection for honors admission is based on high school class rank; high school GPA; SAT and ACT scores; strength of high school course load (AP, IB, and honors courses); demonstration of intellectual engagement through academic awards, leadership, and school/community involvement; honors application essay; and honors application interview. For students entering later than their freshman year, additional factors are considered, including faculty recommendation, college GPA, and college course load. Median credentials for the current honors freshman class are as follows: median unweighted high school GPA of 4.0, median combined SAT score of 1320, and median class rank in the top 2 percent. Admissions deadline is rolling, but students are strongly encouraged to submit applications to the Honors Program by February 1.

Scholarship Availability: Every entering freshman student invited to join the Meredith Honors Program receives an academic scholarship, which is renewable for all four years of a student's undergraduate career, provided she remains in good academic standing with the program. The most outstanding 2 or 3 scholars in each class are awarded the Presidential scholarship–a fully renewable four-year grant that offers the College's most generous academic award. Included in this package is an opportunity to study abroad, an extensive enrichment program, and an active mentoring relationship with the College President.

Campus Overview

Independent comprehensive, founded 1891 • **Urban** 225-acre campus • **Women only** 2,009 undergraduate students, 79% full-time.

Undergraduates 1,578 full-time, 431 part-time. Students come from 33 states and territories, 20 other countries, 12% are from out of state, 9% African American, 2% Asian American or Pacific Islander, 2% Hispanic American, 0.4% Native American, 1% international, 8% transferred in, 46% live on campus.

Faculty *Total:* 262, 49% full-time, 56% with terminal degrees. *Student/faculty ratio:* 10:1.

Academic Programs *Special study options:* academic remediation for entering students, accelerated degree program, adult/continuing education programs, advanced placement credit, cooperative education, double majors, honors programs, independent study, internships, off-campus study, part-time degree program, services for LD students, student-designed majors, study abroad, summer session for credit. *ROTC:* Army (c), Air Force (c).

Athletics Member NCAA. All Division III. *Intercollegiate sports:* basketball W, cross-country running W(c), soccer W, softball W, tennis W, volleyball W. *Intramural sports:* swimming and diving W(c).

Costs (2004–05) *Comprehensive fee:* $24,350 includes full-time tuition ($19,000) and room and board ($5350). Part-time tuition: $500 per credit hour.

Financial Aid 518 Federal Work-Study jobs (averaging $1217). 4 state and other part-time jobs (averaging $1387). In 2004, 91 non-need-based awards were made. *Average percent of need met:* 73%. *Average financial aid package:* $14,010. *Average need-based loan:* $3906. *Average need-based gift aid:* $10,068. *Average non-need-based aid:* $4730.

Contact: Dr. Cynthia Edwards, Ph.D., Professor of Psychology and Director of the Honors Program, Meredith College, 3800 Hillsborough Street, Raleigh, North Carolina 27607-5298; *Telephone:* 919-760-8604; *E-mail:* honors@meredith.edu; *Web site:* http://www.meredith.edu/honors/

North Carolina Agricultural and Technical State University
Honors Program
Greensboro, North Carolina

The Honors Program of North Carolina Agricultural and Technical State University (A&T) exemplifies the institution's commitment to excellence in teaching and learning. The program offers high-achieving students a challenging but supportive academic, cultural, and leadership environment that stimulates them to reach their full potential as independent learners and future decision makers. Its approach to education stresses close interaction between faculty members and students, supports intellectual experimentation, raises students' commitment to demanding work, provides opportunities for leadership development, and stimulates cross-cultural awareness and appreciation. The Honors Program also provides a stimulus for faculty members who teach honors courses to rethink old approaches and experiment with new ones, thus contributing to improved instruction across the curriculum. The program currently has nearly 400 members.

Participation Requirements: There are two tracks that students can pursue in the A&T Honors Program. The Honors in General Education track requires at total of 24 hours of classes. Of these, a minimum of 9 hours must be earned in low-enrollment honors sections of regular general education classes. Students may take a maximum of 9 hours in regular general education classes for honors credit by making arrangements with the instructor to carry out additional activities that enrich the academic experience beyond that of a non-honors student taking the same class. These enrichment activities must be identified in an Honors Contract. Finally, students must take 6 hours of low-enrollment honors seminars that are usually interdisciplinary in nature and always approach topics from a broad viewpoint. Students must maintain a 3.5 cumulative GPA to remain in and graduate from the Honors in General Education track.

The second track is Honors in the Major. It, too, is a 24-hour program. Students are required to take 18 hours of major classes for honors credit, either by enrolling in low-enrollment honors courses or by earning honors credit through the contract process. Students in the Honors in the Major track must also take 6 hours of honors seminars. Finally, they must complete a senior thesis or creative project and present their work in a public setting. To remain in and graduate from the Honors in the Major track, students must maintain a 3.5 cumulative GPA.

Students who complete both tracks of the Honors Program are required to take only 6 hours of honors seminars, which may be earned while enrolled in either or both honors tracks.

Students who join the Honors Program as incoming freshmen must complete 12 hours of honors courses by the end of their first year in order to remain in the program. Likewise, a student in the program must pursue a minimum of one course for honors credit each semester to remain in the program. A minimum cumulative GPA of 3.5 is also required at all times. Students who fall below a 3.5 have one semester to bring their grades back up. Students whose cumulative GPA falls below 3.5 for two semesters in a row are dismissed from the program.

Admission Process: Entering freshmen are invited to join the Honors Program if they have a cumulative weighted GPA of at least 3.7 on a 4.0 scale and an SAT combined score of at least 1575 or an ACT composite score of 22. Some entering students, including high school valedictorians and salutatorians, National Merit and Achievement Scholarship finalists, and graduates of the North Carolina School of Science and Mathematics, are automatically invited to join the program. Students who score 1800 on the SAT or 29 on the ACT are also automatically eligible to join the Honors Program. Students already at A&T are eligible to join the Honors Program once they have compiled a cumulative GPA of 3.5 and completed a minimum of 12 hours of classes. Transfer students who were members of the honors program at another accredited institution are immediately eligible to join the A&T Honors Program. Transfer students who were not in an honors program can join the A&T Honors Program as soon as they complete a minimum of 12 A&T hours of classes with a cumulative GPA of 3.5.

Scholarship Availability: The University awards a wide range of Chancellor and other merit-based scholarships. Many of the awardees are members of the Honors Program.

Campus Overview

State-supported university, founded 1891, part of University of North Carolina System • **Coed** 7,982 undergraduate students, 90% full-time, 52% women, 48% men.

Undergraduates 7,197 full-time, 785 part-time. Students come from 42 states and territories, 20% are from out of state, 92% African American, 1% Asian American or Pacific Islander, 0.6% Hispanic American, 0.4% Native American, 0.8% international, 6% transferred in, 29% live on campus.

Faculty *Total:* 458. *Student/faculty ratio:* 17:1.

Academic Programs *Special study options:* academic remediation for entering students, adult/continuing education programs, advanced placement credit, cooperative education, honors programs, internships, off-campus study, part-time degree program, services for LD students, study abroad, summer session for credit. *ROTC:* Army (b), Air Force (b).

Athletics Member NCAA. All Division I except football (Division I-AA). *Intercollegiate sports:* baseball M(s), basketball M(s)/W(s), cross-country running M(s)/W(s), softball W, swimming and diving W(s), tennis M(s)/W(s), track and field M(s)/W(s), volleyball W(s). *Intramural sports:* baseball M/W, basketball M/W, bowling W, cross-country running M/W, football M, golf M/W, racquetball M/W, soccer M/W, softball M/W, swimming and diving M/W, table tennis M/W, tennis M/W, track and field M/W, volleyball M/W, weight lifting M/W.

Costs (2004–05) *Tuition:* state resident $1769 full-time, $362 per credit hour part-time; nonresident $11,211 full-time, $1542 per credit hour part-time. *Required fees:* $1297 full-time. *Room and board:* $5070; room only: $2700.

Financial Aid In 2003, 309 non-need-based awards were made. *Average percent of need met:* 54%. *Average financial aid package:* $5238. *Average need-based loan:* $4913. *Average need-based gift aid:* $3287. *Average non-need-based aid:* $4169.

Contact: Director of the A&T Honors Program: Dr. Peter Meyers, 329 Gibbs Hall, North Carolina Agricultural and Technical State University, 1601 East Market Street, Greensboro, North Carolina 27411; *Telephone:* 336-256-0277; *Fax:* 336-334-7837; *E-mail:* peterm@ncat.edu; *Web site:* http://www.ncat.edu/~honors

North Carolina State University
University Honors Program
Raleigh, North Carolina

The University Honors Program (UHP) at North Carolina State University (NC State) is a highly selective program of great expectations that is designed to encourage and enable outstanding students to engage in the full range of scholarly experiences that are possible at a major research, land-grant university. It is an opportunity for motivated students to craft for themselves a unique undergraduate education. Prospective students should understand that the emphasis of the UHP is on research and scholarship.

The UHP is just one of many honors or honors-like experiences at NC State. There are thirty-two honors programs based in colleges and departments that invite NC State students in their sophomore and junior years. Joining the UHP in targeting entering students is the University Scholars Program (USP), a program that emphasizes cultural enrichment but also has an academic component. To increase the number of entering students who can benefit from special opportunities, students must choose to participate in either the USP or the UHP; they cannot participate in both.

Students are invited to apply for admission to the UHP. The largest group of students enters the program upon their arrival at NC State as first-year students. However, invitations are also issued to students after their first and second semesters at NC State, based on their academic record at NC State. The UHP is not appropriate for students transferring to NC State as sophomores or juniors. Instead, those students should contact the relevant college or departmental Honors Program.

Students in the University Honors Program must complete a minimum of four honors seminars. These are low-enrollment courses featuring inquiry-guided learning and innovative instruction by award-winning professors. Most of the seminars satisfy one of the general education requirements, so for many students they do not represent additional courses, although this varies depending on the specific curriculum of each student. The seminars are designed to help students see how knowledge is generated; think about the ethical, historical, and societal implications of new knowledge; and to think across disciplinary boundaries. The goal is to use the relatively familiar environment of a course to introduce students to research and to prepare them for engaging in research in their own disciplines.

University Honors Program students are encouraged to engage in experiential learning. Credit courses exist for honors independent study, honors extension and engagement, and honors cooperative education. Special workshops and information sessions introduce students to these and other opportunities, including study abroad and undergraduate research experiences. The UHP offers its participants study-abroad scholarships and undergraduate research awards.

The culmination of the University Honors Program experience is the Honors Capstone research. Under the supervision of a faculty member, students engage in a two-semester independent project that results in a public presentation appropriate to the discipline. University Honors Program students may choose to participate in one or more college or departmental honors programs. These generally involve an independent research project, which can also serve as the UHP Capstone.

The Honors Village living-learning community is a partnership of the UHP and University Housing. Located in the historic Quad residence halls, the Honors Village was renovated in 2004–05. It was part of a $17-million project that included the construction of a new building, the Honors Village Commons. The Honors Village is immediately adjacent to the offices of the UHP and one of the campus dining halls. First-year students are strongly encouraged, but not required, to live in the Honors Village. They are placed into small groups, each under the leadership of an Honors Village mentor, a *returning student who provides guidance and advice and seeks to build group camaraderie by arranging social events and group meals. Students can elect to enroll in a 1-credit-hour thematic honors colloquium, designed to introduce students to various aspects of life in the Research Triangle (e.g., the Raleigh Visual Arts Scene, the Raleigh Literary Scene, and the Triangle Outdoors). The Honors Village features a faculty-member apartment, which is occupied by a scholar who interacts with the students and offers special programming.*

The UHP houses the Office of Undergraduate Fellowship Advising, which supports students competing for nationally competitive scholarships and fellowships, including the Rhodes, Marshall, Mitchell, Goldwater, and Gates-Cambridge Scholarships.

The University Honors Program was established in 2000, adopting its research-focused mission in 2003. There are currently 400–500 active participants.

Participation Requirements: Participants must complete four 3-credit honors seminars and a 6-credit honors capstone research project while maintaining a GPA of 3.25 or higher. Students participating in one of the college or disciplinary honors programs must complete an additional 9 or more hours of honors course work in the discipline, and most require some kind of research project; minimum GPA requirements vary by program.

Admission Process: Students are invited to apply for admission to the University Honors Program. Automatic invitations are issued based on high school GPA and SAT scores. However, any student may request and submit an application. The program seeks students who are motivated to partake of the resources of a major land-grant, research institution and who plan to engage in some kind of research or other scholarly activity as undergraduates. Applications are reviewed by faculty members and campus professionals, with a major emphasis placed on student essays. In recent years, the UHP has received 400 applications for 125–150 places. Invitations to apply are also issued to NC State students, based solely on their academic record at NC State in their first semester or first year. These supplemental entry groups each number between 25 and 40 students.

Scholarship Availability: The University Honors Program has no scholarships of its own. However, NC State is committed to meeting the demonstrated financial need for all incoming first-year students who have elected to participate in the University Honors Program and who meet the Financial Aid Preference deadline.

The NC State Merit Scholarship Competition includes both University-wide (noncurriculum specific) scholarships and merit scholarships given by the individual colleges and academic departments for students planning to enter their specific majors. In addition, the Park Scholarship Program, supported by the Roy Park Foundation, awards full scholarships to 45–50 students each year. These four-year awards cover tuition and fees, room and board, textbooks, academic supplies, and living expenses, plus a stipend for a personal computer and opportunities for enrichment activities.

Campus Overview

State-supported university, founded 1887, part of University of North Carolina System • **Coed** 22,754 undergraduate students, 83% full-time, 42% women, 58% men.

Undergraduates 18,890 full-time, 3,864 part-time. Students come from 52 states and territories, 54 other countries, 7% are from out of state, 10% African American, 5% Asian American or Pacific Islander, 2% Hispanic American, 0.7% Native American, 0.9% international, 5% transferred in, 33% live on campus.

Faculty *Total:* 1,825, 90% full-time, 89% with terminal degrees. *Student/faculty ratio:* 16:1.

Academic Programs *Special study options:* academic remediation for entering students, accelerated degree program, adult/continuing education programs, advanced placement credit, cooperative education, distance learning, double majors, honors programs, independent study, internships, off-campus study, part-time degree program, services for LD students, student-designed majors, study abroad, summer session for credit. *ROTC:* Army (b), Navy (b), Air Force (b).

Athletics Member NCAA. All Division I except football (Division I-A). *Intercollegiate sports:* badminton M(c)/W(c), baseball M(s), basketball M(s)/W(s), bowling M(c)/W(c), cheerleading M/W, crew M(c)/W(c), cross-country running M(s)/W(s), equestrian sports M(c)/W(c), fencing M/W, field hockey M(c)/W(c), golf M(s)/W, gymnastics W(s), ice hockey M(c)/W(c), lacrosse M(c)/W(c), racquetball M(c)/W(c), riflery M/W, rugby M(c)/W(c), sailing M(c)/W(c), skiing (downhill) M(c)/W(c), soccer M(s)/W(s), softball W(s), swimming and diving M(s)/W(s), table tennis M(c)/W(c), tennis M(s)/W(s), track and field M(s)/W(s), ultimate Frisbee M(c)/W(c), volleyball M(c)/W(s), water polo M(c)/W(c), wrestling M(s). *Intramural sports:* badminton M/W, baseball M, basketball M/W, bowling M/W, cheerleading W(c), crew M/W, cross-country running M/W, equestrian sports M/W, fencing M/W, field hockey W, football M/W, golf M/W, gymnastics W, ice hockey M, lacrosse M/W, racquetball M/W, rugby M/W, sailing M/W, skiing (downhill) M/W, soccer M/W, softball M/W, swimming and diving M/W, table tennis M/W, tennis M/W, track and field M/W, volleyball M/W, water polo M/W, wrestling M.

Costs (2005–06) *Tuition:* state resident $3505 full-time; nonresident $15,403 full-time. Full-time tuition and fees vary according to program. Part-time tuition and fees vary according to course load and program. *Required fees:* $1162 full-time. *Room and board:* $6851; room only: $4183. Room and board charges vary according to board plan and housing facility.

Financial Aid 582 Federal Work-Study jobs (averaging $1448). 218 state and other part-time jobs (averaging $5712). In 2004, 3900 non-need-based awards were made. *Average percent of need met:* 82%. *Average financial aid package:* $8410. *Average need-based loan:* $3155. *Average need-based gift aid:* $5925. *Average non-need-based aid:* $7306.

Contact: Director: Richard L. Blanton, Campus Box 8610, North Carolina State University, Raleigh, North Carolina 27695; *Telephone:* 919-513-4078; *Fax:* 919-513-4392; *E-mail:* university_honors@ncsu.edu; *Web site:* http://honors.ncsu.edu

---

The University of North Carolina at Asheville
University Honors Program
Asheville, North Carolina

*T*he University of North Carolina at Asheville's (UNCA) University Honors Program offers special educational opportunities to academically talented and motivated students. The college-wide program welcomes freshmen, transfers, and continuing students from all academic departments.

The Honors Program offers courses as well as cocurricular activities designed to extend learning beyond the classroom. Courses include special sections of many general education requirements, such as freshman composition and humanities, and challenging junior and senior honors seminars. The Honors Program emphasizes both breadth and depth in liberal education. The breadth comes through special emphasis on interdisciplinary courses. Depth, or excellence in a particular field, is encouraged through undergraduate research with a faculty mentor in the academic major. Additional educational opportunities include independent study and internships.

The Honors Program also offers a range of extracurricular activities designed to foster community and leadership among participants.

The 15-year-old program currently enrolls 300 students.

Participation Requirements: Students who complete requirements of the Honors Program graduate with Distinction as a University Scholar. Those requirements include completion of 15 hours of honors credit (including the Senior Honors Colloquium and an honors special topics course) with a GPA of at least 3.5, a minimum 3.5 GPA in the last 60 hours of credit, and completion of a research or creative project.

Admission Process: Freshmen apply directly to the Honors Program. Participants are chosen on the basis of SAT scores, rank in class, and leadership activities. Transfer students may also apply for admission, provided they have earned a GPA of at least 3.5 on all transfer hours. Continuing UNCA students may apply if they have earned a GPA of at least 3.25. Students must maintain a GPA of at least 3.25 and must complete at least one 3-hour honors course during their first four semesters in order to remain a member of the Honors Program.

Scholarship Availability: The Honors Program itself does not offer scholarships but cooperates closely with the University Laurels Academic Merit Scholarship Program. Students interested in those academic scholarships apply as part of the UNCA application process. Students identified as merit scholarship candidates are invited to the campus for Interview Day, which is usually scheduled in February. Many candidates for the University Laurels Academic Merit Scholarships are also considered for admission to the University Honors Program.

Campus Overview

State-supported comprehensive, founded 1927, part of University of North Carolina System • **Coed** 3,572 undergraduate students, 81% full-time, 57% women, 43% men.

Undergraduates 2,909 full-time, 663 part-time. Students come from 41 states and territories, 28 other countries, 14% are from out of state, 3% African American, 1% Asian American or Pacific Islander, 2% Hispanic American, 0.3% Native American, 1% international, 6% transferred in, 39% live on campus.

Faculty *Total:* 312, 58% full-time, 64% with terminal degrees. *Student/faculty ratio:* 14:1.

Academic Programs *Special study options:* academic remediation for entering students, adult/continuing education programs, advanced placement credit, distance learning, double majors, honors programs, independent study, internships, off-campus study, part-time degree program, student-designed majors, study abroad, summer session for credit. *Unusual degree programs:* 3-2 chemistry and textile chemistry with North Carolina State University.

Athletics Member NCAA. All Division I. *Intercollegiate sports:* baseball M(s), basketball M(s)/W(s), cheerleading M/W, cross-country running M(s)/W(s), soccer M(s)/W(s), tennis M(s)/W(s), track and field M(s)/W(s), volleyball W(s). *Intramural sports:* badminton M/W, basketball M/W, football M, golf M/W, racquetball M/W, soccer M/W, softball M/W, table tennis M/W, tennis M/W, ultimate Frisbee M/W, volleyball M/W, water polo M/W.

Costs (2004–05) *Tuition:* state resident $1897 full-time; nonresident $11,097 full-time. Part-time tuition and fees vary according to course load. *Required fees:* $1495 full-time. *Room and board:* $5212; room only: $2722. Room and board charges vary according to housing facility.

Financial Aid 101 Federal Work-Study jobs (averaging $1234). 637 state and other part-time jobs (averaging $1407). In 2003, 250 non-need-based awards were made. *Average percent of need met:* 79%. *Average financial aid package:* $7383. *Average need-based loan:* $3539. *Average need-based gift aid:* $3365. *Average non-need-based aid:* $2891.

Contact: Kathleen Peters, Ph.D., Director, Honors Program, 141 Karpen Hall, CPO 2150, The University of North Carolina at Asheville, One University Heights, Asheville, North Carolina 28804; *Telephone:* 828-251-6607; *Fax:* 828-251-6614; *E-mail:* kpeters@unca.edu

The University of North Carolina at Chapel Hill
Honors Program
Chapel Hill, North Carolina

The Honors Program at the University of North Carolina (UNC) at Chapel Hill offers a challenging curriculum of small classes and seminars at one of the nation's premier research universities. The more than 100 honors courses taught during each academic year are designed primarily for freshmen and sophomores. For juniors, the program offers two interdisciplinary colloquia, one each semester, focused on changing topics selected by students. The colloquia allow for wide-ranging interaction with leading faculty members and visiting experts from around the nation. Recent topics have included America the World, Business Ethics, and The Law and Social Justice. The senior Honors Program centers on writing a thesis or completing an original artistic project in a student's major department.

Honors courses are small, usually limited to no more than 15 to 20 students, and they are taught by regular members of the faculty, including many who have won teaching awards. The courses cover a wide variety of topics in the humanities, social sciences, natural sciences, and fine arts. The Honors Office awards course development grants each year to enable faculty members to create seminars that are interdisciplinary or incorporate new approaches to teaching. Some seminars provide opportunities for service in order to apply classroom principles and theory to real-world challenges. For example, one civic arts seminar combines the study of urban education and the policy debates surrounding it with hands-on experience mentoring junior high school students from the nearby city of Durham.

The Honors Program considers study abroad an essential component of a high-quality undergraduate education. To that end, it operates its own UNC faculty-led programs in London, Rome, and Cape Town. The semester in Cape Town is built around internships with local agencies involved in the social and economic reconstruction of post-apartheid South Africa. The Honors Program also administers the Burch Field Research Seminars, which place UNC faculty members and students in different locations around the globe to work on shared research and artistic projects. Recent seminars have offered theater internships in New York, opportunities to study astronomy at UNC's new telescope high atop the Chilean Andes, hands-on experience with documentary filmmaking in Bangkok, and foreign-policy internships in Washington, D.C. In addition, individual students may apply for a Burch Fellowship for their sophomore or junior summers. The Burch Fellowships provide a stipend of up to $6000 for students to "pursue an intellectual passion" through a self-designed learning experience.

Honors advisers help students plan their curricula in light of their educational and career goals. The Honors Student Advisory Board organizes an array of activities outside the classroom. These include service projects, social events, and Food for Thought, a series of informal dinner discussions with faculty members.

One distinctive feature of the Honors Program at UNC is its accessibility. Indeed, the Fiske Guide to Colleges called the Honors Program at Chapel Hill one of the "most accessible in the country." Students not initially invited into the Honors Program may apply after arriving on campus. Moreover, students who are not in the Honors Program may take honors courses on a space-available basis if they have an overall B average or better.

The Honors Program is located in the James M. Johnston Center for Undergraduate Excellence. The Johnston Center serves as an intellectual crossroads for the entire Carolina campus. Students visit the center to enjoy a variety of cocurricular programming, including films, lectures, musical performances, and art and photography exhibitions. With its state-of-the-art technology, the Johnston Center also serves as a laboratory for innovation in teaching and learning.

The center's teleconferencing facilities connect UNC programs abroad back to the campus and give students in Chapel Hill access to academic experts from all parts of the world. A number of other programs are also housed in the Johnston Center, including the Office for Undergraduate Research, the Office of Distinguished Scholarships, and the Robertson Scholars Program. The Office for Undergraduate Research assists students in identifying opportunities to work with faculty members on cutting-edge research. In 2004, more than a third of all Carolina undergraduates, many of them first-year students, were engaged in such faculty-mentored projects. The Office of Distinguished Scholarships assists students in identifying and applying for prestigious scholarship awards. In 2003–04, UNC joined Harvard and Stanford universities as the only schools to have winners of each of the most highly esteemed awards: Rhodes, Luce, Truman, and Goldwater. The Robertson Scholars Program is a collaborative program that enrolls outstanding students at UNC and Duke University each year.

The Honors Program was created in 1954 and maintains an enrollment of approximately 650 first-year students, sophomores, and juniors as well as approximately 300 seniors working on honors theses in their major departments. More than 300 other students take advantage of honors course offerings each year.

Participation Requirements: After entering the Honors Program, students must maintain a cumulative GPA of at least 3.0 and take at least two honors courses per academic year in order to remain in the program through the junior year. Students receive a notation on their official transcripts for each academic year in which they complete the Honors Program requirements.

In the senior year, the successful completion and defense of an honors thesis under the direction of a faculty mentor qualifies a student for graduation with Honors or Highest Honors and to have this distinction designated on the diploma. To begin work on an honors thesis, a student must have a minimum overall GPA of 3.2 and permission of her or his major department. A student may write a thesis without having previously participated in the Honors Program.

Admission Process: There is no separate application for the Honors Program for incoming first-year students. Students are selected for invitation into the program in two separate rounds—mid-January and late March—from the pool of high school students admitted to UNC. Two hundred students, about 6 percent of the first-year class, join the program each fall. A faculty committee selects invitees on the basis of their academic credentials and a qualitative evaluation of other application materials, including required essays and letters of recommendation. The Honors Program seeks to identify students who are likely to thrive in, and actively contribute to, a rigorous interdisciplinary learning environment.

First-year students who do not receive an honors invitation at the time of enrollment may apply to join the program at the beginning of their second semester, and sophomores may apply at the start of their fall semester. Students who transfer to UNC as sophomores may apply at the start of their first academic year.

Scholarship Availability: The UNC Honors Office has no scholarships to distribute directly to students; however, need-based scholarships and several types of merit-based awards are available through the University's Office of Student Aid and Scholarships. Because of the high academic accomplishment of Honors Program participants, many receive merit awards.

Campus Overview

State-supported university, founded 1789, part of University of North Carolina System • **Coed** 16,144 undergraduate students, 95% full-time, 59% women, 41% men.

Undergraduates 15,355 full-time, 789 part-time. Students come from 52 states and territories, 102 other countries, 18% are from out of state, 11% African American, 6% Asian American or Pacific Islander, 2% Hispanic American, 0.8% Native American, 1% international, 5% transferred in, 44% live on campus.

Faculty Total: 1,460, 92% full-time, 81% with terminal degrees. Student/faculty ratio: 14:1.

Academic Programs Special study options: advanced placement credit, distance learning, double majors, freshman honors college, honors programs, independent study, internships, off-campus study, services for LD students, student-designed majors, study abroad, summer session for credit. ROTC: Army (b), Navy (b), Air Force (b).

Athletics Member NCAA. All Division I except football (Division I-A). Intercollegiate sports: baseball M(s)/W(c), basketball M(s)/W(s), crew M(c)/W(s), cross-country running M(s)/W(s), equestrian sports M(c)/W(c), fencing M/W, field hockey W(s), golf M(s)/W(s), gymnastics W(s), lacrosse M(s)/W(s), racquetball M(c)/W(c), rugby M(c)/W(c), sailing M(c)/W(c), soccer M(s)/W(s), softball W(s), swimming and diving M(s)/W(s), tennis M(s)/W(s), track and field M(s)/W(s), ultimate Frisbee M(c)/W(c), volleyball M(c)/W(s), wrestling M(s). Intramural sports: badminton M/W, basketball M/W, bowling M/W, cross-country running M/W, field hockey M(c)/W(c), football M/W, golf M(c)/W(c), gymnastics M(c)/W(c), ice hockey M(c)/W(c), lacrosse M(c)/W(c), racquetball M/W, soccer M/W, softball M/W, squash M(c)/W(c), swimming and diving M/W, table tennis M/W, tennis M/W, track and field M/W, ultimate Frisbee M/W, volleyball M/W, water polo M/W, weight lifting M/W, wrestling M(c).

Costs (2004–05) Tuition: state resident $3205 full-time; nonresident $16,303 full-time. Full-time tuition and fees vary according to program. Part-time tuition and fees vary according to course load and program. Required fees: $1246 full-time. Room and board: $6245; room only: $3420. Room and board charges vary according to board plan, housing facility, and location.

Financial Aid 824 Federal Work-Study jobs (averaging $1691). In 2002, 2170 non-need-based awards were made. Average percent of need met: 100%. Average financial aid package: $8983. Average need-based loan: $3719. Average need-based gift aid: $5325. Average non-need-based aid: $5451.

Contact: Associate Dean for Honors: James Leloudis; Assistant Dean for Honors: Ritchie Kendall, Honors Program, Graham Memorial, CB#3510, University of North Carolina at Chapel Hill, Chapel Hill, North Carolina 27599-3510; Telephone: 919-966-5110; Fax: 919-962-1548; Web site: http://honors.unc.edu

The University of North Carolina at Charlotte
Honors College
Charlotte, North Carolina

The Honors College comprises several distinct programs, each with its own standards for admission and requirements for graduation. Students may enroll in more than one program. Unique enrichment opportunities, including scholarships, study abroad, community service, executive shadowing, special lectures, and individualized senior projects, are also available. A special honors residence option is also available for all students in the Honors College. The Honors College Web site is: http://www.honorscollege.uncc.edu, which has links to all programs described below. There are also links to several scholarships.

The four principle programs are the University Honors Program, the Business Honors Program, the Teaching Fellows Program, and Department Honors Programs. A summary of each is provided below.

The University Honors Program (UHP) is open to talented and highly motivated students of all majors. It is designed to challenge and broaden the intellectual growth of UNC Charlotte's most gifted students. A series of interdisciplinary core courses focus on global issues, including war and peace, economics and the international community, science and values, and human rights. Cultural enrichment opportunities, a strong commitment to citizenship and service, and an individually designed senior project provide UHP *students unique opportunities to customize their honors curriculum to meet their own specific goals. For more information about admission, curriculum, UHP courses, and activities, students should visit http://www.uhonors.uncc.edu/ or contact the UHP Director, Connie Rothwell, at crothwll@email.uncc.edu.*

The Business Honors Program (BHP) offers talented students exceptional opportunities in the field of business. BHP students enroll in small sections of required business courses at the sophomore and junior levels. In addition, significant extracurricular opportunities are provided to enhance student leadership and professional business skills. For more information about admission, curriculum, BHP courses, and the BHP activities, students should visit http://www.uncc.edu/colleges/business/bus_honors/ or contact the BHP assistant director, Kristine Hopkins, at kdhopkin@email.uncc.edu.

The Teaching Fellows Program (TF) at UNC Charlotte fosters scholastic achievement and professional leadership through personal attention and enrichment experiences. Teaching Fellows participate in special activities that complement their involvement in the regular teacher education program. All students enrolled in the UNC Charlotte Teaching Fellows program must apply for, and be awarded, a North Carolina Teaching Fellows Scholarship, which provides $6500 per year for four years to 400 outstanding North Carolina high school seniors. Applications for this award must be made while students are in their senior year of high school. To learn more about the TF program, students should visit http://www.uncc.edu/tfellows/ or contact Dr. Misty Hathcock at mchathco@email.uncc.edu.

Department Honors Programs, offered by many academic departments at UNC Charlotte, enable students to graduate with honors in their academic discipline. Currently, departments with honors programs include anthropology, art, biology, chemistry, geography and earth science, history, Latin American studies, mathematics, philosophy, physics, political science, and psychology. Graduation with honors within an academic discipline may be combined with graduation with University Honors distinction. Generally the curriculum for students in a Department Honors Program focuses on upper-division course work, culminating in a senior thesis or self-directed project completed within a student's academic major. To learn more about Department Honors Programs, students should visit http://www.honorscollege.uncc.edu/departments.htm or contact the individual department honors program directors listed on that Web site.

The Honors College was established July 2003.

Participation Requirements: Participation varies among programs; however, information is available either from the Honors College Web site or from links to each program. It is important for students in the Honors College to be active not only in specified classes but also in seminars, program-sponsored events, and social activities. University Honors, Business Honors, and Departmental Honors programs require students to complete senior projects to graduate with honors. Upon completion of select course work and the project, diplomas are engraved and the student transcript shows each distinction. Medals are awarded by some programs and departments for the graduation ceremony.

Scholarship Availability: Information about University scholarships for merit is available through admissions at http://www.uncc.edu/admissions.

Campus Overview

State-supported university, founded 1946, part of University of North Carolina System • **Coed** 15,875 undergraduate students, 80% full-time, 54% women, 46% men.

Undergraduates 12,728 full-time, 3,147 part-time. Students come from 48 states and territories, 80 other countries, 9% are from out of state, 15% African American, 5% Asian American or Pacific Islander, 3% Hispanic American, 0.4% Native American, 2% international, 11% transferred in, 27% live on campus.

Faculty *Total:* 1,164, 70% full-time, 69% with terminal degrees. *Student/faculty ratio:* 15:1.

Academic Programs *Special study options:* adult/continuing education programs, advanced placement credit, cooperative education, distance learning, double majors, English as a second language, freshman honors college, honors programs, internships, off-campus study, part-time degree program, services for LD students, study abroad, summer session for credit. *ROTC:* Army (b), Air Force (b).

Athletics Member NCAA. All Division I. *Intercollegiate sports:* baseball M(s), basketball M(s)/W(s), cross-country running M(s)/W(s), golf M(s), soccer M(s)/W(s), softball W(s), tennis M(s)/W(s), track and field M(s)/W(s), volleyball W(s). *Intramural sports:* archery M(c)/W(c), badminton M(c)/W(c), baseball M(c)/W(c), basketball M/W, bowling M(c)/W(c), fencing M(c)/W(c), football M/W, golf M/W, ice hockey M(c)/W(c), lacrosse M(c)/W(c), racquetball M(c)/W(c), rock climbing M/W, rugby M(c)/W(c), soccer M(c)/W(c), softball M(c)/W(c), swimming and diving M(c)/W(c), table tennis M/W, tennis M(c)/W(c), track and field M/W, volleyball M(c)/W(c), water polo M/W, wrestling M(c)/W(c).

Costs (2004–05) *Tuition:* state resident $2129 full-time, $533 per term part-time; nonresident $12,241 full-time, $3061 per term part-time. Full-time tuition and fees vary according to course load. Part-time tuition and fees vary according to course load. *Required fees:* $1344 full-time, $398 per term part-time. *Room and board:* $5304; room only: $2724. Room and board charges vary according to board plan and housing facility.

Financial Aid 530 Federal Work-Study jobs (averaging $1282). 1,825 state and other part-time jobs (averaging $1611). In 2004, 1916 non-need-based awards were made. *Average percent of need met:* 64%. *Average financial aid package:* $8527. *Average need-based loan:* $3862. *Average need-based gift aid:* $4083. *Average non-need-based aid:* $5772.

Contact: Associate Dean: Dr. Al Maisto, Honors College, 317 Cato, The University of North Carolina at Charlotte, 9201 University City Boulevard, Charlotte, North Carolina 28223-0001; *Telephone:* 704-687-4824; *Fax:* 704-687-3116; *E-mail:* amaisto@email.uncc.edu; *Web site:* http://www.honorscollege.uncc.edu

The University of North Carolina at Greensboro
International Honors College
Greensboro, North Carolina

The International Honors College at the University of North Carolina at Greensboro (UNCG) provides outstanding undergraduate students with an enhanced and supportive intellectual and social experience that acculturates them to the life of the mind and helps them to become critical, independent thinkers who are active in the design and pursuit of their own education and prepared to lead successful and fulfilling professional, civic, and personal lives.

Students choose from a wide range of small, often interdisciplinary courses that provide greater depth and breadth than regular courses. Honors courses are taught by faculty members who are among the best at UNCG, who are deeply engaged with their disciplines, and who are dedicated to helping students achieve their greatest potential. Honors courses typically have fewer than 20 students and foster discussion, collaboration, and mutual discovery among students and faculty members. The variety of honors courses, and particularly the chance to customize one's curriculum through honors contract courses and independent studies, means that students have considerable control over their own education. If a desired course is not in the catalog, students may work with professors to design their own. Moreover, many of the advanced honors courses, such as the Senior Honors Project, allow students to do original, sophisticated work and are an excellent preparation for graduate school, professional training, and other postgraduation endeavors.

The International Honors College believes that all its students, whether earning degrees in the College of Arts and Sciences or in one of UNCG's professional schools, should have a solid liberal education and that, in today's world, this includes being internationally aware and competent. As a result, students in the International Honors College are required to reach an intermediate level of competency in a language that is not their native language (ancient and sign languages are permissible) and to have a substantive international experience that complements their broader educational goals. For most students, this international experience is a semester of study abroad at one of UNCG's many exchange partners. However, for some students, the best international experience may be a different experience, such as an internship with an international firm or a service-learning project involving an immigrant population.

The International Honors College also believes that a college education is too important to be limited to the classroom. As a result, it has an honors residence hall for those students who are interested and sponsors events such as student symposia, debates, guest lectures, dinners with faculty members, and informal coffees in which students and faculty members have the chance to mix and enjoy the camaraderie that comes from sharing ideas and honest talk. The Honors Student Advisory Board is active in the planning and the running of many of these events.

The International Honors College has its origins in a collection of special programs first established in the late 1940s. In 1962, these programs were organized into the Honors Program, and, in 2005, the Honors Program was transformed into the International Honors College. In 2005, there were approximately 400 students enrolled in the International Honors College.

Participation Requirements: Students in the International Honors College have a choice of three programs. The General-Education Honors Program requires 14 hours of honors course work. Students must also reach an intermediate level of competency in a language that is not their native one (ancient and sign languages are permissible) and complete a substantive international experience that complements their broader educational goals. Most required course work can be satisfied by replacing regular courses with honors courses that satisfy the same general-education requirements. The Disciplinary Honors Program requires at least 9 hours of honors course work and a Senior Honors Project. The Senior Honors Project is typically completed through a designated 3-hour course. However, students may earn additional academic credit if warranted or complete the project through an Undergraduate Research Assistantship rather than receive academic credit. The Full University Honors Program requires that students complete both the General-Education Honors and the Disciplinary Honors Programs. For all programs, students must maintain at least a 3.3 GPA to participate. Students who fulfill program requirements and have at least a 3.3 GPA at graduation are recognized at graduation and at the annual Honors Banquet. The accomplishment is also noted on the student's transcript along with the title of the Senior Honors Project (if appropriate).

Admission Process: Prospective freshmen who have at least a 3.8 weighted high school grade point average or a score of at least 1200 on the SAT (27 on the ACT) may apply for admission to the International Honors College. Admission decisions are based on the student's weighted high school grade point average, SAT (or ACT) score, a personal statement, and a description of additional academic and extracurricular activities that the student has engaged in. Students who are already at UNCG or who are transferring from other colleges or universities may apply if they have an aggregate grade point average of at least 3.3. Admission decisions are based on the aggregate grade point average, a personal statement, and a description of additional academic and extracurricular activities that the student has engaged in. In all cases, admission decisions are made on a rolling basis by a committee of honors faculty members drawn from the Honors Council, the International Honors College's governing board.

Scholarship Availability: In addition to the full range of scholarships open to all UNCG students (prospective honors students should visit UNCG's scholarships Web page at http://fia.dept.uncg.edu/scholarships for more details), the International Honors College administers the prestigious Undergraduate Scholars Program, a merit scholarship program based on superior scholastic performance, personal achievement, and potential. The International Honors College also awards the Lichtin Family Honors Scholarship, given to a rising junior or senior honors student with exemplary academic performance and future promise in honors, and (beginning with students entering in fall 2006) $1000 travel grants for students who fulfill their international experience requirement by studying abroad for a semester at one of UNCG's many exchange partners. Finally, for students interested in competing for nationally competitive undergraduate and graduate scholarships and fellowships, many of which provide support for study abroad, the International Honors College provides in-depth advice and support. Students who wish to complete an application are given hands-on coaching to ensure that their application is of the highest quality. Among the scholarships and fellowships that students may compete for are the Cooke, Fulbright, Goldwater, Madison, Marshall, Mellon, Mitchell, Rhodes, Truman, and Udall. Recent UNCG students have received awards for study in such diverse locations as Germany, Mali, and Sri Lanka.

Campus Overview

State-supported university, founded 1891, part of University of North Carolina System • **Coed** 11,106 undergraduate students, 84% full-time, 68% women, 32% men.

Undergraduates 9,317 full-time, 1,789 part-time. Students come from 41 states and territories, 55 other countries, 8% are from out of state, 20% African American, 3% Asian American or Pacific Islander, 1% Hispanic American, 0.3% Native American, 0.9% international, 9% transferred in, 34% live on campus.

Faculty *Total:* 947, 75% full-time, 71% with terminal degrees. *Student/faculty ratio:* 14:1.

Academic Programs *Special study options:* academic remediation for entering students, accelerated degree program, adult/continuing education programs, advanced placement credit, distance learning, double majors, English as a second language, freshman honors college, honors programs, independent study, internships, off-campus study, part-time degree program, services for LD students, student-designed majors, study abroad, summer session for credit. *ROTC:* Army (c), Air Force (c). *Unusual degree programs:* 3-2 business administration with North Carolina State University, University of North Carolina at Charlotte.

Athletics Member NCAA. All Division I. *Intercollegiate sports:* baseball M(s), basketball M(s)/W(s), cross-country running M(s)/W(s), golf M(s)/W(s), soccer M(s)/W(s), softball W(s), tennis M(s)/W(s), volleyball W(s), wrestling M(s). *Intramural sports:* badminton M/W, basketball M/W, bowling M/W, equestrian sports M(c)/W(c), fencing M(c)/W(c), football M/W, golf M/W, ice hockey M(c), lacrosse M(c)/W(c), racquetball M/W, rugby M(c)/W(c), soccer M/W, softball M/W, swimming and diving M/W, table tennis M/W, tennis M/W, track and field M/W, volleyball M/W.

Costs (2004–05) *Tuition:* state resident $2028 full-time, $253 per hour part-time; nonresident $12,996 full-time, $1625 per hour part-time. Part-time tuition and fees vary according to course load. *Required fees:* $1407 full-time, $2838 per term part-time. *Room and board:* $5000; room only: $2800. Room and board charges vary according to board plan and housing facility.

Financial Aid 565 Federal Work-Study jobs (averaging $1801). In 2004, 763 non-need-based awards were made. *Average percent of need met:* 70%. *Average financial aid package:* $6655. *Average need-based loan:* $3433. *Average need-based gift aid:* $2105. *Average non-need-based aid:* $3533.

Contact: Director: Dr. Dennis Patrick Leyden, International Honors College, 205 Foust Building, The University of North Carolina at Greensboro, P.O. Box 26170, Greensboro, North Carolina 27402-6170; *Telephone:* 336-334-5538; *E-mail:* askhonors@uncg.edu; *Web site:* http://www.uncg.edu/hss

The University of North Carolina at Pembroke
University Honors College
Pembroke, North Carolina

The University Honors College (UHC) at The University of North Carolina at Pembroke (UNC Pembroke or UNCP) recognizes and promotes the scholarly and personal growth of academically accomplished students in an intellectually stimulating environment with greater curricular flexibility and close interaction with faculty. The UHC learning community includes six interdisciplinary seminars within the General Education curriculum, a leadership program, cultural and service opportunities, and a senior research project. The University Honors College provides opportunities for supplemental cultural experiences and supports student participation in relevant academic conferences within the state, regionally, and nationally. Honors students are encouraged to consider study abroad and to pursue graduate or professional education upon graduation. The University Honors College is located in Old Main, the signature building on campus, and includes a computer lab and lounge for UHC students. University Honors College students may elect to live in shared residential facilities. Graduates receive a special diploma at commencement and the designation of University Honors College graduate on all transcripts. The University Honors College was inaugurated during the 2001–02 academic year. It supplants the longstanding Chancellor's Scholars Program. Approximately 20–25 freshmen are accepted each year. Continuing students may also be accepted..

Participation Requirements: Students who enter the University Honors College as freshmen begin with an intensive learning community experience, taking four general education core courses together, to support relationship building and program identification. The UHC curriculum includes a total of four interdisciplinary seminars, of which one is generally taken each semester. A two-semester sequence of guided research, with a faculty member in the major field, provides an opportunity to undertake an independent creative project or research endeavor that is presented to the members of the academic community. Research throughout the collegiate experience is supported through funding and opportunities for participation in conferences and research endeavors.

The University Honors College meets on a bi-monthly basis to support a sense of community. Members of the University Honors College participate in cultural activities on campus and develop a University service project annually. Generally during the freshman year, UHC students are part of LSOP (Leadership and Service Opportunities Program), designed to enhance leadership development and to support community involvement. University Honors College students receive recognition in a number of formal and informal ways including priority registration, honors advising, special encouragement for study abroad programs and graduate study and selected research opportunities. In a relatively small institution, University Honors College students are well known and well regarded.

Continuation in the University Honors College requires a minimum GPA of 3.0 at the end of the freshman year, 3.25 at the end of the sophomore year and 3.50 at the end of the junior year, as well as successful completion of required course work, the research sequence and other program expectations.

Admission Process: University Honors College students are accepted through a special application process. Students are selected based upon documented academic ability and demonstrated leadership. Motivated students with strong SAT (1100) or ACT (24) scores and superior academic records (minimum 3.5 GPA) are invited to submit an application to the University Honors College. Admission decisions are made by the program director with the assistance of the advisory committee.

Scholarship Availability: Admission to the UHC is independent of financial assistance. However, fully two thirds of the University student body receives some form of financial assistance and all students admitted to the University Honors College are considered for financial assistance. Sources of aid include need-based grants, federal and state loan programs, and endowed specialized and general scholarships. Some financial assistance programs carry a work/service requirement of 8 hours weekly in a University or community placement.

Campus Context: UNC Pembroke is one of the sixteen campuses in the University of North Carolina system. Founded in 1887 to educate American Indians, the University is now one of the most culturally diverse institutions in the southeast. The 126-acre campus is located on the coastal plains of southeastern North Carolina near I-95 and U.S. Highway 74. The University is approximately 1½ hours south of Raleigh and 1½ hours north of the North and South Carolina beaches and 2 hours east of Charlotte.

A regional public comprehensive university, UNC Pembroke awards a broad range of baccalaureate and master's degrees accredited by the Commission on Colleges of the Southern Association of Colleges and Schools. The University is organized around one college and three schools: the College of Arts and Sciences and the Schools of Business, Education, and Graduate Studies. University Honors College students elect course work from among fifty-five majors and more than 100 concentrations, interdisciplinary programs, and academic minors. The most popular majors among all students are education and business.

Campus Overview

State-supported comprehensive, founded 1887, part of University of North Carolina System • **Coed** 4,508 undergraduate students, 74% full-time, 64% women, 36% men.

Undergraduates 3,344 full-time, 1,164 part-time. Students come from 33 states and territories, 20 other countries, 3% are from out of state, 24% African American, 2% Asian American or Pacific Islander, 2% Hispanic American, 21% Native American, 0.7% international, 11% transferred in, 27% live on campus.

Faculty Total: 355, 64% full-time, 54% with terminal degrees. Student/faculty ratio: 15:1.

Academic Programs Special study options: academic remediation for entering students, accelerated degree program, adult/continuing education programs, advanced placement credit, cooperative education, distance learning, double majors, English as a second language, honors programs, independent study, internships, off-campus study, part-time degree program, services for LD students, study abroad, summer session for credit. ROTC: Army (b), Air Force (b).

Athletics Member NCAA. All Division II. Intercollegiate sports: baseball M(s), basketball M(s)/W(s), cross-country running M(s)/W(s), golf M(s), soccer M(s)/W(s), softball W(s), tennis W(s), track and field M(s), volleyball W(s), wrestling M(s). Intramural sports: basketball M/W, bowling M/W, cheerleading M/W, football M/W, golf M/W, racquetball M/W, soccer M/W, softball M/W, tennis M/W, track and field M/W, volleyball M/W, water polo M/W, weight lifting M/W, wrestling M/W.

Costs (2004–05) Tuition: state resident $1696 full-time; nonresident $11,128 full-time. Full-time tuition and fees vary according to course load and location. Part-time tuition and fees vary according to course load and location. Required fees: $1136 full-time. Room and board: $4560; room only: $2610. Room and board charges vary according to board plan and housing facility.

Financial Aid 383 Federal Work-Study jobs (averaging $1500). 27 state and other part-time jobs (averaging $1500). In 2004, 114 non-need-based awards were made. Average percent of need met: 68%. Average financial aid package: $6598. Average need-based loan: $3438. Average need-based gift aid: $4118. Average non-need-based aid: $1313.

Contact: Contact Person: Dr. Carolyn R. Thompson, University Honors College, The University of North Carolina at Pembroke, P.O.

Box 1510, Pembroke, North Carolina 28272-1510; *Telephone:* 910-521-6841; *Fax:* 910-521-6606; *E-mail:* honors@uncp.edu; *Web site:* http://www.uncp.edu/honors_college

The University of North Carolina at Wilmington
Honors Scholars Program
Wilmington, North Carolina

*T*he Honors Scholars Program at the University of North Carolina at Wilmington (UNCW) provides academically talented students with a variety of innovative and unique educational experiences both in and out of the classroom. The program encourages curiosity, critical thinking, and independent work skills by offering exciting academic and cultural activities as well as the opportunity for close working and social relationships with the faculty members. The program includes academics, cocurricular activities, and the opportunity to reside in a designated honors residence. In fall 2004, there were a total of 360 students in the program, including 105 freshmen, 95 sophomores, and 160 juniors and seniors.

Participation Requirements: Honors students take a 3-credit freshman interdisciplinary honors seminar in their first semester and a 3-credit honors topical seminar in their second year. In addition, students take 2 credits of honors enrichment seminars and 12 hours of honors sections of basic studies in their first two years. Honors classes are small—usually 20 students or fewer—to encourage discussion and independent work. If eligible, students may achieve Departmental Honors in their major in their last two years, culminating in a 6-credit senior project. The University Honors designation requires the full four-year participation, with honors in a discipline.

Admission Process: Students may enter the program as incoming freshmen (by invitation based on high school grades, SAT/ACT scores, and class rank) or as sophomores based on earned GPA. Students enter Departmental Honors based on an earned GPA of 3.2 or better.

Scholarship Availability: A limited number of merit scholarships are available on a competitive basis for students accepted into the Honors Scholars Program. In addition, several academic departments have scholarship funds for majors in their disciplines.

Campus Overview

State-supported comprehensive, founded 1947, part of University of North Carolina System • **Coed** 10,353 undergraduate students, 91% full-time, 60% women, 40% men.

Undergraduates 9,394 full-time, 959 part-time. Students come from 49 states and territories, 28 other countries, 14% are from out of state, 4% African American, 2% Asian American or Pacific Islander, 2% Hispanic American, 0.9% Native American, 0.5% international, 12% transferred in, 23% live on campus.

Faculty *Total:* 686, 68% full-time, 66% with terminal degrees. *Student/faculty ratio:* 19:1.

Academic Programs *Special study options:* academic remediation for entering students, accelerated degree program, adult/continuing education programs, advanced placement credit, cooperative education, distance learning, double majors, English as a second language, honors programs, independent study, internships, part-time degree program, services for LD students, study abroad, summer session for credit.

Athletics Member NCAA. All Division I. *Intercollegiate sports:* baseball M(s), basketball M(s)/W(s), cheerleading M/W, cross-country running M(s)/W(s), golf M(s)/W(s), soccer M(s)/W(s),

softball W(s), swimming and diving M(s)/W(s), tennis M(s)/W(s), track and field M(s)/W(s), volleyball W(s). *Intramural sports:* badminton M/W, baseball M(c), basketball M/W, crew M(c)/W(c), cross-country running M/W, equestrian sports M(c)/W(c), field hockey W(c), golf M(c)/W, gymnastics M(c)/W(c), lacrosse M(c)/W(c), rugby M(c), sailing M(c)/W(c), soccer M(c)/W(c), softball M/W(c), swimming and diving M(c)/W(c), table tennis M/W, tennis M(c)/W(c), ultimate Frisbee M(c)/W(c), volleyball M(c)/W.

Costs (2004–05) *Tuition:* state resident $1928 full-time; nonresident $11,638 full-time. Full-time tuition and fees vary according to course load. Part-time tuition and fees vary according to course load. *Required fees:* $1698 full-time. *Room and board:* $5800. Room and board charges vary according to board plan and housing facility.

Financial Aid 279 Federal Work-Study jobs (averaging $3000). In 2004, 122 non-need-based awards were made. *Average percent of need met:* 88%. *Average financial aid package:* $6693. *Average need-based loan:* $4046. *Average need-based gift aid:* $3852. *Average non-need-based aid:* $1369.

Contact: Director: Dr. Kate Bruce, The University of North Carolina at Wilmington, Wilmington, North Carolina 28403-3297; *Telephone:* 910-962-4181; *Fax:* 910-962-7020; *E-mail:* honors@uncw.edu; *Web site:* http://www.uncw.edu/honors/

Western Carolina University
Honors College
Cullowhee, North Carolina

*T*he Honors College is a fully interdisciplinary undergraduate College designed to enhance the academic and social experience of outstanding students at Western Carolina University (WCU). A chief aim of the program is to connect these students with excellent faculty members. The academic center of the College provides meeting space for students, free copying, and computer access. The honors residence is Reynolds Hall, an air-conditioned facility with seminar rooms and study spaces. The College is student-centered. The Honors Board of Directors is a student organization that advises the dean in setting goals and determining priorities. The Board of Directors organizes College social activities and participates in recruitment. Students also manage the Honors College Web site.

Both honors students and the College administration believe the Honors College should support the efforts of all students at WCU. All honors activities are open events. In addition, the College is responsible for the following activities, which are for all students: an annual Undergraduate Expo where students present results of research or artistic activities, travel to the National Conference on Undergraduate Research, the Undergraduate Research Grant Program, and the Mountain Heritage Day 5-K Road Race. Service activities include participation in the annual Tuckaseegee River Clean-up and sponsorship of campus blood drives.

The WCU Honors College is one of the few that grants its own diploma. This is available for Honors College students in any degree program offered at the University.

There are more than 800 students enrolled in the Honors College.

Participation Requirements: To receive the Honors College diploma, students must complete 30 hours in honors classes and graduate with a minimum cumulative GPA of 3.33. Honors classes include liberal studies classes available only to students enrolled in the College. Students may also earn honors credit through honors contracts or independent projects in upper-level courses.

Admission Process: Students must be accepted to Western Carolina University before applying to the Honors College. To be considered for admission, at least one of the following criteria must be met: 3.5 high school GPA or above, SAT I of 1200 or higher or ACT of 30 or higher, or high school class rank in the top 10 percent. The more of these criteria that are met, the more likely a student is to be accepted. Students who achieve a minimum 3.5 GPA in their first semester at WCU are also eligible. Those currently enrolled at WCU and transfer students must apply to the Honors College for admission consideration.

Scholarship Availability: Several merit-based scholarship programs are administered by the Admissions Office at WCU, including full scholarships for National Merit Scholars. There are also some scholarship funds available through the Honors College.

Campus Overview

State-supported comprehensive, founded 1889, part of University of North Carolina System • **Coed** 6,785 undergraduate students, 86% full-time, 53% women, 47% men.

Undergraduates 5,802 full-time, 983 part-time. Students come from 46 states and territories, 43 other countries, 9% are from out of state, 5% African American, 0.7% Asian American or Pacific Islander, 1% Hispanic American, 2% Native American, 3% international, 10% transferred in, 50% live on campus.

Faculty *Total:* 608, 62% full-time, 61% with terminal degrees. *Student/faculty ratio:* 16:1.

Academic Programs *Special study options:* academic remediation for entering students, accelerated degree program, adult/continuing education programs, advanced placement credit, cooperative education, distance learning, double majors, English as a second language, honors programs, independent study, internships, part-time degree program, services for LD students, student-designed majors, study abroad, summer session for credit.

Athletics Member NCAA. All Division I except football (Division I-AA). *Intercollegiate sports:* baseball M(s), basketball M(s)/W(s), cheerleading M/W, cross-country running M(s)/W(s), golf M(s)/W(s), soccer W(s), tennis W(s), track and field M(s)/W(s), volleyball W(s). *Intramural sports:* badminton M/W, basketball M/W, bowling M/W, cross-country running M/W, equestrian sports M/W, football M/W, lacrosse M/W, racquetball M/W, rugby M, soccer M/W, softball M/W, swimming and diving M/W, table tennis M/W, tennis M/W, track and field M/W, ultimate Frisbee M/W, volleyball M/W, water polo M/W, weight lifting M/W, wrestling M.

Costs (2004–05) *Tuition:* state resident $1651 full-time; nonresident $11,087 full-time. Part-time tuition and fees vary according to course load. *Required fees:* $1798 full-time. *Room and board:* $4028; room only: $2128. Room and board charges vary according to board plan and housing facility.

Financial Aid 335 Federal Work-Study jobs (averaging $1378). In 2004, 819 non-need-based awards were made. *Average percent of need met:* 76%. *Average financial aid package:* $7904. *Average need-based loan:* $3421. *Average need-based gift aid:* $4149. *Average non-need-based aid:* $2576.

Contact: Brian Railsback, G-55 Stillwell, The Honors College, Western Carolina University, Cullowhee, North Carolina 28723; *Telephone:* 828-227-7383; *Fax:* 828-227-7011; *E-mail:* ghnassia@wcu. edu; *Web site:* http://www.wcu.edu/honorscollege

NORTH DAKOTA

Dickinson State University
Theodore Roosevelt Honors Leadership Program
Dickinson, North Dakota

Dickinson State University's Theodore Roosevelt Honors Leadership Program (TR Program), an innovative Honors Program themed along the lines of leadership, seeks academically inclined students who wish to hone their leadership skills no matter what their career paths may be. Its mission is to challenge high-caliber students to become excited about learning and achieving personal goals and to prepare leaders for service in the community, the nation, and the world. The manner in which the program balances scholarship and servant leadership challenges participants with a curriculum that goes beyond the expectations of their major.

Dickinson State University's unique Honors Leadership Program is inspired by President Theodore Roosevelt and how his character was formed while ranching and leading the strenuous life near Medora, North Dakota, during the 1880s. Roosevelt once said, "Had it not been for the years spent in North Dakota, and what I learned here, I would not have become President of the United States."

Students study the qualities and practices of effective leaders, leadership theory, global leadership, leadership and change, and twenty-first century leadership and take other honors courses in a learning community comprising 100 TR Scholars from across the United States and the globe. The TR Program curriculum culminates in a leadership studies minor. The TR Program experience includes a personal enhancement retreat, leadership satellite seminars, invited authors and speakers, national and regional honors conference participation, service and study-abroad opportunities, enhanced internships and study tours, and the privilege of living in honors housing. Those who take full advantage of the TR Program distinguish themselves academically and through service and equip themselves for excellence in graduate school or any vocation.

Participation Requirements: In order to qualify for the Theodore Roosevelt Honors Leadership Program, incoming freshmen must have an ACT score of 26 or higher or a GPA of 3.5 or higher in high school. It is possible to transfer in as a sophomore with a college GPA of at least 3.25, an ACT score of 26 or higher, and a letter of recommendation expressing the candidate's suitability for the TR Program.

In order to maintain their status as TR Scholars, students must complete at least 24 semester hours per academic year, maintain at least a 3.25 cumulative GPA, and actively participate in TR Program learning opportunities and initiatives. TR Scholars are eligible to receive a scholarship for up to ten consecutive fall and spring semesters. TR Program students graduate with honors distinction and a leadership studies minor, which gives them a distinct advantage as they pursue graduate school or enter the workforce.

Admission Process: Applicants must complete and submit the Dickinson State University Scholarship form by December 1, along with the following: a two-to-three-page page essay; a resume featuring extracurricular activities, community service, and leadership positions; two letters of recommendation; and a high school transcript. Prospective students should visit http://www.dickinsonstate.com/TR_ home.asp for complete details on how to apply.

Scholarship Availability: All freshmen accepted to the TR Program receive a Theodore Roosevelt Honors Leadership Program Scholarship. The current value of the scholarship is $2000 per academic year. International students are eligible for $500 per year on top of a generous Global Awareness Initiative Scholarship. Native American students are invited to apply for a Cultural Diversity tuition waiver in addition to the TR Program Scholarship.

More than 80 percent of Dickinson State University students qualify for financial aid. This year more than $1 million was awarded in scholarships.

Campus Overview

State-supported 4-year, founded 1918, part of North Dakota University System • **Coed** 2,479 undergraduate students, 71% full-time, 58% women, 42% men.

Undergraduates 1,749 full-time, 730 part-time. Students come from 22 states and territories, 23 other countries, 29% are from out of state, 2% African American, 0.4% Asian American or Pacific Islander, 1% Hispanic American, 1% Native American, 4% international, 9% transferred in, 30% live on campus.

Faculty *Total:* 205, 45% full-time, 28% with terminal degrees. *Student/faculty ratio:* 19:1.

Academic Programs *Special study options:* academic remediation for entering students, accelerated degree program, adult/continuing education programs, advanced placement credit, cooperative education, distance learning, double majors, external degree program, honors programs, independent study, internships, off-campus study, part-time degree program, services for LD students, student-designed majors, study abroad, summer session for credit.

Athletics Member NAIA. *Intercollegiate sports:* badminton M/W, baseball M(s), basketball M(s)/W(s), cheerleading M/W, cross-country running M(s)/W(s), football M(s), golf M(s)/W(s), softball W(s), track and field M(s)/W(s), volleyball W(s), wrestling M(s). *Intramural sports:* badminton M/W, basketball M/W, football M/W, soccer M/W, softball W, squash M/W, table tennis M/W, tennis M/W, volleyball M/W, water polo M/W.

Costs (2004–05) *Tuition:* state resident $3800 full-time, $127 per credit part-time; nonresident $8877 full-time, $338 per credit part-time. Full-time tuition and fees vary according to location, program, and reciprocity agreements. Part-time tuition and fees vary according to course load, location, program, and reciprocity agreements. *Required fees:* $759 full-time, $31 per credit part-time. *Room and board:* Room and board charges vary according to board plan.

Financial Aid 176 Federal Work-Study jobs (averaging $1116). 225 state and other part-time jobs (averaging $1199).

Contact: Director: Dr. James M. Tallmon, 291 Campus Drive, Dickinson, North Dakota 58601-4896; *Telephone:* 800-279-HAWK (toll-free); *Fax:* 701-483-2025; *E-mail:* j.tallmon@dickinsonstate.edu; *Web site:* http://www.dickinsonstate.com/TR_home.asp

North Dakota State University
University Honors Program
Fargo, North Dakota

An interdisciplinary alternative for highly motivated students, the North Dakota State University (NDSU) Honors Program provides an opportunity for the lively exchange of ideas within and outside the classroom. Students enroll in a colloquium (small discussion class) each of the first three years. Though the themes vary, the basic structure and format of the colloquia in all three years remain the same: discussion, reading, and writing focused on topics and ideas that can be explored through several different disciplines. During the fourth year, students complete an independent study project or senior thesis, usually in their major field, with the guidance of a faculty member in the discipline and an Honors Program adviser.

Honors students have primary majors in the range of disciplines offered at North Dakota State, such as engineering, chemistry, computer science, pharmacy, and architecture. The program also has a Student Council that organizes a variety of cocurricular and social activities, including a series of lectures by faculty members outside the Honors Program, trips to galleries and theaters, volunteer activities, and informal social activities.

Begun in 1969, the program currently has 100 active students.

Participation Requirements: Students must take one 3-credit colloquium each of the first six semesters of the program. A senior thesis is required in the fourth year.

Admission Process: First-year students are selected on the basis of high school grades, a writing sample, and/or recommendations and interviews. After the first semester, students from any college within the University may apply to join the program. The deadline for applying to the program is April 1.

Scholarship Availability: Two $1000 scholarships are available to students having majors within the College of Humanities and Social Sciences.

Campus Overview

State-supported university, founded 1890, part of North Dakota University System • **Coed** 10,549 undergraduate students, 89% full-time, 45% women, 55% men.

Undergraduates 9,359 full-time, 1,190 part-time. Students come from 44 states and territories, 67 other countries, 46% are from out of state, 1% African American, 1% Asian American or Pacific Islander, 0.5% Hispanic American, 1% Native American, 1% international, 7% transferred in, 29% live on campus.

Faculty *Total:* 609, 83% full-time, 76% with terminal degrees. *Student/faculty ratio:* 19:1.

Academic Programs *Special study options:* academic remediation for entering students, advanced placement credit, cooperative education, distance learning, double majors, English as a second language, honors programs, independent study, internships, part-time degree program, services for LD students, student-designed majors, study abroad, summer session for credit. *ROTC:* Army (b), Air Force (b).

Athletics Member NCAA. All Division I. *Intercollegiate sports:* archery M(c)/W(c), baseball M(s), basketball M(s)/W(s), bowling M(c)/W(c), cheerleading M(c)/W(c), cross-country running M(s)/W(s), football M(s), golf M/W(s), ice hockey M(c), riflery M(c)/W(c), rugby M(c)/W(c), soccer M(c)/W(s), softball W(s), track and field M(s)/W(s), volleyball M(c)/W(s), wrestling M(s). *Intramural sports:* basketball M/W, football M/W, softball M/W, volleyball M/W, wrestling M.

Costs (2004–05) *One-time required fee:* $45. *Tuition:* area resident $3981 full-time, $166 per credit part-time; nonresident $10,629 full-time, $443 per credit part-time. Full-time tuition and fees vary according to reciprocity agreements. Part-time tuition and fees vary according to course load and reciprocity agreements. Minnesota resident, $4,476 per year. *Required fees:* $794 full-time, $31 per credit part-time. *Room and board:* $4727; room only: $1882. Room and board charges vary according to board plan and housing facility.

Financial Aid 853 Federal Work-Study jobs (averaging $1774). In 2004, 1439 non-need-based awards were made. *Average percent of need met:* 72%. *Average financial aid package:* $5487. *Average need-based loan:* $3838. *Average need-based gift aid:* $2944. *Average non-need-based aid:* $1703.

Contact: Director: Paul Homan, P.O. Box 5075, Fargo, North Dakota 58105; *Telephone:* 701-231-8852; *Fax:* 701-231-1047; *E-mail:* paul.homan@ndsu.edu; *Web site:* http://www.ndsu.nodak.edu/honors/

OHIO

Case Western Reserve University
College Scholars Program
Cleveland, Ohio

The College Scholars Program is designed for a small group of outstanding undergraduates in the arts, humanities, sciences, engineering, nursing, mathematics and natural sciences, and the social sciences, who are interested in exploring how academic learning can address larger world concerns. The program includes opportunities to develop communication and leadership skills, sessions with renowned leaders and experts, and the design, conduct, and presentation of a senior project that applies individual expertise to a social or significant issue important to the surrounding community. The program gives students the chance to learn in a community, work closely with faculty members, meet distinguished speakers, and help shape curriculum in ways not possible in other academic programs. Guest speakers have included writers Susan Sontag, Kurt Vonnegut, Richard Rodriguez, and Harlan Ellison; journalists Anthony Lewis and Katha Pollitt; physician and health-care advocate Paul Farmer; political activists Ralph Nader and Dr. Howard Zinn; scholars Cornel West and Mary Catherine Bateson; and Lech Walesa, former president of Poland, among others.

Participation Requirements: The two-year, 12-credit program is open to Case Western Reserve University sophomores with a diversity of interests and perspectives. Applications are accepted once a year, at the beginning of the spring semester. First-semester sophomores focus on communication skills, leadership, and ethics. Juniors and first-semester seniors choose interdisciplinary topics to study and teach in depth. By their second semester, seniors must complete and defend a significant independent project and then graduate with the term College Scholar on their diploma.

Admission Process: Acceptance to the College Scholars Program is based on an application, essays, and an interview. Generally, applications and supporting materials must be submitted by mid-February, and late applications are not accepted. Acceptance into the College Scholars Program is not based solely on grades or test scores.

Scholarship Availability: Scholarships are available through the University; there are no special scholarships available through the College Scholars Program.

Campus Overview

Independent university, founded 1826 • **Coed** 3,516 undergraduate students, 92% full-time, 40% women, 60% men.

Undergraduates 3,252 full-time, 264 part-time. Students come from 50 states and territories, 28 other countries, 40% are from out of state, 5% African American, 15% Asian American or Pacific Islander, 2% Hispanic American, 0.4% Native American, 4% international, 3% transferred in, 75% live on campus.

Faculty *Total:* 592, 100% full-time, 96% with terminal degrees. *Student/faculty ratio:* 8:1.

Academic Programs *Special study options:* accelerated degree program, adult/continuing education programs, advanced placement credit, cooperative education, double majors, English as a second language, honors programs, independent study, internships, off-campus study, part-time degree program, services for LD students, student-designed majors, study abroad, summer session for credit. *ROTC:* Army (c), Air Force (c). *Unusual degree programs:* 3-2 astronomy, biochemistry.

Athletics Member NCAA. All Division III. *Intercollegiate sports:* archery M(c)/W(c), baseball M, basketball M/W, cheerleading M(c)/W(c), crew M(c)/W(c), cross-country running M/W, fencing M(c)/W(c), football M, ice hockey M(c)/W(c), soccer M/W, softball W, swimming and diving M/W, tennis M/W, track and field M/W, ultimate Frisbee M(c)/W(c), volleyball M(c)/W, wrestling M. *Intramural sports:* badminton M/W, basketball M/W, bowling M/W, cross-country running M/W, football M/W, golf M/W, racquetball M/W, soccer M/W, softball M/W, squash M/W, swimming and diving M/W, table tennis M/W, tennis M/W, track and field M/W, ultimate Frisbee M/W, volleyball M/W, water polo M/W, weight lifting M/W, wrestling M.

Costs (2004–05) *Comprehensive fee:* $35,264 includes full-time tuition ($26,500), mandatory fees ($562), and room and board ($8202). Part-time tuition: $1104 per credit hour. Part-time tuition and fees vary according to course load. *College room only:* $5110. Room and board charges vary according to board plan, housing facility, and student level.

Financial Aid 1,248 Federal Work-Study jobs (averaging $2070). In 2003, 977 non-need-based awards were made. *Average percent of need met:* 87%. *Average financial aid package:* $25,758. *Average*

need-based loan: $3445. Average need-based gift aid: $17,506. Average non-need-based aid: $12,650.

Contact: Dr. Jonathan Sadowsky, College Scholars Program, Department of History, Case Western Reserve University, 10900 Euclid Avenue, Cleveland, Ohio 44106-7120; *Telephone:* 216-368-0528; *E-mail:* jas34@case.edu; *Web site:* http://www.case.edu/artsci/scholars

---

Cincinnati State Technical and Community College
The Honors Experience
Cincinnati, Ohio

The Cincinnati State Technical and Community College Honors Experience is designed to provide academically talented, highly motivated students the opportunity to reach their potential by offering enhanced learning opportunities. The Honors Experience emphasizes a broad-based foundation of educational disciplines with the goal of enabling the student to transfer to a senior institution or enter a professional field at a high skill level with the capacity for continuous learning and responsible citizenship. The Honors Experience values creativity and intellectual curiosity; establishes a community among students and faculty members; provides unique course work, enrichment activities, and honors advising; and nurtures individual development and leadership.

The Honors Experience is dedicated to providing students challenging alternatives to completing core courses, as well as specialized courses in both academic and technical fields. All students participate in Honors Orientation and timely multidisciplinary colloquiums. Honors course design favors creative approaches to problem solving, meaningful research and communication, and appreciation of cultural diversity and the arts. The Honors Experience, started in 1999, currently offers fourteen core curriculum courses, with additional classes offered in the divisional curriculum.

Participation Requirements: Honors scholars must meet all requirements of the College and degree program, maintaining a GPA of 3.25 or better. In order to graduate as an Honors Experience Scholar, students must complete a minimum of eight honors courses, including Honors Orientation and at least one honors colloquium. Any Cincinnati State student may take an honors course with the permission of the instructor or the Honors Chair.

Admission Process: Incoming students are identified through admissions testing, a high school GPA of 3.25 or better, high school class rank in the top 20th percentile, and SAT or ACT scores. Existing or transfer students may be considered for admission with 18 credit hours of work and a GPA of 3.25 or better. Two letters of recommendation and a personal essay are required with an application to the Honors Experience.

Scholarship Availability: Six full merit scholarships, paying for tuition, books, and fees, are awarded each year to graduates of local high schools. Recipients must meet all College requirements for academic scholarships and complete a separate honors scholarship application in order to be considered for scholarships.

Campus Overview

State-supported 2-year, founded 1966, part of Ohio Board of Regents • **Coed** 8,472 undergraduate students, 39% full-time, 57% women, 43% men.

Undergraduates 3,296 full-time, 5,176 part-time. Students come from 9 states and territories, 62 other countries, 11% are from out of state, 27% African American, 0.8% Asian American or Pacific Islander, 0.7% Hispanic American, 0.1% Native American, 2% international.

Faculty *Total:* 577, 31% full-time. *Student/faculty ratio:* 16:1.

Academic Programs *Special study options:* academic remediation for entering students, advanced placement credit, cooperative education, distance learning, double majors, English as a second language, honors programs, internships, off-campus study, part-time degree program, services for LD students, student-designed majors, summer session for credit.

Athletics Member NJCAA. *Intercollegiate sports:* basketball M/W, golf M/W, soccer M. *Intramural sports:* cheerleading W.

Costs (2005–06) *Tuition:* state resident $4152 full-time, $71 per credit hour part-time; nonresident $8019 full-time, $143 per credit hour part-time. Full-time tuition and fees vary according to reciprocity agreements. Part-time tuition and fees vary according to reciprocity agreements. *Required fees:* $155 full-time, $31 per term part-time.

Financial Aid 100 Federal Work-Study jobs (averaging $3500).

Contact: Honors Chair: Marcha L. Hunley, Humanities and Sciences Division, Cincinnati State Technical and Community College, 3520 Central Parkway, Cincinnati, Ohio 45223-2690; *Telephone:* 513-569-1732; *E-mail:* marcha.hunley@cincinnatistate.edu

Cleveland State University
Cleveland State University Honors Program
Cleveland, Ohio

In fall 2004, Cleveland State University launched its Honors Program to attract academically talented and highly motivated students. The first class, consisting of 40 first-year students, had an average high school GPA of 3.9. Beginning in fall 2005, the Honors Program is accepting applications from first-year students and students entering their junior year. The junior applicants may be transfers from two- and four-year academic institutions or current Cleveland State University students who have distinguished themselves academically. When fully operational, the program will have 250 to 300 students.

The central mission of Cleveland State University Honors Program is to attract and to better serve the educational needs of academically talented and highly motivated students at Cleveland State University. The Honors Program's primary mission parallels the first goal of Cleveland State University's Functional Mission Statement, which is to "recruit, instruct, retain and graduate a diverse student population" and to "provide opportunities for students to fulfill additional educational aspirations."

The program encourages the participation of the broadest possible range of talented students, including traditional first-year students, transfer students from two- or four-year academic institutions, continuing Cleveland State University students who were not originally admitted to the Honors Program, and students returning to complete their undergraduate education after a hiatus in their studies. The Honors Program achieves these goals by providing students admitted to the program with a challenging, enriched, or interdisciplinary curriculum model during their first two years; a specially tailored honors course of study during their final two years; and substantial financial support from sources outside the University's normal operating budget.

Participation Requirements: To continue participation in the program, students must make satisfactory progress toward graduation, complete at least four general education honors courses, participate in the 1-credit-hour universal honors course each term, and maintain a cumulative grade point average of 3.5 or higher. Students who complete the Honors Program are recognized at graduation as Cleveland State University Honors Scholars.

Admission Process: Prospective first-year students must apply separately to the program. Application materials are available at the program's Web site. Applicants should have a composite ACT score of at least 27, a total SAT score of at least 1220 on the old test or 1830 on the new test, or a place in the top 10 percent of their high school class. A 1,000-word autobiographical essay is required with the application. Students are expected to complete a college-preparatory curriculum in high school. High schools vary in the advanced courses they offer; honors applicants are expected to complete the most rigorous curriculum available at their high school. Applicants who participate in Ohio's Post-Secondary Educational Opportunity Program are expected to have completed the standard high school college-preparatory curriculum in addition to their college work. Preferred applicants should have four years of high school English; four years of high school mathematics, including precalculus and, in some cases, calculus; at least three years of natural science (usually biology, physics, and chemistry); at least three years of social science courses; and three or more years of a foreign language, along with additional classes in the visual or performing arts. There will be students admitted who have not met all of these criteria; however, it should be noted that a student without high school physics, for example, is generally not prepared for a college-level course in the subject. Preference in admission to the Honors Program is given to students whose high school transcript indicates they are prepared for a wide variety of possible college majors.

Applicants entering the program as juniors should have a cumulative grade point average of 3.5 or higher. They must submit three academic letters of reference and a 1,000-word autobiographical essay. Preferred applicants should be on track to graduate in two years (for those whose major is in a four-year program). College transcripts should reflect a rigorous course of study both in the student's preferred major and in his or her choices for general education and elective courses. Students should have made good progress toward completion of general education course requirements and lower-division prerequisites for courses in the major.

Scholarship Availability: First-year-entry and junior-entry honors program students are eligible for renewable scholarships covering full tuition, books, and academic fees. Additional scholarships to cover all or part of room and board may be available. Funding for Honors Scholarships comes from a variety of sources. To allow the University to fund as many students as possible, all students must file a Free Application for Federal Student Aid (FAFSA). Further information is available at the program's Web site.

Campus Overview
State-supported university, founded 1964 • **Coed** 9,842 undergraduate students, 68% full-time, 55% women, 45% men.

Undergraduates 6,706 full-time, 3,136 part-time. Students come from 21 states and territories, 63 other countries, 1% are from out of state, 21% African American, 3% Asian American or Pacific Islander, 3% Hispanic American, 0.2% Native American, 2% international, 10% transferred in, 4% live on campus.

Faculty *Total:* 957, 59% full-time, 56% with terminal degrees. *Student/faculty ratio:* 16:1.

Academic Programs *Special study options:* academic remediation for entering students, accelerated degree program, adult/continuing education programs, advanced placement credit, cooperative education, English as a second language, freshman honors college, honors programs, independent study, internships, off-campus study, part-time degree program, student-designed majors, study abroad, summer session for credit. *ROTC:* Army (c), Navy (c), Air Force (c).

Athletics Member NCAA. All Division I. *Intercollegiate sports:* baseball M(s), basketball M(s)/W(s), cross-country running W(s), fencing M(s)/W(s), golf M(s), soccer M(s), softball W(s), swimming and diving M(s)/W(s), tennis W(s), track and field W(s), volleyball W(s), wrestling M(s). *Intramural sports:* badminton M/W, basketball M/W, bowling M/W, cross-country running M/W, fencing M/W, field hockey M/W, football M, golf M/W, racquetball M/W, sailing M/W, soccer M/W, swimming and diving M/W, tennis M/W, track and field M/W, volleyball M/W, water polo M/W, weight lifting M(c)/W(c), wrestling M.

Costs (2004–05) *Tuition:* state resident $6792 full-time, $283 per semester hour part-time; nonresident $9216 full-time, $384 per semester hour part-time. Full-time tuition and fees vary according to program and student level. Part-time tuition and fees vary according to program and student level. *Room and board:* $6610; room only: $3972. Room and board charges vary according to board plan and housing facility.

Financial Aid In 2004, 627 non-need-based awards were made. *Average percent of need met:* 51%. *Average financial aid package:* $7070. *Average need-based loan:* $3975. *Average need-based gift aid:* $4772. *Average non-need-based aid:* $7464.

Contact: Dr. Barbara Margolius, 2121 Euclid Avenue, LB-246, Cleveland, Ohio 44115; *Telephone:* 216-687-5559; *Fax:* 216-687-5552; *E-mail:* b.margolius@csuohio.edu; *Web site:* http://www.csuohio.edu/honors/

College of Mount St. Joseph
Honors Program
Cincinnati, Ohio

The Honors Program is designed to meet the needs and interests of highly motivated students who are able to take responsibility for their own learning under the guidance of experienced faculty members. The program stresses the relatedness of the various disciplines and challenges students to make connections among them and between these learnings and life in society as they gain an integrated view of the world around them. Classes are limited to 15 to 20 students and are conducted in a seminar format. All courses have an interdisciplinary focus while at the same time fulfilling in part the core liberal arts and sciences component of the College's curriculum. The program is, therefore, compatible with all undergraduate majors. Faculty members who teach in the Honors Program come from a variety of departments and disciplines and are selected because of their demonstrated excellence in teaching as well as their interest and expertise in interdisciplinary study. In addition to a departmental academic adviser, honors students receive additional advising and consultation from the Director of the Honors Program. Students are encouraged to participate in service learning opportunities and other community service projects on and off campus as a means of developing a global perspective and of seeing connections among cultures, people, and nations.

A comfortable study/lounge area adjacent to an open computer lab is provided for honors students. There is space for quiet study as well as for conversation and group work.

There are approximately 60 students enrolled in the Honors Program, which was founded in 1994.

Participation Requirements: Students must complete a Freshman Seminar, at least five honors courses, and a Senior Seminar, which includes a capstone project of the student's design. Honors students must maintain a GPA of 3.2 or higher. Upon completion of the requirements, students are listed in the graduation program as graduates of the Honors Program. This designation is also noted on their diplomas.

Admission Process: Admission to the Honors Program requires that students score in the 75th percentile or above on the SAT or ACT, that they be in the upper 25 percent of their high school graduating class, and that they be recommended by a teacher or counselor. Students must also submit a personal essay before they are admitted to the Freshman Seminar. Final admission to the program is contingent upon successful completion of this seminar.

Scholarship Availability: Several categories of scholarships are available to students who qualify for the Honors Program. Administration of these is through the College Office of Admission.

Campus Overview
Independent Roman Catholic comprehensive, founded 1920 • **Coed** 1,858 undergraduate students, 70% full-time, 69% women, 31% men.

Undergraduates 1,297 full-time, 561 part-time. Students come from 21 states and territories, 12% are from out of state, 9% African American, 0.5% Asian American or Pacific Islander, 0.6% Hispanic American, 0.2% Native American, 0.1% international, 10% transferred in, 23% live on campus.

Faculty *Total:* 225, 52% full-time, 42% with terminal degrees. *Student/faculty ratio:* 11:1.

Academic Programs *Special study options:* academic remediation for entering students, accelerated degree program, adult/continuing education programs, advanced placement credit, cooperative education, distance learning, double majors, honors programs, independent study, internships, off-campus study, part-time degree program, services for LD students, study abroad, summer session for credit. *ROTC:* Army (c), Air Force (c).

Athletics Member NCAA. All Division III. *Intercollegiate sports:* baseball M, basketball M/W, cheerleading W, cross-country running M/W, football M, golf M/W, soccer M/W, softball W, tennis M/W, track and field M/W, volleyball W, wrestling M. *Intramural sports:* basketball M/W, racquetball M/W, soccer M/W, softball M/W, table tennis M/W, tennis M/W, volleyball M/W.

Costs (2005–06) *Comprehensive fee:* $24,860 includes full-time tuition ($18,400), mandatory fees ($390), and room and board ($6070). Full-time tuition and fees vary according to course load, program, and reciprocity agreements. Part-time tuition: $430 per semester hour. Part-time tuition and fees vary according to course load, location, program, and reciprocity agreements. *Required fees:* $65 per term part-time. *College room only:* $3000. Room and board charges vary according to board plan and housing facility.

Financial Aid 115 Federal Work-Study jobs (averaging $1500). 109 state and other part-time jobs (averaging $1501). In 2004, 176 non-need-based awards were made. *Average percent of need met:* 89%. *Average financial aid package:* $16,473. *Average need-based loan:* $4156. *Average need-based gift aid:* $9000. *Average non-need-based aid:* $3800.

Contact: Director: Dr. Jim Bodle, Department of Behavioral Sciences, 5701 Delhi Road, Cincinnati, Ohio 45233-1670; *Telephone:* 513-244-4862; *E-mail:* jim_bodle@mail.msj.edu; *Web site:* http://www.msj.edu/academics/majors/honors/index.asp

Cuyahoga Community College
Honors Program
Cleveland, Ohio

The Cuyahoga Community College (CCC) (Cleveland, Ohio) Honors Program serves a diverse group of talented, self-motivated students who benefit from an intellectually challenging and enriching college experience. The program emphasizes participatory and experiential learning through a variety of activities, including cultural events, seminars and conferences, community service, service learning, and research. The Honors Program curriculum and pedagogy encourage students to assume responsibility for their own learning, by stressing scholarship, leadership, research, creativity, and critical thinking.

The Cuyahoga Community College Honors Program offers a substantive, attractive local college experience for the area's high-potential students and future leaders. It is part of Cuyahoga Community College's mission to provide a cost-effective and academically sound alternative for many students who would otherwise lack access to higher education. The Honors Program provides a pathway for students to earn an associate degree in an appropriately challenging environment, with the opportunity to transfer to a four-year college or university to obtain a bachelor's degree. One aim of the program is to develop honors students in a way that results in their being more engaged in and knowledgeable about the community in which they live, increasing the probability they will remain in the area after completing their education. To this end, the College has transfer agreements that enable program graduates to enter directly into the honors programs of local four-year colleges and universities.

In addition, understanding that almost all Honors Program graduates expect to continue their studies after graduating from Cuyahoga Community College, the program is designed to produce graduates with advanced communication and critical-thinking skills who are better prepared to meet their continuing education needs. These same skills also serve them well in their eventual careers, helping them become leaders in their professions and communities.

One of the purposes of the service-oriented learning activities that are an integral part of the program is to develop graduates who have a heightened appreciation for diverse cultures and points of view. The College is a multicampus institution with sites in the urban center of a major city and in suburban settings, thus enabling partnering with community organizations serving the needs of a wide range of individuals and groups. Engaging in service activities with these community partners, both with service learning integrated into the curriculum and with volunteer community service, helps develop program graduates who are civically engaged in their communities.

There are currently more than 150 students taking honors courses each semester.

Participation Requirements: Students who have been admitted to the Honors Program must maintain an overall GPA of 3.25 or higher. Students must complete a minimum of 15 honors credits. Upon graduation, honors students are recognized at commencement and are identified on their diplomas and transcripts as Honors Program graduates of Cuyahoga Community College.

The Cuyahoga Community College Honors Program is continuing to develop articulation agreements with honors programs of regional colleges and universities. Graduates are currently participating in honors programs in four-year colleges and universities, including Kent State University and Akron University.

Admission Process: To be admitted to the Cuyahoga Community College Honors Program, students must complete an Honors Program application, which is reviewed by the Honors Program Advisory Committee or the assigned representative. The application documents those criteria the student has met.

Applicants who are first-time college attendees must qualify for admission in English 1010 and Math 1060 and have proof of one or more of the following: an overall minimum 3.5 GPA or equivalent in high school (on a 4.0 scale); an ACT composite minimum score of 26; an SAT combined score of at least 1800 (1200 if graduated before May 2006); and graduation or anticipated graduation in the top 10 percent of their high school class.

Applicants who are continuing CCC students and those not entering directly from high school must have earned a minimum 3.5 GPA in at least 12 college-level credits, or a student may enter the program upon the recommendation of a CCC faculty member and the concurrence of the Honors Program Director.

Scholarship Availability: Participants in the Honors Program are eligible for scholarships. Scholarship awards are coordinated with financial aid when available.

Campus Overview

State and locally supported 2-year, founded 1963 • **Coed** 25,214 undergraduate students, 40% full-time, 64% women, 36% men.

Undergraduates 10,169 full-time, 15,045 part-time. Students come from 21 states and territories, 63 other countries, 30% African American, 2% Asian American or Pacific Islander, 4% Hispanic American, 0.7% Native American, 2% international, 3% transferred in.

Faculty *Total:* 1,667, 20% full-time, 6% with terminal degrees. *Student/faculty ratio:* 19:1.

Academic Programs *Special study options:* adult/continuing education programs, advanced placement credit, cooperative education, distance learning, English as a second language, external degree program, independent study, part-time degree program, services for LD students, summer session for credit.

Athletics Member NJCAA. *Intercollegiate sports:* baseball M(s), basketball M(s), cross-country running M(s)/W(s), soccer M(s), softball W(s). *Intramural sports:* basketball M, tennis M/W, track and field M/W, volleyball M/W.

Costs (2005–06) *Tuition:* area resident $2301 full-time, $77 per credit hour part-time; state resident $3042 full-time, $101 per credit hour part-time; nonresident $6228 full-time, $208 per credit hour part-time.

Financial Aid 802 Federal Work-Study jobs (averaging $3300).

Contact: Dr. Linda Simmons, VP of Academic and Student Affairs, 700 Carnegie Avenue, Cleveland, Ohio 44115; *Telephone:* 216-987-4867; *Fax:* 216-566-5977; *E-mail:* linda.simmons@tri-c.edu

Denison University
Honors Program
Granville, Ohio

The Denison Honors Program is designed especially for outstanding students in the college. At its heart are twenty to twenty-five interdisciplinary and experimental seminars each semester that are especially challenging and exciting for highly motivated and academically gifted students. Honors Seminars occur across all four divisions of the college and at both the introductory and advanced levels. The Honors Program does not constitute a separate track or Honors College; most seminars fulfill general education and/or requirements within individual majors or minors. Seminar offerings (and instructors) continually change to reflect new intellectual and artistic opportunities and questions.

The Honors Program is located in Gilpatrick House, a lovely Victorian house on campus. The first floor contains a fully electronic seminar room and a commons area for events and informal discussion as well as the administrative offices of the program. The upstairs serves as a residence area for 10 honors students (with additional honors housing in another residence hall). The Gilpatrick Fellow assists in planning extracurricular activities for students in the program; these include subsidized cultural events in nearby Columbus (such as musical or dance performances or films), intellectual and arts venues, and many service or other social opportunities.

The Honors Program also oversees student applications for many prestigious undergraduate grants—such as the Truman, Udall, or Goldwater Science Scholarships—and postgraduate scholarships—the Rhodes, Marshall, Fulbright, and many other programs. Denison is proud of its many alumni who have received such honors, and we work closely with students throughout the application process.

Participation Requirements: Denison students with a 3.4 GPA or above are eligible to register for Honors Seminars. Students may graduate "with Honors" (*cum laude, magna cum laude,* and *summa cum laude*) by completing the following requirements: achieving a 3.4, 3.6, or 3.8 GPA, respectively; completing a senior honors research project, and completing other requirements in some departments.

Honors students at Denison also have a second option of graduating "in the Honors Program." These students must complete the following requirements: achieve and maintain at least a 3.4 GPA by the end of the sophomore year, declare intention to the Director of the Program to complete the requirement in the Honors Program no later than preregistration time in the fall of the junior year, complete at least two Honors Seminars during the first four semesters, complete at least four Honors Seminars during the Denison career, and complete a two-term research and senior Honors Project in the department or program of their majors. Students wishing to declare the intention to complete the Honors Program requirements should discuss this option with the Director of the Honors Program no later than the end of the sophomore year.

Scholarship Availability: Denison University is committed to enrolling academically talented individuals, which is evidenced by its comprehensive scholarship program. Entering first-year students invited to participate in the Honors Program are eligible for Denison's full range of academic scholarships. To be assured of consideration, the complete Denison application must be received by the Admissions Office by January 1 of the applicant's senior year of high school.

Information on all awards is available from the Denison Admissions Office. The profile for students receiving award offers in recent years has been a class rank in the top decile, strong test scores, and evidence of significant extracurricular achievement and essay writing ability.

Campus Overview

Independent 4-year, founded 1831 • **Coed** 2,229 undergraduate students, 99% full-time, 56% women, 44% men.

Undergraduates 2,200 full-time, 29 part-time. Students come from 49 states and territories, 28 other countries, 58% are from out of state, 5% African American, 3% Asian American or Pacific Islander, 3% Hispanic American, 0.2% Native American, 5% international, 0.8% transferred in, 98% live on campus.

Faculty *Total:* 196, 92% full-time, 91% with terminal degrees. *Student/faculty ratio:* 11:1.

Academic Programs *Special study options:* advanced placement credit, cooperative education, double majors, honors programs, independent study, internships, off-campus study, part-time degree program, services for LD students, student-designed majors, study abroad. *ROTC:* Army (c). *Unusual degree programs:* 3-2 engineering with Case Western Reserve University, Columbia University, Rensselaer Polytechnic Institute, Washington University in St. Louis; forestry with Duke University; natural resources with University of Michigan; occupational therapy with Washington University in St. Louis; environmental management, dentistry with Case Western Reserve University; medical technology with Rochester General Hospital.

Athletics Member NCAA. All Division III. *Intercollegiate sports:* baseball M, basketball M/W, crew M(c), cross-country running M/W, equestrian sports M(c)/W(c), field hockey W, football M, golf M, ice hockey M(c), lacrosse M/W, riflery M(c)/W(c), rugby M(c)/W(c), sailing M(c)/W(c), skiing (downhill) M(c)/W(c), soccer M/W, softball W, squash M(c)/W(c), swimming and diving M/W, tennis M/W, track and field M/W, volleyball W. *Intramural sports:* badminton M(c)/W(c), basketball M/W, cheerleading M/W, crew W(c), fencing M(c)/W(c), football M/W, golf M/W, lacrosse M(c), racquetball M/W, soccer M/W, softball M/W, squash M/W, table tennis M/W, tennis M/W, ultimate Frisbee M/W, volleyball M(c)/W, water polo M/W, weight lifting M/W.

Costs (2004–05) *Comprehensive fee:* $34,980 includes full-time tuition ($26,600), mandatory fees ($710), and room and board ($7670). Part-time tuition: $830 per semester hour. Part-time tuition and fees vary according to course load. *College room only:* $4220. Room and board charges vary according to housing facility.

Financial Aid 559 Federal Work-Study jobs (averaging $1793). 1,111 state and other part-time jobs (averaging $1979). In 2004, 1085 non-need-based awards were made. *Average percent of need met:* 96%. *Average financial aid package:* $23,968. *Average need-based loan:* $4828. *Average need-based gift aid:* $17,873. *Average non-need-based aid:* $11,507.

Contact: Director: Dr. Kent Maynard, Granville, Ohio 43023; *Telephone:* 740-587-6573; *Fax:* 740-587-5688; *E-mail:* sunkle@ denison.edu; *Web site:* http://www.denison.edu/honors/

Heidelberg College
Heidelberg College Honors Program
Tiffin, Ohio

The Heidelberg College Honors Program, Life of the Mind, is designed to challenge exceptional, highly motivated students to reach their potential. Life of the Mind is a comprehensive approach to reaching the brightest students by empowering them to explore their abilities within a supportive community of scholars and learners. The program comprises four intellectual areas that are each complemented by an honors seminar. They are the Scholar, the Scientist, the Artist, and the Citizen. Typically, the first year emphasizes the skills needed by the emerging scholar; the second year stresses the scientific method and empirical processes of inquiry; the third year focuses on the aesthetic experience and creative endeavors; and the fourth year requires participants to reflect on the meaning of citizenship and underscores the values of participation in local, national, and global issues.

Recognizing a need for involvement in the greater community, the Honors Program expects students to share their time and talents. A service-learning seminar and 40 hours of service placement are required. Students are also required to compose and present a senior project. After the approval of the Honors Committee and with the guidance of a faculty mentor of the student's choice, a senior project is developed and the results are presented in a public forum. The topic may be related to the student's major or in an area of special interest.

There are many benefits to being in Life of the Mind. The program provides a separate, 24-hour-access study center that includes a lounge, Computer Lab, seminar room, and program office. The honors students also have priority registration each term. In place of approximately 40 hours of general education requirements, the students complete the required seminars along with ten self-selected support courses. The increased flexibility of requirements enables students to more easily engage in additional educational opportunities, such as the completion of a second major, study abroad, or an internship. During the four years, the honors students also compile a portfolio that provides documentation of distinguished accomplishments and credentials.

The Heidelberg College Honors Program, Life of the Mind, was established in 1994. There are approximately 125 students currently enrolled.

Participation Requirements: To graduate from the Honors Program with an Honors Diploma, a student must successfully complete a senior project, four honors seminars, a portfolio, and the service-learning component. In addition, each student must complete the requirements of a major and support courses as well as earn a minimum cumulative GPA of 3.3. Graduates of the program are designated by distinctive academic regalia at graduation and receive an Honors Diploma that notes honors courses taken.

Admission Process: First-year entering students are invited to join the Honors Program on the basis of a minimum high school cumulative GPA of a 3.5 or ranking in the top 10 percent of their graduating class and a minimum ACT score of 27 or a minimum SAT I combined score of 1210 (not yet adjusted for 2005 changes). Entering first-year students who do not meet the above criteria may apply for admission to the program after completing 15 semester hours while achieving a minimum GPA of 3.5. Transfer students must meet the above high school requirements and have at least a 3.3 cumulative GPA from an accredited college or university or have at least a 3.5 college GPA based on a minimum of 15 semester hours or 22.5 quarter hours and permission of the Program Director.

Scholarship Availability: Scholarships of various amounts are awarded through the Office of Admissions based on academic performance and a scholarship competition held on campus in February. Most honors students are recipients of academic scholarships.

Campus Overview

Independent comprehensive, founded 1850, affiliated with United Church of Christ • **Coed** 1,189 undergraduate students, 96% full-time, 51% women, 49% men.

Undergraduates 1,144 full-time, 45 part-time. Students come from 22 states and territories, 10 other countries, 20% are from out of state, 4% African American, 0.2% Asian American or Pacific Islander, 0.6% Hispanic American, 0.1% Native American, 2% international, 3% transferred in, 87% live on campus.

Faculty *Student/faculty ratio:* 12:1.

Academic Programs *Special study options:* academic remediation for entering students, accelerated degree program, adult/continuing education programs, advanced placement credit, double majors, English as a second language, honors programs, internships, off-campus study, part-time degree program, services for LD students, study abroad, summer session for credit. *ROTC:* Army (c), Air Force (c). *Unusual degree programs:* 3-2 engineering with Case Western Reserve University; nursing with Case Western Reserve University; environmental management with Duke University.

Athletics Member NCAA. except baseball (Division III), men's and women's basketball (Division III), men's and women's cross-country running (Division III), football (Division III), men's and women's golf (Division III), men's and women's soccer (Division III), softball (Division III), men's and women's tennis (Division III), men's and women's track and field (Division III), men's and women's volleyball (Division III), wrestling (Division III) *Intercollegiate sports:* baseball M, basketball M/W, cross-country running M/W, football M, golf M/W, soccer M/W, softball W, tennis M/W, track and field M/W, volleyball M/W, wrestling M. *Intramural sports:* archery M/W, badminton M/W, cheerleading M/W, football M, golf M/W, racquetball M/W, skiing (cross-country) M/W, softball W, table tennis M/W.

Costs (2004–05) *Comprehensive fee:* $21,610 includes full-time tuition ($14,575), mandatory fees ($325), and room and board ($6710). Full-time tuition and fees vary according to course load and location. Part-time tuition and fees vary according to location. *College room only:* $3080. Room and board charges vary according to board plan and housing facility.

Financial Aid 600 Federal Work-Study jobs (averaging $927). 13 state and other part-time jobs (averaging $3130). In 2003, 147 non-need-based awards were made. *Average percent of need met:* 89%. *Average financial aid package:* $15,836. *Average need-based loan:* $4280. *Average need-based gift aid:* $9800. *Average non-need-based aid:* $5316.

Contact: Dean of Honors Program: Dr. Jan Younger, 310 East Market Street, Tiffin, Ohio 44883-2462; *Telephone:* 419-448-2157; or 800-925-9250 (toll-free) *Fax:* 419-448-2124; *E-mail:* jyounger@mail.heidelberg.edu; *Web site:* http://www.heidelberg.edu

John Carroll University
Honors Program
University Heights, Ohio

*T**he Honors Program at John Carroll University provides exceptional students the opportunity to expand and amplify their educational experience during college. The Honors Program, in conjunction with the Liberal Arts Core, seeks not only to prepare students for a lifetime of learning and to provide them with specific academic content, but also to foster in students a love of learning and the problem-solving and critical-thinking abilities essential for excellence.*

The John Carroll University Honors Program is a University-based honors program, rather than a departmentally based honors program or a separate honors college. Thus, students take honors courses as part of the basic Liberal Arts Core. The University, as well as the Honors Program, believes a strong liberal arts background is essential for all bachelor degrees, so students take a selection of courses from different discipline areas designed to provide such a broad base to the undergraduate educational experience. The Honors Program is integrated into the University Core Curriculum and allows honors students to satisfy the core curriculum in ways consistent with their academic abilities and preparation.

In concert with the tradition of Jesuit education, the goal of the Honors Program is to pursue excellence in an environment that promotes the development and understanding of values and emphasizes freedom of inquiry, integration of knowledge, and social responsibility. These themes manifest themselves not just in the academic arena, but also in the development of the whole person.

Through small classes and close contact with faculty members, the Honors Program provides opportunities for greater depth and mastery in a student's education. Through interdisciplinary classes and the cross-disciplinary study of topics and issues, the Honors Program builds a broader perspective out of which a student can reflect on the world and its needs. Through the latitude to construct self-designed majors, the program encourages students to be creative in their college program. Through foreign language study and honors seminars, the Honors Program fosters a better understanding of a global society. Finally, through the community of honors students, who meet together and share social, cultural, and artistic events and have continual contact in classes, the Honors Program develops a camaraderie that strengthens students' ability to participate in the world.

The Honors Program endeavors to prepare a person to be a constructive, thoughtful, and active participant in the local and world communities. An honors graduate is one who values learning, service, and excellence, and thus will continue to learn, serve, and excel in whatever he or she does in life. The modern Honors Program at John Carroll was instituted in 1989–90. The first Honors Program began in 1963. There are approximately 180 students participating in the program.

Participation Requirements: Requirements include competency in English composition, demonstrated by one year of English Composition, or, if a student is exempt through AP credit or testing, one additional course in English that emphasizes writing; competency in oral communication as demonstrated by a one semester course specially designed for honors students or by testing out; competency in foreign language or calculus, demonstrated by two years of a language or by one year of calculus; six H or HP courses that fulfill portions of University Core Curriculum (H courses are honors sections of regularly taught courses; HP courses are special interdisciplinary or team-taught courses designed for honors students); participation in the Honors Colloquium (taken in the first year), which uses an interdisciplinary approach to explore a general topic (this seminar is team-taught by 3 faculty members, with each faculty member bringing his or her expertise to bear on the topic); and participation in a Senior Honors Seminar or Senior Honors Project.

The seminar uses an interdisciplinary approach to explore a specific topic. This course is jointly taught and usually continues the topic from the Honors Colloquium taken by these students in their first year. The Senior Honors Project requires at least 3 hours of independent research under the direction of an adviser.

Honors participants must maintain a minimum 3.5 GPA, and must have a GPA of at least 3.5 at graduation. Students who graduate from the Honors Program are identified by the words Honors Scholar on their transcripts and by a special gold seal on their diplomas. In addition, at graduation, Honors Students are recognized by a gold cord worn with their academic gown.

Admission Process: Entering freshmen seeking admission to the Honors Program should normally have a minimum combined score of at least 1270 on the SAT (Parts I and II) or at least a 28 composite score on the ACT, rank in the top 10 percent of their high school class, and have at least a 3.5 GPA in their high school college-preparatory courses. In short, the program is seeking students who rank above the 90th percentile of first-year students throughout the nation. Students in their sophomore and junior years, transfer students, and nontraditional students are also welcome to apply to the program. Currently enrolled students should have a minimum 3.5 GPA in college prior to applying to the Honors Program.

Scholarship Availability: The Honors Program does not administer any scholarships or financial aid. However, the University provides solid financial assistance to honors students. As an indication of that support, virtually all first-year honors students who entered between 1990 and 2004 and who requested financial assistance received merit and/or need-based scholarships. These grants included such awards as American Values Scholarships ($1000–$3000 per year, renewable, based on merit and/or demonstrated leadership or volunteerism, consideration given to need), President's Honor Awards (amounts vary up to $10,000, renewable, merit-based), Mastin Scholarships in the sciences ($10,000 per year, renewable, merit-based), John Carroll grants (amount varies, renewable, merit- and need-based), National Merit Scholarships (sponsored by John Carroll, merit-based, up to full tuition, for National Merit Finalists).

Campus Overview

Independent Roman Catholic (Jesuit) comprehensive, founded 1886 • **Coed** 3,350 undergraduate students, 95% full-time, 54% women, 46% men.

Undergraduates 3,184 full-time, 166 part-time. Students come from 35 states and territories, 27% are from out of state, 4% African American, 2% Asian American or Pacific Islander, 3% Hispanic American, 0.1% Native American, 5% transferred in, 57% live on campus.

Faculty *Total:* 409, 59% full-time. *Student/faculty ratio:* 15:1.

Academic Programs *Special study options:* accelerated degree program, adult/continuing education programs, advanced placement credit, cooperative education, double majors, honors programs, independent study, internships, off-campus study, part-time degree program, student-designed majors, study abroad, summer session for credit. *ROTC:* Army (b). *Unusual degree programs:* 3-2 engineering with Case Western Reserve University, University of Detroit Mercy; nursing with Case Western Reserve University.

Athletics Member NCAA. All Division III. *Intercollegiate sports:* baseball M, basketball M/W, crew M(c)/W(c), cross-country running M/W, football M, golf M/W, ice hockey M(c), lacrosse M(c)/W(c), rugby M(c)/W(c), sailing M(c)/W(c), skiing (downhill) M(c)/W(c), soccer M/W, softball W, swimming and diving M/W, tennis M/W, track and field M/W, volleyball M(c)/W, wrestling M. *Intramural sports:* basketball M/W, football M/W, racquetball M/W, softball M/W, swimming and diving M/W, tennis M/W, volleyball M/W, water polo M/W.

Costs (2005–06) *Comprehensive fee:* $31,156 includes full-time tuition ($23,380), mandatory fees ($250), and room and board ($7526). Part-time tuition: $708 per credit hour.

Financial Aid *Average financial aid package:* $14,104.

Contact: Director: Dr. John R. Spencer, 20700 North Park Boulevard, University Heights, Ohio 44118; *Telephone:* 216-397-4677; *Fax:* 216-397-4478; *E-mail:* honors@jcu.edu; *Web site:* http://www.jcu.edu/honors

---

Kent State University
Honors College
Kent, Ohio

Honors at Kent State University began in the 1933–34 academic year when the first senior honors thesis was written. In 1960 the program attained University-wide status and in 1965 became a collegial unit headed by a dean.

The Honors College, open to students of all majors, is at the center of Kent State University's long tradition of providing special attention to undergraduates with outstanding intellectual and creative ability. Within the framework of the larger University, with its diverse academic programs and excellent research and library facilities, the Honors College offers students enriched and challenging courses and programs, opportunities for close relationships with peers and faculty members, and careful advising to meet their interests and goals.

The Honors College is guided by two basic principles. The first is a responsibility to provide academic work that offers intellectual challenge to the best students in the University and demands of them the best effort of which they are capable. To this end courses are designed to stretch the mind, sharpen skills, and encourage high standards of performance.

The second principle is the belief that regardless of degree program, students should be liberally educated. That is, they should understand and appreciate the language, literature, and history of cultures; the social, political, and economic structure of societies; the creative achievements that enrich lives; and the basic assumptions and substance of the natural sciences. In keeping with this belief, the College provides honors sections of many of the University's Liberal Education Requirement courses. Honors students are also encouraged to enrich their major programs by enrolling in related courses across disciplinary boundaries, e.g., studying foreign languages to complement degree programs in business. In addition, honors students pursue double majors in unusual combinations such as mathematics and theater, physics and English, and elementary education and dance.

Honors courses are available throughout the undergraduate years and can be used to meet requirements in all the degree-granting colleges and schools of the University.

All honors freshmen are enrolled in the year-long Freshman Honors Colloquium. The colloquium is a rigorous course in reading, thinking, and writing about literature and ideas. The goal of the course is to develop habits of inquiry, understanding, and communication to serve the student through the college years and beyond.

In addition to the Freshman Honors Colloquium, many honors courses are taught each semester by distinguished faculty members throughout the University. Although these courses differ in content from art to zoology, they share a common form. Class enrollments are small (no more than 20), and students get to know each other and their professors in an environment that encourages learning through discussion, reading, individual work, and writing.

Honors students are also encouraged to study on a one-to-one basis with members of the faculty. The Individual Honors Work course is available from the freshman through senior years and can take many forms. For example, it has been used by students to create a course not available in the regular curriculum, to study off campus, or to undertake a specialized scholarly or creative project. Seniors are strongly encouraged to complete the Senior Honors Thesis/Project.

Honors students are advised by the dean and a professional advising staff and by collegial and faculty advisers in their majors. Honors students must meet with their honors adviser at least once each semester in order to register for the following term. Honors students then have priority registration.

Enrollment is currently about 1,100, with an additional 200 students at the regional campuses.

Participation Requirements: Two categories of graduation recognition are possible: one with a thesis (graduation with honors) and one with course work only (graduation as an Honors College Scholar). Graduation with honors exists in three categories—University, General, and Departmental—and includes a certificate announcing Distinction in the student's major. Each category carries specific course and GPA requirements. The normal expectation is that students complete eight honors courses, with adjustments made for entrance after the freshman year. Students graduating from the Honors College are recognized at commencement and the Senior Honors Brunch; in addition, thesis students are recognized at the annual Forum for Undergraduate Scholars and Artists and in a published booklet.

Admission Process: Students apply directly to the Honors College by having guidance counselors send a copy of their high school transcript (showing class rank, GPA, ACT/SAT scores, and senior courses). Admission and scholarship decisions are made on an ongoing basis. Students who apply after the freshman year are evaluated on the basis of actual college performance. Students may apply as late as the end of the junior year.

Scholarship Availability: The Honors College directly distributes renewable merit scholarships, ranging from $1500 to full in-state tuition, room, and board, to approximately 65 percent of the freshman honors class. Also included are some discipline-specific awards. Minimum requirements are usually the top 10 percent in both class rank and national test scores.

Campus Overview

State-supported university, founded 1910, part of Kent State University System • **Coed** 19,060 undergraduate students, 84% full-time, 60% women, 40% men.

Undergraduates 15,925 full-time, 3,135 part-time. Students come from 47 states and territories, 60 other countries, 9% are from out of state, 8% African American, 1% Asian American or Pacific Islander, 1% Hispanic American, 0.4% Native American, 0.8% international, 5% transferred in, 35% live on campus.

Faculty Total: 1,395, 59% full-time, 46% with terminal degrees. Student/faculty ratio: 20:1.

Academic Programs *Special study options:* academic remediation for entering students, accelerated degree program, adult/continuing education programs, advanced placement credit, cooperative education, distance learning, double majors, English as a second language, external degree program, freshman honors college, honors programs, independent study, internships, off-campus study, part-time degree program, services for LD students, student-designed majors, study abroad, summer session for credit. *ROTC:* Army (b), Air Force (b). *Unusual degree programs:* 3-2 international relations.

Athletics Member NCAA. All Division I except football (Division I-A). *Intercollegiate sports:* baseball M(s), basketball M(s)/W(s), cross-country running M(s)/W(s), field hockey W(s), golf M(s)/W(s), gymnastics W(s), soccer W(s), softball W(s), track and field M(s)/W(s), volleyball W(s), wrestling M(s). *Intramural sports:* badminton M(c)/W(c), baseball M(c), basketball M/W, bowling M(c)/W(c), equestrian sports M(c)/W(c), fencing M(c)/W(c), field hockey W(c), football M/W, golf M(c)/W(c), ice hockey M(c), lacrosse M(c), racquetball M(c)/W(c), rugby M(c)/W(c), sailing M(c)/W(c), skiing (downhill) M(c)/W(c), soccer M(c)/W(c), softball M/W, swimming and diving M(c)/W(c), table tennis M/W, tennis M/W, ultimate Frisbee M/W, volleyball M(c)/W(c), water polo M/W, wrestling M.

Costs (2004–05) *One-time required fee:* $100. *Tuition:* state resident $7504 full-time, $343 per credit hour part-time; nonresident $14,516 full-time, $663 per credit hour part-time. Full-time tuition and fees vary according to course level, course load, degree level, location, program, reciprocity agreements, and student level. Part-time tuition and fees vary according to course level, course load, degree level, location, program, reciprocity agreements, and student level. *Room and board:* $6410; room only: $3890. Room and board charges vary according to board plan and housing facility.

Financial Aid 1,042 Federal Work-Study jobs (averaging $2316). In 2004, 1241 non-need-based awards were made. *Average percent of need met:* 56%. *Average financial aid package:* $6943. *Average need-based loan:* $3894. *Average need-based gift aid:* $4439. *Average non-need-based aid:* $3588.

Contact: Dean: Dr. Larry R. Andrews, P.O. Box 5190, Kent, Ohio 44242; *Telephone:* 330-672-2312; *Fax:* 330-672-3327; *E-mail:* landrews@kent.edu; *Web site:* http://www.kent.edu/honors

---

Malone College
Honors Program
Canton, Ohio

The Honors Program at Malone College exists to support intellectually gifted and highly motivated students as they move to transform themselves and their world as followers of Jesus Christ. The program challenges students to fulfill their intellectual and personal potential through enriching and stimulating experiences in and out of the classroom. It cultivates an esprit de corps *among its students and provides occasion to pursue ideas more deeply and develop closer relationships with faculty and each other. Students are prepared for the pursuit of original and advanced research, scholarship, and/or artistic performance.*

The Honors Program core curriculum of general education courses and upper-level interdisciplinary seminars is based on the belief in the virtues of a liberal arts education and seeks to develop students' understanding of the unity of knowledge and the interrelationship of the academic disciplines. The students write an honors thesis in an area of their choice and work closely with a faculty advisor during the process. Some funding for research is available, and students are encouraged to participate in academic conferences through subsidies for honors students. Cocurricular activities offer free cultural and social opportunities not generally available to others. Honors students have taken leadership roles in all aspects of campus life, including organizing their own service projects. Faculty are selected from among the best professors on campus and participate in the cocurricular activities.

The Honors Program began in the fall of 2000 and graduated its first cohort in spring of 2004. Approximately 75 students are involved in the program annually.

Participation Requirements: Students may complete as much of the program as they choose, but to graduate with Honors Program designation, they must have a 3.6 cumulative GPA and complete a minimum of 9 hours in honors general education courses, 6 hours of upper-level interdisciplinary seminars, and an honors thesis, for a total of 19 credits in honors coursework. Honors graduates receive medallions at the Senior Recognition banquet and wear them at graduation. Their achievement is also noted on their transcript.

Admission Process: Malone's Honors Program is open to students of all majors. Incoming freshmen are invited to apply to the Honors Program if they have a high school GPA of 3.6 and an ACT composite score of 26 or higher or an SAT combined score of 1170 or higher. Transfer and continuing students who have a college GPA of at least 3.6 are also eligible to apply to the program. Application includes an essay and two references. All applications are reviewed by the Honors

Program committee beginning in mid-March. Students are admitted on a rolling basis until the cohort is full.

Scholarship Availability: Students with at least a 3.6 GPA and 26 ACT/1170 SAT who complete the admission process by January 15 of the senior year will be invited to the Brehme Scholars Day Competition in February. Three full-tuition and twenty half-tuition scholarships will be awarded. All honors students qualify for the prestigious J. Walter and Emma Malone academic scholarship although participation in the Honors Program is not a condition for these awards. Details are available through the Malone College Admissions Center.

Campus Overview

Independent comprehensive, founded 1892, affiliated with Evangelical Friends Church–Eastern Region • **Coed** 1,936 undergraduate students, 88% full-time, 62% women, 38% men.

Undergraduates 1,698 full-time, 238 part-time. Students come from 24 states and territories, 12 other countries, 10% are from out of state, 6% African American, 0.5% Asian American or Pacific Islander, 0.6% Hispanic American, 0.9% international, 4% transferred in, 51% live on campus.

Faculty *Total:* 195, 53% full-time, 41% with terminal degrees. *Student/faculty ratio:* 14:1.

Academic Programs *Special study options:* academic remediation for entering students, accelerated degree program, adult/continuing education programs, advanced placement credit, cooperative education, distance learning, double majors, honors programs, independent study, internships, off-campus study, part-time degree program, services for LD students, student-designed majors, study abroad, summer session for credit. *ROTC:* Army (c), Air Force (c).

Athletics Member NAIA, NCCAA. *Intercollegiate sports:* baseball M(s), basketball M(s)/W(s), cheerleading M/W, cross-country running M(s)/W(s), football M(s), golf M(s)/W(s), soccer M(s)/W(s), softball W(s), tennis M(s)/W(s), track and field M(s)/W(s), volleyball W(s). *Intramural sports:* badminton M/W, basketball M/W, bowling M/W, cross-country running M/W, football M/W, racquetball M/W, skiing (cross-country) M/W, soccer M/W, softball M/W, table tennis M/W, tennis M/W, ultimate Frisbee M/W, volleyball M/W, weight lifting M/W.

Costs (2004–05) *Comprehensive fee:* $22,000 includes full-time tuition ($15,630), mandatory fees ($250), and room and board ($6120). Part-time tuition: $320 per semester hour. Part-time tuition and fees vary according to course load. *Required fees:* $63 per term part-time. *College room only:* $3250. Room and board charges vary according to board plan.

Financial Aid 294 Federal Work-Study jobs (averaging $1914). 71 state and other part-time jobs (averaging $2355). In 2004, 159 non-need-based awards were made. *Average percent of need met:* 74%. *Average financial aid package:* $11,799. *Average need-based loan:* $3610. *Average need-based gift aid:* $8038. *Average non-need-based aid:* $4364.

Contact: Director: Dr. Diane Chambers, Honors Program Director, Malone College, 515 25th St. NW, Canton, Ohio 44709; *Telephone:* 330-471-8183; *Fax:* 330-471-8527; *E-mail:* dchambers@malone.edu or honors@malone.edu; *Web site:* http://www.malone.edu

Miami University

Honors & Scholars Program

Oxford, Ohio

Miami University's Honors and Scholars Program embraces three different programs for exceptional students: Harrison Scholars, University Honors, and Oxford Scholars Programs. All three programs aim to provide and create an environment that enhances students' success in scholarship, leadership, and service. Miami's Harrison Scholars Program, established in 1984, enrolls approximately 100 students and provides students with a full-ride scholarship for four years, as well as automatic admission into the University Honors Program. The University Honors Program, established in 1964, enrolls approximately 750 students and provides a variety of learning opportunities: more than 100 small, highly interactive courses each year; a faculty mentorship program for first-year students; three optional residence halls with purposeful programming for honors students; a summer tuition waiver; special professional advising for prestigious scholarships and other enriching opportunities; and grants for research and creative activity. The Oxford Scholars Program offers its approximately 1,200 students the opportunity to live in the Honors and Scholars residence halls, support for conference travel, 1-credit special seminars, and cocurricular programs.

Participation Requirements: Harrison and University Honors students are required to complete ten Honors Experiences and receive at least a 3.5 GPA in order to graduate with University Honors. Honors Experiences encompass a broad array of learning opportunities. They consist of honors courses as well as other experiences such as study abroad, summer research projects, internships, graduate courses, intensive leadership and service-learning experiences, and independent studies. Of the required ten Honors Experiences, eight must be honors courses. In addition to program requirements, students may select to complete an honors thesis. These students graduate with the notation University Honors with Distinction on their transcripts.

First-year students have the option to participate in a Faculty Mentor Program that gives them the opportunity to interact closely with faculty members outside the classroom. This program encourages students to engage in intellectual inquiry by providing a variety of venues for discussions and reflection.

Admission Process: Admission to the Harrison Scholars and University Honors Program is highly selective. Students must submit a special application that includes two essays, a letter of recommendation, a list of achievements, and transcripts. Applications are reviewed for multiple academic and contextual variables. In 2005–06, students selected for the Harrison Scholars Program had an average ACT score of 33, an average GPA of 4.3, and an average class rank in the top of 1 percent. They also typically received recognition for their academic, artistic, service, and athletic accomplishments at the national level. Students selected for the University Honors Program had an average ACT score of 31, ranked in the top 3 percent of their graduating class, and had an average GPA of 4.1, in addition to outstanding accomplishments at the national, state, or regional level. All students who apply to Miami University are automatically considered for the Oxford Scholars Program. The average criteria for Oxford Scholars in 2005–06 were an ACT of 30, a GPA of 3.9, a graduating rank in the top 6 percent, and strong leadership and service accomplishments. Current Miami students may also apply for the University Honors Program after completing 15 Miami credit hours with a minimum earned GPA of 3.5. A limited number of spaces are also available to transfer students.

Scholarship Availability: All students selected for the Harrison Scholars Program receive a four-year renewable scholarship consisting of full tuition plus room and board. Students selected for the University Honors Program receive an annual renewable scholarship of $1500. Oxford Scholars Program students receive a four-year renewable scholarship of $1000. In addition, awards are available to assist Harrison and University Honors students with research expenses, travel to professional conferences, and other academic and enrichment endeavors. All Harrison and University Honors students have the opportunity to earn up to eight free tuition credits that can be used for summer study at Miami or in one of Miami's many international summer workshops.

The Honors and Scholars Program also administers the Joanna Jackson Goldman Memorial Prize, one of the largest awards of its kind in the nation. This award annually supports a graduating Miami senior for a year of independent scholarship or creative activity. The amount of the prize is approximately $25,000. Eligibility for the award includes an outstanding academic record, demonstrated capacity for independent work, and creative initiative in some field of scholarship or the arts.

In addition, the program administers an Urban Leadership Internship Program in which 20 students design their own ten-week summer internship and service-learning experience in one of five urban areas and receive a stipend for support. Finally, the program offers support for an internship at MTV in New York City.

Campus Overview

State-related university, founded 1809, part of Miami University System • **Coed** 15,059 undergraduate students, 98% full-time, 54% women, 46% men.

Undergraduates 14,727 full-time, 332 part-time. Students come from 50 states and territories, 32 other countries, 28% are from out of state, 3% African American, 3% Asian American or Pacific Islander, 2% Hispanic American, 0.5% Native American, 0.4% international, 1% transferred in, 45% live on campus.

Faculty *Total:* 1,161, 73% full-time, 75% with terminal degrees. *Student/faculty ratio:* 17:1.

Academic Programs *Special study options:* adult/continuing education programs, advanced placement credit, cooperative education, double majors, honors programs, independent study, internships, off-campus study, services for LD students, student-designed majors, study abroad, summer session for credit. *ROTC:* Army (c), Navy (b), Air Force (b). *Unusual degree programs:* 3-2 engineering with Case Western Reserve University, Columbia University; forestry with Duke University.

Athletics Member NCAA. All Division I except football (Division I-A). *Intercollegiate sports:* archery M(c)/W(c), baseball M(s), basketball M(s)/W(s), cross-country running M(s)/W(s), equestrian sports M(c)/W(c), fencing M(c)/W(c), field hockey W(s), golf M(s), gymnastics M(c)/W(c), ice hockey M(s), lacrosse M(c), racquetball M(c)/W(c), rugby M(c), sailing M(c)/W(c), soccer M(c)/W(s), softball W(s), swimming and diving M(s)/W(s), tennis M(c)/W(s), track and field M(s)/W(s), volleyball M(c)/W(s), wrestling M(c). *Intramural sports:* archery M/W, badminton M(c)/W(c), basketball M/W, cheerleading M(c)/W(c), crew M(c)/W(c), cross-country running M(c)/W(c), equestrian sports M(c)/W(c), fencing M(c)/W(c), field hockey W, football M/W, golf M(c)/W(c), gymnastics M(c)/W(c), ice hockey M(c)/W(c), lacrosse M(c)/W(c), racquetball M(c)/W(c), rugby M(c), sailing M/W, skiing (cross-country) M/W, skiing (downhill) M(c)/W(c), soccer M(c)/W(c), softball M/W, squash M(c)/W(c), swimming and diving M/W, table tennis M(c)/W(c), tennis M(c)/W(c), track and field M/W, ultimate Frisbee M(c)/W(c), volleyball M(c)/W(c), water polo M(c)/W(c), weight lifting M(c)/W(c), wrestling M(c).

Costs (2004–05) *Tuition:* state resident $8236 full-time, $760 per credit hour part-time; nonresident $18,236 full-time. Ohio residents receive $9,750 in resident scholarships. *Required fees:* $1406 full-time, $59 per credit hour part-time. *Room and board:* $7010; room only: $3510. Room and board charges vary according to board plan and housing facility.

Financial Aid 951 Federal Work-Study jobs (averaging $1650). In 2004, 5816 non-need-based awards were made. *Average percent of need met:* 77%. *Average financial aid package:* $15,358. *Average need-based loan:* $3825. *Average need-based gift aid:* $4350. *Average non-need-based aid:* $11,132.

Contact: Director, Honors & Scholars Program, Bishop Hall, Oxford, Ohio 45056; *Telephone:* 513-529-3399; *Fax:* 513-529-4920; *E-mail:* honors@muohio.edu; *Web site:* http://www.muohio.edu/honors

Mount Vernon Nazarene University
Honors Program
Mount Vernon, Ohio

The Honors Program at Mount Vernon Nazarene University (MVNU) is designed to provide rewarding challenges for high achievers in the way of specific courses, seminars, and other out-of-the-ordinary experiences both on and off campus. Honors students have access to exceptional learning opportunities that strengthen competence in liberal arts subjects as well as the students' major fields. The mission of the MVNU Honors Program is to develop within academically advanced students a greater understanding of what it means to be a Christian intellectual, integrating faith with learning through the development of critical-thinking skills. In the end, the goal of the program is to foster exposure to diverse views and a reasoned and Christian approach to personal, school, and global issues.

The Honors Program facilitates exploration of issues of interest with other academically motivated students as well as senior faculty members in small class settings that are discussion and participation oriented and intellectually stimulating. What sets the MVNU program apart from other Honors Programs is the Honors Seminar, which provides a forum for all four classes of honors students to interact on the basis of presentations in various fields of the liberal arts. In addition, students are required to complete an Honors Project by their fourth year. The participation with other academically advanced students in the seminar as well as an independent study project creates a balance that provides the student with a challenging and well-rounded education experience.

Currently in its tenth year, the program has developed into a high-quality program. Approximately 50 students are enrolled in the MVNU Honors Program.

Participation Requirements: Students must be involved in the Honors Seminar each semester they are on campus. They are expected to achieve at least 3 credit hours of honors work in general core courses either in honors sections or through a system of contracting to complete extra or advanced work by agreement with the professor. They must also complete 1 credit of Service Learning and an Honors Project (HP), which comprises 4 credit hours of research within the major field of the student. The student working on an HP is mentored by a faculty member within the major department and the final work is examined by a committee of three faculty members.

To remain in the program, students must maintain a minimum 3.5 GPA. Upon completion of all the requirements, the student graduates with University Honors and Departmental Honors, which is noted on the diploma and transcript.

Admission Process: First-time freshmen may apply with two letters of recommendation attesting to the student's academic ability, an interview with the Honors Program Committee either in person or on the telephone, a score of at least 27 on the ACT (or 1210 on the SAT), a minimum high school GPA of 3.4 (on a 4.0 scale), and any other information the applicant or committee deems necessary or helpful. Students applying after their second semester at the College must have completed 26 credit hours with at least a 3.5 cumulative GPA, two letters of recommendation from college professors, and an interview with the Honors Committee. Transfer students must have at least a 3.5 GPA, an ACT composite score of 27 or above, letters of recommendation from two professors, and an interview with the Honors Committee.

Scholarship Availability: An annual scholarship ranging from $250 (freshmen) to $400 (seniors) is awarded to all honors students. In addition, significant scholarships are awarded through the Office of Admissions based on academic performance and can be renewed over the course of a four-year degree program.

Campus Overview

Independent Nazarene comprehensive, founded 1964 • **Coed** 2,166 undergraduate students, 87% full-time, 57% women, 43% men.

Undergraduates 1,893 full-time, 273 part-time. Students come from 24 states and territories, 11 other countries, 9% are from out of state, 3% African American, 0.6% Asian American or Pacific Islander, 0.8% Hispanic American, 0.2% Native American, 0.6% international, 2% transferred in, 74% live on campus.

Faculty *Total:* 230, 39% full-time, 43% with terminal degrees. *Student/faculty ratio:* 18:1.

Academic Programs *Special study options:* academic remediation for entering students, adult/continuing education programs, advanced placement credit, cooperative education, double majors, freshman honors college, honors programs, independent study, internships, off-campus study, part-time degree program, services for LD students, study abroad, summer session for credit.

Athletics Member NAIA, NCCAA. *Intercollegiate sports:* baseball M(s), basketball M(s)/W(s), golf M(s), soccer M(s)/W(s), softball W(s), volleyball W(s). *Intramural sports:* basketball M/W, bowling M/W, cheerleading M/W, football M/W, skiing (downhill) M/W, soccer M/W, softball M/W, table tennis M/W, volleyball M/W.

Costs (2004–05) *Comprehensive fee:* $19,710 includes full-time tuition ($14,482), mandatory fees ($494), and room and board ($4734). Full-time tuition and fees vary according to course load, program, and reciprocity agreements. Part-time tuition: $517 per credit hour. Part-time tuition and fees vary according to course load, program, and reciprocity agreements. *College room only:* $2619. Room and board charges vary according to housing facility.

Financial Aid 180 Federal Work-Study jobs (averaging $1472). 317 state and other part-time jobs (averaging $1534). In 2003, 815 non-need-based awards were made. *Average percent of need met:* 83%. *Average financial aid package:* $10,581. *Average need-based loan:* $831. *Average need-based gift aid:* $5355. *Average non-need-based aid:* $1406.

Contact: Director: Dr. Thomas Beutel, 800 Martinsburg Road, Mount Vernon, Ohio 43050; *Telephone:* 740-392-6868 Ext. 3225; *Fax:* 740-397-2769; *E-mail:* tbeutel@mvnu.edu; *Web site:* http://www.mvnu.edu

Ohio Dominican University
The Ohio Dominican University Honors Program
Columbus, Ohio

*S*ince its introduction, the Honors Program at Ohio Dominican University (ODU) has been successful in attracting the top students enrolled at the institution. Based on the Seven ODU Learning Outcomes, honors-designated courses are offered to specifically challenge and engage talented and motivated students. Through the curriculum, the program provides learning experiences that explore the integration of concepts within and among disciplines; empower students to become intentional learners; engage students actively in the learning process; encourage students to interact with faculty members and with one another, both inside and outside the classroom; and emphasize depth and thoroughness of understanding.

Participation in the Honors Program provides unique opportunities not available to other students. Honors courses are small, taught by honors faculty members, and designed to stimulate creativity, critical thinking, collaboration, and analytical skills. In addition, honors students enjoy special events and are frequently invited to attend VIP receptions with dignitaries and speakers who come to the campus. Honors students receive a great deal of mentoring guidance

and companionship throughout their time at Ohio Dominican. The Senior Honors Project enables a student to work closely with a faculty member on a significant piece of work and frequently serves as a springboard to graduate or professional schools, as well as satisfying employment.

The Honors Program plans a variety of activities throughout the school year, including performances, scholarly presentations, poetry readings, writing groups, films, discussions and pizza parties, and informal discussions with professors to discuss everything from animation to zoology.

In addition to academic, cultural, and social advantages, Ohio Dominican University also offers Siena Hall, a residence dedicated to its community of scholars. Siena Hall provides an atmosphere conducive to study, creativity, and collaboration among the honors students who live there. Activities such as field trips to cultural events, discussions, and movies are offered, and students are also encouraged to develop programming of their own.

While the program has been in existence for many years, a newly launched curriculum is scheduled to be implemented beginning in fall 2005. This new curriculum presents courses designed to develop students' research and writing skills in an interdisciplinary context toward the successful completion of a Senior Honors Project. It is a growing program, with 47 students currently active. Competitive applications are accepted on an annual basis, and review results in the invitation to 25 incoming freshmen.

Participation Requirements: Once in the program, students remain in good standing by maintaining a GPA of at least 3.0 and fulfilling the requirements of the Honors Program. The Ohio Dominican University Honors Program requires the completion of four honors courses and a Senior Honors Project. Honors courses, which are designed for and limited to honors students, include Introduction to Critical Thinking, Critical Writing and Research, Honors Seminar: Issues in the Disciplines, and Senior Honors Project. Students who successfully complete the Honors Program receive a designation on their transcript and special recognition at commencement.

Admission Process: Students who qualify for the Honors Program are invited to apply on a rolling admission schedule. Those students who achieve a high school GPA of at least 3.7 and an ACT score of at least 26 are invited to complete an application and submit it along with an essay and a recommendation from one high school teacher.

Campus Overview

Independent Roman Catholic comprehensive, founded 1911 • **Coed** 2,545 undergraduate students, 67% full-time, 64% women, 36% men.

Undergraduates 1,694 full-time, 851 part-time. Students come from 19 states and territories, 11 other countries, 3% are from out of state, 24% African American, 1% Asian American or Pacific Islander, 1% Hispanic American, 0.3% Native American, 0.7% international, 8% transferred in, 29% live on campus.

Faculty *Total:* 192, 33% full-time, 51% with terminal degrees. *Student/faculty ratio:* 16:1.

Academic Programs *Special study options:* academic remediation for entering students, adult/continuing education programs, advanced placement credit, distance learning, English as a second language, honors programs, independent study, internships, off-campus study, part-time degree program, student-designed majors, study abroad, summer session for credit. *ROTC:* Army (c).

Athletics Member NAIA. *Intercollegiate sports:* baseball M(s), basketball M(s)/W(s), cheerleading M/W, cross-country running M/W, football M(s), golf M(s)/W(s), soccer M(s)/W(s), softball W(s), tennis M(s)/W(s), volleyball W(s). *Intramural sports:* badminton M/W, basketball M/W, bowling M/W, golf M/W, lacrosse M/W, soccer M/W, softball M/W, table tennis M/W, tennis M/W, volleyball M/W.

Costs (2004–05) *Comprehensive fee:* $24,250 includes full-time tuition ($18,000), mandatory fees ($50), and room and board ($6200). Part-time tuition: $370 per credit hour. *Required fees:* $100 per term part-time. *Room and board:* Room and board charges vary according to board plan and housing facility.

Financial Aid 200 Federal Work-Study jobs (averaging $2000). *Average percent of need met:* 92%. *Average financial aid package:* $12,467.

Contact: Dr. Valerie Staton, Honors Director, 1216 Sunbury Road, Columbus, Ohio 43219; *Telephone:* 614-251-4685; *Fax:* 614-252-0776; *E-mail:* statonv@ohiodominican.edu; *Web site:* http://www.ohiodominican.edu/honors/honorsprogram.shtml

The Ohio State University
University Honors Program
Columbus, Ohio

Within the context of a major research institution, the Ohio State University Honors Program offers outstanding students a variety of exciting learning opportunities, including more than 325 honors sections of courses each year. Honors courses average 18 students in size, are generally limited to 25 students, and are taught by top faculty members with a strong commitment to undergraduate education.

Honors students have many opportunities for research and scholarship under the guidance of faculty. Typically research experiences culminate in a senior honors thesis and graduation with distinction in the major area. Grants and scholarships are awarded competitively to students pursuing individual research projects. Each year, selected students participate in the Denman Undergraduate Research Forum on campus and an international research symposium at the University of Sao Paulo, Brazil.

Honors students have the option of residing in one of five honors residence halls, which provide special honors living-learning communities for students. Four halls house all levels of students while the fifth is an apartment-style residence for upper-class honors students. The halls provide rooms in a variety of sizes and configurations, comfortably furnished study areas, fully equipped kitchens, and recreational areas for socializing. Computer labs are located within walking distance of all five honors residence halls.

A wide array of cocurricular activities designed to connect students to faculty are available for honors students, including fireside chats that expose students to topics ranging from involvement in undergraduate research to the Harry Potter literary phenomenon; short term honors study-abroad programs featuring quarter-long honors courses that culminate in abroad experiences in London, England, and Athens, Greece; and UNITY, which coordinates cultural excursions to various cities, a Dinner & Dialogue program where faculty members facilitate discussions with students over ethnic cuisine, and subsidized tickets to area cultural events.

The 20-year old program currently enrolls 6,500 students.

Participation Requirements: To retain the honors designation, all honors students must complete 6 honors or approved upper-division courses during the first two years of enrollment and maintain a minimum 3.4 cumulative GPA. Additional requirements vary by program of study.

Admission Process: Students with at least 29 ACT or 1300 SAT composite scores who rank in the top 10 percent of their graduating high school class are automatically offered University Honors Program affiliation based upon their application to the University. Outstanding students who do not meet these criteria are encouraged to complete the Honors & Scholars common application, which allows them to be considered for both the University Honors Program and the Ohio State Scholars Programs.

Scholarship Availability: The Ohio State University offers a competitive merit aid program. Scholarships are awarded based upon students' high school records, ACT or SAT scores, and the results of scholarship competitions such that every honors student has at least one merit scholarship ranging in amount from $750 per year to a full-ride at in-state value; scholarships are awarded for twelve quarters provided students maintain at minimum a 3.2 GPA.

National Merit, National Achievement, and National Hispanic Scholarships are awarded to most National Merit finalists who designate Ohio State as their first choice institution by March 1 and to National Achievement/Hispanic Finalists who apply to Ohio State by February 1. Such students may also receive the Distinguished Scholarship, which covers full in-state tuition plus $4500 per year for 12 quarters.

Other financial assistance, including scholarships, research support, grants, loans, and part-time employment, is available to qualified students at the Ohio State University.

Campus Overview

State-supported university, founded 1870 • **Coed** 37,509 undergraduate students, 90% full-time, 47% women, 53% men.

Undergraduates 33,584 full-time, 3,925 part-time. Students come from 53 states and territories, 121 other countries, 11% are from out of state, 8% African American, 5% Asian American or Pacific Islander, 2% Hispanic American, 0.4% Native American, 3% international, 5% transferred in, 24% live on campus.

Faculty *Total:* 3,782, 74% full-time. *Student/faculty ratio:* 14:1.

Academic Programs *Special study options:* academic remediation for entering students, accelerated degree program, adult/continuing education programs, advanced placement credit, cooperative education, distance learning, double majors, English as a second language, freshman honors college, honors programs, independent study, internships, off-campus study, part-time degree program, services for LD students, student-designed majors, study abroad, summer session for credit. *ROTC:* Army (b), Navy (b), Air Force (b).

Athletics Member NCAA. All Division I except football (Division I-A). *Intercollegiate sports:* baseball M(s), basketball M(s)/W(s), cheerleading M/W, cross-country running M(s)/W(s), fencing M(s)/W(s), field hockey W(s), golf M(s)/W(s), gymnastics M(s)/W(s), ice hockey M(s)/W(s), lacrosse M(s)/W(s), riflery M/W, soccer M(s)/W(s), softball W(s), swimming and diving M(s)/W(s), tennis M(s)/W(s), track and field M(s)/W(s), volleyball M(s)/W(s), wrestling M(s). *Intramural sports:* badminton M(c)/W(c), baseball M(c), basketball M/W, bowling M(c)/W(c), crew M(c)/W, cross-country running M/W, equestrian sports M(c)/W(c), fencing M(c)/W(c), field hockey W, football M/W, golf M/W, gymnastics M(c)/W(c), ice hockey M(c)/W(c), lacrosse M(c)/W(c), racquetball M(c)/W(c), riflery M(c)/W(c), rock climbing M/W, rugby M(c)/W(c), sailing M(c)/W(c), skiing (downhill) M(c)/W(c), soccer M(c)/W(c), softball W(c), squash M(c)/W(c), swimming and diving M(c)/W(c), table tennis M/W, tennis M/W, track and field M(c)/W(c), ultimate Frisbee M(c)/W(c), volleyball M(c)/W(c), water polo M(c)/W(c), weight lifting M(c), wrestling M/W.

Costs (2004–05) *Tuition:* state resident $7479 full-time; nonresident $18,066 full-time. Full-time tuition and fees vary according to course load, program, reciprocity agreements, and student level. Part-time tuition and fees vary according to course load, program, reciprocity agreements, and student level. *Room and board:* $6909. Room and board charges vary according to board plan and housing facility.

Financial Aid 4,303 Federal Work-Study jobs (averaging $3322). In 2004, 5432 non-need-based awards were made. *Average percent of need met:* 68%. *Average financial aid package:* $9149. *Average need-based loan:* $4254. *Average need-based gift aid:* $4917. *Average non-need-based aid:* $3816.

Contact: Dr. Linda Harlow, Associate Provost, University Honors and Scholars Center, 220 West Twelfth Avenue, Columbus, Ohio 43210; *Telephone:* 614-292-3135; *Fax:* 614-292-6135; *E-mail:* osuhons@osu.edu; *Web site:* http://www.honors.osu.edu

Ohio University
Honors Tutorial College
Athens, Ohio

Ohio University's Honors Tutorial College is not a standard honors college; it is first and foremost a tutorial college based on the tutorial model of collaborative learning developed at Oxford and Cambridge Universities. A tutorial consists of either a one-on-one course with a professor or a small seminar with a professor and a handful of Honors Tutorial students. Tutorials are quarter-long conversations in which students and tutors explore issues and ideas that are fundamental to a specified disciplinary area. In order for the conversation to be substantive, tutees are given substantial reading assignments and are often asked to complete papers and/or problem sets, design projects, and undertake creative activities. Through these conversations, students gain knowledge, hone essential skills, and develop an understanding of what inspires them. The tutorial method of instruction is one of the most exciting, challenging, and rewarding ways to acquire an undergraduate education.

The level of expectation for tutorial performance is high. Successful tutorial students tend to exhibit a clear capacity for self-motivation, maturity, self-discipline, and creativity. In tutorials, tutors expect application and effort beyond the norm. In particular, they look for signs of a commitment to intellectual exploration and growth. Within this framework, intellectual risks are encouraged and necessary.

The Honors Tutorial College was founded in 1972 and is a full degree-granting college headed by an academic dean. The College has more than 900 alumni. They hold positions of responsibility in academia, law firms, corporations, government, and medical fields. In this group are Emmy, Pulitzer, Grammy, and Clio winners and individuals who have been recognized by their discipline or institution for their achievements and leadership. Graduates of the Honors Tutorial College credit the tutorial method of education as a critical factor in providing them with the tools and experience they needed to succeed.

Approximately 200 faculty members participate as tutors each year, giving service, in most cases, to the College in addition to their normal teaching loads. Tutors are full-time faculty members with outstanding teaching and research credentials. Each program of study is headed by a faculty member known as the director of studies. This individual administers the program at the department or school level and serves as the primary academic adviser for Honors Tutorial students in that particular discipline. Because of the close working relationship that tutees form with their tutors and the nationally recognized level of educational challenge inherent in the Honors Tutorial College, students have an outstanding track record of acceptance to the premier graduate and professional programs in their fields.

Because Ohio University genuinely believes in the capacity of high-caliber students to enrich the intellectual life of the campus, it provides resources and privileges to Honors Tutorial College students that are not granted to other undergraduates. Some of those benefits include priority registration, graduate library privileges, special research opportunities, and automatic eligibility for scholar housing. The University is willing to make these investments as long as the recipients of these benefits maintain a high level of academic excellence and campus/community involvement. This quid pro quo is probably best captured by the oft-repeated quotation: "Of those to whom much is given, much is required." Consequently the College expects its students to undertake leadership roles and to contribute substantively to the cultural and academic realms of the university.

To assist students in making the most of their talents and in taking the greatest enjoyment out of their time as undergraduates, the Honors Tutorial College strives to create a close-knit community among its members. This is not to say that the College encourages exclusivity (quite the contrary), but it does provide a home base that promotes interaction between students and a homelike atmosphere in its offices, which are located in a house built in the 1930s in the center of campus. The staff members at the College take great pride in knowing each Honors Tutorial student and in encouraging them to develop their interests and potential. Students in the College are also highly supportive of each other and frequently form the type of friendships that extend far beyond graduation.

Participation Requirements: In general, tutees enroll in one tutorial per term. The remainder of their course work consists of traditional classes, generally at an advanced level. For the most part, Honors Tutorial students are not subject to the prerequisites established for traditional courses and are allowed, with the approval of their academic adviser and the course instructor, to take graduate courses that count toward their undergraduate degrees.

Currently, the College offers programs of study in disciplines ranging from anthropology to physics, journalism to dance. These programs are separate and distinct from the traditional undergraduate degrees offered at Ohio University. Each program has a core curriculum consisting of tutorials and collateral course work. There is no credit-hour minimum for graduation; students must fulfill the program of study requirements, demonstrate competencies through high-quality writing and critical thinking, and complete a research thesis or project that is presented publicly before graduation.

Honors Tutorial students are the only students at Ohio University who are not subject to general education requirements, save freshman English and junior composition (the latter may be waived with the approval of a director of studies). Since Honors Tutorial students are not responsible for general education requirements, sufficient flexibility exists to allow students to study abroad without causing delays in graduation. Most programs are four years in duration, and in some cases, students may qualify to pursue a joint B.A./M.A. or B.S./M.S. program that allows them to complete two degrees in the span of four years. Students in the social sciences and journalism may also apply to the graduate sequence in contemporary history offered through Ohio University's prestigious Contemporary History Institute.

Admission Process: Due to the faculty-intensive nature of the tutorial program, each entering class consists of only 55 to 60 students. The application process is thorough and highly competitive. Every successful applicant to the College passes through three levels of review. The first consists of a review of an applicant's file by the assistant dean or the dean of the College. The second is conducted by the director of studies in the program(s) to which the student has applied. The third review takes place after the on-campus personal interview (which is a required element of the admission process). Prospective students are allowed to apply for admission for up to three programs of study.

Students who are successful in gaining admission to the Honors Tutorial College possess a wide variety of academic backgrounds. On the whole, however, they tend to demonstrate some or all of the following characteristics: excellent high school grades, strong standardized test scores, and notable scholarly, literary, and/or artistic accomplishments. All applicants to the College are urged to submit a portfolio containing letters of recommendation and examples of substantive academic and/or creative work. Some programs of study, such as film and journalism, require applicants to prepare a portfolio. Applicants should check the Honors Tutorial College Web site at http://www.ouhtc.org for information about portfolio submission.

The personal interview, which marks the final stage of the admission process, helps the College to determine if a student can thrive in a tutorial-based setting. Because of the highly interactive and personal nature of a tutorial education, the importance of attitude cannot be overestimated. The purpose of the interview is to determine if an individual possesses traits most likely to assist them as a tutee, including a deep-seated passion for learning, an ability to concentrate, a willingness to obtain a thorough grounding in fundamentals, the capacity to be a fearless questioner, an understanding that true learning never takes place within a comfort zone, and a sense of humor. In cases where lack of financial resources makes travel difficult, the College, upon request, can sometimes provide assistance in bringing an individual to campus for the interview.

Scholarship Availability: Ohio University offers a variety of scholarships. Some are based on merit; others require a combination of merit and demonstrated need. Information about scholarship options can be found on the Ohio University Admission Office Web site at http://www.ohio.edu/admissions/scholfinaid/. In addition to financial aid packages provided by the University, the College possesses some scholarship funding provided by its alumni and friends. While not technically scholarships, one of the features of the Honors Tutorial College is its ability to support unique educational opportunities and research for its students. Using funding donated by alumni and friends, the College invests between $25,000 and $30,000 per annum in the research and educational endeavors of its students.

Campus Overview

State-supported university, founded 1804, part of Ohio Board of Regents • **Coed** 16,937 undergraduate students, 94% full-time, 53% women, 47% men.

Undergraduates 15,968 full-time, 969 part-time. Students come from 52 states and territories, 109 other countries, 8% are from out of state, 3% African American, 0.9% Asian American or Pacific Islander, 1% Hispanic American, 0.2% Native American, 2% international, 3% transferred in, 43% live on campus.

Faculty *Total:* 1,162, 74% full-time, 81% with terminal degrees. *Student/faculty ratio:* 18:1.

Academic Programs *Special study options:* academic remediation for entering students, accelerated degree program, adult/continuing education programs, advanced placement credit, cooperative education, distance learning, double majors, English as a second language, external degree program, honors programs, independent study, internships, off-campus study, part-time degree program, services for LD students, student-designed majors, study abroad, summer session for credit. *ROTC:* Army (b), Air Force (b).

Athletics Member NCAA. All Division I except football (Division I-A). *Intercollegiate sports:* baseball M(s), basketball M(s)/W(s), cheerleading M/W, cross-country running M(s)/W(s), equestrian sports M(c)/W(c), field hockey W(s), golf M(s)/W(s), ice hockey M(c), lacrosse M(c)/W(c), rugby M(c)/W(c), soccer M(c)/W(s), softball W(s), swimming and diving M(s)/W(s), track and field M(s)/W(s), volleyball M(c)/W(s), water polo M(c)/W(c), weight lifting M(c), wrestling M(s). *Intramural sports:* baseball M, basketball M/W, bowling M/W, cross-country running M/W, football M, racquetball M/W, soccer M/W, softball M/W, swimming and diving M/W, tennis M/W, track and field M/W, volleyball M/W.

Costs (2004–05) *Tuition:* state resident $7770 full-time, $248 per quarter hour part-time; nonresident $16,734 full-time, $543 per quarter hour part-time. *Room and board:* $7539; room only: $3708. Room and board charges vary according to board plan.

Financial Aid In 2004, 1309 non-need-based awards were made. *Average percent of need met:* 54%. *Average financial aid package:* $7430. *Average need-based loan:* $4018. *Average need-based gift aid:* $3726. *Average non-need-based aid:* $4317.

Contact: Assistant Dean: Jan Hodson, 35 Park Place, Athens, Ohio 45701; *Telephone:* 740-593-2723; *Fax:* 740-593-9521; *E-mail:* honors.college@ohiou.edu; *Web site:* http://www.ouhtc.org

Sinclair Community College
Honors Program
Dayton, Ohio

The Sinclair Honors Program is designed to meet the needs of academically superior students who seek intellectual challenge and are willing to assume more responsibility for the learning experience. The aim of the program is to identify, stimulate, and recognize Sinclair's best students. Honors courses cultivate critical-thinking skills, encourage individual inquiry, and demand high-quality performance and responsibility. Honors works closely with Phi Theta Kappa and the Ohio Fellows Program. The Honors Director presides over an Honors Council made up of faculty members, students, and counselors.

Started in the 1980s, the program enrolls about 100 students each quarter in honors classes, and about 20 honors scholars are currently active. It is affiliated with the National Collegiate Honors Council and the Mid-East Honors Association.

Participation Requirements: Any Sinclair student may take an honors course with permission from the instructor or Honors Director. Honors scholars must maintain a minimum 3.25 GPA (or a 3.5 to be eligible for quarterly $400 scholarships). Honors scholars must complete five honors courses in three different disciplines, and one of those courses must be interdisciplinary. They must also complete a service learning project, a requirement that may or may not earn credit.

Admission Process: Students are identified through admissions testing as possible honors participants and are invited to apply. However, any student who meets the criteria may apply at any point while at Sinclair. Two letters of reference and a personal essay are required in addition to at least a 3.25 GPA and an interview with the Honors Council.

Scholarship Availability: Honors scholars with a GPA of 3.5 or better are eligible to apply for Honors Scholarships up to six times (six quarters) while attending the College. These scholarships, provided by the Sinclair Foundation, are for $400 maximum per quarter and may be used for tuition, fees, and bookstore charges. An application with letters of reference is required, and students must apply in writing for renewal each quarter.

Campus Overview

State and locally supported 2-year, founded 1887, part of Ohio Board of Regents • **Coed** 19,563 undergraduate students, 39% full-time, 57% women, 43% men.

Undergraduates 7,550 full-time, 12,013 part-time. Students come from 31 states and territories, 4% are from out of state, 16% African American, 1% Asian American or Pacific Islander, 1% Hispanic American, 0.4% Native American, 0.7% international, 6% transferred in.

Faculty *Total:* 1,117, 42% full-time, 61% with terminal degrees. *Student/faculty ratio:* 23:1.

Academic Programs *Special study options:* academic remediation for entering students, adult/continuing education programs, cooperative education, distance learning, English as a second language, external degree program, honors programs, independent study, internships, off-campus study, part-time degree program, services for LD students, student-designed majors, summer session for credit. *ROTC:* Army (c), Air Force (c).

Athletics Member NJCAA. *Intercollegiate sports:* baseball M(s), basketball M(s)/W(s), golf M(s), tennis M(s)/W(s), volleyball W(s).

Costs (2004–05) *Tuition:* area resident $1803 full-time, $40 per credit part-time; state resident $2943 full-time, $65 per credit part-time; nonresident $5310 full-time, $118 per credit part-time. Full-time tuition and fees vary according to course load. Part-time tuition and fees vary according to course load.

Financial Aid 50 Federal Work-Study jobs (averaging $800).

Contact: Director: Dr. Thomas Martin, 444 West Third Street, Dayton, Ohio 45402-1460; *Telephone:* 937-512-5189; *E-mail:* thomas.martin6057@sinclair.edu; *Web site:* http://www.sinclair.edu/departments/honors/

The University of Akron
University Honors Program
Akron, Ohio

Since its beginning in 1975, the University Honors Program has supported high-achieving and highly motivated students with its special curriculum opportunities. More than 1,400 students have achieved graduation as University Scholars during the history of the program. Challenging curricular options, honors classes, scholarships, and priority registration are only a few of the many benefits honors students receive.

The University of Akron Honors Program spans the entire University. Students complete the requirements for a major in one of more than 200 bachelor's degree programs across the campus. An honors faculty adviser from each of the majors is assigned to an incoming student and works closely with the student as an adviser throughout his or her course of study. Honors sections of courses are provided in many areas in order to ensure an enriching experience of studying and interacting with other high-achieving students. In place of the General Education requirements of the University, honors students complete an individually selected set of courses to meet the honors distribution requirements. The 38-hour requirement (including physical education) incorporates course work in humanities, languages and the arts, social sciences, and natural sciences and mathematics.

Honors Program students participate in three 2-credit colloquia over the course of their sophomore, junior, and senior years. These interdisciplinary seminars are open only to honors students and they provide a small class size for increased discussion and interaction among students. The three colloquia are topical courses in humanities, social sciences, and natural sciences.

Students are required to complete a Senior Honors Project. This capstone experience begins during the junior year with a student selecting a sponsor, topic, and committee and developing a proposal. The student's completion of the Senior Honors Project is considered to be a unique opportunity to apply their learning and test their abilities. Students are encouraged to focus on an interdisciplinary topic for their study and then present their research in the annual University Student Research Forum. Upon completion of the Senior Honors Project and course work requirements while maintaining a GPA of at least 3.4, students are recognized at graduation with the designation of University Honors Scholar.

Scholarship opportunities are available within the Honors Program and across the University. The program provides ongoing academic and career counseling to students in all disciplines of study. The newly built Honors Complex is the special residence hall for more than 400 honors students and houses a computer lab for honors students, classrooms, and the Honors Program offices. The program is currently increasing in size, as seen by the doubling of honors students in the past five years. Approximately 800 students are in the Honors Program, representing a range of local, national, and international students.

Participation Requirements: Students who are accepted as honors students complete an individually designed course of study in collaboration with their faculty adviser. Students are required to complete a minimum of 128 credits, including major requirements, honors distribution requirements, colloquia, and their Senior Honors Project. The project, an integral part of the honors experience, may take the form of a research report, a senior thesis, or an artistic or creative work.

GPA levels must be maintained to be an honors scholarship recipient. These levels are two semesters or 32 credits, 3.25; four semesters or 64 credits, 3.3; and six semesters or 96 credits, 3.4. In order to complete the undergraduate degree with the University Honors Scholar designation, the final GPA must be 3.4 or higher.

Admission Process: A special application process is required for honors students. High school performance criteria, as well as standardized test scores, are considered. Students must achieve two of the three following criteria for admission to the program: ACT composite score or SAT combined score in the top 10 percent, minimum GPA of 3.5, and rank in top 10 percent in class. Essays are required for admission.

Students who qualify are invited for an interview by University faculty members and administrators. This experience provides an opportunity for the student to come to the campus and meet with faculty members while applying for acceptance into the program. For students entering as transfer students, as continuing students at the University of Akron, or as students who have delayed the start of their college studies, similar evidence of academic excellence and potential is required. There are two application deadlines for the Honors Program (and scholarship support): the early application deadline is November 15 and the regular deadline is February 1.

Scholarship Availability: Honors program students are eligible for generous academic scholarships awarded for merit. The Lisle M. Buckingham Scholarships and the Zeigler Scholarship guarantee sufficient funds to cover tuition and fees, residence hall costs, and meal plans. Two levels of honors scholarships are the Honors Merit Scholarship (approximately $3000) and the Honors Recognition Scholarship ($1500). Other generous scholarship opportunities are available to high-achieving students. Additional information on scholarships, deadlines, and qualifications is available from the Office of Student Financial Aid.

Campus Overview

State-supported university, founded 1870 • **Coed** 19,245 undergraduate students, 71% full-time, 55% women, 45% men.

Undergraduates 13,633 full-time, 5,612 part-time. Students come from 42 states and territories, 84 other countries, 2% are from out of state, 14% African American, 2% Asian American or Pacific Islander, 0.8% Hispanic American, 0.4% Native American, 0.8% international, 4% transferred in, 13% live on campus.

Faculty *Total:* 1,580, 46% full-time, 57% with terminal degrees. *Student/faculty ratio:* 19:1.

Academic Programs *Special study options:* academic remediation for entering students, accelerated degree program, adult/continuing education programs, advanced placement credit, cooperative education, distance learning, double majors, English as a second language, honors programs, independent study, internships, part-time degree program, services for LD students, student-designed majors, study abroad, summer session for credit. *ROTC:* Army (b), Air Force (b).

Athletics Member NCAA. All Division I except football (Division I-A). *Intercollegiate sports:* baseball M(s), basketball M(s)/W(s), cheerleading M/W, cross-country running M(s)/W(s), golf M(s), riflery M/W, soccer M(s)/W, softball W(s), tennis M(s)/W(s), track and field M(s)/W(s), volleyball W(s). *Intramural sports:* archery M/W, basketball M/W, bowling M/W, cross-country running M/W, football M, golf M/W, lacrosse M/W, racquetball M/W, riflery M(c)/W(c), rock climbing M/W, skiing (cross-country) M(c)/W(c), skiing (downhill) M(c)/W(c), soccer M/W, softball M/W, swimming and diving W, table tennis M/W, tennis M/W, track and field M/W, volleyball M/W, weight lifting M, wrestling M.

Costs (2004–05) *Tuition:* state resident $6424 full-time, $268 per credit part-time; nonresident $14,654 full-time, $542 per credit part-time. Full-time tuition and fees vary according to course load, degree level, and location. Part-time tuition and fees vary according to course load, degree level, and location. *Required fees:* $1086 full-time, $45 per credit part-time. *Room and board:* $6660; room only: $4240. Room and board charges vary according to board plan and housing facility.

Financial Aid 740 Federal Work-Study jobs (averaging $1919). 2,374 state and other part-time jobs (averaging $1758). In 2003, 1787 non-need-based awards were made. *Average percent of need met:* 41%. *Average financial aid package:* $5999. *Average need-based loan:* $3655. *Average need-based gift aid:* $4415. *Average non-need-based aid:* $1807.

Contact: Contact: Dr. Dale H. Mugler, Director, University Honors Program, Honors Complex 178, University of Akron, Akron, Ohio 44325-1803; *Telephone:* 330-972-5365; *E-mail:* dmugler@uakron.edu; or Dr. Karyn Bobkoff Katz, Associate Director, University Honors Program, Honors Complex 178, University of Akron, Akron, Ohio 44325-1803; *Telephone:* 330-972-8679; *E-mail:* kkatz@uakron.edu; *Web site:* http://www.uakron.edu/honors

University of Cincinnati
University Honors Scholars Program
Cincinnati, Ohio

The University Honors Scholars Program is an all-University program open to academically talented and motivated students enrolled in any of the University of Cincinnati's (UC) colleges. The mission of the Honors Scholars Program is to enrich the educational experience of academically talented students through curriculum and cocurricular programs focused in the following areas: interdisciplinary studies, leadership, global studies, research and creative arts, and community engagement. These areas of emphasis are in alignment with the University's strategic plan, UC\21 (http://www.uc.edu/uc21/).

Honors students can select honors sections of general education or major courses to fulfill requirements. Honors special topics courses allow students to earn general education credit in courses focused around the curricular emphases of interdisciplinary studies, leadership, global studies, research and creative arts, and community engagement. Students also have the option of earning honors credit through experiential learning and contracts. Honors courses are smaller than nonhonors sections of courses, with a typical enrollment limit of 25.

Honors students have access to a broad range of social, cultural, and educational events sponsored by the Honors Scholars Program. These events are focused around the curricular emphases of the program and provide students the opportunity to interact with honors students from different colleges and majors. Students also have access to honors housing where honors students serve as resident assistants.

Honors-PLUS is a demanding undergraduate business honors curriculum operating in conjunction with the Honors Scholars Program. By combining academic and work experiences, the program integrates the resources of the university, the College of Business, and greater Cincinnati businesses to provide graduates with the knowledge and skills necessary for immediate and productive employment and position them for advancement as business and community leaders.

The Honors Scholars Program has been in existence at UC since the 1960s. It became university-wide in 1991. Currently, the there are 2,000 students in the program.

Participation Requirements: Students must earn 24 credit hours to earn a lower-division honors distinction. Students who wish to earn full University Honors must earn 36 honors credits prior to graduation. Of the 36 credits, 9 must come from specially designated honors special-topics courses. Students can earn credit in the following ways: honors sections of introductory or intermediate courses, honors special-topics courses, honors contracts for nonhonors courses, experiential learning, honors individually guided study, departmental honors courses, and departmental senior capstones/theses. In order to maintain membership in the program, students must maintain a minimum 3.2 cumulative GPA and make reasonable progress toward completion of the hours requirements. Upon graduation with 36 hours of honors credit, students receive special recognition at an honors graduation ceremony. Students who graduate with a GPA of 3.2 to 3.74 receive special notation on both the transcript and diploma as an Honors Scholar. Students who graduate with a GPA of 3.75 or higher receive special notation as a Distinguished Honors Scholar.

Admission Process: Applicants are evaluated using the following criteria: test scores, high school rank, high school GPA, writing skills, strength of the high school schedule (AP, honors classes, etc.), academic awards or honors, leadership, activities, and service. The typical honors student has an SAT score of 1300, an ACT composite of 29, and a high school GPA of 3.8. Applications are accepted at any time; however, for priority consideration, application materials must be received by March 1. Students already at UC may apply after accumulating 12 hours of credit with a minimum GPA of 3.2.

Scholarship Availability: Financial aid is administered through the Office of Financial Aid. Of special interest to potential honors students is the Cincinnatus Scholarship Competition, which is open to prospective students who apply to the University of Cincinnati and meet eligibility criteria similar to admission to the Honors Program, including academic excellence, community service, and performance during the competition itself. Four-year awards range from $8000 to $64,000. On average, 90 percent of honors students receive Cincinnatus scholarship awards.

In addition, many colleges offer specific college-based scholarship funds. For example, the College of Business provides scholarship funds to students under the Honors-PLUS program. It offers total financial support, co-op experience, and a personal mentor.

Honors Undergraduate Research Awards are given to promote research and scholarly or creative activity among honors students at UC. These awards enable honors students to undertake projects of an original nature within their major field of study.

Campus Overview

State-supported university, founded 1819, part of University of Cincinnati System • **Coed** 19,128 undergraduate students, 83% full-time, 49% women, 51% men.

Undergraduates 15,858 full-time, 3,270 part-time. Students come from 52 states and territories, 123 other countries, 8% are from out of state, 14% African American, 3% Asian American or Pacific Islander, 1% Hispanic American, 0.4% Native American, 4% international, 6% transferred in, 18% live on campus.

Faculty *Total:* 1,193, 96% full-time, 70% with terminal degrees. *Student/faculty ratio:* 15:1.

Academic Programs *Special study options:* academic remediation for entering students, accelerated degree program, adult/continuing education programs, advanced placement credit, cooperative education, distance learning, double majors, English as a second language, honors programs, independent study, internships, off-campus study, part-time degree program, services for LD students, study abroad, summer session for credit. *ROTC:* Army (b), Air Force (b).

Athletics Member NCAA. All Division I except football (Division I-A). *Intercollegiate sports:* baseball M, basketball M(s)/W(s), cheerleading M/W, crew M(c)/W(c), cross-country running M(s)/W(s), golf M(s), rugby M(c), soccer M(s)/W(s), swimming and diving M(s)/W(s), tennis M(s)/W(s), track and field M(s)/W, volleyball W(s). *Intramural sports:* archery W, badminton M/W, baseball M, basketball M/W, bowling M/W, crew M(c)/W(c), football M, golf M/W, gymnastics W, ice hockey M, racquetball M/W, soccer M/W, squash M/W, swimming and diving M/W, tennis M/W, track and field M/W, volleyball M/W, weight lifting M, wrestling M.

Costs (2004–05) *Tuition:* state resident $7005 full-time, $233 per credit hour part-time; nonresident $19,977 full-time, $594 per credit hour part-time. Full-time tuition and fees vary according to course load, degree level, location, program, and reciprocity agreements. Part-time tuition and fees vary according to course load, degree level, location, program, and reciprocity agreements. *Required fees:* $1374 full-time. *Room and board:* $8004; room only: $5142. Room and board charges vary according to board plan and housing facility.

Financial Aid In 2003, 694 non-need-based awards were made. *Average percent of need met:* 54%. *Average financial aid package:* $7790. *Average need-based loan:* $3652. *Average need-based gift aid:* $4039. *Average non-need-based aid:* $4013.

Contact: Director, University Honors Scholars Program, University of Cincinnati, P.O. Box 210007, Cincinnati, Ohio 45221-0007; *Telephone:* 513-556-6274; *Fax:* 513-556-2890; *E-mail:* honors@uc.edu; *Web site:* http://www.uc.edu/honors

University of Dayton
Honors and Berry Scholars Programs
Dayton, Ohio

The University of Dayton has two distinct University-wide programs: the University Honors Program and the John W. Berry Sr. Scholars Program. The Honors Program admits selected beginning and transfer students. Honors Program students take 9 credits of honors sections and may elect to complete an Honors Thesis Project and earn an Honors Program–designated diploma. Those not admitted as incoming students may later earn entry. Honors students comprise approximately 10 percent of the undergraduate student population.

The John W. Berry Sr. Scholars Program is the University of Dayton's most selective academic program, limited to 30 entering first-year University Honors students from across all divisions of the University who, over the course of their years together, take a defined series of seminars. They participate in summer leadership and service programs and an international or cultural immersion experience. They also complete an Honors Thesis Project in order to earn a designated Berry Scholars Program diploma. There are currently 120 Berry Scholars.

Certain library and housing benefits, as well as cultural and social opportunities, are available to Berry Scholars and University Honors students. Among other types of integrated learning and living programs, incoming honors students also take a special one-semester English course. Connected with this course is the visit to the campus of the annual Honors Author, one of whose books the first-year students will have studied in their Honors English class. The most up to date information about both programs is found at the Honors Program Web site (http://honors.udayton.edu).

The University Honors and Berry Scholars Programs were founded in 1979 and graduated the first class of students in 1983. There are more than 700 alumni of the Berry Scholars Program, among whom more than 500 have advanced degrees, many from the most prestigious postgraduate programs nationally and internationally. The University Honors and Berry Scholars Programs currently operate with an endowment of $15 million that supports special programming, international study, and four-year full-tuition John W. Berry Sr. Scholarships for incoming Berry Scholars.

Participation Requirements: Berry Scholars together take a series of small-section seminars in English, religious studies, history, social science, philosophy, and engineering systems design over the course of three years. These seminars satisfy most University-wide general education requirements. In the final required seminar, the entire third-year Berry Scholars class works as a team on a complex project using a systems approach. Students then complete an Honors Thesis Project of their choosing under the guidance of 1 or more faculty members. An optional concluding Colloquium on Faith and Reason is offered in their last semester. Berry Scholars participate in a summer leadership program prior to arriving on campus as first-year students. They also participate in a summer service project after their first, second, or third years. Finally, Berry Scholars are also required to participate in an international or cultural-immersion learning experience. Summer study abroad, international research, and international study opportunities during spring break in the history and social science seminars are the typical methods of completing this requirement. Graduates of the John W. Berry Sr. Scholars Program earn a designated diploma, as well as a Berry Scholars key.

Honors Program students take 18 credits of honors-designated classes and choose to complete an Honors Thesis Project if they wish to earn the Honors Program–designated diploma. Students who earn the 18 honors credits and maintain a minimum 3.5 GPA, but who choose not to complete a thesis project, remain in the program but do not receive the designated diploma.

Admission Process: For strongest consideration, students aspiring for admission to the Berry Scholars Program should apply to the University for admission by January 1 and to the Berry Scholars Program by February 1. The Office of Admission designates honors student status, and only students admitted to the Honors Program may apply to the Berry Scholars Program. Admission to the Berry Scholars Program is a two-step process. After reviewing Berry Scholar applications, only a certain number of applicants are invited to interview with the program director or associate director and selected faculty and staff members. Out of these, 30 students are chosen.

Invitations to interview for the Berry Scholars Program are extended, usually beginning in February, and interviews continue well into March. While applications are accepted until April 1, applicants should be aware that February 1 is the deadline for strongest consideration. Invitations for most of the thirty places in the program are usually extended by April 1, and May 1 is the final deadline for acceptance. Current application deadlines and procedures can be found at the Web site.

Scholarship Availability: The Office of Scholarship awards scholarships to incoming students, and admission to the Honors Program enhances those opportunities. In addition, the Berry Scholars Program awards to those students admitted as Berry Scholars a special John W. Berry Sr. Scholarship that increases their scholarship awards to full tuition over the course of four years. Berry Scholars may also take more than the allowed 17 credit hours without further cost, allowing for multiple majors and/or degrees. In addition, generous funding is available to Berry Scholars for the required international study and to Honors and Berry students for research related to their Honors Thesis projects.

Campus Overview

Independent Roman Catholic university, founded 1850 • **Coed** 7,158 undergraduate students, 93% full-time, 50% women, 50% men.

Undergraduates 6,675 full-time, 483 part-time. Students come from 49 states and territories, 25 other countries, 34% are from out of state, 4% African American, 1% Asian American or Pacific Islander, 2% Hispanic American, 0.2% Native American, 0.6% international, 2% transferred in, 79% live on campus.

Faculty *Total:* 823, 48% full-time. *Student/faculty ratio:* 14:1.

Academic Programs *Special study options:* academic remediation for entering students, accelerated degree program, adult/continuing education programs, advanced placement credit, cooperative education, distance learning, double majors, English as a second language, honors programs, independent study, internships, off-campus study, part-time degree program, services for LD students, student-designed majors, study abroad, summer session for credit. *ROTC:* Army (b), Air Force (c).

Athletics Member NCAA. All Division I except football (Division I-AA). *Intercollegiate sports:* baseball M(s), basketball M(s)/W(s), crew W, cross-country running M(s)/W(s), golf M(s)/W(s), soccer M(s)/W(s), softball W(s), tennis M(s)/W(s), track and field W(s), volleyball W(s). *Intramural sports:* archery M(c)/W(c), baseball M(c), basketball M/W, crew M(c), football M/W, ice hockey M(c), lacrosse M(c)/W(c), racquetball M/W, rugby M(c)/W(c), soccer M(c)/W(c), softball M/W, tennis M/W, track and field M(c), ultimate Frisbee M(c)/W(c), volleyball M(c)/W(c), water polo M(c).

Costs (2004–05) *One-time required fee:* $1200. *Comprehensive fee:* $26,550 includes full-time tuition ($19,570), mandatory fees ($680), and room and board ($6300). Full-time tuition and fees vary according to program. Part-time tuition: $652 per credit hour. Part-time tuition and fees vary according to course load and program.

Required fees: $25 per term part-time. *College room only:* $3600. Room and board charges vary according to board plan, housing facility, and student level.

Financial Aid 972 Federal Work-Study jobs (averaging $1290). 2,616 state and other part-time jobs (averaging $1380). In 2003, 2009 non-need-based awards were made. *Average percent of need met:* 82%. *Average financial aid package:* $13,325. *Average need-based loan:* $4152. *Average need-based gift aid:* $8340. *Average non-need-based aid:* $4988.

Contact: Director, 125 Alumni Hall, Dayton, Ohio 45469-0311; *Telephone:* 937-229-4615; *Fax:* 937-229-4298; *E-mail:* honorsinfo@ notes.udayton.edu

The University of Findlay
Honors Program
Findlay, Ohio

The University of Findlay Honors Program provides a challenging educational experience that enriches and accelerates a student's academic growth. The program encourages and stimulates students beyond general academic excellence by providing opportunities for independent research, individual guidance, and specially designed courses and seminars. Students design their own honors curriculum by virtue of the projects they develop and the honors classes they choose.

Admission to the Honors Program requires a certain GPA for semester hours earned. Freshmen, however, may be admitted to the program during the first semester on the basis of their high school GPA and ACT score. Students must also obtain the recommendations of 2 faculty members for admission to the program.

Students who choose to develop their own projects do so through either a 1-hour contract or an independent research project. Both options allow students to pursue individual academic interests in conjunction with a professor who works with the student on the project. The projects are approved by the Honors Advisory Board on the basis of academic scope and depth and creativity. Students may also enroll in honors seminars that are developed by faculty members and are offered each semester on a one-time basis. These seminars are intense courses challenging the highest level of academic excellence within various fields of the liberal arts curriculum, offering honors students the opportunity to study beyond the regular curriculum. In addition, honors students may enroll in graduate classes in the Liberal Studies Program for honors credits.

Since its beginning in 1984, the Honors Program has enjoyed continuous growth and currently enrolls 150 students. In 1995, the faculty adopted new goals for the program. Whereas previous goals emphasized independent study, present goals now include more freshman participation, more opportunities that challenge the highest level of academic excellence, more opportunities for faculty development and collaborative faculty-student research, and an environment that encourages the aspirations and the achievement of superior students. The Honors Program sponsors Academic Excellence Day each year to give students the opportunity to present papers and projects to the entire campus.

Participation Requirements: In order to graduate as an Honors Scholar in a particular field, a student must have accumulated 16 hours of honors credits, 4 of which are a senior major independent research project, with grades of B or above in all honors endeavors. The student must also have accumulated a 3.5 or higher GPA. Honors Scholars are recognized by designation in the graduation program, the University of Findlay bachelor's hood, and a special diploma from the Honors Program.

Scholarship Availability: The University of Findlay offers numerous scholarships to students of exceptional ability.

Campus Overview

Independent comprehensive, founded 1882, affiliated with Church of God • **Coed** 3,460 undergraduate students, 76% full-time, 59% women, 41% men.

Undergraduates 2,622 full-time, 838 part-time. Students come from 45 states and territories, 34 other countries, 13% are from out of state, 3% African American, 1% Asian American or Pacific Islander, 1% Hispanic American, 0.3% Native American, 3% international, 4% transferred in, 41% live on campus.

Faculty *Total:* 356, 47% full-time. *Student/faculty ratio:* 19:1.

Academic Programs *Special study options:* academic remediation for entering students, accelerated degree program, adult/continuing education programs, advanced placement credit, cooperative education, distance learning, double majors, English as a second language, honors programs, independent study, internships, off-campus study, part-time degree program, services for LD students, student-designed majors, study abroad, summer session for credit. *ROTC:* Army (c), Air Force (c). *Unusual degree programs:* 3-2 nursing with Mount Carmel College of Nursing.

Athletics Member NCAA. All Division II. *Intercollegiate sports:* baseball M(s), basketball M(s)/W(s), cross-country running M(s)/W(s), football M(s), golf M(s)/W(s), ice hockey M(c)/W(c), soccer M(s)/W(s), softball W(s), swimming and diving M(s)/W(s), tennis M(s)/W(s), track and field M(s)/W(s), volleyball M(s)/W(s), water polo M(c)/W(c), wrestling M(s). *Intramural sports:* basketball M/W, volleyball M/W.

Costs (2004–05) *Comprehensive fee:* $28,188 includes full-time tuition ($19,996), mandatory fees ($918), and room and board ($7274). Full-time tuition and fees vary according to location and program. Part-time tuition: $440 per semester hour. Part-time tuition and fees vary according to location and program. *Required fees:* $120 per term part-time. *College room only:* $3646. Room and board charges vary according to housing facility.

Financial Aid 300 Federal Work-Study jobs (averaging $830). In 2003, 400 non-need-based awards were made. *Average percent of need met:* 84%. *Average financial aid package:* $14,150. *Average need-based loan:* $4000. *Average need-based gift aid:* $9100. *Average non-need-based aid:* $7200.

Contact: Director: Dr. Marie Louden-Hanes, Assistant Vice President, Academic Enhancement, The University of Findlay, 1000 North Main Street, Findlay, Ohio 45840-3695; *Telephone:* 419-434-4504; 800-472-9502 (toll-free) *Fax:* 419-434-4675; *E-mail:* louden-hanes@findlay.edu; *Web site:* http://www.findlay.edu

The University of Toledo
University Honors Program
Toledo, Ohio

The Honors Program at the University of Toledo provides an academically stimulating environment that encourages students to make the most of their University education. Students meet other students with similar interests, become involved in research or creative projects, work with honors faculty members, attend conferences, and receive help in preparing for future career or professional goals.

The University Honors Program is available across all colleges and in all majors, including interdepartmental programs such as Africana studies and women's and gender studies. Honors courses are offered within various departments as well as in the Honors Program itself, providing a wide range of selections for students in the program.

Among the many advantages of honors participation is the option of taking courses designed with honors students in mind. These *courses are smaller in size, focus on student-faculty interaction, may be set up as interdisciplinary seminars, and give students an opportunity to get to know their peers and their professors. Honors seminars cover a range of disciplines and issues; recent examples include The Legacy of Vietnam, Archaeology of Ancient Egypt, and Political Leadership.*

In addition to a range of stimulating courses, honors students have the chance to meet other honors students through participation in the Student Honors Society, attendance at student Brown Bag Presentations, and participation in service learning, as well as through many other intellectual, social, and community events.

The Honors Program also encourages student participation at regional and national research conferences. Many students present their research, read or perform creative work, or exhibit artwork and other projects to academic audiences. Students also receive help and advice in applying for various scholarships, internships, or travel-abroad programs.

Honors students have priority advanced registration when enrolling in their courses, and the honors staff and departmental advisers provide personal attention in academic advising, including advice about overall educational and personal objectives, assistance in graduate and professional school selection, and the preparation of letters of recommendation.

Students graduating from the Honors Program receive a citation on their diplomas and special recognition at graduation. In addition, students are awarded an honors medallion upon graduation.

The 41-year-old program currently enrolls more than 800 students.

Admission Process: Admission to the Honors Program is based on high school GPA, ACT or SAT I scores, an extracurricular résumé, and references. Students entering directly from high school with a 3.75 GPA or higher and an ACT composite of 28 or higher (or SAT I combined score of 1260 or higher) are encouraged to apply. Highly motivated students with at least a 3.5 GPA and an ACT composite of at least 25 (or minimum SAT I combined score of 1140) are also considered for admission to the program.

Scholarship Availability: Many honors students receive University-sponsored scholarships, such as the Founders Scholarship and the Tower Excellence Scholarship. The minimal application standards for many other scholarships are the same as for the Honors Program. The Huebner Scholarship, available through the Honors Program, offers short-term aid to honors students in need. Sullivan Fellowships are available to support honors student research.

Campus Overview

State-supported university, founded 1872 • **Coed** 16,366 undergraduate students, 80% full-time, 51% women, 49% men.

Undergraduates 13,146 full-time, 3,220 part-time. Students come from 36 states and territories, 93 other countries, 8% are from out of state, 12% African American, 2% Asian American or Pacific Islander, 2% Hispanic American, 0.2% Native American, 2% international, 7% transferred in, 18% live on campus.

Faculty *Total:* 1,281, 59% full-time, 54% with terminal degrees. *Student/faculty ratio:* 19:1.

Academic Programs *Special study options:* academic remediation for entering students, adult/continuing education programs, advanced placement credit, cooperative education, distance learning, double majors, honors programs, independent study, internships, off-campus study, part-time degree program, services for LD students, student-designed majors, study abroad, summer session for credit. *ROTC:* Army (b), Air Force (c).

Athletics Member NCAA. All Division I. *Intercollegiate sports:* baseball M(s), basketball M(s)/W(s), cross-country running M(s)/W(s), football M(s), golf M(s)/W(s), ice hockey M(s)/W(s), lacrosse M(s)/W(s), soccer W(s), softball W(s), swimming and diving M(s)/W(s), tennis M(s)/W(s), track and field M(s)/W(s), volleyball W(s). *Intramural sports:* badminton M/W, basketball M/W, bowling M/W, crew M(c)/W(c), fencing M(c)/W(c), football M/W, golf M/W, lacrosse M/W, racquetball M/W, sailing M(c)/W(c), skiing (cross-country) M(c)/W(c), skiing (downhill) M(c)/W(c), soccer M(c)/W(c), softball M/W, swimming and diving M/W, table tennis M/W, tennis M/W, track and field M/W, volleyball M/W, water polo M/W, weight lifting M/W.

Costs (2004–05) *Tuition:* state resident $5990 full-time, $294 per semester hour part-time; nonresident $14,801 full-time, $661 per semester hour part-time. Full-time tuition and fees vary according to course load, program, and reciprocity agreements. Part-time tuition and fees vary according to course load, program, and reciprocity agreements. *Required fees:* $1064 full-time. *Room and board:* $7488. Room and board charges vary according to board plan, housing facility, and location.

Financial Aid 520 Federal Work-Study jobs (averaging $2333). In 2004, 1466 non-need-based awards were made. *Average percent of need met:* 52%. *Average financial aid package:* $6583. *Average need-based loan:* $3526. *Average need-based gift aid:* $4577. *Average non-need-based aid:* $3079.

Contact: Director: David Hoch, Sullivan Hall, Mailstop #504, The University of Toledo, Toledo, Ohio 43606-3390; *Telephone:* 419-530-6030; *Fax:* 419-530-6032; *E-mail:* honors@utoledo.edu; *Web site:* http://honors.utoledo.edu

Walsh University
General Honors Program
North Canton, Ohio

The Honors Program at Walsh University engages top students in a uniquely cohesive and personally empowering educational experience. The honors curriculum consists of a sequence of interdisciplinary courses, including team-taught seminars and an original thesis project, all focused on the unifying theme of "Bridging Analysis and Creativity." Students are encouraged to amplify their scholarly research with creative projects engaging their own personal interests and talents. Outside of the classroom, honors students have the advantage of enriching cultural and social activities planned especially for them. As members of the Walsh University Honors Society, honors students join with faculty, administrators, and peers in fostering a community of learners with a shared sense of purpose in the pursuit of academic excellence.

The program began in the 1993–94 academic year. There are currently 65 students in the program, which can accommodate up to 30 students in each of the freshman, sophomore, junior, and senior classes.

Participation Requirements: In their freshman year, students in the General Honors Program take special sections of history and English. In their sophomore year, they take two special sections of honors world literature. Qualified transfer and second-year students can join the Honors Program under the Track II option with Honors 200.

In their junior year, honors students take two team-taught, interdisciplinary courses with rotating topics and complete a junior honors project in one of their regularly scheduled upper-division courses, usually in their major.

The capstone of the Honors Program is the senior honors thesis, an independent research project of either 3 or 6 credits that allows students to investigate issues of significance while working closely with a supportive faculty mentor. Honors projects are modeled on the types of research, writing, and creativity typical of graduate schools and are meant to serve as preparation for such study. The project includes an oral presentation in a final celebration with faculty members and peers in fulfilling the final requirements of the program.

All honors courses except the senior thesis fulfill either core or major requirements. Students completing the General Honors Program graduate with 27 to 30 credit hours of honors courses. Track II students graduate with 18 to 21 credit hours.

Admission Process: To be eligible to apply for the General Honors Program, students must meet any two of the following three criteria: a high school GPA of 3.5 or above, a minimum ACT score of 27 or a minimum SAT I score of 1200, and graduation in the top 10 percent of one's high school class. Students who apply and meet these criteria are invited to be interviewed on Scholarship Days, which take place in February. Track II candidates must have completed at least 30 credit hours of undergraduate work with at least a 3.3 GPA. Students remain in good standing in the Honors Program with a 3.3 cumulative GPA and at least a grade of B in all honors courses.

Scholarship Availability: The University offers a limited number of full-tuition Presidential Scholarships to incoming freshmen. Presidential Scholars are automatically part of the Honors Program. To apply for a Presidential Scholarship a student must meet two of the following three criteria: 4.0 GPA, rank in the upper 1 percent of the graduating class, and a minimum score of 31 on the ACT or 1230 on the SAT I. All other students accepted into the Honors Program receive a $1500 Honors Program Scholarship in addition to other scholarships they may qualify for. Honors Program Scholarships are renewable each year a student remains eligible for the program.

Campus Overview

Independent Roman Catholic comprehensive, founded 1958 • **Coed** 1,694 undergraduate students, 74% full-time, 61% women, 39% men.

Undergraduates 1,261 full-time, 433 part-time. Students come from 17 states and territories, 8 other countries, 3% are from out of state, 6% African American, 0.3% Asian American or Pacific Islander, 0.8% Hispanic American, 0.5% Native American, 2% international, 8% transferred in, 50% live on campus.

Faculty *Total:* 172, 45% full-time, 56% with terminal degrees. *Student/faculty ratio:* 14:1.

Academic Programs *Special study options:* academic remediation for entering students, accelerated degree program, adult/continuing education programs, advanced placement credit, double majors, English as a second language, freshman honors college, honors programs, independent study, internships, off-campus study, part-time degree program, services for LD students, study abroad, summer session for credit. *Unusual degree programs:* 3-2 forestry with University of Michigan; behavioral science/counseling; biology/physical therapy.

Athletics Member NAIA. *Intercollegiate sports:* baseball M(s), basketball M(s)/W(s), cheerleading W, cross-country running M(s)/W(s), football M(s), golf M(s)/W(s), soccer M(s)/W(s), softball W(s), tennis M(s)/W(s), track and field M(s)/W(s), volleyball W(s). *Intramural sports:* basketball M/W, bowling M/W, football M/W, soccer M/W, softball M/W, table tennis M/W, volleyball M/W.

Costs (2004–05) *One-time required fee:* $165. *Comprehensive fee:* $23,310 includes full-time tuition ($15,100), mandatory fees ($510), and room and board ($7700). Full-time tuition and fees vary according to course load. Part-time tuition: $500 per credit. *Required fees:* $17 per credit part-time. *College room only:* $4500. Room and board charges vary according to board plan and housing facility.

Financial Aid 182 Federal Work-Study jobs (averaging $1480). 30 state and other part-time jobs (averaging $1418). In 2003, 157 non-need-based awards were made. *Average percent of need met:* 81%. *Average financial aid package:* $10,364. *Average need-based loan:* $2424. *Average need-based gift aid:* $5602. *Average non-need-based aid:* $4312.

Contact: Director: Dr. John Kandl, 2020 East Maple Street, NW, North Canton, Ohio 44720; *Telephone:* 330-490-7127; *Fax:* 330-499-8518; *E-mail:* jkandl@walsh.edu

Wittenberg University
University Honors Program
Springfield, Ohio

*T*he Wittenberg University Honors Program, which was created in 1978, heightens and enhances the rich variety of intellectual experiences possible in a liberal arts education. The program provides an academic and social climate in which students of high academic potential can find a community of classmates and teachers engaged in intellectual inquiry at the highest level. The program brings students together in special, often interdisciplinary seminars during the sophomore and junior years and affords mutual support as each student undertakes independent work culminating in a senior honors thesis or project within the major. Housed in the beautiful historic Matthies House, the program invites students to use the study and social facilities in the house.

Participation Requirements: Since fall 2002, students awarded the Smith and Matthies scholarships are inducted into the University Honors Program and enjoy full membership privileges as soon as they have registered for classes. Other students who achieve a grade-point average of 3.5 or higher in the course of their first and second years are automatically invited to apply early in spring semester each year. The application, which may vary in content from year to year, generally consists of a critical reaction to one of a number of scholarly articles chosen by the Honors Committee from different disciplines in order to appeal to the greatest number of possible applicants. Candidates are also asked to provide the names of two faculty members familiar with their work whom members of the committee might contact as references.

To graduate with University Honors, students must complete at least two Honors seminars, complete and successfully defend an Honors Thesis in the department of their major area of study, and maintain a minimum 3.5 cumulative grade-point average.

Admission Process: No students are automatically admitted to the program but, instead, must apply for admission in January of their first year at Wittenberg.

Scholarship Availability: The University awards substantial scholarships based on academic excellence, but none are awarded through the Honors Program. Small grants help senior honors students with costs of the senior honors thesis/project.

Campus Overview

Independent comprehensive, founded 1845, affiliated with Evangelical Lutheran Church • **Coed** 2,177 undergraduate students, 92% full-time, 57% women, 43% men.

Undergraduates 2,013 full-time, 164 part-time. Students come from 38 states and territories, 14 other countries, 25% are from out of state, 6% African American, 0.9% Asian American or Pacific Islander, 1% Hispanic American, 0.4% Native American, 2% international, 1% transferred in, 86% live on campus.

Faculty *Total:* 202, 73% full-time, 77% with terminal degrees. *Student/faculty ratio:* 13:1.

Academic Programs *Special study options:* academic remediation for entering students, accelerated degree program, adult/continuing education programs, advanced placement credit, cooperative education, double majors, English as a second language, freshman honors college, honors programs, independent study, internships, off-campus study, part-time degree program, student-designed majors, study abroad, summer session for credit. *ROTC:* Army (c), Air Force (c). *Unusual degree programs:* 3-2 engineering with Georgia Institute of Technology, Washington University in St. Louis, Case Western Reserve University; forestry with Duke University; nursing with Case Western Reserve University, Johns Hopkins University; occupational therapy with Washington University in St. Louis.

Athletics Member NCAA. All Division III. *Intercollegiate sports:* baseball M, basketball M/W, cheerleading M/W, crew M(c)/W(c), cross-country running M/W, equestrian sports W(c), field hockey W, football M, golf M/W, ice hockey M(c), lacrosse M/W, rugby M(c)/W(c), soccer M/W, softball W, swimming and diving M/W, tennis M/W, track and field M/W, volleyball M(c)/W. *Intramural sports:* archery M/W, badminton M/W, basketball M/W, fencing M/W, football M/W, golf M/W, racquetball M/W, sailing M/W, skiing (downhill) M/W, soccer M/W, softball M/W, swimming and diving M/W, table tennis M/W, tennis M/W, track and field M/W, ultimate Frisbee M/W, volleyball M/W, water polo M/W, weight lifting M/W.

Costs (2004–05) *Comprehensive fee:* $32,882 includes full-time tuition ($26,040), mandatory fees ($156), and room and board ($6686). Part-time tuition: $826 per hour. Part-time tuition and fees vary according to course load. *College room only:* $3454. Room and board charges vary according to board plan.

Financial Aid 690 Federal Work-Study jobs (averaging $1545). 791 state and other part-time jobs (averaging $1486). In 2003, 514 non-need-based awards were made. *Average financial aid package:* $20,750. *Average need-based loan:* $4564. *Average need-based gift aid:* $16,355. *Average non-need-based aid:* $10,047.

Contact: Director: Dr. Timothy L. Wilderson, Wittenberg University, P.O. Box 720, Springfield, Ohio 45501-0720; *Telephone:* 937-327-6357; *Fax:* 937-327-6340; *E-mail:* twilkerson@wittenberg.edu; *Web site:* http://www4.wittenberg.edu/academics/honors/

Wright State University
University Honors Program
Dayton, Ohio

The Wright State University Honors Program was created in 1972 to meet the needs of the University's brightest, most ambitious students. It is open to students of all majors and provides a varied curriculum consisting of honors sections of general education courses; service-learning courses; interdisciplinary core courses in the humanities, social sciences, and natural sciences; and broadly interdisciplinary topical senior seminars. Departments are also free to propose honors sections of regular courses at both the introductory and advanced level. First-year students are able to participate in learning communities of linked courses in which the same 20 students enroll. Most majors offer students the opportunity for intense honors work in the major during the senior year. Students may choose from three honors designations, which are noted on the transcript and in the Commencement program: University Honors Scholar, General Studies Honors, and Departmental Honors.

The primary mission of the Honors Program is to produce a body of graduates who are well-educated, socially conscious, and capable of assuming leadership roles in society. The Honors Program is responsible for providing undergraduates with all the tools and every opportunity to create a stimulating, well-rounded, solidly grounded, and socially responsible education. The program currently has approximately 1,500 alumni, disproportionately distributed in the medical, legal, and academic professions, where many of them are beginning to move into leadership roles. Alumni surveys indicate that the program is fulfilling its mission.

The Honors Program encourages diversity in its student body, faculty members, course content, and extracurricular activities. Transfer students and nontraditional students are particularly welcome additions to the student mix. Students who complete honors work at another NCHC institution receive honors credit at Wright State for those courses.

Honors classes are small—between 15 and 24 students. Faculty members are encouraged to try innovative, student-centered teaching styles. Honors classes usually feature discussion, collaboration, creative projects, or extensive research papers. Most honors courses are writing-intensive. Ongoing assessment indicates that students are happy with their honors courses, often citing them as the only undergraduate courses that challenged them to think analytically. To recognize and encourage outstanding teaching, the students select a faculty member as Honors Teacher of the Year.

About 9 percent (345 members) of each incoming class enter the University as honors students. The overall number of active participants averages about 900. Honors students may elect to live in the 384-bed Honors Community, which features one 25-station computer classroom and another twenty-five-seat electronic classroom as well as social and commercial space. The Honors Faculty in Residence lives in the building and sponsors academically oriented programming.

Participation Requirements: To remain active, students must maintain a minimum 3.0 GPA and make progress toward graduation with honors. Approximately 90 students complete one of the honors degree options each year. To meet their requirements, students choose from sixty to seventy courses each year. Students who complete University Honors take a minimum of eight honors courses plus a departmental program. General Studies Honors requires eight courses and a minimum cumulative GPA of 3.4. Many departmental programs also require students to complete at least one University Honors seminar.

Admission Process: Students are admitted to the program based on high school or college performance.

Scholarship Availability: Honors students are supported by a comprehensive scholarship program. Up to 60 incoming students receive substantial Honors Scholarships that commit them to four years of participation in the Honors Program. Continuing students compete for awards of varying amounts. Several modest awards are usually offered each quarter. Upper-division honors students are recognized with Distinguished Senior Awards, research grants, and the Heritage and Salsburg Scholarships. An Honors Program Development Fund exists to help students with travel to conferences, international study, and other extracurricular opportunities.

Campus Overview
State-supported university, founded 1964 • **Coed** 12,128 undergraduate students, 85% full-time, 57% women, 43% men.

Undergraduates 10,281 full-time, 1,847 part-time. Students come from 49 states and territories, 66 other countries, 3% are from out of state, 12% African American, 2% Asian American or Pacific Islander, 1% Hispanic American, 0.4% Native American, 1% international, 7% transferred in, 22% live on campus.

Faculty Total: 756, 96% full-time. *Student/faculty ratio:* 20:1.

Academic Programs *Special study options:* academic remediation for entering students, adult/continuing education programs, advanced placement credit, cooperative education, English as a second language, honors programs, internships, off-campus study, part-time degree program, services for LD students, student-designed majors, study abroad, summer session for credit. *ROTC:* Army (b), Air Force (b).

Athletics Member NCAA. All Division I. *Intercollegiate sports:* baseball M(s), basketball M(s)/W(s), cross-country running M(s)/W(s), golf M(s), soccer M(s)/W(s), softball W(s), swimming and diving M(s)/W(s), tennis M(s)/W(s), track and field W(s), volleyball W(s). *Intramural sports:* baseball M, basketball M/W, cheerleading M/W, cross-country running M/W, football M/W, golf M/W, racquetball M(c)/W(c), rugby M(c)/W(c), skiing (downhill) M(c)/W(c), soccer M/W, softball M/W, squash M/W, table tennis M(c)/W(c), tennis M/W, volleyball M(c)/W.

Costs (2004–05) *Tuition:* state resident $6477 full-time, $197 per hour part-time; nonresident $12,492 full-time, $381 per hour part-time. *Room and board:* $6328. Room and board charges vary according to board plan and housing facility.

Financial Aid In 2002, 4027 non-need-based awards were made. *Average financial aid package:* $7857.

Contact: Director: Dr. Susan Carrafiello, 3640 Colonel Glenn Highway, Dayton, Ohio 45435; *Telephone:* 937-775-2660; *E-mail:* honors@wright.edu; *Web site:* http://www.wright.edu/academics/honors

Youngstown State University
University Scholars and Honors Programs
Youngstown, Ohio

The Honors Program is designed to create a continuing community of intellectual excellence. Exceptional students brought together from diverse disciplines and challenged with extraordinary courses and learning experiences outside the classroom can find in the program opportunities to develop their full cultural and intellectual potential, with their unique academic achievements being recognized with an honors degree. Intended to foster interdisciplinary interaction, self-expression, experimentation, leadership, and academic excellence, the Honors Program serves as a tangible emblem of Youngstown State University's (YSU) commitment to education, teaching innovation, and cultural enrichment.

The 25-year-old program currently enrolls 400 students.

Participation Requirements: To graduate from the Honors Program, students must have a minimum 3.4 GPA overall and have completed 24 credit hours of honors courses, with 12 hours from the general education requirement, 6 hours of upper-division credits, 1 credit of honors seminars, and a senior thesis. Students wear an honors medal at Commencement, and, upon graduation, students are distinguished by a diploma recognizing their honors degree.

Admission Process: First-quarter students either in the top 15 percent of their high school graduating class or with a minimum ACT score of 26 (or minimum combined SAT I score of 1160) as well as other interested students may apply. University Scholars who have an ACT score of at least 28 or an SAT I score of at least 1260 are automatically enrolled in the program. Students who have completed at least 12 hours with a minimum GPA of 3.4 are also encouraged to join the Honors Program.

Scholarship Availability: The University Scholarship is YSU's most prestigious scholarship. These are awarded to first-year students who have graduated from high school in the same year that they will enroll at YSU as full-time students. Candidates must have, as minimum criteria for award consideration, a score of 28 or better on the ACT or 1220 or better on the SAT I and be recognized as National Merit or Achievement Semifinalist or rank in the upper 15 percent of high school class pursuing a college-preparatory curriculum. The value of the scholarship (estimated at $14,000) includes all fees and tuition up to 16 hours per semester, plus campus room and board fees and a $360 academic-year book allowance. If renewed for four years of study, the estimated value of the scholarship is $56,000.

Forty new University scholarships are awarded annually for a total of 160.

Campus Overview

State-supported comprehensive, founded 1908 • **Coed** 11,796 undergraduate students, 79% full-time, 56% women, 44% men.

Undergraduates 9,372 full-time, 2,424 part-time. Students come from 35 states and territories, 56 other countries, 9% are from out of state, 11% African American, 0.9% Asian American or Pacific Islander, 2% Hispanic American, 0.4% Native American, 0.5% international, 5% transferred in, 10% live on campus.

Faculty *Total:* 989, 43% full-time, 47% with terminal degrees. *Student/faculty ratio:* 18:1.

Academic Programs *Special study options:* academic remediation for entering students, accelerated degree program, adult/continuing education programs, advanced placement credit, cooperative education, distance learning, double majors, English as a second language, honors programs, internships, off-campus study, part-time degree program, services for LD students, student-designed majors, study abroad, summer session for credit. *ROTC:* Army (b), Air Force (c). *Unusual degree programs:* 3-2 chemistry.

Athletics Member NCAA. All Division I except football (Division I-AA). *Intercollegiate sports:* baseball M(s), basketball M(s)/W(s), cross-country running M(s)/W(s), golf M(s)/W, soccer W, softball W(s), swimming and diving W, tennis M(s)/W(s), track and field M(s)/W(s), volleyball W(s). *Intramural sports:* badminton M/W, basketball M/W, bowling M/W, golf M/W, ice hockey M/W, lacrosse M/W, racquetball M/W, soccer M/W, softball M/W, swimming and diving M/W, table tennis M/W, tennis M/W, ultimate Frisbee M/W, volleyball M/W, water polo M/W.

Costs (2004–05) *Tuition:* state resident $5655 full-time, $236 per credit part-time; nonresident $10,863 full-time, $453 per credit part-time. Full-time tuition and fees vary according to course load. Part-time tuition and fees vary according to course load. *Required fees:* $229 full-time, $10 per credit part-time. *Room and board:* $6100. Room and board charges vary according to board plan and housing facility.

Financial Aid 657 Federal Work-Study jobs (averaging $1896).

Contact: Assistant Director: Amy Cossentino; *Telephone:* 330-941-2772; *Fax:* 330-941-4743; *E-mail:* alcossentino@ysu.edu; *Web site:* http://www.ysu.edu/honors/index.htm

OKLAHOMA

East Central University
Scholastic Honors Program
Ada, Oklahoma

The East Central University (ECU) Scholastic Honors Program embodies high ideals of academic excellence through which students are provided challenging college experiences and enriched opportunities. Honors students are nurtured through vibrant and distinctive seminar-type classes that are mature in scope, content, and student application. An honors course does not accomplish this by simply increasing the quantitative workload beyond that expected of a nonhonors student but by establishing an environment of scholarly interchange between students and faculty members. Small class size, flexible teaching and learning styles, independent research and presentation, critical-thinking skill development, community involvement, and student collaboration are essential in the honors student's growth and degree progress. There are approximately 250 active honors students in the program.

Participation Requirements: The Honors Program consists of honors courses offered throughout the student's college career. A student who wishes to graduate with University Honors completes a minimum of 26 hours of honors-designated course work as follows: a 1-hour freshman colloquium required during the first semester at ECU and essential in the preparation of honors study, 6 hours from Honors General Humanities I and II or Early and Modern Western Civilization, 9 or more additional hours in honors general education course work, 6 hours contracted in the student's specialized major or senior thesis, and a 3-hour senior interdisciplinary capstone experience. Specialized honors courses are offered in the fields of communication, Western literature, philosophy, critical thinking, and ethics. Students wishing to have the honors designation on their diploma and transcript must maintain at least a 3.0 throughout their college career, and a completed portfolio of the student's research must be on file in the Honors Office.

Transfer students or upperclass students may be admitted to honors and graduate with Departmental Honors. This 9-hour minimum option requires students to complete honors research in their major field and the senior capstone course. Transfer students may include in their degree plan honors courses taken at other institutions but must be approved by the Honors Board.

Students completing all honors degree requirements are recognized at commencement, and final transcripts note their graduation with scholastic honors. The Honors Student Association, a student-led service organization on campus, provides monetary awards each year for the best original research. This student organization participates in many community service projects, funds student presentations at professional conferences, and chaperones and advises incoming freshman scholarship students as they are oriented and enrolled on campus.

Admission Process: Incoming freshmen with a high school GPA of at least 3.5 and a composite ACT score of 24 (with a letter of recommendation) or a composite ACT score of 26 or higher are invited by the Honors Board to apply for admission to the program. Admission is based on academic experience, a demonstration of writing skills, and extracurricular activities. Any continuing or transfer students may petition for admission if their GPA is 3.5 or greater or if they are recommended by other faculty members.

Scholarship Availability: Scholarships of various amounts are awarded through the Office of Student Services based on academic performance and include the Regents, Presidential, Dean's, Academic, and Human Diversity Scholarships. While scholarships are not directly offered through honors, most honors students are recipients of academic scholarships, and participation in honors enhances the student's ability to obtain financial assistance.

Campus Overview

State-supported comprehensive, founded 1909, part of Oklahoma State Regents for Higher Education • **Coed** 3,870 undergraduate students, 83% full-time, 61% women, 39% men.

Undergraduates 3,215 full-time, 655 part-time. Students come from 24 states and territories, 32 other countries, 4% are from out of state, 5% African American, 0.9% Asian American or Pacific Islander, 3% Hispanic American, 19% Native American.

Faculty *Total:* 203, 77% full-time. *Student/faculty ratio:* 19:1.

Academic Programs *Special study options:* academic remediation for entering students, adult/continuing education programs, advanced placement credit, distance learning, double majors, honors programs, independent study, internships, off-campus study, part-time degree program, services for LD students, summer session for credit.

Athletics Member NCAA, NAIA. All NCAA Division II. *Intercollegiate sports:* baseball M(s), basketball M(s)/W(s), cheerleading M/W, cross-country running M(s)/W(s), football M(s), golf M(s)/W, soccer W(s), softball W(s), tennis M(s)/W(s), track and field M/W. *Intramural sports:* basketball M/W, football M/W, racquetball M/W, soccer M/W, softball M/W, tennis M/W, volleyball M/W.

Costs (2004–05) *Tuition:* state resident $2996 full-time, $100 per semester hour part-time; nonresident $7169 full-time, $239 per semester hour part-time. Full-time tuition and fees vary according to course load. Part-time tuition and fees vary according to course load. *Required fees:* $956 full-time, $30 per semester hour part-time, $24 per term part-time. *Room and board:* $2910; room only: $1040. Room and board charges vary according to board plan and housing facility.

Financial Aid 181 Federal Work-Study jobs (averaging $2272). 401 state and other part-time jobs (averaging $6138). In 2004, 276 non-need-based awards were made. *Average percent of need met:* 66%. *Average financial aid package:* $8013. *Average need-based loan:* $3762. *Average need-based gift aid:* $5359. *Average non-need-based aid:* $3189.

Contact: Director: Dr. Dennis L. Boe, Box W-3, Ada, Oklahoma 74820; *Telephone:* 580-332-8000 Ext. 599; *Fax:* 580-436-3329 ; *E-mail:* dboe@mailclerk.ecok.edu; *Web site:* http://www.ecok.edu/acaddept/honors/

Northeastern State University
Honors Program
Tahlequah, Oklahoma

The Honors Program at Northeastern State University (NSU) is a challenging educational option for academically talented students who enjoy learning. Honors students work with distinguished faculty members and peers in enhanced courses, pursue independent research, and participate in cocurricular cultural experiences.

Benefits of being an honors student include academic scholarships through the Academic Scholars Program, Baccalaureate Scholars Program, or selected Collegiate Scholars; special honors courses; priority enrollment; enrichment activities, cultural events, and field trips; faculty mentorship on individual research projects; use of exclusive honors facilities; Honors Scholar recognition at graduation; and designation on the diploma.

The Honors Program at NSU offers a unique opportunity for gifted students to grow academically in an intellectually stimulating student-friendly environment.

Participation Requirements: To maintain honors eligibility, students must maintain a minimum GPA and follow the approved Honors Program contract.

Admission Process: Students must have an ACT composite score of 30 or higher with a high school GPA of 3.5 or higher, an ACT composite score of 29 with a high school GPA of 3.65 or higher, or an ACT composite score of 28 with a high school GPA of 3.8 or higher; a high school ranking within the upper 10 percent; and a written essay read and approved by the Honors Committee. Students must also complete and submit an approved Application for Admission to Northeastern State University and the Northeastern State University Honors Program.

Scholarship Availability: One goal at NSU is to seek the best and brightest students. Each year, NSU awards many of these students scholarships based on merit and talent. All freshmen who meet the ACT score and/or GPA criteria are eligible to be considered for admission to the Honors Program. Students must remain in good academic standing to receive the eight-semester scholarship.

Campus Overview

State-supported comprehensive, founded 1846, part of Oklahoma State Regents for Higher Education • **Coed** 8,543 undergraduate students, 78% full-time, 60% women, 40% men.

Undergraduates 6,677 full-time, 1,866 part-time. Students come from 27 states and territories, 44 other countries, 0.1% are from out of state, 6% African American, 0.7% Asian American or Pacific Islander, 2% Hispanic American, 29% Native American, 2% international, 16% transferred in.

Faculty *Total:* 480. *Student/faculty ratio:* 24:1.

Academic Programs *Special study options:* academic remediation for entering students, adult/continuing education programs, advanced placement credit, distance learning, double majors, English as a second language, honors programs, internships, part-time degree program, services for LD students, summer session for credit. *ROTC:* Army (b).

Athletics Member NCAA. All Division II. *Intercollegiate sports:* baseball M(s), basketball M(s)/W(s), cheerleading M/W, football M(s), golf M(s)/W(s), soccer M(s)/W(s), softball W(s), tennis W(s). *Intramural sports:* basketball M/W, bowling M/W, football M, golf

M/W, racquetball M/W, soccer M/W, softball M/W, swimming and diving M/W, tennis W, track and field M, volleyball M/W, water polo M/W, weight lifting M, wrestling M.

Costs (2004–05) *Tuition:* state resident $3000 full-time, $100 per credit hour part-time; nonresident $7350 full-time, $245 per credit hour part-time. Full-time tuition and fees vary according to course level, course load, and location. Part-time tuition and fees vary according to course level and course load. *Room and board:* $3080. Room and board charges vary according to board plan and housing facility.

Financial Aid 314 Federal Work-Study jobs (averaging $2600). 761 state and other part-time jobs (averaging $3000). In 2002, 1080 non-need-based awards were made. *Average percent of need met:* 69%. *Average financial aid package:* $8100. *Average need-based loan:* $4100. *Average need-based gift aid:* $4050. *Average non-need-based aid:* $900.

Contact: Director: Dr. Karen Carey, Northeastern State University, 600 North Grand, Tahlequah, Oklahoma 74464; *Telephone:* 918-456-5511 Ext. 2236; *E-mail:* careyka@nsuok.edu; *Web site:* http://nsuok.edu/admissions/honors.html or http://arapaho.nsuok.edu/~honors

Oklahoma Baptist University
Honors Program
Shawnee, Oklahoma

The Oklahoma Baptist University (OBU) Honors Program offers academic enhancement and opportunities for independent study and fellowship with other academically outstanding students in all majors. The Honors Program curriculum includes some common classes and multiple opportunities for independent study, service, and travel. Students in the Honors Program are asked to complete two of three capstones—extended volunteer service, study abroad, and a senior thesis. Additional costs and course requirements above those required for normal graduation are minimal.

It is also possible to complete an honors degree by writing a thesis under the guidelines and direction of the University honors committee.

In the freshman year, Honors Program students complete a 3-hour Introduction to Honors (Critical Skills) course and a 3-hour honors version of Composition and Classical Literature in lieu of normal freshman English requirements. After the freshman year, students complete at least four honors colloquia (0–1 hour each), an honors biblical ethics course (in lieu of another required course in religion), a contracted study course in the major (1–2 hours), and two of three capstone experiences. Service internship requires a minimum of 80 clock hours on an approved project. Travel/study abroad requires at least four weeks of immersion in a non-U.S. cultural setting. The thesis requires an extended research and independent writing project completed under direction of a faculty adviser; thesis completion involves registration for a 3-hour independent study course. Students must maintain a 3.25 GPA overall to remain active in the program.

Students inside or outside of the Honors Program may elect to complete only the thesis for honors graduation. They must have a 3.5 GPA overall and in the major at the time of application (mid-junior year) and at completion. Students work with a faculty adviser, an off-campus reader, and the University honors committee, presenting several progress reports and eventually a public presentation/defense and a final document.

Participation Requirements: Participation is offered to all entering freshmen with a high school GPA of 3.5 or higher and scores of 29 (composite) on the ACT or 1300 (combined) on the SAT. Students with slightly lower test scores and high motivation are encouraged to apply as space is available. Occasionally other highly successful and motivated freshmen are allowed to join the program after the first semester of the freshman year. Transfer students who come to OBU after having been active in an honors program are admitted, but their experiences are assessed and requirements are adjusted individually.

Scholarship Availability: Many OBU students are awarded academic scholarships, but no scholarship aid is given simply for participation in the Honors Program. Some awards are made by the program to assist honors students to complete study abroad or thesis research.

Campus Overview
Independent Southern Baptist comprehensive, founded 1910 • **Small-town** 125-acre campus with easy access to Oklahoma City • **Coed**

Faculty *Student/faculty ratio:* 15:1.

Athletics Member NAIA.

Costs (2004–05) *Comprehensive fee:* $16,962 includes full-time tuition ($12,286), mandatory fees ($876), and room and board ($3800). Full-time tuition and fees vary according to course load. Part-time tuition: $385 per credit hour. Part-time tuition and fees vary according to course load. *College room only:* $1750. Room and board charges vary according to board plan and housing facility.

Financial Aid 303 Federal Work-Study jobs (averaging $834). In 2003, 432 non-need-based awards were made. *Average percent of need met:* 70. *Average financial aid package:* $10,644. *Average need-based loan:* $3834. *Average need-based gift aid:* $3301. *Average non-need-based aid:* $4398.

Contact: Contact: Director: Dr. Karen Youmans, OBU Box 61244, 500 West University, Shawnee, Oklahoma 74804; *E-mail:* karen.youmans@mail.okbu.edu; *Web site:* http://www.okbu.edu/honors

Oklahoma City University
University Honors Program
Oklahoma City, Oklahoma

Oklahoma City University (OCU) established the University Honors Program in 1990 to meet the special interests and needs of intellectually gifted students. Open to qualified undergraduates of all majors, the University Honors Program offers honors sections of general education courses as well as the opportunity to complete Honors contracts and research. Honors students may choose from a wide variety of these courses, which include psychology, biology, literature and philosophy, history, and many others. During their first semester in the Honors Program, all new students enroll in the 1-hour Honors Colloquium, a course designed to help each class of honors students become better acquainted with each other and the Honors Program. The capstone honors course is the Junior-Senior Seminar, which is offered with varying topics each semester.

At Oklahoma City University, an honors course generally covers the same material as a traditional course, but honors sections are smaller and more often use a seminar format. The requirements differ from those of regular classes, not so much in the amount of work demanded as in the type of work. Honors classes typically involve extensive class participation, and written work is often in the form of essays or individual research projects. The program also hosts an annual Undergraduate Research Day.

In addition to the academic advantages of the University Honors Program, OCU honors students enjoy other benefits as well. Honors students have the benefit of priority semester enrollment and an additional .25 added to each credit hour of honors courses. Honors students have opportunities to meet with visiting scholars and attend special events, both social and academic. A special Honors Study in the library is the center for many Honors Program activities. As part of a network of the National Collegiate Honors Council, OCU honors students may present papers at regional and national conferences and participate in exciting summer and semester programs.

There are 120 students in the program.

Participation Requirements: In order to be a University Honors Program graduate, students must complete 25 hours in honors courses while maintaining at least a 3.5 cumulative university GPA and a 3.25 cumulative GPA in honors courses.

Two courses, the Honors Colloquium and the Junior-Senior Seminar, are required for all students in the program. Students may select from a variety of courses, including independent research, to complete the balance of the 25-hour requirement. Upon successful completion of the requirements, honors students receive special recognition upon graduation, a gold stole to wear at the Commencement ceremony with their cap and gown, and a special designation on their diplomas.

Admission Process: Admission to the Honors Program is separate from admission to the University. First-year students must have a minimum ACT score of 27 or a minimum high school GPA of 3.75. Transfer students must have a GPA of at least 3.5; up to 6 hours of honors credit from another college or university counts toward OCU's Honors Program requirements. Enrolled OCU students must have a minimum GPA of 3.5 based on a minimum of 12 credit hours at the University. Qualified students must submit an application and write two essays selected from a list of three. The Honors Committee reviews the essays based on substance and content, grammatical correctness, demonstrated conceptual thinking, balanced viewpoint, development of ideas, organization, and originality.

Scholarship Availability: OCU offers a wide variety of scholarships, both academic and need-based, to students of exceptional ability and promise.

Campus Overview

Independent United Methodist comprehensive, founded 1904 • **Coed** 1,869 undergraduate students, 76% full-time, 60% women, 40% men.

Undergraduates 1,419 full-time, 450 part-time. Students come from 49 states and territories, 65 other countries, 34% are from out of state, 7% African American, 2% Asian American or Pacific Islander, 4% Hispanic American, 3% Native American, 22% international, 6% transferred in, 39% live on campus.

Faculty *Total:* 285, 58% full-time. *Student/faculty ratio:* 14:1.

Academic Programs *Special study options:* academic remediation for entering students, accelerated degree program, adult/continuing education programs, advanced placement credit, cooperative education, double majors, English as a second language, external degree program, honors programs, independent study, internships, off-campus study, part-time degree program, services for LD students, student-designed majors, study abroad, summer session for credit. *ROTC:* Army (c), Air Force (c).

Athletics Member NAIA. *Intercollegiate sports:* baseball M(s), basketball M(s)/W(s), cheerleading M(s)/W(s), crew M/W, golf M(s)/W(s), soccer M(s)/W(s), softball W(s). *Intramural sports:* badminton M/W, basketball M/W, bowling M/W, crew M/W, fencing M/W, football M, golf M/W, softball M/W, table tennis M/W, volleyball M/W.

Costs (2004–05) *Comprehensive fee:* $21,990 includes full-time tuition ($15,200), mandatory fees ($840), and room and board ($5950). Full-time tuition and fees vary according to program. Part-time tuition: $518 per semester hour. Part-time tuition and fees vary according to program. *Required fees:* $100 per term part-time. *College room only:* $2900. Room and board charges vary according to board plan and housing facility.

Financial Aid 190 Federal Work-Study jobs (averaging $1842). 55 state and other part-time jobs (averaging $2214). In 2003, 130 non-need-based awards were made. *Average percent of need met:* 79%. *Average financial aid package:* $11,702. *Average need-based loan:* $3547. *Average need-based gift aid:* $8155. *Average non-need-based aid:* $7046.

Contact: Dr. Virginia McCombs, Director, University Honors Program, Oklahoma City University, 2501 North Blackwelder, Oklahoma City, Oklahoma 73106; *Telephone:* 405-208-5457; *Fax:* 405-208-5200; *E-mail:* vmccombs@okcu.edu; *Web site:* http://www.okcu.edu/honors/

Oklahoma State University
The Honors College
Stillwater, Oklahoma

The Honors College provides many opportunities and challenges for outstanding undergraduate students in a supportive learning environment. Special honors sections of general education courses, interdisciplinary honors courses, and special honors projects allow students to enhance their learning experience. Classes are small (typically 20–22 students, but frequently smaller), and a wide range of honors courses is offered each semester. Honors courses are taught by members of the faculty who are experienced and known for excellence in the classroom and in their academic fields. Frequent interaction with other honors students and faculty members helps honors students develop a "sense of belonging" in the small-college atmosphere of the Honors College while being able to take advantage of the opportunities offered by a comprehensive research university.

Active participants in the Honors College (6 honors credit hours per semester during the freshman and sophomore years, 3 hours per semester thereafter) earn use of the Honors College Study Lounge and computer lab, early enrollment for the following semester, and extended semester-long library checkout privileges. They also have the option to live on the honors floors in Stout Hall on a space-available basis.

Special honors advising is provided by Honors Advisors, who themselves have earned Honors Program or Honors College degrees.

Honors College students regularly participate in conferences of the Great Plains Honors Council and the National Collegiate Honors Council, as do members of the faculty and professional honors staff. Opportunities for community service are available, as are research opportunities with faculty members that lead to the senior honors thesis or senior honors report.

In the past ten years, Honors College students have won Rhodes, Marshall, Truman, Goldwater, Udall, Pickering, Gates Cambridge, National Science Foundation, and Fulbright Scholarships. Honors College students work closely with the OSU Office of Scholar Development and Recognition for fellowship advice. Approximately two thirds of Honors College degree students continue their education in graduate and professional schools, including some of the most prestigious in the nation, while others seek immediate entry into their chosen career fields.

In the 1995 decennial accreditation review of Oklahoma State University by the North Central Association of Colleges and Schools, the University Honors Program, which is currently known as The Honors College, was found to be one of the major strengths of the university. The OSU Honors Director is a past President of the National Collegiate Honors Council.

Honors opportunities have been in existence since 1965 in the College of Arts and Sciences and since 1989 on a University-wide basis. There are currently 869 active participants.

Participation Requirements: The Honors College degree is the highest distinction that may be earned by an undergraduate student at Oklahoma State University (OSU). Requirements include completion of the General Honors Award (21 honors credit hours with a distribution requirement over four of six broad subject-matter areas and including a minimum of two honors seminars or special interdisciplinary honors courses), completion of the Departmental or College Honors Award (12 upper-division honors credit hours, including a senior honors thesis or senior honors project), a total of 39 honors credit hours, and both OSU and cumulative GPAs of at least 3.5. Transfer students may count up to 15 transfer honors credit hours toward the General Honors Award. The honors hood is conferred on Honors College degree recipients at Commencement, along with a special Honors College degree diploma.

Admission Process: Freshmen are eligible for admission to the University Honors College on the basis of an ACT composite score of 27 or higher (SAT I 1210 or higher) and a high school GPA of 3.75 or higher. January 15 is the application deadline for automatic acceptance. Continuing students are eligible according to the following OSU and cumulative GPAs: 0–59 credit hours, 3.3; 60–93 credit hours, 3.4; 94 or more credit hours, 3.5.

Scholarship Availability: The Honors College does not award scholarships. For information about scholarships, interested students should contact the Office of Financial Aid at OSU.

Campus Overview

State-supported university, founded 1890, part of Oklahoma State University System • **Coed** 18,789 undergraduate students, 88% full-time, 49% women, 51% men.

Undergraduates 16,628 full-time, 2,161 part-time. Students come from 50 states and territories, 82 other countries, 14% are from out of state, 4% African American, 2% Asian American or Pacific Islander, 2% Hispanic American, 9% Native American, 4% international, 9% transferred in, 40% live on campus.

Faculty *Total:* 1,184, 75% full-time, 78% with terminal degrees. *Student/faculty ratio:* 20:1.

Academic Programs *Special study options:* academic remediation for entering students, accelerated degree program, adult/continuing education programs, advanced placement credit, cooperative education, distance learning, double majors, English as a second language, freshman honors college, honors programs, independent study, internships, off-campus study, part-time degree program, services for LD students, student-designed majors, study abroad, summer session for credit. *ROTC:* Army (b), Air Force (b). *Unusual degree programs:* 3-2 accounting.

Athletics Member NCAA. All Division I except football (Division I-A). *Intercollegiate sports:* baseball M(s), basketball M(s)/W(s), cross-country running M(s)/W(s), equestrian sports W(s), golf M(s)/W(s), soccer W(s), softball W(s), tennis M(s)/W(s), track and field M(s)/W(s), wrestling M(s). *Intramural sports:* archery M/W, badminton M/W, basketball M/W, bowling M/W, crew M(c)/W(c), cross-country running M/W, football M/W, golf M/W, ice hockey M(c)/W(c), lacrosse M(c)/W(c), racquetball M/W, riflery M(c)/W(c), rugby M(c)/W(c), sailing M(c)/W(c), soccer M(c)/W(c), softball M/W, squash M/W, swimming and diving M/W, table tennis M/W, tennis M/W, track and field M/W, ultimate Frisbee M(c)/W(c), volleyball M/W, water polo M/W, weight lifting M/W, wrestling M.

Costs (2004–05) *Tuition:* state resident $2910 full-time, $97 per credit hour part-time; nonresident $10,200 full-time, $340 per credit hour part-time. Full-time tuition and fees vary according to course level. Part-time tuition and fees vary according to course level. *Required fees:* $1161 full-time, $46 per credit hour part-time. *Room and board:* $5602; room only: $2602. Room and board charges vary according to board plan, housing facility, and location.

Financial Aid 600 Federal Work-Study jobs (averaging $1750). 2,750 state and other part-time jobs (averaging $2205). In 2003, 3710 non-need-based awards were made. *Average percent of need met:* 78%. *Average financial aid package:* $8307. *Average need-based loan:* $3891. *Average need-based gift aid:* $3439. *Average non-need-based aid:* $2832.

Contact: Director: Robert L. Spurrier Jr., 510 Edmon Low Library, Stillwater, Oklahoma 74078-1073; *Telephone:* 405-744-6799; *Fax:* 405-744-6839; *E-mail:* robert.spurrier@okstate.edu; *Web site:* http://www.okstate.edu/honors

Oklahoma State University–Oklahoma City
Honors Program
Oklahoma City, Oklahoma

The Honors Program at Oklahoma State University–Oklahoma City (OSU–OKC) is in the developing stage. Because of an intensive promotional effort and a change in the requirements to participate, the program has established itself on campus and in the metro area of Oklahoma City. Since 1998, any student who wants to enroll in an honors course or complete an honors contract in a college course can do so, regardless of GPA. To get the honors credit on their transcripts, students have to earn an A or B in the course. Opening the Honors Program in this way to all interested students has resulted in increased numbers of active students and a greater awareness of the Honors Program on the campus and in the community. In the past two years, the number of students enrolled in honors courses and those who have contracted for honors projects has increased every semester. Currently, there are more than 50 active honors students, and this number is expected to grow to 100 by the next year.

The Honors Program at OSU–OKC, a two-year college, is concerned with preparing students to transfer to four-year institutions with credible academic records. Participation helps students in raising their GPAs, and students meet other honors students at area and regional honors conferences. The Central Oklahoma Two-Year College Honors Council's Colloquium every fall and the Great Plains Honors Conference every spring have become popular and well-attended opportunities for students to present their projects. They gain confidence in their own scholarship and look forward to being a part of a university honors program or honors college when they graduate from OSU–OKC.

Honors students work closely with faculty sponsors. Most projects are presented to the class and provide research and study beyond the scope of the course, which benefits all students enrolled.

Since OSU–OKC is a commuter campus and most students have families and jobs, it is not possible to hold regular meetings. However, along with the conferences, students are recognized each semester and they receive certificates, pins, and awards, and they share with faculty members and other students the types of projects they have done in the past semester. These events have brought about a sense of community and continuity among honors students and their faculty sponsors.

Participation Requirements: Honors hours are earned by enrolling in an honors course, usually English, humanities, or math, or contracting for individual honors projects in a college course of the student's choice. There is no specific GPA required, but in order for the honors credits to appear on the student's transcript, a grade of A or B must be earned in the course. The first 3 hours of honors credit earn a certificate; pins showing total hours earned are given for 6, 9, and 12 hours; and a student receives the Graduate Honors Scholar award for 15 hours of honors credit and a GPA of at least 3.5.

Admission Process: Students are considered members of the OSU–OKC Honors Program upon completion of their first 3 hours of honors work. Honors contracts are prepared by providing a description of the project and submitting it for approval to the honors committee by the end of the fourth week of the semester. After approval, the contracts are returned to the sponsors to be completed by the fourteenth week.

Scholarship Availability: Fee waiver scholarships are awarded each semester to applicants who have earned 6 hours of honors credit, hold a GPA of at least 3.5, and are active students in the current semester.

Campus Overview

State-supported 2-year, founded 1961, part of Oklahoma State University • **Coed** 5,654 undergraduate students.

Undergraduates Students come from 18 states and territories, 15 other countries, 1% are from out of state, 13% African American, 3% Asian American or Pacific Islander, 3% Hispanic American, 6% Native American, 0.8% international.

Faculty *Total:* 250, 26% full-time. *Student/faculty ratio:* 20:1.

Academic Programs *Special study options:* academic remediation for entering students, advanced placement credit, distance learning, double majors, honors programs, independent study, part-time degree program, services for LD students, summer session for credit.

Athletics *Intramural sports:* basketball M/W, volleyball M/W.

Costs (2004–05) *Tuition:* state resident $2304 full-time, $77 per credit hour part-time; nonresident $5754 full-time, $192 per credit hour part-time. *Required fees:* $35 full-time.

Financial Aid 75 Federal Work-Study jobs (averaging $2500).

Contact: Robert L. Spurrier Jr., The Honors College, 510 Edmon Low Library, Oklahoma State University, Oklahoma City, Oklahoma 74078-1073; *Telephone:* 405-744-6796; *Fax:* 405-945-9141; *E-mail:* robert.spurrier@okstate.edu

---

Oral Roberts University
Honors Program
Tulsa, Oklahoma

The purpose of Oral Roberts University's (ORU) Honors Program is to provide academically gifted students an educational experience at a level that both transcends the rigor and scope of the general curriculum and integrates the ethical responsibilities of using God's intellectual gifts for the healing of humanity into the concept of the "whole person" education. The program is designed for students and faculty members who possess the mental resources to plan, create, and implement strategies and programs that further fulfill the University's Statement of Purpose. This program continues the University's tradition of instilling character in students and preparing them for a lifetime of leadership and service to their community and world.

Successful, innovative faculty members are actively recruited to teach honors classes. These courses are designed to promote classroom discussion and allow opportunities to continue the learning process outside of class through field trips and extracurricular activities. Class enrollment is normally limited to 18 to 24 students. Social events are planned monthly, beginning with an orientation reception at the start of the year and a luncheon with the President of ORU. Honors dormitory housing is available, which promotes quiet hours and a high-quality academic atmosphere.

Founded in 2000, the program currently includes 220 students.

Participation Requirements: ORU's Honors Program is two-tiered, with 16 to 18 Fellows and approximately 60 Scholars accepted each year. Fellows must have exceptionally high academic credentials (e.g., National Merit Scholars) and outstanding application packets. Scholars have high academic credentials and strong application packets. All Honors Program students must complete a minimum of 24 hours of honors courses at the 100 to 200 level, plus any unique requirements within selected majors. Fellows take one special interdisciplinary honors seminar during each of the first six semesters. Each of these seminars is taught by 2 faculty members from separate departments to promote interdisciplinary exchange. Senior Papers that display outstanding academic scholarship are required as the capstone course for all Honors Program students. Graduating students who fulfill these requirements and have a cumulative GPA of at least 3.45 receive special recognition at an honors reception, during their department's hooding ceremony, and during commencement. Transcripts designate whether they graduated with honors as a Fellow or as a Scholar.

Admission Process: Honors-caliber high school students who have strong test scores (at least 1280 on the SAT or 29 on the ACT), excellent academic records (minimum 3.45 GPA), demonstrated leadership skills and church and community service, and supportive letters of recommendation are encouraged to apply to the Honors Program by the deadline in early March. Students from this pool are selected by the end of March as either Fellows or Scholars. Transfer students and current ORU students can apply to be Scholars if they meet the above requirements.

Scholarship Availability: All of ORU's Honors Program students receive merit-based scholarships. ORU offers Presidential Awards by invitation only to students who have a minimum unweighted GPA of 3.45 and minimum scores of 31 on the ACT or 1360 on the SAT. Academic tuition scholarships are awarded automatically to students scoring at least 24 on the ACT or 1100 on the SAT.

Campus Overview

Independent interdenominational comprehensive, founded 1963 • **Coed** 3,303 undergraduate students, 92% full-time, 58% women, 42% men.

Undergraduates 3,038 full-time, 265 part-time. Students come from 41 other countries, 61% are from out of state, 16% African American, 2% Asian American or Pacific Islander, 6% Hispanic American, 2% Native American, 5% international, 5% transferred in, 71% live on campus.

Faculty *Total:* 267, 67% full-time, 36% with terminal degrees. *Student/faculty ratio:* 16:1.

Academic Programs *Special study options:* academic remediation for entering students, adult/continuing education programs, advanced placement credit, distance learning, double majors, English as a second language, external degree program, freshman honors college, honors programs, independent study, internships, off-campus study, part-time degree program, services for LD students, student-designed majors, study abroad, summer session for credit. *ROTC:* Air Force (c). *Unusual degree programs:* 3-2 education.

Athletics Member NCAA. All Division I. *Intercollegiate sports:* baseball M(s), basketball M(s)/W(s), cross-country running M(s)/W(s), golf M(s)/W(s), soccer M(s)/W(s), tennis M(s)/W(s), track and field M(s)/W(s), volleyball W(s). *Intramural sports:* badminton M/W, basketball M/W, bowling M/W, football M/W, racquetball M/W, soccer M/W, softball M/W, table tennis M/W, tennis M/W, volleyball M/W.

Costs (2005–06) *Comprehensive fee:* $22,410 includes full-time tuition ($15,400), mandatory fees ($480), and room and board ($6530). Part-time tuition: $642 per credit hour. *College room only:* $3280. Room and board charges vary according to board plan and housing facility.

Financial Aid 313 Federal Work-Study jobs (averaging $1590). 750 state and other part-time jobs (averaging $1500). In 2002, 445 non-need-based awards were made. *Average percent of need met:* 89%. *Average financial aid package:* $14,950. *Average need-based loan:* $8629. *Average need-based gift aid:* $7577. *Average non-need-based aid:* $7029.

Contact: Director: Dr. John Korstad, Professor of Biology, Oral Roberts University, 7777 South Lewis Avenue, Tulsa, Oklahoma 74171; *Telephone:* 918-495-6942; *Fax:* 918-495-6297; *E-mail:* jkorstad@oru.edu; *Web site:* http://honors.oru.edu

Redlands Community College
Honors Program
El Reno, Oklahoma

The Redlands Community College (RCC) Honors Program consists of course work that offers academically talented students stimulating class experiences and interaction with other exceptional students. The benefits that the students receive are recognition by faculty members and administrators of their academic abilities and achievements, enhanced opportunities for acceptance in honors programs at four-year institutions, participation in a challenging and enriching curriculum, interaction with other honor students, and special recognition at their graduation ceremonies.

The designated honors courses, the interdisciplinary seminars, and the contracted courses are taught by faculty members who have exhibited excellence in teaching and who have shown a distinct interest in working with honors students. The honors faculty and the Honors Directors are available to the students to aid them in their research and presentations at the Great Plains NCHC Regional Conference and the University of Oklahoma Undergraduate Research Day.

Because Redlands Community College is a small school, honors students have access to all campus facilities and an honors study room with a reference library, a multimedia computer, and access to the Internet. Students graduating with honors must have a 3.25 GPA. In addition to being recognized at their graduation ceremonies, honors students have their accomplishment noted on their transcripts.

In existence for twelve years, the program currently enrolls 30 students.

Participation Requirements: After acceptance, honors students must successfully complete 15 credit hours of honors work to graduate with honors. Twelve of the hours may be completed through a contract with an individual instructor or by taking designated honors courses. Three credit hours must be earned through interdisciplinary honors seminars. Honors students are also encouraged to participate in the Great Plains NCHC Regional Honors Conference and in the Central Oklahoma Two-Year College Honors Council's annual colloquium. In order to get honors credit for a contracted course, honors students must complete an honors project and receive at least a B in the course. The honors project does not affect the student's grade in a contracted course. Students who graduate with honors are given special recognition at the graduation ceremony and receive a medallion at an honors dinner.

Admission Process: Students applying to the RCC Honors Program for the first time as freshmen must meet requirements based on ACT scores and high school GPAs. Other students may rely on their college GPAs and a successful interview with an Honors Director.

Scholarship Availability: Incoming freshmen are eligible for tuition waiver scholarships, and all other honors students may apply for the Faculty Honors Scholarships, which are given at the end of every fall term. These are based on the number of honors credit hours, GPA, and participation in honors activities on campus.

Campus Overview

State-supported 2-year, founded 1938, part of Oklahoma State Regents for Higher Education • **Coed** 2,323 undergraduate students, 25% full-time, 63% women, 37% men.

Undergraduates 583 full-time, 1,740 part-time. Students come from 4 states and territories, 7 other countries, 6% African American, 2% Asian American or Pacific Islander, 3% Hispanic American, 8% Native American, 2% international, 15% transferred in.

Faculty Total: 125, 26% full-time, 7% with terminal degrees. Student/faculty ratio: 18:1.

Academic Programs Special study options: academic remediation for entering students, accelerated degree program, adult/continuing education programs, advanced placement credit, cooperative education, distance learning, double majors, external degree program, honors programs, internships, part-time degree program, services for LD students, summer session for credit.

Athletics Member NJCAA. Intercollegiate sports: baseball M(s), basketball M(s)/W(s), volleyball W(s). Intramural sports: basketball M/W, volleyball W.

Costs (2004–05) Tuition: state resident $1320 full-time, $44 per credit hour part-time; nonresident $3570 full-time, $119 per credit hour part-time. Required fees: $870 full-time, $29 per credit hour part-time.

Financial Aid 25 Federal Work-Study jobs (averaging $2000). 70 state and other part-time jobs (averaging $2000).

Contact: Joel Figgs, 1300 South Country Club Road, Box 370, El Reno, Oklahoma 73036; Telephone: 405-262-2552; E-mail: figgsj@redlandscc.edu

Southeastern Oklahoma State University
Southeastern Honors Program
Durant, Oklahoma

The Southeastern Honors Program, built on the foundation of the Parsons Scholars Program, has a long and honorable tradition that goes back to 1978, when David L. Parsons, a 1928 Southeastern alumnus, endowed the Parsons Scholars scholarship.

Today, the Southeastern Honors Program is committed to the ongoing growth and development of a culturally diverse and academically talented group of honors students. With a focus on educational excellence as well as cultural and technological literacy, the program challenges high caliber students with special talents and outstanding academic abilities to develop local and global awareness and to achieve their full potential.

Students selected for the program receive a four year renewable academic scholarship to attend Southeastern Oklahoma State University.

Southeastern honors students are enrolled in honors sections of liberal arts courses as part of their general education curriculum. Honors courses are designed to provide an opportunity for honors students to take a more in-depth study of the subject. To make this possible, enrollment in each course is limited. The courses are generally more discussion oriented, and, in some instances, attendance at campus cultural events is included as a requirement of the course. In addition to honors courses, honors students receive numerous other special benefits, including access to specially designated housing, priority enrollment, field trips, cultural events, and enrichment activities as well as faculty mentorship in individual scholarly projects, opportunities to attend honors conferences, and recognition upon graduation and notation on the transcript. More than 140 students are currently enrolled in the Southeastern Honors Program.

Participation Requirements: The honors curriculum consists of nine required general education honors courses scheduled over the four-year period. There are also five designated honors electives, and students may receive honors credit by contract in any of the fifty-two major fields available at Southeastern. Honors Program graduates receive special recognition upon graduation, and completion is noted on the transcript.

Admission Process: Honors applicants must have an ACT composite of 25 or SAT of 1130 or higher from a national test date. Applicants must submit a letter of recommendation from a high school faculty member or administrator who is familiar with the student's character, accomplishments, and potential. Applicants must also submit an original, typed, single-spaced, one-page letter, addressed to the Southeastern faculty, outlining student qualifications, including academic achievements (GPA, ACT, etc.), leadership activities, and community service. Students must also explain why they will be an asset to the honors community at Southeastern. Students should note that, since this letter is evaluated on its own merit, without supporting documents, it should comprehensively present all student achievements. All applications must include an approved application for admission to Southeastern Oklahoma State University as well as a completed application for the Southeastern Honors Program. A seven-semester transcript is required by Honors Day. All applicants who fulfill the preceding requirements are eligible to participate in interviews and essay-writing competition on Honors Day, after which scholarships are awarded.

Scholarship Availability: The Honors Program administers six types of scholarships, which vary in requirements and awards. The Academic Scholars award is available to applicants with an ACT score of 31 or higher. Recipients must maintain a cumulative GPA of 3.25 or higher and complete at least 24 hours per year. The Regional University Scholars award is available to Oklahoma residents with an ACT composite of 30 or higher. Recipients must maintain a cumulative GPA of 3.25 or higher and complete at least 24 hours per year. The Parsons Scholars award is available to Oklahoma applicants with an ACT composite of 25 or higher. Recipients must maintain a cumulative GPA of 3.0 or higher and complete at least 30 hours per year. The Academic Scholars by Nomination award is available to applicants with a minimum ACT of 30 (or SAT equivalent) or minimum GPA of 3.8 and high school class ranking in the top 4 percent or GPA pf 4.0 and first in class ranking. Recipients must maintain a cumulative GPA of 3.25 or higher and complete at least 24 hours per year. The Presidential Honors Scholars award is available to applicants with an ACT composite of 25 or higher. Recipients must maintain a cumulative GPA of 3.0 or higher and complete at least 24 hours per year. The Out-of-State Scholars award is available to applicants with an ACT composite of 25 or higher. Recipients must maintain a cumulative GPA of 3.0 or higher and complete at least 24 hours per year.

Campus Overview

State-supported comprehensive, founded 1909, part of Oklahoma State Regents for Higher Education • **Coed** 3,738 undergraduate students, 79% full-time, 54% women, 46% men.

Undergraduates 2,966 full-time, 772 part-time. Students come from 35 states and territories, 28 other countries, 22% are from out of state, 5% African American, 0.6% Asian American or Pacific Islander, 2% Hispanic American, 29% Native American, 2% international, 12% transferred in, 20% live on campus.

Faculty *Total:* 223, 69% full-time, 54% with terminal degrees. *Student/faculty ratio:* 20:1.

Academic Programs *Special study options:* academic remediation for entering students, accelerated degree program, adult/continuing education programs, advanced placement credit, distance learning, double majors, honors programs, independent study, internships, off-campus study, part-time degree program, services for LD students, summer session for credit.

Athletics Member NCAA. All Division II. *Intercollegiate sports:* baseball M(s), basketball M(s)/W(s), cross-country running W(s), football M(s), softball W(s), tennis M(s)/W(s), volleyball W(s). *Intramural sports:* basketball M/W, football M.

Costs (2004–05) *Tuition:* state resident $2126 full-time, $71 per credit hour part-time; nonresident $6455 full-time, $215 per credit hour part-time. Full-time tuition and fees vary according to course level. Part-time tuition and fees vary according to course level and course load. *Required fees:* $997 full-time, $29 per semester hour part-time, $68 per term part-time. *Room and board:* $3470; room only: $1850. Room and board charges vary according to board plan and housing facility.

Financial Aid 362 Federal Work-Study jobs (averaging $1189). 857 state and other part-time jobs (averaging $1665). In 2003, 274 non-need-based awards were made. *Average percent of need met:* 75%. *Average financial aid package:* $1254. *Average need-based loan:* $1898. *Average need-based gift aid:* $1217. *Average non-need-based aid:* $1024.

Contact: Director: Dr. Lisa L. Coleman, PMB 4066, 1405 North 4th Avenue, PMB 4066, Durant, Oklahoma 74701; *Telephone:* 580-745-2770; *E-mail:* lcoleman@sosu.edu; *Web site:* http://www.sosu.edu/honor/

Tulsa Community College
Honors Program
Tulsa, Oklahoma

*T*he Tulsa Community College (TCC) Honors Program offers honors courses to curious and self-motivated students who wish to grow personally and academically. The goal of the program is to provide students with an enriched academic environment through more direct involvement in their own learning experience. Classes are smaller, interaction with peers and professors is lively, and opportunities for independent study are provided. The Honors Program was developed in 1985. TCC currently has 120 Honors Scholars.

Admission Process: All students are welcome to take honors courses; however, a 3.0 GPA is recommended. In order to become an Honors Scholar, the student must meet two of the following criteria: combined score of 1100 on the SAT I (or the equivalent on the new SAT) or composite ACT score of 25 or above; a high school GPA of at least 3.5; ranking in the upper 10 percent of the high school graduating class, or equivalent GED score, or membership in the high school honor society; a 3.5 GPA on a minimum of 12 credit hours; demonstration of special abilities or awards in writing or other significant projects; or completion of two honors-credit courses at TCC with a grade of B or A. Students must also submit a writing sample and a letter of recommendation from a qualified instructor, and they must be approved by all honors coordinators.

Scholarship Availability: Honors Scholars qualify for the TCC Honors Scholar State Regents Tuition Waiver; the University of Tulsa also offers partial scholarships to TCC Honors Scholar graduates. In addition, the TCC Honors Program awards the TCC Foundation Honor Award each year to Honors students; honors faculty members recommend students for the award. Academic Scholars Scholarships, which provide eight semesters of support, are awarded to 5 Honors Scholars each year.

Campus Overview

State-supported 2-year, founded 1968, part of Oklahoma State Regents for Higher Education • **Coed** 22,866 undergraduate students.

Undergraduates Students come from 16 states and territories, 1% are from out of state, 9% African American, 2% Asian American or Pacific Islander, 3% Hispanic American, 7% Native American.

Faculty *Total:* 1,285, 33% full-time. *Student/faculty ratio:* 20:1.

Academic Programs *Special study options:* academic remediation for entering students, accelerated degree program, adult/continuing education programs, advanced placement credit, cooperative education, distance learning, English as a second language, external degree program, freshman honors college, honors programs, internships, part-time degree program, services for LD students, summer session for credit.

Athletics *Intramural sports:* basketball M/W, bowling M/W, cross-country running M/W, football M/W, golf M/W, racquetball M/W, soccer M/W, tennis M/W, track and field M/W, volleyball M/W.

Costs (2004–05) *Tuition:* state resident $1918 full-time, $40 per credit hour part-time; nonresident $4918 full-time, $140 per credit hour part-time. *Required fees:* $715 full-time, $24 per credit hour part-time.

Financial Aid 200 Federal Work-Study jobs (averaging $1500).

Contact: Director: David Lawless, 909 South Boston MC510, Tulsa, Oklahoma 74119-2095; *Telephone:* 918-595-7378; *Fax:* 918-595-8378; *E-mail:* dlawless@tulsacc.edu

University of Oklahoma
Honors College
Norman, Oklahoma

The Honors College incorporates a curricular program dedicated to providing academically talented students with the opportunity to develop their intellectual potential to the fullest. The Honors College utilizes the Honors College faculty as well as the best research and teaching faculty members from all undergraduate colleges of the University to offer special honors courses at both the upper-division and lower-division levels. The courses are limited to approximately 22 students, with enrollment restricted to members of the Honors College. This gives each honors course a rich environment of academically talented students. The lower-division honors courses include courses that fulfill the University of Oklahoma (OU) general education requirements. The upper-division courses include special-topic seminars, team-taught colloquia, and independent study and research with faculty members in the student's major discipline. Students in the Honors College may elect to enroll in up to 9 credit hours of honors courses each semester. Honors students must complete a minimum of 20 hours of honors-designated course work: 12 credit hours including a 3-credit-hour freshman seminar, 5 hours of honors reading and research, and a 3-credit–hour honors colloquium.

The program began in 1962, went through a major reorganization in 1987, and became an Honors College in 1997. There are approximately 1,900 students currently enrolled.

Participation Requirements: Continued membership in the Honors College requires both maintaining an OU cumulative GPA of 3.4 and exhibiting continued progress toward completion of the curricular requirements of an honors degree. Progress is defined as completing at least one honors course during every 30 credit hours earned at the University, or approximately one honors course per academic year for full-time students. Most honors students take two or three honors courses per year.

Students successfully completing the honors curriculum with a 3.4–3.59 GPA have a cum laude designation on their diploma, with a 3.6–3.79 GPA a magna cum laude designation, or with a 3.8 GPA or higher a summa cum laude designation.

Admission Process: Freshmen entering the University of Oklahoma are eligible to apply to the Honors College if they have a composite ACT score of 29 or higher or an SAT total of 1280 or higher and they rank in the top 10 percent of graduates in their high school class or they have a high school GPA of 3.75. Transfer students who come to the University of Oklahoma with 15 or more college credit hours and a transfer GPA of 3.4 or higher are eligible to apply. OU students who have earned 15 or more hours of OU credit and have maintained a cumulative GPA of 3.4 or higher are eligible to apply. Final admission into the Honors College is determined by an evaluation of the Honors College application form, which includes a written essay of 400–500 words.

Campus Overview
State-supported university, founded 1890 • **Coed** 20,297 undergraduate students, 88% full-time, 49% women, 51% men.

Undergraduates 17,866 full-time, 2,431 part-time. Students come from 50 states and territories, 74 other countries, 23% are from out of state, 5% African American, 5% Asian American or Pacific Islander, 4% Hispanic American, 7% Native American, 3% international, 7% transferred in, 20% live on campus.

Faculty *Total:* 1,204, 81% full-time, 79% with terminal degrees. *Student/faculty ratio:* 21:1.

Academic Programs *Special study options:* academic remediation for entering students, accelerated degree program, adult/continuing education programs, advanced placement credit, cooperative education, distance learning, double majors, English as a second language, external degree program, freshman honors college, honors programs, independent study, internships, off-campus study, part-time degree program, services for LD students, student-designed majors, study abroad, summer session for credit. *ROTC:* Army (b), Navy (b), Air Force (b).

Athletics Member NCAA. All Division I except football (Division I-A). *Intercollegiate sports:* baseball M(s), basketball M(s)/W(s), cross-country running M(s)/W(s), golf M(s)/W(s), gymnastics M(s)/W(s), soccer W(s), softball W(s), tennis M(s)/W(s), track and field M(s)/W(s), volleyball W(s), wrestling M(s). *Intramural sports:* badminton M/W, basketball M/W, bowling M/W, crew M(c)/W(c), cross-country running M/W, football M/W, golf M/W, ice hockey M(c)/W(c), lacrosse M, racquetball M/W, rock climbing M/W, rugby M(c)/W(c), sailing M(c)/W(c), soccer M/W, softball M/W, squash M/W, swimming and diving M/W, table tennis M/W, tennis M/W, track and field M/W, ultimate Frisbee M(c)/W(c), volleyball M/W.

Costs (2004–05) *Tuition:* state resident $2778 full-time, $93 per credit hour part-time; nonresident $10,296 full-time, $343 per credit hour part-time. Full-time tuition and fees vary according to course load, location, program, and reciprocity agreements. Part-time tuition and fees vary according to course load, location, program, and reciprocity agreements. *Required fees:* $1362 full-time, $38 per credit hour part-time, $107 per term part-time. *Room and board:* $5814; room only: $2924. Room and board charges vary according to board plan and housing facility.

Financial Aid 657 Federal Work-Study jobs (averaging $2324). In 2003, 1906 non-need-based awards were made. *Average percent of need met:* 81%. *Average financial aid package:* $8180. *Average need-based loan:* $4282. *Average need-based gift aid:* $3662. *Average non-need-based aid:* $1107.

Contact: Dean: Dr. Robert Con Davis-Undiano, Honors House, 1300 Asp Avenue, Norman, Oklahoma 73019; *Telephone:* 405-325-5291; *Fax:* 405-325-7109; *E-mail:* rcdavis@ou.edu; *Web site:* http://www.ou.edu/honors

OREGON

Eastern Oregon University
Honors Program
La Grande, Oregon

The pursuit of an Eastern Oregon University (EOU) honors baccalaureate degree can enrich the educational opportunities available to EOU students and promote an environment for intellectual and personal achievement. EOU's Honors Program is designed to nurture talent by providing opportunities to go further in an academic discipline and broaden or deepen an education beyond the usual required work. EOU's program was founded in 2001 and averages 50 students.

Participation Requirements: The student submits all the honors contracts, with endorsing faculty members' signatures, before being identified as an honors student. In addition to all regular degree requirements, required components for completion of the honors baccalaureate degree include the following: three academic projects, campus leadership, community service learning, and one preprofessional conference presentation/participation, such as the spring symposium. A total of five contracts that outline the degree requirements are to be submitted. Honors seminars are also offered.

An academic honors project should cover the material in greater depth than in regular class assignments. The student is responsible for the greater share of learning and discovery and should have unusual opportunities to explore the subject matter in exciting ways.

The honors student completes three contracts for three academic projects that are to be submitted in the format that is most appropriate to the discipline and subject matter–for example, art, a research paper, an experiment, a performance, or multiproject.

The three academic project contracts can comprise an expanded project based on an upper-division course's content. For example, a student may write a 25-page paper for a course that requires a 15-page paper of all students. Extra course credits will not be awarded for this extra honors effort. The second project choice involves students who choose to work on a unique project in their field of specialization. Field research is strongly encouraged. If the discipline is not a research-oriented area, then a unique project that is not normally carried out in EOU's regular offerings is recommended. The project should be conceptualized by the student in consultation with faculty members. The honors student may receive upper-division credits for their work, which is to be determined by endorsing faculty members. The final project choice is an interdisciplinary project that incorporates the student's major field and one other discipline. The honors student may receive upper-division credits for their work, which is to be determined by endorsing faculty members.

The campus leadership component requires substantial involvement in any aspect of campus service, which demonstrates individual initiative on the part of the student. For example, a regular tutoring assignment through the Learning Center does not fulfill this requirement, even if it is performed without pay. However, a tutoring assignment combined with the production of a supplement to course materials, such as a collection of original study aids to be kept on hand for future use, or a tutoring assignment combined with the offering of extra sessions that demonstrate a commitment and effort beyond what is normally expected of tutors, does fulfill this requirement.

The community service learning project requires that the student seek out, independently or with the help of the Cornerstones Office, a service opportunity. This opportunity is preferably not directly related to the student's major and takes place in the community beyond the EOU campus. This is not an internship; it is engagement in service to others. Also, the student must complete at least 40 hours of unpaid service of any nature appropriate to the agency and complete two brief papers or projects in other formats to be approved in advance with the Cornerstones Office, including a "preflection," and a final "reflection" linking the service experience with the academic experience.

Admission Process: An honors scholar may be any individual possessing motivation to nominate himself or herself. All students are encouraged to consider the prospect of earning an honors baccalaureate degree. To apply to the program, students must have completed a minimum of 44 credits with a minimum 3.25 GPA. Students submit five honors contracts with endorsing faculty members' signatures that outline the academic, leadership, and service learning components of their program. EOU's Honors Program does accept transfer students. Early admission is offered to outstanding incoming freshmen.

Scholarship Availability: EOU does not offer scholarships for honors scholars.

Campus Overview

State-supported comprehensive, founded 1929, part of Oregon University System • **Coed** 3,069 undergraduate students, 60% full-time, 58% women, 42% men.

Undergraduates 1,831 full-time, 1,238 part-time. Students come from 42 states and territories, 30 other countries, 31% are from out of state, 2% African American, 3% Asian American or Pacific Islander, 3% Hispanic American, 2% Native American, 2% international, 15% transferred in, 15% live on campus.

Faculty *Total:* 110, 85% full-time. *Student/faculty ratio:* 15:1.

Academic Programs *Special study options:* adult/continuing education programs, advanced placement credit, cooperative education, distance learning, double majors, English as a second language, external degree program, honors programs, independent study, internships, off-campus study, part-time degree program, services for LD students, student-designed majors, study abroad, summer session for credit. *ROTC:* Army (b). *Unusual degree programs:* 3-2 engineering with Oregon State University; nursing with Oregon Health Sciences University; agriculture with Oregon State University.

Athletics Member NCAA, NAIA. All NCAA Division III. *Intercollegiate sports:* baseball M, basketball M/W, cross-country running M/W, football M, skiing (cross-country) M(c)/W(c), skiing (downhill) M(c)/W(c), soccer W, softball W, track and field M/W, volleyball M(c)/W. *Intramural sports:* baseball M/W, basketball M/W, cheerleading M/W, football M/W, racquetball M/W, soccer M/W, softball M/W, volleyball M/W, weight lifting M/W.

Costs (2004–05) *Tuition:* state resident $4257 full-time; nonresident $4257 full-time. Full-time tuition and fees vary according to course load. Part-time tuition and fees vary according to course load. *Required fees:* $1260 full-time. *Room and board:* $6099. Room and board charges vary according to board plan and housing facility.

Financial Aid 245 Federal Work-Study jobs (averaging $1553). In 2004, 37 non-need-based awards were made. *Average percent of need met:* 59%. *Average financial aid package:* $11,762. *Average need-based loan:* $3751. *Average need-based gift aid:* $3698. *Average non-need-based aid:* $1298.

Contact: Coordinator: Dr. Jeff Woodford, Chair, EOU Honors Committee, One University Boulevard, Badgley Hall 303J, La Grande, Oregon 97850; *Telephone:* 541-962-3321; *E-mail:* jwoodford@eou.edu; *Web site:* http://www.eou.edu/honors/

Oregon State University
University Honors College
Corvallis, Oregon

The University Honors College (UHC) is a campuswide degree-granting college, one of twelve at Oregon State University (OSU). It awards the Honors Baccalaureate of Science, Arts, or Fine Arts in the academic discipline, designating one of two tracks within the UHC. Students may major in any academic discipline and complete either the 30-credit "Honors Scholar" or the 15-credit "Honors Associate" track. The goal of the UHC is to provide a small college environment within a larger university and to stress education that focuses on relationships rather than subjects or disciplines. UHC classes are limited to 20 at the lower division and 12 at the upper division, and a writing-intensive skills requirement is included in the "Honors Scholar" track.

UHC courses are transcript visible and denoted by a departmental prefix and an H suffix or HC prefix. All courses are proposed by interested faculty members or by other nomination and are screened by the UHC Council. UHC courses are not automatically renewed and are assumed to be taught on a one-time-only basis that requires a renewal application. UHC courses may be regular quarter-length classes or offered in a compressed, weekend, or evening-course format. About three quarters of UHC offerings parallel the general education requirement of the institution; the remainder are UHC colloquia designed especially for UHC students. A study-abroad option is available, either independently or as part of OSU's unique concurrent degree requirements for an International Degree.

The University Honors College at OSU currently has approximately 500 students (80 percent are from Oregon, 47 percent are women, and 22 percent are members of minority groups). The program draws students from across the country and around the world. Honors students may elect to live in the Honors Residence Hall.

Participation Requirements: Once admitted, UHC students must maintain a minimum GPA of 3.25 to remain in good standing. Sub-par performance results in a probationary window to improve academic performance prior to dismissal from the UHC portion of OSU.

Admission Process: Applicants to the UHC must be admitted or applying to OSU. An application form is available upon request from the UHC or via its Web site. There are two deadlines a year: November 1 and February 1 for the following fall admission. Admission criteria are rigorous but include an opportunity to "write in" thorough responses to a series of essay questions. Transfer students may be admitted on a space-available basis.

Scholarship Availability: UHC students are supported by scholarships from their academic colleges or by Presidential, Achievement, and Provost (merit-based) Scholarships. Additional scholarship support is available through the Honors College, and other decentralized support is available.

Campus Overview

State-supported university, founded 1868, part of Oregon University System • **Coed** 15,713 undergraduate students, 89% full-time, 47% women, 53% men.

Undergraduates 13,966 full-time, 1,747 part-time. Students come from 50 states and territories, 93 other countries, 10% are from out of state, 1% African American, 8% Asian American or Pacific Islander, 3% Hispanic American, 1% Native American, 2% international, 7% transferred in, 22% live on campus.

Faculty *Total:* 808, 87% full-time, 75% with terminal degrees. *Student/faculty ratio:* 24:1.

Academic Programs *Special study options:* academic remediation for entering students, advanced placement credit, cooperative education, distance learning, double majors, English as a second language, external degree program, freshman honors college, honors programs, internships, off-campus study, part-time degree program, services for LD students, student-designed majors, study abroad, summer session for credit. *ROTC:* Army (b), Navy (b), Air Force (b).

Athletics Member NCAA. All Division I except football (Division I-A). *Intercollegiate sports:* baseball M(s), basketball M(s)/W(s), crew M/W, golf M(s)/W(s), gymnastics W(s), soccer M(s)/W(s), softball W(s), swimming and diving W(s), volleyball W(s), wrestling M(s). *Intramural sports:* archery M/W, badminton M/W, basketball M/W, bowling M/W, crew M/W, cross-country running M/W, equestrian sports M(c)/W(c), fencing M(c)/W(c), football M, golf M/W, lacrosse M(c)/W(c), racquetball M/W, riflery M(c)/W(c), rugby M(c)/W(c), sailing M(c)/W(c), skiing (cross-country) M(c)/W(c), skiing (downhill) M(c)/W(c), soccer M/W, softball M/W, squash M(c), swimming and diving M/W, table tennis M(c)/W(c), tennis M/W, track and field M/W, volleyball M/W, water polo M/W, wrestling M.

Costs (2004–05) *Tuition:* state resident $4113 full-time, $108 per credit part-time; nonresident $16,461 full-time, $451 per credit part-time. Part-time tuition and fees vary according to course load. *Required fees:* $1206 full-time. *Room and board:* $6786. Room and board charges vary according to board plan and housing facility.

Financial Aid In 2004, 36 non-need-based awards were made. *Average percent of need met:* 66%. *Average financial aid package:* $8673. *Average need-based loan:* $3213. *Average need-based gift aid:* $2646. *Average non-need-based aid:* $2716.

Contact: Dean: Dr. Jon Hendricks, Assistant Dean: William Bogley, Academic Advisors: LeeAnn Baker and Rebekah Lancelin, 229 Strand Hall, Corvallis, Oregon 97331-2221; *Telephone:* 541-737-6400; *Fax:* 541-737-6401; *E-mail:* honors.college@orgegonstate.edu

Portland State University
University Honors Program
Portland, Oregon

The Honors Program at Portland State University (PSU) is a small, degree-granting program primarily meant for students who plan to go on to graduate or professional school. Students admitted to the program receive the extraordinary privilege of a waiver of general University requirements for the baccalaureate; instead, they work with faculty members in the program and academic departments to design degree programs tailored specifically to fit their plans and interests. Thus, the resident faculty members of the Honors Program have designed a core of course work that emphasizes training in research and writing as well as introducing students to key problems of current intellectual culture. Honors Program students may pursue any of the departmental majors offered at Portland State.

Many take the opportunity offered of the Washington, D.C., internship project; students live for an academic quarter in a group accommodation (provided by the University) in Washington, while taking part in internships appropriate to their career plans. The choice of possibilities in Washington is, of course, quite large; students from this program have successfully undertaken internships in the array of Smithsonian-associated institutions; carefully selected nongovernmental organizations (NGOs), such as Common Cause and others; many of the federal offices and agencies in the capital; and, for premedical students, valuable internships in the National Institutes of Health and the National Institute of Mental Health.

Students from the program share, in addition to their commitment to excellence, a remarkable level of achievement. A recent self-study shows that roughly 75 percent of Honors Program graduates have gone on to one or more advanced degrees, whether a professional degree (e.g., M.D. J.D., or M.B.A.) or one of the academic degrees (e.g., Ph.D.).

Participation Requirements: Honors Program students come from as diverse a range of backgrounds and pursue as wide a variety of majors as do students in the general University (which is Oregon's largest university.) The program is limited in size to 200 students overall to ensure the kind of close mentoring relationship with faculty members that leads to student success. While most—better than 80 percent—of students come directly from high school, the program also admits a number of returning and transfer students (although it is generally not possible to accept applications from students with more than about 60 quarter hours of credit). Students in the program share a commitment to learning and an equal commitment to excellence, which is reflected in their achievements.

Admission Process: Applications are accepted on a rolling basis. Students should contact the office of the University Honors Program directly for information, either by telephone at 503-725-4928 or 800-547-8887, Ext. 4928, or by e-mail at hon@pdx.edu.

Scholarship Availability: Some limited tuition-remission scholarships are available.

Campus Overview

State-supported university, founded 1946, part of Oregon University System • **Coed** 17,355 undergraduate students, 61% full-time, 54% women, 46% men.

Undergraduates 10,609 full-time, 6,746 part-time. Students come from 47 states and territories, 67 other countries, 13% are from out of state, 3% African American, 10% Asian American or Pacific Islander, 4% Hispanic American, 1% Native American, 3% international, 15% transferred in.

Faculty *Total:* 1,199, 59% full-time, 53% with terminal degrees. *Student/faculty ratio:* 18:1.

Academic Programs *Special study options:* academic remediation for entering students, accelerated degree program, adult/continuing

education programs, advanced placement credit, cooperative education, distance learning, double majors, English as a second language, honors programs, independent study, internships, off-campus study, part-time degree program, services for LD students, student-designed majors, study abroad, summer session for credit. *ROTC:* Army (b), Air Force (c).

Athletics Member NCAA. All Division I except football (Division I-AA). *Intercollegiate sports:* baseball M(s), basketball M(s)/W(s), cross-country running M(s)/W(s), golf M(s)/W(s), soccer W(s), softball W(s), tennis M(s)/W(s), track and field M(s)/W(s), volleyball W(s), wrestling M(s). *Intramural sports:* archery M/W, basketball M/W, bowling M(c)/W(c), crew M(c)/W(c), fencing M(c)/W(c), football M, golf M/W, racquetball M/W, sailing M(c)/W(c), skiing (downhill) M(c)/W(c), soccer M(c)/W, softball M/W, table tennis M(c)/W(c), tennis M(c)/W(c), volleyball M/W, water polo M(c)/W(c).

Costs (2004–05) *Tuition:* state resident $3240 full-time, $90 per credit part-time; nonresident $12,636 full-time, $90 per credit part-time. Full-time tuition and fees vary according to program. *Required fees:* $1071 full-time, $17 per credit part-time, $40 per term part-time. *Room and board:* $8310; room only: $6210. Room and board charges vary according to board plan and housing facility.

Financial Aid 547 Federal Work-Study jobs (averaging $3738). In 2004, 166 non-need-based awards were made. *Average percent of need met:* 56%. *Average financial aid package:* $7486. *Average need-based loan:* $4353. *Average need-based gift aid:* $3939. *Average non-need-based aid:* $2318.

Contact: Director: Professor Lawrence Wheeler, Portland State University, P.O. Box 751, Portland, Oregon 97202-0751; *Telephone:* 503-725-4928 or 800-547-8887 Ext. 4928 (toll-free); *Fax:* 503-725-5363; *E-mail:* hon@pdx.edu; *Web site:* http://www.honors.pdx.edu

Southern Oregon University

Honors Program

Ashland, Oregon

The Honors Program at Southern Oregon University (SOU) aims to provide challenging, stimulating learning-and-living environments for students who are interested in high-quality academic growth and achievement. The program give selected, qualified students an educational experience of superior quality, tailored to their individual needs. The Honors Program emphasizes student choice from a variety of different honors opportunities.

Honors options are designed to meet the needs of students who can learn quickly, who seek intellectual challenge and stimulation, who want to delve deeply into learning, who enjoy sharing and discussing ideas, and who like—or want to try—to think outside the box. Special features of the Honors Program at SOU include the following: honors courses satisfy specific graduation requirements, either in general education, the major, or a minor; honors courses are small (about 12 to 15 students and always under 20 students), with an emphasis on writing and class discussion; and all courses are taught by experienced, fully qualified faculty members.

The Honors Program approaches the fundamental issues and content of college courses in a way that stresses concepts and encourages students to see connections and applications. Courses are not more difficult in the sense that the same level of achievement earns a lower grade, but honors courses do generally involve more reading and writing than the regular courses. Most students who choose honors do not mind the extra reading assignments because they really like to read.

The program has several curricular and noncurricular components.

For students beginning their University education, the Honors Program provides small sections of courses that satisfy requirements all students must meet for graduation. For example, since all students

must demonstrate competencies in writing, speaking, and critical thinking, the Honors Program provides the Honors Colloquium (the central course for first-year students), which teaches these skills in a context stressing class discussion, challenging writing assignments, and individualized learning goals. Honors courses are available to satisfy general education or "breadth" requirements in mathematics, sciences, social sciences, and arts and letters.

Students at the junior level or above in some programs may also consider Honors in the Major program. Beginning with the Honors in Mathematics, Honors in Biology, and Honors in Chemistry programs, SOU is building additional programs for Honors in the Major in disciplines in social sciences, arts and letters, and business. New programs are added as they are developed. Honors in the Major varies from discipline to discipline, but it typically involves an extended senior project, an internship, or service learning, with extended opportunities for achievement in academic course work.

Students at the sophomore level or above may enroll in the Churchill Honors Program, a sequence of courses leading to a minor in interdisciplinary ethics. The sequence begins with a year-long seminar on the Western ethical tradition, from the Greeks to the present. Junior-year students take courses in global ethics or ethics applications. During the senior year, students work on an individual or collaborative senior project in applied ethics. The Churchill Program includes students from across the University, from music to chemistry, engaging them in discussions with top-level faculty members about ethical theory and applications. The program builds a cohort experience in which the strong interpersonal relationships are among the outcomes most valued by participants.

Noncurricular aspects of the program include honors floors in the residence halls, social activities, and the Honors Club. The honors floors and the Honors Program sponsor social activities for honors students (including regular "tea parties") and provide a living environment that supports academic achievement. The Honors Club sponsors a variety of activities, but it typically organizes discussions of ethical issues, speakers, and other programs involving issues of social responsibility and/or social service.

The Honors Program for first-year students began in 2002 and enrolls more than 150 students each year. The Churchill Honors Program, named after SOU President Julius A. Churchill, admits about 20 students annually at the sophomore level. The number of students pursuing Honors in the Major varies.

Participation Requirements: Each curricular component of the Honors Program may be taken independently of the others. The Honors Program office provides individualized academic advising for each student to ensure that course selections meet the student's particular needs.

Students completing three years of the Churchill Honors Program graduate as Churchill Honors Scholars, following the presentation of their senior project to faculty and community members. Those students who complete two of the three years in this program graduate as Churchill Honors Associates.

Admission Process: Students apply separately for each curricular component. Entering first-year students, transfer students, and others seeking honors-level work in general education apply to the Honors Program to receive authorization to enroll in honors courses. The program invites all entering students with a record of achievement and aptitude to apply. Admission to the Churchill Honors Program typically occurs at the end of the freshman year; an essay and interview are required. Admission to Honors in the Major is accomplished by application to the specific department. Admission at unusual times is possible for students at all stages of undergraduate study.

Scholarship Availability: Southern Oregon University offers hundreds of scholarships that assist students in pursuing their academic goals for almost every major and category of student. Academic achievement, outstanding service or performance, and financial need form the basis for selection. While some scholarships require a combination of qualifications, others may have only one requirement. Scholarships may be automatically renewable as long as criteria are met, or they may be awarded on a one-time basis. Other scholarships may require recipients to reapply and be considered along with all other applicants. SOU's scholarships range in amounts from $100 to full tuition and fees, with room, board, and book allowances and with an average award of approximately $1000.

Of the 161 scholarships available, 100 accept the online scholarship application hosted by the Oregon Student Assistance Commission. Incoming freshmen and new transfer students need to complete their applications and send materials to SOU by February 16 each year to be considered for the Laurels, Diversity, Incentive, Presidentials, Ruth Kneass Memorial, and RAIFA Educational Scholarships. All other scholarships that accept the online form have a due date of March 1.

Southern Oregon University has local chapters of the following interdisciplinary honors societies: Alpha Lambda Delta, National Residence Hall Honorary, Omicron Delta Epsilon, and Phi Kappa Phi.

Campus Overview

State-supported comprehensive, founded 1926, part of Oregon University System • **Coed** 4,672 undergraduate students, 79% full-time, 56% women, 44% men.

Undergraduates 3,693 full-time, 979 part-time. Students come from 45 states and territories, 33 other countries, 20% are from out of state, 2% African American, 4% Asian American or Pacific Islander, 4% Hispanic American, 2% Native American, 2% international, 10% transferred in, 24% live on campus.

Faculty Total: 312, 62% full-time. *Student/faculty ratio:* 19:1.

Academic Programs *Special study options:* academic remediation for entering students, accelerated degree program, adult/continuing education programs, advanced placement credit, cooperative education, distance learning, double majors, English as a second language, freshman honors college, honors programs, independent study, internships, off-campus study, part-time degree program, services for LD students, student-designed majors, study abroad, summer session for credit. *Unusual degree programs:* 3-2 engineering with Oregon State University.

Athletics Member NAIA. *Intercollegiate sports:* basketball M(s)/W(s), cross-country running M(s)/W(s), football M(s), skiing (downhill) M/W, soccer W(s), softball W(s), tennis W(s), track and field M(s)/W(s), volleyball W(s), wrestling M(s). *Intramural sports:* basketball M/W, bowling M/W, cheerleading M/W, crew M/W, football M/W, golf M/W, racquetball M/W, rugby M/W, sailing M/W, skiing (cross-country) M/W, soccer M/W, softball M/W, swimming and diving M/W, table tennis M/W, tennis M/W, track and field M/W, ultimate Frisbee M/W, volleyball M/W, water polo M/W.

Costs (2005–06) *Tuition:* state resident $3738 full-time, $98 per credit part-time; nonresident $14,565 full-time, $98 per credit part-time. Full-time tuition and fees vary according to course load, location, and reciprocity agreements. Part-time tuition and fees vary according to course load, location, and reciprocity agreements. *Required fees:* $1125 full-time, $25 per credit part-time. *Room and board:* $7560; room only: $4536. Room and board charges vary according to board plan and housing facility.

Financial Aid 371 Federal Work-Study jobs (averaging $899). In 2004, 387 non-need-based awards were made. *Average percent of need met:* 56%. *Average financial aid package:* $7587. *Average need-based loan:* $4013. *Average need-based gift aid:* $4961. *Average non-need-based aid:* $8113.

Contact: Director: Dr. Sandra Coyner, Honors Program, Southern Oregon University, 1250 Siskiyou Boulevard, Ashland, Oregon 97520; *Telephone:* 541-552-6150; *E-mail:* coyner@sou.edu; *Web site:* http://www.sou.edu/honors

University of Oregon
Robert D. Clark Honors College
Eugene, Oregon

Robert D. Clark Honors College, located within the University of Oregon (UO), offers the advantages of a small, liberal arts college and a major research university. Clark Honors College grants both the Bachelor of Arts and Bachelor of Science degrees.

Clark Honors College provides an extensive, balanced curriculum of interrelated courses in the humanities, social sciences, natural sciences, and mathematics, which complements students' work in their chosen majors. This core curriculum is designed to foster creative, critical thinking and accounts for about one third of students' credits toward graduation. Clark Honors College aims to reach beyond professional or specialized training to inspire students to a full lifetime of intellectual curiosity and personal growth. Students work closely with Clark Honors College professors to establish a broad knowledge base and develop skills that cross all boundaries. Each student is an integral part of this exciting learning community with other highly motivated students, award-winning faculty members, mentoring alumni, and a supportive staff. Discussion-centered classes are limited to 25 students and are taught by skilled faculty members. Students also participate in seminars and colloquia that will help them merge education with real-world experiences. Close advising is an important aspect of Clark Honors College, from summer or fall orientation preceding the first year to faculty supervision of the honors thesis in the senior year.

In their senior year, students prepare an advanced research or creative project and present it orally before a faculty committee. Throughout the honors thesis process, students work individually with professors from their major field. As the culminating experience of their undergraduate career, the senior thesis and oral presentation give students an opportunity to demonstrate both the breadth of learning attained at Clark Honors College and the specialized knowledge gained from their major.

Participation Requirements: Robert D. Clark Honors College, established in 1960, is the oldest Honors College in the United States. About 650 students are currently enrolled, representing interests in all scholarly disciplines. Students come from all over the nation and the world and every year the student body increases in ethnic and geographic diversity.

Admission Process: High school seniors who have demonstrated academic excellence are encouraged to apply to Clark Honors College. A small number of transfer students are also accepted each year. Students must apply both to the University for general admission as well as to Clark Honors College. A complete Clark Honors College application consists of an application form, two teacher recommendations, transcripts, SAT or ACT scores, an activity summary, and an essay, all of which must be sent in one packet directly to Clark Honors College. Application materials are available online (http://honors.uoregon.edu).

The early notification deadline is November 1 and the regular application deadline is January 15. Students who complete their application by November 1 or January 15 are guaranteed full consideration by the Clark Honors College admissions committee. Students who apply by November 1 are notified of the committee's decision by December 15; students who apply by January 15 are notified by April 1. Late applications and transfers are considered individually on a space-available basis.

Scholarship Availability: Scholarships are awarded through the University, academic departments, and private sources. Oregon Presidential Scholarships are designated for promising students from Oregon. The University of Oregon is the only public institution in Oregon to sponsor National Merit Scholarships. The general University scholarships application is due January 15. Clark Honors College awards a generous number of need-based scholarships to cover all or part of the resource fees. Clark Honors College also participates in the Western Undergraduate Exchange program. To be eligible for these awards, students should complete their Clark Honors College and University of Oregon applications by November 1 or January 15 and submit a Free Application for Federal Student Aid (FAFSA).

Campus Overview

State-supported university, founded 1872, part of Oregon University System • **Coed** 16,349 undergraduate students, 91% full-time, 53% women, 47% men.

Undergraduates 14,890 full-time, 1,459 part-time. Students come from 56 states and territories, 87 other countries, 20% are from out of state, 2% African American, 6% Asian American or Pacific Islander, 3% Hispanic American, 1% Native American, 4% international, 9% transferred in, 21% live on campus.

Faculty *Total:* 1,116, 70% full-time, 95% with terminal degrees. *Student/faculty ratio:* 19:1.

Academic Programs *Special study options:* academic remediation for entering students, accelerated degree program, adult/continuing education programs, advanced placement credit, distance learning, double majors, English as a second language, freshman honors college, honors programs, independent study, internships, off-campus study, part-time degree program, services for LD students, student-designed majors, study abroad, summer session for credit. *ROTC:* Army (b), Air Force (c).

Athletics Member NCAA. All Division I except football (Division I-A). *Intercollegiate sports:* badminton M(c)/W(c), baseball M(c), basketball M(s)/W(s), bowling M(c)/W(c), cheerleading M(s)(c)/W(s)(c), crew M(c)/W(c), cross-country running M(s)/W(s), equestrian sports M(c)/W(c), fencing M(c)/W(c), golf M(s)/W(s), ice hockey M(c), lacrosse M(c)/W(s), racquetball M(c)/W(c), rugby M(c)/W(c), sailing M(c)/W(c), skiing (downhill) M(c)/W(c), soccer M(c)/W(s), softball W(s), swimming and diving M(c)/W(c), table tennis M(c)/W(c), tennis M(s)/W(s), track and field M(s)/W(s), ultimate Frisbee M(c)/W(c), volleyball M(c)/W(s), water polo M(c)/W(c), wrestling M(s). *Intramural sports:* badminton M/W, baseball M, bowling M/W, crew M/W, cross-country running M/W, equestrian sports M/W, fencing M/W, ice hockey M, lacrosse M/W, racquetball M/W, rugby M/W, sailing M/W, skiing (downhill) M/W, soccer M/W, softball W, swimming and diving M/W, table tennis M/W, tennis M/W, track and field M/W, ultimate Frisbee M/W, volleyball M/W, water polo M/W.

Costs (2004–05) *Tuition:* state resident $4071 full-time, $103 per credit hour part-time; nonresident $15,501 full-time, $407 per credit hour part-time. Full-time tuition and fees vary according to class time, course load, degree level, program, and reciprocity agreements. Part-time tuition and fees vary according to class time, course load, degree level, and program. *Required fees:* $1479 full-time, $346 per term part-time. *Room and board:* $7331. Room and board charges vary according to board plan and housing facility.

Financial Aid In 2003, 816 non-need-based awards were made. *Average percent of need met:* 77%. *Average financial aid package:* $8054. *Average need-based loan:* $4243. *Average need-based gift aid:* $3779. *Average non-need-based aid:* $1753.

Contact: Director: Richard Kraus, Clark Honors College, 1293 University of Oregon, Eugene, Oregon 97403-1293; *Telephone:* 541-346-5414; *E-mail:* honors@uoregon.edu; *Web site:* http://honors.uoregon.edu

University of Portland
Honors Program
Portland, Oregon

The Honors Program at the University of Portland is designed to enhance the intellectual life of the University community by the close mentoring of high achieving and intrinsically motivated students who will serve as the intellectual catalysts at the University and beyond. The program features specialized core experiences for the first two years. Each student forms a close bond with a faculty mentor and shares in a variety of reflection opportunities. At the end of each semester the student, after numerous discussions/consultations with his or her mentor, writes a paper in which she or he reflects on the year's academic experiences. These reflection responses are guided by the core questions of the University. At the end of the freshman year, the mentor meets with the student and discusses the personal reflection statement. At the end of the sophomore year, honors students attend a reflective retreat during which they review their personal development over the first two years at the University and explore and create personal mission statements. In the last two years, students meet the honors requirements within their majors, complete an Honors Capstone Experience, and participate in at least two seminar offerings. Beyond the curriculum, honors students are encouraged to participate in a wide range of opportunities from listening to and interacting with guest speakers, to study abroad, to innovative projects.

Participation Requirements: All students in the Honors Program take a course that is specifically designated as an honor's course each semester for the first two years. The sophomore-year courses, however, integrate honors students into a core class setting that includes other students interested in greater intellectual challenges. In this course, honors students are expected to become models for other students by demonstrating their passion for learning. The junior and senior years offer honors requirements within the major, concluding with an Honors Capstone Experience adjudicated by a team of interdisciplinary professors. The last two years are also enriched with interdisciplinary reading and discussion seminars, of which each honors student must take two. Additional opportunities to listen to and interact with various speakers who come to campus are an expectation of the honors students.

Admission Process: Application for admission to the Honors Program is by invitation from the Director of the Honors Program. Those initially invited to apply are identified by having a grade point average of 3.75 or above and a SAT cumulative score of 1300 or above (if revised SAT is taken with essay portion included, minimal score is 1950). Other students interested in the program are encouraged to apply and will be evaluated on an individual basis. Students interested in the program are expected to complete an honors application. Applications along with the materials submitted as part of the general application process to the University are reviewed by a panel of University faculty members and administrators directly connected with the Honors Program. Decisions regarding acceptance into the Honors Program commence in the late fall of the year preceding the start of the student at the University.

Scholarship Availability: While the University offers a wide variety of scholarship opportunities, there are, at this time, no scholarships specifically related to the Honors Program.

Campus Overview

Independent Roman Catholic comprehensive, founded 1901 • **Coed** 2,829 undergraduate students, 96% full-time, 60% women, 40% men.

Undergraduates 2,721 full-time, 108 part-time. Students come from 40 states and territories, 19 other countries, 56% are from out of state, 2% African American, 9% Asian American or Pacific Islander, 4% Hispanic American, 0.6% Native American, 2% international, 4% transferred in, 54% live on campus.

Faculty *Total:* 305, 59% full-time, 54% with terminal degrees. *Student/faculty ratio:* 13:1.

Academic Programs *Special study options:* adult/continuing education programs, advanced placement credit, double majors, honors programs, independent study, internships, off-campus study, part-time degree program, services for LD students, study abroad, summer session for credit. *ROTC:* Army (b), Air Force (b).

Athletics Member NCAA. All Division I. *Intercollegiate sports:* baseball M(s), basketball M(s)/W(s), cross-country running M(s)/W(s), golf M(s)/W(s), rugby M(c), soccer M(s)/W(s), tennis M(s)/W(s), track and field M(s)/W(s), volleyball W(s). *Intramural sports:* basketball M/W, crew M/W, cross-country running M/W, football M/W, rugby M, skiing (cross-country) M/W, skiing (downhill) M/W, soccer M(c)/W, softball M/W, swimming and diving M/W, tennis M/W, track and field M/W, volleyball M/W, water polo M/W, weight lifting M/W.

Costs (2004–05) *Comprehensive fee:* $30,570 includes full-time tuition ($23,200), mandatory fees ($320), and room and board ($7050). Full-time tuition and fees vary according to program. Part-time tuition: $735 per credit hour. Part-time tuition and fees vary according to program. *College room only:* $3525. Room and board charges vary according to board plan and housing facility.

Financial Aid 900 Federal Work-Study jobs (averaging $1750). 9 state and other part-time jobs (averaging $1660). In 2003, 973 non-need-based awards were made. *Average percent of need met:* 83%. *Average financial aid package:* $20,606. *Average need-based loan:* $5277. *Average need-based gift aid:* $13,764. *Average non-need-based aid:* $15,934.

Contact: Associate Dean: Dr. Edward K. Bowen, University of Portland, 5000 North Willamette Boulevard, Portland, Oregon 97203; *Telephone:* 503-943-7388; *Fax:* 503-943-8079; *E-mail:* bowen@up.edu

PENNSYLVANIA

Alvernia College

Honors Program

Reading, Pennsylvania

*T*he purpose of the Honors Program at Alvernia College is to assist students of outstanding intellectual promise and high motivation who are seeking increased challenge at the undergraduate level and/or who are interested in future graduate or professional study. The program is designed to recognize and encourage academic excellence, to stimulate students to work at their own pace, and to facilitate the exchange of idea and information among students and faculty members with varied interests in different disciplines. Alvernia College's Honors Program is guided by the same Franciscan values that guide the College as a whole: service, humility, peacemaking, contemplation, and collegiality. The Honors Program provides a collegial environment in which students feel comfortable engaging in contemplative work. Honors students are encouraged to give back to their communities and to embrace the College's core values in everything they do. The Honors Program gives academically gifted students of all majors a college experience that helps them develop their talents and skills. Students comment that being involved in the Honors Program allows them to form a peer group of similarly talented individuals who are dedicated to academic inquiry and success.

Honors classes typically have less than 20 students and are taught by professors who have a real passion for the subject they are teaching. The program features interdisciplinary, interactive classes with innovative topics and methods of teaching. In the past few years, courses have included: CSI: Fact and Fiction; Religion, War and Politics; The Human Genome; Mind, Brains, and Computers; Alvernia College Radio; World Music; and Peace and Justice. Traditional lecture-style courses are discouraged, and students can expect to be involved in discussions and debates, out-of-class experiences or in-class simulations, and other types of experiential learning. In the first year seminar, students typically have the opportunity to participate as a group in a service-learning project. Students in the Honors Program have flexibility in which courses they take; typically, courses help students meet the general education requirements of the College. To complete the program, students complete a two-semester thesis on a topic of their choice. Honors students frequently present their research at local undergraduate research conferences.

The program offers extracurricular opportunities, such as cultural events and social gatherings. In the recent past, students have attended a variety of regional theater performances, gone to museums and historical sites, and attended on-campus lectures and events. The Director has hosted a picnic at her house to mark the end of the academic year, and there is a special ceremony for students who complete all of the Honors Program requirements. Honors students tend to be highly involved in all aspects of campus life.

The Honors Program was founded in 1999. Each year, about 60 first-year students are automatically enrolled in the program. Transfers may apply for admission, as may students past their first semester at the College. At any given time, there are between 150 and 200 students in the program. Faculty members from almost every department have offered courses in the Honors Program.

Participation Requirements: Graduation from the Alvernia College Honors Program requires that students complete the following: the First-Year Honors Seminar (may be waived for transfer students), 9 additional credits of Honors course work, and a 6-credit thesis. Students are required to attain a cumulative grade point average of 3.3 in both the major and general course work by graduation. Completion of the Honors Program is recognized by a cord at graduation, noted on the commencement program, and designated on a student's transcript.

Admission Process: Admission to the Alvernia College Honors Program requires SAT I scores of 1100 or higher (1650 on the three-part SAT), a minimum high school grade point average of 3.5, and students should be in the top 25 percent of their high school class. Students who meet two of the three criteria are considered for admission to the program. Students with a 3.3 GPA or higher at Alvernia or transferring from another institution may petition the Director of the Program for admission. Such petitions should include a letter of intent, proof of current GPA, and a meeting with the Director. Admission to the program is rolling and automatic. Students not admitted automatically may petition for admission.

Scholarship Availability: While there are no scholarships available independently through the Honors Program, there is a high correlation between Honors Program membership and the top two levels of academic scholarship recipients at the College. Therefore, almost all Honors Program participants receive merit-based scholarships.

Campus Overview

Independent Roman Catholic comprehensive, founded 1958 • **Coed** 1,848 undergraduate students, 75% full-time, 67% women, 33% men.

Undergraduates 1,384 full-time, 464 part-time. Students come from 13 states and territories, 4 other countries, 8% are from out of state, 10% African American, 2% Asian American or Pacific Islander, 5% Hispanic American, 1% international, 4% transferred in, 26% live on campus.

Faculty *Total:* 133, 49% full-time. *Student/faculty ratio:* 18:1.

Academic Programs *Special study options:* academic remediation for entering students, accelerated degree program, adult/continuing education programs, advanced placement credit, double majors, honors programs, independent study, internships, off-campus study, part-time degree program, services for LD students, summer session for credit. *ROTC:* Army (c). *Unusual degree programs:* 3-2 occupational therapy.

Athletics Member NCAA. All Division III. *Intercollegiate sports:* baseball M, basketball M/W, cross-country running M/W, field hockey W, golf M, lacrosse M/W, soccer M/W, softball W, tennis M/W, volleyball W. *Intramural sports:* basketball M/W, ice hockey M(c)/W(c), lacrosse M/W, skiing (downhill) M(c)/W(c), volleyball M(c).

Costs (2004–05) *Comprehensive fee:* $25,005 includes full-time tuition ($17,500), mandatory fees ($175), and room and board ($7330). Full-time tuition and fees vary according to class time and reciprocity agreements. Part-time tuition: $515 per credit. Part-time tuition and fees vary according to class time and course load. *College room only:* $3690. Room and board charges vary according to board plan and housing facility.

Financial Aid 620 Federal Work-Study jobs (averaging $1950). In 2003, 130 non-need-based awards were made. *Average percent of need met:* 81%. *Average financial aid package:* $17,907. *Average need-based loan:* $3552. *Average need-based gift aid:* $9245. *Average non-need-based aid:* $15,489.

Contact: Director of Honors Program: Victoria Williams, Ph.D., 400 Saint Bernardine Street, Reading, Pennsylvania 19607; *Telephone:* 610-796-5511; *Fax:* 610-796-8396; *E-mail:* victoria.williams@alvernia.edu; *Web site:* http://www.alvernia.edu/honors

Arcadia University
Honors Program
Glenside, Pennsylvania

The mission of the Arcadia University Honors Program is to offer intellectually challenging and enriching educational opportunities to highly motivated, talented, and creative students in all majors. The program offers scholars occasions to interact collaboratively and form a sense of community through both on- and off-campus learning activities. Honors courses average 10 to 20 students in a class, offering the opportunity to interact with faculty members from a variety of academic departments. Students accepted into the Honors Program are encouraged to study abroad during their academic program. All honors students are invited to go to London or Scotland during spring break for free, while all other full-time freshmen in good academic standing may attend for $245. The Honors Program was founded in the early 1970s and enhanced and broadened in the fall of 1996. The program presently accommodates 100 students.

Participation Requirements: The Honors Program offers four types of academic activities. The first are honors sections of the freshman writing courses, EN 101: Thought and Expression I and EN 102: Thought and Expression II. The second are Honors Readings (HN 201) and Honors Project (HN 202)—courses that are typically taken during the sophomore year. The third activity involves upper-level courses adapted for honors credit. The fourth type is Honors Colloquia (HN 390), which are investigative seminars addressing open-ended topics. They connect at least two disciplines and blend readings in classic texts with innovative learning styles.

Honors Program students must maintain a GPA of at least 3.25 to remain in good standing. Students who complete the Honors Program requirements have the designation Honors Scholar appear on their transcripts.

Admission Process: Students are accepted into the Honors Program on a rolling basis. Freshman applicants to the University with a score of at least 1200 on the SAT who rank in the top 10 percent of their graduating class are evaluated for acceptance into the program based upon the strength of their admissions application (high school average, rank, essay, recommendations, etc.). Transfer applicants with a minimum transfer GPA of 3.25 are reviewed for acceptance into the program as well. Students seeking to enter the program after being

enrolled at Arcadia University may be nominated or may self-nominate for consideration if they have an overall GPA of 3.25 or higher.

Scholarship Availability: All students accepted to Arcadia University are automatically reviewed for scholarships. The University's Distinguished Scholarships range from $3000 a year to full tuition, and Achievement Awards range from $1000 to $6000 a year.

Campus Overview

Independent comprehensive, founded 1853, affiliated with Presbyterian Church (U.S.A.) • **Coed** 1,929 undergraduate students, 88% full-time, 73% women, 27% men.

Undergraduates 1,706 full-time, 223 part-time. Students come from 27 states and territories, 15 other countries, 27% are from out of state, 9% African American, 3% Asian American or Pacific Islander, 2% Hispanic American, 0.3% Native American, 1% international, 5% transferred in, 68% live on campus.

Faculty *Total:* 347, 30% full-time. *Student/faculty ratio:* 12:1.

Academic Programs *Special study options:* adult/continuing education programs, advanced placement credit, cooperative education, distance learning, double majors, English as a second language, honors programs, independent study, internships, off-campus study, part-time degree program, services for LD students, student-designed majors, study abroad, summer session for credit. *ROTC:* Army (c). *Unusual degree programs:* 3-2 engineering with Columbia University; environmental studies; optometry with Pennsylvania College of Optometry.

Athletics Member NCAA. All Division III. *Intercollegiate sports:* baseball M, basketball M/W, cross-country running M/W, equestrian sports M/W, field hockey W, golf M/W, lacrosse W, soccer M/W, softball W, swimming and diving M/W, tennis M/W, volleyball W. *Intramural sports:* basketball M/W, cheerleading W(c), equestrian sports M/W, field hockey W, rock climbing M/W, soccer M/W, swimming and diving M, tennis M/W, volleyball M/W, weight lifting M/W.

Costs (2005–06) *Comprehensive fee:* $33,570 includes full-time tuition ($23,990), mandatory fees ($280), and room and board ($9300). Full-time tuition and fees vary according to course load, degree level, and program. Part-time tuition: $420 per credit. *Room and board:* Room and board charges vary according to board plan.

Financial Aid 914 Federal Work-Study jobs (averaging $1294). 224 state and other part-time jobs (averaging $870). In 2004, 143 non-need-based awards were made. *Average percent of need met:* 79%. *Average financial aid package:* $16,465. *Average need-based loan:* $5120. *Average need-based gift aid:* $11,566. *Average non-need-based aid:* $7142.

Contact: Director: Collene Hare, 450 South Easton Road, Glenside, Pennsylvania 19038-3295; *Telephone:* 877-ARCADIA (toll-free); *Fax:* 215-572-4049; *E-mail:* admiss@arcadia.edu; *Web site:* http://www.arcadia.edu

Bloomsburg University of Pennsylvania
Honors Program
Bloomsburg, Pennsylvania

The University Honors Program (UHP) at Bloomsburg University (BU) offers students who have demonstrated exceptional academic talents and achievements an opportunity to reach their full potential as scholars. Listed as a "first-rate honors program" by the Money Advisor (1995, Time, Inc.), the program challenges students through specially designed honors courses, providing an alternative to Bloomsburg's general education curriculum. Students select classes from a varying menu of humanities, social science, and math/science courses, followed by a selection of junior-level seminars in areas of special concern (values, diversity, quantitative/analytical, and interdisciplinary studies). Honors classes are small (average size is fewer than 20 students) and are taught by outstanding faculty members who are committed to helping their students achieve intellectual depth, pursue creative discovery, and produce finished scholarly work. Honors faculty members must submit course proposals for review by an Honors Advisory Committee consisting of faculty members, students, and the program director. The core program culminates in a two-semester Honors Independent Study (HIS) project. The topic or subject area is chosen by the student, and both theses and creative projects are encouraged. Students are guided and advised during their HIS project by a faculty mentor of their choice. This amounts to an apprenticeship with a practicing scholar and provides an invaluable experience for the exceptional undergraduate student. Students are encouraged to start their HIS projects in their junior year such that they have an opportunity to present their findings at regional and national meetings.

In addition to exceptional classes and specialized, advanced study, the UHP fosters and maintains an active community of scholarly students. Through small classes, class and program trips, social activities, and group-oriented service projects, honors students develop and engage in a rewarding community of like-minded students sharing ideas, working together, and supporting one another in their personal and intellectual endeavors. To further encourage community, students have the option of selecting honors interest housing, in which they live on a dormitory floor with other honors students. The students have a self-determined governing body and are deeply involved in helping to shape the Honors Program. Honors students serve as interviewers during recruiting, encourage top-notch faculty members to submit course proposals, design and maintain the Honors Program Web site, plan service and social activities, and serve on the Honors Advisory Committee and their own Honors Executive Board.

Approximately 120 students are enrolled in the UHP. Students and faculty members out of all four colleges (Liberal Arts, Science and Technology, Business, and Professional Studies) participate in the Honors Program at Bloomsburg. The overall program meets the guidelines developed by the National Collegiate Honors Council, of which the program is a member.

Participation Requirements: The honors curriculum is a four-year program that follows the basic structure of the University's general education curriculum. Students are required to take a minimum of 25 credits of honors courses, including at least one honors humanities, one honors social science, one honors math/science with a laboratory component, and one 300-level honors seminar plus the 1-credit Introduction to Honors Research and two semesters of Honors Independent Study. Students are placed in Honors Composition in the spring of their freshman year after completing or testing out of Composition 1. Students are also required to be active in service. UHP students must maintain a minimum overall 3.0 QPA. Graduates who successfully complete the program are awarded a bachelor's degree with University Honors. They are individually recognized at the Awards Banquet prior to commencement and receive special honors tassels for their graduation caps and recognition in the commencement program. Each honors course completed is designated on the students' transcripts, as is successful completion of the UHP.

Admission Process: Admission of freshmen to the program is by application. Applicants must have a minimum combined SAT score of 1150 (neither the verbal nor math score may fall below 550) and rank in the top 20 percent of their high school class. Students are asked to submit an essay on a topic chosen by the Honors Advisory Committee, a letter of recommendation from a high school faculty member or counselor, and an example of their best written or creative work. Each student is interviewed by a faculty member and 2 current honors students. Selection of successful applicants is overseen by the Honors Advisory Committee based on the criteria listed above.

Matriculated and transfer students are admitted on an individual basis. Acceptance is determined based on the student's college or university record (minimum GPA of 3.25), a letter of recommendation from a faculty member, an essay, and a completion plan.

Within BU guidelines, the UHP accepts Advanced Placement credits to fulfill the Honors Composition requirement.

Scholarship Availability: The UHP has a two-tiered scholarship program. Each year, the program awards approximately twenty freshman scholarships and about twelve smaller scholarships for students above the freshman year. These are merit scholarships. Funds to support students working on their Honors Independent Study projects are routinely available. BU also has a number of University, college, and departmental merit scholarships available.

Campus Overview

State-supported comprehensive, founded 1839, part of Pennsylvania State System of Higher Education • **Coed** 7,524 undergraduate students, 93% full-time, 60% women, 40% men.

Undergraduates 7,029 full-time, 495 part-time. Students come from 26 states and territories, 33 other countries, 10% are from out of state, 5% African American, 1% Asian American or Pacific Islander, 2% Hispanic American, 0.1% Native American, 0.5% international, 5% transferred in, 42% live on campus.

Faculty *Total:* 395, 88% full-time, 76% with terminal degrees. *Student/faculty ratio:* 21:1.

Academic Programs *Special study options:* academic remediation for entering students, adult/continuing education programs, advanced placement credit, cooperative education, distance learning, double majors, freshman honors college, honors programs, independent study, internships, off-campus study, part-time degree program, services for LD students, study abroad, summer session for credit. *ROTC:* Army (b), Air Force (c). *Unusual degree programs:* 3-2 engineering with Pennsylvania State University, Wilkes University.

Athletics Member NCAA. All Division II except wrestling (Division I). *Intercollegiate sports:* baseball M(s), basketball M(s)/W(s), cheerleading M/W, cross-country running M(s)/W(s), equestrian sports M(c)/W(c), field hockey W(s), football M(s), lacrosse W, soccer M(s)/W(s), softball W(s), swimming and diving M(s)/W(s), tennis M(s)/W(s), track and field M(s)/W(s), volleyball W, wrestling M(s). *Intramural sports:* archery M(c)/W(c), basketball M/W, fencing M(c)/W(c), field hockey W, football M/W, lacrosse M(c), racquetball M/W, rock climbing M(c)/W(c), rugby M(c)/W(c), skiing (downhill) M(c)/W(c), soccer M/W, softball M/W, tennis M/W, ultimate Frisbee M(c)/W(c), volleyball M/W, water polo M(c)/W(c), weight lifting M(c), wrestling M.

Costs (2004–05) *Tuition:* state resident $4810 full-time, $200 per credit part-time; nonresident $12,026 full-time, $501 per credit part-time. Full-time tuition and fees vary according to course load. Part-time tuition and fees vary according to course load. *Required fees:* $1279 full-time. *Room and board:* $5200; room only: $3012. Room and board charges vary according to board plan and housing facility.

Financial Aid 1,141 Federal Work-Study jobs (averaging $2553). 1,073 state and other part-time jobs (averaging $2609). *Average percent of need met:* 65%. *Average financial aid package:* $10,465. *Average need-based loan:* $3541. *Average need-based gift aid:* $3897.

Contact: Director: Dr. Emeric Schultz, University Honors Program, B12 Luzerne Hall, Bloomsburg University, 400 East Second Street, Bloomsburg, Pennsylvania 1781; *Telephone:* 570-389-4713; *Fax:* 570-389-2049; *E-mail:* eschultz@bloomu.edu

Cabrini College

Honors Program

Radnor, Pennsylvania

The Honors Program at Cabrini College recognizes that students have various reasons for being interested in honors education. Some students see college as the beginning of a process of life-long learning and a desire to engage in new subjects, stimulating discussions, and active learning. Other students are interested in becoming scholars, researchers, and public intellectuals. Our program helps both types of students achieve their goals. We like to think of our Honors Program as providing a university experience within the college context.

The Honors Program is curricular, residential, and experiential. Based in the College's core curriculum, honors courses fulfill general degree requirements as well as honors program requirements. Honors classes are small and characterized by enthusiastic discussions and/or inquiry-based projects. Courses are taught by full-time faculty and approach the relevant content area in unique and interesting ways. For example, rather than simply taking a U.S. history course, honors students have the option of learning about the scope of American history through studying the culture of baseball. Rather than simply taking an introduction to business course, honors students have the option of learning about micro- and macro-economics in a course analyzing the context of the Great Depression.

First-year students are given preferential housing on the top floor of the College's new residence hall. This floor includes a study area for honors students. Sophomore students are given the opportunity to live in an honors house on campus, if they want to continue living in an honors environment. Finally, honors students have the opportunity to participate in a wide range of experiential opportunities offered through the College generally or the Honors Program specifically. These include study-abroad experiences and internships, cultural activities, and special interactions with visiting scholars as well as off-campus excursions, hikes, and concerts.

Participation Requirements: Honors students are required to complete at least 4 honors courses beyond the first-year Honors Seminar to have honors noted on their diploma and their transcript. All of these courses fulfill core curriculum or general education requirements in addition to fulfilling the requirements of the honors program. Students must maintain at least a 3.0 in their honors courses.

Admission Process: Admission to the honors program for first year students is by invitation only. Generally speaking, the Admissions office sends out these invitations to students with a combined SAT score of 1080 or higher and who had a minimum 3.5 high school GPA. Students not invited to join the program during the admissions process are eligible to join the program with the recommendation of a faculty member and an interview with the director of the honors program.

Scholarship Availability: Of all first year students, 92 percent receive some type of financial aid. In 2004–05, first year students received an average of $11,800 in total aid, with $9,278 in total grant money.

Campus Overview

Independent Roman Catholic comprehensive, founded 1957 • **Coed** 1,649 undergraduate students, 87% full-time, 65% women, 35% men.

Undergraduates 1,434 full-time, 215 part-time. Students come from 20 states and territories, 12 other countries, 47% are from out of state, 7% African American, 2% Asian American or Pacific Islander, 2% Hispanic American, 0.1% Native American, 1% international, 4% transferred in, 61% live on campus.

Faculty *Total:* 216, 29% full-time, 39% with terminal degrees. *Student/faculty ratio:* 15:1.

Academic Programs *Special study options:* academic remediation for entering students, accelerated degree program, adult/continuing education programs, advanced placement credit, cooperative education, double majors, honors programs, independent study, internships, off-campus study, part-time degree program, services for LD students, student-designed majors, study abroad, summer session for credit. *ROTC:* Army (c). *Unusual degree programs:* 3-2 physical therapy, occupational therapy with Thomas Jefferson University.

Athletics Member NCAA. All Division III. *Intercollegiate sports:* basketball M/W, cross-country running M/W, field hockey W, golf M, lacrosse M/W, soccer M/W, softball W, swimming and diving W, tennis M/W, track and field M/W, volleyball W. *Intramural sports:* badminton M/W, basketball M/W, cheerleading W(c), football M/W, racquetball M/W, rugby M/W, skiing (downhill) M/W, soccer M/W, softball M/W, squash M/W, swimming and diving M/W, tennis M/W, ultimate Frisbee M/W, volleyball M/W.

Costs (2004–05) *Comprehensive fee:* $31,230 includes full-time tuition ($21,450), mandatory fees ($800), and room and board ($8980). Part-time tuition: $380 per credit hour. Part-time tuition and fees vary according to course load. *Required fees:* $45 per term part-time. *Room and board:* Room and board charges vary according to board plan and housing facility.

Financial Aid 203 Federal Work-Study jobs (averaging $765). In 2003, 322 non-need-based awards were made. *Average financial aid package:* $12,877. *Average need-based loan:* $5269. *Average need-based gift aid:* $5253. *Average non-need-based aid:* $4260.

Contact: Director: Dr. Leonard Norman Primiano, 610 King of Prussia Road, Radnor, Pennsylvania 19087-3698; *Telephone:* 601-902-8330; *Fax:* 610-902-8285; *E-mail:* lprimiano@cabrini.edu

California University of Pennsylvania

Honors Program

California, Pennsylvania

The Honors Program has a flexible curriculum, which allows students in any major to participate and complete both their individual major and their Honors Program. The specific mission of the Honors Program is to help students prepare for the next phase in their lives after graduation. The Honors Program provides an enhanced educational experience for the most talented students and faculty members in small courses and a personalized environment. Each spring, the Honors Program sponsors a grouping of courses from several academic disciplines that are arranged to give students a truly interdisciplinary experience. The spring curriculum is rotated each year through a varying emphasis on science, arts and humanities, and social sciences. The program includes an extended field-trip experience at significant locales.

The Honors Program has existed since 1980, admits approximately 75 students each year, and has 190 students currently enrolled in the program.

Participation Requirements: The Honors Program is a four-year program that culminates in the writing and oral presentation of a thesis project. Typically, first-year students take two semesters of honors composition courses (6 credits) and the Honors Program orientation course, which functions as a first-year seminar. The Honors Program minimally requires the successful completion of 24 honors credits (eight courses), which includes the senior thesis project. Honors Program students are required to maintain at least a 3.25 (Dean's list) overall cumulative GPA. The transcript of the Honors Program is imprinted with a special indication and designation upon granting of the degree. Honors Program students are given special recognition similar to graduate students in the commencement booklet, and they receive a specific and special recognition on their University transcript.

Admission Process: Program participation is by invitation only. Generally, all incoming students to the University are screened on the basis of their SAT or ACT scores as well as their high school GPA, which generates the invitation. The minimum SAT score is 1100 (composite verbal and math) and must be accompanied by a high school cumulative GPA of at least 3.0. An SAT score of at least 1200 (composite verbal and math) requires no specific high school GPA. A student who achieves a GPA of 3.75 or higher after accruing 30 University credits may seek admission to the program.

Scholarship Availability: The Honors Program receives one annual scholarship, although nearly all academic scholarships at the University are awarded to Honors Program students. Each summer, California University of Pennsylvania participates in the Pennsylvania Summer Honors Program, which provides two Honors Program students the opportunity to study at one of the State System of Higher Education's institutions. Frequently, the scholarship provides a rewarding experience.

Campus Overview

State-supported comprehensive, founded 1852, part of Pennsylvania State System of Higher Education • **Coed** 5,455 undergraduate students, 89% full-time, 52% women, 48% men.

Undergraduates 4,830 full-time, 625 part-time. Students come from 22 states and territories, 15 other countries, 4% are from out of state, 5% African American, 0.3% Asian American or Pacific Islander, 0.5% Hispanic American, 0.2% Native American, 0.7% international, 37% transferred in, 25% live on campus.

Faculty *Total:* 364, 76% full-time, 46% with terminal degrees. *Student/faculty ratio:* 19:1.

Academic Programs *Special study options:* academic remediation for entering students, accelerated degree program, adult/continuing education programs, advanced placement credit, cooperative education, distance learning, double majors, honors programs, independent study, internships, off-campus study, part-time degree program, services for LD students, study abroad, summer session for credit. *ROTC:* Army (b).

Athletics Member NCAA. All Division II. *Intercollegiate sports:* baseball M(s), basketball M(s)/W(s), cheerleading M/W, cross-country running M(s)/W(s), fencing M/W, football M(s), golf M(s)/W(s), soccer M(s)/W(s), softball W(s), swimming and diving W(s), tennis W(s), track and field M(s)/W(s), volleyball M/W(s). *Intramural sports:* archery M/W, baseball M, basketball M/W, cheerleading M/W, cross-country running M/W, equestrian sports M/W, fencing M/W, football M, golf M, ice hockey M/W, lacrosse M/W, rugby M/W, soccer M/W, softball M/W, track and field M/W, volleyball M/W.

Costs (2004–05) *Tuition:* state resident $4810 full-time, $200 per credit part-time; nonresident $7216 full-time, $301 per credit part-time. Full-time tuition and fees vary according to location. Part-time tuition and fees vary according to location. *Required fees:* $1441 full-time. *Room and board:* $7280; room only: $4590. Room and board charges vary according to board plan.

Financial Aid *Average financial aid package:* $7025.

Contact: Director: Dr. Edward J. Chute or Assistant Director: Professor Erin E. Mountz or Honors Program Secretary: Kimberly L. Orslene, California University of Pennsylvania, 250 University Avenue, Box 100, California, Pennsylvania 15419-1394; *Telephone:* 724-938-4535 or 1544; *Fax:* 724-938-5710; *E-mail:* honors@cup.edu

Clarion University of Pennsylvania
Honors Program
Clarion, Pennsylvania

*C*larion University's Honors Program is a "close knit" group of talented students preparing for the future. Honors courses satisfy general educational requirements and include field experiences. The twenty-one-course curriculum promotes development of essential life skills targeted for successful career outcomes. The honors experience extends beyond the walls of the traditional classroom and has included visits with archaeologists in Italy, with psychologists and anthropologists at a primate center, with large corporate firms and small businesses, and with molecular biologists in laboratories. Honors students have studied twentieth-century music, learned the art of problem solving, and pondered the ethical implications of research. In addition, curricular and cocurricular themes prepare Clarion Honors Program students to assume leadership roles. The program has formed learning partnerships with high school programs for the gifted. Academically talented students from these high schools visit the campus for theater performances, environmental science field trips, and debate tournaments. The Honors Program is not for all students—it's only for those individuals who desire professional success, demand academic excellence, and expect to create the future.

The program, which has been in existence since 1986, selects 50 freshmen each year. Currently, there are 200 students in the program. Honors students major in every department and college within the University and participate in preprofessional planning.

Participation Requirements: The Honors Program is a four-year program. In the freshman year, students take a 6-credit modes of discourse (linked English and speech class) and a 3-credit humanities course in the spring semester. In the sophomore year, students take a 3-credit mathematics or science class and a 3-credit social sciences course. In the junior year, students take a junior seminar that develops a project (typically within the major) for the senior presentation. Honors 450 is the capstone experience that culminates in a University-wide presentation. This senior project is developed individually with a faculty adviser. Honors courses are taught as special topics and faculty instructors are recruited for their scholarly expertise.

To remain in the program, students must maintain at least a 3.4 cumulative GPA. Successful completion of the program is recognized at commencement and is also noted on the official transcript.

Admission Process: High school students are recruited on the basis of applications. Application sets require SAT I scores of 1150 or higher or equivalent ACT scores, graduation in the top 15 percent of the high school class, activities, a short written statement, and an interview with the Program Admissions Committee. Students may apply for admission to the Honors Program after the first or second semester of the freshman year. Students may major in any discipline within the University.

Scholarship Availability: Scholarships of various amounts are awarded based on academic performance while in high school. Sophomores, juniors, and seniors may receive renewable awards based on academic performance and service. Most honors students are recipients of academic scholarships.

Campus Overview

State-supported comprehensive, founded 1867, part of Pennsylvania State System of Higher Education • **Coed** 5,943 undergraduate students, 89% full-time, 62% women, 38% men.

Undergraduates 5,277 full-time, 666 part-time. Students come from 29 states and territories, 40 other countries, 5% African American,

0.7% Asian American or Pacific Islander, 0.9% Hispanic American, 0.2% Native American, 0.9% international, 6% transferred in, 34% live on campus.

Faculty *Total:* 313, 87% full-time. *Student/faculty ratio:* 19:1.

Academic Programs *Special study options:* academic remediation for entering students, accelerated degree program, adult/continuing education programs, advanced placement credit, distance learning, double majors, honors programs, internships, part-time degree program, services for LD students, study abroad, summer session for credit. *Unusual degree programs:* 3-2 engineering with University of Pittsburgh, Case Western Reserve University.

Athletics Member NCAA. All Division II except wrestling (Division I). *Intercollegiate sports:* baseball M(s), basketball M(s)/W(s), cross-country running M(s)/W(s), football M(s), golf M(s), softball W(s), swimming and diving M(s)/W(s), tennis W(s), track and field M(s)/W(s), volleyball W(s), wrestling M(s). *Intramural sports:* badminton M/W, basketball M/W, bowling M/W, cross-country running M/W, football M, golf M/W, racquetball M/W, soccer M/W, swimming and diving M/W, tennis M/W, track and field M/W, volleyball M(c)/W, weight lifting M/W, wrestling M.

Costs (2004–05) *Tuition:* state resident $4810 full-time, $200 per credit hour part-time; nonresident $9620 full-time, $401 per credit hour part-time. *Room and board:* $4816; room only: $3194.

Financial Aid 300 Federal Work-Study jobs (averaging $1540). In 2001, 297 non-need-based awards were made. *Average percent of need met:* 93%. *Average financial aid package:* $6654. *Average need-based loan:* $3401. *Average need-based gift aid:* $6493. *Average non-need-based aid:* $2577.

Contact: Contact: Director: Dr. Hallie E. Savage, 840 Wood Street, Clarion, Pennsylvania 16214-1232; *Telephone:* 814-393-2585; *Fax:* 814-393-2430; *E-mail:* hsavage@clarion.edu; *Web site:* http://www. clarion.edu/honors

College Misericordia
College Honors Program
Dallas, Pennsylvania

The Honors Program at College Misericordia is an interdisciplinary learning community of students and faculty members working together to create an intellectually stimulating and challenging environment for learning. The academic portion of the Honors Program consists of three components: alternative courses, monthly Explorations Seminars, and the Capstone Seminar. The first is a sequence of core courses in the humanities and social sciences designed specifically for honors students. Honors classes are small (usually fewer than 15 students), emphasize discussion and critical analysis of material, use primary sources in addition to traditional textbooks, and focus on developing students' communication skills, particularly in writing. In addition, honors courses are linked by common principles and ideas so that they are strongly interdisciplinary. The program also offers elective honors courses in math, science, and the health sciences. The second academic component of the Honors Program requires student participation in the Honors Explorations Seminar, which usually meets three times each semester. The seminar takes many different forms, including debates, roundtables, or guest lectures, but it always involves discussion among students and faculty members on a topic of general interest. The final academic component of the Honors Program is the required Honors Capstone Seminar. Within this seminar, students are guided through a process of self-directed research and writing and produce a professional-quality research paper that is presented to the College community and published in the College Misericordia honors journal, Honorus.

The Honors Program also sponsors a variety of additional academic and social programs and opportunities for honors students.

Field trips to local and regional historical and cultural venues are often incorporated into honors classes, as are service-learning opportunities. Annual honors trips are planned in consultation with students and have included trips to Philadelphia; Washington, D.C.; and Montreal. Interested honors students are also encouraged to participate in conferences sponsored by the National Collegiate Honors Council and other colleges and universities. Honors students are integrally involved in making program-related decisions and in planning honors activities and events. This is accomplished primarily through the College Misericordia Honors Student Council, which consists of student representatives from each of the classes.

The College Misericordia Honors Program was founded in 1999 and currently enrolls 60 students.

Participation Requirements: Honors students must complete an alternative 36-credit core sequence of honors courses in the humanities and social sciences similar to the College's required core sequence. Each semester, honors students must successfully participate in the Honors Exploration Seminar. They must also complete the Honors Capstone Seminar, which is usually taken in the senior year.

To remain in the program, honors students must achieve at least a 3.0 GPA in their freshman and sophomore years and a 3.25 GPA thereafter; they must also receive grades of C or better in all honors classes.

Graduating honors students who have fulfilled the requirements of the program receive recognition on their diploma, at College awards ceremonies, and at commencement.

Admission Process: Students are admitted to the Honors Program by application only. Admissions decisions are based on evidence of intellectual curiosity, which can be reflected in a number of different ways, including high school academic record, SAT scores, writing ability, interest in current events, and involvement in extracurricular activities. Students should contact the directors to request application materials.

Scholarship Availability: College Misericordia offers a variety of academic scholarships to qualified students. There are no scholarships specifically reserved for students in the Honors Program.

Campus Overview

Independent Roman Catholic comprehensive, founded 1924 • **Coed** 2,071 undergraduate students, 68% full-time, 74% women, 26% men.

Undergraduates 1,410 full-time, 661 part-time. Students come from 21 states and territories, 2 other countries, 16% are from out of state, 2% African American, 1% Asian American or Pacific Islander, 1% Hispanic American, 0.3% Native American, 0.1% international, 6% transferred in, 39% live on campus.

Faculty *Total:* 261, 36% full-time, 38% with terminal degrees. *Student/faculty ratio:* 11:1.

Academic Programs *Special study options:* academic remediation for entering students, accelerated degree program, adult/continuing education programs, advanced placement credit, cooperative education, distance learning, double majors, English as a second language, honors programs, independent study, internships, off-campus study, part-time degree program, services for LD students, student-designed majors, study abroad, summer session for credit. *ROTC:* Army (c), Air Force (c). *Unusual degree programs:* 3-2 occupational therapy, physical therapy, speech-language pathology.

Athletics Member NCAA. All Division III. *Intercollegiate sports:* baseball M, basketball M/W, cheerleading W, cross-country running M/W, field hockey W, golf M, lacrosse M/W, soccer M/W, softball W, swimming and diving M/W, tennis W, track and field M/W, volleyball W. *Intramural sports:* basketball M/W, bowling M/W, cross-country running M/W, football M/W, golf M/W, lacrosse M/W, racquetball M/W, soccer M/W, softball M/W, table tennis M/W, tennis M/W, ultimate Frisbee M/W, volleyball M/W.

Costs (2004–05) *Comprehensive fee:* $26,650 includes full-time tuition ($17,850), mandatory fees ($950), and room and board

($7850). Part-time tuition: $395 per credit. *College room only:* $4500. Room and board charges vary according to board plan and housing facility.

Financial Aid 245 Federal Work-Study jobs (averaging $1000). In 2004, 120 non-need-based awards were made. *Average percent of need met:* 76%. *Average financial aid package:* $13,740. *Average need-based loan:* $6992. *Average need-based gift aid:* $9635. *Average non-need-based aid:* $5789.

Contact: Directors: Dr. Marnie Hiester, College Misericordia, Lake Street, Dallas, Pennsylvania 18612; *Telephone:* 570-674-6316; *E-mail:* mhiester@misericordia.edu; Dr. Cathy Turner, College Misericordia, Lake Street, Dallas, Pennsylvania 18612; *Telephone:* 570-674-6777; *E-mail:* cturner@misericordia.edu; *Web site:* http://www.misericordia.edu

Drexel University
Pennoni Honors College
Philadelphia, Pennsylvania

The Drexel University Pennoni Honors College enriches the university experience for students with demonstrated academic achievements. The Honors College is in its fourteenth year of operation. In the Honors College, students from all majors receive individual attention throughout their academic progress and participate in a variety of courses that engage small groups of students with Drexel's best faculty members, special trips and cultural events, and social gatherings. The College offers the advantages of an elite liberal arts college within a major technological university. Incoming students are selected for admission based upon their superior intellectual strengths, accomplishments, and motivation. Current students who meet these criteria are also invited to apply.

The following three types of courses carry honors credits: honors sections of courses offered by various departments; interdisciplinary honors colloquia, sponsored by the Honors College; and honors options, the individual enrichment of nonhonors courses for particular students, which must be approved in advance by the instructor and the Assistant Dean.

Currently, there are approximately 1,500 students in the Honors College. About 350 to 400 entering freshmen are admitted each year.

Participation Requirements: Students are required to take a 1-credit honors seminar in the freshman year and two additional 3-credit courses prior to completion of the sophomore year. To remain in the Honors College, students must maintain a minimum 3.2 GPA. Qualified honors students may graduate with distinction from the Honors College. These students must complete 32 honors credits, which may include their senior design project or senior thesis, and maintain an overall GPA of 3.5 or higher. The design project or thesis must be judged worthy of honors credit.

Admission Process: Students apply directly to the Assistant Dean of the Honors College. The application requires standard information and includes a brief essay. Qualified Drexel students with a minimum 3.5 GPA may apply through the pre-junior year.

Scholarship Availability: Need-based and merit scholarships as well as grants, loans, and work-study programs are available through the Admissions Office. Some co-op positions and faculty research assistant positions are also available to students. The University makes approximately $60 million available annually for scholarship aid. In addition, a six-month co-op typically pays a Drexel student an average of $12,000. The Honors College itself does not offer scholarships.

Campus Overview

Independent university, founded 1891 • **Coed** 11,960 undergraduate students, 82% full-time, 40% women, 60% men.

Undergraduates 9,844 full-time, 2,116 part-time. Students come from 44 states and territories, 96 other countries, 42% are from out of state, 10% African American, 12% Asian American or Pacific Islander, 3% Hispanic American, 0.2% Native American, 6% international, 9% transferred in, 37% live on campus.

Faculty *Total:* 1,308, 50% full-time. *Student/faculty ratio:* 10:1.

Academic Programs *Special study options:* academic remediation for entering students, accelerated degree program, adult/continuing education programs, advanced placement credit, cooperative education, distance learning, double majors, English as a second language, freshman honors college, honors programs, independent study, internships, part-time degree program, services for LD students, study abroad, summer session for credit. *ROTC:* Army (b), Air Force (c).

Athletics Member NCAA. All Division I. *Intercollegiate sports:* baseball M(s), basketball M(s)/W(s), crew M(s)/W(s), field hockey W(s), golf M(s), lacrosse M(s)/W(s), soccer M(s)/W(s), softball W(s), swimming and diving M(s)/W(s), tennis M(s)/W(s), volleyball W(s), wrestling M(s). *Intramural sports:* badminton M/W, basketball M/W, fencing M/W, football M, ice hockey M, riflery M/W, rugby M/W, sailing M/W, softball M, squash M/W, table tennis M/W, tennis M/W, volleyball M/W, water polo M/W.

Costs (2004–05) *Comprehensive fee:* $32,070 includes full-time tuition ($20,800), mandatory fees ($1220), and room and board ($10,050). Full-time tuition and fees vary according to course load, program, and student level. Part-time tuition: $480 per credit. Part-time tuition and fees vary according to course load and program. *Required fees:* $95 per term part-time. *College room only:* $5970. Room and board charges vary according to board plan and housing facility.

Financial Aid In 2004, 1458 non-need-based awards were made. *Average percent of need met:* 58%. *Average financial aid package:* $13,735. *Average need-based loan:* $4507. *Average need-based gift aid:* $4518. *Average non-need-based aid:* $8347.

Contact: Director: Mark L. Greenberg, Dean, Antonia Mcmenamin, Assistant Dean, Honors Center, 5016 MacAlister Hall, Philadelphia, Pennsylvania 19104; *Telephone:* 215-895-1267; *Fax:* 215-895-6813; *E-mail:* mcmenaab@mail.drexel.edu; *Web site:* http://www.honors.drexel.edu

Duquesne University
The Honors College
Pittsburgh, Pennsylvania

The Honors College is a select group of students who enjoy living and learning together. These students share a commitment to their studies and come from all of Duquesne University's many schools, from Pharmacy to Business Administration to Liberal Arts, Music, Health Sciences, Natural and Environmental Sciences, and Education. Students in the Honors College constitute a select learning community, as the Honors College students share special CORE curriculum classes, but the social, service, and living dimensions of the Honors College are as important as the academic component. Students in the Honors College find wonderful opportunities of all sorts: for learning, for making friends, for contributing to the University and the community, and for forming lifelong bonds with one another.

Honors College students share a CORE curriculum of seven courses that are required of all students. These courses are distinguished by their small size (20–30 students), their outstanding faculty members, and their interactive character. Learning is lively, personal, stimulating, and enriching in Honors CORE courses. Honors students are also encouraged to engage in special research and study projects under the guidance of their faculty members.

Honors College students can live in the Assumption Living-Learning Center, where the rooms are spacious and each floor has a lounge, a kitchen area, and a computer facility specifically for the use of Honors College students. At the heart of the Honors College experience lies the opportunity for students to become good friends with their classmates. This is particularly important during those first difficult weeks of college, and the Honors College creates a stable base that supports students as they create friendships, academic connections, and lasting memories.

Honors College students have their own Integrated Honors Society, an organization that arranges social outings and activities and identifies and coordinates service projects in the local community. While Honors College students enjoy each other's company and provide service in the community, the students also have the opportunity to learn the leadership skills of running their own organization.

There are many benefits to being in the Honors College: students learn through extraordinary teaching; get early, preferred registration status; live in special quarters that provide academic and social advantages; and receive a special designation on their transcript that identifies them as Honors College students. This designation may enhance employment opportunities and admission to graduate schools.

The Honors College, founded in 1997, grew out of the Integrated Honors Program, which was started in 1984. The program currently enrolls almost 400 students.

Participation Requirements: Honors College students must maintain a minimum GPA and complete the Honors CORE curriculum. The final or capstone course in the Honors CORE sequence is an Honors Seminar.

Admission Process: High school students with strong academic records (minimum 3.5 GPA) and combined SAT scores of 1200 (minimum 620 verbal) or an ACT score of at least 28 are invited to join the Honors College.

Scholarship Availability: Duquesne University offers a full range of competitive merit scholarships. While no scholarships are tied directly to the Honors College, many Honors College students are recipients of merit-based scholarships.

Campus Overview

Independent Roman Catholic university, founded 1878 • **Coed** 5,584 undergraduate students, 94% full-time, 59% women, 41% men.

Undergraduates 5,239 full-time, 345 part-time. Students come from 46 states and territories, 57 other countries, 19% are from out of state, 4% African American, 1% Asian American or Pacific Islander, 1% Hispanic American, 0.1% Native American, 2% international, 4% transferred in, 54% live on campus.

Faculty *Total:* 874, 47% full-time. *Student/faculty ratio:* 15:1.

Academic Programs *Special study options:* accelerated degree program, adult/continuing education programs, advanced placement credit, distance learning, double majors, English as a second language, external degree program, freshman honors college, honors programs, independent study, internships, off-campus study, part-time degree program, services for LD students, student-designed majors, study abroad, summer session for credit. *ROTC:* Army (b), Navy (c), Air Force (c). *Unusual degree programs:* 3-2 engineering with Case Western Reserve University, University of Pittsburgh.

Athletics Member NCAA. All Division I except football (Division I-AA). *Intercollegiate sports:* baseball M(s), basketball M(s)/W(s), cheerleading M(c)/W(c), crew M(c)/W(s), cross-country running M(s)/W(s), golf M(s), ice hockey M(c), lacrosse W(s), soccer M(s)/W(s), swimming and diving M(s)/W(s), tennis M(s)/W(s), track and field M/W(s), volleyball W(s), wrestling M(s). *Intramural sports:* badminton M/W, basketball M/W, bowling M/W, football M/W, racquetball M/W, soccer M/W, softball M/W, squash M/W, table tennis M/W, tennis M/W, volleyball M/W, water polo M/W.

Costs (2004–05) *Comprehensive fee:* $28,180 includes full-time tuition ($18,693), mandatory fees ($1667), and room and board

($7820). Full-time tuition and fees vary according to program. Part-time tuition: $608 per credit. Part-time tuition and fees vary according to program. *Required fees:* $65 per credit part-time. *College room only:* $4266. Room and board charges vary according to board plan and housing facility.

Financial Aid 1,773 Federal Work-Study jobs (averaging $2448). In 2003, 1025 non-need-based awards were made. *Average percent of need met:* 83%. *Average financial aid package:* $15,179. *Average need-based loan:* $4478. *Average need-based gift aid:* $10,303. *Average non-need-based aid:* $8113.

Contact: Director: Dr. Michael Cahall, 214 College Hall, Duquesne University, Pittsburgh, Pennsylvania 15282; *Telephone:* 412-396-1142; *E-mail:* honorscollege@duq.edu; *Web site:* http://www.honorscollege.duq.edu

Eastern University
Templeton Honors College
St. Davids, Pennsylvania

*T*he Templeton Honors College (THC) is Eastern University's "college within the university," designed to challenge and prepare the most academically gifted undergraduate students for leadership and service as individuals of influence in culture, society, and in their professions by providing a holistic program focused on the life of the mind, character formation, and skill development.

The THC curriculum, which replaces a majority of Eastern University's existing core curriculum, involves intensive reading, writing, and discussion in both the Great Books and major current books and ideas. Throughout their education, Templeton Honors students receive a thorough grounding in the humanities and sciences through a learning experience comprised of specific THC seminars, a broad selection of honors electives, and diverse cultural experiences, such as visiting the Philadelphia Chamber Orchestra and the Philadelphia Art Museum. THC scholars take courses in the Honors College while concurrently majoring in any of the regular majors and programs of Eastern University.

Each year, the entering cohort of the Templeton Honors College is limited to no more than 24 students. Participation in the Templeton Honors College becomes part of the student's academic record.

The Templeton Honors College has been made possible through the generosity of Drs. John and Josephine Templeton Jr.

Participation Requirements: THC scholars register for three Honors College seminars/tutorials in each semester of their first year, two seminars/tutorials in each semester of their second year, and then choose two courses from a broad selection of honors electives during the course of their final two years. First-year students participate in the Adirondacks camping trip the week before commencing classes and produce and participate in either an Oxford-style debate or a mock trial at the end of their freshman year. Usually in their junior year, THC scholars satisfy their THC requirements by participating for one semester in a study outside program. The THC offers off-campus study either abroad in places like Salzburg and Oxford or domestically in places like Washington, D.C.; Gettysburg; and Oregon. In the senior year, a senior honors thesis is the final requirement that must be submitted before graduation. Honors College students must maintain a minimum 3.3 GPA throughout their first year and at least a 3.5 GPA in subsequent years to remain in good standing in the THC.

Admission Process: Admission to the Templeton Honors College is based on acceptance into the overall undergraduate program at Eastern University, a combined SAT I score of 1300 or higher or an ACT score of 30 or higher, graduation in the top 9 percent of one's high school class, or extraordinary leadership abilities. Students who transfer to Eastern with a GPA of not less than 3.5 and with not more than 36 hours of undergraduate credit are eligible for admission to the THC with the permission of the Dean. The admissions process involves two stages: a written application and a formal interview with the THC Dean and staff.

Scholarship Availability: All THC scholars are awarded an honors grant of $3000. Separate endowed scholarships provide grants for students majoring in specific disciplinary areas.

Campus Overview

Independent American Baptist Churches in the USA comprehensive, founded 1952 • **Coed** 2,200 undergraduate students, 88% full-time, 66% women, 34% men.

Undergraduates 1,946 full-time, 254 part-time. Students come from 38 states and territories, 26 other countries, 40% are from out of state, 13% African American, 2% Asian American or Pacific Islander, 5% Hispanic American, 0.3% Native American, 1% international, 3% transferred in, 74% live on campus.

Faculty *Total:* 343, 24% full-time. *Student/faculty ratio:* 13:1.

Academic Programs *Special study options:* academic remediation for entering students, accelerated degree program, adult/continuing education programs, advanced placement credit, English as a second language, honors programs, independent study, internships, off-campus study, part-time degree program, student-designed majors, summer session for credit. *ROTC:* Army (c), Air Force (c).

Athletics Member NCAA. All Division III. *Intercollegiate sports:* baseball M, basketball M/W, field hockey W, golf M, lacrosse M/W, soccer M/W, softball W, volleyball W. *Intramural sports:* basketball M/W, soccer M/W, volleyball W.

Costs (2005–06) *Comprehensive fee:* $26,670 includes full-time tuition ($18,830) and room and board ($7840). *College room only:* $4280.

Financial Aid 347 Federal Work-Study jobs (averaging $1050). 811 state and other part-time jobs (averaging $500). In 2002, 228 non-need-based awards were made. *Average percent of need met:* 74%. *Average financial aid package:* $11,892. *Average need-based loan:* $3505. *Average need-based gift aid:* $9959. *Average non-need-based aid:* $14,048.

Contact: Dr. Christopher A. Hall, Dean, Templeton Honors College, Heritage House, 106 Heritage House, 1300 Eagle Road, St. Davids, Pennsylvania 19087; *Telephone:* 610-341-5880; *Fax:* 610-341-1790; *E-mail:* chall@eastern.edu. Ms. Lauren Arnold, Assistant to the Dean and THC Admissions Counselor; *Telephone:* 610-225-5022; *Fax:* 610-341-1790; *E-mail:* larnold@eastern.edu

East Stroudsburg University of Pennsylvania
University Honors Program
East Stroudsburg, Pennsylvania

The Honors Program at East Stroudsburg University (ESU) offers the superior student an opportunity to be challenged beyond the ordinary university education.

At the center of the program are special honors general education courses that feature small class size (15 to 20 students), close student-faculty interaction, and expanded activities outside the classroom, allowing time for creativity and explorations of intellectual depth and breadth. These classes introduce the honors students to various aspects of social, cultural, and scientific heritage and encourage the students to draw connections between the different fields and perspectives studied as well as between the academy and the greater world in which they live.

The classroom experiences are enriched by a variety of field trips and opportunities to attend summer seminars abroad as well as regional and national conventions. Finally, the honor students are encouraged to engage in independent learning and research.

ESU provides an Honors Floor in one of the residence halls for those who choose to reside there. The floor includes kitchen and lounge areas as well as free Internet access from the student rooms.

The program has been in existence since 1989 and admits approximately 35 freshmen and transfer students each year. There are approximately 120 students currently enrolled in the program.

Participation Requirements: In their freshman year, honors students are encouraged to participate in a learning community of two or three honors classes. All honors students are expected to complete a minimum of 18 credits in honors general education classes followed by a multidisciplinary upper-level seminar. After successful completion of their course work, the students choose a thesis adviser in their major, develop a prospectus, and complete an honors thesis in their major.

To remain in the program, students must maintain a minimum 3.3 cumulative GPA and participate in enrichment and service activities. Successful completion of the program is recognized at commencement and is also noted on the official transcript.

Admission Process: Admission to the program is by recruitment from admissions, invitation from the Honors Director, or student-initiated application via the Internet or other media.

Freshmen or transfer students with fewer than 30 credits are expected to place in the 85th percentile of their high school class and achieve 1150 or higher on the SAT. Transfer students with more than 30 credits may be eligible on the basis of a minimum GPA of 3.3.

Scholarship Availability: Honors scholarships of various amounts are awarded each spring based on academic performance and active participation in the Honors Program. There are also scholarships each year for 2 students to participate in a special Pennsylvania State System of Higher Education summer honors seminar abroad. A variety of other University scholarships are also available to Honors Students; approximately 65 percent of ESU full-time students receive scholarship aid.

Campus Overview

State-supported comprehensive, founded 1893, part of Pennsylvania State System of Higher Education • **Coed** 5,409 undergraduate students, 91% full-time, 59% women, 41% men.

Undergraduates 4,933 full-time, 476 part-time. Students come from 19 states and territories, 16 other countries, 21% are from out of state, 4% African American, 1% Asian American or Pacific Islander, 4% Hispanic American, 0.2% Native American, 0.4% international, 7% transferred in, 44% live on campus.

Faculty *Total:* 308, 82% full-time, 67% with terminal degrees. *Student/faculty ratio:* 21:1.

Academic Programs *Special study options:* academic remediation for entering students, adult/continuing education programs, advanced placement credit, double majors, honors programs, independent study, internships, off-campus study, part-time degree program, services for LD students, student-designed majors, study abroad, summer session for credit. *ROTC:* Army (c), Air Force (c). *Unusual degree programs:* 3-2 engineering with Pennsylvania State University - University Park Campus, University of Pittsburgh; podiatric medicine with Pennsylvania College of Podiatric Medicine.

Athletics Member NCAA. All Division II except wrestling (Division I). *Intercollegiate sports:* baseball M(s), basketball M(s)/W(s), cross-country running M(s)/W(s), field hockey W(s), football M(s), lacrosse W(s), soccer M(s)/W(s), softball W(s), swimming and diving W(s), tennis M(s)/W(s), track and field M(s)/W(s), volleyball M(s)/W(s), wrestling M(s). *Intramural sports:* badminton M/W, basketball M/W, equestrian sports M/W, golf M/W, ice hockey M/W, lacrosse M, racquetball M/W, rugby M/W, soccer M/W, softball W, tennis M/W, track and field M/W, ultimate Frisbee M/W, volleyball M/W, water polo M/W.

Costs (2004–05) *Tuition:* state resident $4810 full-time; nonresident $12,026 full-time, $501 per credit part-time. Part-time tuition and fees vary according to course load. *Required fees:* $1414 full-time, $55 per credit part-time. *Room and board:* $4506; room only: $2864. Room and board charges vary according to board plan and housing facility.

Financial Aid 386 Federal Work-Study jobs (averaging $1042). 624 state and other part-time jobs (averaging $1379). In 2003, 866 non-need-based awards were made. *Average percent of need met:* 87%. *Average financial aid package:* $5237. *Average need-based loan:* $3594. *Average need-based gift aid:* $3332. *Average non-need-based aid:* $7025.

Contact: Directors: Dr. Kenneth M. Mash and Dr. Peter Pruim, University Honors Program, East Stroudsburg University of Pennsylvania, East Stroudsburg, Pennsylvania 18301; *E-mail:* honors@ po-box.esu.edu; *Web site:* http://www.esu.edu/honors

Edinboro University of Pennsylvania

Dr. Robert C. Weber Honors Program

Edinboro, Pennsylvania

The two-part academic program introduces the core curriculum through general education honors, and concludes with upper-division honors and the departmental senior honors project. The comprehensive program offers motivated students ample opportunities to develop independence and initiative, as well as enabling them to work closely with outstanding University professors. In general education honors, students pursue their chosen academic course of study while completing a series of core honors courses. Of the total required number of credit hours in general education, 25 percent of the total are taken as honors courses. Honors students who complete general education honors receive an award for excellence in general education. Upper-division honors link general education to the more specialized areas of study and culminates with a departmental senior honors project. Senior projects are designed in consultation with academic departments as the most appropriate culminating experience in the individual majors. As a final step in upper-division honors, the senior project is presented in an appropriate public forum, such as journal publication, academic conference, online journal, art gallery, or recital hall. With the successful completion of upper-division honors, including the senior project, the honors student receives the Upper-Division Honors Award.

Honors students attain honors credit hours by taking courses designated as honors courses. Students may also contract courses. A contract is an agreement between an honors student in good standing, a faculty member, and the honors director. In a contracted course, the honors student agrees to do additional course work for honors credit. Students may also choose a curricular link contract. In this type of contract, the honors student initiates a project that links two courses from different departments that are not in themselves interdisciplinary. One of the two courses serves as the contract course of record with that professor issuing the course evaluation. The professor of the other course serves as a reader of the final project. The curricular link contract is particularly appropriate to the student nearing the end of general education honors or at the beginning of upper-division honors. Honors Program students may also attain honors credits by taking courses that are designated as graduate courses.

Honors students enroll in independent study to work on projects that are not in topic areas typically offered in the undergraduate curriculum. For example, the senior honors project is a 6-semester hour project, consisting of two 3-hour independent studies that encourages honors students to develop expertise on a specific topic and to gain research and practical experience. Under the guidance of

a faculty mentor, the student is responsible for researching, experimenting, documenting, and presenting in public various components of the chosen project.

Honors students are encouraged to study abroad and are given opportunities that are not available to other university students. There are three major awards in the Honors Program: the General Education Honors Award, the Upper-Division Honors Award, and the Honors Program Diploma.

Students qualify for admission to general education honors based on academic achievement, aptitude test scores, class rank, and teacher recommendations. Historically, entering freshmen honors students have averaged 1225 on the Scholastic Aptitude Test (SAT) or 27 on the American College Test (ACT) and have ranked in the top 10 perecnt of their graduating classes. Students interested in the challenges and rewards of an Honors Program and near or above the historical averages may apply for admission.

A student already attending Edinboro University must be a full-time student with a GPA of 3.5 or higher. As part of the application process, the student must register for an honors course. During the semester of that course, the application semester, the student must provide letters of support from two faculty members, secure the approval of the academic adviser, and complete a plan-of-study in consultation with the honors director and academic advisor. Students qualify for admission to upper-division honors based on academic achievement at Edinboro University of Pennsylvania. Application may be made by any full-time Edinboro University student who has completed 63 credit hours with an overall GPA of 3.4 or higher.

Participation Requirements: An honors student must complete a minimum of 6 honors credits each academic year with a grade of A or B to remain in good standing. To receive the General Education Honors Award, a student must complete 15 honors credit hours. Upper-division honors requires the completion of 9 honors credit hours, including 6 credit hours for the senior honors project. To receive an Honors Program diploma, an honors student must complete both portions of the Honors Program, a total of 24 credit honors. To remain eligible for scholarships, a student must maintain a GPA of 3.5.

Scholarship Availability: Edinboro University has developed a sizable scholarship program to assist students in the Dr. Robert C. Weber Honors Program. Students entering the Honors Program as freshmen may make application for scholarships at the time of application to general education honors. In 2001–02, more than thirty partial scholarships were awarded to entering freshman and fifty scholarships were awarded to continuing honors students. To be eligible for a scholarship after the freshman year, a student must be in good standing with a GPA of 3.5.

Campus Overview

State-supported comprehensive, founded 1857, part of Pennsylvania State System of Higher Education • **Coed** 6,735 undergraduate students, 90% full-time, 58% women, 42% men.

Undergraduates 6,030 full-time, 705 part-time. Students come from 41 states and territories, 39 other countries, 11% are from out of state, 7% African American, 0.7% Asian American or Pacific Islander, 1% Hispanic American, 0.2% Native American, 2% international, 7% transferred in, 27% live on campus.

Faculty *Total:* 405, 93% full-time, 58% with terminal degrees. *Student/faculty ratio:* 17:1.

Academic Programs *Special study options:* academic remediation for entering students, adult/continuing education programs, advanced placement credit, distance learning, double majors, freshman honors college, honors programs, independent study, internships, off-campus study, part-time degree program, services for LD students, student-designed majors, study abroad, summer session for credit. *ROTC:* Army (b). *Unusual degree programs:* 3-2 engineering with Pennsylvania State University - University Park Campus, University of Pittsburgh, Case Western Reserve University, Pennsylvania State University at Erie, The Behrend College; pre-pharmacy, 2+3 at Lake Erie College of Osteopathic Medicine and School of Pharmacy.

Athletics Member NCAA. All Division II except wrestling (Division I). *Intercollegiate sports:* basketball M(s)/W(s), cross-country running M(s)/W(s), football M(s), ice hockey M(c), soccer W(s), softball W(s), swimming and diving M(s)/W(s), track and field M(s)/W(s), volleyball W(s), wrestling M(s). *Intramural sports:* badminton M/W, basketball M/W, football M/W, racquetball M/W, soccer M/W, softball M/W, table tennis M/W, volleyball M/W, wrestling M.

Costs (2005–06) *Tuition:* $200 per credit part-time; state resident $4810 full-time; nonresident $9620 full-time, $401 per credit part-time. Part-time tuition and fees vary according to course load. *Required fees:* $1279 full-time, $47 per credit part-time, $25 per term part-time. *Room and board:* $5338; room only: $3320. Room and board charges vary according to board plan.

Financial Aid 556 Federal Work-Study jobs (averaging $1122). 815 state and other part-time jobs (averaging $1524). In 2003, 690 non-need-based awards were made. *Average percent of need met:* 83%. *Average financial aid package:* $6569. *Average need-based loan:* $3227. *Average need-based gift aid:* $1867. *Average non-need-based aid:* $2120.

Contact: Director: Dr. Tim Cordell, Dr. Robert C. Weber Honors Program, 103 Earp Hall, Edinboro University of Pennsylvania, Edinboro, Pennsylvania 16444; *Telephone:* 814-732-2981; *Fax:* 814-732-2982; *E-mail:* cordell@edinboro.edu; Web site: honors.edinboro.edu

---

Elizabethtown College

Honors Program

Elizabethtown, Pennsylvania

Elizabethtown College Honors Program, sponsored by a grant from The Hershey Company, reflects the College's commitment to providing customized learning opportunities for its students. In the case of the Honors Program, the focus of this customization is on students with excellent academic records, superior academic abilities, intellectual promise, and demonstrated initiative. Consistent with the mission of the College, the Honors Program seeks to promote high standards of scholarship and leadership among those students selected for the program. Excellence has been identified as a core value of the College and is a hallmark of the Honors Program. In general, class size is deliberately kept small at Elizabethtown; this is universally so in the Honors Program. Rarely, if ever, do honors classes exceed 15 students.

The opportunity to work closely with faculty mentors from the first to the senior year is an explicit goal of everyone associated with the program. In order to foster even greater involvement between faculty-scholars and honors students, cocurricular activities are planned on a regular basis. Events such as field trips to nearby cultural sites (such as New York City and Washington, D.C.) are routine. In addition, international travel is both encouraged and valued. Semester-long study-abroad opportunities are expected, and there are opportunities for students to visit other countries in an annual intersession trip (e.g., Austria, Ecuador, Costa Rica and Iceland).

To facilitate academic and scholarship opportunities, the Honors Program offers each qualified student up to $500 as support toward research for the honors senior thesis. In order to help foster a deeper sense of community within the students in the program, an honors office, a lounge, private study rooms, and a computer lab are part of the program's facilities.

The Honors Program was established in 1999 and currently has nearly 200 students.

Participation Requirements: Students entering the program in the first year take a two-course sequence focusing primarily on critical-thinking and foundational skills. The second of these courses

includes an interdisciplinary perspective. In the sophomore and junior years, two additional honors courses are taken. In the junior/senior year a leadership development course and a capstone thesis requirement must be completed. At any time, students may upgrade a 200-level or higher regular course to an honors course on the basis of a written contract with a professor and the Honors Director by conducting an honors component, such as a research project suitable for publication in a professional journal. A total of 24 credits must be acquired in honors courses in order to fulfill the program's requirements and graduate as a recognized honors scholar. In order to remain in good standing within the program, students must maintain a GPA of at least 3.5 overall.

Admission Process: Admission to the Honors Program is normally at the beginning of the first year, although a small number of sophomores may be admitted to the extent that they can be accommodated. Sophomore admission comes upon demonstrated excellence in the first year, the recommendations of at least 2 professors, and the concurrence of the honors committee. For freshmen, the minimum standard for admission is a combined score of at least 1200 on the SAT (with neither the verbal nor the math score below 550) or other standardized test, rank in the top 10 percent of one's high school graduating class, and review by the honors committee acting on the recommendation of the admissions office. Application to the Honors Program must be received by January 15.

Scholarship Availability: Scholarships are routinely offered to Honors Program students through the College's Financial Aid Office. These scholarships currently range between $9000 and $13,000 annually. Normal progress within the program permits the student to retain this grant every year for four years.

Campus Overview

Independent comprehensive, founded 1899, affiliated with Church of the Brethren • **Coed** 2,113 undergraduate students, 88% full-time, 65% women, 35% men.

Undergraduates 1,859 full-time, 254 part-time. Students come from 32 states and territories, 33 other countries, 31% are from out of state, 1% African American, 2% Asian American or Pacific Islander, 1% Hispanic American, 0.2% Native American, 4% international, 3% transferred in, 85% live on campus.

Faculty *Total:* 215, 59% full-time, 55% with terminal degrees. *Student/faculty ratio:* 12:1.

Academic Programs *Special study options:* adult/continuing education programs, advanced placement credit, double majors, English as a second language, external degree program, honors programs, independent study, internships, off-campus study, part-time degree program, services for LD students, study abroad, summer session for credit. *Unusual degree programs:* 3-2 engineering with Pennsylvania State University - University Park Campus; forestry with Duke University; nursing with Thomas Jefferson University; allied health programs with Thomas Jefferson University, Widener University, University of Maryland at Baltimore.

Athletics Member NCAA. All Division III. *Intercollegiate sports:* baseball M, basketball M/W, cheerleading M(c)/W(c), cross-country running M/W, field hockey W, golf M, lacrosse M/W, soccer M/W, softball W, swimming and diving M/W, tennis M/W, track and field M/W, volleyball M(c)/W, wrestling M. *Intramural sports:* basketball M/W, racquetball M/W, soccer M/W, softball M/W, tennis M/W, volleyball M/W.

Costs (2004–05) *Comprehensive fee:* $30,310 includes full-time tuition ($23,710) and room and board ($6600). Full-time tuition and fees vary according to course load. Part-time tuition: $600 per credit hour. Part-time tuition and fees vary according to class time and course load. *College room only:* $3300. Room and board charges vary according to board plan and housing facility.

Financial Aid 893 Federal Work-Study jobs (averaging $1268). In 2004, 174 non-need-based awards were made. *Average percent of need met:* 87%. *Average financial aid package:* $17,750. *Average* *need-based loan:* $3881. *Average need-based gift aid:* $13,750. *Average non-need-based aid:* $14,620.

Contact: Director: Dr. Dana Gulling Mead, One Alpha Drive, Elizabethtown, Pennsylvania 17022; *Telephone:* 717-361-3758; *Fax:* 717-361-1390; *E-mail:* honors@etown.edu; *Web site:* http://www.etown.edu

Gannon University
University Honors Program
Erie, Pennsylvania

*T*he student-centered and student-governed Gannon University Honors Program is designed to provide a challenging educational experience to talented and highly motivated students willing to accept the challenge. The program is open to students of all majors and consists primarily of honors sections of courses that are required of all students. The honors courses are limited to 15 students, are conducted as seminars, and are highly interactive. The faculty members who teach in the program are encouraged to be creative in the content discussed as well as in the manner in which it is presented. A hallmark of the program is the community that exists—students with students, as well as faculty members with students. The program is governed by a 15-member Student Advisory Board, which is responsible for suggesting courses, and faculty members, who are responsible for planning cultural, social, and intellectual outside-the-classroom activities. The Gannon program is a member of the National Collegiate Honors Council, the Northeast Region of the National Collegiate Honors Council, and the Mid-East Honors Association; students are encouraged to attend conferences sponsored by each of the associations. The Honors Program at Gannon began in 1988 and now has 175 students in the program.*

Participation Requirements: To graduate as Honors Scholars, students must take 24 credits of honors courses and 6 credits of a foreign language. To graduate as Associate Honors Scholars, they must take 18 credits of honors courses. They must also achieve an overall GPA of 3.25 or above. Honors students complete the same number of credits for graduation as any other Gannon student. Honors students receive special recognition at graduation and their honors courses are documented on their transcripts.

Along with the academic requirements for the program, students are expected to participate in social, cultural, and intellectual activities provided by the program. They are also expected to be involved in some service activity.

Admission Process: Entering freshmen are selected on the basis of their SAT I scores, class rank, GPA, and extracurricular activities. Students already attending Gannon and transfer students must have at least a 3.5 GPA to be considered.

Campus Overview

Independent Roman Catholic comprehensive, founded 1925 • **Coed** 2,430 undergraduate students, 87% full-time, 59% women, 41% men.

Undergraduates 2,114 full-time, 316 part-time. Students come from 30 states and territories, 11 other countries, 20% are from out of state, 5% African American, 1% Asian American or Pacific Islander, 0.9% Hispanic American, 0.2% Native American, 2% international, 3% transferred in, 54% live on campus.

Faculty *Total:* 298, 58% full-time, 49% with terminal degrees. *Student/faculty ratio:* 10:1.

Academic Programs *Special study options:* academic remediation for entering students, accelerated degree program, adult/continuing education programs, advanced placement credit, cooperative education, distance learning, double majors, English as a second language, external degree program, honors programs, independent study, internships, off-campus study, part-time degree program, services for LD students, study abroad, summer session for credit. *ROTC:* Army (b). *Unusual degree programs:* 3-2 engineering with University of Akron, University of Pittsburgh, University of Detroit Mercy; law with Duquesne University.

Athletics Member NCAA. All Division II. *Intercollegiate sports:* baseball M(s), basketball M(s)/W(s), cross-country running M(s)/W(s), football M, golf M(s)/W(s), lacrosse W(s), soccer M(s)/W(s), softball W(s), swimming and diving M(s)/W(s), volleyball W(s), wrestling M(s). *Intramural sports:* badminton M/W, basketball M/W, bowling M/W, cross-country running M/W, football M, golf M/W, racquetball M/W, soccer M/W, softball M/W, swimming and diving M/W, tennis M/W, volleyball M(c)/W, water polo M, weight lifting M, wrestling M.

Costs (2004–05) *Comprehensive fee:* $24,490 includes full-time tuition ($17,030), mandatory fees ($470), and room and board ($6990). Full-time tuition and fees vary according to class time and program. Part-time tuition: $530 per credit hour. Part-time tuition and fees vary according to class time and program. *Required fees:* $15 per credit hour part-time. *College room only:* $3760. Room and board charges vary according to board plan and housing facility.

Financial Aid 501 Federal Work-Study jobs (averaging $1170). 190 state and other part-time jobs (averaging $1700). In 2003, 311 non-need-based awards were made. *Average percent of need met:* 80%. *Average financial aid package:* $12,740. *Average need-based loan:* $3002. *Average need-based gift aid:* $10,140. *Average non-need-based aid:* $5940.

Contact: Director: Rev. Robert Susa, Gannon University, 109 University Square, Erie, Pennsylvania 16541; *Telephone:* 814-871-5628; *Fax:* 814-871-5630; *E-mail:* susa001@gannon.edu

Gwynedd-Mercy College
Honors Program
Gwynedd Valley, Pennsylvania

*T*he Honors Program at Gwynedd-Mercy offers excellent students in baccalaureate degree programs enhanced educational opportunities through an integrated curriculum, combining an enriched general education in liberal studies with study in the major. Honors program courses are taught by teams of faculty members who have a strong commitment to interdisciplinary and collaborative teaching and learning. Classes are small, 8 to 10 students on the average, and are conducted in a seminar style.*

The Honors Program at Gwynedd-Mercy consists of a series of liberal arts courses that are interdisciplinary in nature. Linked through the exploration of a very broad master theme, The Quest for Community and Freedom: The Individual and Society, the courses examine and explore the contributions made by the Western Tradition and the American experience to people's understanding of human freedom, responsibility in the community, and their relation to nature, giving attention as well to cross-cultural comparisons to these traditions. A capstone course, Towards Global Community, explores global trends from 1945 into the twenty-first century. Aimed toward developing a shared intellectual experience, the program seeks to foster the collegiality and community of learning crucial to intellectual growth and encourages students to reflect on the values and principles central to the visions of civility and community of Western democratic, Judeo-Christian, and other traditions.

Courses are writing-intensive and concentrate on close readings of primary texts. They are enriched by field trips to museums, theaters, and spots of historical and cultural interest.

Founded in 1995, the program currently enrolls 30 students.

Participation Requirements: Students admitted to the program complete six honors courses. With the exception of transfer students, program participants tend to take one course per semester, following a prescribed sequence through the program: three courses in the Western tradition, two in the American Experience, and a capstone course, Towards Global Community, at the conclusion. To remain in the program, students must maintain a minimum 3.0 GPA in honors courses. Upon completion of the six courses, students are awarded a Certificate of Completion that goes into their academic record. Achieving at least a 3.0 GPA in the six honors courses and a minimum 3.35 GPA overall for the bachelor's degree entitles students to their degree with honors, with recognition at commencement and a special diploma.

Admission Process: Enrollment in the Honors Program is by invitation only. For entering freshmen it is based on SAT I or ACT scores, rank in class, faculty member/guidance counselor recommendations, a personal interview, and high school average. For transfer students, GPA from transfer institution(s), letters of recommendation from faculty members at previous institution(s), an interview, and SAT I scores are evaluated. Admission is on a rolling basis.

Scholarship Availability: Merit-based academic scholarships of various amounts are awarded through the Admissions Office. The Honors Program does not award scholarships as such. However, most participants in the program are recipients of academic awards.

Campus Overview

Independent Roman Catholic comprehensive, founded 1948 • **Coed** 2,160 undergraduate students, 58% full-time, 76% women, 24% men.

Undergraduates 1,263 full-time, 897 part-time. Students come from 8 states and territories, 49 other countries, 5% are from out of state, 13% African American, 3% Asian American or Pacific Islander, 2% Hispanic American, 0.1% Native American, 2% international, 10% transferred in, 20% live on campus.

Faculty *Total:* 280, 29% full-time, 33% with terminal degrees. *Student/faculty ratio:* 13:1.

Academic Programs *Special study options:* academic remediation for entering students, accelerated degree program, adult/continuing education programs, advanced placement credit, cooperative education, double majors, English as a second language, freshman honors college, honors programs, independent study, internships, part-time degree program, summer session for credit.

Athletics Member NCAA. All Division III. *Intercollegiate sports:* basketball M/W, field hockey W, lacrosse W, soccer M, softball W(c), tennis M/W, volleyball W.

Costs (2004–05) *Comprehensive fee:* $24,900 includes full-time tuition ($16,900), mandatory fees ($500), and room and board ($7500). Full-time tuition and fees vary according to program. Part-time tuition: $340 per credit. Part-time tuition and fees vary according to program. *Required fees:* $10 per credit part-time. *Room and board:* Room and board charges vary according to board plan and housing facility.

Financial Aid 356 Federal Work-Study jobs (averaging $1330). 10 state and other part-time jobs (averaging $2230). In 2003, 220 non-need-based awards were made. *Average percent of need met:* 82%. *Average financial aid package:* $14,448. *Average need-based loan:* $5076. *Average need-based gift aid:* $11,224. *Average non-need-based aid:* $6482.

Contact: Director: Dr. Carol Breslin, Gwynedd-Mercy College, Gwynedd Valley, Pennsylvania 19437; *Telephone:* 215-646-7300 Ext. 136; *E-mail:* breslin.c@gmc.edu

Harrisburg Area Community College
Honors Program
Harrisburg, Pennsylvania

Harrisburg Area Community College's (HACC) Honors Program offers an integrated, coherent alternative to a major portion of the College's general education curriculum. The Honors Program is designed for bright, self-motivated students who actively wish to expand their intellectual horizons, challenge their abilities, and develop their originality in an environment that nurtures the whole student academically, socially, emotionally, and intellectually.

In honors courses, the intellectual atmosphere is supportive and cordial, emphasizing each student's power of reasoning, creative inquiry, and communication. Honors courses are small, and enrollment is limited, usually to no more than 15 students. They are often conducted as seminars and tutorials where students do independent research. In addition, they are intense, with depth and rigor of instruction stressed. Honors courses are also student centered, making individuals responsible for the pace and direction of their studies. Finally they are discussion based, interdisciplinary (linking developments in the arts, humanities, sciences, and technologies to focus on contemporary social and intellectual questions), and diverse (exploring multiple points of view).

The full Honors Program is only available on the Harrisburg campus, but limited honors classes are offered on all campuses.

The Honors Program sponsors the Honors Lecture Series, open to the College and the community. At least 6 distinguished scholars are invited each year to address the campus community on issues of current interest. Topic choices are coordinated with the Phi Theta Kappa honors study topics; such choices include popular culture and health care.

Pizza parties, holiday gatherings, and coffees and teas are a regular feature in the HACC honors classes, as are regularly scheduled field trips to Washington, D.C., and New York City.

The Harrisburg Area Community College Honors Program was founded in 1990 and has 85 students currently enrolled.

Participation Requirements: Honors courses are identified in the *Schedule of Classes*. Four to six honors classes are offered on a convenient schedule each fall and spring semester.

The total number of college credits required to earn an associate degree—61 credits—is the same as for nonhonors students. The critical difference is in the depth and content of the four required honors courses. Three of the four required courses may be chosen from honors sections of the college core classes, other college requirements, or special honors courses. Honors core courses are offered every fall and spring semester. All honors students must complete the Honors Seminar, a broad interdisciplinary course with rotating topics, offered every spring semester, which includes a substantial original project. Early Admission Honors students should also take the 1-credit Introduction to Honors offered in the fall semester.

Students must maintain a 3.0 average to remain in the Honors Program. Students who complete the program receive recognition on transcripts and are eligible to wear the Honors Braid at graduation.

Admission Process: Students should submit the single page application, available online, from any HACC admissions office, from advisers, in the brochure, on bulletin boards, or from the Director, along with any required support materials to the admissions office at their primary campus.

To be admitted to the Honors Program, a student must meet at least one of the following criteria: Have a high school GPA of at least 3.5 (on a 4.0 scale) or rank in the top 10 percent of their high school graduating class; show a combined score of at least 1200 on the SAT test (or 1100 if prior to April 1995) or an ACT score of 25 or higher;

have completed 12 or more college credit courses with a GPA of at least 3.25; be a member of Phi Theta Kappa National Honor Society; demonstrate special academic abilities or talents by submitting projects, portfolios, papers, awards, or reports of auditions; or be strongly recommended by faculty members.

All pertinent transcripts and test scores are independently verified. A letter of acceptance is sent to all qualifying honors students. Students may apply to the Honors Program at any time, as there is a policy of rolling admissions. Qualified new students may sign up for a single course if they complete the formal application process within the opening weeks of the term.

Interested and motivated students who nearly qualify under the above criteria may, with the instructor's permission, take one individual honors class. If the student is successful, receives an A or B in the class, and is enthusiastic about continuing, that student may apply for full admission to the Honors Program.

Scholarship Availability: There are currently no scholarships dedicated to Honors Students. However, there are numerous scholarships for which honors students are eligible, and for which they are encouraged to apply. Prospective students may visit http://www.hacc.edu and then follow the link through Student Services to the Financial Aid page for scholarship information.

Campus Overview

State and locally supported 2-year, founded 1964 • **Coed** 16,109 undergraduate students, 40% full-time, 65% women, 35% men.

Undergraduates 6,413 full-time, 9,696 part-time. Students come from 14 states and territories, 8 other countries, 1% are from out of state, 10% African American, 3% Asian American or Pacific Islander, 6% Hispanic American, 0.3% Native American, 0.9% international, 30% transferred in.

Faculty *Total:* 955, 27% full-time, 5% with terminal degrees. *Student/faculty ratio:* 23:1.

Academic Programs *Special study options:* academic remediation for entering students, adult/continuing education programs, advanced placement credit, distance learning, double majors, English as a second language, honors programs, independent study, internships, part-time degree program, services for LD students, student-designed majors, study abroad, summer session for credit. *ROTC:* Army (b).

Athletics *Intercollegiate sports:* basketball M/W, soccer M/W, swimming and diving M/W, tennis M/W, volleyball M/W. *Intramural sports:* basketball M/W, football M/W, golf M/W, racquetball M/W, skiing (downhill) M/W, soccer M, softball M/W, squash M/W, tennis M/W, volleyball W.

Costs (2004–05) *Tuition:* area resident $2625 full-time, $76 per credit hour part-time; state resident $4950 full-time, $151 per credit hour part-time; nonresident $7275 full-time, $226 per credit hour part-time. *Required fees:* $360 full-time, $12 per credit hour part-time.

Contact: Director: Yvonne J. Milspaw, Ph.D., Professor of English and Humanities, CASS Division, Harrisburg Area Community College, 1 HACC Drive, Harrisburg, Pennsylvania 17110; *Telephone:* 717-780-2555; *E-mail:* yjmilspa@hacc.edu; *Web site:* http://www.hacc.edu

Indiana University of Pennsylvania

Robert E. Cook Honors College

Indiana, Pennsylvania

The Robert E. Cook Honors College at Indiana University of Pennsylvania (IUP) is a residential Honors College designed to give talented students a graduate student atmosphere during their

undergraduate education. Students engage in a learning community that blends their academics, social service learning, and residential lives.

The curriculum focuses on critical thinking, communication skills, and problem solving as a group. An interdisciplinary core course serves as the backbone of the curriculum, with other honors courses available in the humanities, sciences, education, and fine arts. This is supplemented through a Social Service program coordinating social service activities with each student's education. Further, a strong study-abroad and internship program provides real settings for further study.

Participation Requirements: Entering freshmen complete a minimum of 24 honors credits. There are two required courses: Honors College Core Course (18 credits, four semesters, HC101, 102, 201, and 202), and an honors section of Senior Synthesis (3 credits). All students must complete 3 additional honors credits that can be met through honors electives, an undergraduate thesis, undergraduate research, or departmental honors programs.

Honors students must maintain a minimum 3.25 QPA, but are granted one semester probation. Successful completion of the College is recognized at commencement and is also noted on the official transcript and diploma.

Admission Process: High school students are admitted on the basis of an application, essays, teacher recommendations, social service, high school average, and SAT I or ACT scores. Transfer students may apply during the first or second semesters. Students may select from any of the more than 100 majors at IUP. There are two decision timelines for applying. The early decision deadline is November 15; regular decision is March 1.

Scholarship Availability: Scholarships of various amounts are reserved specifically for honors students based on application merit and academic performance. Scholarship competition is heavy; however, many students receive some form of support.

Campus Overview

State-supported university, founded 1875, part of Pennsylvania State System of Higher Education • **Coed** 12,163 undergraduate students, 92% full-time, 56% women, 44% men.

Undergraduates 11,230 full-time, 933 part-time. Students come from 38 states and territories, 74 other countries, 4% are from out of state, 6% African American, 1% Asian American or Pacific Islander, 0.9% Hispanic American, 0.2% Native American, 2% international, 5% transferred in, 32% live on campus.

Faculty *Total:* 689, 91% full-time, 83% with terminal degrees. *Student/faculty ratio:* 17:1.

Academic Programs *Special study options:* academic remediation for entering students, accelerated degree program, adult/continuing education programs, advanced placement credit, cooperative education, distance learning, double majors, English as a second language, freshman honors college, honors programs, independent study, internships, off-campus study, part-time degree program, services for LD students, study abroad, summer session for credit. *ROTC:* Army (b). *Unusual degree programs:* 3-2 engineering with Drexel University, University of Pittsburgh; forestry with Duke University.

Athletics Member NCAA. All Division II. *Intercollegiate sports:* baseball M(s), basketball M(s)/W(s), cross-country running M(s)/W(s), field hockey W(s), football M(s), golf M(s), lacrosse W(s), soccer W(s), softball W(s), swimming and diving M/W(s), tennis W(s), track and field M(s)/W(s), volleyball W(s). *Intramural sports:* archery M/W, badminton M/W, basketball M/W, bowling M/W, cross-country running M(c)/W(c), equestrian sports M(c)/W(c), fencing M(c), football M/W, golf M/W, ice hockey M(c), racquetball M/W, riflery M(c)/W(c), sailing M(c)/W(c), skiing (downhill) M(c)/W(c), soccer M(c)/W(c), softball M(c)/W(c), swimming and diving M/W, table tennis M/W, tennis M/W, track and field M/W, volleyball M/W, water polo M/W, weight lifting M/W, wrestling M.

Costs (2004–05) *Tuition:* state resident $4810 full-time, $200 per credit hour part-time; nonresident $12,026 full-time, $501 per credit hour part-time. Full-time tuition and fees vary according to course load, location, and reciprocity agreements. Part-time tuition and fees vary according to course load, location, and reciprocity agreements. *Required fees:* $1275 full-time, $20 per credit hour part-time, $233 per term part-time. *Room and board:* $4868; room only: $2940. Room and board charges vary according to board plan, housing facility, and location.

Financial Aid 1,600 Federal Work-Study jobs (averaging $1267). 1,779 state and other part-time jobs (averaging $1161). In 2002, 379 non-need-based awards were made. *Average percent of need met:* 76%. *Average financial aid package:* $7067. *Average need-based loan:* $3483. *Average need-based gift aid:* $3639. *Average non-need-based aid:* $2286.

Contact: Director: Dr. Janet E. Goebel, 136 Whitmyre Hall, Indiana University of Pennsylvania, 290 Pratt Drive, Indiana, Pennsylvania 15705; *Telephone:* 800-487-9122; *Fax:* 724-357-3906; *E-mail:* honors@iup.edu; *Web site:* http://www.iup.edu/honors

Keystone College
Honors Program
LaPlume, Pennsylvania

*T*he Honors Program at Keystone College benefits students of intellectual promise and high motivation who seek increasing challenge at the undergraduate level. The program is designed to recognize and encourage academic excellence, to stimulate students to work at their own pace, and to facilitate the exchange of ideas and information among students with different interests and in different disciplines. The Honors Program provides cocurricular activities, service opportunities, and intellectual and social support, adding significant dimensions to the student's academic program. Students are placed in a challenging yet supportive environment within which they can develop their critical and creative thinking skills and find ways to use these skills to make a difference in the larger community.

All incoming honors students are enrolled in a special section of English 101 (College Writing I–Academic Writing). Workshops for peer editing and revision complement teacher-student interaction both in and outside the classroom. The honors section contains an enriched curriculum and is taught by a senior faculty member.

Each semester, students select courses to be taken with honors designation. A contract is signed by the student and faculty member for each honors-designated course, outlining more in-depth, enriched requirements. Most of the College's courses can be taken for honors designation.

The Honors Program provides students with intellectual enrichment outside of the classroom as well. The Honors Council assigns one book each semester for outside reading, culminating in a formal discussion with Keystone College's President, Dr. Edward G. Boehm Jr. Each semester also brings a schedule of new guest speakers, cultural events, and/or other activities to Honors Program students. Recent guests have included playwright and Oscar-nominated screenwriter Mark Medoff, historian William Kashatus, and writer Mark Mathabane, author of Kaffir Boy.

Participation Requirements: Sudents are required to successfully complete 21 honors-designated credits in addition to the enriched English 101 course. (Students pursuing an associate degree are required to successfully complete 9 honors-designated credits.) In addition, all honors students complete a senior thesis project and presentation.

Admission Process: To qualify for the College's Honors Program, students must place in the top 10 percent of their high school graduating class or have a minimum 3.3 (out of 4.0) high school GPA. Students must achieve a minimum 1100 combined SAT score or 24 composite ACT score.

The Director of Admissions invites students to participate in the Honors Program once formal acceptance to the College is granted. Students who desire to participate must submit a complete application for admission no later than April 1 of their senior year.

Scholarship Availability: Honors Program students enrolled on a full-time basis may be eligible for scholarships totaling between half tuition and full tuition plus fees. Students are evaluated for merit-based awards upon application.

Campus Overview

Independent primarily 2-year, founded 1868 • **Coed** 1,658 undergraduate students, 74% full-time, 62% women, 38% men.

Undergraduates 1,231 full-time, 427 part-time. Students come from 12 states and territories, 7 other countries, 6% are from out of state, 4% African American, 0.6% Asian American or Pacific Islander, 2% Hispanic American, 0.5% Native American, 0.7% international, 10% transferred in, 24% live on campus.

Faculty *Total:* 206, 30% full-time, 13% with terminal degrees. *Student/faculty ratio:* 12:1.

Academic Programs *Special study options:* academic remediation for entering students, adult/continuing education programs, advanced placement credit, cooperative education, distance learning, external degree program, freshman honors college, honors programs, independent study, internships, part-time degree program, services for LD students, student-designed majors, summer session for credit. *ROTC:* Army (c), Air Force (c).

Athletics Member NCAA. *Intercollegiate sports:* baseball M, basketball M/W, cross-country running M/W, golf M, soccer M/W, softball W, tennis M/W, track and field M/W, volleyball W. *Intramural sports:* basketball M/W, cheerleading M(c)/W(c), equestrian sports M(c)/W(c), football M/W, lacrosse M/W, skiing (downhill) M(c)/W(c), soccer M/W, softball M/W, table tennis M/W, tennis M/W, volleyball M/W, weight lifting M/W.

Costs (2005–06) *Comprehensive fee:* $22,810 includes full-time tuition ($14,100), mandatory fees ($920), and room and board ($7790). Part-time tuition: $325 per credit. *Required fees:* $110 per term part-time. *Room and board:* Room and board charges vary according to board plan and housing facility.

Financial Aid 125 Federal Work-Study jobs (averaging $1000). 100 state and other part-time jobs (averaging $1000).

Contact: David L. Elliott, Ph.D., Honors Program Director, Professor, Division of Communication Arts and Humanities, Keystone College, One College Green, LaPlume, Pennsylvania 18440; *Telephone:* 570-945-8453, 877-4COLLEGE (toll free); *E-mail:* david.elliott@keystone.edu; *Web site:* http://www.keystone.edu

Kutztown University of Pennsylvania
Honors Program
Kutztown, Pennsylvania

*F*ounded in 1986, the Kutztown University Honors Program is designed to provide academic and leadership opportunities for the University's most proficient and highly motivated students. The undergraduate program is open to full-time students. It requires a minimum of 21 credits in honors courses that stress in-depth study, research, and challenging exploration of various areas of study. The 21 honors credits also count toward the 120 credits for graduation. Students may earn these honors credits through a variety of methods, including honors courses, internships, course by contract, and by independent study (thesis).

In addition to honors course work, students in the Honors Program also complete two units of service, which do not carry academic credit allocation (one for the community and one for the University). Service opportunities in the community are offered through a variety of official University sources under the auspices of the off-campus Student Life Center, and an agreement to serve a minimum of 30 hours of service, approved by the Honors Director and the Honors Council, is established between the student and the community agency in advance of the term that the service is to be completed. For the second unit, students may select from a variety of services to the University, approved by the Honors Director and Honors Council in advance of student participation. The service component of the Honors Program should begin in the student's sophomore year at Kutztown University.

There are currently 225 students enrolled in the program.

Participation Requirements: An honors diploma is awarded to those students in the program who have met all college requirements, have completed at least 21 credits in honors course work through any variety of the methods described above, have attained a minimum cumulative quality point average of 3.25, and have completed a two-unit service component.

Admission Process: Freshmen who have been identified as potential honors students based on their high school record and SAT scores, transfer students from other honors programs, and incumbent students who have earned a cumulative QPA of 3.25 or higher are invited to join the Honors Program. Undergraduate students who are not members of the Honors Program may take an honors course if they have a quality point average of 3.0 or higher in 15 credits taken at the University. These students do not receive honors credits for the course. Permission of the Honors Program Director is required.

Applications for the Honors Program must be submitted in the spring semester.

Scholarship Availability: Scholarships based upon merit are available to entering freshmen and to upperclassmen who participate in the Honors Program.

Campus Overview

State-supported comprehensive, founded 1866, part of Pennsylvania State System of Higher Education • **Coed** 8,527 undergraduate students, 90% full-time, 59% women, 41% men.

Undergraduates 7,676 full-time, 851 part-time. Students come from 21 states and territories, 29 other countries, 8% are from out of state, 7% African American, 1% Asian American or Pacific Islander, 3% Hispanic American, 0.3% Native American, 0.6% international, 7% transferred in, 52% live on campus.

Faculty *Total:* 432, 68% full-time, 54% with terminal degrees. *Student/faculty ratio:* 20:1.

Academic Programs *Special study options:* academic remediation for entering students, accelerated degree program, adult/continuing education programs, advanced placement credit, distance learning, double majors, external degree program, honors programs, independent study, internships, off-campus study, part-time degree program, services for LD students, student-designed majors, study abroad, summer session for credit. *ROTC:* Army (c), Air Force (c). *Unusual degree programs:* 3-2 engineering with Pennsylvania State University - University Park Campus.

Athletics Member NCAA. All Division II. *Intercollegiate sports:* baseball M(s), basketball M(s)/W(s), cheerleading W(s), cross-country running M(s)/W(s), equestrian sports M(c)/W(c), field hockey W(s), football M(s), golf W(s), ice hockey M(c), lacrosse M(c)/W(c), riflery M(c)/W(c), rugby M(c)/W(c), skiing (downhill) M(c)/W(c), soccer M(s)/W(s), softball W(s), swimming and diving M(s)/W(s), tennis M(s)/W(s), track and field M(s)/W(s), volleyball M(c)/W(s), wrestling M(s). *Intramural sports:* badminton M/W, basketball M/W, equestrian sports M/W, football M/W, golf M/W, ice hockey M, lacrosse M/W, riflery M/W, rugby M/W, skiing (cross-country) M/W, skiing (downhill) M/W, soccer M/W, softball M/W, tennis M/W, ultimate Frisbee M/W, volleyball M/W, water polo M/W, weight lifting M/W.

Costs (2004–05) *Tuition:* state resident $4810 full-time, $200 per credit part-time; nonresident $12,026 full-time, $501 per credit part-time. Part-time tuition and fees vary according to course load. *Required fees:* $1446 full-time, $74 per credit part-time. *Room and board:* $5274; room only: $3792. Room and board charges vary according to board plan and housing facility.

Financial Aid 425 Federal Work-Study jobs (averaging $1017). In 2003, 244 non-need-based awards were made. *Average percent of need met:* 64%. *Average financial aid package:* $6204. *Average need-based loan:* $3403. *Average need-based gift aid:* $3773. *Average non-need-based aid:* $1817.

Contact: Director: Dr. Andrea Mitnick, Speech Communication Associate Professor, P.O. Box 730, Kutztown, Pennsylvania 19530; *Telephone:* 610-683-1391; *Fax:* 610-683-1393; *E-mail:* vigoda@kutztown.edu

La Salle University
University Honors Program
Philadelphia, Pennsylvania

The pedagogical philosophy of La Salle University emphasizes the need for a strong basis in the humanities for all undergraduates and, for this reason, requires everyone to complete a set of courses that focus on these humanities. Individual academic departments offer students a more intensive study in a specific discipline, but only after the majority of the requirements in this humanistically based core have been completed.

The curricular structure of the honors program follows this general University model, but with modifications that recognize the needs and abilities of the highly motivated and intellectually gifted student. These modifications are primarily in the manner in which the honors program student satisfies these essential University-wide requirements.

In the first year of studies, the honors program student completes three honors courses each term. These courses are in the disciplines of history, literature, and philosophy, and over the course of the year, take the student from the ancient world to the contemporary period. The professors teaching this first-year program make every attempt to coordinate their readings and assignments so that at any particular time during the academic year, the students are viewing the same period of civilization through the perspective of three different disciplines.

A typical week has the student spending 3 hours of class time in each of the three disciplines and 3 hours of time in a special situation in which an attempt is made to integrate the three seemingly distinct disciplines. This last 3-hour period of time brings together all of the first-year students in the program and their professors in a variety of experiences. Some of the sessions are held on campus, and others make use of the many museums and resources of the Philadelphia area. In recent years this has meant afternoons or evenings spent at the Academy of Music with the Philadelphia Orchestra, at the Philadelphia Museum of Art with the curator of the medieval collection, at the Arden Theater with the artistic director, or at the Franklin Institute. Each activity is designed to complement and supplement the work of the classroom—a humanities lab, in effect.

Total enrollment in the honors program is approximately 210 students from the four class years.

Participation Requirements: The total number of courses required in honors is a minimum of fourteen, including the independent project. One of the courses must be an ethical issues seminar in the student's major. In addition to the curricular requirements, students are required to maintain a cumulative GPA of 3.0 and a GPA of 3.0 in honors courses to remain active in the honors program.

After having successfully completed the first year of studies, the honors program student is then offered a wide variety of seminars in honors. These seminars allow the student to study topics, time periods, and areas of interest in considerably more depth, using the broad overview of the first year as a solid foundation upon which to build. Serving as the substitutes for the regular core requirements of the University, these seminars are often cross-disciplinary. They can be single course offerings or multiple course offerings (e.g., with teachers team teaching a course). In addition, each honors program student is required to complete an independent study project that is the equivalent of one 3-credit course. This is done on a topic of the student's choosing (not necessarily in the major) and is directed by a faculty member.

Students who complete all of the requirements of the honors program are graduated from La Salle with the special distinction of General University Honors. This distinction is noted on the official transcript, on the diploma, and in a special listing in the Commencement program.

Admission Process: Each year approximately 60 students are admitted to the honors program (from a freshman class of approximately 800 students). Invitations are extended to students who have been accepted for admission by the University, who have combined SAT I scores of approximately 1250, and who rank in the first quintile of their graduating class.

The application deadline is May 1.

Scholarship Availability: Each year La Salle awards approximately thirty full-tuition scholarships to high school seniors. The Scholarship Selection Committee looks for students with a combined SAT I score of approximately 1300 or higher and who rank in the top 10 percent of the graduating class. A separate application for a scholarship must be submitted in addition to the application for admission to the University. Scholarship applications may be obtained by contacting the office of the director of the honors program or through the Office of Admissions.

Campus Overview

Independent Roman Catholic comprehensive, founded 1863 • **Coed** 4,338 undergraduate students, 79% full-time, 59% women, 41% men.

Undergraduates 3,438 full-time, 900 part-time. Students come from 36 states and territories, 36 other countries, 37% are from out of state, 14% African American, 4% Asian American or Pacific Islander, 6% Hispanic American, 0.2% Native American, 0.9% international, 9% transferred in, 63% live on campus.

Faculty *Total:* 492, 42% full-time, 67% with terminal degrees. *Student/faculty ratio:* 16:1.

Academic Programs *Special study options:* accelerated degree program, adult/continuing education programs, advanced placement credit, cooperative education, double majors, freshman honors college, honors programs, independent study, internships, off-campus study, part-time degree program, services for LD students, student-designed majors, study abroad, summer session for credit. *ROTC:* Army (c), Air Force (c). *Unusual degree programs:* 3-2 occupational therapy with Thomas Jefferson University, speech pathology.

Athletics Member NCAA. All Division I except football (Division I-AA). *Intercollegiate sports:* baseball M(s), basketball M(s)/W(s), crew M(s)/W(s), cross-country running M(s)/W(s), field hockey W(s), golf M(s)/W(s), lacrosse W(s), soccer M(s)/W(s), softball W(s), swimming and diving M(s)/W(s), tennis M(s)/W(s), track and field M(s)/W(s), volleyball W(s). *Intramural sports:* baseball M, basketball M/W, crew M/W, field hockey W, football M/W, golf M/W, ice hockey M(c), lacrosse M(c), rugby M(c)/W(c), soccer M/W, softball W, swimming and diving M/W, tennis M/W, track and field M/W, volleyball M/W.

Costs (2005–06) *Comprehensive fee:* $35,600 includes full-time tuition ($25,880), mandatory fees ($310), and room and board ($9410). Full-time tuition and fees vary according to program. Part-time tuition and fees vary according to class time and course load. *College room only:* $4920. Room and board charges vary according to board plan, housing facility, and location.

Financial Aid In 2003, 575 non-need-based awards were made. *Average percent of need met:* 74%. *Average financial aid package:* $15,998. *Average need-based loan:* $4340. *Average need-based gift aid:* $11,273. *Average non-need-based aid:* $9222.

Contact: Director: John S. Grady, LaSalle University, 1900 West Olney Avenue, Philadelphia, Pennsylvania 19141-1199; *Telephone:* 215-951-1360; *Fax:* 215-951-1488; *E-mail:* grady@lasalle.edu

Lock Haven University of Pennsylvania
Honors Program
Lock Haven, Pennsylvania

*T*he Honors Program expresses Lock Haven University's commitment to academic excellence by providing faculty members and students alike with challenging opportunities for creative intellectual growth. The honors curriculum combines a rigorous subject matter grounded in the broad sweep of human civilization and an integrated four-year program for the development of sophisticated intellectual abilities. A spirit of inquiry in the tradition of the liberal arts inspires the program and fosters in each student the capacity for independent learning. Honors courses share an interdisciplinary approach, heavy reliance on classic sources, intensive writing, small size (usually 15–20 students), and active student involvement.*

The Honors Program began in 1988 with an entering freshman class of 20 students. The program's growing reputation made possible an expansion to 40 freshmen for fall 1996. Total enrollment is expected to increase gradually from 100 to 125. This expansion has been carefully designed to ensure that the small learning communities of 20 freshmen will remain intact. With the expansion will come a greater variety of honors courses and cocurricular activities.

Participation Requirements: The heart of the Honors Program is a 27-hour program of studies providing students with a uniquely challenging and rewarding educational experience while meeting University requirements both in general education and in the student's major. The particular strength of the honors curriculum lies in its integration of these courses into a cohesive and developmentally sequenced program of study culminating in a senior project and the oral presentation of that project in the honors colloquium.

Honors freshmen form learning communities of 18 to 20 students and take two classes together each semester: Honors Composition and Literature I and II and Honors Historical and Philosophical Studies I and II. Navigating the sometimes difficult transition from high school to university is made easier by 4 hours per week of cocurricular activities that provide the supportive mentoring of upperclass honors students and faculty members who show freshmen the way to success and help them develop their own voices as adult learners.

After the freshman year, students take one course for honors credit each semester, either an honors course that satisfies a general education requirement or an honors augmentation of a nonhonors course, usually in the student's major. Augmentation projects are planned to build a foundation for the honors senior project, the culmination of the student's academic program. These projects provide excellent preparation and credentials for graduate and professional schools. Honors students are also encouraged to take advantage of the University's extensive study-abroad and internship opportunities.

Cocurricular activities are an important part of the honors experience throughout the four years, although the minimum requirement drops to 2 hours per week after the first year. However, many honors students decide to take up leadership opportunities by becoming Freshman Discussion Group leaders, Activity Group leaders, or even Student Associate Directors.

Honors students may earn official recognition in one of two categories: university honors (completed in four years) or university honors with distinction (completed in four years, including completion of a senior honors project). Honors graduation in each of these categories requires completion of honors curricular requirements with a minimum GPA of 3.2 in honors courses and overall as well as active participation in honors cocurricular activities.

Admission Process: Entering freshmen are selected on the basis of high school grades, SAT I scores, essays, recommendations, and high school activities. Continuation in the Honors Program requires a minimum GPA of 3.0 (overall and in honors) at the end of the first year and a minimum GPA of 3.2 thereafter. Lock Haven University students may also enter the Honors Program after one to three semesters of study; a minimum GPA of 3.2 is required.

Scholarship Availability: Three forms of merit-based financial aid are available to honors students. The Lock Haven University Foundation currently awards five Presidential Scholarships of $2000 and thirteen Academic Honors Scholarships of $1500 to entering freshmen enrolling in the Honors Program. The Presidential Scholarships are renewable for up to three years. A limited number of Academic Honors Scholarships are awarded to continuing students on a competitive basis. All scholarship renewals and awards after the first year require a minimum GPA of 3.2. Continuation in the Honors Program is optional. In addition to these scholarships, many honors students are employed in the Honors Center for 2 to 5 hours per week.

Campus Overview

State-supported comprehensive, founded 1870, part of Pennsylvania State System of Higher Education • **Coed** 4,875 undergraduate students, 91% full-time, 59% women, 41% men.

Undergraduates 4,435 full-time, 440 part-time. Students come from 32 states and territories, 39 other countries, 11% are from out of state, 4% African American, 0.8% Asian American or Pacific Islander, 2% Hispanic American, 0.3% Native American, 1% international, 5% transferred in, 36% live on campus.

Faculty *Total:* 259, 91% full-time, 61% with terminal degrees. *Student/faculty ratio:* 20:1.

Academic Programs *Special study options:* academic remediation for entering students, adult/continuing education programs, advanced placement credit, cooperative education, distance learning, double majors, English as a second language, honors programs, independent study, internships, off-campus study, part-time degree program, services for LD students, student-designed majors, study abroad, summer session for credit. *ROTC:* Army (b). *Unusual degree programs:* 3-2 engineering with Pennsylvania State University - University Park Campus; nursing with Clarion University of Pennsylvania.

Athletics Member NCAA. All Division II except wrestling (Division I). *Intercollegiate sports:* baseball M(s), basketball M(s)/W(s), cross-country running M(s)/W(s), field hockey W(s), football M(s), lacrosse W(s), soccer M(s)/W(s), softball W(s), swimming and diving W(s), track and field M(s)/W(s), volleyball W(s), wrestling M(s). *Intramural sports:* badminton M/W, basketball M/W, cross-country running M/W, fencing M/W, field hockey W, football M, golf M/W, ice hockey M, lacrosse M/W, racquetball M/W, rugby M/W, skiing (cross-country) M/W, skiing (downhill) M/W, soccer M/W, softball M/W, swimming and diving M/W, tennis M/W, track and field M/W, ultimate Frisbee M/W, volleyball M/W, water polo M, weight lifting M/W, wrestling M.

Costs (2004–05) *Tuition:* state resident $4810 full-time, $200 per credit part-time; nonresident $10,026 full-time, $418 per credit part-time. Full-time tuition and fees vary according to course load and location. Part-time tuition and fees vary according to course load and location. *Required fees:* $1290 full-time, $63 per credit part-time. *Room and board:* $5516; room only: $3140. Room and board charges vary according to board plan and housing facility.

Financial Aid 253 Federal Work-Study jobs (averaging $1174). 951 state and other part-time jobs (averaging $711). In 2003, 95 non-need-based awards were made. *Average percent of need met:* 77%. *Average financial aid package:* $6120. *Average need-based loan:* $3767. *Average need-based gift aid:* $4568. *Average non-need-based aid:* $1575.

Contact: Director: Dr. Joseph P. McGinn, 401 North Fairview Street, Lock Haven, Pennsylvania 17745; *Telephone:* 570-893-2165; *Fax:* 570-893-2711; *E-mail:* jmcginn@lhup.edu; *Web site:* http://www.lhup.edu/honors

Mansfield University of Pennsylvania
Honors Program
Mansfield, Pennsylvania

The Honors Program at Mansfield University is a 24-credit multidisciplinary academic program that features innovative course work, challenging subjects, and opportunities for cultural enrichment. This program is designed for students with a strong record of academic achievement and desire for new learning experiences. The Honors Program enables students to explore subjects that interest them in greater depth than may be possible in traditional courses, and it also allows students to apply their knowledge across academic fields. It is the goal of the Honors Program to provide students with the knowledge, skills, and opportunities to achieve their full potential during their academic career at Mansfield University. Mansfield University is a member of the National Collegiate Honors Council (NCHC) and the Northeast Region National Collegiate Honors Council (NE-NCHC).

The Honors Program offers a dynamic learning environment that includes small classes, unique courses, collaborative and individual research projects, and field-based educational experiences. All Honors Program students are required to complete five specially designed core courses, two honors electives, and one senior honors research project presentation. The electives, representing a cross-section of the liberal arts and sciences, change each semester.

Benefits of the Honors Program include priority scheduling and scholarship awards, including M.U. Foundation Awards, Highest QPA by Class Book Awards, and full scholarships to attend the five-week Summer Honors Program of the State System of Higher Education, which earns each participant 6 University honors credits. Past destinations have included Moscow, Vienna, Scotland, South Africa, Ecuador, and Oxford. In addition, specific honors students are recognized at the University honors banquet. Honors students are presented with honors medallions, receive an honors sweater, attend the private press conference for the featured campus speaker, have their own study area, attend senior honors research project presentations, and have the opportunity to attend many cultural events. Graduating honors students' transcripts list their honors accomplishments. Students in nursing, music, elementary education, or special education have the option of choosing either the standard Honors Program requirements or a specialized sequence.

Participation Requirements: Honors students must maintain a QPA of at least 3.0 both in their honors courses and overall. A student who falls below 3.0 is placed on honors probation. The student is given one semester to improve their QPA and/or honors course grades. Should the QPA not be raised to at least 3.0 by the following semester, the student is dismissed from the program. There are three required meetings during the academic year, one during the fall semester and two during the spring semester.

Admission Process: Enrollment in the Honors Program is accomplished in three ways. Students who demonstrate superior high school achievement, as reflected by SAT scores and a high class rank, are invited to accept early admission into the Honors Program during freshman orientation. Freshmen who exhibit strong academic potential during their first semester are invited to join the program on the basis of a faculty recommendation. Students who have completed their freshman year and demonstrate strong academic achievement can forward a written request to the Honors Program Director to be considered for admission.

After their admission to the Honors Program, students are assigned an honors adviser, who assists them with their progress in the program. The honors adviser also helps with the student's general education program so that it is challenging and relevant to the student's interests. The Honors Program is compatible with all Mansfield University departmental majors without any extra courses. All honors courses count in fulfilling the general education block requirements, dependent upon content. Students who decide to leave the Honors Program do not lose any of the credits they have earned. All credits still appear on the student's transcript and count as fulfilling their general education requirements.

Campus Overview

State-supported comprehensive, founded 1857, part of Pennsylvania State System of Higher Education • **Coed** 3,127 undergraduate students, 90% full-time, 61% women, 39% men.

Undergraduates 2,813 full-time, 314 part-time. Students come from 17 states and territories, 23 other countries, 19% are from out of state, 6% African American, 0.6% Asian American or Pacific Islander, 1% Hispanic American, 1% Native American, 3% international, 8% transferred in, 50% live on campus.

Faculty *Total:* 208, 80% full-time, 57% with terminal degrees. *Student/faculty ratio:* 18:1.

Academic Programs *Special study options:* academic remediation for entering students, accelerated degree program, adult/continuing education programs, advanced placement credit, distance learning, double majors, freshman honors college, honors programs, independent study, internships, off-campus study, part-time degree program, services for LD students, student-designed majors, study abroad, summer session for credit.

Athletics Member NCAA. All Division II. *Intercollegiate sports:* baseball M(s), basketball M(s)/W(s), cross-country running M(s)/W(s), field hockey W(s), football M(s), soccer W(s), softball W(s), swimming and diving W, track and field M(s)/W(s). *Intramural sports:* badminton M/W, basketball M/W, bowling M/W, cheerleading W, cross-country running M/W, equestrian sports M/W, football M/W, golf M/W, racquetball M/W, skiing (cross-country) M/W, skiing (downhill) M/W, soccer M/W, softball M/W, swimming and diving M/W, tennis M/W, track and field M/W, volleyball M/W, water polo M/W, weight lifting M/W.

Costs (2004–05) *Tuition:* state resident $4810 full-time, $200 per credit part-time; nonresident $12,026 full-time, $501 per credit part-time. Part-time tuition and fees vary according to course load. *Required fees:* $1420 full-time, $74 per credit part-time. *Room and board:* $5456. Room and board charges vary according to board plan.

Contact: Director: Dr. Sharon Carrish, 307 Hemlock Manor, Mansfield, Pennsylvania 16933; *Telephone:* 570-662-4371; *E-mail:* scarrish@mansfield.edu

Marywood University
Honors Program
Scranton, Pennsylvania

The Honors Program at Marywood University allows students to supplement their undergraduate education through honors work and activities in an open program set up. All students who meet certain academic requirements are eligible to enroll for honors courses at any time, but certain highly motivated students may opt to pursue a Citation in Honors, which denotes full participation in and completion of the Honors Program. Participation does not require extra courses or fees; the program is simply designed to enhance the liberal arts curriculum at Marywood, and students from all majors and disciplines are welcome.

At Marywood, honors students enjoy small-seminar courses based in the liberal arts (class size generally ranges from 10 to 15 students). These honors course sections move at a quicker pace, offer more opportunity for discussion and class participation, and cover more material in more depth than the regular sections of the course. The program also allows students to complete honors courses via Honors Enrichment—the student makes a regular section of a course honors through an independent study contract with the professor and the Director of Honors and Fellowships. Students who pursue the Citation in Honors also complete an honors thesis during their senior year. This comprehensive capstone project combines a topic in the student's major and a specific focus in the liberal arts to fully encapsulate his or her undergraduate experience. Each student's thesis is published annually in Scientia, the Journal of Marywood's Honors Program.

Honors students are encouraged to participate in undergraduate research and pursue scholarships and fellowships for study abroad and graduate and professional programs through the Office of Honors and Fellowships. Along with support from the Director of Honors and Fellowships, this office gives students access to Marywood's Undergraduate Research Review Committee, the Scholarships and Fellowships Committee (each of whose members are responsible for helping students apply for specific awards), and the Honors and Fellowships Advisory Board.

The Office of Honors and Fellowships also works closely with other Marywood offices and venues to serve students in various educational and cocurricular capacities. It sponsors and supports programs for honors students and for the University community at large. These activities include information sessions, guest speakers, recognition events, and student presentation forums. The main goal of both the Honors Program and the Office of Honors and Fellowships is to help students take an active role in their education—to challenge their minds and expand their horizons so that they may succeed and thrive in today's demanding world.

Marywood's Honors Program was officially founded and launched in the fall of 1983. Approximately 50 honors students are pursuing a Citation in Honors.

Participation Requirements: To be eligible to take honors courses, students must maintain a Quality Point Average (QPA) of 3.0 or better. To graduate with a Citation in Honors, students must maintain a QPA of 3.25 or better and complete a minimum of 24 honors credits: 15–21 credits in the core liberal arts curriculum, up to 6 credits in their major, and 3 credits for the thesis. Honors theses are published annually in *Scientia*, the Journal of Marywood's Honors Program. Participation in honors courses is noted on all official transcripts, and attainment of the Citation in Honors is noted on all official transcripts and the student's diploma upon graduation.

Admission Process: Marywood's Honors Program is open, so any student with a QPA of 3.0 or better can enroll for honors courses during any semester with permission from the Director of Honors and Fellowships. Incoming freshman with an SAT score of 1100 or higher are invited to enroll in honors courses at the start of their undergraduate career. Freshman with lower SAT scores who feel that they are still qualified to take honors courses based on other academic criteria may meet with the Director of Honors and Fellowships to receive special permission to participate if desired. There is no deadline to elect for formal participation in the Honors Program; however, students are encouraged to declare their intent to pursue a Citation in Honors early so that the Director of Honors and Fellowships may assist them with academic planning.

Scholarship Availability: Nearly $11 million of institutional aid is offered to qualified students through the University every year. Requirements and conditions vary by award.

Campus Overview

Independent Roman Catholic comprehensive, founded 1915 • **Coed** 1,811 undergraduate students, 88% full-time, 74% women, 26% men.

Undergraduates 1,598 full-time, 213 part-time. Students come from 28 states and territories, 18 other countries, 20% are from out of state, 2% African American, 0.9% Asian American or Pacific Islander, 2% Hispanic American, 0.3% Native American, 2% international, 7% transferred in, 38% live on campus.

Faculty *Total:* 313, 45% full-time, 35% with terminal degrees. *Student/faculty ratio:* 12:1.

Academic Programs *Special study options:* academic remediation for entering students, accelerated degree program, adult/continuing education programs, advanced placement credit, distance learning, double majors, English as a second language, external degree program, honors programs, independent study, internships, off-campus study, part-time degree program, services for LD students, student-designed majors, study abroad, summer session for credit. *ROTC:* Army (c), Air Force (c). *Unusual degree programs:* 3-2 physician assistant, communication sciences disorders.

Athletics Member NCAA. All Division III. *Intercollegiate sports:* baseball M, basketball M/W, cross-country running M/W, field hockey W, soccer M/W, softball W, tennis M/W, volleyball W. *Intramural sports:* badminton M/W, baseball M, basketball M/W, cheerleading W(c), field hockey W, football M, golf M/W, lacrosse M(c)/W, racquetball M(c), skiing (downhill) M(c)/W(c), soccer M(c)/W(c), softball M/W, swimming and diving M/W, table tennis M/W, tennis M/W, ultimate Frisbee W(c), volleyball M/W.

Costs (2005–06) *Comprehensive fee:* $30,740 includes full-time tuition ($20,700), mandatory fees ($940), and room and board ($9100). Part-time tuition: $643 per credit. Part-time tuition and fees vary according to course load. *Required fees:* $190 per term part-time. *College room only:* $5152. Room and board charges vary according to board plan and housing facility.

Financial Aid 643 Federal Work-Study jobs (averaging $1724). In 2003, 228 non-need-based awards were made. *Average percent of need met:* 75%. *Average financial aid package:* $14,499. *Average need-based loan:* $4185. *Average need-based gift aid:* $10,319. *Average non-need-based aid:* $6929.

Contact: Christina Marie Elvidge, Director of Honors and Fellowships, Marywood University, 2300 Adams Avenue, Scranton, Pennsylvania 18509; *Telephone:* 570-340-6045 Ext. 2107; *Fax:* 570-340-6028; *E-mail:* elvidge@marywood.edu; *Web site:* http://www.marywood.edu/www2/Honors/honors_web_page.htm

Mercyhurst College
Honors Program
Erie, Pennsylvania

The Mercyhurst College Honors Program (MCHP) has a rich assortment of curricular and extracurricular opportunities for academically accomplished students who seek extraordinary intel-

lectual stimulation. Selected entering freshmen and transfer students are invited to participate in the Honors Preparation Year (HPY). In this trial year, the HPY students have the opportunity to sample the MCHP before formally joining in the spring term. During the HPY, students take at least one honors course, attend intellectual and/or cultural events on campus, and perform service learning. They are invited to numerous out-of-classroom events, such as service learning excursions, trips to regional art museums, and gatherings with their MCHP mentors. At the end of the HPY, students who wish to join the MCHP must submit an admission portfolio to the director. Students must have a minimum QPA of 3.0 at the College, attend at least ten events that are intellectual or cultural in nature, perform 10 hours of community service, and secure two letters of recommendation from faculty members at the College as part of the admission process. In the spring, students are officially inducted into the MCHP. MCHP students continue attending intellectual and cultural events on campus; by their junior and senior years, they are often creating and/or participating in these events. MCHP students also continue taking honors courses. By graduation, they have taken at least nine honors courses. At least six of these courses must be honors classes that also satisfy the College-wide liberal studies core requirement, while the others may be courses in which the student completes an honors contract. Honors courses offered at Mercyhurst are lively and small (fewer than 20) and often feature student-led discussions; they are more student centered and student driven than non-honors courses. The courses are often designed to allow students more freedom in their education; this format is outstanding preparation for graduate school. Honors students have input into the creation of honors courses at the College. As the capstone to their experience in the MCHP, all honors students must write a senior honors thesis, which they present at the College-wide research symposium in the spring.

Extracurricular activities and professional development are major components of the MCHP experience. Honors students at Mercyhurst College create many of the events that define the intellectual and cultural life of the College, from discussion on timely issues to performing arts presentations. In addition, MCHP students play a prominent role in national, regional, and College-wide conferences, symposia, shows, and performances. Honors students at Mercyhurst College have read papers at national professional meetings, been successful in major national scholarship competitions, had their papers published in a variety of journals, and had their work shown in regional exhibits. MCHP graduates study at some of the most prestigious graduate and professional schools. The College works with advisers and students to prepare them for candidacy for graduate school.

Approximately 90 honors students are in the MCHP. There are an additional 100 students who are eligible to enroll in honors courses despite not being in the program.

Participation Requirements: To graduate with College Honors, students must maintain a 3.5 QPA, complete a total of nine honors courses (three of which may have been honors contracts), attend fifteen events of intellectual or cultural interest each year, perform 15 hours of service each year, and write an approved senior thesis (in chosen major) or an honors thesis.

Admission Process: Participating in the MCHP requires an invitation from the Director. Each year about 120 entering freshmen are invited to join the program. Invitations are based on SAT I or ACT scores, high school records, and recommendations. Transfer students are eligible to join the MCHP and invitations are based on former college or university performance. Students already at Mercyhurst who have a record of academic achievement are also encouraged to consider the MCHP, particularly if recommended by a faculty member.

Scholarship Availability: While the MCHP Director supervises the awarding of just one academic scholarship, many are available through the College's Office of Financial Aid.

Campus Overview

Independent Roman Catholic comprehensive, founded 1926 • **Coed** 3,807 undergraduate students, 87% full-time, 61% women, 39% men.

Undergraduates 3,296 full-time, 511 part-time. Students come from 38 states and territories, 26 other countries, 38% are from out of state, 3% African American, 0.5% Asian American or Pacific Islander, 1% Hispanic American, 0.3% Native American, 4% international, 2% transferred in, 73% live on campus.

Faculty *Total:* 237, 67% full-time, 40% with terminal degrees. *Student/faculty ratio:* 19:1.

Academic Programs *Special study options:* academic remediation for entering students, accelerated degree program, adult/continuing education programs, advanced placement credit, cooperative education, double majors, honors programs, independent study, internships, off-campus study, part-time degree program, services for LD students, student-designed majors, study abroad, summer session for credit. *ROTC:* Army (c), Air Force (c). *Unusual degree programs:* law with Duquesne University.

Athletics Member NCAA, NCCAA. All NCAA Division II. *Intercollegiate sports:* baseball M(s), basketball M(s)/W(s), crew M(s)/W(s), cross-country running M(s)/W(s), field hockey W(s), football M(s), golf M(s)/W(s), ice hockey M(s)/W(s), lacrosse M(s)/W(s), soccer M(s)/W(s), softball W(s), tennis M(s)/W(s), volleyball M(s)/W(s), water polo M(s)/W(s), wrestling M(s). *Intramural sports:* basketball M/W, football M, skiing (cross-country) M/W, skiing (downhill) M/W, volleyball M/W.

Costs (2005–06) *Comprehensive fee:* $26,187 includes full-time tuition ($17,760), mandatory fees ($1353), and room and board ($7074). Full-time tuition and fees vary according to course load, degree level, and location. Part-time tuition: $592 per credit. Part-time tuition and fees vary according to course load and degree level. *College room only:* $3576. Room and board charges vary according to board plan and location.

Financial Aid 271 Federal Work-Study jobs (averaging $1372). 1,250 state and other part-time jobs (averaging $1171). In 2004, 574 non-need-based awards were made. *Average percent of need met:* 91%. *Average financial aid package:* $12,094. *Average need-based loan:* $3766. *Average need-based gift aid:* $8617. *Average non-need-based aid:* $8220.

Contact: Director: Dr. Joseph M. Morris, 501 East 38th Street, Erie, Pennsylvania 16546; *Telephone:* 814-824-2154; *Fax:* 814-824-3041; *E-mail:* hondir@mercyhurst.edu; *Web site:* http://www.mercyhurst.edu

Messiah College
Honors Program
Grantham, Pennsylvania

The Messiah College Honors Program was inaugurated in the fall of 1998. The mission of the Honors Program is to foster academic excellence and to cultivate an intellectually rigorous Christian world view, thus equipping young men and women for lives of leadership and service.

Students in the Honors Program take several interdisciplinary honors courses beginning in their freshman year and continuing through their junior year. These small, seminar-type courses are taught by senior faculty members and cover topics such as Art of the Ancient Americas, Darwin and Darwinism, and The Writer's Call to Fidelity: Wallace Stegner's Example. In their fourth year, students participate in a two-semester Senior Honors Project and Colloquium, culminating in a public presentation. In addition to these credit-bearing experiences, students meet each semester outside of the classroom in the Honors Congress to discuss timely issues. Throughout the academic year students also have opportunities to interact with special campus guests as part of the Honors Discourse. The College's proximity to the academic and cultural centers of

Washington, Philadelphia, Baltimore, and New York provide additional opportunities for students in the Honors Program.

Students from all of the college's applied and liberal arts majors are eligible to participate in the Honors Program. Moreover, in keeping with College's commitment to educating the whole person, students in the Honors Program are strongly encouraged to participate in the college's many cocurricular opportunities, including those in athletics, music, theater, student government, campus publications, and off-campus ministries.

Program enrollment is 250 students.

Participation Requirements: Students in the Honors Program must take an honors section of First Year Seminar, honors sections of three other interdisciplinary general education courses, and complete a two-semester Senior Honors Project. Students in the Honors Program must maintain a minimum cumulative 3.3 GPA as first-year students and at least a 3.6 GPA for each following year. Upon graduation, recognition of the student's completion of the Honors Program is noted at commencement and on the student's college transcript.

Admission Process: No special application is required. As part of the regular college admissions process, students who meet minimum eligibility requirements are considered for the program. Minimum requirements for the Honors Program are an SAT I score of at least 1300 and graduation in the top 10 percent of the student's high school class. From the eligible pool of candidates, 150 students are selected for on-campus interviews. After the on-campus interview and evaluation of all other application materials, approximately 75 students are selected each year for the Honors Program.

Scholarship Availability: All students who are selected for the Honors Program receive scholarship aid. Each year, 6 freshman students are awarded a full-tuition Trustees Scholarship, while all other freshmen in the Honors Program receive scholarships covering at least two-thirds tuition.

Campus Overview

Independent interdenominational 4-year, founded 1909 • **Coed** 2,917 undergraduate students, 98% full-time, 63% women, 37% men.

Undergraduates 2,860 full-time, 57 part-time. Students come from 41 states and territories, 29 other countries, 48% are from out of state, 3% African American, 2% Asian American or Pacific Islander, 2% Hispanic American, 0.1% Native American, 2% international, 3% transferred in, 89% live on campus.

Faculty *Total:* 310, 55% full-time. *Student/faculty ratio:* 13:1.

Academic Programs *Special study options:* academic remediation for entering students, accelerated degree program, adult/continuing education programs, advanced placement credit, double majors, English as a second language, honors programs, independent study, internships, off-campus study, part-time degree program, services for LD students, student-designed majors, study abroad, summer session for credit.

Athletics Member NCAA. All Division III. *Intercollegiate sports:* baseball M, basketball M/W, cross-country running M/W, field hockey W, golf M, lacrosse M/W, soccer M/W, softball W, tennis M/W, track and field M/W, volleyball W, wrestling M. *Intramural sports:* basketball M/W, soccer M/W, softball M/W, ultimate Frisbee M/W, volleyball M/W.

Costs (2004–05) *Comprehensive fee:* $27,350 includes full-time tuition ($20,120), mandatory fees ($670), and room and board ($6560). Part-time tuition: $840 per credit. *Required fees:* $28 per credit part-time. *College room only:* $3400. Room and board charges vary according to board plan, housing facility, and location.

Financial Aid 755 Federal Work-Study jobs (averaging $1821). 734 state and other part-time jobs (averaging $2296). In 2004, 512 non-need-based awards were made. *Average percent of need met:* 66%. *Average financial aid package:* $13,585. *Average need-based loan:* $4011. *Average need-based gift aid:* $4738. *Average non-need-based aid:* $5372.

Contact: Director: Dr. Dean C. Curry, Grantham, Pennsylvania 17055; *Telephone:* 717-766-2511; *E-mail:* dcurry@messiah.edu; *Web site:* http://www.messiah.edu

Millersville University of Pennsylvania
University Honors College
Millersville, Pennsylvania

The University Honors College provides challenging and enriching educational experiences for Millersville University's most talented and motivated students. Those who elect to join the College are encouraged and guided by their faculty mentors to fully realize their academic and professional potential and to raise their sights and ambitions beyond what they felt was possible for them to accomplish. The College is designed to give the students the knowledge, skills, and self-confidence they need to prosper in graduate and professional school as well as in the world of business.

Designed to fulfill the University-wide general education requirements, the College is open to undergraduate students in all majors. It provides honors students with a core of stimulating and demanding liberal arts courses. These courses are intended to introduce honors students to the intellectual underpinnings of Western culture while developing their ability to think critically, do independent research, and write in a style that is both lucid and analytical. The core requirements explore the evolution of the Western intellectual and literary traditions, mathematical theory and applications, scientific methods in theory and practice, and multicultural/interdisciplinary studies. These requirements include an honors composition course and an advanced writing experience in the form of a senior thesis. The core courses are intended to encourage a commitment to academic pursuits while providing a common intellectual bond. The core is augmented with a variety of honors general education electives from which the student may choose. The majority of these courses put emphasis on research and writing.

Honors courses have limited enrollments. This creates an intimate and stimulating learning environment where students from varied backgrounds and disciplines can develop a sense of intellectual camaraderie. While honors courses involve both depth and breadth of study and stress independent research and writing, the workloads required are manageable. The primary concern of the faculty members who teach in the College is the cultivation of the academic talents of the honors students. Through formal study and informal advisement, the University Honors College prepares and encourages Millersville University's finest students to continue their education in graduate and professional schools. Honors graduates compete for entrance into the nation's finest graduate programs.

The University Honors Program was founded in 1980. The Honors Program became the Honors College in 2001. There are approximately 300 students enrolled in the College.

Participation Requirements: Completion of the program requires that students achieve a grade of B– or better in a minimum of 30 hours of honors credits; write and submit a thesis, which must be approved by the Honors College Committee; and attain a final GPA of 3.35 or higher. Students graduating in the program receive the University Honors Baccalaureate and normally graduate with departmental honors in their respective majors.

Admission Process: Students must apply separately to the University Honors College. A one-page essay on one of a number of designated topics must accompany the application. A letter of recommendation is also required. Admission is rolling. Entering freshmen who have combined SAT I scores of 1200 or better and are in the top 10 percent of their high school graduating class are recruited to join the University Honors College. As motivation,

enthusiasm, and commitment to learning are often better predictors of success than test scores, students who do not meet these formal criteria but who are seriously interested in participating in the program are encouraged to apply to the Director for admission.

Scholarship Availability: The University Honors College administers a limited number of four-year scholarships restricted to students enrolled in the University Honors College. These scholarships can be combined with scholarships awarded by both admissions and academic departments.

Campus Overview

State-supported comprehensive, founded 1855, part of Pennsylvania State System of Higher Education • **Coed** 6,991 undergraduate students, 91% full-time, 56% women, 44% men.

Undergraduates 6,378 full-time, 613 part-time. Students come from 23 states and territories, 4% are from out of state, 6% African American, 2% Asian American or Pacific Islander, 3% Hispanic American, 0.2% Native American, 0.4% international, 5% transferred in, 37% live on campus.

Faculty *Total:* 468, 68% full-time, 70% with terminal degrees. *Student/faculty ratio:* 18:1.

Academic Programs *Special study options:* academic remediation for entering students, accelerated degree program, adult/continuing education programs, advanced placement credit, cooperative education, distance learning, double majors, honors programs, independent study, internships, off-campus study, part-time degree program, services for LD students, study abroad, summer session for credit. *ROTC:* Army (b). *Unusual degree programs:* 3-2 engineering with Pennsylvania State University - University Park Campus, University of South Carolina.

Athletics Member NCAA. All Division II except wrestling (Division I). *Intercollegiate sports:* baseball M(s), basketball M(s)/W(s), cross-country running M(s)/W(s), field hockey W(s), football M(s), golf M(s), lacrosse W(s), soccer M(s)/W(s), softball W(s), swimming and diving W(s), tennis M(s)/W(s), track and field M(s)/W(s), volleyball W(s), wrestling M(s). *Intramural sports:* archery M(c)/W(c), badminton M/W, basketball M/W, bowling M(c)/W(c), cheerleading W, fencing M(c)/W(c), golf M/W, ice hockey M(c), lacrosse M(c), racquetball M/W, rock climbing M/W, rugby M(c)/W(c), soccer M/W, softball M/W, tennis M/W, ultimate Frisbee M/W, volleyball M(c)/W, water polo M(c)/W(c).

Costs (2004–05) *Tuition:* state resident $4810 full-time, $200 per credit part-time; nonresident $12,026 full-time, $501 per credit part-time. Part-time tuition and fees vary according to course load. *Required fees:* $1271 full-time, $74 per credit part-time. *Room and board:* $5642; room only: $3308. Room and board charges vary according to board plan.

Financial Aid 395 Federal Work-Study jobs (averaging $839). 1,791 state and other part-time jobs (averaging $1282). In 2003, 166 non-need-based awards were made. *Average percent of need met:* 83%. *Average financial aid package:* $6171. *Average need-based loan:* $3373. *Average need-based gift aid:* $3654. *Average non-need-based aid:* $2342.

Contact: Dr. Steven Miller, University Honors College, Millersville University, P.O. Box 1002, Millersville, Pennsylvania 17551-0302; *Telephone:* 717-872-3571; *Fax:* 717-871-2216; *E-mail:* steven.miller@millersville.edu; *Web site:* http://www.millersv.edu/~honors/

Neumann College
Honors Program
Aston, Pennsylvania

Founded in 1989, the Honors Program is two-tiered, including a Freshman Honors and a College Honors Program. There are 40 students currently enrolled in the program.

Freshman Honors consists of two 6-credit multidisciplinary seminars that are team-taught and two 3-credit honors courses that are team-taught, one in the fall and the other in the spring semester. The seminars incorporate aspects from the disciplines of philosophy, history, political science, psychology, literature, and communication arts. College Honors consists of a series of three multidisciplinary seminars that are offered to sophomore, junior, and senior students. The seminar topics are selected primarily through student input.

The focus of the Honors Program is on innovative, experimental methodologies that seek new ways to develop critical thinking and communication skills. All honors seminars are discussion-oriented with small group work and in-class exercises devoted to critical thinking skill development. There are no lectures and no essay examinations, but rather students are evaluated on the development of strong oral and written communication and critical-thinking skills. The Director of Honors is also the adviser to honors students during their first year.

Participation Requirements: Completion of the College Honors Program requires an overall GPA of 3.6 or above in 9 credits of honors seminars. Those who successfully complete the program are awarded a certificate of completion at the Honors Convocation.

Admission Process: Freshman Honors usually consists of 20 students selected for their academic, extracurricular, and leadership achievements in high school; candidates must also be interviewed by the Director of Honors. While SAT scores and class rank are considered, emphasis is given to those students who have demonstrated a potential for leadership and academic excellence. Entrance into College Honors requires an overall GPA of 3.4 or above and an interview with the Director of Honors. College honors seminars are limited to 20 students.

Scholarship Availability: Neumann College offers scholarships to students based on merit. All Honors students are on scholarship.

Campus Overview

Independent Roman Catholic comprehensive, founded 1965 • **Coed** 2,197 undergraduate students, 78% full-time, 67% women, 33% men.

Undergraduates 1,709 full-time, 488 part-time. Students come from 18 states and territories, 8 other countries, 27% are from out of state, 13% African American, 1% Asian American or Pacific Islander, 1% Hispanic American, 0.1% Native American, 0.6% international, 3% transferred in, 46% live on campus.

Faculty *Total:* 218, 36% full-time, 33% with terminal degrees. *Student/faculty ratio:* 16:1.

Academic Programs *Special study options:* academic remediation for entering students, accelerated degree program, adult/continuing education programs, advanced placement credit, cooperative education, distance learning, double majors, freshman honors college, honors programs, independent study, internships, off-campus study, part-time degree program, services for LD students, student-designed majors, study abroad, summer session for credit. *ROTC:* Army (c).

Athletics Member NCAA. All Division III. *Intercollegiate sports:* baseball M, basketball M/W, field hockey W, golf M, ice hockey M/W, lacrosse M/W, soccer M/W, softball W, tennis M/W, volleyball W. *Intramural sports:* basketball M/W, lacrosse M, softball W, tennis M/W, volleyball M/W.

Costs (2004–05) *Comprehensive fee:* $24,930 includes full-time tuition ($16,590), mandatory fees ($600), and room and board ($7740). Part-time tuition: $380 per credit. *College room only:* $4600.

Financial Aid 120 Federal Work-Study jobs (averaging $1200). *Average percent of need met:* 65%. *Average financial aid package:* $17,000. *Average need-based loan:* $7500. *Average need-based gift aid:* $17,000.

Contact: Director: Thomas Marshall, One Neumann Drive, Aston, Pennsylvania 19014-1298; *Telephone:* 610-558-5624; *Fax:* 610-361-5314; *E-mail:* tmarshal@neumann.edu

Northampton Community College
Northampton Community College Honors Program
Bethlehem, Pennsylvania

Northampton Community College's (NCC) Honors Program will begin in the Fall semester of the 2006-07 academic year. The program is designed to meet the needs of its most academically prepared students. It will do so by providing an enriched educational environment in which students will be challenged to reach their full intellectual potential and to better prepare themselves for the academic demands of the four-year college or university of their choice. The program will feature designated general education honors course sections as well as opportunities to take many courses throughout the college for honors credit.

The overall goal of the program is to provide an academic atmosphere in which students learn to think critically, creatively, and independently, to grow intellectually, and to take responsibility for their own learning. Emphasis is on encouraging students to present scholarly papers and projects, to use primary sources, to participate in alternative learning strategies, and to experience related cultural and social activities both within and beyond NCC.

Honors faculty members are dedicated to inspiring and challenging students with innovative and exciting pedagogical strategies. Many honors courses will include a service learning component, allowing students to relate and apply the content of their course to community service projects outside the college. Cultural excursions and other extracurricular activities within the courses will always be encouraged by the Honors Program.

The Honors Program at NCC will begin in Fall 2006 and anticipates an enrollment of between 20 and 50 students.

Participation Requirements: Students must take a minimum of four honors courses (12 credits) to complete the program and attain a cumulative 3.5 GPA. To remain within the program, students must maintain a minimum of a 3.5 GPA, but are given one semester of probation if they fail to do so.

Admission Process: Students must complete the NCC application forms and the NCC Honors Program application form. Applicants must meet at least one of the following criteria to qualify for the Honors Program: a minimum high school GPA of 3.5 on a 4.0 scale; a minimum college or university GPA of 3.5 taking 12 credits of coursework; graduated from the top 20% of high school class; secured a recommendation letter from a high school faculty member, counselor or other appropriate designate approved by the honors director. Students choosing the recommendation option will need to complete an interview with the Director of the Honors Program. In addition, all students must meet the requirements for admission into English I.

Scholarship Availability: Northampton Community College offers a number of merit based scholarships.

Campus Overview

State and locally supported 2-year, founded 1967 • **Coed** 8,246 undergraduate students, 43% full-time, 63% women, 37% men.

Undergraduates 3,565 full-time, 4,681 part-time. Students come from 22 states and territories, 39 other countries, 3% are from out of state, 6% African American, 2% Asian American or Pacific Islander, 9% Hispanic American, 0.3% Native American, 1% international, 35% transferred in, 3% live on campus.

Faculty *Total:* 512, 20% full-time, 21% with terminal degrees. *Student/faculty ratio:* 21:1.

Academic Programs *Special study options:* academic remediation for entering students, accelerated degree program, adult/continuing education programs, advanced placement credit, cooperative education, distance learning, double majors, English as a second language, internships, part-time degree program, services for LD students, student-designed majors, study abroad, summer session for credit.

Athletics *Intercollegiate sports:* baseball M, basketball M/W, bowling M/W, golf M/W, ice hockey M/W, soccer M/W, softball W, tennis M/W, volleyball M/W, wrestling M(c). *Intramural sports:* basketball M/W, bowling M/W, football M/W, golf M/W, racquetball M/W, soccer M/W, volleyball M/W.

Costs (2004–05) *Tuition:* area resident $2070 full-time, $69 per credit hour part-time; state resident $4140 full-time, $138 per credit hour part-time; nonresident $6210 full-time, $207 per credit hour part-time. *Required fees:* $660 full-time, $22 per credit hour part-time. *Room and board:* $5604; room only: $3262. Room and board charges vary according to board plan and housing facility.

Financial Aid 300 Federal Work-Study jobs (averaging $2800). 130 state and other part-time jobs (averaging $1500).

Contact: Director: Ken Burak, Assistant Professor of Philosophy, 3835 Green Pond Road, Bethlehem, Pennsylvania 18020; *Telephone:* 610-332-6128; *Fax:* 610-861-4167; *E-mail:* kburak@northampton.edu

Pennsylvania State University
Schreyer Honors College
University Park, Pennsylvania

The Schreyer Honors College is Penn State's University-wide undergraduate honors program. Selected students in all of Penn State's academic colleges may simultaneously be members of the Schreyer Honors College and pursue a broad range of opportunities for study, research, and scholarly exploration. The goal of the Schreyer Honors College is to provide an environment in which students of high ability can achieve their academic potential, while they develop as responsible civic leaders and global citizens. In short, the Schreyer Honors College has a three-part mission: achieving academic excellence, building a global perspective, and creating opportunities for leadership and civic engagement.

The Schreyer Honors College's hallmark is flexibility in accommodating the diverse intellectual interests of highly talented students. The curriculum is designed to challenge, enrich, and broaden students' general education and to deepen their preparation for graduate study or a profession. Schreyer Scholars may choose from a wide variety of special honors courses and sections to satisfy their degree requirements. A Scholar's progress in his or her field of specialization is enhanced by honors courses, independent study and research, access to graduate-level courses, and honors-option work in regular courses. The Schreyer Honors College encourages and facilitates the creation of individualized programs by providing maximum flexibility to students and advisers.

A fundamental element of the best undergraduate education is the interaction between outstanding faculty members and motivated students. The Schreyer Honors College fosters such interaction through courses of reduced size (usually 15–25) and extensive non-classroom programming in its two residence halls. An honors thesis is the capstone experience for Schreyer Scholars and leads to

an honors diploma from Penn State. The College thus provides students with the advantages often identified with small liberal arts colleges along with the libraries, laboratories, and research opportunities of one of the world's great universities.

The Schreyer Honors College was founded as the University Scholars Program in 1980 and became a college in 1997. It currently has approximately 1,800 students, of whom 300 are first-year students.

Participation Requirements: Schreyer Scholars must take at least three honors courses or sections during their first year (one of which must be Honors First-Year Composition) and at least three honors courses or sections during the sophomore year. During their remaining time at Penn State, they must complete at least 14 credits of honors work. The Schreyer Honors College expects that Scholars will take their honors work in both general education and the major(s), but there are no requirements about the precise distribution of honors work. Scholars who enter after the first year are subject to these requirements from the time they join the Schreyer Honors College. Scholars must maintain at least a 3.33 cumulative average each semester and must file an Annual Academic Plan.

All Scholars must complete an honors thesis in order to graduate with an honors diploma from Penn State. Before each commencement, graduating Schreyer Scholars receive the Scholars medal at a special awards ceremony.

Admission Process: First-year Schreyer Scholars are selected through a special application process. Students with exceptional high school records and excellent SAT scores are encouraged to apply. Selection is highly competitive as the number of first-year places is set at a maximum of 300. While many factors weigh heavily in the selection process, including essays and teacher recommendations, first-year students entering in 2005 had an average SAT score of 1428 and an average high school GPA of 4.08. The College is looking for students who will thrive as members of an intellectual community: students who will be active participants in all their courses (including those outside their major) and who are interested in the range of opportunities offered by the Schreyer Honors College.

Applications received by the priority deadline of November 30 are given first consideration. After that date, applications are considered on a rolling basis until mid-March. All applicants must also complete the standard Penn State application, which has the same priority and final deadlines.

Penn State students may be nominated for entry into the Schreyer Honors College by their major department after the fourth semester, based upon outstanding academic performance and research potential. Junior-year entrants to the Schreyer Honors College do not receive the Academic Excellence Scholarship, but they receive all other benefits of the program from the time they enter. Transfer students can be evaluated for membership in the Schreyer Honors College after their complete academic record from their previous institution is available.

Scholarship Availability: All first-year entrants to the Schreyer Honors College are awarded the Academic Excellence Scholarship (AES), renewable for eight semesters provided they remain Scholars in good standing. The current value of the AES is $2500 per year. In addition, many Scholars receive merit scholarships from their Penn State major or academic college.

Campus Overview

State-related university, founded 1855, part of Pennsylvania State University • **Coed** 34,824 undergraduate students, 96% full-time, 46% women, 54% men.

Undergraduates 33,376 full-time, 1,448 part-time. Students come from 54 states and territories, 23% are from out of state, 4% African American, 6% Asian American or Pacific Islander, 3% Hispanic American, 0.1% Native American, 2% international, 1% transferred in, 38% live on campus.

Faculty *Total:* 2,543, 87% full-time, 71% with terminal degrees. *Student/faculty ratio:* 17:1.

Academic Programs *Special study options:* academic remediation for entering students, accelerated degree program, adult/continuing

education programs, advanced placement credit, cooperative education, distance learning, double majors, English as a second language, external degree program, freshman honors college, honors programs, independent study, internships, part-time degree program, services for LD students, student-designed majors, study abroad, summer session for credit. *ROTC:* Army (b), Navy (b), Air Force (b). *Unusual degree programs:* 3-2 nursing with Lincoln University (PA); earth science, mineral science.

Athletics Member NCAA. All Division I except football (Division I-A). *Intercollegiate sports:* archery M(c)/W(c), badminton M(c)/W(c), baseball M(s), basketball M(s)/W(s), bowling M(c), cross-country running M(s)/W(s), equestrian sports M(c)/W(c), fencing M(s)/W(s), field hockey W(s), golf M(s)/W(s), gymnastics M(s)/W(s), ice hockey M(c)/W(c), lacrosse M(s)/W(s), rugby M(c)/W(c), skiing (downhill) M(c)/W(c), soccer M(s)/W(s), softball W, swimming and diving M(s)/W(s), table tennis M(c), tennis M(s)/W(s), track and field M(s)/W(s), volleyball M(s)/W(s), water polo M(c)/W(c), weight lifting M(c)/W(c), wrestling M(s). *Intramural sports:* badminton M/W, basketball M/W, bowling M/W, crew M(c)/W(c), cross-country running M/W, fencing M(c)/W(c), field hockey W, football M, golf M/W, gymnastics M(c)/W(c), lacrosse M(c)/W(c), racquetball M/W, riflery M(c)/W(c), sailing M(c)/W(c), soccer M/W, softball M/W, squash M/W, tennis M/W, track and field M/W, ultimate Frisbee M(c)/W(c), volleyball M/W, wrestling M.

Costs (2004–05) *Tuition:* state resident $10,408 full-time, $434 per credit part-time; nonresident $20,336 full-time, $847 per credit part-time. *Required fees:* $448 full-time, $75 per term part-time. *Room and board:* $6230; room only: $3250.

Financial Aid 2,125 Federal Work-Study jobs (averaging $1327). 286 state and other part-time jobs (averaging $4845). In 2003, 3627 non-need-based awards were made. *Average percent of need met:* 70%. *Average financial aid package:* $12,802. *Average need-based loan:* $4221. *Average need-based gift aid:* $4381. *Average non-need-based aid:* $3887.

Contact: Schreyer Honors College, 10 Schreyer Honors College, The Pennsylvania State University, University Park, Pennsylvania 16802-3905; *Telephone:* 814-865-2060; *E-mail:* scholars@psu.edu; *Web site:* http://www.shc.psu.edu

Philadelphia Biblical University

Honors Program

Langhorne, Pennsylvania

The Honors Program at Philadelphia Biblical University (PBU) seeks to develop Christian scholars who integrate their biblical studies with their general and professional education. With the study of the Bible at the center of all University education, the Honors Program is, accordingly, interdisciplinary in nature.

The Honors Program emphasizes the conversation between the Bible and the Great Books that has shaped the Western tradition. Through reading and studying foundational texts in Western philosophy, political science, church history, and literature, students develop their skills of reasoning and shaping oral and written arguments. The approach is text centered, student focused, and writing intensive. In the four honors courses, with enrollment in each limited to 15 students, classes consist of discussion-based seminars complemented by tutorials that present the historical-cultural-intellectual context for the texts read. Essay examinations ascertain the student's development in the course.

In addition to the honors courses, the honors community of faculty members and students meets biweekly for a meal and a colloquium. Honors colloquia include student or faculty presentations and open

discussion of selected topics under the direction of the honors faculty. Each semester, one of the colloquia is designated a university-wide forum. The honors forums cover a broad range of interdisciplinary topics and foster intellectual stimulation and collegiality within the larger university community. To provide the students with extracurricular learning experiences, the Honors Program plans special activities twice per semester. These educational opportunities open the student to the historical, cultural, artistic, and academic world of Philadelphia and the surrounding region.

The capstone of the Honors Program is the honors project. The students choose a research topic designed to bring together all of their education. Working closely with an adviser, the students learn and apply the fundamentals of researching and writing a thesis.

The honors faculty members are aggressively involved in mentoring the students from their freshman year to graduation. The development of student-faculty relationships provides an important scaffolding for the student's intellectual development. Faculty members advise students in course work, colloquium topics, and the honors project. They also teach courses, plan colloquia and activities, and accompany the students on extracurricular activities.

Participation Requirements: Students must take the four designated honors courses (philosophy, history of Christianity, political science, and literature), participate in the honors colloquia and special activities every semester in the program, and submit a thesis or special project at the end of their senior year. The honors student must maintain a cumulative GPA of at least 3.5 to continue in and graduate from the program. Successful completion of the program requirements is recognized with a special seal on the diploma and notation on all official transcripts.

Admission Process: The honors committee selects from each entering class up to 10 students who have proven their ability to participate in study and dialogue requiring advanced levels of critical thinking. Students with SAT scores of 1250 or higher (or the ACT equivalent) and with a cumulative GPA or 3.5 or higher (on a 4.0 scale) have a higher probability of being admitted into the program, but no applicant is accepted or refused solely on the basis of these scores. With the application to the program the student must submit an essay, which is evaluated by the whole committee. Applicants must have a formal interview with the committee during the summer or early in the fall semester. The application deadline for incoming freshman students is April 1. It is customary for the honors committee to reserve room in the program for transfer students or other exceptional students who may not have had the opportunity to submit their applications as incoming freshmen or who may not have been ready for the program's intellectual rigor right out of high school. These applicants are reviewed by the committee, and the applicants are invited to an interview. Underclassmen not initially accepted into the Honors Program may reapply during a subsequent semester if they feel that the merit of their application has been enhanced since their previous attempt.

Scholarship Availability: Students with at least a 3.6 GPA and an SAT score of 1350 (30 on the ACT) or higher are eligible for consideration for the Honors Academic Scholarships of $8000 per year.

Campus Overview

Independent nondenominational comprehensive, founded 1913 • **Coed** 1,022 undergraduate students, 89% full-time, 54% women, 46% men.

Undergraduates 909 full-time, 113 part-time. Students come from 38 states and territories, 49% are from out of state, 11% African American, 2% Asian American or Pacific Islander, 2% Hispanic American, 0.2% Native American, 2% international, 9% transferred in, 52% live on campus.

Faculty Total: 147, 35% full-time, 40% with terminal degrees. *Student/faculty ratio:* 13:1.

Academic Programs *Special study options:* academic remediation for entering students, accelerated degree program, adult/continuing

education programs, advanced placement credit, double majors, honors programs, independent study, internships, off-campus study, part-time degree program, services for LD students, study abroad, summer session for credit. *ROTC:* Air Force (c).

Athletics Member NCAA, NCCAA. All NCAA Division III. *Intercollegiate sports:* baseball M, basketball M/W, field hockey W, golf M, soccer M/W, softball W, tennis M/W, volleyball M/W. *Intramural sports:* basketball M/W, soccer M/W, table tennis M/W, tennis M/W, volleyball M/W.

Costs (2005–06) *Comprehensive fee:* $20,600 includes full-time tuition ($14,180), mandatory fees ($320), and room and board ($6100). Full-time tuition and fees vary according to course load, location, and program. Part-time tuition: $427 per credit. Part-time tuition and fees vary according to course load, location, and program. *College room only:* $3000. Room and board charges vary according to board plan, housing facility, and location.

Financial Aid 96 Federal Work-Study jobs (averaging $1247). In 2004, 139 non-need-based awards were made. *Average percent of need met:* 70%. *Average financial aid package:* $10,811. *Average need-based loan:* $4126. *Average need-based gift aid:* $7796. *Average non-need-based aid:* $7064.

Contact: Dr. Brian G. Toews, Administrator, Honors Program, Philadelphia Biblical University, 200 Manor Avenue, Langhorne, Pennsylvania 19047-2990; *Telephone:* 215-702-4227, 800-366-0049 (toll-free) Ext. 4227; *Fax:* 215-702-4342; *E-mail:* btoews@pbu.edu; *Web site:* http://www.pbu.edu/academic/honors/index.htm

Philadelphia University

Honors Program

Philadelphia, Pennsylvania

The Honors Program at Philadelphia University was established in 1985 to bring together highly motivated students and dedicated faculty members in a program that is both challenging and supportive. Overall, the program aims to reach beyond professional or specialized training and to inspire students to a full lifetime of broad and intellectual curiosity, self-sustained inquiry, and personal growth. It attempts to develop critical thinking and leadership skills and widen awareness of global issues.

The program is a combination of accelerated, enriched courses and cocurricular activities designed to challenge selected students at the University. The program's core of 22 credits is composed of honors work in both College Studies and career-specific courses. There are an optional community service learning component and opportunities for enrollment in graduate-level courses. Honors credit is available during study abroad and through co-op and internship programs.

Participating faculty members from across campus often teach enriched sections of existing courses or supervise independent study or research projects. These faculty members are dedicated teachers and scholars respected for their effectiveness in the classroom and for original contributions to their field of specialty. The Honors Program not only challenges students, but also demands an extension of faculty roles beyond customary professional expectations. These are the roles of the catalyst and mentor as well as of one who perceives and understands shifting pressures on students and student energies as the term progresses.

The program enrolls approximately 150 active students.

Participation Requirements: Students are expected to maintain a B/B+ average and enroll in at least one honors course per year. Students receive the full honors awards if they have a 3.3 or better GPA and have completed the required 22 honors credits.

Any student enrolled at the University may enroll in honors courses as a noncertificate honors student if their overall GPA is above 3.0. Honors courses are noted on student transcripts, and completion of the program is cited on the diploma at Commencement.

Admission Process: The program is offered each year, by invitation, to a select number of qualified students. Admission to the Honors Program is based upon proof of a student's potential for high academic achievement. A majority of honors students are identified by their high school performance. The University may evaluate the student's GPA, class rank, SAT/ACT scores, and extracurricular activities. All entering freshmen and/or transfer students may apply for admission to the Honors Program. Although there is an attempt to identify eligible students before admission to the University, students who have demonstrated academic excellence during their first and second term may also be invited to join the program.

A student may be admitted to the Honors Program at one of the following times in their baccalaureate experience: prior to matriculation as either a freshman or a transfer student, if admission criteria for the Honors Program have been met (based on high school rank, standard test scores, interviews, etc.) or after one term of work at the University, with a faculty recommendation and GPA above 3.1.

Scholarship Availability: The University offers a number of faculty grants and scholarships to freshmen and transfer students, based on academic merit. Many students receiving these scholarships and grants are also in the Honors Program.

Campus Overview

Independent comprehensive, founded 1884 • **Coed** 2,695 undergraduate students, 88% full-time, 69% women, 31% men.

Undergraduates 2,362 full-time, 333 part-time. Students come from 47 states and territories, 29 other countries, 49% are from out of state, 9% African American, 4% Asian American or Pacific Islander, 3% Hispanic American, 0.1% Native American, 2% international, 4% transferred in, 51% live on campus.

Faculty *Total:* 428, 24% full-time. *Student/faculty ratio:* 12:1.

Academic Programs *Special study options:* academic remediation for entering students, accelerated degree program, adult/continuing education programs, advanced placement credit, cooperative education, English as a second language, freshman honors college, honors programs, independent study, internships, off-campus study, part-time degree program, services for LD students, study abroad, summer session for credit.

Athletics Member NCAA. All Division II except soccer (Division I). *Intercollegiate sports:* baseball M(s), basketball M(s)/W(s), field hockey W(s), golf M(s), lacrosse W(s), soccer M(s)/W(s), softball W(s), tennis M(s)/W(s), volleyball W(s). *Intramural sports:* basketball M/W, cross-country running M/W, football M, skiing (downhill) M(c)/W(c), soccer M/W, softball M/W, swimming and diving M/W, table tennis M/W, tennis M/W, volleyball M/W, weight lifting M/W.

Costs (2004–05) *Comprehensive fee:* $28,792 includes full-time tuition ($20,940), mandatory fees ($70), and room and board ($7782). Full-time tuition and fees vary according to program. Part-time tuition: $676 per credit. Part-time tuition and fees vary according to class time and program. *College room only:* $3834. Room and board charges vary according to board plan and housing facility.

Financial Aid 850 Federal Work-Study jobs (averaging $2000). In 2004, 592 non-need-based awards were made. *Average percent of need met:* 71%. *Average financial aid package:* $14,862. *Average need-based loan:* $4057. *Average need-based gift aid:* $9499. *Average non-need-based aid:* $4058.

Contact: Director: Dr. Marcella L. McCoy, School House Lane and Henry Avenue, Philadelphia, Pennsylvania 19144-5497; *Telephone:* 215-951-5367; *Fax:* 215-951-6888; *E-mail:* honors@philau.edu

Point Park University
Point Park University Honors Program
Pittsburgh, Pennsylvania

Honors at Point Park University is a program designed specifically for academically talented students. It includes innovative teaching methods which extend beyond the classroom. Students have access to stimulating seminars, research opportunities, service projects, and unique cultural and social events to enhance their academic experience. Eligible students from all majors are encouraged to apply.

Honors courses are small—no more than 15 students, usually less. This creates an intimate learning environment with plenty of open discussions between students and instructors. There is more give and take between students and instructors, greater opportunities for independent research intellectual growth, creativity, and pursuing individual goals.

Along with the academic advantages—learning with other inquisitive students, freedom to explore topics and subjects of special interest—personal attention from instructors—students participating in the Honors Program build resumes for life after graduation. Founded in 1997, the Honors Program has 136 students currently enrolled.

Participation Requirements: Honors Program students are required to take six honors courses with at least two at the 300 or 400 levels and maintain a 3.5 cumulative QPA in honors courses (no grade of C or lower). In some majors, a senior honors thesis or performance project may fulfill part of the Honors Program requirements.

Students completing the program requirements receive a special honors certificate upon graduation.

Admission Process: Once admitted to Point Park, any student may apply for the Honors Program at any time during his of her college career. Once accepted, a student must maintain a 3.5 QPA. There is no additional charge for participation in the Honors Program.

Scholarship Availability: Point Park University offers a variety of scholarships to students that recognize academic achievement, community service, athletic and artistic ability.

Campus Overview

Independent comprehensive, founded 1960 • **Coed** 2,844 undergraduate students, 74% full-time, 59% women, 41% men.

Undergraduates 2,111 full-time, 733 part-time. Students come from 45 states and territories, 34 other countries, 16% are from out of state, 17% African American, 0.6% Asian American or Pacific Islander, 1% Hispanic American, 0.3% Native American, 1% international, 17% transferred in, 22% live on campus.

Faculty Total: 343, 26% full-time, 33% with terminal degrees. Student/faculty ratio: 15:1.

Academic Programs Special study options: academic remediation for entering students, accelerated degree program, adult/continuing education programs, advanced placement credit, distance learning, double majors, honors programs, independent study, internships, off-campus study, part-time degree program, services for LD students, student-designed majors, study abroad, summer session for credit. ROTC: Army (c), Air Force (c).

Athletics Member NAIA. Intercollegiate sports: baseball M(s), basketball M(s)/W(s), cross-country running M(s)/W(s), soccer M(s), softball W(s), volleyball W(s). Intramural sports: basketball M, football M, golf M, tennis M/W, volleyball M/W, weight lifting M/W.

Costs (2004–05) Comprehensive fee: $22,960 includes full-time tuition ($15,500), mandatory fees ($460), and room and board ($7000). Full-time tuition and fees vary according to program. Part-time tuition: $422 per credit. Part-time tuition and fees vary according to program. Required fees: $10 per credit part-time. College room only: $3300. Room and board charges vary according to board plan.

Financial Aid 213 Federal Work-Study jobs (averaging $2205). 264 state and other part-time jobs (averaging $1965). In 2004, 345 non-need-based awards were made. Average percent of need met: 68%. Average financial aid package: $12,451. Average need-based loan: $5024. Average need-based gift aid: $6939. Average non-need-based aid: $7994.

Contact: Heather Offner, Assistant to the Director of Institutional Research, Point Park University, 201 Wood Street, Pittsburgh, Pennsylvania 15222; Telephone: 412-392-3906; Fax: 412-392-6164; E-mail: hoffner@pointpark.edu

Saint Francis University
Honors Program
Loretto, Pennsylvania

The Saint Francis University (SFU) Honors Program is designed to challenge highly motivated students by making them part of a community of learners while at the same time affording them the opportunity to devise a personal program of study.

Students are introduced to the Honors Program through a yearlong learning-community experience consisting of a four-course sequence with intense critical-thinking, writing, and speaking components. Successful completion of this sequence waives the University's speech requirement for the honors student.

All other honors requirements are fulfilled at the student's own pace and with the student's personal academic interests in mind. For example, honors students develop individual Direct Readings Tutorials with faculty mentors. The disciplines and scope of the tutorials are left up to the student but must be outside his or her major field of study.

Based upon the Franciscan ideal of concern for others above self, service-learning activities are built into all upper-level honors seminars. An original research project is the program's capstone requirement.

Those participating in the Honors Program are the only students granted priority registration at the University. The program also offers innovative course work, extensive faculty-student interaction, individualized honors advising, and opportunities for independent study.

The Bach Family Honors House opens in January 2006. The facility, which covers more than 6,000 square feet, includes a conference room with state-of-the-art audiovisual equipment for seminars and honors core courses, a residence for 8 honors students per year, a 24-hour study space for all honors students, and meeting, lecture, and movie space.

Founded in 1984, the program currently enrolls 100 students.

Participation Requirements: All courses completed for honors credit are duly designated on the student's transcript. Students who complete all honors curricular requirements and achieve at least a 3.25 cumulative GPA receive the Honors Program diploma—a large, hand-lettered parchment diploma presented in traditional rolled fashion—at commencement. Honors Program graduates receive special velvet diploma bags during the annual awards convocation hosted by the President. The notation Honors Program Graduate appears on the transcript and in the commencement program.

Admission Process: Enrollment is by application. Applicants must place within the first quintile of their high school graduating class and must have at least a 3.25 GPA and SAT scores of 1150 or above, with emphasis on the verbal score. An interview is required. The deadline for application is March 1.

Scholarship Availability: Six Founders' (full-tuition) Scholarships are awarded annually to incoming Honors Program students. Saint Francis University offers a variety of scholarships, and most are based on academic accomplishment, not on financial need. Some are based on service to the University or on other criteria determined by the donors. All Honors Program members are scholarship recipients.

Campus Overview

Independent Roman Catholic comprehensive, founded 1847 • **Coed** 1,332 undergraduate students, 87% full-time, 61% women, 39% men.

Undergraduates 1,163 full-time, 169 part-time. Students come from 34 states and territories, 33 other countries, 22% are from out of state, 6% African American, 0.6% Asian American or Pacific Islander, 0.9% Hispanic American, 0.1% Native American, 0.6% international, 8% transferred in, 72% live on campus.

Faculty *Total:* 164, 54% full-time, 61% with terminal degrees. *Student/faculty ratio:* 14:1.

Academic Programs *Special study options:* academic remediation for entering students, accelerated degree program, adult/continuing education programs, advanced placement credit, distance learning, double majors, external degree program, freshman honors college, honors programs, internships, off-campus study, part-time degree program, student-designed majors, study abroad, summer session for credit. *ROTC:* Army (c). *Unusual degree programs:* 3-2 engineering with Pennsylvania State University - University Park Campus, University of Pittsburgh, Clarkson University; forestry with Duke University; occupational therapy, physical therapy, physician assistant.

Athletics Member NCAA. All Division I except football (Division I-AA). *Intercollegiate sports:* basketball M(s)/W(s), cross-country running M(s)/W(s), field hockey W(s), golf M(s)/W(s), lacrosse W(s), soccer M(s)/W(s), softball W(s), swimming and diving M(s)/W(s), tennis M(s)/W(s), track and field M(s)/W(s), volleyball M(s)/W(s). *Intramural sports:* basketball M/W, bowling M/W, cheerleading M/W, cross-country running M/W, football M, golf M/W, lacrosse W, racquetball M/W, skiing (cross-country) M/W, skiing (downhill) M/W, soccer M/W, softball W, swimming and diving M/W, table tennis M/W, tennis M/W, track and field M/W, ultimate Frisbee M/W, volleyball M/W, weight lifting M/W.

Costs (2004–05) *Comprehensive fee:* $27,860 includes full-time tuition ($19,390), mandatory fees ($1050), and room and board ($7420). Full-time tuition and fees vary according to program. Part-time tuition: $606 per credit hour. *Required fees:* $295 per credit hour part-time, $36 per term part-time. *College room only:* $3600. Room and board charges vary according to board plan, housing facility, and location.

Financial Aid 724 Federal Work-Study jobs (averaging $1000). 30 state and other part-time jobs (averaging $991). In 2003, 138 non-need-based awards were made. *Average percent of need met:* 82%. *Average financial aid package:* $17,128. *Average need-based loan:* $4531. *Average need-based gift aid:* $12,421. *Average non-need-based aid:* $9562.

Contact: Director: Donna M. Menis, St. Francis University, 117 Evergreen, Loretto, Pennsylvania 15940; *Telephone:* 814-472-3065; *Fax:* 814-472-3937; *E-mail:* dmenis@francis.edu; *Web site:* http://www.francis.edu

Saint Joseph's University

Honors Program

Philadelphia, Pennsylvania

The Saint Joseph's University (SJU) Honors Program seeks to produce well-educated, articulate citizens who exemplify the highest standards of academic, professional, and personal achievement. It offers an enriched general education curriculum that broadens cultural interests, integrates knowledge, sharpens writing skills, and encourages student involvement in the learning process.

The curriculum is composed of intellectually rigorous courses that satisfy both general education and major requirements. The honors core consists of a group of yearlong, interdisciplinary, team-taught courses in arts, sciences, and business that appear in a regular cycle. These sequence courses are complemented by one-semester courses in a wide range of disciplines at various levels of entry.

There are distinctive benefits attached to belonging to the Saint Joseph's Honors Program. Team-taught courses allow distinguished faculty members to share their knowledge and expertise with students in a challenging academic environment. Individual honors courses stress a detailed and thoroughly scholarly exploration of different fields of knowledge. The student-faculty ratio in the Honors Program is 10:1. Honors students register ahead of other students.

Honors suites in the residence halls allow like-minded students to live together, even as freshmen. Honors students are provided with free tickets and transportation to concerts and performances by world-renowned institutions such as the Arden Theater Company, the Curtis Institute of Music, the Philadelphia Orchestra, the Pennsylvania Ballet, the Academy of Vocal Arts, the Philadelphia Museum of Art, and the Franklin Science Institute. Receptions, concerts, and lectures are regularly sponsored by the Honors Program for honors students.

Student peer mentors report to the program directors about social activities, class work, registration, and other student concerns. Students have access to Claver House, a quiet retreat where honors students can study, work with personal computers, and attend receptions. Students have opportunities to present research and creative work at national conferences and seminars; they are also kept informed about scholarship and funding opportunities for graduate and professional work.

Participation Requirements: Students may enroll in General Honors, which is awarded upon successful completion of eight honors courses. Because all honors courses fulfill other curricular requirements of the University, the Honors Program imposes no courses over and above those required of non-honors students. Students are required to maintain a cumulative average of 3.5 or better in order to graduate with the General Honors Certificate.

Students may also participate in Departmental Honors, which is awarded upon successful completion of the general curriculum and a two-semester research project in their senior year. Students of exceptional caliber may apply for the University Scholar designation. Those who qualify are freed from four to ten of their senior-year course requirements in order to complete an independent project of unusual breadth, depth, and originality.

General Honors Certificate is noted on the student's permanent record and is awarded upon successful completion of General Honors. An Honors Degree, noted on the permanent record and acknowledged on a distinctive diploma, is awarded to students who have completed General Honors and the Departmental Honors project. University Honors, noted on the permanent record and acknowledged on a distinctive diploma, is awarded to students who have completed General Honors and the University Scholar research project.

Admission Process: Incoming students are invited into the Honors Program if their combined SAT combined score is above 1350 (or the equivalent on the new SAT) and they have a high school grade point average of at least 3.75. Freshmen who achieve a GPA of 3.5 or better in their first semester at SJU are also invited to join the Honors Program.

Scholarship Availability: Each year, Saint Joseph's University awards merit-based scholarships to freshman candidates who have outstanding academic and achievement records. Students are selected by a scholarship committee. A formal application is not required for merit-based scholarships; however, for any additional assistance, candidates must apply. Instructions are given in detail at the time of the candidate's application. Students who are awarded these scholarships are automatically invited to join the Honors Program. Board of Trustees' Scholarships are awarded to freshman recipients who have superior academic records. Candidates typically rank at or near the top of their high school class, have an "A" GPA, and SAT scores in the 1400-and-above range. These scholars must maintain a 3.2 GPA in order to retain their scholarship each year.

Presidential Scholarships are awarded to candidates who achieve significant results in their high school class and have SAT scores of 1300 and above. The value of this scholarship ranges from one-half to three-quarter tuition. These scholars must maintain a 3.2 GPA in order to retain their scholarship each year.

University Scholarships are awarded to incoming freshmen who rank in the top 10 percent of their high school graduating class and have SAT scores in the 1200-and-above range. The value of this scholarship ranges from one-fourth to one-half tuition.

Campus Overview

Independent Roman Catholic (Jesuit) comprehensive, founded 1851 • **Coed** 4,978 undergraduate students, 83% full-time, 52% women, 48% men.

Undergraduates 4,112 full-time, 866 part-time. Students come from 38 states and territories, 48 other countries, 45% are from out of state, 7% African American, 2% Asian American or Pacific Islander, 2% Hispanic American, 0.1% Native American, 1% international, 2% transferred in, 59% live on campus.

Faculty *Total:* 569, 46% full-time. *Student/faculty ratio:* 15:1.

Academic Programs *Special study options:* academic remediation for entering students, accelerated degree program, adult/continuing education programs, advanced placement credit, cooperative education, distance learning, double majors, English as a second language, honors programs, independent study, internships, off-campus study, part-time degree program, services for LD students, student-designed majors, study abroad, summer session for credit. *ROTC:* Army (c), Navy (c), Air Force (b).

Athletics Member NCAA. All Division I. *Intercollegiate sports:* baseball M(s), basketball M(s)/W(s), crew M(s)(c)/W(s)(c), cross-country running M(s)/W(s), field hockey W(s), golf M(s), lacrosse M(s)/W(s), soccer M(s)/W(s), softball W(s), tennis M(s)/W(s), track and field M(s)/W(s). *Intramural sports:* basketball M/W, field hockey W(c), golf M, ice hockey M(c), racquetball M/W, rugby M(c)/W(c), tennis M/W, volleyball M(c).

Costs (2004–05) *Comprehensive fee:* $35,515 includes full-time tuition ($25,770), mandatory fees ($135), and room and board ($9610). Full-time tuition and fees vary according to student level. Part-time tuition: $390 per credit. *College room only:* $6100. Room and board charges vary according to board plan and housing facility.

Financial Aid 350 Federal Work-Study jobs (averaging $949). In 2002, 737 non-need-based awards were made. *Average percent of need met:* 80%. *Average financial aid package:* $11,862. *Average need-based loan:* $4890. *Average need-based gift aid:* $7590. *Average non-need-based aid:* $6580.

Contact: Dr. Samuel Smith, Director or Dr. David R. Sorensen, Associate Director, Saint Joseph's University, 5600 City Avenue, Philadelphia, Pennsylvania 19103; *Telephone:* 610-660-1795; *E-mail:* smith@sju.edu or dsorense@sju.edu; *Web site:* http://www.sju.edu/honors

Shippensburg University of Pennsylvania
Honors Program
Shippensburg, Pennsylvania

The Honors Program at Shippensburg University is dedicated to promoting scholarship, leadership, and service. Honors students benefit from small classes, excellent teaching, and exciting research, study-abroad, and internship opportunities. Students in the program also participate in special social, cultural, and community service activities. The Honors Program involves students in every major and every class level. They come from a variety of backgrounds and have diverse academic and social interests. What they share is their desire to make the most of all the opportunities available to them at Shippensburg University.

The Honors Program curriculum is designed for academically motivated students who thrive in an atmosphere of creative learning and intellectual exploration. The program offers courses within the general education curriculum, including literature, history, philosophy, geography, sociology, and biology. Other honors elective courses are focused on topics that encourage in-depth and independent exploration of a central theme.

The Honors Program provides students with numerous opportunities to expand their honors academic experience beyond the Shippensburg campus. Honors classes frequently include field trips to New York, Baltimore, and Washington, D.C. The Honors Program encourages its students to study abroad, and students can earn honors credits for the courses they complete while studying abroad. The Honors Program also sponsors one-week and three-week Honors Abroad seminars during spring and summer breaks. And each year, 2 Shippensburg University Honors students receive full scholarships to participate in a 6-credit summer Honors Program sponsored by the Pennsylvania State System of Higher Education.

All honors students are members of the Honors Student Organization (HSO). The HSO is led by 4 officers and the chairs of six standing committees: Community Service, Excitement in Education, Freshmen Orientation, Recreation, Media, and Recruitment. The HSO coordinates the program's service projects, which have included a mentoring program for middle school students and Rails-to-Trails cleanups, and sponsors recreational activities. Honors students also participate in the program's governance by serving with Honors faculty on the Honors Program Steering Committee.

The program began in 1984 and currently enrolls 150 students.

Participation Requirements: To graduate from the Honors Program, students must complete 24 credit hours of honors general education courses. Students are expected to maintain a minimum 3.25 overall QPA and a minimum 3.25 QPA in honors courses. Successful completion of the Honors Program is noted at graduation and is recorded on the student's transcript. Students also receive a Certificate of Graduation from the Honors Program.

Admission Process: Shippensburg University's Honors Program accepts 50 students for each entering class from those who formally apply. Entering University students should have a minimum SAT I score of 1200 (25 on the ACT), be in the upper fifth of their high school class, and have participated in a variety of extracurricular activities. If an entering freshman is not admitted to the program because of limited space but obtains a QPA of 3.25 the first semester, the student is encouraged to reapply for acceptance. The Director of Honors interviews interested, currently enrolled students to determine if they meet the criteria for admission and are able to complete 24 credits of general education honors courses. Interested high school seniors, transfer students, and undergraduates enrolled at Shippensburg University may obtain an application form from the Honors Program Web site, listed in this description. Applications must be submitted by March 1.

Scholarship Availability: The University offers many scholarships for qualified students.

Campus Overview

State-supported comprehensive, founded 1871, part of Pennsylvania State System of Higher Education • **Coed** 6,579 undergraduate students, 96% full-time, 52% women, 48% men.

Undergraduates 6,291 full-time, 288 part-time. Students come from 28 states and territories, 21 other countries, 6% are from out of state, 4% African American, 1% Asian American or Pacific Islander, 1% Hispanic American, 0.3% Native American, 0.3% international, 5% transferred in, 34% live on campus.

Faculty *Total:* 378, 82% full-time, 76% with terminal degrees. *Student/faculty ratio:* 19:1.

Academic Programs *Special study options:* academic remediation for entering students, accelerated degree program, advanced placement credit, cooperative education, distance learning, double majors, honors programs, independent study, internships, off-campus study, part-time degree program, services for LD students, study abroad, summer session for credit. *ROTC:* Army (b). *Unusual degree programs:* 3-2 engineering with Pennsylvania State University - University Park and Harrisburg Campus, University of Maryland College Park.

Athletics Member NCAA. All Division II. *Intercollegiate sports:* baseball M(s), basketball M(s)/W(s), cross-country running M(s)/W(s), field hockey W(s), football M(s), lacrosse W(s), soccer M(s)/W(s), softball W(s), swimming and diving M(s)/W(s), tennis W(s), track and field M(s)/W(s), volleyball W(s), wrestling M(s). *Intramural sports:* basketball M/W, bowling M(c)/W(c), cross-country running M, football M, ice hockey M(c)/W(c), lacrosse M(c), racquetball M/W, rugby M(c)/W(c), soccer M/W, softball M/W, swimming and diving M/W, table tennis M, tennis M/W, volleyball M(c)/W, water polo M(c)/W(c), wrestling M.

Costs (2004–05) *Tuition:* state resident $4810 full-time, $200 per credit hour part-time; nonresident $12,026 full-time, $501 per credit hour part-time. *Required fees:* $1176 full-time, $20 per credit hour part-time, $127 per term part-time. *Room and board:* $5274; room only: $3190. Room and board charges vary according to board plan and housing facility.

Financial Aid 294 Federal Work-Study jobs (averaging $1463). 432 state and other part-time jobs (averaging $1276). In 2004, 1876 non-need-based awards were made. *Average percent of need met:* 69%. *Average financial aid package:* $6059. *Average need-based loan:* $3410. *Average need-based gift aid:* $3840. *Average non-need-based aid:* $695.

Contact: Director: Dr. Kim Klein, Honors Program, 1871 Old Main Drive, Shippensburg, Pennsylvania 17257; *Telephone:* 717-477-1604; *Fax:* 717-477-4096; *E-mail:* honors@ship.edu; *Web site:* http://www.ship.edu/~honors

Susquehanna University
University Honors Program
Selinsgrove, Pennsylvania

The Honors Program at Susquehanna University offers a challenging program of study for the exceptional student interested in a more independent and interdisciplinary approach than that usually offered to an undergraduate. The program is especially well suited to the aggressively curious, active learner who values breadth of study, multiple perspectives, and answers that go beyond the superficial. It has been recognized as a model for other honors programs throughout the country.

Limited to 50 students in each entering class, the program includes a series of special courses and projects throughout all four undergraduate years. Discussion groups, lectures, off-campus visits, and residential programs complement Honors Program courses.

The University's Scholars' House, a small, comfortable residence for students involved in academically challenging projects, serves as the center of many Honors Program activities, including fireside chats, a film series, and practice sessions for the University's College Bowl team. Many of the Scholars' House residents are members of the Honors Program. Some of their projects include the establishment of a campus jazz society, the development of a World Wide Web connection for the Scholars' House, an economic and ecological study of the tradeoffs facing the logging industry in Maine, a comparison of Christianity and Buddhism, and a children's book.

As a member of the National Collegiate Honors Council, Susquehanna regularly participates in or hosts special events for honors program students from throughout the Northeast and other regions. Honors students also have access to a variety of special off-campus projects at locations ranging from the Woods Hole Oceanographic Institution in Massachusetts and the United Nations in New York to Pueblo Indian sites in New Mexico.

The first honors class enrolled in 1982. Approximately 150 students are currently enrolled.

Participation Requirements: Participating students take an honors course during three of their first four semesters. The first course, "Thought," focuses on ideas and their expression. "Thought and the Social Sciences" or "Thought and the Natural Sciences" are cross-disciplinary views of the social and natural sciences. "Thought and Civilization" is an interdisciplinary look at literature and cultures. These Thought courses replace required Core courses.

In the sophomore year, honors students write a research-supported essay developing a topic of their choice. This experience offers students an opportunity to work one-on-one with faculty members early in their undergraduate studies.

As juniors and seniors, honors students select 8 semester hours from a series of 300-level interdisciplinary honors seminars that also fulfill the University's Core requirements or that serve as especially interesting and challenging electives. As seniors they also engage in a senior honors seminar that fulfills the Core requirement for a "Futures" course and a senior research project.

Students normally must maintain a cumulative GPA of 3.3 or higher at the end of each semester to remain in the Honors Program. Candidates who successfully complete all the requirements of the Honors Program graduate with University Honors.

Scholarship Availability: Scholarships are held by many students in the University Honors Program, but are not tied to the program in any way. Honors Program enrollees typically qualify for one of the top scholarships awarded by Susquehanna. A description of these scholarships and their value during the 1999–2000 academic year follows.

University Assistantships, Susquehanna's most prestigious academic scholarships, are awards of $10,500 that include a professional work experience (about 10 hours a week on average) with a member of the University faculty or administrative staff. Recipients typically rank in the top 5 percent of their high school classes and score in the top 10 percent nationally on standardized tests.

The other four scholarships are valued at $8500 annually. Recipients of these scholarships typically rank in the top 10 percent of their high school classes and score in the top 15 percent nationally on standardized tests. Valedictorian/Salutatorian Scholarships are given to students who rank first or second in their high school classes in a demanding academic program. Degenstein Scholarships, funded by the Charles B. Degenstein Scholars Program, are given to exceptionally able students with preference to those intending to major or minor in programs within Susquehanna's Sigmund Weis School of Business. Scholarships for Distinguished Achievement in Science and Mathematics are awarded to students planning majors in the sciences, computer science, or mathematics; recipients are chosen on the basis of outstanding academic achievement. Presidential Scholarships are awarded on a competitive basis to new students who have demonstrated superior academic achievement and personal promise.

Campus Overview

Independent 4-year, founded 1858, affiliated with Evangelical Lutheran Church in America • **Coed** 2,071 undergraduate students, 95% full-time, 56% women, 44% men.

Undergraduates 1,961 full-time, 110 part-time. Students come from 25 states and territories, 10 other countries, 40% are from out of state, 2% African American, 2% Asian American or Pacific Islander, 2% Hispanic American, 0.2% Native American, 0.6% international, 1% transferred in, 80% live on campus.

Faculty *Total:* 182, 66% full-time, 73% with terminal degrees. *Student/faculty ratio:* 13:1.

Academic Programs *Special study options:* accelerated degree program, adult/continuing education programs, advanced placement credit, distance learning, double majors, honors programs, independent study, internships, off-campus study, part-time degree program, student-designed majors, study abroad, summer session for credit. *ROTC:* Army (c). *Unusual degree programs:* 3-2 forestry with Duke University; environmental management with Duke University, allied health programs with Thomas Jefferson University, dentistry with Temple University.

Athletics Member NCAA. All Division III. *Intercollegiate sports:* baseball M, basketball M/W, cheerleading M(c)/W(c), crew M(c)/W(c), cross-country running M/W, equestrian sports M(c)/W(c), field hockey W, football M, golf M/W, lacrosse M/W, rugby M(c)/W(c), soccer M/W, softball W, swimming and diving M/W, tennis M/W, track and field M/W, volleyball M(c)/W. *Intramural sports:* basketball M/W, bowling M/W, football M/W, racquetball M/W, soccer M/W, softball M/W, table tennis M/W, tennis M/W, ultimate Frisbee M, volleyball M/W.

Costs (2004–05) *Comprehensive fee:* $31,650 includes full-time tuition ($24,500), mandatory fees ($310), and room and board ($6840). Part-time tuition: $780 per semester hour. *College room only:* $3620.

Financial Aid 905 Federal Work-Study jobs (averaging $1574). 64 state and other part-time jobs (averaging $3816). In 2004, 550 non-need-based awards were made. *Average percent of need met:* 83%. *Average financial aid package:* $17,743. *Average need-based loan:* $3737. *Average need-based gift aid:* $13,961. *Average non-need-based aid:* $11,878.

Contact: Simona Hill, Susquehanna University, 514 University Avenue, Selinsgrove, Pennsylvania 17870-1001; *Telephone:* 570-372-4263; *Fax:* 570-372-2722 (Admissions/Financial Aid); *E-mail:* hill@susqu.edu; *Web site:* http://www.susqu.edu

Temple University
Honors Program
Philadelphia, Pennsylvania

The Temple University Honors Program began as the College of Arts and Sciences Honors Program in 1967. In 1988, the program was expanded to include outstanding students enrolled in all twelve undergraduate schools and colleges at the University. The Honors Program offers these academically talented, motivated, and interesting students a place of their own in the context of a major research university.

The heart of the program is a set of courses open only to honors students and taught by designated honors faculty members, many of whom have won the Temple University Great Teacher Award. The program features small classes of about 20 students and encourages a lively, seminar-style classroom atmosphere. Students (representing nearly every major in the university) can complete university general education requirements through their honors courses. In addition, they may take unique lower- and upper-level electives created for the program. (University honors students enrolled in the Fox School of Business and Management participate concurrently in Business Honors, a four-year program.)

Students may also participate in an upper-division Honors Program with a focus on individual research under the supervision of a faculty mentor, leading to an honors thesis. Honors students may apply for the TempleMed and TempleLaw Scholars program. Following freshmen year they may apply to be a Diamond Scholar, which affords a summer research fellowship that comes with a stipend and 3 semester credit hours. The Temple Undergraduate Research Forum–Creative Works Symposium (TURF–CWS) is a juried conference where students from across the university present original

research. Students are encouraged to apply for Research Incentive Funds to support undergraduate research projects and/or presentation of their research at professional conferences.

The University Honors Program, in collaboration with the Honors Activities Board, arranges special lectures, poetry readings, community service, political panels, career talks, field trips, and information sessions on major scholarships (Udall, Truman, Rhodes, Marshall, etc.). The honors listserv keeps students abreast of internship opportunities, scholarships, jobs, free tickets to concerts, and the like. Students spend time in the honors lounge where computers and companionship are available. During their freshmen and sophomore years they are eligible to live in honors housing in "1300"—the newest residence hall on campus, with suite-style accommodations for freshmen and apartments for sophomores—and take classes down the hall in a state-of-the-art Honors classroom.

Honors has its own orientation in the summer prior to freshmen year. The honors staff is committed to helping students throughout their Temple careers. Working closely with departmental advisers, the honors staff helps students with course selection, decisions about majors, careers, scholarship and graduate school applications, job and internship opportunities, preparation for medical school interviews, and more.

Participation Requirements: Honors students receive an honors certificate after completing eight honors courses, usually within the first two years. This is recorded on their official transcripts. To earn the certificate they must maintain a minimum 3.0 GPA. Students are encouraged to continue taking upper-division honors courses and, as well, apply for the upper-division Honors Program, which includes a thesis requirement.

Admission Process: During the normal application process, all students are screened for honors. No separate application for the Honors Program is required. Selection criteria include high school record, essay, recommendations, and SAT scores. Temple will require the writing section of the new SAT and the ACT for fall 2006, but will not use it in admissions or honors decisions until at least fall 2007 after admissions has analyzed the data and how to use it. Approximately 300 students enter the Honors Program each year. Most are offered financial aid based on merit and/or need. Transfer students and freshmen or sophomores already enrolled at Temple who have outstanding credentials may apply for admission into Honors by filling out an application available in the honors office, 204 Tuttleman Learning Center.

Scholarship Availability: Scholarships are held by many students in the University Honors Program, but they are not tied to the program in any way. Merit-based awards range from $1000 to $10,000 per year and are renewable for four years based upon academic eligibility. All admitted students are considered for scholarships at the time they apply; there is no separate application.

Campus Overview

State-related university, founded 1884 • **Coed** 23,429 undergraduate students, 86% full-time, 57% women, 43% men.

Undergraduates 20,183 full-time, 3,246 part-time. Students come from 46 states and territories, 105 other countries, 23% are from out of state, 20% African American, 8% Asian American or Pacific Islander, 3% Hispanic American, 0.3% Native American, 3% international, 11% transferred in, 26% live on campus.

Faculty *Total:* 2,361, 56% full-time. *Student/faculty ratio:* 18:1.

Academic Programs *Special study options:* academic remediation for entering students, adult/continuing education programs, advanced placement credit, cooperative education, distance learning, double majors, English as a second language, honors programs, independent study, internships, off-campus study, part-time degree program, services for LD students, student-designed majors, study abroad, summer session for credit. *ROTC:* Army (b), Navy (c), Air Force (c). *Unusual degree programs:* 3-2 physical therapy, pharmacy.

Athletics Member NCAA. All Division I except football (Division I-A). *Intercollegiate sports:* baseball M(s), basketball M(s)/W(s),

crew M(s)/W(s), fencing W(s), field hockey W(s), golf M(s), gymnastics M(s)/W(s), lacrosse W(s), soccer M(s)/W(s), softball M(s)/W(s), tennis M(s), track and field M(s)/W(s), volleyball W(s). *Intramural sports:* basketball M/W, bowling M/W, football M/W, golf M/W, lacrosse M, racquetball M/W, rugby M, soccer M/W, softball M, tennis M/W, volleyball M/W, water polo M/W.

Costs (2004–05) *Tuition:* state resident $8622 full-time, $334 per credit hour part-time; nonresident $15,788 full-time, $562 per credit hour part-time. Full-time tuition and fees vary according to course load, location, program, and reciprocity agreements. Part-time tuition and fees vary according to course load, location, program, and reciprocity agreements. *Required fees:* $480 full-time. *Room and board:* $7522; room only: $4876. Room and board charges vary according to board plan and housing facility.

Financial Aid In 2004, 3729 non-need-based awards were made. *Average percent of need met:* 89%. *Average financial aid package:* $12,190. *Average need-based loan:* $3527. *Average need-based gift aid:* $4452. *Average non-need-based aid:* $3818.

Contact: Director: Dr. Ruth Ost, 204 Tuttleman Learning Center, 1809 North 13th Street, Philadelphia, Pennsylvania 19122-6073; *Telephone:* 215-204-0710; *Fax:* 215-204-0711; *E-mail:* honors@temple.edu; *Web site:* http://www.temple.edu/honors

Thiel College
Honors Program
Greenville, Pennsylvania

The purpose of the Thiel College Honors Program is to provide an integrative education designed to enhance the student's critical thinking, to enable the student to make connections among disciplines, and to challenge the student in an atmosphere of seminar-style discussion. In order to provide a sound educational structure within which honors students may exercise significant choice, the Honors Program requires completion of a separate Honors Core as a substitute for the College's general education requirements. Distinctive to this core are interdisciplinary courses that emphasize multiple ways of seeing and knowing, the complex interrelatedness among elements in the cultural and natural worlds, techniques of information gathering, gaining skill in problem solving, gaining experiences in the process of making value choices among alternatives, and openness to accepting the criticism of ideas.

The program was founded in 1981, and there are approximately 60 current student participants.

Participation Requirements: The Honors Program core consists of 38 to 45 credit hours, depending upon the student's foreign language placement. Requirements include a yearlong sophomore interdisciplinary course and a yearlong junior capstone course in which the student completes an original creative or problem-solving project under the direction of a faculty mentor. These courses are distinctive to the Honors Program, having no equivalents elsewhere in the curriculum. The student also completes a year of Western humanities with honors sections and honors sections of freshman composition and religion.

To remain in the program, a student must maintain at least a 3.0 cumulative GPA with no more than one semester below 3.0. Successful completion of the program is recognized in the commencement program and by the wearing of an honors cord at graduation. It is also noted on the student's official transcript and by a gold seal attached to the diploma.

Admission Process: Applicants to the College who have an 1140 or higher SAT I score or a 25 or higher ACT score and a minimum 3.3 high school GPA are automatically invited to join the program. There are no application deadlines, since all students are admitted to the College on a rolling basis. All students may participate in the program

regardless of their majors or fields of study. All decisions about admission or retention within the program are subject to review by the Honors Program Committee.

Scholarship Availability: Freshmen entering the program are eligible to compete for a variety of academic scholarships. Upper-class students are eligible to apply for a number of other scholarships, one of which is restricted to Honors Program students and provides several awards each year. Most program participants receive academic scholarships.

Campus Overview

Independent 4-year, founded 1866, affiliated with Evangelical Lutheran Church in America • **Coed** 1,245 undergraduate students, 95% full-time, 49% women, 51% men.

Undergraduates 1,185 full-time, 60 part-time. Students come from 19 states and territories, 15 other countries, 27% are from out of state, 6% African American, 0.6% Asian American or Pacific Islander, 0.6% Hispanic American, 0.2% Native American, 5% international, 4% transferred in, 82% live on campus.

Faculty *Total:* 120, 50% full-time, 41% with terminal degrees. *Student/faculty ratio:* 16:1.

Academic Programs *Special study options:* academic remediation for entering students, adult/continuing education programs, advanced placement credit, cooperative education, double majors, English as a second language, freshman honors college, honors programs, internships, off-campus study, part-time degree program, services for LD students, study abroad, summer session for credit. *Unusual degree programs:* 3-2 engineering with Case Western Reserve University, Point Park College, University of Pittsburgh; forestry with Duke University.

Athletics Member NCAA. All Division III. *Intercollegiate sports:* baseball M, basketball M/W, cheerleading M/W, cross-country running M/W, football M, golf M/W, lacrosse M/W, soccer M/W, softball W, tennis M/W, track and field M/W, volleyball W, wrestling M. *Intramural sports:* badminton M/W, basketball M/W, football M, soccer M, softball M/W, volleyball M/W.

Costs (2004–05) *Comprehensive fee:* $22,974 includes full-time tuition ($15,000), mandatory fees ($1390), and room and board ($6584). Full-time tuition and fees vary according to course load. Part-time tuition: $400 per credit hour. Part-time tuition and fees vary according to course load. *College room only:* $3396. Room and board charges vary according to board plan and housing facility.

Financial Aid 154 Federal Work-Study jobs (averaging $1013). 416 state and other part-time jobs (averaging $1014). In 2004, 143 non-need-based awards were made. *Average percent of need met:* 81%. *Average financial aid package:* $14,916. *Average need-based loan:* $4236. *Average need-based gift aid:* $10,025. *Average non-need-based aid:* $4676.

Contact: Director: Dr. Beth Parkinson, Professor of Psychology, 75 College Avenue, Greenville, Pennsylvania 16125-2181; *Telephone:* 724-589-2070; *Fax:* 724-589-2021; *E-mail:* bparkins@thiel.edu; *Web site:* http://www.thiel.edu/Academics/honors/honors.htm

University of Pittsburgh
University Honors College
Pittsburgh, Pennsylvania

The University of Pittsburgh Honors College (UHC) is dedicated to high attainment among able and motivated undergraduates University-wide. In addition to approximately eighty science and humanities courses each year offering small class sizes with special depth and challenge, UHC's broad portfolio of academic offerings *includes concentrated academic advising, undergraduate teaching and research fellowships, a distinguished and demanding degree option, summer research and field programs, and a wide variety of cocurricular activities created and run by students themselves. The latter include a professionally refereed undergraduate scholarly journal (*The Pittsburgh Undergraduate Review*), Pittsburgh's singular undergraduate literary journal (*The Three Rivers Review*), a creative nonfiction journal (*Collision*), a political journal (*Pittsburgh Political Review*), the University Mock Trial team, and a College Bowl team.*

In effect, UHC provides a rich palette of selections from which discerning students can choose as they please. Its location in award-winning architecture atop Pitt's historic Cathedral of Learning is also a 24-hour home-away-from-home for quiet study and academic exchange that commands a 50-mile panoramic view of western Pennsylvania.

The availability of a special degree for qualified students—the Bachelor of Philosophy (B. Phil.)—distinguishes UHC from an honors "program." This special competency-based baccalaureate degree is available to students in any undergraduate school of the University. Its general requirements include demonstrated academic performance, completion of degree requirements in the home school of admission, and accomplishment of a distinctive program of study approved by UHC advising that typically reflects broad scope across the disciplines and depth within a discipline. The special requirement of the B. Phil. is the completion and defense of a thesis during the junior and senior years under the tutelage of a faculty adviser. By the last term in residence, the student must publicly present the results of this independent scholarship to a Faculty Examination Committee, including one external examiner from outside the University of Pittsburgh who is selected by the faculty adviser to spend several days on campus.

The University Honors College provides special academic and career advising to complement the formal advising programs offered by schools and departments. Through unlimited individualized advising, UHC brokers the University of Pittsburgh's wealth of resources to the undergraduate level, helping ambitious students network to attain opportunities and expertise they would otherwise miss. UHC's advising staff is especially experienced in helping talented students combine diverse academic interests into educationally sound and appealing plans of study. Considerations include the University's full range of certificates, majors, and other degree plans as well as national scholarships and fellowships for undergraduates. Due to UHC, Pitt is a leading winner of the nation's most prestigious undergraduate awards—the Rhodes and Marshall scholarships—among public and private colleges and universities in Pennsylvania.

The University of Pittsburgh dedicated UHC during its 1987 bicentennial ceremonies. Headcount enrollment in UHC courses now tops 700 students each year, including many students from the College of Business Administration and nearly 100 students from the School of Engineering.

Participation Requirements: UHC is a flexible, nonmembership personalized operation whose many varied offerings respond to the individual initiative of interested students rather than any fixed participation criteria. There is no required level of participation in UHC; qualified students choose involvement in as many or as few opportunities as they wish. In some cases, students may "try out" for the select few positions available in an activity, such as editorial positions on one of the four journals. In other cases, such as open musical performances, poetry readings, and literary discussion groups, space for involvement is not generally a problem. Requirements for course work participation are indicated below.

Admission Process: The University Honors College is not a membership organization. There is no separate application for admission to UHC beyond the student's application to his or her targeted undergraduate college. Permission for involvement in UHC offerings, such as UHC courses, proceeds on the ongoing basis of a student's immediate past achievement. Entering freshmen having a combined SAT I score above 1350 and ranking in the top 5 percent of their high school graduating class are automatically qualified to take any UHC course whose particular prerequisites have been satisfied.

The same goes for continuing students having a QPA of at least 3.25 (B+) in their prior term. Students who do not meet this threshold may make their case to a member of the UHC staff or to their academic adviser for qualification to enroll in any particular UHC course.

Scholarship Availability: Freshman applicants for the fall term who file a complete admissions application by January 15 of their senior year are automatically considered for merit-based academic scholarships. These scholarships are based on high school performance, the degree of difficulty of the curriculum, class rank, and college entrance examination test results. Out of a freshman class of about 3,100, close to 600 scholarships are awarded, varying in the amount from $1000 to full tuition, room, and board.

UHC oversees the awarding of the Chancellor's Undergraduate Scholarship, which covers full tuition, room, and board for four and sometimes five years. Competition for the Chancellor's is by invitation following nominations by the Office of Admissions and entails written work as well as a possible interview. UHC also makes available in some cases upper-class merit scholarships from its private endowment.

Campus Overview

State-related university, founded 1787, part of Commonwealth System of Higher Education • **Coed** 17,181 undergraduate students, 88% full-time, 52% women, 48% men.

Undergraduates 15,080 full-time, 2,101 part-time. Students come from 53 states and territories, 49 other countries, 6% are from out of state, 9% African American, 4% Asian American or Pacific Islander, 1% Hispanic American, 0.2% Native American, 0.7% international, 4% transferred in, 36% live on campus.

Academic Programs *Special study options:* academic remediation for entering students, accelerated degree program, adult/continuing education programs, advanced placement credit, cooperative education, distance learning, double majors, English as a second language, external degree program, freshman honors college, honors programs, independent study, internships, off-campus study, part-time degree program, services for LD students, student-designed majors, study abroad, summer session for credit. *ROTC:* Army (b), Navy (c), Air Force (b). *Unusual degree programs:* 3-2 statistics.

Athletics Member NCAA. All Division I except football (Division I-A). *Intercollegiate sports:* baseball M(s), basketball M(s)/W(s), cross-country running M(s)/W(s), gymnastics W(s), soccer M(s)/W(s), softball W(s), swimming and diving M(s)/W(s), tennis W(s), track and field M(s)/W(s), volleyball W(s), wrestling M(s). *Intramural sports:* badminton M/W, basketball M/W, bowling M(c)/W(c), crew M(c)/W(c), equestrian sports M(c)/W(c), football M, ice hockey M(c)/W(c), lacrosse M(c)/W(c), racquetball M/W, skiing (downhill) M(c)/W(c), soccer M/W, softball M/W, squash M/W, swimming and diving M/W, table tennis M(c)/W(c), tennis M(c)/W(c), ultimate Frisbee M(c)/W(c), volleyball M/W, water polo M(c)/W(c), wrestling M.

Costs (2004–05) *Tuition:* state resident $10,130 full-time, $361 per credit part-time; nonresident $19,500 full-time, $696 per credit part-time. Full-time tuition and fees vary according to degree level and program. Part-time tuition and fees vary according to degree level and program. *Required fees:* $700 full-time, $164 per term part-time. *Room and board:* $7090; room only: $4260. Room and board charges vary according to board plan and housing facility.

Financial Aid 1,643 Federal Work-Study jobs (averaging $1722). In 2003, 1882 non-need-based awards were made. *Average percent of need met:* 77%. *Average financial aid package:* $10,003. *Average need-based loan:* $4641. *Average need-based gift aid:* $5183. *Average non-need-based aid:* $7188.

Contact: G. Alec Stewart, Dean, University Honors College, University of Pittsburgh, Pittsburgh, Pennsylvania 15260; *Telephone:* 412-624-6880; *Fax:* 412-624-6885; *E-mail:* uhchome@pitt.edu; *Web site:* http://www.pitt.edu/~uhchome

The University of Scranton

Honors Program

Scranton, Pennsylvania

The Honors Program at the University of Scranton provides an exceptional opportunity for selected students to receive an education of greater depth and breadth. It is open to full-time students in all majors and requires no extra fees.

The program is carefully designed to lead students to progressively more sophisticated and independent work, both in and out of their majors. Unlike most honors programs, it admits students in their sophomore year and concentrates not on honors sections of courses but on one-on-one work with faculty members. This carefully mentored work provides an exceptional opportunity for honors students to know and work with committed faculty members.

The most distinctive element of Scranton's Honors Program is the tutorials it makes available to upperclass students. Honors students satisfy three to five major and nonmajor course requirements with honors tutorials. These provide intensive interaction with faculty members and move the student from participating in carefully designed courses to working under the direction of a faculty member to explore a personally chosen subject. These tutorials are often interdisciplinary and are frequently designed to correlate with other honors work. Their flexibility includes the availability of any subject a faculty member is willing to teach, such as a tutorial on French philosophy conducted in French, and the possibility of responding to new discoveries or circumstances, such as a tutorial on terrorism, which was reconceptualized after September 11, 2001.

The independent work of the tutorials is extended in the senior honors project. This involves the intensive exploration under a mentor's direction of a specialized topic, which is either academic or professional. The finished projects are defended before a 3-person panel, bound, and placed in the library.

In addition to the tutorials and project, where the student is the only pupil, the program also includes an interdisciplinary course limited to honors students, with an average size of 22 students, and two seminars limited to no more than 14 students. Periodic social events provide informal opportunities to extend the friendships formed in the course and seminars.

The Honors Program at the University of Scranton was established in 1966 and currently has an enrollment of 112 students.

Participation Requirements: Admitted as sophomores, honors students must take an interdisciplinary honors course that satisfies a general education requirement. Recent offerings include Victorian Studies, which uses Victorian literature to examine such topics as social class, the role of women, and religion; Public Policy and Family Issues, which is a service-learning course; and Science and Public Policy, which addresses such issues as the human genome policy.

As juniors and seniors, honors students must take three tutorials, one of which must be in their major and one in their second major or out of their major. These can satisfy major, cognate, or general education requirements. Honors students must participate in two seminars; one is based on an interdisciplinary reading list and the second on the senior projects. These semester-long seminars, which each meet for an hour weekly, are free of tuition charge but satisfy only honors graduation requirements. Finally, honors students must complete a two-semester, 6-credit project in their major, which ordinarily satisfies a major's elective requirements. They must successfully defend this project before a 3-person panel.

Continued participation in the program requires appropriate progress toward completion of the honors curriculum and toward the minimum 3.5 GPA that is required for graduation. Honors students are recognized at graduation, and their diploma and transcript note their completion of the program.

Admission Process: Students ordinarily apply to the Honors Program in their sophomore year. The application deadline is October 1. Freshmen or transfer students who expect to graduate in three years may also apply if they have a minimum of 18 credits. Exceptional juniors are occasionally admitted to the program.

Applicants must demonstrate a reasonable possibility of achieving the minimum 3.5 GPA (cum laude) required for honors graduation; ordinarily this means at least a 3.3 GPA. In addition to the GPA, acceptance is based on an application and essay, faculty recommendations, high school and college records, interviews, and SAT or ACT scores.

Scholarship Availability: The University gives substantial academic scholarships, but none through the Honors Program.

Campus Overview

Independent Roman Catholic (Jesuit) comprehensive, founded 1888 • **Coed** 4,045 undergraduate students, 94% full-time, 58% women, 42% men.

Undergraduates 3,811 full-time, 234 part-time. Students come from 30 states and territories, 12 other countries, 49% are from out of state, 1% African American, 2% Asian American or Pacific Islander, 4% Hispanic American, 0.1% Native American, 0.5% international, 1% transferred in, 52% live on campus.

Faculty *Total:* 391, 63% full-time, 60% with terminal degrees. *Student/faculty ratio:* 13:1.

Academic Programs *Special study options:* academic remediation for entering students, accelerated degree program, adult/continuing education programs, advanced placement credit, distance learning, double majors, external degree program, honors programs, independent study, internships, off-campus study, part-time degree program, services for LD students, student-designed majors, study abroad, summer session for credit. *ROTC:* Army (b), Air Force (c). *Unusual degree programs:* 3-2 engineering with University of Detroit Mercy, Widener University.

Athletics Member NCAA. All Division III. *Intercollegiate sports:* baseball M, basketball M/W, bowling M(c)/W(c), crew M(c)/W(c), cross-country running M/W, equestrian sports M(c)/W(c), field hockey W, golf M, ice hockey M, lacrosse M/W(c), rugby M(c)/W(c), skiing (downhill) M(c)/W(c), soccer M/W, softball W, swimming and diving M/W, tennis M/W, track and field M(c)/W(c), volleyball M(c)/W, wrestling M. *Intramural sports:* badminton M/W, baseball M, basketball M/W, bowling M/W, cross-country running M/W, football M, golf M/W, racquetball M/W, soccer M/W, softball M/W, swimming and diving M/W, table tennis M/W, tennis M/W, ultimate Frisbee M/W, volleyball M/W, water polo M/W, weight lifting M/W, wrestling M.

Costs (2004–05) *Comprehensive fee:* $31,998 includes full-time tuition ($22,214), mandatory fees ($260), and room and board ($9524). Part-time tuition: $618 per credit. *Required fees:* $25 per term part-time. *College room only:* $5564. Room and board charges vary according to board plan and housing facility.

Financial Aid 1,005 Federal Work-Study jobs (averaging $1800). 255 state and other part-time jobs (averaging $1500). In 2004, 211 non-need-based awards were made. *Average percent of need met:* 72%. *Average financial aid package:* $15,558. *Average need-based loan:* $4375. *Average need-based gift aid:* $11,250. *Average non-need-based aid:* $7813.

Contact: Director: Ellen Miller Casey, Ph.D. English Department, University of Scranton, Scranton, Pennsylvania 18510; *Telephone:* 570-941-7426; *Fax:* 570-941-6657; *E-mail:* caseye1@scranton.edu

Villanova University
Honors Program
Villanova, Pennsylvania

The Villanova University Honors Program is a distinctive academic community comprised of students and faculty members who particularly enjoy the experience of intellectual growth. The program is designed to provide exceptional opportunities for critical and independent thinking, for the creative exchange of ideas, and for the synthesis of intellectual insights into lived experiences. Honors enhances the academic life central to a Villanova education by bringing together talented students and faculty members in challenging seminars, individual research projects, and cocurricular activities. Members of the program enjoy the benefits of a small college environment, while taking full advantage of the many resources of the broader University community.

Through the Faculty Mentors Program, Academic Peer Advisors, and Alumni Network, honors students receive excellent academic advisement throughout their college careers in selecting courses and majors, preparing for summer and postgraduate opportunities, and learning to identify and develop their own intellectual voices. Of special note, the Honors Program houses the Office of Undergraduate Grants and Awards, which administers the University's programs for the Presidential Scholarship, the Connelly-Delouvrier International Scholarship, the Undergraduate Collaborative Research Awards, and all of the nationally competitive fellowships and scholarships (Rhodes, Marshall, Fulbright, Truman, Goldwater, etc.). The Honors Program also administers the Bryn Mawr College–Villanova University Tuition Exchange Program. Villanova Honors Program graduates are frequently elected to Phi Beta Kappa and other prestigious honor societies, often receive the medallions awarded for academic excellence at graduation, and are highly successful in their pursuit of prestigious fellowships, graduate and professional school acceptances, and career opportunities.

Students can major, concentrate, or take individual courses in the Honors Program. An academic division within the College of Liberal Arts and Sciences, the program currently offers courses in the humanities, social sciences, and natural sciences, which are required areas of study for all of the University's majors. In full partnership with the College of Commerce and Finance, the program also offers courses that satisfy core and major requirements for honors business students. Honors courses are taught by faculty members who have distinguished themselves as dynamic teachers and scholars. These small seminars emphasize interdisciplinary approaches, extensive reading and writing, and the development of critical skills of judgment and analysis in a climate of mutual respect and cooperation. Innovative courses in the program include team-taught seminars and seminars given by visiting professors. All honors courses are enriched by a variety of lectures, cultural events, and social activities.

Faculty members and students meet outside of class individually, as a class, and as part of larger program events. The student-run Honors Events Committee invites speakers and organizes trips to cultural events in New York and Washington, D.C. Local Philadelphia highlights like the Philadelphia Orchestra, Independence Hall, and South Street are a short train ride away, with a regional rail-line stop on campus. Students present their own research in the informal atmosphere of Friday Colloquia and share their musical and artistic talents in recitals and exhibitions. All students are invited to contribute to The Polis, the program's literary magazine. Honors students also coordinate a number of service initiatives, including a sophomore service-learning community, which integrates volunteer experience with academic course work and residence hall community development. In addition, students participate equally with faculty members in setting policy and selecting new courses for the program. Every year is different depending on the special interests and initiatives of students themselves.

Honors students participate actively in all aspects of the Villanova community; honors is only one aspect of their campus life. Averaging two to three courses (the standard course load is five) in the program per semester, honors students bring to the program their own diversity of talents, interests, and experiences. They often hold leadership positions in student government, campus publications, musical and theatrical performance groups, and volunteer service projects, both on and off campus.

Founded forty-five years ago, the Villanova Honors Program has grown from a core of interdisciplinary humanities seminars into a four-year curriculum, which serves approximately 500 students from all of the University's colleges: Liberal Arts and Sciences, Commerce and Finance, Engineering, and Nursing. Currently, 450 students are registered with the Honors Program. There are a total of 120 majors and 240 concentrations across the four years (approximately thirty majors and sixty concentrations in each graduating class).

Participation Requirements: To remain active in the program, honors students must earn a minimum GPA of 3.33. Students who complete the program requirements may graduate with a Bachelor of Arts, Honors Program (B.A.,Honors); Bachelor of Natural and Math Science, Honors Program (B.S.,Honors); or a Bachelor of Science Business Honors (B.S.,B.Honors). Each of the honors degrees may be combined with a second major in another discipline. Each of these four-year comprehensive majors culminates in a year-long senior thesis project. The Honors Program Sequence in Liberal Studies (honors concentration) is another option. All Honors Program certifications require a minimum GPA of 3.33.

Admission Process: Incoming students are invited to apply to the program in the June immediately prior to their enrollment at Villanova based on their SAT I scores (at least 1330, with a minimum of 630 on both math and verbal sections), high school record (rank in the top 10 percent), and/or a previously expressed interest in the program. Current undergraduate students apply upon the recommendation of a faculty member or through their own initiative.

Scholarship Availability: Villanova University offers a number of merit-based scholarships to members of each incoming class. Designed to recognize distinctive achievement and to attract superior students to the University, these scholarships include the four-year full-tuition Presidential Scholarship administered by the Honors Program, sizable partial-tuition Villanova Scholar Awards, Commuting Scholar Awards, Augustinian Scholarships, and college-specific scholarships that are administered through the Office of University Admission.

All of the students who receive scholarships to Villanova are invited to participate in the courses and activities of the Honors Program.

Campus Overview

Independent Roman Catholic comprehensive, founded 1842 • **Coed** 7,292 undergraduate students, 90% full-time, 51% women, 49% men.

Undergraduates 6,585 full-time, 707 part-time. Students come from 51 states and territories, 29 other countries, 71% are from out of state, 3% African American, 6% Asian American or Pacific Islander, 5% Hispanic American, 0.2% Native American, 2% international, 1% transferred in, 65% live on campus.

Faculty *Total:* 892, 58% full-time, 70% with terminal degrees. *Student/faculty ratio:* 12:1.

Academic Programs *Special study options:* accelerated degree program, adult/continuing education programs, advanced placement credit, distance learning, double majors, English as a second language, honors programs, independent study, internships, off-campus study, part-time degree program, services for LD students, study abroad, summer session for credit. *ROTC:* Army (c), Navy (b), Air Force (c). *Unusual degree programs:* 3-2 allied health programs with Thomas Jefferson University, MCP Hahnemann, University of Pennsylvania, Philadelphia College of Optometry.

Athletics Member NCAA. All Division I except football (Division I-A). *Intercollegiate sports:* baseball M(s), basketball M(s)/W(s),

cheerleading M/W, crew M(c)/W(s), cross-country running M(s)/ W(s), field hockey W(s), golf M, ice hockey M(c), lacrosse M/W, rugby M(c), sailing M(c)/W(c), skiing (downhill) M(c)/W(c), soccer M(s)/W(s), softball W(s), swimming and diving M/W(s), tennis M/W, track and field M(s)/W(s), volleyball M(c)/W(s), water polo M(c)/W, weight lifting M(c)/W(c). *Intramural sports:* basketball M/W, football M/W, soccer M/W, softball M/W, tennis M/W, track and field M/W, ultimate Frisbee M/W, volleyball M/W.

Costs (2004–05) *Comprehensive fee:* $36,917 includes full-time tuition ($27,175), mandatory fees ($675), and room and board ($9067). Full-time tuition and fees vary according to program and student level. Part-time tuition: $580 per credit hour. Part-time tuition and fees vary according to class time, course level, and program. *Required fees:* $280 per term part-time. *College room only:* $4787. Room and board charges vary according to board plan and housing facility.

Financial Aid 1,975 Federal Work-Study jobs (averaging $2052). In 2004, 331 non-need-based awards were made. *Average percent of need met:* 77%. *Average financial aid package:* $20,271. *Average need-based loan:* $4774. *Average need-based gift aid:* $15,101. *Average non-need-based aid:* $10,648.

Contact: Director: Dr. Edwin L. Goff, 800 Lancaster Avenue, Villanova, Pennsylvania 19085; *Telephone:* 610-519-4650; *Fax:* 610-519-5405; *E-mail:* honorsprogram@villanova.edu; *Web site:* http://www.honorsprogram.villanova.edu

West Chester University of Pennsylvania

Honors Program

West Chester, Pennsylvania

The aim of the Honors Program at West Chester University (WCU) is to provide an exciting environment for academically gifted and highly motivated students to interact in a learning community of peers, faculty members, administrators, and staff members that will challenge and enrich the students' college experience. Grounded in the liberal arts tradition, the Honors Program seeks cross-disciplinary connections to develop students' natural intellectual abilities and challenge them to employ those gifts on behalf of the larger community. To that end, the Honors Program seeks to build character and foster a commitment to lifelong learning that prepares leaders for the twenty-first century. The program's aim is summarized best in its motto: To be honorable is to serve.

The Honors Program's curricular focus fosters this aim. During the first five semesters, a core of nine sequenced courses will familiarize students with defining and addressing leadership challenges facing today's communities. These courses, designed by dedicated, enthusiastic honors faculty members, are usually team-taught. Classes foster discussion and afford opportunities for off-campus service-learning experiences. Upon completion of the honors core, the culminating experience, a student-designed senior project mentored by a faculty member, provides students with the opportunity to identify, investigate, and address creatively a problem in a community business, nonprofit agency, or research laboratory. Many students have found their senior projects to be effective springboards to future academic or professional aspirations.

Throughout their years in the West Chester Honors Program, students experience many benefits beyond the strictly academic. They receive support from both fellow students and honors faculty and staff members, who are always available for additional advising. WCU honors students also enjoy the substantial benefits of priority scheduling and honors housing in Killinger Hall, which is fully wired for individual computer connection to the University system and has a

film/video editing laboratory. Honors students qualify for honors scholarship awards and have the opportunity to participate in the International Summer Honors Program, whose locations rotate annually. Finally, students qualify for membership in the very active Honors Student Association and have the opportunity to serve on the Honors Council and governance committees.

The program also has a partnership with Scholars in South Africa, where summer study opportunities exist and with the Bonner Foundation, which supports civic engagement and service-learning events through awarding Bonner-AmeriCorps educational awards.

WCU's Honors Program, which was founded in 1978, admits 40 freshmen each year. There are approximately 160 students currently enrolled in the program.

Participation Requirements: By the end of their fifth semester, all honors students must complete a 27-hour honors core that includes 100-, 200-, and 300-level cross-disciplinary courses. These courses, plus one additional mathematics or science course, fulfill the University's general education requirements for honors students. The 100- and 200-level core courses focus on personal development, including physical and psychological well-being, communication, and ethics and morality in a technological age. Courses at the 300 level build upon the learner's knowledge of self and address broader perspectives of community and social change. Program members are expected to maintain a minimum 3.25 GPA, progress through the honors core, and actively participate in campus community life to remain in good standing with the program. After completion of the honors core, students complete a 3-credit senior project. Each spring, the WCU Honors Program honors its graduates with an Awards Banquet attended by the honors faculty and top University officials; special awards and certificates are distributed at this time. Medallions are presented to graduates.

Admission Process: Membership in honors is competitive, with a maximum of forty seats open each fall. Invited students are asked to submit an application form involving short essays. Current membership includes students from forty-four different academic majors; 72 percent women, 28 percent men, and 12 percent multicultural. Incoming freshmen and transfer students are normally invited to apply to the program if they demonstrate at least two of the following: a minimum high school GPA of 3.5; a minimum SAT I score of 1200; rank in the top 20 percent of their graduating class; a record of achievement in high school Honors/AP courses. Candidates are reviewed by committee and selected on the basis of commitment to service, leadership potential, and their fit with the program's philosophy. WCU employs a rolling admissions policy.

Scholarship Availability: The Honors Program awards the Mynn Diefenderfer White Honors Scholarship, a $1000 renewable tuition scholarship, to an outstanding junior in the Honors Program and the Charles Ernst Scholarship of $1000 to an outstanding senior. In addition, WCU has many merit scholarship programs at the departmental, college, and University level. Honors students are among the most frequent recipients of these awards.

Campus Overview

State-supported comprehensive, founded 1871, part of Pennsylvania State System of Higher Education • **Coed** 10,644 undergraduate students, 88% full-time, 61% women, 39% men.

Undergraduates 9,407 full-time, 1,237 part-time. Students come from 35 states and territories, 11% are from out of state, 8% African American, 2% Asian American or Pacific Islander, 2% Hispanic American, 0.3% Native American, 0.4% international, 9% transferred in, 30% live on campus.

Faculty *Total:* 787, 72% full-time, 43% with terminal degrees. *Student/faculty ratio:* 18:1.

Academic Programs *Special study options:* academic remediation for entering students, accelerated degree program, adult/continuing education programs, advanced placement credit, distance learning, double majors, English as a second language, honors programs, independent study, internships, off-campus study, part-time degree program, services for LD students, student-designed majors, study abroad, summer session for credit. *ROTC:* Army (c), Air Force (c). *Unusual degree programs:* engineering with Pennsylvania State University.

Athletics Member NCAA. All Division II except field hockey (Division I). *Intercollegiate sports:* baseball M(s), basketball M(s)/W(s), cheerleading W(c), cross-country running M(s)/W(s), equestrian sports M(c)/W(c), fencing M/W, field hockey W(s), football M(s), golf M(s), gymnastics W(s), ice hockey M(c), lacrosse W(s), rugby M(c)/W(c), soccer M(s)/W(s), softball W(s), swimming and diving M(s)/W(s), tennis M(s)/W(s), track and field M(s)/W(s), volleyball W(s), water polo M(c)/W(c). *Intramural sports:* basketball M/W, fencing M(c)/W(c), football M/W, lacrosse M/W, soccer M/W, softball M/W, tennis M/W, volleyball M/W.

Costs (2005–06) *Tuition:* state resident $4810 full-time, $200 per credit part-time; nonresident $12,026 full-time, $501 per credit part-time. Full-time tuition and fees vary according to course load. Part-time tuition and fees vary according to course load. *Required fees:* $1196 full-time, $46 per credit part-time. *Room and board:* $5782; room only: $3098. Room and board charges vary according to board plan and housing facility.

Contact: Dr. Kevin W. Dean, Director or Donna Carney, Administrative Assistant, Honors Program, 131 Francis Harvey Green Library, West Chester University, West Chester, Pennsylvania 19383-2981; *Telephone:* 610-436-2996; *Fax:* 610-436-2620; *E-mail:* dcarney@wcupa.edu; *Web site:* http://www.wcupa.edu/_ACADEMICS/cae.hon/default.htm

Widener University
Honors Program in General Education
Chester, Pennsylvania

Guided by the principle that serious students create opportunities to learn from one another as well as from faculty members, Widener's honors classes are limited to a maximum of 15 students and are conducted as seminars. Faculty members encourage student involvement in setting the direction of courses. Participants in Widener's Honors Program also attend a minimum of eight outside-of-class events, including performances, lectures, and art museum receptions on campus; cultural events in Philadelphia and Wilmington; presentations at nearby schools and cultural centers; and various social events. Students in the Honors Program find that they have joined a community of mutual support and friendship in which the educational experience is exceptional.

Honors courses are not necessarily more demanding than regular classes in terms of the amount of work required. Rather, they are structured to allow for spirited discussion and interaction. A sampling of the courses that have been offered include Race, Violence and Memory; World War and Cinema; Environmental Challenges and Current Solutions; Seeing Others Seeing Ourselves; Philosophy of Sex and Love; Sociology of Everyday Life; and Literature and Medicine. The usual course distribution is freshman honors English, one honors colloquium, and at least three other honors courses. However, students are encouraged to take as many additional honors courses as they wish. Honors courses are taught by faculty members selected for their ability to stimulate and challenge inquisitive students.

All honors courses count toward the University's general education requirements, which must be met by all students for graduation. Thus, students enrolled in any of Widener's undergraduate majors may participate in the program. Founded in 1988, the Honors Program in General Education currently has 220 student participants.

The Honors Program in General Education is part of Widener's Honors Council. This body comprises more than thirty academic honors societies and hosts Honors Week every spring. The purpose of

Honors Week is threefold: to recognize the members of the honors societies, to foster the spirit of academic achievement, and to engage the campus community in a series of academic lectures and student presentations culminating in an Honors Convocation.

Participation Requirements: In order to continue in the Honors Program, each participant must maintain a minimum overall GPA of 3.0 and a minimum GPA of 3.0 in all honors courses taken. A Certificate of Honors in General Education is awarded at graduation to students who successfully complete at least five honors courses. Those who also complete a second honors colloquium or an honors independent study earn a Certificate of Advanced Honors in General Education.

Admission Process: High school students who apply to Widener are invited to participate in the Honors Program based on SAT scores and high school records. Applicants selected for the Honors Program are given priority consideration for Widener's Presidential Scholarships. After the first and second semesters of the freshman year, other students displaying excellence in college work may apply for admission to the program.

Campus Overview

Independent comprehensive, founded 1821 • **Coed** 2,501 undergraduate students, 95% full-time, 50% women, 50% men.

Undergraduates 2,378 full-time, 123 part-time. Students come from 26 states and territories, 38 other countries, 35% are from out of state, 12% African American, 2% Asian American or Pacific Islander, 2% Hispanic American, 0.2% Native American, 2% international, 5% transferred in, 61% live on campus.

Faculty *Total:* 398, 56% full-time. *Student/faculty ratio:* 12:1.

Academic Programs *Special study options:* academic remediation for entering students, accelerated degree program, adult/continuing education programs, advanced placement credit, cooperative education, distance learning, double majors, English as a second language, honors programs, independent study, internships, off-campus study, part-time degree program, services for LD students, student-designed majors, study abroad, summer session for credit. *ROTC:* Army (b), Navy (c), Air Force (c). *Unusual degree programs:* 3-2 physical therapy, education.

Athletics Member NCAA. All Division III. *Intercollegiate sports:* baseball M, basketball M/W, cheerleading W, cross-country running M/W, field hockey W, football M, golf M, lacrosse M/W, soccer M/W, softball W, swimming and diving M/W, tennis M/W, track and field M/W, volleyball W. *Intramural sports:* crew M, ice hockey M(c), rugby M(c)/W(c), skiing (downhill) M(c)/W(c), soccer M, volleyball M(c), water polo M(c)/W(c).

Costs (2004–05) *Comprehensive fee:* $31,100 includes full-time tuition ($22,800), mandatory fees ($200), and room and board ($8100). Full-time tuition and fees vary according to class time and program. Part-time tuition: $760 per credit. *Required fees:* $100 per semester part-time. *College room only:* $3700. Room and board charges vary according to board plan and housing facility.

Financial Aid In 2003, 276 non-need-based awards were made. *Average percent of need met:* 91%. *Average financial aid package:* $18,668. *Average need-based loan:* $5781. *Average need-based gift aid:* $11,379. *Average non-need-based aid:* $8117.

Contact: Director: Dr. Ilene D. Lieberman, One University Place, Chester, Pennsylvania 19013; *Telephone:* 610-499-4349; *Fax:* 610-499-4578; *E-mail:* honors.program@widener.edu

York College of Pennsylvania
York College Honors Program
York, Pennsylvania

*Y*ork College's Honors Program seeks to provide challenging and engaging experiences for academically motivated and accomplished students. The program offers course work, special academic and career advising, and extracurricular enrichment activities to its small group of undergraduate students. Students find that the community of scholars created by the Honors Program stimulates and supports their intellectual growth and interests while providing recognition for their extra efforts. The honors curriculum supplements the student's regular academic program by replacing a portion of the College's general education requirements with enhanced honors courses. The students belong to an Honors Club, in which they enjoy the fellowship of the honors community. The club has a great deal of autonomy in designing the activities of the group, such as trips to Baltimore, Maryland; New York City; and Washington, D.C. A key characteristic of the College as a whole, and the Honors Program in particular, is individual attention to students' whole development as a person. Small and innovative classes with enthusiastic and talented faculty members, regular contact with several advisers, and a fun and engaging orientation give the College the opportunity to meet the students' needs for intellectual and personal growth.

The program was developed in 2000 and enrolled its first class of approximately 20 students in the fall of 2001. The program currently has 55 members.

Co-Coordinators of the Honors Program are Dr. Perri B. Druen, Psychology, and Dr. Jim Kearns, Mechanical Engineering.

Participation Requirements: In order to become an Honors Program Graduate and receive special recognition at the Commencement Ceremony, students must complete a minimum of 20 honors credits in such courses as honors core courses (English and Information Literacy, Critical Thinking); honors-area courses (e.g., History); honors special-topics courses, which may be interdisciplinary or particularly timely (such as Elections in America or Youth Violence); and honors-by-contract courses, in which a student may add an honors component to any regular course by working with the instructor of the course to customize projects for the student. Students complete an honors project, which is typically in the student's major area and may include research studies, performances or recitals, design projects, or works of fine art or poetry; complete a service component, in which students contribute to the academic culture at the College and in the community by organizing activities such as field trips, tutoring services, York College's own student conference, or service learning in courses; and attain an overall GPA of 3.3.

Admission Process: To be eligible for participation, students must apply to and be accepted by York College. The criteria for acceptance into the program are not solely based upon measures of previous academic performance. All interested students are encouraged to apply and are evaluated individually on the basis of their preparedness and motivation for honors study. Preference is given to students who have achieved a combined SAT score of 1200 or higher and who rank in the top 20 percent of their high school graduating class. Interested students who are accepted to the College may request an application at the address listed below. The application includes a list of honors and awards, extracurricular and leadership activities, and a prompted essay. Students who apply early are notified of acceptance in late March or early April; after that, admission is on a rolling basis.

Scholarship Availability: Incoming students with a minimum SAT score of 1200 and a rank in the top 20 percent of their high school class are invited to apply for Trustee and Presidential Scholarships. A competition on campus, held early in the spring semester, determines the winners.

Campus Overview

Independent comprehensive, founded 1787 • **Coed** 5,379 undergraduate students, 81% full-time, 60% women, 40% men.

Undergraduates 4,344 full-time, 1,035 part-time. Students come from 36 states and territories, 45% are from out of state, 2% African American, 1% Asian American or Pacific Islander, 2% Hispanic American, 0.1% Native American, 6% transferred in, 45% live on campus.

Faculty *Total:* 404, 32% full-time, 38% with terminal degrees. *Student/faculty ratio:* 15:1.

Academic Programs *Special study options:* academic remediation for entering students, accelerated degree program, adult/continuing education programs, advanced placement credit, cooperative education, distance learning, double majors, honors programs, independent study, internships, part-time degree program, student-designed majors, study abroad, summer session for credit. *ROTC:* Army (c).

Athletics Member NCAA. All Division III. *Intercollegiate sports:* baseball M, basketball M/W, cheerleading W, cross-country running M/W, field hockey W, golf M, ice hockey M(c), lacrosse M/W, soccer M/W, softball W, swimming and diving M/W, tennis M/W, track and field M/W, volleyball M(c)/W, wrestling M. *Intramural sports:* badminton M/W, basketball M/W, football M/W, lacrosse M(c)/W(c), rugby M(c)/W(c), skiing (downhill) M(c)/W(c), soccer M/W, softball M/W, swimming and diving M/W, table tennis M, tennis M/W, track and field M/W, volleyball M/W, water polo M/W, weight lifting M(c)/W(c), wrestling M.

Costs (2004–05) *Comprehensive fee:* $15,434 includes full-time tuition ($8600), mandatory fees ($584), and room and board ($6250). Full-time tuition and fees vary according to course load and program. Part-time tuition: $260 per credit hour. Part-time tuition and fees vary according to course load and program. *College room only:* $3475. Room and board charges vary according to housing facility.

Financial Aid 252 Federal Work-Study jobs (averaging $1375). 62 state and other part-time jobs (averaging $1209). In 2004, 381 non-need-based awards were made. *Average percent of need met:* 72%. *Average financial aid package:* $6773. *Average need-based loan:* $3617. *Average need-based gift aid:* $3809. *Average non-need-based aid:* $3068.

Contact: Admissions Office, York College of Pennsylvania, York, Pennsylvania 17405; *Telephone:* 717-849-1600 or 800-455-8018 (toll-free); *Web site:* http://www.ycp.edu

PUERTO RICO

University of Puerto Rico, Río Piedras
Honors Program
San Juan, Puerto Rico

*T*he Honors Program, established in 1961, answered directly to the Chancellor's Office but has undergone fundamental changes since its inception. Currently, the Honors Program answers to the Office of the Dean of Academic Affairs (Certification No. 122 (1993–94) of the Academic Senate).

The Honors Program offers students the opportunity to achieve an integrated undergraduate education of excellence in an innovative and creative atmosphere. Integrated education provides an open and flexible approach to the learning process, in which not only the incorporation of diverse areas of knowledge is favored, but also the necessary specialization to master a given field. The Honors Program aspires to cultivate an environment in keeping with the dynamic spirit of professors and students interested in exploring new possibilities and new horizons in terms of the content as well as the focus of academic offerings. The Honors Program creates an alternative for those students who wish an individualized study environment and flexible and varied curricular offerings that enrich their majors.

Although the Honors Program does not offer academic degrees, students who have fulfilled all Honors Program requirements receive a Certificate of Recognition. This information is also registered in the academic transcript, where the title of the honors thesis appears.

The Honors Program enriches the University experience and helps integrate knowledge in an interdisciplinary way. The student has access to a series of special academic benefits, namely, small classes, direct contact with professors, independent research, interdisciplinary and research seminars, and association with similarly motivated undergraduate students. Available to the students are seminar and study rooms as well as a lounge for academic and social interaction.

Participation Requirements: Each student is assigned an academic adviser or mentor who guides and counsels in the formation of a study plan.

In addition to taking the courses required by their respective Colleges, the students must fulfill the following Honors Program requirements: learn a third language in addition to Spanish and English, take a tutorial and a research seminar, and prepare an honors thesis. The Governing Board, in consultation with the student, has the discretion to make adjustments in these requirements through substitutions, equivalencies, or additions. This depends upon a student's particular needs. All of the Honors Program's academic offerings respond to the demands of the highest academic standards.

Admission Process: In order to be admitted to the Honors Program students must have completed at least one semester of University studies with a full-time program; have a 3.5 GPA or higher at the time of applying for admission to the Honors Program; submit two or three letters of recommendation; and demonstrate, through interviews with the Directors of Studies and the Governing Board, the capacity and interest to satisfactorily meet Honors Program requirements. After this process, the Governing Board decides which candidates are accepted into the Honors Program.

Campus Overview

Commonwealth-supported university, founded 1903, part of University of Puerto Rico System • **Coed** 17,746 undergraduate students, 82% full-time, 67% women, 33% men.

Undergraduates 14,564 full-time, 3,182 part-time. Students come from 4 states and territories, 9 other countries, 1% are from out of state, 100% Hispanic American, 0.2% international, 4% transferred in.

Faculty *Total:* 1,793, 79% full-time, 42% with terminal degrees. *Student/faculty ratio:* 22:1.

Academic Programs *Special study options:* academic remediation for entering students, accelerated degree program, adult/continuing education programs, advanced placement credit, English as a second language, honors programs, part-time degree program, services for LD students, study abroad, summer session for credit. *ROTC:* Army (b), Air Force (b).

Athletics Member NCAA, NAIA. All NCAA Division II. *Intercollegiate sports:* basketball M(s)/W(s), cross-country running M(s)/W(s), soccer M(s), swimming and diving M(s)/W(s), table tennis M(s)/W(s), tennis M(s)/W(s), track and field M(s)/W(s), volleyball M(s)/W(s), water polo M(s), weight lifting M(s). *Intramural sports:* basketball M/W, cross-country running M/W, soccer M, swimming and diving M/W, table tennis M/W, tennis M/W, track and field M/W, volleyball M/W, water polo M, weight lifting M.

Costs (2004–05) *Tuition:* commonwealth resident $790 full-time, $30 per credit part-time; nonresident $2470 full-time, $100 per credit part-time. Part-time tuition and fees vary according to degree level. *Room and board:* $4940.

Contact: Carlos G. Ramos Bellido, University of Puerto Rico, Río Piedras Campus, P.O. Box 21847, UPR Station, San Juan, Puerto Rico 00931-1847; *Telephone:* 787-764-0000 Ext. 3288, 787-764-2221, 787-764-4945; *Fax:* 787-764-3044; E-mail: cramos1@rrpac.upr.clu.edu

RHODE ISLAND

Bryant University
Honors Program
Smithfield, Rhode Island

The current Honors Program at Bryant University represents an expansion and a new focus for the small program that was previously in place. It is designed to be a community of scholars, excellent students who are interested in a career in business but who also want a strong grounding in the liberal arts. Honors courses are offered in both business subjects and humanities, in small classes (usually 8 to 18 students) taught by the University's best instructors.

Honors Program members may also participate in a variety of off-campus excursions to events of cultural, historical, or business interest, and special on-campus dinners are arranged each semester. Forty-three freshmen are enrolled in the program. An optional honors residence floor is a strong possibility for the future.

Participation Requirements: Students must complete at least eight 3-credit honors courses in order to become Honors Program graduates, recognized at commencement and on transcripts and diplomas. The final course is a capstone course, a seminar that requires an independent, term-long project, supervised by a panel of instructors. Students must achieve a minimum overall GPA of 3.5, with at least a 3.2 in honors courses, to graduate in the program.

Admission Process: Freshman applicants for the Honors Program must have a minimum total SAT I score of 1200 (or equivalent ACT) and must rank in the top 20 percent of their high school class. Students who are not ranked by their high schools need a high school GPA of at least 3.5. Other students may apply to join the program later if they have earned at least a 3.5 GPA during their time at Bryant or another college.

Scholarship Availability: Although the Honors Program does not offer scholarships directly, virtually all Honors Program members receive academic scholarships from the University.

Campus Overview

Independent comprehensive, founded 1863 • **Coed** 3,047 undergraduate students, 93% full-time, 40% women, 60% men.

Undergraduates 2,826 full-time, 221 part-time. Students come from 30 states and territories, 28 other countries, 78% are from out of state, 3% African American, 3% Asian American or Pacific Islander, 3% Hispanic American, 0.3% Native American, 2% international, 4% transferred in, 78% live on campus.

Faculty *Total:* 256, 53% full-time, 60% with terminal degrees. *Student/faculty ratio:* 16:1.

Academic Programs *Special study options:* adult/continuing education programs, advanced placement credit, double majors, honors programs, independent study, internships, part-time degree program, services for LD students, study abroad, summer session for credit. *ROTC:* Army (b).

Athletics Member NCAA. All Division II. *Intercollegiate sports:* baseball M, basketball M(s)/W(s), bowling M(c)/W(c), cheerleading M(c)/W(c), cross-country running M/W, field hockey W, football M, golf M(c)/W(c), ice hockey M(c), lacrosse M/W, racquetball M(c)/W(c), rugby M(c)/W(c), soccer M/W, softball W, squash M(c)/W(c), swimming and diving M(c)/W(c), tennis M/W, track and field M/W, ultimate Frisbee M(c)/W(c), volleyball W, wrestling M(c).

Intramural sports: basketball M/W, field hockey W, football M, lacrosse M, soccer M/W, softball M/W, volleyball M/W, water polo M/W.

Costs (2005–06) *Comprehensive fee:* $34,330 includes full-time tuition ($24,762) and room and board ($9568). Full-time tuition and fees vary according to course load. Part-time tuition: $891 per course. Part-time tuition and fees vary according to course load. Full-time tuition includes cost of personal laptop computer. *College room only:* $5550. Room and board charges vary according to board plan and housing facility.

Financial Aid 286 Federal Work-Study jobs (averaging $1120). 1,011 state and other part-time jobs (averaging $1494). In 2003, 462 non-need-based awards were made. *Average percent of need met:* 74%. *Average financial aid package:* $12,628. *Average need-based loan:* $4850. *Average need-based gift aid:* $8688. *Average non-need-based aid:* $7482.

Contact: Honors Program Coordinator: Dr. Ranjan Karri, Smithfield, Rhode Island 02917; *Telephone:* 401-232-6069; *E-mail:* rkarri@bryant.edu

Johnson & Wales University
Honors Program
Providence, Rhode Island

The Johnson & Wales University Honors Program is designed to provide scholarly challenges for academically talented students. The university-wide program allows students to enroll in honors sections of their freshmen courses and to make various other courses Honors Options (H-Option) by completing additional assignments, such as papers, presentations, research, or multimedia projects, in addition to their required course work. Honors students culminate their senior year by completing a scholarly paper in their major, community leadership, or another School of Arts and Sciences topic.

The benefits available to honors students are numerous. These students are eligible for membership in the Chancellor's Circle and Collegiate Honors Society (CHS), and they have the opportunity to receive Presidential and Chancellor Scholarships. Honors students are involved in leadership activities and community service learning opportunities. In addition, they may attend presentations by visiting speakers, participate in social events sponsored by CHS, be invited to the annual Honors Banquet, take advantage of the benefits of living in the wellness dorms, and graduate early by taking accelerated courses.

The Johnson & Wales University Honors Program was established in 1994. It currently enrolls 695 students and is still growing.

Participation Requirements: Students within the Honors Program must maintain a minimum 3.4 GPA and complete the required number of honors courses and projects for their respective schools and degrees. Those within the Colleges of Business, Hospitality, and Technology are required to complete a minimum of six courses within the Honors Program for an associate-level degree and twelve courses within the program for a bachelor's-level degree. Students within the Culinary College are required to complete nine honors-level courses and/or labs for an associate degree and sixteen honors-level courses and/or labs for a bachelor's degree. Students in all colleges must complete a final honors project under the guidance of a faculty adviser and submit that project at least one term prior to graduation in order to fulfill the bachelor's degree requirements.

All students meeting these requirements receive the Honors Program designation upon graduation.

Admission Process: Admissions to the Honors Program is offered to entering first-year students and to transfer students who have earned fewer than 30 credits or were enrolled in an Honors Program at the college they previously attended. Eligibility is based on graduation within the top 25 percent of the high school class, minimum scores of 500 on both math and verbal sections of the SAT I, and a minimum GPA of 3.4 for transfer students. The Admissions Office also takes into consideration the strength of the secondary school curriculum, letters of recommendation, leadership activities, and school or community involvement.

Scholarship Availability: Honors students are eligible to receive Chancellor's Scholarships ranging from $10,000 to full tuition or Presidential Scholarships ranging from $2500 to $5000. Both scholarships are renewable for up to four years for continuous, full-time, day-school students, provided the recipient's GPA does not fall below 2.75 for the Presidential Scholarship or 3.4 for the Chancellor's Scholarship. All other requirements for the scholarship must also be met.

Campus Overview
Independent comprehensive, founded 1914 • **Coed** 9,246 undergraduate students.

Undergraduates Students come from 50 states and territories, 51 other countries, 72% are from out of state, 11% African American, 3% Asian American or Pacific Islander, 6% Hispanic American, 0.2% Native American, 5% international.

Faculty *Total:* 398, 70% full-time. *Student/faculty ratio:* 27:1.

Academic Programs *Special study options:* academic remediation for entering students, accelerated degree program, adult/continuing education programs, advanced placement credit, cooperative education, double majors, English as a second language, freshman honors college, honors programs, independent study, internships, part-time degree program, services for LD students, study abroad, summer session for credit.

Athletics Member NCAA. All Division III. *Intercollegiate sports:* baseball M(c), basketball M/W, cross-country running M/W, equestrian sports M(c)/W(c), golf M/W, ice hockey M(c), sailing M/W, soccer M/W, softball W, tennis M/W, volleyball M/W, wrestling M. *Intramural sports:* badminton M/W, basketball M/W, bowling M(c)/W(c), cheerleading M/W, football M/W, skiing (downhill) M(c)/W(c), soccer M/W, softball M/W, table tennis M/W, tennis M(c)/W(c), volleyball M/W.

Costs (2005–06) *Comprehensive fee:* $27,645 includes full-time tuition ($19,200), mandatory fees ($900), and room and board ($7545). Part-time tuition: $355 per quarter hour.

Financial Aid In 2003, 393 non-need-based awards were made. *Average percent of need met:* 69%. *Average financial aid package:* $11,459. *Average need-based loan:* $5250. *Average need-based gift aid:* $4065. *Average non-need-based aid:* $3239.

Contact: Director: Dr. Jim Brosnan, 10 Abbott Park Place, Providence, Rhode Island 02903; *Telephone:* 401-598-1796; *Fax:* 401-598-1821; *E-mail:* pvd.honors@jwu.edu

Rhode Island College
College Honors Program
Providence, Rhode Island

Designed for motivated students with superior academic records, the College Honors Program offers opportunities for individualized study, special classes, and extracurricular intellectual and social activities. The College Honors Program has two parts: General Education and Departmental Honors.

Students admitted to the program take the majority of their General Education requirements in specially designed honors sections. Those sections are limited to about 15 students in order to promote class participation and to encourage relationships among students and between students and teachers. Honors classes are taught by professors chosen for their commitment to undergraduate education, their abilities in the classroom, and their scholarly credentials. While the honors sections normally do not demand a greater amount of work and are not graded on a higher scale than nonhonors sections, they are meant to be more intellectually challenging and often make use of innovative pedagogical methods.

Students who complete General Education Honors have the option of doing honors in a particular academic major. Such Departmental Honors experiences involve the completion of a Senior Honors Project in which students work one-on-one with a professor of their choice on a topic of their choice. The Senior Honors Project is especially important for students who plan to go on to graduate or professional school. There are a Junior Honors Colloquium and Seminar to help prepare students to do Senior Honors Projects.

Honors students have access to an honors lounge and are encouraged to participate in various extracurricular activities, both social and cultural. Those who live on campus may opt to reside in special quiet suites reserved for students in the program. The College Honors Program was founded in 1982. It admits about 50 freshmen each year and currently has about 220 active students.

Participation Requirements: Students take at least six of their ten required general education classes in honors sections, normally including the four core courses on culture and critical thinking. They must maintain a minimum 3.0 cumulative GPA to remain in the program. Those choosing to stop with General Education Honors are so recognized at commencement and on their official transcripts. Students choosing to go on to a Senior Honors Project in a department are recognized for General Education Honors, Departmental Honors, and College Honors if they also complete the Junior Colloquium and Seminar. Senior Honors Projects may be done in virtually any academic area and may be of different kinds, e.g., research, critical, creative, or performative. They are normally done over the two semesters of the senior year and are awarded 6 credit hours toward graduation.

Admission Process: Students are invited into the program as freshmen on the basis of high-school records, SAT I scores, personal essays, and other supporting materials. There is no special application form for honors, only a box to check on the regular college application. Applications are reviewed individually on a rolling basis by a faculty honors committee. Students may also apply to the program after their first semester at the college.

Scholarship Availability: The College Honors Program awards the only merit-based academic scholarships at the College. Honors scholarships are renewable for a total of eight semesters. In addition, the College makes every effort to meet the financial need of students in the program with nonrepayable grants.

Campus Overview

State-supported comprehensive, founded 1854 • **Coed** 7,287 undergraduate students, 69% full-time, 68% women, 32% men.

Undergraduates 5,045 full-time, 2,242 part-time. Students come from 10 states and territories, 12% are from out of state, 4% African American, 2% Asian American or Pacific Islander, 5% Hispanic American, 0.3% Native American, 0.3% international, 9% transferred in, 12% live on campus.

Faculty *Total:* 306. *Student/faculty ratio:* 16:1.

Academic Programs *Special study options:* academic remediation for entering students, adult/continuing education programs, advanced placement credit, double majors, freshman honors college, honors programs, independent study, internships, off-campus study, part-time degree program, services for LD students, student-designed majors, study abroad, summer session for credit. *ROTC:* Army (c).

Athletics Member NCAA. All Division III. *Intercollegiate sports:* baseball M, basketball M/W, cross-country running M/W, gymnastics W, soccer M/W, softball W, tennis M/W, track and field M/W, volleyball W, wrestling M. *Intramural sports:* basketball M/W, football M, golf M, tennis M/W, volleyball M/W.

Costs (2005–06) *Tuition:* state resident $3888 full-time, $168 per credit part-time; nonresident $11,200 full-time, $466 per credit part-time. Part-time tuition and fees vary according to course load. *Required fees:* $788 full-time, $21 per credit part-time, $60 per term part-time. *Room and board:* $7010; room only: $3740. Room and board charges vary according to board plan and housing facility.

Contact: Director: Dr. Spencer Hall, English Department, Providence, Rhode Island 02908; *Telephone:* 401-456-8671; *Fax:* 401-456-8379; *E-mail:* shall@ric.edu; *Web site:* http://www.ric.edu/honors

Roger Williams University
University Honors Program
Bristol, Rhode Island

The University Honors Program, established in 1994, enrolls approximately 5 percent of the freshman class. There is a total annual participation of nearly 150 full-time students, representing the breadth of the University's undergraduate programs. The University Honors Program holds an institutional membership in the National Collegiate Honors Council. Learning on the collegiate level encourages independent and original thinking in all course work. These qualities are particularly characteristic of the University Honors Program. Students and faculty members in the program share a passion for learning. The University Honors Program supplements a student participant's undergraduate education, distinguishing them as superior scholars and active participants in the University community.

Participation Requirements: The University Honors Program curriculum is writing intensive. It consists of six prescribed courses in the first two years of study, including special sections of the University core course requirements; a community service or leadership experience in the junior year; and a final major-related project for performance or presentation in the student's year of graduation. These requirements usually engage the student in research and written assignments. In addition, they provide opportunities for students to mentor freshmen in the University Honors Program, while conceiving and implementing a leadership or service project with the support of the Honors Advisory Council and the Feinstein Service Learning Program. Drawing upon major-related interests (and, if required in the major, the senior thesis), graduating honors students are able to share some aspect of their undergraduate study and research with the academic community.

Admission Process: SAT, ACT, and TOEFL scores are used as admissions criteria. High school average, strength of high school curriculum, rank in class, academic recommendations, personal essay, and extracurricular activities are all factors considered by the honors admissions committee. For maximum consideration for merit-based scholarships and those particularly for honors scholarships, applications should be received on or before February 1.

Scholarship Availability: Students must maintain a minimum cumulative 3.3 GPA in order to retain an annual scholarship for consecutive years of undergraduate study (full-time day status) and remain active in the Honors Program. In addition, all academic requirements for the Honors Program must be achieved.

Campus Overview

Independent comprehensive, founded 1956 • **Coed** 4,190 undergraduate students, 85% full-time, 50% women, 50% men.

Undergraduates 3,569 full-time, 621 part-time. Students come from 44 states and territories, 37 other countries, 89% are from out of state, 1% African American, 2% Asian American or Pacific Islander, 2% Hispanic American, 0.2% Native American, 2% international, 3% transferred in, 79% live on campus.

Faculty *Total:* 383, 44% full-time, 57% with terminal degrees. *Student/faculty ratio:* 16:1.

Academic Programs *Special study options:* adult/continuing education programs, advanced placement credit, cooperative education, distance learning, double majors, English as a second language, external degree program, freshman honors college, honors programs, independent study, internships, part-time degree program, services for LD students, student-designed majors, study abroad, summer session for credit. *ROTC:* Army (b).

Athletics Member NCAA. All Division III. *Intercollegiate sports:* baseball M, basketball M/W, cheerleading W(c), crew M(c)/W(c), cross-country running M/W(c), equestrian sports M/W, lacrosse M/W, rugby M(c), sailing M/W, soccer M/W, softball W, tennis M/W, track and field M(c)/W(c), volleyball M/W, wrestling M. *Intramural sports:* badminton M/W, basketball M/W, field hockey M/W, football M/W, golf M/W, lacrosse M/W, racquetball M/W, soccer M/W, softball M/W, squash M/W, swimming and diving M/W, table tennis M/W, tennis M/W, ultimate Frisbee M/W, volleyball M/W.

Costs (2005–06) *Comprehensive fee:* $33,103 includes full-time tuition ($21,848), mandatory fees ($1018), and room and board ($10,237). Full-time tuition and fees vary according to class time, course load, and program. Part-time tuition: $910 per credit. Part-time tuition and fees vary according to class time. *College room only:* $5355. Room and board charges vary according to board plan and housing facility.

Financial Aid 434 Federal Work-Study jobs (averaging $1783). 598 state and other part-time jobs (averaging $1714). In 2003, 270 non-need-based awards were made. *Average percent of need met:* 83%. *Average financial aid package:* $14,260. *Average need-based loan:* $4187. *Average need-based gift aid:* $8067. *Average non-need-based aid:* $5865.

Contact: Director: Dr. Peter Deekle; *Telephone:* 401-254-3063; *E-mail:* pdeekle@rwu.edu

SOUTH CAROLINA

The Citadel, The Military College of South Carolina

Honors Program

Charleston, South Carolina

The Citadel's Honors Program is a specially designed educational experience meeting the needs of students with an outstanding record of academic achievement and a sense of intellectual adventure. While pursuing any one of seventeen degree programs offered by The Citadel, honors students take a series of Core Curriculum Honors Courses—for example, studies based in literature and writing, history, and mathematics—concentrated in their first two years, and an occasional Honors Seminar or Honors Research Project in their third and fourth years. There are approximately 65 students in the 9-year-old program.

Although The Citadel's Honors Program has many facets, the essential character of the program can be found in three aspects. First, there is a tutorial foundation. All honors courses, from freshman-level courses through senior-level seminars, have attached to them a regularly scheduled, one-on-one meeting between the student and the professor. These are not just check-in meetings to see if the student has any problems; rather, the professor and the student prearrange to work together on one of the assignments of the course.

Second, there is preprofessional counseling. All honors students take a three-semester sequence of courses entitled Personal and Professional Development. Taught entirely in tutorial, it directs students in a three-year period of research, reflection, and writing on the subject of their professional goals, encouraging them to envision their leadership in their future profession and guiding them in exploring, through research and writing, the ideals as well as the facts of that profession.

Finally, there is leadership. The Citadel encourages students to take full advantage of the many leadership opportunities afforded by the military environment of the school. Year after year, the chain of command at The Citadel is heavily populated from top to bottom by Honors Program students. The Citadel has an honors brand of leadership based on the concept of service, which has enabled honors students to consistently earn positions of leadership. The deadline for applying to the program is January 15.

Participation Requirements: Students majoring in one of the sciences or engineering are required to complete the following honors courses: Honors Personal and Professional Development I, II, and III; Honors English I, II, III, and IV; Honors History I and II; Honors Social Science Project; and one Honors Seminar or Research Project. Students majoring in one of the liberal arts or social sciences are required to complete the following honors courses: Honors Personal and Professional Development I, II, and III; Honors English I, II, III, and IV; Honors History I and II; Honors Social Science Project; and two Honors Seminars or Research Projects (or one of each). Students who complete all Honors Program requirements are recognized as Honors Program Graduates in the College Commencement ceremony. They receive an Honors Program certificate as well as a gold honors seal on their diploma. A notation is added to the official College transcript to indicate that they have completed the requirements of the Honors Program and to explain what those requirements are. This note comes at the very beginning of the transcript to assist future employers or graduate/professional school admissions committees in understanding what the Honors Program means at The Citadel.

Scholarship Availability: No scholarships are awarded through the Honors Program, although the Honors Director is a member of the College Scholarships Committee.

Campus Overview

State-supported comprehensive, founded 1842 • **Urban** 130-acre campus • **Coed, primarily men,** 2,177 undergraduate students, 95% full-time, 8% women, 92% men.

Undergraduates 2,061 full-time, 116 part-time. Students come from 48 states and territories, 29 other countries, 51% are from out of state, 8% African American, 3% Asian American or Pacific Islander, 4% Hispanic American, 0.1% Native American, 2% international, 4% transferred in, 100% live on campus.

Faculty *Total:* 230, 67% full-time, 79% with terminal degrees. *Student/faculty ratio:* 15:1.

Academic Programs *Special study options:* adult/continuing education programs, advanced placement credit, cooperative education, double majors, English as a second language, honors programs, independent study, internships, off-campus study, part-time degree program, services for LD students, study abroad, summer session for credit. *ROTC:* Army (b), Navy (b), Air Force (b).

Athletics Member NCAA. All Division I except football (Division I-AA). *Intercollegiate sports:* baseball M(s), basketball M(s), crew M(c)/W(c), cross-country running M(s)/W(s), golf M(s)/W(s), ice hockey M(c)/W(c), lacrosse M(c)/W(c), riflery M(c)/W(c), rugby M(c)/W(c), sailing M(c)/W(c), soccer M(s)/W(s), tennis M(s), track and field M(s)/W(s), volleyball M(c)/W(s), weight lifting M(c)/W(c), wrestling M(s). *Intramural sports:* badminton M/W, basketball M/W, football M/W, racquetball M/W, softball M/W, swimming and diving M/W, table tennis M/W, tennis M/W, track and field M/W, volleyball M/W, water polo M/W, weight lifting M/W, wrestling M/W.

Costs (2004–05) *Tuition:* state resident $5900 full-time, $182 per credit hour part-time; nonresident $14,518 full-time, $365 per credit hour part-time. *Required fees:* $928 full-time, $15 per term part-time. *Room and board:* $4684.

Financial Aid 19 Federal Work-Study jobs (averaging $863). In 2002, 172 non-need-based awards were made. *Average percent of need met:*

78%. *Average financial aid package:* $7992. *Average need-based loan:* $5000. *Average need-based gift aid:* $4980. *Average non-need-based aid:* $7438.

Contact: Director: Jack W. Rhodes, Honors Program, The Citadel, The Military College of South Carolina, 171 Moultrie Street, Charleston, South Carolina 29409-6370; *Telephone:* 843-953-3708; *Fax:* 843-953-7084; *E-mail:* rhodesj@citadel.edu

Claflin University
The Alice Carson Tisdale Honors College
Orangeburg, South Carolina

A prestigious college within the University, the Alice Carson Tisdale Honors College is one of Claflin's Centers of Excellence. Established in 1995, the enriched curriculum focuses around a core of required courses and rigorous academic criteria that is set by each school. The program includes coherent learning experiences, intense academic advising, cultural enrichment activities, community service activities, and other experiences designed to enhance and develop a student's academic and leadership potential. Currently the Honors College enrolls 241 undergraduates or about 14 percent of the student body.

The faculty members who teach honors courses encourage increased student participation, require more original writing, and demand a greater amount of reflective thinking. Honors College students are required to participate in four years of weekly Honors Leadership Seminars. These seminars are designed to allow students to learn about the nature, practice, and responsibility of leadership. Courses are offered from a variety of disciplines in order to give honors students opportunities to fulfill many general education requirements and earn honors credit at the same time. These courses may come from the natural sciences, humanities, social sciences, and the arts. A special Honors Center with a seminar room, computer lab, and a lounge offer honors students reserved facilities for studying, holding seminars, and meeting informally. All honors students live in special honors facilities with computer and study labs.

Participation Requirements: In order to remain in the Honors College, a student must maintain a semester and annual CGPA of 3.25 or higher, follow the approved honors curriculum, participate in weekly Honors Leadership Seminars and Honors Week activities, and exhibit exemplary moral and ethical conduct. Scholars are responsible for adhering to the requirement of 70 community service hours per academic year and are expected to complete eight consecutive semesters at the institution. Honors College students must also prepare, present, and defend a research project/thesis to the University community during Honors Week of their senior year. The honors research project/thesis is listed in the graduation program, and an Alice Carson Tisdale Honors Scholar is noted on the graduating student's diploma.

Admission Process: An incoming freshman who has already been granted admission to Claflin University may apply to the Honors College during his or her senior year of high school. The applicant must possess a minimum high school GPA of 3.25, a score of at least 1100 on the SAT (or a score of 24 or higher on the ACT), graduate in the top 10 percent of his or her graduating class, complete a specific level of high school course work, exhibit leadership qualities and/or special talents, and demonstrate participation in school and community-service learning projects and programs. The process for the selection of students is both competitive and selective.

Sophomore and junior students matriculating at Claflin University are also invited and encouraged to apply to the Honors College. Students who have a cumulative earned college GPA of 3.3 or higher and have demonstrated outstanding leadership qualities and/or talents while attending Claflin University are eligible to apply for membership. Based on an applicant's profile, the Honors College Selection Committee makes recommendations to the University during the spring semester of each year.

Scholarship Availability: The Claflin University Presidential Scholarship is awarded to outstanding high school seniors who are committed to academic excellence and who plan to pursue graduate or professional studies after graduating from the University. Awards are made on the basis of academic achievement, a score of 1200 or higher on the SAT (or an equivalent score on the ACT), leadership potential, and exemplary character. The award includes tuition, room and board, books, and a monthly sustenance allowance. The Presidential Scholarship selection is determined by the University's president.

The second scholarship offered is the Honors College Scholarship. This scholarship is awarded for four years and ranges in value from $2000 to the full cost of tuition, fees, and room and board. These scholarships are awarded to selected incoming freshmen on the basis of academic achievement, SAT scores of 1100 or higher (or an equivalent score on the ACT), and demonstrated leadership ability.

Both the Presidential and Honors College scholarships are competitive and selective.

Campus Overview

Independent United Methodist 4-year, founded 1869 • **Coed** 1,772 undergraduate students, 96% full-time, 66% women, 34% men.

Undergraduates 1,698 full-time, 74 part-time. Students come from 29 states and territories, 19 other countries, 15% are from out of state, 93% African American, 0.1% Asian American or Pacific Islander, 0.1% Hispanic American, 0.1% Native American, 5% international, 2% transferred in, 65% live on campus.

Faculty *Total:* 121, 77% full-time. *Student/faculty ratio:* 14:1.

Academic Programs *Special study options:* academic remediation for entering students, adult/continuing education programs, advanced placement credit, cooperative education, freshman honors college, honors programs, independent study, internships, off-campus study, part-time degree program, study abroad, summer session for credit. *ROTC:* Army (c). *Unusual degree programs:* 3-2 engineering with South Carolina State University, Clemson University; occupational therapy at the Medical University of South Carolina; chiropractic medicine at Sherman College of Straight Chiropractic.

Athletics Member NAIA. *Intercollegiate sports:* baseball M/W, basketball M(s)/W(s), cross-country running M/W, softball W, tennis M/W, track and field M/W, volleyball W. *Intramural sports:* basketball M/W, table tennis M/W, tennis M/W, volleyball M/W.

Costs (2005–06) *Comprehensive fee:* $18,492 includes full-time tuition ($10,900), mandatory fees ($1684), and room and board ($5908). Part-time tuition: $384 per credit hour. *Required fees:* $63 per credit hour part-time. *College room only:* $2632. Room and board charges vary according to housing facility.

Financial Aid In 2002, 300 non-need-based awards were made. *Average percent of need met:* 70%. *Average financial aid package:* $9000.

Contact: Director: Alice Carson Tisdale, The Alice Carson Tisdale Honors College, Claflin University, 400 Magnolia Street, Orangeburg, South Carolina 29115; *Telephone:* 803-535-5094; *Fax:* 803-535-5385; *E-mail:* mail:actisdale@claflin.edu

Clemson University
Calhoun Honors College
Clemson, South Carolina

Established in 1962, the Calhoun Honors College provides highly motivated, academically talented students unique opportunities for scholarship and research. The purpose of honors at Clemson is to foster continued intellectual growth, cultivate a lifelong love of learning, and prepare students for lives as leaders and change agents.

More than 1,000 students participate in the Honors College, including approximately 300 freshmen who join the program each year. Thirty percent of Clemson's honors students graduated from high school with a class rank of number one; approximately 40 percent scored more than 1400 on the SAT I.

In addition to the intellectual challenge, advantages of membership include early course registration, extended library loan privileges, and the option of honors housing in Holmes Hall. The Calhoun Honors College also sponsors an annual lecture series that brings to the campus scholars of national and international acclaim. Honors students are provided admission to concerts, plays, and other cultural events at Clemson's Brooks Center for the Performing Arts. Under the New York Times Readership Program, honors students are provided free daily copies of the newspaper. The Calhoun Honors College and the graduate school sponsor a University-wide Research Forum every April, giving honors students an opportunity to present their research.

Honors students may apply for grants to support their Departmental Honors research projects. These competitive grants may be used for equipment, supplies, and travel to research facilities. Also, Educational Enrichment Awards of up to $3000 help provide life-changing educational experiences outside the classroom and away from the Clemson campus. These experiences may be internships, international study, public-service projects, or other significant undertakings consistent with the student's educational and career goals.

Students with the academic ability and leadership potential to compete for major fellowships, such as the Rhodes, Marshall, Truman, and Goldwater Scholarships, are provided guidance under the auspices of the Dixon Fellows Program. Admission to this program of approximately 70 students is highly selective and requires the submission of a personal statement, curriculum vitae, and other written materials.

Beginning in the summer of 2005, the Honors College features a four-week study-abroad program in Brussels, Belgium, for up to 25 honors students. The program includes two courses, one on the economic and political integration of Europe, and one on the culture of Belgium, with emphasis on art and architectural history. Also, the new Duckenfield Scholars Program, administered by the Honors College, enables 1 honors student to study during the summer at St. Peters College of the University of Oxford. The student selected as the Duckenfield Scholar is provided with funding to cover the cost of tuition, fees, room, and board.

Beginning in the 2006–07 academic year, the Honors College will feature a new research program that will enable up to 40 entering students to participate in mentored research projects during the summer prior to the fall semester. The program will cover costs of room and board for up to six weeks.

Participation Requirements: General Honors requires at least six honors courses of no less than 3 credits each. General Honors courses include the interdisciplinary Calhoun Honors Seminars that satisfy general education requirements in the humanities, social science, science and technology in society, and cross-cultural awareness. Average enrollment in these courses is 19 students.

Departmental Honors involves in-depth study within the student's major. Although specific requirements are set by individual departments, all students are expected to complete an honors thesis or capstone project. Departmental Honors theses and research projects have resulted in publications, postgraduate grants, and patents.

In addition to honors courses, students may complete up to two 300- or 400-level courses under the Honors Contract option. Subject to the approval of the Honors Director and the department chair, graduate courses may substitute for honors requirements.

Students who complete General and Departmental Honors are recognized at an awards ceremony where they are awarded the B.C. Inabinet medallion. Completion of honors requirements is recognized on the student's transcript, diploma, and in the graduation program.

To receive credit for General and Departmental Honors, all honors courses must be completed with a grade of A or B. Honors students must maintain an overall GPA of 3.4 or greater.

Admission Process: For entering freshmen, admission is by invitation and is based on a combination of academic performance indicators, including high school grade point average, class rank, and SAT or ACT scores. No one factor alone is sufficient for admission. In considering candidates for admission, the Honors Office extends invitations to those students who show the promise of meeting the high academic standards of the Calhoun Honors College. Typically, honors freshmen rank in the top 2 percent of their high school class and present SAT scores of 1380 and higher. Students who are not admitted to the program as entering freshmen may become members by earning a cumulative GPA of at least 3.5, provided that they have at least four semesters remaining to complete degree requirements.

Scholarship Availability: Scholarships for Clemson University are administered through the Office of Student Financial Aid. Except for the Clemson University National Scholars Program (NSP), as described in the following paragraph, there are no specific scholarships associated with membership in the Calhoun Honors College. However, many honors students receive scholarships because of their superior academic qualifications.

The Clemson National Scholars Program is Clemson's premier scholarship program for undergraduates, offering a full-tuition and fees scholarship plus an extensive array of educational enrichment activities. Consideration for NSP is based exclusively on merit and entails a highly selective review process that includes personal interviews and considers proven and potential academic excellence, leadership, and service. The scholarship covers all costs, including tuition, fees, room, board, books, and incidental expenses, and it is renewable for four years. The program offers use of a laptop computer, summer study abroad, several seminars, and an extensive selection of educational enrichment opportunities. An out-of-state fee waiver is offered if applicable. The Clemson National Scholarship is awarded without regard to place of residence or academic major.

Campus Overview

State-supported university, founded 1889 • **Coed** 13,936 undergraduate students, 94% full-time, 45% women, 55% men.

Undergraduates 13,066 full-time, 870 part-time. Students come from 53 states and territories, 62 other countries, 32% are from out of state, 7% African American, 2% Asian American or Pacific Islander, 1% Hispanic American, 0.2% Native American, 0.5% international, 5% transferred in, 47% live on campus.

Faculty Total: 1,105, 85% full-time, 82% with terminal degrees. Student/faculty ratio: 16:1.

Academic Programs Special study options: academic remediation for entering students, accelerated degree program, advanced placement credit, cooperative education, distance learning, double majors, honors programs, internships, part-time degree program, services for LD students, study abroad, summer session for credit. ROTC: Army (b), Air Force (b).

Athletics Member NCAA. All Division I except football (Division I-A). Intercollegiate sports: baseball M, basketball M(s)/W(s), bowling M(c)/W(c), cheerleading M/W, crew M(c)/W(s), cross-country running M(s)/W(s), equestrian sports M(c)/W(c), fencing M(c)/W(c), field hockey M(c)/W(c), golf M(s), ice hockey M(c)/W(c), lacrosse M(c)/W(c), riflery M(c)/W(c), rugby M(c)/W(c), sailing M(c)/W(c), soccer M(s)/W(s), softball W(c), swimming and diving M(s)/W(s), tennis M(s)/W(s), track and field M(s)/W(s), ultimate Frisbee M(c)/W(c), volleyball M(c)/W(s), weight lifting M(c)/W(c), wrestling M(c). *Intramural sports:* basketball M/W, golf M/W, racquetball M/W, soccer M/W, softball M/W, swimming and diving M(c)/W(c), table tennis M/W, tennis M(c)/W(c), volleyball M/W, water polo M/W.

Costs (2004–05) *Tuition:* state resident $7840 full-time, $324 per hour part-time; nonresident $16,404 full-time, $676 per hour part-time. *Required fees:* $234 full-time, $6 per term part-time. *Room and board:* $5292; room only: $3094. Room and board charges vary according to board plan and housing facility.

Financial Aid 563 Federal Work-Study jobs (averaging $1790). 3,152 state and other part-time jobs (averaging $2478). In 2004, 1688 non-need-based awards were made. *Average percent of need met:* 43%. *Average financial aid package:* $8707. *Average need-based loan:* $4161. *Average need-based gift aid:* $3308. *Average non-need-based aid:* $3720.

Contact: Director: Dr. Stephen H. Wainscott, Clemson University, Clemson, South Carolina 29634; *Telephone:* 864-656-4762; *Fax:* 864-656-1472; *E-mail:* shwns@mail.clemson.edu

---

College of Charleston
Honors Program
Charleston, South Carolina

The Honors Program at the College of Charleston was created in 1978 to provide a program and a community for talented and motivated students who enjoy active participation in small stimulating classes and like to investigate ideas. The Honors Program is dedicated to providing these students with a place where they can flourish and grow; it is a true learning community of teachers and students. In addition to receiving exciting and unique educational experiences, students can participate with their fellow Honors Program students in social, cultural, and intellectual events on the campus and in historic Charleston, South Carolina.

The Honors Program challenges intellectually talented students to make the most of the opportunities available to them and to become actively involved in their own education. In honors classes, students take responsibility for their own learning through class discussions, interaction with faculty members and fellow students, and independent research. Honors students are advised by specially chosen faculty advisers, receive priority registration, and have the opportunity to room with other honors students in special honors residence halls. Classes, seminars, and student gatherings are held in the Honors Center, the historic William Aiken House built by Governor William Aiken in 1839.

Participation Requirements: All students take Honors English, the Colloquium in Western Civilization, and at least three other honors courses, one of which must be interdisciplinary. They also take one semester of calculus and a math course at the 200-level or above. Each student undertakes an independent study under the supervision of a faculty tutor and a senior research project, which culminates in a written paper (the Bachelor's Essay). A student must have a GPA of 3.4 or higher to graduate from the program.

Admission Process: There are about 600 students in the program. Approximately 200 entering students are accepted each year by a faculty/student committee on the basis of applications submitted directly to the program or as part of their online application to the Admissions Office of the College of Charleston. The successful candidate is typically in the top 10 percent of his/her class, has taken numerous honors and/or AP or IB courses, and is active in extracurricular and/or service activities. While there is no minimum SAT score required, the SAT scores of entering freshmen (excluding the new writing portion) average above 1320 (29 or above on the ACT). A student may apply for admission to the program at any time but is encouraged to apply to both the College of Charleston and the Honors Program (separate applications) before November 1 to maximize the possibility of being accepted to the program and being considered for all available scholarships. Transfer students and currently enrolled students with a GPA of 3.6 or greater may also apply to the program.

Scholarship Availability: The vast majority of the students in the Honors Program receive some form of academic scholarship. More than 85 percent of the honors students who enrolled in the last two years received merit scholarships. Students are considered for all available College of Charleston merit scholarships on the basis of their admission application credentials, provided that they are admitted before January 15 preceding the fall term of freshmen enrollment.

Campus Overview

State-supported comprehensive, founded 1770 • **Coed** 9,866 undergraduate students, 92% full-time, 64% women, 36% men.

Undergraduates 9,034 full-time, 832 part-time. Students come from 52 states and territories, 76 other countries, 35% are from out of state, 8% African American, 1% Asian American or Pacific Islander, 2% Hispanic American, 0.4% Native American, 2% international, 5% transferred in, 29% live on campus.

Faculty *Total:* 836, 60% full-time, 64% with terminal degrees. *Student/faculty ratio:* 14:1.

Academic Programs *Special study options:* accelerated degree program, adult/continuing education programs, advanced placement credit, cooperative education, distance learning, double majors, English as a second language, honors programs, independent study, internships, off-campus study, part-time degree program, services for LD students, study abroad, summer session for credit. *ROTC:* Air Force (c). *Unusual degree programs:* 3-2 engineering with Case Western Reserve University, Clemson University, Georgia Institute of Technology, University of South Carolina; biometry with Medical University of South Carolina, marine engineering with University of Michigan.

Athletics Member NCAA. All Division I. *Intercollegiate sports:* baseball M(s), basketball M(s)/W(s), cross-country running M(s)/W(s), equestrian sports W, golf M(s)/W(s), sailing M/W, soccer M(s)/W(s), softball W(s), swimming and diving M(s)/W(s), tennis M(s)/W(s), volleyball W(s). *Intramural sports:* badminton M/W, basketball M/W, crew M/W, equestrian sports W, fencing M/W, football M/W, racquetball M/W, rugby W, soccer M/W, softball M/W, tennis M/W, volleyball M/W, weight lifting M/W.

Costs (2004–05) *Tuition:* state resident $6202 full-time, $258 per semester hour part-time; nonresident $14,140 full-time, $589 per semester hour part-time. Part-time tuition and fees vary according to course load. *Room and board:* $6506; room only: $4446. Room and board charges vary according to board plan and housing facility.

Financial Aid In 2004, 836 non-need-based awards were made. *Average percent of need met:* 62%. *Average financial aid package:* $8820. *Average need-based loan:* $3527. *Average need-based gift aid:* $2877. *Average non-need-based aid:* $10,003.

Contact: Dr. John H. Newell, Director of the Honors Program, College of Charleston, Charleston, South Carolina 29424; *Telephone:* 843-953-7154; *Fax:* 843-953-7135; *E-mail:* newellj@cofc.edu; *Web site:* http://www.cofc.edu/~honors

Columbia College (South Carolina)

Honors Program

Columbia, South Carolina

*F*or more than fifteen years, the Columbia College Honors Program has provided an enriched academic experience for the outstanding student committed to excellence. The fundamental assumption of honors education is that honors students should continually challenge their intellectual limits, working creatively and seriously to reach their highest potential as scholars, reflective learners, individual thinkers, and leaders. The program emphasizes risk, independent learning, and a spirited exchange of ideas in a stimulating classroom environment that encourages students to develop their own ideas in a knowledgeable and reasoned framework.

The Honors Program Center offers an attractive and appropriate place for students to study and relax as a collaborative community of learners. The center includes computers fully networked to campus technology, printers, copy and fax machines, a library of honors materials, a seminar table, and comfortable furniture. In addition, new and continuing students may choose honors residential opportunities in selected residence halls.

Approximately 120 students are currently enrolled in the program.

Participation Requirements: Each student must complete 24 hours in honors courses, including the honors seminar and project. A student may enroll in up to 3 hours of honors independent study courses and one honors choice up to 4 hours. Students must maintain at least a 3.4 GPA in the cumulative average. Failure to maintain at least a 3.4 GPA results in one semester of academic probation. Only two semesters of probation are permissible in a student's undergraduate career.

Seniors are honored with a reception prior to graduation at which time they present their honors projects and receive their honors medallions to be worn at graduation. Seniors who complete the honors requirements graduate *cum honore* with an achievement noted on their diplomas.

Admission Process: Students are invited into honors in the freshman year based on their high school GPA, level of courses taken (AP, IB, and honors), SAT or ACT score, class rank, leadership experience, extracurricular involvement, and application essay. Recently, GPAs have averaged above 3.8 and SAT scores have averaged above 1250, but any motivated, capable student is encouraged to apply. Students may petition for admission past the freshman year with recommendations from College faculty members.

Scholarship Availability: The outstanding rising senior honors student is awarded the prestigious Tull Scholarship. A select group of outstanding honors students from each class also receive honors scholarships. These scholarships are based on GPA, involvement in the Honors Program, and leadership in the College and community.

Campus Overview

Independent United Methodist comprehensive, founded 1854 • **Suburban** 33-acre campus • **Women only** 1,149 undergraduate students, 78% full-time.

Undergraduates 893 full-time, 256 part-time. Students come from 12 states and territories, 17 other countries, 6% are from out of state, 45% African American, 0.9% Asian American or Pacific Islander, 2% Hispanic American, 0.3% Native American, 1% international, 10% transferred in, 63% live on campus.

Faculty *Total:* 168, 55% full-time. *Student/faculty ratio:* 11:1.

Academic Programs *Special study options:* academic remediation for entering students, adult/continuing education programs, advanced placement credit, distance learning, double majors, honors programs, independent study, internships, off-campus study, part-time degree program, student-designed majors, study abroad, summer session for credit. *ROTC:* Army (c), Navy (c), Air Force (c).

Athletics Member NAIA. *Intercollegiate sports:* basketball W(s), soccer W(s), tennis W(s), volleyball W(s). *Intramural sports:* crew W.

Costs (2004–05) *Comprehensive fee:* $23,660 includes full-time tuition ($17,690), mandatory fees ($350), and room and board ($5620). Part-time tuition: $475 per credit hour. Part-time tuition and fees vary according to course load. *College room only:* $2930. Room and board charges vary according to board plan and housing facility.

Financial Aid 200 Federal Work-Study jobs (averaging $1000). In 2003, 79 non-need-based awards were made. *Average percent of need met:* 66%. *Average financial aid package:* $19,176. *Average need-based loan:* $4094. *Average need-based gift aid:* $8995. *Average non-need-based aid:* $6826.

Contact: Director: Dr. John Zubizarreta, Columbia, South Carolina 29203; *Telephone:* 803-786-3014; *Fax:* 803-786-3315; *E-mail:* jzubizarreta@colacoll.edu; *Web site:* http://www.columbiacollegesc.edu/academics/honors.html

Converse College

Nisbet Honors Program

Spartanburg, South Carolina

*T*he Nisbet Honors Program began in 2000 through an endowment from alumna Marian McGowan Nisbet, '62, and her husband, Olin. The program seeks to offer the academically gifted student the challenge and community in which she may grow to her full potential. The Honors Program includes opportunities to do independent research with faculty mentors, to take honors courses with other academically gifted students, to meet nationally known visiting scholars, and to meet socially to discuss intellectually challenging topics.

One of the most unusual features of the program is its emphasis on interdisciplinary learning. The interdisciplinary seminars have 2 faculty members from different fields in the classroom throughout the entire course, and students learn how different branches of learning approach the tasks of collecting and interpreting evidence and of making sense of the complex world. Topics for interdisciplinary seminars over the past few years have included the history of disease, with a historian and a biologist teaching together; human sexuality and the literature of love, marriage, and birth, with a biologist and an English professor; the new South in history and literature, with a historian and an English professor; and psychological and political aspects of American musicals, with a political scientist and a psychologist.

More than 100 students are currently enrolled, and the program continues to expand.

Participation Requirements: To graduate from the program, students must successfully complete a freshman honors seminar (or another honors course if they enter after the fall of the freshman year), one interdisciplinary honors seminar, a 1-credit junior honors seminar, a 1-credit senior honors seminar, and either two more honors experiences (such as two additional honors courses, a yearlong honors course, an honors-directed independent study, or some combination of these) or a senior honors thesis in their major. Students must maintain a GPA of at least 3.0 and receive at least a B- in honors courses to continue in the program.

The senior honors thesis represents a substantial independent research or creative project. Students may begin preparing for this project by applying for summer research grants as early as the summer after the freshman year. With faculty member and peer support, sophomores and juniors explore areas for independent research. They work closely with a faculty mentor during the junior and senior years. The senior honors seminar provides a forum in which students can share their work with others doing honors theses.

Students who complete a thesis and other program requirements graduate with honors in their field and with the designation Graduate of the Nisbet Honors Program. Students who complete the program only through course work graduate with the latter designation alone.

Admission Process: To be invited into the Honors Program as incoming freshmen, students must have applied to and been admitted to the College. A select number of entering freshmen are invited into the program based on their outstanding high school performance and their potential for success in college. To be considered, students generally must have SAT scores of at least 1250 and comparably strong high school records. Students who do well once they have begun their studies at Converse are also considered for the program; freshmen and sophomores must earn at least a 3.3 GPA after taking 12 hours at the College to be invited to apply.

Scholarship Availability: Most students invited into the Honors Program as incoming freshmen are eligible for the College's top scholarships, which range up to full comprehensive fee coverage (tuition, room, and board).

Campus Overview

Independent comprehensive, founded 1889 • **Urban** 70-acre campus • **Women only** 756 undergraduate students, 83% full-time.

Undergraduates 629 full-time, 127 part-time. Students come from 30 states and territories, 8 other countries, 28% are from out of state, 10% African American, 0.4% Asian American or Pacific Islander, 1% Hispanic American, 0.4% Native American, 3% international, 3% transferred in, 90% live on campus.

Faculty *Total:* 165, 45% full-time, 46% with terminal degrees. *Student/faculty ratio:* 14:1.

Academic Programs *Special study options:* accelerated degree program, adult/continuing education programs, advanced placement credit, distance learning, double majors, English as a second language, honors programs, independent study, internships, off-campus study, part-time degree program, study abroad, summer session for credit. *ROTC:* Army (c).

Athletics Member NCAA. All Division II. *Intercollegiate sports:* basketball W(s), cheerleading W, cross-country running W(s), soccer W(s), tennis W(s), volleyball W(s). *Intramural sports:* archery W, basketball W, bowling W, equestrian sports W, fencing W, field hockey W, gymnastics W, soccer W, softball W, swimming and diving W, tennis W, volleyball W, weight lifting W.

Costs (2004–05) *Comprehensive fee:* $26,070 includes full-time tuition ($19,960) and room and board ($6110). Full-time tuition and fees vary according to program. Part-time tuition and fees vary according to program.

Financial Aid 159 Federal Work-Study jobs (averaging $1501). 60 state and other part-time jobs (averaging $1000). In 2004, 156 non-need-based awards were made. *Average percent of need met:* 86%. *Average financial aid package:* $17,050. *Average need-based loan:* $4073. *Average need-based gift aid:* $14,296. *Average non-need-based aid:* $17,244.

Contact: Co-directors: Dr. Laura Feitzinger Brown, Assistant Professor of English; *Telephone:* 864-596-9115; *E-mail:* laura.brown@converse.edu. Dr. John Theilmann, Professor of History and Politics; *Telephone:* 864-596-9703; *E-mail:* john.theilmann@converse.edu; Converse College, 580 East Main Street, Spartanburg, South Carolina 29302; *Telephone:* 800-766-1125 (toll-free); *Web site:* http://www.converse.edu/Academics/NisbetHonorsProgram.asp

Francis Marion University
Honors Program
Florence, South Carolina

The Honors Program at Francis Marion University offers higher education that includes extra value. It gives gifted and ambitious students in all majors the opportunity to work with the University's most challenging faculty members in small but stimulating classes, engage in interdisciplinary study that synthesizes knowledge from different disciplines, and achieve their full intellectual potential in preparation for careers and/or graduate or professional school. Participants in the Honors Program are encouraged to take an active role in the learning process and to enter into dialogue with their professors and classmates.

Most honors classes at Francis Marion University are chosen from basic courses that meet general education requirements but employ different, more collaborative, interactive, and interdisciplinary methods and are limited to an enrollment of 15 students per course. Eleven to fifteen honors courses (some including labs) are usually offered each fall and spring semester. There are always some upper-division courses. Three special classes, the Freshman Honors Seminar and the Honors Colloquium and the Honors Independent Study (which may offer credit in the discipline) for upperclassmen, are exciting and engaging offerings that are available only to Honors Program students. Many honors classes meet in the Honors Room, a pleasant seminar-style space, with room to lounge and study when classes are finished. Coffee and hot chocolate are provided, and the room is decorated with framed posters from past Fall Honors Trips. Honors classes often incorporate field trips, dinners, or other special events, and the Honors Program itself offers periodic receptions and other opportunities for honors students and faculty members to meet.

An important feature of the Honors Program is the Honors Student Association (HSA). Membership is open to all honors-eligible students but is optional. HSA coordinates social and academic activities, including receptions, Play Nights, visits with state legislators in Columbia, fund-raising and service activities, and social events. Since 1996, the Honors Program and HSA have sponsored an annual fall trip in November. Groups of 35 students, accompanied by 6 faculty members, have enjoyed fall trips to Washington, D.C.; New York City; Boston; and Orlando (to attend an NCHC Conference). The cost of the fall trips for students is minimal, thanks to University subsidy.

Honors students in their junior year can apply for admission to the Washington Semester Program coordinated by the University of South Carolina's Honors College. Students accepted as fellows live and work in Washington, D.C., for a semester while earning 15 hours of honors credit.

Of the approximately 750 honors-eligible students, 150 are usually enrolled in one to three honors classes in a given semester. The Honors Program was founded in 1985.

Participation Requirements: Initial eligibility for the Honors Program is determined by SAT or ACT scores. A minimum score of 1100 on the SAT or 24 on the ACT qualifies an entering student for the Honors Program. Second-semester freshmen must earn an overall GPA of 3.0 or better in order to become or remain eligible for the Honors Program. Sophomores, juniors, and seniors must earn an overall GPA of 3.25 or better in order to become or remain eligible for the Honors Program.

To graduate With University Honors, students must complete 21 semester hours of honors classes with a minimum GPA of 3.25. Courses taken for at least 9 of these 21 semester hours must be numbered 300 or above. In addition, students must achieve a grade of B or higher in the Honors Colloquium, which deals with a special topic from an interdisciplinary perspective, and successfully complete an Honors Independent Study project. Students graduating With University Honors are awarded a gold Honors Cord at commencement. Each year, the University gives a cash prize to the recipient of the Duane P. Myers Honors Award and the Honors Student Association Award.

Admission Process: Students applying to Francis Marion University with a minimum SAT score of 1100 or a minimum ACT score of 24 are automatically eligible to participate in the Honors Program. The Honors Director and faculty members advise these students as a group, with assistance from current honors students, at their orientation and registration sessions. Students may earn or lose honors eligibility, as described in the section above, while enrolled at Francis Marion University.

Scholarship Availability: Francis Marion University gives substantial academic scholarships, but none through the Honors Program. The honors budget provides funding to support students' research projects and student travel to present papers or panels at conferences.

Campus Overview

State-supported comprehensive, founded 1970 • **Coed** 3,227 undergraduate students, 90% full-time, 63% women, 37% men.

Undergraduates 2,918 full-time, 309 part-time. Students come from 31 states and territories, 21 other countries, 5% are from out of state, 40% African American, 1% Asian American or Pacific Islander, 1% Hispanic American, 0.6% Native American, 1% international, 7% transferred in, 44% live on campus.

Faculty *Total:* 213, 80% full-time, 72% with terminal degrees. *Student/faculty ratio:* 17:1.

Academic Programs *Special study options:* accelerated degree program, adult/continuing education programs, advanced placement credit, distance learning, double majors, honors programs, independent study, internships, off-campus study, part-time degree program, services for LD students, study abroad, summer session for credit. *Unusual degree programs:* 3-2 engineering with Clemson University; forestry with Clemson University.

Athletics Member NCAA. All Division II. *Intercollegiate sports:* baseball M(s), basketball M(s)/W(s), cheerleading M/W, cross-country running M(s)/W(s), golf M(s), soccer M(s)/W(s), softball W(s), tennis M(s)/W(s), track and field M/W, volleyball W(s). *Intramural sports:* basketball M/W, bowling M/W, cheerleading M(c)/W(c), football M/W, golf M/W, racquetball M/W, soccer M/W, softball M/W, table tennis M/W, tennis M/W, track and field M/W, ultimate Frisbee M/W, volleyball M/W.

Costs (2004–05) *Tuition:* state resident $5405 full-time, $270 per credit hour part-time; nonresident $10,810 full-time, $540 per credit hour part-time. Part-time tuition and fees vary according to course load. *Required fees:* $135 full-time, $2 per credit hour part-time. *Room and board:* $4656; room only: $2500. Room and board charges vary according to board plan and housing facility.

Financial Aid 131 Federal Work-Study jobs (averaging $1388).

Contact: Director: Dr. Pamela Rooks, Professor of English, Francis Marion University, Post Office Box 100547, Florence, South Carolina 29501-0547; *Telephone:* 843-661-1526; *Fax:* 843-661-4676; *E-mail:* prooks@fmarion.edu; *Web site:* http://www.fmarion.edu/academics/Honors

Greenville Technical College

Honors Program, Division of Arts and Sciences

Greenville, South Carolina

The Honors Program is designed to enhance the Greenville Tech experience for bright, highly motivated students. It is designed for students who want the most out of college. The program's faculty members welcome the opportunity to help these students stretch their intellectual limits.

The honors classes are modeled after graduate seminars. They are small, allowing maximum interaction between the students and the instructor. Lecturing is minimal. Instead, students are expected to be well-prepared for class to encourage a highly participatory process.

Central to the Honors Program's philosophy is the idea that honors education does not mean more work for students; it means different work. Different in this case means more give and take between the student and the instructor, greater opportunities for independent research, more difficult materials, and enhanced opportunities for creativity and meeting individual goals.

Participation Requirements: An Honors Program graduate must maintain a 3.0 GPA or higher, complete a service requirement, complete at least one seminar course, and complete at least six courses with honors designation.

Admission Process: Current Greenville Tech students and students transferring to Greenville Tech Honors from other colleges must have a GPA of at least 3.4, no less than 9 transferable credit hours, and two letters of recommendation from individuals familiar with their academic performance, at least one of whom is an instructor at the college level. In addition, the honors applicant must submit an essay and have an interview.

High school students entering Greenville Tech Honors must have a high school GPA of at least 3.5 or a score of 1150 or above on the SAT or a score of 26 or above on the ACT. In addition, high school students must submit two letters of recommendation from individuals familiar with their academic performance, at least one of whom is a high school teacher. Students must also interview with Dr. Frank Provenzano, the Honors Program Director.

Scholarship Availability: Many honors students qualify for the LIFE Scholarship (Legislative Incentives for Future Education), recently established by the South Carolina General Assembly and available to students attending South Carolina colleges, in the amount of $1000 each year for students in a two-year college. In addition, scholarships are available to honors students based on academic performance. To apply for these scholarships, students should contact Greenville Tech's Financial Aid Office at 864-250-8128.

Campus Overview

State-supported 2-year, founded 1962, part of South Carolina State Board for Technical and Comprehensive Education • **Coed** 13,000 undergraduate students.

Undergraduates Students come from 6 other countries.

Faculty *Total:* 478, 52% full-time.

Academic Programs *Special study options:* academic remediation for entering students, adult/continuing education programs, advanced placement credit, cooperative education, part-time degree program, summer session for credit.

Athletics *Intramural sports:* basketball M/W, bowling M/W, tennis M/W, volleyball M/W.

Financial Aid 120 Federal Work-Study jobs (averaging $3270).

Contact: Director: Dr. Frank J. Provenzano, P.O. Box 5616, Greenville, South Carolina 29606; *Telephone:* 864-250-8786, 800-922-1183 Ext. 8786 (toll-free in South Carolina), 800-723-0673 Ext. 8786 (toll-free out-of-state); *E-mail:* frank.provenzano@gvltec.edu; *Web site:* http://www.greenvilletech.com

Newberry College

Summerland Honors Program

Newberry, South Carolina

At Newberry College, students and faculty members walk together on the path of knowledge, and along the way they bring to life a distinctive learning community. The Summerland Honors Program accentuates all that is best about living and studying at Newberry College, a place where people are willing to seek innovative and memorable educational opportunities and experiences by taking risks inside and outside of the classroom. The Summerland Honors community is a perfect haven for students to search for understanding and to consider myriad questions, old and new.

In many ways the human story has been and will continue to be a quest for identity. How have we understood what it means to be human? The Summerland Honors Program is structured upon the theme, Quest for Identity, and affords opportunities to explore this essential question from a number of vantage points. Indeed, each of the three years of paired, interdisciplinary, and team-taught seminars focuses on a particular perspective concerning this quest for identity. Year one studies the question from the perspective of the arts and humanities. Year two examines the question through the lens of the natural sciences. The third year probes the quest for identity from the perspective of the social sciences.

In each of the six honors seminars, students also participate in enrichment activities designed to engage them actively in their learning and to provide opportunities for them to apply their knowledge in service to the campus and the local community. Finally, an integrative capstone course in the senior year asks students to reflect and build on the preceding three-year experience. Courses taken in the Honors Program fulfill core requirements in the humanities, natural sciences, and social sciences, as appropriate.

Members of the Summerland Honors community learn to weave a tapestry of understanding around any topic and to layer insight upon insight thereby achieving a breadth and a depth of understanding. Participants become independent learners who take responsibility for leading and sustaining study and discussion on any topic. The service-learning component provides even greater opportunities for growth and rewards. Summerland Honors Program graduates are prepared and motivated for active citizenship, empowered and ready to assume positions of advocacy for social change as a way to make life more productive and meaningful.

An innovative curriculum and a spirited learning community enable participants to realize Newberry College's institutional goals. While educating the whole person, the Summerland Honors Program promotes the development of communication skills (oral and written), the development of critical-thinking skills, and emphasizes an awareness of ethical concerns.

Fall 1996 marked the inaugural year of the program, which is limited each year to 20 participants in the freshmen class. There are a total of 45 to 50 students currently enrolled in the program.

Participation Requirements: In order to graduate from the Honors Program, a student must hold a cumulative 3.25 GPA in the Honors Program and in the general curriculum. Six Summerland Honors Seminars are required to graduate from the program. Students must also complete the Senior Capstone Experience. Successful completion of the Honors Program requirements is noted at graduation, recorded on the student's transcript, and designated on the student's diploma.

Admission Process: Admission to the Summerland Honors Program is based on multidimensional criteria, including high school GPA, high school class rank, SAT/ACT equivalent scores, and interviews with members of the Newberry College community. Applications are received from February to May.

Scholarship Availability: Most Summerland Honors students receive Founder Scholarships and Presidential Scholarships; however, they are eligible for other Newberry College scholarships.

Campus Overview

Independent Evangelical Lutheran 4-year, founded 1856 • **Coed** 771 undergraduate students, 96% full-time, 43% women, 57% men.

Undergraduates 742 full-time, 29 part-time. Students come from 26 states and territories, 13 other countries, 20% are from out of state, 27% African American, 0.1% Asian American or Pacific Islander, 1% Hispanic American, 0.8% Native American, 2% international, 8% transferred in, 87% live on campus.

Faculty *Total:* 69, 67% full-time, 45% with terminal degrees. *Student/faculty ratio:* 12:1.

Academic Programs *Special study options:* adult/continuing education programs, advanced placement credit, cooperative education, double majors, honors programs, independent study, internships, part-time degree program, student-designed majors, study abroad, summer session for credit. *ROTC:* Army (c). *Unusual degree programs:* 3-2 engineering with Clemson University; forestry with Duke University.

Athletics Member NCAA. All Division II. *Intercollegiate sports:* baseball M(s), basketball M(s)/W(s), cheerleading W(s), cross-country running M(s)/W(s), football M(s), golf M(s)/W(s), soccer M(s)/W(s), softball W(s), tennis M(s)/W(s), volleyball W(s), wrestling M(s). *Intramural sports:* basketball M/W, football M.

Costs (2004–05) *Comprehensive fee:* $23,991 includes full-time tuition ($17,470), mandatory fees ($631), and room and board ($5890). Part-time tuition: $300 per credit hour. *Room and board:* Room and board charges vary according to board plan and housing facility.

Financial Aid 52 Federal Work-Study jobs (averaging $804). 45 state and other part-time jobs (averaging $518). In 2002, 104 non-need-based awards were made. *Average percent of need met:* 79%. *Average financial aid package:* $13,886. *Average need-based loan:* $3866. *Average need-based gift aid:* $10,899. *Average non-need-based aid:* $11,851.

Contact: Director: Dr. Charles N. Horn, 2100 College Street, Newberry, South Carolina 29108; *Telephone:* 803-321-5257; *Fax:* 803-321-5636; *E-mail:* chorn@newberry.edu; *Web site:* http://www.newberry.edu

University of South Carolina
South Carolina Honors College
Columbia, South Carolina

*S*outh Carolina Honors College represents the University of South Carolina's (USC's) tangible commitment to providing its finest undergraduates with a superlative education consonant with their abilities and potential. The College serves as a visible and vital academic unit intended to attract the best high school students in the state, region, and country and provide them with a firm foundation for their future achievements.

Over the past three decades, the administrations of five University presidents created and sustained the Honors Program and its successor College. Their efforts resulted in an Honors College offering a peerless academic experience unifying the benefits of a small liberal arts college with the opportunities of a comprehensive university. It fuses these qualities in a unique synthesis, offering complementary combinations and counteracting the potential negatives of each academic environment. Everything that is done reflects the integration, not separation, of these educational alternatives.

As in a fine liberal arts college, Honors College classes are limited in size, populated by talented students, and taught by faculty members dedicated to designing courses that involve these students more actively in their own education. Honors students, however, are not set apart from the University but are a part of it. This simple change in preposition makes a world of difference for the students; it opens to them the world of the comprehensive University, with its research resources, diverse programs and curriculum, and rich campus culture.

The goals of the College are best represented by the type of student it hopes to attract and fulfill: leaders who are scholars; young men and women with a love of learning and faith in the role of reason; students who combine those elements common to all educated people, namely, the ability to use language with clarity and grace;

appreciation of experimental sciences and scientific method; and insight into their own and other cultures through history, literature, and the arts, as well as the social sciences.

The Honors College sets high standards for its students and, therefore, for itself. Success is measured not only by the quality of the students attracted to the College but by the quality of the academic program the College offers them. Graduation with Honors from the South Carolina Honors College involves more than earning good grades; it stands for a substantive experience that challenges the students across the breadth of their academic endeavors.

Each semester, the Honors College offers approximately 125 courses across the undergraduate curriculum. In addition, the graduate schools of law, medicine, and public health also offer honors courses. In the lower division, the College provides courses that may be used to fulfill the general education requirements of all the undergraduate colleges in the University. In addition, upper-division courses are offered in areas with sufficient majors or general interest. Honors courses consist of honors sections of existing University courses or special classes developed especially for and existing only in the Honors College. The Honors College also provides extensive avenues and support for students to participate in undergraduate research and scholarship.

The Honors College office is located on the historic Horseshoe, the antebellum campus of the University. Honors facilities include classrooms, student lounges, and honors housing for up to 700 students.

The College has approximately 1,100 students.

Participation Requirements: Students who wish to earn honors from South Carolina Honors College must complete 45 credits of honors course work, including a 29- to 30-credit core and a 3- to 15-credit senior thesis. Honors core requirements consist of 6 credits of English, 8 of science, 6 of history of civilization, 6 of humanities/social sciences, and at least 3 credits of math/analytical.

Graduation with Honors from South Carolina Honors College is an official University honor that appears on the diploma and the transcript of each student who fulfills the requirements. In addition to formal recognition at each University Commencement, the Honors College holds its own ceremony to recognize those students completing all the requirements.

The College also offers its own interdisciplinary degree, the *Baccalaureus Artium et Scientiae.* In order to be admitted, applicants must be fourth-semester Honors College students with a minimum GPA of 3.6. They must develop a program of study approved by a panel consisting of the Associate Dean and Dean of the Honors College and 2 faculty advisers. They must take the maximum general education requirements of both the Division of Science and Math and the Division of Liberal Arts of the College of Arts and Sciences; complete an advanced foreign language course; take at least 69 credits of honors course work, including at least a 9-credit senior thesis; and maintain a minimum 3.5 GPA.

Admission Process: Entering freshmen generally score more than 1300 on the SAT and rank in the top 5 percent of their high school class. They are selected on the basis of a separate application that includes both academic and extracurricular criteria. Students who have completed at least one semester of college (at USC or elsewhere) may also apply. To remain in the Honors College, students must maintain a minimum GPA that is set at 3.0 their first semester and rises to 3.3 by their senior year. The deadline for applying is December 1.

Scholarship Availability: Two scholarships, the South Carolina Honors College Scholarship and the William A. Mould Scholarship, are administered through the Honors College. The South Carolina Honors College Scholarship is awarded to out-of-state honors students with no other scholarship support. The Mould Scholarship is awarded to deserving students on the basis of need. Recipients are selected based on their enrollment in the Honors College.

The vast majority of honors students hold scholarships granted by the University of South Carolina. Students complete the same application for the University's major merit scholarships as for the Honors College.

Campus Overview

State-supported university, founded 1801, part of University of South Carolina System • **Coed** 17,690 undergraduate students, 88% full-time, 54% women, 46% men.

Undergraduates 15,548 full-time, 2,142 part-time. Students come from 54 states and territories, 66 other countries, 12% are from out of state, 15% African American, 3% Asian American or Pacific Islander, 2% Hispanic American, 0.3% Native American, 1% international, 6% transferred in, 46% live on campus.

Faculty *Total:* 1,520, 73% full-time, 75% with terminal degrees. *Student/faculty ratio:* 17:1.

Academic Programs *Special study options:* accelerated degree program, adult/continuing education programs, advanced placement credit, cooperative education, distance learning, double majors, English as a second language, external degree program, freshman honors college, honors programs, independent study, internships, part-time degree program, services for LD students, student-designed majors, study abroad, summer session for credit. *ROTC:* Army (b), Air Force (b).

Athletics Member NCAA. All Division I except football (Division I-A). *Intercollegiate sports:* baseball M(s), basketball M(s)/W(s), cross-country running W(s), equestrian sports W(s), golf M(s)/W(s), soccer M(s)/W(s), softball W(s), swimming and diving M(s)/W(s), tennis M(s)/W(s), track and field M(s)/W(s), volleyball W(s). *Intramural sports:* badminton M/W, basketball M/W, bowling M/W, football M/W, golf M/W, racquetball M/W, soccer M/W, softball M/W, swimming and diving M/W, table tennis M/W, tennis M/W, track and field M/W, volleyball M/W, weight lifting M(c)/W(c), wrestling M(c).

Costs (2004–05) *Tuition:* state resident $5548 full-time, $260 per credit hour part-time; nonresident $14,886 full-time, $677 per credit hour part-time. Full-time tuition and fees vary according to program and reciprocity agreements. *Required fees:* $230 full-time, $10 per credit hour part-time. *Room and board:* $5590; room only: $3280. Room and board charges vary according to board plan, housing facility, and location.

Financial Aid 726 Federal Work-Study jobs (averaging $2016). In 2003, 4684 non-need-based awards were made. *Average percent of need met:* 80%. *Average financial aid package:* $9188. *Average need-based loan:* $3471. *Average need-based gift aid:* $3352. *Average non-need-based aid:* $5990.

Contact: Dean: Dr. Davis Baird, Harper College, Columbia, South Carolina 29208; *Telephone:* 803-777-8102; *Fax:* 803-777-2214; *E-mail:* db@sc.edu; *Web site:* http://schc.sc.edu

Winthrop University

Honors Program

Rock Hill, South Carolina

The Winthrop University Honors Program has evolved into one of the University's most exciting offerings. The program is designed to enrich the college experience for highly talented and motivated students. Through interactions with outstanding faculty members and peers, a vital community of scholars is created that embraces the pursuit of knowledge for the enhancement of intellectual and personal growth.

Winthrop University's Honors Program encourages learning through a variety of settings, including seminars, independent directed study, interdisciplinary courses, a senior thesis, and a selection of 1-credit intensive symposia centered on great works or current events. The student's course program is constructed by the student with the consultation of his or her adviser and the Director of the Honors Program. After completing the Honors Program at

Winthrop, students not only have a deeper, richer understanding of the content studied, they retain the joy of learning, the strength of independent thought, and the ability to direct their own learning.

Participation Requirements: The Winthrop University Honors Program requires completion of at least 23 hours of honors courses and a service-learning course/project. Students must maintain a minimum cumulative GPA of 3.3 in order to graduate with an Honors Program degree. To receive honors credit for a course, students must complete the course with a minimum grade of B. Any Winthrop University student with a cumulative GPA of 3.3, whether formally admitted into the Honors Program or not, is allowed to enroll in honors courses. In addition to the required service-learning project, students must enroll in courses GNED102H and CRTW201H. They must also take at least 6 credit hours of honors course work inside the major and 3 credit hours of honors course work outside the major, one honors symposium, an honors thesis, and HONR451H. Graduation with an Honors Program degree with international experience requires completion of the above requirements plus and extended experience in a learning environment outside the U.S.

In addition to the honors courses offered each semester through the Honors Program Office, students also have the option of taking a course through contracted study, which involves a student contracting with the professor of a regularly scheduled course to take that course for honors credit.

Admission Process: Incoming freshman students are invited by the Honors Program Director to participate based on their SAT or ACT scores and high school grade point average. All other students are eligible for the Honors Program after they have achieved a GPA of 3.3 or higher. The Honors Program is open to students in all majors at Winthrop University. A Winthrop University Honors Program application form must be completed for consideration and admittance into the program.

Scholarship Availability: Scholarships of various types are offered through the Office of Admissions based on academic performance. The Honors Program Office does not offer any scholarships; however, most honors students are the recipients of academic scholarships.

Campus Overview

State-supported comprehensive, founded 1886, part of South Carolina Commission on Higher Education • **Coed** 5,213 undergraduate students, 89% full-time, 70% women, 30% men.

Undergraduates 4,617 full-time, 596 part-time. Students come from 41 states and territories, 30 other countries, 13% are from out of state, 28% African American, 1% Asian American or Pacific Islander, 1% Hispanic American, 0.4% Native American, 2% international, 7% transferred in, 43% live on campus.

Faculty *Total:* 485, 53% full-time, 54% with terminal degrees. *Student/faculty ratio:* 15:1.

Academic Programs *Special study options:* adult/continuing education programs, advanced placement credit, cooperative education, distance learning, double majors, honors programs, independent study, internships, off-campus study, part-time degree program, services for LD students, study abroad, summer session for credit.

Athletics Member NCAA. All Division I. *Intercollegiate sports:* baseball M(s), basketball M(s)/W(s), cheerleading M(c)/W(c), cross-country running M(s)/W(s), fencing M(c)/W(c), golf M(s)/W(s), lacrosse M(c)/W(c), rugby M(c), soccer M(s), softball W(s), tennis M(s)/W(s), track and field M(s)/W(s), volleyball W(s). *Intramural sports:* badminton M/W, basketball M/W, cross-country running M/W, equestrian sports M(c)/W(c), football M/W, golf M/W, racquetball M/W, soccer M/W, softball M/W, swimming and diving M/W, table tennis M/W, tennis M/W, ultimate Frisbee M/W, volleyball M/W, water polo M/W, weight lifting M/W.

Costs (2004–05) *Tuition:* state resident $7816 full-time, $326 per semester hour part-time; nonresident $14,410 full-time, $601 per semester hour part-time. Full-time tuition and fees vary according to degree level. Part-time tuition and fees vary according to degree level.

Required fees: $20 full-time, $10 per term part-time. *Room and board:* $4992; room only: $3060. Room and board charges vary according to board plan and housing facility.

Financial Aid 250 Federal Work-Study jobs (averaging $880). In 2003, 519 non-need-based awards were made. *Average percent of need met:* 64%. *Average financial aid package:* $8945. *Average need-based loan:* $4884. *Average need-based gift aid:* $5819. *Average non-need-based aid:* $6545.

Contact: Director: Dr. Kathy A. Lyon, 139 Bancroft, Rock Hill, South Carolina 29733; *Telephone:* 803-323-2320; *Fax:* 803-323-3910; *E-mail:* lyonk@winthrop.edu

SOUTH DAKOTA

South Dakota State University
Honors College
Brookings, South Dakota

*T*he South Dakota State University (SDSU) Honors College was not inaugurated until 1999, but the University has offered honors courses since the 1960s and supported a formal University Honors Program for approximately twenty years. The SDSU Honors College is the newest approach to the University's long-standing commitment to excellence in education. It is an investment in the goal to graduate students who are globally aware and competitive, gifted in communication skills, exceptionally knowledgeable in their disciplines, active in community affairs, and motivated to excel in their professional pursuits.

Students participating in the SDSU Honors College benefit in many ways. Learning is enhanced when students form communities and complete limited-enrollment honors courses together. Students grow intellectually as a result of their relationships with faculty mentors on campus and with external mentors drawn from a variety of professions and enterprises. On-campus students have the opportunity to be grouped in a shared housing area, making it easier to form student support and study groups. Students may participate in sponsored undergraduate research under the supervision of University faculty members and are encouraged to participate in a variety of course-centered and Honors College–sponsored enrichment programs. Students receive faculty guidance in seeking highly competitive international, national, and institutional fellowships or scholarships for graduate or professional studies. Graduate study and career opportunities are broadened through the Honors College networking with other universities and public and private-sector employers.

Honors College courses have limited enrollments of no more than 25 students. The courses emphasize student responsibilities for course quality and outcomes and further emphasize active student participation in the learning process. Honors College courses are dedicated to developing the highest level of proficiency in communication skills, critical-thinking skills, and creativity. The Honors Colloquium and the directed study requirement place special emphasis on integration and synthesis of ideas.

Honors College enrichment opportunities, an integral part of Honors College courses, are required beyond academic expectations. These enrichment opportunities are designed to contribute to the social and cultural maturity of students as well as to serve as an alternative means of teaching and learning. Participation in enrichment programs is required in some instances and encouraged in other instances. Enrichment opportunities take many forms, including campus lectures, theater performances, field trips, conference attendance, social gatherings, and study abroad.

Campus residential hall space is dedicated to a residential life program for freshman and sophomore Honors College students on a request basis. Honors College programming, computer usage, and *study areas are included. The residential life program seeks to promote a sense of unity among Honors College students and seeks to facilitate the promotion of Honors College academic and enrichment objectives.*

Current student enrollment in honors courses is approximately 250 students.

Participation Requirements: The Honors College curriculum is a four-year program. The curriculum includes 15 credit hours of honors general education courses, 3- to 6-credit courses of Honors Colloquium, 3 to 6 credit hours of honors directed study, and 6 credit hours of honors contract course work. Participation in enrichment opportunities is also required. A total of 27 honors course credits and a minimum cumulative 3.5 GPA are required to graduate with Honors College distinction.

Admission Process: Incoming freshmen with an ACT score of 27 or above or the equivalent SAT score and/or rank in the upper 10 percent of their high school class are invited to enroll for general education honors sections. Exceptions are made for other students who have demonstrated high academic ability, exceptional motivation, or extraordinary talents. Eligible students who wish to continue in the Honors College must apply for full admission toward the end of their first year. Admission exceptions are made for transfer students. Once accepted for continued enrollment, students must earn a minimum 3.0 GPA for a given semester, complete minimum enrichment opportunities, enroll in Honors courses, and maintain continued enrollment status. There is no additional cost for initial or continued Honors College enrollment.

Scholarship Availability: Honors College students are eligible to apply for one or more of the nearly 2,000 achievement-based University, college, and departmental scholarships. Nearly all Honors students are eligible for a University Foundation–sponsored $1000 four-year renewable scholarship.

Campus Overview

State-supported university, founded 1881 • **Coed** 9,572 undergraduate students, 80% full-time, 53% women, 47% men.

Undergraduates 7,703 full-time, 1,869 part-time. Students come from 33 states and territories, 21 other countries, 25% are from out of state, 0.7% African American, 0.8% Asian American or Pacific Islander, 0.6% Hispanic American, 1% Native American, 0.2% international, 8% transferred in, 28% live on campus.

Faculty *Total:* 547, 75% full-time, 57% with terminal degrees. *Student/faculty ratio:* 19:1.

Academic Programs *Special study options:* academic remediation for entering students, accelerated degree program, adult/continuing education programs, advanced placement credit, cooperative education, distance learning, double majors, freshman honors college, honors programs, independent study, internships, off-campus study, part-time degree program, services for LD students, study abroad, summer session for credit. *ROTC:* Army (b), Air Force (b). *Unusual degree programs:* 3-2 economics.

Athletics Member NCAA. All Division I. *Intercollegiate sports:* baseball M(s), basketball M(s)/W(s), cross-country running M(s)/W(s), equestrian sports W, football M(s), golf M(s)/W(s), ice hockey M(c)/W(c), rugby M(c)/W(c), soccer M(c)/W(s), softball W(s), swimming and diving M(s)/W(s), tennis M(s)/W(s), track and field M(s)/W(s), volleyball W(s), wrestling M(s). *Intramural sports:* badminton M/W, basketball M/W, fencing M(c)/W(c), football M/W, golf M/W, ice hockey M(c)/W, racquetball M/W, softball M/W, swimming and diving M/W, table tennis M/W, tennis M/W, track and field M/W, volleyball M/W, water polo M/W, wrestling M.

Costs (2005–06) *Tuition:* state resident $2291 full-time, $76 per credit part-time; nonresident $7278 full-time, $243 per credit part-time. Full-time tuition and fees vary according to course load and program. Part-time tuition and fees vary according to course load and program. *Required fees:* $2441 full-time, $81 per credit part-time. *Room and board:* $4769; room only: $2113. Room and board charges vary according to board plan and housing facility.

Financial Aid 705 Federal Work-Study jobs (averaging $1039). 2,173 state and other part-time jobs (averaging $1332). In 2004, 932 non-need-based awards were made. *Average percent of need met:* 86%. *Average financial aid package:* $7182. *Average need-based loan:* $4392. *Average need-based gift aid:* $3095. *Average non-need-based aid:* $982.

Contact: Dean of Honors College and Distinguished Professor Robert Burns, SDSU Admin. 315, Box 2201, Brookings, South Dakota 57007; *Telephone:* 605-688-4913; *Fax:* 605-688-6540; *E-mail:* robert.burns@sdstate.edu

The University of South Dakota
University Honors Program
Vermillion, South Dakota

The University of South Dakota's (USD) Honors Program provides especially motivated, creative, and thoughtful students an enriched undergraduate experience and prepares them well for life after college. The program is grounded in the liberal arts and promotes lifelong learning, responsible citizenship, and cultural appreciation. Honors students benefit from a special curriculum of smaller, more challenging classes that complements work done in their chosen major field(s). Honors students participate in a wide array of special events and opportunities sponsored by the Honors Program. Many of USD's honors graduates have won prestigious national scholarships, and the majority go on to pursue graduate and professional training at some of the best institutions across the United States.

The heart and soul of the University Honors Program is the special honors curriculum. Students complete an integrated honors core curriculum instead of the University's general core curriculum. The honors core does not add any additional credit hours. During their freshman and sophomore years, students take a course based on a canon of "great books" and then spend two semesters in an interdisciplinary civilization course taught by at least 4 faculty members from different disciplines. As upperclassmen, honors students complete three honors seminars, courses that join 15 honors students with 1 or more USD professors in a setting that permits intensive interaction on special topics. The seminars promote thoughtful discussion and give students expanded opportunities to exhibit their oral and written communication skills as well as to express themselves in creative projects. Professors from the graduate and professional schools at USD (such as medicine, law, and business) regularly offer honors seminars.

As seniors, honors students choose a committee of professors with whom they design and complete an honors project in an area of personal interest. Honors projects range from original compositions of literature to artistic performances to specialized scientific experiments. Nearly all culminate in a written honors thesis. These projects permit students to enjoy a one-on-one mentoring relationship with professors from all segments of the University.

Honors students come from across the region. They have a wide variety of academic majors. The group makes up about 5 percent of the total student body, but they have a much higher representation in leadership positions across campus. Students have the opportunity to choose to live on the honors floor, a high-energy community of committed scholars. The honors community is further enriched by its student-run Honors Association, which offers fun, yet somewhat educational, programs.

The University Honors Program is housed in three magnificently restored rooms in Old Main—the oldest public higher education building in South Dakota, which was restored and rededicated in 1997. A computerized card entry lock gives Honors Students access to the area after hours. Three desktop computers are available exclusively for use by Honors Students. Students often meet here after classes to check e-mail, chat, or complete papers.

The University Honors Program, which has been open to students in all undergraduate majors since 1968, currently enrolls about 270 students. It is administered by a Faculty Director, a full-time Associate Director, and a secretary.

Participation Requirements: The honors core curriculum includes both honors classes (specially designed courses only for honors students) and honors requirements (regularly scheduled courses open to all students). Required honors courses include English composition, speech, Ideas in History, interdisciplinary civilization, and three seminars, as well as a thesis. Honors requirements include 1 year of a laboratory science, one semester of calculus (or a semester of trigonometry or precalculus and honors logic), 1 year of a foreign language, and a course in the fine arts. Advanced Placement and transfer credits are usually accepted for all honors requirements and for honors English composition.

Admission Process: Students must submit an application form, high school transcript, ACT or SAT I scores, and a resume of high school awards and activities. The honors staff evaluates the students' test scores, high school grades, class rank, choice of high school courses, and honors/awards/activities. Successful applicants usually have test scores and high school grades in the 90th percentile or above. However, the committee also considers evidence of exceptional ability and/or motivation that may not be shown by test scores or grades.

Most students apply for admission as first-year students, but students in the first two or three semesters of college are encouraged to apply as well. For these students, the committee looks for evidence of undergraduate success. Applications are considered on a rolling basis.

Scholarship Availability: USD offers several major merit-based scholarships for talented students, most of whom participate in the Honors Program. National Merit Finalists who specify USD as their first college of choice are automatically eligible for resident tuition, fees, and room and board for four years. USD's prestigious Presidential Alumni Scholarship provides four years of resident tuition and fees. The USD School of Medicine offers up to six early admissions to the School of Medicine to superior South Dakota applicants who enter the Honors Program, and the Law School has a similar program for up to 5 South Dakota applicants.

Campus Overview

State-supported university, founded 1862 • **Coed** 6,024 undergraduate students, 68% full-time, 62% women, 38% men.

Undergraduates 4,088 full-time, 1,936 part-time. Students come from 41 states and territories, 18 other countries, 27% are from out of state, 0.8% African American, 0.7% Asian American or Pacific Islander, 1% Hispanic American, 2% Native American, 1% international, 11% transferred in, 31% live on campus.

Faculty *Total:* 345, 97% full-time, 78% with terminal degrees. *Student/faculty ratio:* 15:1.

Academic Programs *Special study options:* advanced placement credit, distance learning, double majors, English as a second language, honors programs, independent study, internships, off-campus study, part-time degree program, services for LD students, study abroad, summer session for credit. *ROTC:* Army (b). *Unusual degree programs:* 3-2 accounting.

Athletics Member NCAA. All Division II. *Intercollegiate sports:* baseball M(s), basketball M(s)/W(s), cross-country running M(s)/W(s), football M(s), softball W(s), swimming and diving M(s)/W, tennis M(s)/W(s), track and field M(s)/W(s), volleyball W(s). *Intramural sports:* badminton M/W, basketball M(c)/W(c), bowling M/W, cross-country running M/W, fencing M(c)/W(c), football M(c)/W(c), golf M/W, ice hockey M(c), racquetball M(c)/W(c), riflery M/W, rugby M(c), soccer M(c)/W(c), softball M(c)/W(c), swimming and diving M/W, table tennis M/W, tennis M/W, track and field M/W, volleyball M/W, water polo M/W.

Costs (2004–05) *Tuition:* state resident $2371 full-time, $74 per credit hour part-time; nonresident $7538 full-time, $236 per credit hour part-time. Full-time tuition and fees vary according to course load and reciprocity agreements. Part-time tuition and fees vary according to course load and reciprocity agreements. *Required fees:* $2378 full-time, $74 per credit hour part-time. *Room and board:* $3741; room only: $1937. Room and board charges vary according to board plan and housing facility.

Financial Aid 650 Federal Work-Study jobs (averaging $1200). In 2003, 831 non-need-based awards were made. *Average percent of need met:* 75%. *Average financial aid package:* $6032. *Average need-based loan:* $3562. *Average need-based gift aid:* $3037. *Average non-need-based aid:* $5643.

Contact: Director: Dr. Doug Peterson, Old Main 120, 414 East Clark Street, Vermillion, South Dakota 57069; *Telephone:* 605-677-5223; *Fax:* 605-677-3137; *E-mail:* honors@usd.edu; *Web site:* http://www.usd.edu/honors

TENNESSEE

Belmont University
Honors Program
Nashville, Tennessee

*T*he Honors Program at Belmont University was created to provide an enrichment opportunity for students who have a potential for superior academic performance and who seek added challenge and breadth in their studies. The program is designed to allow students to advance as fast as their ability permits and to encourage a range and depth of learning in their study, in keeping with faculty members' expectations of excellence for honors students.

Students are offered a creative curriculum, flexibility and individualization in the formation of their degree plans, the collegiality of like-minded and equally dedicated peers, and academic and personal support from a tutorial relationship with a faculty member in the student's major field.

The honors curriculum is an alternative general education curriculum core that substitutes for the regular general education core for any baccalaureate degree. The 47 hours include 24 hours of interdisciplinary courses arranged around time frames in the development of Western culture, 8 hours of interdisciplinary math and science, 6 hours of courses outside the usual curriculum, 6 hours of tutorial study with a faculty member in the student's major, and a 3-hour thesis.

Successful completion of Belmont's Honors Program gives the student the designation of Belmont Scholar at graduation, which is noted orally, in the bulletin, and on the diploma.

There are approximately 125 students in the program, with the entering class limited to 36 students per year. The deadline for applying is February 15.

Admission Process: Students applying to the Honors Program should have both an outstanding high school record and a composite entrance examination score (ACT or SAT I) predictive of their ability to do honors work. In addition, students submit samples of their writing and are interviewed by the director.

Scholarship Availability: Belmont offers many types of financial awards and scholarships to academically superior students. Many students with these awards are also Honors Program students, but no financial aid is linked to participation in the program.

Campus Overview

Independent Baptist comprehensive, founded 1951 • **Coed** 3,317 undergraduate students, 90% full-time, 62% women, 38% men.

Undergraduates 2,973 full-time, 344 part-time. Students come from 48 states and territories, 27 other countries, 51% are from out of state, 3% African American, 2% Asian American or Pacific Islander, 2% Hispanic American, 0.4% Native American, 1% international, 9% transferred in, 57% live on campus.

Faculty *Total:* 437, 46% full-time, 33% with terminal degrees. *Student/faculty ratio:* 12:1.

Academic Programs *Special study options:* accelerated degree program, adult/continuing education programs, advanced placement credit, cooperative education, distance learning, double majors, honors programs, independent study, internships, off-campus study, part-time degree program, student-designed majors, study abroad, summer session for credit. *ROTC:* Army (c), Navy (c). *Unusual degree programs:* 3-2 engineering with Auburn University, Georgia Institute of Technology, University of Tennessee.

Athletics Member NCAA. All Division I. *Intercollegiate sports:* baseball M(s), basketball M(s)/W(s), cross-country running M(s)/W(s), golf M(s)/W(s), soccer M(s)/W(s), softball W(s), tennis M(s)/W(s), track and field M(s)/W(s), volleyball W(s). *Intramural sports:* basketball M/W, bowling M/W, football M, golf M, racquetball M/W, table tennis M/W, tennis M/W, volleyball M/W.

Costs (2004–05) *Comprehensive fee:* $22,376 includes full-time tuition ($15,360), mandatory fees ($860), and room and board ($6156). Full-time tuition and fees vary according to class time and course load. Part-time tuition: $585 per credit hour. Part-time tuition and fees vary according to course load. *Required fees:* $290 per term part-time. *College room only:* $2950. Room and board charges vary according to board plan, housing facility, and location.

Financial Aid 197 Federal Work-Study jobs (averaging $1382). In 2003, 516 non-need-based awards were made. *Average percent of need met:* 37%. *Average financial aid package:* $3527. *Average need-based loan:* $3765. *Average need-based gift aid:* $2463. *Average non-need-based aid:* $6503.

Contact: Director: Devon Boan, Professor, 1900 Belmont Blvd., Nashville, Tennessee 37212; *Telephone:* 615-460-6472; *E-mail:* boand@mail.belmont.edu; *Web site:* http://www.belmont.edu/honors/

Chattanooga State Technical Community College

Honors Program

Chattanooga, Tennessee

The Chattanooga State Honors Program is an offering of courses and related educational activities designed to provide an enriched collegiate experience for able and highly motivated students. Sections are smaller, offering more individual attention from instructors and more opportunities for independent and original work by students. Class offerings represent a variety of disciplines and areas of focused study: engineering, statistics, English composition, English literature, American literature, world literature, Shakespeare, calculus, leadership development, world history, U.S. history, general psychology, sociology, creative writing (fiction and poetry sections), creative writing on line, Southern culture, folklore, public speaking, religions of the world, Western philosophy, contemporary women artists and writers, and others.

An atmosphere of camaraderie is promoted within the Honors Program; thus, faculty members and students attend local cultural events, such as concerts, operas, and theater productions, or they may visit art museums, historical sites, and other related sites. These events are coordinated with the classroom experience and enhance the development of the student both academically and socially. Students may also be eligible to present outstanding papers or projects at Honors Conferences or participate in conference activities. As with all reputable Honors Programs at other community colleges, universities, and four-year colleges in Tennessee, the Honors Program at Chattanooga State is a member of the National Collegiate Honors Council, the Southern Regional Honors Council, and the Tennessee Honors Council.

Honors students have priority enrollment in the annual spring break trip to Europe. Sponsored by the Honors Program, this trip provides an exceptional learning experience for honors students, who visit London, Paris, Rome, Amsterdam, Athens, and many other European cities. Students may receive up to 6 hours of credit in honors course work during the trip.

Chattanooga State is one of seventeen community colleges in the country to be selected as a site of the Phi Theta Kappa Leadership Development Program. The program's central focus is on the development of skills that aid students in increasing their understanding of themselves and of the theories and techniques of leadership and of group processes. The key course in this program, Leadership Development, is offered through the Chattanooga State Honors Program.

The Chattanooga State Honors Program has been in existence for about fifteen years.

Participation Requirements: To graduate with an honors diploma and to have the honors designation on the transcript, students must complete a total of four honors classes and satisfy the other course requirements of their respective majors. In the process, they must maintain a minimum 3.5 GPA.

Admission Process: To be eligible for the Honors Program, presently enrolled students must have completed a minimum of 15 semester hours of course work (excluding transitional studies) and have a GPA of at least 3.5, unless granted conditional acceptance by the coordinator. Incoming freshmen must have an ACT composite score of 25 or higher or a high school GPA of 3.5 or greater, unless they have been granted conditional acceptance by the coordinator. In addition to meeting the eligibility requirements, prospective honors students must complete each element of the honors application and secure two letters of recommendation for their entry into the program.

Scholarship Availability: A number of Honors Program scholarships are available to eligible full-time honors students (both incoming students and those currently enrolled). These scholarships cover full tuition and $150 of book expenses for up to four semesters (fall and spring). To retain an honors scholarship for the four semesters, recipients must maintain a minimum 3.5 GPA, must maintain full-time status, and must be enrolled in at least one honors course per semester.

Campus Overview

State-supported 2-year, founded 1965, part of Tennessee Board of Regents • **Coed** 8,121 undergraduate students, 47% full-time, 62% women, 38% men.

Undergraduates 3,782 full-time, 4,339 part-time. Students come from 5 states and territories, 19% African American, 1% Asian American or Pacific Islander, 1% Hispanic American, 0.4% Native American, 22% transferred in.

Faculty *Total:* 626, 32% full-time. *Student/faculty ratio:* 22:1.

Academic Programs *Special study options:* academic remediation for entering students, accelerated degree program, adult/continuing education programs, advanced placement credit, cooperative education, distance learning, English as a second language, honors programs, independent study, internships, part-time degree program, services for LD students, summer session for credit.

Athletics Member NJCAA. *Intercollegiate sports:* baseball M(s), basketball M(s)/W(s), softball W(s). *Intramural sports:* softball W.

Costs (2004–05) *Tuition:* state resident $1952 full-time; nonresident $6072 full-time. *Required fees:* $339 full-time.

Financial Aid 377 Federal Work-Study jobs (averaging $652).

Contact: Coordinator of the Honors Program: Jeff McEwen, 4501 Amnicola Highway, Chattanooga, Tennessee 37406; *Telephone:* 423-697-4739; *Fax:* 423-697-4430; *E-mail:* jeff.mcewen@ chattanoogastate.edu

Christian Brothers University
Honors Program
Memphis, Tennessee

The Christian Brothers University (CBU) Honors Program offers an enriched academic experience to gifted and highly motivated students in all disciplines. Members of the Honors Program take a series of special-topics courses with limited enrollment, usually about 20 students. These courses are offered in a variety of disciplines and fulfill general education requirements for all majors. The program offers students the opportunity to explore challenging topics in small groups led by faculty members chosen for their interest in developing courses especially designed for the Honors Program and for their commitment to teaching honors students. The program offers special-topics courses in English, history, philosophy, political science, psychology, economics, sociology, and religion as well as a senior seminar. Program-sponsored social and cultural events provide opportunities for extracurricular enrichment and create a sense of community among honors students and faculty members.

The CBU Honors Program is now in its fifteenth year. Currently, there are 120 students in the Honors Program.

Participation Requirements: Students participate in the program at two levels. Some students earn Honors Program Diplomas by taking at least six honors courses, including the senior seminar, and maintaining at least a 3.2 GPA. Others take fewer honors courses, selecting those most closely related to their academic interests.

Admission Process: First-year students are invited to apply for admission to the Honors Program during the spring before they enroll at CBU. Invitation to the program is based on high school grades and ACT or SAT I scores. A personal interview is also part of the selection process. Transfer students and students who are not initially selected for membership may also apply for admission, usually after completing one semester at CBU.

Campus Overview

Independent Roman Catholic comprehensive, founded 1871 • **Coed** 1,572 undergraduate students, 78% full-time, 55% women, 45% men.

Undergraduates 1,228 full-time, 344 part-time. Students come from 31 states and territories, 22 other countries, 16% are from out of state, 36% African American, 5% Asian American or Pacific Islander, 2% Hispanic American, 2% international, 3% transferred in, 31% live on campus.

Faculty *Total:* 176, 60% full-time, 67% with terminal degrees. *Student/faculty ratio:* 12:1.

Academic Programs *Special study options:* accelerated degree program, advanced placement credit, double majors, honors programs, internships, off-campus study, part-time degree program, study abroad, summer session for credit. *ROTC:* Army (c), Navy (c), Air Force (c).

Athletics Member NCAA. All Division II. *Intercollegiate sports:* baseball M(s), basketball M(s)/W(s), cross-country running M/W, golf M, soccer M(s)/W(s), softball W(s), tennis M/W, volleyball W(s). *Intramural sports:* basketball M/W, bowling M/W, cross-country running M/W, football M/W, golf M, racquetball M/W, soccer M/W, softball M/W, swimming and diving M/W, table tennis M/W, volleyball M/W.

Costs (2004–05) *Comprehensive fee:* $23,530 includes full-time tuition ($17,710), mandatory fees ($520), and room and board

($5300). Full-time tuition and fees vary according to class time. Part-time tuition: $555 per credit hour. Part-time tuition and fees vary according to class time. *College room only:* $2390. Room and board charges vary according to board plan and housing facility.

Financial Aid 289 Federal Work-Study jobs (averaging $1050). 313 state and other part-time jobs (averaging $1000). In 2004, 327 non-need-based awards were made. *Average percent of need met:* 75%. *Average financial aid package:* $13,967. *Average need-based loan:* $4195. *Average need-based gift aid:* $5832. *Average non-need-based aid:* $9410.

Contact: Director: Dr. Tracie Burke, 650 East Parkway South, Memphis, Tennessee 38104-5581; *Telephone:* 901-321-3357; *Fax:* 901-321-4340

East Tennessee State University
Honors College
Johnson City, Tennessee

East Tennessee State University (ETSU) offers a variety of honors programs designed to provide special educational curricula for academically talented students and a variety of honors opportunities designed to encourage all students to pursue their studies outside the classroom. Within this mission, the goals focus on recruiting exceptional students; nurturing their intellectual growth through challenging curricula; promoting their commitment to active lifelong learning, leadership, and service; and instilling in them a desire to advance knowledge in their chosen fields. In order to accomplish these goals, a series of formal, application-based honors programs are offered, and grant and scholarship awards to support study abroad, international educational exchange, and undergraduate research and creative activities are available to all qualified students. Honors programs enlist exceptional faculty members who promote innovative and creative approaches to teaching in their classrooms and laboratories. Honors courses are small and provide special enrichment opportunities. Honors Scholars collaborate with professors in research and scholarly activities and receive assistance in the pursuit of fellowships, awards, and access to continued studies in graduate and professional programs.

Honors programs available include the University Honors Scholars Program, Midway Scholars Program, Arts Scholars Program, and a variety of Honors-in-Discipline programs based in colleges and departments. Discipline-specific programs are designed for students majoring in a specific area and currently are available in the Colleges of Business & Technology; Education; and Nursing (junior admission only); and in the Departments of Biological Sciences; Chemistry; Criminal Justice & Criminology; English; Environmental Health; History; Mathematics; Philosophy; Physics, Astronomy & Geology; and Psychology. New honors-in-discipline programs are added each year. University Honors Scholars and Midway Scholars may major in any of the 115 academic programs available at ETSU. Arts Scholars typically major in the fine arts, graphic design, digital media, music, bluegrass, theater, or broadcasting. Special colloquia are offered for all honors programs, and workshops assist students with applications to named scholarship/ fellowship programs and to graduate and professional schools.

The four-year University Honors Scholars Program, founded in 1993, is specially designed for incoming freshmen (22 each year) who desire an interdisciplinary approach to general education in addition to their chosen fields of interest. Most general education requirements in this program are provided by yearlong interdisciplinary seminars that emphasize active learning through writing, discussion, and service-learning projects. Students take each honors general education seminar with their own honors class. Faculty teams from *different disciplines, each with established teaching and scholarly reputations, design these courses to integrate information across traditional academic boundaries. For their senior theses, students work in their major or minor interest in collaboration with a faculty member in a significant creative research project. University Scholars have unlimited access to Honors House, including computer facilities and study and meeting rooms. Students are encouraged to participate actively in the Honors Student Council and Honors Advisory Committee in addition to other campus organizations. A variety of social and cultural events are arranged each year for University Honors Scholars.*

The Midway Scholars Program provides honors programming for 20 exceptional transfer students each year. In this new program, students take honors classes specific to their fields of study, an orientation to research class, and complete a senior research project and honors thesis. Students also have opportunity to apply for a one-time award to fund a study abroad or a fifth semester of study at ETSU. Midway Scholars have access to computers, study areas, and seminar and meeting rooms in the new Honors College facility on campus.

The Arts Scholars program admits 25 freshmen each year who participate in a program designed to support an interdisciplinary group of student artists who share the experience of learning about art together. Students share their endeavors and part of their course work with their incoming class and participate with other Arts Scholars in a Roving Artists company designed to bring mini-productions and special exhibits to the campus and region. The program provides a special colloquium, Artistic Vision course, an arts diversity requirement (two courses outside the area of expertise), and a community service requirement (10 hours per semester). Students work closely with exceptional faculty artists in a variety of areas. Arts Scholars have access to computers, study areas, and seminar and meeting rooms in the new Honors College facility on campus, as well as a dedicated production facility for the Roving Arts company.

Participation Requirements: All Honors Scholars must complete a major senior project in research or creative activities and an honors thesis appropriate to their area of expertise. University Honors Scholars must successfully complete a minimum of 15 hours per semester, attain a GPA of at least 3.0 by their second semester, and maintain a minimum GPA of 3.25 for their fourth and all remaining semesters. Required honors courses include a calculus (one semester), U.S. history (two semesters), and 24 hours of honors general education seminars. Probationary status may be granted for one semester only before scholarship support is withdrawn. University Honors Scholar status is designated on all diplomas and transcripts; special regalia and ceremonies also are provided. Discipline-specific honors programs include a minimum of 12 credits of honors courses in the discipline plus the capstone senior honors project and thesis. GPA requirements vary, but graduates must have a 3.2 or better. Midway Scholars must enroll in 15 credit hours per semester, attain at least a 3.0 GPA in their first semester at ETSU and at least a 3.25 GPA each semester thereafter, and successfully complete all curriculum requirements, including the capstone senior project and thesis. Students not meeting these requirements are provided one probationary semester with financial support and one semester without support. Arts Scholars must maintain a minimum overall GPA of 2.5 and successfully meet all service and curriculum requirements, including the capstone senior honors project and thesis.

Admission Process: Candidates for any ETSU honors program must submit a special application; deadlines currently vary, so students should check the Web site. Scholarships are awarded on a competitive basis, and all applications are evaluated by teams of faculty members and advisers specialized to each program. The University Honors Scholars Program admits 22 incoming freshmen each fall (transfer students are not accepted to this program); minimum requirements for application include an ACT score of at least 29 or an SAT score of 1280 or higher and a minimum high school GPA of 3.5 (4.0 scale). Information on high school curriculum, extracurricular activities, previous scholastic honors, letters of recommendation, and submission of a essay to a standardized question are evaluated. The Midway

Scholars Program admits 20 transfer students (minimum 30 credit hours) each year; minimum requirements are a 3.5 GPA and at least 30 earned credit hours from the previous school. Information on extracurricular activities, letters of recommendation, and response to a standardized essay question are evaluated. The Arts Scholars Program admits 25 freshmen each year; minimum requirements are 2.8 high school GPA, a 22 ACT or 1050 SAT, and documentation of exceptional expertise in an artistic area. Information on extacurricular activities, letters of recommendation, and a narrative response to a standardized essay are required, as well as submission of a portfolio representing the quality and range of artistic endeavors. Special guidelines for contents and format of the artistic portfolio are provided on the Web site. Honors-in-discipline programs often require special application, either for incoming freshmen, transfer students, or students already enrolled. Minimum qualifications include at least a 3.2 high school GPA and 25 ACT/1160 SAT or a minimum 3.2 college GPA for transfer students.

Scholarship Availability: All students not currently residents of Tennessee who are accepted in any ETSU honors program receive a scholarship equivalent to out-of-state tuition. Limited numbers of scholarships equivalent to in-state tuition and fees are available for students in all honors programs. Honors-in-Discipline programs offer scholarships ranging from two to eight semesters, dependent on when the student is accepted. University Honors Scholars receive support for eight regular semesters, including full tuition and fees, book allowance, and costs of standard room and board. University Honors Scholars are expected to live on campus for their freshman and sophomore years. Midway Scholars receive a scholarship providing full tuition and fees and book allowance for four semesters of study and a chance to apply for funds to assist with research expenses, study abroad, or a fifth semester of study. Arts Scholars receive a scholarship for eight regular semesters; Tennessee residents receive in-state tuition and fees and out-of-state students receive a scholarship equivalent to out-of-state tuition.

Campus Overview

State-supported university, founded 1911, part of State University and Community College System of Tennessee, Tennessee Board of Regents • **Coed** 9,672 undergraduate students, 83% full-time, 58% women, 42% men.

Undergraduates 7,988 full-time, 1,684 part-time. Students come from 44 states and territories, 52 other countries, 9% are from out of state, 4% African American, 1% Asian American or Pacific Islander, 1% Hispanic American, 0.4% Native American, 1% international, 9% transferred in, 21% live on campus.

Faculty *Total:* 760, 63% full-time, 53% with terminal degrees. *Student/faculty ratio:* 17:1.

Academic Programs *Special study options:* accelerated degree program, adult/continuing education programs, advanced placement credit, cooperative education, distance learning, double majors, freshman honors college, honors programs, independent study, internships, off-campus study, part-time degree program, services for LD students, study abroad, summer session for credit. *ROTC:* Army (b).

Athletics Member NCAA. All Division I. *Intercollegiate sports:* baseball M(s), basketball M(s)/W(s), cross-country running M(s)/W(s), golf M(s)/W(s), soccer W(s), softball W(s), tennis M(s)/W(s), track and field M(s)/W(s), volleyball W(s). *Intramural sports:* basketball M/W, cross-country running M/W, football M/W, golf M/W, racquetball M/W, softball M/W, tennis M/W, volleyball W, weight lifting M.

Costs (2004–05) *Tuition:* state resident $3352 full-time, $147 per hour part-time; nonresident $11,840 full-time, $515 per hour part-time. Full-time tuition and fees vary according to course load and program. *Required fees:* $707 full-time, $45 per hour part-time, $4 per term part-time. *Room and board:* $4858; room only: $2200. Room and board charges vary according to board plan and housing facility.

Financial Aid 751 Federal Work-Study jobs (averaging $1183). 426 state and other part-time jobs (averaging $916). In 2003, 1150 non-need-based awards were made. *Average percent of need met: 82%. Average financial aid package:* $4895. *Average need-based loan:* $3343. *Average need-based gift aid:* $3228. *Average non-need-based aid:* $3267.

Contact: Dean: Dr. Rebecca Pyles, 914 West Maple Street, P.O. Box 70294, Johnson City, Tennessee 37614-0294; *Telephone:* 423-439-6456; *Fax:* 423-439-6191; *E-mail:* honors@etsu.edu; *Web site:* http://www.etsu.edu/honors

Freed–Hardeman University
Honors College
Henderson, Tennessee

The Freed-Hardeman University (FHU) Honors College seeks to provide the optimum educational experience for the talented student in the setting of a Christian university. In honors, attention is given to oral and written communication skills and to the ability to think and respond quickly under pressure. The program blends a strong emphasis on a liberal arts education with the opportunity to pursue guided, independent study in technical or specialized areas. Graduates of the program not only have the necessary theoretical knowledge for success in their field, but also possess problem-solving and communication skills.

Since 1974, the program has served to enhance the undergraduate experience of Freed-Hardeman's best students. Students in honors represent every department in the University having earned H grades (A with honors) in 336 different courses. The Honors Student Association has approximately 135 members.

Participation Requirements: Continued participation in the program or association requires that students maintain at least a 3.3 GPA. Honors College membership and recognition at graduation requires a higher GPA and a special application process, including a faculty interview.

Admission Process: Entry into the program is by invitation after an application process for incoming freshmen or by invitation based on GPA for students with more than 30 semester hours of completed work at FHU. Students transferring from honors programs at accredited colleges and universities are welcomed into honors at Freed-Hardeman and their prior honors work may count as much as 40 percent of the total requirements for graduation with honors. Honors College admission requires success in honors course work at FHU, appropriate GPA, letters of recommendation, and a personal interview.

Scholarship Availability: Freed-Hardeman offers a number of scholarships to students of exceptional ability. Many students receiving these scholarships are also in honors. The Joe and Malinda Ivey College Scholarship provides special assistance to students who are members of minority groups.

Campus Overview

Independent comprehensive, founded 1869, affiliated with Church of Christ • **Coed** 1,440 undergraduate students, 95% full-time, 54% women, 46% men.

Undergraduates 1,367 full-time, 73 part-time. Students come from 35 states and territories, 18 other countries, 48% are from out of state, 4% African American, 0.5% Asian American or Pacific Islander, 0.4% Hispanic American, 0.6% Native American, 2% international, 4% transferred in, 81% live on campus.

Faculty *Total:* 135, 73% full-time, 69% with terminal degrees. *Student/faculty ratio:* 15:1.

Academic Programs *Special study options:* academic remediation for entering students, accelerated degree program, advanced placement credit, cooperative education, double majors, honors programs, independent study, internships, off-campus study, part-time degree program, services for LD students, student-designed majors, study abroad, summer session for credit. *Unusual degree programs:* 3-2 engineering with Tennessee Technological University, Auburn University, Vanderbilt University, University of Tennessee, Oklahoma Christian University, The University of Memphis.

Athletics Member NAIA. *Intercollegiate sports:* baseball M(s), basketball M(s)/W(s), cheerleading M/W(s), soccer M(s)/W(s), softball W(s), tennis M(s)/W(s), volleyball W(s). *Intramural sports:* basketball M/W, football M/W, racquetball M/W, softball M/W, table tennis M/W, tennis M/W, volleyball M/W.

Costs (2005–06) *Comprehensive fee:* $18,640 includes full-time tuition ($10,500), mandatory fees ($1940), and room and board ($6200). Full-time tuition and fees vary according to course load and degree level. Part-time tuition: $350 per semester hour. Part-time tuition and fees vary according to course load and degree level. *Required fees:* $72 per semester hour part-time. *College room only:* $3440. Room and board charges vary according to board plan and housing facility.

Financial Aid In 2003, 251 non-need-based awards were made. *Average percent of need met:* 59%. *Average financial aid package:* $9025. *Average need-based loan:* $3689. *Average need-based gift aid:* $5761. *Average non-need-based aid:* $10,088.

Contact: Dean: Dr. Rolland W. Pack, 158 East Main Street, Henderson, Tennessee 38340; *Telephone:* 731-989-6057; *Fax:* 731-983-3112; *E-mail:* rpack@fhu.edu; *Web site:* http://www.fhu.edu

Lipscomb University
Honors Program
Nashville, Tennessee

The Lipscomb University Honors Program offers additional and unique opportunities for academically talented students to enrich their college academic and cultural experience. The program is open to all majors and requires no additional fees. Students enroll in classes which have fewer students and which are taught by faculty recognized in their departments as outstanding at stimulating discussion, independent thought, and interdisciplinary approaches to course content. Students are encouraged to develop research for presentation at state, regional and national conferences and to pursue innovative internships and study abroad opportunities.

Many honors students take advantage of the university study abroad programs in Vienna and in Greece and the overseas summer internship program in London. In addition, students have participated in the Oxford Honors Program sponsored by the Council of Christian Colleges and Universities as well as in the film studies semester and the Russian history experience offered through CCCU.

In addition to the academic experience, students in the honors program participate in a number of cultural activities each year. Since Lipscomb is located in Nashville, Tennessee, students have opportunities to attend major theater productions, Broadway musicals, symphonies and to visit the exhibits of major art collections at three large area museums. Students can also hear a great selection of blues, jazz, bluegrass, and ethnic music performed at several venues in and around Nashville.

Participation Requirements: Students select honors sections of general education courses for the majority of the 25 hours required for graduation. In addition they must take an interdisciplinary seminar and write a thesis, typically in their major field of study. Recent seminars have focused on mythology, the intersection of religion and literature, social consequences of communications technology, and cosmology. To finish the program, students must have a 3.5 cumulative GPA. Students who do graduate with honors are so noted both in the commencement ceremony bulletin and on their official university transcript.

Admission Process: Admission to the program is guaranteed for students who score 27 and above on the ACT or 1220 and above on the SAT. Students who do not meet these requirements in their first semester can enter the program after they have achieved a 3.5 GPA. Transfer students who have been in an honors program on their campuses and who have a 3.5 GPA are also eligible to enter the program. Students seeking admission to the program can find an on-line application at http://honors.lipscomb.edu or they can write to the director at the address provided in this description.

Scholarship Availability: Lipscomb awards more than $11.5 million in institutional scholarships and grants. Lipscomb offers tuition scholarships to National Merit Finalists and to students with outstanding scores on the ACT or SAT.

Campus Overview

Independent comprehensive, founded 1891, affiliated with Church of Christ • **Coed** 2,316 undergraduate students.

Undergraduates 5% African American, 0.1% Asian American or Pacific Islander, 2% Hispanic American, 0.2% Native American, 2% international.

Faculty *Total:* 201, 61% full-time. *Student/faculty ratio:* 13:1.

Academic Programs *Special study options:* academic remediation for entering students, accelerated degree program, adult/continuing education programs, advanced placement credit, distance learning, double majors, honors programs, independent study, internships, part-time degree program, services for LD students, study abroad, summer session for credit. *ROTC:* Army (c), Air Force (c). *Unusual degree programs:* 3-2 engineering with Auburn University, Vanderbilt University, Tennessee Technical University, University of Tennessee; nursing with Vanderbilt University, Belmont University.

Athletics Member NCAA. All Division I. *Intercollegiate sports:* baseball M(s), basketball M(s)/W(s), cross-country running M(s)/W(s), golf M(s)/W(s), soccer M(s)/W(s), softball W(s), tennis M(s)/W(s), volleyball W(s). *Intramural sports:* basketball M/W, football M/W, racquetball M/W, soccer M/W, softball M/W, table tennis M/W, tennis M/W, volleyball M/W.

Costs (2004–05) *Comprehensive fee:* $19,576 includes full-time tuition ($13,022), mandatory fees ($464), and room and board ($6090). Full-time tuition and fees vary according to degree level and location. Part-time tuition: $475 per hour. Part-time tuition and fees vary according to class time, degree level, and location. *Room and board:* Room and board charges vary according to board plan, housing facility, and location.

Financial Aid 124 Federal Work-Study jobs (averaging $1545). In 2003, 804 non-need-based awards were made. *Average percent of need met:* 79%. *Average financial aid package:* $8909. *Average need-based loan:* $5755. *Average need-based gift aid:* $1698. *Average non-need-based aid:* $5826.

Contact: Director, Dr. Paul Prill, Lipscomb University, 3901 Granny White Pike, Nashville, Tennessee 37204; *Telephone:* 615-279-5805; *Fax:* 615-269-1830; *E-mail:* Paul.Prill@lipscomb.edu; *Web site:* http://honors.lipscomb.edu

Middle Tennessee State University
Honors College
Murfreesboro, Tennessee

*T*he 26-year-old MTSU Honors College is a 31-semester-hour integrated enrichment program offering courses in all five of the University colleges.

The Honors College commitment to enrichment extends beyond the classroom. The Honors Student Association participates in University events, and the College hosts weekly cultural activities. Also offered is the Honors Lecture Series, an interdisciplinary approach to a single topic where faculty members, administrators, and guest speakers lecture from their discipline's perspective. In addition, the Honors College features an Honors Living and Learning Residential Center.

Outstanding class recognition, a 15-hour certificate after meeting the general studies requirement, and an Honors Medallion awarded to graduating seniors are several ways superior students are recognized. To graduate with University Honors, students must achieve at least a 3.25 GPA.

There are more than 1,000 students enrolled in the Honors College.

Participation Requirements: The first 15 hours of the honors curriculum consist of lower-division/general studies courses. Enrollment is limited to 20 or fewer students. The 16 hours of upper-division requirements include 6 hours of specially crafted upper-division courses, a 6-hour interdisciplinary colloquia requirement, a thesis tutorial, and the capstone honors thesis. These courses are limited to 15 or fewer students. The final requirement for graduation with University Honors is an honors thesis/creative project. Each thesis writer selects an adviser and is assigned committee members. After the thesis defense and public presentation, theses are bound and become part of the permanent holdings of the MTSU library. The University is very proud of its emphasis on undergraduate research as it prepares seniors for advanced study.

Admission Process: Entering freshmen can enroll in honors courses if they have a minimum ACT composite score of 26 and a high school GPA of at least 3.0 on a 4.0 scale, or a minimum ACT composite score of 24 and a high school GPA of at least 3.5 on a 4.0 scale. Returning students and transfers must have a minimum 3.0. Students whose GPA falls below a 3.0 will be unable to register for honors classes.

Scholarship Availability: Scholarship opportunities exist for in-state entering freshmen and those who have achieved outstanding academic records while participating in the Honors College. In particular, three academic achievement scholarships ($1000) are awarded by the honors scholarship committee.

Campus Overview

State-supported university, founded 1911, part of Tennessee Board of Regents • **Coed** 20,288 undergraduate students, 84% full-time, 53% women, 47% men.

Undergraduates 17,130 full-time, 3,158 part-time. Students come from 47 states and territories, 8% are from out of state, 12% African American, 3% Asian American or Pacific Islander, 2% Hispanic American, 0.4% Native American, 10% transferred in, 20% live on campus.

Faculty *Total:* 1,054, 73% full-time. *Student/faculty ratio:* 24:1.

Academic Programs *Special study options:* academic remediation for entering students, accelerated degree program, adult/continuing education programs, advanced placement credit, cooperative education, distance learning, double majors, English as a second language, freshman honors college, honors programs, independent study, internships, off-campus study, part-time degree program, services for LD students, student-designed majors, study abroad, summer session for credit. *ROTC:* Army (b), Air Force (c). *Unusual degree programs:* 3-2 engineering with University of Tennessee, Knoxville; Georgia Institute of Technology; Tennessee Technological University; The University of Memphis; Tennessee State University; Vanderbilt University.

Athletics Member NCAA. All Division I except football (Division I-A). *Intercollegiate sports:* baseball M(s), basketball M(s)/W(s), cheerleading M(s)/W(s), cross-country running M(s)/W(s), equestrian sports M/W, golf M(s), soccer W(s), softball W(s), tennis M(s)/W(s), track and field M(s)/W(s), volleyball W(s). *Intramural sports:* basketball M/W, bowling M(c)/W(c), fencing M(c)/W(c), field hockey M(c)/W(c), football M, lacrosse M(c)/W(c), racquetball M(c)/W(c), riflery M, rugby M(c)/W(c), soccer M(c)/W, softball M/W, swimming and diving M/W, tennis M/W, ultimate Frisbee M(c)/W(c), volleyball M(c)/W(c), wrestling M(c)/W(c).

Costs (2004–05) *Tuition:* state resident $3352 full-time, $147 per semester hour part-time; nonresident $11,840 full-time, $515 per semester hour part-time. Part-time tuition and fees vary according to course load. *Required fees:* $878 full-time. *Room and board:* $4814; room only: $2576. Room and board charges vary according to board plan and housing facility.

Financial Aid 377 Federal Work-Study jobs (averaging $2237). In 2003, 3075 non-need-based awards were made. *Average percent of need met:* 78%. *Average financial aid package:* $4318. *Average need-based loan:* $4444. *Average need-based gift aid:* $2156. *Average non-need-based aid:* $2330.

Contact: University Honors College, Paul W. Martin Sr. Honors Building, MTSU Box 267, Murfreesboro, Tennessee 37132; *Telephone:* 615-898-2152; *Fax:* 615-904-8263; *E-mail:* honors@mtsu.edu; *Web site:* http://honors.web.mtsu.edu/

Motlow State Community College
Honors Scholar Program
Lynchburg, Tennessee

The Honors Scholar Program provides a path to excellence for academically talented students who want to derive maximum benefit from their educational experience. This college-wide curriculum helps students achieve their goals through intensive individual and group study and through interaction with other equally well-qualified students, under the guidance of qualified faculty members. Any eligible student may take any honors course without committing to the Honors Scholar Program as a whole.

Participation Requirements: After admission to honors course(s) and successful completion of said course(s) with a 3.0 or better, students are eligible for continued enrollment in specific sequential honors courses.

Admission Process: Students under 21 years of age must present an ACT composite score of 23 or higher with documented eligibility for all collegiate-level courses and a high school GPA of 3.0 or higher.

Students who are 21 years of age or older must take the English, reading, and mathematics portions of the COMPASS test and score high enough to be exempt from basic or developmental course requirements.

Students who have taken collegiate courses in dual- and/or joint-enrollment arrangements and maintained a minimum 3.0 collegiate average or students who have advanced standing credit in English, Advanced Placement credit, or CLEP credit may enter the

Honors Scholar Area of Emphasis but are required to complete the same number of honors hours as other honors scholar.

Students who fail to meet the requirements may still enroll in honors courses upon the recommendation of a faculty member.

There are two ways to complete the Honors Scholar Program: eligible students may complete the Honors Scholar Area of Emphasis and graduate with a minimum 3.3 grade point average, or eligible students may choose to complete a requisite number of honors courses without completing the Honors Scholar Area of Emphasis. Students may satisfy the requirements for any Area of Emphasis, graduate with a minimum 3.3 grade point average, and earn 18 hours from honors courses with at least 6 hours in English honors and 3 hours in interdisciplinary studies honors courses.

Scholarship Availability: At least fifteen scholarships of $750 per semester (renewable for up to four semesters) are available for Honors Scholars Program students. Students should visit the Honors Scholar program Web site for scholarship applications and other information (http://www.mscc.edu/honors).

Campus Overview

State-supported 2-year, founded 1969, part of Tennessee Board of Regents • **Coed** 3,540 undergraduate students, 58% full-time, 63% women, 37% men.

Undergraduates 2,041 full-time, 1,499 part-time. Students come from 11 states and territories, 8 other countries, 0.9% are from out of state, 7% African American, 1% Asian American or Pacific Islander, 1% Hispanic American, 0.4% Native American, 0.3% international, 7% transferred in.

Faculty *Total:* 187, 40% full-time. *Student/faculty ratio:* 32:1.

Academic Programs *Special study options:* academic remediation for entering students, adult/continuing education programs, advanced placement credit, cooperative education, distance learning, double majors, honors programs, independent study, part-time degree program, services for LD students, summer session for credit.

Athletics Member NJCAA. *Intercollegiate sports:* baseball M(s), basketball M(s)/W(s), softball W(s). *Intramural sports:* archery M/W, badminton M/W, basketball M/W, bowling M/W, golf M/W, tennis M/W, volleyball M/W.

Costs (2004–05) *Tuition:* state resident $1952 full-time, $83 per credit part-time; nonresident $7798 full-time, $336 per credit part-time. Full-time tuition and fees vary according to program. Part-time tuition and fees vary according to course load and program. *Required fees:* $247 full-time, $144 per credit part-time.

Financial Aid 66 Federal Work-Study jobs (averaging $12,185).

Contact: Wes Spratlin, Honors Scholar Program Coordinator, Motlow State Community College, P.O. Box 8500, Lynchburg, Tennessee 37352-8500; *Telephone:* 931-393-1537; *Fax:* 931-393-1748; *E-mail:* wspratlin@mscc.edu; *Web site:* http://www.mscc.edu/honors

Northeast State Technical Community College
Honors Program
Blountville, Tennessee

The Northeast State Technical Community College (NSTCC) Honors Program offers honors sections of regular courses in English composition and literature, U.S. history, speech, astronomy, myth and tradition, psychology, philosophy, biology, history, and women's studies. These classes offer challenging, stimulating opportunities for increased knowledge and personal growth for students as they are small, discussion- and writing-based classes with a high level of teacher-student interaction.

Students must fulfill a requirement to attend and write about one Lyceum lecture per semester. These lectures, presented by both program faculty members and guests, are designed to not only impart information but also generate critical thinking and discussion on campus about important issues.

The Honors Program was implemented in 1991–92 and has a current enrollment of 40 students.

Participation Requirements: To receive an honors diploma, students must complete 18 hours of honors courses. Successful completion of Honors Program requirements is noted on the student's diploma and transcript.

Admission Process: Students may enter the program in one of two ways: they may enter as first-semester freshmen with an ACT composite of 25 or better or an SAT I combined score of 1140, or transfer/returning students may be enrolled after completion of 12 hours of college-level course work with a minimum 3.25 GPA.

Scholarship Availability: There are scholarship opportunities available to NSTCC honors students through the NSTCC Foundation. Scholarships of $200 are awarded to honors students each semester. All students enrolled in the program full-time who meet the minimum GPA requirement and fulfill the Lyceum requirement are eligible to receive the scholarship until graduation.

Campus Overview

State-supported 2-year, founded 1966, part of Tennessee Board of Regents • **Coed** 5,084 undergraduate students, 55% full-time, 55% women, 45% men.

Undergraduates 2,798 full-time, 2,286 part-time. Students come from 3 states and territories, 3% are from out of state, 3% African American, 0.7% Asian American or Pacific Islander, 0.7% Hispanic American, 0.3% Native American, 5% transferred in.

Faculty *Total:* 241, 40% full-time, 12% with terminal degrees. *Student/faculty ratio:* 22:1.

Academic Programs *Special study options:* academic remediation for entering students, advanced placement credit, cooperative education, distance learning, double majors, honors programs, part-time degree program, services for LD students, summer session for credit.

Athletics *Intramural sports:* basketball M/W, golf M/W, volleyball M/W.

Costs (2004–05) *Tuition:* state resident $1952 full-time, $83 per credit hour part-time; nonresident $7798 full-time, $336 per credit hour part-time. Full-time tuition and fees vary according to course load. Part-time tuition and fees vary according to course load. *Required fees:* $260 full-time, $12 per credit hour part-time, $18 per credit hour part-time.

Financial Aid 109 Federal Work-Study jobs (averaging $1318). 35 state and other part-time jobs.

Contact: Coordinator: James Whorton, Associate Professor of English, P.O. Box 246, Blountville, Tennessee 37617-0246; *Telephone:* 423-354-2427; *Fax:* 423-323-3083; *E-mail:* jwhorton@northeaststate.edu; *Web site:* http://www.northeaststate.edu

Tennessee Technological University
Honors Program
Cookeville, Tennessee

Emphasizing a broad range of cocurricular activities, leadership training, communication skills, preprofessional research, and creative problem solving, the Tennessee Technological University

(TTU) Honors Program strives to create an atmosphere in which young scholars can discuss their ideas and experiences in a supportive yet challenging environment. The program encourages students not only to participate in existing activities, but also to create and organize workshops, committees, presentations, and other projects that expand their own range of expertise and draw on individual initiative and teamwork.

In addition to offering smaller class sections and greater opportunities for in-depth study, the TTU Honors Program matches incoming students with Big Sibs (experienced Honors students who serve as peer advisers, publishes two student-produced newsletters and an annual Honors Handbook, offers several annual leadership retreats, participates in community service activities, and maintains a host of student-run committees that plan and facilitate social events, make Honors Program policy decisions, and organize a variety of social service and recreational projects. These include active intramural sports teams, weekly movies and lively discussions, visits to faculty homes, interdisciplinary luncheon fora, jam sessions, reading groups, and daily gatherings in the Honors Lounge. The Honors dorm features roommate matching and has a close-knit community atmosphere.

TTU honors students participate enthusiastically in honors conferences at the state, regional, and national levels, typically sending one of the largest delegations in the nation. Other opportunities for experience in scholarly research and career skills include mentorships with professors in a student's major field, resume building and preparation, and collaborative/interdisciplinary projects in which honors faculty members and students work together. As a result, each year the University is able to prepare and recommend TTU honors graduates successfully for graduate fellowships and competitive graduate school programs.

Participation Requirements: There are three categories of membership in the TTU Honors Program. A full member has a cumulative QPA of at least 3.5 (except first-semester members who may drop to a 3.1) and is making progress toward graduation with honors. An associate member is one who has been admitted to the Honors Program but whose QPA is temporarily lower than 3.5, but remains at least 3.1. He or she continues to be an active participant in the program and must continue to take honors courses. An affiliate member is a student who enrolls in one or more honors courses but who has not yet met full membership requirements. This three-tiered approach encourages students to continue challenging themselves intellectually as well as in their leadership and service in the community.

Honors 1010, a ten-week introductory honors seminar, is required of all full members. The purpose of the course is to promote understanding of diverse views, collaborative learning, collegial exchange, and a lifelong love of learning and service.

Honors Colloquia are interdisciplinary seminars on topics that are not offered as part of the regular University curriculum. The colloquia explore relationships among social, cultural, historical, scientific, economic, and other concerns. Recent topics include a team-taught environmental field study, the politics of the Middle East, space-time physics, human rights and the law, a cross-cultural survey of mysticism, privilege and prejudice, the ethnomusicology of China, recombinant DNA, brain chemistry, and artificial intelligence.

Directed Studies allow a student, in collaboration with a faculty member, to explore an area of interest not ordinarily covered in regular classes. The Honors Thesis is an optional two-semester sequence for those wishing to undertake rigorous academic research on an advanced and focused topic.

In addition to all relevant University, college, and departmental requirements of the student's chosen curriculum, *in cursu honorum* students must successfully complete the following requirements: Honors 1010 (1 semester hour), at least two honors colloquia or one colloquium and one Directed Study or Research for Thesis semester, at least 15 additional semester hours in honors courses in at least three different disciplines, and achievement of a minimum cumulative QPA of 3.5.

Admission Process: Incoming freshmen must have an ACT composite of 26 or higher or the SAT I equivalent of 1170. As full members of the Honors Program, they may attend early registration and are assigned a Big Sibling (an established honors student who serves as a mentor). Transfer students, or students enrolled at Tech more than one semester, may enter the Honors Program by completing one honors course and achieving a cumulative QPA of 3.5 or higher.

Scholarship Availability: The TTU Honors Program does not fund scholarships directly. However, due to an agreement with the Tennessee Board of Regents, the Honors Program provides Enrichment Options (HPEO) in place of the 75 hours of work Financial Aid attaches to its scholarships. Full members of the Honors Program participate in other activities, such as the Big Sibling Program, in which students are trained as mentors for incoming freshmen; service activities; work with a mentoring professor on research or a special project; presentations (both attending and giving); workshops; attending state, regional, and national honors conferences (TTU routinely sends a large delegation); participating in campus clubs and/or interest groups; playing intramural sports; and many other intellectual and social activities.

Campus Overview

State-supported university, founded 1915, part of Tennessee Board of Regents • **Coed** 7,224 undergraduate students, 89% full-time, 46% women, 54% men.

Undergraduates 6,448 full-time, 776 part-time. Students come from 38 states and territories, 45 other countries, 4% are from out of state, 4% African American, 1% Asian American or Pacific Islander, 0.9% Hispanic American, 0.3% Native American, 0.6% international, 9% transferred in, 28% live on campus.

Faculty *Total:* 556, 67% full-time, 65% with terminal degrees. *Student/faculty ratio:* 18:1.

Academic Programs *Special study options:* academic remediation for entering students, accelerated degree program, adult/continuing education programs, advanced placement credit, cooperative education, distance learning, double majors, English as a second language, honors programs, independent study, internships, off-campus study, part-time degree program, services for LD students, study abroad, summer session for credit. *ROTC:* Army (b), Air Force (c).

Athletics Member NCAA. All Division I except football (Division I-AA). *Intercollegiate sports:* baseball M(s), basketball M(s)/W(s), cheerleading M(s)/W(s), cross-country running M(s)/W(s), golf M(s)/W(s), riflery M(s)/W(s), soccer W(s), softball W(s), tennis M(s)/W(s), track and field W(s), volleyball W(s). *Intramural sports:* basketball M/W, bowling M/W, fencing M(c)/W(c), football M/W, golf M/W, racquetball M/W, rugby M(c)/W(c), soccer M/W, softball M/W, tennis M/W, ultimate Frisbee M/W, volleyball M/W, wrestling M.

Costs (2004–05) *Tuition:* state resident $3998 full-time, $147 per hour part-time; nonresident $12,486 full-time, $515 per hour part-time. Full-time tuition and fees vary according to program. Part-time tuition and fees vary according to course load and program. *Required fees:* $42 per hour part-time. *Room and board:* $5270; room only: $2520. Room and board charges vary according to board plan and housing facility.

Financial Aid 553 Federal Work-Study jobs (averaging $1350). In 2003, 1215 non-need-based awards were made. *Average percent of need met:* 77%. *Average financial aid package:* $3870. *Average need-based loan:* $3061. *Average need-based gift aid:* $2768. *Average non-need-based aid:* $3030.

Contact: Director: Dr. Connie Hood, Box 5124, TJ Farr 204, Cookeville, Tennessee 38505; Associate Director: Dr. Rita Barnes; *Telephone:* 615-372-3797; *E-mail:* honors@tntech.edu; *Web site:* http://www.tntech.edu/honors/

The University of Memphis
University Honors Program
Memphis, Tennessee

The University of Memphis Honors Program is a University-wide academic program that offers a unique opportunity to experience both the wide-ranging opportunities of a metropolitan research university and the nurturing environment of a small liberal arts college. Similar to classes at a liberal arts college, honors classes are limited in size, populated by academically ambitious and talented students, and taught by distinguished faculty members noted for both their teaching and research accomplishments.

The program offers special curricular options and the opportunity to earn honors distinction. Classes within the program span the entire range of the University. The honors curriculum includes sections of general education program courses and other courses that fulfill core curriculum requirements. In addition to honors sections of regularly offered courses, the Honors Program also offers interdisciplinary courses designed to explore a particular topic intensively and creatively.

The University Honors Program encourages and supports opportunities that are designed to enhance the educational experiences of its members, providing administrative and financial support for independent scholarship, internships, and study abroad and other student exchange experiences. The Honors Program also coordinates special academic, social, and cultural events for honors students. Through these events, students can become part of a community of friends and fellow scholars that provides an atmosphere that is conducive to studying and a place where friendships are easily established. Because of the special nature of their contribution to the University, honors students enjoy other privileges as well, including priority registration, an honors computer lab and student lounge, and special ceremonies that recognize outstanding students.

Participation Requirements: The program consists of a minimum of 24 credits of honors course work. Students must take at least 12 credits of honors courses during their first two years, including two interdisciplinary, team-taught honors seminars that are required for all first-year students. Students must maintain a minimum GPA of 3.25 to remain in good standing and graduate with University Honors distinction on their transcripts and diplomas.

Admission Process: Qualified students admitted to the University of Memphis are invited to apply to the University Honors Program. Most students admitted to the program have at least a 3.5 high school GPA and a score of 27 or higher on the ACT or 1200 or higher on the SAT. Transfer students are also eligible for the Honors Program if they have earned an overall grade point average of at least 3.25.

Scholarship Availability: The University of Memphis provides more than $4 million in scholarships to high-ability students. Many students who receive scholarships are members of the University Honors Program. The Honors Program also provides a limited number of Non-Resident Honors Student Awards that cover out-of-state tuition for nonresident students.

Campus Overview

State-supported university, founded 1912, part of Tennessee Board of Regents • **Coed** 15,928 undergraduate students, 74% full-time, 61% women, 39% men.

Undergraduates 11,722 full-time, 4,206 part-time. Students come from 44 states and territories, 83 other countries, 7% are from out of state, 38% African American, 2% Asian American or Pacific Islander, 1% Hispanic American, 0.3% Native American, 2% international, 16% live on campus.

Faculty *Total:* 1,183, 66% full-time, 67% with terminal degrees. *Student/faculty ratio:* 19:1.

Academic Programs *Special study options:* academic remediation for entering students, accelerated degree program, adult/continuing education programs, advanced placement credit, cooperative education, distance learning, double majors, English as a second language, external degree program, honors programs, independent study, internships, off-campus study, part-time degree program, services for LD students, student-designed majors, study abroad, summer session for credit. *ROTC:* Army (b), Navy (b), Air Force (b).

Athletics Member NCAA. All Division I except football (Division I-A). *Intercollegiate sports:* baseball M(s), basketball M(s)/W(s), cheerleading M(s)/W(s), cross-country running M(s)/W(s), golf M(s)/W(s), racquetball M(c)/W(c), riflery M(s)/W(s), soccer M(s)/W(s), swimming and diving M(c)/W(c), tennis M(s)/W(s), track and field M(s)/W(s), volleyball W(s). *Intramural sports:* archery M/W, badminton M/W, basketball M/W, bowling M/W, fencing M, golf M/W, rugby M/W, soccer M, softball M/W, swimming and diving M/W, table tennis M/W, tennis M/W, track and field M/W, volleyball M/W.

Costs (2004–05) *Tuition:* state resident $3748 full-time, $209 per credit hour part-time; nonresident $12,472 full-time, $573 per credit hour part-time. Full-time tuition and fees vary according to program and reciprocity agreements. Part-time tuition and fees vary according to course load and program. *Required fees:* $732 full-time. *Room and board:* $4920; room only: $2840. Room and board charges vary according to housing facility.

Financial Aid 287 Federal Work-Study jobs (averaging $2122). In 2002, 416 non-need-based awards were made. *Average percent of need met:* 76%. *Average financial aid package:* $3816. *Average need-based loan:* $3598. *Average need-based gift aid:* $3361. *Average non-need-based aid:* $2963.

Contact: Director: Dr. Melinda Jones, University Honors Program, 204 Scates Hall, University of Memphis, Memphis, Tennessee 38152; *Telephone:* 901-678-2690; *Fax:* 901-678-5367; *Web site:* http://www.memphis.edu/honors

The University of Tennessee
University Honors Program
Knoxville, Tennessee

The University Honors Program at the University of Tennessee (UT), Knoxville, is a campuswide program open to students pursuing any of approximately 120 academic majors in ten colleges. The goals of the University Honors Program are to provide enhanced academic opportunities, to foster intellectual development, and to promote campus and community involvement to high-ability students. The 20-year-old program currently enrolls a total of 650 students. Other honors opportunities on campus include honors courses and departmental honors concentrations.

University Honors Scholars select from a wide variety of specially designed interdisciplinary seminars offered by University Honors as well as honors classes offered by numerous departments to fulfill many of their general education requirements. Seminars are designed for 15 students, while departmental honors classes vary in size but are much smaller than their nonhonors counterparts. Students later enroll in at least two upper-division honors classes in their majors. Finally, a senior seminar helps to prepare Honors Scholars to complete their Senior Project, a capstone experience developed with the guidance of a faculty mentor. The best among these are archived by the University's library, and a select few are chosen for awards of distinction.

Students receive a number of benefits. They attend early orientation sessions, are assigned a peer mentor (an honors student of similar interests), and have the opportunity to live in the Honors Learning Community in Morrill Hall. Honors Scholars receive priority in course and housing selection and have enhanced library privileges. During the academic year, students have unlimited access to the honors study areas and to a large, state-of-the-art computer facility. Social events are held on a regular basis each year, and evening information sessions feature a wide range of academic and extracurricular opportunities. Academic and career advising is customized to each student's interests and includes discussion of academic issues, professional opportunities, and the Senior Project.

Honors students are leaders in all areas of campus life, from the classroom to the community. The University Honors Program facilitates their pursuits of independent research and creative work and off-campus study. Honors study-abroad opportunities exist in Cambridge, Vienna, and Sicily, and other sites are being explored. On campus, Honors Scholars are elected leaders of student government and other campus organizations, appointed as members of deans' student-advisory committees, and work each year to make improvements to the campus. The Honors Student Council pursues an active agenda, providing a strong voice for student desires and concerns. Finally, honors students are encouraged to be active and creative volunteers in organizations that serve the broader off-campus community.

A distinctive feature of the University Honors Program is its emphasis on original work, demonstrated through opportunities for students to become engaged in faculty-sponsored research. Students are encouraged to participate in professional organizations and activities; the annual Exhibition of Undergraduate Research and Creative Achievement provides a public forum for presentation of original works. The Honors Program furthermore assists students in the pursuit of major competitive fellowships, scholarships, and internships, and honors students have been recipients of Rhodes, Fulbright, Truman, Goldwater, and National Science Foundation awards.

Participation Requirements: All first-year University Honors Program students complete a 1-credit seminar focusing on various aspects of the undergraduate experience (study abroad, computer skills, service learning, etc.). A minimum of 26 credit hours must be in honors course work, and a minimum 3.25 GPA is required to maintain full standing in the program. Honors courses are indicated on transcripts; honors degrees are indicated on the transcript and diploma.

Admission Process: To apply for admission, students should have at least a 3.75 high school GPA and a minimum 29 ACT score or 1280 SAT score (composite math and verbal scores). Applications are also accepted from students with a 3.75 GPA who want to transfer from other NCHC-member Honors Programs. A limited number of students may be admitted each year following completion of the first year at UT with a superior academic record, including honors courses.

Scholarship Availability: Interested students are encouraged to complete the University's Entering Freshman Scholarship Application (November 1 postmark deadline) or the Transfer Scholarship Application (February 1 postmark deadline) to be considered for competitive scholarships. Interviews for selection of the top competitive awards, the Oldham and Manning, are held early in the spring semester. Scholarships awarded based on certified grades and scores (Presidential–National Merit, Volunteer, University, African American Achiever) require admission by February 1.

Campus Overview

State-supported university, founded 1794, part of University of Tennessee System • **Coed** 19,634 undergraduate students, 92% full-time, 51% women, 49% men.

Undergraduates 18,065 full-time, 1,569 part-time. Students come from 59 states and territories, 101 other countries, 14% are from out of state, 8% African American, 3% Asian American or Pacific Islander, 1% Hispanic American, 0.4% Native American, 0.9% international, 6% transferred in, 37% live on campus.

Faculty *Total:* 1,557, 95% full-time, 82% with terminal degrees. *Student/faculty ratio:* 15:1.

Academic Programs *Special study options:* accelerated degree program, adult/continuing education programs, advanced placement credit, cooperative education, distance learning, double majors, English as a second language, honors programs, independent study, internships, off-campus study, part-time degree program, services for LD students, student-designed majors, study abroad, summer session for credit. *ROTC:* Army (b), Air Force (b).

Athletics Member NCAA. All Division I except football (Division I-A). *Intercollegiate sports:* baseball M(s), basketball M(s)/W(s), cheerleading M(s)/W(s), crew W(s), cross-country running M(s)/W(s), golf M(s)/W(s), soccer W(s), softball W(s), swimming and diving M(s)/W(s), tennis M(s)/W(s), track and field M(s)/W(s), volleyball W(s). *Intramural sports:* badminton M/W, basketball M/W, bowling M/W, crew M(c)/W(c), cross-country running M/W, equestrian sports M(c)/W(c), fencing M(c)/W(c), field hockey M/W, football M/W, golf M/W, gymnastics M(c)/W(c), ice hockey M(c)/W(c), lacrosse M(c)/W(c), racquetball M/W, riflery M(c)/W(c), rugby M(c)/W(c), sailing M(c)/W(c), skiing (downhill) M(c)/W(c), soccer M/W, softball M/W, swimming and diving M/W, table tennis M/W, tennis M/W, track and field M/W, volleyball M(c)/W, water polo M/W, weight lifting M(c)/W(c).

Costs (2004–05) *Tuition:* state resident $5376 full-time, $291 per semester hour part-time; nonresident $10,442 full-time, $835 per semester hour part-time. Full-time tuition and fees vary according to location and program. Part-time tuition and fees vary according to location and program. *Room and board:* $5398; room only: $2710. Room and board charges vary according to board plan and housing facility.

Financial Aid In 2003, 126 non-need-based awards were made. *Average percent of need met: 64%. Average financial aid package:* $6954. *Average need-based loan: $3523. Average need-based gift aid:* $5115. *Average non-need-based aid: $8931.*

Contact: Director: Professor Mark Luprecht, University Honors Program, Melrose Hall, F101, University of Tennessee, 1616 Melrose Place, Knoxville, Tennessee 37996-4352; *Telephone:* 865-974-7875; *Fax:* 865-974-4784; *E-mail:* honors@utk.edu; *Web site:* http://honors.utk.edu

The University of Tennessee at Chattanooga
University Honors Program
Chattanooga, Tennessee

The University Honors (UHON) Program at UTC is a four-year interdisciplinary program that stresses the importance of a global perspective through the study of great literature, fine art, and profound ideas. The UHON seminars are designed especially for small groups of honors students and are intended to encourage intellectual, moral, and social growth. The program's goal is to foster a community of scholars who benefit from each other's work and who provide the University with new ideas and ways to achieve excellence.

In order to achieve this goal, the program provides the honors students with special benefits, including exclusive 24-hour access to a 2,200-square-foot reading room and adjacent computer lab, intensive academic advisement, priority registration for classes, a stipend for local symphony and theater performances, and substantial funding for annual study trips abroad.

The UHON Program was privately endowed in 1977 and expanded to its current size in 1986 through a grant from the National Endowment for the Humanities. The program currently includes about 150 students, 15 select faculty members, and 4 adviser-administrators.

Participation Requirements: The required UHON curriculum consists of 33 semester hours (Humanities I and II; Classical and Medieval Historical and Political Thought; Development of Scientific Thought; Origins of Social Science; Contemporary Social Science; one course from Chinese and Japanese Traditions, Traditions of India, Traditions of Latin America, or African Traditions; and two courses from film, music, art, or theater history and aesthetics). During the senior year, each UHON student undertakes an independent departmental honors project with the guidance of a faculty member in the major. The project carries 4 hours of academic credit and usually results in a research paper of substantial length and quality that must be defended before a committee from the major department. All UHON courses replace the University's general education requirements.

Students must maintain at least a 3.5 cumulative GPA for all college course work, earn at least 24 hours toward graduation each academic year, and complete the sequence of UHON seminars. They are also expected to participate in the social, cultural, and service life of the University.

UHON students receive designations on their diplomas and in the commencement program as University Honors Scholars. Students also receive engraved medallions at commencement as recognition of their achievement in completing the program.

Admission Process: Prospective freshmen must submit a separate application, which is available from the UHON Office or Web site, to the UHON Program by February 1. There is no minimum high school GPA or test score required, but successful applicants present average ACT scores of 29 and high school GPAs of 3.8. Applications include a creative essay, a report of extracurricular activities, and recommendations from teachers. Promising candidates are invited for a two-day conference at UTC, where they are able to explore the campus, attend University classes and a special seminar, visit with faculty representatives from various departments, and socialize with current UHON students and other applicants. The visit also gives the UHON staff a chance to evaluate applicants by means of interviews, informal discussions, and observed classroom interaction. Final selections are completed by March 20.

Students not admitted as freshmen may apply to become Associate Honors Scholars if they have completed at least 24 hours of course work with a cumulative GPA of 3.5 or better. Associate Honors Scholars are eligible for all benefits of the UHON Program except the Honors Program Scholarships.

Scholarship Availability: About twenty new scholarships are awarded each year to freshmen selected for the UHON Program, including sixteen William E. Brock, Jr. Scholarships; two Paul Koblentz Memorial Scholarships; and two Roberta M. "Bobbie" Yates Scholarships. Those students not receiving UHON scholarships are considered for all other merit-based awards offered by the University. Virtually all UHON students receive scholarships. In 2004–05, UHON students received about $270,000 in state scholarship funds and $498,000 in exclusive UHON scholarships—an average of more than $7000 per year per student.

Campus Overview

State-supported comprehensive, founded 1886, part of University of Tennessee System • **Coed** 7,405 undergraduate students, 85% full-time, 57% women, 43% men.

Undergraduates 6,266 full-time, 1,139 part-time. Students come from 40 states and territories, 52 other countries, 9% are from out of state, 22% African American, 2% Asian American or Pacific Islander, 0.9% Hispanic American, 0.3% Native American, 1% international, 8% transferred in, 33% live on campus.

Faculty *Total:* 668, 55% full-time, 53% with terminal degrees. *Student/faculty ratio:* 17:1.

Academic Programs *Special study options:* academic remediation for entering students, adult/continuing education programs, advanced placement credit, cooperative education, distance learning, double majors, English as a second language, honors programs, independent study, internships, off-campus study, part-time degree program, services for LD students, study abroad, summer session for credit. *Unusual degree programs:* 3-2 engineering with Georgia Institute of Technology, University of Tennessee, Knoxville.

Athletics Member NCAA. All Division I except football (Division I-AA). *Intercollegiate sports:* basketball M(s)/W(s), crew M/W, cross-country running M(s)/W(s), golf M(s)/W, soccer M(s)/W(s), softball W(s), tennis M(s)/W(s), track and field M/W, volleyball W(s), wrestling M(s). *Intramural sports:* badminton M/W, basketball M/W, bowling M/W, cross-country running M/W, fencing M, football M, golf M, racquetball M/W, swimming and diving M/W, tennis M/W, volleyball W, weight lifting M, wrestling M.

Costs (2004–05) *Tuition:* state resident $4128 full-time, $221 per hour part-time; nonresident $12,350 full-time, $565 per hour part-time. *Required fees:* $800 full-time. *Room and board:* $5808; room only: $3360. Room and board charges vary according to housing facility.

Financial Aid 220 Federal Work-Study jobs (averaging $1795). 400 state and other part-time jobs (averaging $1875). In 2004, 825 non-need-based awards were made. *Average percent of need met:* 80%. *Average financial aid package:* $8450. *Average need-based loan:* $4450. *Average need-based gift aid:* $3600. *Average non-need-based aid:* $3400.

Contact: Director: Gregory O'Dea, 615 McCallie Avenue, Chattanooga, Tennessee 37403; *Telephone:* 423-425-4128; *Fax:* 423-425-2128; *E-mail:* gregory-o'dea@utc.edu; *Web site:* http://www.utc.edu/univhon/

The University of Tennessee at Martin

Honors Programs

Martin, Tennessee

Honors Programs at the University of Tennessee at Martin (UTM) comprise the University Scholars Program and the Honors Seminar Program. Together these programs involve approximately 300 students annually in honors courses, seminars with visiting speakers, independent research and creative projects, cultural activities, and service projects.

The University Scholars Program, founded in 1981, is a sequence of courses and extracurricular activities for a select group of talented and motivated students. The major goal is to provide special academic opportunities that help these students to perform with distinction in their careers and as citizens. Interdisciplinary inquiry and independent study and research characterize this program. The program currently is limited to 60 undergraduate students at all levels in the University. Scholars students enroll every semester in one University Scholars course, accumulating a four-year total of 10 hours toward graduation with the designation University Scholar.

The Honors Seminar Program, founded in 1984, brings together students and distinguished campus visitors (scholars, leaders, or artists) in seminars to discuss and examine issues and ideas. Approximately 240 students are currently active in the program. Honors Seminar students attend a series of public presentations by visiting speakers. They select 1 speaker with whom to study in more depth in two special seminars. Up to 4 hours of elective credit toward the degree may be earned.

Participation Requirements: All honors students complete an honors core curriculum consisting of 12 credit hours in interdisciplinary honors courses and honors sections of University core courses.

Admission Process: Students with a minimum ACT composite score of 28 or a minimum SAT score of 1240 and a minimum high school GPA of 3.5 may apply for University Scholars Program admission prior to their freshman year. A few students with outstanding freshman college records at UTM or who are transferring from another institution may also be invited to apply. A minimum 3.3 GPA is required for good standing. Students qualify for the Honors

Seminar Program by having an ACT composite score of 28 or higher or an SAT score of 1240 or higher and a high school GPA of 3.5 or higher. Students apply for the program by completing the regular applications for admission and financial aid at UTM. A minimum 3.2 GPA is required for good standing.

Scholarship Availability: Students invited into the University Scholars Program are assured of a scholarship package of at least $5000 per year for up to four years of their participation. Honors Seminar students are assured of a scholarship package of at least $3000 per year for up to four years of their participation.

Campus Overview

State-supported comprehensive, founded 1900, part of University of Tennessee System • **Coed** 5,667 undergraduate students, 85% full-time, 56% women, 44% men.

Undergraduates 4,791 full-time, 876 part-time. Students come from 41 states and territories, 28 other countries, 3% are from out of state, 16% African American, 0.5% Asian American or Pacific Islander, 1% Hispanic American, 0.4% Native American, 2% international, 7% transferred in, 37% live on campus.

Faculty *Total:* 387, 63% full-time, 48% with terminal degrees. *Student/faculty ratio:* 17:1.

Academic Programs *Special study options:* academic remediation for entering students, accelerated degree program, adult/continuing education programs, advanced placement credit, cooperative education, distance learning, double majors, English as a second language, honors programs, independent study, internships, off-campus study, part-time degree program, services for LD students, student-designed majors, study abroad, summer session for credit. *ROTC:* Army (b).

Athletics Member NCAA. All Division I except football (Division I-AA). *Intercollegiate sports:* baseball M(s), basketball M(s)/W(s), cheerleading M/W, cross-country running M(s)/W(s), golf M(s), riflery M(s)/W(s), soccer W(s), softball W(s), tennis M(s)/W(s), volleyball W(s). *Intramural sports:* basketball M/W, football M/W, golf M/W, rock climbing M/W, soccer M/W, softball M/W, swimming and diving M/W, table tennis M/W, tennis M/W, track and field M/W, ultimate Frisbee M/W, volleyball M/W.

Costs (2004–05) *Tuition:* state resident $4134 full-time, $183 per credit hour part-time; nonresident $12,388 full-time, $197 per credit hour part-time. *Room and board:* $4100; room only: $1960. Room and board charges vary according to board plan and housing facility.

Financial Aid 265 Federal Work-Study jobs (averaging $2019). In 2003, 1044 non-need-based awards were made. *Average percent of need met:* 75%. *Average financial aid package:* $8183. *Average need-based loan:* $3687. *Average need-based gift aid:* $4036. *Average non-need-based aid:* $3901.

Contact: Director, Honors Program, 15 Holland McCombs Center, The University of Tennessee at Martin, Martin, Tennessee 38238; *Telephone:* 731-881-7436; *Fax:* 731-881-1082; *E-mail:* honors@utm.edu; *Web site:* http://www.utm.edu/honors

TEXAS

Abilene Christian University

Honors Program

Abilene, Texas

The Honors Program at Abilene Christian University offers academic enrichment and fellowship for highly motivated students in all majors. It requires no extra courses or fees and can be tailored for students with multiple majors or degrees.

In addition to the stimulating classes, Honors Program students enjoy honors social events, an honors common room, and early

registration privileges. Student representatives attend conferences of the National Collegiate Honors Council and the Great Plains Honors Council. Grants are available for study abroad.

Founded in 1984, the program involves an average of 350 to 400 students. Planning is underway to convert it to an honors college.

Participation Requirements: Within the program, students pursue either the University Honors track (four years, 30 semester hours), the General Honors track (three years, 21 semester hours), or the Departmental Honors track (two years, 12 semester hours). Those who finish the requirements and have a cumulative GPA of at least 3.5 receive a note on their transcript, special recognition at Commencement, and a certificate of achievement.

The University and General Honors tracks include 18 hours of freshman and sophomore honors classes. These include special versions of core curriculum courses— English, Bible, sciences, communications—as well as honors humanities and the honors seminar in social sciences. All honors classes emphasize breadth, flexibility, and critical thinking. The classes are kept small (limited to honors students) and are taught by selected faculty members. Collaborative learning, service learning, study abroad, credit by examination, and other options can help meet this requirement.

At the junior and senior level, the University and Departmental Honors tracks stress professional competence, interdisciplinary thinking, and preparation for graduate study or a career. The upper-division requirement (12 hours) includes 6 hours by honors contract in junior- and senior-level courses and a 3-hour Capstone Project, all of which fit into majors' requirements. Also required are three 1-hour interdisciplinary colloquia. Each colloquium features discussion and a position paper. Topics have included Leonardo's Notebooks, Science and Religion, Islam, Wagner's Ring, The Sixties, and Photography and Society. Course credit fits into elective hours.

Admission Process: Admission to the program is guaranteed for students who meet three criteria: a combined SAT score of 1220 (total of Math and Critical Reading scores) or an ACT composite score of 27, a high school GPA of 3.75 or rank in the top 10 percent of the class, and a satisfactory personal essay. For details and an online application, students should visit http://www.acu.edu/academics/honors/application.html. No essay is required for students who have received a National Merit Finalist Scholarship or a Presidential Scholarship from ACU. Applicants whose scores are lower may be granted provisional admission on the basis of high school records or other evidence of high motivation and ability.

Scholarship Availability: The University gives more than $42 million in financial aid, including substantial academic scholarships. Ninety percent of freshmen receive financial aid.

Campus Overview

Independent comprehensive, founded 1906, affiliated with Church of Christ • **Coed** 4,209 undergraduate students, 95% full-time, 55% women, 45% men.

Undergraduates 4,010 full-time, 199 part-time. Students come from 48 states and territories, 50 other countries, 18% are from out of state, 7% African American, 1% Asian American or Pacific Islander, 7% Hispanic American, 0.5% Native American, 4% international, 6% transferred in, 42% live on campus.

Faculty Total: 347, 62% full-time, 59% with terminal degrees. Student/faculty ratio: 17:1.

Academic Programs Special study options: adult/continuing education programs, advanced placement credit, distance learning, double majors, English as a second language, external degree program, honors programs, independent study, internships, off-campus study, part-time degree program, services for LD students, student-designed majors, study abroad, summer session for credit. Unusual degree programs: 3-2 engineering with The University of Texas at Dallas, The University of Texas at Arlington.

Athletics Member NCAA. All Division II. Intercollegiate sports: baseball M(s), basketball M(s)/W(s), cross-country running M(s)/

W(s), football M(s), golf M(s), soccer M(c)/W(c), softball W(s), tennis M(s)/W(s), track and field M(s)/W(s), volleyball W(s). Intramural sports: badminton M/W, basketball M/W, bowling M/W, cross-country running M/W, football M/W, racquetball M/W, soccer M/W, softball M/W, table tennis M/W, tennis M/W, track and field M/W, volleyball M/W, water polo M.

Costs (2004–05) Comprehensive fee: $19,470 includes full-time tuition ($13,650), mandatory fees ($550), and room and board ($5270). Full-time tuition and fees vary according to course load. Part-time tuition: $455 per semester hour. Part-time tuition and fees vary according to course load. Required fees: $27 per semester hour part-time, $10 per semester part-time. College room only: $2240. Room and board charges vary according to board plan and housing facility.

Financial Aid 440 Federal Work-Study jobs (averaging $1454). In 2003, 1026 non-need-based awards were made. Average percent of need met: 74%. Average financial aid package: $10,751. Average need-based loan: $4034. Average need-based gift aid: $7406. Average non-need-based aid: $5084.

Contact: Director: Dr. Chris Willerton, ACU Box 29142, Abilene, Texas 79699-9142; Telephone: 325-674-2728; Fax: 325-674-6581; E-mail: chris.willerton@acu.edu; Web site: http://www.acu.edu/honors

Angelo State University
Honors Program
San Angelo, Texas

The Honors Program at Angelo State University (ASU) is a collection of courses and opportunities that provide honors students with an enriched educational experience. Key characteristics of the program are an honors lounge in the Porter Henderson Library, access to external speakers, and the opportunity to join the Honors Student Association. The honors lounge contains six computer workstations, a study area, a social area, a conference room, and the honors director's office.

The Honors Program at Angelo State University is intended to provide students with the opportunity to achieve a deeper understanding of course material, be exposed to cultural and intellectual events that broaden their appreciation of the world that surrounds them, develop leadership qualities that help them through their careers and personal lives, and nurture an understanding and appreciation of the diverse needs of society and how their personal service can enhance the quality of life for their family and others. The Honors Program achieves these goals through course offerings and extracurricular activities designed to challenge and enhance the intellectual and personal abilities of honors students. Additional information may be found at http://www.angelo.edu/dept/honors/.

Participation Requirements: A listing of the formal courses offered in the program appears below. These requirements result in a total of 30 credit hours of work taken by each honors student. Most of the courses required in the program are honors sections of regularly offered courses. During the last two years, students receive honors credit for two courses within their major discipline. These courses can be standard sections, with the honors student being required to complete additional assignments not given to regular students. Alternatively, these major discipline courses may be special courses, such as individual research. Requirements for the Honors Program include Introduction to Honors Study (2 hours, taken as HONR 1201), History 1301 (3 hours), English 1302 (3 hours), Government 2301 (3 hours), humanities (Great Books Courses HONR 2301 and HONR 2302, 6 hours total; two courses, including a 3-hour course toward the humanities requirement and a 3-hour course toward the visual and performing arts requirement—art, drama, or music), a lab science course (3 hours), Introduction to Honors Research (2 hours), Honors Seminar (1 hour; this class is open to honors students only during their senior year), and department/major discipline courses (6 hours). In future years of the program, class substitutions will be possible for transfer students or existing students who enter the program after their freshman year. These substitutions will be made on an individual basis and will take into account whether the student meets existing requirements for students entering the program. Students will still have to complete 20 hours in residence.

Students must maintain a minimum 3.25 overall GPA. Students who complete all of these requirements receive a separate designation on their diploma and transcript and are recognized at graduation.

Admission Process: Students who meet the criteria below and complete an application form are considered for admission into the Honors Program. Admission into the program is on a rolling basis. To be accepted into the program, freshmen must be in the top 10 percent of their high school class, have a minimum score of 1200 on the SAT or 27 on the ACT, complete an application, provide two completed reference forms, and have a solid record of participation in extracurricular activities. To be admitted after the freshman year, students must have a minimum GPA of 3.25, score at least 1200 on the SAT or 27 on the ACT, be in the top 10 percent of their high school class, complete an application, provide two completed reference forms, and have a solid record of participation in extracurricular activities.

Scholarship Availability: Scholarships are available to all honors students after their first full year in the program. Also, students who meet the admission requirements for the Honors Program are eligible to apply for the Carr Academic Scholarship. Information concerning this scholarship and other scholarships may be obtained at http://www.angelo.edu/services/financial_aid/.

Campus Overview

State-supported comprehensive, founded 1928, part of Texas State University System • **Coed** 5,712 undergraduate students, 83% full-time, 55% women, 45% men.

Undergraduates 4,755 full-time, 957 part-time. Students come from 40 states and territories, 25 other countries, 2% are from out of state, 6% African American, 1% Asian American or Pacific Islander, 23% Hispanic American, 0.3% Native American, 1% international, 8% transferred in, 25% live on campus.

Faculty *Total:* 337, 74% full-time, 55% with terminal degrees. *Student/faculty ratio:* 20:1.

Academic Programs *Special study options:* academic remediation for entering students, accelerated degree program, adult/continuing education programs, advanced placement credit, distance learning, double majors, honors programs, independent study, internships, off-campus study, part-time degree program, services for LD students, study abroad, summer session for credit. *ROTC:* Air Force (b). *Unusual degree programs:* 3-2 engineering with University of Texas at El Paso, Texas A&M University; agriculture education with Texas A&M University.

Athletics Member NCAA, NAIA. All NCAA Division II. *Intercollegiate sports:* baseball M(s), basketball M(s)/W(s), cross-country running M(s)/W(s), football M(s), rugby M(c), soccer W(s), softball W(s), track and field M(s)/W(s), volleyball W(s). *Intramural sports:* archery M/W, badminton M/W, basketball M/W, bowling M/W, football M/W, golf M/W, racquetball M/W, rugby M, soccer M/W, softball M/W, swimming and diving M/W, table tennis M/W, tennis M/W, ultimate Frisbee M/W, volleyball M/W, weight lifting M/W.

Costs (2004–05) *Tuition:* state resident $2208 full-time, $92 per credit part-time; nonresident $8400 full-time, $350 per credit part-time. Full-time tuition and fees vary according to course load. Part-time tuition and fees vary according to course load. *Required fees:* $918 full-time, $35 per credit part-time, $93 per term part-time. *Room and board:* $4696; room only: $3024. Room and board charges vary according to board plan and housing facility.

Financial Aid In 2002, 202 non-need-based awards were made. *Average percent of need met:* 60%. *Average financial aid package:* $4299. *Average need-based loan:* $2500. *Average need-based gift aid:* $2193. *Average non-need-based aid:* $1872.

Contact: Director: Dr. Nick Flynn, Honors Program Director, Angelo State University, San Angelo, Texas 76909; *Telephone:* 325-942-2722; *Fax:* 325-942-2716; *E-mail:* honors@angelo.edu; Web site: http://www.angelo.edu/dept/honors

Baylor University
Honors College
Waco, Texas

*T*he Honors College at Baylor University comprises four innovative interdisciplinary undergraduate programs: the Honors Program, the University Scholars Program, the Baylor Interdisciplinary Core, and the Great Texts Program. What unites the four programs is their shared commitment to providing students the opportunity to pursue the sorts of questions that often fall between the cracks of the specialized disciplines and to investigate the writings of scientists along with the writings of poets, historians, and philosophers. The Honors Program supplements traditional degree requirements and majors with a focus on classroom discussion, independent readings and research, and interdisciplinary approaches to learning. The hallmark of the program is an honors thesis, researched during the junior and senior years and defended before graduation. Honors Program students from across the University's colleges and schools work on such projects in collaboration with faculty members in their fields of interest. The University Scholars Program allows select high-achieving students in the arts and sciences the opportunity to design personalized curricula with the help of faculty advisers. The resulting flexibility allows University Scholars to broaden their background in the liberal arts while remaining focused on at least one, and usually several, academic areas of interest. Requirements also include a reading list and a senior thesis project. Many University Scholars also participate in the Honors Program, and all program graduates receive a B.A. degree with a major in University Scholars. The Baylor Interdisciplinary Core (BIC) provides an alternative core curriculum that takes the place of Baylor's traditional general studies requirements. Innovative, team-taught course sequences allow BIC students to engage the humanities, the social sciences, and the physical sciences, in conversation with diverse faculty members affiliated with the relevant disciplines. BIC students move from their alternative core classes into the requirements for their declared majors. The Great Texts Program teaches required courses for Honors Program and University Scholars students, and it also offers an interdisciplinary major and minor. Great Texts majors study a sustained curriculum in great works of literature and the arts, theology, philosophy, science, and leadership; their study proves to lay a foundation for graduate work in any humanities discipline or to complement other educational and preprofessional pursuits. All of the program's courses are taught in a seminar format.

Students in one or more of these programs may apply for on-campus housing in the Honors College Living-Learning Center, whose purpose is to integrate intellectual pursuits into the fabric of student life and to foster among its students a community of engagement. Other features of the Honors College include team teaching, seminar-style classes (often capped at 20 students), book and film clubs, activities and lectures, student leadership groups, and emphases on primary texts inside the classroom and outside of it in activities that bring together Honors College students and faculty members.

The Honors Program was established in 1959 and currently enrolls approximately 700 students. A total of nearly 200 students are University Scholars, thirty years after this program's founding in

1975. The Interdisciplinary Core's inaugural class entered Baylor in 1995, and about 700 current students are involved in this program. The Honors College was established in 2002 and brought together these three existing programs and the new Great Texts unit, which is now home to forty majors and minors.

Participation Requirements: The Honors Program requires students to complete 21 credit hours of honors courses during their first two years of study, including two required Great Texts courses. During the junior and senior years, honors students complete 4 credit hours of colloquium, an interdisciplinary reading and discussion sequence, and 6 credit hours toward the honors thesis, all while maintaining at least a 3.2 GPA. Graduates' accomplishments are noted both on the Baylor diploma and at commencement. University Scholars must complete a series of three Great Texts courses and an individualized reading list, which culminates in an exit interview. University Scholars must maintain a minimum 3.5 GPA to stay in the program, and they must also complete and submit an extended research project before graduation. Students in the Baylor Interdisciplinary Core must complete five course sequences (30–44 credit hours, depending on the degree): Examined Life, World Cultures, World of Rhetoric, Social World, and Natural World. These sequences count toward the alternative core curriculum, and no minimum GPA is required during the first two years of study, when the majority of these courses are taken. Great Texts majors must complete 30 credit hours of course work in the major, including two introductory courses, five required upper-division courses, and three upper-division elective courses in Great Texts.

Admission Process: The Honors Program usually invites students with combined SAT scores of 1270 or above (excluding the new writing test) or composite ACT scores of 29 or above, as well as students graduating in the top 5 percent of their classes, to apply. A brief essay is also required. The University Scholars Program has no required minimum SAT score, but admitted students' scores usually average at or above 1400 (verbal plus math). The application consists of an information form, a one- or two-page essay, three letters of reference, and a one- to two-page resume. The Baylor Interdisciplinary Core requires no minimum test scores, but students interested in the program submit an online application, which includes several short essays and a required follow-up phone interview. There are no specific requirements for admission into the Great Texts Program. Students may declare a Great Texts major before or upon arriving at Baylor.

Scholarship Availability: Scholarships are granted through Baylor's Office of Academic Scholarships and Financial Aid.

Campus Overview

Independent Baptist university, founded 1845 • **Coed** 11,580 undergraduate students, 96% full-time, 58% women, 42% men.

Undergraduates 11,162 full-time, 418 part-time. Students come from 50 states and territories, 90 other countries, 16% are from out of state, 7% African American, 6% Asian American or Pacific Islander, 8% Hispanic American, 0.6% Native American, 1% international, 4% transferred in, 34% live on campus.

Faculty *Total:* 883, 87% full-time. *Student/faculty ratio:* 16:1.

Academic Programs *Special study options:* accelerated degree program, advanced placement credit, double majors, honors programs, internships, part-time degree program, services for LD students, student-designed majors, study abroad, summer session for credit. *ROTC:* Air Force (b). *Unusual degree programs:* 3-2 forestry with Duke University; architecture with Washington University in St. Louis, medical technology and biology, medicine, dentistry, optometry.

Athletics Member NCAA. All Division I except football (Division I-A). *Intercollegiate sports:* badminton M(c)/W(c), baseball M(s), basketball M(s)/W(s), crew M(c)/W(c), cross-country running M(s)/W(s), fencing M(c)/W(c), golf M(s)/W(s), ice hockey M(c), lacrosse M(c)/W(c), rugby M(c)/W(c), sailing M(c)/W(c), soccer M(c)/W(s), softball W(s), tennis M(s)/W(s), track and field M(s)/W(s), volleyball

M(c)/W(s), water polo M(c)/W(c). *Intramural sports:* basketball M/W, bowling M/W, football M/W, golf M/W, racquetball M/W, soccer M/W, softball M/W, swimming and diving M/W, table tennis M/W, tennis M/W, track and field M/W, volleyball M/W, weight lifting M/W.

Costs (2005–06) *Comprehensive fee:* $27,555 includes full-time tuition ($19,050), mandatory fees ($2020), and room and board ($6485). Part-time tuition: $794 per semester hour. *Required fees:* $78 per semester hour part-time. *College room only:* $3346. Room and board charges vary according to board plan and housing facility.

Financial Aid 2,998 Federal Work-Study jobs (averaging $2535). In 2004, 3215 non-need-based awards were made. *Average percent of need met:* 68%. *Average financial aid package:* $14,153. *Average need-based loan:* $2494. *Average need-based gift aid:* $9743. *Average non-need-based aid:* $6412.

Contact: Honors College Dean: Dr. Thomas S. Hibbs, Baylor University, One Bear Place, #97181, Waco, Texas 76798-7181; *Telephone:* 254-710-7689; *Fax:* 254-710-7782; *Web site:* http://www.baylor.edu/honors_college/

Blinn College
Honors Program
Brenham, Texas

The Blinn College Honors Program began in 2001. It is designed for students seeking enhanced academic challenges in a stimulating learning environment. The reading- and writing-intensive program gives qualified students the opportunity for more in-depth study than may be possible in the traditional classroom. Honors contracts are available in the following academic disciplines: humanities, mathematics and engineering, social science, and natural science. Additional offerings will be added as the program expands. Students should check the program Web site for the most current list of honors offerings. The Blinn College Honors Program is affiliated with the National Collegiate Honors Council, the Great Plains Honors Council, and the Gulf Coast Intercollegiate Honors Council.

Participation Requirements: To be an Honors Program graduate, students must earn 18 hours minimum of honors credit, including at least one course from English, mathematics, social sciences, and natural sciences. Hours are earned through honors contracts in which students complete activities above the normal course expectations with specially designated faculty mentors. Students are limited to 6 to 8 hours of honors credit per semester. On their transcripts, students receive an honors designation for each 3–4 hours of honors credit earned as well as transcript recognition for being an Honors Program graduate. Students also receive special recognition at spring Commencement exercises.

Admission Process: To qualify for admission to the program, incoming freshmen must have a minimum of 1200 on the SAT or 27 on the ACT and be THEA exempt or THEA complete. Current or returning students must have a cumulative 3.5 GPA or higher in all classes and have passed THEA or be THEA exempt.

All applicants must submit a completed Honors Program application, separate from the application for admission to Blinn; a 500-word minimum essay that explains why they seek acceptance into the program; and three letters of recommendation, two of which must come from high school or college faculty members that are familiar with the student's academic ability. There is a rolling deadline for submitting an application packet to the Honors Program. Tentative deadlines for each long semester will be posted on the program's Web site.

Scholarship Availability: Students accepted into the Honors Program who successfully meet the conditions for honors credit and who maintain a cumulative 3.5 GPA in all their classes qualify for a

$250 scholarship (one honors contract) or a $500 scholarship (two honors contracts) each semester they participate in the program.

Campus Overview

State and locally supported 2-year, founded 1883 • **Coed** 14,057 undergraduate students.

Undergraduates Students come from 36 states and territories, 42 other countries, 1% are from out of state, 8% African American, 2% Asian American or Pacific Islander, 10% Hispanic American, 0.4% Native American, 1% international, 9% live on campus.

Faculty *Total:* 546, 48% full-time, 22% with terminal degrees. *Student/faculty ratio:* 27:1.

Academic Programs *Special study options:* academic remediation for entering students, adult/continuing education programs, advanced placement credit, distance learning, double majors, English as a second language, freshman honors college, honors programs, part-time degree program, services for LD students, summer session for credit.

Athletics Member NJCAA. *Intercollegiate sports:* baseball M(s), basketball M(s)/W(s), cheerleading M(s)/W(s), football M(s), softball W(s), volleyball W(s). *Intramural sports:* basketball M/W, bowling M/W, football M, golf M, softball W, table tennis M/W, volleyball M/W, weight lifting M/W.

Costs (2004–05) *Tuition:* state resident $1728 full-time, $67 per hour part-time; nonresident $4000 full-time, $135 per hour part-time. *Room and board:* $3700. Room and board charges vary according to board plan, gender, and housing facility.

Contact: Director: Jeffrey K. Scott, Blinn College, 902 College Avenue, Brenham, Texas 77833; *Telephone:* 979-830-4414; *Fax:* 979-830-4185; *E-mail:* blinnhonors@blinn.edu; *Web site:* http://www.blinn.edu/HonorsProgram/index.htm

Grayson County College
Presidential Scholars Program

Denison, Texas

Grayson County College's Presidential Scholars honor program is founded on the belief that pursuing one's dreams by aiming high is essential to academic success, and that support is necessary to achieve those lofty goals. Scholars study together in an honor's section of a core humanities subject each year. Honors courses are participatory in nature, emphasizing active learning inside and outside the classroom setting, with a focus upon inquiry-driven research. As ambassadors for the college, scholars participate in service learning, seeking volunteer opportunities to encourage others. Scholars enjoy their honors studies in seminar-format, communication-intensive, collaborative learning environment. Each year, scholars take a field trip to enjoy their shared interest in learning. Scholars host a two-day symposium each spring semester where they present their research findings to the college and the community. Thus the Presidential Scholars is primarily a small group of students dedicated to the generous enterprise of learning, of sharing and promoting academic excellence in the first two years of post-secondary education. In addition to the counseling offered by GCC's administrative staff and faculty, scholars are assisted by their coordinator in their academic pursuits and transfer plans. The program began in 1989 and serves fifteen students. Planning is underway to convert this highly selective program to an honors college allowing greater participation from students and faculty in honors sections of all the core courses.

Participation Requirements: Students must be enrolled full-time at GCC and enrolled in the Scholars' section of the core humanities

course offered that year. Scholars must maintain a 3.4 GPA. They are recognized at the Honors and Awards Assembly, a college-wide celebration of students' greatest achievements at GCC. At graduation, Scholars wear a red stole. Freshman scholars, who are not themselves graduating that year, assist with graduation as ushers and servers. Scholars' transcripts are marked to reflect their participation in the honors program.

Admission Process: Students must complete an admissions form to the Presidential Scholars program, which includes essay writing, completion of GCC's General Scholarship Application (2 forms for recommendations), official high school and college transcripts, and copies of test scores. Students need a cumulative B+ high school average and a 3.4 GPA for any college work completed. ACT scores of 23+ and SAT I scores of 1070 are required minimums if these tests have been taken.

Scholarship Availability: All Presidential Scholars receive $700/semester for tuition and books and if desired, free residential housing on campus with their purchase of the college's meal plan. These scholarships may be added to any of the 250 general scholarships also awarded by GCC.

Campus Overview

State and locally supported 2-year, founded 1964 • **Coed** 3,344 undergraduate students, 51% full-time, 58% women, 42% men.

Undergraduates 1,697 full-time, 1,647 part-time. Students come from 3 states and territories, 2 other countries.

Faculty *Total:* 219, 43% full-time. *Student/faculty ratio:* 16:1.

Academic Programs *Special study options:* academic remediation for entering students, adult/continuing education programs, advanced placement credit, English as a second language, honors programs, part-time degree program, summer session for credit.

Athletics Member NJCAA. *Intercollegiate sports:* baseball M(s), basketball M(s)/W(s), softball W(s). *Intramural sports:* baseball M, basketball M/W, football M, soccer M, softball W.

Contact: Coordinator: Dr. Jean Sorensen, Presidential Scholars Honor Program, Grayson County College, 6101 Grayson Drive, Denison, Texas 75020-8299; *Telephone:* 903-463-8660; *Fax:* 903-463-5284; *E-mail:* sorensenj@grayson.edu

Hardin-Simmons University
Hardin-Simmons Honors Program

Abilene, Texas

In order to attract and challenge the best academic students, Hardin-Simmons University inaugurated its current Honors Program in 2004. The honors offerings, divided between general core and subject area courses, are held to a minimum of 18 hours; thus, students selected into the program are encouraged to integrate more fully in the larger University community. In addition to the central components of interactive learning and scholarly research, there is the further commitment to spiritual growth.

The program provides an enriched educational environment for undergraduate students of exceptional promise who have a wide variety of interests and seek an enhanced learning opportunity. In keeping with the University's Christian mission, the program promotes creative and critical-thinking skills to equip individuals for success in today's world. Courses are taught by selected faculty members interested in working with highly motivated students. Participants are expected to strive for excellence and assume personal accountability for their intellectual growth.

Beyond the classroom, the program offers outstanding academic and extracurricular opportunities designed for intellectually curious, self-motivated students who want to optimize their University experience. Members of the Honors Council and professors participating in the program are dedicated to assisting students in establishing and reaching their personal, scholastic, and career goals.

Students admitted to the program choose from several limited-enrollment honors classes and are able to schedule individual courses for honors credit both on campus and through international studies. The honors experience includes the privilege of working within an inner circle of fellow scholars who possess similar inclinations toward excellence and success in the pursuit of knowledge. Students may anticipate exposure to intensive reading, guided research, focused writing, group activities, interactive learning, introduction to developing technologies, and a senior capstone project. The completed capstone project is presented within a public forum requiring the attendance of all honors peers.

Honors courses are not intended simply to be harder or to demand more work than standard classes; rather, they are designed to maximize student initiative in learning more independently, more intensely, and with greater freedom to explore ideas than might be practical in the usual classroom environment. Honors students are encouraged to integrate what they are learning throughout their University studies. They are also encouraged to look beyond their books, labs, and classwork and to engage actively in the broader University experience.

Participation Requirements: Continuation in the program requires a minimum GPA of 3.5 in honors classes, 3.65 in the major, and 3.5 overall, as well as a senior capstone course with public presentation of research findings. Graduates of the program earn special recognition during graduation ceremonies, along with honors designation on the transcript and diploma.

Admission Process: During the spring and summer, applicants are admitted who meet three of the following four requirements: secondary school rank in the top 10 percent, minimum GPA of 3.75 on 4.0 scale, minimum ACT of 25 or SAT of 1140, and evidence of participation in extracurricular activities. Transfer and other students may also apply. Students leaving the program for legitimate reasons may petition to be readmitted.

Scholarship Availability: Students admitted to the Honors Program normally receive the Presidential Scholarship—the most prestigious academic award offered to entering freshmen. Additional scholarships for honors students are awarded and administered by the Director of the Honors Program.

Campus Overview

Independent Baptist comprehensive, founded 1891 • **Coed** 1,942 undergraduate students, 88% full-time, 56% women, 44% men.

Undergraduates 1,705 full-time, 237 part-time. Students come from 27 states and territories, 4% are from out of state, 5% African American, 1% Asian American or Pacific Islander, 9% Hispanic American, 0.6% Native American, 10% transferred in, 44% live on campus.

Faculty *Total:* 179, 72% full-time, 61% with terminal degrees. *Student/faculty ratio:* 15:1.

Academic Programs *Special study options:* academic remediation for entering students, accelerated degree program, adult/continuing education programs, advanced placement credit, distance learning, double majors, honors programs, independent study, internships, off-campus study, part-time degree program, services for LD students, study abroad, summer session for credit.

Athletics Member NCAA. All Division III. *Intercollegiate sports:* baseball M, basketball M/W, cheerleading M(c)/W(c), football M, golf M/W, soccer M/W, softball W, tennis M/W, volleyball W. *Intramural sports:* badminton M/W, basketball M/W, bowling M/W, cross-country running M(c)/W(c), football M/W, golf M/W, racquetball M/W, soccer M/W, softball M/W, table tennis M(c)/W(c), tennis M/W, ultimate Frisbee M(c)/W(c), volleyball M/W, weight lifting M(c)/W(c).

Costs (2004–05) *Comprehensive fee:* $17,298 includes full-time tuition ($12,600), mandatory fees ($776), and room and board ($3922). Full-time tuition and fees vary according to program. Part-time tuition: $420 per semester hour. Part-time tuition and fees vary according to course load and program. No tuition increase for student's term of enrollment. *Required fees:* $96 per term part-time. *College room only:* $1953. Room and board charges vary according to board plan and housing facility.

Financial Aid 191 Federal Work-Study jobs (averaging $1554). 381 state and other part-time jobs (averaging $1199). In 2003, 140 non-need-based awards were made. *Average percent of need met:* 66%. *Average financial aid package:* $11,521. *Average need-based loan:* $3913. *Average need-based gift aid:* $4733. *Average non-need-based aid:* $3111.

Contact: Director: Robert D. Hamner, Box 15915, Hardin-Simmons University, Abilene, Texas 79698; *Telephone:* 325-670-1310; *Fax:* 325-677-8351; *E-mail:* rdh@hsutx.edu; *Web site:* http://www.hsutx.edu/academics/honors

---

Kingwood College
Community of Scholars
Kingwood, Texas

The Community of Scholars and Kingwood College take pride in their values-centered curriculum, a highly accessible faculty, and commitment to community. The Mission Statement identifies knowledge as the result of a lifelong pursuit of learning, wisdom as the result of the integration of reflection and action, justice as the promotion of the values that seek a better world, and association that promotes the development of a community of learners. Kingwood believes that these components create an excellent environment for teaching and learning. These components complement the aims of the Community of Scholars program, which are to foster the academic life and liberal education of intellectually able students, to give recognition to outstanding students, and to enhance the intellectual and academic life of the College for the benefit of all students and the College.

The Community of Scholars offers its members excellent instruction and preparation for transfer to a four-year institution. Community of Scholars courses are kept small in size (maximum of 15 students) to ensure close contact with the instructor and a ready exchange of ideas. All Community of Scholars courses are designed to promote knowledge acquisition through reading and discussion rather than by rote learning.

The Community of Scholars program fosters an approach to learning that it labels the Community of Scholars Mentality. The Community of Scholars Mentality includes the following characteristics, among others: a curiosity about the world and a desire to study it in the spirit of critical inquiry, an interest in the academic organization and presentation of knowledge, a willingness to lay the foundations for lifelong learning, an appreciation for the transforming power as well as the practical uses of the liberal arts, an eagerness to understand and improve upon one's own learning styles, and an ability to work independently as well as collaboratively with student scholars and Community of Scholars faculty members.

Community of Scholars faculty members model the characteristics of the liberally trained and educated person who is curious about the world, committed to lifelong learning, respectful yet critical of tradition, and tolerant of the opinions of others while possessing firm convictions based on study and experience. They personally demonstrate and foster in others the ability to take multiple perspectives on an issue and to make connections creatively across disciplines. They create the conditions in which students feel enough trust to take risks as they engage in analytical thinking and creative activity that may be unfamiliar to them. Creativity occurs best when teachers place an emphasis on student autonomy and encourage student experimentation. Creativity serves to reinvent, transform, and regenerate the person. Faculty members are also student centered. In addition to teaching course content, they are interested in teaching students certain ways of knowing (e.g., thinking skills, political awareness, intellectual empathy, value identification, and experimentation that links thinking with acting) that are transferable to other learning situations. They believe in values-centered education.

Participation Requirements: Students who complete 12 hours of honors credit with A's or B's are awarded the Kingwood College Honors Certificate. Students who complete 9 hours of honors credit with a minimum overall 3.5 GPA and 25 hours of community service receive the designation of Honors Scholar. Students who complete 15 hours of honors credit with a minimum overall 3.5 GPA are recognized at commencement and receive the designation of Honors Program Graduate on their diplomas and transcripts. Students who complete 15 hours of honors credit with a minimum overall 3.5 GPA and 25 hours of community service are recognized at commencement and receive the designation of Honors Scholar with Distinction.

Admission Process: Any student can register for an honors course. Students may apply for admission into the Community of Scholars program after the first semester of the freshman year. To qualify for admission, a student must have at least a 3.5 overall GPA and take at least one honors course per semester.

Scholarship Availability: Scholarships (ten per full semester) of $250 each are offered through the Community of Scholars program based on academic performance. High school seniors are eligible, as are currently enrolled Kingwood College students.

Campus Overview

State and locally supported 2-year, founded 1984, part of North Harris Montgomery Community College District • **Coed** 6,403 undergraduate students, 21% full-time, 65% women, 35% men.

Undergraduates 1,343 full-time, 5,060 part-time. Students come from 44 other countries, 0.7% are from out of state, 8% African American, 3% Asian American or Pacific Islander, 14% Hispanic American, 0.6% Native American, 2% international, 4% transferred in.

Faculty *Total:* 331, 29% full-time. *Student/faculty ratio:* 16:1.

Academic Programs *Special study options:* academic remediation for entering students, accelerated degree program, advanced placement credit, cooperative education, distance learning, double majors, English as a second language, external degree program, honors programs, independent study, internships, part-time degree program, services for LD students, summer session for credit.

Athletics *Intramural sports:* baseball M.

Costs (2005–06) *Tuition:* area resident $984 full-time, $52 per credit part-time; state resident $1944 full-time, $92 per credit part-time; nonresident $2304 full-time, $220 per credit part-time. Full-time tuition and fees vary according to course load and program. Part-time tuition and fees vary according to course load.

Financial Aid 13 Federal Work-Study jobs, 4 state and other part-time jobs.

Contact: Cindy Baker, Kingwood College, 20000 Kingwood Drive, Kingwood, Texas 77339; *Telephone:* 281-312-1623; *E-mail:* bongiorni@nhmccd.edu; *Web site:* http://kcweb.nhmccd.edu/employee/bongiorni/hon_prg.htm

Lamar University
University Honors Program
Beaumont, Texas

The University Honors Program at Lamar is attentive to the energy and curiosity of emerging scholars, providing an enhanced curriculum and access to additional scholarships and grants. The program is designed to bring out the best in academically talented students and to serve as a core of academic excellence within the University community. Lamar's honors students enjoy the privilege of small classes taught by some of the best professors Lamar has to offer. Students also have opportunities to work with these professors on special projects and independent study. Lamar's honors students are encouraged to do research—including an honors thesis—and to publish and present their work regionally and nationally. McMaster Scholarships and grants-in-aid support students in off-campus internships, field study, and study-abroad programs. The Scholars Development Program prepares students bound for graduate-level study to compete for fellowships. Through the Honors Student Association, students engage in service projects and are active in campus life. Students also have the opportunity to associate with other University Honors Program students in Lamar's newest residence hall in Cardinal Village, which opened in fall 2004. On the Lamar campus, the University Honors Program is housed in the ROTC Building. Facilities include offices (Rooms 102 and 106), as well as a student lounge (103 and 104). The University Honors Program also has access to a large meeting/classroom in the ROTC Building. The University Honors Program is administered by a Director and Assistant Director and governed by the University Honors Council, which has faculty representatives from all colleges of the University. The Executive Council of the Honors Student Association serves as an advisory board to the Honors Program Director.

The Honors Program has served the needs of Lamar's intellectually gifted students since the mid-1960s. More than 220 students are active participants in the Honors Program.

Participation Requirements: University Honors Program students should take one or more honors classes each semester during their first two years at Lamar. The majority of the University's core curriculum requirements may be completed as honors, and advanced interdisciplinary seminars are available. Many students also choose to take an Honors Independent Study class, which enables them to conduct research or engage in creative activity under the supervision of a faculty member of their choice. Continued enrollment in the Honors Program requires that the student maintain at least a 3.2 GPA.

All students entering the University Honors Program are encouraged to work toward becoming University Honors Program graduates. There are two ways to achieve this distinction. The student may complete 24 hours of honors classes, including 6 hours of the honors thesis. The thesis represents original research or creative work produced by the student under the direction of a faculty supervisor. Alternatively, the student may complete 27 hours of honors classes, at least 9 hours of which are upper-level honors classes. University Honors Program graduates must also collect a specified number of "honor points" through community service and participation in cultural events and campus activities.

Special recognition is given to University Honors Program graduates at University commencement, including the opportunity to wear the University Honors Program medallion. The status of each University Honors Program graduate is also permanently affixed to the individual's official University transcript.

Admission Process: Incoming freshmen desiring to participate in the University Honors Program at Lamar must complete an application form and forward it, along with an official copy of the high school transcript indicating class rank and SAT or ACT score, to the Director of the University Honors Program. The application must be accompanied by two letters of recommendation from the student's teachers, counselors, administrators, or supervisors and a brief resume of the student's high school activities and achievements. Entering freshmen must have an SAT I score of at least 1200 (ACT 27) or a ranking in the top 10 percent of their graduating class. Students are also expected to exhibit a record of academic achievement and community involvement. (The expected score on the three-part SAT is 1800.)

Continuing Lamar students and transfer students from other colleges or Universities must have at least a 3.5 GPA on a minimum of 12 credit hours of academic work. A separate application form is available for these students, who are strongly encouraged to contact the Director for guidance in accessing University Honors Program opportunities.

To be considered for scholarships, students should submit their applications for admission to the University Honors Program by February 1 in the year the student expects to enter Lamar in the fall semester. Others seeking participation in the program may apply at any time. Application forms are available from the University Honors Program offices or on the Lamar University Web site.

Scholarship Availability: The McMaster Honors Scholarships at Lamar were instituted in 1976 in memory of Mr. and Mrs. M. W. McMaster of Beaumont. This fund now has an endowment of nearly $2 million. The program offers financial support to students both in the form of McMaster Honors Scholarships and in the form of grants-in-aid of research and creative activity. McMaster Scholarships range from $500 to $1250 per semester and may be received in combination with other scholarships from the University or the student's major department. In addition, the Tom Jones Memorial Fund provides several thousand dollars annually for honors scholarships.

Both incoming freshmen and honors students already enrolled at Lamar may apply for honors scholarships. Eligibility for honors scholarships requires an SAT I score of at least 1200 (ACT 27) and a ranking in the top 10 percent of the graduating class for incoming freshmen and a GPA of 3.6 or higher for current Lamar University Honors Program students. Recipients of the scholarships must complete at least one honors class each semester, maintain a minimum 3.2 GPA, perform volunteer service, and participate in University Honors Program activities, including the Honors Student Association.

Incoming students applying for honors scholarships must so indicate on their University Honors Program application and append a letter or essay as described on the application form. Current Lamar students must submit a separate scholarship application form accompanied by two faculty member recommendation forms. The priority deadline for all scholarship applications is February 1. Scholarships are allocated by the Lamar University Honors Council, and notification letters are mailed out before the end of March. Application forms for the McMaster Honors Scholarships are available from the Honors Program Office or on the Honors Web site. Receiving a University Honors Program scholarship does not prevent students from applying for other Lamar University scholarships. Students should contact the Scholarships Office at 409-880-1714.

Campus Overview

State-supported university, founded 1923, part of Texas State University System • **Coed** 9,620 undergraduate students, 70% full-time, 60% women, 40% men.

Undergraduates 6,771 full-time, 2,849 part-time. Students come from 30 states and territories, 27 other countries, 1% are from out of state, 24% African American, 3% Asian American or Pacific Islander, 5% Hispanic American, 0.6% Native American, 0.6% international, 7% transferred in.

Faculty Total: 525, 71% full-time, 45% with terminal degrees. Student/faculty ratio: 20:1.

Academic Programs Special study options: academic remediation for entering students, accelerated degree program, adult/continuing education programs, advanced placement credit, cooperative education, English as a second language, honors programs, internships, off-campus study, part-time degree program, services for LD students, student-designed majors, study abroad, summer session for credit.

Athletics Member NCAA. All Division I except football (Division I-AA). Intercollegiate sports: baseball M(s), basketball M(s)/W(s), cheerleading M/W, cross-country running M(s)/W(s), golf M(s)/W(s), tennis M(s)/W(s), track and field M(s)/W(s), volleyball W(s). Intramural sports: basketball M/W, cross-country running M/W, football M, golf M/W, gymnastics W, racquetball M/W, rugby M/W, sailing M/W, soccer M/W, swimming and diving M/W, table tennis M, tennis M/W, track and field M/W, volleyball M/W, weight lifting M/W.

Costs (2004–05) Tuition: $864 per term part-time; state resident $2304 full-time; nonresident $9552 full-time, $3582 per term part-time. Part-time tuition and fees vary according to course load. Required fees: $852 full-time, $374 per term part-time. Room and board: $5706; room only: $3225. Room and board charges vary according to board plan and housing facility.

Financial Aid 94 Federal Work-Study jobs (averaging $3000). 21 state and other part-time jobs (averaging $3000). In 2004, 1500 non-need-based awards were made. Average percent of need met: 23%. Average financial aid package: $1855. Average non-need-based aid: $1300.

Contact: Dr. Donna B. Birdwell, Director, Dr. Kevin Dodson, Assistant Director, University Honors Program, Lamar University, P.O. Box 10968, Beaumont, Texas 77710; Telephone: 409-880-8658; Fax: 409-880-2325; E-mail: donna.birdwell@.lamar.edu; Web site: http://dept.lamar.edu/honors/

Laredo Community College
Laredo Community College Honors Program
Laredo, Texas

*T*he Laredo Community College (LCC) Honors Program serves academically gifted students from the Laredo area. The program is unique in that it provides full scholarships covering tuition, fees, and books to 25 freshman students based on merit. Students who maintain eligibility continue to receive the scholarship their sophomore year.

The LCC Honors Program is guided by its mission to encourage students to become outstanding independent learners, capable of critical thinking and self-expression; provide students with opportunities to engage in meaningful teamwork; allow students to explore facets of learning and materials that are usually unavailable in regular courses; increase opportunities for reading and writing at an advanced level; enhance mathematical, scientific, and technological skills; provide for a higher degree of student participation and involvement; and increase the opportunity for academically gifted students to transfer to a major university.

The honors curriculum includes all component areas of the LCC core curriculum. It offers designated courses in the humanities, social and behavioral sciences, and mathematics, with contract courses available in the natural sciences and other disciplines. Honors classes are taught by faculty members who are dedicated to presenting students with the most stimulating educational experience and environment possible. Small classes (10–25 students) allow optimum interaction between faculty members and students.

In addition to their classroom experiences, honors students participate in a variety of student development activities. Honors students meets regularly to plan distinguished-speaker programs, leadership seminars, field trips, community service activities, fund-raisers, and other social events. Each year two sophomore students recognized for their outstanding achievement by Honors Program coordinators are provided with funding to attend the National Collegiate Honors Council (NCHC) national conference.

Also, sophomore students (on a rotation basis) have the distinction of serving as student representatives at the College's Board of Trustees meetings. An honors lounge located adjacent to the Honors Office in the Kazen College Center is a gathering place for students to study or just relax and socialize.

Founded in 1988, the program has a maximum enrollment of 50 students.

Participation Requirements: Honors students must successfully complete a minimum of 24 semester credit hours of honors courses. Students take designated honors courses and contract courses to fulfill this requirement. They must maintain an overall GPA of 3.0 and earn no grade lower than C in any course. All honors classes are indicated on official transcripts. Honors Program graduates receive a special diploma, wear the honors stole, and are personally recognized during the graduation ceremony by the College president who dons each student with the honors medallion.

Admission Process: To qualify for the Honors Program, a student must meet at least one of the following requirements: ACT composite score of 23, SAT composite score of 1070, academic recognition on the Texas Assessment of Knowledge and Skills (TAKS), or rank in the top 10 percent of the high school class. Final selection is based upon an interview with the Honors Program coordinators. Application forms are available at the LCC Web site at http://www.laredo.edu/honors or at the LCC Honors Office. The deadline for submitting applications is February 15. A current high school transcript and two letters of recommendation must be included with the application.

Scholarship Availability: The Honors Program provides full scholarships covering tuition, fees, and books. Scholarships are limited to fall and spring semesters, up to 66 semester credit hours.

Campus Overview

State and locally supported 2-year, founded 1946 • **Coed** 9,032 undergraduate students, 33% full-time, 59% women, 41% men.

Undergraduates 3,018 full-time, 6,014 part-time. Students come from 4 states and territories, 5 other countries, 0.2% African American, 0.2% Asian American or Pacific Islander, 94% Hispanic American, 3% international.

Faculty *Total:* 376, 55% full-time, 10% with terminal degrees. *Student/faculty ratio:* 19:1.

Academic Programs *Special study options:* academic remediation for entering students, adult/continuing education programs, advanced placement credit, distance learning, double majors, English as a second language, freshman honors college, honors programs, independent study, internships, part-time degree program, services for LD students, summer session for credit.

Athletics Member NJCAA. *Intercollegiate sports:* baseball M(s), tennis M(s)/W(s), volleyball W(s). *Intramural sports:* cross-country running M/W, gymnastics M/W, swimming and diving M/W, tennis M/W, track and field M/W, volleyball M/W.

Costs (2005–06) *Tuition:* area resident $1188 full-time, $32 per credit hour part-time; state resident $1904 full-time, $64 per credit hour part-time; nonresident $2628 full-time, $96 per credit hour part-time. *Required fees:* $24 per credit hour part-time, $28 per term part-time. *Room and board:* $4000.

Financial Aid 282 Federal Work-Study jobs (averaging $1854). 127 state and other part-time jobs (averaging $1884).

Contact: Honors Program Coordinators: Dr. Jacinto P. Juarez and Jose D. Compean, Laredo Community College Honors Program, Box 172, West End Washington Street, Laredo, Texas 78040; *Telephone:* 956-764-5956; *Fax:* 956-721-5807; *E-mail:* honors@laredo.edu; *Web site:* http://www.laredo.edu/honors

Lee College
Honors Program
Baytown, Texas

*T*he Honors Program at Lee College serves academically talented and highly motivated students. Honors at Lee College reflects the College's mission statement by providing high-quality instruction for its students and preparing them for success in higher education or employment. The program also promotes the College's goals of continued review and revitalization of existing curricula, academic programs, and course offerings while improving recruitment and retention.

Historically, the program has been faculty and student inspired with individual faculty members or students proposing courses. The Honors Program presently consists of team-taught interdisciplinary courses in American studies (offering credit in American history and American literature), environmental science and chemistry, and freshman composition and humanities. Honors contracts, which provide students the opportunity to work on a one-to-one-basis with faculty members, are presently available in eighteen disciplines including accounting, allied health, applied music, biology, chemistry, English, environmental science, government, history, humanities, journalism, kinesiology, literature, philosophy, physics, psychology, sociology, and theater arts. The nature of the contractual arrangements varies from course to course according to the characteristics of the discipline involved.

In addition to the intellectual challenge, honors offers students the following educational advantages: scholarship opportunities, classes limited to 14 students, an honors study suite with computers dedicated exclusively to honors, participation in the governance of the Honors Program, counseling and transfer advisement, college financial support for student travel for presentations at scholarly conferences and conventions, and opportunities to publish. Students enrolled in honors belong to the Student Honors Council, which serves to support the Honors Program and sponsors a fall retreat to promote esprit de corps among honors students. A spring lyceum offers honors students the opportunity to present their work to the College community. Students also participate in the spring and fall symposiums of the Gulf Coast Intercollegiate Honors Conference (GCIHC) and the annual meeting of the Great Plains Honors Conference. Students who present papers at symposiums and conferences or who publish have it so noted on transcripts. The Lee College Honors Program publishes Touchstone, the Texas State Historical Association's journal of undergraduate research. Lee College has articulation agreements in honors with a number of public and private universities throughout the state of Texas.

Honors at Lee College began thirty-six years ago with a team-taught, interdisciplinary American studies course. However, the program has recently undergone considerable expansion as the consequence of the appointment of an honors coordinator in 1994. Currently, approximately 70 students are either enrolled in interdisciplinary honors courses or are pursuing honors contracts.

Participation Requirements: The Lee College Honors Program is designed to be an open-ended program that offers students the option of pursuing either full participation or a limited number of hours. Each honors course or contract completed with a grade of B or better is designated honors on transcripts; "completed Honors Program" is noted on the permanent transcript of students who earn 15 hours of more in honors with a cumulative GPA of at least 3.25 on a 4.0 scale.

Admission Process: Students desiring to enroll in honors must meet any two of the following requirements: minimum ACT scores of 26, SAT I scores of 1100 and above (for English honors, must also have a verbal score of 500 and above), 9 or more hours of college-level work with a GPA of 3.5 or better, a minimum score of 6 on the Lee College English placement test and 13 on the reading test (or CPT 82 or above), rank in top 10 percent of high school class, interview with and approval of the honors instructor teaching the class or offering the contract, and recommendation(s) from previous instructor(s).

Scholarship Availability: There are twenty-six scholarships available in general honors and six in American Studies. Honors students are also eligible for other scholarships offered by the Lee College Foundation.

Campus Overview

Suburban 35-acre campus with easy access to Houston • **Coed** 5,906 undergraduate students, 27% full-time, 44% women, 56% men.

Undergraduates 1,624 full-time, 4,282 part-time. Students come from 10 other countries, 12% African American, 1% Asian American or Pacific Islander, 22% Hispanic American, 0.2% Native American, 0.9% international.

Faculty *Total:* 363, 47% full-time, 9% with terminal degrees. *Student/faculty ratio:* 16:1.

Academic Programs *Special study options:* academic remediation for entering students, adult/continuing education programs, advanced placement credit, cooperative education, distance learning, English as a second language, honors programs, independent study, internships, part-time degree program, summer session for credit. *ROTC:* Army (c).

Athletics Member NJCAA. *Intercollegiate sports:* basketball M(s), tennis W(s), volleyball W(s). *Intramural sports:* basketball M, bowling M/W, football M, racquetball M/W, table tennis M/W, volleyball W.

Financial Aid 30 Federal Work-Study jobs (averaging $3130).

Contact: Honors Program Coordinator: John C. Britt, Lee College, P.O. Box 818, Baytown, Texas 77522-0818; *Telephone:* 281-425-6375; *Fax:* 832-556-4023; *E-mail:* jbritt@lee.edu+

LeTourneau University

Honors Program

Longview, Texas

The Honors Program at LeTourneau University challenges academically talented and highly motivated students to reach their full intellectual, social, spiritual, and leadership potential in a global society. Within an active learning environment, the Honors Program fosters ingenuity in independent and collective problem solving, enabling the students to relate learning to experiential practice. The Honors Program offers opportunities to integrate faith and learning; to analyze, synthesize, and evaluate ideas; to express concepts and research effectively; to broaden intellectual horizons through interdisciplinary collaboration; and to explore their major fields with greater depth.

Participation in and completion of the Honors Program require no additional fees, and the program is available to qualified students regardless of their chosen major. In addition to the academic challenges, Honors Program students participate in various social events and community service opportunities. Honors Program students may also become involved with the University's Center for the Development of Christian Leadership. The purpose of the Center is to prepare students to lead transformational change in their local and global communities.

Following two years of careful planning by a University-wide committee, the Honors Program was initiated in 2001. Approximately 25 students are admitted to the program each fall.

Participation Requirements: LeTourneau University Honors Program participants must complete at least 17 credits of honors courses. During the freshman year, students must enroll in three

honors courses: Honors Seminar, Biblical Worldview, and either Communication in the Information Age or Creativity: Birth of a Notion.

Students must take two 3-hour honors courses and two 1-hour honors seminars during the sophomore and junior years. The Honors Program student and their academic adviser choose from honors courses offered each semester.

During the senior year, two 1-hour seminar honors classes serve as capstone experiences for the students. The courses move the student into dealing with postgraduation issues and life and are required of all Honors Program students.

Upon completion of the Honors Program, students receive an honors degree, wear an honors cord, and are recognized at commencement. In addition, the students' permanent academic records at LeTourneau University reflect participation in the program.

Admission Process: Participants in the LeTourneau University Honors Program are selected through a specific application process. Students with outstanding academic achievement (high ACT/SAT scores, exceptional high school GPA) and a record of extracurricular involvement are invited to apply. Selection is highly competitive. The initial cohort of honors students at LeTourneau had an average ACT score, SAT score, and high school GPA of 31, 1410, and 3.99 respectively.

Scholarship Availability: Honors-caliber students may apply for one of several academic scholarships that are awarded on the bases of standardized test scores and high school cumulative GPAs. Early application is encouraged. These scholarships include Heritage Scholarships, Presidential Scholarships, and Dean's Scholarships.

Campus Overview

Independent nondenominational comprehensive, founded 1946 • **Coed** 3,388 undergraduate students, 37% full-time, 54% women, 46% men.

Undergraduates 1,241 full-time, 2,147 part-time. Students come from 50 states and territories, 27 other countries, 49% are from out of state, 20% African American, 1% Asian American or Pacific Islander, 8% Hispanic American, 0.4% Native American, 0.9% international, 3% transferred in, 76% live on campus.

Faculty *Total:* 301, 23% full-time, 44% with terminal degrees. *Student/faculty ratio:* 16:1.

Academic Programs *Special study options:* academic remediation for entering students, adult/continuing education programs, advanced placement credit, cooperative education, distance learning, double majors, honors programs, independent study, internships, off-campus study, part-time degree program, services for LD students, study abroad, summer session for credit.

Athletics Member NCAA, NCCAA. All NCAA Division III. *Intercollegiate sports:* baseball M, basketball M/W, cross-country running M/W, golf M/W, soccer M/W, softball W, tennis M/W, volleyball W. *Intramural sports:* badminton M/W, basketball M/W, bowling M/W, cross-country running M/W, football M/W, golf M/W, racquetball M/W, soccer M/W, softball M/W, swimming and diving M/W, table tennis M/W, tennis M/W, volleyball M/W.

Costs (2005–06) *Comprehensive fee:* $22,176 includes full-time tuition ($15,710), mandatory fees ($180), and room and board ($6286). Part-time tuition: $280 per hour. Part-time tuition and fees vary according to course load. *Room and board:* Room and board charges vary according to board plan.

Financial Aid In 2003, 220 non-need-based awards were made. *Average percent of need met:* 74%. *Average financial aid package:* $12,078. *Average need-based loan:* $4199. *Average need-based gift aid:* $7874. *Average non-need-based aid:* $4002.

Contact: Contact: Dr. J. Dirk Nelson, Assistant Vice President for Academic Affairs, LeTourneau University, P.O. Box 7001, Longview, Texas 75607-7001; *Telephone:* 903-233-3230; *Fax:* 903-233-3259; *E-mail:* dirknelson@letu.edu.

Lubbock Christian University

University Honors Program

Lubbock, Texas

The University Honors Program provides students of high academic ability an opportunity to enhance their college educational experience with challenging and stimulating courses. Although it does not require its students to take any more courses or hours than they would take otherwise, the program provides more depth and breadth of study within the courses they do take. The emphasis is on quality and not quantity—that is, honors classes, smaller than their nonhonors counterparts, typically are discussion-based and student-centered, dealing with meaningful ideas rather than just adding extra volumes of work to the course load.

Honors faculty members, the Honors Director, the University's Academic Vice President, and honors student representatives comprise the Honors Advisory Council, which makes policy and offers guidance to the program. Elected student representatives comprise the Student Honors Advisory Council, which plans and executes extracurricular activities for honors students and also runs freshman orientation, mentoring, and recruiting programs. Students also participate in monthly informal luncheons with the Director and honors faculty members; occasional dinners in faculty members' homes; various service projects; and excursions to concerts, theatrical performances, and museums and other field trips relevant to honors classes.

Benefits of the program include honors academic scholarships, preferred dorm placement, interesting and challenging courses, small class size, the collegiality of like-minded students and professors in academic as well as social settings, the distinction of an honors designation on the transcript and diploma, honors recognition at graduation, enhanced marketability of being an honors graduate, study-abroad opportunities, travel scholarships to regional and national conferences, and affiliation with the National Collegiate Honors Council and the Great Plains Honors Council.

The program began in fall 2000 with its first cohort of 15 students and has continued to add one or two new cohorts each fall.

Participation Requirements: The University Honors Program is open to students of any major. The program consists of 30 hours of required honors credit. Twelve of these 30 semester hours are taken in an honors core of four courses during the first year. These core courses are English, Bible, history, and science, and they satisfy either University or departmental core requirements. All honors students take these courses as the foundation of the honors experience.

An additional 18 hours of the 30 required may be chosen from among courses designated for honors credit. The University presently offers an additional 21 hours of honors courses on a variety of topics, and it plans to continue to add courses as the program grows and develops. Included in these 21 hours is a senior capstone course, HON 4380, Senior Research, designed to give honors students an opportunity to engage in an extensive research project on an issue or problem in their major field of study. Students fulfill hours of required honors credit by entering into honors contracts with instructors of a variety of primarily upper-division classes, usually in their majors. In these classes, faculty members give honors students more challenging work to earn the honors designation.

Continuation in the honors program is based on a 3.5 or higher GPA in all honors courses and a 3.25 or higher GPA in all courses. Honors students who successfully complete the 30 hours of honors course work and maintain the GPA requirements receive honors recognition at graduation as well as the distinction of an honors designation on their transcripts and diplomas.

Admission Process: Acceptance in the honors program is based on an ACT composite score of 27 or higher or SAT I composite score of 1210 or higher.

Scholarship Availability: Lubbock Christian University offers significant scholarship assistance to deserving students, including an annually renewable $1000 Honors Scholarship to students whose ACT/SAT scores qualify them for the University Honors Program. This Honors Scholarship is in addition to other academic scholarships awarded by the University. Continuation of the Honors Scholarship is based on students successfully meeting the honors program's GPA and course requirements. Entering students with an ACT score of 30 or higher or an SAT I score of 1320 or higher or an SAT score of 1980 or higher are eligible for an additional Helen DeVitt Jones Scholarship of $1500. The University awards approximately five of these Jones Scholarships annually on first-come, first-served basis. These awards are annually renewable to recipients who continue to meet the Honors Program's minimum GPA standards.

Campus Overview

Independent comprehensive, founded 1957, affiliated with Church of Christ • **Coed** 1,778 undergraduate students, 77% full-time, 56% women, 44% men.

Undergraduates 1,376 full-time, 402 part-time. Students come from 33 states and territories, 13 other countries, 10% are from out of state, 6% African American, 0.6% Asian American or Pacific Islander, 14% Hispanic American, 0.5% Native American, 0.1% international, 16% transferred in, 30% live on campus.

Faculty Total: 155, 51% full-time, 45% with terminal degrees. Student/faculty ratio: 15:1.

Academic Programs Special study options: academic remediation for entering students, accelerated degree program, adult/continuing education programs, advanced placement credit, distance learning, double majors, honors programs, internships, part-time degree program, services for LD students, student-designed majors, study abroad, summer session for credit. ROTC: Army (c), Air Force (c). Unusual degree programs: 3-2 engineering with Texas Tech University.

Athletics Member NAIA. Intercollegiate sports: baseball M(s), basketball M(s)/W(s), cheerleading M/W, golf M/W, soccer M, track and field M/W, volleyball W(s). Intramural sports: badminton M/W, basketball M/W, bowling M/W, cross-country running M/W, football M/W, golf M/W, racquetball M/W, soccer M/W, softball M/W, table tennis M/W, tennis M/W, track and field M/W, volleyball M/W.

Costs (2004–05) Comprehensive fee: $16,124 includes full-time tuition ($11,088), mandatory fees ($906), and room and board ($4130). Full-time tuition and fees vary according to program. Part-time tuition and fees vary according to course load and program. Room and board: Room and board charges vary according to board plan and housing facility.

Financial Aid 926 Federal Work-Study jobs (averaging $2000). 91 state and other part-time jobs (averaging $303). In 2004, 165 non-need-based awards were made. Average percent of need met: 73%. Average financial aid package: $11,134. Average need-based loan: $3809. Average need-based gift aid: $7049. Average non-need-based aid: $10,018.

Contact: Director: Dr. Jim Bullock, 5601 19th Street, Lubbock, Texas 79407-2099; Telephone: 806-720-7603; Fax: 806-720-7255; E-mail: jim.bullock@lcu.edu; Web site: http://www.lcu.edu/LCU/academics/honors

Midwestern State University

Honors Program

Wichita Falls, Texas

First established in 1964 and developed upon Midwestern State University's (MSU) Tradition of Excellence, the University Honors Program offers high-achieving MSU students a challenging premier undergraduate learning experience. From the Honors Introductory

Seminar at the beginning, through honors designated classes taught by outstanding faculty members, to the Honors Capstone Course and graduation with honors at the end, the MSU Honors Program serves as a powerful program from start to finish.

Midwestern State University is a member of the National Collegiate Honors Council and the regional Great Plains Honors Council. These affiliations broaden the scope of opportunities available for honors students. By enriching the educational experience of MSU's honors students, the MSU Honors Program creates an atmosphere of intellectual fellowship that enhances the University-wide quality of education and promotes Midwestern State University as the center of intellectual growth and development in north-central Texas.

Participation Requirements: Participation in the Honors Program recognizes the student's potential to work in a more challenging educational framework, guided by some of Midwestern's most outstanding faculty members. In order to graduate with Honors Program distinction, students are required to successfully complete eight honors designated courses. The selection of honors designated courses includes an Honors Introductory Seminar at the beginning and an Honors Capstone Course at the end. In order to remain in good standing in the program, honors students must take at least one honors designated class each fall and spring semester and maintain a minimum cumulative GPA of 3.25 at all times. In addition to these curricular requirements, the Honors Program requires participation in a variety of cocurricular components, such as a guest speaker series, participation in professional conferences, field trips, community service, leadership, and a choice of undergraduate research projects, internships, or study abroad. Honors housing offers students a supportive living/learning environment. Finally, honors experiences and achievements better prepare students for success and leadership in graduate and professional schools, in the job market, and as citizens of the global community.

Admission Process: Admission to the Honors Program is by application and is based upon a minimum SAT score of 1200 or ACT score of 27, a written essay, and a faculty letter of recommendation. Individuals may under special circumstances be granted provisional status based on alternate requirements. Students, including transfer students, may not enter the Honors Program later than their sophomore year.

Scholarship Availability: Honors students in good standing receive a yearly honors scholarship until graduation. Participation in the Honors Program is also an important consideration for selection of Midwestern's coveted Clark and Hardin Scholars, MSU's highest undergraduate honors.

Campus Overview

State-supported comprehensive, founded 1922 • **Coed** 5,606 undergraduate students, 71% full-time, 57% women, 43% men.

Undergraduates 3,992 full-time, 1,614 part-time. Students come from 42 states and territories, 37 other countries, 6% are from out of state, 11% African American, 3% Asian American or Pacific Islander, 9% Hispanic American, 1% Native American, 5% international, 11% transferred in, 14% live on campus.

Faculty *Total:* 315, 69% full-time, 54% with terminal degrees. *Student/faculty ratio:* 20:1.

Academic Programs *Special study options:* academic remediation for entering students, accelerated degree program, adult/continuing education programs, advanced placement credit, distance learning, English as a second language, honors programs, internships, part-time degree program, services for LD students, study abroad, summer session for credit. *ROTC:* Air Force (c).

Athletics Member NCAA. All Division II. *Intercollegiate sports:* basketball M(s)/W(s), cheerleading M(s)(c)/W(s)(c), fencing M(c)/W(c), football M(s), soccer M(s)/W(s), softball W(s), tennis M(s)/W(s), volleyball W(s). *Intramural sports:* archery M/W, badminton M/W, basketball M/W, bowling M/W, football M/W, golf M/W, rugby M(c), soccer M/W, softball M/W, table tennis M/W, tennis M/W, volleyball M/W, weight lifting M/W.

Costs (2004–05) *Tuition:* state resident $1440 full-time, $48 per credit hour part-time; nonresident $9180 full-time, $306 per credit hour part-time. Part-time tuition and fees vary according to course load. *Required fees:* $2300 full-time, $132 per credit hour part-time. *Room and board:* $4844; room only: $2400. Room and board charges vary according to board plan and housing facility.

Financial Aid 56 Federal Work-Study jobs (averaging $1200). 15 state and other part-time jobs (averaging $897). In 2003, 639 non-need-based awards were made. *Average percent of need met:* 60%. *Average financial aid package:* $4035. *Average need-based loan:* $4715. *Average need-based gift aid:* $3937. *Average non-need-based aid:* $3932.

Contact: Director: Dr. Mark Farris, 3410 Taft Boulevard, Wichita Falls, Texas 76308; *Telephone:* 940-397-4534; *Fax:* 940-397-4042; *E-mail:* honors@mwsu.edu

---

Montgomery College
Honors Program
Conroe, Texas

In recent years, enrollment in honors classes has reached 1,300 students and includes humanities, social sciences, sciences, business, math, applied technology, and arts. In addition to the general Honors Program, the College offers several admission-by-application specialty honors programs: Macklin Scholars, Millennium Scholars, Montgomery Scholars, and Takoma Park Scholars. Information can be obtained on the College's Honors Program Web site, www.montgomerycollege.edu.

Participation Requirements: The general Honors Program is open to students who meet the eligibility requirements. There is no minimum number of courses. Awards include the Honors Scholar Award, which is given to those who have completed twelve honors courses, taken in more than one discipline, and earned a minimum 3.4 GPA. Honors students who receive this award are recognized at each campus's academic honors award convocation held each spring. Montgomery College is currently developing an honors track that it plans to implement in fall 2006. In addition, each campus has honors student clubs that promote honors activities at the College, sponsor fundraisers, and support the honor programs.

Admission Process: Students, either current Montgomery College students or other college students with a minimum GPA of 3.2 and 12 earned academic credits, including a grade of A or B in Techniques of Writing (En101/a or EN102), are eligible for the Honors Program. Recent high school graduates or currently enrolled high school seniors may be admitted on the basis of an evaluation of their high school grade reports. Board of Trustee scholarship recipients who have had a transcript review to verify their English placement are also eligible. In addition, returning adult students who have demonstrated academic excellence are eligible.

Scholarship Availability: Both the Montgomery College Foundation and the Board of Trustees offer a limited number of scholarships to students demonstrating high academic potential. Scholarships are competitive. Specialized honors programs offer a variety of other scholarship opportunities for qualified students who are accepted into these programs.

Campus Overview

State and locally supported 2-year, founded 1995, part of North Harris Montgomery Community College District • **Coed** 6,524 undergraduate students, 36% full-time, 61% women, 39% men.

Undergraduates 2,380 full-time, 4,144 part-time. 0.7% are from out of state, 6% African American, 2% Asian American or Pacific Islander, 11% Hispanic American, 0.6% Native American, 0.6% international.

Faculty *Total:* 399, 25% full-time.

Academic Programs *Special study options:* academic remediation for entering students, adult/continuing education programs, advanced placement credit, English as a second language, internships, part-time degree program, services for LD students, summer session for credit.

Costs (2004–05) *Tuition:* area resident $984 full-time; state resident $1944 full-time; nonresident $2304 full-time.

Financial Aid 25 Federal Work-Study jobs (averaging $2500). 4 state and other part-time jobs.

Contact: Contact: Professor Dedee Aleccia, Director of the College-Wide Honors Program, Montgomery College, 3200 College Park Drive, Conroe, Texas 77384; *Telephone:* 301-251-7417; *E-mail:* dedee.aleccia@montgomerycollege.edu

North Harris College

Honors Program

Houston, Texas

The mission of the North Harris College Honors Program is to augment existing programs and reaffirm the College's commitment to excellence by identifying, recruiting, and challenging academically motivated students and providing enrichment and flexibility to develop full-student potential while offering faculty members the opportunity for renewal and innovation. The Honors Program offers enrichment of course materials and the freedom to work independently and collaboratively with faculty members who encourage lively, engaging discourse and activity outside the classroom.

Honors credit is earned through special contracts and classes with a coordinator who is committed to an open-ended approach to learning. Students are encouraged to contribute extensively and creatively through small group interaction, seminars, laboratories, oral reports, special research projects, informal discussions, and both individual and group projects.

The Honors Student Organization (HSO) is in charge of workshop presentations, debates, and seminars each semester. The organization selects and coordinates presentations for Honors Day each semester. In addition, its members operate the Honors Program booth at Oktoberfest and Spring Fling and write the honors newsletter, The Honors Scholar. Representatives from the organization serve on the honors committee.

In addition to the Honors Student Organization's activities, interaction among honors students is promoted through attendance at honors conventions, cultural events off campus, and the pizza luncheon each midsemester.

The Honors Scholar Community Service Program provides an opportunity for honors students to make a difference in their communities by volunteering their time in a community service activity. Any honors student who has or plans to complete at least 9 hours of honors credit is eligible to participate in the program.

The program began in 1993 and averages 80 students each semester.

Participation Requirements: Upon successfully completing 15 hours of honors-contract credit with a GPA of 3.5 or better, students receive the designation Honors Program Graduate on their diploma and transcript, special recognition at graduation, and a medallion commemorating the event.

To graduate as an honors scholar, a student must complete at least 9 honors credit hours with at least a 3.5 GPA as well as 25 hours of community service. With the completion of 15 honors credit hours with a minimum 3.5 GPA and completion of 25 hours of community service, a student may qualify to graduate as an Honors Scholar with Distinction.

Admission Process: The Honors Program is open to all students. Any student may attempt an honors contract any semester he or she is enrolled at North Harris College with permission of the instructor in his or her regularly scheduled class and acceptance by the honors coordinator for that contract.

Scholarship Availability: Any student in the Honors Program who is carrying 6 or more College credit hours, has at least a 3.5 GPA, and is attempting at least one honors class or contract, is eligible for the Honors Program scholarship after the completion of 12 hours of college credit. The scholarships are awarded to the top students who apply, based on their GPAs. The scholarship may be used for tuition, books, or fees and related educational expenses for the following semester. The Honors Program scholarship is renewable for an additional two semesters with reapplication.

Campus Overview

State and locally supported 2-year, founded 1972, part of North Harris Montgomery Community College District • **Coed** 10,591 undergraduate students.

Undergraduates 0.5% are from out of state, 21% African American, 7% Asian American or Pacific Islander, 23% Hispanic American, 0.3% Native American, 4% international.

Faculty *Total:* 534, 36% full-time.

Academic Programs *Special study options:* academic remediation for entering students, adult/continuing education programs, advanced placement credit, cooperative education, distance learning, double majors, English as a second language, external degree program, honors programs, independent study, internships, off-campus study, part-time degree program, services for LD students, summer session for credit. *ROTC:* Army (c).

Athletics *Intramural sports:* badminton M/W, baseball M/W, basketball M/W, bowling M/W, football M/W, golf M/W, gymnastics M/W, racquetball M/W, soccer M/W, softball M/W, table tennis M/W, tennis M/W, track and field M/W, volleyball M/W, weight lifting M/W.

Costs (2004–05) *Tuition:* area resident $1236 full-time; state resident $2436 full-time; nonresident $2886 full-time. *Required fees:* $276 full-time.

Financial Aid 61 Federal Work-Study jobs (averaging $1390). 9 state and other part-time jobs (averaging $1153).

Contact: Director: Sandy Deabler, Honors Office A-168, North Harris College, 2700 W. W. Thorne Drive, Houston, Texas 77073; *Telephone:* 281-618-5528; *Fax:* 281-618-5574; *E-mail:* sandy.deabler@nhmccd.edu; *Web site:* http://www.northharriscollege.com/Templates/content.aspx?pid=12748

Prairie View A&M University

University Scholars Program

Prairie View, Texas

The University Scholars Program responds to the need for more highly competent leaders and practitioners in all fields. Selection of students for the Scholars Program is based on outstanding academic achievement, participation in extracurricular activities and/or community-based outreach programs, expressed interest in eventual pursuit and completion of the doctorate or other professional degree, and a commitment to fulfilling a service-learning project as part of the degree-completion requirements.

Advanced Placement (AP) credit in core courses, especially English and mathematics, is awarded to qualified scholars. Students are encouraged to enroll in honors sections, attend intellectually challenging seminars and workshops, travel to special culturally enriching events, and participate in research projects. Scholars are provided broad options in selecting elective courses. Students are encouraged to participate fully in the life of the campus and to seek opportunities to develop strong leadership and communication skills.

Upon completion of the program, students receive a University Scholars Program cord. Students completing at least 18 hours of honors course work with a grade of no less than C in any honors course graduate with the designation of University Scholar. Those completing a research thesis graduate with the designation of Research Fellow. The expectation is that students who remain in the program until graduation will graduate with, at minimum, cum laude honors. A notation of University Scholars Program completion is indicated on the transcript.

Admission Process: Students are required to have the following high school qualifications in order to be eligible to participate: a minimum 3.5 GPA on a 4.0 scale; an SAT I score of at least 1100 (or the equivalent on the new SAT) or an ACT score of at least 23; a strong college-preparatory background in mathematics, science, and English; recommendations from high school teachers, including rating of academic performance, motivation, and self-discipline; and passage of any state-mandated examination used as a high school exit examination. Transfer students with a college GPA of 3.5 or higher may apply for admission to the University Scholars Program.

Scholarship Availability: University Scholars Program applicants are encouraged to apply for the Presidential Scholarships and/or the Regents Scholarship by March 1. Employment opportunities, primarily of the work-study variety, are available.

Campus Overview

State-supported comprehensive, founded 1878, part of Texas A&M University System • **Coed** 6,324 undergraduate students, 91% full-time, 56% women, 44% men.

Undergraduates 5,758 full-time, 566 part-time. Students come from 21 states and territories, 21 other countries, 6% are from out of state, 92% African American, 0.9% Asian American or Pacific Islander, 3% Hispanic American, 0.1% Native American, 1% international, 6% transferred in, 52% live on campus.

Faculty *Total:* 467, 82% full-time, 3% with terminal degrees. *Student/faculty ratio:* 18:1.

Academic Programs *Special study options:* academic remediation for entering students, accelerated degree program, advanced placement credit, cooperative education, distance learning, double majors, English as a second language, honors programs, independent study, internships, off-campus study, part-time degree program, services for LD students, study abroad, summer session for credit. *ROTC:* Army (b), Navy (b).

Athletics Member NCAA. All Division I except football (Division I-AA). *Intercollegiate sports:* baseball M(s), basketball M(s)/W(s), cross-country running M(s)/W(s), golf M(s)/W(s), soccer W(s), softball W(s), tennis M(s)/W(s), track and field M(s)/W(s), volleyball W(s). *Intramural sports:* baseball M, basketball M/W, bowling W, cross-country running M/W, golf M/W, soccer W, softball W, tennis M/W, track and field M/W, volleyball M/W.

Costs (2004–05) *Tuition:* state resident $1440 full-time, $48 per credit hour part-time; nonresident $9180 full-time, $306 per credit hour part-time. Full-time tuition and fees vary according to course load and degree level. Part-time tuition and fees vary according to course load and degree level. *Required fees:* $2762 full-time. *Room and board:* $6068; room only: $3788. Room and board charges vary according to board plan and housing facility.

Financial Aid 732 Federal Work-Study jobs (averaging $1934). 328 state and other part-time jobs (averaging $1146). In 2002, 271 non-need-based awards were made. *Average percent of need met:* 75%. *Average financial aid package:* $6920. *Average need-based loan:* $4000. *Average need-based gift aid:* $3300. *Average non-need-based aid:* $1400.

Contact: Director: Wash A. Jones, Ph.D., University Scholars Program, Prairie View A&M University, P. O. Box 2879, Prairie View, Texas 77446; *Telephone:* 936-857-4116; *Fax:* 936-857-2994; *E-mail:* wajones@pvamu.edu

St. Edward's University
Honors Program
Austin, Texas

The Honors Program is designed for students who are academically talented and passionate about learning. Students from all majors in the traditional undergraduate program are accepted. The program offers small classes (about 15 per class) with other highly motivated students and distinguished professors who enjoy serving as mentors. Most honors classes fulfill general education requirements. Honors students especially appreciate the high level of participation expected of them through wide-ranging discussions, class presentations, and group and individual projects. Classes are interdisciplinary, and the program emphasizes writing and critical thinking. The Honors Program is closely associated with the University's Fellowship Office to provide support for students applying for major national and postgraduate scholarships.

One of the highlights of the program is the Honors Senior Thesis project, which students may substitute for the university's capstone requirement. The thesis project allows students to work closely with a faculty mentor on a project based on their individual interests and talents. Recent projects include a business plan, an analysis of ethics in the workplace, a photodocumentary, a poetry chapbook, and a rhetorical analysis of the war speeches of American presidents.

The program is designed to work best for students who are accepted to the Honors Program as incoming freshmen, but some openings are available for students to join the program before completing 45 hours. Transfer applicants are considered on an individual basis.

The Honors Program was founded in 1987 and currently has 150 students.

Participation Requirements: To complete the Honors Program, students must take seven honors seminars and complete an Honors Senior Thesis project, for a total of 24 credits. They must maintain a minimum GPA of 3.50 in honors courses and a cumulative GPA of at least 3.25. Many honors classes may be substituted for general education requirements. Students may take no more than two honors courses a semester. Completion of the Honors Program is designated on the diploma. Each spring at the University's Honors Night program, graduating seniors are awarded a medallion, and they are given special recognition at commencement.

Admission Process: Students selected to be part of the Honors Program generally rank in at least the top 15 percent of their graduating class and have scores of at least 1200 on the SAT or 27 on the ACT. They are also outstanding writers and are typically involved in academically oriented extracurricular activities such as debate, UIL competition, academic decathlon, literary magazine, or science competition.

Approximately 30 students are admitted each fall, and applications are considered throughout the year until the program fills. Therefore, it is to a student's advantage to apply for honors at the same time as applying for admission or shortly thereafter.

Scholarship Availability: Most students who meet the criteria for the Honors Program are also eligible for four-year scholarship awards ranging from $4500 to $8500.

Campus Overview

Independent Roman Catholic comprehensive, founded 1885 • **Coed** 3,731 undergraduate students, 72% full-time, 57% women, 43% men.

Undergraduates 2,692 full-time, 1,039 part-time. Students come from 40 states and territories, 39 other countries, 5% are from out of state, 5% African American, 2% Asian American or Pacific Islander, 30% Hispanic American, 0.7% Native American, 2% international, 7% transferred in, 39% live on campus.

Faculty *Total:* 410, 34% full-time, 52% with terminal degrees. *Student/faculty ratio:* 15:1.

Academic Programs *Special study options:* academic remediation for entering students, adult/continuing education programs, advanced placement credit, double majors, honors programs, internships, part-time degree program, services for LD students, study abroad, summer session for credit. *ROTC:* Army (c), Air Force (c).

Athletics Member NCAA. All Division II. *Intercollegiate sports:* baseball M(s), basketball M(s)/W(s), cross-country running M/W, golf M(s)/W(s), soccer M(s)/W(s), softball W(s), tennis M(s)/W(s), volleyball W(s). *Intramural sports:* basketball M/W, football M/W, golf M/W, lacrosse M(c), racquetball M/W, soccer M/W, softball M/W, tennis M/W, volleyball M/W.

Costs (2005–06) *Tuition:* $17,320 full-time, $578 per hour part-time. *Room only:* Room and board charges vary according to board plan and housing facility.

Financial Aid 350 Federal Work-Study jobs (averaging $1523). 17 state and other part-time jobs (averaging $1882). In 2004, 240 non-need-based awards were made. *Average percent of need met:* 71%. *Average financial aid package:* $12,340. *Average need-based loan:* $4232. *Average need-based gift aid:* $9141. *Average non-need-based aid:* $5550.

Contact: Director: Barbara Filippidis, Campus Box 779, St. Edward's University, 3001 South Congress Avenue, Austin, Texas 78704-6489; *Telephone:* 512-448-8558; *Fax:* 512-44-8492; *E-mail:* barbaraf@admin. stedwards.edu; *Web site:* http://www.stedwards.edu

---

Sam Houston State University

Elliott T. Bowers Honors Program

Huntsville, Texas

The Honors Program at Sam Houston State University was initiated in 1990 to attract highly motivated and academically talented students. Based on the active involvement of select faculty members, the program seeks to create an intellectual and social climate that encourages students to develop their potential both in and out of the classroom. To this end, the program creates a community of scholars, wherein both students and professors interact and challenge each other in developing their abilities. Specifically, the program provides personalized instruction and mentorship opportunities in supporting the University's overall mission of maintaining high academic standards and fostering community service.

The Honors Program provides these achievement-oriented individuals, through financial support and opportunities to interact with other similarly motivated students, special course offerings leading to an unusually broad educational experience, limited-enrollment classes, closer contact with the faculty, the opportunity to participate in early registration, and access to distinctively designed facilities, including Spivey House, the honors residence hall.

Approximately 275 students are actively involved in the Honors Program. Honors students are found in every department and college at Sam Houston State University.

Participation Requirements: The honors curriculum is a four-year program that requires the same number of credits as the general educational program. To remain in the Honors Program, students must maintain at least a 3.25 GPA. To graduate with the Honors Program designation, students must complete at least 24 hours of honors credit, including two multidisciplinary seminar classes. To graduate with highest honors, students must complete an additional 6-hour honors thesis. The designation With Honors in the Honors Program or With Highest Honors in the Honors Program is recorded on the student's transcript and is noted during the graduation ceremony. Honors graduates are also provided with a distinctive honors medallion for the graduation ceremony.

Admission Process: To be considered for admission to the Honors Program, students must submit a special application. Incoming freshmen are eligible to apply if they have a combined SAT score (verbal and math) of 1200 or above or a composite ACT score of 27 or above or if they have graduated in the top 10 percent of their high school class. For transfer or continuing students, eligibility is based upon a college cumulative GPA of 3.4 or better. All applicants must submit transcripts, a written essay, and letters of reference. Admission is competitive. A panel of faculty members reviews all applications to determine which students will be invited to participate in the program.

Scholarship Availability: The Honors Program administers a $2.5-million endowment that provides funds for scholarships and student development activities. Incoming freshman honors students are eligible to apply for Richard A. Cording Scholarships, and junior and senior honors students are also eligible to complete for Augusta Lawrence Scholarships. In addition, Sam Houston State University has other scholarships at the departmental, college, and University levels. Typically, honor students compete well for these scholarships.

Campus Overview

State-supported university, founded 1879, part of The Texas State University System • **Coed** 12,297 undergraduate students, 85% full-time, 58% women, 42% men.

Undergraduates 10,402 full-time, 1,895 part-time. Students come from 45 states and territories, 47 other countries, 3% are from out of state, 15% African American, 1% Asian American or Pacific Islander, 11% Hispanic American, 0.7% Native American, 0.8% international, 13% transferred in, 27% live on campus.

Faculty *Total:* 584, 71% full-time, 70% with terminal degrees. *Student/faculty ratio:* 22:1.

Academic Programs *Special study options:* academic remediation for entering students, adult/continuing education programs, advanced placement credit, distance learning, double majors, English as a second language, honors programs, independent study, internships, off-campus study, part-time degree program, services for LD students, study abroad, summer session for credit. *ROTC:* Army (b). *Unusual degree programs:* 3-2 engineering with Texas A&M University.

Athletics Member NCAA. All Division I except football (Division I-AA). *Intercollegiate sports:* baseball M(s), basketball M(s)/W(s), cross-country running M(s)/W(s), equestrian sports M/W, golf M(s)/W(s), lacrosse M(c), riflery M(c)/W(c), rugby M(c), soccer M(c)/W(s), softball M(s)/W(s), tennis M(s)/W(s), track and field M(s)/W(s), volleyball W(s). *Intramural sports:* basketball M/W, bowling M/W, football M, gymnastics W(c), racquetball M/W, soccer M/W, softball M/W, swimming and diving M/W, tennis M/W, volleyball M/W, water polo M/W.

Costs (2004–05) *Tuition:* state resident $3030 full-time, $101 per hour part-time; nonresident $10,770 full-time, $359 per hour part-time. Full-time tuition and fees vary according to course load. Part-time tuition and fees vary according to course load. *Required fees:* $1230 full-time, $444 per term part-time. *Room and board:* $4336; room only: $2224. Room and board charges vary according to board plan and housing facility.

Financial Aid In 2004, 416 non-need-based awards were made. *Average percent of need met:* 83%. *Average financial aid package:* $14,534. *Average need-based loan:* $4552. *Average need-based gift aid:* $4016. *Average non-need-based aid:* $6297.

Contact: Director: Glenn M. Sanford, Ph.D., P.O. Box 2479, Huntsville, Texas 77341; *Telephone:* 936-294-1477; *Fax:* 936-294-1090; *E-mail:* honors@shsu.edu

San Jacinto College South

Honors Program

Houston, Texas

The San Jacinto College South Honors Program offers academically talented and highly motivated students special opportunities for enriched learning and recognition. The program provides a stimulating range and depth of scholarly pursuits within an interdisciplinary context.

The program offers three types of academic experiences. First is the interdisciplinary course, which combines freshman English and History courses for two semesters. Combining writing, literature, and history, these two courses, one offered in the fall semester and one offered in the spring semester, challenge students to blur the lines of distinction between academic fields. This course is limited to 18 students. Next, the honors program offers honors courses in other specific departments, including anthropology, archaeology, business, government, history, mathematics, English, psychology, sociology, economics, and speech. These courses are also limited to 18 students. Finally, the program offers Honors by Contract in virtually every other academic department, where students work on independent projects with selected faculty members.

Two hundred to 250 students have accepted the San Jacinto College South Honors Program challenge.

Participation Requirements: Members are expected to enroll in at least 3 hours each semester they are in the Honors Program. In addition, members are encouraged to participate in the campus Honors Program retreat and in the Annual Gulf Coast Intercollegiate Honors Council Retreat as well as in local, state, and national research and writing contests.

Admission Process: Graduating high school seniors, returning students, and transfer students can are recruited based on their SAT I or ACT scores, TAAS scores, San Jacinto College GPA, or high school GPA.

Scholarship Availability: Each year the Honors Program awards more than $7000 in scholarships to entering and returning students based on their academic potential and achievements.

Campus Overview

State and locally supported 2-year, founded 1961 • **Coed**

Undergraduates Students come from 17 states and territories, 12 other countries.

Contact: Eddie Weller, Ph.D., Professor of History, Honors Program Director, San Jacinto College South, 13735 Beamer Road, Houston, Texas 77089-6099; *Telephone:* 281-484-1900 Ext. 3505; *Fax:* 281-929-4693; *E-mail:* eddie.weller@scjd.edu; *Web site:* http://www.sjcd.edu

Schreiner University

Schreiner University Honors Program

Kerrville, Texas

The Schreiner University Honors Program values its members' unique histories and recognizes each individual in the quest to interpret his or her place in this world. The program intends to provide personalized learning experiences to meet the needs and interests of academically aggressive college students by offering honors courses designed to engage students in a dynamic liberal arts education; cocurricular opportunities to develop academically, socially, and spiritually; recognition of such students as "Schreiner Honors Scholars"; and standards that are advantageous for graduate school admission.

Students are provisionally accepted into the program. At the end of their fall semester, students who persist in their desire to become Schreiner University Honors Program members and who fulfill the expectations of honors students are, by full faculty vote, nominated for formal induction into the program during its annual January ceremony. Seniors are honored with their honors rings during this ceremony.

Schreiner University expects its honors students to be actively involved in the program by taking ownership of it through planning and engaging in program activities and by exploring avenues for experiential learning. In addition, honors students should strive toward these ideals: exercising greater initiative and independence in order to foster a community of scholars, displaying an eagerness to learn in and out of the classroom, exhibiting integrity and ethical conduct, being willing to accept intellectual risks, and acknowledging an Aristotelian treatise that asserts that happiness is achieved through contemplation of philosophic truth rather than through the pursuit of pleasure, fame, and wealth.

Each semester, the Schreiner University Honors Program sponsors excursions designed to provide personal, social, and/or cultural enrichment for its students. In the past, these activities have included private luncheons with distinguished guests such as Joy Harjo, poet, or Millard Fuller, founder of Habitat for Humanity; star gazing at a local observatory; overnight excursions to the Renaissance Festival and the Seminole Canyon area to view ancient rock art; and cultural events in San Antonio and surrounding areas.

Honors students have priority class registration, monthly luncheons focused on a group activity, and the above-mentioned opportunities for extracurricular involvement.

Each year, the program reserves a moderate portion of its budget to fund scholarship opportunities such as presenting papers at regional and national conferences. Written proposals requesting funds for such scholarship are considered each semester at midterm by the Honors Committee.

The University provides opportunities to spend a semester, a year, or a miniterm in a structured program at a college or university abroad and/or in the United States. A written proposal due the year prior to the intended study experience is required of all students seeking study outside of the campus.

Founded in 1989, the program involves an average of 60 students.

Participation Requirements: All honors students enroll in one honors course each semester. An interdisciplinary sequence beginning with the First-Year Honors Seminar comprises the mandatory honors-designated courses, with these sections offering enhanced curriculum and experiential learning opportunities. Such curricula may require students to complete up to 7 more credit hours beyond the requirements for their degree plans. By their senior year, most honors students have completed this sequence and contract an honors course within their major to satisfy their honors course requirement.

To remain in good standing in the Schreiner University Honors Program, students must meet minimum cumulative GPA requirements based on the following sliding scale. Freshmen must maintain a minimum cumulative GPA of 3.25; sophomores, 3.35; juniors, 3.45; and seniors, 3.5. Students must also exhibit academic and social integrity. A breach in acceptable conduct will, upon the recommendation of the Honors Committee, be cause for dismissal from the program. Examples of such cause for dismissal include academic dishonesty, i.e., plagiarism, cheating, or serious violations of state or federal law. In addition, students must complete honors courses. Either a grade of F for an honors-designated course or failure to complete the honors component of contracted course is grounds for probation or dismissal.

To be recognized as a Schreiner Honors Scholar, a student must have a minimum cumulative GPA of 3.5, have participated in the honors program for at least the last four consecutive semesters, and have completed one semester in the Honors Colloquium.

Admission Process: The Admissions Office automatically notifies the Honors Program Director of all first-year freshmen and transfer students who meet the quantitative standards noted below. Through written correspondence, the director invites qualified candidates to apply. The final deadline for honors application process is July 15.

Students are invited to become first-semester provisional honors candidates based on the following criteria: a high school GPA of at least 3.5; the level of courses taken, including AP and honors; class rank; SAT/ACT score (minimum 1100/25); leadership experience; extracurricular activities; and a Presidential essay.

If applicants believe their scores and GPA do not reflect their abilities well, they may present other indicators of their promise, such as recommendations from teachers or creative work, or they may request a personal interview.

Each fall and spring, the Schreiner University Honors Program invites current students who have proven to be aggressive learners and who have yet to complete four consecutive, full-time semesters at Schreiner University to be considered for admission into honors. The deadline for application is September 30 for the following spring and January 31 for the fall.

Current students and transfer students are invited to become first-semester provisional honors candidates based on the following criteria: a cumulative GPA of at least 3.25; leadership experience; extracurricular activities; a Presidential essay; and an interview with the Honors Committee.

Scholarship Availability: The University offers substantial academic scholarships ranging from $6000 to $10,000.

Campus Overview

Independent Presbyterian comprehensive, founded 1923 • **Coed** 793 undergraduate students, 90% full-time, 60% women, 40% men.

Undergraduates 717 full-time, 76 part-time. Students come from 8 states and territories, 2 other countries, 1% are from out of state, 3% African American, 0.9% Asian American or Pacific Islander, 17% Hispanic American, 1% Native American, 0.8% international, 12% transferred in, 58% live on campus.

Faculty *Total:* 82, 60% full-time, 49% with terminal degrees. *Student/faculty ratio:* 13:1.

Academic Programs *Special study options:* academic remediation for entering students, accelerated degree program, advanced placement credit, cooperative education, double majors, honors programs, independent study, internships, part-time degree program, services for LD students, student-designed majors, study abroad, summer session for credit. *Unusual degree programs:* 3-2 engineering with University of Texas at Austin, Texas A&M University.

Athletics Member NCAA. All Division III. *Intercollegiate sports:* baseball M, basketball M/W, cheerleading W, golf M/W, soccer M/W, softball W, tennis M/W, volleyball W. *Intramural sports:* basketball M/W, cross-country running M(c)/W(c), football M/W, golf M/W, racquetball M/W, rock climbing M/W, skiing (downhill) M/W, soccer M/W, table tennis M/W, tennis M/W, ultimate Frisbee M/W, volleyball M/W.

Costs (2004–05) *Comprehensive fee:* $21,323 includes full-time tuition ($14,043), mandatory fees ($400), and room and board ($6880). Part-time tuition: $599 per credit. *College room only:* $3580. Room and board charges vary according to board plan and housing facility.

Financial Aid 110 Federal Work-Study jobs (averaging $897). 170 state and other part-time jobs (averaging $638). In 2004, 118 non-need-based awards were made. *Average percent of need met:* 73%. *Average financial aid package:* $12,868. *Average need-based loan:* $3224. *Average need-based gift aid:* $9911. *Average non-need-based aid:* $13,913.

Contact: Honors Program Director, 2100 Memorial Boulevard, Kerrville, Texas 78028; *Telephone:* 830-896-5411

Stephen F. Austin State University
School of Honors
Nacogdoches, Texas

The School of Honors offers no courses of its own. It provides honors sections of many basic courses, and in areas where there are no courses offered, students may complete unique projects and gain special credit through honors contracts. Students must complete 25 hours of honors course work (in any areas) during their four years of college. Those who successfully do so are able to graduate with a separate School of Honors diploma in addition to the regular college diploma. Normally an incoming freshman is expected to take a 1-credit-hour SFA 101 honors course (Introduction to College Life) and 24 additional hours in any areas of their choosing. The SFA 101 course requirement is waived for any transfer student who has amassed at least one semester of college course work.

The average class size for honors sections is fewer than 25, and some classes are as small as 12 students. The courses are usually taught by the most able and distinguished professors at the University, and they are designed to foster independent thinking and comradeship among the participants. Honors students who maintain a GPA of 3.25 or higher are eligible to live at Wisely Hall, designated as the Academic Excellence Dorm for the University. It is centrally located and is designated a Quiet Dorm. There are several private rooms on the ground floor for students with physical disabilities. Admission to Wisely Hall requires an SAT score of at least 1220 (not yet adjusted for the new system) or an ACT score of at least 27 plus class standing in the top 25 percent. There is also a suite of rooms, conveniently located, that houses the offices of the School of Honors Director and the Honors Administrative Assistant and a meeting and seminar room. This room also contains desktop computers, laser-jet printers, and a high-speed scanner.

The School of Honors makes available a number of laptop computers that can be checked out during the week or on weekends. There is also a copying machine available for honors student use as well as a fax machine. School of Honors students have the privilege of registering first at the University, at the same time as graduating seniors. This virtually guarantees that they will get the courses and hours that best meet their schedule. There are currently about 700 students in the program, which was created thirteen years ago. A number of these students explore extracurricular activities through their own Honor Student Association. They are involved in projects ranging from raising money for impoverished children to assisting mothers and their young ones in the Women's Shelter to volunteering for Habitat for Humanity. Each fall, the School of Honors takes an out-of-town tour to Houston to attend an off-Broadway show at one of the city's leading theaters. Individual colleges and departments of the University offer membership in local, regional, and national honors societies. The Honor Student Association was named Student Organization of the Year for 2000 by vote of the Student Government of the University.

Participation Requirements: Students may take their required 24 hours of course work in any area they wish. There are no standard academic courses or capstone courses at this time, although the University Honors Council has been considering adding a capstone honors course to further enrich the experience. Continued participation requires that students maintain an overall GPA of at least 3.25 plus a 3.0 average or higher in the honors courses. No more than two course grades of 2.0 in honors courses are permitted. If the student fails to achieve this minimum 3.25 average, they have up to two semesters to lift their grades back up to standards. Should they not improve their average, they must become inactive in the program and lose their honors privileges. At graduation time, the Registrar stamps the transcripts of all those who successfully completed the program with a statement that the student has earned their degree "through the

School of Honors." A separate diploma is presented, signed by the President of the University, the Dean of the appropriate college, and the Director of the School of Honors. All honors courses completed are designated on the transcript with the word Honors.

Admission Process: Admission to the program requires an SAT score of at least 1220 (not yet adjusted for the new system) or an ACT score of at least 27. The program also seeks students in the top 15 percent of their graduating class, and consideration is given to students whose national test scores are slightly lower than required but whose high school grades and class ranking are very high. Those with the appropriate SAT or ACT scores may rank below the top 15 percent in their graduating class. Some small or private schools do not rank graduates; class ranking is waived for those students and home-educated applicants. Extracurricular activities are factored in, as are letters of recommendation. Admission dates are not critical, as this is a state university that has a rolling admission process.

Scholarship Availability: The School of Honors offers several major scholarships based solely on achievement. Three Vera Dugas Scholarships are awarded each year. Awards range from $2500 to $4000 per semester ($20,000 for four years to $32,000 for four years) depending on returns from the invested funds. This should provide considerable support for tuition as well as part of other college expenses. In addition, the School of Honors provides eleven University Scholars awards each year. They pay $1000 per semester for a maximum of eight semesters, or a possible total of $8000. These are divided among the seven colleges of the University. Receipt of scholarship aid of $1000 or more per year entitles recipients to in-state tuition if they are not residents of Texas or an adjacent state. Information and most forms may be downloaded from the Web site listed in the Contact section of this description. The absolute University-wide deadline for any year's applications for financial support is February 1.

Campus Overview

State-supported comprehensive, founded 1923 • **Coed** 9,568 undergraduate students, 86% full-time, 59% women, 41% men.

Undergraduates 8,206 full-time, 1,362 part-time. Students come from 34 states and territories, 42 other countries, 2% are from out of state, 16% African American, 1% Asian American or Pacific Islander, 7% Hispanic American, 0.8% Native American, 0.5% international, 8% transferred in, 38% live on campus.

Faculty Total: 582, 75% full-time, 67% with terminal degrees. Student/faculty ratio: 18:1.

Academic Programs Special study options: academic remediation for entering students, accelerated degree program, adult/continuing education programs, advanced placement credit, distance learning, double majors, freshman honors college, honors programs, independent study, internships, off-campus study, part-time degree program, services for LD students, student-designed majors, study abroad, summer session for credit. ROTC: Army (b).

Athletics Member NCAA. All Division I except football (Division I-AA). Intercollegiate sports: basketball M(s)/W(s), cross-country running M(s)/W(s), golf M(s), soccer W(s), softball W(s), tennis W(s), track and field M(s)/W(s), volleyball W(s). Intramural sports: badminton M/W, baseball M(c), basketball M/W, cross-country running M/W, football M/W, lacrosse M(c)/W(c), racquetball M(c)/W(c), rugby M(c)/W(c), soccer M(c), softball M/W, table tennis M/W, tennis M/W, volleyball M(c)/W(c), water polo M/W, wrestling M(c)/W(c).

Costs (2004–05) Tuition: state resident $3360 full-time, $145 per credit hour part-time; nonresident $11,100 full-time, $403 per credit hour part-time. Full-time tuition and fees vary according to course load. Part-time tuition and fees vary according to course load. Required fees: $938 full-time, $33 per credit hour part-time. Room and board: $5012. Room and board charges vary according to board plan and housing facility.

Financial Aid 421 Federal Work-Study jobs (averaging $1539). 100 state and other part-time jobs (averaging $1102). In 2003, 369

non-need-based awards were made. Average percent of need met: 67%. Average financial aid package: $4506. Average need-based loan: $2066. Average need-based gift aid: $1626. Average non-need-based aid: $3012.

Contact: Director: School of Honors, SFASU, Box 6114 SFA Station, Nacogdoches, Texas 75962; Telephone: 936-468-2813; Web site: http://www.sfasu.edu/honors

Texas A&M University
University Honors Programs
College Station, Texas

*T*he University Honors Program at Texas A&M University (TAMU) offers special opportunities for high-achieving students to pursue academic work that challenges their interests and abilities. The program is campuswide, encompassing all undergraduate colleges within the University. As a result, honors students have access to the entire spectrum of educational resources available at Texas A&M. Honors courses and individualized research programs bring together outstanding students and faculty members in an environment designed to encourage initiative, creativity, and independent thinking.

Honors courses have limited enrollment in order to facilitate participatory learning through the interchange of ideas between students and professors and among students themselves. Honors students have the opportunity to work one-on-one with some of the University's most distinguished faculty members and receive individual attention and special services typically available only on smaller campuses. At the same time, students enjoy the resources of one of the nation's major research universities, including state-of-the-art laboratory, library, and computing facilities. Texas A&M is among the top twenty-five public universities in the nation.

Honors students at Texas A&M pursue regular majors in any one of the 151 degree plans available to undergraduates through the Colleges of Agriculture and Life Sciences, Architecture, Education and Human Development, Geosciences, Liberal Arts, Science, Veterinary Medicine and Biomedical Sciences, Dwight Look College of Engineering, and Mays Business School. Students customize their honors experience by selecting from more than 300 honors course sections a year, completing course work in the University core curriculum and/or within their disciplines. Honors advisers assist students in their pursuit of honors sequences that may be departmental, college, or University level.

The University Honors Program, in conjunction with its scholarship program, attracts successful, confident, and motivated students from across the nation. Texas A&M is among the top ten public institutions for enrollment of National Merit Scholars and among the top twenty-five for enrollment of National Achievement Scholars. Scholarships are available for students with a proven academic record who also show promise of leadership. There are two honors residence halls at Texas A&M; both halls are coed. Lechner Hall houses freshman honors and scholarship students, whereas Clements Hall is open to all honors students regardless of classification or scholarship status.

Honors students may take advantage of a number of services offered by the University Honors Program: a community newsletter and listserv, special events designed to enhance their honors experience, national scholarship competition advising, and help accessing the resources of the University and beyond.

More than 2,500 students enroll in honors courses each semester. Recently, honors students have won the prestigious Goldwater, Marshall, National Science Foundation, Rhodes, and Udall scholarships. Texas A&M University recently installed a chapter of Phi Beta Kappa.

Participation Requirements: While participation is flexible, students receive the University-level honors designation on their transcripts by completing the following requirements: 36 honors hours over a defined distribution requirement for University Honors students; 19 honors hours across the core curriculum for Foundation Honors students; or 9 honors hours, 6 research hours, and a senior thesis for University Undergraduate Research Fellows. Students completing departmental or collegiate honors tracks receive an Honors Certificate from the corresponding unit. College honors tracks are available through the College of Liberal Arts, the Dwight Look College of Engineering, and the Mays Business School. Advantages include interdisciplinary seminars and contact with industry professionals.

Admission Process: No application is necessary to participate in the University Honors Program. Incoming freshmen with a minimum 1250 on the SAT (28 ACT) and top 10 percent class rank are automatically admitted to the University Honors Program. Thereafter, any student who maintains a minimum 3.5 cumulative GPR may take honors courses. Transfer students are admitted on a case-by-case basis, usually with a minimum 3.5 GPR. Students generally register for 3 to 9 honors hours each semester.

Scholarship Availability: The Office of Honors Programs and Academic Scholarships are also responsible for the selection and administration of all the major four-year academic scholarships. Each spring the office makes about 1,000 award offers to students with exemplary academic records and a proven record of leadership and community involvement. The average SAT I score of students receiving the top scholarship award is 1460. The Texas A&M academic scholarships are for $2500 or $3000 a year and are renewable for four years by meeting specific renewal criteria. Texas A&M University also sponsors any National Merit Finalist with a scholarship through the National Merit Corporation. National Merit Finalist packages range from $36,500 to $66,900. To encourage study abroad among the honors community, a $1000 award is offered to students who participate in a Texas A&M–sponsored study-abroad program. The University Scholar Program rewards academic scholarship recipients who distinguish themselves during their freshman year with their academic and leadership record. University Scholars receive an additional scholarship while serving as ambassadors of Texas A&M. Currently enrolled honors students who are not academic scholarship recipients may compete for one-year Honors Incentive Award scholarships of $1000.

Campus Overview

State-supported university, founded 1876, part of Texas A&M University System • **Coed** 35,732 undergraduate students, 91% full-time, 49% women, 51% men.

Undergraduates 32,374 full-time, 3,358 part-time. Students come from 52 states and territories, 128 other countries, 3% are from out of state, 2% African American, 3% Asian American or Pacific Islander, 10% Hispanic American, 0.5% Native American, 1% international, 4% transferred in, 25% live on campus.

Faculty *Total:* 2,232, 85% full-time, 87% with terminal degrees. *Student/faculty ratio:* 20:1.

Academic Programs *Special study options:* academic remediation for entering students, accelerated degree program, advanced placement credit, cooperative education, distance learning, double majors, English as a second language, honors programs, independent study, internships, off-campus study, part-time degree program, services for LD students, study abroad, summer session for credit. *ROTC:* Army (b), Navy (b), Air Force (b).

Athletics Member NCAA. All Division I except football (Division I-A). *Intercollegiate sports:* archery W(s), baseball M(s), basketball M(s)/W(s), cross-country running M(s)/W(s), equestrian sports W(s), golf M(s)/W(s), soccer W(s), softball W(s), swimming and diving M(s)/W(s), tennis M(s)/W(s), track and field M(s)/W(s), volleyball W(s). *Intramural sports:* archery M/W, badminton M/W, basketball M/W, bowling M/W, cross-country running M/W, fencing M(c)/W(c), field hockey M(c)/W(c), football M/W, golf M/W, gymnastics M(c)/W(c), lacrosse M(c)/W(c), racquetball M(c)/W(c), riflery M/W,

rugby M(c)/W(c), sailing M(c)/W(c), soccer M/W, softball M/W, squash M/W, swimming and diving M/W, table tennis M/W, tennis M/W, track and field M/W, ultimate Frisbee M(c)/W(c), volleyball M/W, water polo M/W, weight lifting M(c)/W(c), wrestling M(c).

Costs (2004–05) *Tuition:* state resident $3675 full-time, $123 per semester hour part-time; nonresident $11,415 full-time, $381 per semester hour part-time. Full-time tuition and fees vary according to course load, location, and program. *Required fees:* $2280 full-time. *Room and board:* $6887; room only: $3704. Room and board charges vary according to board plan, housing facility, and location.

Financial Aid 1,047 Federal Work-Study jobs (averaging $1278). 4,500 state and other part-time jobs (averaging $2599). In 2003, 10248 non-need-based awards were made. *Average percent of need met:* 64%. *Average financial aid package:* $8781. *Average need-based loan:* $4153. *Average need-based gift aid:* $8880. *Average non-need-based aid:* $6370.

Contact: Executive Director: Dr. Edward A. Funkhouser, 101 Academic Building, 4233 TAMU, College Station, Texas 77843-4233; *Telephone:* 979-845-6774; *Fax:* 979-845-0300; *E-mail:* honors@tamu.edu; *Web site:* http://honors.tamu.edu

Texas A&M University–Corpus Christi
University Honors Program
Corpus Christi, Texas

During its inaugural year in 2005–06, the Honors Program at Texas A&M University–Corpus Christi (A&M–Corpus Christi) welcomes its first cohort of sophomore students in fall 2005 and recruits during that same semester for its initial cohort of first-year students, who are scheduled to enter the program in spring 2006. Building on its nationally recognized first-year learning-community program, the University invites students who have the ability to excel academically, the motivation to engage in active and collaborative learning, and the desire to interact with the world beyond the classroom. Honors students come from all undergraduate programs within the University and have their choice of two tracks: the Professional Track (requiring 17–26 honors credit hours) and the University Track (requiring at least 26 honors credit hours). Students in both tracks enroll in a rich array of core-required honors courses during their first two years. Upper-division University Track students participate in linked honors seminars in multiple disciplines; students in both tracks may pursue individual research interests, independent study, service-learning projects, and enriching extracurricular and cocurricular opportunities. The capstone of the honors experience is the Project of Excellence during the senior year of study. Anticipated enrollment at the end of spring 2006 is 100 students.

Participation Requirements: Beginning in fall 2006, the Honors Program will accept students as entering first-year students, students who have 15–30 credit hours at Texas A&M University–Corpus Christi, or transfer students. Students in both the Professional and University Tracks are expected to enroll in 13 to 22 hours of core-required honors courses, which are reserved for honors students. All honors students are also required to complete a Project of Excellence during their senior year. The project may take the form of a composition, exhibit, performance, thesis, or presentation of field research and culminates in a document housed in the University's Mary and Jeff Bell Library. Diplomas designate Graduate of the Professional Honors Track or Graduate of the University Honors Track upon successful completion of all requirements in the Honors Program and major field of study.

Admission Process: Application to the Honors Program involves a portfolio process in addition to University admission requirements.

Applicants may either self-nominate or be invited to apply after nomination by a faculty member. The admission portfolio must include a letter of application, three letters of recommendation, high school and college transcripts, and two examples of academic work, one of which is an extensive writing sample. An admission subcommittee of the Honors Council reviews the portfolios and occasionally may request an interview with the student.

Scholarship Availability: Students are eligible for the full range of University scholarships if they apply before the deadline. More information is available from Lindsey Johnson, Scholarship Coordinator (telephone: 361-825-2522; e-mail: lindsey.johnson@island.tamucc.edu).

Campus Overview

State-supported comprehensive, founded 1947, part of Texas A&M University System • **Coed** 6,581 undergraduate students, 80% full-time, 61% women, 39% men.

Undergraduates 5,255 full-time, 1,326 part-time. Students come from 37 states and territories, 23 other countries, 2% are from out of state, 3% African American, 2% Asian American or Pacific Islander, 37% Hispanic American, 0.6% Native American, 0.8% international, 20% transferred in, 16% live on campus.

Faculty *Total:* 446, 57% full-time. *Student/faculty ratio:* 21:1.

Academic Programs *Special study options:* academic remediation for entering students, advanced placement credit, cooperative education, distance learning, double majors, independent study, internships, off-campus study, part-time degree program, services for LD students, summer session for credit. *ROTC:* Army (b).

Athletics Member NCAA. *Intercollegiate sports:* baseball M(s), basketball M(s)/W(s), golf W, softball W, tennis M/W, track and field M/W, volleyball W. *Intramural sports:* baseball M, basketball M/W, cross-country running M/W, golf W, racquetball M/W, softball W, tennis M/W, track and field M/W, volleyball W.

Costs (2004–05) *Tuition:* state resident $3176 full-time, $100 per semester hour part-time; nonresident $10,916 full-time, $368 per semester hour part-time. Full-time tuition and fees vary according to course load. Part-time tuition and fees vary according to course load. *Required fees:* $1103 full-time, $33 per semester hour part-time, $90 per term part-time. *Room only:* $5355. Room and board charges vary according to housing facility.

Financial Aid 6 state and other part-time jobs (averaging $2400). In 2002, 510 non-need-based awards were made. *Average percent of need met:* 69%. *Average financial aid package:* $6202. *Average need-based loan:* $3644. *Average need-based gift aid:* $3659. *Average non-need-based aid:* $4281.

Contact: Director: Dr. Janis Haswell, c/o Department of English, 6300 Ocean Drive, Corpus Christi, Texas 78412-5813; *Telephone:* 361-825-5981; *E-mail:* jhaswell@falcon.tamucc.edu; *Web site:* http://falcon.tamucc.edu/~jhaswell/Honorsfolder/Honorsindex.htm

Texas Christian University
Honors Program
Fort Worth, Texas

At present, the Honors Program membership numbers approximately 400 from an undergraduate student body of 6,300.

The Honors Council is the Honors Program's primary governing body. It develops program goals and philosophies and approves new honors courses. The council is an official University committee consisting of both faculty members and honors students. The Honors Week Committee is also a University committee consisting of both professors and students. It plans and supervises the activities of Honors Week. The Honors Cabinet is the student governing body of the Honors Program. It serves as an advisory body to the Director by addressing student concerns about program policy, classes, and activities.

One of the Cabinet's primary goals is to build a sense of community in the Honors Program. Cabinet members plan both academic and social extracurricular activities such as the Fall Escape, firesides, trips to museums and plays, and dinners, as well as other activities designed to provide opportunities for students and professors to get to know one another. Cabinet members elect the Cabinet Chair, Vice-Chair, and Secretary at their first meeting in January. The Chair is an ex officio member of the Honors Council and the Honors Week Committee and also serves on Intercom, a committee of TCU student leaders.

Participation Requirements: Students in the Honors Program must remain in good academic standing by meeting certain grade requirements and fulfilling honors curriculum requirements. Freshmen and sophomores are expected to participate in at least one honors class each semester until they have fulfilled the Lower Division honors requirements. They must, however, complete these requirements no later than the end of their sophomore year. Continuance in the program past the freshman year requires a cumulative TCU GPA of 3.0; to continue past the sophomore year requires a cumulative TCU GPA of 3.4. After completing the Lower Division honors requirements, juniors and seniors are eligible to engage in Departmental and University Honors courses. Honors degrees are conferred upon Honors Program graduates who complete the Lower Division requirements, meet the specific Departmental and/or University Honors criteria, achieve an overall TCU and cumulative GPA of 3.5 or higher, and complete at least 60 credit hours at TCU exclusive of credit by examination.

During their freshman and sophomore years, honors students must complete either the Honors Intellectual Traditions Track or the Honors Western Civilization Track to fulfill the Lower Division requirements. Both tracks emphasize the history of Western civilization and are comprised of 15 credit hours.

The Honors Intellectual Traditions Track requires an Honors Freshman Seminar (or another 3-hour honors class) in the first semester of the freshman year, three semesters (9 hours) of Honors Intellectual Traditions (HHIT 1113, 2123, 2133), and an additional honors class (3 hours) of the student's choice. The HHIT sequence explores interrelationships among history, religion, literature, philosophy, and art from the ancient Greek, Hebrew, and Roman worlds through the twentieth century. The Honors Western Civilization Track requires 15 hours of courses, consisting of 6 hours of History of Civilization (HIST 2003, 2013) plus 9 hours of honors classes. The 9 hours of honors classes are chosen from specially designated honors sections of UCR courses offered each semester.

Students who complete the Lower Division honors curriculum requirements and achieve a cumulative GPA of 3.4 by the end of their sophomore year are invited to begin work toward one or both tracks for graduation with honors. The distinctions of University Honors and Departmental Honors are an official part of the student's degree and are listed on the student's academic transcript. University Honors are awarded to students who complete four Honors Colloquia (The Nature of Society, On Human Nature, The Nature of Values, and The Nature of the Universe or Origins). Additionally, students must show evidence of proficiency in a foreign language at the sophomore level either through completion of 6 hours of 2000-level foreign language courses or through credit by examination.

Departmental Honors are awarded to students who engage in honors courses involving significant research in their major. Requirements typically consist of a junior-level seminar and a Senior Honors Project. Since these are research courses, their descriptions are intentionally broad. Although the form of a project is not restricted, and may include compositions, exhibits, or performances, the project must culminate in a document that is housed in the Special Collections Department of the Mary Couts Burnett Library, with its 1.85 million volumes.

Admission Process: Admission to the TCU Honors Program, founded in 1962, is by invitation and is separate from admission to the University. Entering freshmen are invited to join on the basis of criteria set each year by the Director and the Honors Council. Generally speaking, these include both SAT I/ACT scores and graduating rank in class. The goal of the invitational criteria is to produce a program membership of the top 10 to 12 percent of the students entering TCU each fall. Since intellectual motivation is a significant factor in determining academic success, those who fall slightly short of test score criteria, but who wish to undertake the challenge, may be admitted at the discretion of the Honors Program Director. Additionally, freshmen achieving at least a 3.4 GPA at the end of the fall semester are eligible to join the program.

Scholarship Availability: Merit-based scholarships range in value from $1500 per semester to forty-two full-tuition scholarships.

Campus Overview

Independent university, founded 1873, affiliated with Christian Church (Disciples of Christ) • **Coed** 7,154 undergraduate students, 93% full-time, 60% women, 40% men.

Undergraduates 6,687 full-time, 467 part-time. Students come from 50 states and territories, 75 other countries, 20% are from out of state, 5% African American, 2% Asian American or Pacific Islander, 6% Hispanic American, 0.5% Native American, 4% international, 6% transferred in, 44% live on campus.

Faculty *Total:* 748, 59% full-time, 60% with terminal degrees. *Student/faculty ratio:* 15:1.

Academic Programs *Special study options:* adult/continuing education programs, advanced placement credit, distance learning, double majors, English as a second language, honors programs, independent study, internships, part-time degree program, services for LD students, study abroad, summer session for credit. *ROTC:* Army (b), Air Force (b). *Unusual degree programs:* 3-2 education.

Athletics Member NCAA. All Division I. *Intercollegiate sports:* baseball M(s), basketball M(s)/W(s), cross-country running M(s)/W(s), football M(s), golf M(s)/W(s), riflery W(s), soccer M/W(s), swimming and diving M(s)/W(s), tennis M(s)/W(s), track and field M(s)/W(s), volleyball W(s). *Intramural sports:* basketball M/W, football M, lacrosse M/W, racquetball M/W, rugby M/W, soccer M/W, softball M/W, table tennis M/W, tennis M/W, ultimate Frisbee M/W, volleyball M/W, weight lifting M/W.

Costs (2004–05) *Comprehensive fee:* $25,620 includes full-time tuition ($19,700), mandatory fees ($40), and room and board ($5880). *College room only:* $3880. Room and board charges vary according to board plan and housing facility.

Financial Aid 1,296 Federal Work-Study jobs (averaging $2313). 25 state and other part-time jobs (averaging $2400). In 2004, 1439 non-need-based awards were made. *Average percent of need met:* 67%. *Average financial aid package:* $14,037. *Average need-based loan:* $5317. *Average need-based gift aid:* $9867. *Average non-need-based aid:* $8209.

Contact: Peggy Watson, TCU Honors Program, TCU Box 297022, Fort Worth, Texas 76129; *Telephone:* 817-257-7125; *Fax:* 817-921-7333; *E-mail:* pwatson@tcu.edu; *Web site:* http://www.tcu.edu

---

Texas Lutheran University
Honors Program
Seguin, Texas

To become a member of the Texas Lutheran Honors Program is to become a part of a group of about 70 TLU students who have been selected because of their superior academic achievement. Some highly qualified students are appointed to the program as incoming freshmen. Additional students are appointed at the end of their freshman year. Honors students have new opportunities for liberal learning beyond the general requirements of students, and are permitted greater flexibility in curriculum planning. Academic requirements for Honors Program members are meant to encourage breadth as well as depth of study, interdisciplinary understanding, and the challenge appropriate to high academic standing.

Honors seminars and the directed readings course provide members with the opportunity to work closely with their professors and with students who are their intellectual peers. Members have the option of a senior honors thesis or performance project to fulfill their honors course requirement; this may be coordinated with one's departmental senior seminar. Members can even write their own curriculum if they choose to. Additional benefits of Honors Program membership include reductions in costs of tickets to cultural events on campus and in the surrounding region. The Honors Student Study Grant program provides research and special project funds for members involved in independent study courses or other research. Informal forums for discussion of student/academic issues or for talking with special guest speakers enhance lunch or supper get-togethers.

In existence for more than twenty years, the program now enrolls 71 students.

Participation Requirements: Honors Program members at Texas Lutheran University must fulfill the University's 124-credit hour requirement for graduation as well as the associated 30 upper-division hour requirement. In addition, they must complete the general education core courses, GEC 131-132 and GEC 134, or be exempted from the former by advanced placement examination. Honors applicants are expected to have completed this requirement by the time of application to the program.

Unique to the program is the requirement of 12 upper-division hours in the subject areas, although members are required to take fewer total hours here. Except for theology (where the 6-hour requirement still applies), they need take only a minimum of 3 hours in each of the other seven subject areas, but four courses must be taken at the junior or senior level.

The honors courses are designed especially for Texas Lutheran University honors students, and only they can register for them. These courses were created to provide members with the kind of intellectual discussions appropriate to their level of academic ability; the seminars are generally interdisciplinary in nature. All program members must fulfill 4 to 6 hours of honors course work to graduate as honors students. Courses include a senior-level directed readings course and a sophomore-level course that focuses on arts and ideas.

Members must maintain a 3.25 GPA. The deadline for applying to the program is April 1.

Campus Overview

Independent 4-year, founded 1891, affiliated with Evangelical Lutheran Church • **Coed** 1,414 undergraduate students, 94% full-time, 55% women, 45% men.

Undergraduates 1,324 full-time, 90 part-time. Students come from 24 states and territories, 12 other countries, 4% are from out of state, 8% African American, 1% Asian American or Pacific Islander, 17% Hispanic American, 0.4% Native American, 1% international, 4% transferred in, 66% live on campus.

Faculty *Total:* 122, 57% full-time, 52% with terminal degrees. *Student/faculty ratio:* 15:1.

Academic Programs *Special study options:* adult/continuing education programs, advanced placement credit, double majors, honors programs, independent study, internships, part-time degree program, services for LD students, study abroad, summer session for credit. *ROTC:* Army (c), Air Force (c). *Unusual degree programs:* 3-2 engineering with Texas A&M University, Texas Tech University, Texas State University.

Athletics Member NCAA. All Division III. *Intercollegiate sports:* baseball M, basketball M/W, cross-country running W, football M, golf M/W, soccer M/W, softball W, tennis M/W, track and field W, volleyball W. *Intramural sports:* basketball M/W, bowling M/W, football M, racquetball M/W, softball M/W, tennis M/W, volleyball M/W.

Costs (2004–05) *Comprehensive fee:* $21,630 includes full-time tuition ($16,480), mandatory fees ($120), and room and board ($5030). Full-time tuition and fees vary according to course load. Part-time tuition: $550 per credit hour. Part-time tuition and fees vary according to course load. *Required fees:* $60 per term part-time. *College room only:* $2340. Room and board charges vary according to board plan, housing facility, and location.

Financial Aid 304 Federal Work-Study jobs (averaging $960). In 2001, 392 non-need-based awards were made. *Average percent of need met:* 91%. *Average financial aid package:* $13,991. *Average need-based loan:* $5051. *Average non-need-based aid:* $5823.

Contact: Deborah Hettinger, Texas Lutheran University, 1000 West Court Street, Seguin, Texas 78155; *Telephone:* 830-372-6069; *E-mail:* dhettinger@tlu.edu

---

Texas Southern University
Frederick Douglass Honors Program
Houston, Texas

The Frederick Douglass Honors Program at Texas Southern University is a highly selective program designed for superior students known as Douglass Scholars to develop in both liberal and specialized undergraduate studies. The program's mission is to promote intellectual curiosity through an in-depth study of a distinctive curriculum. The program is structured to broaden a student's knowledge base through the study of oral and written discourse, philosophy and logic, literature and aesthetics, the natural and physical sciences, higher mathematics, world cultures, political systems, and classical rhetoric. Through methodologies, such as conceptual analysis, critical thinking, and empirical and analytical reasoning, learning strategies are employed, fostering a sense of current realities and promoting a reflective and introspective foresight toward the future. Humanitarian attitudes and insights are delivered through a study of the application of great ideas and their culminating manifestations in the history of civilization. Being a member of the Honors Program is very prestigious at Texas Southern University.

The Honors Program curriculum offers advanced and challenging classes and seminars that are specially designed for highly motivated Douglass Scholars. Each semester, Scholars enroll in their prospective major and minor courses along with courses designated as honors. Scholars can major in any field of study. In order to graduate as a Douglass Scholar, the honors curriculum must be fulfilled. Honors distinction is printed on the transcripts of Douglass Scholars.

Participation Requirements: Frederick Douglass Scholars are required to demonstrate exemplary academic skills in their studies. Scholars are required to maintain a minimum 3.2 semester grade point average and a minimum 3.2 cumulative grade point average each semester to remain in good academic standing. Scholars must complete the minimum credit hours each semester (15 hours per semester or 30 hours per academic year) to meet the required classification status at the end of each academic year. Freshman Scholars must attend daily study sessions. Participation in all collegiate and extracurricular activities sponsored or endorsed by the program is mandatory.

Scholars are required to participate in internships and summer research programs. The Honors Program has membership with numerous national honor societies and professional organizations. In addition, Douglass Scholars enhance their leadership skills by participating in campus organizations.

Admission Process: Admission to the Honors Program is very selective and highly competitive. All selection criteria must be met to qualify for an award. The selection process begins in the spring semester (March) and continues until spaces are filled. Admission is based on high school grades, class rank, recommendation letters from three instructors, standardized test scores, and a 200-word essay. In addition to these factors, consideration is given to the applicant's high school curriculum, demonstrated leadership ability, and community and extracurricular activities. Admission and enrollment for the Honors Program occurs only in the fall semester of each academic school year.

Scholarship Availability: Honor scholarships are only offered to recent high school graduates who are entering college for the first time. Students admitted to the Honors Program who remain in good academic standing receive scholarship awards to cover the cost of tuition and fees each semester. In general, the Honors Program scholarship averages from $6000 to $8000 each academic year for four years. Scholarships are awarded in two categories: Residential Scholarships and Commuter Scholarships. Residential Scholarships are awarded to students who choose to reside on campus and live in honors housing. Commuter Scholarships are awarded to students who choose not to reside on campus.

Campus Overview

State-supported university, founded 1947, part of Texas Higher Education Coordinating Board • **Coed** 9,585 undergraduate students, 85% full-time, 58% women, 42% men.

Undergraduates 8,179 full-time, 1,406 part-time. Students come from 36 states and territories, 42 other countries, 12% are from out of state, 90% African American, 2% Asian American or Pacific Islander, 3% Hispanic American, 0.1% Native American, 4% international, 10% transferred in, 15% live on campus.

Faculty *Total:* 630, 59% full-time. *Student/faculty ratio:* 25:1.

Academic Programs *Special study options:* academic remediation for entering students, accelerated degree program, adult/continuing education programs, cooperative education, distance learning, English as a second language, honors programs, internships, part-time degree program, services for LD students, summer session for credit. *ROTC:* Army (c), Navy (c).

Athletics Member NCAA. All Division I except football (Division I-AA). *Intercollegiate sports:* baseball M(s), basketball M(s)/W(s), bowling W(s), cross-country running M(s)/W(s), golf M(s), soccer M/W(s), softball W(s), tennis M(s)/W(s), track and field M(s)/W(s), volleyball M/W(s). *Intramural sports:* softball M/W, swimming and diving M/W, tennis M/W, volleyball M/W.

Costs (2004–05) *Tuition:* state resident $1152 full-time, $48 per hour part-time; nonresident $7344 full-time, $350 per hour part-time. Full-time tuition and fees vary according to course load and program. Part-time tuition and fees vary according to course load and program. *Required fees:* $2580 full-time. *Room and board:* $5824; room only: $2316. Room and board charges vary according to board plan and housing facility.

Financial Aid 225 Federal Work-Study jobs (averaging $4000). 29 state and other part-time jobs (averaging $4000). *Average percent of need met:* 48%. *Average financial aid package:* $14,065. *Average need-based loan:* $6625. *Average need-based gift aid:* $9050.

Contact: Dr. Richard Pitre, Associate Provost for Academic Affairs or Linda Coach-Riley, Program Coordinator, Frederick Douglass Honors Program, Texas Southern University, 3100 Cleburne, Houston, Texas 77004; *Telephone:* 713-313-7458 or 7534; *Fax:* 713-313-1879; *E-mail:* Pitre_Rx@tsu.edu or Coach_Lf@tsu.edu; *Web site:* http://www.tsu.edu

Texas State University–San Marcos

Mitte Honors Program

San Marcos, Texas

The Mitte Honors Program at Texas State University–San Marcos combines the rich experience of a small, liberal arts college with the resources of a premier public, student-centered, and doctoral-granting institution. As a core community of scholars dedicated to the highest purposes of university education, the Mitte Honors Program attracts and retains the most highly qualified students and provides a living embodiment of collegiate ideals and thereby enriches the institution in its entirety.

The program offers a diversity of curricula in small, seminar-type classes, where honors students discuss ideas and raise questions stimulated by readings, field trips, and presentations. Dedicated faculty members provide an interdisciplinary atmosphere that promotes curiosity, creativity, and a lifetime love of learning. Recent course offerings include Art and Artists: Catalysts of Social Change, New and Old World Philosophy, Baseball and the American Experience, Elementary Number Theory, Religion, Science and the Quest for Meaning, the Theory of Language, Astronomy in Art, History and Literature, and a course on French cinema taught entirely in Paris.

The Texas State Honors Program has grown exponentially since its founding by history professor Emmie Craddock in 1967. Today, the program directly involves more than 600 of Texas State's best and brightest students. In addition, the program serves a broader student population (nearly 27,000) through several widespread initiatives: 1) the Scholars of Promise recruiting initiative to recruit the best high school students from across the state, 2) the Scholars of Promise development initiative to groom Texas State students for nationally competitive scholarships, including the Rhodes, Fulbright, and Rockefeller competitions, 3) the Common Experience, a campuswide, sustained common conversation that integrates across academic departments, student affairs, and the broader community, and 4) high-quality study-abroad opportunities, including a new program offered in residence at Oxford University.

Participation Requirements: To graduate in the Mitte Honors Program, students complete at least five honors courses (15 hours), including the Honors Thesis. Honors courses can substitute for general education courses, individual requirements, or electives. Honors students must maintain a minimum GPA of 3.25.

Participation in the Mitte Honors Program allows students to become part of a community within the University. Students receive special advising and support for student organizations and engagement initiatives. Honors facilities include four seminar rooms, a student lounge, student organization offices, a media room, a computer lab, and a thesis library. Honors students are eligible to register early each semester. Many students present their honors theses research at national conferences and publish work in regional and national publications. Students can apply for an Honors Thesis Grant to fund up to $500 of their thesis research. In addition, they can present their theses at the undergraduate Honors Thesis Forum, which is held at the end of each semester.

Admission Process: Entering freshman with a minimum composite ACT score of 27 or SAT I score of 1180 or who are in the top 10 percent of their high school graduating class are eligible for the program. Currently enrolled and transfer students with a GPA of at least 3.25 are also eligible. Students can submit applications online or as hard copy at any time during their college careers and can withdraw from the program without penalty.

Scholarship Availability: Freshman, continuing students, and transfer students can apply for more than $100,000 in scholarships annually, including the Mitte Scholarships, Terry Scholarships, University Honors Program Scholarships, Craddock Scholarships, Friedman Scholarship, Camp Scholarship, and Honors Study Abroad Scholarships.

Campus Overview

State-supported university, founded 1899, part of Texas State University System • **Coed** 22,402 undergraduate students, 81% full-time, 55% women, 45% men.

Undergraduates 18,046 full-time, 4,356 part-time. Students come from 46 states and territories, 55 other countries, 1% are from out of state, 5% African American, 2% Asian American or Pacific Islander, 19% Hispanic American, 0.7% Native American, 1% international, 13% transferred in, 22% live on campus.

Faculty *Total:* 1,077, 65% full-time, 57% with terminal degrees. *Student/faculty ratio:* 26:1.

Academic Programs *Special study options:* academic remediation for entering students, accelerated degree program, adult/continuing education programs, advanced placement credit, distance learning, double majors, English as a second language, honors programs, independent study, internships, off-campus study, part-time degree program, services for LD students, study abroad, summer session for credit. *ROTC:* Army (b), Air Force (b). *Unusual degree programs:* 3-2 engineering with University of Texas at Austin, Texas A&M University, Texas Tech University, University of Texas at San Antonio; dentistry with University of Texas Health Science Center at San Antonio.

Athletics Member NCAA. All Division I except football (Division I-AA). *Intercollegiate sports:* baseball M(s), basketball M(s)/W(s), cheerleading M/W, cross-country running M(s)/W(s), equestrian sports M(c)/W(c), fencing M(c)/W(c), golf M(s)/W(s), gymnastics M(c)/W(c), lacrosse M(c)/W(c), rugby M(c)/W(c), soccer M(c)/W(s), softball M(c)/W(s), tennis M(c)/W(s), track and field M(s)/W(s), ultimate Frisbee M(c)/W(c), volleyball W(s), water polo M(c)/W(c), weight lifting M(c)/W(c), wrestling M(c)/W(c). *Intramural sports:* basketball M/W, bowling M/W, cross-country running M/W, football M/W, golf M/W, racquetball M/W, soccer M/W, softball M/W, tennis M/W, ultimate Frisbee M, volleyball M/W.

Costs (2004–05) *Tuition:* state resident $3270 full-time, $109 per semester hour part-time; nonresident $11,010 full-time, $367 per semester hour part-time. Full-time tuition and fees vary according to course load. Part-time tuition and fees vary according to course load. *Required fees:* $1410 full-time, $36 per semester hour part-time, $247 per term part-time. *Room and board:* $5456; room only: $3370. Room and board charges vary according to board plan and housing facility.

Financial Aid 737 Federal Work-Study jobs (averaging $1646). 126 state and other part-time jobs (averaging $789). In 2004, 2465 non-need-based awards were made. *Average percent of need met:* 66%. *Average financial aid package:* $8997. *Average need-based loan:* $3820. *Average need-based gift aid:* $3814. *Average non-need-based aid:* $7617.

Contact: Director: Dr. Christopher Frost, San Marcos, Texas 78666; *Telephone:* 512-245-2266; *Fax:* 512-245-8959; *E-mail:* honors@txstate.edu

Texas Tech University

University Honors College

Lubbock, Texas

An element that distinguishes Texas Tech University (TTU) is its University Honors College, which is available to serve the interests of students from all disciplines, as well as students majoring in the honors arts and letters (HAL) and the honors multidisciplinary natural history and humanities (NHH) Bachelor of Arts degrees.

Accepting only the most academically motivated students, the College is dedicated to examining life and society and to broadening its participants through unusual classes, challenging reading, wide-ranging discussions, and stimulating instruction. Moreover, the University Honors College strives to prepare its participants for a lifetime of self-education.

Several features add to the ideal of educating the honors students at Texas Tech University. The University Honors College produces a wide variety of interdisciplinary classes, where professors especially strive to meet the objective of providing the broadest possible undergraduate educational experience. In addition, the University Honors College sponsors and cooperates with an extensive array of undergraduate research initiatives. Honors advisers provide personal counseling for students who are interested in securing national and international scholarships. The program financially supports study abroad and provides students with information and programs of particular interest. It has special entry and early decision programs for undergraduates who are interested in medical school, law school, and graduate business study. It is also through the honors office that incoming students receive scholarship support at the University—a scholarship program that is among the most generous in the region. Finally, there are special and superior residence hall accommodations available to honors participants. In combination with a number of cocurricular activities and University privileges accorded especially to honors students, the University Honors College is recognized as the ideal opportunity on campus for meeting the special needs and providing the special opportunities that high-end students have and want.

Another unique feature of the Texas Tech University Honors College is its extensive student involvement. Students sit on committees, engage in recruiting, help make decisions on course content and textbooks, and evaluate faculty members. Honors students are members of their own student organization, Eta Omicron Nu, which provides social, service, and other extracurricular opportunities. Honors students also represent the University at national and regional honors conventions, and Honors Ambassadors represent the program at a variety of special events.

Currently, there are approximately 1,000 students at the University Honors College.

Participation Requirements: The University Honors College requires that students maintain a GPA of at least 3.25 to remain in good standing and exhibit meaningful progress toward attaining an honors degree. The honors degree requires 24 hours of honors course work to graduate with "honors" and 30 hours, including a senior thesis, to graduate with "highest honors."

Admission Process: There are several different routes to admission into the Honors College, but in the final analysis, students must be formally accepted before they can take advantage of the various benefits and advantages that the program offers. The minimum requirement for application to the University Honors College consists of one or more of the following: a cumulative SAT I score of at least 1200 or a cumulative ACT score of at least 28, graduation within the top 10 percent of the high school class, or submission of a written essay (in addition to the essays required in the application itself) in which compelling reasons are provided for why the above criteria have not been met and an explanation of why the student thinks that he or she would especially benefit by belonging to the University Honors College. Continuing Texas Tech students or transfer students must have a GPA of at least 3.4. Other factors that are considered in the admission process are the nature and extent of extracurricular activities, grades in college-preparatory high school classes, qualities reflected in two letters of recommendation, and written essays. Complete and current application information and forms are available on the Web site listed in the Contact section of this description.

Because there are limits on the number of students that can be admitted, students must apply to the University Honors College as soon as they are reasonably sure that they will be attending Texas Tech. Applications are accepted each year from about September 1 to April 1. An early decision option allows students to apply by December 15 to receive notice of acceptance by February 1. Students are admitted on a rolling basis as applications are received. Applicants are generally not admitted outside of these enrollment dates unless there are exceptional circumstances.

Scholarship Availability: A large number of significant scholarships are available; nonresident students who qualify for at least $1000 in scholarship awards from Texas Tech University pay Texas resident tuition, as do students from New Mexico, Oklahoma, and Arkansas who reside in counties bordering Texas. (Residents from non-bordering counties of New Mexico and Oklahoma also pay a greatly reduced rate.) Information and forms are available on the Web at http://www.fina.ttu.edu.

Campus Overview

State-supported university, founded 1923, part of Texas Tech University System • **Coed** 23,329 undergraduate students, 90% full-time, 45% women, 55% men.

Undergraduates 20,903 full-time, 2,426 part-time. Students come from 52 states and territories, 87 other countries, 4% are from out of state, 3% African American, 2% Asian American or Pacific Islander, 11% Hispanic American, 0.7% Native American, 1% international, 9% transferred in, 22% live on campus.

Faculty *Total:* 1,111, 92% full-time, 88% with terminal degrees. *Student/faculty ratio:* 19:1.

Academic Programs *Special study options:* academic remediation for entering students, accelerated degree program, advanced placement credit, cooperative education, distance learning, double majors, English as a second language, external degree program, freshman honors college, honors programs, independent study, internships, off-campus study, part-time degree program, services for LD students, student-designed majors, study abroad, summer session for credit. *ROTC:* Army (b), Air Force (b). *Unusual degree programs:* 3-2 architecture.

Athletics Member NCAA. All Division I except football (Division I-A). *Intercollegiate sports:* baseball M(s), basketball M(s)/W(s), cross-country running M(s)/W(s), golf M(s)/W(s), soccer W(s), softball W(s), tennis M(s)/W(s), track and field M(s)/W(s), volleyball W(s). *Intramural sports:* badminton M/W, baseball M, basketball M/W, bowling M/W, cross-country running M, equestrian sports M, fencing M(c)/W(c), football M/W, golf M/W, gymnastics W, ice hockey M(c), lacrosse M(c)/W(c), racquetball M/W, rock climbing M(c)/W(c), rugby M(c)/W(c), soccer M/W, softball M/W, swimming and diving M/W, table tennis M/W, tennis M/W, track and field M/W, ultimate Frisbee M(c)/W(c), volleyball M/W, water polo M/W, weight lifting M, wrestling M(c).

Costs (2004–05) *Tuition:* state resident $3720 full-time, $124 per credit hour part-time; nonresident $11,460 full-time, $382 per credit hour part-time. Full-time tuition and fees vary according to course load, program, and reciprocity agreements. Part-time tuition and fees vary according to course load, program, and reciprocity agreements. *Required fees:* $2128 full-time, $54 per credit hour part-time, $284 per semester part-time. *Room and board:* $6421; room only: $3631. Room and board charges vary according to board plan and housing facility.

Financial Aid 445 Federal Work-Study jobs (averaging $1555). In 2003, 5641 non-need-based awards were made. *Average financial aid package:* $6485. *Average need-based loan:* $3662. *Average need-based gift aid:* $3281. *Average non-need-based aid:* $2204.

Contact: Dean: Gary M. Bell, Associate Dean: Gary Elbow, McClellan Hall, P.O. Box 41017, Lubbock, Texas 79409-1017; *Telephone:* 806-742-1828; *Fax:* 806-742-1805; *E-mail:* honors@ttu.edu; *Web site:* http://www.honr.ttu.edu

Texas Woman's University
Honors Scholar Program
Denton, TEXAS

The Honors Scholar Program at Texas Woman's University (TWU) provides talented and motivated students in all majors an enriched academic and cultural environment. The three-fold emphasis upon the development of skills in writing, research, and technology provides students with preparation that will be useful to them throughout their careers.

While its students strive for academic excellence in the classroom, they also enjoy ample cultural and social opportunities throughout the year. Students in the program organize cultural activities that include attendance at theatrical performances, music recitals, dance performances, and tours of various art galleries and museums. The University's proximity to the Dallas–Ft. Worth Metroplex offers program participants a wide variety of cultural and social experiences. Students regularly attend and present at the National Collegiate Honors Council and the Great Plains Honors Council conferences. The program sponsors a trip abroad each year; past destinations included London, northern Spain, Ireland, Paris, Rome, and Athens.

The program was begun in 2000 and currently has 200 students. The TWU honors program is diverse, with 14 percent Hispanic and 11 percent African-American students. Enrollment is limited to 5 percent of the undergraduate student body in order to provide participants with individualized assistance in areas ranging from advising to career planning to the preparation of scholarship and graduate school applications.

Currently, there are three honors floors in the residence halls, each with a study lounge and kitchenette. Students in the program enjoy membership in the Athenian Honor Society (the cultural, social, and representative organization for participants) and a number of campus privileges, including early registration and extended library privileges.

Upon completion, students graduate as TWU honors scholars and receive recognition at commencement, an honors scholar medallion, a certificate, and an acknowledgment of participation on both the diploma and University transcripts.

Participation Requirements: The Honors Scholar Program accepts students either as new freshmen or as transfer students. All students must complete 25 hours of honors-designated course work, which includes a three-hour capstone project in the senior year. These hours may be fulfilled through a combination of honors course work, honors contract work, or select graduate courses in the student's major field. Students are allowed to select any combination of honors courses being offered and consult with the Director and academic advisers to tailor a program of honors study to their particular major. Students must maintain a minimum GPA of 3.30 throughout.

Admission Process: Students must apply to the Honors Scholar Program for admission. The application requires students to provide basic information about their academic preparation and their leadership, creative, athletic, or service experiences. Applicants are also asked to provide three references and a brief personal statement. Telephone or in-person interviews are conducted by the program's director.

Freshmen are admitted on the basis of SAT scores, high school grades and rank, and extracurricular activities. While admissions decisions are based on a combination of factors, generally the admissions committee gives preference to students with a minimum SAT score of 1220 (Verbal and Math) and to those who are in the top 5 percent of their high school class. New freshmen seeking admission for the fall semester should submit applications no later than April 1.

Transfer students are accepted on the basis of college GPA and extracurricular activities. As with freshman applicants, the admissions committee considers more than grades alone but gives preference to candidates with a GPA of 3.5 or higher. Applicants must have between 24 and 48 college credit hours at the time of application, or they must have completed an honors program at a school with which TWU has an articulation agreement. Up to 12 hours of honors credit may be accepted from honors programs that are NCHC-member institutions. Transfer students may apply at any time.

Scholarship Availability: Texas Woman's University provides substantial academic scholarship support to qualified candidates, including several scholarships for honors program participants each year. In addition, the Honors Scholars Program provides assistance for all participants in identifying and applying for departmental, university-wide, and external scholarships. The University's international study scholarships provide assistance for those seeking to study abroad.

Campus Overview

State-supported university, founded 1901 • **Suburban** 270-acre campus with easy access to Dallas–Fort Worth • **Coed primarily women** 5,826 undergraduate students, 75% full-time, 94% women, 6% men.

Undergraduates 4,352 full-time, 1,474 part-time. Students come from 19 states and territories, 47 other countries, 1% are from out of state, 22% African American, 5% Asian American or Pacific Islander, 13% Hispanic American, 0.9% Native American, 3% international, 14% transferred in, 25% live on campus.

Faculty Total: 700, 57% full-time. Student/faculty ratio: 14:1.

Academic Programs Special study options: academic remediation for entering students, accelerated degree program, adult/continuing education programs, advanced placement credit, cooperative education, distance learning, double majors, honors programs, independent study, internships, off-campus study, part-time degree program, services for LD students, study abroad, summer session for credit. ROTC: Army (c), Air Force (c). Unusual degree programs: 3-2 engineering with The University of Texas at Dallas, Texas A&M University at College Station; physical therapy, human biology, kinesiology, nursing.

Athletics Member NCAA. All Division II. Intercollegiate sports: basketball W(s), gymnastics W(s), soccer W(s), softball W(s), volleyball W(s). Intramural sports: badminton M(c)/W(c), basketball M(c)/W(c), bowling M(c)/W(c), football M(c)/W(c), golf M(c)/W(c), soccer M(c)/W(c), softball M(c)/W(c), volleyball M(c)/W(c).

Costs (2004–05) Tuition: state resident $2616 full-time, $109 per semester hour part-time; nonresident $8808 full-time, $367 per semester hour part-time. Full-time tuition and fees vary according to course load, degree level, location, program, and reciprocity agreements. Part-time tuition and fees vary according to course load, degree level, location, program, and reciprocity agreements. Required fees: $779 full-time, $157 per semester hour part-time. Room and board: $5094; room only: $2480. Room and board charges vary according to board plan and housing facility.

Financial Aid 131 Federal Work-Study jobs (averaging $1702). 481 state and other part-time jobs (averaging $3144). In 2003, 174 non-need-based awards were made. Average percent of need met: 98%. Average financial aid package: $10,412. Average need-based loan: $3720. Average need-based gift aid: $3934. Average non-need-based aid: $2100.

Contact: Director: Dr. Guy Litton, P.O. Box 425678, Texas Woman's University, Denton, Texas 76204-5678; Telephone: 940-898-2337; Fax: 940-898-2835; E-mail: alitton@twu.edu; Web site: http://www.twu.edu

Tyler Junior College
Scholars Academy
Tyler, Texas

*S*cholars Academy provides a variety of enriched academic *experiences for talented and motivated students. Within a system that combines rigorous course work with creative instruction, Scholars Academy students are challenged to become responsible leaders. The primary goals are the development of a commitment to honest inquiry, an atmosphere of cooperative relationships with faculty members and fellow students, and a willingness to serve humanity. Scholars Academy courses are smaller than traditional courses, and faculty members are committed to providing a dynamic and interactive classroom experience. Several courses feature service learning components, and the program provides extracurricular opportunities. Scholars Academy was established in 1999, and it currently has approximately 80 students enrolled in honors courses.*

Participation Requirements: In order to graduate from Tyler Junior College with Scholars Academy Distinction, students must complete all general graduation requirements for the degree sought, as specified in the applicable Tyler Junior College catalog; complete at least 18 hours of Scholars Academy courses, including at least 3 hours of ENGL 2353 (Leadership) and a total of at least 3 hours of the 1-hour seminar courses; maintain a 3.3 or higher cumulative grade point average for courses completed at Tyler Junior College; and complete all 48 hours of community service.

Admission Process: Entering freshmen should meet at least one of the following criteria: score 1070 or higher on the SAT; score 23 composite or higher on the ACT; or complete all sections of the Texas Success Initiative. Transfer students or continuing students should have a 3.3 or higher cumulative grade point average on at least 12 hours of college course work and pass all sections of TASP or its equivalent and complete all sections of the Texas Success Initiative.

Admission is rolling, but scholarship deadlines are March 1.

Scholarship Availability: Honors scholarships are available for selected sophomore students who are on the honors graduation track. These awards are based GPA, professor recommendation, volunteer hours completed, and honors credit hours completed. The number of honors scholarships awarded each year varies.

Campus Overview

State and locally supported 2-year, founded 1926 • **Coed** 9,591 undergraduate students.

Undergraduates Students come from 30 states and territories, 25 other countries, 1% are from out of state, 19% African American, 1% Asian American or Pacific Islander, 8% Hispanic American, 0.5% Native American, 0.5% international, 8% live on campus.

Faculty *Total:* 456, 51% full-time. *Student/faculty ratio:* 21:1.

Academic Programs *Special study options:* academic remediation for entering students, accelerated degree program, adult/continuing education programs, advanced placement credit, distance learning, English as a second language, freshman honors college, honors programs, part-time degree program, services for LD students, summer session for credit.

Athletics Member NJCAA. *Intercollegiate sports:* baseball M, basketball M(s)/W(s), football M(s), golf M/W, soccer M(s), tennis M(s)/W(s), volleyball W. *Intramural sports:* basketball M/W, racquetball M/W, volleyball M/W, weight lifting M/W.

Costs (2004–05) *Tuition:* area resident $1460 full-time, $44 per semester hour part-time; state resident $2330 full-time, $73 per semester hour part-time; nonresident $2630 full-time, $83 per semester hour part-time. *Required fees:* $70 per term part-time. *Room and board:* $3700.

Financial Aid 39 Federal Work-Study jobs (averaging $1117). 23 state and other part-time jobs (averaging $992).

Contact: Coordinator: Ms. Joan Bruckwicki, Tyler Junior College, P.O. Box 9020, Tyler, Texas 75711; *Telephone:* 903-510-2896; 903-510-6581 *E-mail:* jbru@tjc.edu; http://www.tjc.edu/scholars/index.htm

University of Houston
The Honors College
Houston, Texas

*T*he Honors College at the University of Houston provides the *careful guidance, flexibility, and personal instruction that nurture excellence. For the 300 students who join us each fall, the Honors College offers the advantages of a small college without sacrificing the resources and rich diversity of a large University. The faculty and staff members believe that a university education should offer more than the acquisition of skills for the workplace. Accordingly, the Honors College aims to challenge its finest students to develop the attributes of mind and character that enhance all facets of life.*

The Honors College draws on the talents of the finest faculty members at the University to provide a wide range of special courses with limited enrollment. Honors courses encourage student participation, interaction, and discussion. Students enjoy special privileges, including Honors College scholarships, priority registration, computer facilities, reserved lounge and study areas, study-abroad opportunities, and special housing in the Honors College residence halls.

Many intangible benefits come with participation in the honors community, most notably friendships that develop in the classroom and carry over into other areas of student life. The students take a lead in fostering an atmosphere of collegiality and a spirit of camaraderie through informal gatherings, social activities, and on- and off-campus cultural events.

Participation Requirements: Honors students are expected to take the Human Situation, a team-taught course designed to introduce students to great books in the Western tradition. In addition, students are expected to take at least one honors course each semester and to maintain a cumulative GPA of at least 3.25.

Admission Process: The priority application deadline is February 1, but the Honors College continues to process and review applications until the fall class is filled. Each applicant to the Honors College is considered individually; admission is based on academic and extracurricular achievement, standardized test scores, and an academic essay. Applications from transfer students are welcome.

Scholarship Availability: Applicants to the Honors College are automatically considered for the sizable number of merit-based scholarships the University awards to new students. The University of Houston awards scholarship support to cover the cost of tuition, required fees, room, board, and a $250 per semester book stipend to National Merit Scholarship finalists who select the University of Houston as their first choice in accordance with the rules and deadlines established by the National Merit Scholarship Corporation (NMSC). Out-of-state students who receive merit-based scholarships worth at least $1000, qualify for in-state tuition. In addition, the Honors College awards smaller scholarships to both entering and continuing students; need-based financial assistance is also available.

Campus Overview

State-supported university, founded 1927, part of University of Houston System • **Coed** 27,312 undergraduate students, 70% full-time, 52% women, 48% men.

Undergraduates 19,088 full-time, 8,224 part-time. Students come from 52 states and territories, 130 other countries, 2% are from out of

state, 15% African American, 21% Asian American or Pacific Islander, 21% Hispanic American, 0.4% Native American, 5% international, 10% transferred in, 10% live on campus.

Faculty *Total:* 1,624, 73% full-time, 74% with terminal degrees. *Student/faculty ratio:* 21:1.

Academic Programs *Special study options:* academic remediation for entering students, accelerated degree program, adult/continuing education programs, advanced placement credit, cooperative education, distance learning, double majors, English as a second language, freshman honors college, honors programs, independent study, internships, off-campus study, part-time degree program, services for LD students, study abroad, summer session for credit. *ROTC:* Army (b), Navy (c).

Athletics Member NCAA. All Division I except football (Division I-A). *Intercollegiate sports:* baseball M(s), basketball M(s)/W(s), cheerleading M/W, cross-country running M(s)/W(s), golf M(s), soccer W(s), softball W(s), swimming and diving W(s), tennis W(s), track and field M(s)/W(s), volleyball W(s). *Intramural sports:* badminton M/W, baseball M, basketball M/W, bowling M(c)/W(c), cheerleading M/W, cross-country running M/W, football M/W, golf M/W, lacrosse M, racquetball M/W, rock climbing M/W, rugby M, soccer M(c), swimming and diving M/W, table tennis M/W, tennis M/W, track and field M/W, ultimate Frisbee M/W, volleyball M/W, water polo M/W, weight lifting M.

Costs (2004–05) *Tuition:* state resident $1440 full-time, $48 per credit hour part-time; nonresident $9180 full-time, $306 per credit hour part-time. Full-time tuition and fees vary according to course level, course load, degree level, location, program, reciprocity agreements, and student level. Part-time tuition and fees vary according to course level, course load, degree level, location, program, reciprocity agreements, and student level. *Required fees:* $3533 full-time. *Room and board:* $6030; room only: $3390. Room and board charges vary according to board plan and housing facility.

Financial Aid In 2002, 3150 non-need-based awards were made. *Average percent of need met:* 80%. *Average financial aid package:* $11,340. *Average need-based loan:* $5300. *Average need-based gift aid:* $6200. *Average non-need-based aid:* $2730.

Contact: The Honors College, 212 M. D. Anderson Library, University of Houston, Houston, Texas 77204-2001; *Telephone:* 888-827-0366 (toll-free); *Fax:* 713-743-9015; *Web site:* http://www.uh.edu/honors

University of North Texas
Honors College
Denton, Texas

The Honors College at the University of North Texas (UNT) promotes academic excellence and intellectual growth for the many talented and motivated students who hold membership. Opportunities within and beyond the classroom are designed to foster intellectual curiosity and assist students in building an intellectual foundation that will serve them in the pursuits of a lifetime, including graduate school and career development.

The Honors College offers both Lower Division and Upper Division Honors Programs, including the Honors Certificate Program, the Honors Scholar Award, and the Distinguished Honors Scholar designation. Students in any major may pursue Honors College membership, as many courses offered for honors credit meet University core requirements. The Honors College also offers a research track through which students can develop research skills, write an honors thesis, and present their scholarly work at UNT's annual University-wide Scholars Day and at regional and national honors and professional conferences.

Although the honors classroom is the heart of the program, students in the Honors College also enjoy many other enrichment opportunities, including informal lunches with professors and deans; free tickets to a variety of cultural events, including jazz and other concerts, plays, and art shows; informational meetings about graduate and professional school and special opportunities on campus; and trips to local museums and lectures. Students who are members of the Honors College may also live in honors housing, which offers special programming for students.

At commencement, graduates are honored at a special reception at which their accomplishments are recognized with the Honors College medallion. Their transcript is also designated to provide a permanent record of their graduation through the Honors College.

Participation Requirements: Once admitted, students activate their Honors College membership by registering for and successfully completing an honors course. Active membership is then maintained until graduation by taking Honors courses and keeping a GPA of at least 3.0. Students in the Honors College are also members of the college or school in which their major is offered, and each semester they enjoy the flexibility of designing a schedule that includes honors, non-honors, and major courses. Honors advising is available to help students make decisions about courses and the most appropriate program in honors for their academic and intellectual goals. Details about each option can be found on the Honors College Web page at www.unt.edu/honors.

Admission Process: A separate application, available at www.unt.edu/honors or by mail from the Honors College, is required. The University's goal is to admit students who already possess the foundation necessary for academic achievement and the motivation to embrace honors opportunities for additional intellectual growth. Freshmen are eligible for admission on the basis of a score of at least 27 on the ACT or 1200 on the SAT (for fall 2005 admission) and an excellent high school record that supports the applicant's commitment to academic excellence. Interested students may print the Honors College application from the Web site and mail it to the Honors College, along with a sample of their written work and a copy of their high school transcript. Continuing UNT students or students transferring to UNT from other institutions of higher learning are eligible to join the program if they have a minimum GPA of 3.25 on at least one full semester of college course work. For more information, students should contact the Honors College Academic Adviser at 940-565-3305.

Scholarship Availability: While the Honors College awards a number of scholarships each year, students are advised to apply through the University's Office of Financial Aid and Scholarships to be considered for all the scholarships for which they are eligible. National Merit Scholars who select UNT as their first choice should contact the Office of Financial Aid and Scholarships or the Honors College for information on the excellent scholarships for which they are eligible.

Campus Overview

State-supported university, founded 1890 • **Coed** 24,274 undergraduate students, 78% full-time, 55% women, 45% men.

Undergraduates 19,055 full-time, 5,219 part-time. 12% African American, 4% Asian American or Pacific Islander, 10% Hispanic American, 0.8% Native American, 3% international, 12% transferred in, 23% live on campus.

Faculty *Total:* 1,520, 60% full-time. *Student/faculty ratio:* 18:1.

Academic Programs *Special study options:* academic remediation for entering students, accelerated degree program, advanced placement credit, cooperative education, distance learning, double majors, English as a second language, external degree program, freshman honors college, honors programs, internships, part-time degree program, services for LD students, study abroad, summer session for credit. *ROTC:* Army (c), Navy (b).

Athletics Member NCAA. All Division I. *Intercollegiate sports:* baseball M(c), basketball M(s)/W(s), bowling M(c)/W(c), cross-country running M(s)/W(s), fencing M(c)/W(c), football M(s), golf M(s)/W(s), ice hockey M(c), lacrosse M(c)/W(c), rugby M(c), sailing M(c)/W(c), soccer W, softball W, swimming and diving M(c)/W(c), tennis M(c)/W(s), track and field M(s)/W(s), ultimate Frisbee M(c)/W(c), volleyball W(s). *Intramural sports:* basketball M/W, bowling M/W, field hockey M/W, football M/W, golf M/W, racquetball M/W, soccer M/W, softball M/W, table tennis M/W, tennis M/W, track and field M/W, volleyball M/W, water polo M/W, weight lifting M(c)/W(c).

Costs (2004–05) *Tuition:* state resident $3690 full-time, $123 per credit hour part-time; nonresident $11,430 full-time, $381 per credit hour part-time. Full-time tuition and fees vary according to course load. Part-time tuition and fees vary according to course load. *Required fees:* $1871 full-time, $483 per term part-time. *Room and board:* $5124; room only: $2890. Room and board charges vary according to board plan.

Financial Aid In 2004, 1046 non-need-based awards were made. *Average percent of need met: 65%. Average financial aid package: $7269. Average need-based loan: $3728. Average need-based gift aid: $3655. Average non-need-based aid: $1482.*

Contact: Dean: Dr. Gloria C. Cox, Honors College, University of North Texas, P.O. Box 310529, Denton, Texas 76203; *Telephone:* 940-565-3305; *Fax:* 940-369-7370; *E-mail:* gcox@unt.edu; *Web site:* http://www.unt.edu/honors

University of St. Thomas
Honors Program
Houston, Texas

The purpose of the Honors Program at the University of St. Thomas (UST) is the creation of virtuous professionals who are makers and preservers of a culture that is not hostile to the virtuous life. This requires two distinct but related educational activities: the tradition or the handing over of artifacts and archetypes of Western culture to students and an apprenticeship in the redeployment of these cultural instruments in the contemporary world, which ideally will result in their reform and transformation. Established in 1989, the Honors Program currently enrolls 50 to 70 students.

Participation Requirements: The program begins with four interdisciplinary, team-taught seminars that have a two-fold purpose: to connect the study of Western culture with the problem of living one's life and to provide structural principles for understanding culture itself and, therefore, of facilitating understanding of non-Western cultures. Team-teaching both furthers the interdisciplinary nature of the courses and encourages collaboration in learning among students and faculty members.

These four courses are the necessary prologue to a course in reflective practical action. This course combines reading and discussion with individual service projects. In this way, students learn how values become incarnate in the world through work and how self-development is connected with service to others.

An undergraduate research project, which culminates in the presentation of results in a University forum, is designed to foster professional creativity and responsibility as well as collaboration with a faculty mentor.

A final team-taught seminar undertakes an interdisciplinary approach to the analysis and solution of some contemporary problem. As they prepare to leave the University, students discover that their education, liberal and professional, has given them the power to understand and transform contemporary society in the light of their values.

Successful completion of the Honors Program is noted on the student's transcript. Graduates of the Honors Program receive a certificate and medallion at Commencement, and Honors Program is printed on their diploma.

Admission Process: In order to be considered for admission, students must complete the University's general scholarship application and arrange for an interview with the program. Students must have a GPA of at least 3.5 on a 4.0 scale, be in the top 15 percent of their graduating class, and have an SAT I score of at least 1220 (recentered) or an ACT score of at least 27.

Scholarship Availability: All members of the UST Honors Program receive scholarships. These include the President's Scholarship, which is valued between $36,000 and is given to students who are in the top 20 percent of their graduating class or have a GPA of at lest 3.5 and an SAT score of at least 1250 (or 28 on the SAT); the St. Thomas Aquinas Scholarship, which is valued between $26,000 and $28,000 and is awarded to students who are in the top 30 percent of their class or a GPA of at least 3.0 and an SAT score of at least 1170 (or 26 on the ACT); and the Frances E. Monaghan Scholarship, which is valued between $8000 and $20,000 and is awarded to students who are in the top 35 percent of their class or have a GPA of at least 2.75 and an SAT score of at least 1100 (or 24 on the ACT).

Campus Overview
Independent Roman Catholic comprehensive, founded 1947 • **Coed** 1,910 undergraduate students, 70% full-time, 63% women, 37% men.

Undergraduates 1,335 full-time, 575 part-time. Students come from 29 states and territories, 40 other countries, 4% are from out of state, 5% African American, 12% Asian American or Pacific Islander, 29% Hispanic American, 0.6% Native American, 3% international, 9% transferred in, 15% live on campus.

Faculty *Total:* 260, 45% full-time, 60% with terminal degrees. *Student/faculty ratio:* 14:1.

Academic Programs *Special study options:* academic remediation for entering students, adult/continuing education programs, advanced placement credit, distance learning, double majors, honors programs, independent study, internships, off-campus study, part-time degree program, services for LD students, study abroad, summer session for credit. *ROTC:* Army (c). *Unusual degree programs:* 3-2 engineering with University of Notre Dame, University of Houston, Texas A&M University.

Athletics *Intramural sports:* baseball M(c), basketball M/W(c), fencing M(c)/W(c), golf M/W, racquetball M/W, rugby M(c), soccer M(c)/W(c), table tennis M/W, tennis M/W, volleyball M/W(c), wrestling M(c).

Costs (2004–05) *Comprehensive fee:* $23,612 includes full-time tuition ($16,200), mandatory fees ($112), and room and board ($7300). Full-time tuition and fees vary according to course load. Part-time tuition: $540 per credit hour. Part-time tuition and fees vary according to course load. *Required fees:* $30 per term part-time. *College room only:* $4000. Room and board charges vary according to board plan and housing facility.

Financial Aid 39 Federal Work-Study jobs (averaging $2931). 5 state and other part-time jobs (averaging $3000). In 2004, 256 non-need-based awards were made. *Average percent of need met: 65%. Average financial aid package: $11,396. Average need-based loan: $3865. Average need-based gift aid: $8250. Average non-need-based aid: $6792.*

Contact: Director: Dr. Terry Hall, 3800 Montrose Boulevard, Houston, Texas 77006; *Telephone:* 713-525-3587; *Fax:* 713-525-2125; *E-mail:* thall@stthom.edu; *Web site:* http://www.stthom.edu/honors

The University of Texas at Arlington

The Honors College

Arlington, Texas

The Honors College is a community of exceptionally capable and highly motivated students who seek the intellectual stimulation offered by major urban university and the individual attention available in an Honors College. The College promotes a spirit of inquiry among students and faculty members and sets standards for academic performance at the University of Texas at Arlington (UTA). Honors students from all disciplines study together in interdisciplinary core courses, honors sections of lower-division University courses, advanced honors courses in their majors, and colloquiums and seminars in special topics. Honors study-abroad programs provide intensive international experiences; in recent years, programs have been offered in Europe, Africa, and Central America. Honors service learning courses provide community service opportunities and support for students interested in volunteering.

Course work in the Honors College is compatible with any major, and all honors courses fulfill core, departmental, and/or college requirements. The Honors College does not grant degrees; rather, honors degrees are awarded in the disciplines of the academic schools and colleges.

Honors College at UTA currently enrolls approximately 600 students.

Participation Requirements: Honors degrees are granted in all disciplines of the University's eight undergraduate schools and colleges (Architecture, Business Administration, Education, Engineering, Liberal Arts, Nursing, Science, and Social Work) and in the Interdisciplinary Studies Program. To graduate with an honors degree, the student must be a member of the Honors College in good standing (maintaining a minimum 3.2 GPA) and must complete the degree requirements in a disciplinary major.

Honors requirements include at least 24 hours of honors course work (all of which may also fulfill University core and disciplinary major requirements) as follows: 3 hours in an approved research methods course, 3 hours in an approved thesis/creative project course, and at least 18 honors hours chosen from special honors sections of University core requirements, other honors interdisciplinary seminars/special topics courses, honors independent study courses, honors electives, honors credit contract courses, and honors courses in the major.

The 24-hour requirement for transfer students may be adjusted in some colleges. Further details regarding the honors curriculum are available at the Honors College Web site or by contacting an honors adviser.

Admission Process: The Honors College seeks students with broad interests, varied talents, and diverse cultural backgrounds. Entering freshman honors applicants must have a minimum combined SAT (Verbal and Quantitative) score of 1200 or a minimum composite ACT score of 27 and/or be in the upper 10 percent of their high school graduating class. Continuing and transfer honors candidates must have a minimum 3.2 GPA. Admission is not based solely on grades or standardized test scores; the Admissions Committee (comprising honors faculty and staff members) also carefully considers faculty recommendations and the applicant's statements of purpose. Applications for admission are available online at the College's Web site or in the Honors College Office.

Scholarship Availability: The Honors College, in conjunction with the UTA Scholarship Office, awards nearly 500 scholarships to honors students each year. Students who maintain the requisite GPA of at least 3.25 may renew their scholarships for up to three additional years. The Honors Undergraduate Research Program, in concert with UTA's other schools and colleges, places students in funded research assistantships in their disciplines. Information on departmental and organizational scholarships and financial aid is available online at http://www.2.uta.edu/fao/. By recent agreement with the UTA Graduate School and the academic units, honors students interested in continuing at UTA for their graduate or professional education (74 master's degree and 34 doctoral degree programs are offered) are eligible for fast-track admission as well as special fellowship support. Students with honors undergraduate degrees from other Great Plains Honors Council institutions are also eligible for fast-track admission.

Campus Overview

State-supported university, founded 1895, part of University of Texas System • **Coed** 19,114 undergraduate students, 72% full-time, 53% women, 47% men.

Undergraduates 13,708 full-time, 5,406 part-time. Students come from 45 states and territories, 139 other countries, 2% are from out of state, 13% African American, 11% Asian American or Pacific Islander, 13% Hispanic American, 0.7% Native American, 5% international, 17% transferred in, 14% live on campus.

Faculty *Total:* 1,081, 70% full-time. *Student/faculty ratio:* 22:1.

Academic Programs *Special study options:* academic remediation for entering students, adult/continuing education programs, advanced placement credit, cooperative education, distance learning, double majors, English as a second language, freshman honors college, honors programs, independent study, internships, part-time degree program, services for LD students, student-designed majors, study abroad, summer session for credit. *ROTC:* Army (b), Air Force (c). *Unusual degree programs:* 3-2 Bachelor of Arts or Bachelor of Science and Master of Science in Psychology with industrial/organized emphasis; Bachelor of Arts in psychology and a Master of Health Care Administration.

Athletics Member NCAA. All Division I. *Intercollegiate sports:* baseball M(s), basketball M(s)/W(s), cross-country running M(s)/W(s), golf M(s), softball W(s), tennis M(s)/W(s), track and field M(s)/W(s), volleyball W(s). *Intramural sports:* badminton M/W, basketball M/W, bowling M/W, football M/W, golf M/W, racquetball M/W, soccer M/W, softball M/W, squash M/W, swimming and diving M/W, ultimate Frisbee M/W, volleyball M/W.

Costs (2004–05) *Tuition:* state resident $3630 full-time, $121 per credit hour part-time; nonresident $12,690 full-time, $423 per credit hour part-time. Full-time tuition and fees vary according to course level, course load, and program. Part-time tuition and fees vary according to course level, course load, and program. *Required fees:* $1670 full-time, $59 per credit hour part-time, $103 per term part-time. *Room and board:* $5212. Room and board charges vary according to board plan and housing facility.

Financial Aid 811 Federal Work-Study jobs (averaging $2118). In 2003, 1628 non-need-based awards were made. *Average percent of need met:* 76%. *Average financial aid package:* $8480. *Average need-based loan:* $5383. *Average need-based gift aid:* $4275. *Average non-need-based aid:* $2397.

Contact: Dean Robert F. McMahon, The University of Texas at Arlington, Box 19222, Arlington, Texas 76019; *Telephone:* 817-272-7215; *Fax:* 817-272-7217; *E-mail:* honors@uta.edu; *Web site:* http://honors.uta.edu

The University of Texas at Austin
Turing Scholars Program
Austin, Texas

The Turing Scholars Program is designed to challenge and inspire the nation's best computer science (CS) students by providing an intensive CS curriculum and an environment that fosters undergraduate research. Housed in the seventh-ranked CS department in the country, as ranked by the National Research Council and U.S. News & World Report, the program combines the best of a small-college experience with the advantages of a large university. Turing Scholars enjoy small class sizes, close interaction with faculty members, honors housing, exciting cutting-edge research, access to a wide variety of undergraduate and graduate courses, and ample opportunities for interdisciplinary studies.

Turing Scholars take a special set of core honors courses in subjects ranging from data structures and algorithms to computer architecture, analysis of algorithms, operating systems, and programming languages. Numerous elective courses are available, including courses in cryptography, networks, artificial intelligence, robotics, graphics, computer games, distributed computing, security, automatic theorem proving, databases, software engineering, and object-oriented programming. Under the guidance of faculty members, students conduct undergraduate research that culminates in an honors thesis. Research typically begins in the junior year but sometimes begins as early as the freshman year.

The Turing Scholars Program is named after Alan Turing, one of the founding fathers of computer science. Turing made seminal contributions in the theory of computing, as well as tremendous practical contributions in his code-breaking efforts of World War II. The honors program is thus aptly named, as its goal is to produce students who are well-grounded in both theoretical and practical aspects of computer science.

The Turing Scholars Program is one of several honors programs at the University of Texas at Austin. As such, Turing Scholars take advantage of University-wide extracurricular activities organized by the University Honors Center. These activities include performances, lectures, and faculty socials. Turing Scholars are also invited to live with other honors students in the Honors Residence Halls (Andrews, Blanton, and Carothers).

The Turing Scholars experience typically extends far off campus. The University's location in a major high-tech city, the national reputation of the CS department, and the excellence of the Turing Scholars Program attract recruiters from across the country. Students completing their freshman year often participate in paid summer internships at companies such as IBM, Microsoft, Lockheed Martin, National Instruments, Intel, and Dell. In addition, Turing Scholars have participated in IBM's Extreme Blue program; interned at NASA's Goddard Space Flight Center; conducted research at the Arecibo Observatory in Puerto Rico; researched numerical analysis at the Royal Institute of Technology in Stockholm, Sweden; and earned patents for work at IBM.

Participation Requirements: The Turing Scholars Program requires completion of 25 credit hours of honors computer science, including a research seminar. Turing Scholars take two years of courses as a cohort prior to selecting computer science electives as their interests diverge.

Turing Scholars must maintain a University grade point average of at least 3.5 and a computer sciences grade point average of at least 3.3. Upon completion of the curriculum and acceptance of the honors thesis by the director, students graduate with a Bachelor of Science in computer sciences, Option II: Turing Scholars Honors. Many Turing Scholars also receive departmental honors based on high grade point averages and exceptional theses.

Admission Process: High school seniors complete an application that includes transcripts, SAT I or ACT scores, AP and SAT II subject-area scores (if taken), educational and career goals, computer science background, and a specified essay. The priority deadline for admissions is February 1. Letters of recommendation are not required but can be helpful if the letters address qualities relevant to academic scholarship. The faculty members on the Turing Scholars committee review applications for evidence of intellectual curiosity, potential for independent research, and evidence of leadership. Strong applicants have taken rigorous courses and performed well in math and science courses. Experience with computer science is desired but not required.

Scholarship Availability: Scholarship funding is based on grants and corporate and private donations. Students admitted to the Turing Scholars Program are invited to apply for scholarships. Scholarship decisions are based upon academic excellence and financial need. In addition, Applied Research Laboratories provides a few paid summer research positions as part of their High School Apprenticeship Program.

Campus Overview

State-supported university, founded 1883, part of University of Texas System • **Coed** 37,377 undergraduate students, 91% full-time, 52% women, 48% men.

Undergraduates 33,888 full-time, 3,489 part-time. Students come from 52 states and territories, 121 other countries, 5% are from out of state, 4% African American, 17% Asian American or Pacific Islander, 15% Hispanic American, 0.4% Native American, 3% international, 5% transferred in, 18% live on campus.

Faculty *Total:* 2,721, 91% full-time, 89% with terminal degrees. *Student/faculty ratio:* 19:1.

Academic Programs *Special study options:* academic remediation for entering students, accelerated degree program, adult/continuing education programs, advanced placement credit, cooperative education, distance learning, double majors, English as a second language, honors programs, independent study, internships, part-time degree program, services for LD students, student-designed majors, study abroad, summer session for credit. *ROTC:* Army (b), Navy (b), Air Force (b). *Unusual degree programs:* 3-2 architecture.

Athletics Member NCAA. All Division I except football (Division I-A). *Intercollegiate sports:* baseball M(s), basketball M(s)/W(s), crew W(s), cross-country running M(s)/W(s), golf M(s)/W(s), soccer W(s), softball W(s), swimming and diving M(s)/W(s), tennis M(s)/W(s), track and field M(s)/W(s), volleyball W(s). *Intramural sports:* archery M(c)/W(c), badminton M/W, baseball M(c), basketball M/W, bowling M/W, crew M(c)/W(c), equestrian sports M(c)/W(c), fencing M(c)/W(c), football M/W, golf M/W, gymnastics M(c)/W(c), ice hockey M(c), lacrosse M(c)/W(c), racquetball M(c)/W(c), rugby M(c), sailing M(c)/W(c), soccer M(c)/W(c), softball M/W, squash M(c)/W(c), swimming and diving M/W, table tennis M(c)/W(c), tennis M(c)/W(c), track and field M/W, ultimate Frisbee M(c)/W(c), volleyball M(c)/W(c), water polo M(c)/W(c), weight lifting M(c)/W(c).

Costs (2004–05) *Tuition:* state resident $4260 full-time; nonresident $12,960 full-time. Full-time tuition and fees vary according to course load and program. Part-time tuition and fees vary according to course load and program. *Required fees:* $1475 full-time. *Room and board:* $6184; room only: $3569. Room and board charges vary according to board plan and housing facility.

Financial Aid 1,370 Federal Work-Study jobs (averaging $1802). 300 state and other part-time jobs (averaging $1227). In 2004, 9660 non-need-based awards were made. *Average percent of need met:* 95%. *Average financial aid package:* $9250. *Average need-based loan:* $4920. *Average need-based gift aid:* $5850. *Average non-need-based aid:* $4280.

Contact: Director: Dr. Calvin Lin, Associate Professor, Turing Scholars Program, College of Liberal Arts, GEB 1.206, Austin, Texas 78712; *Telephone:* 512-471-9509; *Fax:* 512-471-8885; *E-mail:* honors@cs.utexas.edu; *Web site:* http://www.cs.utexas.edu/honors

The University of Texas at Dallas

Collegium V Honors Program

Richardson, Texas

Collegium V (CV) is a four-year honors program that blends the resources of a research university with the advantages of a selective liberal arts college. The program offers special opportunities for academic and personal growth. Students become part of a supportive community of professors and scholars who interact frequently with one another inside and outside the classroom. Classes are limited to 20 students and taught by the University's most accomplished teachers. Research opportunities are encouraged and supported. A wide range of extracurricular events enables students to explore ideas outside the traditional classroom.

Collegium V classes are among the most innovative and popular classes on campus. More than thirty CV classes are offered every year, covering a wide range of topics, including computer science, electrical engineering, law and government, economics, psychology, cognitive science, history, art history, and literature. Drawing upon the opportunities available in the Dallas–Fort Worth metroplex, CV classes have helped to forge a closer relationship between the University and community organizations such as the Dallas Museum of Art and the Natural History Museum. CV students have also been active participants in the semester-long Bill Archer Washington Internship Program.

Members have special access to the Collegium V lounge, which houses two computer rooms, individual and group study rooms, and a TV/video room. The lounge is a meeting ground for honors students who are seeking a place to work, relax, and make new friends. The lounge is available 24 hours a day, seven days a week. Many extracurricular events take place in the lounge, including a weekly coffee social (Java Friday), frequent guest speakers, and occasional movie nights. Members also receive tickets to on-campus and off-campus cultural events, including the Dallas Symphony, the Dallas Ballet, the Dallas Opera, and other local concerts, performances, exhibits, and plays.

Collegium V was founded in 1997. There are 338 students currently enrolled in the program from across the University. The most popular majors among members are electrical engineering, computer science, management, premedicine, and prelaw. Ninety students are admitted to the incoming freshman class.

Participation Requirements: To complete the Collegium V curriculum, students are expected to take 12 credit hours (approximately one course per semester) of lower-level CV classes during the freshman and sophomore years and an additional 12 credit hours during their junior and senior years. Lower-level classes are generally in the core curriculum. Upper-level classes may include specially designed CV classes, honors work in a major, research and independent study, internships, and graduate work. During their senior year, students are expected to complete a senior thesis or project and make their results public. Students are also expected to participate in a certain number of extracurricular events every semester and to graduate with a GPA of at least 3.5.

Students graduating with Collegium V honors receive special recognition on their diploma and a certificate of achievement at graduation. All honors work is designated as CV Honors on a student's transcript.

Admission Process: Incoming freshmen to the University of Texas at Dallas (UTD) with an SAT score of at least 2025 (or an ACT score of at least 30) and a high school grade point average of at least 3.6 are encouraged to apply to Collegium V. The average SAT score for the freshman class is 2130. Students must be accepted to UTD before their applications are considered. Applications require a brief essay, a list of AP and IB courses, a list of extracurricular activities, and two letters of recommendation. Reviews of applications begin on February 1. The freshman class size is limited to 90.

Scholarship Availability: The University of Texas at Dallas offers a large number of academic excellence scholarships available to students applying to the University and Collegium V.

Campus Overview

State-supported university, founded 1969, part of University of Texas System • **Coed** 9,070 undergraduate students, 70% full-time, 48% women, 52% men.

Undergraduates 6,372 full-time, 2,698 part-time. Students come from 48 states and territories, 156 other countries, 3% are from out of state, 7% African American, 19% Asian American or Pacific Islander, 10% Hispanic American, 0.7% Native American, 5% international, 15% transferred in, 21% live on campus.

Faculty *Total:* 627, 69% full-time, 81% with terminal degrees. *Student/faculty ratio:* 23:1.

Academic Programs *Special study options:* academic remediation for entering students, accelerated degree program, adult/continuing education programs, advanced placement credit, cooperative education, distance learning, double majors, freshman honors college, honors programs, independent study, internships, part-time degree program, services for LD students, student-designed majors, study abroad, summer session for credit. *ROTC:* Army (c), Air Force (c). *Unusual degree programs:* 3-2 engineering with Abilene Christian University, Austin College, Paul Quinn College, Texas Woman's University.

Athletics Member NCAA. All Division III. *Intercollegiate sports:* baseball M, basketball M/W, cross-country running M/W, golf M/W, soccer M/W, softball W, tennis M/W, volleyball W. *Intramural sports:* badminton M/W, basketball M/W, cheerleading M/W, cross-country running M/W, football M/W, golf M/W, ice hockey M, lacrosse M, racquetball M/W, rugby M, soccer M/W, softball M/W, squash M/W, swimming and diving M/W, table tennis M/W, tennis M/W, ultimate Frisbee M/W, volleyball M/W, weight lifting M/W, wrestling M.

Costs (2004–05) *Tuition:* state resident $1440 full-time, $48 per credit part-time; nonresident $9180 full-time, $306 per credit part-time. Full-time tuition and fees vary according to course load, degree level, program, and student level. Part-time tuition and fees vary according to course load, degree level, program, and student level. *Required fees:* $4923 full-time, $160 per credit part-time, $167 per term part-time. *Room and board:* $6244. Room and board charges vary according to board plan and housing facility.

Financial Aid 305 Federal Work-Study jobs (averaging $6520). In 2003, 859 non-need-based awards were made. *Average percent of need met:* 66%. *Average financial aid package:* $11,349. *Average need-based loan:* $6729. *Average need-based gift aid:* $6638. *Average non-need-based aid:* $8774.

Contact: Director of Collegium V: Edward J. Harpham, Professor of Political Science and Associate Dean of Undergraduate Education, Collegium V, Office of Undergraduate Education, MP 1.6, The University of Texas at Dallas, Box 830688, Richardson, Texas 75083-0688; *Telephone:* 972-883-4297; *Fax:* 972-883-2487; *E-mail:* harpham@utdallas.edu; *Web site:* http://cv.utdallas.edu

The University of Texas at El Paso

University Honors Program

El Paso, Texas

The University of Texas at El Paso (UTEP) Honors Program, open to students of all majors, is designed for the academically motivated student who seeks an intellectual challenge and a more personal focus in education. The program provides an environment conducive to intellectual growth through honors courses, group activities, and interaction in the Honors Lounge, which is available for study, conversation with other honors students, and Honors Council meetings. The Honors Lounge is a home for honors students and facilitates a sense of community among students and faculty members.

Honors classes are small, theoretically oriented, and taught by outstanding faculty members in a personalized classroom environment. Creative thinking, writing, verbal, and reading skills are emphasized. During the first two years, honors classes encourage students to broaden their academic horizons, while the last two years emphasize depth. For some students, this depth will culminate in an honors senior thesis, a year-long research project that is bound and placed in the library as a permanent record of the student's achievement. Students graduating with the University Honors Certificate, University Honors Degree, and/or a cumulative GPA of 4.0 receive a certificate(s) designating their respective honor or honors. Students who join the Honors Council participate in an induction ceremony and receive a certificate of membership.

Each semester, a variety of honors sections are offered at the lower- and upper-division levels. These courses can be used to meet requirements for the bachelor's degree as well as the University Honors Degree (e.g., English, history, accounting, or biology). Departments offering courses include accounting, anthropology, biological sciences, chemistry, English, finance, geological sciences, history, languages and linguistics, philosophy, physics, political science, sociology, and theater arts. Well before registration, the Honors Program publishes descriptions of honors courses and biographical data on honors faculty members for the students' information. Students may also contract for honors credit in nonhonors courses. All honors courses completed are designated with honors on the student's academic transcript. Students must apply to participate in the program. The program is 20 years old and currently enrolls 400 students.

Participation Requirements: The Honors Program offers two options: the University Honors Degree and the University Honors Certificate. The Honors Degree requires the student to complete a minimum of 30 hours of honors courses and have a minimum GPA of 3.3 upon graduation. These include honors courses in all basic education areas and 6 hours of upper-division honors hours and/or 6 hours of honors thesis. The graduate will have University Honors Degree on the diploma and on the permanent academic transcript. The Honors Certificate requires 18 hours of honors courses, 6 hours of which must be upper-division, and a minimum cumulative 3.3 GPA upon graduation. Such students will have University Honors Certificate recorded on their diploma and permanent transcript. A University Honors Certificate will also be awarded.

All students who satisfactorily complete the Honors Program requirements graduate with special recognition. Graduating with honors adds a special distinction to transcripts and diplomas and therefore, to graduate and/or professional school applications. In addition, honors graduates are publicly recognized at the annual Honors Convocation and at Commencement ceremonies.

The Honors Program hosts faculty and campus visitors to speak on topics of interest to honors students. Such speakers have included judicial persona and journalists as well as mayoral and city council candidates.

Honors students are invited to join the Honors Council and so interact with other honors students and assist in the planning of honors activities according to their interests. Students who join the Honors Council participate in an induction ceremony and receive a certificate of membership.

Admission Process: Freshman students may apply to the program if they have a superior score on the SAT or ACT or rank in the top 15 percent of their high school graduation class. A cumulative GPA of 3.3 is required for admission of current or transfer students. Once admitted to the program, students must maintain a 3.3 GPA.

Scholarship Availability: UTEP offers many scholarships to students of exceptional ability, ranging in amounts of $150 to $4000. In addition, ten Houston Endowment, Inc., scholarships of $5000 each are awarded annually to University Honors Program members.

Campus Overview

State-supported university, founded 1913 • **Coed** 15,592 undergraduate students, 70% full-time, 54% women, 46% men.

Undergraduates 10,938 full-time, 4,654 part-time. Students come from 47 states and territories, 67 other countries, 2% are from out of state, 2% African American, 1% Asian American or Pacific Islander, 75% Hispanic American, 0.2% Native American, 11% international, 7% transferred in, 3% live on campus.

Faculty *Total:* 949, 67% full-time. *Student/faculty ratio:* 19:1.

Academic Programs *Special study options:* academic remediation for entering students, accelerated degree program, adult/continuing education programs, advanced placement credit, cooperative education, distance learning, English as a second language, honors programs, independent study, internships, off-campus study, part-time degree program, services for LD students, summer session for credit. *ROTC:* Army (b), Air Force (b).

Athletics Member NCAA. All Division I except football (Division I-A). *Intercollegiate sports:* basketball M(s)/W(s), cross-country running M(s)/W(s), golf M(s), riflery M/W, tennis W(s), track and field M(s)/W(s), volleyball W(s). *Intramural sports:* archery M/W, badminton M/W, basketball M/W, bowling M/W, fencing M/W, field hockey M, golf M/W, gymnastics M/W, racquetball M/W, skiing (downhill) M, soccer M/W, squash M/W, swimming and diving M/W, tennis M/W, track and field M/W, volleyball M/W, water polo M/W, weight lifting M, wrestling M/W.

Costs (2005–06) *Tuition:* state resident $3930 full-time, $131 per credit hour part-time; nonresident $12,210 full-time. Part-time tuition and fees vary according to course load. *Required fees:* $1134 full-time. *Room only:* $4095. Room and board charges vary according to housing facility.

Financial Aid 854 Federal Work-Study jobs (averaging $2097). 63 state and other part-time jobs (averaging $2563). In 2003, 702 non-need-based awards were made. *Average percent of need met:* 87%. *Average financial aid package:* $8482. *Average need-based loan:* $4556. *Average need-based gift aid:* $4310. *Average non-need-based aid:* $1890.

Contact: Director: Gary Edens, Honors House, El Paso, Texas 79968-0607; *Telephone:* 915-747-5858; *Fax:* 915-747-5841; *E-mail:* gedens@utep.edu; *Web site:* http://www.utep.edu

The University of Texas at San Antonio

Honors College

San Antonio, Texas

The mission of the Honors College at the University of Texas at San Antonio (UTSA) is to provide enhanced educational opportunities for selected, motivated, enthusiastic, diverse, and inquisitive students and to foster the pursuit of excellence in undergraduate higher education. A second mission of the Honors College is to increase the number of outstanding students at UTSA and to assist in retaining those students through all four years of their undergraduate experience. As a result, Honors College students make a visible and positive impact on the entire University community.

In order to accomplish its mission, the UTSA Honors College (1) creates opportunities for honors students to work closely with faculty members who are dedicated to providing superior instruction for honors students and who attempt to encourage lively and engaging discourse; (2) provides opportunities for honors students to engage in supervised research and other creative work; (3) offers personalized academic advising, guidance, referrals for scholarships and internships, and support to honors students as a manifestation of the interest the University has in their academic progress; (4) provides opportunities for honors students to learn from other highly motivated students in small, interactive classes of 20 to 30 students; and (5) attempts to create a social and cultural environment to support the formation of a well-rounded individual, confident of his or her place in the community and the world.

The Honors College is open to students in all academic majors. The program, which was founded in 1985, admits up to 200 students each year. There are approximately 550 students currently enrolled in the Honors College.

Participation Requirements: To graduate with honors from the Honors College, all students must have a minimum GPA of 3.25. There are three types of honors students can earn: Business Honors, Tier 1 Honors, and Tier 2 (highest) Honors. Students in the College of Business earn Business Honors by completing five of the courses in the Common Body of Knowledge (CBK) for Business in honors sections. Students who enter the Honors College with less than 30 hours may earn Tier 1 Honors by completing 21 hours of honors course work, including at least two courses from the honors core (i.e., Honors World and Society and Honors Seminars). Students earn Tier 2 Honors by completing 30 hours of honors course work, including at least three courses from the honors core, and by writing an honors thesis. Students who enter the Honors College with 50 or more hours completed may waive 6 of the 30 hours of honors course work required for Tier 2 Honors. Students who do not intend to graduate with honors are welcome to join the Honors College as well. To be considered an active member eligible for preferential honors registration, members of the Honors College must complete a minimum of 3 hours course work per academic year.

Admission Process: Applicants to the program are required to submit an application form, an essay, two letters of recommendation, and high school and/or college transcripts. High school seniors, transfer students, and enrolled UTSA students are encouraged to apply for admission. General guidelines for admission to the program are a class standing in the top 10 percent and a minimum SAT-R score of 1000 or an ACT score of 22; or a class standing in the top 20 percent and a minimum SAT-R score of 1200 or an ACT score of 27; or a college GPA of 3.3 or better for a minimum of 12 hours. The admissions committee evaluates each student individually, weighing intellectual promise, seriousness of purpose, and writing skills, so students who fall close to these guidelines are encouraged to apply.

There is rolling admission to the Honors College, but incoming transfer students and new freshman applicants who wish to receive honors scholarships must mail their applications by February 1.

Scholarship Availability: The Honors College offers approximately 150 honors scholarships each year. The largest of these scholarships are one Catto Endowed Scholarship ($3500 a year for up to four years), the two Peter T. Flawn Presidential Honors Scholarships ($2500 a year for up to four years), and the twenty Presidential Honors Scholarships ($1500 a year for up to four years) awarded to new UTSA students each year. Out-of-state and international students who receive honors scholarships of $1000 or more are eligible to pay in-state tuition rates. To be eligible for honors scholarships, incoming freshmen and transfer students must apply by February 1. Other honors scholarships require no special application and are awarded to students already enrolled and in good standing with the Honors College.

Campus Overview

State-supported university, founded 1969, part of University of Texas System • **Coed** 22,537 undergraduate students, 85% full-time, 53% women, 47% men.

Undergraduates 19,175 full-time, 3,362 part-time. Students come from 50 states and territories, 72 other countries, 20% are from out of state, 6% African American, 5% Asian American or Pacific Islander, 46% Hispanic American, 0.6% Native American, 2% international, 11% transferred in.

Faculty *Total:* 1,089, 55% full-time, 65% with terminal degrees. *Student/faculty ratio:* 24:1.

Academic Programs *Special study options:* academic remediation for entering students, accelerated degree program, adult/continuing education programs, advanced placement credit, cooperative education, distance learning, double majors, English as a second language, freshman honors college, honors programs, independent study, internships, part-time degree program, services for LD students, study abroad, summer session for credit. *ROTC:* Army (b), Air Force (b).

Athletics Member NCAA. All Division I. *Intercollegiate sports:* baseball M(s), basketball M(s)/W(s), cross-country running M(s)/W(s), golf M(s), softball W(s), tennis M(s)/W(s), track and field M(s)/W(s), volleyball W(s). *Intramural sports:* badminton M/W, baseball M, basketball M/W, cross-country running M/W, football M/W, golf M, soccer M/W, softball M/W, table tennis M/W, tennis M/W, track and field M/W, volleyball M/W, weight lifting M/W.

Costs (2004–05) *Tuition:* state resident $3720 full-time, $124 per hour part-time; nonresident $11,460 full-time, $382 per hour part-time. *Required fees:* $1552 full-time. *Room and board:* $5306; room only: $3114.

Financial Aid 393 Federal Work-Study jobs (averaging $4000). 293 state and other part-time jobs (averaging $4000). In 2003, 537 non-need-based awards were made. *Average percent of need met:* 59%. *Average financial aid package:* $6136. *Average need-based loan:* $3579. *Average need-based gift aid:* $3584. *Average non-need-based aid:* $1466.

Contact: Dean: Dr. Richard Diem, Office of the Honors College, 6900 North Loop 1604 West, San Antonio, Texas 78249; *Telephone:* 210-458-4106; *Fax:* 210-458-5730; *E-mail:* richard.diem@utsa.edu.

The University of Texas–Pan American

University Honors Program

Edinburg, Texas

Through the University Honors Program, the University of Texas–Pan American (UT-PA) demonstrates its strong commitment to providing an exceptional educational experience for academically talented undergraduate students. Small classes, innovative teaching techniques, individualized instruction, research opportunities, academic recognition, and a wide variety of extracurricular activities are just some of the benefits of this outstanding program.

Participants in the University Honors Program are eligible to enroll in honors classes. Because they are typically small in size—usually 20 students or less—these classes provide a comfortable forum for in-depth discussion and interaction among students and faculty members. Enrichment, rather than acceleration, is the main objective. Students find that honors classes are not necessarily more difficult than others, but rather more stimulating and interesting.

Beginning the sophomore year, University Honors Program students have an opportunity to select a topic that is of particular interest and undertake an independent studies project under the one-on-one guidance of a knowledgeable faculty mentor. This project is designed to offer honors students invaluable experience in independent research and creative design, critical thinking, and problem solving that prepares them for future graduate and career challenges. Honors faculty members and honors thesis/senior project mentors are especially selected for their commitment to undergraduate education and for their skills in mentoring students.

The 40-year-old program currently enrolls more than 200 students.

Participation Requirements: All honors students are to complete 13 hours of honors core requirements. The Honors Council, the advisory group that oversees the University Honors Program, has recommended that students complete a minimum of 6 additional honors hours.

Admission Process: Entering freshmen may gain admission to the program in any one of the following three ways: have a composite ACT score of at least 24 (or the SAT equivalent); graduate in the top 10 percent of his or her high school class; or graduate from high school with a grade average of 90 or above in academic courses.

Students who have earned 12 or more hours of college credit with at least a 3.3 GPA are also eligible to apply to the program. The applicant's college grades and recommendations from professors determine his or her admission to the program.

In addition to the summa, magna, and cum laude recognition awarded to students by the University, the University Honors Program awards students who successfully complete a thesis/senior project with certification of honors graduation. The certification also specifies the student's level of distinction.

Scholarship Availability: Currently, there are three competitive scholarship funds administered through the University Honors Program. Interested students first must be accepted into the program. Applications for these scholarships are available by February 1 of each year; deadline for priority consideration is March 1 of each year. These scholarships are awarded for the following academic year. Depending on fund availability, scholarships are also awarded to assist students participating in the Honors Study-Abroad Program. Small research scholarships are also available to assist students with the completion of the thesis/senior project.

Entering freshmen who have been accepted to the Honors Program may also apply for an Honors Learning Community Scholarship through the Residence Life Office. More information can be found on the Web site at http://www.utpa.edu/reslife/hlc.html.

Other financial assistance, including grants, University scholarships, loans, and part-time employment, is available to qualified students through the Office of Student Financial Aid.

Campus Overview

State-supported comprehensive, founded 1927, part of University of Texas System • **Coed** 14,788 undergraduate students, 72% full-time, 58% women, 42% men.

Undergraduates 10,662 full-time, 4,126 part-time. Students come from 25 states and territories, 27 other countries, 0.5% are from out of state, 0.2% African American, 1% Asian American or Pacific Islander, 89% Hispanic American, 0.1% Native American, 3% international, 6% transferred in, 1% live on campus.

Faculty *Total:* 730, 78% full-time. *Student/faculty ratio:* 21:1.

Academic Programs *Special study options:* academic remediation for entering students, adult/continuing education programs, advanced placement credit, cooperative education, distance learning, double majors, honors programs, independent study, internships, part-time degree program, services for LD students, study abroad, summer session for credit. *ROTC:* Army (b). *Unusual degree programs:* accounting.

Athletics Member NCAA. All Division I. *Intercollegiate sports:* baseball M(s), basketball M(s)/W(s), cross-country running M(s)/W(s), golf M(s)/W(s), tennis M(s)/W(s), track and field M(s)/W(s), volleyball W(s). *Intramural sports:* basketball M/W, bowling M/W, cheerleading M/W, football M/W, racquetball M/W, soccer M/W, softball M/W, tennis M/W, volleyball M/W.

Costs (2004–05) *Tuition:* state resident $2504 full-time, $86 per semester hour part-time; nonresident $10,244 full-time, $344 per semester hour part-time. *Required fees:* $648 full-time, $75 per semester hour part-time. *Room and board:* $4233; room only: $2406. Room and board charges vary according to board plan and housing facility.

Financial Aid 848 Federal Work-Study jobs (averaging $1939). 133 state and other part-time jobs (averaging $1170). In 2003, 387 non-need-based awards were made. *Average percent of need met:* 82%. *Average financial aid package:* $6950. *Average need-based loan:* $3382. *Average need-based gift aid:* $7001. *Average non-need-based aid:* $4082.

Contact: Director: Dora E. Saavedra, Ph.D., SBSC Building, Room 104, The University of Texas–Pan American, 1201 West University Drive, Edinburg, Texas 78541-2999; *Telephone:* 956-381-3461; *Fax:* 956-381-2484; *E-mail:* honors@panam.edu; *Web site:* http://www.panam.edu/honors

UTAH

Brigham Young University
University Honors Program
Provo, Utah

*T*he Brigham Young University (BYU) Honors Program, founded in 1960, provides an unusually rich and challenging experience for capable and motivated undergraduate students. Honors education is not merely a more intensive general education or a more strenuous program in a major; rather, it attempts to link the broad university perspective with the specific concentration associated with a major. Students who pursue honors education at BYU are offered the challenge of honors courses that form a part of their general education, as well as an intensive experience in their major. Honors education is open to all capable and motivated students and only requires that students have a formal commitment of intent to graduate with University Honors and maintain a minimum 3.5 GPA.

The most important advantage of enrolling in honors is the opportunity to participate in demanding, high-quality courses taught by some of the University's best professors. In addition, honors provides a stimulating learning environment outside formal honors course settings, including honors colloquia, seminars, and departmental honors courses that provide a variety of experiences for honors students in the historical development of ideas, cultures, arts, letters, and the sciences. Recent colloquia have included Use and Misuse of Human and Natural Resources: Man's Role in Changing the Face of the Earth, The Pen and the Sword: A Study of Writing About How Human Civilization Seeks Peace and Suffers War, The Daedalus Project, Memoir and Imagination, and Shaping the Modern Mind. Recent seminars have included Women's Issues in the Natural Sciences, Wilderness Writing, and Bioethics.

Students in honors benefit most directly from their association with fellow honors students and with honors faculty members. To encourage interaction among students outside the classroom, special on-campus housing for honors students is available. In addition, honors students also have a center in the Karl G. Maeser Memorial Building, which provides them with a quiet study hall, a commons room for informal meetings and discussion, an advisement center, and classrooms. HSAC, the Honors Student Advisory Council, plans many activities for honors students throughout the semester, including lectures, dances, retreats, and outings. The Honors Program publishes the scholarly work of students in Insight, *an intellectual journal with an all-student staff. A special series of art exhibitions are sponsored in the Maeser Building.*

There are approximately 3,000 committed honors students, with more than 8,000 students participating in some aspect of honors.

Participation Requirements: There are certain requirements for students to graduate with University Honors. Students must take 22 credit hours of honors courses (including some required courses), two semesters of foreign language, and calculus, principles of statistics, or advanced logic; meet with an Honors Program representative for advisement at least once each year; demonstrate familiarity with the great works of literature, art, music, theater, and film by turning in a portfolio of written responses to the works and also submitting a portfolio of work representing each semester of undergraduate study and a one-page description of ongoing service to the community for review by the Honors Deans; submit a proposal for an honors thesis during the junior year; and submit a finished honors thesis and pass a thesis defense with a committee of Honors Deans and faculty members during the senior year.

Scholarship Availability: The Honors Program itself offers one named scholarship, and most honors students hold, or are eligible for, some kind of University scholarship. The Honors Program coordinates information and advisement for many graduate scholarships, grants, and fellowships. Money is available directly from the Honors Program to aid in thesis research.

Campus Overview

Independent university, founded 1875, affiliated with The Church of Jesus Christ of Latter-day Saints, part of Church Education System (CES) of The Church of Jesus Christ of Latter-day Saints • **Coed** 30,847 undergraduate students, 81% full-time, 49% women, 51% men.

Undergraduates 24,948 full-time, 5,899 part-time. Students come from 57 states and territories, 125 other countries, 76% are from out of state, 0.4% African American, 3% Asian American or Pacific Islander, 3% Hispanic American, 0.7% Native American, 4% international, 5% transferred in, 20% live on campus.

Faculty *Total:* 1,744, 75% full-time. *Student/faculty ratio:* 20:1.

Academic Programs *Special study options:* academic remediation for entering students, accelerated degree program, adult/continuing education programs, advanced placement credit, cooperative education, distance learning, double majors, English as a second language, external degree program, freshman honors college, honors programs, independent study, internships, off-campus study, part-time degree program, services for LD students, study abroad, summer session for credit. *ROTC:* Army (b), Air Force (b).

Athletics Member NCAA. All Division I except football (Division I-A). *Intercollegiate sports:* baseball M(s), basketball M(s)/W(s), cheerleading M(s)/W(s), cross-country running M(s)/W(s), golf M(s)/W(s), gymnastics W(s), lacrosse M(c), racquetball M/W, rugby M(c), soccer M(c)/W(s), softball W(s), swimming and diving M(s)/W(s), tennis M(s)/W(s), track and field M(s)/W(s), volleyball M(s)/W(s). *Intramural sports:* badminton M/W, basketball M/W, field hockey M, football M/W, golf M/W, racquetball M/W, soccer M/W, softball M/W, table tennis M/W, tennis M/W, ultimate Frisbee M/W, volleyball M/W, water polo M/W, wrestling M.

Costs (2004–05) *Comprehensive fee:* $10,490 includes full-time tuition ($4920) and room and board ($5570). Full-time tuition and fees vary according to reciprocity agreements. Part-time tuition: $252 per credit hour. Part-time tuition and fees vary according to course load and reciprocity agreements. Latter Day Saints full-time student $3280 per year; part-time student $168 per credit hour. *Room and board:* Room and board charges vary according to board plan and housing facility.

Financial Aid 234 state and other part-time jobs (averaging $636). In 2003, 9766 non-need-based awards were made. *Average percent of need met:* 42%. *Average financial aid package:* $4168. *Average need-based loan:* $1737. *Average need-based gift aid:* $2431. *Average non-need-based aid:* $2882.

Contact: Coordinator: J. Scott Miller, Honors Program, 350 MSRB, Brigham Young University, Box 22600, Provo, Utah 84602-2600; *Telephone:* 801-422-5225; *Fax:* 801-422-0263; *E-mail:* honors@byu.edu; *Web site:* http://www.byu.edu/honors

Southern Utah University
Honors Program
Cedar City, Utah

*S*outhern Utah University (SUU) understands the need to challenge students who love learning and to place them in environments that further this hunger for knowledge. SUU's Honors Program provides enrichment opportunities for exceptionally talented, creative, and academically committed students in a friendly, informal, and interdisciplinary undergraduate experience. The program was created in 1999. Currently the Honors Program enrolls approximately 200 students and is open to freshmen, sophomores, juniors, and seniors.*

The program connects students with SUU's best faculty members through small classes and participation in out-of-class activities. Students learn in a collaborative environment where their ideas and research carry respect. All honors classes have a limit of 20 students to enhance the mentoring process and provide more one-on-one learning opportunities.

As a community of scholars, students and faculty members work enthusiastically to understand complex issues from diverse perspectives and to develop skills in self-expression, critical thinking, information gathering, and problem solving. In addition, they learn to process similarities and differences in how scholars in science, fine arts, humanities, and the social sciences see their world. Honors students are required to write analytical or scientific papers of substantial length and depth.

As often as possible, honors students attend colloquia featuring artists, academics, native people, and political leaders. They participate in roundtable discussions and social events with faculty members and other honors students.

Recently the Honors Program instituted a program called Maymester Gone Wild! *During the Maymester, interested students can study at SUU's Mountain Center, where they live and learn for three weeks with the professors, getting hands-on learning in the areas of biology, art, and English. Hikes and field studies are also conducted during that time.*

Honors Hall is a dormitory reserved for honors students who are interested in living on campus. In Honors Hall the students meet new friends and create bonds that remain throughout their college careers.

Participation Requirements: Students can graduate with University Honors if they complete 10 lower-division credits and 10 upper-division credits, totaling 20 honors credits, and complete HONR 4971 (Senior Thesis).

Honors credit can be earned in three ways. For many general education classes, there is a designated honors section that is only open to honors students. These sections are taught by selected faculty members and have a higher expectation than other sections. Another approach encourages students to create honors contracts with participating honors faculty members. If the student discovers a particular interest in a certain class that he or she is taking, a contract can be made between the professor and the student, stating that the completion of additional requirements will result in the changing of that class to an honors class for the particular student. Finally, each honors student is required to write a senior thesis. This is normally done during the student's senior year and is the capstone of their education at Southern Utah University. A faculty mentor is involved, as is the honors adviser, who makes sure that the student is on track and progressing.

Admission Process: Students must complete an application, write a 500-word essay on a topic of their choice, and earn at least a 3.5 grade point average and a 25 ACT composite score to be admitted to the Honors Program.

Scholarship Availability: The Honors Program has a housing/meal plan scholarship that is awarded on a first-come, first-served basis.

Campus Overview

State-supported comprehensive, founded 1897, part of Utah System of Higher Education • **Coed** 6,381 undergraduate students, 70% full-time, 57% women, 43% men.

Undergraduates 4,480 full-time, 1,901 part-time. Students come from 40 states and territories, 14 other countries, 12% are from out of state, 0.7% African American, 2% Asian American or Pacific Islander, 2% Hispanic American, 1% Native American, 0.6% international, 8% transferred in, 13% live on campus.

Faculty *Total:* 290, 75% full-time, 53% with terminal degrees. *Student/faculty ratio:* 21:1.

Academic Programs *Special study options:* academic remediation for entering students, adult/continuing education programs, advanced placement credit, cooperative education, distance learning, double majors, English as a second language, honors programs, independent study, internships, part-time degree program, services for LD students, summer session for credit. *ROTC:* Army (b).

Athletics Member NCAA. All Division I except football (Division I-AA). *Intercollegiate sports:* baseball M(s), basketball M(s)/W(s), cross-country running M/W, golf M(s), gymnastics W(s), softball W(s), tennis W(s), track and field M(s)/W(s). *Intramural sports:* basketball M/W, football M, golf M/W, soccer M/W, tennis M/W, track and field M/W, volleyball M/W.

Costs (2004–05) *Tuition:* state resident $2588 full-time, $129 per credit hour part-time; nonresident $8542 full-time, $427 per credit hour part-time. Part-time tuition and fees vary according to course load. *Required fees:* $466 full-time. *Room and board:* $5400; room only: $2400. Room and board charges vary according to board plan and housing facility.

Financial Aid In 2004, 652 non-need-based awards were made. *Average percent of need met:* 84%. *Average financial aid package:* $3699. *Average need-based loan:* $3481. *Average need-based gift aid:* $3020. *Average non-need-based aid:* $3507.

Contact: Professor Matthew Nickerson, Southern Utah University, 351 West University Boulevard, Cedar City, Utah 84720; *Telephone:* 435-586-1955; *Fax:* 435-865-8152; *E-mail:* nickerson@suu.edu

Utah State University

Honors Program

Logan, Utah

In the Honors Program, Utah State University's (USU) goal is to help students achieve. The Honors Program is a community of scholars whose curiosity, creativity, and enthusiasm for learning foster educational achievement and personal growth. USU students are going places—to graduate school, to professional school, or to outstanding jobs. Experience has shown us that honors students enter the job force a step ahead of students who do not participate in the Honors Program. At the same time, the honors experience enhances students' undergraduate experience, allowing them to immerse themselves in their discipline and explore avenues usually reserved for graduate students.

Honors offers undergraduate students intensive seminars, experimental and interdisciplinary courses, writing projects, leadership opportunities, and artistic and social activities. Honors classes are also smaller, allowing students to get to know more professors and encouraging classroom interaction and discussion. The University allows students to define their own interests and pursue them through "contracts" with professors, thus fostering close contact.

Honors students also benefit from a community of peers, namely, students who enjoy learning, who support one another's intellectual growth, and who participate actively in their own education. Honors is designed to serve students who work hard, raise questions, and seek answers. The curriculum encourages students who want to go beyond minimum requirements and narrow specialties. The program helps those who want to make the most of their University experience.

Students generally begin with Honors in University Studies, which includes 12 total credit hours. Some of these are from specifically designed honors seminars. Scholars Forum, Honors Enrichment, and Honors Inquiry have all been created to meet the needs of honors students and are taken in the first two years of study. Students also take some breadth and depth courses through honors, and USU has special sections of math and English just for honors students.

Once students begin upper-division classes in the major, they merge onto Departmental Honors, which entails 15 credit hours. Through Departmental Honors, students complete honors contracts with professors. These regular meetings enable students to pursue their own interests and research agendas while fostering strong relationships with professors, who mentor students and can thus write stronger letters of recommendation to graduate schools and/or the professional world. All of this work and thinking and research culminate in the honors thesis or project, which is completed in the junior or senior year. This capstone experience provides an opportunity to apply the research techniques of the Departmental Honors program and prepares students for the kind of work expected in graduate or professional school and in employment.

The program is 38 years old and currently enrolls 650 students.

Participation Requirements: Students may work toward one of three honors degree options. These are Honors in University Studies with Department Honors, which requires 27 total honors credits in lower-division courses selected from the honors course list and upper-division courses within an official department honors plan and includes the creation and presentation of a senior thesis/project/ seminar; Department Honors, which requires 15 total honors credits in upper-division courses within an official department honors plan and includes the creation and presentation of a senior thesis/project and seminar; and University Honors, which requires 27 total honors credits in lower-division courses selected from the honors course list and an individually designed upper-division plan and includes the creation and presentation of a senior thesis/project and seminar.

Admission Process: A limited number of entering freshmen are invited to join the Honors Program each year based on a combination of high school GPA and ACT or SAT scores. These are generally students who have been awarded scholarships and/or otherwise recognized for their academic abilities and ambitions. Students with university transcripts (transfer or re-entry students or students with concurrent enrollment credit) must have a minimum cumulative GPA of 3.5 to join the program. There are no extra fees. Once they are in the program, honors students must maintain a minimum GPA of 3.3 to be in good standing.

Students admitted to the program are eligible to register for honors classes. Those who plan to complete honors degrees should plan to take at least one honors course every semester to fulfill the degree requirements.

Scholarship Availability: The Helen B. Cannon Award, named in honor of a former English graduate instructor who encouraged learning through different aspects of the world, is available only to active honors students. Criteria is based on GPA, intended senior thesis, an intellectual biography, and honors program completed. The award, totaling $1000, is given to the recipient at a luncheon in April honoring the student and his or her family. A $500 installment is given at the luncheon and the other $500 is given upon graduation.

Campus Overview

State-supported university, founded 1888, part of Utah System of Higher Education • **Coed** 13,585 undergraduate students, 85% full-time, 49% women, 51% men.

Undergraduates 11,506 full-time, 2,079 part-time. Students come from 53 states and territories, 52 other countries, 27% are from out of state, 0.6% African American, 1% Asian American or Pacific Islander, 2% Hispanic American, 0.4% Native American, 2% international, 7% transferred in.

Faculty *Total:* 764, 95% full-time, 84% with terminal degrees. *Student/faculty ratio:* 19:1.

Academic Programs *Special study options:* academic remediation for entering students, accelerated degree program, adult/continuing education programs, advanced placement credit, cooperative education, distance learning, double majors, English as a second language, freshman honors college, honors programs, independent study, internships, off-campus study, part-time degree program, services for LD students, student-designed majors, study abroad, summer session for credit. *ROTC:* Army (b), Air Force (b).

Athletics Member NCAA. All Division I except football (Division I-A). *Intercollegiate sports:* baseball M(c), basketball M(s)/W(s), cross-country running M(s)/W(s), equestrian sports M(c)/W(c), golf M(s), gymnastics W(s), ice hockey M(c), rugby M(c)/W(c), soccer M(c)/W(c), softball W(s), tennis M(s)/W(s), track and field M(s)/W(s), volleyball M(c)/W(s). *Intramural sports:* badminton M/W, basketball M/W, cross-country running M/W, fencing M(c)/W(c), football M/W, golf M/W, ice hockey W(c), lacrosse M(c), racquetball M(c)/W(c), skiing (cross-country) M(c)/W(c), skiing (downhill) M(c)/W(c), soccer M/W, softball M/W, squash M/W, swimming and diving M/W, table tennis M/W, tennis M/W, ultimate Frisbee M(c)/W(c), volleyball M/W, water polo M(c)/W(c).

Costs (2004–05) *Tuition:* state resident $2850 full-time; nonresident $9178 full-time. Full-time tuition and fees vary according to course load and student level. Part-time tuition and fees vary according to course load and student level. *Required fees:* $524 full-time. *Room and board:* $4230; room only: $1550. Room and board charges vary according to board plan and housing facility.

Financial Aid 458 Federal Work-Study jobs (averaging $2406). 113 state and other part-time jobs (averaging $2406). In 2003, 1228 non-need-based awards were made. *Average percent of need met:* 58%. *Average financial aid package:* $5000. *Average need-based loan:* $3850. *Average need-based gift aid:* $3100. *Average non-need-based aid:* $2800.

Contact: Honors Director: Dr. Christie Fox, 3015 Old Main Hill, Utah State University, Logan, Utah 84322-3015; *Telephone:* 435-797-2715; *Fax:* 435-797-3941; *E-mail:* honors@cc.usu.edu; *Web site:* http://www.usu.edu/honors

Utah Valley State College
Honors Program
Orem, Utah

*T*he Honors Program at Utah Valley State College is designed to challenge motivated students. Students who enter honors are deeply committed to realizing their academic, professional, and human potential. Honors courses facilitate this goal by providing small classes (no more than 20 students) that encourage an intimate, intensive, and stimulating learning experience. Students interact with each other and distinguished faculty members who have been carefully selected on the basis of scholarship, teaching ability, and rapport with students. The emphasis is on the development of reading, writing, and discussion skills that lead to productive analysis in all areas of the human experience. There are approximately 300 honors students currently enrolled.

Participation Requirements: Honors graduates complete honors courses that fulfill general education requirements and compose a thesis. They must graduate with a GPA of at least 3.5. Upon graduation, an honors seal is placed on the diploma and the transcript.

Admission Process: To enter the Honors Program, a candidate must meet GPA and ACT or SAT requirements and be interviewed by the honors director.

Scholarship Availability: Graduates have preferred transfer and access to scholarships at all Utah universities.

Campus Overview

State-supported 4-year, founded 1941, part of Utah System of Higher Education • **Coed** 24,149 undergraduate students, 51% full-time, 42% women, 58% men.

Undergraduates 12,229 full-time, 11,920 part-time. Students come from 50 states and territories, 78 other countries, 13% are from out of state, 0.4% African American, 2% Asian American or Pacific Islander, 3% Hispanic American, 1% Native American, 3% international, 9% transferred in.

Faculty *Total:* 1,172, 33% full-time, 14% with terminal degrees. *Student/faculty ratio:* 19:1.

Academic Programs *Special study options:* academic remediation for entering students, accelerated degree program, advanced placement credit, cooperative education, distance learning, English as a second language, honors programs, independent study, internships, off-campus study, part-time degree program, services for LD students, student-designed majors, study abroad, summer session for credit. *ROTC:* Army (b), Air Force (c).

Athletics Member NCAA. All Division I. *Intercollegiate sports:* baseball M(s), basketball M(s)/W(s), cross-country running M(s)/W(s), golf M(s), soccer W(s), softball W(s), track and field M(s)/W(s), volleyball W(s), wrestling M(s). *Intramural sports:* basketball M/W, bowling M/W, football M/W, golf M/W, racquetball M/W, soccer M/W, softball M/W, table tennis M/W, tennis M/W, volleyball M/W, weight lifting M/W.

Costs (2004–05) *Tuition:* state resident $2788 full-time; nonresident $8718 full-time. Full-time tuition and fees vary according to course level. Part-time tuition and fees vary according to course level and course load.

Financial Aid In 2003, 536 non-need-based awards were made. *Average percent of need met:* 66%. *Average financial aid package:* $6477. *Average need-based loan:* $1965. *Average need-based gift aid:* $2278. *Average non-need-based aid:* $1603.

Contact: Director: JaNae Brown Haas, History Department, Mailcode 185, 800 West 1200 University Parkway, Orem, Utah 84058; *Telephone:* 801-863-6262; *Fax:* 801-863-7013; *E-mail:* haasja@uvsc.edu; *Web site:* http://www.uvsc.edu

Weber State University
Honors Program
Ogden, Utah

The Honors Program fosters the growth of intellectual independence and initiative, invites a sophisticated level of classroom and extracurricular interaction, and examines complex issues from diverse perspectives. The chief goal of the Honors Program is to help students become competitive with graduates of any undergraduate institution. To do this, the Honors Program believes that each student should be well grounded in the liberal arts, engage in exploration and research, develop and articulate personal perspectives through strong written and oral communication skills, develop an understanding of global issues through travel-study opportunities, become an active participant in the campus and local community through community service and volunteerism, and join in the creation of an undergraduate community of scholars.

Honors Program classes are limited to a maximum of 15 students and are taught by a select faculty. Honors faculty members are distinguished by their commitment to academic excellence and their ability to work and communicate with highly motivated undergraduates. The University's teaching method emphasizes reading original sources, writing essays, and Socratic dialogue. The Honors Program also creates a learning community of student and faculty members through extracurricular social and cultural activities, guest speakers, study groups, participation in national and regional conferences, and travel-abroad opportunities.

There are three honors designations in the Weber State University Honors Program: University Honors, Departmental Honors, and General Honors. University Honors is available to all Honors Program students graduating with a bachelor's degree. Departmental Honors is available to students majoring in a department with designated Departmental Honors options. General Honors is available to students when they complete their associate degree. The new honors student begins taking University Honors classes to satisfy their general education requirements, starting with Introduction to Honors.

Established in 1969, the program currently enrolls 162 students (57 seniors, 30 juniors, 43 sophomores, and 32 freshmen).

Participation Requirements: To graduate with University Honors, a student must complete a minimum of 27 University Honors credits, including 21 honors core credits. The 27 hours may also include honors components and general education courses offered through the Honors Program. Honors core classes include Introduction to Honors (3 credits), Great Ideas of the East (3 credits), and Great Ideas of the West (3 credits); two Honors Colloquium courses (3 credits each); and the Honors Senior Project (1–6 credits, taken over a two-semester period, normally during the last two semesters of the senior year).

The requirements for graduation with Departmental Honors vary depending on the student's major. Most departments require students graduating with Departmental Honors to complete 9 hours of University Honors classes and 9–12 hours of upper-division classes in their major, with an honors component, and maintain a minimum cumulative 3.3 GPA. Students completing General Honors must complete their associate degree and12 credit hours of honors courses. The 12 credit hours may include honors courses taken for general education credit.

Students are expected to take an honors class every semester until general education requirements are completed, after which they are expected to take at least one course every other semester. No grades below B are accepted for credit toward graduation with University, Departmental, or General Honors. Student progress is reviewed each semester. An honors student who has difficulty maintaining these standards is offered counseling and assistance from members of the Honors Program staff.

Official recognition is given for the completion of University Honors, Departmental Honors, and General Honors. Notation of these achievements is made on the graduating honors student's transcript, diploma, and commencement program.

Admission Process: A student may apply for entrance into the Honors Program anytime after formal acceptance by the Weber State Admissions Office. However, to take advantage of the many options available, early entrance is recommended. An application form is available in the honors office or online at http://programs.weber.edu/honors. The applicant is asked to provide evidence of a cumulative GPA of at least 3.5 or minimum ACT score of 26 or SAT score of 1150. New students are required to attend an honors orientation with the Honors Adviser and register for Honors 1110, Introduction to Honors.

Scholarship Availability: Each year the Weber State University Honors Program has several tuition waiver scholarships that are awarded to deserving students. These waivers are based on both GPA and involvement and activity within the Honors Program. There are also several leadership scholarship tuition waivers for students who serve on the Honors Student Advisory Board. Students apply for leadership waivers in March in the Honors Center only. Tuition waiver scholarship information is available online, and students may apply online or in person in the Honors Center.

Campus Overview

State-supported comprehensive, founded 1889, part of Utah System of Higher Education • **Coed** 18,132 undergraduate students, 59% full-time, 50% women, 50% men.

Undergraduates 10,669 full-time, 7,463 part-time. Students come from 52 states and territories, 37 other countries, 5% are from out of state, 0.7% African American, 1% Asian American or Pacific Islander, 4% Hispanic American, 0.5% Native American, 0.9% international, 9% transferred in, 3% live on campus.

Faculty *Total:* 454, 100% full-time, 98% with terminal degrees. *Student/faculty ratio:* 22:1.

Academic Programs *Special study options:* academic remediation for entering students, accelerated degree program, adult/continuing education programs, advanced placement credit, cooperative education, distance learning, double majors, English as a second language, external degree program, freshman honors college, honors programs, independent study, internships, off-campus study, part-time degree program, services for LD students, student-designed majors, study abroad, summer session for credit. *ROTC:* Army (b), Navy (b), Air Force (b).

Athletics Member NCAA. All Division I except football (Division I-AA). *Intercollegiate sports:* baseball M(c), basketball M(s)/W(s), bowling M(c)/W(c), cheerleading M(s)/W(s), cross-country running M(s)/W(s), fencing M(c)/W(c), golf M(s)/W(s), ice hockey M(c), lacrosse M(c)/W(c), racquetball M(c)/W(c), rugby M(c)/W(c), skiing (downhill) M(c)/W(c), soccer M(c)/W(c), softball W(c), swimming and diving M(c)/W(c), tennis M(s)/W(s), track and field M(s)/W(s), volleyball W(s), water polo M(c)/W(c). *Intramural sports:* baseball M/W, basketball M/W, bowling M/W, cross-country running M/W, football M/W, golf M/W, racquetball M/W, soccer M/W, softball M/W, tennis M/W, volleyball M/W.

Costs (2004–05) *Tuition:* state resident $2344 full-time; nonresident $8204 full-time. Part-time tuition and fees vary according to course load. *Required fees:* $532 full-time. *Room and board:* $6400; room only: $3200. Room and board charges vary according to board plan and housing facility.

Financial Aid In 2001, 2470 non-need-based awards were made. *Average percent of need met:* 87%. *Average financial aid package:* $5300. *Average need-based loan:* $2620. *Average need-based gift aid:* $3750. *Average non-need-based aid:* $1420.

Contact: Dr. Robert Mondi, 2904 University Circle, Ogden, Utah 84404-2904; *Telephone:* 801-626-6230; *Fax:* 801-626-7568; *E-mail:* rmondi@weber.edu; *Web site:* http://programs.weber.edu/honors

Westminster College

Honors Program

Salt Lake City, Utah

The Honors Program provides Westminster College students who are academically and intellectually prepared with the opportunity to satisfy their College-wide Liberal Education (LE) Skills and Liberal Education Distribution course requirements in an alternative and unique manner. By completing a seven-course sequence of interdisciplinary, team-taught, discussion-oriented honors courses, students earn an honors certificate while satisfying these requirements. Moreover, by understanding their historical, scientific, and intellectual heritage, honors students are prepared to be articulate and responsible members of society and defenders of their own ideas. The classes are restricted in size, employ seminar-style approaches, and emphasize study of primary texts.

The Honors Program also provides an enhanced educational experience for students by giving them access to supplementary resources like the "Pizza with Profs" lecture series; the Honors Program resource library; special enriched learning experiences, such as attendance at cultural events and other field study; funding to attend and give papers at academic conferences; three $2300 awards to fund student research during the summer; leadership training opportunities like the student Honors Council; special recognition opportunities like the honors seminar book awards; and opportunities to participate in special meetings with distinguished visiting scholars and lecturers.

The program was founded in 1987 and currently enrolls approximately 100 students. It is housed in historic Nunemaker Place, located on the banks of Emigration Creek. This three-story building gives honors students a place to study, write papers on networked computers, attend social events or meetings, or hang out with friends.

Participation Requirements: Students admitted to the program must maintain a GPA of at least 3.25 overall and 3.0 in honors courses. If an honors student falls below these GPA minimums, a probationary semester is used to allow the student to return to the minimum GPA standards for continued participation. Students who complete seven courses in the honors LE sequence are awarded a special certificate recognizing this achievement (contingent on Westminster graduation).

To be awarded the Honors Degree, students must satisfy the following requirements at graduation: maintain a minimum GPA of 3.0 in all honors course work, including those courses listed below for the honors degree, and a minimum GPA of 3.25; complete seven LE courses, with no more than one of these courses taken CR/NC; complete four semesters of college-level instruction in a single foreign language (or the equivalent); complete 6 credit hours of course work in Honors 300 or 400 seminars; and complete a senior project in the student's major for a minimum of 3 credit hours. The nature of this project is determined in conjunction with the Director of Honors and the student's major adviser.

Admission Process: Incoming students expressing a desire to enroll in the Honors Program are ranked according to the following criteria: ACT scores, high school GPA, and the quality of a written statement that explains why the student wishes to participate and why he or she feels qualified for participation in the program. The top 35 students are invited to enroll in honors courses. If accepted students decline the offer, the invitation process continues until a class of 35 students is formed. In the past, a typical incoming honors student has had a 3.8 GPA and a 29 composite ACT score. Students who fall near or above these guidelines and who sincerely wish to be in the program are encouraged to apply. Application forms are available on the program's Web site.

Since a number of high-achieving, upperclass Westminster College students may not have applied to the Honors Program as incoming freshmen but may still wish to participate in some of its classes, any undergraduate in good standing with a GPA of 3.5 or higher is eligible to enroll in 300- and 400-level honors seminars. The Honors Program is an active part of the larger College community and welcomes the energy, intellect, and diversity that students bring to the Honors Program from different disciplines across the campus.

Scholarship Availability: The Honors Program administers the Alvin and Helene Richer Academic Excellence scholarship, which makes up the difference between the highest College-awarded scholarship and Westminster tuition. Students must have an ACT score of 30 or higher to apply and must show particular promise in the areas of academic excellence, campus leadership, and undergraduate research. The College also has a wide range of financial support available. Ninety-seven percent of freshmen at Westminster receive financial aid, averaging approximately $15,750 per student annually. Merit-based scholarships are available to incoming freshmen and transfer students as well as to continuing students, thanks to a generous endowment program and institutional aid program. Every full-time student admitted to Westminster is automatically considered for merit-based scholarships awarded by the College, which are based on GPA from previous academic (high school or college) course work. In addition, the Westminster College Award for Exemplary Achievement recognizes students who have achieved excellence in any activity or endeavor of significance. Ten awards of $60,000 ($15,000 per year) are awarded; a separate application is required. More than $9.6 million was awarded in institutional scholarships in 2003–04.

Campus Overview

Independent comprehensive, founded 1875 • **Coed** 1,896 undergraduate students, 89% full-time, 60% women, 40% men.

Undergraduates 1,678 full-time, 218 part-time. Students come from 35 states and territories, 18 other countries, 9% are from out of state, 0.6% African American, 3% Asian American or Pacific Islander, 4% Hispanic American, 0.8% Native American, 2% international, 12% transferred in, 26% live on campus.

Faculty *Total:* 281, 42% full-time, 33% with terminal degrees. *Student/faculty ratio:* 10:1.

Academic Programs *Special study options:* academic remediation for entering students, accelerated degree program, advanced placement credit, cooperative education, double majors, English as a second language, external degree program, honors programs, independent study, internships, part-time degree program, services for LD students, student-designed majors, study abroad, summer session for credit. *ROTC:* Army (c), Navy (c), Air Force (c). *Unusual degree programs:* 3-2 engineering with University of Southern California, Washington University in St. Louis.

Athletics Member NAIA. *Intercollegiate sports:* basketball M/W, golf M/W, soccer M, volleyball W. *Intramural sports:* basketball M/W, cross-country running M/W, football M/W, skiing (cross-country) M/W, soccer M/W, table tennis M/W, tennis M/W, volleyball M/W, weight lifting M/W.

Costs (2004–05) *Comprehensive fee:* $24,112 includes full-time tuition ($18,192), mandatory fees ($284), and room and board ($5636). Full-time tuition and fees vary according to course load. Part-time tuition: $758 per credit hour. *Required fees:* $107 per term part-time. *Room and board:* Room and board charges vary according to board plan.

Financial Aid 321 Federal Work-Study jobs (averaging $2200). In 2003, 451 non-need-based awards were made. *Average percent of need met:* 89%. *Average financial aid package:* $14,130. *Average need-based loan:* $3921. *Average need-based gift aid:* $9761. *Average non-need-based aid:* $7385.

Contact: Director: Dr. Richard Badenhausen, Honors Program, Westminster College, 1840 South 1300 East, Salt Lake City, Utah 84105; *Telephone:* 801-832-2460; *Fax:* 801-832-3102; *E-mail:* rbadenhausen@westminstercollege.edu; *Web site:* http://www.westminstercollege.edu/honors/

VERMONT

Champlain College
Champlain College Honors Program
Burlington, Vermont

Champlain College, founded in 1878, began its Honors Program in 1999. In its history, the College evolved from a two-year business college to a four-year institution. It now offers four-year bachelor's degrees and has recently begun offering advanced degree programs. Into this environment of an evolving and rapidly changing program, the Champlain College Honors Program was born.

The primary characteristic of Champlain College's Honors Program is its energetic beginning that aims to introduce the most motivated learners of the College's first-year class each year to other students who share that enthusiasm. In their first year in the program, students take the special Honors Program sections of the two-semester sequence called Critical Reading and Expository Writing I and II (nicknamed CREW I and CREW II). In those classes where the discussions are very lively, students meet their Honors Program peers. Outside of class, students communicate in the online Honors Program lounge, a virtual environment created to enable students to have discussions beyond the classroom. The design of the lab took eighteen months of planning, but it now offers students most of the features available in a real lounge, with the exception of a working fireplace. Related outside activities include trips to art or history museums in Montreal.

Beyond the first year, Champlain offers Honors Program sections of classes in its second-year history sequence of four required semesters, which the College proudly points to as quite intense for a career-oriented college. Beyond the second year, students typically arrange an Honors Contract to take a course in their major for Honors Program credit by working individually with a faculty member. Fourth-year students are offered an honors section of the Seminar in Contemporary World Issues, a course that is required of all graduates of the College.

After a trial period of five years, the College intends to change its honors curriculum, beginning in 2006. Seniors are scheduled to take part in an honors internship of community service. In some curriculum areas, plans are for Honors Program students to write a senior thesis, and, for others, an Honors senior thesis is scheduled to become part of the regular requirements.

Faculty members who volunteer to teach Honors Program classes report that they find the teaching more demanding and more rewarding when compared to other classes at the College. Classes for Honors Program students tend to be small (fewer than 20 students); however it is important to note that the average class size is only 22 students. Nevertheless, faculty members do find an extra measure of authenticity in Honors Program teaching. For example, in a regular class in business or psychology, students might read about seminal studies or famous articles in the field; in the Honors Program classes, students read the specific study or article.

Founded in September 1999, there are currently 92 students enrolled in the Honors Program.

Participation Requirements: Once invited into the Honors Program as part of the admissions process, students are automatically enrolled in the program beginning in their first semester, unless they request to decline the invitation. Students must take at least one Honors Program course (3 credits) per year and maintain a minimum GPA of 3.5 to stay in the program. Each Honors Program course taken appears marked with an H on the student's transcript. At commencement, students who have maintained Honors Program status for four years receive an Honors Program certificate in addition to their diploma. Beginning in 2005–06, students need to complete an internship in community service and complete an Honors thesis or Honors project in order to receive the Honors Program certificate at graduation.

Admission Process: Champlain College does not require specific SAT scores for admission into the Honors Program, and there is no numerical cutoff set at a particular GPA on a high school transcript. Rather, the Admissions Office (not the Honors Program Director) makes invitations to prospective students to join the Honors Program, based on the high school curriculum, extracurricular activities, and letters of recommendation. The Admissions Office seeks students who are motivated learners as the main criterion in selecting students for the Champlain College Honors Program. In its revised format, the program will select some candidates from the incoming first-year class. Those candidates and other students interested in the Honors Program will apply to be admitted during their third year.

Scholarship Availability: No scholarship award accompanies participation in Champlain College's Honors Program. Beginning in the 2005–06 academic year, Honors Program students are inducted into a nationally recognized scholastic honor society.

Campus Overview
Independent comprehensive, founded 1878 • **Coed** 2,491 undergraduate students, 68% full-time, 50% women, 50% men.

Undergraduates 1,704 full-time, 787 part-time. Students come from 28 states and territories, 26 other countries, 60% are from out of state, 0.8% African American, 2% Asian American or Pacific Islander, 1% Hispanic American, 0.9% Native American, 0.4% international, 6% transferred in, 41% live on campus.

Faculty Total: 256, 25% full-time, 29% with terminal degrees. Student/faculty ratio: 17:1.

Academic Programs Special study options: advanced placement credit, cooperative education, distance learning, double majors, freshman honors college, honors programs, internships, off-campus study, part-time degree program, services for LD students, study abroad, summer session for credit. ROTC: Army (c).

Athletics Intramural sports: basketball M/W, bowling M/W, cross-country running M/W, golf M/W, ice hockey M/W, lacrosse M, sailing M/W, skiing (cross-country) M/W, skiing (downhill) M/W, soccer M/W, ultimate Frisbee M/W, volleyball M/W.

Costs (2005–06) Comprehensive fee: $24,605 Canadian dollars includes full-time tuition ($14,660 Canadian dollars), mandatory fees ($250 Canadian dollars), and room and board ($9695 Canadian dollars). Full-time tuition and fees vary according to course load. Part-time tuition: $420 Canadian dollars per credit hour. Part-time tuition and fees vary according to course load. College room only: $5855 Canadian dollars. Room and board charges vary according to board plan and housing facility.

Financial Aid 228 Federal Work-Study jobs (averaging $2200). In 2004, 14 non-need-based awards were made. Average percent of need met: 64%. Average financial aid package: $9229. Average need-based loan: $5201. Average need-based gift aid: $5195. Average non-need-based aid: $46,000.

Contact: Director: Nancy Nahra, Ph.D., Professor of Humanities, Champlain College Honors Program, Mailbox 34, Champlain College, Burlington, Vermont 05402; Telephone: 802-651-5920; Fax: 802-860-2750; E-mail: nahra@champlain.edu; Web site: http://www.champlain.edu/majors/honors.php

University of Vermont
The Honors College
Burlington, Vermont

Fall 2004 saw the opening of the new Honors College at the University of Vermont (UVM). The Honors College is an enrichment program, bringing together outstanding students from all seven undergraduate schools and colleges. It is also a residential college, with administrative, residential, and academic facilities located in the new University Heights North Quad complex. Members are strongly encouraged to live in the Honors College residence and participate in the College's extracurricular and cocurricular activities.

First-year Honors College students take a two-semester, 6-credit seminar, Making Ethical Choices: Personal, Public, and Professional. This class combines study of classical philosophical works of ethical and political theory with a discussion of case studies and problems in applied ethics. Sophomores take two 3-credit special-topics seminars, one in the fall and one in the spring. These sophomore courses vary from year to year and span an academic landscape as rich and diverse as the interests and specialties of the faculty members who teach them. In the junior year, students typically take one 3-credit seminar in their home college or school, which prepares them for the senior-year honors project. Senior students complete a two-semester, 6-credit research thesis or senior project approved by their home school or college. Students who satisfy all the requirements of the Honors College graduate as University Scholars.

Honors College students are granted early enrollment for their courses and receive graduate student borrowing privileges at the library. The Honors College sponsors both cocurricular and extracurricular programs, from lectures and dinners with faculty members to weekly social gatherings. The Honors College provides intensive advising for students, including preparation for competition for prestigious postgraduation scholarships, such as the Rhodes and Marshall Scholarships. When the Honors College reaches full capacity in fall 2007, it will have up to 700 students.

Participation Requirements: Students in the Honors College are "dual citizens" of the Honors College and their home academic school or college. They satisfy distributive and general requirements in their home units, as well as major requirements and any other program requirement relevant to their course of studies. In addition, they take a two-semester, 6-credit course during their first year; two 3-credit special topics in their sophomore year; a 3-credit seminar designed for Honors College students in their home school or college in their junior year; and a two semester, 3-credit thesis or project in their senior year. Students must maintain a GPA of 3.2 or better to retain their membership in the Honors College. Students who complete these requirements graduate as University Scholars and receive special recognition at commencement.

Admission Process: Admission to the Honors College is based on prior academic performance. There is no application required for first-year admission; rather, the Honors College reviews the academic records of the University's entering class and invites top performers to enroll. Up to 100 first-year students are admitted each year. The Honors College also welcomes applications for sophomore admission from students who were not in the Honors College as freshmen. Sophomore admission requires an application form, a grade point average of 3.4 or above at the end of the first year, a faculty letter of recommendation, and a brief essay. Up to 100 sophomores are admitted to the Honors College annually.

Scholarship Availability: There are a small number of scholarships tied to the Honors College. Honors College students are also eligible for scholarship funds distributed more generally by the University. The Dean of the Honors College has a discretionary fund to help students with mini-scholarships to cover the cost of special events and projects.

Campus Overview

State-supported university, founded 1791 • **Coed** 9,235 undergraduate students, 86% full-time, 56% women, 44% men.

Undergraduates 7,956 full-time, 1,279 part-time. Students come from 50 states and territories, 30 other countries, 63% are from out of state, 1% African American, 2% Asian American or Pacific Islander, 2% Hispanic American, 0.2% Native American, 0.7% international, 4% transferred in, 52% live on campus.

Faculty Total: 691, 80% full-time, 77% with terminal degrees. Student/faculty ratio: 15:1.

Academic Programs Special study options: advanced placement credit, cooperative education, distance learning, double majors, English as a second language, freshman honors college, honors programs, independent study, internships, off-campus study, part-time degree program, services for LD students, student-designed majors, study abroad, summer session for credit. ROTC: Army (b). Unusual degree programs: 3-2 computer science.

Athletics Member NCAA. All Division I. Intercollegiate sports: baseball M(s), basketball M(s)/W(s), cheerleading M(c)/W(c), crew M(c)/W(c), cross-country running M(s)/W(s), equestrian sports M(c)/W(c), fencing M(c)/W(c), field hockey W(s), gymnastics M(c)/W(c), ice hockey M(s)/W(s), lacrosse M(s)/W(s), rugby M(c)/W(c), sailing M(c)/W(c), skiing (cross-country) M(s)/W(s), skiing (downhill) M(s)/W(s), soccer M(s)/W(s), softball W(s), swimming and diving W(s), table tennis M(c)/W(c), track and field M(s)/W(s), ultimate Frisbee M(c)/W(c), volleyball M(c)/W(c), water polo M(c)/W(c). Intramural sports: basketball M/W, bowling M/W, football M/W, ice hockey M/W, lacrosse M/W, racquetball M/W, soccer M/W, softball M/W, tennis M/W, volleyball M/W, water polo M/W.

Costs (2004–05) One-time required fee: $300. Tuition: state resident $9088 full-time, $379 per credit part-time; nonresident $22,728 full-time, $947 per credit part-time. Part-time tuition and fees vary according to course load. Required fees: $1138 full-time. Room and board: $7016; room only: $4710. Room and board charges vary according to board plan.

Financial Aid 1,786 Federal Work-Study jobs (averaging $2004). In 2003, 896 non-need-based awards were made. Average percent of need met: 82%. Average financial aid package: $14,960. Average need-based loan: $5980. Average need-based gift aid: $10,079. Average non-need-based aid: $2132.

Contact: Dean: Bob Pepperman Taylor, Assistant to the Dean: Patricia Redmond, The Honors College, North Quad, University Heights, University of Vermont, Burlington, Vermont 05405; Telephone: 802-656-4289 or 9100; Fax: 802-656-9009; E-mail: robert.taylor@uvm.edu or patricia.redmond@uvm.edu

VIRGINIA

Hampden-Sydney College
Honors Program
Hampden-Sydney, Virginia

The Honors Program at Hampden-Sydney College is designed specifically for the student who gives evidence of intellectual curiosity, independence of thought, excitement in learning, and appreciation of knowledge. It is for young men who spark the enthusiasm of fellow students and challenge the best in their teachers.

Participants in the program are encouraged to take an active role in the learning process, entering into dialogue with their professors and classmates, rather than just listening to lectures. The size of Hampden-Sydney and its excellent faculty make it well-suited to provide a learning environment for such motivated students.

Hampden-Sydney is proud that 18 percent of its students are honors scholars, young men who are recognized for distinguished achievement in secondary school and for their promise of successful careers both in college and in life. Honors scholarships are awarded in four categories. Stipends vary, but all four categories provide a scholarship to meet the recipient's College-determined need.

For such men, Hampden-Sydney has created its Honors Program, which gives participants in the program latitude for intellectual challenge and independent study, broadening their perspective and *complementing their formal academic pursuits. Special courses for honors scholars boost curricular breadth. Honors scholars also receive tickets and transportation to attend plays, concerts, and other performances in Richmond, Virginia. On campus, honors scholars occasionally have dinner with visiting dignitaries and are invited to special colloquia. They may themselves hold symposia for other honors students in the region. In addition, participants in the Honors Program at Hampden-Sydney may attend the annual conventions of the Virginia Collegiate Honors Council or the National Collegiate Honors Council.*

The Honors Program at Hampden-Sydney was founded in 1978 and admits more than 50 freshmen each year. Other students join the Honors Program as sophomores, juniors, or seniors. There are approximately 200 students currently enrolled in the program.

Participation Requirements: Freshmen honors scholars are invited to participate in a two-semester interdisciplinary seminar that is team taught by two faculty members from different academic divisions of the College. Other honors seminars are taught to upperclassmen. Honors scholars and other strong students are encouraged to apply to participate in the College's Summer Research program during at least one of the summers of their college years. Honors scholars and other qualified students are encouraged to pursue Departmental Honors during their senior year. This program, available in each academic department of the College, includes a semester or yearlong independent research project under the supervision of a faculty mentor. Students who successfully complete the Departmental Honors project graduate with honors in their field of study. An optional Senior Fellowship program provides a more intense interdisciplinary research experience. There is also a limited honors housing option.

Admission Process: High school students are recruited for the Honors Program on the basis of their high school class rank, their SAT or ACT scores, their application essay, their letters of recommendation from college counselors and teachers, and, in some instances, a personal interview. The Honors Council also looks closely at the range of activities in which applicants to the program have been involved during their high school years and is particularly impressed by those applicants who have had leadership roles in their extracurricular activities. The application deadline is March 1.

Sophomores and transfer students who perform well during their first year at Hampden-Sydney are eligible to compete for an in-course honors scholarship during the fall of their second year at the College. Other qualified students who are not honors scholars may participate in the summer research and the departmental honors programs.

Scholarship Availability: The Honors Program, with the help of the College's admissions office, awards honors scholarships of various amounts to incoming freshmen based on their academic performance during high school. The Honors Program also awards competitive academic scholarships to sophomores and transfer students who perform well during their first year at the College.

Campus Overview

Independent 4-year, founded 1776, affiliated with Presbyterian Church (U.S.A.) ● **Rural** 660-acre campus with easy access to Richmond ● **Men only** 1,082 undergraduate students, 100% full-time.

Undergraduates 1,080 full-time, 2 part-time. Students come from 36 states and territories, 6 other countries, 33% are from out of state, 4% African American, 0.9% Asian American or Pacific Islander, 2% Hispanic American, 0.5% Native American, 1% international, 2% transferred in, 93% live on campus.

Faculty *Total:* 106, 87% full-time. *Student/faculty ratio:* 11:1.

Academic Programs *Special study options:* academic remediation for entering students, accelerated degree program, advanced placement credit, double majors, honors programs, independent study, internships, off-campus study, study abroad, summer session for credit. *ROTC:* Army (c). *Unusual degree programs:* 3-2 engineering with University of Virginia.

Athletics Member NCAA. All Division III. *Intercollegiate sports:* baseball M, basketball M, crew M(c), cross-country running M,

fencing M(c), football M, golf M, lacrosse M, riflery M(c), rugby M(c), soccer M, tennis M, ultimate Frisbee M(c). *Intramural sports:* basketball M, football M, soccer M, softball M, volleyball M.

Costs (2005–06) *Comprehensive fee:* $30,316 includes full-time tuition ($21,878), mandatory fees ($1068), and room and board ($7370). Part-time tuition: $704 per credit hour. *College room only:* $3116. Room and board charges vary according to board plan and housing facility.

Financial Aid 247 Federal Work-Study jobs (averaging $1276). In 2004, 491 non-need-based awards were made. *Average percent of need met:* 83%. *Average financial aid package:* $16,542. *Average need-based loan:* $4113. *Average need-based gift aid:* $12,876. *Average non-need-based aid:* $14,853.

Contact: Director: Katherine J. Weese, Box 169, Hampden-Sydney, Virginia 23943; *Telephone:* 434-223-6254; *Fax:* 434-223-6045; *E-mail:* kweese@hsc.edu; *Web site:* http://www.hsc.edu/academics/honors/

Hampton University
Honors Program
Hampton, Virginia

Honors College (HC), the primary component of Hampton University's Honors Program, is a special honors track for motivated, high-achieving students who are willing to seek success rather than avoid failure, who have the courage to take intellectual risks, and who are able to see the world in a "grain of sand." Honors College, established on Hampton University's campus in fall 1986, is designed to promote the development of intellectual, ethical leadership skills while fostering excellence in education, commitment to the learning process, experimentation, and a sense of a learning community. Honors College involves all academic units of the University and includes experiences from the freshman through the senior years. It includes an innovative curriculum; individualized advising and support services; special options, opportunities, and financial incentives; and extracurricular activities.

The honors faculty is made up of teachers who have demonstrated excellence in teaching, who are interested in interdisciplinary applications, who are committed to working with students to facilitate learning and discovery, and who are willing to work with other faculty members to improve the academic environment of the University as a whole.

In addition to participating in enriched courses with others of a similar scholastic aptitude, the student may receive or take advantage of Honors College perquisites, which include the HC pin; priority in course selection at each semester's registration; individualized advising; eligibility for scholarships and internships; participation in special events, field trips, and social activities; a fee waiver for transcripts; individualized assistance in preparing resumes and/or applications for fellowships and postgraduate study; special recognition during Honors Day Convocation; the honors designation on transcripts, Commencement certificates, and the Commencement programs; special honors cords and a medallion to be worn with graduation regalia; subsidized honors program and honors conference expenses; and the honors newsletter, Word of Honor. There are currently 176 students enrolled in Honors College.

Participation Requirements: The Honors College requires students to complete 12 hours of honors credit in the general education courses and 12 hours of honors credit in the major, usually by contract. In addition, the Honors College student must take Argumentation and Debate or Logic and Ethics plus four University honors seminars, including UNV 200 Honors Service Learning Seminar, UNV 290 and 390 University Honors Seminar I and II, and UNV 400 Honors

Independent Study Capstone Seminar. For the independent study, students are encouraged to choose a topic of interest that is not directly related to their major.

Admission Process: Entering freshmen, transfer students, and other students who are interested in pursuing an honors experience must apply for admission to Honors College after completing at least 15 hours of course work at the University. A student in Honors College is required to maintain a minimum GPA of 3.2. Other additional requirements are to perform at least 150 hours of community service, serve on an HC Committee for at least one semester, participate in a conference experience, and take the appropriate exam for graduate study.

Scholarship Availability: Hampton University offers a number of Presidential and Merit Scholarships. Many students who receive these scholarships are in the Honors College program.

Campus Overview

Independent university, founded 1868 • **Coed** 5,317 undergraduate students, 92% full-time, 63% women, 37% men.

Undergraduates 4,903 full-time, 414 part-time. Students come from 38 states and territories, 85% are from out of state, 95% African American, 0.8% Asian American or Pacific Islander, 0.9% Hispanic American, 0.2% Native American, 8% transferred in, 59% live on campus.

Faculty *Total:* 463, 71% full-time. *Student/faculty ratio:* 16:1.

Academic Programs *Special study options:* academic remediation for entering students, accelerated degree program, adult/continuing education programs, advanced placement credit, cooperative education, distance learning, double majors, honors programs, independent study, internships, off-campus study, part-time degree program, services for LD students, study abroad, summer session for credit. *ROTC:* Army (b), Navy (b).

Athletics Member NCAA. All Division I. *Intercollegiate sports:* basketball M(s)/W(s), bowling W(s), cross-country running M(s)/W(s), football M(s), golf M(s)/W(s), sailing M(s)/W(s), softball W(s), tennis M(s)/W(s), track and field M(s)/W(s), volleyball W(s). *Intramural sports:* basketball M/W, bowling W, football M, sailing M/W, soccer M/W, softball M/W, volleyball W.

Costs (2004–05) *Comprehensive fee:* $21,420 includes full-time tuition ($13,506), mandatory fees ($1490), and room and board ($6424). Part-time tuition: $305 per credit. *College room only:* $3340. Room and board charges vary according to housing facility.

Financial Aid 342 Federal Work-Study jobs (averaging $1800). In 2004, 227 non-need-based awards were made. *Average percent of need met:* 50%. *Average financial aid package:* $3266. *Average need-based loan:* $3265. *Average need-based gift aid:* $3437. *Average non-need-based aid:* $5767.

Contact: Director: Dr. Freddye Davy, Box 6174, Hampton, Virginia 23668; *Telephone:* 757-727-5076; *Fax:* 757-728-6711

James Madison University
Honors Program
Harrisonburg, Virginia

The James Madison University (JMU) Honors Program enhances the intellectual, cultural, social, and career opportunities for the most motivated, enthusiastic, and curious students. It offers rigorous and creative courses and interdisciplinary seminars that are taught by outstanding professors in small classes to facilitate discussion and critical thinking. In addition, the program organizes outside lectures, field trips to galleries, concerts and theater, and other special events to stimulate and challenge intellectual and social development. The University also provides opportunities for significant independent research and creative work with faculty mentors. First- and second-year honors students enjoy priority registration.

The Honors Program began in 1961 as 6 hours of independent study culminating in a senior thesis. In 1975, it offered honors sections and seminars to highly qualified first- and second-year students. The first program director was named in 1982, and 50 honors scholars were admitted. The current three-mode structure was instituted in 1986. Today, academically talented JMU students may participate in one of three honors programs: the honors scholars, subject-area honors, or the senior honors project. There are 600 students in the program, which is approximately 5 percent of undergraduates.

Participation Requirements: Honors scholars participate in four years of honors study in a bachelor's degree program in any major. They complete 27 hours of honors work—a combination of honors courses, seminars, and independent study—and earn fifty points as a part of the Honors Opportunities Program, which is designated to encourage first-year honors students to get involved in learning outside the traditional classroom setting. They are also required to maintain a 3.25 cumulative GPA. Subject-area honors students enter the program in their second, third, or fourth semesters at JMU. They complete 24 hours of honors work—a combination of honors courses, seminars, and independent study—and maintain a cumulative GPA of 3.25 or higher. Senior honors project students enter the program in the second semester of their junior year and complete 6 hours of independent study over three semesters, culminating in documents of significant research or creative work. Each program is designed to prepare students for graduate or professional schools, enhance their opportunities for a rewarding career, and expand their knowledge of themselves, others, and the world.

Honors organizations provide activities and support. The Honors Student Advisory Council advises staff members on the program, policies, and student needs. Honors Publications oversees the publication of the *Honors News* and the *FUGUE*, which is an annual journal of the arts. The Honors Scholars Society plans social activities building community and providing a support network. The Madison Honors Club provides opportunities for honors students to build community and develop leadership while serving others. The student-led organization provides service to at-risk children, families in need, the sick, and the elderly in the community.

Junior and senior honors students in good standing receive honors pins at an annual awards ceremony. Seniors completing the honors scholars or subject-area honors programs receive a medallion to wear at commencement. All seniors completing a senior honors project and, thus, graduating with distinction, receive a certificate and have their names, project titles, and project directors listed in the commencement program. The most coveted awards are the Phi Beta Kappa Award for the most outstanding honors project and the Service Award for exceptional service to the program.

Admission Process: To participate in the honors scholars program, a student must apply and be invited to join the program during the senior year in high school. Applicants are evaluated on SAT I scores (the minimum combined score is 1300), unweighted GPA and strength of high school program, participation in school and community activities, two letters of recommendation, and an analytical essay in response to a common text. Admission is competitive; approximately 200 entering freshmen are admitted as honors scholars.

To apply for subject-area honors, a student must have earned at least a 3.25 GPA at JMU and must submit a recommendation from a faculty member and an application, including a personal statement. All qualified applicants are accepted. To qualify for participation in the senior honors project, a student must have a cumulative GPA of at least 3.25 and submit a project proposal with the approval of a project director; two readers; the department head and dean; and the director of the Honors Program. Transfer students from recognized honors programs are admitted as subject-area or senior honors project students.

Scholarship Availability: Honors students are eligible to apply for all scholarships and grants offered by the University. Most of these are need-based (FAFSA required). A limited number of merit-based awards are available. These include departmental awards and the James Madison Scholar Awards, which are three four-year awards to National Merit Finalists. The Honors Program has very limited scholarship funds. Honors Scholarships, typically $500, are awarded to returning students to assist in international study. Edythe Rowley Scholarships, typically $1000, are awarded to returning students to meet unanticipated financial needs.

Campus Overview

State-supported comprehensive, founded 1908 • **Coed** 14,954 undergraduate students, 95% full-time, 60% women, 40% men.

Undergraduates 14,275 full-time, 679 part-time. Students come from 47 states and territories, 47 other countries, 29% are from out of state, 3% African American, 5% Asian American or Pacific Islander, 2% Hispanic American, 0.2% Native American, 0.8% international, 4% transferred in, 39% live on campus.

Faculty *Total:* 1,110, 67% full-time, 64% with terminal degrees. *Student/faculty ratio:* 17:1.

Academic Programs *Special study options:* accelerated degree program, adult/continuing education programs, advanced placement credit, distance learning, double majors, freshman honors college, honors programs, independent study, internships, part-time degree program, services for LD students, study abroad, summer session for credit. *ROTC:* Army (b), Air Force (c). *Unusual degree programs:* engineering with University of Virginia; forestry with Virginia Tech.

Athletics Member NCAA. All Division I except football (Division I-AA). *Intercollegiate sports:* archery M/W, baseball M(s), basketball M(s)/W(s), cross-country running M(s)/W(s), fencing W, field hockey W(s), golf M/W, gymnastics M/W, lacrosse W(s), soccer M(s)/W(s), softball W(s), swimming and diving M/W, tennis M/W, track and field M(s)/W(s), volleyball W(s), wrestling M. *Intramural sports:* badminton M/W, baseball M(c), basketball M/W, bowling M/W, cheerleading W(c), cross-country running M(c)/W(c), equestrian sports M(c)/W(c), fencing M(c)/W(c), field hockey M(c)/W(c), football M/W, golf M/W, gymnastics M(c)/W(c), lacrosse M(c)/W(c), racquetball M/W, rugby M(c)/W(c), soccer M/W, softball M/W, swimming and diving M(c)/W(c), table tennis M/W, tennis M/W, ultimate Frisbee M/W, volleyball M/W, water polo M(c)/W(c).

Costs (2004–05) *Tuition:* state resident $5476 full-time; nonresident $14,420 full-time. Part-time tuition and fees vary according to course load. *Room and board:* $6116; room only: $3166. Room and board charges vary according to board plan and housing facility.

Financial Aid 2,022 Federal Work-Study jobs (averaging $1280). In 2004, 228 non-need-based awards were made. *Average percent of need met:* 30%. *Average financial aid package:* $6342. *Average need-based loan:* $3670. *Average need-based gift aid:* $4029. *Average non-need-based aid:* $1525.

Contact: Director: Dr. Joanne V. Gabbin, Hillcrest 107, MSC 1501, James Madison University, 800 South Main Street, Harrisonburg, Virginia 22807; *Telephone:* 540-568-6310; *Fax:* 540-568-8079; *E-mail:* gabbinjv@jmu.edu; *Web site:* http://www.jmu.edu/honorsprog

Longwood University
Honors Program
Farmville, Virginia

Initiated in 1983, the Longwood Honors Program offers courses in a wide variety of majors to academically oriented students seeking intellectual challenge. Honors courses emphasize discussion and writing, regardless of discipline. The small classes (no more than 18 students) encourage teacher-student interaction and opportunities for hands-on learning. For example, the honors section of Introduction to

Anthropology includes a three-day dig, allowing students to apply the principles and terms learned in the classroom. Currently 150 full-time undergraduates participate in the Honors Program.

In addition to honors sections of general education courses, classes of general interest (e.g., Surviving Hard Times, The Civil Rights Struggle in Virginia, and Issues of Sex and Gender) and independent study in a student's major are available.

Incoming honors students may choose to live on the freshman honors floor of the Academic Residence Community (ARC), Longwood's newest residence hall.

Participation Requirements: To graduate from the Honors Program, students complete eight honors courses (three at the 300 level or above) with a minimum 3.25 cumulative GPA average in honors and overall. Students successfully completing the Honors Program are recognized at graduation and on their transcripts.

Admission Process: Incoming students are offered admission to the Honors Program based on a review of their high school records, including an unweighted average of their core academic courses; profiles of their college-credit courses, especially through AP and I.B.; and SAT or ACT scores. Successful honors applicants in the class of 2008 had median SATs in the high-1200s and a median unweighted GPA of more than 3.8. Transfer students with a minimum cumulative 3.25 GPA are also eligible. Freshmen with a Longwood GPA of at least 3.25 after the first semester are also encouraged to apply.

Scholarship Availability: A number of renewable, merit-based scholarships are awarded on a competitive basis to students in each entering class. Three Citizen Scholars each receive a $6400 annual award; two Longwood Scholars each receive $2200; one Lush Scholar receives $4800; and six Hull Scholars each receive $6300. In addition, two renewable, merit-based Advanced Honors Scholarships of $3000 each are awarded every year, one to a rising junior and one to a rising senior.

Campus Overview

State-supported comprehensive, founded 1839, part of The State Council of Higher Education for Virginia (SCHEV) • **Coed** 3,739 undergraduate students, 96% full-time, 66% women, 34% men.

Undergraduates 3,604 full-time, 135 part-time. Students come from 25 states and territories, 11 other countries, 10% are from out of state, 6% African American, 2% Asian American or Pacific Islander, 2% Hispanic American, 0.4% Native American, 0.5% international, 4% transferred in, 67% live on campus.

Faculty *Total:* 242, 79% full-time. *Student/faculty ratio:* 20:1.

Academic Programs *Special study options:* accelerated degree program, advanced placement credit, distance learning, double majors, honors programs, independent study, internships, off-campus study, part-time degree program, services for LD students, study abroad, summer session for credit. *ROTC:* Army (b). *Unusual degree programs:* 3-2 engineering with University of Virginia, Old Dominion University, University of Tennessee, Virginia Polytechnic Institute and University, Christopher Newport University.

Athletics Member NCAA. All Division I. *Intercollegiate sports:* baseball M(s), basketball M(s)/W(s), cross-country running M(s)/W(s), equestrian sports M(c)/W(c), field hockey W(s), golf M(s)/W(s), lacrosse W(s), rugby M(c)/W(c), soccer M(s)/W(s), softball W(s), swimming and diving M(c)/W(c), tennis M(s)/W(s), track and field M(c)/W(c), volleyball M(c)/W(c), wrestling M(c). *Intramural sports:* badminton M/W, basketball W, bowling M/W, cheerleading M/W, football M/W, golf M/W, racquetball M/W, soccer M/W, softball M/W, table tennis M/W, tennis M/W, ultimate Frisbee M/W, volleyball M/W.

Costs (2004–05) *Tuition:* state resident $3320 full-time, $139 per credit hour part-time; nonresident $9780 full-time, $408 per credit hour part-time. *Required fees:* $3121 full-time. *Room and board:* $5424; room only: $3176. Room and board charges vary according to board plan.

Financial Aid 314 Federal Work-Study jobs (averaging $916). 435 state and other part-time jobs (averaging $771). In 2003, 958

non-need-based awards were made. *Average percent of need met: 77%. Average financial aid package: $7013. Average need-based loan: $4102. Average need-based gift aid: $3880. Average non-need-based aid: $4298.*

Contact: Director: Dr. Geoffrey Orth, Honors Program, Longwood University, Farmville, Virginia 23909; *Telephone:* 434-395-2789, 434-395-2157; *E-mail:* honors@longwood.edu

Lynchburg College
Westover Honors Program
Lynchburg, Virginia

The Westover Honors Program offers exceptional undergraduates an alternative to the College's traditional general education curriculum. The honors curriculum makes heavy use of the seminar format and places strong emphasis on collaborative learning and problem solving. The multidisciplinary curriculum is designed to break down intellectual barriers and expose students to new ways of looking at old problems. The faculty members strive to build bridges across the curriculum in order to facilitate the integration of ideas from a variety of disciplines and to form a coherent body of knowledge.

Because of their maturity, self-discipline, and heightened intellectual ability, Westover Fellows take on a significant share of the responsibility for their own education. The seminar format requires high-quality student participation in the classroom and considerable preparation before class. Group projects, research papers, and oral presentations are required in most honors courses. As active members of a vital learning community, students and faculty members engage one another in open discussion as they explore new avenues of inquiry together. The program's maxim is "Question. Doubt. Challenge."

Recognizing that the sharing of ideas and potentially unpopular opinions is a risky endeavor, participants and leaders of the program make every effort to promote a classroom environment characterized by trust and mutual respect. A freshman orientation retreat allows incoming fellows to develop strong bonds before the academic year begins. A freshman seminar introduces students to basic principles of interpersonal communication, conflict resolution, critical thinking, and argumentation. Weekly lunches (attended by honors faculty members and students), freshman honors housing, membership in the Society of Westover Fellows, student representation on the program's advisory council, and a variety of social and educational activities all help to forge a true sense of community.

The program, established in 1987, seeks to admit 40 freshmen annually. There are approximately 100 students currently enrolled.

Participation Requirements: In their freshman year, fellows take 16 credits in honors (Advanced English Composition, Mathematics Seminar, Social Science Seminar, a two-semester Humanities Seminar, and the 1-credit Freshman Seminar), which constitute approximately half of their academic course load. Fellows take 12 credits of honors courses in their sophomore year and an additional 15 credits over the next two years. Examples of recent junior/senior colloquia include America in Vietnam, Manifestations of Anger in Contemporary Society, and Heroes as Persuasive Figures. All students must satisfy the College's foreign language and wellness requirements.

During the first two years in the program, students acquire and refine the essential skills and competencies needed to complete the required Senior Honors Project. This project, normally in the student's major concentration and guided by a faculty committee, culminates in a formal defense that is open to the entire Westover community.

To remain in the program, fellows must maintain both a semester and cumulative GPA of at least 3.0. Successful completion of the program is recognized at commencement, and the designation of Westover Honors Graduate is noted on the diploma.

Admission Process: To be eligible for participation as a freshman, students must have a combined SAT score of at least 1200 and a cumulative high school GPA of at least 3.5. Eligible students are invited to join the program upon their acceptance to the College. Others may contact the Director for special consideration of their qualifications. While most students enter the program as freshmen, some students are invited to enter as sophomores. Invitations are based on the student's freshman year academic performance, recommendations from faculty members, and a personal interview.

Scholarship Availability: Lynchburg College offers academic (merit) scholarships on the basis of high school GPA and SAT scores. For the 2002–03 academic year, scholarships for freshmen in the Westover ability group were $10,000. High school class valedictorians or salutatorians received an additional $2000. Students may qualify for additional aid based on need and other criteria.

Campus Overview

Independent comprehensive, founded 1903, affiliated with Christian Church (Disciples of Christ) • **Coed** 1,934 undergraduate students, 95% full-time, 59% women, 41% men.

Undergraduates 1,839 full-time, 95 part-time. Students come from 36 states and territories, 13 other countries, 36% are from out of state, 8% African American, 2% Asian American or Pacific Islander, 3% Hispanic American, 0.6% Native American, 0.7% international, 4% transferred in, 81% live on campus.

Faculty *Total:* 209, 64% full-time, 61% with terminal degrees. *Student/faculty ratio:* 13:1.

Academic Programs *Special study options:* accelerated degree program, adult/continuing education programs, advanced placement credit, double majors, honors programs, independent study, internships, off-campus study, part-time degree program, services for LD students, study abroad, summer session for credit. *Unusual degree programs:* 3-2 engineering with Old Dominion University, University of Virginia.

Athletics Member NCAA. All Division III. *Intercollegiate sports:* baseball M, basketball M/W, cheerleading M/W, cross-country running M/W, equestrian sports M/W, field hockey W, golf M, lacrosse M/W, soccer M/W, softball W, tennis M/W, track and field M/W, volleyball W. *Intramural sports:* badminton M/W, baseball M, basketball M/W, bowling M/W, equestrian sports M/W, football M, golf M, racquetball M/W, rugby M/W, soccer M/W, softball W, tennis M/W, track and field M/W, volleyball M/W.

Costs (2004–05) *Comprehensive fee:* $27,885 includes full-time tuition ($22,640), mandatory fees ($245), and room and board ($5000). Part-time tuition: $325 per credit hour. Part-time tuition and fees vary according to course load. *College room only:* $2900. Room and board charges vary according to board plan.

Financial Aid 479 Federal Work-Study jobs (averaging $1064). In 2004, 596 non-need-based awards were made. *Average percent of need met:* 87%. *Average financial aid package:* $16,994. *Average need-based loan:* $3459. *Average need-based gift aid:* $12,938. *Average non-need-based aid:* $7856.

Contact: Director: Dr. Edward DeClair, or Vice President for Enrollment Management: Ms. Rita Detwiler, 1501 Lakeside Drive, Lynchburg, Virginia 24501; *Telephone:* 434-544-8481; *E-mail:* seymann@lynchburg.edu; *Web site:* http://www.lynchburg.edu/westover/

Marymount University
Honors Program
Arlington, Virginia

The Honors Program at Marymount University draws on all facets of the curriculum to offer highly motivated students an enriched learning experience. The program is highly selective, and only 20 undergraduates are accepted each year in order to ensure an environment that supports animated classroom discussion and one-on-one faculty mentoring.

This year's honors class is made up of students pursuing a variety of academic disciplines. The curriculum requires at least 21 honors credits, beginning with an introductory seminar that examines how scholars from different disciplines strive for knowledge. The students then complete at least four honors courses adapted from the University's liberal arts core curriculum, and their course of study culminates with an honors thesis.

Marymount's Honors Program utilizes a research-based model that is consistent with the University's longtime emphasis on undergraduate research. In their junior year, honors students develop and propose original research projects in their specialized field of study under the guidance of a faculty member. In their senior year, the students conduct their research and then write, present, and defend their thesis. Students also have the opportunity to present their scholarly work at regional and national conferences, such as the annual National Conference on Undergraduate Research.

Benefits of the Honors Program include substantial scholarship support; one-on-one faculty mentoring; studies and activities that draw on the rich resources of Washington, D.C.; direct involvement in program governance; travel support for professional conferences; and special recognition at graduation and on diplomas and transcripts. Honors Program students also enjoy group outings to performances and exhibits and discussion dinners with faculty members and guest speakers. Each year, special opportunities are made available to honors students, as well. During the 2004 election campaign, for example, several traveled to Cleveland, Ohio, to watch the Vice Presidential Debate from the press center. They were also on hand for all the action in "Spin Alley," which followed the debate, thanks to Marymount Communications Professor Paul Byers, who was the official timekeeper for the Presidential and Vice Presidential Debates.

Honors students can gain an added sense of community by living on an academic floor, which offers extended quiet hours for study and special programs related to academic fields and interest. Very much a part of the greater Marymount community, honors students are active in clubs, student government, and athletics. They have also formed an honors organization that is open to everyone on campus who enjoys learning. Marymount and the Honors Program are dedicated to providing all students with the opportunity to expand their intellectual horizons, while gaining the knowledge and skills necessary for personal and professional success.

Participation Requirements: The Honors Program consists of seven specialized classes (21 credits), many of which satisfy the University's liberal arts core requirements. The required courses are an introductory freshman seminar, four intermediate honors courses, an honors thesis proposal, and the honors thesis.

Following the successful completion of the honors introductory seminar, the secondary honors courses (totaling at least 12 credits) may be fulfilled in special sections of liberal arts core classes. Students can also fulfill this requirement by arranging independent study, taking contract or graduate courses, or studying abroad. Upper-level classes relate to the honors thesis. Students develop a proposal and conduct original research in their specialized field of study under the guidance of a faculty member. They then write, present, and defend their thesis in the senior year. Honors Program students must maintain a minimum overall GPA of 3.5 and earn at least a B in all honors courses. The transcripts of students who successfully complete all program requirements have the designation Honors Scholar.

Admission Process: Marymount's Honors Program is for students who are seeking significant challenges and rewards. All current high school seniors and college freshmen are eligible to apply; students beyond freshman rank but currently in an honors program at another institution are also eligible to apply. Admission is competitive and limited to 20 students each year.

In addition to the University's general admission requirements, the following credentials are recommended for those seeking admission to the Honors Program: a high school or college GPA of at least 3.5 and a minimum combined (math and verbal) SAT score of 1200 or composite ACT score of 26. International students must present a TOEFL score of at least 617 on the paper-based test or 260 on the computer-based test. All materials, including an essay and additional letters of recommendation, should be submitted by February 1. Students should also apply for general admission before submitting their Honors Program application or concurrently with it.

Scholarship Availability: The University awards approximately $7 million annually in financial aid, including substantial academic scholarships. All Honors Program students are eligible for a Presidential Scholarship, as well as other academic and need-based aid. Combined academic scholarships cover most, if not all, tuition expenses.

Campus Overview

Independent comprehensive, founded 1950, affiliated with Roman Catholic Church • **Coed** 2,227 undergraduate students, 80% full-time, 74% women, 26% men.

Undergraduates 1,778 full-time, 449 part-time. Students come from 42 states and territories, 62 other countries, 42% are from out of state, 16% African American, 8% Asian American or Pacific Islander, 10% Hispanic American, 0.2% Native American, 8% international, 15% transferred in, 30% live on campus.

Faculty *Total:* 387, 33% full-time, 56% with terminal degrees. *Student/faculty ratio:* 13:1.

Academic Programs *Special study options:* academic remediation for entering students, advanced placement credit, double majors, English as a second language, honors programs, independent study, internships, off-campus study, part-time degree program, services for LD students, student-designed majors, study abroad, summer session for credit. *ROTC:* Army (c).

Athletics Member NCAA. All Division III. *Intercollegiate sports:* basketball M/W, cross-country running M/W, golf M, lacrosse M/W, soccer M/W, swimming and diving M/W, volleyball W. *Intramural sports:* basketball M/W, cheerleading W, football M/W, golf M, soccer M/W, softball M/W, swimming and diving M/W, volleyball M/W.

Costs (2004–05) *Comprehensive fee:* $24,610 includes full-time tuition ($16,952), mandatory fees ($138), and room and board ($7520). Part-time tuition: $549 per credit hour. *Required fees:* $6 per credit hour part-time.

Financial Aid 180 Federal Work-Study jobs (averaging $1763). In 2004, 298 non-need-based awards were made. *Average percent of need met:* 73%. *Average financial aid package:* $13,276. *Average need-based loan:* $3846. *Average need-based gift aid:* $6584. *Average non-need-based aid:* $7407.

Contact: Director: Dr. Scott Carnicom, Honors Program, Marymount University, 2807 North Glebe Road, Arlington, Virginia 22207; *Telephone:* 703-284-1665; *E-mail:* scott.carnicom@marymount.edu; *Web site:* http://www.marymount.edu/academic/honors/

Norfolk State University
Honors Program
Norfolk, Virginia

*T*he Honors Program, now in its second decade, offers an enriched and challenging program of study for full-time students who show exceptional academic potential. All students taking special Honors (H) courses are considered part of the program, which is open to all majors. Students completing 15 or 30 hours of honors courses receive special diplomas inscribed "Parsons Vice Presidential Scholar" and "Parsons Presidential Scholar," respectively.

Benefits of the program include the following: small enriched courses taught in-depth; the opportunity to work closely with top faculty members; seminars and lectures given by visiting scholars; opportunities to present original research at state, regional, and national collegiate honors council meetings; invitations to civic and cultural events, with opportunities to meet famous leaders and artists; recognition of work at the annual Honors Luncheon; a computer lab; and rewards in employment and graduate school.

Honors courses are generally taught seminar-style in the Parsons Honors Center. Most require more independent work from students and all offer participation in cocurricular and extracurricular trips and activities.

The program currently enrolls about 200 students.

Participation Requirements: Most honors courses are core curriculum offerings required for all majors (e.g., English 101 H). There are also major courses in specific departments (e.g., Accounting 201 H) and interdisciplinary seminars (e.g., GST 345/346 H and 445/446 H), with topics that change each semester. Students graduating as Parsons Vice Presidential Scholars (15 hours) or Parsons Presidential Scholars (30 hours) must take at least one such seminar and have a minimum 3.0 GPA upon graduation (with no grade lower than a C in an honors course and at least a 3.0 GPA for all honors courses taken). Parsons Presidential Scholars are also required to participate in community service for academic credit. Parsons Vice Presidential Scholar and Parsons Presidential Scholar are both diploma citations.

Admission Process: Students may be invited to enter the Honors Program in the following circumstances: upon admission as freshmen according to high school records (3.0 GPA minimum and at least 900 combined SAT I score) and other indicators of academic proficiency (these students are expected to complete the 30-hour sequence of courses and required seminars) or as sophomores, juniors, or seniors having achieved a 3.5 or above GPA for all courses completed in the curriculum (or 3.0 by permission of the instructor).

Scholarship Availability: The Honors Program currently offers $250 per semester to eligible students. Students who participate in the program also have an advantage in competing for regular University scholarships. Students accepting Presidential Scholarships or Board of Visitor Scholarships from the University are required to participate in the Honors Program. For complete information, students should contact the Financial Aid Office directly.

Campus Overview

State-supported comprehensive, founded 1935, part of State Council of Higher Education for Virginia • **Urban** 134-acre campus • **Coed**

Faculty *Student/faculty ratio:* 17:1.

Athletics Member NCAA. All Division I except football (Division I-AA).

Costs (2004–05) *Tuition:* state resident $2220 full-time, $74 per credit hour part-time; nonresident $12,180 full-time, $406 per credit hour part-time. Full-time tuition and fees vary according to course load. Part-time tuition and fees vary according to course load. *Required fees:* $2075 full-time, $116 per credit hour part-time. *Room and board:* $6236; room only: $3942. Room and board charges vary according to board plan.

Financial Aid *Average percent of need met:* 87. *Average financial aid package:* $8884. *Average need-based loan:* $3977. *Average need-based gift aid:* $5020.

Contact: Director: Dr. Page R. Laws, 700 Park Avenue, Norfolk, Virginia 23504; *Telephone:* 757-823-8208, 757-823-2303; *Fax:* 757-823-2302; *E-mail:* honors@nsu.edu; *Web site:* http://www.nsu.edu/honors/

Old Dominion University
Honors College
Norfolk, Virginia

Established in 1986, the Academic Honors Program was renamed the Honors College in 1996. It administers the Undergraduate Research Program, the award-winning President's Lecture Series, degrees with honors for the academic departments, and a program of study for honors students. This four-year program offers specially designed, low-enrollment courses exclusively to honors students. In the first two years, the majority of these courses is used to fulfill the University's lower division General Education requirements. To complete the course of study in the Honors College, students must take a minimum of six general education honors courses, two upper-division courses as honors, a junior tutorial, and a senior colloquium. Academic degrees are earned in any of the six colleges of the University.

With an emphasis on teaching, innovation, and small classes, the Honors College offers the experience of a small liberal arts college within the framework of a large university. After four years of such an experience, students are better equipped to structure their lives and careers to meet their individual needs and strengths. A program that offers the best of both a small college and a large university naturally promotes greater sensitivity to self and society.

There are approximately 550 students in the Honors College.

Participation Requirements: Currently enrolled students and transfer students who have completed their lower-division general education requirements may participate in the honors experience by taking upper-division courses as honors (open to any student with a GPA of 3.25), earning a degree with honors in their major, or competing for a $1000 undergraduate research grant (open to all juniors and seniors with minimum GPAs of 3.4). Students must maintain an overall GPA of 3.25. Each spring at the Honors College awards banquet, graduates receive a certificate, a medal to wear on their gown, and a silver tassel for their mortar board. Their names are listed separately in the graduation program, and note of their accomplishment is made on their student transcripts.

Admission Process: Criteria used to select the 150 first-year students admitted annually include high school GPA and curriculum, SAT scores, class rank, and a written personal statement. Other students are admitted on the basis of a 3.5 college GPA, completion of at least four remaining general education courses as honors courses, and two letters of recommendation from University faculty members.

Scholarship Availability: All Honors College students receive an annual $500 stipend. The College also has an endowed scholarship, the Cranmer/Skinner Scholarship, which provides two awards each year. The Brock Foundation Honors Scholarship funds an additional 2 honors students each year. Students who opt for the dual-degree program between the College of Arts and Letters and the College of Engineering and Technology are eligible to apply for the endowed Sumitoma Scholarship. This scholarship also requires that the student study Japanese and do an internship at the Sumitoma Corporation in Japan (expenses paid).

Campus Overview

State-supported university, founded 1930 • **Coed** 14,417 undergraduate students, 71% full-time, 58% women, 42% men.

Undergraduates 10,235 full-time, 4,182 part-time. Students come from 37 states and territories, 79 other countries, 7% are from out of state, 23% African American, 6% Asian American or Pacific Islander, 3% Hispanic American, 0.7% Native American, 2% international, 11% transferred in, 24% live on campus.

Faculty *Total:* 900, 67% full-time, 54% with terminal degrees. *Student/faculty ratio:* 17:1.

Academic Programs *Special study options:* accelerated degree program, adult/continuing education programs, advanced placement credit, cooperative education, distance learning, double majors, English as a second language, freshman honors college, honors programs, independent study, internships, off-campus study, part-time degree program, services for LD students, student-designed majors, study abroad, summer session for credit. *ROTC:* Army (b), Navy (b). *Unusual degree programs:* 3-2 international studies, dental hygiene, communications/humanities, English, English/applied linguistics, history, interdisciplinary studies/humanities, health science/community health, biology, chemistry, geology, oceanography, history, women's studies.

Athletics Member NCAA. All Division I. *Intercollegiate sports:* baseball M(s), basketball M(s)/W(s), cheerleading M(s)/W(s), crew M(c)/W(c), fencing M(c)/W(c), field hockey M(c)/W(s)(c), golf M(s)/W, lacrosse M(c)/W(s), rugby M(c)/W(c), sailing M/W, soccer M(s)(c)/W(s), softball W(c), swimming and diving M(s)/W(s), tennis M(s)/W(s), volleyball M(c)/W(c), wrestling M(s). *Intramural sports:* badminton M/W, basketball M/W, bowling M/W, cross-country running M/W, golf M/W, sailing M, soccer M/W, softball M/W, swimming and diving M/W, table tennis M/W, tennis M/W, ultimate Frisbee M/W, volleyball M/W, water polo M/W, wrestling M/W.

Costs (2004–05) *Tuition:* state resident $5100 full-time, $170 per credit hour part-time; nonresident $14,520 full-time, $484 per credit hour part-time. Full-time tuition and fees vary according to course level, course load, and location. Part-time tuition and fees vary according to course level, course load, and location. *Required fees:* $168 full-time, $84 per term part-time. *Room and board:* $5802; room only: $3342. Room and board charges vary according to board plan and housing facility.

Financial Aid In 2004, 458 non-need-based awards were made. *Average percent of need met:* 69%. *Average financial aid package:* $6313. *Average need-based loan:* $3721. *Average need-based gift aid:* $3676. *Average non-need-based aid:* $3296.

Contact: Dean: Dr. Louis H. Henry, 218 Education Building, Norfolk, Virginia 23529-0076; *Telephone:* 757-683-4865; *Fax:* 757-683-4970; *E-mail:* lhhenry@odu.edu; *Web site:* http://www.odu.edu/ao/honors

Radford University
Honors Academy
Radford, Virginia

*T*he Honors Academy provides academic enrichment opportunities for talented students and recognizes outstanding student achievement. The Academy includes the honors curriculum and a residential component, Floyd Hall, which has been designated as the honors living and learning community. As a designated Center of Excellence, the Honors Academy is a focal point for the promotion and recognition of academic excellence at Radford University (RU), and it provides a stimulating academic environment and intellectual challenges for students and faculty members. Campus projects sponsored by the Honors Academy include the campus College Bowl tournament, the Undergraduate/Graduate Forum, the Senior Academic Recognition Banquet for members of academic honor fraternities and leadership organizations, and the Highlander Academy, a summer academic enrichment experience for middle and high school students that also provides leadership experience for Honors Academy members, who serve as teaching assistants.

Through participation in the Honors Academy, students can customize and enhance their undergraduate experience as they interact with peers who are motivated to achieve academic excellence and with faculty members whose professional passions are teaching and learning. Honors Academy members who fulfill an Honors Plan of Study (HPS) and maintain required GPAs are designated as

Highlander Scholars. New Highlander Scholars are inducted and graduating Highlander Scholars are recognized at the Spring Honors Banquet every April. Highlander Scholars complete honors course work in three areas: general education honors-designated courses, their academic major, and a capstone project that they present at the RU Undergraduate/Graduate Forum. General education honors-designated courses emphasize the development of critical-thinking skills, as well as excellence in written and oral communication, and have 20 or fewer students enrolled. These courses are enhanced with interactive, seminar-style teaching; field trips; guest speakers; and enrichment assignments that allow students to take more responsibility for their own learning.

Honors courses in a major are accomplished through an honors contract and mentoring with a faculty member. The honors contract customizes a course based on the specific interests and academic aspirations of the student. Highlander Scholars accomplish a senior capstone project with the supervision of a faculty adviser. Examples of capstone projects include original laboratory research, a thesis, a portfolio of creative works, international travel, an internship, student teaching, and a clinical experience. The Honors Academy Student Organization is the social component for Honors Academy members, and it provides opportunities for leadership as well as campus and community service.

The Radford University Honors Academy is affiliated with the National Collegiate Honors Council (NCHC), the Southern Regional Honors Council (SRHC), and the Virginia Collegiate Honors Council (VCHC). These affiliations allow Highlander Scholars the opportunity to participate in conferences and events with other honors students from across the United States.

The Honors Program at Radford University was founded in 1980, and the transition to the Honors Academy was completed in 1998. Currently there are 264 Honors Academy members; 111 of them have earned the coveted title of Highlander Scholar. More information about the Radford University Honors Academy is available at the Web site at http://www.radford.edu/~honors.

Participation Requirements: The following minimum GPAs are required for Honors Academy membership: 3.0 for freshman class standing, 3.3 for sophomore class standing, 3.4 for junior class standing, and 3.5 for senior class standing. To retain membership in the program, Highlander Scholars must continue to meet these GPA eligibility requirements and make progress toward completing their HPS.

To graduate from the Honors Academy as a Highlander Scholar, students must have a minimum 3.5 overall GPA and complete at least 27 hours of honors course work from the following three areas in accordance with their HPS: 6–12 hours of general education honors-designated courses, 12–15 hours of honors courses in the academic major or related courses, and 3–6 hours in a capstone project. All Highlander Scholars are required to present the results of their capstone project at the Undergraduate/Graduate Forum. Highlander Scholars who fulfill all requirements necessary to graduate from the Honors Academy are awarded a certificate and a Distinctive Honors stole at the Spring Honors Banquet and are recognized in the Honors Academy newsletter and by the University President at the commencement ceremony.

Admission Process: High school students who possess two of the following three credentials are invited to join the Honors Academy at the time they are admitted to Radford University: SAT scores of 1100 or above or an ACT score of 24 or above, a high school GPA of 3.5 or above, and a rank in the top 20 percent of their graduating class.

Highlander Scholars are members of the Honors Academy who have an approved HPS, which is the agreement that outlines how the student will satisfy the curriculum requirements of the Honors Academy. Students who were not invited into the Honors Academy as entering students are invited to join and may apply to become Highlander Scholars after they have completed at least one semester at Radford University and meet the eligibility requirements.

Scholarship Availability: The Radford University Foundation awards full and partial Presidential Scholarships to new students based on high school credentials, an application process, and competitive interviews held during the spring. Recipients of these scholarships are invited to join the Honors Academy. The RU Foundation also awards approximately 400 partial scholarships to students enrolled at Radford University based on an application process during the spring. The Honors Academy office nominates all interested and qualified Honors Academy members for prestigious national scholarships and awards, such as the Rhodes, British Marshall, Goldwater, and Truman Scholarships, and mentors those nominees through the application process.

Campus Overview

State-supported comprehensive, founded 1910 • **Coed** 8,356 undergraduate students, 94% full-time, 59% women, 41% men.

Undergraduates 7,870 full-time, 486 part-time. Students come from 39 states and territories, 43 other countries, 8% are from out of state, 6% African American, 2% Asian American or Pacific Islander, 2% Hispanic American, 0.2% Native American, 0.7% international, 9% transferred in, 39% live on campus.

Faculty *Total:* 533, 67% full-time. *Student/faculty ratio:* 21:1.

Academic Programs *Special study options:* accelerated degree program, adult/continuing education programs, advanced placement credit, distance learning, double majors, English as a second language, honors programs, independent study, internships, off-campus study, part-time degree program, services for LD students, student-designed majors, study abroad, summer session for credit. *ROTC:* Army (b), Navy (c).

Athletics Member NCAA. All Division I. *Intercollegiate sports:* baseball M(s), basketball M(s)/W(s), cross-country running M(s)/W(s), field hockey W(s), golf M(s)/W(s), soccer M(s)/W(s), softball W(s), swimming and diving W(s), tennis M(s)/W(s), track and field M(s)/W(s), volleyball W(s). *Intramural sports:* basketball M/W, bowling M/W, cross-country running M/W, equestrian sports W(c), football M/W, ice hockey M(c), racquetball M/W, rock climbing M/W, rugby M(c)/W(c), skiing (downhill) M(c)/W(c), soccer M/W, softball M/W, tennis M/W, ultimate Frisbee M(c), volleyball M/W, weight lifting M/W, wrestling M/W.

Costs (2004–05) *Tuition:* state resident $4762 full-time, $198 per credit hour part-time; nonresident $11,762 full-time, $490 per credit hour part-time. *Room and board:* $5886; room only: $3154. Room and board charges vary according to board plan and housing facility.

Financial Aid 518 Federal Work-Study jobs (averaging $1086). 600 state and other part-time jobs (averaging $1097). In 2003, 1763 non-need-based awards were made. *Average percent of need met:* 73%. *Average financial aid package:* $7736. *Average need-based loan:* $3257. *Average need-based gift aid:* $3717. *Average non-need-based aid:* $5566.

Contact: Director: Joseph King, Honors Academy, Box 6971, Radford, Virginia 24142; *Telephone:* 540-831-6125; *Fax:* 540-831-5004; *E-mail:* honors@radford.edu; *Web site:* http://www.radford.edu/~honors. Individuals with disabilities needing accommodation should call 540-831-5128 or 540-831-6125 (voice).

Roanoke College

Honors Program

Salem, Virginia

The Roanoke College Honors Program provides distinctive educational opportunities and challenges for students who possess a strong academic background, broad extracurricular interests, and leadership abilities. Superior faculty members, engaged students, and outstanding curricular and cocurricular programs all contribute to an environment in which students can realize their full personal, moral, and intellectual potential. The program also encourages service to the community and active involvement in the life of the College.

The honors curriculum consists of a sequence of dynamic interdisciplinary courses that substitute for the College's general studies requirements throughout the four years. Students begin with a freshman seminar that provides a foundation in critical thinking and written and oral communication. As sophomores, they take a two-semester sequence that focuses on the central themes and issues in human civilization. Juniors select from topical courses in the humanities, sciences, and social sciences that emphasize diverse cultures and perspectives. Seniors bring all the fields of study to focus on selected contemporary issues in a capstone course. Students also work closely with one or more faculty members to complete an honors project, usually a research project or artistic creation related to their major field of study.

The outside of class and service components of the Honors Program are as enriching as the curriculum. Through the Plenary Enrichment Program (PEP), students attend a range of events, such as plays, concerts, operas, films, lectures, and discussions, both on and off campus. Students also participate in service activities each semester, donating time and energy to the campus and local communities. These events give students a broader view of intellectual life outside the classroom and provide wonderful opportunities for discussions and thought. An annual reflective paper completes the PEP requirement.

Participation Requirements: To graduate with the Honors Program designation, students must complete the honors curriculum and an honors project; complete distribution requirements in mathematics, foreign language, and the social, physical, and life sciences; and participate in the Plenary Enrichment Program each semester they are studying on campus. Students may major in any discipline and participate in the Honors Program but must maintain at least a 3.2 cumulative GPA to remain in the program and to graduate with the honors designation. Successful completion of the program is recognized at commencement and is noted on the diploma.

Admission Process: Most students enter the Honors Program as freshmen, and students should apply to the program when applying for admission to the College. Applications are considered on the basis of academic performance, extracurricular interests, and leadership abilities as evidenced by high school grades and course work, class rank, SAT or ACT scores, extracurricular activities, and responses to questions on the application form. Letters of recommendation and a personal interview are recommended. The application deadline is March 15.

It is also possible to enter the Honors Program at the beginning of the sophomore year; transfer students who will be entering their sophomore year are encouraged to apply.

Scholarship Availability: Honors students receive a Davis Honors Scholarship of $2000 each year they participate in the program. The Davis Honors Scholarship is in addition to other aid or scholarships they may receive.

Campus Overview

Independent 4-year, founded 1842, affiliated with Evangelical Lutheran Church in America • **Coed** 1,850 undergraduate students, 94% full-time, 58% women, 42% men.

Undergraduates 1,742 full-time, 108 part-time. Students come from 40 states and territories, 25 other countries, 40% are from out of state, 4% African American, 2% Asian American or Pacific Islander, 2% Hispanic American, 0.6% Native American, 1% international, 4% transferred in, 60% live on campus.

Faculty *Total:* 168, 74% full-time, 71% with terminal degrees. *Student/faculty ratio:* 14:1.

Academic Programs *Special study options:* accelerated degree program, adult/continuing education programs, advanced placement credit, double majors, English as a second language, honors programs, independent study, internships, off-campus study, part-time degree program, services for LD students, study abroad, summer session for credit. *Unusual degree programs:* 3-2 engineering with Washington University in St. Louis, Virginia Polytechnic Institute and State University, University of Tennessee–Knoxville.

Athletics Member NCAA. All Division III. *Intercollegiate sports:* baseball M, basketball M/W, cross-country running M/W, field hockey W, golf M/W(c), ice hockey M(c), lacrosse M/W, soccer M/W, softball W, tennis M/W, track and field M/W, volleyball M(c)/W. *Intramural sports:* badminton M/W, basketball M/W, cheerleading M/W, field hockey W, football M/W, ice hockey M, lacrosse M, racquetball M/W, soccer M/W, softball M/W, table tennis M/W, tennis M/W, volleyball M/W, water polo M/W.

Costs (2004–05) *Comprehensive fee:* $29,021 includes full-time tuition ($21,504), mandatory fees ($605), and room and board ($6912). Part-time tuition: $1020 per course. *College room only:* $3350. Room and board charges vary according to housing facility.

Financial Aid 620 Federal Work-Study jobs (averaging $1409). In 2003, 412 non-need-based awards were made. *Average percent of need met:* 88%. *Average financial aid package:* $18,394. *Average need-based loan:* $4307. *Average need-based gift aid:* $14,459. *Average non-need-based aid:* $9187.

Contact: Admissions; *Telephone:* 540-375-2270; *Fax:* 540-375-2267; *E-mail:* admissions@roanoke.edu; *Web site:* http://www.roanoke.edu

Sweet Briar College
Honors Program
Sweet Briar, Virginia

The Sweet Briar College Honors Program is dedicated to enriching the intellectual life of the entire College community and to providing integrated and interdisciplinary experiences that enhance students' creative and critical-thinking abilities. It offers recognition to those students who perform academically on an honors level but also encourages all students to participate in honors activities. The Honors Program seeks to synthesize curricular and cocurricular activities, to create a sense of community in academic endeavors, and to emphasize the connections between disciplines and departments. The Honors Program, through honors seminars, honors variants and sections, honors colloquiums, and other activities and events, provides a space in which academically excellent students can meet, share ideas, interact with faculty members, and contribute to the intellectual life of the College.

Each year, faculty members design new courses for the Honors Program. These courses are usually interdisciplinary and frequently team taught. In honors seminars, students examine a topic from a wide range of perspectives and take responsibility for presentations and discussions in class. Honors seminars emphasize the development of critical-thinking abilities.

Honors variants challenge students by encouraging greater rigor, depth, and breadth in their studies. At the student's request, an honors variant may be added to a regularly offered course. Honors variants allow students to undertake different kinds of work in a tutorial setting. Departments may offer a special section of a regularly offered course as an honors section.

The Senior Honors Thesis Project provides the honors student with the opportunity to design and complete a long-term research project in her major department. The thesis project consists of 3 credit hours of independent study completed prior to the start of the senior year and 6 credit hours of independent-study course work in the student's major department during the fall and spring semester of the senior year. The thesis project is the culmination of an honors course of study at Sweet Briar.

Honors colloquiums are scheduled every other week during the fall and spring semesters, and they feature faculty members, and occasionally students, presenting on topics of current interest and

discussing their research interests and findings. Noted scholars and speakers are also invited to campus throughout the year to participate in the colloquiums.

Students may participate in many honors activities and take advantage of program opportunities. The Honors Journal, published online, features works of a high caliber produced by students. Honors-on-the-Road (HOTR) organizes off-campus day trips to plays, festivals, and nearby cultural events and an annual bus trip to Washington, D.C. The Honors Lunch Table meets once a week. Honors students and faculty members meet for lunch in the dining hall to discuss current topics of interest and academic issues and to plan for upcoming honors events.

The Sweet Briar College Honors Program was established in 1989. This year, approximately 60 students are active in the program.

Participation Requirements: Students in the Honors Program should complete one honors course per year and participate in honors-sponsored cocurricular activities. Students who plan to graduate with an honors degree must take six honors courses, at least three of which are honors seminars, and successfully complete the Senior Honors Thesis Project. Students who would like to graduate with departmental honors must successfully complete the Senior Honors Thesis Project.

The award of the honors degree is noted on both the student's transcript and diploma. The honors degree has four major requirements: successful completion of the honors thesis; successful completion of at least six honors courses, in which at least three must be honors seminars with the grade achieved no less than a B; a GPA of 3.3 or higher in the major department at graduation; and a cumulative GPA of 3.0 or higher at graduation.

In order to receive departmental honors at graduation, a student must successfully complete 9 credits of honors work in her major department and produce an appropriate thesis or project as approved by the major department and the Honors Committee.

Admission Process: First-year students holding the top merit awards offered by Sweet Briar to incoming students are invited to join the program. These include the Commonwealth, Founders, Prothro, Betty Bean Black, and selected Sweet Briar Scholars awards. Other entering students showing academic promise based on their high school record may also be invited into the program. Matriculating students are evaluated at the end of each term. Those with a GPA of 3.3 or higher are considered honors students and are invited to participate fully in the Honors Program, although all students are encouraged to take advantage of the opportunities offered by the Honors Program.

Scholarship Availability: Honors scholarships recognize excellence in academic work and contributions to College and community life by Sweet Briar's most motivated and highest-achieving students. Recipients are selected each spring from the freshman, sophomore, and junior classes. A student may receive up to $7000 toward tuition and a book shop credit. Eligible students are notified and invited to apply. Selection is made based on academic performance, breadth of study, faculty recommendations, and GPA.

Each year, the Honors Program awards fellowships to enable undergraduates to conduct independent research projects under the supervision of a faculty sponsor in the Honors Summer Research Program. The Honors Program has Honors Student Travel Grants available for students for academic travel and research expenses.

Campus Overview

Independent 4-year, founded 1901 • **Rural** 3250-acre campus • **Women only** 728 undergraduate students, 94% full-time.

Undergraduates 682 full-time, 46 part-time. Students come from 44 states and territories, 14 other countries, 53% are from out of state, 2% African American, 2% Asian American or Pacific Islander, 2% Hispanic American, 0.4% Native American, 3% international, 2% transferred in, 90% live on campus.

Faculty *Total:* 105, 66% full-time, 79% with terminal degrees. *Student/faculty ratio:* 7:1.

Academic Programs *Special study options:* accelerated degree program, adult/continuing education programs, advanced placement credit, double majors, honors programs, independent study, internships, off-campus study, part-time degree program, services for LD students, student-designed majors, study abroad, summer session for credit. *Unusual degree programs:* 3-2 engineering with Virginia Polytechnic Institute and State University, University of Virginia, Columbia University, Washington University in St. Louis.

Athletics Member NCAA. All Division III. *Intercollegiate sports:* equestrian sports W(c), fencing W(c), field hockey W, lacrosse W, soccer W, softball W(c), swimming and diving W, tennis W, volleyball W.

Costs (2005–06) *Comprehensive fee:* $31,460 includes full-time tuition ($22,230), mandatory fees ($200), and room and board ($9030). Full-time tuition and fees vary according to program. Part-time tuition: $740 per credit hour. Part-time tuition and fees vary according to program. *College room only:* $3630.

Financial Aid 67 Federal Work-Study jobs (averaging $929). *Average percent of need met:* 92%. *Average financial aid package:* $14,878. *Average need-based loan:* $4961. *Average need-based gift aid:* $13,088. *Average non-need-based aid:* $10,040.

Contact: Director: Dr. Cathy Gutierrez, Associate Dean of Academic Affairs and Assistant Professor of Religion, Sweet Briar College, Sweet Briar, Virginia 24595; *Telephone:* 434-381-6206; *E-mail:* cgutierrez@sbc.edu; *Web site:* http://www.honors.sbc.edu

Virginia Commonwealth University

Honors Program

Richmond, Virginia

The Virginia Commonwealth University (VCU) Honors Program is designed to meet the needs of academically talented undergraduate students through a challenging and exciting program with high academic standards. The University Honors Program offers students an opportunity to exchange ideas, ask questions, participate in research, and explore values with fellow students and teachers who have been carefully selected for their scholarship and teaching excellence. The University Honors Program offers the opportunity for students to expand their creative and intellectual horizons and to benefit from small classes in which there is greater interaction between students and faculty members and among students themselves. Some honors courses are special sections of regular classes open only to honors students. Class size is limited (usually to 20 or fewer students) to maximize student participation and interaction with the instructor. In these special sections, subjects are discussed in-depth, and discussions often continue after class.

Other courses are unique to the Honors Program. Of particular interest among these are the modules. These are single-focus courses that occupy only one third of a semester. The modules are often interdisciplinary and strive to connect the student's studies. Honors students receive personal and careful advising from both the Honors Program faculty and faculty members in their major field of study. This allows them to devise courses of study that meet academic requirements while allowing for the development of individual educational objectives.

Honors students, while benefiting from their association with a smaller unit within the University, also have the benefit of the resources of a major research university. Virginia Commonwealth University is located on two Richmond campuses: the Academic Campus and the Medical College of Virginia Campus. The University offers a wide range of academic opportunities and is committed to its mission of excellence in teaching as well as to the expansion of knowledge through research.

The Honors Program offers a variety of intellectual, cultural, and social activities as important supplements to classroom study. Among these are weekly brown bag lunches, honors seminars, an outstanding lecturer series, and the Honors Idea Exchange, which is a registered student campus organization composed of honors students. The center of activities and community for the University Honors Program is the Honors Center at West Grace Street. In the center, students have meeting rooms, quiet study rooms, a computer laboratory, a copy machine, and recreation areas. The Honors Center is open during the day and at night for study. In addition, many honors students are housed in the building containing the Honors Center, and some of the classes are also conducted there.

The Honors Program is committed to enriching the student's academic and personal endeavors. Since those in the Honors Program are serious students, special privileges are provided beyond the vast resources available to all VCU students. These privileges include access to early registration the week before the rest of the student body, graduate student library privileges, and honors housing in specific wings of the residence halls. Guaranteed admission programs with professional-level health sciences programs and graduate programs in basic health sciences, business, education, and others represent other opportunities for qualified honors students.

The Honors Program at Virginia Commonwealth University began in 1983 and has grown over the years to currently serve more than 1,600 students.

Participation Requirements: Successful completion of the Honors Program leads to graduation with University Honors, an accomplishment that is documented on official transcripts and diplomas. Graduation requirements for completing the Honors Program differ according to school or major. In addition to completing at least six module courses and maintaining a minimum cumulative GPA of 3.5 and a minimum 3.2 GPA in honors courses, honors students present a dossier documenting how they have met the University's expectations for an honors education.

Admission Process: The Honors Program is open to entering freshmen with SAT scores of 1270 or higher who rank in the upper 15 percent of their graduating class and to transfer students and continuing students with an overall GPA of 3.5 or higher with 30 college semester hours. Students may also be admitted on an individual basis with evidence of sufficient personal commitment to do honors-level work.

Scholarship Availability: In addition to a significant number of merit-based scholarships awarded by the University, the Honors Program recognizes continuing VCU students who demonstrate academic achievement in the Honors Program with approximately $60,000 in scholarship aid. Honors Program Scholarships are awarded by the Honor Council, an advisory board to the Honors Program. Honors Program scholarships worth $500–$2500 are open to continuing honors students in all majors.

Campus Overview

State-supported university, founded 1838 • **Coed** 19,180 undergraduate students, 79% full-time, 60% women, 40% men.

Undergraduates 15,100 full-time, 4,080 part-time. Students come from 48 states and territories, 75 other countries, 20% African American, 9% Asian American or Pacific Islander, 3% Hispanic American, 0.6% Native American, 2% international, 10% transferred in, 22% live on campus.

Faculty *Total:* 2,147, 55% full-time. *Student/faculty ratio:* 14:1.

Academic Programs *Special study options:* academic remediation for entering students, accelerated degree program, adult/continuing education programs, advanced placement credit, cooperative education, distance learning, double majors, English as a second language, honors programs, independent study, internships, off-campus study, part-time degree program, services for LD students, student-designed majors, study abroad, summer session for credit. *ROTC:* Army (c).

Athletics Member NCAA. All Division I. *Intercollegiate sports:* baseball M(s), basketball M(s)/W(s), cross-country running M(s)/W(s), field hockey W(s), golf M(s), soccer M(s)/W(s), tennis M(s)/W(s), track and field M(s)/W(s). *Intramural sports:* basketball M/W, cheerleading M/W, fencing M(c)/W(c), golf M(c)/W(c), ice hockey M(c), lacrosse M(c)/W(c), rugby M(c)/W(c), soccer M(c), table tennis M/W, tennis M(c)/W(c), ultimate Frisbee M(c)/W(c), volleyball W(c).

Costs (2005–06) *Tuition:* state resident $3969 full-time, $165 per credit part-time; nonresident $16,732 full-time, $668 per credit part-time. *Required fees:* $1416 full-time, $52 per credit part-time. *Room and board:* $7042; room only: $4102. Room and board charges vary according to board plan.

Financial Aid 936 Federal Work-Study jobs (averaging $1816). In 2003, 822 non-need-based awards were made. *Average percent of need met:* 51%. *Average financial aid package:* $7172. *Average need-based loan:* $3834. *Average need-based gift aid:* $3508. *Average non-need-based aid:* $4156.

Contact: Director: Dr. Timothy L. Hulsey, 701 West Grace Street, P.O. Box 843010, Richmond, Virginia 23284-3010; *Telephone:* 804-828-1803; *Fax:* 804-827-1669; *E-mail:* tlhulsey@vcu.edu; *Web site:* http://www.pubinfo.vcu.edu/honorsprogram

---

Virginia Military Institute
Institute Honors Program
Lexington, Virginia

The Institute Honors Program exists primarily to enrich the academic experience of Virginia Military Institute's (VMI) most outstanding cadets through activities that encourage an affinity for intellectual inquiry and develop the capacity for sophisticated engagement of issues and problems, whether ethical, civic, or professional. In all of its elements, the program stresses peer leadership, strong oral and written communication skills, and the highest standards of academic integrity and excellence.

While several of VMI's academic departments offer programs leading to honors in the major, the Institute Honors Program is intended to recognize a broader range of achievement than honors earned in any particular major. Attainment of Institute Honors is viewed as the highest academic achievement at VMI.

Cadets who are admitted to the program participate each semester in an Honors Forum, where a faculty moderator encourages serious conversation about current events and issues of significance. Sections of the forum meet weekly, and students are provided with free subscriptions to major newspapers and periodicals (e.g., the Economist*) to stimulate discussion.*

Typically offered at the sophomore and junior levels, specially designated honors courses present the opportunity for cadets to broaden their academic and intellectual horizons across the disciplines. These courses are taught as seminars, with much emphasis on student participation. Enrollment is strictly limited, allowing ample time for individual attention from the professor in tutorials, which are required in addition to regular class meetings. Several honors courses are offered each semester on topics such as literature and politics in German history; environmental myth, ethics, and justice; chemistry in a cultural context; Africa in modern times; and Paris, a course that included a class field trip to the city during break.

The crowning achievement of the Institute Honors candidate at VMI is the completion of a senior honors project or thesis under the supervision of a faculty member in the major department. The senior honors project/thesis concludes with a public presentation by the cadet, *open to faculty members and other students as well as interested members of the college community. A copy of the final document is bound and shelved in a special section of the VMI library.*

Participants in the Institute Honors Program are viewed as prime candidates and receive a regular flow of information, encouragement, and assistance in applying for prestigious national awards such as the Rhodes, Marshall, Fulbright, and Goldwater Scholarships. In addition, they are eligible for many special local resources, opportunities, and awards. An ample fund is available to encourage individuals or groups of cadets in the program to plan special projects, trips, and guest speakers. Grants to support research for the senior project/thesis are available through VMI's progressive and well-endowed Undergraduate Research Initiative. Several prizes are given for outstanding papers and other work produced in honors courses.

Each semester, honors cadets are invited to participate in events organized especially for them. In 2004–05, for example, they met in small seminars with Nobel laureate Elie Wiesel, legal scholar Martha Nussbaum, and cultural critic Elaine Scarry when these distinguished guests visited the campus. In addition to the opportunities available at VMI, cadets in the program benefit from programs offered by a close neighbor Washington and Lee University and other nearby institutions such as the University of Virginia and James Madison University as well as from Lexington's proximity to major cities like Richmond and Washington, DC.

Participation Requirements: Honors cadets must participate in a section of the Honors Forum each semester they are enrolled at VMI and are in the program. The program also requires two honors courses. To provide broad exposure to the disciplines, one course is required in each of two academic groups: Engineering/Science and Liberal Arts/Leadership. The final requirement is a senior project/thesis, completed under the direction of a faculty mentor and concluding with a public presentation of that project. Cadets must maintain a cumulative GPA of 3.5 or better in order to remain in the program. Institute Honors Scholars lead the processional at commencement and are presented with a personalized certificate accompanying their diplomas. Attainment of Institute Honors is registered on the official VMI transcript.

Admission Process: Admission is guaranteed for all Institute Scholars. On a rolling basis, the program is open by application to other matriculating freshmen whose high school records suggest strong academic potential; those who end the freshman year with a minimum cumulative GPA of 3.5; and others who meet the minimum GPA requirement and who can demonstrate the ability to meet all of the program requirements in a timely, reasonable manner. Applications for admission to the program are evaluated by the Institute Honors Review Committee.

Scholarship Availability: Through the Admissions Office, VMI offers approximately twenty generous academic Institute Scholarships annually to outstanding entering cadets, including a number of full scholarships. Financial need is not a criterion for selection. Institute Scholars are automatically admitted to the Institute Honors Program.

Campus Overview

State-supported 4-year, founded 1839 • **Small-town** 134-acre campus • **Coed primarily men** 1,362 undergraduate students, 100% full-time, 6% women, 94% men.

Undergraduates 1,362 full-time. Students come from 45 states and territories, 17 other countries, 48% are from out of state, 5% African American, 3% Asian American or Pacific Islander, 3% Hispanic American, 0.4% Native American, 2% international, 2% transferred in, 100% live on campus.

Faculty *Total:* 151, 73% full-time, 79% with terminal degrees. *Student/faculty ratio:* 11:1.

Academic Programs *Special study options:* accelerated degree program, advanced placement credit, double majors, honors programs, independent study, internships, services for LD students, study abroad, summer session for credit. *ROTC:* Army (b), Navy (b), Air Force (b).

Athletics Member NCAA. All Division I except football (Division I-AA). *Intercollegiate sports:* baseball M(s), basketball M(s), cross-country running M(s)/W(s), fencing M(c)/W(c), golf M(s), ice hockey M(c), lacrosse M(s), racquetball M(c)/W(c), riflery M(s)/W(s), rugby M(c)/W(c), soccer M(s), swimming and diving M(s)/W, tennis M(s), track and field M(s)/W(s), volleyball M(c)/W(c), water polo M(c)/W(c), weight lifting M(c)/W(c), wrestling M(s). *Intramural sports:* basketball M/W, football M/W, soccer M/W, softball M/W.

Costs (2004–05) *One-time required fee:* $1525. *Tuition:* state resident $4050 full-time; nonresident $17,512 full-time. *Required fees:* $2479 full-time. *Room and board:* $5474.

Financial Aid 56 Federal Work-Study jobs (averaging $883). In 2003, 250 non-need-based awards were made. *Average percent of need met:* 93%. *Average financial aid package:* $12,502. *Average need-based loan:* $3619. *Average need-based gift aid:* $7661. *Average non-need-based aid:* $6421.

Contact: Dr. Robert L. McDonald Associate Dean for Academic Affairs and Chair, Institute Honors Advisory Committee, 213 Smith Hall, Virginia Military Institute, Lexington, Virginia 24450; *Telephone:* 540-464-7212; *Fax:* 540-464-7779; *E-mail:* mcdonaldrl@mail.vmi.edu; *Web site:* http://www.vmi.edu

---

Virginia Polytechnic Institute and State University
University Honors Program
Blacksburg, Virginia

While the University Honors Program offers a significant complement of honors core curriculum courses, a colloquia series, and research opportunities, the major focus for the program is to encourage each student to seek a superior education consisting of the following elements: significant accomplishment in the instructional arena, participation in intellectual life beyond the instructional level, leadership/service activity, and extensive interaction with members of the faculty.

To these ends, such activities as a summer reading program leading to student-faculty conversation groups, special classes taught by senior faculty members, special classes concerning research methodologies, participation in major scholarship competitions, and seeking one of four honors degrees become tools students use. Because of the high quality of entering students, freshman honors courses are designed to assist students with Advanced Placement and International Baccalaureate, and other earned college credits link students to the broader curriculum of the University. A personal statement, curriculum vita project, and course of study planner assist students in preparing to use the curriculum to their advantage. Honors students are encouraged to seek diversity, and, as a result, many choose multiple majors and minors, often across college boundaries. The Honors Program and Graduate School maintain a five-year bachelor's/master's program.

The staff consists of a director, an associate director, two assistant directors, an office manager, and a secretary. The faculty members participating in the program are drawn from the University at large, but the Academy of Teaching Excellence (made up of about 80 faculty members who have won major teaching awards) oversees the program. Faculty participation is both high (typically 200 faculty members participate in some aspect of the program) and enthusiastic. Working with the faculty, honors students have participated in research that has led to participation in professional meetings and publication in academic journals.

Honors provides access to the major facilities of the University, including some (such as graduate library privileges) not open to other undergraduate students. The Honors Program offers special lectures, faculty teas, and special leadership seminars in a not-for-credit environment. These activities are all integral to the education of the whole person.

The University Honors Program also administers advising for students who are planning a career in medicine or dentistry. A full-time faculty member counsels students individually and oversees the preparation and submission of letters of evaluation at the time of their application to professional school. The emphasis in premedical planning is on a broad education combined with a strong foundation in the natural sciences.

The University Honors Program is more than 25 years old. There are about 1,800 students in the program.

Admission Process: Entering students must score 1300 or higher on the SAT I (620 verbal, 600 math) and must be in the top 10 percent of their graduating high school class. Students must attain GPA of at least 3.5 if the SAT I is 1400 or above or at least 3.7 if the SAT I is 1300–1399.

Scholarship Availability: The Honors Program offers merit-based scholarships as well as others that are both need- and merit-based. The honors application serves as the application for these scholarships.

Campus Overview

State-supported university, founded 1872 • **Coed** 21,272 undergraduate students, 97% full-time, 41% women, 59% men.

Undergraduates 20,729 full-time, 543 part-time. Students come from 52 states and territories, 104 other countries, 29% are from out of state, 6% African American, 7% Asian American or Pacific Islander, 2% Hispanic American, 0.3% Native American, 3% international, 3% transferred in, 41% live on campus.

Faculty *Total:* 1,490, 86% full-time. *Student/faculty ratio:* 16:1.

Academic Programs *Special study options:* accelerated degree program, adult/continuing education programs, advanced placement credit, cooperative education, distance learning, double majors, English as a second language, honors programs, independent study, internships, part-time degree program, services for LD students, study abroad, summer session for credit. *ROTC:* Army (b), Navy (b), Air Force (b).

Athletics Member NCAA. All Division I except football (Division I-A). *Intercollegiate sports:* baseball M(s), basketball M(s)/W(s), bowling M(c)/W(c), crew M(c)/W(c), cross-country running M(s)/W(s), equestrian sports M(c)/W(c), fencing M(c)/W(c), field hockey M(c)/W(c), golf M(s), gymnastics M(c)/W(c), ice hockey M(c)/W(c), lacrosse M(c)/W(s), rugby M(c)/W(c), skiing (downhill) M(c)/W(c), soccer M(s)/W(s), softball W, swimming and diving M(s)/W(s), tennis M(s)/W(s), track and field M(s)/W(s), ultimate Frisbee M/W, volleyball M(c)/W(s), water polo M(c)/W(c), weight lifting M(c)/W(c), wrestling M(s). *Intramural sports:* badminton M/W, basketball M/W, cross-country running M/W, football M/W, golf M/W, ice hockey M/W, racquetball M/W, riflery M/W, skiing (downhill) M/W, soccer M/W, softball W, squash M/W, swimming and diving M/W, table tennis M/W, tennis M/W, track and field M/W, ultimate Frisbee M/W, volleyball M/W, wrestling M.

Costs (2004–05) *Tuition:* state resident $4512 full-time, $188 per credit hour part-time; nonresident $15,206 full-time, $634 per credit hour part-time. *Required fees:* $1324 full-time, $156 per term part-time. *Room and board:* $4288; room only: $2150. Room and board charges vary according to board plan and location.

Financial Aid 923 Federal Work-Study jobs (averaging $1177). 3,940 state and other part-time jobs (averaging $1482). In 2003, 1016 non-need-based awards were made. *Average percent of need met:* 75%. *Average financial aid package:* $7035. *Average need-based loan:* $3743. *Average need-based gift aid:* $4371. *Average non-need-based aid:* $1615.

Contact: Virginia Tech University Honors, Hillcrest Hall (0427), Blacksburg, Virginia 24061; *Telephone:* 540-231-4591; *E-mail:* honors@vt.edu; *Web site:* http://www.univhonors.vt.edu

WASHINGTON

Eastern Washington University
Honors Program
Cheney, Washington

*S*ince *1983, the Honors Program has been one of the most successful and highly regarded academic units at Eastern Washington University (EWU). Each June, exceptional honors seniors receive an honors designation at a University-wide convocation the night before commencement.*

Freshman Honors Program benefits include satisfying six of the eight general education core requirements, priority registration, and a variety of cultural events. It takes a special student to be among the 75 freshmen and 20 transfer students admitted each fall. The Honors Program is open to all motivated sophomores; talented upper-division students may complete the Departmental Honors track if they have at least a 3.3 college GPA and do outstanding honors work in their major.

The Honors Program is for students who like puzzle-solving, who think education should be diverse in terms of subject matter, and who enjoy a smaller, interactive classroom. It is fast-paced in terms of the learning process, and it allows access to top professors during the freshman year and beyond.

Students in graduate or professional schools credit the EWU Honors Program for early access to experiences and research most university students do not enjoy as undergraduates.

Participation Requirements: Freshmen are required to complete at least 16 credits (two 8-credit Honors 100 series courses). Students must earn a minimum 3.3 GPA in honors courses and may select one of the following tracks: *Lower Division Honors,* 16 credits of honors freshman courses; *University Honors,* freshman courses, two Honors 398 courses, and the departmental capstone; *Transfer Honors,* Honors 398-01, a specific fall semester course, and the departmental capstone; *Departmental Honors,* three departmental honors courses in the major, two Honors 398 courses, and the departmental capstone; or *Departmental Honors* and *University Honors,* 16 credits of honors-sequence courses, three departmental honors-enriched courses, three Honors 398 courses, and the departmental capstone.

Admission Process: Freshmen with a minimum 3.6 high school cumulative GPA and transfer students with a 3.7 or higher GPA are encouraged to apply. Students are required to include the senior-year transcript, all Running Start or transfer credit and/or anticipated AP credit, a brief letter describing the student's academic interest area(s), and a letter of recommendation from a teacher or counselor.

Acceptance into Honors Program at EWU is competitive, and applicants are reviewed on a rolling basis. Students are encouraged to visit the campus, although an Honors Program interview is not required.

Scholarship Availability: Students must complete the EWU Scholarship Application, which can be found online at http://financialaid.ewu.edu and check the Honors box.

Freshman awards for students who participate in the Honors Program include the Orland B. Killin award for freshmen in the top 2 percent of their graduating class; the Academic Honors award, which is renewable for one year with a minimum 3.7 cumulative EWU GPA; the Scholastic Honors award, which is renewable for one year with a minimum 3.7 cumulative EWU GPA; the Honors Assistantship, a directed work experience where freshmen are placed in jobs that match their interests and abilities and may earn up to $2500; and the National Merit and Washington Scholar awards.

Campus Overview

State-supported comprehensive, founded 1882 • **Coed** 9,390 undergraduate students, 86% full-time, 58% women, 42% men.

Undergraduates 8,038 full-time, 1,352 part-time. Students come from 46 states and territories, 34 other countries, 9% are from out of state, 3% African American, 4% Asian American or Pacific Islander, 6% Hispanic American, 2% Native American, 1% international, 12% transferred in, 20% live on campus.

Faculty *Total:* 561, 71% full-time, 97% with terminal degrees. *Student/faculty ratio:* 24:1.

Academic Programs *Special study options:* academic remediation for entering students, advanced placement credit, cooperative education, distance learning, double majors, English as a second language, honors programs, independent study, internships, off-campus study, part-time degree program, services for LD students, student-designed majors, study abroad, summer session for credit. *ROTC:* Army (b).

Athletics Member NCAA. All Division I except football (Division I-AA). *Intercollegiate sports:* badminton M(c), baseball M(c), basketball M(s)/W(s), cross-country running M(s)/W(s), golf M/W(s), ice hockey M(c), soccer W(s), tennis M(s)/W(s), track and field M(s)/W(s), volleyball W(s). *Intramural sports:* baseball M/W, basketball M/W, bowling M/W, cross-country running M/W, football M/W, golf W, racquetball M/W, rugby W(c), soccer M/W, softball M/W, tennis M/W, track and field M/W, volleyball M/W, wrestling M(c).

Costs (2004–05) *Tuition:* state resident $3822 full-time, $127 per credit part-time; nonresident $13,299 full-time, $443 per credit part-time. Full-time tuition and fees vary according to course load. Part-time tuition and fees vary according to course load. *Required fees:* $234 full-time. *Room and board:* $5460. Room and board charges vary according to board plan and housing facility.

Financial Aid 360 Federal Work-Study jobs (averaging $2100). 503 state and other part-time jobs (averaging $2061). In 2003, 93 non-need-based awards were made. *Average percent of need met:* 42%. *Average financial aid package:* $10,485. *Average need-based loan:* $3713. *Average need-based gift aid:* $4793. *Average non-need-based aid:* $2480.

Contact: Dr. Perry Higman, Director or Mary Benham, Coordinator and Academic Adviser, Honors Program, 204 Hargreaves Hall, Eastern Washington University, Cheney, Washington 99004; *Telephone:* 509-359-2822; *Fax:* 509-359-2823; *E-mail:* honors@mail.ewu.edu; *Web site:* http://honors.ewu.edu

Seattle Pacific University
University Scholars
Seattle, Washington

*T*he *University Scholars program at Seattle Pacific University (SPU) is an alternative general education program for selected students who are highly motivated to pursue an intense academic program studying great works of art, literature, philosophy, social science, and natural science in their historical contexts. In their first three years, students are part of a cohort that progresses through a curriculum of great works, examines the relationship of science and faith, and considers the West's relationship to the world. In their senior year, students work individually with faculty mentors to produce an honors paper or project in a discipline.*

University Scholars courses are team-taught and rigorously interdisciplinary and offer intensive peer discussion. The program's goal is to create a faithful community of self-motivated scholars engaged in thoughtful cross-disciplinary conversation, writing, and action on issues facing the church and the world. Scholars gather for social events several times a year, including presentations and a celebration of the senior honors projects each spring.

Founded in 1970, the program enrolls a maximum of 40 students in each cohort, for a total of approximately 150–160 University Scholars.

Participation Requirements: During their first two years, University Scholars take the Honors University Seminar and then a sequence of courses called Texts and Contexts. In their junior year, they take a sequence of courses in Faith and Science, and their capstone experience begins with a seminar on Christianity and Scholarship, followed by 4 credits of work in an honors project or thesis. A total of 36 credits in University Scholars courses is required for graduation, and students must maintain a minimum 3.2 cumulative GPA in order to remain in the program. At commencement, University Scholars receive special recognition and an indication on their transcripts that they have completed the University Scholars program.

Special service to the University community is a high priority for University Scholars. Each year, the graduating senior who most exemplifies the high ideals of the program is honored with the Wesley E. Lingren Award in honor of the founding director.

Admission Process: University Scholars are selected through a special application process. Students with excellent SAT or ACT scores and exceptional high school GPAs are invited to apply by writing an honors entrance essay. The average high school GPA of entering freshmen is 3.62. Students who are highly motivated or who are specially gifted in a particular field are urged to contact the director if they find they have not received an invitation to apply. While many factors contribute to the selection process, most first-year students entering in 2004 had an SAT (or ACT equivalent) score of above 1300.

Scholarship Availability: The University gives substantial academic scholarships, but they are not directly tied to the University Scholars program.

Campus Overview

Independent Free Methodist comprehensive, founded 1891 • **Coed** 2,934 undergraduate students, 94% full-time, 66% women, 34% men.

Undergraduates 2,754 full-time, 180 part-time. Students come from 47 states and territories, 15 other countries, 35% are from out of state, 2% African American, 6% Asian American or Pacific Islander, 2% Hispanic American, 1% Native American, 1% international, 9% transferred in, 58% live on campus.

Faculty *Total:* 310, 57% full-time. *Student/faculty ratio:* 15:1.

Academic Programs *Special study options:* academic remediation for entering students, adult/continuing education programs, advanced placement credit, cooperative education, distance learning, double majors, English as a second language, external degree program, honors programs, independent study, internships, off-campus study, part-time degree program, services for LD students, student-designed majors, study abroad, summer session for credit. *ROTC:* Army (c), Navy (c), Air Force (c).

Athletics Member NCAA. All Division II. *Intercollegiate sports:* basketball M(s)/W(s), crew M/W, cross-country running M(s)/W(s), gymnastics W(s), soccer M(s)/W, track and field M(s)/W(s), volleyball W(s). *Intramural sports:* badminton M/W, basketball M/W, bowling M/W, cross-country running M/W, football M/W, golf M/W, skiing (cross-country) M(c)/W(c), skiing (downhill) M(c)/W(c), soccer M/W(c), softball M/W, swimming and diving M/W, table tennis M/W, tennis M/W, track and field M/W, volleyball M(c)/W(c), weight lifting M/W, wrestling M.

Costs (2004–05) *Comprehensive fee:* $27,834 includes full-time tuition ($20,139), mandatory fees ($327), and room and board ($7368). Part-time tuition: $560 per credit. Part-time tuition and fees vary according to course load. *College room only:* $3951. Room and board charges vary according to board plan and housing facility.

Financial Aid 375 Federal Work-Study jobs (averaging $1442). 413 state and other part-time jobs (averaging $1923). In 2004, 711 non-need-based awards were made. *Average percent of need met:* 81%. *Average financial aid package:* $16,829. *Average need-based loan:* $5584. *Average need-based gift aid:* $13,868. *Average non-need-based aid:* $8208.

Contact: Director: Dr. Luke M. Reinsma, Marston Hall, Seattle Pacific University, 3307 Third Avenue West, Seattle, Washington 98119; *Telephone:* 206-281-2093; *Fax:* 206-281-2335; *E-mail:* lreinsma@spu.edu; *Web site:* http://www.spu.edu/acad/univ-scholars

University of Washington
University Honors Program
Seattle, Washington

The University Honors Program was founded in 1961 in the College of Arts and Sciences and subsequently extended to the College of Engineering. Believing in the ancient Greek notion that the goal of education is to prepare citizens for intelligent action in the world, the University Honors Program exists to meet the educational needs of the ablest and most highly motivated undergraduates at the University of Washington (UW). It seeks to identify and recruit exceptional students and to provide them with special academic advising, close contact with honors faculty members, and the opportunity to build a learning community among honors faculty members and students.

The program provides a formal curricular structure that extends across the full span of undergraduate study by combining honors general education with advanced honors courses in the major. The honors interdisciplinary core curriculum brings dedicated students and faculty members together in small classes (the average size is 30) that address several concerns: methods of inquiry in the natural sciences, social sciences, and humanities; historical and cross-cultural perspectives; and effective communication. Critical-thinking and writing skills are emphasized across the honors curriculum. Research methods and the presentation of individual research findings are particularly emphasized in the final, departmental phase of an honors degree. In all, some 300 honors courses and sections of courses are offered each year.

Approximately 1,400 students are enrolled in the Honors Program, which is housed in Mary Gates Hall, a center for undergraduate education.

Participation Requirements: The honors core curriculum (which replaces the general education/breadth requirement) consists of interdisciplinary courses taught by diverse faculty members from across the campus and scholars from Seattle's intellectual community. An honors housing option is also available in McCarty Hall. Business and Nursing follow the Arts and Sciences model; honors options are also available in the College of Forestry and the College of Ocean and Fishery Sciences. To maintain good standing in and graduate from the Honors Program, students must achieve a minimum overall GPA of 3.3 and are normally required to present a GPA of 3.5 or better in their major subject. Completing the honors general education core as well as departmental honors requirements results in the degree With College Honors. Students who enter into and complete only the honors requirements in the major graduate With Distinction. This option is particularly suited to transfer students and those students who enter the University with a very substantial number of college credits earned while still in high school and through such options as AP examinations and I.B. credits.

Admission Process: Students apply for the University Honors Program as part of their application for UW admission, providing an Honors Essay and a school evaluation letter in addition to the regular admission materials. Admission is competitive and conducted on a rolling basis. Applicants are selected on the basis of several factors, including grades, curriculum, test scores, essay, activities, and school recommendation. Candidates are most apt to be given consideration for one of the 200 entering places if they present a GPA of 3.8 or better and SAT scores well above 1300. GPA adjustments are made for schools whose grading practices more closely approximate those of the University of Washington. Freshmen can also apply for late admission into honors through a competitive application process during the spring quarter of their freshman year. Eligibility for late admission is based on a minimum GPA of 3.5 and written essays, as well as demonstrable knowledge of honors requirements.

Scholarship Availability: The University of Washington offers a number of merit-based scholarships (UW Undergraduate Scholars, for state residents; President's Scholars; and Mary Gates Scholars), and the University Honors Program offers several Mary Gates Endowment Honors Scholarships, as well as the Campbell, Lovstead, and Eberhardter scholarships (prospective students should see the program's Web site for more information), to entering students. Exceptional students are automatically considered based on their admission applications and their honors applications. National Merit Scholarships are awarded to the most qualified candidates from among those who have designated the University of Washington as their first-choice institution. A variety of financial aid offers, scholarships, research and leadership grants, and campus employment opportunities are also available to undergraduates.

Campus Overview

State-supported university, founded 1861 • **Coed** 28,362 undergraduate students, 83% full-time, 52% women, 48% men.

Undergraduates 23,552 full-time, 4,810 part-time. Students come from 52 states and territories, 59 other countries, 13% are from out of state, 3% African American, 24% Asian American or Pacific Islander, 3% Hispanic American, 1% Native American, 3% international, 6% transferred in, 17% live on campus.

Faculty *Total:* 3,383, 82% full-time, 93% with terminal degrees. *Student/faculty ratio:* 11:1.

Academic Programs *Special study options:* academic remediation for entering students, accelerated degree program, adult/continuing education programs, advanced placement credit, cooperative education, distance learning, double majors, English as a second language, external degree program, honors programs, independent study, internships, part-time degree program, services for LD students, student-designed majors, study abroad, summer session for credit. *ROTC:* Army (b), Navy (b), Air Force (b).

Athletics Member NCAA. All Division I except football (Division I-A). *Intercollegiate sports:* baseball M(s), basketball M(s)/W(s), crew M(s)/W(s), cross-country running M(s)/W(s), golf M(s)/W(s), gymnastics W(s), soccer M(s)/W, softball W(s), swimming and diving M(s)/W(s), tennis M(s)/W(s), track and field M(s)/W(s), volleyball W(s), wrestling M(c). *Intramural sports:* archery M(c)/W(c), badminton M/W, basketball M/W, bowling M/W, crew M(c)/W(c), fencing M(c)/W(c), field hockey M(c)/W(c), football M/W, golf M/W, gymnastics M(c)/W(c), ice hockey M(c), lacrosse M(c)/W(c), racquetball M(c)/W(c), rugby M(c), sailing M(c)/W(c), skiing (cross-country) M(c)/W(c), skiing (downhill) M(c)/W(c), soccer M(c)/W(c), squash M(c)/W(c), swimming and diving M/W, table tennis M/W, tennis M/W, track and field M/W, volleyball M/W, water polo M(c)/W(c), wrestling M.

Costs (2004–05) *Tuition:* state resident $5286 full-time; nonresident $17,916 full-time. *Room and board:* $7017. Room and board charges vary according to board plan and housing facility.

Financial Aid 855 Federal Work-Study jobs (averaging $2690). 156 state and other part-time jobs (averaging $3000). In 2004, 400 non-need-based awards were made. *Average percent of need met:* 86%. *Average financial aid package:* $10,400. *Average need-based loan:* $5000. *Average need-based gift aid:* $7000. *Average non-need-based aid:* $3300.

Contact: Associate Director: Dr. Julie Villegas, Box 352800, 211 Mary Gates Hall, Seattle, Washington 98195-4300; *Telephone:* 206-543-7444; *Fax:* 206-543-6469; *E-mail:* villegas@u.washington.edu; *Web site:* http://depts.washington.edu/uwhonors

University of Washington, Tacoma
Global Honors Program
Tacoma, Washington

The University of Washington, Tacoma (UWT) Global Honors Program serves students in all undergraduate majors who wish to enter careers directed toward the real needs of the Puget Sound region and the world at a time when the emerging global economy is transforming the planet. The Global Honors Program appeals to students transferring to UWT as juniors who recognize the need for a more complete and sophisticated understanding of world problems than would be available to them in their academic majors. The program builds on the strengths of UWT's exceptional faculty members from all academic units. With the Global Honors Program's core courses organized as seminars (between 12 and 15 students enrolled in each), its international experience component, and its culminating project/thesis, it adds substantially to options available to the best students at UWT.

Faculty members in the program come from all academic units on campus, are selected competitively, and are actively engaged in the design and implementation of the program. Global Honors is housed in its own suite, with a student lounge, staff adviser, and faculty director. Special funding is made available to support study-abroad participation and involvement in scholarly conferences and research projects. A range of cultural activities is supported by the program as well.

The Global Honors Program admits its first students in the fall of 2005 on a cohort basis. The first group of 15 to 20 students is a small subset of the UWT student body, but the program is expected to double and triple in size as the campus grows. Students are accepted from among those admitted to UWT as juniors, and applicants are evaluated on the basis of GPA, an application letter and personal statement, a writing sample, letters of recommendation, and a personal interview. The Global Honors Program is interested, in particular, in attracting students with the potential to bring unique perspectives and make exceptional contributions to the program and the campus.

Participation Requirements: The core of the program is three seminars with content varying according to the expertise of the instructor, though each includes extensive reading lists, rigorous writing and research assignments, and the expectation of active participation and engagement by students. The first course deals with twentieth- and twenty-first-century history, economic philosophies, and political systems. The second course examines twentieth- and twenty-first-century literature, art, and music. The third core course considers future threats and opportunities, including such issues as poverty and the distribution of resources, the global environment, public health and pandemics, and religious, national, and ethnic conflicts.

A senior honors thesis/project is completed in the student's academic major and includes a public presentation at a special culminating event held at the end of each academic year. Students are also required to complete a meaningful study-abroad program before or during their senior year

Students must maintain a minimum 3.5 GPA during their enrollment in the program. They must complete 15 credits in their core courses, 5 to 10 credits of thesis/project courses with participation in a culminating conference, and a study-abroad experience. Students receive a special Global Honors designation on their transcripts as well as a special certificate at graduation.

Admission Process: Students are admitted as juniors transferring to the University of Washington, Tacoma. Admission decisions are based on GPA, personal essay, letters of recommendation, and interviews. Students can only enter the program each fall quarter.

Scholarship Availability: Students are eligible for the full range of the University of Washington, Tacoma's scholarships if they apply according to the University's schedule. More information is available at the University's financial aid Web site at http://www.tacoma.washington.edu/finaid/. The Global Honors Program also offers study-abroad grants to all students successfully involved in the program and assists them with other costs related to the program.

Campus Overview

State-supported upper-level, founded 1990 • **Coed**

Faculty *Total:* 131, 75% full-time. *Student/faculty ratio:* 16:1.

Costs (2004–05) *Tuition:* state resident $5190 full-time; nonresident $17,820 full-time.

Contact: Director: Dr. William Richardson, Global Honors Program, University of Washington, Tacoma, 1900 Commerce Street, Tacoma, Washington 98402; *Telephone:* 253-692-4450; *Fax:* 253-692-5718; *E-mail:* glhonors@u.washington.edu; *Web site:* http://www.tacoma.washington.edu/honors/

Washington State University
University Honors College
Pullman, Washington

The University Honors College (UHC) at Washington State University (WSU) is one of the oldest (founded in 1960) and best known honors programs in the nation. A free-standing academic unit, the UHC offers highly motivated and talented students a four-year general education curriculum. The UHC has as its primary goal the fostering of genuine intellectual curiosity and the encouragement of lifelong learning among its students. The UHC aims to support the best possible teaching and learning opportunities for participating faculty members and students. Honors courses are small and are taught by faculty members who have a commitment to teaching undergraduate students. The capstone experience of the four-year curriculum is an honors thesis, including an oral presentation. The UHC has a tradition of encouraging students to study a foreign language and to study abroad. Approximately half of the honors students complete a foreign language through the intermediate level; one third study abroad in one of the University's special Honors Exchanges or Education Abroad programs. The Certificate of Global Competencies is an elective certificate for honors students whose international interests and/or career objectives can be enhanced by an integrated program of language study, academic course work, and study abroad.

Several special programs are available to WSU honors students. These include the Honors/Veterinary Medicine Program, which enables eligible students to complete a B.S./D.V.M. in seven years rather than eight; the 4-1 program, which allows students to obtain a B.A. in a liberal arts major and an M.B.A. in five years rather than six; special honors exchanges to Wales and Denmark; and the opportunity to live in WSU's Scholars Residence Hall or Honors Hall.

Approximately 600 students are enrolled in the UHC. Honors students major in every department and college at WSU.

Participation Requirements: The honors curriculum is a four-year program that requires the same number of credits as the general education program. To graduate from the UHC, students must have a minimum 3.2 overall GPA. Each semester, the UHC honors its graduates before commencement when certificates, awards, and special honors medallions are distributed. Completion of the honors curriculum also is noted on students' transcripts.

Admission Process: Admission of first-year students to the UHC is determined by a separate application to honors. Honors College faculty members review student applications and select students based upon their high school grades, test scores (SAT or ACT), recommendations from high school faculty members, and an essay prepared by the applicant. Transfer and international students are admitted on an individual basis after eligibility has been determined.

Within WSU guidelines, the UHC accepts Advanced Placement, International Baccalaureate, and Running Start credits to fulfill Honors requirements.

Scholarship Availability: The Honors College administers many scholarships. In addition, WSU has many merit scholarship programs at the departmental, college, and university level. Honors students are among the most frequent recipients of these awards. Select Regents Scholars receive a full-ride University scholarship for four years and are automatically admitted to the UHC.

Campus Overview

State-supported university, founded 1890 • **Coed** 19,280 undergraduate students, 86% full-time, 53% women, 47% men.

Undergraduates 16,545 full-time, 2,735 part-time. Students come from 53 states and territories, 65 other countries, 9% are from out of state, 3% African American, 6% Asian American or Pacific Islander, 4% Hispanic American, 1% Native American, 3% international, 13% transferred in, 37% live on campus.

Faculty *Total:* 1,297, 84% full-time, 81% with terminal degrees. *Student/faculty ratio:* 18:1.

Academic Programs *Special study options:* academic remediation for entering students, adult/continuing education programs, advanced placement credit, cooperative education, distance learning, double majors, English as a second language, external degree program, honors programs, independent study, internships, off-campus study, part-time degree program, services for LD students, student-designed majors, study abroad, summer session for credit. *ROTC:* Army (b), Navy (b), Air Force (b). *Unusual degree programs:* 3-2 architecture, doctor of veterinary medicine, doctor of pharmacy.

Athletics Member NCAA, NAIA. All NCAA Division I except football (Division I-A). *Intercollegiate sports:* baseball M(s), basketball M(s)/W(s), bowling M(c)/W(c), crew M(c)/W(s), cross-country running M(s)/W(s), equestrian sports M(c)/W(c), golf M(s)/W(s), ice hockey M(c)/W(c), lacrosse M(c)/W(c), rugby M(c)/W(c), skiing (cross-country) M(c)/W(c), skiing (downhill) M(c)/W(c), soccer M(c)/W(s), softball W(c), swimming and diving W(s), tennis W(s), track and field M(s)/W(s), volleyball M(c)/W(s), water polo M(c). *Intramural sports:* badminton M/W, basketball M/W, bowling M/W, cheerleading M/W, cross-country running M/W, fencing M(c)/W(c), football M/W, golf M/W, racquetball M/W, soccer M/W, softball M/W, table tennis M/W, tennis M/W, track and field M/W, volleyball M/W, wrestling M.

Costs (2004–05) *Tuition:* state resident $4745 full-time, $258 per credit part-time; nonresident $13,163 full-time, $679 per credit part-time. Part-time tuition and fees vary according to course load. *Required fees:* $613 full-time. *Room and board:* $6450; room only: $3622. Room and board charges vary according to board plan and housing facility.

Financial Aid 639 Federal Work-Study jobs (averaging $1316). 1,080 state and other part-time jobs (averaging $1425). In 2003, 796 non-need-based awards were made. *Average percent of need met:* 95%. *Average financial aid package:* $9702. *Average need-based loan:* $4497. *Average need-based gift aid:* $5292. *Average non-need-based aid:* $3401.

Contact: Dean: Dr. Mary Wack, Honors Hall, Room 130, P.O. Box 642012, Pullman, Washington 99164-2012; *Telephone:* 509-335-4505; *Fax:* 509-335-3784; *E-mail:* honors@wsu.edu

Western Washington University
University Honors Program
Bellingham, Washington

The Western Washington University Honors Program was created in 1962 to offer selected students of high academic achievement the opportunity to participate in a challenging intellectual enterprise. Since then, honors has grown to offer a wide variety of courses in general education, more specialized seminars, and the opportunity to work one-on-one with a faculty member in the completion of a senior project.

Honors courses are rigorous and stress active participation, writing, and independent thinking. Honors faculty members come from programs and departments throughout the University and are known campuswide for their excellence as classroom teachers.

Honors students come from every college in the University, but the largest number major in the natural sciences, including programs such as premedicine and environmental science. Students in honors must fulfill all the requirements set forth in the University's Bulletin, *including those for general education and the major. Students with AP credit, work in the International Baccalaureate program, or other forms of credit that award them advanced standing may be able to count that work toward completion of the requirements for the program.*

The program admits up to 100 freshmen each year and has a total enrollment of about 300.

Graduation through honors is a mark of distinction, and students are recognized at Commencement and receive notations on their transcripts indicating they have completed the program.

Participation Requirements: Students who enter the program as freshmen complete a yearlong sequence of courses that introduces them to the Western and non-Western cultural traditions and other general education courses and specialized seminars. Seminar topics change annually and cover all the major disciplinary areas (natural sciences, humanities, and social sciences). Honors classes are always small and are open only to honors students. Sections of the freshman sequence and other general education courses have enrollments of not more than 25 to 30, while seminars enroll 12 or fewer. All students who graduate through the program must complete a senior project, where they work individually with a professor or, in some instances, more than one professor. The project is usually in the major, but in some cases it may be in an auxiliary area. Students are encouraged to think creatively about the project, and while many elect to write a traditional thesis, recitals, shows, and other creative works have all been offered to fulfill this requirement. To graduate through honors, students must maintain a minimum 3.5 GPA for the last 90 graded credits of academic work and fulfill specific departmental requirements where they exist. Students in the program have gone on to graduate and professional programs at the finest institutions in the nation.

Admission Process: Admission to the program is competitive. Entering freshmen, transfer students, and already enrolled Western students may apply directly or answer an invitation from the program. Honors does not use set formulas for admission. Rather, candidates are evaluated according to a number of factors in order to determine the likelihood of their success in the program. When reviewing an applicant, the program considers previous academic achievement, including GPA and class rank; a detailed letter of recommendation; scores on appropriate tests; and the applicant's writing. In considering students for admission, the program regards a demonstrated commitment to serious academic work to be at least as important as aptitude. Applications should be received by March 15.

Campus Overview

State-supported comprehensive, founded 1893 • **Coed** 12,862 undergraduate students, 91% full-time, 56% women, 44% men.

Undergraduates 11,677 full-time, 1,185 part-time. Students come from 44 states and territories, 29 other countries, 6% are from out of state, 2% African American, 8% Asian American or Pacific Islander, 3% Hispanic American, 2% Native American, 0.8% international, 8% transferred in, 30% live on campus.

Faculty *Total:* 616, 74% full-time, 75% with terminal degrees. *Student/faculty ratio:* 22:1.

Academic Programs *Special study options:* accelerated degree program, advanced placement credit, cooperative education, distance learning, double majors, English as a second language, honors programs, independent study, internships, off-campus study, services for LD students, student-designed majors, study abroad, summer session for credit.

Athletics Member NCAA. All Division II. *Intercollegiate sports:* basketball M(s)/W(s), cheerleading M/W, crew M(s)/W(s), cross-country running M(s)/W(s), football M(s), golf M(s)/W(s), soccer M(s)/W(s), softball W(s), track and field M(s)/W(s), volleyball W(s). *Intramural sports:* badminton M/W, baseball M, basketball M/W, ice hockey M, lacrosse M/W, racquetball M/W, rugby M/W, sailing M/W, skiing (downhill) M/W, soccer M/W, softball M/W, swimming and diving M/W, table tennis M/W, tennis M/W, volleyball M/W, water polo M/W, wrestling M.

Costs (2004–05) *Tuition:* state resident $3885 full-time, $130 per credit part-time; nonresident $13,272 full-time, $442 per credit part-time. Full-time tuition and fees vary according to location. Part-time tuition and fees vary according to location. *Required fees:* $567 full-time, $189 per term part-time. *Room and board:* $6242; room only: $4101. Room and board charges vary according to board plan and housing facility.

Financial Aid 264 Federal Work-Study jobs (averaging $2677). 312 state and other part-time jobs (averaging $3306). In 2004, 190 non-need-based awards were made. *Average percent of need met:* 85%. *Average financial aid package:* $8681. *Average need-based loan:* $4150. *Average need-based gift aid:* $5170. *Average non-need-based aid:* $1633.

Contact: Director: Dr. George Mariz, 228 Miller Hall, Bellingham, Washington 98225-9089; *Telephone:* 360-650-3446; *Fax:* 360-650-7789; *E-mail:* george.mariz@wwu.edu

WEST VIRGINIA

Marshall University
Honors Program
Huntington, West Virginia

The Honors Program at Marshall University, which is open to students of all majors, was established in the early 1960s to provide maximum educational opportunities for students of high ability. Honors students are encouraged to raise their expectations of themselves by pursuing enriched courses within and beyond the regular curriculum. The centerpiece of the program is the team-taught, interdisciplinary seminar that brings together outstanding, motivated students and stimulating professors. The program typically offers three or four of these 4-semester-hour seminars per semester. Each seminar is limited to 15 students.

The mission of the Honors Program is to offer an enhanced educational experience to academically talented and highly motivated students; to design, in collaboration with faculty members who are recognized for excellence in teaching, an innovative, interdisciplinary, and multidisciplinary curriculum that emphasizes critical thinking, communications skills, and collaborative learning; and to supplement that curriculum with enriched academic opportunities that consist of outside lectures, fieldwork, or course-related travel. Students participating in the Honors Program develop confidence in their abilities to understand and discuss complex ideas and texts as well as to engage in problem solving and research design. They learn to apply this new knowledge in meaningful ways that can help them succeed in their professional and personal lives following college, strengthen their written and oral communication skills, work effectively in groups of diverse people, make connections between disciplines, and enjoy a range of supplemental experiences of an academic and social nature with similarly motivated and talented students.

The Honors Program is housed in the John R. Hall Center for Academic Excellence (CAE), which brings together all honors and scholarship programs at Marshall. The CAE facilities include a computer lab, scholarship library, student lounge, and two seminar classrooms. The CAE also contains the offices of the Executive Director of the CAE, the Assistant Director, and two program assistants. In 1995, honors students formed the Marshall University Honors Student Association (MUHSA), which is open to all eligible students. MUHSA sponsors academic and social events on campus, and it advises the faculty committee that oversees the Honors Program through its three seats on that committee, ensuring honors students a voice in deciding the direction of the program.

The number of students in the program is approximately 300.

Participation Requirements: Students who wish to graduate with University Honors on their diplomas must complete 24 hours of honors classes, consisting of HON 101 (the freshman-year orientation class), 4 hours of a 100-level seminar, 8 hours of upper-level seminars, and 11 hours of honors credit made up of departmental honors classes or independent study in honors. They must do this while maintaining at least a 3.3 GPA in all courses and a minimum cumulative 3.3 GPA in honors courses. In the past, interdisciplinary seminars have included such topics as Poetry and the Condition of Music, War in the Twentieth Century, Plagues and Epidemics, and Primatology and Human Evolution. Honors students are advised by the CAE Director and by faculty members in the student's major field of study.

Admission Process: Students may begin honors work at any stage in their college careers, although many begin as freshmen. Entering freshmen with an ACT minimum composite score of 26 (or SAT equivalent) and at least a 3.3 GPA can enroll in any honors course. Transfer students or students already enrolled with a minimum 3.3 GPA can enroll in any honors course.

Scholarship Availability: Superior high school or transfer students (minimum 3.5 GPA and minimum ACT composite score of 25) can apply for academic scholarships or tuition waivers, the John Marshall Scholarship Program (minimum 30 ACT), the Erma Byrd Scholars Program, the Charles and Mary Jo Locke Hedrick Scholarship (minimum 28 ACT), and the Society of Yeager Scholars Program (minimum 28 ACT). The Honors Program also offers an annual $1000 travel-abroad scholarship and a $500 award for domestic study.

Campus Overview

State-supported university, founded 1837, part of University System of West Virginia • **Coed** 9,859 undergraduate students, 84% full-time, 57% women, 43% men.

Undergraduates 8,275 full-time, 1,584 part-time. Students come from 41 states and territories, 29 other countries, 17% are from out of state, 5% African American, 0.9% Asian American or Pacific Islander, 0.8% Hispanic American, 0.3% Native American, 0.9% international, 5% transferred in, 20% live on campus.

Faculty Total: 711, 64% full-time, 55% with terminal degrees. Student/faculty ratio: 20:1.

Academic Programs Special study options: academic remediation for entering students, accelerated degree program, adult/continuing education programs, advanced placement credit, cooperative education, distance learning, double majors, English as a second language,

honors programs, independent study, internships, off-campus study, part-time degree program, services for LD students, study abroad, summer session for credit. *ROTC:* Army (b). *Unusual degree programs:* 3-2 forestry with Duke University.

Athletics Member NCAA. All Division I except football (Division I-A). *Intercollegiate sports:* baseball M(s), basketball M(s)/W(s), cross-country running M(s)/W(s), golf M(s)/W(s), lacrosse M(c), rugby M(c)/W(c), soccer M(s)/W(s), softball W(s), swimming and diving W(s), tennis W(s), track and field M(s)/W(s), volleyball W(s). *Intramural sports:* basketball M/W, bowling M/W, football M/W, golf M/W, racquetball M/W, soccer M/W, softball M/W, swimming and diving M/W, tennis M/W, track and field M/W, volleyball M/W.

Costs (2004–05) *Tuition:* state resident $3818 full-time, $151 per semester hour part-time; nonresident $10,128 full-time, $414 per semester hour part-time. Full-time tuition and fees vary according to program and reciprocity agreements. Part-time tuition and fees vary according to program and reciprocity agreements. *Required fees:* $478 full-time, $12 per semester hour part-time. *Room and board:* $6060. Room and board charges vary according to board plan and housing facility.

Financial Aid 330 Federal Work-Study jobs (averaging $1600). 54 state and other part-time jobs (averaging $6617). In 2004, 1501 non-need-based awards were made. *Average percent of need met:* 58%. *Average financial aid package:* $6769. *Average need-based loan:* $4683. *Average need-based gift aid:* $3930. *Average non-need-based aid:* $4758.

Contact: Director: Dr. Edwina Pendarvis, Honors Program, John R. Hall Center for Academic Excellence, Marshall University, Huntington, West Virginia 25755; *Telephone:* 304-696-2475; *Fax:* 304-696-7102; *Web site:* http://www.marshall.edu/cae/

Shepherd University
Honors Program
Shepherdstown, West Virginia

The mission of the Honors Program at Shepherd University is to create an academic environment in which gifted students can experience education in a dynamic and interactive way. Through seminars that promote active engagement in the subject area, independent research, a student-centered curriculum, and innovative teaching techniques, students in the Honors Program have the opportunity to become more self-directed in their learning. In the Honors Program, education does not simply take place in the classroom or through texts. Students become directly involved in the area of study through international and domestic travel, field trips, one-to-one interaction with professors and classmates, and a variety of activities outside the classroom that enhance the learning experience.

In addition to expanding the students' academic horizons, the Honors Program encourages student leadership and service to the community. The aim is to create graduates who are independent thinkers, insatiable learners, and responsible, socially conscious citizens. Honors students will leave Shepherd equipped to attend the finest graduate schools in the country and to be successful as solid contributors in their chosen professional careers. Graduates of the Honors Program are given recognition at graduating ceremonies.

The Honors Center at Shepherd University is located in the Miller Hall residence building. The Center includes the Office of the Director, the study lounges, and a computer lab. Miller is also the honors residence hall, allowing students to take full advantage of these facilities.

The fourteen-year-old program currently enrolls 130 students.

Participation Requirements: During the freshman year, honors students must participate in the honors core: Honors Written English and Honors History of Civilization. This team-taught learning community introduces freshman honors students to major types of expository and critical writing in conjunction with the study of Western civilization. Topics focus on philosophical thought throughout history with emphasis on changes in government, economics, arts, science, and literature.

After completing the freshman core, honors students may choose an honors course in a specific discipline or a special topics course. Special topics courses are team-taught seminars that cover interdisciplinary studies. In the past, these courses have included analysis of environmental issues; an exploration of the arts through theater, fine art, music, and dance; and the study of the history and culture of regions both within the United States and on an international level.

In their sophomore year, students take the sophomore honors core, a learning community that includes honors-level world literature and a second section of honors history of civilization.

During their junior year, honors students begin research toward a major thesis to be completed as a graduation requirement. Each student chooses a mentor from the faculty and begins to formulate a reading list that would contribute to a thesis proposal. In collaboration with the thesis director, the student develops an original idea about the chosen topic and then analyzes the information using research to substantiate this idea.

Scholarship Availability: Shepherd University Presidential Scholarships are awarded to freshmen who have demonstrated outstanding academic potential based on both their high school grades in a college-preparatory program and their scores on either the ACT or the SAT I. The quality of high school courses as well as extracurricular activities both within and outside of high school are also considered. Scholarships may also be awarded to transfer students who have demonstrated outstanding academic progress based on their previous college work and grades.

The Honors Program awards several Presidential Scholarships to candidates who stand out for their high academic achievements, leadership in high school activities, and community service. These $1500 scholarships may be renewed yearly for a total of four years as long as the recipient maintains a cumulative yearly Shepherd GPA of at least 3.2 and completes at least 15 semester hours of course work per semester. For consideration for the Presidential Scholarships, students must complete the admissions application process by the stated application deadlines.

The Rubye Clyde Scholarship has been set up by the Shepherd University Foundation in recognition of Rubye Clyde McCormick and is designed for outstanding West Virginia students with solid academic credentials. Full tuition and fees as well as room and board for one year (about $5000) are provided through the scholarship. This scholarship is renewable if the student meets academic criteria established by the Shepherd University Foundation. In order to renew the scholarship, the student must have a 3.5 GPA or above with a course load of 15 credit hours per semester. This scholarship is open to a student in any major or field of study.

One Ralph and Margaret Burkhart Scholarship is awarded to an Honors Program candidate each year. This scholarship provides $5000 per academic year for tuition and fees, room and board, and books and supplies. Minimum selection criteria include a high school GPA of 3.5, a score of 1270 on the SAT I or 30 on the ACT, a personal interview with the Director of the Honors Program, and an essay that is part of the honors admission process. This scholarship is renewable each year based on the following criteria: enrollment in and completion of a minimum of 15 credit hours per semester and a GPA of at least 3.5.

The Hearst Foundation, Inc., was founded in 1945 by publisher and philanthropist William Randolph Hearst. In 1948, Mr. Hearst established the California Charities Foundation. Soon after Mr. Hearst's death in 1951, the name was changed to the William Randolph Hearst Foundation. Both foundations are independent private philanthropies operating separately from the Hearst Corporation. The charitable goals of the two foundations are essentially the same, reflecting the philanthropic interests of William Randolph

Hearst—education, health, human services, and culture. Any student applying to the Honors Program is eligible for an award from these foundations. Potential recipients are judged on leadership, community service, and a superior academic record.

Campus Overview

State-supported comprehensive, founded 1871, part of West Virginia Higher Education Policy Commission • **Coed** 5,141 undergraduate students, 63% full-time, 57% women, 43% men.

Undergraduates 3,262 full-time, 1,879 part-time. Students come from 49 states and territories, 21 other countries, 30% are from out of state, 5% African American, 1% Asian American or Pacific Islander, 2% Hispanic American, 0.5% Native American, 0.8% international, 7% transferred in, 25% live on campus.

Faculty *Total:* 310, 38% full-time, 43% with terminal degrees. *Student/faculty ratio:* 21:1.

Academic Programs *Special study options:* academic remediation for entering students, accelerated degree program, adult/continuing education programs, advanced placement credit, cooperative education, double majors, honors programs, independent study, internships, part-time degree program, services for LD students, study abroad, summer session for credit.

Athletics Member NCAA. All Division II. *Intercollegiate sports:* baseball M(s), basketball M(s)/W(s), football M(s), golf M, soccer M(s)/W(s), softball W(s), tennis M(s)/W(s), volleyball W(s). *Intramural sports:* basketball M/W, bowling M/W, football M/W, racquetball M/W, soccer M/W, softball M/W, swimming and diving M/W, tennis M/W, ultimate Frisbee M/W, volleyball M/W, weight lifting M/W, wrestling M/W.

Costs (2004–05) *Tuition:* state resident $3654 full-time; nonresident $9234 full-time. Full-time tuition and fees vary according to degree level, program, and reciprocity agreements. Part-time tuition and fees vary according to degree level and program. *Room and board:* $5574. Room and board charges vary according to board plan and housing facility.

Financial Aid 183 Federal Work-Study jobs (averaging $1500). 325 state and other part-time jobs (averaging $3000). In 2004, 500 non-need-based awards were made. *Average percent of need met:* 73%. *Average financial aid package:* $7797. *Average need-based loan:* $3552. *Average need-based gift aid:* $3444. *Average non-need-based aid:* $7490.

Contact: Director: Dr. Stephanie Slocum-Schaffer, 201 Miller Hall, Shepherdstown, West Virginia 25443; *Telephone:* 304-876-5244; *Fax:* 304-876-5311; *E-mail:* sslocums@shepherd.edu

---

West Virginia University
University Honors Program
Morgantown, West Virginia

The University Honors Program incorporates a style of learning and living at West Virginia University (WVU) that is tailored to the highly motivated, excelling student's special requirements. Honors courses, designed to stimulate creativity, provoke in-depth discussion, and expand the experience of the student beyond the normal curriculum, are offered in sections of 20 or fewer students. Faculty members noted for their outstanding instruction teach these classes. These same professors and other faculty members serve as honors advisers, guiding students from the moment they set foot on campus through both the University's liberal arts studies and general education curricula and their own individual academic programs. Live-and-learn communities in the residence halls give students in similar degree programs an opportunity to share living and learning experiences together; first-year honors students have the exclusive opportunity to live in Stalnaker Hall. Honors students are also privy to priority registration, allowing them the first pick of classes above all other students at the University and allowing them to academically tailor each semester to their individual needs. The Honors Program provides its students with excellent opportunities for study abroad, research experience, and internships by both promoting and hosting events that cater to these.

To meet the needs of an ever-growing student body, the University Honors Program has recently added two elected leadership positions for students in the heart of the honors administration; these are the Student Academic and Community Ambassadors. Working hand in hand with the honors administration, the holders of these two positions carry great responsibility, serve as voices of student concern within the program, and are representatives of the University and the Honors Program. The Academic Ambassador heads up recruitment and admissions efforts as well as coordinates all aspects of honors orientation, a 1-hour course required of all entering honors students in their first semester. This ambassador also leads student delegations at both regional and national honors conventions. The Community Ambassador tends to the extracurricular aspects of the program, ensuring an increased sense of community within the honors student body. With the Director and his assistant, this ambassador plans and executes social events, field trips, guest lectures, themed dinners, and community service projects in which the honors students take part.

Upon graduation and successful completion of the program, the students' diplomas and transcripts indicate their designation as a University Honors Scholar. Two graduating seniors receive the Joginder and Charlotte Nath Award, which is geared toward students in scientific research. The Dennis O'Brien Award recognizes 2 outstanding seniors who have exemplified service to the community, University, and Honors Program itself. Graduates also have the opportunity to join the University Honors Program Alumni Society.

Participation Requirements: To graduate as a University Honors Scholar, students must complete a minimum of 24 honors credit hours. Beginning in fall 2005, there are two tracks that students may elect to follow. The 21st Century Scholar track follows a liberal arts curriculum and is aimed at those students in majors that facilitate honors involvement; students are required to take two integrated learning courses and a research methods course in the junior year. The Professional Scholar track focuses on students in highly specialized, structured majors, such as physical therapy, education, engineering, and the fine and performing arts; students are allowed to pursue their traditional curricula with specialized honors courses in their major fields of study. All students are expected to complete a 6-hour honors senior capstone course. This usually takes the form of a thesis or research project, but senior design projects, internships, and senior recitals are commonly completed for honors credit, depending on the major.

All students are expected to save their course work during their undergraduate career and prepare a portfolio, including reflection papers on each honors course and the honors experience as a whole. Potential graduates from the program must make an appointment for an exit interview with either the Director or his assistant during the student's final semester, at which time the portfolio is reviewed.

To remain in the program, students must maintain a minimum overall GPA of 3.2 during the freshman year and a minimum 3.3 GPA during the sophomore and junior years; they must graduate with at least a 3.4 GPA. In this way, all University Honors Scholars also receive University honors of at least cum laude.

All first-year students must take a 1-hour honors orientation class, which fulfills the University's orientation requirement. These courses are taught and largely designed by upperclass honors students. Honors engineers complete a specialized honors engineering orientation.

Admission Process: Entering freshmen are considered for admission to the program on the basis of their ACT composite or SAT combined standard scores and their high school GPA or status as National Merit Semifinalists. WVU students with fewer than 34 credit hours and at least a 3.7 GPA with no grades of I or W may also apply. There is no deadline for application to the program. Transfer students who have accrued 34 or fewer college credit hours and have maintained an overall GPA of 3.7 or better with no grades of I or W from an accredited institution may be accepted as a WVU honors student. In addition, honors students with college GPAs that meet WVU standards for regularly admitted honors students are accepted if the honors admissions standards at the University from which the student is transferring are similar to those at WVU.

Scholarship Availability: Most scholarships are offered through the WVU Scholars Program, a comprehensive awards program ranging from the full cost of an undergraduate education to several hundred dollars. Many students in the Scholars Program are also in the Honors Program, although acceptance into one of the programs does not automatically qualify students for the other. If students have no other aid of any kind (scholarships, grants, or loans), the Honors Program does offer a small stipend for full-time honors students.

Campus Overview

State-supported university, founded 1867, part of West Virginia Higher Education Policy Commission • **Coed** 18,653 undergraduate students, 94% full-time, 47% women, 53% men.

Undergraduates 17,614 full-time, 1,039 part-time. Students come from 51 states and territories, 59 other countries, 40% are from out of state, 4% African American, 2% Asian American or Pacific Islander, 1% Hispanic American, 0.3% Native American, 2% international, 5% transferred in, 27% live on campus.

Faculty *Total:* 1,073, 72% full-time, 68% with terminal degrees. *Student/faculty ratio:* 22:1.

Academic Programs *Special study options:* academic remediation for entering students, accelerated degree program, adult/continuing education programs, advanced placement credit, distance learning, double majors, English as a second language, external degree program, honors programs, independent study, internships, off-campus study, part-time degree program, services for LD students, student-designed majors, study abroad, summer session for credit. *ROTC:* Army (b), Air Force (b). *Unusual degree programs:* 3-2 education, business foreign language, occupational therapy, physical therapy, social work.

Athletics Member NCAA. All Division I except football (Division I-A). *Intercollegiate sports:* baseball M(s), basketball M(s)/W(s), cheerleading M(s)/W(s), crew W(s), cross-country running W(s), gymnastics W(s), riflery M(s)/W(s), soccer M(s)/W(s), swimming and diving M(s)/W(s), tennis W(s), track and field W(s), volleyball W(s), wrestling M(s). *Intramural sports:* archery M(c)/W(c), badminton M(c)/W(c), basketball M/W, bowling M(c)/W(c), equestrian sports M(c)/W(c), fencing M(c)/W(c), field hockey W(c), football M, golf M/W(c), ice hockey M(c), lacrosse M(c), racquetball M/W, riflery M/W, rugby M(c)/W(c), skiing (cross-country) M(c)/W(c), skiing (downhill) M(c)/W(c), soccer M/W(c), softball W(c), swimming and diving M/W, tennis W, track and field W, ultimate Frisbee M(c)/W(c), volleyball M/W, wrestling M.

Costs (2004–05) *Tuition:* state resident $3938 full-time, $167 per credit hour part-time; nonresident $12,060 full-time, $506 per credit hour part-time. Full-time tuition and fees vary according to location, program, and reciprocity agreements. Part-time tuition and fees vary according to course load, location, program, and reciprocity agreements. *Room and board:* $6084; room only: $3212. Room and board charges vary according to board plan, housing facility, and location.

Financial Aid 2,000 Federal Work-Study jobs (averaging $1480). 1,230 state and other part-time jobs (averaging $1142). In 2004, 6517 non-need-based awards were made. *Average percent of need met:* 88%. *Average financial aid package:* $6837. *Average need-based loan:* $3975. *Average need-based gift aid:* $3209. *Average non-need-based aid:* $3019.

Contact: Director: Dr. Keith Garbutt, University Honors Program, 248 Stalnaker Hall, West Virginia University, P.O. Box 6635, Morgantown, West Virginia 26506-6635; *Telephone:* 304-293-2100; *Fax:* 304-293-7569; *E-mail:* uhp@mail.wvu.edu; *Web site:* http://www.honors.wvu.edu

WISCONSIN

Carthage College
Honors Program
Kenosha, Wisconsin

The Honors Program at Carthage College offers students with excellent high school or transfer records a program of study that is tailored to their individual needs. Anyone admitted into the program may take advantage of any or all of the extra academic challenges and support the program offers, and those who complete all requirements graduate with All-College Honors.

Students in the Honors Program encounter a variety of classes. All students enroll in honors sections of Carthage's required first-year seminar courses. They may also receive honors credit for a variety of introductory-level courses by completing the requirements on enhanced honors syllabi for those courses. In advanced courses in their majors, students work closely with their professors to design and complete honors contracts that allow students to examine more closely aspects of that topic that are of greatest interest to them. The honors experience also includes an interdisciplinary Senior Honors Colloquium, in which students from a variety of disciplines gather to examine a common question using the lenses they have developed in their majors. By teaching and learning from each other in this colloquium, students gain a greater understanding not only of the course's central question, but also of the ways in which different individuals and different disciplines might approach such questions and of possible connections between disciplines. Honors courses rarely have more than 16 students and often have between 5 and 10.

Small class size, honors sections, and honors contracts foster close contact between students and professors, one of the hallmarks of the Honors Program. Outside of class, students regularly attend national and regional conventions with their professors to share their work and to learn from others. Students and faculty members also cooperate in several groups to select honors courses and to plan events and activities for students in the program. Because of this contact, professors are better able to identify highly motivated and qualified students and help prepare them for careers, graduate school, and competitive scholarships. In addition, this contact allows students insight into the work and thought of scholars in various academic disciplines.

A student-run Honors Council acts as the students' voice in planning and revising aspects of the Honors Program. The Honors Council also helps plan extracurricular events both on campus and in the Chicago-Milwaukee corridor. These events include speakers, workshops, and visits to museums, plays, operas, and concerts. The Honors Council organizes a peer mentoring program and a yearly forum at which students present their senior theses.

The Carthage Honors Program was originally founded in 1970 and currently has approximately 90–100 students.

Participation Requirements: Students admitted into Carthage's Honors Program may take advantage of any or all of the program's offerings. All requirements for honors (except for the Senior Honors Colloquium) parallel regular college requirements, and students may move into and out of the honors track as they wish.

The full honors curriculum includes three components. The Foundation Component (four courses) includes honors sections of the first-year seminars and enhanced honors syllabi in introductory-level courses. The Concentration Component includes two honors contracts in advanced courses in the major and an exemplary senior thesis in the major presented to an audience outside of the major department. The Integration Component of the Carthage Honors Program asks students to make connections between disciplines by taking a three-course Honors Junior Symposium and by completing the Senior Honors Colloquium.

Students must maintain a cumulative GPA of at least 3.5 to graduate with Honors. Those who complete all requirements earn All-College Honors, but others may choose to earn Honors in the major.

Admission Process: Each year, after examining the ACT scores and GPAs of the incoming class, approximately the top 10 percent of the group are sent invitations to the Honors Program. In addition to test scores and grades, the College may also consider performance in its Lincoln Scholarship Competition, which consists of an interview with faculty members and an essay. Both first-year and transfer students are considered for admission into the Honors Program.

Scholarship Availability: Carthage College offers substantial scholarships totaling more than $1 million to incoming and transfer students through its Lincoln Scholarship and Transfer Scholarship Competitions, with awards ranging from full tuition to full tuition with room and board. Most winners of these awards are in the Honors Program, although the program itself does not offer any scholarships of its own.

Campus Overview

Independent comprehensive, founded 1847, affiliated with Evangelical Lutheran Church in America • **Coed** 2,560 undergraduate students, 81% full-time, 60% women, 40% men.

Undergraduates 2,061 full-time, 499 part-time. Students come from 31 states and territories, 11 other countries, 58% are from out of state, 5% African American, 1% Asian American or Pacific Islander, 4% Hispanic American, 0.6% Native American, 0.6% international, 3% transferred in, 68% live on campus.

Faculty *Total:* 183, 63% full-time, 60% with terminal degrees. *Student/faculty ratio:* 17:1.

Academic Programs *Special study options:* accelerated degree program, adult/continuing education programs, advanced placement credit, cooperative education, double majors, honors programs, independent study, internships, off-campus study, part-time degree program, services for LD students, student-designed majors, study abroad, summer session for credit. *ROTC:* Army (c), Air Force (c). *Unusual degree programs:* 3-2 engineering with Case Western Reserve University, University of Wisconsin-Madison, University of Minnesota; occupational therapy with Washington University in St. Louis.

Athletics Member NCAA. All Division III. *Intercollegiate sports:* baseball M, basketball M/W, bowling W(c), cross-country running M/W, football M, golf M/W, ice hockey M(c), soccer M/W, softball W, swimming and diving M/W, tennis M/W, track and field M/W, volleyball M/W, water polo W(c). *Intramural sports:* badminton M/W, basketball M/W, bowling M/W, cheerleading M/W, football M/W, racquetball M/W, rock climbing M/W, soccer M/W, softball M/W, table tennis M/W, tennis M/W, volleyball M/W, weight lifting M/W.

Costs (2005–06) *Comprehensive fee:* $29,000 includes full-time tuition ($22,500) and room and board ($6500). Part-time tuition: $330 per credit hour. Part-time tuition and fees vary according to class time and course load. *Room and board:* Room and board charges vary according to board plan.

Financial Aid In 2002, 213 non-need-based awards were made. *Average percent of need met:* 39%. *Average financial aid package:* $8222. *Average need-based loan:* $4043. *Average need-based gift aid:* $4262. *Average non-need-based aid:* $7185.

Contact: Director: Dr. Gregory Baer, Carthage College, 2001 Alford Park Drive, Kenosha, Wisconsin 53140; *Telephone:* 262-551-5742; *Fax:* 262-551-6208; *E-mail:* gbaer@carthage.edu; *Web site:* http://www.carthage.edu/honors

Marquette University

Honors Program

Milwaukee, Wisconsin

Founded in 1963, the Marquette University Honors Program is designed for intellectually impassioned students who love to learn. Through an innovative curriculum that complements all majors on campus, the Honors Program aims to provide students with a small college experience amid the benefits of a large university setting. By offering students an education rooted in a classical humanities curriculum, particularly as it is shaped by the Jesuit ideal of rigorous academic inquiry, the University Honors Program seeks to develop graduates who make a habit of reflecting on knowledge and experience, and growing from this, who work to bring about justice in the world.

The curriculum is designed for a diverse body of motivated students from a range of racial, ethnic, religious, and education backgrounds who are well prepared with respect to interest, commitment, and skills. Marquette delivers this curriculum through small seminars, individual tutorials, an undergraduate research program, integrated capstone courses, close student-faculty interaction, study-abroad opportunities, residential community living and learning experiences, and cultural activities.

Participation Requirements: Two basic elements define the Honors curriculum: Honors Program Foundation Courses and the Honors Program Seminar Series. The foundation courses consist of eight courses in English, history, theology, and philosophy and are designed to develop in students the fundamental abilities to think critically, reason analytically, and express themselves coherently, both orally and in writing. Honors Program Seminars are characterized by topic-driven inquiry conducted from a communal perspective that requires the efforts, insights, and perspectives of all individuals participating. These seminars build progressively on one another from year to year, beginning with a 1-credit intellectual immersion during a student's first semester at college and culminating with a 3-credit capstone experience the senior year. During the sophomore year, students are challenged to engage in nontraditional academic approaches that work toward integration of their intellectual and affective sides (more details are available on the Web site), while the junior year brings the opportunity to conduct independent research with a faculty member. This 33-credit curriculum enhances all majors on campus. Students are required to maintain a minimum 3.2 GPA in order to earn the University honors degree.

Admission Process: The Honors Program is open to academically qualified students in any of Marquette's six colleges—Arts and Sciences, Business, Communication, Engineering, Health Sciences, or Nursing. Students apply during their senior year in high school. Applications can be obtained through the Office of Admissions at Marquette University or online. A total of 100 students enter the program as freshmen each year; the total enrollment is 400.

The selection committee looks for students who are motivated to learn, willing to work hard, and interested in taking intellectual risks. High school performance, test scores, and letters of recommendation are used as general guidelines for admission, but the most important part of the application is the student's essay. The selection committee looks for creativity, imagination, and originality. Typically, high school graduates who enter the Honors Program average at least 30 on the English ACT, but this should not be considered an inflexible standard. The University's goal is to develop a community of scholars whose academic interests and experiences contribute to the learning enterprise of all students; accordingly, Marquette admits a diverse body of students whose single shared characteristic is intellectual passion.

Scholarship Availability: All scholarships are awarded by applications to the Office of Financial Aid.

Campus Overview

Independent Roman Catholic (Jesuit) university, founded 1881 • **Coed** 7,923 undergraduate students, 93% full-time, 55% women, 45% men.

Undergraduates 7,392 full-time, 531 part-time. Students come from 50 states and territories, 82 other countries, 58% are from out of state, 5% African American, 4% Asian American or Pacific Islander, 4% Hispanic American, 0.3% Native American, 2% international, 2% transferred in, 50% live on campus.

Faculty *Total:* 1,001, 59% full-time, 70% with terminal degrees. *Student/faculty ratio:* 15:1.

Academic Programs *Special study options:* adult/continuing education programs, advanced placement credit, cooperative education, double majors, English as a second language, honors programs, internships, off-campus study, part-time degree program, services for LD students, study abroad, summer session for credit. *ROTC:* Army (b), Navy (b), Air Force (b).

Athletics Member NCAA. All Division I. *Intercollegiate sports:* baseball M(c), basketball M(s)/W(s), cheerleading M/W, crew M(c)/W(c), cross-country running M(s)/W(s), fencing M(c)/W(c), football M(c), golf M(s), lacrosse M(c), rugby M(c)/W(c), skiing (downhill) M(c)/W(c), soccer M(s)/W(s), softball W(c), swimming and diving M(c)/W(c), tennis M(s)/W(s), track and field M(s)/W(s), volleyball M(c)/W(c). *Intramural sports:* badminton M/W, basketball M/W, football W, golf M/W, racquetball M/W, soccer M/W, softball M/W, squash M/W, tennis M/W, track and field M/W, ultimate Frisbee M/W, volleyball M/W, water polo M/W, weight lifting M/W.

Costs (2004–05) *Comprehensive fee:* $29,822 includes full-time tuition ($21,550), mandatory fees ($382), and room and board ($7890). Full-time tuition and fees vary according to course load and reciprocity agreements. Part-time tuition: $635 per credit. Part-time tuition and fees vary according to course level and program. *Required fees:* $191 per semester part-time. *College room only:* $5130. Room and board charges vary according to board plan, housing facility, and location.

Financial Aid 300 Federal Work-Study jobs (averaging $2500). In 2003, 1498 non-need-based awards were made. *Average percent of need met:* 86%. *Average financial aid package:* $16,853. *Average need-based loan:* $5591. *Average need-based gift aid:* $10,774. *Average non-need-based aid:* $6674.

Contact: Director: Dr. Anthony Peressini, Coughlin Hall 001, P.O. Box 1881, Milwaukee, Wisconsin 53201-1881; *Telephone:* 414-288-7516; *Fax:* 414-288-1957; *E-mail:* honors.program@marquette.edu; *Web site:* http://www.marquette.edu/as/programs/honors.shtml

University of Wisconsin–Eau Claire

University Honors Program

Eau Claire, Wisconsin

The University Honors Program provides an extra measure of challenge and enrichment for students in any of the colleges at the University of Wisconsin–Eau Claire campus. It strives to enhance their critical thinking and communication skills, capacity for independent learning as well as working in teams, and leadership abilities. Courses are limited to a maximum of 20 students and are highly interactive. Students receive individual attention from faculty members in ways that cannot be done in larger courses. Almost all honors courses apply to credits needed for general education and provide a special means of meeting graduation requirements. The program does not increase the number of courses students are required to take as an undergraduate.

Colloquia courses change from semester to semester, and some are team-taught. They are usually offered during several semesters, but new ones are added each year and some are dropped. Departmental courses are predictably scheduled each semester and include basic courses in accounting, art, biology, chemistry, communications, economics, history, mathematics, music, philosophy, physics, political science, psychology, religious studies, and sociology. The first-year seminar is team-taught by honors seniors who enroll in Mentoring in Honors and are supervised by the director. The course provides an introduction to the baccalaureate degree, the purpose of a liberal education, and the nature of academic disciplines. The senior honors seminar is a retrospective, integrative experience. Some departments offer students the opportunity to earn departmental honors in their majors. Students may pursue departmental honors without being participants in the University Honors Program. Admissions to departmental programs generally require a 3.5 GPA in the major and in total credits.

The physical location of the program provides a classroom; a student study area with computers, a refrigerator, and a microwave; a conference room; a reception area; and the director's office. A student organization arranges trips to museums, theaters, and concerts as well as a variety of service and social activities. Outside of classes there are weekly Breakfasts with a Professor, monthly Pizzas with a Professor, special speakers, and support for attending state, regional, and national honors conferences.

The University Honors Council establishes policies for the program, approves honors courses, and selects honors faculty. This council consists of faculty representatives from each of the colleges as well as two student representatives. More than 140 faculty members have taught honors courses.

The 22-year-old University Honors Program currently enrolls 375 students.

Participation Requirements: To earn University Honors, students must complete at least the following: a 1-credit first-year honors seminar, 12 credits of interdisciplinary honors colloquia (or 9 credits of colloquia if a senior 1-credit Mentoring in Honors is completed), 12 credits of departmental courses limited to honors program students, and a 1-credit senior-level honors seminar. They must have at least a 3.5 GPA at graduation. This totals 24–26 credits of honors courses out of the 120 needed for graduation.

Students completing the requirements for University Honors receive special recognition during the Commencement ceremonies. They wear an honors medallion on a gold ribbon along with gold cord, and they stand to be recognized. Their achievement is noted on their permanent records and transcripts. They each receive a special certificate. *

Admission Process: Students are invited to participate in the honors program in several ways. Most are recruited as incoming first-year students based on two criteria: they must be in the top 5 percent of their high school graduating class and they must have an ACT composite of at least 28 or an SAT I score of at least 1280. Because these criteria miss a number of outstanding students, some are invited based on faculty recommendations and placement test scores. Finally, students are invited after they have completed 15 credits if they have a 3.67 GPA or better and an ACT composite score of at least 26. Transfer students who have been participating in honors programs at other college or universities are admitted and given credit for previous honors courses toward meeting the program's requirements for graduation with University Honors.

Scholarship Availability: Students eligible to participate in the University Honors Program are awarded at least a $500 freshman honors scholarship. Larger scholarships are also available and awarded competitively.

Campus Overview

State-supported comprehensive, founded 1916, part of University of Wisconsin System • **Coed** 10,034 undergraduate students, 92% full-time, 59% women, 41% men.

Undergraduates 9,280 full-time, 754 part-time. Students come from 21 states and territories, 45 other countries, 21% are from out of state, 0.5% African American, 3% Asian American or Pacific Islander, 0.9% Hispanic American, 0.6% Native American, 1% international, 5% transferred in, 38% live on campus.

Faculty *Total:* 506, 81% full-time, 76% with terminal degrees. *Student/faculty ratio:* 20:1.

Academic Programs *Special study options:* academic remediation for entering students, adult/continuing education programs, advanced placement credit, cooperative education, distance learning, double majors, English as a second language, honors programs, independent study, internships, off-campus study, part-time degree program, services for LD students, study abroad, summer session for credit.

Athletics Member NCAA. All Division III. *Intercollegiate sports:* basketball M/W, cross-country running M/W, football M, golf M/W, gymnastics W, ice hockey M/W, soccer W, softball W, swimming and diving M/W, tennis M/W, track and field M/W, volleyball W, wrestling M. *Intramural sports:* badminton M/W, baseball M, basketball M/W, bowling M/W, football M/W, golf M/W, ice hockey M/W, racquetball M/W, rugby M/W, skiing (cross-country) M/W, skiing (downhill) M/W, soccer M/W, softball M/W, swimming and diving M/W, table tennis M/W, tennis M/W, volleyball M/W, water polo M, weight lifting M/W.

Costs (2004–05) *Tuition:* state resident $4864 full-time, $203 per credit part-time; nonresident $14,910 full-time, $621 per credit part-time. Full-time tuition and fees vary according to reciprocity agreements. Part-time tuition and fees vary according to reciprocity agreements. *Room and board:* $4310; room only: $2480. Room and board charges vary according to board plan.

Financial Aid 1,725 Federal Work-Study jobs (averaging $1743). 2,120 state and other part-time jobs (averaging $1115). In 2003, 851 non-need-based awards were made. *Average percent of need met:* 96%. *Average financial aid package:* $6593. *Average need-based loan:* $3845. *Average need-based gift aid:* $4108. *Average non-need-based aid:* $1675.

Contact: Director: Dr. Paul J. Hoff, 209 Schneider Hall, Eau Claire, Wisconsin 54702-4004; *Telephone:* 715-836-3621; *Fax:* 715-836-2380; *E-mail:* hoffpj@uwec.edu; *Web site:* http://www.uwec.edu/Admin/Honors/honors.htm

---

University of Wisconsin–Madison
College of Letters and Science Honors Program
Madison, Wisconsin

The College of Letters and Science (L&S) Honors Program began in 1960 in response to a petition from 172 students asking the faculty to help challenge them more fully. The faculty legislation chartering the program states: "At the heart of our proposals is the creation of more challenge and opportunity, especially in terms of increased depth and breadth, and more freedom of initiative, for the top-notch students at all stages of their career." The profile of current honors students includes the following: 70 percent are from in state and 30 percent are from out of state, the average class rank is the 96th percentile, the average GPA is 3.87 on a scale of 4.0, the average ACT is 30, and the average SAT I is 1410. Beyond the raw statistics, students have participated in soccer, cross-country, tennis, track, football, basketball, skiing, and Tae Kwon Do; hiked 500 miles of the Appalachian Trail; acted in Shakespeare's plays; sung in musicals; played all the instruments in orchestra and band; performed service in Mexico and the altiplano of Bolivia; and conducted workshops for

SADD. Honors students are represented and led by their official Honors Student Organization, which organizes extracurricular field trips to the theater and to tour Frank Lloyd Wright homes in Oak Park and service activities for disadvantaged and minority students in the community. A weekly e-mail news bulletin apprises students of events and scholastic opportunities, such as funds for sophomore research apprenticeships and senior honors theses. Approximately 1,400 students are enrolled in the Letters and Science Honors Program.

Participation Requirements: Honors students work to complete the requirements for three different kinds of honors degrees that are available to students in the College of Letters and Science: Honors in the Liberal Arts, Honors in the Major, and Comprehensive Honors. Honors in the Liberal Arts is likely to be the primary focus for most first- and second-year students before they begin to concentrate on their majors. Honors in the Liberal Arts requires students to earn at least 24 honors credits (with a GPA of 3.3 or higher) in broadly distributed subjects ranging from the humanities to the social and natural sciences. Honors in the Major is the second type of honors offered by the College of Letters and Science. Its requirements can be completed independently from Honors in the Liberal Arts; neither is a prerequisite for the other. The curriculum for Honors in the Major is established by each academic department and program in the College. Students must apply to their major department for permission to enter this phase of the Honors Program. Requirements vary a great deal from department to department, but all are designed to culminate in a senior-year experience in which students are exposed to the cutting edge of that particular field. Many Honors in the Major students write an original research thesis, but, in some departments, students produce an original work of art, put on a performance, or complete a practicum in which they begin to act as professionals in their chosen field. Finally, Comprehensive Honors is awarded to those students who complete the requirements for both Honors in the Liberal Arts and Honors in the Major. Comprehensive Honors is the highest recognition that the College of Letters and Science can award an undergraduate, and students entering the program are urged to work toward this goal.

Admission Process: Admission to the Honors Program (which, for first-year students, means being admitted to pursue Honors in the Liberal Arts) is highly competitive. To apply, students should submit the L&S Honors application along with a 500-word essay. Applications are accepted and read on a rolling basis, but there is normally a mid-April deadline. Because positions in the program are limited and the quality of applicants has been rising in recent years, the honors staff carefully considers all aspects of an applicant's record, including extracurricular activities. It is thus not possible to identify any one criterion that ensures admission to the program. In past years, the average honors student has ranked in the 95th percentile of his or her high school class, has had a GPA of 3.9, and has had standardized test scores of 31 on the ACT and 1410 on the SAT I. Applications are encouraged from students who rank in the top 10 percent of their high school class. Students from unranked high schools should have the appropriate test scores and a minimum high school GPA of 3.6 on a 4.0 scale. Sophomores, juniors, and transfer students with a minimum 3.3 GPA are considered for admission to Honors in the Liberal Arts based on their undergraduate course work, an essay, and a letter of recommendation from an instructor; in some cases, the Honors Director may grant exceptions to these admissions criteria. Students applying to complete Honors in the Major must consult with the honors adviser in their major department to learn the admissions process and requirements. Students must maintain at least a 3.3 cumulative GPA to remain in the Honors Program.

Scholarship Availability: The Honors Program annually administers a number of awards and scholarships in support of undergraduate research. Burack Scholarships help support honors students in the University of Wisconsin (UW) Academic Year Abroad program, and students can earn honors credit for course work done on UW study-abroad programs. Every summer, Sophomore Research Apprenticeship grants support 40 undergraduates, who learn how to conduct original scholarly and scientific investigations while working alongside some of UW's outstanding research faculty members. Trewartha and Honors Thesis Research Grants support research during the academic year and also in the summer, when students often have more time to concentrate on their projects. In addition, many honors students win prestigious, University-wide Hilldale Research Fellowships.

Campus Overview

State-supported university, founded 1848, part of University of Wisconsin System • **Coed** 29,766 undergraduate students, 91% full-time, 53% women, 47% men.

Undergraduates 27,014 full-time, 2,752 part-time. Students come from 54 states and territories, 110 other countries, 29% are from out of state, 2% African American, 5% Asian American or Pacific Islander, 3% Hispanic American, 0.6% Native American, 3% international, 4% transferred in, 24% live on campus.

Faculty *Total:* 2,984, 80% full-time, 87% with terminal degrees. *Student/faculty ratio:* 15:1.

Academic Programs *Special study options:* accelerated degree program, adult/continuing education programs, advanced placement credit, cooperative education, distance learning, double majors, English as a second language, honors programs, independent study, internships, part-time degree program, services for LD students, student-designed majors, study abroad, summer session for credit. *ROTC:* Army (b), Navy (b), Air Force (b). *Unusual degree programs:* 3-2 accounting, pharmacy.

Athletics Member NCAA. All Division I except football (Division I-A). *Intercollegiate sports:* basketball M(s)/W(s), cheerleading M/W, cross-country running M(s)/W(s), golf M(s)/W(s), ice hockey M(s)/W(s), sailing M(c)/W(c), soccer M(s)/W(s), softball W(s), swimming and diving M(s)/W(s), tennis M(s)/W(s), track and field M(s)/W(s), ultimate Frisbee M(c)/W(c), volleyball W(s), water polo M(c)/W(c), wrestling M(s).

Costs (2004–05) *Tuition:* state resident $5860 full-time; nonresident $19,860 full-time. Full-time tuition and fees vary according to degree level and reciprocity agreements. Part-time tuition and fees vary according to course load, degree level, and reciprocity agreements. *Room and board:* $6250. Room and board charges vary according to board plan, housing facility, and location.

Financial Aid 3,894 Federal Work-Study jobs (averaging $2640). In 2004, 3750 non-need-based awards were made. *Average financial aid package:* $10,740. *Average need-based loan:* $4397. *Average need-based gift aid:* $6689. *Average non-need-based aid:* $2762.

Contact: Director: Christopher Kleinhenz, 420 South Hall, 1055 Bascom Mall, Madison, Wisconsin 53706; *Telephone:* 608-262-2984; *Fax:* 608-263-7116; *E-mail:* honors@honors.ls.wisc.edu; *Web site:* http://www.honors.ls.wisc.edu

University of Wisconsin–Milwaukee
University Honors Program
Milwaukee, Wisconsin

*T*he University Honors Program brings together outstanding students and faculty members from all University of Wisconsin–Milwaukee (UWM) schools and colleges. Committed to the importance of the liberal arts, the program offers small discussion seminar classes that provide many of the benefits of a small liberal arts college at a large metropolitan university. It attracts some of the most talented students from the University's various schools and colleges.

Honors classes differ from regular classes at UWM in that they are small, interactive seminars. With a maximum of about fifteen students each, honors seminars are conducted in an atmosphere of openness and intellectual exchange. Exploring fundamental works in the humanities, arts, natural sciences, and social sciences, the seminars generate lively discussion of major issues and problems. No examinations are given. Instead, students are encouraged to think critically about important questions and to explore these questions through writing. Grades are based on the quality of each student's written and oral work.

The Honors Program employs five instructional staff members; two permanent lecturers and three visiting assistant professors teach exclusively in the program for three-year terms. These instructors have strengthened a strong undergraduate teaching program by providing continuity for the curriculum and personal attention to students. In addition to the honors instructional staff, some of UWM's best teachers and scholars teach regularly in the program, offering undergraduates the opportunity of working with faculty members often available only to graduate students. The Honors Program seeks to bring to a public institution the same level of excellence in liberal arts that is associated with the country's best private colleges.

The Honors Program was established in the College of Letters and Science in 1960 and became University-wide in 1983. Approximately 450 students are currently participating in the program.

Participation Requirements: The honors curriculum comprises introductory humanities seminars with variable topics; honors calculus; upper-level seminars in humanities, social and natural sciences, and the arts; independent study; research; study abroad; and an optional senior thesis or project. Students can major in any area. Honors students fulfill many of their general education requirements (GER) through honors seminars. They can also use upper-level honors credits to fulfill major requirements.

In order to graduate with an honors degree, students must have a minimum 3.5 GPA overall at the time of graduation and complete at least 21 honors credits. All UWM undergraduate schools and colleges now offer the honors degree, a special diploma awarded to students who complete Honors Program requirements. Students who complete a senior thesis receive the special distinction of "honors with thesis."

Admission Process: The Honors Program is open to students from all schools and colleges within the University. New freshmen are admitted on the basis of their high school rank in class, ACT scores, and Wisconsin English Placement Test scores. Continuing and transfer students are invited to apply if they have achieved a minimum 3.5 GPA for at least 12 credits of college work.

Scholarship Availability: The Honors Program offers several annual awards. The Honors Program Scholarship, made available by anonymous donation, is awarded annually to a junior or senior; the Herman Weil Senior Thesis Award funds research expenses associated with completion of a senior thesis; and the KleinOsowski Scholarship is awarded to a freshman or sophomore student with a cumulative GPA of 3.5 or higher.

Honors Program students are also given preference for several other UWM scholarships and awards. These include the Fred Miller/Milwaukee Braves Scholarship, awarded every four years to an incoming freshman, and the William F. Halloran Scholarship, awarded annually to a freshman

Campus Overview

State-supported university, founded 1956, part of University of Wisconsin System • **Coed** 22,307 undergraduate students, 80% full-time, 54% women, 46% men.

Undergraduates 17,922 full-time, 4,385 part-time. Students come from 53 states and territories, 2% are from out of state, 7% African American, 5% Asian American or Pacific Islander, 4% Hispanic American, 0.7% Native American, 0.6% international, 7% transferred in, 13% live on campus.

Academic Programs *Special study options:* academic remediation for entering students, accelerated degree program, adult/continuing education programs, advanced placement credit, cooperative education, distance learning, double majors, English as a second language, honors programs, independent study, internships, off-campus study, part-time degree program, services for LD students, student-designed majors, study abroad, summer session for credit. *ROTC:* Army (c), Air Force (c).

Athletics Member NCAA. All Division I. *Intercollegiate sports:* baseball M, basketball M(s)/W(s), cross-country running M(s)/W(s), soccer M(s)/W(s), swimming and diving M(s)/W(s), tennis M(s)/W(s), track and field M(s)/W(s), volleyball M/W(s). *Intramural sports:* badminton M/W, basketball M/W, bowling M(c)/W(c), fencing M(c)/W(c), field hockey M/W, football M, golf M/W, racquetball M/W, riflery M(c)/W(c), rugby M(c)/W(c), sailing M(c)/W(c), skiing (downhill) M(c)/W(c), soccer M/W, swimming and diving M/W, tennis M/W, volleyball M/W, water polo M/W, weight lifting M/W, wrestling M.

Costs (2004–05) *Tuition:* state resident $5138 full-time, $214 per credit part-time; nonresident $17,890 full-time, $745 per credit part-time. Full-time tuition and fees vary according to location, program, and reciprocity agreements. Part-time tuition and fees vary according to course load, location, program, and reciprocity agreements. *Required fees:* $697 full-time. *Room and board:* $4505; room only: $2670. Room and board charges vary according to board plan and housing facility.

Financial Aid In 2002, 324 non-need-based awards were made. *Average percent of need met:* 69%. *Average financial aid package:* $7300. *Average need-based loan:* $3443. *Average need-based gift aid:* $4337. *Average non-need-based aid:* $1771.

Contact: Director: Professor Lawrence Baldassaro, 302 Garland Hall, University of Wisconsin–Milwaukee, P.O. Box 413, Milwaukee, Wisconsin 53201; *Telephone:* 414-229-4658, 414-229-4636; *Fax:* 414-229-6070; *E-mail:* honorweb@uwm.edu; *Web site:* http://www.uwm.edu/Dept/Honors

University of Wisconsin–Oshkosh
University Honors Program
Oshkosh, Wisconsin

The University Honors Program at the University of Wisconsin–Oshkosh offers a challenging and enriching academic experience to undergraduates who have clearly demonstrated their commitment to academic excellence. The curriculum of the University Honors Program has a 19-credit requirement built around several interdisciplinary courses and designated general education courses taught by selected faculty members.

Courses in the University Honors Program are limited to 25 students but average about half that number. About twelve honors courses are offered each semester to University Honors Program students, who have early registration privileges. Special orientation and registration workshops are held for all University Honors Program students.

Honors courses and the faculty members who teach them are selected by the University Honors Program Committee, composed of faculty representatives from the four colleges and students in the University Honors Student Association. All University Honors Program students must also attend a cultural event and file an activities report each semester they are in the program.

In addition to this curriculum, the University Honors Program emphasizes participation in the broader life of the University and community. The University Honors Student Association organizes recreational programs, a lecture series (Pizza with Professors), and *field trips to cultural sites in the region. Students in the program are encouraged to participate in the Upper Midwest Honors Conference, held each spring.*

The program has been in operation since 1981. There are currently 300 active students in the program. The University limits the number of University Honors Program students to no more than 5 percent of the undergraduate student enrollment.

Participation Requirements: All University Honors Program students enroll in the following courses, a total of 7 academic credits: honors seminar (3 credits), a thematic interdisciplinary seminar for new University Honors Program students; Culture Connection (1 credit), a cultural activities course modeled on a tutorial that involves writing assignments under the direction of honors readers; and either an honors senior thesis (3 credits), a thesis or project unique to the University Honors Program but earning credit in a student's major field of study, or an honors senior seminar (3 credits), an interdisciplinary capstone course. The remaining 12 academic credits are earned in sections of general education courses that are offered exclusively for University Honors Program students.

University Honors Program students must maintain a minimum GPA (out of a 4.0 scale) to remain in good standing: first-year students must maintain a minimum 3.2 GPA, sophomores 3.3 GPA, and juniors and seniors 3.4 GPA; students must maintain a minimum 3.5 GPA to receive University Honors. Graduating students present their senior-thesis projects at an Honors Thesis Symposium. At an awards ceremony held at the end of each semester, graduates receive a University Honors Program medallion, which they wear at the University's graduation ceremony. The University Chancellor presents the medallion to each University Honors Program graduate in an assembly of University faculty and staff members, administrators, and students' families and friends. The designation of Scholar Graduate–University Honors Program appears on the graduate's official transcript.

Admission Process: All students who are in the top 10 percent of their high school graduating class and who have an ACT composite score of 26 or better are automatically eligible for admission, as are all high school valedictorians and National Merit Scholars. Entering students who meet only one of these criteria may send a letter to the director requesting admission to the program explaining why special consideration is warranted in their case and enclosing a copy of their high school transcript. Second-semester students who achieved a specific GPA requirement during their first semester are invited to participate in the University Honors Program without regard to high school standing or ACT score. Approximately 70 students per year enter the program by means of their grade point averages.

Scholarship Availability: There are no scholarships specifically for University Honors Program students, though University Honors Program students receive a wide range of academic achievement scholarships. As of 2002, the University has increased the number of scholarships.

Campus Overview

State-supported comprehensive, founded 1871, part of University of Wisconsin System • **Coed** 9,812 undergraduate students, 88% full-time, 59% women, 41% men.

Undergraduates 8,586 full-time, 1,226 part-time. Students come from 30 states and territories, 32 other countries, 2% are from out of state, 0.9% African American, 2% Asian American or Pacific Islander, 1% Hispanic American, 0.8% Native American, 0.9% international, 10% transferred in, 34% live on campus.

Faculty *Total:* 566, 71% full-time, 67% with terminal degrees. *Student/faculty ratio:* 21:1.

Academic Programs *Special study options:* academic remediation for entering students, accelerated degree program, adult/continuing education programs, advanced placement credit, cooperative education, distance learning, double majors, English as a second language, honors programs, independent study, internships, part-time degree program, services for LD students, student-designed majors, study abroad, summer session for credit. *ROTC:* Army (b).

Athletics Member NCAA. All Division III. *Intercollegiate sports:* baseball M, basketball M/W, cross-country running M/W, football M, golf W, gymnastics W, riflery M/W, soccer M/W, softball W, swimming and diving M/W, tennis M/W, track and field M/W, volleyball W, wrestling M. *Intramural sports:* basketball M/W, bowling M(c)/W(c), cross-country running M/W, football M/W, golf M/W, gymnastics M(c), ice hockey M(c), lacrosse M(c)/W(c), racquetball M/W, skiing (downhill) M/W, soccer M/W, softball M/W, tennis M/W, volleyball M(c)/W, wrestling M.

Costs (2004–05) *Tuition:* state resident $4616 full-time, $194 per credit hour part-time; nonresident $14,662 full-time, $612 per credit hour part-time. Full-time tuition and fees vary according to reciprocity agreements. Part-time tuition and fees vary according to reciprocity agreements. *Room and board:* $4630; room only: $2530. Room and board charges vary according to board plan and housing facility.

Financial Aid In 2003, 60 non-need-based awards were made. *Average percent of need met:* 53%. *Average financial aid package:* $3080. *Average need-based loan:* $3500. *Average need-based gift aid:* $2000. *Average non-need-based aid:* $3333.

Contact: Director: Dr. Roberta Maguire, University Honors Program, Polk 9, University of Wisconsin–Oshkosh, 800 Algoma Boulevard, Oshkosh, Wisconsin 54901; *Telephone:* 920-424-7364; *E-mail:* maguire@uwosh.edu; *Web site:* http://www.uwosh.edu/honors

---

University of Wisconsin–Stout
University Honors Program
Menomonie, Wisconsin

*T*he University Honors Program (UHP) at the University of Wisconsin–Stout (UW–Stout) aims to enhance the undergraduate experience of highly motivated and talented students. Four Honors Seminars, four Honors Contracts, and biannual Honors Colloquia provide a framework in which students deepen and broaden their general education and their major studies in concert with other engaged students and committed faculty members. In the seminars, students use primary sources to explore fundamental problems in the disciplines; the capstone Seminar in Service explicitly challenges students to connect their learning with their responsibilities as educated citizens. In Honors Contracts, students select a professor with whom they design a project based on their own interest and curiosity. In Honors Colloquia, students and faculty members of the UHP join to study and debate issues that intersect scholarship and civic responsibility. The UHP Student Association conducts social activities and aids in UHP policy formation. Involvement in state, regional, and national honors activities provides students with opportunities to present and discuss their research and to meet other motivated students. UHP students bring diverse personal, intellectual, and professional interests to the program; through their participation in the UHP, they bridge their differences and create a sense of community within the University.*

The UHP began in 1994. Approximately 130 students, representing each of Stout's major programs, are enrolled in the University Honors Program.

Participation Requirements: The University Honors Program requires 23 honors credits. Students earn 11 of these credits in Honors Seminars and 12 through Honors Contracts. All but 3 of these honors credits fulfill the University's general education requirements. Students also join with faculty members in Honors Colloquia held each semester. To graduate from the UHP, students must maintain a minimum 3.0 GPA in Honors Seminars. UHP graduates are recognized at graduation, and successful completion of the UHP is noted on each student's diploma and transcript.

Admission Process: First-year students who rank in the top 10 percent of their high school class and those who rank in the top 10 percent of Stout's ACT scores are invited to join the UHP upon acceptance to the University. Other first-year, transfer, and nontraditional students may apply for admission. Factors considered in application admissions decisions include the student's special skills and accomplishments, motivation for learning, teacher recommendations, and past academic performance. Applications are considered up to the sixth week of class each semester. Admissions decisions are made by the UHP Director and the UHP Advisory Committee.

Scholarship Availability: The UHP does not administer scholarships. The UW–Stout Foundation does, however, award a number of scholarships for which UHP students are uniquely qualified.

Campus Overview

State-supported comprehensive, founded 1891, part of University of Wisconsin System • **Coed** 6,972 undergraduate students, 89% full-time, 49% women, 51% men.

Undergraduates 6,229 full-time, 743 part-time. Students come from 26 states and territories, 28% are from out of state, 1% African American, 2% Asian American or Pacific Islander, 0.7% Hispanic American, 0.4% Native American, 0.6% international, 8% transferred in, 38% live on campus.

Faculty *Total:* 397, 73% full-time, 64% with terminal degrees. *Student/faculty ratio:* 20:1.

Academic Programs *Special study options:* academic remediation for entering students, accelerated degree program, adult/continuing education programs, advanced placement credit, cooperative education, distance learning, double majors, external degree program, honors programs, independent study, internships, off-campus study, part-time degree program, services for LD students, study abroad, summer session for credit.

Athletics Member NCAA. All Division III. *Intercollegiate sports:* baseball M, basketball M/W, cross-country running M/W, football M, gymnastics W, ice hockey M/W(c), soccer M(c)/W, softball W, tennis W, track and field M/W, volleyball M(c)/W. *Intramural sports:* baseball M, basketball M/W, bowling M(c)/W(c), football M/W, golf M/W, ice hockey M/W, racquetball M/W, rugby M(c)/W(c), skiing (cross-country) M(c)/W(c), skiing (downhill) M(c)/W(c), softball M/W, ultimate Frisbee M/W, volleyball M/W.

Costs (2004–05) *Tuition:* state resident $4455 full-time, $186 per credit part-time; nonresident $14,780 full-time, $530 per credit part-time. Full-time tuition and fees vary according to reciprocity agreements. Part-time tuition and fees vary according to reciprocity agreements. *Required fees:* $1807 full-time, $23 per credit part-time. *Room and board:* $4334; room only: $2500. Room and board charges vary according to board plan.

Financial Aid 1,352 Federal Work-Study jobs (averaging $1448). In 2004, 373 non-need-based awards were made. *Average percent of need met:* 90%. *Average financial aid package:* $7107. *Average need-based loan:* $4031. *Average need-based gift aid:* $4230. *Average non-need-based aid:* $2140.

Contact: Director: Dr. Robert Horan, 42 Harvey Hall, Menomonie, Wisconsin 54751-0790; *Telephone:* 715-232-1455; *Fax:* 715-232-2093; *E-mail:* horanr@uwstout.edu

University of Wisconsin–Whitewater
University Honors Program
Whitewater, Wisconsin

*T*he University Honors Program at the University of Wisconsin–Whitewater (UW–W) is an academic enrichment program aimed at providing opportunities for motivated students who seek a highly challenging and intellectually enriched learning environment. General studies honors courses consist of smaller groups of students and are led by some of the University's most accomplished teachers and scholars. The honors option allows students to individualize and enhance their academic program beyond general studies. In addition to small classes and seminars, the program encourages research and other creative activities, study abroad, internships, and summer-scholar opportunities. University Honors Program students also have access to a comfortable on-campus facility that offers sophisticated computer equipment, state-of-the art meeting rooms, student work areas, and other amenities.

University Honors Program students must complete 21 credits in honors courses or honors option work. The expectation is that these credits will include honors in general studies, service learning, participation in research, a creative activity, or undergraduate teaching experiences. Honors in the major track is currently undergoing curriculum development and is only available in some departments.

Participation Requirements: Entering freshmen students must meet one of the following high school graduation criteria: students should be in the top 10 percent of their high school class, with a minimum ACT composite score of 24; or students should be in the top 25 percent of their high school class, with a minimum ACT score of 28; or students should be highly recommended, with letters of nomination by their high school counselor and at least one instructor. Eligible students wishing to enroll in the University Honors Program must complete and file an application, which can be obtained at the University Honors Program Office or online at http://acadaff.uww.edu/Honors/honorsforms.htm.

Students already enrolled at UW–W may apply for admission when they have completed at least 12 credits of academic work at the University, with a minimum grade point average of 3.4.

Transfer students who have a minimum 3.4 grade point average may apply to the program. Honors credits from other accredited institutions may be accepted following the review of an official transcript by the University Honors Program director. Final admission to the program is dependent on developing a plan for completion of at least half of the requisite honors credits and program expectations for graduation.

To remain in good standing, a student must maintain a UW–W cumulative grade point average of at least 3.4. Students whose grade point average falls below the minimum are suspended from the program. Reinstatement may be achieved at the end of any ensuing semester when the student attains the minimum 3.4 cumulative grade point average. Students qualifying for reinstatement must contact the University Honors Program Office. Honors courses and honors option work must be completed according to the distribution outlined in the course of study.

Admission Process: Freshmen who meet the eligibility requirements are automatically invited to attend the preview for the University Honors Program at the time of their registration. Other students meeting eligibility requirements must apply to the program directly and meet with the University Honors Program director.

Scholarship Availability: Incoming freshmen scholarships are awarded through the Office of Admissions. Continuing students have the opportunity to apply for various University scholarships and national competitions, if applicable.

Campus Overview

State-supported comprehensive, founded 1868, part of University of Wisconsin System • **Coed** 9,533 undergraduate students, 91% full-time, 52% women, 48% men.

Undergraduates 8,708 full-time, 825 part-time. Students come from 29 states and territories, 26 other countries, 4% are from out of state, 4% African American, 3% Asian American or Pacific Islander, 2% Hispanic American, 0.5% Native American, 0.5% international, 6% transferred in, 40% live on campus.

Faculty *Total:* 503, 76% full-time, 72% with terminal degrees. *Student/faculty ratio:* 20:1.

Academic Programs *Special study options:* academic remediation for entering students, accelerated degree program, adult/continuing education programs, advanced placement credit, cooperative education, distance learning, double majors, English as a second language, external degree program, honors programs, independent study, internships, part-time degree program, services for LD students, student-designed majors, study abroad, summer session for credit. *ROTC:* Army (b), Air Force (b).

Athletics Member NCAA. All Division III. *Intercollegiate sports:* baseball M, basketball M/W, bowling M(c)/W, cheerleading M(c)/W(c), cross-country running M/W, football M, golf W, gymnastics W, ice hockey M(c)/W(c), lacrosse M(c), rugby M(c)/W(c), soccer M/W, softball W, swimming and diving M/W, tennis M/W, track and field M/W, volleyball M(c)/W, weight lifting M(c), wrestling M. *Intramural sports:* basketball M/W, football M/W, golf M/W, racquetball M/W, rock climbing M(c)/W(c), skiing (downhill) M(c)/W(c), soccer M, softball M/W, table tennis M/W, tennis M/W, ultimate Frisbee M(c)/W(c), volleyball M/W, water polo M/W.

Costs (2005–06) *One-time required fee:* $100. *Tuition:* state resident $4370 full-time, $186 per credit part-time; nonresident $14,965 full-time, $663 per credit part-time. Full-time tuition and fees vary according to degree level and reciprocity agreements. *Required fees:* $710 full-time, $29 per credit part-time. *Room and board:* $4210; room only: $2460. Room and board charges vary according to board plan.

Financial Aid 575 Federal Work-Study jobs (averaging $1210). 2,100 state and other part-time jobs (averaging $1860). In 2004, 707 non-need-based awards were made. *Average percent of need met:* 75%. *Average financial aid package:* $6080. *Average need-based loan:* $3739. *Average need-based gift aid:* $4199. *Average non-need-based aid:* $2254.

Contact: Director: Roxanne DePaul, Ph.D., University Honors Program, University of Wisconsin–Whitewater, 800 West Main Street, Whitewater, Wisconsin 53190; *Telephone:* 262-472-1268; *E-mail:* honors@mail.uww.edu; *Web site:* http://acadaff.uww.edu/Honors/

WYOMING

University of Wyoming
University Honors Program
Laramie, Wyoming

For students with wide-ranging curiosity and a passion for learning, the University of Wyoming Honors Program offers a sequence of five challenging core courses (including the popular elective study-abroad courses, Shakespeare in England and Italy and Modern Japanese Society and Culture), a senior independent research project, a variety of extracurricular activities, and optional housing within a campus residence hall or in the newly remodeled Honors House. Additional benefits include substantial scholarships for resident and nonresident students and for study abroad, support for travel to conferences, support for undergraduate research, and special recognition on the transcript and at graduation.

Honors core courses are limited to 18 or 20 students, taught by some of the University's best faculty members, and designed to bring together talented students from all majors. Courses are innovative and interdisciplinary, set up to encourage a sense of community among the participants. Like other UW students, an Honors Program participant follows a course of study leading to a degree in one of the six undergraduate colleges and eighty-five majors. Honors courses count toward general education requirements.

The honors senior research project, initiated in the junior year and developed through the senior year, focuses on a topic chosen by the student and explored with the help of a faculty specialist. Projects in the creative arts, as well as more traditional experiments and analyses, are encouraged. By developing a strong competence in research or an area in the creative arts, an honors student gives his or her undergraduate education a highly individual stamp. The senior project often leads directly into graduate studies or a special career path.

Honors courses and faculty members are selected each year by the student-faculty Honors Advisory Committee from proposals invited from all faculty at the University. Honors faculty members need to demonstrate a strong record of innovative and effective teaching. The Wyoming Honors Program was initiated in 1958 and now enrolls 632 students.

Participation Requirements: In order to graduate with the University Honors Program, a student must maintain a 3.25 GPA and complete five seminars and the senior independent project, totaling 18 semester credit hours. Students who complete the program are recognized at graduation with a gold stole and a designation on their transcript and diploma.

Admission Process: To join the program as a freshman, a student must meet one of three criteria: a composite ACT score of 28, a combined SAT score of 1240, or a high school GPA of 3.7. Strong students who do not meet one of these criteria should write to the program director and explain their reasons for wishing to participate.

Transfer students may join the program if they have two years or more of course work remaining. They must have a transfer GPA of 3.25.

All applications are reviewed, and priority is given to those received before February 10.

Scholarship Availability: Scholar's Stipends in the amount of resident tuition and fees are awarded for four years to 18 incoming freshmen, regardless of residency. Nonresident and nontraditional students may compete for University of Wyoming Dr. Scholl Foundation Scholarships. Boyd Special Academic Opportunities Scholarships assist enrolled students who plan to study in an off-campus setting, such as international exchanges, internships, exchanges at other U.S. universities, and independent research travel. Several other scholarships are awarded every year.

Campus Overview

State-supported university, founded 1886 • **Coed** 9,589 undergraduate students, 81% full-time, 53% women, 47% men.

Undergraduates 7,762 full-time, 1,827 part-time. Students come from 53 states and territories, 46 other countries, 27% are from out of state, 1% African American, 1% Asian American or Pacific Islander, 4% Hispanic American, 1% Native American, 1% international, 11% transferred in, 20% live on campus.

Faculty *Total:* 692, 93% full-time, 82% with terminal degrees. *Student/faculty ratio:* 16:1.

Academic Programs *Special study options:* accelerated degree program, advanced placement credit, distance learning, double majors, English as a second language, external degree program, honors programs, independent study, internships, off-campus study, part-time degree program, services for LD students, student-designed majors, study abroad, summer session for credit. *ROTC:* Army (b), Air Force (b).

Athletics Member NCAA. All Division I except football (Division I-A). *Intercollegiate sports:* badminton M(c)/W(c), baseball M(c), basketball M(s)/W(s), cheerleading M(s)/W(s), cross-country running M(s)/W(s), fencing M(c)/W(c), golf M(s)/W(s), ice hockey M(c)/W(c), riflery M(c)/W(c), rugby M(c)/W(c), skiing (downhill) M(c)/W(c), soccer M(c)/W(c), swimming and diving M(s)/W(s), tennis W(s), track and field M(s)/W(s), ultimate Frisbee M(c)/W(c), volleyball W(s), wrestling M(s). *Intramural sports:* archery M/W, badminton M/W, baseball M, basketball M/W, bowling M/W, cross-country running M/W, football M/W, golf M/W, racquetball M/W, rock climbing M/W, skiing (downhill) M/W, soccer M/W, softball M/W, table tennis M/W, tennis M/W, track and field M/W, volleyball M/W, water polo M/W, weight lifting M/W, wrestling M/W.

Costs (2004–05) *Tuition:* $87 per credit part-time; state resident $2610 full-time, $87 per credit hour part-time; nonresident $8640 full-time, $288 per credit hour part-time. Full-time tuition and fees vary according to course load, location, program, and reciprocity agreements. Part-time tuition and fees vary according to course load, location, program, and reciprocity agreements. *Required fees:* $633 full-time, $153 per term part-time. *Room and board:* $5953; room only: $2590. Room and board charges vary according to board plan and housing facility.

Financial Aid 464 Federal Work-Study jobs (averaging $1299). In 2003, 1973 non-need-based awards were made. *Average percent of need met:* 75%. *Average financial aid package:* $7910. *Average need-based loan:* $3526. *Average need-based gift aid:* $1932. *Average non-need-based aid:* $1435.

Contact: Director: Duncan Harris, Honors Center, Merica Hall 102, Department 3413, 1000 East University Avenue, University of Wyoming, Laramie, Wyoming 82071; *Telephone:* 307-766-4110; *Fax:* 307-766-4298; *E-mail:* honors@uwyo.edu; *Web site:* http://www.uwadmnweb.uwyo. edu.Honors/default.htm

Western Wyoming Community College
Honors Program
Rock Springs, Wyoming

The Honors Program at Western Wyoming Community College (WWCC) was designed for students with superior academic records, above-average enthusiasm for learning, and intellectual curiosity. The Honors Program's mission is to challenge bright students by encouraging learning communities within the classroom and opportunities for intellectual growth outside the classroom. Through field trips and classroom interaction, students form lifelong friendships with others who share their commitment to learning.

Organized in 1991, the Honors Program accepts 10 incoming first-year students and 10 second-year students, so that each fall a mixed group of 20 students begins the program together. This system allows the program to attract excellent freshmen and to include nontraditional students who have proved themselves to be academically superior in their first year of college. The 20 Honors Program students are chosen each spring through a process of application and an essay. Freshmen must submit an application, an essay, and ACT scores; WWCC faculty members must nominate sophomores, who must submit an essay and a college GPA.

As part of the Honors Program, students participate in two special honors colloquiums in humanities and environmental science. The humanities colloquium incorporates cultural field trips into the course content, as students examine the role of the arts and humanities in the human experience. Students travel to symphonies, operas, art galleries, plays, and museums at the program's expense as part of this course. The environmental science colloquium uses current local

environmental issues as a gateway to exploration of the science behind the issue. Topics vary from year to year.

Honors Program students also pursue an individual research project, working closely with a faculty mentor. This project allows them to investigate a topic of their choice, become familiar with research methods, and develop their own expertise on a topic of personal interest, giving their education a highly individual stamp.

Honors Program students are also eligible to enroll in any of ten honors courses offered yearly. Most of these challenging courses are seminar style, with limited enrollment. Taught by some of Western's most dedicated faculty members, these courses encourage participation and bring together talented students from all majors. While they are intended for academically motivated students, honors courses are not simply more work with stiffer competition. They are innovative, intellectually stimulating, and designed to develop a community of scholars among the participants.

Participation Requirements: Students participating in the Honors Program are expected to maintain a GPA of at least 3.25 in 15 credit hours. They must also enroll in two honors courses per academic year, including the two honors colloquiums in humanities and environmental science. Students who have participated in the WWCC Honors Program are automatically accepted into the honors programs at the University of Wyoming, Utah State University, and Weber State University. In addition, colleges and universities throughout the nation recognize the Honors Program designation on a student's transcript as a sign of superior work.

Admission Process: To be admitted to the Honors Program, first-year students must have a score of at least 25 on the ACT or 1100 on the SAT, complete the WWCC admissions process, and complete an Honors Program application. To be admitted as sophomores, students must be nominated by a faculty member who has had them in class, have attained at least a 3.75 GPA in their freshman year, submit an Honors Program application in March, and plan to enroll full-time for two more semesters. Twenty students are selected on the basis of academic records, letters of recommendation, and application essays. Honors Program participants are screened and selected during the spring for the following academic year.

Scholarship Availability: Although specific Honors Program scholarships are not offered, most students selected for the program receive some type of scholarship from the College. Institutional scholarships may be awarded for academics, special abilities (art, dance, music, and theater), occupational programs, and athletics. Academic scholarships may be awarded to high school seniors with a minimum 3.1 cumulative GPA on a 4.0 scale and a score of at least 18 on the ACT or 870 on the SAT. Two continuing students in each of seven WWCC divisions may be selected for academic division scholarships after nomination by each division. Students with a minimum 3.0 cumulative GPA and at least 12 credit hours at WWCC are eligible for consideration. Additional grants may be awarded to students through WWCC's foundation grant program, including Civic Grants, Whisenand II Grants, and Anna Baird Williams Grants, and through the Western Wyoming College Foundation.

Campus Overview

State and locally supported 2-year, founded 1959 • **Coed** 2,654 undergraduate students, 41% full-time, 63% women, 37% men.

Undergraduates 1,099 full-time, 1,555 part-time. Students come from 12 states and territories, 17 other countries, 7% are from out of state, 0.6% African American, 0.5% Asian American or Pacific Islander, 7% Hispanic American, 0.8% Native American, 3% international, 3% transferred in, 13% live on campus.

Faculty *Total:* 195, 33% full-time. *Student/faculty ratio:* 17:1.

Academic Programs *Special study options:* academic remediation for entering students, adult/continuing education programs, advanced placement credit, cooperative education, distance learning, English as a second language, freshman honors college, honors programs, independent study, internships, part-time degree program, services for LD students, summer session for credit.

Athletics Member NJCAA. *Intercollegiate sports:* basketball M(s)/W(s), cheerleading M(s)/W(s), soccer M(s)(c)/W(s)(c), volleyball W(s), wrestling M(s). *Intramural sports:* badminton M/W, basketball M/W, bowling M/W, football M/W, rock climbing M/W, skiing (downhill) M/W, soccer M/W, softball M/W, table tennis M/W, tennis M/W, ultimate Frisbee M/W, volleyball M/W, water polo M/W.

Costs (2005–06) *Tuition:* state resident $1658 full-time, $70 per credit hour part-time; nonresident $4418 full-time, $185 per credit hour part-time. Full-time tuition and fees vary according to reciprocity agreements. Part-time tuition and fees vary according to course load and reciprocity agreements. *Room and board:* $3033; room only: $1474. Room and board charges vary according to board plan and housing facility.

Financial Aid 20 Federal Work-Study jobs (averaging $1500).

Contact: Honors Program Director: Karen Love, 2500 College Drive, Rock Springs, Wyoming 82901; *Telephone:* 307-382-1733; *E-mail:* klove@wwcc.wy.edu; *Web site:* http://www.wwcc.wy.edu/programs/honors.htm. Director of Admissions: Laurie Watkins, P.O. Box 428, Rock Springs, Wyoming 82902-0428; *Telephone:* 307-382-1647, 800-226-1181 (toll-free); *Fax:* 307-382-1636; *E-mail:* admissions@wwcc.wy.edu; *Web site:* http://www.wwcc.wy.edu

CANADA

University of Victoria
Honors Program
Victoria, British Columbia

The Honours Program at the University of Victoria (UVic) offers academic enrichment for highly motivated students. More than 25 academic units offer Honours Programs with a number of opportunities for combined programs, satisfying the requirements for two departments. More than 200 students are registered in Honours programs.

Participation Requirements: Students must maintain a minimum GPA to continue in the program. Students in an honours program must normally complete an honours thesis or graduating essay to fulfill the requirements of the degree. Each academic unit has an honours adviser. Academic advice is also available from the Faculty Advising Centres. Students who achieve a minimum graduating GPA in required courses graduate with an honours degree "with distinction."

Admission Process: Students normally apply for admission to an Honours Program at the end of their second year of University study. Admission is based on completion of specified prerequisites and a minimum GPA.

Scholarship Availability: The University of Victoria offers a competitive merit aid program with awarded scholarships based on a student's high school record at admission and on course work completed at the University for continuing students. Other financial assistance, including bursaries, loans, and part-time employment, is also available to qualified students. UVic awards more than Can$2 million each year in merit-based scholarships.

Campus Overview

Province-supported university, founded 1963 • **Coed** 15,910 undergraduate students, 65% full-time, 60% women, 40% men.

Undergraduates 10,418 full-time, 5,492 part-time. Students come from 13 provinces and territories, 92 other countries, 13% are from out of state, 11% transferred in, 16% live on campus.

Faculty *Total:* 698, 95% full-time. *Student/faculty ratio:* 22:1.

Academic Programs *Special study options:* academic remediation for entering students, adult/continuing education programs, advanced placement credit, cooperative education, distance learning, double majors, English as a second language, honors programs, independent study, internships, off-campus study, part-time degree program, services for LD students, student-designed majors, study abroad, summer session for credit.

Athletics Member NAIA, CIS. *Intercollegiate sports:* basketball M(s)/W(s), crew M(s)/W(s), cross-country running M(s)/W(s), field hockey W(s), golf M/W, rugby M(s)/W, soccer M(s)/W(s), swimming and diving M(s)/W(s). *Intramural sports:* badminton M/W, baseball W, basketball M/W, cross-country running M/W, fencing M/W, field hockey M/W, football M/W, golf M/W, ice hockey M/W, racquetball M/W, rock climbing M(c)/W(c), rugby M/W, sailing M/W, skiing (downhill) M/W, soccer M/W, softball M/W, squash M/W, swimming and diving M/W, table tennis M/W, tennis M/W, ultimate Frisbee M/W, volleyball M/W, water polo M/W, weight lifting M/W.

Costs (2004–05) *Tuition:* province resident $4239 Canadian dollars full-time, $282 Canadian dollars per unit part-time; International tuition $12,495 Canadian dollars full-time. Full-time tuition and fees vary according to course load and program. Part-time tuition and fees vary according to course load and program. *Required fees:* $586 Canadian dollars full-time, $586 Canadian dollars per year part-time. *Room and board:* $5790 Canadian dollars; room only: $3400 Canadian dollars. Room and board charges vary according to board plan and housing facility.

Contact: Assistant Dean and Director: Dr. Michael C. R. Edgell, Advising Centre for Humanities, Science and Social Sciences, P.O. Box 3025 STN CSC, Victoria, British Columbia V8W 3P2, Canada; *Telephone:* 250-721-7565; *Fax:* 250-472-5145; *E-mail:* dadv@uvic.ca; *Web site:* http://www.uvic.ca

NETHERLANDS

University of Amsterdam
Interdisciplinary Honors Modules
Amsterdam, The Netherlands

The Institute for Interdisciplinary Studies offers several Interdisciplinary Honors Modules. Students can include these in their University or departmental honors program. Interdisciplinary Honors Modules now include Masters of Suspicion: Darwin, Marx, Nietzsche, and Freud (level A); Creativity: From Algorithm to History of Art (level B); and Big History (level A).

Interdisciplinary Honors Modules have as their primary educational goals learning to approach a subject from different scientific perspectives while acknowledging the relationship between the sciences as well as developing academic skills. The academic skills, which are practiced, include presenting, taking minutes, debating, and self-reflection. Interdisciplinary classes, seminars, tutorials, and assignments serve to realize these goals.

Classes and seminars are given to small groups of students (maximum of 15) by 4 tutors who have completed their studies in a different discipline. Besides attending the honors classes, honors students are also invited to join excursions, attend plays or workshops, and have dinner at the end of the module with staff members of the Honors Modules. Students who have completed these modules have shown themselves to be highly motivated and to have wide academic interests.

The University of Amsterdam started its Honors Program in 2004. During the 2005–06 year, approximately 120 students are participating in the Interdisciplinary Honors Modules.

Participation Requirements: An honors student applies for honors education in his or her discipline and follows extra honors modules—in addition to his or her normal study load. One or more of these modules should preferably be interdisciplinary and can be taken at the Institute for Interdisciplinary Studies. These modules have a value of 6 ECTS each. The bachelor's degree should be finished in three or four years, with an average grade of 7 out of 10. The student then receives an Honors-Bachelor diploma.

Admission Process: Selection is made on the basis of disciplinary exam scores, study progress, and motivation, and it is done either by the supervisor of the students' regular discipline or by the supervisor of the Institute for Interdisciplinary Studies. Students who want to follow a B-level module should already have some experience in interdisciplinary (honors) education. An essay and an interview are part of the application process.

Campus Overview

State-supported university, founded 1635. • **Coed** 23,861 undergraduate students.

Faculty *Total:* 3,000.

Costs (2004–05) *Tuition:* tuition fees differ per program, ranging from 500 euros to 21,000 euros.

Contact: Drs. Machiel Keestra, Assistant Professor, Head of the Interdisciplinary Honors Modules, Institute for Interdisciplinary Studies, University of Amsterdam, Sarphatistraat 104, Kamer 1.10, 1018 GV Amsterdam,The Netherlands; *Telephone:* +31-20-525-5507 secr. 5190; *Fax:* +31-20-525-5505; *E-mail:* M.Keestra@uva.nl; *Web site:* http://www.iis.uva.nl

University of Utrecht
Department of Social Geography and Planning
Honours Programme
Utrecht, The Netherlands

The Department of Social Geography and Planning has been gathering experience since 1995 with types of education especially developed for the 5 to 10 percent of the best performing students. Within the current Honours Programme a lot of emphasis is laid upon the personal initiatives of the students regarding the enrichment and intensity of their study, naturally also under the supervision of excellent teachers/professors. This approach has proved successful: the "excellent tracé" was awarded the national ISO prize for educational innovation due to the inspiring education and the offered personal freedom. Many participants become successful assistants in training or get rewarding jobs outside University.

The added value of the programme in terms of services provided to the students is more intensive guidance by extremely qualified professors; broader, more intense, and in-depth courses; space for personal initiative of the participants; and a stimulating academic context for students in the shape of "Socratic workshops." The added value of content is increased demands regarding the international character of the program, small scale, connections with the research programs and topics being followed within the faculty's prestige programs, and a heavier study load. Added value regarding external effects is increased output and guidance towards selective and prestigious master's programs.

The program is developed in such a way that its shape and content create a balance in supply (by the University) and demand (by students). Active learning is its main concern; group-forming is stimulated and development of responsibility (leadership, initiative, ethical reflection, carrying out one's profession in order to benefit society) takes centre stage.

Senior teacher-researchers and professors discuss the state of the art in these subjects; students start working actively with the extra, in-depth literature (discussions, presentations, papers, etc.). The seminars are connected to the faculty members' research interests and thus provide for an embedding of the Honours Programme into the faculty members' main tracks of research. The programme also has a strong international component.

Honours students do a heavier empirical research exercise more independently than "regular" students, which is embedded in a seminar—Geo-research—in which the assistants in training present their research (designs). In the third year, students write an honours thesis of 15 ECTS, for which considerably higher demands are made than for a regular bachelor's thesis. This individual project is embedded in a workshop on conceptualization and design of research supervised by professors.

Furthermore, all students in the Honours Programme, during the entire duration of the programme, participate in the so-called "Socratic workshops," held once every four weeks, in which the participants (of all years) discuss their honors activities, experience leadership courses, and develop activities of their own accord (such as inviting guest lecturers). These workshops are there for identification (group-forming) and serve as a forum for important initiatives.

Participation Requirements: The full Honours Programme comprises 60 ECTS, of which 30 ECTS are "replacements" (other or differently organized study components) and 30 ECTS are "intensifying," which means extra ECTS (students do not pay extra for extra ECTS). A student has to submit every year again. To obtain an honours bachelor's or an honours testimonium, a student has to fulfil the whole programme, including a research project, an honours thesis, an international experience, at least two capstone projects, and all the Socratic workshops. Currently, the exact needed number of ECTS to obtain a testimonium is determined by the honours director and the study board.

Admission Process: On the basis of their study results during their first semester, students are invited to participate. The program is aimed at the 10 percent of the students who have achieved the best study results. At the beginning of each consecutive academic year, it is established whether students are able to apply to the program on the basis of their study results and motivation. Naturally, the Faculty of Geosciences maintains a policy of nondiscrimination during the selection process, which guarantees the equal treatment of all students. Students may petition for admission past the requirements.

Students have to write a letter of motivation, including a learning portfolio, a CV, and a personal essay. Their average CPA should be 7 or higher (7 out of 10). For freshmen, the GPA of the first University semester is the criterion; for second years, their freshmen GPA; and, for seniors, the average of their full University career. In addition, high school average and recommendation of tutors or faculty members may be requested. The deadline dates change every year, but are mostly in November.

Campus Overview

Public university founded 1635 • **Coed** 26,787 undergraduate students.

Undergraduates 5,216 full-time.

Faculty *Total:* 8,224.

Academic Programs *Special study options:* study abroad.

Athletics Students can join olympos—see www.olympos.nl.

Costs (2004–05) *Tuition:* The tuition for one year, full-time studies is 1500 euros. For recent information, see www.qdesk.uu.nl.

Contact: Honours Director: Drs. Marca V. C. Wolfensberger, Faculty of Geoscience, University of Utrecht, Heidelberglaan 2, 3508 TC Utrecht, The Netherlands; *Telephone:* 31 (0) 30 2531396, 31 (0)30 2532086; *Fax:* 31 (0)30 253 20 37; *E-mail:* m.wolfensberger@geo.uu.nl; *Web site:* http://www.geo.uu.nl/25380main.html

Index

Alphabetical Listing of Schools

Mississippi University for Women (MS)	288
Missouri Southern State University (MO)	293
Missouri State University (MO)	294
Missouri Western State University (MO)	295
Monmouth University (NJ)	317
Monroe College (NY)	354
Montana State University (MT)	301
Montgomery College (TX)	503
Morehouse College (GA)	162
Motlow State Community College (TN)	487
Mott Community College (MI)	273
Mount Mercy College (IA)	213
Mt. San Antonio College (CA)	104
Mount Vernon Nazarene University (OH)	403
Mount Wachusett Community College (MA)	255
Murray State University (KY)	225
Nassau Community College (NY)	355
Neosho County Community College (KS)	219
Neumann College (PA)	451
Newberry College (SC)	476
New Jersey Institute of Technology (NJ)	318
New Mexico State University (NM)	325
Norfolk State University (VA)	537
Northampton County Area Community College (PA)	451
North Carolina Agricultural and Technical State University (NC)	383
North Carolina State University (NC)	384
North Central College (IL)	183
North Dakota State University (ND)	393
Northeastern Illinois University (IL)	184
Northeastern State University (OK)	416
Northeastern University (MA)	256
Northeast State Technical Community College (TN)	487
Northern Arizona University (AZ)	79
Northern Illinois University (IL)	185
Northern Kentucky University (KY)	226
Northern Michigan University (MI)	274
North Harris College (TX)	504
North Hennepin Community College (MN)	280
Northwestern State University of Louisiana (LA)	231
Northwood University (MI)	274
Nova Southeastern University (FL)	140
Oakton Community College (IL)	186
Ohio Dominican University (OH)	404
The Ohio State University (OH)	405
Ohio University (OH)	406
Oklahoma Baptist University (OK)	417
Oklahoma City University (OK)	417
Oklahoma State University (OK)	418
Oklahoma State University, Oklahoma City (OK)	419
Old Dominion University (VA)	538
Oral Roberts University (OK)	420
Orange County Community College (NY)	356
Oregon State University (OR)	424
Pace University (NY)	357
Palm Beach Atlantic University (FL)	141
Palm Beach Community College (FL)	142
Paradise Valley Community College (AZ)	80
Parkland College (IL)	187
The Pennsylvania State University University Park Campus (PA)	452
Philadelphia Biblical University (PA)	453
Philadelphia University (PA)	454
Pittsburg State University (KS)	219
Point Park University (PA)	455
Polytechnic University, Brooklyn Campus (NY)	358
Portland State University (OR)	425
Prairie State College (IL)	187
Prairie View A&M University (TX)	504
Prince George's Community College (MD)	243
Pueblo Community College (CO)	117
Purdue University (IN)	205
Queens College of the City University of New York (NY)	359
Quinnipiac University (CT)	123
Radford University (VA)	539
Ramapo College of New Jersey (NJ)	319
Redlands Community College (OK)	421
Reinhardt College (GA)	162
Rhode Island College (RI)	468
The Richard Stockton College of New Jersey (NJ)	320
Roanoke College (VA)	540
Rochester Community and Technical College (MN)	280
Rochester Institute of Technology (NY)	360
Roger Williams University (RI)	469
Rollins College (FL)	142
Roosevelt University (IL)	188
Rowan University (NJ)	321
Russell Sage College (NY)	361
Rutgers, The State University of New Jersey, Camden (NJ)	322
Rutgers, The State University of New Jersey, New Brunswick/Piscataway (NJ)	323
Sacred Heart University (CT)	124
Sage College of Albany (NY)	361
Saint Anselm College (NH)	310
St. Edward's University (TX)	505
Saint Francis University (PA)	455
Saint John's University (MN)	281
Saint Joseph College (CT)	125
Saint Joseph's University (PA)	456
Saint Leo University (FL)	143
St. Mary's College of Maryland (MD)	244
Saint Xavier University (IL)	188
Salem State College (MA)	257
Salisbury University (MD)	245
Sam Houston State University (TX)	506
San Diego City College (CA)	104
San Diego Mesa College (CA)	105
San Diego State University (CA)	106
San Jacinto College District (TX)	507
Santa Clara University (CA)	107
Santa Fe Community College (FL)	144
Sauk Valley Community College (IL)	189
Schreiner University (TX)	507
Scottsdale Community College (AZ)	80
Seattle Pacific University (WA)	545
Seminole Community College (FL)	145
Shepherd University (WV)	550
Shippensburg University of Pennsylvania (PA)	457
Simmons College (MA)	257
Sinclair Community College (OH)	407
Skyline College (CA)	108
South Dakota State University (SD)	479
Southeastern Louisiana University (LA)	232
Southeastern Oklahoma State University (OK)	421
Southeast Missouri State University (MO)	296
Southern Arkansas University–Magnolia (AR)	87
Southern Connecticut State University (CT)	126
Southern Illinois University Carbondale (IL)	190
Southern New Hampshire University (NH)	311
Southern Oregon University (OR)	426
Southern Polytechnic State University (GA)	163
Southern University and Agricultural and Mechanical College (LA)	233
Southern Utah University (UT)	526
South Florida Community College (FL)	145
South Mountain Community College (AZ)	81
Southwestern Illinois College (IL)	191
Southwest Minnesota State University (MN)	282